GRUBER'S COMPLETE SAT* GUIDE 2014

17th Edition

*SAT® is a registered trademark of the College Entrance Examination Board. The College Entrance Examination Board is not associated with and does not endorse this book.

GARY R. GRUBER, PHD

sourcebooks edu

Published by Sourcebooks, Inc.
P.O. Box 4410, Naperville, Illinois 60567-4410
(630) 961-3900
Fax: (630) 961-2168
www.sourcebooks.com

Library of Congress Cataloging-in-Publication Data is on file with the publisher.

Printed and bound in the United States of America.
DR 10 9 8 7 6 5 4 3 2 1

Recent and Forthcoming Study Aids from Dr. Gary Gruber Include

Gruber's Complete PSAT/NMSQT Guide 2014

Gruber's Complete ACT Guide 2014

Gruber's Complete GRE Guide 2014

Gruber's SAT 2400

Gruber's Complete SAT Math Workbook

Gruber's Complete SAT Critical Reading Workbook

Gruber's Complete SAT Writing Workbook

Gruber's SAT Word Master

Gruber's Essential Guide to Test Taking: Grades 3–5

Gruber's Essential Guide to Test Taking: Grades 6–9

www.collegecountdown.com

www.sourcebooks.com

www.drgarygruber.com

www.mymaxscore.com

Important Note About This Book and Its Author

This book is the most up-to-date and complete book on the current SAT. EVERY EXAM is patterned after the SAT, and *all* the strategies and techniques deal with the SAT. The SAT incorporates all the Gruber Critical Thinking Strategies.

This book was written by Dr. Gary Gruber, the leading authority on the SAT, who knows more than anyone else in the test-prep market exactly what is being tested on the SAT. In fact, the procedures to answer the SAT questions rely more heavily on the Gruber Critical Thinking Strategies than ever before, and this is the only book that has the exact thinking strategies you need to use to maximize your SAT score. Gruber's SAT books are used by the nation's school districts more than any other books and are proven to get the highest documented school district SAT scores.

Dr. Gruber has published more than 35 books with major publishers on test-taking and critical thinking methods, with more than 7 million copies sold. He has also authored more than 1,000 articles on his work in scholarly journals and nationally syndicated newspapers, has appeared on numerous television and radio shows, and has been interviewed in hundreds of magazines and newspapers. He has developed major programs for school districts and for city and state educational agencies for improving and restructuring curriculum, increasing learning ability and test scores, increasing motivation and developing a "passion" for learning and problem solving, and decreasing the student dropout rate. For example, PBS (Public Broadcasting System) chose Dr. Gruber to train the nation's teachers on how to prepare students for the SAT through a national satellite teleconference and videotape. His results have been lauded by people throughout the country from all walks of life.

Dr. Gruber is recognized nationally as the leading expert on standardized tests. It is said that no one in the nation is better at assessing the thinking patterns of how a person answers questions and providing the mechanism to improve faulty thinking approaches. SAT score improvements by students using Dr. Gruber's techniques have been the highest in the nation.

Gruber's unique methods have been and are being used by PBS, by the nation's learning centers, by international encyclopedias, by school districts throughout the country, in homes and workplaces across the nation, and by a host of other entities.

His goal and mission is to get people's potential realized and the nation "impassioned" with learning and problem solving so that they don't merely try to get a fast uncritical answer, but actually enjoy and look forward to solving the problem and learning.

For more information on Gruber courses and additional Gruber products, visit www.drgarygruber.com.

Important: Many books do not reflect the current SAT questions. Don't practice with questions that misrepresent the actual questions on the SAT. For example, the math questions created by the test makers are oriented to allow someone to solve many problems without a calculator as fast as he or she could with one, and some can be solved faster without a calculator. This book reflects the SAT more accurately than any other commercial book, and the strategies contained in it are exactly those needed to be used on the SAT. It is said that only Dr. Gruber has the expertise and ability to reflect the exam far more closely than any competitor! Don't trust your future with less than the best material.

The Author Has Something Important to Tell You About How to Raise Your SAT Score

What Are Critical Thinking Skills?

First of all, I believe that intelligence can be taught. Intelligence, simply defined, is the aptitude or ability to reason things out. I am convinced that *you can learn to think logically* and figure things out better and faster, *particularly in regard to SAT Math and Verbal problems.* But someone must give you the tools. Let us call these tools *strategies.* And that's what Critical Thinking Skills are all about—*strategies.*

Learn the Strategies to Get More Points

The Critical Thinking Skills (beginning on page 60) will sharpen your reasoning ability so that you can increase your score dramatically on each part of the SAT.

These Critical Thinking Skills—5 General Strategies, 19 Math Strategies, and 16 Verbal Strategies—course right through this book. The Explanatory Answers for the 5 Practice Tests in the book direct you to those strategies that may be used to answer specific types of SAT questions. We can readily prove that the strategies in Part 4 of this book are usable for more than 90 percent of the questions that will appear on your SAT. *Each additional correct answer gives you approximately 10 points.* It is obvious, then, that your *learning* and *using* the 40 easy-to-understand strategies in this book will very likely raise your SAT score substantially.

Are the Practice Tests in This Book Like an Actual SAT?

If you compare any one of the 5 Practice Tests in this book with an actual SAT, you will find the book test very much like the *actual* test in regard to *format, question types,* and *level of difficulty.* Compare our book tests with one of the official tests published by the College Board!

Building Your Vocabulary Can Make a Big Difference on Your Test

Although Antonyms no longer appear on the SAT, Vocabulary will still be tested, especially on Sentence Completions and Reading Comprehension. This book includes five vital sections to build your vocabulary:

1. 3,400-Word List
2. 100 Vocabulary Tests
3. Latin and Greek Roots, Prefixes, and Suffixes
4. The Most Important/Frequently Used SAT Words
5. The Hot Prefixes and Roots

If you have time, it is important for you to study this word-building instructional material. You will find that *many, many words* in the 3,400-Word List will actually show up in the Sentence Completion and Reading Comprehension sections of the Verbal part of your SAT. We repeat that each additional correct answer adds approximately 10 points to your score. Knowing the meanings of the words in the 3,400-Word List will, therefore, help you considerably to "rake in" those precious points.

Study the Latin and Greek Roots, Prefixes, and Suffixes

We have developed a list that contains roots, prefixes, and suffixes that give you the meaning of more than 150,000 words. Learning all 366 will increase your vocabulary immensely. You may also wish to study the Hot Prefixes and Roots in Appendix A.

Study the Most Important/Frequently Used SAT Words

We have developed a list of the most frequently used words and their opposites related to specific categories for easy memorization. Study these words.

Study the Mini-Math Refresher

If you believe you are weak in basic math skills, study the Mini-Math Refresher. The material in this section is keyed to the Complete Math Refresher section for more thorough instruction.

Take the 101 Most Important Math Questions Test

To see what your weak basic math skills are, take the 101 Most Important Math Questions Test and look at the solutions to the questions. The questions are keyed to the Complete Math Refresher so you can further brush up on your weak areas by referring to those pages in the Complete Math Refresher that are relevant for any questions you missed.

The Explanatory Answers to Questions Are Keyed to Specific Strategies and Basic Skills

The Explanatory Answers in this book are far from skimpy—unlike those of other SAT books. Our detailed answers will direct you to the strategy that will help you to arrive at a correct answer quickly. In addition, the Math solutions in the book refer directly to the Complete Math Refresher section, particularly useful in case your Math skills are rusty.

Lift That SAT Score

By using the material in this book—that is, by taking the tests, learning the specific strategies, and refreshing your basic skills, as described above—you should increase your SAT score substantially.

—Gary Gruber

Contents

INTRODUCTION xiv

I. Important Facts About the SAT / xiv

II. The Inside Track on How SAT Questions Are Developed and How They Vary from Test to Test / xxi

III. What Are Critical Thinking Skills? / xxii

IV. Multi-Level Approaches to the Solution of Problems / xxiv

V. A 4-Hour Study Program for the SAT / xxvii

VI. Longer-Range Study Program and Helpful Steps for Using This Book / xxviii

VII. Format of the SAT / xxix

VIII. Questions Recently Asked of Dr. Gruber in Interviews / xxxi

IX. What You Can Do as a Parent to Help Your Child / xxxiv

PART 1

STRATEGY DIAGNOSTIC TEST FOR THE SAT 1

Directions for Taking the Diagnostic Test / 2

Strategy Diagnostic Test Answer Sheet / 3

Section 1: Verbal Ability / 4

Section 2: Math Ability / 12

Strategy Diagnostic Test Answer and Diagnostic Table / 18

PART 2

THE WORLD'S SHORTEST PRACTICE TEST—18 QUESTIONS TO APPROXIMATE YOUR SAT SCORE 23

Verbal (Critical Reading) / 24

Math / 25

Writing / 26

Answers / 27

Explanatory Answers / 28

PART 3

THE 101 MOST IMPORTANT MATH QUESTIONS YOU NEED TO KNOW HOW TO SOLVE 31

101 Math Questions Answer Sheet / 32

101 Math Questions Test / 34

101 Math Questions: Answers, Diagnoses, Solutions, Generalizations, and Rules / 45

101 Math Questions: Answers / 46

Basic Skills Math Diagnosis / 48

Solutions, Generalizations, and Rules / 49

PART 4

STRATEGY SECTION 59

5 General Strategies / 60

35 Easy-to-Learn Strategies / 62

How to Learn the Strategies / 62

Important Note on the Allowed Use of Calculators on the SAT / 62

Important Note on Math Questions on the SAT / 63

The Grid-Type Math Question / 63

Use of a Calculator in the Grid-Type Question / 67

19 Math Strategies / 69

16 Verbal (Critical Reading) Strategies / 119

4 Sentence Completion Strategies / 120

Critical Reading Strategies / 127

What Reading Comprehension Questions Ask / 127

Getting Involved with the Passage / 127

Introductory Passage 1 / 128

Breakdown and Underlining of the Passage / 128

How to Answer Reading Comprehension Questions Most Effectively / 129

Introductory Passage 2 / 130

Introductory Passage 3 / 132

Summary / 134

About the Double-Reading Passages / 134

9 Reading Comprehension Strategies / 135

3 Vocabulary Strategies / 150

PART 5

MINI-MATH REFRESHER 157

Algebra and Arithmetic / 158

Geometry / 161

PART 6

COMPLETE SAT MATH REFRESHER 167

Session 1—Fractions, Decimals, Percentages, etc. / 169

Fractions, Decimals, Percentages / 170

Deviations / 173

Ratios and Proportions / 174

Variations / 175

Comparison of Fractions / 176

Practice Test 1 / 178

Answer Key for Practice Test 1 / 187

Answers and Solutions for Practice Test 1 / 187

Session 2—Rate Problems / 191

Word Problem Setup / 192

Distance and Time / 194

Work / 195

Mixture / 196

Cost / 196

Practice Test 2 / 198

Answer Key for Practice Test 2 / 207

Answers and Solutions for Practice Test 2 / 207

Session 3—Area, Perimeter, and Volume Problems / 217

Area, Perimeter, and Volume / 218

Practice Test 3 / 226

Answer Key for Practice Test 3 / 235

Answers and Solutions for Practice Test 3 / 235

Session 4—Algebra Problems / 241

Algebraic Properties / 242

Fundamental Laws of Our Number System / 242

Algebraic Expressions / 243

Equations / 243

Algebra of Graphs / 245

Inequalities / 252

Exponents and Roots / 257

Practice Test 4 / 258

Answer Key for Practice Test 4 / 266

Answers and Solutions for Practice Test 4 / 266

Session 5—Geometry Problems / 271

Basic Definitions / 272

Triangles / 274

Properties of Triangles / 275

Four-Sided Figures / 278

Many-Sided Figures / 279

Circles / 279

Practice Test 5 / 282

Answer Key for Practice Test 5 / 291

Answers and Solutions for Practice Test 5 / 291

Session 6—Miscellaneous Problems / 301

Averages, Medians, and Modes / 302

Standard Deviation / 303

Properties of Integers / 304

Approximations / 306

Combinations / 307

Permutations / 308

Probability / 308

The Absolute Value Sign / 308

Functions / 309

Practice Test 6 / 310

Answer Key for Practice Test 6 / 316

Answers and Solutions for Practice Test 6 / 316

Session 7—Tables, Charts, and Graphs / 320

Charts and Graphs / 321

Tables and Charts / 321

Graphs / 322

Bar Graphs / 323

Circle Graphs / 324

Line Graphs / 325

Practice Test 7 and Solutions / 326

Session 8—Modern Math / 331

Sets / 332

Relations / 333

Solution Sets / 333

Axioms / 334

Closed Sets / 334

Mathematical Symbols / 334

Practice Test 8 and Solutions / 335

PART 7

VOCABULARY BUILDING THAT IS GUARANTEED TO RAISE YOUR SAT SCORE 343

Knowing Word Meanings Is Essential for a Higher SAT Score / 344

8 Steps to Word Power / 345

The Gruber Prefix-Root-Suffix List That Gives You the Meanings of More Than 150,000 Words / 348

Roots / 349

Prefixes / 351

Suffixes / 352

A List of SAT Words Appearing More Than Once on Actual SAT Exams / 353

The Most Important/Frequently Used SAT Words and Their Opposites / 355

The Gruber SAT 3,400-Word List / 359

100 Tests to Strengthen Your Vocabulary / 408

Answers to Vocabulary Tests / 451

PART 8

GRAMMAR AND USAGE REFRESHER 455

The Parts of Speech / 457

Clauses and Phrases / 460

The Sentence and Its Parts / 463

Verbs / 469

Nouns and Pronouns / 473

Subject-Verb Relationship / 480

Tense / 483

Verbals / 487

Mood and Voice / 491

Modifiers—Adjectives, Adjective Phrases, and Clauses / 494

Modifiers (Continued)—Adverbs, Adverbial Phrases, and Clauses / 500

Connectives / 504

Correct Usage—Choosing the Right Word / 509

Grammar and Usage Index / 513

PART 9

THE SAT WRITING TEST 517

The SAT Writing Section / 518

Content of the Writing Test / 518

The Essay on the SAT Writing Test / 519

The SAT Essay Scoring Guide / 522

The Writing Sample / 523

Sample Essays / 523

Important Tips on How to Write the Best Essay / 525

Other Types of Questions on the SAT Writing Test / 533

Identifying Errors / 533

Sample Questions with Answers / 533

Improving Sentences / 536

Sample Questions with Answers / 536

Improving Paragraphs / 540

Sample Test with Answers / 542

The Writing Questions Most Students Get Wrong / 544

PART 10

FIVE SAT PRACTICE TESTS 553

5 Important Reasons for Taking These Practice Tests / 554

10 Tips for Taking the Practice Tests / 555

SAT Practice Test 1 Introduction / 556

Answer Sheet for Practice Test 1 / 557

SAT Practice Test 1 / 563

How Did You Do on This Test? / 609

Answer Key for Practice Test 1 / 610

SAT Score Conversion Table / 615

Chart for Self-Appraisal Based on the Practice Test You Have Just Taken / 618

Explanatory Answers for Practice Test 1 / 621

What You Must Do Now to Raise Your SAT Score / 653

Answer Sheet for Practice Test 2 / 655

SAT Practice Test 2 / 661

How Did You Do on This Test? / 709

Answer Key for Practice Test 2 / 710

SAT Score Conversion Table / 715

Chart for Self-Appraisal Based on the Practice Test You Have Just Taken / 718

Explanatory Answers for Practice Test 2 / 721

What You Must Do Now to Raise Your SAT Score / 752

Answer Sheet for Practice Test 3 / 754

SAT Practice Test 3 / 760

How Did You Do on This Test? / 807

Answer Key for Practice Test 3 / 808

SAT Score Conversion Table / 813

Chart for Self-Appraisal Based on the Practice Test You Have Just Taken / 816

Explanatory Answers for Practice Test 3 / 819

What You Must Do Now to Raise Your SAT Score / 852

Answer Sheet for Practice Test 4 / 854

SAT Practice Test 4 / 860

How Did You Do on This Test? / 907

Answer Key for Practice Test 4 / 908

SAT Score Conversion Table / 913

Chart for Self-Appraisal Based on the Practice Test You Have Just Taken / 916

Explanatory Answers for Practice Test 4 / 919

What You Must Do Now to Raise Your SAT Score / 948

Answer Sheet for Practice Test 5 / 950

SAT Practice Test 5 / 956

How Did You Do on This Test? / 1003

Answer Key for Practice Test 5 / 1004

SAT Score Conversion Table / 1009

Chart for Self-Appraisal Based on the Practice Test You Have Just Taken / 1012

Explanatory Answers for Practice Test 5 / 1015

What You Must Do Now to Raise Your SAT Score / 1047

APPENDIXES 1049

Appendix A: Hot Prefixes and Roots / 1049

Appendix B: Words Commonly Mistaken for Each Other / 1054

INTRODUCTION

I. Important Facts About the SAT

What Is on the SAT?

It will include a student-written essay and a multiple-choice writing section testing students' ability to identify sentence errors, improve sentences, and improve paragraphs. Although grammar and usage will be tested, students will not be asked to define or use grammatical terms, and spelling and capitalization will not be tested. The essay section will be the first part of the test. The Math section will include arithmetic, geometry, Algebra I, and some advanced math covering topics in Algebra II, statistics, probability, and data analysis. The test will measure reasoning ability and problem-solving skills. The other parts of the test will contain some long and shorter reading passages, a long paired passage, a short paired passage, and sentence completion questions.

How Will the Test Be Scored?

There will be a range of three scores each from 200–800 for the Writing, Math, and Critical Reading sections.

How Long Will the Test Be?

The total time of the test will be 3 hours and 45 minutes.

What Verbal Background Must I Have?

The reading and vocabulary level is at the 10th- to 12th-grade level, but strategies presented in this book will help you even if you are at a lower grade level.

What Math Background Must I Have?

The Math part will test first- and second-year algebra (Algebra I and II) and geometry. However, if you use common sense, rely on just a handful of geometrical formulas, and learn the strategies and thinking skills presented in this book, you don't need to take a full course in geometry or memorize all the theorems. If you have not taken algebra, you should still be able to answer many of the math questions using the strategies presented in this book.

SAT vs. ACT: How Should Students Decide Which Test to Take?

The correlation happens to be very high for both tests; if you score well on one, you will likely score about as well on the other. They cover a lot of the same material. Both exams test grammar, math, and critical reading skills. However, the ACT includes a whole section on scientific data interpretation (the SAT has a few similar questions in its Math section); fortunately, you don't have to have a scientific background to excel on the ACT.

The ACT is more *memory*-oriented, while the SAT is more *strategy*-oriented. If you memorize quickly and retain facts well under pressure, I recommend the ACT. If you are more prone to strategizing or you like puzzles, I would take the SAT. In any event, I would check with the schools that you are applying to and find out which test they prefer.

Is Guessing Advisable?

Although there is a small penalty for wrong answers ($\frac{1}{4}$ point for 5-choice questions), in the long run, you *break even* if you guess *or* leave the answer blank. For a full explanation of why, see page 61, Strategy 3. So it really will not affect your score in the long run if you guess or leave answers out. And, if you can eliminate an incorrect choice, it is imperative that you do not leave the answer blank.

Can I Use a Calculator on the Math Portion of the Test?

Students can use a four-function, scientific, or graphing calculator. While it is possible to solve every question without the use of a calculator, it is recommended that you use a calculator if you don't immediately see a faster way to solve the problem without one.

Should I Take an Administered Actual SAT for Practice?

Yes, but only if you will learn from your mistakes by recognizing the strategies you should have used on your exam. Taking the SAT merely for its own sake is a waste of time and may in fact reinforce bad methods and habits. Note that the SAT is released to students on the *Question and Answer Service* three times a year, usually in the January, May, and October administrations. It is wise to take exams on these dates if you wish to see your mistakes and correct them.

Can I Get Back the SAT with My Answers and the Correct Ones After I Take It? How Can I Make Use of This Service?

The disclosed SAT is sent back to the student on request with an $18.00 payment. You can also order a copy of your answer sheet for an additional $25.00 fee. Very few people take advantage of this fact or use the disclosed SAT to see what mistakes they've made and what strategies they could have used on the questions.

Check in your SAT information bulletin or log on to www.collegeboard.com for the dates this Question and Answer Service is available.

A Table of What's on the SAT

Math	
Time	70 min. (Two 25 min. sections, One 20 min. section)
Content	Multiple-Choice Items Student-Produced Responses Measuring: Numbers and Operations Algebra I, II, and Functions Geometry, Statistics, Probability, and Data Analysis
Score	M 200–800
Critical Reading	
Time	70 min. (Two 25 min. sections, One 20 min. section)
Content	Sentence Completion Critical Reading: Short and Long Reading Passages with one Double Long Passage and one Double Short Passage
Score	CR 200–800
Writing	
Time	60 min. (25 min. essay, 35 min. multiple-choice exam in two sections)
Content	Multiple-Choice: Identifying Errors Improving Sentences and Paragraphs Student-Written Essay Effectively Communicating a Viewpoint, Defining and Supporting a Position
Score	W 200–800 Essay Subscore: 0–12 Multiple-Choice Subscore: 20–80

Note: There is an experimental section that does not count toward your SAT score. This section can contain any of the SAT item types (writing [multiple-choice], critical reading, or math) and can appear in any part of the test. Do not try to outguess the test maker by trying to figure out which of the sections are experimental on the actual test (believe me, you won't be able to)—treat every section as if it counts toward your SAT score.

A Table of What's on the PSAT

Math	
Time	50 min. (Two 25 min. sections)
Content	Multiple-Choice Items Student-Produced Responses Measuring: Numbers and Operations Algebra I and Functions Geometry and Measurement; Statistics, Probability, and Data Analysis
Score	20–80

Critical Reading	
Time	50 min. (Two 25 min. sections)
Content	Sentence Completion Critical Reading: Short and Long Reading Passages, with one Double Long Passage and one Double Short Passage
Score	20–80
Writing	
Time	30 min. (one section)
Content	Multiple-Choice: Identifying Errors Improving Sentences and Paragraphs Measuring: Grammar, Usage, Word Choice
Score	20–80

Should I Use Scrap Paper to Write on and to Do Calculations?

Always use your test booklet (not your answer sheet) to draw on. Many of my strategies expect you to label diagrams, draw and extend lines, circle important words and sentences, etc., so feel free to write anything in your booklet. The booklets aren't graded—just the answer sheets (see General Strategy 4, page 61).

Should I Be Familiar with the Directions to the Various Items on the SAT Before Taking the SAT?

Make sure you are completely familiar with the directions to each of the item types on the SAT—the directions for answering the Sentence Completions, the Reading, the Writing, the Regular Math, and especially the Grid-Type (see General Strategy 2, page 60).

What Should a Student Bring to the Exam on the Test Date?

You should bring a few sharpened #2 pencils with erasers and also your ID.

Bring a calculator to the test, but be aware that every math question on the SAT can be solved without a calculator; in many questions, it's actually easier not to use one.

Acceptable calculators: Graphing calculators, scientific calculators, and four-function calculators (the last is not recommended) are all permitted during testing. If you have a calculator with characters that are one inch or higher, or if your calculator has a raised display that might be visible to other test takers, you will be seated at the discretion of the test supervisor.

Unacceptable calculators: Laptops or portable/handheld computers; calculators that have a QWERTY keyboard, make noise, use an electrical outlet, or have a paper tape; electronic writing pads or stylus-driven devices; pocket organizers; and cell phone calculators will not be allowed during the test.

How Should a Student Pace Himself/Herself on the Exam? How Much Time Should One Spend on Each Question?

Calculate the time allowed for the particular section. For example, 25 minutes. Divide by the number of questions. For example, 20. That gives you an average of spending $1\frac{1}{4}$ minutes per question in this example. However, the first set of questions within an item type in a section is easier, so spend less than a minute on the first set of questions and perhaps more than a minute on the last set. With the reading passages you should give yourself only about 30 seconds a question and spend the extra time on the reading passages. Also, more difficult reading questions may take more time.

How Is the Exam Scored? Are Some Questions Worth More Points?

Each question is worth the same number of points. After getting a raw score—the number of questions right minus a penalty for wrong answers—this is equated to a "scaled" score from 200 to 800 in each of the Critical Reading, Math, and Writing sections. A scaled score of 500 in each part is considered average.

It's 3 Days Until the SAT; What Can a Student Do to Prepare?

Make sure you are completely familiar with the structure of the test (page xxix), the basic math skills needed (pages 157–165), and the basic verbal skills, such as prefixes and roots (pages 348–352). Take a few practice tests and refresh your understanding of the strategies used to answer the questions (see page xxvii for the 4-Hour Study Program).

What Percentage of SAT Study Time Should I Spend Learning Vocabulary Words?

A student should not spend too much time on this—perhaps 4 hours at most. To build your word recognition quickly, learn the Prefixes and Roots I have compiled, as well as the 3 Vocabulary Strategies. Students might also want to learn the Most Frequently Used SAT Words and Their Opposites, a list that I have developed based on research of hundreds of actual SATs.

What Is the Most Challenging Type of Question on the Exam and How Does One Attack It?

Many questions on the test, especially at the end of a section, can be challenging. You should always attack challenging questions by using a specific strategy or strategies and common sense.

What Should a Student Do to Prepare on Friday Night? Cram? Watch TV? Relax?

On Friday night, I would just refresh my knowledge of the structure of the test, some strategies, and some basic skills (verbal or math). You want to do this to keep the thinking going so that it is continual right up to the exam. Don't overdo it; just do enough so that it's somewhat continuous—this will also relieve some anxiety, so that you won't feel you are forgetting things before the exam.

The Test Is Given in One Booklet. Can a Student Skip Between Sections?

No—you cannot skip between the sections. You have to work on the section until the time is called. If you get caught skipping sections or going back to earlier sections, then you risk being asked to leave the exam.

Should a Student Answer All Easy Questions First and Save Difficult Ones for Last?

The easy questions usually appear at the beginning of the section, the medium difficulty ones in the middle, and the hard ones toward the end. So I would answer the questions as they are presented to you, and if you find you are spending more than 30 seconds on a question and not getting anywhere, go to the next question. You may, however, find that the more difficult questions toward the end are actually easy for you because you have learned the strategies in this book.

What Is the Recommended Course of Study for Those Retaking the Exam?

Try to get a copy of the exam that you took if it was a disclosed one—the disclosed ones, which you have to send a payment for, are usually given in October, January, and May. Try to learn from your mistakes by seeing what strategies you could have used to get questions right. Certainly learn the specific strategies for taking your next exam.

What Are the Most Crucial Strategies for Students?

All specific Verbal (Critical Reading) and Math Strategies are crucial, including the general test-taking strategies (described starting on page 60): guessing, writing and drawing in your test booklet, and being familiar with question-type directions. The key Reading Strategy is to know the four general types of questions that are asked in reading—main idea, inference, specific details, and tone or mood. In math, it's the translations strategy—words to numbers, drawing of lines, etc. Also make sure you know the basic math skills cold (see pages 157–165 for these rules—*make sure you know them*).

I Know There Is an Experimental Section on the Exam That Is Not Scored. How Do I Know Which Section It Is?

The SAT people have now made it so difficult to tell which is the experimental section, I would not take a chance second-guessing them and leaving it out. It will look like any of the other sections. It is true that if there are, for example, two of the same sections, such as two sections that both deal with grid questions, one of them is experimental—but you won't know which one it is. Also, if there are two sections with a long double reading passage, one of those sections is experimental, but again you won't know which one it is.

Can I Take the Test More Than Once, and If So, How Will the Scores Be Reported to the Schools of My Choice? Will All Scores Be Reported to the Schools, and How Will They Be Used?

Check with the schools to which you are applying to see how they use the reported scores, e.g., whether they average them or whether they take the highest. Ask the schools whether they see unreported scores; if they do, find out how the individual school deals with single and multiple unreported scores.

How Do Other Exams Compare with the SAT? Can I Use the Strategies and Examples in This Book for Them?

Most other exams are modeled after the SAT, so the strategies used here are definitely useful when taking them. For example, the GRE (Graduate Record Examinations, for entrance into graduate school) has questions that use the identical strategies used on the SAT. The questions are just worded at a slightly higher level. The ACT (American College Testing Program), another college entrance exam, reflects more than ever strategies that are used on the SAT. For the ACT, you can get *Gruber's Complete ACT Guide 2014*. For the GRE, you can get *Gruber's Complete GRE Guide 2014*.

How Does the Gruber Preparation Method Differ from Other Programs and SAT Books?

Many other SAT programs try to use "quick fix" methods or subscribe to memorization. So-called quick fix methods can be detrimental to effective preparation because the SAT people constantly change questions to prevent "gimmick" approaches. Rote memorization methods do not enable you to answer a variety of questions that appear in the SAT exam. In more than thirty years of experience writing preparation books for the SAT, Dr. Gruber has developed and honed the Critical Thinking Skills and Strategies that are based on all standardized tests' construction. So, while his method immediately improves your performance on the SAT, it also provides you with the confidence to tackle problems in all areas of study for the rest of your life. He remarkably enables you to be able to look at a problem or question without panic, extract something curious or useful from the problem, and move on to the next step and finally to a solution, without rushing into a wrong answer or getting lured into a wrong choice. It has been said that test taking through his methodology becomes enjoyable rather than painful.

II. The Inside Track on How SAT Questions Are Developed and How They Vary from Test to Test

When an SAT question is developed, it is based on a set of criteria and guidelines. Knowing how these guidelines work should demystify the test-making process and convince you why the strategies in this book are so critical to getting a high score.

Inherent in the SAT questions are Critical Thinking Skills, which present strategies that enable you to solve a question by the quickest method with the least amount of panic and brain-racking, and describe an elegance and excitement in problem solving. Adhering to and using the strategies (which the test makers use to develop the questions) will let you "sail" through the SAT. This is summed up in the following statement:

> *Show me the solution to a problem, and I'll solve that problem. Show me a Gruber strategy for solving the problem, and I'll solve hundreds of problems.*
>
> —Gary Gruber

Here's a sample of a set of guidelines presented for making up an SAT-type question in the Math area:

The test maker is to make up a hard math problem in the regular math multiple-choice area, which involves

(A) algebra
(B) two or more equations
(C) two or more ways to solve: one way being standard substitution, the other, faster way using the *strategy* of merely *adding* or *subtracting* equations.*

Previous examples given to the test maker for reference:

1. If $x + y = 3$, $y + z = 4$, and $z + x = 5$, find the value of $x + y + z$.

(A) 4
(B) 5
(C) 6
(D) 7
(E) 8

Solution: *Add* equations and get $2x + 2y + 2z = 12$; divide both sides of the equation by 2 and we get $x + y + z = 6$. (Answer C)

2. If $2x + y = 8$ and $x + 2y = 4$, find the value of $x - y$.

(A) 3
(B) 4
(C) 5
(D) 6
(E) 7

Solution: *Subtract* equations and get $x - y = 4$. (Answer B)

Here's an example from a recent SAT.

If $y - x = 5$ and $2y + z = 11$, find the value of $x + y + z$.

(A) 3
(B) 6
(C) 8
(D) 16
(E) 55

Solution: *Subtract* equation $y - x = 5$ from $2y + z = 11$.
We get $2y - y + z - (-x) = 11 - 5$.
So, $y + z + x = 6$. (Answer B)

* *Note:* See Math Strategy #13 on page 100.

III. What Are Critical Thinking Skills?

Critical Thinking Skills, a current buzz phrase, are generic skills for finding the most creative and effective way of solving a problem or evaluating a situation. The most effective way of solving a problem is to extract some piece of information or observe something curious from the problem and then use one or more of the specific strategies or Critical Thinking Skills (together with basic skills or information you already know) to get to the next step in the problem. This next step will catapult you toward a solution with further use of the specific strategies or thinking skills.

1. EXTRACT OR OBSERVE SOMETHING CURIOUS 2. USE SPECIFIC STRATEGIES TOGETHER WITH BASIC SKILLS

These specific strategies will enable you to "process" think rather than just be concerned with the end result; the latter usually gets you into a fast, rushed, and wrong answer. The Gruber strategies have been shown to make test takers more comfortable with problem solving and to make the process enjoyable. The skills will last a lifetime, and you will develop a passion for problem solving. These Critical Thinking Skills show that conventional "drill and practice" is a waste of time unless the practice is based on these generic thinking skills.

Here's a simple example of how these Critical Thinking Skills can be used in a math problem:

Which is greater, $7\frac{1}{7} \times 8\frac{1}{8} \times 6\frac{1}{6}$ or $8\frac{1}{8} \times 6\frac{1}{6} \times 7$?

Long and tedious way: Multiply $7\frac{1}{7} \times 8\frac{1}{8} \times 6\frac{1}{6}$ and compare it with $8\frac{1}{8} \times 6\frac{1}{6} \times 7$.

Error in doing the problem the "long way": You don't have to *calculate;* you just have to *compare,* so you need a *strategy* for *comparing* two quantities.

Critical Thinking Way:

1. *Observe:* Each expression contains $8\frac{1}{8}$ and $6\frac{1}{6}$.
2. *Use Strategy:* Since both $8\frac{1}{8}$ and $6\frac{1}{6}$ are just weighting factors, like the same quantities on both sides of a balance scale, just *cancel* them from both multiplied quantities above.
3. You are then left comparing $7\frac{1}{7}$ with 7, so the first quantity, $7\frac{1}{7}$, is greater. Thus $7\frac{1}{7} \times 8\frac{1}{8} \times 6\frac{1}{6}$ is greater than $8\frac{1}{8} \times 6\frac{1}{6} \times 7$.

Here's a simple example of how Critical Thinking Skills can be used for a Verbal problem:

If you see a word such as DELUDE in a sentence or in a reading passage, you can assume that the word DELUDE is negative and probably means "taking away from something" or "distracting," since the prefix DE- means "away from" and thus has a negative connotation. Although you may not get the exact meaning of the word (in this case the meaning is to "deceive" or "mislead"), you can see how the word may be used in the context of the sentence it appears in, and thus get the flavor or feeling of the sentence, paragraph, or sentence completion. I have researched and developed more than 50 prefixes and roots (present in this book) that can let you make use of this context strategy.

Notice that the Critical Thinking approach gives you a fail-safe and exact way to the solution without superficially trying to solve the problem or merely guessing at it. This book contains all the Critical Thinking Strategies you need to know for the SAT test.

Dr. Gruber has researched hundreds of SAT tests (thousands of SAT questions) and documented 40 Critical Thinking Strategies (all found in this book) common to every test. These strategies can be used for any Math, Verbal, or Logical Reasoning problem.

In short, you can learn how to solve a specific problem and thus find how to answer that specific problem, or you can learn a powerful strategy that will enable you to answer hundreds of problems.

IV. Multi-Level Approaches to the Solution of Problems

How a student answers a question is more important than the answer given by the student. For example, the student may have randomly guessed, the student may have used a rote and unimaginative method for solution, or the student may have used a very creative method. It seems that one should judge the student by the way he or she answers the question and not just by the answer to the question.

Example:

Question: Without using a calculator, which is greater: 355 × 356 or 354 × 357?

Case 1: **Rote Memory Approach** (a completely mechanical approach not realizing the fact that there may be a faster method that takes into account patterns or connections of the numbers in the question): The student multiplies 355 × 356, gets 126,380, and then multiplies 354 × 357 and gets 126,378.

Case 2: **Observer's Rote Approach** (an approach that makes use of a mathematical strategy that can be memorized and tried for various problems): The student does the following:
He or she divides both quantities by 354.
He or she then gets $\frac{355 \times 356}{354}$ compared with $\frac{354 \times 357}{354}$.
He or she then divides these quantities by 356 and then gets $\frac{355}{354}$ compared with $\frac{357}{356}$.
Now he or she realizes that $\frac{355}{354} = 1\frac{1}{354}$; $\frac{357}{356} = 1\frac{1}{356}$.
He or she then reasons that since the left side, $1\frac{1}{354}$, is greater than the right side, $1\frac{1}{356}$, the left side of the original quantities, 355 × 356, is greater than the right side of the original quantities, 354 × 357.

Case 3: **The Pattern Seeker's Method** (the most mathematically creative method—an approach in which the student looks for a pattern or sequence in the numbers and then is astute enough to represent the pattern or sequence in more general algebraic language to see the pattern or sequence more clearly):
Look for a pattern. Represent 355 × 356 and 354 × 357 by symbols.
Let $x = 354$.
Then $355 = x + 1$, $356 = x + 2$, $357 = x + 3$.
So $355 \times 356 = (x + 1)(x + 2)$ and $354 \times 357 = x(x + 3)$.
Multiplying the factors, we get
$355 \times 356 = x^2 + 3x + 2$ and $354 \times 357 = x^2 + 3x$.
The difference is $355 \times 356 - 354 \times 357 = x^2 + 3x + 2 - x^2 - 3x$, which is just 2.
So 355 × 356 is greater than 354 × 357 by 2.

Note: You could have also represented 355 by x. Then $356 = x + 1$; $354 = x - 1$; $357 = x + 2$. We would then get $355 \times 356 = (x)(x + 1)$ and $354 \times 357 = (x - 1)(x + 2)$. Then we would use the method above to compare the quantities.
—OR—
You could have written 354 as a and 357 as b. Then $355 = a + 1$ and $356 = b - 1$. So $355 \times 356 = (a + 1)(b - 1)$ and $354 \times 357 = ab$. Let's see what $(355 \times 356) - (354 \times 357)$ is. This is the same as $(a + 1)(b - 1) - ab$, which is $(ab + b - a - 1) - ab$, which is in turn

$b - a - 1$. Since $b - a - 1 = 357 - 354 - 1 = 2$, the quantity $355 \times 356 - 354 \times 357 = 2$, so 355×356 is greater than 354×357 by 2.

Case 4: **The Astute Observer's Approach** (the simplest approach—an approach that attempts to figure out a connection between the numbers and uses that connection to figure out the solution):
$355 \times 356 = (354 + 1) \times 356 = (354 \times 356) + 356$ and
$354 \times 357 = 354 \times (356 + 1) = (354 \times 356) + 354$
One can see that the difference is just 2.

Case 5: **The Observer's Common Relation Approach** (the approach that people use when they want to connect two items to a third to see how the two items are related):
355×356 is greater than 354×356 by 356.
354×357 is greater than 354×356 by 354.
So this means that 355×356 is greater than 354×357.

Case 6: **Scientific, Creative, and Observational Generalization Method** (a highly creative method and the most scientific method, as it spots a critical and curious aspect of the sums being equal and provides for a generalization to other problems of that nature):
Represent $354 = a$, $357 = b$, $355 = c$, and $356 = d$
We have now that (1) $a + b = c + d$
(2) $|b - a| > |d - c|$
We want to prove: $ab < dc$
Proof:
Square inequality (2): $(b - a)^2 > (d - c)^2$
Therefore: (3) $b^2 - 2ab + a^2 > d^2 - 2dc + c^2$
Multiply (3) by (-1) and this reverses the inequality sign:
$-(b^2 - 2ab + a^2) < -(d^2 - 2dc + c^2)$
or
(4) $-b^2 + 2ab - a^2 < -d^2 + 2dc - c^2$
Now square (1): $(a + b) = (c + d)$ and we get:
(5) $a^2 + 2ab + b^2 = c^2 + 2dc + d^2$
Add inequality (4) to equality (5) and we get:
$4ab < 4dc$
Divide by 4 and we get:
$\boldsymbol{ab < dc}$
The generalization is that for any positive numbers a, b, c, d when $|b - a| > |d - c|$ and $a + b = c + d$, then $ab < dc$.
This also generalizes in a geometrical setting where for two rectangles whose perimeters are the same $(2a + 2b = 2c + 2d)$, the rectangle whose absolute difference in sides $|d - c|$ is least has the greatest area.

Case 7: **Geometric and Visual Approach*** (the approach used by visual people or people who have a curious geometric bent and possess "out-of-the-box" insights):

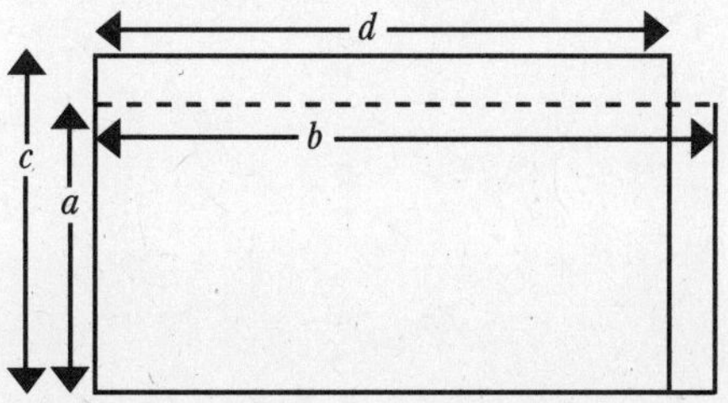

Where $a = 354$, $b = 357$, $c = 355$, and $d = 356$, we have two rectangles where the first one's length is d and width is c, and the second one's length is b (dotted line) and width is a.

**This method of solution was developed by and sent to the author from Dr. Eric Cornell, a Nobel laureate in Physics.*

Now the area of the first rectangle (dc) is equal to the area of the second (ab) minus the area of the rectangular slab, which is $(b - d)a$ plus the area of the rectangular slab $(c - a)d$. So we get: $cd = ab - (b - d)a + (c - a)d$. Since $b - d = c - a$, we get $cd = ab - (c - a)a + (c - a)d = ab + (d - a)(c - a)$.
Since $d > a$ and $c > a$, $cd > ab$. So $355 \times 356 > 354 \times 357$.

Note: Many people have thought that by multiplying units digits from one quantity and comparing that with the multiplication of the units digits from the other quantity that they'd get the answer. For example, they would multiply $5 \times 6 = 30$ from 355×356, then multiply $4 \times 7 = 28$ from 354×357, and then say that 355×356 is greater than 354×357 because $5 \times 6 > 4 \times 7$. They would be lucky. That works if the sum of units digits of the first quantity is the same as or greater than the sum of units digits of the second quantity. However, if we want to compare something like $354 \times 356 = 126{,}024$ with $352 \times 359 = 126{,}368$, that method would not work.

V. A 4-Hour Study Program for the SAT

For those who have only a few hours to spend in SAT preparation, I have worked out a *minimum* study program to get you by. It tells you what basic Math skills you need to know, what vocabulary practice you need, and the most important strategies to focus on, from the 40 in this book.

General

Study General Strategies, pages 60–61.

Critical Reading

Study the following Verbal Strategies beginning on page 120 (first 3 questions for each strategy):

Sentence Completion Strategies 1, 2, pages 120–123
Vocabulary Strategies 1, 2, and 3, pages 150–155
Reading Comprehension Strategies 1 and 2, pages 135–139

Study the Most Important/Frequently Used SAT Words and Their Opposites, page 355.

Math

Study the Mini-Math Refresher beginning on page 157.
Study the following Math Strategies beginning on page 69* (first 3 questions for each strategy):

Strategy 2, page 71
Strategy 4, page 80
Strategy 8, page 90
Strategy 12, page 98
Strategy 13, page 100
Strategy 14, page 103
Strategy 17, page 111
Strategy 18, page 114

If you have time, take Practice Test 1 starting on page 563. Do sections 1–10. Check your answers with the explanatory answers starting on page 621, and look again at the strategies and basic skills that apply to the questions you missed.

Writing

Look through the material in Part 9—The SAT Writing Test starting on page 517.

*Make sure you read pages 62–68 before you study Math Strategies.

VI. Longer-Range Study Program and Helpful Steps for Using This Book

1. Learn the 5 General Strategies for test taking on pages 60–61.
2. Take the Strategy Diagnostic SAT test on page 1 and follow the directions for diagnosis in (2).
3. Take the SAT Practice Test 1 on page 563 and score yourself according to the instructions.
4. For those problems or questions that you answered incorrectly or were uncertain of, see the explanatory answers, beginning on page 621, and make sure that you learn the strategies keyed to the questions, beginning on page 59. For complete strategy development, it is a good idea to study *all* the strategies beginning on page 59 (in the Strategy section), and learn how to do all the problems within each strategy.
5. If you are weak in basic Math skills, take the 101 Most Important Math Questions Test beginning on page 31 and follow the directions for diagnosis.
6. To see if you are making use of the strategies you've learned, you should take the World's Shortest Practice Test on page 23 and follow the directions for diagnosis.

For Vocabulary Building

7. Learn the special Latin and Greek prefixes, roots, and suffixes beginning on page 348. This will significantly build your vocabulary. You may also want to study the Hot Prefixes and Roots in Appendix A beginning on page 1049.
8. Study 100 words per day from the 3,400-Word List beginning on page 359.
9. Optional: Take the vocabulary tests beginning on page 408.
10. Study the Most Important/Frequently Used SAT Words and Their Opposites beginning on page 355.

For Math-Area Basic Skills Help

11. For the basic Math skills keyed to the questions, study the Complete SAT Math Refresher beginning on page 167, or for a quicker review, look at the Mini-Math Refresher, beginning on page 157.

For Writing Help

12. Look through Part 9—The SAT Writing test beginning on page 517. You may also wish to refresh your grammar ability by looking through the Grammar and Usage Refresher starting on page 455.

Now

13. Take the remaining four Practice SAT tests beginning on page 661, score yourself, and go over your answers with the explanatory answers. Always refer to the associated strategies and basic skills for questions you answered incorrectly or were not sure how to do.

VII. Format of the SAT

Total time for "counted" (not experimental) CRITICAL READING: 70 minutes—67 questions
Total time for "counted" (not experimental) MATH: 70 minutes—54 questions
Total time for "counted" (not experimental) WRITING (Multiple-Choice): 35 minutes—49 questions
Total time for WRITING (Essay): 25 minutes—1 or 2 prompts
Total time for experimental, pre-test items: 25 minutes—number of questions varies

Note: The following represents a form of an SAT. The SAT has many different forms, so the order of the sections may vary and the experimental section* may not be the third section as we have here. However, the first section will always be the Essay and the last section will be a 10-minute Multiple-Choice Writing section.

10 Sections of the SAT*	***Number of Questions***	***Number of Minutes***
Section 1: WRITING (Essay)	**1**	**25**
Section 2: MATH	**20**	**25**
Regular Math	20	
		5 minute break
Section 3: EXPERIMENTAL*	**varies**	**25**
Could be Writing, Critical Reading, or Math		
Section 4: CRITICAL READING	**24**	**25**
Sentence Completion	8	
1 short passage (60–125 wds)	2	
1 short passage (60–125 wds)	2	
1 passage (650–850 wds)	11–13	
OR		
Double reading passage (350–450 wds each)	11–13	
		1 minute break
Section 5: WRITING (Multiple-Choice)	**35**	**25**
Improving Sentences	11	
Identifying Errors	18	
Improving Paragraphs	6	
Section 6: MATH	**18**	**25**
Regular Math	8	
Student-Produced ("grid type")	10	
		5 minute break
Section 7: CRITICAL READING	**24**	**25**
Sentence Completions	5	
1 paired short passage (about 130 wds each)	4	
1 passage (400–550 wds)	5–7	
1 passage (550–700 wds)	8–10	

*10 Sections of the SAT**	*Number of Questions*	*Number of Minutes*
Section 8: MATH	**16**	**20**
Regular Math	16	
Section 9: CRITICAL READING	**19**	**20**
Sentence Completion	6	
Double reading passage (350–450 wds each)	13	
OR		
1 passage (650–850 wds)	13	
Section 10: WRITING (Multiple Choice)	**14**	**10**
Improving Sentences	14	
	TOTAL MINUTES = 225 ($3\frac{3}{4}$ hours)	

*The order of the sections on the actual test varies since the SAT has several different forms. There will be passages on Humanities, Social Sciences, Natural Sciences, and Narrative (fiction or nonfiction). Total number of counted reading questions will be 48.

Note: One of the sections is experimental. An experimental section does not count in your SAT score. You cannot tell which of the sections of the test is experimental.

VIII. Questions Recently Asked of Dr. Gruber in Interviews

How Did You Get Started in Test Prep? Do You Still Personally Train Students?

When I was in fifth grade, I received a 90 IQ (below average) on an IQ test. My father, who was a high school teacher at the time, was concerned, so he was able to get me an IQ test, hoping I could study it and increase my score. However, when I looked at the test, I was so fascinated at what the questions were trying to assess, I started to figure out what strategies and thinking could have been used for the questions and saw interesting patterns for what the test maker was trying to test.

I increased my IQ to 126 and then to 150. The initial experience of scoring so low on my first IQ test and being branded as "dull minded" actually sparked my fascination and research with standardized tests. I was determined to help all other students obtain my knowledge and experience so they would be able to reach their full potential, as I had. So I constantly write books, newspaper and magazine articles and columns, and software, and I personally teach students and teachers.

What Is the "Gruber Method" and How Does It Differ from Other Test Prep Methods?

The unique aspect of my method is that I provide a mechanism and process in which students internalize the use of the strategies and thinking skills I've developed and honed over thirty years. The method reinforces those strategies and skills so that students can answer questions on the SAT or ACT without panic or brain-racking. This is actually a fun process. The Gruber Method focuses on the students' patterns of thinking and how each student should best answer the questions. I have even developed a nationally syndicated test—the only one of its kind—that actually tracks a student's thinking approach for the SAT (and ACT) and directs the student to exactly which strategies are necessary for him or her to learn. Instead of just learning how to solve one problem at a time, if you learn a Gruber strategy you can use it to solve thousands of problems.

How Do You Ensure That the Practice Tests in Your Books Are Accurate Reflections of What Students Will See on the Actual Tests?

There are two processes for this. First, I am constantly critically reviewing and analyzing all the current questions and patterns on the actual tests. The second process is that I am directly in touch with the research development teams for any new items or methods used in the questions on any upcoming tests, so I am probably the only one besides the actual SAT or ACT staff who knows exactly what is being tested and why it is being tested on current and upcoming exams.

What Percentage of Test Prep Study Time Should Students Spend Learning Vocabulary Words?

Students should not spend too much time on this—perhaps 4 hours at most. The rest of the time should be invested in learning the Hot Prefixes and Roots list (page 1049).

What Advice Can You Give to Students Suffering from Test Anxiety?

I find that when students learn specific strategies, they see how a strategy can be used for a multitude of questions. And when they see a question on an actual SAT that uses the strategy, it reinforces their self-confidence and reduces their sense of panic. Students can also treat the SAT as a game by using my strategic approaches, and this also reduces panic.

SAT vs. ACT: How Should Students Decide Which Test to Take?

The correlation happens to be very high for both tests, so if you score well on one, you will score equivalently on the other. The material is about the same; for example, there is grammar on both tests. Math is about the same, except the ACT is less strategically oriented. There is reading on both tests, and those sections test about the same things. However, on the ACT there is a whole section on scientific data interpretation (the SAT has some questions on this topic in the Math section). And the ACT is more memory-oriented than the SAT. If you are more prone to using memory, I would take the ACT. If you are more prone to strategizing or if you like puzzles, I would take the SAT. In any event, I would check with the schools to which you're applying to find out which test they prefer.

What Is the Single Most Important Piece of Advice You Can Give to Students Taking the SAT or ACT?

Learn some specific strategies, which can be found in my books. This will let you think mechanically without racking your brain. When answering the questions, don't concentrate on or panic about finding the answer. Try to extract something in the question that is curious and/or will lead you to the next step in the question. Through this, you will process the question, enabling you to reach an answer.

What Is the Single Most Important Piece of Advice You Can Give to Tutors Teaching the SAT or ACT?

Make sure you learn the strategies. Teach students those strategies by using many different questions that employ each strategy, so students will see variations on how each particular strategy is used.

What Recommendations Can You Give to Tutors Who Want to Use Your Books in Their Test Prep Programs?

In sections VI and VII in the Introduction to this book, there are programs for 4 hours and longer for studying for the SAT. You can use this information to create a program for teaching the student. Always try to reinforce the strategic approach, where the student can focus on and internalize strategies so he or she can use them for multitudes of questions.

Apparently, Very Few People Know the Answer to This Important Question: When Should Students Take the SAT or ACT?

Students should find out from the school to which they are applying the preferred test dates for the SAT or ACT that they need to register for. However, if a student wants to take an SAT or ACT for practice, he or she should take it only on the test dates where the exam is disclosed, which means that the test answers and the students' answers are given back to them. For the SAT, check out the College Board's website (www.collegeboard.com), and for the ACT, check www.actstudent.org. By getting the test and the results for each question back, students can learn from their mistakes by going through the questions they got wrong and then working on the strategies and basic skills they could have used to solve those questions.

IX. What You Can Do as a Parent to Help Your Child

First, you should be aware of what the SAT tests and why it is important.

What Is the Importance of the SAT and What Background Is Required to Do Well on It?

A good score on the SAT is needed to get into a good college. Your child will need to have taken courses in geometry and algebra (elementary and intermediate). Some topics in advanced algebra are good to know, and trigonometry is not needed. Your child should know writing skills and grammar, and know how to understand what he or she is reading.

What Should My Child Know Before Taking or Practicing SAT Tests?

It is important for your child to develop a way of answering questions on the test without panic and without tediously racking his or her brain. In order to answer questions in the most efficient manner, your child needs to be sure of basic skills, including math, the meaning of certain vocabulary words, the best ways to understand a passage in reading, and grammar rules. Then he or she must learn specific strategies in the math and reading areas.

What Does My Child Need for the Test?

Your child should have a calculator—a simple one is all that is necessary. He or she should also have a watch to keep track of time.

Very Important: When Should My Child Take the SAT If He or She Takes it for Practice?

Your child should take the SAT for practice in either January, May, or October, and you should make sure you subscribe to the College Board's Question and Answer Service (see www.collegeboard.com) so you can get the test and your child's answers back for those dates.

How Should My Child Study for the Test?

Depending on when he or she will take the test, your child should brush up on his or her basic skills (math, vocabulary, writing, and reading) and learn specific strategies. Then he or she should take some practice tests. It is important that you tell your child that quality not quantity is important. So if he or she can spend two hours a day learning some strategies and taking only two sections of the test and effectively learning from his or her mistakes, that is much better than learning all the strategies or taking a whole test and superficially learning from his or her mistakes. The best way is to do a little each day, so that the strategies and methods are internalized.

What If My Child Wants to Guess at Questions?

Even though there is a penalty for a wrong answer, it is okay for your child to guess at an answer. Statistically, he or she will break even. But let your child know that if he or she learns the strategies, he or she will have a much better chance of getting the questions right and his or her guess may be more accurate by using some test-taking strategies.

How Can I Work with My Child?

You can go over some of the strategies with your child and some practice questions. You may enjoy the strategies and questions and even learn something yourself. You may want to try to answer some of the questions and see how your child does with the same questions. And then both of you should figure out the best approach or strategies for the questions. Many parents have commented to me that they never realized there were such powerful strategies for the math and verbal areas and that they wished they had learned these strategies when they were in high school.

PART 1

STRATEGY DIAGNOSTIC TEST FOR THE SAT

Take This Test to Find Out What Strategies You Don't Know

The purpose of this test is to find out *how* you approach SAT problems of different types and to reveal your understanding and command of the various strategies and Critical Thinking Skills. After checking your answers in the table at the end of the test, you will have a profile of your performance. You will know exactly what strategies you must master and where you may learn them.

Directions for Taking the Diagnostic Test

For each odd-numbered question (1, 3, 5, 7, etc.), choose the best answer. In the even-numbered questions (2, 4, 6, 8, etc.), you will be asked how you solved the preceding odd-numbered question. Make sure that you answer the even-numbered questions carefully, as your answers will determine whether or not you used the right strategy. Be completely honest in your answers to the even-numbered questions, since you do want an accurate assessment in order to be helped. *Note*: Only the odd-numbered questions are SAT-type questions that would appear on the actual exam. The even-numbered questions are for self-diagnosis purposes only.

EXAMPLE:

1. The value of $17 \times 98 + 17 \times 2 =$

(A) 1,550
(B) 1,600
(C) 1,700
(D) 1,800
(E) 1,850

(The correct answer is Choice C.)

2. How did you get your answer?

(A) I multiplied 17×98 and added that to 17×2.
(B) I approximated and found the closest match in the choices.
(C) I factored 17 to get $17(98 + 2)$.
(D) I guessed.
(E) By none of the above methods.

In question 2:

- If you chose A, you did the problem the long way unless you used a calculator.
- If you chose B, you probably approximated 98 by 100 and got 1,700.
- If you chose C, you factored out the 17 to get $17(98 + 2) = 17(100) = 1{,}700$. This was the best strategy to use.
- If you chose D, you probably didn't know how to solve the problem and just guessed.
- If you chose E, you did not use any of the methods above but used your own different method.

Note: In the even-numbered questions, you may have used a different approach from what will be described in the answer to that question. It is, however, a good idea to see if the alternate approach is described, as you may want to use that approach for solving other questions. Now turn to the next page to take the test.

Strategy Diagnostic Test Answer Sheet

SECTION 1

Verbal Ability

1 Ⓐ Ⓑ Ⓒ Ⓓ Ⓔ	15 Ⓐ Ⓑ Ⓒ Ⓓ Ⓔ	29 Ⓐ Ⓑ Ⓒ Ⓓ Ⓔ	43 Ⓐ Ⓑ Ⓒ Ⓓ Ⓔ
2 Ⓐ Ⓑ Ⓒ Ⓓ Ⓔ	16 Ⓐ Ⓑ Ⓒ Ⓓ Ⓔ	30 Ⓐ Ⓑ Ⓒ Ⓓ Ⓔ	44 Ⓐ Ⓑ Ⓒ Ⓓ Ⓔ
3 Ⓐ Ⓑ Ⓒ Ⓓ Ⓔ	17 Ⓐ Ⓑ Ⓒ Ⓓ Ⓔ	31 Ⓐ Ⓑ Ⓒ Ⓓ Ⓔ	45 Ⓐ Ⓑ Ⓒ Ⓓ Ⓔ
4 Ⓐ Ⓑ Ⓒ Ⓓ Ⓔ	18 Ⓐ Ⓑ Ⓒ Ⓓ Ⓔ	32 Ⓐ Ⓑ Ⓒ Ⓓ Ⓔ	46 Ⓐ Ⓑ Ⓒ Ⓓ Ⓔ
5 Ⓐ Ⓑ Ⓒ Ⓓ Ⓔ	19 Ⓐ Ⓑ Ⓒ Ⓓ Ⓔ	33 Ⓐ Ⓑ Ⓒ Ⓓ Ⓔ	47 Ⓐ Ⓑ Ⓒ Ⓓ Ⓔ
6 Ⓐ Ⓑ Ⓒ Ⓓ Ⓔ	20 Ⓐ Ⓑ Ⓒ Ⓓ Ⓔ	34 Ⓐ Ⓑ Ⓒ Ⓓ Ⓔ	48 Ⓐ Ⓑ Ⓒ Ⓓ Ⓔ
7 Ⓐ Ⓑ Ⓒ Ⓓ Ⓔ	21 Ⓐ Ⓑ Ⓒ Ⓓ Ⓔ	35 Ⓐ Ⓑ Ⓒ Ⓓ Ⓔ	49 Ⓐ Ⓑ Ⓒ Ⓓ Ⓔ
8 Ⓐ Ⓑ Ⓒ Ⓓ Ⓔ	22 Ⓐ Ⓑ Ⓒ Ⓓ Ⓔ	36 Ⓐ Ⓑ Ⓒ Ⓓ Ⓔ	50 Ⓐ Ⓑ Ⓒ Ⓓ Ⓔ
9 Ⓐ Ⓑ Ⓒ Ⓓ Ⓔ	23 Ⓐ Ⓑ Ⓒ Ⓓ Ⓔ	37 Ⓐ Ⓑ Ⓒ Ⓓ Ⓔ	51 Ⓐ Ⓑ Ⓒ Ⓓ Ⓔ
10 Ⓐ Ⓑ Ⓒ Ⓓ Ⓔ	24 Ⓐ Ⓑ Ⓒ Ⓓ Ⓔ	38 Ⓐ Ⓑ Ⓒ Ⓓ Ⓔ	52 Ⓐ Ⓑ Ⓒ Ⓓ Ⓔ
11 Ⓐ Ⓑ Ⓒ Ⓓ Ⓔ	25 Ⓐ Ⓑ Ⓒ Ⓓ Ⓔ	39 Ⓐ Ⓑ Ⓒ Ⓓ Ⓔ	53 Ⓐ Ⓑ Ⓒ Ⓓ Ⓔ
12 Ⓐ Ⓑ Ⓒ Ⓓ Ⓔ	26 Ⓐ Ⓑ Ⓒ Ⓓ Ⓔ	40 Ⓐ Ⓑ Ⓒ Ⓓ Ⓔ	54 Ⓐ Ⓑ Ⓒ Ⓓ Ⓔ
13 Ⓐ Ⓑ Ⓒ Ⓓ Ⓔ	27 Ⓐ Ⓑ Ⓒ Ⓓ Ⓔ	41 Ⓐ Ⓑ Ⓒ Ⓓ Ⓔ	55 Ⓐ Ⓑ Ⓒ Ⓓ Ⓔ
14 Ⓐ Ⓑ Ⓒ Ⓓ Ⓔ	28 Ⓐ Ⓑ Ⓒ Ⓓ Ⓔ	42 Ⓐ Ⓑ Ⓒ Ⓓ Ⓔ	56 Ⓐ Ⓑ Ⓒ Ⓓ Ⓔ

SECTION 2

Math Ability

1 Ⓐ Ⓑ Ⓒ Ⓓ Ⓔ	10 Ⓐ Ⓑ Ⓒ Ⓓ Ⓔ	19 Ⓐ Ⓑ Ⓒ Ⓓ Ⓔ	28 Ⓐ Ⓑ Ⓒ Ⓓ Ⓔ
2 Ⓐ Ⓑ Ⓒ Ⓓ Ⓔ	11 Ⓐ Ⓑ Ⓒ Ⓓ Ⓔ	20 Ⓐ Ⓑ Ⓒ Ⓓ Ⓔ	29 Ⓐ Ⓑ Ⓒ Ⓓ Ⓔ
3 Ⓐ Ⓑ Ⓒ Ⓓ Ⓔ	12 Ⓐ Ⓑ Ⓒ Ⓓ Ⓔ	21 Ⓐ Ⓑ Ⓒ Ⓓ Ⓔ	30 Ⓐ Ⓑ Ⓒ Ⓓ Ⓔ
4 Ⓐ Ⓑ Ⓒ Ⓓ Ⓔ	13 Ⓐ Ⓑ Ⓒ Ⓓ Ⓔ	22 Ⓐ Ⓑ Ⓒ Ⓓ Ⓔ	31 Ⓐ Ⓑ Ⓒ Ⓓ Ⓔ
5 Ⓐ Ⓑ Ⓒ Ⓓ Ⓔ	14 Ⓐ Ⓑ Ⓒ Ⓓ Ⓔ	23 Ⓐ Ⓑ Ⓒ Ⓓ Ⓔ	32 Ⓐ Ⓑ Ⓒ Ⓓ Ⓔ
6 Ⓐ Ⓑ Ⓒ Ⓓ Ⓔ	15 Ⓐ Ⓑ Ⓒ Ⓓ Ⓔ	24 Ⓐ Ⓑ Ⓒ Ⓓ Ⓔ	33 Ⓐ Ⓑ Ⓒ Ⓓ Ⓔ
7 Ⓐ Ⓑ Ⓒ Ⓓ Ⓔ	16 Ⓐ Ⓑ Ⓒ Ⓓ Ⓔ	25 Ⓐ Ⓑ Ⓒ Ⓓ Ⓔ	34 Ⓐ Ⓑ Ⓒ Ⓓ Ⓔ
8 Ⓐ Ⓑ Ⓒ Ⓓ Ⓔ	17 Ⓐ Ⓑ Ⓒ Ⓓ Ⓔ	26 Ⓐ Ⓑ Ⓒ Ⓓ Ⓔ	35 Ⓐ Ⓑ Ⓒ Ⓓ Ⓔ
9 Ⓐ Ⓑ Ⓒ Ⓓ Ⓔ	18 Ⓐ Ⓑ Ⓒ Ⓓ Ⓔ	27 Ⓐ Ⓑ Ⓒ Ⓓ Ⓔ	36 Ⓐ Ⓑ Ⓒ Ⓓ Ⓔ

Section 1: Verbal Ability

Each of the following sentences has one or two blanks, each blank indicating that something has been omitted. Beneath the sentence are five lettered words or sets of words. Choose the word or set of words that *best* fits the meaning of the sentence as a whole.

EXAMPLE:

Although its publicity has been ________, the film itself is intelligent, well-acted, handsomely produced, and altogether ________.

(A) tasteless...respectable
(B) extensive...moderate
(C) sophisticated...amateur
(D) risqué...crude
(E) perfect...spectacular

● Ⓑ Ⓒ Ⓓ Ⓔ

1. He believed that because there is serious unemployment in our auto industry, we should not ________ foreign cars.

(A) build
(B) repair
(C) review
(D) import
(E) consolidate

2. How did you get your answer?

(A) I tried the word from each choice in the blank and came up with the best answer.
(B) I chose a word from the choices that "sounded good" but that I am really not sure is correct.
(C) I tried to figure out, *before* looking at the choices, what word would fit into the blank. Then I matched that word with the choices.
(D) I guessed.
(E) None of these.

3. The salesmen in that clothing store are so ________ that it is impossible to even look at a garment without being ________ by their efforts to convince you to purchase.

(A) offensive...considerate
(B) persistent...irritated
(C) extensive...induced
(D) immune...aided
(E) intriguing...evaluated

4. How did you get your answer?

(A) I tried each choice (two words at a time) in the blanks to see which made for the best sentence.
(B) I tried to see what words I could come up with for the blanks *before* looking at the choices.
(C) I tried the first word from each of the choices in the first blank in the sentence to see which made the most sense. Then I eliminated the choices whose first words didn't make sense in the sentence. Finally, I tried both words in the remaining choices to further eliminate incorrect choices.
(D) I guessed.
(E) None of these.

5. Many buildings with historical significance are now being ______ instead of being torn down.
(A) built
(B) forgotten
(C) destroyed
(D) praised
(E) repaired

6. How did you get your answer?
(A) I tried each of the choices in the blank.
(B) I tried to find my own word that would fit the blank *before* looking at the choices. Then I matched one of the choices with my word.
(C) I looked for a word that meant the opposite of "being torn down."
(D) I guessed.
(E) None of these.

7. Being ______ person, he insisted at the conference that when he spoke he was not to be interrupted.
(A) a successful
(B) a delightful
(C) a headstrong
(D) an understanding
(E) a solitary

8. How did you get your answer?
(A) I tried all the choices in the sentence and selected the best one.
(B) I realized, from the word *Being* and from the phrase after the comma, that there was a connection between the two parts of the sentence.
(C) I looked for the most difficult-sounding word.
(D) I guessed.
(E) None of these.

9. In spite of the ______ of her presentation, many people were ______ with the speaker's concepts and ideas.
(A) interest...enthralled
(B) power...taken
(C) intensity...shocked
(D) greatness...gratified
(E) strength...bored

10. How did you get your answer?
(A) I tried both words from each choice in the blanks to see which choice made the sentence sound best.
(B) I tried the first word from each choice in the first blank of the sentence to eliminate choices. Then I tried both words from the remaining choices to further eliminate choices.
(C) I realized that the words *in spite of* would create an opposition or contrast between the two parts of the sentence and therefore looked for words in the choices that were opposites.
(D) I guessed.
(E) None of these.

11. Richard Wagner was frequently intolerant; moreover, his strange behavior caused most of his acquaintances to ______ the composer whenever possible.
(A) contradict
(B) interrogate
(C) shun
(D) revere
(E) tolerate

12. How did you get your answer?
(A) I tried all the choices in the blank and selected the best one.
(B) I realized that the word *moreover* indicated support, so I looked for a choice that would represent a *support* of what was in the first part of the sentence.
(C) I tried to find my own word to fit the blank. Then I matched that word with a word in one of the choices.
(D) I guessed.
(E) None of these.

Each of the following questions consists of a word in capital letters, followed by five lettered words or phrases. Choose the word or phrase that is most nearly *opposite* in meaning to the word in capital letters. Since some of the questions require you to distinguish fine shades of meaning, consider all the choices before deciding which is best.

EXAMPLE:

GOOD: (A) sour (B) bad (C) red
(D) hot (E) ugly

Ⓐ ● Ⓒ Ⓓ Ⓔ

Note: Although antonyms are no longer a part of the SAT, we are still testing vocabulary through antonyms on this particular test, since it is important for you to develop vocabulary strategies for the Sentence Completions and Reading Comprehension parts of the SAT.

13. TENACIOUS:

(A) changing
(B) stupid
(C) unconscious
(D) poor
(E) antagonistic

14. How did you get your answer?

(A) I knew the meaning of the word TENACIOUS.
(B) I knew what the root TEN meant and looked for the opposite of that root.
(C) I did not know what TENACIOUS meant but knew a word that sounded like TENACIOUS.
(D) I guessed.
(E) None of these.

15. PROFICIENT:

(A) antiseptic
(B) unwilling
(C) inconsiderate
(D) retarded
(E) awkward

16. How did you get your answer?

(A) I knew what the prefix PRO meant and used it to figure out the capitalized word, but I didn't use any root of PROFICIENT.
(B) I used the meaning of the prefix PRO and the meaning of the root FIC to figure out the meaning of the word PROFICIENT.
(C) I knew from memory what the word PROFICIENT meant.
(D) I guessed.
(E) None of these.

17. DELUDE:

(A) include
(B) guide
(C) reply
(D) upgrade
(E) welcome

18. How did you get your answer?

(A) I knew what the prefix DE meant and used it to figure out the meaning of the word DELUDE, but I didn't use any root of DELUDE.
(B) I used the meaning of the prefix DE and the meaning of the root LUD to figure out the meaning of the word DELUDE.
(C) I knew from memory what the word DELUDE meant.
(D) I guessed.
(E) None of these.

19. POTENT:

(A) imposing
(B) pertinent
(C) feeble
(D) comparable
(E) frantic

20. How did you get your answer?

(A) I knew what the capitalized word meant.
(B) I knew a word or part of a word that sounded the same as POTENT or had a close association with the word POTENT.
(C) I knew a prefix or root of the capitalized word, which gave me a clue to the meaning of the word.
(D) I knew from a part of the capitalized word that the word had a negative or positive association. Thus, I selected a choice that was opposite in flavor (positive or negative).
(E) None of these.

21. RECEDE:

(A) accede
(B) settle
(C) surrender
(D) advance
(E) reform

22. How did you get your answer?

(A) I found a word opposite in meaning to the word RECEDE, *without* looking at the choices. Then I matched my word with the choices.
(B) I used prefixes and/or roots to get the meaning of the word RECEDE.
(C) I looked at the choices to see which word was opposite to RECEDE. I *did not* try first to get my own word that was opposite to the meaning of RECEDE, as in Choice A.
(D) I guessed.
(E) None of these.

23. THERMAL:

(A) improving
(B) possible
(C) beginning
(D) reduced
(E) frigid

24. How did you get your answer?

(A) I knew what the capitalized word meant.
(B) I knew a word or part of a word that sounded the same as THERMAL or had a close association with the word THERMAL.
(C) I knew a prefix or root of the capitalized word, which gave me a clue to the meaning of the word.
(D) I knew from a part of the capitalized word that the word had a negative or positive association. Thus, I selected a choice that was opposite in flavor (positive or negative).
(E) None of these.

25. SLOTHFUL:

(A) permanent
(B) ambitious
(C) average
(D) truthful
(E) plentiful

26. How did you get your answer?

(A) I knew what the capitalized word meant.
(B) I knew a word or part of a word that sounded the same as SLOTH or had a close association with the word SLOTH.
(C) I knew a prefix or root of the capitalized word, which gave me a clue to the meaning of the word.
(D) I knew from a part of the capitalized word that the word had a negative or positive association. Thus, I selected a choice that was opposite in flavor (positive or negative).
(E) None of these.

27. MUNIFICENCE:

(A) disloyalty
(B) stinginess
(C) dispersion
(D) simplicity
(E) vehemence

28. How did you get your answer?

(A) I knew what the capitalized word meant.
(B) I knew a word or part of a word that sounded the same as MUNIFICENCE or had a close association with the word MUNIFICENCE.
(C) I knew a prefix or root of the capitalized word, which gave me a clue to the meaning of the word.
(D) I knew from a part of the capitalized word that the word had a negative or positive association. Thus, I selected a choice that was opposite in flavor (positive or negative).
(E) None of these.

29. FORTITUDE:

(A) timidity
(B) conservatism
(C) placidity
(D) laxness
(E) ambition

30. How did you get your answer?

(A) I knew what the capitalized word meant.
(B) I knew a word or part of a word that sounded the same as FORTITUDE or had a close association with the word FORTITUDE.
(C) I knew a prefix or root of the capitalized word, which gave me a clue to the meaning of the word.
(D) I knew from a part of the capitalized word that the word had a negative or positive association. Thus, I selected a choice that was opposite in flavor (positive or negative).
(E) None of these.

31. DETRIMENT:

(A) recurrence
(B) disclosure
(C) resemblance
(D) enhancement
(E) postponement

32. How did you get your answer?

(A) I knew what the capitalized word meant.
(B) I knew a word or part of a word that sounded the same as DETRIMENT or had a close association with the word DETRIMENT.
(C) I knew a prefix or root of the capitalized word, which gave me a clue to the meaning of the word.
(D) I knew from a part of the capitalized word that the word had a negative or positive association. Thus, I selected a choice that was opposite in flavor (positive or negative).
(E) None of these.

33. CIRCUMSPECT:

(A) suspicious
(B) overbearing
(C) listless
(D) determined
(E) careless

34. How did you get your answer?

(A) I knew what the capitalized word meant.
(B) I knew a word or part of a word that sounded the same as CIRCUMSPECT or had a close association with the word CIRCUMSPECT.
(C) I knew a prefix or root of the capitalized word, which gave me a clue to the meaning of the word.
(D) I knew from a part of the capitalized word that the word had a negative or positive association. Thus, I selected a choice that was opposite in flavor (positive or negative).
(E) None of these.

35. LUCID:

(A) underlying
(B) complex
(C) luxurious
(D) tight
(E) general

36. How did you get your answer?

(A) I knew what the capitalized word meant.
(B) I knew a word or part of a word that sounded the same as LUCID or had a close association with the word LUCID.
(C) I knew a prefix or root of the capitalized word, which gave me a clue to the meaning of the word.
(D) I knew from a part of the capitalized word that the word had a negative or positive association. Thus, I selected a choice that was opposite in flavor (positive or negative).
(E) None of these.

Each of the following passages is followed by questions based on its content. Answer all questions following a passage on the basis of what is *stated* or *implied* in that passage.

She walked along the river until a policeman stopped her. It was one o'clock, he said. Not the best time to be walking alone by the side of a half-frozen river. He smiled at her, then offered to walk her home. It was the first day of the new year, 1946, eight and a half months after the British tanks had rumbled into Bergen-Belsen.

That February, my mother turned twenty-six. It was difficult for strangers to believe that she had ever been a concentration camp inmate. Her face was smooth and round. She wore lipstick and applied mascara to her large dark eyes. She dressed fashionably. But when she looked into the mirror in the mornings before leaving for work, my mother saw a shell, a mannequin who moved and spoke but who bore only a superficial resemblance to her real self. The people closest to her had vanished. She had no proof that they were truly dead. No eyewitnesses had survived to vouch for her husband's death. There was no one living who had seen her parents die. The lack of confirmation haunted her. At night before she went to sleep and during the day as she stood pinning dresses she wondered if, by some chance, her parents had gotten past the Germans or had crawled out of the mass grave into which they had been shot and were living, old and helpless, somewhere in Poland. What if only one of them had died? What if they had survived and had died of cold or hunger after she had been liberated, while she was in Celle* dancing with British officers?

She did not talk to anyone about these things. No one, she thought, wanted to hear them. She woke up in the morning, went to work, bought groceries, went to the Jewish Community Center and to the housing office like a robot.

*Celle is a small town in Germany.

37. The policeman stopped the author's mother from walking along the river because

(A) the river was dangerous
(B) it was the wrong time of day
(C) it was still wartime
(D) it was too cold
(E) she looked suspicious

38. Which part of the passage gives you the best clue for getting the right answer?

(A) Line 2: "It was one o'clock, he said."
(B) Lines 2–3: "It was one o'clock, he said. Not the best time to be walking alone."
(C) Lines 2–3: "It was one o'clock, he said. Not the best time to be walking alone by the side of a half-frozen river."
(D) None of these.
(E) I don't know.

39. The author states that his mother thought about her parents when she

(A) walked along the river
(B) thought about death
(C) danced with the officers
(D) arose in the morning
(E) was at work

40. Which part of the passage gives you the best clue for getting the right answer?

(A) Line 19: "At night before she went to sleep..."
(B) Lines 19–20: "...and during the day as she stood pinning dresses she wondered..."
(C) Lines 11–12: "But when she looked into the mirror in the mornings..."
(D) Lines 24–26: "What if they had survived and died of cold...while she was...dancing with British officers?"
(E) I don't know.

41. When the author mentions his mother's dancing with the British officers, he implies that his mother

(A) compared her dancing to the suffering of her parents
(B) had clearly put her troubles behind her
(C) felt it was her duty to dance with them
(D) felt guilty about dancing
(E) regained the self-confidence she once had

42. Which words expressed in the passage lead us to the right answer?

(A) Line 24: "had survived"
(B) Lines 24–25: "had died of cold or hunger"
(C) Line 21: "gotten past the Germans"
(D) Line 30: "like a robot"
(E) I don't know.

That one citizen is as good as another is a favorite American axiom, supposed to express the very essence of our Constitution and way of life. But just what do we mean when we utter that platitude? One surgeon is not as good as another. One plumber is not as good as another. We soon become aware of this when we require the attention of either. Yet in political and economic matters we appear to have reached a point where knowledge and specialized training count for very little. A newspaper reporter is sent out on the street to collect the views of various passersby on such a question as "Should the United States defend El Salvador?" The answer of the barfly who doesn't even know where the country is located, or that it is a country, is quoted in the next edition just as solemnly as that of the college teacher of history. With the basic tenets of democracy—that all men are born free and equal and are entitled to life, liberty, and the pursuit of happiness—no decent American can possibly take issue. But that the opinion of one citizen on a technical subject is just as authoritative as that of another is manifestly absurd. And to accept the opinions of all comers as having the same value is surely to encourage a cult of mediocrity.

43. Which phrase best expresses the main idea of this passage?

(A) the myth of equality
(B) a distinction about equality
(C) the essence of the Constitution
(D) a technical subject
(E) knowledge and specialized training

44. Which is the best title for this passage?

(A) "Equality—for Everyone, for Every Situation?"
(B) "Dangers of Opinion and Knowledge"
(C) "The American Syndrome"
(D) "Freedom and Equality"
(E) I don't know.

45. The author most probably included the example of the question on El Salvador (lines 11–12) in order to

(A) move the reader to rage
(B) show that he is opposed to opinion sampling
(C) show that he has thoroughly researched his project
(D) explain the kind of opinion sampling he objects to
(E) provide a humorous but temporary diversion from his main point

46. The distinction between a "barfly" and a college teacher (lines 12–15) is that

(A) one is stupid, the other is not
(B) one is learned, the other is not
(C) one is anti-American, the other is not
(D) one is pro-El Salvadoran, the other is not
(E) I don't know.

47. The author would be most likely to agree that

(A) some men are born to be masters; others are born to be servants
(B) the Constitution has little relevance for today's world
(C) one should never express an opinion on a specialized subject unless he is an expert in that subject
(D) every opinion should be treated equally
(E) all opinions should not be given equal weight

48. Which lines give the best clue to the answer to this question?

(A) Lines 3–5
(B) Lines 4–6
(C) Lines 14–17
(D) Lines 18–22
(E) I don't know.

Mist continues to obscure the horizon, but above us the sky is suddenly awash with lavender light. At once the geese respond. Now, as well as their cries, a beating roar rolls across the water as if five thousand housewives have taken it into their heads to shake out blankets all at one time. Ten thousand housewives. It keeps up—the invisible rhythmic beating of all those goose wings—for what seems a long time. Even Lonnie is held motionless with suspense.

Then the geese begin to rise. One, two, three hundred—then a thousand at a time—in long horizontal lines that unfurl like pennants across the sky. The horizon actually darkens as they pass. It goes on and on like that, flock after flock, for three or four minutes, each new contingent announcing its ascent with an accelerating roar of cries and wingbeats. Then gradually the intervals between flights become longer. I think the spectacle is over, until yet another flock lifts up, following the others in a gradual turn toward the northeastern quadrant of the refuge.

Finally the sun emerges from the mist; the mist itself thins a little, uncovering the black line of willows on the other side of the wildlife preserve. I remember to close my mouth—which has been open for some time—and inadvertently shut two or three mosquitoes inside. Only a few straggling geese oar their way across the sun's red surface. Lonnie wears an exasperated, proprietary expression, as if he had produced and directed the show himself and had just received a bad review. "It would have been better with more light," he says; "I can't always guarantee just when they'll start moving." I assure him I thought it was a fantastic sight. "Well," he rumbles, "I guess it wasn't too bad."

49. In the descriptive phrase "shake out blankets all at one time" (line 5), the author is appealing chiefly to the reader's

(A) background
(B) sight
(C) emotions
(D) thoughts
(E) hearing

50. Which words preceding the descriptive phrase "shake out blankets all at one time" (line 5) give us a clue to the correct answer to the previous question (question 49)?

(A) "into their heads"
(B) "lavender light"
(C) "across the water"
(D) "a beating roar"
(E) I don't know.

51. The mood created by the author is one of

(A) tranquility
(B) excitement
(C) sadness
(D) bewilderment
(E) unconcern

52. Which word in the passage is most closely associated with the correct answer?

(A) mist
(B) spectacle
(C) geese
(D) refuge
(E) I don't know.

53. The main idea expressed by the author about the geese is that they

(A) are spectacular to watch
(B) are unpredictable
(C) disturb the environment
(D) produce a lot of noise
(E) fly in large flocks

54. Which line(s) gives us a clue to the correct answer?

(A) Line 1
(B) Lines 16–17
(C) Line 19
(D) Line 30
(E) I don't know.

55. Judging from the passage, the reader can conclude that

(A) the speaker dislikes nature's inconveniences
(B) the geese's timing is predictable
(C) Lonnie has had the experience before
(D) both observers are hunters
(E) the author and Lonnie are the same person

56. Which gives us a clue to the right answer?

(A) Lines 9–10
(B) Line 19
(C) Lines 21–22
(D) Lines 28–29
(E) I don't know.

Section 2: Math Ability

Directions: For this section, solve each problem and decide which is the best of the choices given. Fill in the corresponding circle on the answer sheet. You may use any available space for scratchwork.

Notes:

1. The use of a calculator is permitted.
2. All numbers used are real numbers.
3. Figures that accompany problems in this test are intended to provide information useful in solving the problems. They are drawn as accurately as possible EXCEPT when it is stated in a specific problem that the figure is not drawn to scale. All figures lie in a plane unless otherwise indicated.
4. Unless otherwise specified, the domain of any function *f* is assumed to be the set of all real numbers *x* for which *f*(*x*) is a real number.

REFERENCE INFORMATION

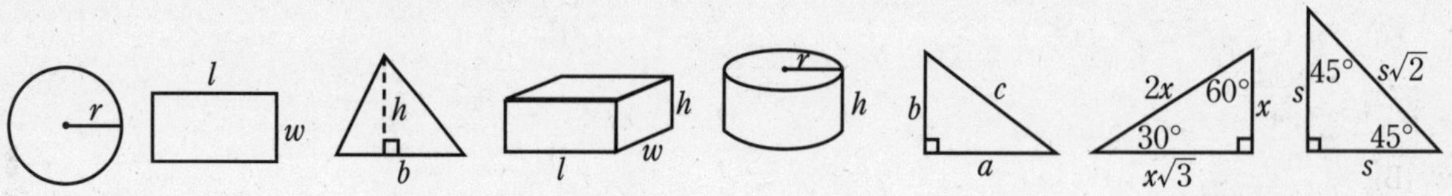

$A = \pi r^2$ $C = 2\pi r$ $A = lw$ $A = \frac{1}{2}bh$ $V = lwh$ $V = \pi r^2 h$ $c^2 = a^2 + b^2$ *Special Right Triangles*

The number of degrees of arc in a circle is 360.
The sum of the measures in degrees of the angles of a triangle is 180.

1. If $P \times \frac{11}{14} = \frac{11}{14} \times \frac{8}{9}$, then $P =$

(A) $\frac{8}{9}$

(B) $\frac{9}{8}$

(C) 8

(D) 11

(E) 14

2. How did you get your answer?

(A) I multiplied $\frac{11}{14}$ by $\frac{8}{9}$, *reducing first.*

(B) I multiplied 11×8 and then divided the product by 14×9.

(C) I canceled $\frac{11}{14}$ from both sides of the equals sign.

(D) I guessed.

(E) None of these.

3. Sarah is twice as old as John. Six years ago, Sarah was 4 times as old as John was then. How old is John now?

(A) 3
(B) 9
(C) 18
(D) 20
(E) Cannot be determined.

4. How did you get your answer?

(A) I substituted S for *Sarah,* = for *is,* and J for *John* in the first sentence of the problem. Then I translated the second sentence into mathematical terms also.
(B) I tried specific numbers for *Sarah* and/or *John.*
(C) I racked my brain to figure out the ages but didn't write any equations down.
(D) I guessed.
(E) None of these.

5. 200 is what percent of 20?

(A) $\frac{1}{10}$
(B) 10
(C) 100
(D) 1,000
(E) 10,000

6. How did you get your answer?

(A) I translated *is* to =, *what* to a variable, *of* to ×, etc. Then I was able to set up an equation.
(B) I just divided the two numbers and multiplied by 100 to get the percent.
(C) I tried to remember how to work with *is-of* problems, putting the *of* over *is* or the *is* over *of.*
(D) I guessed.
(E) None of these.

7. In the diagram below, ΔXYZ has been inscribed in a circle. If the circle encloses an area of 64, and the area of ΔXYZ is 15, then what is the area of the shaded region?

(A) 25
(B) 36
(C) 49
(D) 79
(E) Cannot be determined.

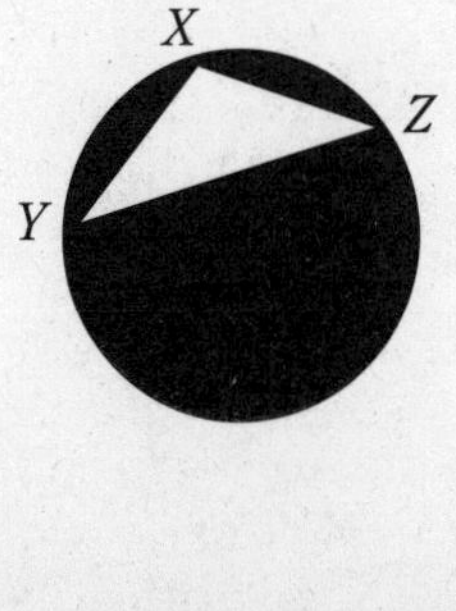

8. How did you get your answer?

(A) I tried to calculate the area of the circle and the area of the triangle.
(B) I used a special triangle or tried different triangles whose area was 15.
(C) I subtracted 15 from 64.
(D) I guessed.
(E) None of these.

9. $66^2 + 2(34)(66) + 34^2 =$

(A) 4,730
(B) 5,000
(C) 9,860
(D) 9,950
(E) 10,000

10. How did you get your answer?

(A) I multiplied 66 × 66, 2 × 34 × 66, and 34 × 34 and added the results.
(B) I approximated a solution.
(C) I noticed that $66^2 + 2(34)(66) + 34^2$ had the form of $a^2 + 2ab + b^2$ and set the form equal to $(a + b)^2$.
(D) I guessed.
(E) None of these.

11. The average height of three students is 68 inches. If two of the students have heights of 70 inches and 72 inches respectively, then what is the height (in inches) of the third student?

(A) 60
(B) 62
(C) 64
(D) 65
(E) 66

12. How did you get your answer?

(A) I used the following equation:

$$(68 + 2) + (68 + 4) + x = 68 + 68 + 68$$

Then I got:
$68 + 68 + (x + 6) = 68 + 68 + 68$, and crossed off the two 68s on both sides of the equation to come up with $x + 6 = 68$.
(B) I was able to eliminate the incorrect choices without figuring out a complete solution.
(C) I got the equation $\frac{(70 + 72 + x)}{3} = 68$, then solved for x.
(D) I guessed.
(E) None of these.

13. If $0 < x < 1$, then which of the following must be true?

I. $2x < 2$
II. $x - 1 < 0$
III. $x^2 < x$

(A) I only
(B) II only
(C) I and II only
(D) II and III only
(E) I, II, and III

14. How did you get your answer?

(A) I plugged in only one number for x in I, II, and III.
(B) I plugged in more than one number for x and tried I, II, and III using each set of numbers.
(C) I used the fact that $0 < x$ and $x < 1$ and manipulated those inequalities in I, II, and III.
(D) I guessed.
(E) None of these.

15. The sum of the cubes of any two consecutive positive integers is always

(A) an odd integer
(B) an even integer
(C) the cube of an integer
(D) the square of an integer
(E) the product of an integer and 3

16. How did you get your answer?

(A) I translated the statement into the form $x^3 + (x + 1)^3 =$ _______ and tried to see what I would get.
(B) I tried numbers like 1 and 2 for the consecutive integers. Then I calculated the sum of the cubes of those numbers. I was able to eliminate some choices and then tried some other numbers for the consecutive integers to eliminate more choices.
(C) I said, of two consecutive positive integers, one is even and therefore its cube is even. The other integer is odd, therefore its cube is odd. An odd + an even is an odd.
(D) I guessed.
(E) None of these.

17. If p is a positive integer, which *could* be an odd integer?

(A) $2p + 2$
(B) $p^3 - p$
(C) $p^2 + p$
(D) $p^2 - p$
(E) $7p - 3$

18. How did you get your answer?

(A) I plugged in a number or numbers for p and started testing all the choices, *starting with Choice A.*
(B) I plugged in a number or numbers for p in each of the choices, *starting with Choice E.*
(C) I looked at Choice E first to see if $7p - 3$ had the form of an even or odd integer.
(D) I guessed.
(E) None of these.

19. In this figure, two points, B and C, are placed to the right of point A such that $4AB = 3AC$. The value of $\frac{BC}{AB}$

(A) equals $\frac{1}{3}$
(B) equals $\frac{2}{3}$
(C) equals $\frac{3}{2}$
(D) equals 3
(E) Cannot be determined.

20. How did you get your answer?

(A) I drew points B and C on the line and labeled AB as a and BC as b and then worked with a and b.
(B) I substituted numbers for AB and AC.
(C) I drew points B and C on the line and worked with equations involving BC and AB.
(D) I guessed.
(E) None of these.

21. A man rode a bicycle a straight distance at a speed of 10 miles per hour. He came back the same way, traveling the same distance at a speed of 20 miles per hour. What was the man's total number of miles for the trip back and forth if his total traveling time was one hour?

(A) 15
(B) $13\frac{1}{3}$
(C) $7\frac{1}{2}$
(D) $6\frac{2}{3}$
(E) $6\frac{1}{3}$

22. How did you answer this question?

(A) I used Rate × Time = Distance and plugged in my own numbers.
(B) I averaged 10 and 20 and worked from there.
(C) I called the times going back and forth by two different unknown variables but noted that the sum of these times was 1 hour.
(D) I guessed.
(E) None of these.

23. If the symbol ϕ is defined by the equation

$$a \phi b = a - b - ab$$

for all a and b, then $\left(-\frac{1}{3}\right) \phi (-3) =$

(A) $\frac{5}{3}$

(B) $\frac{11}{3}$

(C) $-\frac{13}{5}$

(D) -4
(E) -5

24. How did you get your answer?

(A) I played around with the numbers $-\frac{1}{3}$ and -3 to get my answer. I didn't use any substitution method.
(B) I substituted in $a \phi b = a - b - ab$, $\left(-\frac{1}{3}\right)$ for a and -3 for b.
(C) I worked backward.
(D) I guessed.
(E) None of these.

25. If $y^8 = 4$ and $y^7 = \frac{3}{x}$, what is the value of y in terms of x?

(A) $\frac{4x}{3}$

(B) $\frac{3x}{4}$

(C) $\frac{4}{x}$

(D) $\frac{x}{4}$

(E) $\frac{12}{x}$

26. How did you get your answer?

(A) I solved for the value of y from $y^8 = 4$. Then I substituted that value of y in $y^7 = \frac{3}{x}$.
(B) I took the seventh root of y in the second equation.
(C) I divided the first equation by the second equation to get y alone in terms of x.
(D) I guessed.
(E) None of these.

27. If $4x + 5y = 10$ and $x + 3y = 8$, then $\frac{5x + 8y}{3} =$

(A) 18
(B) 15
(C) 12
(D) 9
(E) 6

28. How did you get your answer?

(A) I solved both simultaneous equations for x and for y, then substituted the values of x and y into $\frac{(5x + 8y)}{3}$.
(B) I tried numbers for x and for y that would satisfy the first two equations.
(C) I added both equations to get $5x + 8y$. Then I divided my result by 3.
(D) I guessed.
(E) None of these.

29. The circle with center A and radius AB is inscribed in the square here. AB is extended to C. What is the ratio of AB to AC?

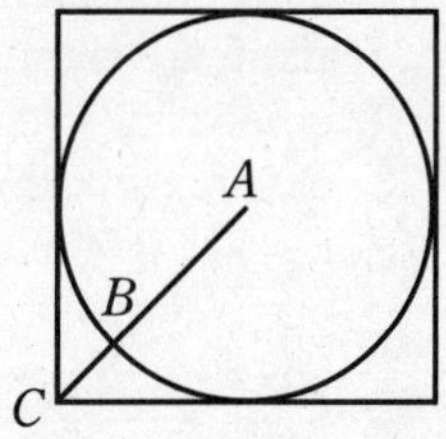

(A) $\sqrt{2}$

(B) $\frac{\sqrt{2}}{4}$

(C) $\frac{\sqrt{2} - 1}{2}$

(D) $\frac{\sqrt{2}}{2}$

(E) None of these.

30. How did you get your answer?

(A) I approximated the solution. I looked to see what the ratio of *AB* to *AC* might be from the diagram. Then I looked through the choices to see which choice was reasonable or to eliminate incorrect choices.
(B) I saw a relationship between *AB* and *AC* but didn't draw any other lines.
(C) I dropped a perpendicular from *A* to one of the sides of the square, then worked with the isosceles right triangle. I also labeled length *AB* by a single letter, and *BC* by another single letter.
(D) I guessed.
(E) None of these.

31. In the accompanying figure, side *BC* of triangle *ABC* is extended to *D*. What is the value of *a*?

(A) 15
(B) 17
(C) 20
(D) 24
(E) 30

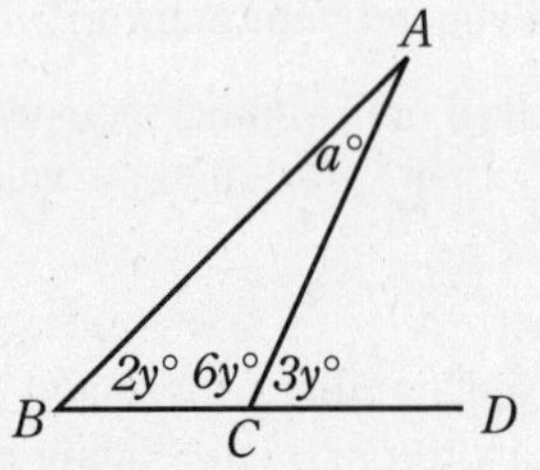

(Note: Figure is not drawn to scale.)

32. How did you get your answer?

(A) I *first* said that $2y + 6y + a = 180$.
(B) I *first* said that $6y + 3y = 180$, then solved for y.
(C) I *first* said $3y = 2y + a$.
(D) I guessed.
(E) None of these.

33. What is the perimeter of the accompanying figure if *B* and *C* are right angles?

(A) 14
(B) 16
(C) 18
(D) 20
(E) Cannot be determined.

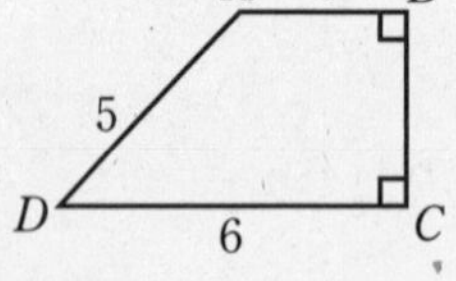

(Note: Figure is not drawn to scale.)

34. How did you get your answer?

(A) I tried to first find angles *A* and *D*.
(B) I drew a perpendicular from *A* to *DC* and labeled *BC* as an unknown (*x* or *y*, etc.).
(C) I labeled *BC* as an unknown (*x* or *y*, etc.) but *did not* draw a perpendicular line from *A* to *DC*.
(D) I guessed.
(E) None of these.

35. Which of the angles below has a degree measure that can be determined?

(A) $\angle WOS$
(B) $\angle SOU$
(C) $\angle WOT$
(D) $\angle ROV$
(E) $\angle WOV$

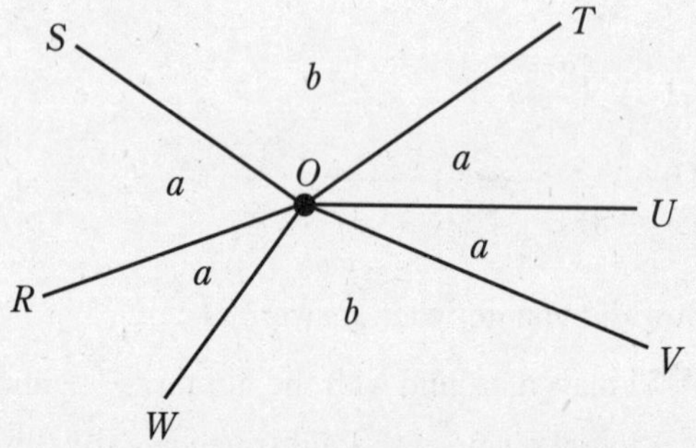

(Note: Figure is not drawn to scale.)

36. How did you get your answer?

(A) I first said that $4a + 2b = 360$, got $2a + b = 180$, and then looked through the choices.
(B) I looked through the choices first.
(C) I knew that the sum of the angles added up to 360 degrees but didn't know where to go from there.
(D) I guessed.
(E) None of these.

This is the end of the Strategy Diagnostic Test for the SAT. You've answered the questions in both the Verbal and Math sections, and you've recorded how you arrived at each answer.

Now you're ready to find out how you did. Go right to the table that follows for answer checking, diagnosis, and prescription.

Remember, the questions are in pairs: the odd-numbered ones are the questions themselves; the even-numbered ones, the approach you used to solve the questions. If either or both of your answers—solution and/or approach—fail to correspond to the answers given in the table, you should study the strategy for that pair.

The table also gives the SAT score increase that's possible if you master that strategy. The approximate time it should take to answer a particular question is also supplied. By using the best strategies throughout the actual SAT, you should increase accuracy, make the best use of your time, and thus improve your score dramatically.

Note: If the even-numbered answer (for questions 2, 4, 6, etc.) does not match with your answer, you may want to look at the approach described in the answer, as you may be able to use that approach with other questions.

STRATEGY DIAGNOSTIC TEST ANSWER AND DIAGNOSTIC TABLE

Section 1 Verbal Ability

Question number	*Answer*	**If either or both of your answers do not match the answers to the left, then refer to this strategy*	*Possible score increase if strategy is learned*	*Estimated time to solve each odd-numbered question (in seconds)*
1 2	D A	Sentence Completion 1, p. 120	70	20
3 4	B C	Sentence Completion 2, p. 121	40	40
5 6	E B	Sentence Completion 3, p. 123	40	30
7 8	C B	Sentence Completion 4, p. 124	100	30
9 10	E C	Sentence Completion 4, p. 124	100	40
11 12	C B	Sentence Completion 4, p. 124	100	30
13 14	A B	Vocabulary 1, p. 150	60	20
15 16	E B	Vocabulary 1, p. 150	60	20
17 18	B B	Vocabulary 1, p. 150	60	20
19 20	C B	Vocabulary 3, p. 154	30	20
21 22	D B	Vocabulary 1, p. 150	60	20
23 24	E B	Vocabulary 3, p. 154	30	20
25 26	B B	Vocabulary 2, p. 152	30	20
27 28	B B, C	Vocabulary 2, p. 152	30	20

STRATEGY DIAGNOSTIC TEST ANSWER AND DIAGNOSTIC TABLE (Continued)

Section 1 Verbal Ability

Question number	*Answer*	**If either or both of your answers do not match the answers to the left, then refer to this strategy*	*Possible score increase if strategy is learned*	*Estimated time to solve each odd-numbered question (in seconds)*
29 30	A B	Vocabulary 3, p. 154	30	20
31 32	D B, C, D	Vocabulary 2, p. 152	30	20
33 34	E B	Vocabulary 1, p. 150	60	30
35 36	B B	Vocabulary 3, p. 154	30	20
37 38	B B	Reading Comprehension 1, 2, pp. 135, 138	200	15
39 40	E B	Reading Comprehension 1, 2, pp. 135, 138	200	20
41 42	D B	Reading Comprehension 1, 2, pp. 135, 138	200	20
43 44	B B	Reading Comprehension 1, 2, pp. 135, 138	200	20
45 46	D B	Reading Comprehension 1, 2, pp. 135, 138	200	30
47 48	E D	Reading Comprehension 1, 2, pp. 135, 138	200	30
49 50	E D	Reading Comprehension 1, 2, pp. 135, 138	200	20
51 52	B B	Reading Comprehension 1, 2, pp. 135, 138	200	20

STRATEGY DIAGNOSTIC TEST ANSWER AND DIAGNOSTIC TABLE (Continued)

Question number	*Answer*	**If either or both of your answers do not match the answers to the left, then refer to this strategy*	*Possible score increase if strategy is learned*	*Estimated time to solve each odd-numbered question (in seconds)*
Section 1 Verbal Ability				
53 54	A B	Reading Comprehension 1, 2, pp. 135, 138	200	20
55 56	C D	Reading Comprehension 1, 2, pp. 135, 138	200	30
Section 2 Math Ability				
1 2	A C	Math 1, p. 69	20	10
3 4	B A	Math 2, p. 71	60	40
5 6	D A	Math 2, p. 71	60	30
7 8	C C	Math 3, p. 77	10	20
9 10	E C	Math 4, p. 80	20	40
11 12	B C	Math 5, p. 83	20	40
13 14	E C	Math 6, p. 86	140	50
15 16	A B or C	Math 7, p. 88	30	40
17 18	E B or C	Math 8, p. 90	20	30
19 20	A A	Math 14, p. 103	50	40
21 22	B C	Math 9, p. 92	10	60
23 24	A B	Math 11, p. 96	30	50

STRATEGY DIAGNOSTIC TEST ANSWER AND DIAGNOSTIC TABLE (Continued)

Section 2 Math Ability

Question number	*Answer*	**If either or both of your answers do not match the answers to the left, then refer to this strategy*	*Possible score increase if strategy is learned*	*Estimated time to solve each odd-numbered question (in seconds)*
25 26	A C	Math 12 or 13, pp. 98, 100	50	30
27 28	E C	Math 13, p. 100	20	20
29 30	D C	Math 14, 18, pp. 103, 114	80	50
31 32	C B	Math 17, 18, pp. 111, 114	160	40
33 34	C B	Math 14, 18, pp. 103, 114	80	30
35 36	C A	Math 17, p. 111	140	40

**Note:* The solution to the odd-numbered question appears in the strategy section listed.

PART 2

THE WORLD'S SHORTEST PRACTICE TEST—18 QUESTIONS TO APPROXIMATE YOUR SAT SCORE

And the Exact Strategies You Need to Improve Your Score

Although it shouldn't take you more than 40 seconds to answer each Verbal (Critical Reading) and Writing question and 1 minute to answer each Math question, you may take this test untimed and still get a fairly accurate prediction.

Note: The PSAT score is approximately calculated by dividing the SAT score by 10 and is used for National Merit Scholarships.

Top schools expect SAT scores in the 75th percentile range. Following is a test that can determine if you have the goods—and it won't take you more than 15 minutes.

Verbal (Critical Reading)

Allow 7 minutes for this part.

Sentence Completions

Fill in the blank(s) with the appropriate choice:

1. The instructor displayed extreme stubbornness; although he ______ the logic of the student's argument, he ______ to acknowledge her conclusion as correct.

    (A) accepted...refused
    (B) concluded...consented
    (C) denounced...decided
    (D) asserted...acceded
    (E) rejected...preferred

2. In spite of the ______ of his presentation, many people were ______ with the speaker's concepts and ideas.

    (A) interest...enthralled
    (B) power...taken
    (C) intensity...shocked
    (D) greatness...gratified
    (E) strength...bored

3. Richard Wagner was frequently intolerant; moreover, his strange behavior caused most of his acquaintances to ______ the composer whenever possible.

    (A) contradict
    (B) interrogate
    (C) shun
    (D) revere
    (E) tolerate

Reading Comprehension

Read the following passage. Then answer the questions:

Sometimes the meaning of glowing water is ominous. Off the Pacific Coast of North America, it may mean that the sea is filled with a minute plant that contains a poison of strange and terrible virulence. About four days after this minute plant comes to alter the coastal plankton, some of the fishes and shellfish in the vicinity become toxic. This is because in their normal feeding, they have strained the poisonous plankton out of the water.

4. Fish and shellfish become toxic when they

    (A) swim in poisonous water
    (B) feed on poisonous plants or animals
    (C) change their feeding habits
    (D) give off a strange glow
    (E) take strychnine into their systems

5. In the context of the passage, the word *virulence* in line 4 means

    (A) strangeness
    (B) color
    (C) calamity
    (D) potency
    (E) powerful odor

6. The paragraph preceding the one in the passage most probably discussed the

    (A) phenomena of the Pacific coastline
    (B) poisons that affect man
    (C) toxic plants in the sea
    (D) characteristics of plankton
    (E) phenomena of the sea

7. It can be assumed that "plankton" in line 5 are

    (A) fish and shellfish
    (B) small plants or animals
    (C) sand deposits
    (D) land parasites
    (E) glacier or rock formations

Math

Allow 7 minutes for this part.

Answer the following questions:

1. If $2x + 3y = 4$ and $y = 2$, find the value of x.

(A) $+2$
(B) $+1$
(C) 0
(D) -1
(E) -2

---

2. Where $a \neq 1$, $\frac{(a^7 - a^6)}{(a - 1)} =$

(A) $\frac{a}{(a - 1)}$
(B) $\frac{1}{(a - 1)}$
(C) $a^6 - a^5$
(D) a^5
(E) a^6

---

3. Sarah is twice as old as John. Six years ago Sarah was four times as old as John was then. In years, how old is John now?

(A) 3
(B) 9
(C) 18
(D) 20
(E) Cannot be determined

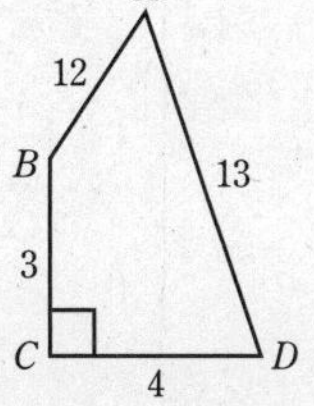

(Note: Figure is not drawn to scale.)

4. The area of the above figure *ABCD*

(A) is 36
(B) is 108
(C) is 156
(D) is 1872
(E) Cannot be determined

In the following questions you must find an answer without referring to choices:

5. If $x + y = 7$ and $xy = 4$, then find the value of $x^2 + y^2$.

---

6. If $y + 2q = 15$, $q + 2p = 5$, and $p + 2y = 7$, then find the value of $p + q + y$.

---

7. On a street with 25 houses, 10 houses have *fewer than 6 rooms,* 10 houses have *more than 7 rooms,* and 4 houses have *more than 8 rooms.* What is the total number of houses on the street that are either 6-, 7-, or 8-room houses?

Writing

Allow 2 minutes for this part.

Identifying Sentence Errors:

Which part (A, B, C, or D) in the sentence is incorrect? Choose E if there is no error.

1. If any signer of the Constitution <u>was</u> to return to life
A
<u>for a day</u>, his opinion <u>of</u> our amendments <u>would be</u>
B C D
interesting. <u>No error</u>.
E

2. <u>After we waited</u> in line <u>for three hours</u>, <u>much to</u>
A B C
<u>our disgust, the tickets had been</u> sold out <u>when</u> we
C D
reached the window. <u>No error</u>.
E

Improving Sentences:

Which choice correctly replaces the sentence?

3. He never has and never will keep his word.

(A) He never has and never will keep his word.
(B) He has never yet and never will keep his word.
(C) He has not ever and will not keep his word.
(D) He never has or will keep his word.
(E) He never has kept and he never will keep his word.

4. In spite of Tom wanting to study, his sister made him wash the dishes.

(A) In spite of Tom wanting to study, his sister made him wash the dishes.
(B) In spite of the fact that Tom wanted to study, his sister made him wash the dishes.
(C) In spite of Tom's need to study, his sister made him wash the dishes.
(D) In spite of Tom's wanting to study, his sister made him wash the dishes.
(E) In spite of Tom studying, his sister made him wash the dishes.

Answers

Verbal (Critical Reading)

1. A

2. E

3. C

4. B

5. D

6. E

7. B

Math

1. D

2. E

3. B

4. A

5. 41

6. 9

7. 11

Writing

1. A

2. C

3. E

4. D

Scoring:

Correct answers for each part	Math SAT	Critical Reading SAT	Writing SAT
1	280–300	270–300	310–400
2	310–400	310–400	410–530
3	410–500	410–480	540–660
4	510–550	490–530	670–800
5	560–600	540–600	
6	610–700	610–700	
7	710–800	710–800	

Explanatory Answers

Explanatory Answers for Verbal (Critical Reading)

1. **(A)** Choice A is correct. This is **Sentence Completion Strategy 4**. I hope you watched for key words like "although" that signal opposites. "Accepted" and "refused" are opposites. Choice B is incorrect. "Concluded" does not sound right or make sense here. Choice C is incorrect. "Denounced" is o.k. but the word "although" signals an opposite and "decided" would not be an opposite of "denounced." Choice D is incorrect. "Although" signals opposites—"asserted" and "accepted" are not opposites. Choice E is incorrect. You are close. "Although" signals opposites. However, "rejected" and "preferred" are not as strong opposites as "accepted" and "refused" in Choice A which is correct.

2. **(E)** Choice E is correct. This is **Sentence Completion Strategy 4.** You needed to notice key words: "In spite of," which signals a contrast or opposite. And "strength" and "bored" do show a contrast. Choice A is incorrect. "Interest" and "enthralled" do not show a real contrast. Choice B is incorrect. "Power" and "taken" do not show a contrast. Choice C is incorrect. "Intensity" and "shocked" do not really show a contrast. Choice D is incorrect. "Greatness" and "gratified" do not show a contrast. In fact one may follow from the other.

3. **(C)** Choice C is correct. This is **Sentence Completion Strategy 4.** I hope you watched for key words, like "moreover." "Moreover" signals something that occurs because of Wagner's strange behavior as being frequently intolerant. "Shun" ("avoid") is the answer. Choice A is incorrect. "Contradict" does not follow. Choice B is incorrect. "Interrogate" does not follow. Choice D is incorrect. You wouldn't "revere" ("look up to" or "admire") a person that has the strange behavior of being frequently intolerant. Choice E is incorrect. If someone is frequently intolerant, his strange behavior wouldn't *moreover* cause you to "tolerate" him.

4. **(B)** Choice B is correct. This is **Reading Comprehension Strategy 2.** The fish feed on the poisonous plankton which can be plants or animals. Choice A is incorrect. It's not that the fish swim in poisonous water—it is that the fish eat the poisonous plankton from the plants. Choice C is incorrect. Don't assume something that is not stated or implied. We have no way of knowing that the fish change their eating habits. Choice D is incorrect. Do not make superficial associations. Just because it says that "the meaning of glowing water is ominous" that does not mean that the fish give off a strange glow and then become toxic. Choice E is incorrect. Although poison is the cause, the specific poison is not mentioned in the passage.

5. **(D)** Choice D is correct. This is **Reading Comprehension Strategy 1 and 5.** "Potency" means "power" or "strength." A "strange and terrible power" does make sense. Choice A is incorrect. If "virulence" meant "strangeness," the segment would read "contains a poison of a strange and terrible strangeness" which would be redundant and not make sense. Choice B is incorrect. What would a "terrible" color mean? Choice C is incorrect. A "calamity" is terrible in itself. So you wouldn't modify "calamity" with "terrible" and say "terrible calamity." Choice E is incorrect. A "powerful odor" would not necessarily make the fish toxic. A strange and powerful poison would.

6. **(E)** Choice E is correct. This is **Reading Comprehension Strategy 2**. Since the first sentence reads "Sometimes the meaning of glowing water is ominous," and the next sentence is specifically about the Pacific Coast of North America, it is probable that the "phenomena of the sea" is discussed in the preceding paragraph. Choice A is incorrect. Most people choose this choice. If the first sentence of the passage were not present, Choice A might be correct. But since the second sentence (and not the first) deals with the Pacific Coast, it is unlikely that the paragraph preceding the one in the passage would deal with the Pacific Coastline because there would be no continuity in the subject matter. Choice B is incorrect. Because we are discussing things about "water," it is unlikely that the paragraph preceding would be about poisons which affect man. Choice C is incorrect. Since

toxic plants are discussed later on in the passage, it is unlikely that "toxic plants in the sea" would be discussed before the passage, especially because the passage is introduced by "Sometimes the meaning of glowing water is ominous." Choice D is incorrect. Since plankton are discussed later on in the passage, it is unlikely that they would be introduced before the passage.

7. **(B)** Choice B is correct. This is **Reading Comprehension Strategy 1 and 5**. Plankton seem to be small plants or animals, and since the fish feed on them, what else could they be? Choice A is incorrect. Watch out for "luring" associations. Plankton seem to come from plants and they are either plants or animals which are attracted to the plant. They would not be fish or shellfish since fish and shellfish are differentiated from coastal plankton in the phrase, "comes to alter the coastal plankton, some of the fishes and shellfish in the vicinity become toxic." If "coastal plankton" were fish and shellfish, the phrase should read, "comes to alter the coastal plankton, some of the coastal plankton in the vicinity become toxic." (You would not substitute "fishes and shellfish" for "coastal plankton"). Choice C is incorrect. How would fish and shellfish feed on "sand deposits?" Choice D is incorrect. Pay attention to the context of the environment that you are in. "Land parasites" would not occur in the water. Choice E is incorrect. How could fish feed on "glacier or rock formations?"

Explanatory Answers for Math

1. **(D)** Choice D is correct. This is **Strategy 7; Basic Skill-Mini-Math Refresher–Equations, Math Refresher (239): Substitute numbers for variables.** *Substitute* $y = 2$ into the equation, $2x + 3y = 4$. You get $2x + 6 = 4$; $2x = -2$ so $x = -1$. Choice A is incorrect. Did you think that if $2x + 6 = 4$ that $2x = 2$ and chose 2 as the answer? Choice B is incorrect. Did you subtract 6 from 4 and get 2? Choice E is incorrect. Did you think that if $2x + 6 = 4$ and $2x = -2$, then $x = -2$?

2. **(E)** Choice E is correct. When dealing with complicated quantities or equations, it is sometimes simpler to factor to see the quantity take a different form. *Factor* out a^6 from the quantity $a^7 - a^6$. You get $a^6(a - 1)$. Thus:

$$\frac{a^7 - a^6}{a - 1} = \frac{a^6(a - 1)}{a - 1} = a^6.$$

This is **Strategy 4; Basic Skill-Mini-Math Refresher–Algebra, Math Refresher (429). Know your math rules.** Choice A is incorrect. Did you think that $a^7 - a^6 = a^1 = a$? Choice B is incorrect. Did you think that $a^7 - a^6 = 1$? Choice C is incorrect. Did you think that $\frac{a^7 - a^6}{a - 1}$ would reduce the exponents and you would get $a^6 - a^5$?

3. **(B)** Choice B is correct. You won't rack your brains if you know how to translate from words to math. *Translate* Sarah to *S*, John to *J*, "is" to =, Six years ago to −6, four times as old as John was then to $4(J - 6)$. Then **Sarah is twice as old as John** translates to **(1)** $S = 2J$. And **Six years ago Sarah was 4 times as old as John was then** translates to **(2)** $S - 6 = 4(J - 6)$, the reason for $J - 6$ being that John was $J - 6$, six years ago. Substituting $S = 2J$ in Equation 1, in Equation 2, we get $2J - 6 = 4(J - 6)$. Then we get: $2J - 6 = 4J - 24$. And then: $-6 + 24 = 4J - 2J = 2J$. So $2J = 18$ **and** $J = 9$. This is **Strategy 2; Basic Skills-Mini-Math Refresher–Rule, Equations; Math Refresher (407).** Choice A is incorrect. Did you translate "four times as old as John was then" to $4J$? You would have gotten $2J - 6 = 4J$ and been careless by saying that $J = 3$. **Wrong translation** and **careless in using math rules**. Choice C is incorrect. Did you solve for Sarah's age (*S*) and get $S = 18$ or did you get for John's age (*J*), $2J = 18$ and choose 18 as the answer? Choice E is incorrect. You can obtain two equations involving Sarah (*S*) and John (*J*). And you have two unknowns ***S*** and ***J***. Unless one equation is a multiple of the other, you can determine the unknowns.

4. **(A)** Choice A is correct. The best way to do the problem is to draw or extend lines to get more information. *Draw BD*, then find length *BD*. $BD = 5$ because triangle *BCD* is a 3-4-5 right triangle. Now triangle *BDA* is also a right triangle because a 5-12-13 triangle is a right triangle. We can then find the area of triangle *BCD* to be $\frac{3 \times 4}{2} = 6$ and the area of triangle *BDA* to be $\frac{5 \times 12}{2} = 30$. So the sum of these areas is the area of the figure *ABCD*. 36 is the answer. This is **Strategy 14; Basic Skills-Mini-Math Refresher–Areas, Right Triangles; Math Refresher (306); (509).** Choice D is incorrect. Did you multiply the sides to get 1872? Now come on, you wouldn't bet $100 on that would you? Choice E is incorrect. Notice that the length of *BD* is determined. This means the area of triangles *BCD* and *BDA* are determined. So the sum of the areas of the two triangles are determined and so the area of figure *ABCD* is determined.

5. The answer is 41. **Don't try to solve for both x and y. You are not asked to do that—you are asked to find the value of $x^2 + y^2$ so try to manipulate the equations to get that quantity.** Remember and use classic forms, like $(x + y)^2 = x^2 + 2xy + y^2$. We have (1) $(x + y)^2 = x^2 + 2xy + y^2 = 7 \times 7 = 49$ and since $xy = 4$, we get $2xy = 8$. Substituting $2xy = 8$ in Equation (1), we get $(x + y)^2 = x^2 + 2xy + y^2 = x^2 + 8 + y^2 = 49$. Subtracting 8 from both sides of the last equation, we get, $x^2 + y^2 = 41$. This is **Strategy 4; Basic Skill-Mini-Math Refresher–Algebra, Math Refresher (409).**

6. The correct answer is 9. I hope you didn't go through the tedium of substitution and solving for q, p, and y. You are *not* asked for the values of *each* of the variables. When you have two or more equations, it is sometimes easier to just *add* or *subtract* them to get a result. *Add* equations, then *divide* by 3.

$$\begin{array}{r} y + 2q = 15 \\ q + 2p = 5 \\ + \quad p + 2y = 7 \\ \hline 3q + 3p + 3y = 27 \end{array}$$

Factor 3: $3(q + p + y) = 27$; $q + p + y = 9$. This is **Strategy 13; Basic Skill-Mini-Math Refresher–Equations, Math Refresher (407).**

7. The correct answer is 11. In many "logic" problems, it is sometimes easier to use an *indirect* approach or use the fact that the *whole equals the sum of its parts.* Use the *indirect* method: Don't try to get the number of 6-7-8 room houses directly. Instead, find houses that have fewer than 6 rooms (10) and more than 8 rooms (4) and what's left is the 6-7-8 room ones. Use the fact that the *whole equals the sum of its parts.* The total number of houses are 25 (given) and this must then equal the parts, 10 that have less than 6 rooms, plus 4 that have more than 8 rooms and whatever is remaining that have 6-7-8 rooms. Thus 25 minus 10 minus 4 equals 11 which is the answer. This is **Strategy 17.**

Explanatory Answers for Writing

1. **(A)** Choice A is correct. "If any signer of the Constitution *were* to return to life…" is correct. The verb in the "if clause" of a present contrary-to-fact conditional statement must have a past subjunctive form (*were*). **See Grammar and Usage Refresher–9d.**

2. **(C)** Choice C is correct. Avoid squinting constructions—that is, modifiers that are so placed that the reader cannot tell whether they are modifying the words immediately preceding the construction or the words immediately following the construction. The correct sentence would read, "After we waited in line for three hours, *much to our disgust, the tickets had been* sold out when we reached the window." That is, as the sentence initially reads, we don't know whether "much to our disgust" modifies "After we were waiting in line for three hours" or modifies "the tickets had been sold out when we reached the window." **See Grammar and Usage Refresher–10u and 11l.**

3. **(E)** Choice E is correct. Avoid improper ellipses. Choices A, B, C, and D are incorrect for this reason. The word "kept" must be included since the second part of the sentence uses another form of the verb ("keep"). **See Grammar and Usage Refresher–10k.**

4. **(D)** Choice D is correct. Choice A is incorrect because the possessive form of the noun ("Toms") must be used to modify the gerund ("wanting"). Choice B is too wordy. Choice C changes the meaning of the original sentence. Choice E is incorrect for the same reason that Choice A is incorrect. Also Choice E changes the meaning of the original sentence. **See Grammar and Usage Refresher–5v.**

PART 3

THE 101 MOST IMPORTANT MATH QUESTIONS YOU NEED TO KNOW HOW TO SOLVE

Take This Test to Determine Your Basic (as Contrasted with Strategic) Math Weaknesses (Diagnosis and Corrective Measures Follow Test)

101 Math Questions Answer Sheet

A. Fractions

1.
2.
3.
4.
5.

B. Even–Odd Relationships

6.
7.
8.
9.
10.
11.
12.

C. Factors

13.
14.
15.
16.
17.
18.
19.
20.
21.

D. Exponents

22.
23.
24.
25.
26.
27.
28.
29.
30.
31.
32.

E. Percentages

33.
34.
35.

F. Equations

36.
37.
38.
39.
40.

G. Angles

41.
42.
43.
44.

H. Parallel Lines

45.
46.
47.
48.
49.
50.
51.

I. Triangles

52.
53.
54.
55.
56.
57.
58.
59.
60.
61.
62.
63.
64.
65.

J. Circles

66.
67.
68.
69.
70.

K. Other Figures

71.
72.
73.
74.
75.
76.
77.
78.
79.
80.

L. Number Lines

81.
82.

M. Coordinates

83.
84.
85.
86.

N. Inequalities

87.
88.
89.
90.
91.
92.

O. Averages

93.
94.

P. Shortcuts

95.
96.
97.
98.
99.
100.
101.

101 Math Questions Test

Following are the 101 most important math questions you should know how to solve. After you take the test, check to see whether your answers are the same as those described, and whether or not you answered the question in the way described. After a solution, there is usually (where appropriate) a rule or generalization of the math concept just used in the solution to the particular problem. Make sure that you understand this generalization or rule, as it will apply to many other questions. Remember that these are the most important basic math questions you need to know how to solve. Make sure that you understand *all of them* before taking any standardized math test such as the SAT.

DO NOT GUESS AT ANY ANSWER! LEAVE THE ANSWER BLANK IF YOU DON'T KNOW HOW TO SOLVE THE PROBLEM.

A. Fractions

1. $\dfrac{a}{\frac{b}{c}} =$

(A) $\frac{ab}{c}$

(B) $\frac{ac}{b}$

(C) $\frac{a}{bc}$

(D) abc

(E) None of these.

---

2. $\dfrac{1}{\frac{1}{y}} =$

(A) y

(B) y^2

(C) $\frac{1}{y}$

(D) infinity

(E) None of these.

---

3. $\dfrac{\frac{a}{b}}{c} =$

(A) $\frac{a}{bc}$

(B) $\frac{ac}{b}$

(C) $\frac{ab}{c}$

(D) abc

(E) None of these.

---

4. $\dfrac{1}{\frac{x}{y}} =$

(A) xy

(B) $\frac{x}{y}$

(C) $\frac{y}{x}$

(D) $\left(\frac{x}{y}\right)^2$

(E) None of these.

---

5. $\dfrac{\frac{a}{b}}{\frac{b}{a}} =$

(A) $\frac{b^2}{a^2}$

(B) $\frac{a^2}{b^2}$

(C) 1

(D) $\frac{a}{b}$

(E) None of these.

B. Even–Odd Relationships

6. ODD INTEGER × ODD INTEGER =

(A) odd integer only

(B) even integer only

(C) even or odd integer

---

7. ODD INTEGER + or − ODD INTEGER =

(A) odd integer only
(B) even integer only
(C) even or odd integer

8. EVEN INTEGER × EVEN INTEGER =

(A) odd integer only
(B) even integer only
(C) even or odd integer

9. EVEN INTEGER + or − EVEN INTEGER =

(A) odd integer only
(B) even integer only
(C) even or odd integer

10. $(\text{ODD INTEGER})^{\text{ODD POWER}} =$

(A) odd integer only
(B) even integer only
(C) even or odd integer

11. $(\text{EVEN INTEGER})^{\text{EVEN POWER}} =$

(A) odd integer only
(B) even integer only
(C) even or odd integer

12. $(\text{EVEN INTEGER})^{\text{ODD POWER}} =$

(A) odd integer only
(B) even integer only
(C) even or odd integer

C. Factors

13. $(x + 3)(x + 2) =$

(A) $x^2 + 5x + 6$
(B) $x^2 + 6x + 5$
(C) $x^2 + x + 6$
(D) $2x + 5$
(E) None of these.

14. $(x + 3)(x - 2) =$

(A) $x^2 - x + 6$
(B) $x^2 + x + 5$
(C) $x^2 + x - 6$
(D) $2x + 1$
(E) None of these.

15. $(x - 3)(y - 2) =$

(A) $xy - 5y + 6$
(B) $xy - 2x - 3y + 6$
(C) $x + y + 6$
(D) $xy - 3y + 2x + 6$
(E) None of these.

16. $(a + b)(b + c) =$

(A) $ab + b^2 + bc$
(B) $a + b^2 + c$
(C) $a^2 + b^2 + ca$
(D) $ab + b^2 + ac + bc$
(E) None of these.

17. $(a + b)(a - b) =$

(A) $a^2 + 2ba - b^2$
(B) $a^2 - 2ba - b^2$
(C) $a^2 - b^2$
(D) 0
(E) None of these.

18. $(a + b)^2 =$

(A) $a^2 + 2ab + b^2$
(B) $a^2 + b^2$
(C) $a^2 + b^2 + ab$
(D) $2a + 2b$
(E) None of these.

19. $-(a - b) =$

(A) $a - b$
(B) $-a - b$
(C) $a + b$
(D) $b - a$
(E) None of these.

20. $a(b + c) =$

(A) $ab + ac$
(B) $ab + c$
(C) abc
(D) $ab + bc$
(E) None of these.

21. $-a(b - c) =$

(A) $ab - ac$
(B) $-ab - ac$
(C) $ac - ab$
(D) $ab + ac$
(E) None of these.

D. Exponents

22. $10^5 =$

(A) 1,000
(B) 10,000
(C) 100,000
(D) 1,000,000
(E) None of these.

23. $107076.5 = 1.070765 \times$

(A) 10^4
(B) 10^5
(C) 10^6
(D) 10^7
(E) None of these.

---

24. $a^2 \times a^5 =$

(A) a^{10}
(B) a^7
(C) a^3
(D) $(2a)^{10}$
(E) None of these.

---

25. $(ab)^7 =$

(A) ab^7
(B) a^7b
(C) a^7b^7
(D) $a^{14}b^{14}$
(E) None of these.

---

26. $\left(\frac{a}{c}\right)^8 =$

(A) $\frac{a^8}{c^8}$
(B) $\frac{a^8}{c}$
(C) $\frac{a}{c^8}$
(D) $\frac{a^7}{c}$
(E) None of these.

---

27. $a^4 \times b^4 =$

(A) $(ab)^4$
(B) $(ab)^8$
(C) $(ab)^{16}$
(D) $(ab)^{12}$
(E) None of these.

---

28. $a^{-3} \times b^5 =$

(A) $\frac{b^5}{a^3}$
(B) $(ab)^2$
(C) $(ab)^{-15}$
(D) $\frac{a^3}{b^5}$
(E) None of these.

---

29. $(a^3)^5 =$

(A) a^8
(B) a^2
(C) a^{15}
(D) a^{243}
(E) None of these.

---

30. $2a^{-3} =$

(A) $\frac{2}{a^3}$
(B) $2a^3$
(C) $2^3\sqrt{a}$
(D) a^{-6}
(E) None of these.

---

31. $2a^m \times \frac{1}{3}a^{-n} =$

(A) $\frac{2}{3}a^{m+n}$
(B) $\frac{2a^m}{3a^n}$
(C) $\frac{2}{3}a^{-mn}$
(D) $-\frac{2}{3}a^{-mn}$
(E) None of these.

---

32. $3^2 + 3^{-2} + 4^1 + 6^0 =$

(A) $8\frac{1}{9}$
(B) $12\frac{1}{9}$
(C) $13\frac{1}{9}$
(D) $14\frac{1}{9}$
(E) None of these.

E. Percentages

33. 15% of 200 =

(A) 3
(B) 30
(C) 300
(D) 3,000
(E) None of these.

34. What is 3% of 5?

(A) $\frac{5}{3}\%$

(B) 15

(C) $\frac{3}{20}$

(D) $\frac{3}{5}$

(E) None of these.

---

35. What percent of 3 is 6?

(A) 50

(B) 20

(C) 200

(D) $\frac{1}{2}$

(E) None of these.

F. Equations

36. If $y^2 = 16$, $y =$

(A) $+4$ only

(B) -4 only

(C) ± 4

(D) ± 8

(E) None of these.

---

37. If $x - y = 10$, $y =$

(A) $x - 10$

(B) $10 + x$

(C) $10 - x$

(D) 10

(E) None of these.

---

38. What is the value of x if $x + 4y = 7$ and $x - 4y = 8$?

(A) 15

(B) $\frac{15}{2}$

(C) 7

(D) $\frac{7}{2}$

(E) None of these.

---

39. What is the value of x and y if $x - 2y = 2$ and $2x + y = 4$?

(A) $x = 2, y = 0$

(B) $x = 0, y = -2$

(C) $x = -1, y = 2$

(D) $x = 0, y = 2$

(E) None of these.

---

40. If $\frac{x}{5} = \frac{7}{12}$, $x =$

(A) $\frac{35}{12}$

(B) $\frac{12}{35}$

(C) $\frac{7}{60}$

(D) $\frac{60}{7}$

(E) None of these.

G. Angles

Questions 41–42 refer to the diagram below:

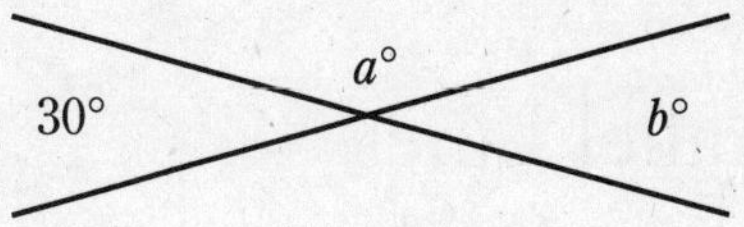

41. $a =$

(A) 30

(B) 150

(C) 45

(D) 90

(E) None of these.

42. $b =$

(A) 30

(B) 150

(C) 45

(D) 90

(E) None of these.

Question 43 refers to the diagram below:

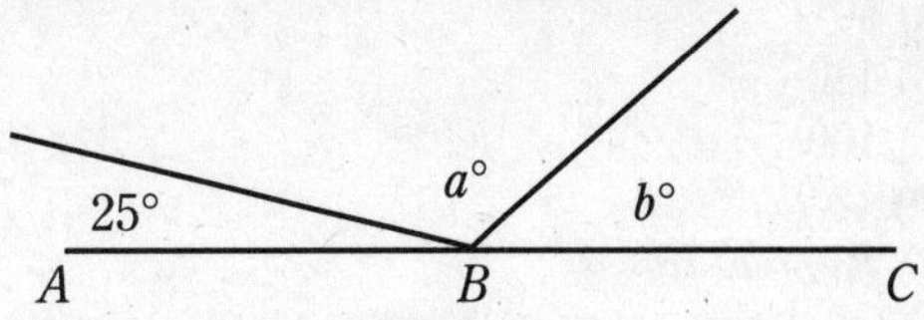

ABC is a straight angle.

43. $a + b =$

(A) 155

(B) 165

(C) 180

(D) 145

(E) None of these.

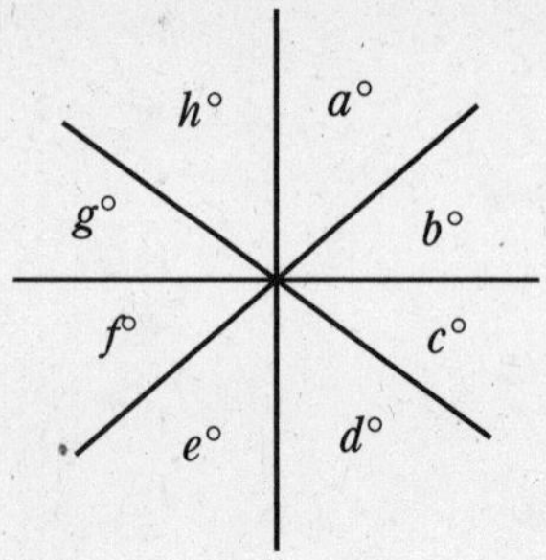

44. What is the value of $a + b + c + d + e + f + g + h$ in the diagram above?

(A) 180
(B) 240
(C) 360
(D) 540
(E) None of these.

H. Parallel Lines

Questions 45–51 refer to the diagram below:

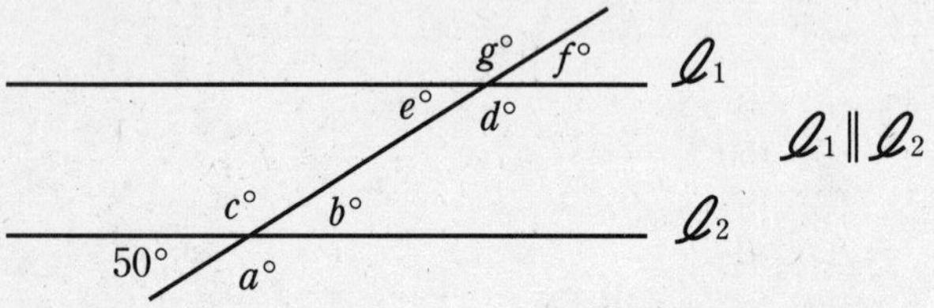

45. $a =$

(A) 50
(B) 130
(C) 100
(D) 40
(E) None of these.

46. $b =$

(A) 50
(B) 130
(C) 100
(D) 40
(E) None of these.

47. $c =$

(A) 50
(B) 130
(C) 100
(D) 40
(E) None of these.

48. $d =$

(A) 50
(B) 130
(C) 100
(D) 40
(E) None of these.

49. $e =$

(A) 50
(B) 130
(C) 100
(D) 40
(E) None of these.

50. $f =$

(A) 50
(B) 130
(C) 100
(D) 40
(E) None of these.

51. $g =$

(A) 50
(B) 130
(C) 100
(D) 40
(E) None of these.

I. Triangles

52.

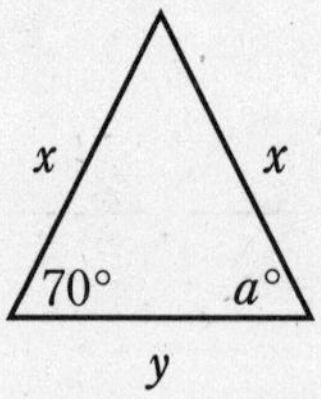

(Note: Figure is not drawn to scale.)

$a =$

(A) 70°
(B) 40°
(C) $\frac{xy}{70°}$
(D) Cannot be determined.
(E) None of these.

53.

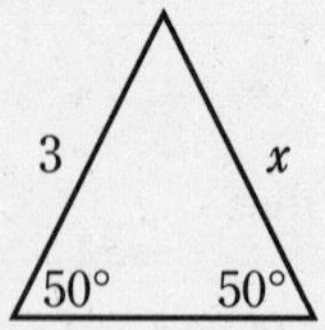

(Note: Figure is not drawn to scale.)

$x =$

(A) 3
(B) $\frac{50}{3}$
(C) $3\sqrt{2}$
(D) Cannot be determined.
(E) None of these.

54.

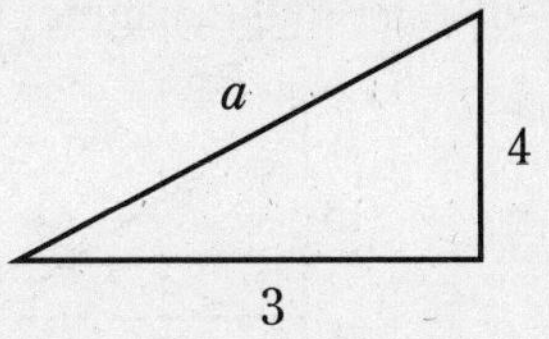

(Note: Figure is not drawn to scale.)

Which is a possible value for a?

(A) 1
(B) 6
(C) 10
(D) 7
(E) 8

55.

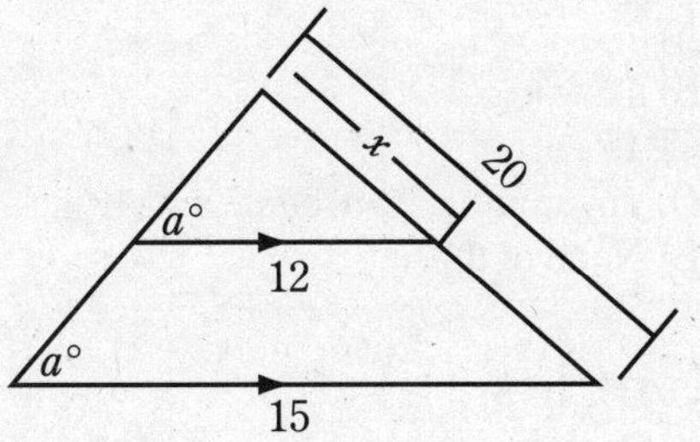

(Note: Figure is not drawn to scale.)

In the triangle above, $x =$

(A) 12
(B) 16
(C) 15
(D) 10
(E) None of these.

56.

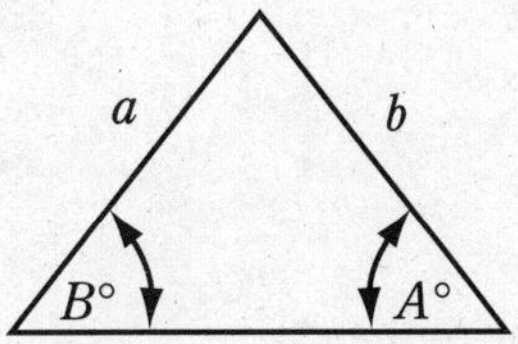

In the triangle above, if $B > A$, then

(A) $b = a$
(B) $b > a$
(C) $b < a$
(D) A relation between b and a cannot be determined.
(E) None of these.

57.

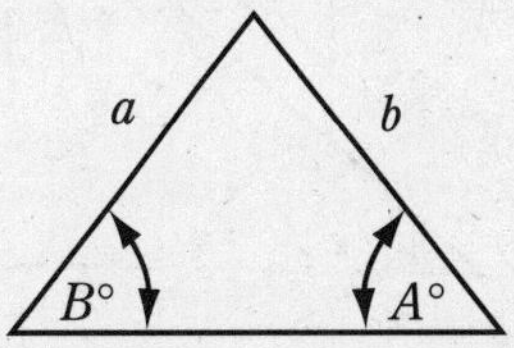

In the triangle above, if $b < a$, then

(A) $B > A$
(B) $B = A$
(C) $B < A$
(D) A relation between B and A cannot be determined.
(E) None of these.

58.

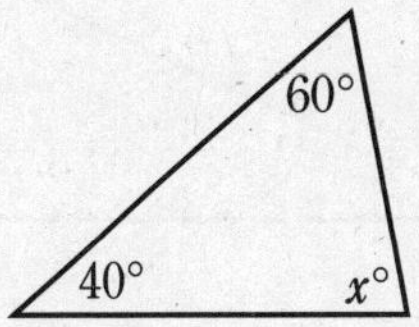

In the triangle above, $x =$

(A) 100
(B) 80
(C) 90
(D) 45
(E) None of these.

59.

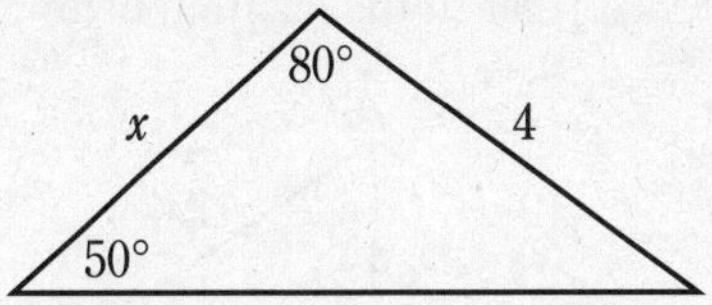

(Note: Figure is not drawn to scale.)

In the triangle above, $x =$

(A) $4\sqrt{2}$
(B) 8
(C) 4
(D) a number between 1 and 4
(E) None of these.

60.

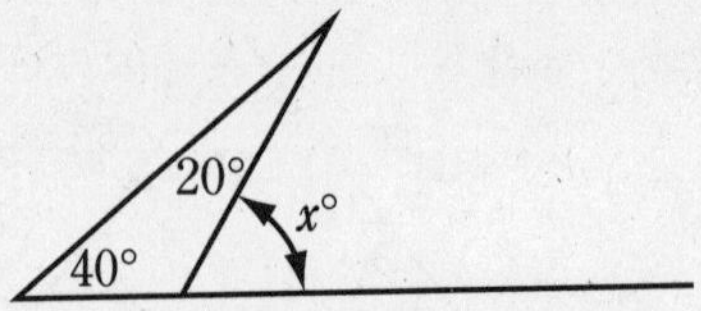

In the diagram above, $x =$

(A) 40
(B) 20
(C) 60
(D) 80
(E) None of these.

61.

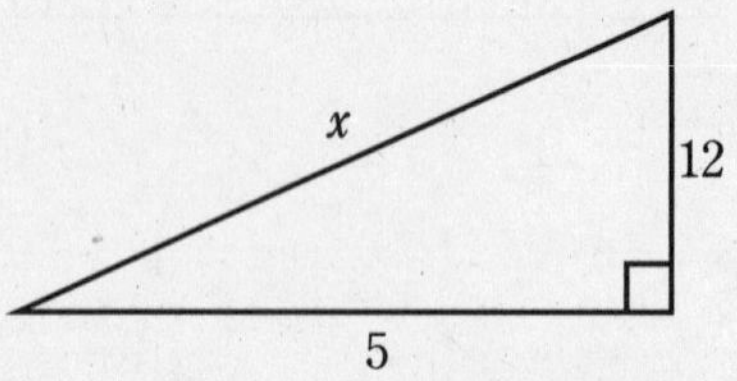

(Note: Figure is not drawn to scale.)

In the right triangle above, $x =$

(A) 17
(B) 13
(C) 15
(D) $12\sqrt{2}$
(E) None of these.

Questions 62–63 refer to the diagram below:

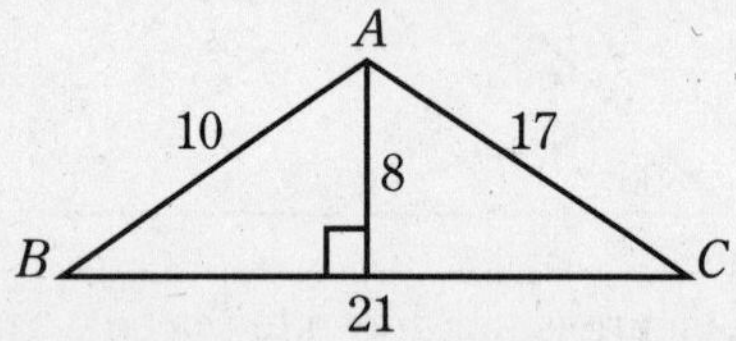

(Note: Figure is not drawn to scale.)

62. The perimeter of the triangle *ABC* is

(A) 16
(B) 48
(C) 168
(D) 84
(E) None of these.

63. The area of triangle *ABC* is

(A) 170
(B) 85
(C) 168
(D) 84
(E) None of these.

Questions 64–65 refer to the diagram below:

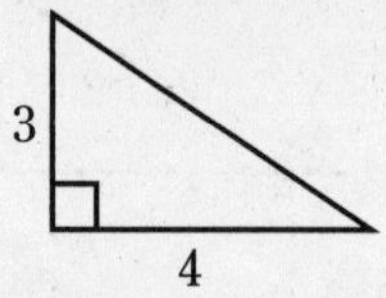

64. The area of the triangle is

(A) 6
(B) 7
(C) 12
(D) any number between 5 and 7
(E) None of these.

65. The perimeter of the triangle is

(A) 7
(B) 12
(C) 15
(D) any number between 7 and 12
(E) None of these.

J. Circles

Questions 66–67 refer to the diagram below:

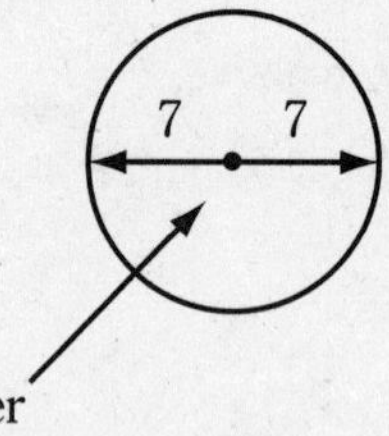

66. The area of the circle is

(A) 49
(B) 49π
(C) 14π
(D) 196π
(E) None of these.

67. The circumference of the circle is

(A) 14π
(B) 7π
(C) 49π
(D) 14
(E) None of these.

68.

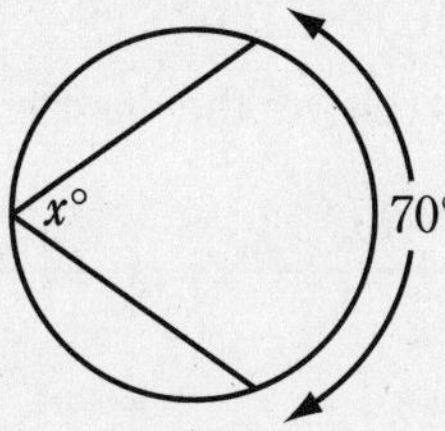

In the diagram above, $x =$

(A) 70°
(B) 35°
(C) 90°
(D) a number that cannot be determined
(E) None of these.

69.

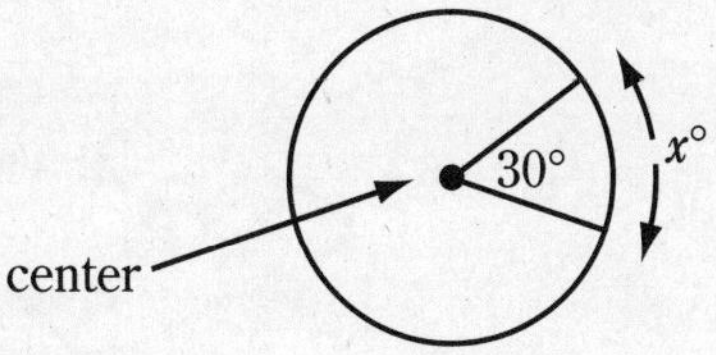

In the diagram above, $x =$

(A) 30°
(B) 60°
(C) 90°
(D) a number that cannot be determined
(E) None of these.

70.

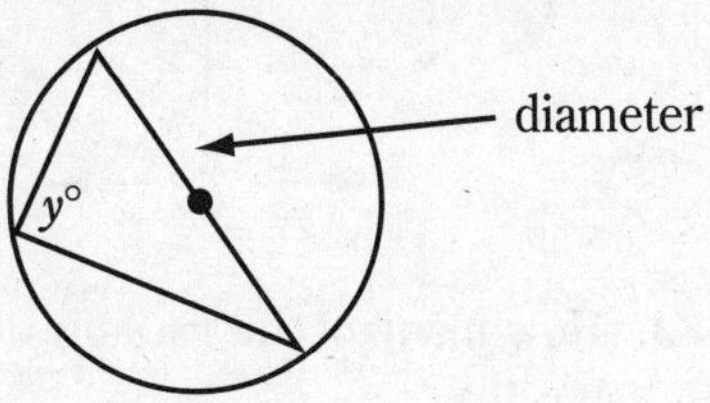

In the diagram above, $y =$

(A) 145°
(B) 60°
(C) 90°
(D) a number that cannot be determined
(E) None of these.

K. Other Figures

Questions 71–72 refer to the diagram below:

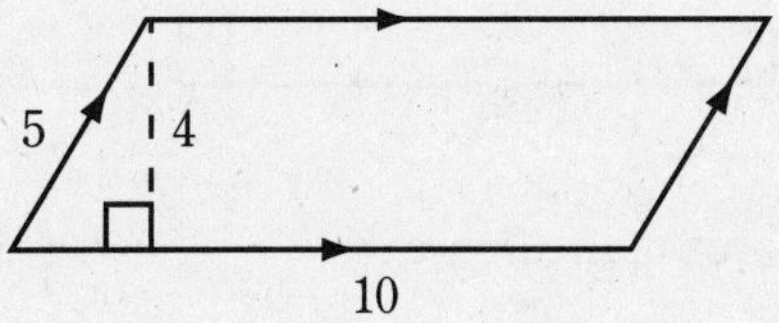

71. The area of the figure is

(A) 15
(B) 20
(C) 40
(D) 50
(E) None of these.

72. The perimeter of the figure is

(A) 15
(B) 30
(C) 40
(D) 50
(E) None of these.

Questions 73–75 refer to the figure below:

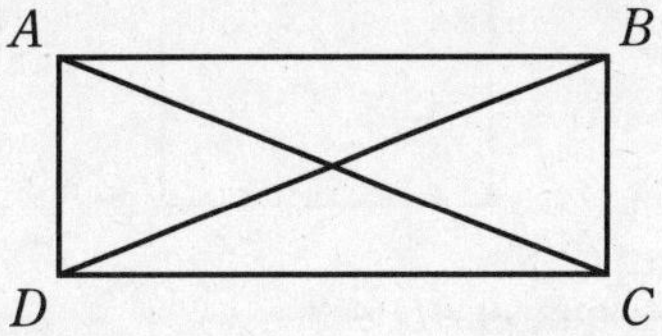

ABCD is a rectangle.

73. What is BC if $AD = 6$?

(A) 4
(B) 6
(C) 8
(D) 10
(E) 12

74. What is DC if $AB = 8$?

(A) 4
(B) 6
(C) 8
(D) 10
(E) 12

75. What is DB if $AC = 10$?

(A) 4
(B) 6
(C) 8
(D) 10
(E) 12

Questions 76–77 refer to the diagram below:

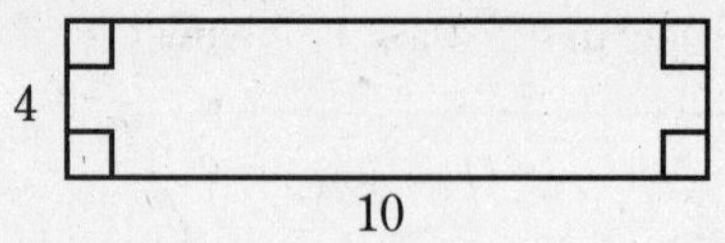

76. The area of the figure is

(A) 14
(B) 40
(C) 80
(D) 28
(E) None of these.

77. The perimeter of the figure is

(A) 14
(B) 28
(C) 36
(D) 40
(E) None of these.

Questions 78–79 refer to the figure below:

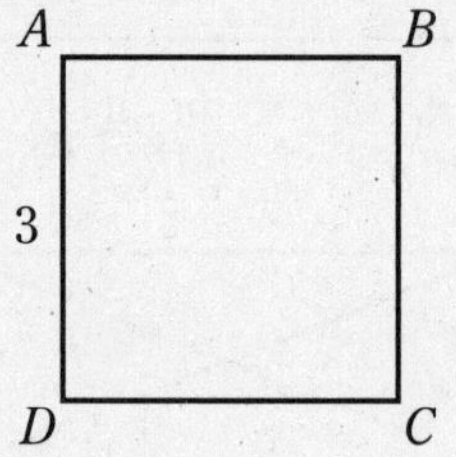

ABCD is a square; *AD* = 3.

78. What is the area of the square?

(A) 9
(B) 12
(C) 16
(D) 20
(E) None of these.

79. What is the perimeter of the square?

(A) 9
(B) 12
(C) 16
(D) 20
(E) None of these.

---

80. The volume of the rectangular solid below is

(A) 48
(B) 64
(C) 128
(D) 72
(E) None of these.

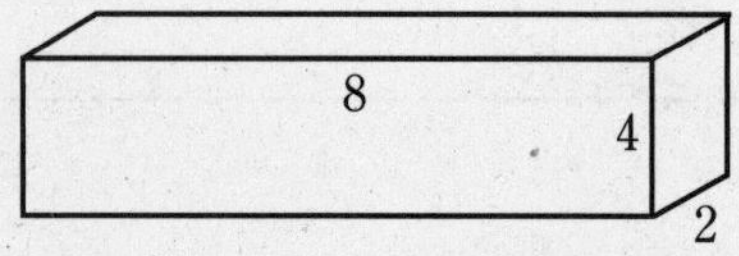

L. Number Lines

Questions 81–82 refer to the diagram below:

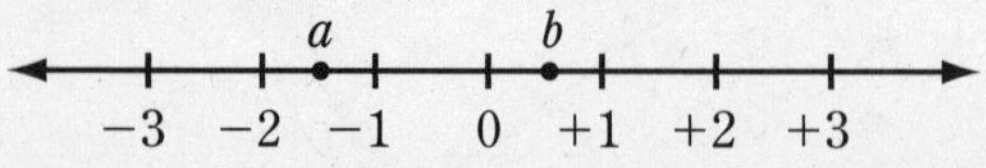

81. Which best defines the range in values of *b*?

(A) $-2 < b < 1$
(B) $0 < b < 2$
(C) $0 < b < 1$
(D) $-3 < b < 3$
(E) $0 < b$

82. Which best defines the range in values of *a*?

(A) $-2 < a$
(B) $-2 < a < -1$
(C) $-2 < a < 0$
(D) $a < -1$
(E) $-3 < a < 0$

M. Coordinates

Questions 83–85 refer to the diagram below:

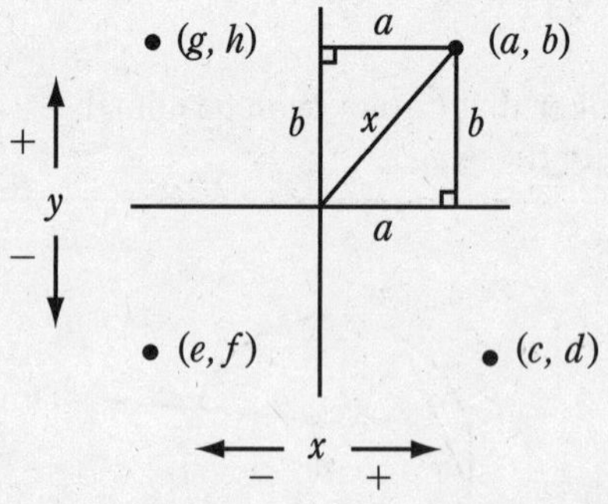

83. How many of the variables *a, b, c, d, e, f, g, h* are positive?

(A) 1
(B) 2
(C) 3
(D) 4
(E) 5

84. How many of the variables *a, b, c, d, e, f, g, h* are negative?

(A) 1
(B) 2
(C) 3
(D) 4
(E) 5

85. If $a = 3$, $b = 4$, what is x?

(A) 3
(B) 4
(C) 5
(D) 6
(E) None of these.

86.

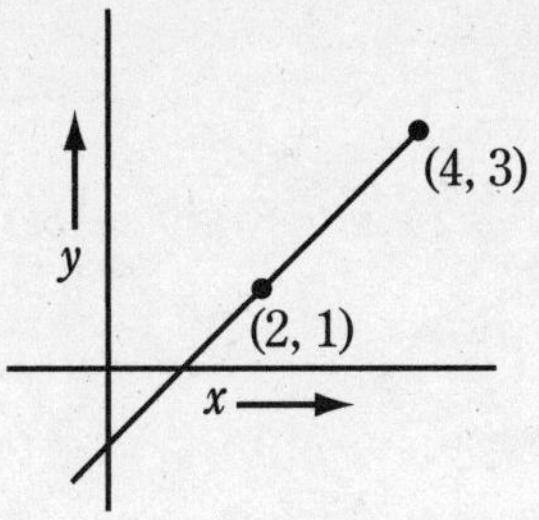

What is the slope of the line above?

(A) −1
(B) 0
(C) +1
(D) +2
(E) +3

N. Inequalities

Note: Any variable can be positive or negative or 0.

87. If $x > y$, then $4x > 4y$

(A) always
(B) sometimes
(C) never

88. If $x + y > z$, then $y > z - x$

(A) always
(B) sometimes
(C) never

89. If $-4 < -x$, then $+4 > +x$

(A) always
(B) sometimes
(C) never

90. If $m > n$, where q is any number, then $qm > qn$

(A) always
(B) sometimes
(C) never

91. If $x > y$ and $p > q$, then $x + p > y + q$

(A) always
(B) sometimes
(C) never

92. If $x > y$ and $p > q$, then $xp > qy$

(A) always
(B) sometimes
(C) never

O. Averages

93. What is the average of 30, 40, and 80?

(A) 150
(B) 75
(C) 50
(D) 45
(E) None of these.

94. What is the average speed in mph of a car traveling 40 miles in 4 hours?

(A) 160
(B) 10
(C) 120
(D) 30
(E) None of these.

P. Shortcuts

95. Which is greater? *Don't calculate a common denominator!*

$$\frac{7}{16} \text{ or } \frac{3}{7}$$

(A) $\frac{7}{16}$

(B) $\frac{3}{7}$

(C) They are equal.
(D) A relationship cannot be determined.

96. Add $\frac{7}{12} + \frac{3}{5} =$

(A) $1\frac{11}{60}$

(B) $1\frac{13}{60}$

(C) $1\frac{15}{60}$

(D) $\frac{10}{17}$

(E) None of these.

97. Subtract $\frac{7}{12} - \frac{3}{5} =$

(A) $-\frac{1}{60}$

(B) $-\frac{3}{60}$

(C) $-1\frac{11}{60}$

(D) $\frac{4}{7}$

(E) None of these.

98. $\frac{4}{250} =$

(A) .016
(B) .04
(C) .004
(D) .025
(E) None of these.

Note: Do not divide 250 into 4 in the above question!

99. What is c if

$$200 = \frac{a+b+c}{2} \text{ and } 80 = \frac{a+b}{3}?$$

(A) 160
(B) 140
(C) 120
(D) 100
(E) None of these.

100. What is the value of $95 \times 75 - 95 \times 74$? (*Don't multiply* 95×75 *or* 95×74*!*)

(A) 65
(B) 75
(C) 85
(D) 95
(E) None of these.

101. Find the value of

$$\frac{140 \times 15}{5 \times 7}$$ (*Don't multiply* 140×15*!*)

(A) 20
(B) 40
(C) 60
(D) 90
(E) None of these.

101 Math Questions: Answers, Diagnoses, Solutions, Generalizations, and Rules

101 Math Questions: Answers

A. Fractions

1. B
2. A
3. A
4. C
5. B

B. Even–Odd Relationships

6. A
7. B
8. B
9. B
10. A
11. B
12. B

C. Factors

13. A
14. C
15. B
16. D
17. C
18. A
19. D
20. A
21. C

D. Exponents

22. C
23. B
24. B
25. C
26. A
27. A
28. A
29. C
30. A
31. B
32. D

E. Percentages

33. B
34. C
35. C

F. Equations

36. C
37. A
38. B
39. A
40. A

G. Angles

41. B
42. A
43. A
44. C

H. Parallel Lines

45. B
46. A
47. B
48. B
49. A
50. A
51. B

I. Triangles

52. A
53. A
54. B
55. B
56. B
57. C
58. B
59. C
60. C
61. B
62. B
63. D
64. A
65. B

J. Circles

66. B
67. A
68. B
69. A
70. C

K. Other Figures

71. C
72. B
73. B
74. C
75. D
76. B
77. B
78. A
79. B
80. B

L. Number Lines

81. C
82. B

M. Coordinates

83. D
84. D
85. C
86. C

N. Inequalities

87. A
88. A
89. A
90. B
91. A
92. B

O. Averages

93. C
94. B

P. Shortcuts

95. A
96. A
97. A
98. A
99. A
100. D
101. C

Basic Skills Math Diagnosis

Math area	*Total questions*	**If you got any of the answers to the following questions wrong, study answers to those questions.*	*Pages in text for review*	*Complete Math Refresher: Refer to the following numbered sections of the Math Refresher (Part 6, starting on page 167) for a refresher on the applicable rules.*
A. Fractions	5	1–5	49	101–112, 123–128
B. Even–Odd Relationships	7	6–12	49	603–611
C. Factors	9	13–21	49–50	409
D. Exponents	11	22–32	50	429–430
E. Percentages	3	33–35	51	106, 107, 114
F. Equations	5	36–40	51	406–409
G. Angles	4	41–44	51–52	500–503
H. Parallel Lines	7	45–51	52	504
I. Triangles	14	52–65	52–54	306–308, 505–516
J. Circles	5	66–70	55	310–311, 524–529
K. Other Figures	10	71–80	55–56	303–305, 309, 312–316, 517–523
L. Number Lines	2	81–82	56	410a
M. Coordinates	4	83–86	56	410b–418
N. Inequalities	6	87–92	57	419–428
O. Averages	2	93–94	57	601
P. Shortcuts	7	95–101	57–58	128, 609

*Answer key is on pages 46–47.

Solutions, Generalizations, and Rules

A. Fractions

1. (B)

$$\frac{a}{\frac{b}{c}} = a \times \frac{c}{b} = \boxed{\frac{ac}{b}}$$

(INVERT TO MULTIPLY)

Alternate way:

$$\frac{a}{\frac{b}{c}} = \frac{a}{\frac{b}{c}} \times \frac{c}{c} = \frac{ac}{\frac{b}{\cancel{c}} \times \cancel{c}} = \boxed{\frac{ac}{b}}$$

---

2. (A)

$$\frac{1}{\frac{1}{y}} = 1 \times \frac{y}{1} = y$$

(INVERT TO MULTIPLY)

---

3. (A)

$$\frac{\frac{a}{b}}{c} = \frac{\frac{a}{b}}{c} \times \frac{b}{b} = \frac{a}{cb} = \boxed{\frac{a}{bc}}$$

---

4. (C)

$$\frac{1}{\frac{x}{y}} = 1 \times \frac{y}{x} = \boxed{\frac{y}{x}}$$

(INVERT TO MULTIPLY)

---

5. (B)

$$\frac{\frac{a}{b}}{\frac{b}{a}} = \frac{a}{b} \times \frac{a}{b} = \boxed{\frac{a^2}{b^2}}$$

(INVERT TO MULTIPLY)

Alternate way:

$$\frac{\frac{a}{b}}{\frac{b}{a}} = \frac{\frac{a}{b} \times a}{\frac{b}{a} \times a} = \frac{\frac{a^2}{b}}{\frac{b}{\cancel{a}}\cancel{a}} = \frac{\frac{a^2}{b}}{b} = \frac{\frac{a^2}{b} \times b}{b \times b} = \boxed{\frac{a^2}{b^2}}$$

B. Even–Odd Relationships

6. (A) ODD × ODD = $\boxed{\text{ODD}}$

$3 \times 3 = 9$; $5 \times 5 = 25$

---

7. (B) ODD + or − ODD = $\boxed{\text{EVEN}}$

$5 + 3 = 8$
$5 - 3 = 2$

---

8. (B) EVEN × EVEN = $\boxed{\text{EVEN}}$

$2 \times 2 = 4$; $4 \times 2 = 8$

---

9. (B) EVEN + or − EVEN = $\boxed{\text{EVEN}}$

$6 + 2 = 8$; $10 - 4 = 6$

---

10. (A) $(\text{ODD})^{\text{ODD}}$ = $\boxed{\text{ODD}}$

$3^3 = 3 \times 3 \times 3 = 27$ (odd)

$1^{27} = 1$ (odd)

---

11. (B) $(\text{EVEN})^{\text{EVEN}}$ = $\boxed{\text{EVEN}}$

$2^2 = 4$ (even); $4^2 = 16$ (even)

---

12. (B) $(\text{EVEN})^{\text{ODD}}$ = $\boxed{\text{EVEN}}$

$2^3 = 2 \times 2 \times 2 = 8$ (even)
$4^1 = 4$ (even)

C. Factors

13. (A) $(x + 3)(x + 2) = x^2 \ldots$

$(x + 3)(x + 2) = x^2 + 2x + 3x \ldots$

$(x + 3)(x + 2) = x^2 + 2x + 3x + 6$

$(x + 3)(x + 2) = \boxed{x^2 + 5x + 6}$

---

14. (C) $(x + 3)(x - 2) = x^2 \ldots$

$(x + 3)(x - 2) = x^2 - 2x + 3x \ldots$

$(x + 3)(x - 2) = x^2 - 2x + 3x - 6$

$(x + 3)(x - 2) = \boxed{x^2 + x - 6}$

15. (B) $(x - 3)(y - 2) = xy \ldots$

$(x - 3)(y - 2) = xy - 2x - 3y \ldots$

$(x - 3)(y - 2) = \boxed{xy - 2x - 3y + 6}$

---

16. (D) $(a + b)(b + c) = ab \ldots$

$(a + b)(b + c) = ab + ac + b^2 \ldots$

$(a + b)(b + c) = \boxed{ab + ac + b^2 + bc}$

---

17. (C) $(a + b)(a - b) =$

$(a + b)(a - b) = a^2$

$(a + b)(a - b) = a^2 - ab + ba \ldots$

$(a + b)(a - b) = a^2 - ab + ba - b^2$

$(a + b)(a - b) = a^2 - \cancel{ab} + \cancel{ba} - b^2$

$\boxed{(a + b)(a - b) = a^2 - b^2}$ MEMORIZE

---

18. (A) $(a + b)^2 = (a + b)(a + b)$

$(a + b)(a + b) = a^2 \ldots$

$(a + b)(a + b) = a^2 + ab + ba \ldots$

$(a + b)(a + b) = a^2 + ab + ba + b^2$

$\boxed{(a + b)^2 = a^2 + 2ab + b^2}$ MEMORIZE

---

19. (D) $-(a - b) = -a - (-b)$
$-(a - b) = -a + b$

$\boxed{-(a - b) = b - a}$ MEMORIZE

---

20. (A) $a(b + c) =$

$a(b + c) = \boxed{ab + ac}$

---

21. (C) $-a(b - c) =$

$-a(b - c) = -ab - a(-c)$

$= -ab + ac = \boxed{ac - ab}$

D. Exponents

22. (C) $10^5 = 100{,}000$

(5 zeros)

---

23. (B) $107076.5 = 1\,0\,7\,0\,7\,6\,.\,5$ (places counted 5 4 3 2 1)

$= 1.070765 \times \boxed{10^5}$

---

24. (B) Add exponents:

$a^2 \times a^5 = \boxed{a^7}$

$a^m \times a^n = a^{m+n}$

---

25. (C) $(ab)^7 = \boxed{a^7b^7}$

$(ab)^m = a^mb^m$

---

26. (A) $\left(\frac{a}{c}\right)^8 = \boxed{\frac{a^8}{c^8}}$; $\left(\frac{a}{c}\right)^m = \frac{a^m}{c^m}$

---

27. (A) $a^4 \times b^4 = \boxed{(ab)^4}$

$a^m \times b^m = (ab)^m$

---

28. (A) $a^{-3} \times b^5 = \boxed{\frac{b^5}{a^3}}$

$a^{-m} \times b^n = \frac{b^n}{a^m}$

---

29. (C) $(a^3)^5 = \boxed{a^{15}}$ $(a^m)^n = a^{mn}$

MULTIPLY EXPONENTS

---

30. (A) $2a^{-3} = \boxed{\frac{2}{a^3}}$

$ax^{-b} = \frac{a}{x^b}$

Since $a^{-n} = \frac{1}{a^n}$

---

31. (B) $2a^m \times \frac{1}{3}a^{-n} = \frac{2}{3}a^ma^{-n}$

$= \frac{2}{3}a^{m-n}$ or $\boxed{\frac{2a^m}{3a^n}}$

---

32. (D) $3^2 + 3^{-2} + 4^1 + 6^0 =$

$3^2 = 3 \times 3 = 9$

$3^{-2} = \frac{1}{3^2} = \frac{1}{9}$

$4^1 = 4$

$6^0 = 1$ (any number to 0 power = 1)

$3^2 + 3^{-2} + 4^1 + 6^0 = 9 + \frac{1}{9} + 4 + 1 = \boxed{14\frac{1}{9}}$

E. Percentages

Translate: is → =

of → × (times)

percent (%) → $\frac{}{100}$

what → x (or y, etc.)

33. (B) 15% of 200 =

$$15\frac{}{100} \times 200 =$$

$$\frac{15}{100} \times 200 =$$

$$\frac{15}{1\not{0}\not{0}} \times 2\not{0}\not{0} = \boxed{30}$$

---

34. (C) What is 3% of 5?

$$x = 3\frac{}{100} \times 5$$

$$x = \frac{3}{100} \times 5$$

$$x = \frac{15}{100} = \boxed{\frac{3}{20}}$$

---

35. (C) What percent of 3 is 6?

$$x \ \frac{}{100} \ \times \ 3 \ = \ 6$$

$$x\frac{}{100} \times 3 = 6$$

$$\frac{x}{100} \times 3 = 6$$

$$\frac{3x}{100} = 6$$

$$3x = 600$$

$$x = \boxed{200}$$

F. Equations

36. (C) $y^2 = 16$

$$\sqrt{y^2} = \pm\sqrt{16}$$

$$y = \boxed{\pm 4}$$

---

37. (A) $x - y = 10$

Add y:

$x - y + y = 10 + y$

$x = 10 + y$

Subtract 10:

$x - 10 = 10 - 10 + y$

$\boxed{x - 10 = y}$

---

38. (B) Add equations:

$$x + 4y = 7$$
$$x - 4y = 8$$

$$2x + \not{4y} - \not{4y} = 15$$

$2x = 15$

$\boxed{x = \frac{15}{2}}$

---

39. (A) $x - 2y = 2$ $\boxed{1}$

$2x + y = 4$ $\boxed{2}$

Multiply $\boxed{1}$ by 2:

$2(x - 2y) = 2(2)$

We get:

$2x - 4y = 4$ $\boxed{3}$

Subtract $\boxed{2}$ from $\boxed{3}$:

$$2x - 4y = 4$$
$$-\ (2x + y = 4)$$

$$0 - 5y = 0$$

$\boxed{y = 0}$ $\boxed{4}$

Substitute $\boxed{4}$ into either $\boxed{1}$ or $\boxed{2}$:

In $\boxed{1}$:

$$x - 2y = 2$$
$$x - 2(0) = 2$$

$\boxed{x = 2}$

---

40. (A) $\frac{x}{5} = \frac{7}{12}$, $x =$

Cross-multiply x:

$$\frac{x}{5} = \frac{7}{12}$$

$$12x = 35$$

Divide by 12:

$$\frac{12x}{12} = \frac{35}{12}$$

$$\boxed{x = \frac{35}{12} = 2\frac{11}{12}}$$

G. Angles

Questions 41–42 refer to the diagram.

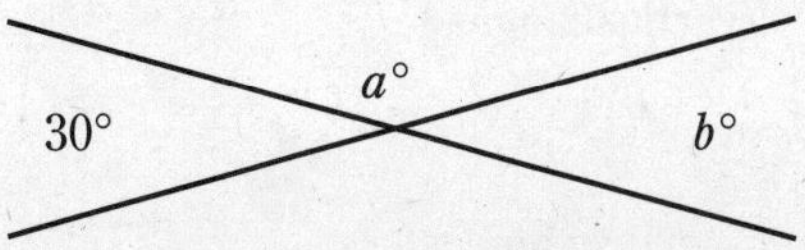

41. (B) $a°$ and 30° are supplementary angles (they add up to 180°).

So $a + 30 = 180$; $a = \boxed{150}$.

42. (A) $b°$ and $30°$ are *vertical* angles (vertical angles are equal).

So $b = \boxed{30}$.

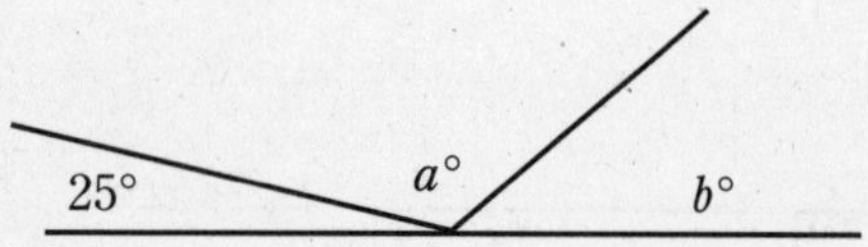

43. (A) $a°$, $b°$, and $25°$ make up a *straight* angle, which is $180°$.
$a + b + 25 = 180$
$a + b = 180 - 25$
$a + b = \boxed{155}$

44. (C) The sum of the angles in the diagram is $\boxed{360°}$, the number of degrees around the circumference of a circle.

H. Parallel Lines

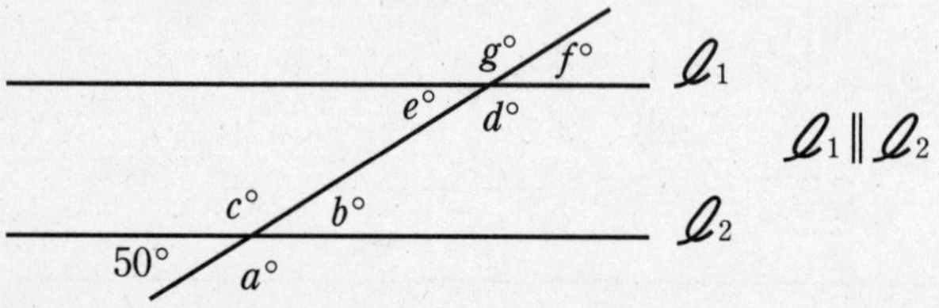

45. (B) $a + 50 = 180$

$a = \boxed{130}$

46. (A) $b = \boxed{50}$ (vertical angles)

47. (B) $c = a$ (vertical angles)

$= \boxed{130}$

48. (B) $d = c$ (alternate interior angles are equal)

$= \boxed{130}$

49. (A) $e = b$ (alternate interior angles)

$= \boxed{50}$

50. (A) $f = e$ (vertical angles)

$= \boxed{50}$

51. (B) $g = d$ (vertical angles)

$= \boxed{130}$

I. Triangles

52. (A)

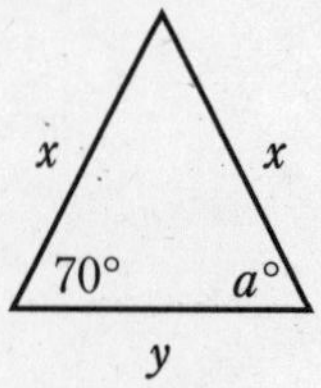

(Note: Figure is not drawn to scale.)

If two sides are equal, base angles are equal. Thus $a = \boxed{70°}$.

53. (A)

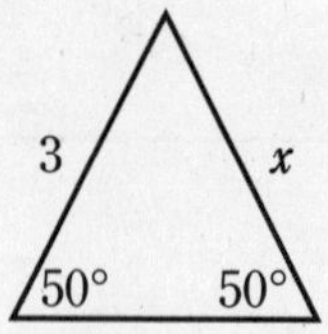

(Note: Figure is not drawn to scale.)

If base angles are equal, then sides are equal, so $\boxed{x = 3}$.

54. (B)

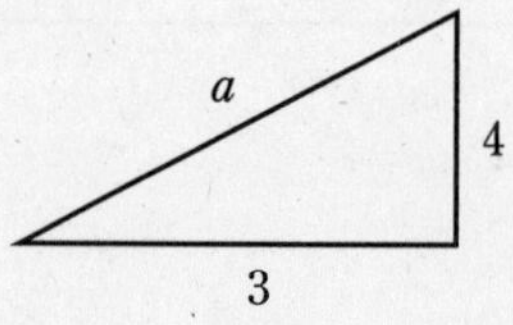

(Note: Figure is not drawn to scale.)

The sum of two sides must be *greater* than the third side. Try choices:

(A) $3 + 4 \not> 1$: (A) is not possible
(B) $3 + 4 > 6$; $6 + 3 > 4$; $4 + 6 > 3$...OK
(C) $3 + 4 \not> 10$: (C) is not possible
(D) $3 + 4 = 7$: (D) is not possible
(E) $3 + 4 \not> 8$: (E) is not possible

55. (B) Using similar triangles, write a *proportion* with x.

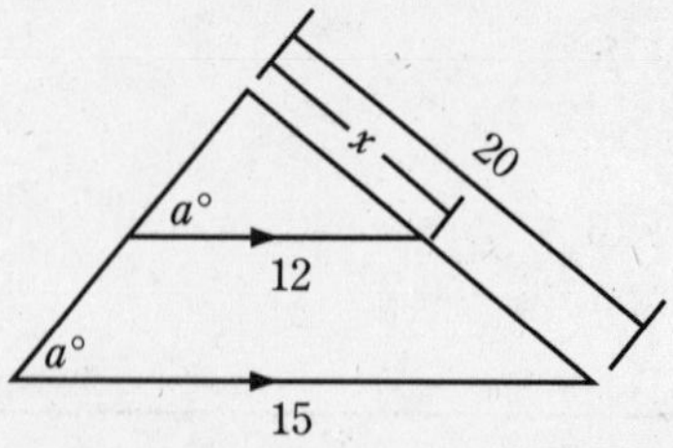

(Note: Figure is not drawn to scale.)

$$\frac{x}{20} = \frac{12}{15}$$
$$15x = 12 \times 20$$
$$x = \frac{12 \times 20}{15}$$
$$x = \frac{\overset{4}{\cancel{12}} \times \overset{4}{\cancel{20}}}{\underset{\cancel{5}}{\cancel{15}}} = \boxed{16}$$

In general:

$$\frac{m}{n} = \frac{q}{p} = \frac{r}{r+s}$$

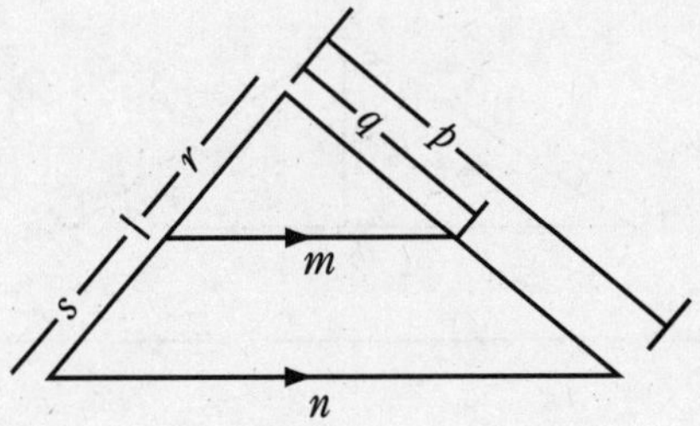

(Note: Figure is not drawn to scale.)

56. (B) The greater angle lies opposite the greater side and vice versa.

If $B > A$, $\boxed{b > a}$

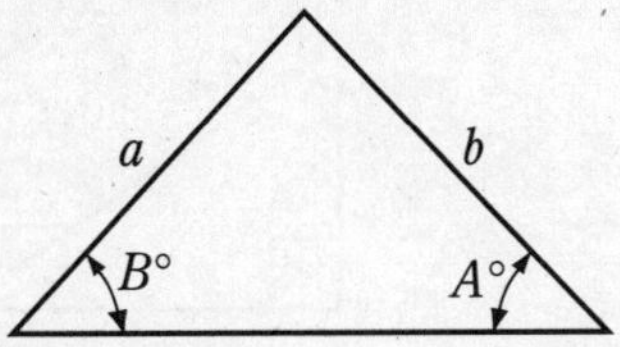

57. (C) The greater side lies opposite the greater angle and vice versa.

If $b < a$, then $\boxed{B < A}$

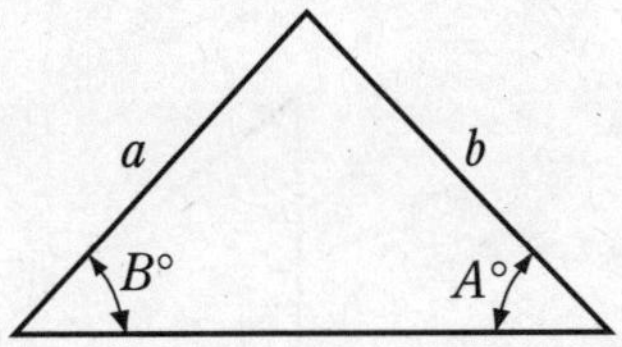

58. (B) Sum of angles of triangle = 180°.

So $40 + 60 + x = 180$

$100 + x = 180$

$\boxed{x = 80}$

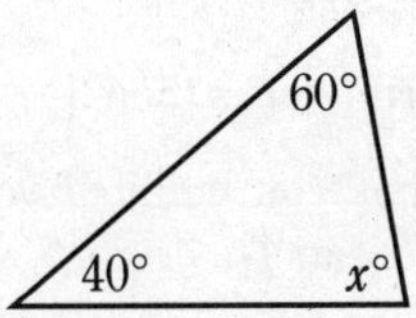

59. (C)

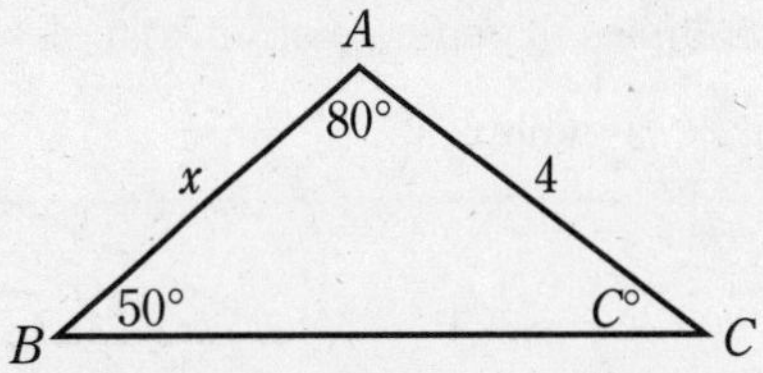

(Note: Figure is not drawn to scale.)

First calculate $\angle C$. Call it y.

$80 + 50 + y = 180$ (Sum of $\angle$s = 180°)

$y = 50$

Since $\angle C = y = 50$ and $\angle B = 50$, side AB = side AC.

$AB = \boxed{x = 4}$

60. (C) $x° = 20° + 40°$ (sum of *remote* interior angles = exterior angle).

$\boxed{x = 60}$

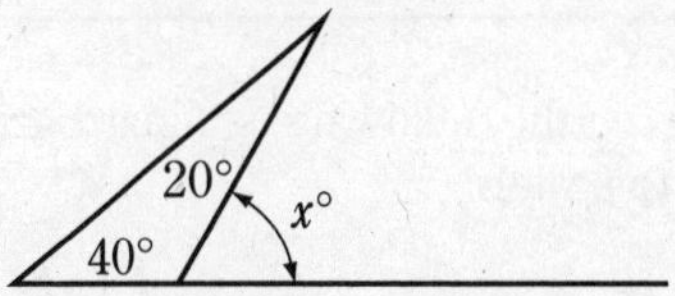

In general,

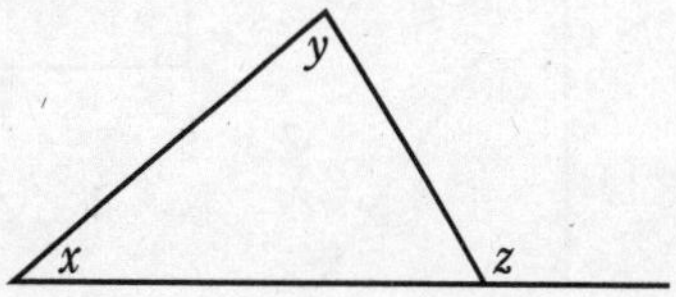

$z = x + y$

61. (B)

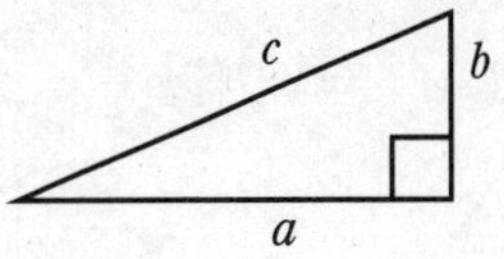

In right Δ, $a^2 + b^2 = c^2$

So for

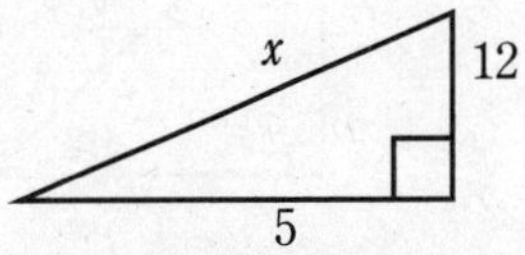

$$5^2 + 12^2 = x^2$$
$$25 + 144 = x^2$$
$$169 = x^2$$
$$\sqrt{169} = x$$
$$\boxed{13} = x$$

Note: Specific right triangles you should memorize; use multiples to generate other triangles.

Example of multiples:

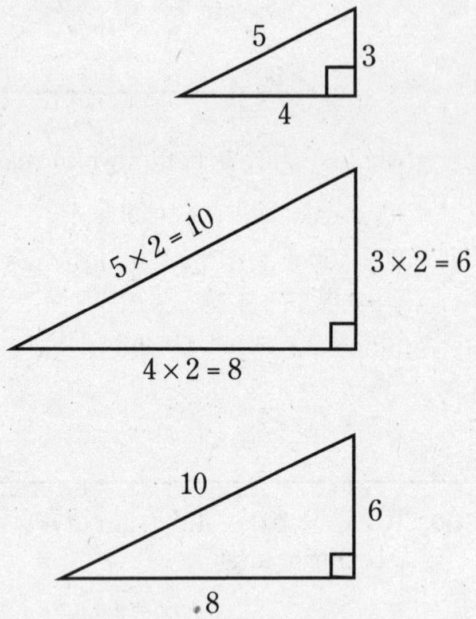

Memorize the following standard triangles (not drawn to scale):

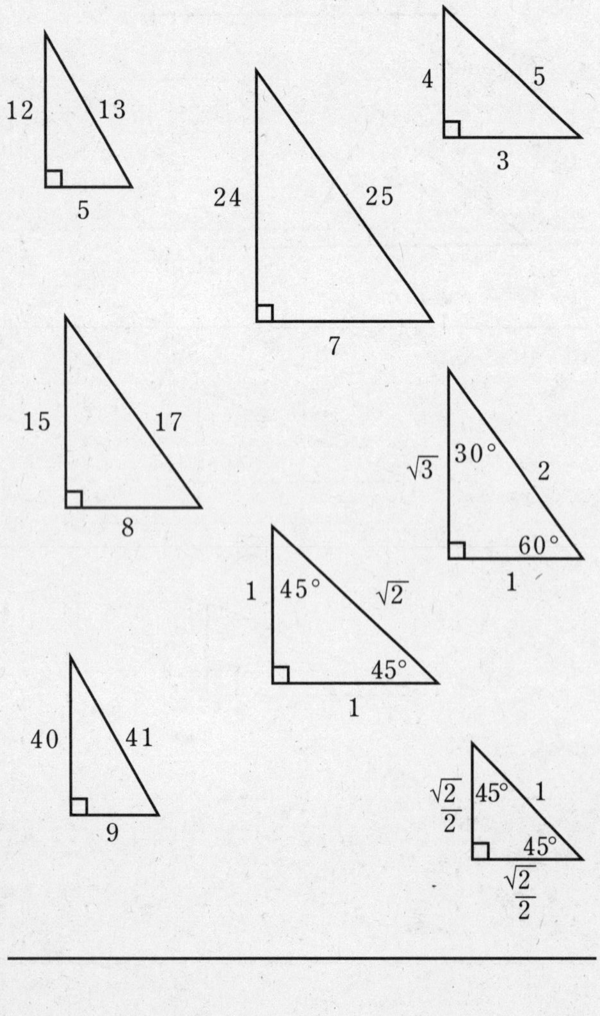

---

62. (B) Perimeter = sum of sides
$10 + 17 + 21 = \boxed{48}$

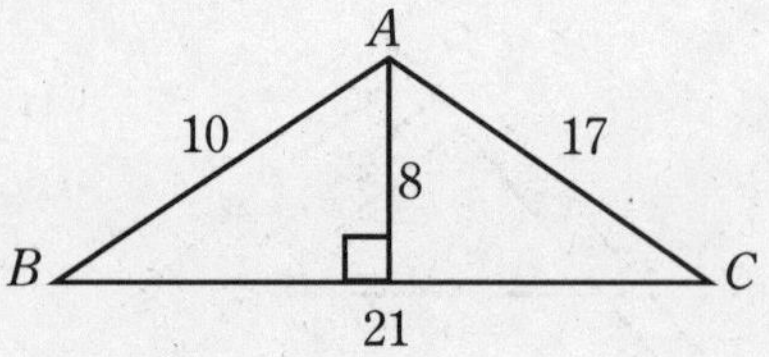

---

63. (D)

Area of $\Delta = \frac{1}{2}bh$

Area of $\Delta = \frac{1}{2}(21)(8) = \boxed{84}$

64. (A) Area of any triangle $= \frac{1}{2}$base × height

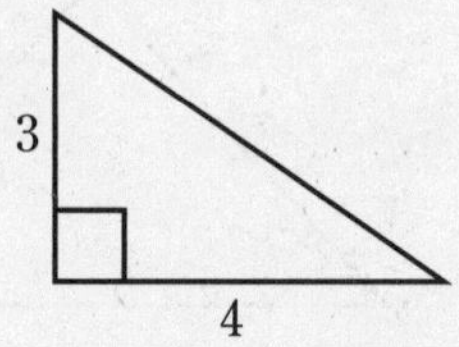

Here 4 is base and 3 is height. So area $= \frac{1}{2}(4 \times 3) = \frac{1}{2}(12) = \boxed{6}$.

---

65. (B)

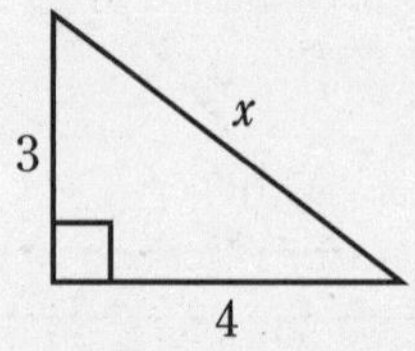

To find perimeter, we need to find the sum of the sides. The sum of the sides is $3 + 4 + x$.

We need to find x. From the solution in Question 61, we should realize that we have a 3–4–5 right triangle, so $x = 5$.

The perimeter is then $3 + 4 + 5 = \boxed{12}$.

Note that you could have found x by using the Pythagorean Theorem:

$3^2 + 4^2 = x^2$; $9 + 16 = x^2$; $25 = x^2$; $\sqrt{25} = x$; $5 = x$.

J. Circles

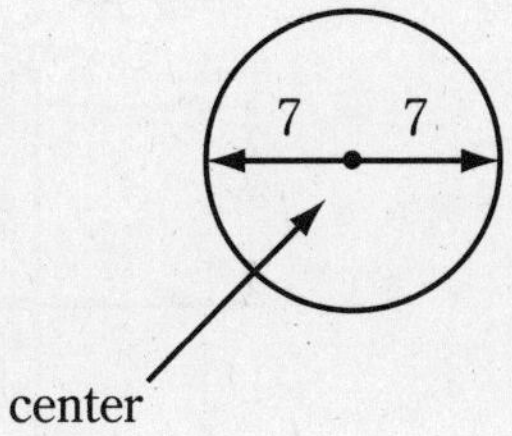

66. (B) Area $= \pi r^2 = \pi(7)^2$
$= \boxed{49\pi}$

---

67. (A) Circumference $= 2\pi r = 2\pi(7)$
$= \boxed{14\pi}$

---

68. (B) Inscribed angle $= \frac{1}{2}$ arc
$x° = \frac{1}{2}(70°)$
$= \boxed{35°}$

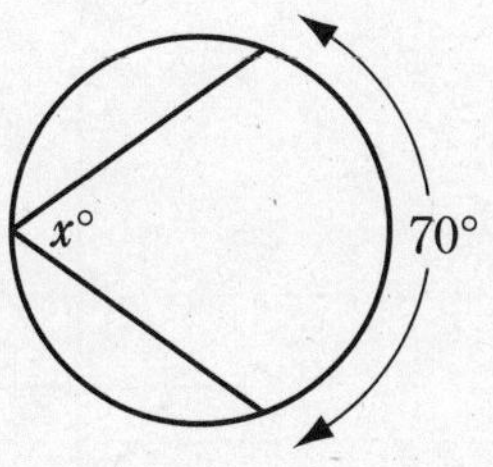

---

69. (A) Central angle = arc
$\boxed{30°} = x°$

Note: The *total* number of degrees around the circumference is 360°. So a central angle of 30°, like the one below, cuts $\frac{30}{360} = \frac{1}{12}$ the circumference.

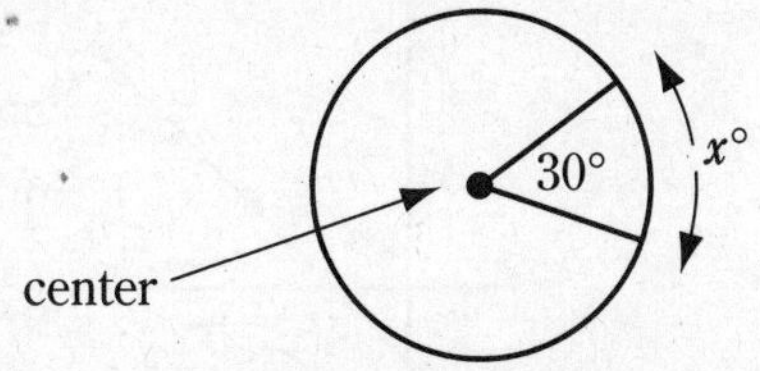

---

70. (C) The diameter cuts a 180° arc on the circle, so an inscribed angle $y = \frac{1}{2}\text{arc} = \frac{1}{2}(180°) = \boxed{90°}$.

Here is a good thing to remember:

Any inscribed angle whose triangle base is a diameter is 90°.

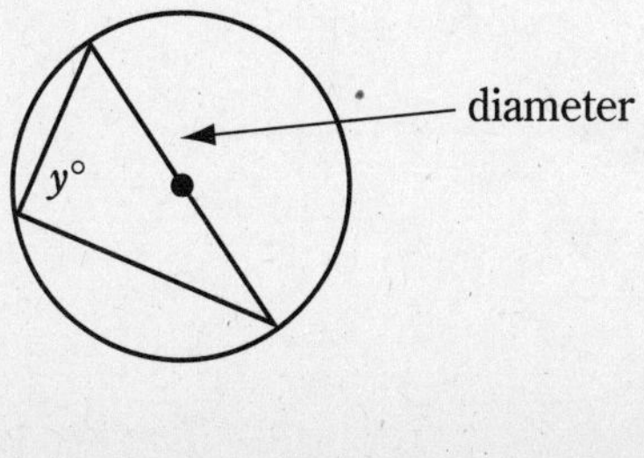

K. Other Figures

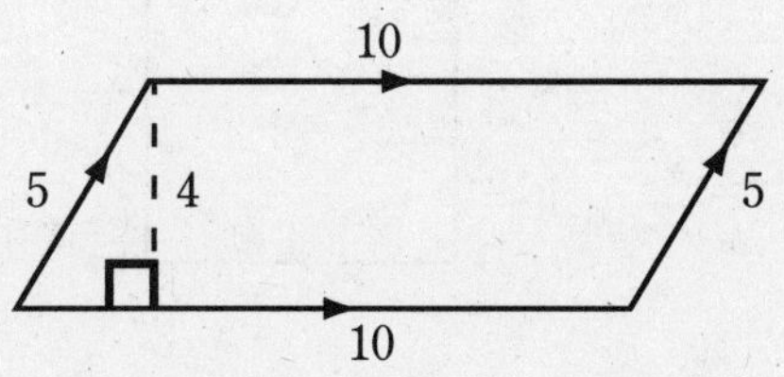

71. (C) Area of parallelogram = base × height = $(10)(4) = \boxed{40}$

72. (B) Perimeter = sum of sides = $5 + 5 + 10 + 10 = \boxed{30}$

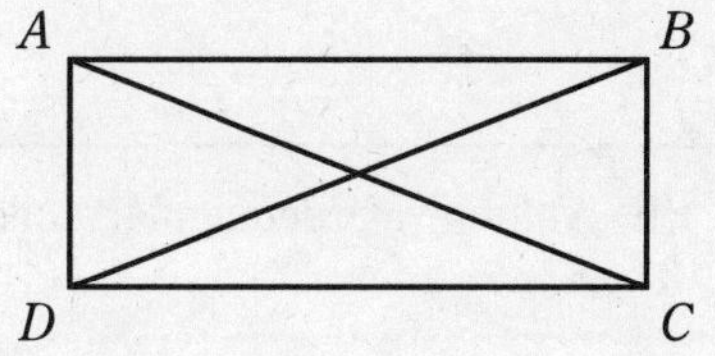

ABCD is a rectangle.

73. (B) In a rectangle (as in a parallelogram), opposite sides are equal.

So $AD = BC = \boxed{6}$.

---

74. (C) In a rectangle (as in a parallelogram), opposite sides are equal.

So $DC = AB = \boxed{8}$.

---

75. (D) In a rectangle (but not in a parallelogram), the diagonals are equal.

So $DB = AC = \boxed{10}$.

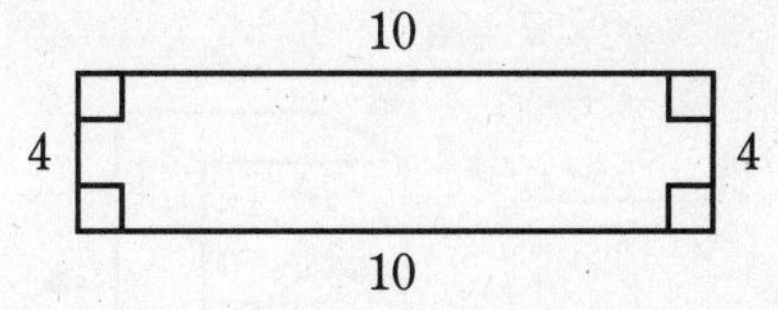

76. (B) Area of rectangle = length × width = $4 \times 10 = \boxed{40}$.

---

77. (B) Perimeter = sum of sides =

$4 + 4 + 10 + 10 = \boxed{28}$.

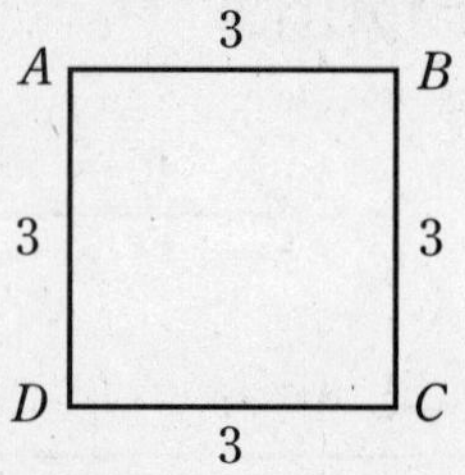

78. (A) Area of a square with side x is x^2. (All sides of a square are equal.) So length = width. Since $x = 3$, $x^2 = \boxed{9}$.

---

79. (B) Perimeter of a square is the sum of all sides of the square. Since all sides are equal, if one side is x, perimeter = $4x$.

$x = 3$, so $4x = \boxed{12}$.

---

80. (B) Volume of rectangular solid shown below = $a \times b \times c$

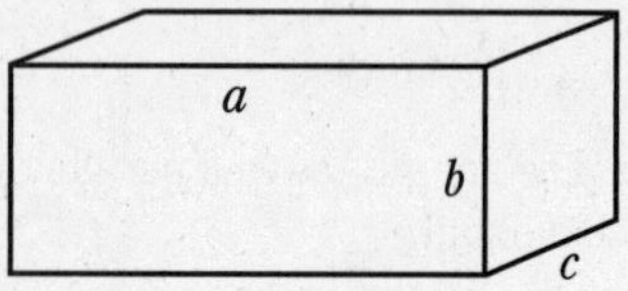

So for:

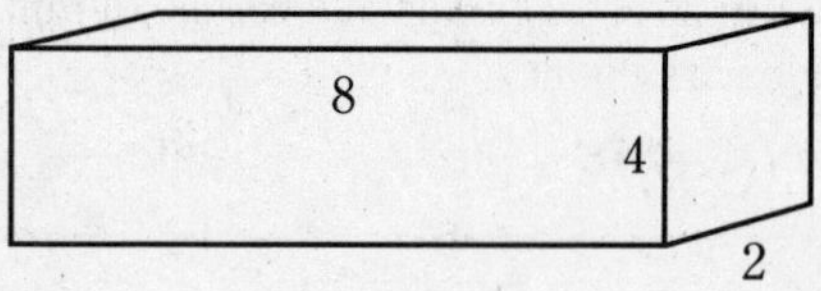

$a = 8$, $b = 4$, $c = 2$

and $a \times b \times c = 8 \times 4 \times 2 = \boxed{64}$.

Note: Volume of cube shown below = $a \times a \times a = a^3$

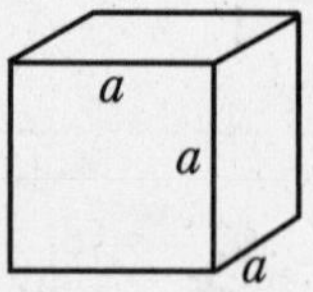

L. Number Lines

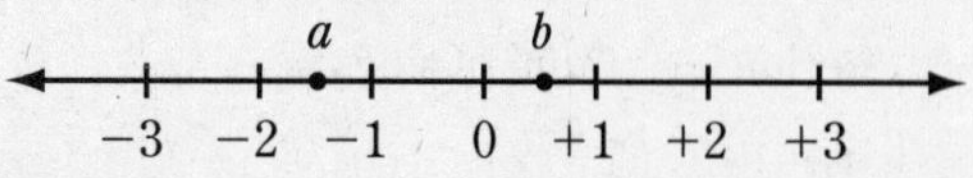

81. (C) b is between 0 and +1 so $\boxed{0 < b < 1}$.

82. (B) a is between −2 and −1 so $\boxed{-2 < a < -1}$.

M. Coordinates

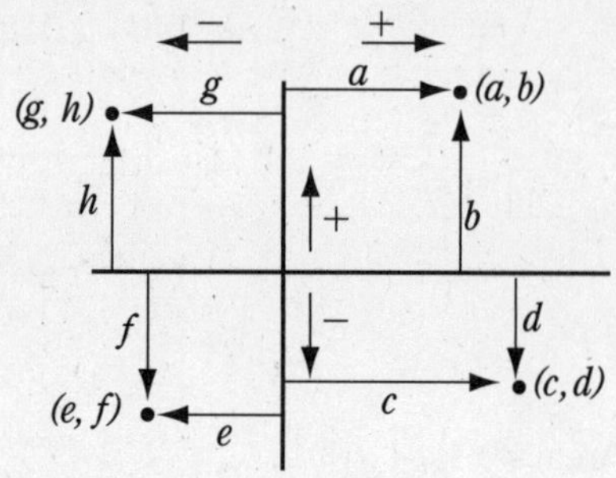

Horizontal right = +
Horizontal left = −
Vertical up = +
Vertical down = −

83. (D) a, b, c, h positive (4 letters)

84. (D) d, e, f, g negative (4 letters)

---

85. (C)

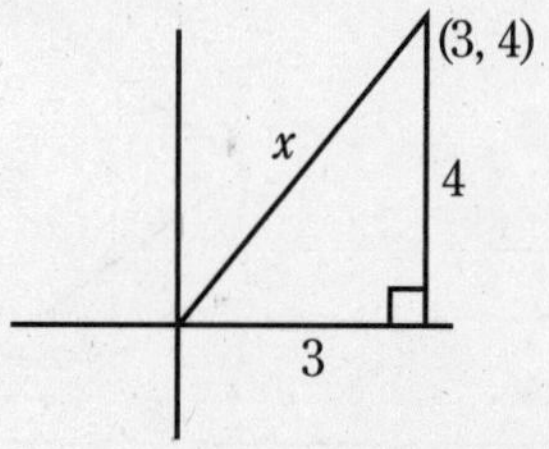

Remember the 3–4–5 right triangle. $\boxed{x = 5}$

You can also use the Pythagorean Theorem:

$3^2 + 4^2 = x^2$; $9 + 16 = x^2$; $x^2 = 25$; $\boxed{x = 5}$

---

86. (C)

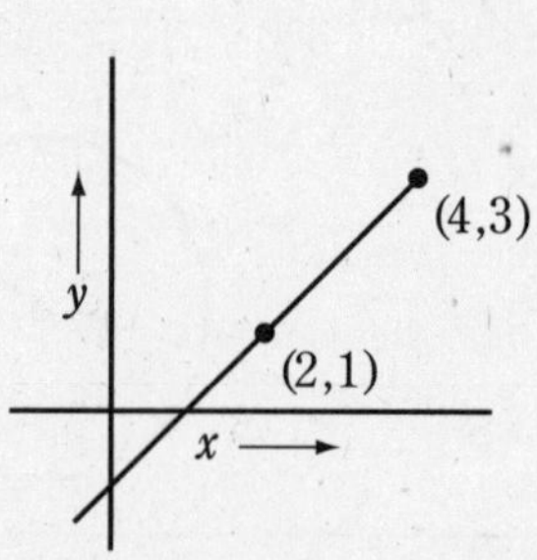

The slope of a line $y = mx + b$ is m. If two points (x_1,y_1) and (x_2,y_2) are on the line, then the slope is

$\frac{y_2 - y_1}{x_2 - x_1} = m$. Here $x_1 = 2$, $y_1 = 1$, $x_2 = 4$, $y_2 = 3$

So $\frac{y_2 - y_1}{x_2 - x_1} = \frac{3-1}{4-2} = \boxed{1}$.

N. Inequalities

87. (A) You can multiply an inequality by a positive number and retain the same inequality:

$x > y$

$\boxed{4x > 4y}$ $\boxed{\text{ALWAYS}}$

---

88. (A) You can subtract the same number from both sides of an inequality and retain the same inequality:

$$x + y > z$$
$$x + y - x > z - x$$

$\boxed{y > z - x}$ $\boxed{\text{ALWAYS}}$

---

89. (A) If you multiply an inequality by a minus sign, you *reverse* the original inequality sign:

$$-4 < -x$$
$$-(-4 < -x)$$

$\boxed{+4 > +x}$ $\boxed{\text{ALWAYS}}$

---

90. (B) If $m > n$,

$qm > qn$ if q is *positive*

$qm < qn$ if q is *negative*

$qm = qn$ if q is *zero*

So, $\boxed{qm > qn}$ $\boxed{\text{SOMETIMES}}$

---

91. (A) You can always add inequality relations to get the same inequality relation:

$$\begin{array}{r} x > y \\ + p > q \\ \hline x + p > y + q \end{array}$$

$\boxed{\text{ALWAYS}}$

---

92. (B) You can't always multiply inequality relations to get the same inequality relation. For example:

$$\begin{array}{r} 3 > 2 \\ \times\ -2 > -3 \\ \hline -6 \not> -6 \end{array} \qquad \begin{array}{r} 3 > 2 \\ \times\ 2 > 1 \\ \hline 6 > 2 \end{array}$$

However, if x, y, p, q are positive, then if $x > y$ and $p > q$, $xp > yq$. $\boxed{\text{SOMETIMES}}$

O. Averages

93. (C) Average of 30, 40, and 80 =

$$\frac{30 + 40 + 80}{3} = \boxed{50}$$

Average of $x + y + z + t + \ldots = \dfrac{x + y + z + t + \ldots}{\textit{number of terms}}$

---

94. (B) Average speed $= \dfrac{\text{total distance}}{\text{total time}}$

Distance = 40 miles, Time = 4 hours

Average speed $= \dfrac{40 \text{ miles}}{4 \text{ hours}} = \boxed{10 \text{ miles per hour}}$

P. Shortcuts

95. (A) Don't get a common denominator if you can do something more easily:

$$\frac{7}{16} \quad \xleftrightarrow{\text{MULTIPLY}} \quad \frac{3}{7}$$

(MULTIPLY, MULTIPLY: cross-multiply)

$$\begin{array}{ccc} 49 & & 48 \\ 49 & > & 48 \\ \text{so } \boxed{\dfrac{7}{16}} & > & \dfrac{3}{7} \end{array}$$

---

96. (A)

$$\frac{7}{12} + \frac{3}{5} = \frac{7 \times 5 + 3 \times 12}{12 \times 5}$$

(MULTIPLY, MULTIPLY)

$$= \frac{35 + 36}{60}$$

$$= \frac{71}{60} = \boxed{1\frac{11}{60}}$$

---

97. (A)

$$\frac{7}{12} - \frac{3}{5} = \frac{7 \times 5 - 3 \times 12}{12 \times 5}$$

(MULTIPLY, MULTIPLY)

$$= \frac{35 - 36}{60}$$

$$= \boxed{-\frac{1}{60}}$$

---

98. (A) Don't divide by 250! Multiply both numerator and denominator by 4:

$$\frac{4}{250} \times \frac{4}{4} = \frac{16}{1{,}000} = \boxed{0.016}$$

---

99. (A) Get rid of denominators!

$200 = \dfrac{a + b + c}{2}$ $\boxed{1}$

Multiply $\boxed{1}$ by 2:

$200 \times 2 = a + b + c$ $\boxed{2}$

$80 = \dfrac{a + b}{3}$ $\boxed{3}$

Multiply $\boxed{3}$ by 3:

$80 \times 3 = a + b$ $\boxed{4}$

Now subtract $\boxed{4}$ from $\boxed{2}$:

$$200 \times 2 - 80 \times 3 = a + b + c - (a + b)$$
$$= \cancel{a} + \cancel{b} + c - \cancel{a} - \cancel{b}$$
$$400 - 240 = c$$
$$\boxed{160} = c$$

100. (D) Don't multiply 95 × 75 or 95 × 74!

Factor *common* 95:

$$\begin{aligned} 95 \times 75 - 95 \times 74 &= 95(75 - 74) \\ &= 95(1) \\ &= \boxed{95} \end{aligned}$$

---

101. (C) $\frac{140 \times 15}{5 \times 7}$

Don't multiply 140 × 15 if you can first *reduce*.

$$\frac{\overset{20}{\cancel{140}} \times 15}{5 \times \underset{1}{\cancel{7}}} = \frac{20 \times 15}{5}$$

Further reduce:

$$\frac{20 \times \overset{3}{\cancel{15}}}{\underset{1}{\cancel{5}}} = \boxed{60}$$

PART 4

STRATEGY SECTION

Using Critical Thinking Skills to Score High on the SAT

5 General Strategies

General Strategies for Taking the SAT Examination

Before studying the 35 specific strategies for the Math and Critical Reading questions, you will find it useful to review the following 5 General Strategies for taking the SAT examination.

Strategy 1:

DON'T RUSH INTO GETTING AN ANSWER WITHOUT THINKING. BE CAREFUL IF YOUR ANSWER COMES TOO EASILY, ESPECIALLY IF THE QUESTION IS TOWARD THE END OF THE SECTION.

Beware of Choice A If You Get the Answer Fast or Without Really Thinking

Everybody panics when they take an exam like the SAT. And what happens is that they rush into getting answers. That's OK, except that you have to think carefully. If a problem looks too easy, beware! And, especially beware of the Choice A answer. It's usually a "lure" choice for those who rush into getting an answer without critically thinking about it. Here's an example:

> Below is a picture of a digital clock. The clock shows that the time is 6:06. Consider all the times on the clock where the hour is the same as the minute like in the clock shown below. Another such "double" time would be 8:08 or 9:09. What is the smallest time period between any two such doubles?
>
> (A) 61 minutes
> (B) 60 minutes
> (C) 58 minutes
> (D) 50 minutes
> (E) 49 minutes
>
> **6:06**

Did you subtract 7:07 from 8:08 and get 1 hour and 1 minute (61 minutes)? If you did you probably chose Choice A: the *lure choice*. Think—do you really believe that the test maker would give you such an easy question? The fact that you figured it out so easily and saw that Choice A was your answer should make you think twice. The thing you have to realize is that there is another possibility: 12:12 to 1:01 gives 49 minutes, and so Choice E is correct.

So, in summary, if you get the answer fast and without doing much thinking, and it's a Choice A answer, think again. You may have fallen for the Choice A lure.

NOTE: Choice A is often a "lure choice" for those who quickly get an answer without doing any real thinking. However, you should certainly realize that Choice A answers can occur, especially if there is no "lure choice."

Strategy 2:

KNOW AND LEARN THE DIRECTIONS TO THE QUESTION TYPES BEFORE YOU TAKE THE ACTUAL TEST.

Never Spend Time Reading Directions During the Test or Doing Sample Questions That Don't Count

All SATs are standardized. For example, all the Regular Math questions have the same directions from test to test, as do the Sentence Completions, etc. So it's a good idea to learn these sets of directions and familiarize yourself with the types of questions early in the game before you take your actual SAT.

Here's an example of a set of SAT directions, together with an accompanying example for the Sentence Completion type of questions.

For each question in this section, select the best answer from among the choices given and fill in the corresponding oval on the answer sheet.

> Directions:
>
> Each sentence below has one or two blanks, each blank indicating that something has been omitted. Beneath the sentence are five words or set of words labeled A through E. Choose the word or set of words that, when inserted in the sentence, *best* fits the meaning of the sentence as a whole.
>
> Example:
>
> Hoping to _______ the dispute, negotiators proposed a compromise that they felt would be _______ to both labor and management.
>
> (A) enforce...useful
> (B) end...divisive
> (C) overcome...unattractive
> (D) extend...satisfactory
> (E) resolve...acceptable
>
> Ⓐ Ⓑ Ⓒ Ⓓ ●

If on your actual test you spend time reading these directions and/or answering the sample question, you will waste valuable time.

As you go through this book, you will become familiar with all the question types so that you won't have to read their directions on the actual test.

Strategy 3:

IT MAY BE WISER NOT TO LEAVE AN ANSWER BLANK.

The Penalty for Guessing Is Much Smaller Than You Might Expect

On the SAT you lose a percentage of points if you guess and get the wrong answers on the multiple-choice questions. Of course, you should always try to eliminate choices. After going through this book, you'll have a better chance of eliminating wrong answers. However, if you cannot eliminate any choice in a question and have no idea of how to arrive at an answer, you might want to pick any answer and go on to the next question.

There are two reasons for this:

1. You don't want to risk mismarking a future answer by leaving a previous answer blank.
2. Even though there is a penalty for guessing, the penalty is much smaller than you might expect, and this way you have at least a chance of getting the question right. Suppose, for example, that you have a five-choice question:

> From a probabilistic point of view, it is very likely that you would get one question right and four wrong (you have a 1 in 5 chance of getting a five-choice question right) if you randomly guess at the answers. Since $\frac{1}{4}$ point is taken off for each wrong five-choice question, you've gotten $1 - \frac{1}{4} \times 4 = 0$ points, because you've gotten 1 question right and 4 wrong. Thus you break even. So the moral is whether you randomly guess at questions you're not sure of at all or whether you leave those question answers blank, it doesn't make a difference in the long run!

Strategy 4:

WRITE AS MUCH AS YOU WANT IN YOUR TEST BOOKLET.

Test Booklets Aren't Graded—So Use Them as You Would Scrap Paper

Many students are afraid to mark up their test booklets. But the booklets are not graded! Make any marks you want. In fact, some of the strategies demand that you extend or draw lines in geometry questions or label diagrams, circle incorrect answers, etc. That's why when I see computer programs that show only the questions on a screen and prevent the student from marking a diagram or circling an answer, I realize that such programs prevent the student from using many powerful strategies. *So write all you want in your test booklet—use your test paper as you would scrap paper.*

Strategy 5:

USE YOUR OWN CODING SYSTEM TO TELL YOU WHICH QUESTIONS TO RETURN TO.

If You Have Extra Time after Completing a Test Section, You'll Know Exactly Which Questions Need More Attention

When you are sure that you have answered a question correctly, mark your question paper with ✓. For questions you are not sure of but for which you have eliminated some of the choices, use **?**. For questions that you're not sure of at all or for which you have not been able to eliminate any choices, use **??**. This will give you a bird's-eye view of what questions you should return to if you have time left after completing a particular test section.

35 Easy-to-Learn Strategies

19 Math Strategies + 16 Verbal (Critical Reading) Strategies

Critical thinking is the ability to think clearly in order to solve problems and answer questions of all types—SAT questions, for example, both Math and Verbal!

Educators who are deeply involved in research on Critical Thinking Skills tell us that such skills are straightforward, practical, teachable, and learnable.

The 19 Math Strategies and 16 Verbal Strategies in this section are Critical Thinking Skills. These strategies have the potential to raise your SAT scores dramatically. Since each correct SAT question gives you an additional 10 points on average, it is reasonable to assume that if you can learn and then use these valuable SAT strategies, you can boost your SAT scores phenomenally!

BE SURE TO LEARN AND USE THE STRATEGIES THAT FOLLOW!

How to Learn the Strategies

1. For each strategy, look at the heading describing the strategy.

2. Try to answer the first example without looking at the EXPLANATORY ANSWER.

3. Then look at the EXPLANATORY ANSWER and if you got the right answer, see if the method described will enable you to solve the question in a better way with a faster approach.

4. Then try each of the next EXAMPLES without looking at the EXPLANATORY ANSWERS.

5. Use the same procedure as in (3) for each of the EXAMPLES.

The MATH STRATEGIES start on page 69, and the VERBAL STRATEGIES start on page 119. However, before you start the Math Strategies, it would be wise for you to look at the *Important Note on the Allowed Use of Calculators on the SAT*, following; the *Important Note on Math Questions on the SAT*, page 62; *The Grid-Type Math Question*, page 63; and *Use of a Calculator in the Grid-Type Question*, page 67.

Important Note on the Allowed Use of Calculators on the SAT

Although the use of calculators on the SAT will be allowed, using a calculator may be sometimes more tedious, when in fact you can use another problem-solving method or shortcut. So you must be selective on when and when not to use a calculator on the test.

Here's an example of when a calculator should *not* be used:

$$\frac{2}{5} \times \frac{5}{6} \times \frac{6}{7} \times \frac{7}{8} \times \frac{8}{9} \times \frac{9}{10} \times \frac{10}{11} =$$

(A) $\frac{9}{11}$

(B) $\frac{2}{11}$

(C) $\frac{11}{36}$

(D) $\frac{10}{21}$

(E) $\frac{244}{360}$

Here the use of a calculator may take some time. However, if you use the strategy of canceling numerators and denominators (Math Strategy 1, Example 3 on page 70) as shown,

Cancel numerators/denominators:

$$\frac{2}{\not{5}} \times \frac{\not{5}}{\not{6}} \times \frac{\not{6}}{\not{7}} \times \frac{\not{7}}{\not{8}} \times \frac{\not{8}}{\not{9}} \times \frac{\not{9}}{\not{10}} \times \frac{\not{10}}{11} = \frac{2}{11}$$

you can see that the answer comes easily as $\frac{2}{11}$.

Later I will show you an example in the *grid-type* question where the use of a calculator will also take you a longer time to solve a problem than without the calculator. Here's an example where using a calculator may get you the solution *as fast as* using a strategy without the calculator:

25 percent of 16 is equivalent to $\frac{1}{2}$ of what number?

(A) 2
(B) 4
(C) 8
(D) 16
(E) 32

Using a calculator, you'd use Math Strategy 2 (page 71) (translating *of* to *times* and *is* to *equals*), first calculating 25 percent of 16 to get 4. Then you'd say 4 = half of what number and you'd find that number to be 8.

Without using a calculator, you'd still use Math Strategy 2 (the translation strategy), but you could write 25 percent as $\frac{1}{4}$, so you'd figure out that $\frac{1}{4} \times 16$ is 4. Then you'd call the number you want to find x, and say $4 = \frac{1}{2}(x)$. You'd find $x = 8$.

Note that both methods, with and without a calculator, are about equally efficient; however, the technique in the second method can be used for many more problems and hones more thinking skills.

Important Note on Math Questions on the SAT

There are two types of math questions on the SAT.

1. The Regular Math (total of 44 counted questions), which has five choices. The strategies for these start on page 69.

2. The Grid-Type Math Question (total of 10 counted questions) is described below.

   Note: The grid-type questions can be solved using the Regular Math Strategies.

The Grid-Type Math Question

There will be 10 questions on the SAT where you will have to grid in your answer rather than choose from a set of five choices. Here are the directions to the grid-type question. Make sure that you understand these directions completely before you answer any of the grid-type questions.

Directions: For Student-Produced Response questions 1–15, use the grids on the following page.

Each of the remaining questions requires you to solve the problem and enter your answer by marking the circles in the special grid, as shown in the examples below. You may use any available space for scratchwork.

Answer: $\frac{7}{12}$ or 7/12

Answer: 2.5

Answer: 201
Either position is correct.

Write answer in boxes. →

Grid in result. →

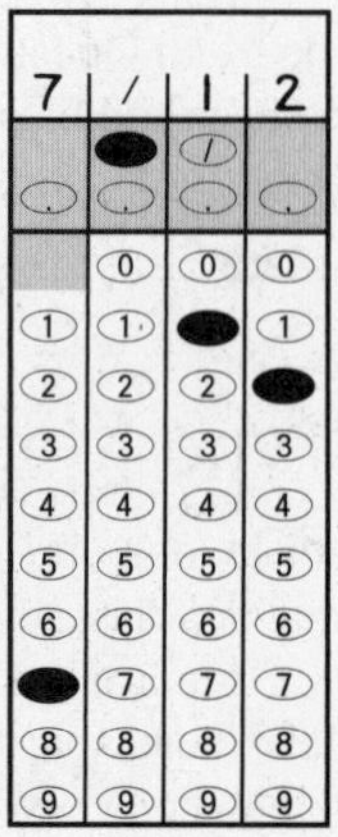

← Fraction line

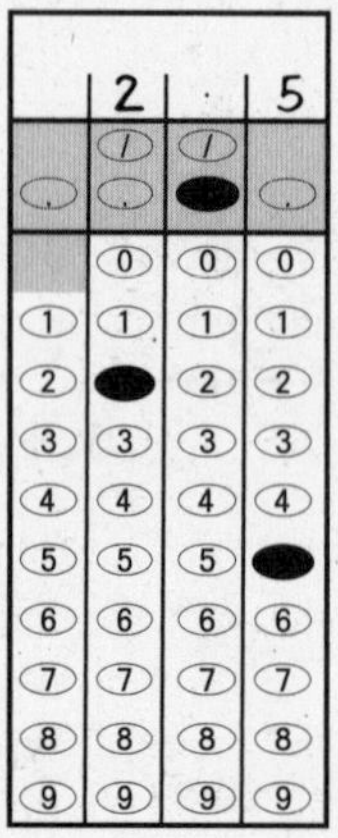

← Decimal point

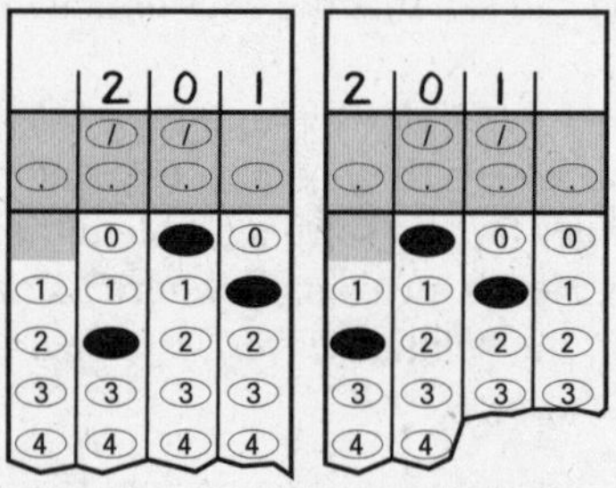

Note: You may start your answers in any column, space permitting. Columns not needed should be left blank.

- Mark no more than one oval in any column.
- Because the answer sheet will be machine-scored, **you will receive credit only if the ovals are filled in correctly.**
- Although not required, it is suggested that you write your answer in the boxes at the top of the columns to help you fill in the ovals accurately.
- Some problems may have more than one correct answer. In such cases, grid only one answer.
- No question has a negative answer.
- **Mixed numbers** such as $2\frac{1}{2}$ must be gridded as 2.5 or 5/2. (If  is gridded, it will be interpreted as $\frac{21}{2}$, not $2\frac{1}{2}$.)

- Decimal Accuracy: If you obtain a decimal answer, **enter the most accurate value the grid will accommodate.** For example, if you obtain an answer such as 0.6666..., you should record the result as .666 or .667. **Less accurate values such as .66 or .67 are not acceptable.**

Acceptable ways to grid $\frac{2}{3}$ = .6666...:

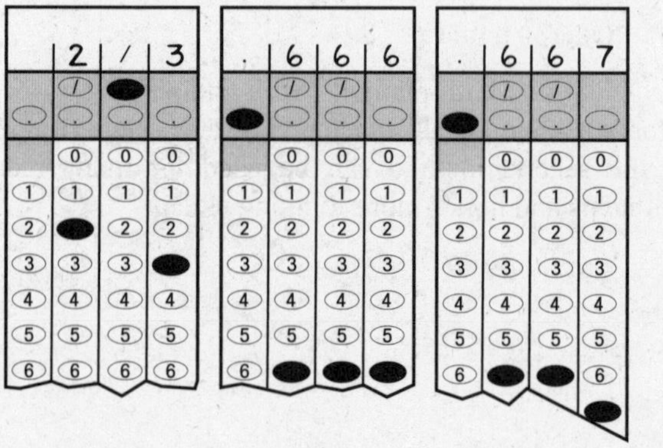

Practice with Grids

According to the directions on the previous page, grid the following values in the grids 1–15:

317

1

4.2

2

.5

3

$\frac{1}{12}$

4
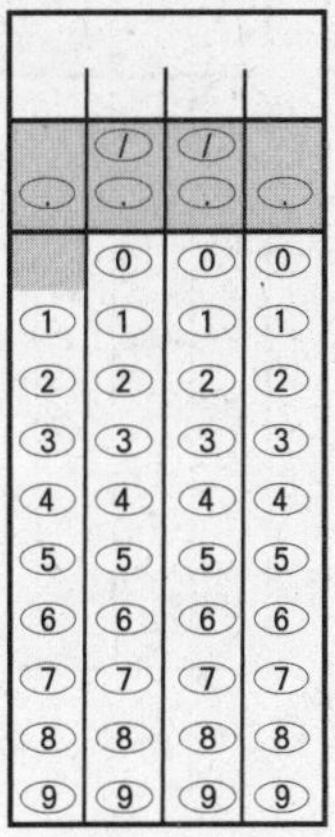

2,474

5

$3\frac{1}{2}$

6
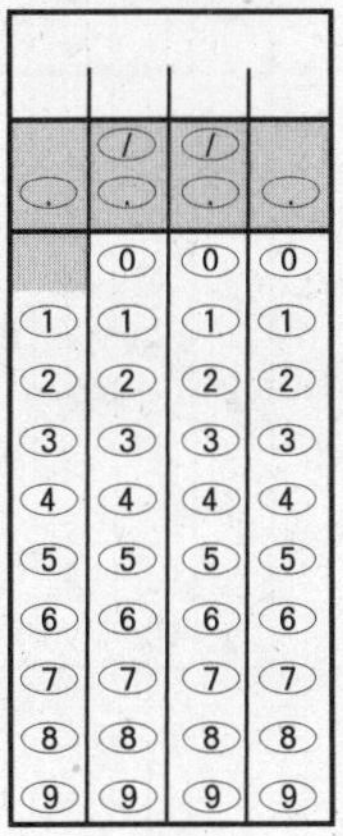

$\frac{57}{3}$

7
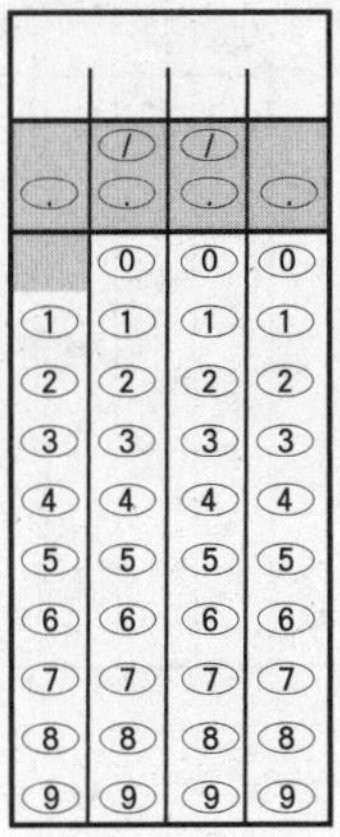

0

8

.346

9

$4\frac{3}{4}$

10

39

11

1

12

$\frac{3}{8}$

13

45.3

14

$8\frac{1}{7}$

15

Answers

317

1
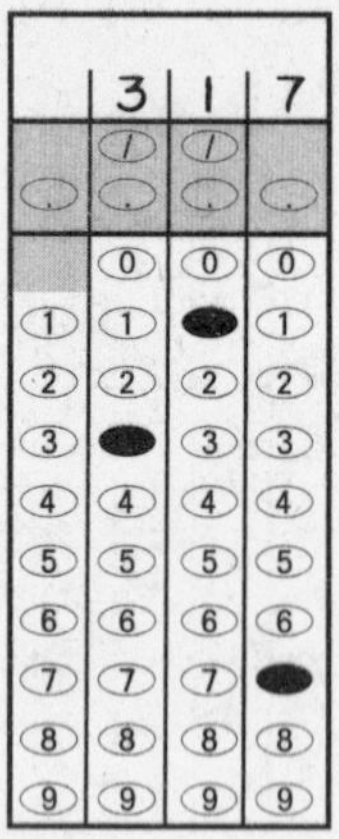

4.2

2

.5

3

$\frac{1}{12}$

4
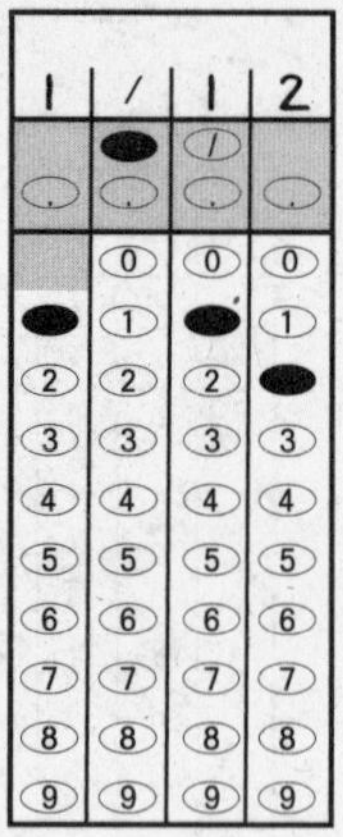

2,474

5

$3\frac{1}{2}$

6
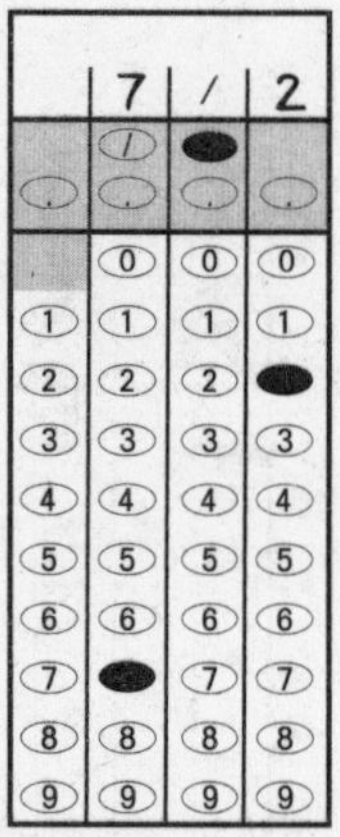

$\frac{57}{3}$

7
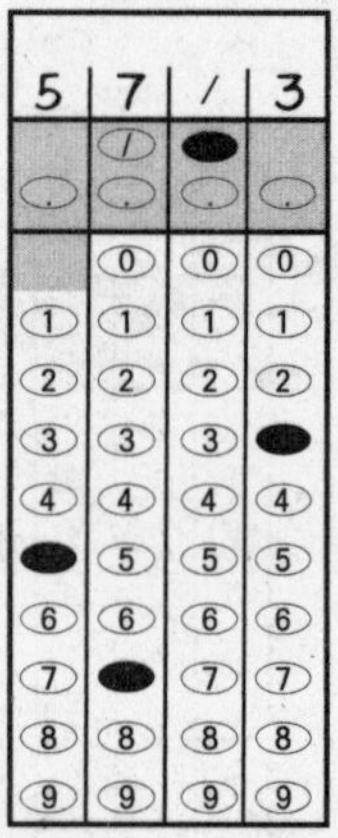

0

8

.346

9
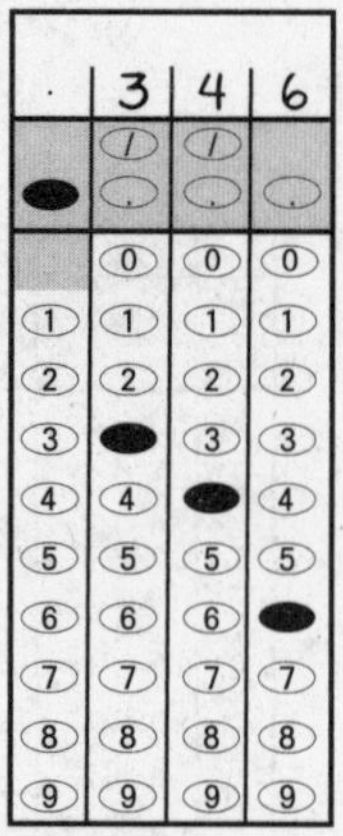

$4\frac{3}{4}$

10
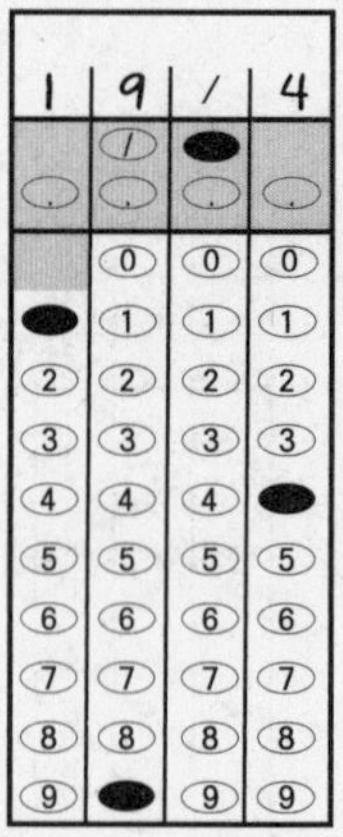

39

11
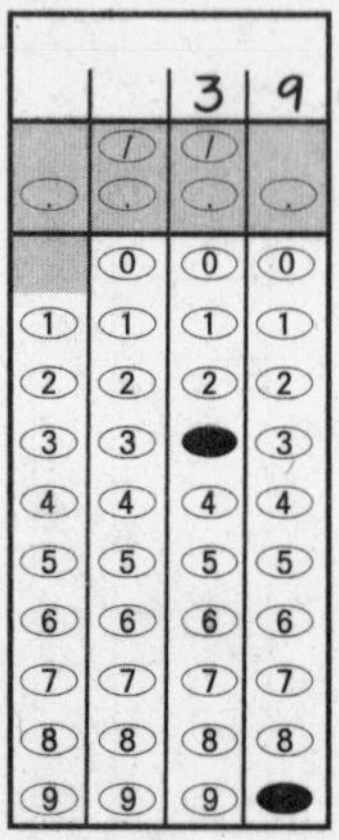

1

12

$\frac{3}{8}$

13
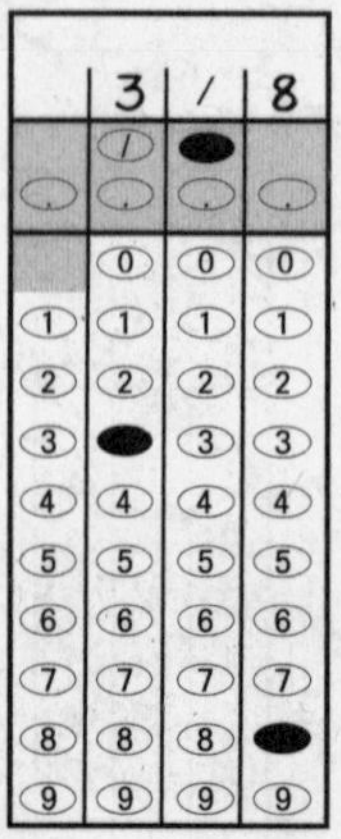

45.3

14
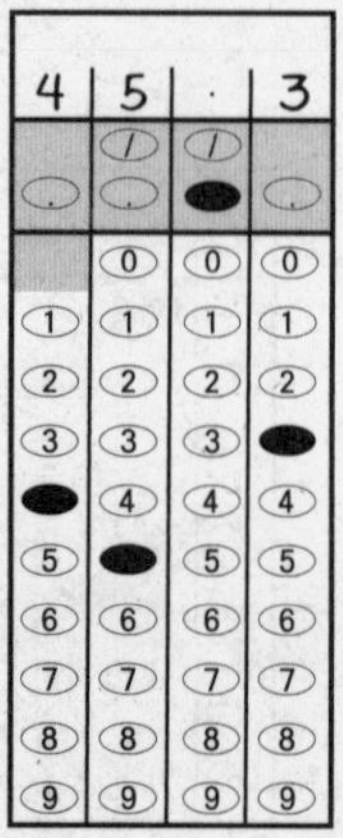

$8\frac{1}{7}$

15

Use of a Calculator in the Grid-Type Question

In the following example, you can either use a calculator or not. However, the use of a calculator will require a different gridding.

EXAMPLE:

If $\frac{2}{7} < x < \frac{3}{7}$ find one value of x.

SOLUTION *WITHOUT* A CALCULATOR:

Get some value between $\frac{2}{7}$ and $\frac{3}{7}$. Write $\frac{2}{7} = \frac{4}{14}$ and $\frac{3}{7} = \frac{6}{14}$.

So we have $\frac{4}{14} < x < \frac{6}{14}$ and x can be $\frac{5}{14}$.

The grid will look like this:

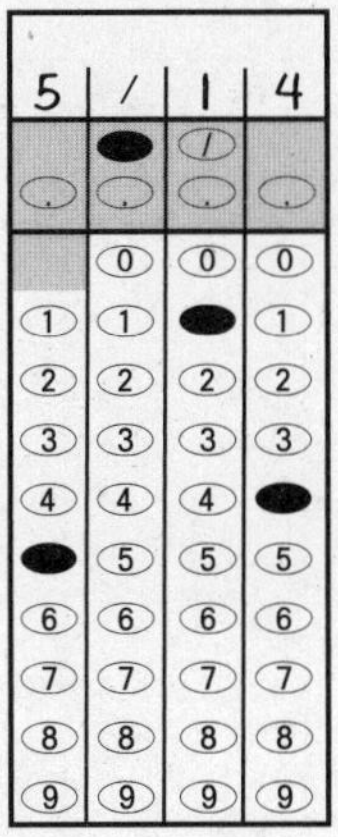

SOLUTION *WITH* A CALCULATOR:

Calculate on a calculator:

$\frac{3}{7} = .4285714...$

$\frac{2}{7} = .2857142...$

So $.2857142 < x < .4285714$.

You could have the grid as follows:

all the way to

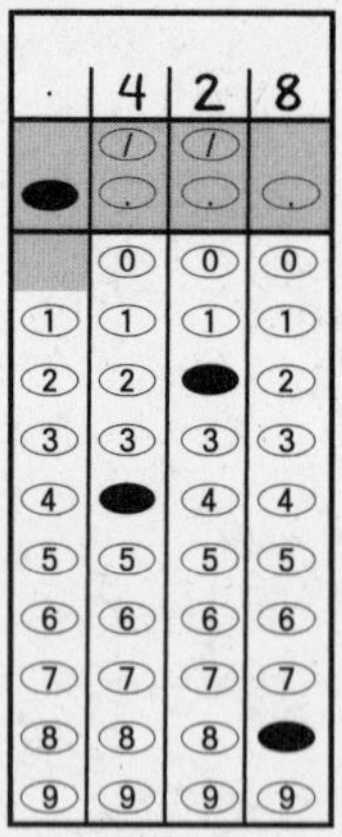

19 Math Strategies

Using Critical Thinking Skills in Math Questions

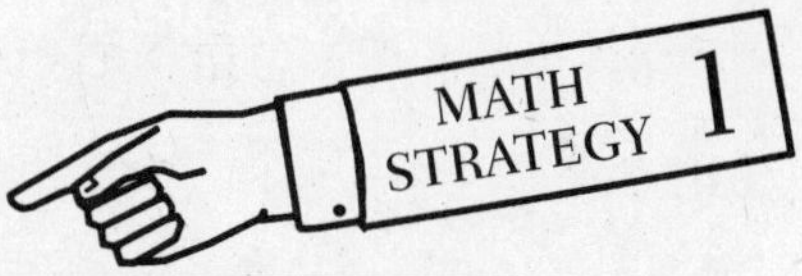

Cancel Quantities to Make the Problem Simpler

Cancel numbers or expressions that appear on both sides of an equation; cancel same numerators and denominators. But make sure that you don't divide by 0 in what you're doing! You will save precious time by using this strategy. You won't have to make any long calculations.

EXAMPLE 1

If $P \times \frac{11}{14} = \frac{11}{14} \times \frac{8}{9}$, then $P =$

(A) $\frac{8}{9}$

(B) $\frac{9}{8}$

(C) 8

(D) 11

(E) 14

Choice A is correct. Do not multiply $\frac{11}{14} \times \frac{8}{9}$!

Cancel the common $\frac{11}{14}$:

$P \times \frac{\cancel{11}}{\cancel{14}} = \frac{\cancel{11}}{\cancel{14}} \times \frac{8}{9}$

$P = \frac{8}{9}$ *(Answer)*

Note: You can cancel the $\frac{11}{14}$ because you are *dividing* both sides by the same nonzero number. Suppose you had a problem like the following:

If $R \times a = a \times \frac{4}{5}$, then $R =$

(A) $\frac{2}{3}$

(B) $\frac{4}{5}$

(C) 1

(D) $\frac{5}{4}$

(E) Cannot be determined.

What do you think the answer is? It's not Choice B! It is Choice E, because you cannot cancel the a, because a may be 0 and you cannot divide by 0. So if $a = 0$, R can be *any* number.

EXAMPLE 2

If $y + \frac{7}{13} + \frac{6}{19} = \frac{3}{5} + \frac{7}{13} + \frac{6}{19}$, then $y =$

(A) $\frac{6}{19}$

(B) $\frac{13}{32}$

(C) $\frac{7}{13}$

(D) $\frac{3}{5}$

(E) $\frac{211}{247}$

Choice D is correct. *Do not add the fractions!*

Don't add $\frac{3}{5}+\frac{7}{13}+\frac{6}{19}$! You waste a lot of time! There is a much shorter way to do the problem. Cancel $\frac{7}{13}+\frac{6}{19}$ from both sides of the equation. Thus,

$$y+\cancel{\frac{7}{13}}+\cancel{\frac{6}{19}}=\frac{3}{5}+\cancel{\frac{7}{13}}+\cancel{\frac{6}{19}}$$

$y=\frac{3}{5}$ *(Answer)*

EXAMPLE 3

$\frac{2}{5}\times\frac{5}{6}\times\frac{6}{7}\times\frac{7}{8}\times\frac{8}{9}\times\frac{9}{10}\times\frac{10}{11}=$

(A) $\frac{9}{11}$
(B) $\frac{2}{11}$
(C) $\frac{11}{36}$
(D) $\frac{10}{21}$
(E) $\frac{244}{360}$

Choice B is correct.

<u>Cancel numerators/denominators:</u>

$$\frac{2}{\cancel{5}}\times\frac{\cancel{5}}{\cancel{6}}\times\frac{\cancel{6}}{\cancel{7}}\times\frac{\cancel{7}}{\cancel{8}}\times\frac{\cancel{8}}{\cancel{9}}\times\frac{\cancel{9}}{\cancel{10}}\times\frac{\cancel{10}}{11}=\frac{2}{11}$$

EXAMPLE 4

If $a + b > a - b$, which must follow?

(A) $a < 0$
(B) $b < 0$
(C) $a > b$
(D) $b > a$
(E) $b > 0$

Choice E is correct.

$a + b > a - b$

<u>Cancel common *a*'s:</u>

$$\cancel{a} + b > \cancel{a} - b$$
$$b > -b$$
Add b: $$b + b > b - b$$
$$2b > 0$$
$$b > 0$$

EXAMPLE 5

If $7\frac{2}{9} = 6 + \frac{y}{27}$, $y =$

(A) 8
(B) 30
(C) 35
(D) 37
(E) 33

Choice E is correct.

<u>Subtract 6 from both sides:</u>

$$7\frac{2}{9} - 6 = 6 + \frac{y}{27} - 6$$
$$1\frac{2}{9} = \frac{y}{27}$$
$$\frac{11}{9} = \frac{y}{27}$$
$$\frac{33}{27} = \frac{y}{27}$$
$$y = 33$$

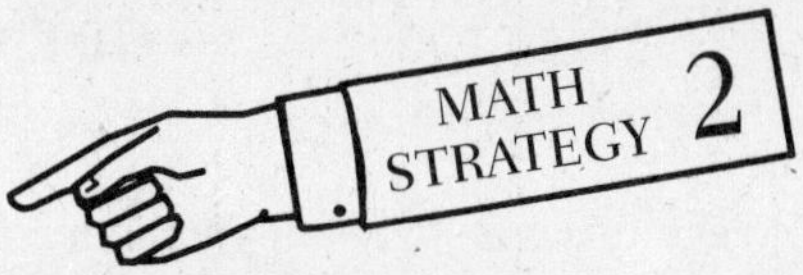

Translate English Words into Mathematical Expressions

Many of the SAT problems are word problems. Being able to translate word problems from English into mathematical expressions or equations will help you to score high on the test. The following table translates some commonly used words into their mathematical equivalents:

TRANSLATION TABLE

Words	*Math Way to Say It*
is, was, has, cost	= (equals)
of	× (times)
percent	/100 (the percent number over 100)
x percent	$x/100$
which, what	x (or any other variable)
x and y	$x + y$
the sum of x and y	$x + y$
the difference between x and y	$x - y$
x more than y	$x + y$
x less than y	$y - x$
the product of x and y	xy
the square of x	x^2
x is greater than y	$x > y$ (or $y < x$)
x is less than y	$x < y$ (or $y > x$)
y years ago	$- y$
y years from now	$+ y$
c times as old as John	$c \times$ (John's age)
x older than y	$x + y$
x younger than y	$y - x$
the increase from x to y	$y - x$
the decrease from x to y	$x - y$
the percent increase from x to y ($y > x$)	$\left(\frac{y - x}{x}\right)100$
the percent decrease from x to y ($y < x$)	$\left(\frac{x - y}{x}\right)100$
the percent of increase	$\left(\frac{\text{amount of increase}}{\text{original amount}}\right) \times 100$
the percent of decrease	$\left(\frac{\text{amount of decrease}}{\text{original amount}}\right) \times 100$
n percent greater than x	$x + \left(\frac{n}{100}\right)x$
n percent less than x	$x - \left(\frac{n}{100}\right)x$

By knowing this table, you will find word problems much easier to do.

OPTIONAL QUIZ ON TRANSLATION TABLE

Take this quiz to see if you understand the translation table before attempting the problems in Strategy #2 that follow.

1. **Mary is five years older than John** translates to:

   (A) $J = 5 + M$
   (B) $M + J = 5$
   (C) $M > 5 + J$
   (D) $M = 5 + J$
   (E) None of these.

   (D) Translate: **Mary** to ***M***; **John** to ***J***; **is** to =; **older than** to +
   So **Mary is five years older than John** becomes:
   ↓ ↓ ↓ ↓ ↓
   $M = 5 + J$

2. **3 percent of 5** translates to:

   (A) 3/5
   (B) 3/100 divided by 5
   (C) (3/100) × 5
   (D) 3 × 100 × 5
   (E) None of these.

   (C) percent or % = /100; of = ×; so

   3% of 5 translates to:
   ↓ ↓↓
   $\frac{3}{100} \times 5$

3. **What percent of 3** translates to:

   (A) $x(100) \times 3$
   (B) $(x/100) \times 3$
   (C) $(x/100)$ divided by 3
   (D) $(3/100)x$
   (E) None of these.

   (B) Translate: what to x; percent to /100. Thus

   What percent of 3 becomes:
   ↓ ↓ ↓↓
   $x \quad /100 \quad \times 3$

4. **Six years ago, Sarah was 4 times as old as John was then** translates to:

   (A) $S - 6 = 4J$
   (B) $6 - S = 4J$
   (C) $6 - S = 4(J - 6)$
   (D) $S - 6 = 4(J - 6)$
   (E) None of these.

   (D) **Six years ago, Sarah was** translates to $S - 6$. **4 times as old as John is** would be $4J$. However, **4 times as old as John *was then*** translates to $4(J - 6)$. Thus **six years ago, Sarah was 4 times as old as John was then** translates to: $S - 6 = 4 \times (J - 6)$

5. **The percent increase from 5 to 10** is

   (A) $[(10 - 5)/5] \times 100$
   (B) $[(5 - 10)/5] \times 100$
   (C) $[(10 - 5)/10] \times 100$
   (D) $[(5 - 10)/10] \times 100$
   (E) None of these.

   (A) Percent increase from a to b is $[(b - a)/a] \times 100$. So **the percent increase from 5 to 10** would be $[(10 - 5)/5] \times 100$.

6. **Harry is older than John and John is older than Mary** translates to:

   (A) $H > J > M$
   (B) $H > J < M$
   (C) $H > M > J$
   (D) $M > H > J$
   (E) None of these.

   (A) **Harry is older than John** translates to: $H > J$. **John is older than Mary** translates to $J > M$. So we have $H > J$ and $J > M$, which, consolidated, becomes $H > J > M$.

7. **Even after Phil gives Sam 6 DVDs, he still has 16 more DVDs than Sam has** translates to:

   (A) $P - 6 = 16 + S$
   (B) $P - 6 = 16 + S + 6$
   (C) $P + 6 = 16 + S + 6$
   (D) $P + 6 + 16 + S$
   (E) None of these.

   (B) **Even after Phil gives Sam 6 DVDs** translates to:
   $P - 6$ [1]
   He still has 16 more DVDs than Sam has translates to:
   $= 16 + S + 6$ [2]
   since Sam has gotten 6 additional DVDs. Thus, combining [1] and [2], we get: $P - 6 = 16 + S + 6$.

8. **q is 10% greater than p** translates to:

(A) $q = (10/100)q + p$
(B) $q > (10/100)p$
(C) $q = (10/100)p + p$
(D) $q = (10/100) + p$
(E) None of these.

(C) (1) **q is** translates to $q =$
(2) **10% greater than p** translates to $(10/100)p + p$ so

q is 10% greater than p
translates to: ↓ ↓
$q = (10/100)p + p$

9. **200 is what percent of 20** translates to:

(A) $200 = x \times 100 \times 20$
(B) $200 = (x/100)$ divided by 20
(C) $200 = (x/100) \times 20$
(D) $200 = x \times 20$
(E) None of these.

(C) Translate **is** to =; **what** to x; **percent** to /100; **of** to × so we get that:
200 is what percent of 20 translates to:
↓ ↓ ↓ ↓ ↓ ↓
$200 \;=\; x \;/100 \;\times 20$

10. **The product of the sums of x and y and y and z is 5** translates to:

(A) $xy + yz = 5$
(B) $x + y + y + z = 5$
(C) $(x + y)(yz) = 5$
(D) $(x + y)(y + z) = 5$
(E) None of these.

(D) **The sum of x and y** is $x + y$. **The sum of y and z** is $y + z$. So the **product of those sums** is $(x + y)(y + z)$.

Thus **The product of the sums of x and y and y and z is 5** translates to:
$(x + y)(y + z) = 5$

STRATEGY 2, EXAMPLE 1

Sarah is twice as old as John. Six years ago, Sarah was 4 times as old as John was then. How old is John now?

(A) 3
(B) 9
(C) 18
(D) 20
(E) impossible to determine

Choice B is correct. Translate:

Sarah is twice as old as John.

$$S = 2 \times J$$

$$S = 2J \quad \boxed{1}$$

Six years ago Sarah was 4 times as old as John was then

$$-6 \quad S = 4 \times (J-6)$$

This becomes $S - 6 = 4(J - 6)$ $\boxed{2}$

Substituting $\boxed{1}$ into $\boxed{2}$:

$$2J - 6 = 4(J - 6)$$
$$2J - 6 = 4J - 24$$
$$18 = 2J$$
$$9 = J \quad \textit{(Answer)}$$

EXAMPLE 2

200 is what percent of 20?

(A) $\frac{1}{10}$
(B) 10
(C) 100
(D) 1,000
(E) 10,000

Choice D is correct. Translate:

200 is what percent of 20

$$200 = x \quad \overline{100} \quad \times 20$$

$$200 = \frac{x}{100}(20)$$

Divide by 20: $10 = \frac{x}{100}$

Multiply by 100: $1{,}000 = x$ *(Answer)*

EXAMPLE 3

If A is 250 percent of B, what percent of A is B?

(A) 125%
(B) $\frac{1}{250}$%
(C) 50%
(D) 40%
(E) 400%

Choice D is correct.

If A is 250 percent of B becomes

$$A = 250 \quad /100 \quad \times B$$

What percent of A is B? becomes

$$x \quad /100 \quad \times A = B$$

Set up the equations:

$$A = \frac{250}{100}B \quad \boxed{1}$$

$$\frac{x}{100}A = B \quad \boxed{2}$$

Divide equation $\boxed{1}$ by equation $\boxed{2}$:

$$\frac{A}{\frac{x}{100}A} = \frac{\frac{250}{100}B}{B}$$

We get:

$$\frac{1}{\frac{x}{100}} = \frac{250}{100}$$

Inverting, we get:

$$\frac{x}{100} = \frac{100}{250}$$

$$x = \frac{10{,}000}{250}$$

To simplify, multiply both numerator and denominator by 4:

$$x = \frac{10{,}000 \times 4}{250 \times 4} = 40$$

$$x = \frac{40{,}000}{1{,}000} = 40$$

Alternate way:

Let $B = 100$ (choose any number for B).
We get (after translation)

$$A = \left(\frac{250}{100}\right)100 \quad \boxed{1}$$

$$\left(\frac{x}{100}\right)A = 100 \quad \boxed{2}$$

From [1],

$$A = 250 \quad \boxed{3}$$

Substituting [3] into [2], we get

$$\left(\frac{x}{100}\right)250 = 100 \quad \boxed{4}$$

Multiplying both sides of [4] by 100,

$$(x)(250) = (100)(100)$$

Dividing by 250:

$$x = \frac{100 \times 100}{250}$$

Simplify by multiplying numerator and denominator by 4:

$$x = \frac{100 \times 100 \times 4}{250 \times 4} = \frac{40{,}000}{1{,}000} = 40$$

EXAMPLE 4

John is now m years old and Sally is 4 years older than John. Which represents Sally's age 6 years ago?

(A) $m + 10$
(B) $m - 10$
(C) $m - 2$
(D) $m - 4$
(E) $4m - 6$

Choice C is correct.

Translate:

John is now m years old
↓ ↓ ↓
J = m

Sally is 4 years older than John
↓ ↓↓ ↓ ↓
S = 4 + J

Sally's age 6 years ago
↓ ↓
S − 6

So we get: $J = m$
$S = 4 + J$

and find: $S - 6 = 4 + J - 6$
$S - 6 = J - 2$
$S - 6 = m - 2$ (substituting m for J)

See Math Strategy 7, Example 2 (page 89) for an alternate approach to solving this problem, using a different strategy: **Use Specific Numerical Examples to Prove or Disprove Your Guess.**

EXAMPLE 5

Phil has three times as many DVDs as Sam has. Even after Phil gives Sam 6 DVDs, he still has 16 more DVDs than Sam has. What was the original number of DVDs that Phil had?

(A) 20
(B) 24
(C) 28
(D) 33
(E) 42

Choice E is correct.

Translate:

Phil has three times as many DVDs as Sam has
↓ ↓ ↓ ↓ ↓
P = 3 × S

Even after Phil gives Sam 6 DVDs, he still has 16
↓ ↓ ↓ ↓ ↓
P − 6 = 16

more DVDs than Sam has
↓ ↓
+ $S + 6$

Sam now has $S + 6$ DVDs because Phil gave Sam 6 DVDs. So we end up with the equations:

$P = 3S$

$P - 6 = 16 + S + 6$

Find P; get rid of S:

$$P = 3S; \qquad \frac{P}{3} = S$$

$$P - 6 = 16 + \frac{P}{3} + 6$$

$$P - 6 = \frac{48 + P + 18}{3}$$

$$3P - 18 = 48 + P + 18$$
$$2P = 84$$
$$P = 42$$

EXAMPLE 6

If q is 10% greater than p and r is 10% greater than y, qr is what percent greater than py?

(A) 1%
(B) 20%
(C) 21%
(D) 30%
(E) 100%

Choice C is correct.

Translate:

If q is $\underbrace{\text{10\% greater than } p}$

$$q = \frac{10}{100}p + p$$

and r is $\underbrace{\text{10\% greater than } y}$

$$r = \frac{10}{100}y + y$$

qr is $\underbrace{\text{what percent greater than } py?}$

$$qr = \frac{x}{100}py + py$$

So we have three equations:

$$q = \frac{10}{100}p + p = \left(\frac{10}{100} + 1\right)p \quad \boxed{1}$$

$$r = \frac{10}{100}y + y = \left(\frac{10}{100} + 1\right)y \quad \boxed{2}$$

$$qr = \frac{x}{100}py + py = \left(\frac{x}{100} + 1\right)py \quad \boxed{3}$$

Multiply $\boxed{1}$ and $\boxed{2}$:

$$qr = \left(\frac{10}{100} + 1\right)^2 py \quad \boxed{4}$$

Now equate $\boxed{4}$ with $\boxed{3}$:

$$qr = \left(\frac{x}{100} + 1\right)py = \left(\frac{10}{100} + 1\right)^2 py \quad \boxed{4}$$

You can see that $\left(\frac{10}{100} + 1\right)^2 = \frac{x}{100} + 1$, canceling py.

So, $\left(\frac{10}{100} + 1\right)^2 = \frac{100}{10{,}000} + 2\left(\frac{10}{100}\right) + 1 = \frac{x}{100} + 1$

$$\frac{100}{10{,}000} + \frac{20}{100} = \frac{21}{100} = \frac{x}{100}$$

$$21 = x$$

The answer is $x = 21$.

Alternate approach: Choose numbers for p and for y:

Let $p = 10$ and $y = 20$

Then, since q is 10% greater than p:

q = 10% greater than 10

$$q = \left(\frac{10}{100}\right)10 + 10 = 11$$

Next, r is 10% greater than y:

r = 10% greater than 20

$$\text{Or, } r = q = \left(\frac{10}{100}\right)10 + 10 = 1120 + 20 = 22$$

Then:

$$qr = 11 \times 22$$

$$\text{and } py = 20 \times 10$$

So, to find what percent qr is greater than py, you would need to find:

$$\frac{qr - py}{py} \times 100 \text{ or}$$

$$\frac{11 \times 22 - 20 \times 10}{20 \times 10} \times 100$$

This is:

$$\frac{42}{200} \times 100 = 21$$

EXAMPLE 7

Sales of Item X
Jan–Jun, 2004

Month	Sales ($)
Jan	800
Feb	1,000
Mar	1,200
Apr	1,300
May	1,600
Jun	1,800

According to the above table, the percent increase in sales was greatest for which of the following periods?

(A) Jan–Feb
(B) Feb–Mar
(C) Mar–Apr
(D) Apr–May
(E) May–Jun

Choice A is correct.

The percent increase from Month A to Month B =

$$\frac{\text{sales (month B)-sales (month A)}}{\text{sales (month A)}} \times 100$$

Month	Sales ($)	Periods	% Increase in Sales
Jan	800	Jan–Feb	$\frac{1{,}000 - 800}{800} \times 100 = \frac{200}{800} \times 100$
Feb	1,000	Feb–Mar	$\frac{1{,}200 - 1{,}000}{1{,}000} \times 100 = \frac{200}{1{,}000} \times 100$
Mar	1,200	Mar–Apr	$\frac{1{,}300 - 1{,}200}{1{,}200} \times 100 = \frac{100}{1{,}200} \times 100$
Apr	1,300	Apr–May	$\frac{1{,}600 - 1{,}300}{1{,}300} \times 100 = \frac{300}{1{,}300} \times 100$
May	1,600	May–Jun	$\frac{1{,}800 - 1{,}600}{1{,}600} \times 100 = \frac{200}{1{,}600} \times 100$
Jun	1,800		

You can see that $\frac{200}{800} \times 100$ (Jan–Feb) is the greatest.

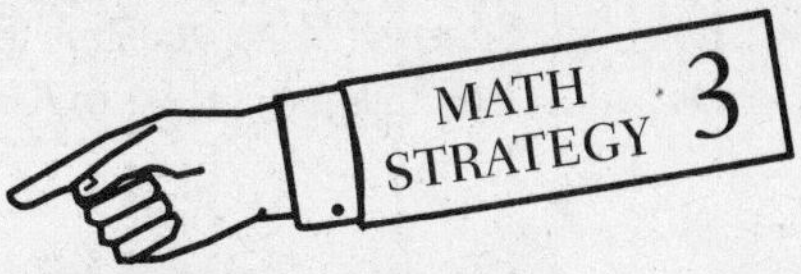

Know How to Find Unknown Quantities (Areas, Lengths, Arc and Angle Measurements) from Known Quantities (the Whole Equals the Sum of Its Parts)

When asked to find a particular area or length, instead of trying to calculate it directly, find it by subtracting two other areas or lengths—a method based on the fact that the whole minus a part equals the remaining part.

This strategy is very helpful in many types of geometry problems. A very important equation to remember is

The whole = the sum of its parts $\boxed{1}$

Equation $\boxed{1}$ is often disguised in many forms, as seen in the following examples:

EXAMPLE 1

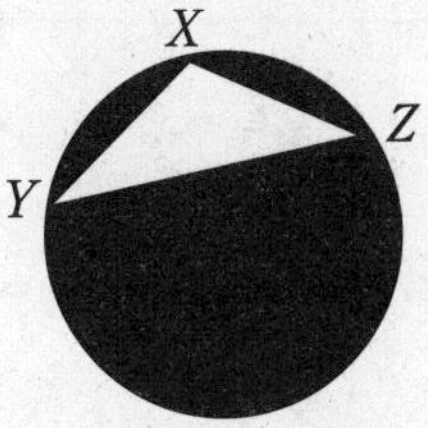

In the diagram above, ΔXYZ has been inscribed in a circle. If the circle encloses an area of 64, and the area of ΔXYZ is 15, then what is the area of the shaded region?

(A) 25
(B) 36
(C) 49
(D) 79
(E) It cannot be determined from the information given.

Choice C is correct. Use equation $\boxed{1}$. Here, the whole refers to the area within the circle, and the parts refer to the areas of the shaded region and the triangle. Thus,

Area within circle =
Area of shaded region +
Area of ΔXYZ

64 = Area of shaded region + 15

or Area of shaded region = 64 − 15 = 49
(Answer)

EXAMPLE 2

In the diagram below, $\overline{AE}$ is a straight line, and F is a point on $\overline{AE}$. Find an expression for $m\angle DFE$.

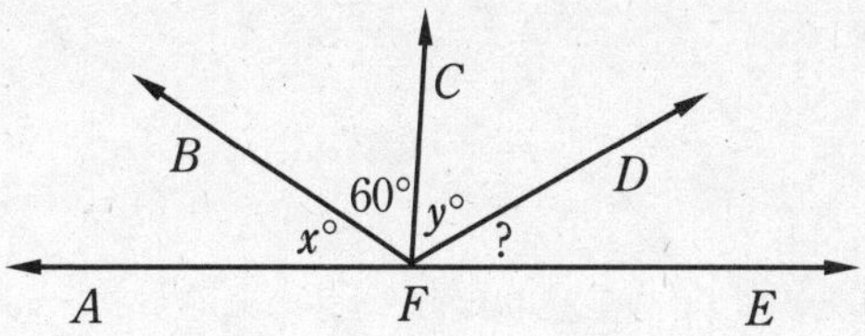

(A) $x + y - 60$
(B) $x + y + 60$
(C) $90 - x - y$
(D) $120 - x - y$
(E) $180 - x - y$

Choice D is correct. Use equation $\boxed{1}$. Here, the whole refers to the straight angle, $\angle AFE$, and its parts refer to $\angle AFB$, $\angle BFC$, $\angle CFD$, and $\angle DFE$. Thus,

$$m\angle AFE = m\angle AFB + m\angle BFC + m\angle CFD + m\angle DFE$$
$$180 = x + 60 + y + m\angle DFE$$
or $$m\angle DFE = 180 - x - 60 - y$$
$$m\angle DFE = 120 - x - y \text{ (Answer)}$$

EXAMPLE 3

In the diagram below, $AB = m$, $BC = n$, and $AD = 10$. Find an expression for CD.

(Note: Diagram represents a straight line.)

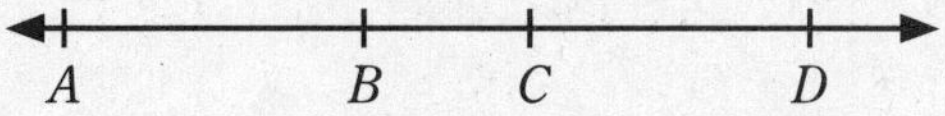

(A) $10 - mn$
(B) $10 - m - n$
(C) $m - n + 10$
(D) $m + n - 10$
(E) $m + n + 10$

Choice B is correct. Use equation $\boxed{1}$. Here, the whole refers to *AD*, and its parts refer to *AB*, *BC*, and *CD*. Thus,

$$AD = AB + BC + CD$$
$$10 = m + n + CD$$
$$\text{or} \quad CD = 10 - m - n \ (\textit{Answer})$$

EXAMPLE 4

The area of triangle $ACE = 64$. The sum of the areas of the shaded triangles *ABF* and *FDE* is 39. What is the side of square *BFDC*?

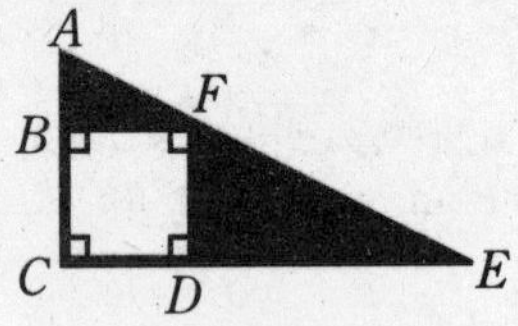

(A) 5
(B) 4
(C) $\sqrt{5}$
(D) $\sqrt{44}$
(E) Cannot be determined.

EXPLANATORY ANSWER

Choice A is correct.

Since we are dealing with areas, let's establish the area of the square *BFDC*, which will then enable us to get its side.

Now, the area of square $BFDC$ = area of triangle ACE – (area of triangles $ABF + FDE$)

Area of square $BFDC = 64 - 39$
$= 25$

Therefore, the side of square $BFDC = 5$.

EXAMPLE 5

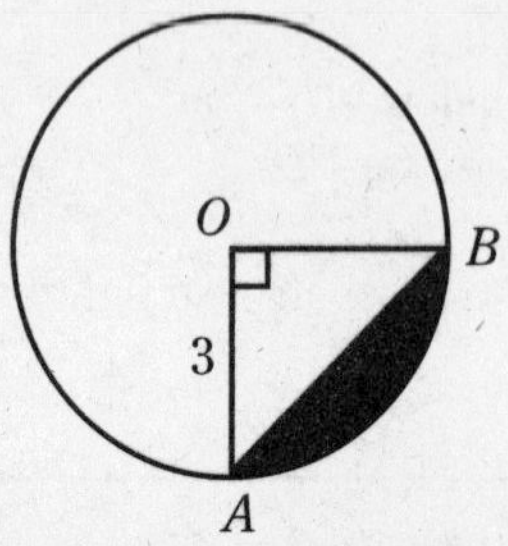

In the figure above, *O* is the center of the circle. Triangle *AOB* has side 3 and angle $AOB = 90°$. What is the area of the shaded region?

(A) $9\left(\frac{\pi}{4} - \frac{1}{2}\right)$

(B) $9\left(\frac{\pi}{2} - 1\right)$

(C) $9(\pi - 1)$

(D) $9\left(\frac{\pi}{4} - \frac{1}{4}\right)$

(E) Cannot be determined.

EXPLANATORY ANSWER

Choice A is correct.

<u>Subtract knowns from knowns</u>:

Area of shaded region = area of quarter circle *AOB* – area of triangle *AOB*

Area of quarter circle $AOB = \frac{\pi(3)^2}{4}$ (since $OA = 3$ and area of a quarter of a circle $= \frac{1}{4} \times \pi \times \text{radius}^2$).

Area of triangle $AOB = \frac{3 \times 3}{2}$ (since $OB = 3$ and area of a triangle $= \frac{1}{2}$ base $\times$ height)

Thus, area of shaded region $= \frac{9\pi}{4} - \frac{9}{2} = 9\left(\frac{\pi}{4} - \frac{1}{2}\right)$.

EXAMPLE 6

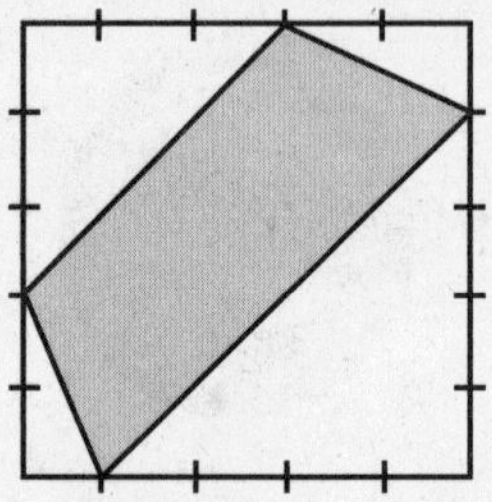

The sides in the square above are each divided into five equal segments. What is the value of

$$\frac{\text{area of square}}{\text{area of shaded region}}?$$

(A) $\frac{50}{29}$

(B) $\frac{50}{21}$

(C) $\frac{25}{4}$

(D) $\frac{29}{25}$

(E) None of these.

EXPLANATORY ANSWER

Choice B is correct.

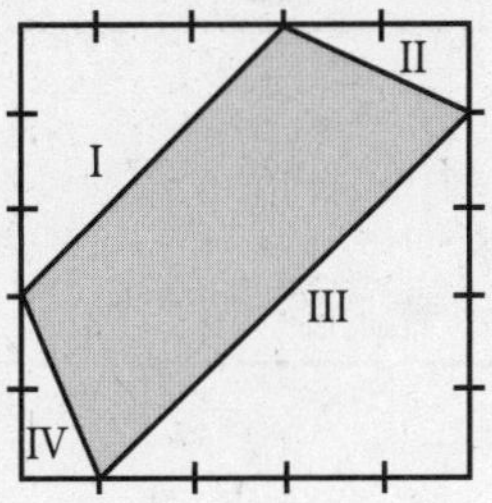

Subtract knowns from knowns:

Area of square $= 5 \times 5 = 25$
Area of shaded region = area of square − area of I − area of II − area of III − area of IV

$$\text{Area of I} = \frac{3 \times 3}{2} = \frac{9}{2}$$
$$\text{Area of II} = \frac{2 \times 1}{2} = 1$$
$$\text{Area of III} = \frac{4 \times 4}{2} = 8$$
$$\text{Area of IV} = \frac{2 \times 1}{2} = 1$$

$$\text{Area of shaded region} = 25 - \frac{9}{2} - 1 - 8 - 1 = \frac{21}{2}$$
$$\frac{\text{area of square}}{\text{area of shaded region}} = \frac{25}{\frac{21}{2}} = 25 \times \frac{2}{21} = \frac{50}{21}$$

EXAMPLE 7

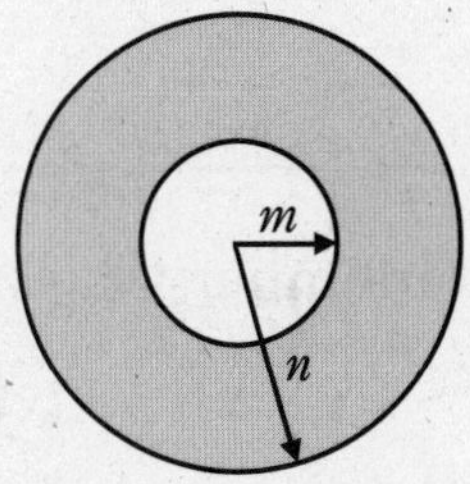

Two concentric circles are shown above with inner radius of m and outer radius of n. What is the area of the shaded region?

(A) $\pi(n - m)^2$
(B) $\pi(n^2 + m^2)$
(C) $\pi(n^2 - m^2)$
(D) $2\pi(n - m)$
(E) $2\pi(n + m)$

EXPLANATORY ANSWER

Choice C is correct.

Subtract knowns from knowns:

Area of shaded region = area of circle of radius n − area of circle of radius m

Area of circle of radius $n = \pi n^2$
Area of circle of radius $m = \pi m^2$

$$\text{Area of shaded region} = \pi n^2 - \pi m^2 = \pi(n^2 - m^2)$$

MATH STRATEGY 4

Remember Classic Expressions Such as

$x^2 - y^2, x^2 + 2xy + y^2, x^2 - 2xy + y^2, \frac{x + y}{xy}$

Memorize the following factorizations and expressions:

$x^2 - y^2 = (x + y)(x - y)$ $\boxed{\text{Equation 1}}$

$x^2 + 2xy + y^2 = (x + y)(x + y) = (x + y)^2$ $\boxed{\text{Equation 2}}$

$x^2 - 2xy + y^2 = (x - y)(x - y) = (x - y)^2$ $\boxed{\text{Equation 3}}$

$\frac{x + y}{xy} = \frac{1}{x} + \frac{1}{y} \quad x, y \neq 0$ $\boxed{\text{Equation 4}}$

$\frac{x - y}{xy} = \frac{1}{y} - \frac{1}{x} \quad x, y \neq 0$ $\boxed{\text{Equation 4A}}$

$xy + xz = x(y + z)$ $\boxed{\text{Equation 5}}$

$xy - xz = x(y - z)$ $\boxed{\text{Equation 5A}}$

Examples 1, 3, and 11 can also be solved with the aid of a calculator and some with the aid of a calculator allowing for exponential calculations. However, to illustrate the effectiveness of Math Strategy 4, we did not use the calculator method of solution for these examples.

Use algebra to see patterns.

EXAMPLE 1

$$66^2 + 2(34)(66) + 34^2 =$$

(A) 4,730
(B) 5,000
(C) 9,860
(D) 9,950
(E) 10,000

Choice E is correct. Notice that there is a 34 and 66 running through the left side of the equality. To see a pattern, *use algebra.* Substitute a for 66 and b for 34. You get:

$$66^2 + 2(34)(66) + 34^2 = a^2 + 2(b)(a) + b^2$$

But from Equation 2,

$$a^2 + 2ab + b^2 = (a + b)(a + b) = (a + b)^2 \qquad \boxed{1}$$

Now substitute the numbers 34 and 66 *back into* $\boxed{1}$ to get:

$$66^2 + 2(34)(66) + 34^2 = (66 + 34)(66 + 34) = 100 \times 100 =$$

$$10{,}000 \quad \textit{(Answer)}$$

EXAMPLE 2

If $(x + y) = 9$ and $xy = 14$, find $\frac{1}{x} + \frac{1}{y}$.

(Note: $x, y > 0$)

(A) $\frac{1}{9}$
(B) $\frac{2}{7}$
(C) $\frac{9}{14}$
(D) 5
(E) 9

Choice C is correct. We are given:

$$(x + y) = 9 \qquad \boxed{1}$$
$$xy = 14 \qquad \boxed{2}$$
$$x, y > 0 \qquad \boxed{3}$$

I hope that you did not solve $\boxed{2}$ for x (or y), and then substitute it into $\boxed{1}$. If you did, you obtained a quadratic equation.

Here is the FAST method. Use Equation 4:

$$\frac{1}{x} + \frac{1}{y} = \frac{x + y}{xy} \qquad \boxed{4}$$

From $\boxed{1}$ and $\boxed{2}$, we find that $\boxed{4}$ becomes

$$\frac{1}{x} + \frac{1}{y} = \frac{9}{14} \quad \textit{(Answer)}$$

EXAMPLE 3

The value of $100 \times 100 - 99 \times 99 =$

(A) 1
(B) 2
(C) 99
(D) 199
(E) 299

Choice D is correct.

Write a for 100 and b for 99 to see a pattern:

$100 \times 100 - 99 \times 99$

$a \times a - b \times b = a^2 - b^2$. Use Equation 1:

Use the fact that $a^2 - b^2 = (a + b)(a - b)$ $\boxed{1}$

Put back 100 for a and 99 for b in $\boxed{1}$:

$a^2 - b^2 = 100^2 - 99^2 = (100 + 99)(100 - 99) = 199$

EXAMPLE 4

Use factoring to make problems simpler.

$$\frac{8^7 - 8^6}{7} =$$

(A) $\frac{8}{7}$
(B) 8^7
(C) 8^6
(D) 8^5
(E) 8^4

Choice C is correct.

Factor: $8^7 - 8^6 = 8^6(8^1 - 1)$ (Equation 5A)
$= 8^6(8 - 1)$
$= 8^6(7)$

So $\frac{8^7 - 8^6}{7} = \frac{8^6(7)}{7} = \frac{8^6(\cancel{7})}{\cancel{7}} = 8^6$

Represented algebraically, the problem would look like this.

Where $a \neq 1$,

$\frac{a^7 - a^6}{a - 1} =$

(A) $\frac{a}{a - 1}$
(B) $\frac{1}{a - 1}$
(C) $a^6 - a^5$
(D) a^5
(E) a^6

Choice E is correct.

Factor: $a^7 - a^6 = a^6(a - 1)$ (Equation 5A)

The expression

$\frac{a^7 - a^6}{a - 1}$

becomes

$\frac{a^6(a - 1)}{a - 1}$

Since $a \neq 1$, this becomes

a^6

EXAMPLE 5

Use factoring to make problems simpler.

$\sqrt{(88)^2 + (88)^2(3)} =$

(A) 88
(B) 176
(C) 348
(D) 350
(E) 352

Choice B is correct. Factor:

$(88)^2 + (88)^2(3) = 88^2(1 + 3) = 88^2(4)$ (Equation 5)

So:

$$\begin{aligned}\sqrt{(88)^2 + (88)^2(3)} &= \sqrt{88^2(4)}\\ &= \sqrt{88^2} \times \sqrt{4}\\ &= 88 \times 2\\ &= 176\end{aligned}$$

EXAMPLE 6

If $y + \frac{1}{y} = 9$, then $y^2 + \frac{1}{y^2} =$

(A) 76
(B) 77
(C) 78
(D) 79
(E) 81

Choice D is correct.

Square $\left(y + \frac{1}{y}\right) = 9$

Substituting y for x and $\frac{1}{y}$ for y in Equation 2, we get:

$$\left(y + \frac{1}{y}\right)^2 = 81 = y^2 + 2(y)\left(\frac{1}{y}\right) + \left(\frac{1}{y}\right)^2$$
$$= y^2 + 2 + \left(\frac{1}{y}\right)^2$$
$$= y^2 + 2 + \frac{1}{y^2}$$
$$79 = y^2 + \frac{1}{y^2}$$

EXAMPLE 7

If $a - b = 4$ and $a + b = 7$, then $a^2 - b^2 =$

(A) $5\frac{1}{2}$
(B) 11
(C) 28
(D) 29
(E) 56

Choice C is correct.

Use $(a - b)(a + b) = a^2 - b^2$ (Equation 1)

$$a - b = 4$$
$$a + b = 7$$
$$(a - b)(a + b) = 28 = a^2 - b^2$$

EXAMPLE 8

If $x^2 - y^2 = 66$ and $x + y = 6$, what is the value of x?

(A) 11

(B) $\frac{21}{2}$

(C) $\frac{17}{2}$

(D) $\frac{13}{2}$

(E) $\frac{11}{2}$

Choice C is correct. Use

$x^2 - y^2 = (x + y)(x - y)$ (Equation 1)

$(x + y)(x - y) = 66$

But we already know $x + y = 6$, so

$6(x - y) = 66$

$x - y = 11$

Now compare your two equations:

$x + y = 6$

$x - y = 11$

Adding these equations (see Strategy 13) gets you

$2x = 17$

$x = \frac{17}{2}$

EXAMPLE 9

What is the least possible value of $\frac{x+y}{xy}$ if $2 \leq x < y \leq 11$ and x and y are integers?

(A) $\frac{22}{121}$

(B) $\frac{5}{6}$

(C) $\frac{21}{110}$

(D) $\frac{13}{22}$

(E) 1

Choice C is correct.

Use $\frac{x+y}{xy} = \frac{1}{x} + \frac{1}{y}$ (Equation 4)

$\frac{1}{x} + \frac{1}{y}$ is *least* when x is *greatest* and y is *greatest*.

Since it was given that x and y are integers and that $2 \leq x < y \leq 11$, the greatest value of x is 10 and the greatest value of y is 11.

So the *least* value of $\frac{1}{x} + \frac{1}{y} = \frac{x+y}{xy} = \frac{10+11}{10 \times 11} = \frac{21}{110}$.

EXAMPLE 10

If $(a + b)^2 = 20$ and $ab = -3$, then $a^2 + b^2 =$

(A) 14
(B) 20
(C) 26
(D) 32
(E) 38

Choice C is correct.

Use $(a + b)^2 = a^2 + 2ab + b^2 = 20$ (Equation 2)

$ab = -3$

So, $2ab = -6$

Substitute $2ab = -6$ in:

$a^2 + 2ab + b^2 = 20$

We get:

$$a^2 - 6 + b^2 = 20$$
$$a^2 + b^2 = 26$$

EXAMPLE 11

If $998 \times 1{,}002 > 10^6 - x$, x could be

(A) 4 but not 3
(B) 4 but not 5
(C) 5 but not 4
(D) 3 but not 4
(E) 3, 4, or 5

Choice C is correct.

Use $(a + b)(a - b) = a^2 - b^2$ (Equation 1)

Write: $998 \times 1{,}002 = (1{,}000 - 2)(1{,}000 + 2) > 10^6 - x$
$= 1{,}000^2 - 4 > 10^6 - x$
$= (10^3)^2 - 4 > 10^6 - x$
$= 10^6 - 4 > 10^6 - x$

Multiply by -1; *reverse inequality sign*:

$$-1(-4 > -x)$$
$$+4 < +x$$

EXAMPLE 12

If $x^2 + y^2 = 2xy$ and $x > 0$ and $y > 0$, then

(A) $x = 0$ only
(B) $y = 0$ only
(C) $x = 1, y = 1$, only
(D) $x > y > 0$
(E) $x = y$

Choice E is correct. In the given equation $x^2 + y^2 = 2xy$, subtract $2xy$ from both sides to get it to look like what you have in Equation 3.

$$x^2 + y^2 - 2xy = 2xy - 2xy = 0$$
$$\text{So, } x^2 - 2xy + y^2 = 0.$$

We have:

$$x^2 - 2xy + y^2 = (x - y)^2 = 0 \quad \text{(Equation 3)}$$
$$x - y = 0, \text{ and thus } x = y.$$

EXAMPLE 13

If $x + y = 7$ and $xy = 4$, then $x^2 + y^2 =$

(A) 16
(B) 28
(C) 41
(D) 49
(E) 65

Choice C is correct. Since we are trying to find $x^2 + y^2$, square $x + y = 7$ to get

$$(x + y)^2 = 49$$

Use Equation 2 to get

$$x^2 + 2xy + y^2 = 49$$

Since $xy = 4$, substitute that quantity into the expanded equation.

We get:

$$x^2 + 8 + y^2 = 49$$

$$x^2 + y^2 = 41$$

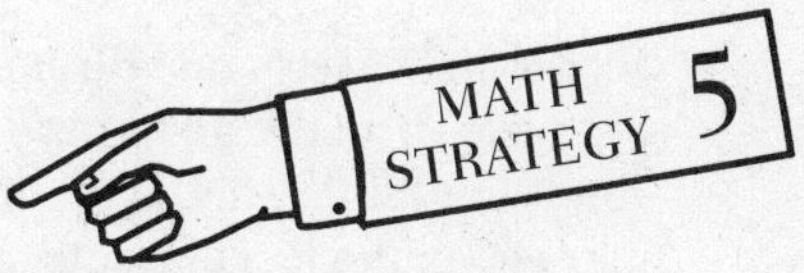

Know How to Manipulate Averages

Almost all problems involving averages can be solved by remembering that

$$\text{Average} = \frac{\text{Sum of the individual quantities or measurements}}{\text{Number of quantities or measurements}}$$

(*Note:* Average is also called Arithmetic Mean.)

EXAMPLE 1

The average height of three students is 68 inches. If two of the students have heights of 70 inches and 72 inches respectively, then what is the height (in inches) of the third student?

(A) 60
(B) 62
(C) 64
(D) 65
(E) 66

Choice B is correct. Recall that

$$\text{Average} = \frac{\text{Sum of the individual measurements}}{\text{Number of measurements}}$$

Let x = height (in inches) of the third student. Thus,

$$68 = \frac{70 + 72 + x}{3}$$

Multiplying by 3,

$$204 = 70 + 72 + x$$
$$204 = 142 + x$$
$$x = 62 \text{ inches}$$

EXAMPLE 2

The average of 30 numbers is 65. If one of these numbers is 65, the sum of the remaining numbers is

(A) 65×64
(B) 30×64
(C) 29×30
(D) 29×64
(E) 29×65

Choice E is correct.

$$\text{Average} = \frac{\text{sum of numbers}}{30}$$

Call the numbers $a, b, c, d,$ etc.

$$\text{So } 65 = \frac{a + b + c + d + \cdots}{30}$$

Now immediately get rid of the fractional part: Multiply by 30 to get: $65 \times 30 = a + b + c + d + \ldots$

Since we were told *one of the numbers is 65,* let $a = 65$:

$65 \times 30 = 65 + b + c + d + \ldots$
So $65 \times 30 - 65 = b + c + d + \ldots$
$b + c + d + \ldots =$ sum of remaining numbers

Factor:

$65 \times 30 - 65 = 65(30 - 1) =$ sum of remaining numbers
$65 \times 29 =$ sum of remaining numbers

EXAMPLES 3–6

3. The average length of 6 objects is 25 cm. If 5 objects are each 20 cm in length, what is the length of the sixth object in cm?

(A) 55
(B) 50
(C) 45
(D) 40
(E) 35

4. Scores on five tests range from 0 to 100 inclusive. If Don gets 70 on the first test, 76 on the second, and 75 on the third, what is the minimum score Don may get on the fourth test to average 80 on all five tests?

(A) 76
(B) 79
(C) 82
(D) 89
(E) 99

5. Eighteen students attained an average score of 70 on a test, and 12 students on the same test scored an average of 90. What is the average score for all 30 students on the test?

(A) 78
(B) 80
(C) 82
(D) 85
(E) Cannot be determined.

6. The average length of 10 objects is 25 inches. If the average length of 2 of these objects is 20 inches, what is the average length of the remaining 8 objects?

(A) $22\frac{1}{2}$ inches
(B) 24 inches
(C) $26\frac{1}{4}$ inches
(D) 28 inches
(E) Cannot be determined.

EXPLANATORY ANSWERS FOR EXAMPLES 3–6

3. (B) *Use the formula:*

$$\text{Average} = \frac{\text{Sum of individual items}}{\text{Number of items}}$$

Now call the length of the sixth item, x. Then:

$$25 = \frac{20 + 20 + 20 + 20 + 20 + x}{6}$$

$$\text{or } 25 = \frac{20 \times 5 + x}{6}$$

Multiply by 6:

$$25 \times 6 = 20 \times 5 + x$$
$$150 = 100 + x$$
$$50 = x$$

4. (B) *Use the formula:*

$$\text{Average} = \frac{\text{Sum of scores on tests}}{\text{Number of tests}}$$

Let x be the score on the fourth test and y be the score on the fifth test.

Then:

$$80 = \text{Average} = \frac{70 + 76 + 75 + x + y}{5}$$

The minimum score x Don can get is the *lowest* score he can get. The higher the score y is, the lower the score x can be. The greatest value of y can be 100. So:

$$80 = \frac{70 + 76 + 75 + x + 100}{5}$$

$$80 = \frac{321 + x}{5}$$

Multiply by 5:

$$400 = 321 + x$$
$$79 = x$$

5. (A) *Use the formula:*

$$\text{Average} = \frac{\text{Sum of scores}}{\text{Number of students}}$$

"Eighteen students attained an average of 70 on a test" translates mathematically to:

$$70 = \frac{\text{sum of scores of 18 students}}{18} \quad \boxed{1}$$

"Twelve students on the same test scored an average of 90" translates to:

$$90 = \frac{\text{sum of scores of other 12 students}}{12} \qquad \boxed{2}$$

Now what you are looking for is the *average score of all 30 students.* That is, you are looking for:

$$\text{Average of 30 students} = \frac{\begin{array}{c}\text{Sum of scores of all}\\ \text{30 students}\end{array}}{30} \qquad \boxed{3}$$

So, if you can find the *sum of scores of all 30 students,* you can find the required average.

Now, the sum of all 30 students = sum of scores of 18 students + sum of scores of other 12 students.

And this can be gotten from $\boxed{1}$ and $\boxed{2}$:

From $\boxed{1}$: 70 × 18 = sum of scores of 18 students

From $\boxed{2}$: 90 × 12 = sum of scores of other 12 students

So adding:

70 × 18 + 90 × 12 = sum of scores of 18 students + sum of scores of other 12 students = sum of scores of 30 students

Put all this in $\boxed{3}$:

$$\begin{aligned}\text{Average of 30 students} &= \frac{70 \times 18 + 90 \times 12}{30}\\ &= \frac{7\cancel{0} \times 18 + 9\cancel{0} \times 12}{3\cancel{0}}\\ &= \frac{7 \times 18 + 9 \times 12}{3}\\ &= \frac{7 \times \overset{6}{\cancel{18}} + \overset{3}{\cancel{9}} \times 12}{\cancel{3}}\\ &= 42 + 36 = 78\end{aligned}$$

6. (C) Denote the lengths of the objects by *a, b, c, d,* etc. Since the average length of 10 objects is given to be 25 inches, establish an equation for the average length:

sum of 10 lengths

$$\text{Average length} = 25 = \frac{a + b + c + d + \cdots + j}{10} \qquad \boxed{1}$$

number of objects

The question also says that the average length of 2 of these objects is 20. Let the lengths of two we choose be *a* and *b*. So,

lengths of 2 objects

$$\text{Average length of } a \text{ and } b = 20 = \frac{a + b}{2} \qquad \boxed{2}$$

number of objects

Now we want to find the average length of the *remaining* objects. There are 8 remaining objects of lengths *c, d, e,…j*. Call the average of these lengths *x*, which is what we want to find.

$$\text{Average length} = x = \frac{c + d + e + \cdots + j}{8}$$

sum of lengths of remaining objects ($a + b$ are not present because only $c + d + \cdots + j$ remain)

number of remaining objects

Use equations $\boxed{1}$ and $\boxed{2}$:

$$25 = \frac{a + b + c + \ldots + j}{10} \qquad \boxed{1}$$

$$20 = \frac{a + b}{2} \qquad \boxed{2}$$

Now, remember, we want to find the value of *x*:

$$x = \frac{c + d + e + \cdots + j}{8}$$

Multiply Equation $\boxed{1}$ by 10 to get rid of the denominator. We get:

$$25 \times 10 = 250 = a + b + c + \cdots + j$$

Now multiply Equation $\boxed{2}$ by 2 to get rid of the denominator:

$$20 \times 2 = 40 = a + b$$

Subtract these two new equations:

$$\begin{array}{rl} & 250 = a + b + c + \cdots + j\\ & -\ [40 = a + b]\\ \hline \text{You get:} & 210 = c + d + \cdots + j\end{array}$$

Now you just have to divide by 8 to get:

$$\frac{210}{8} = \frac{c + d + \ldots + j}{8} = x$$

$$= 26\tfrac{1}{4}$$

MATH STRATEGY 6

Know How to Manipulate Inequalities

Most problems involving inequalities can be solved by remembering one of the following statements.

If $x > y$, then $x + z > y + z$ — Statement 1

If $x > y$ and $w > z$, then $x + w > y + z$ — Statement 2

(Note that Statement 1 and Statement 2 are also true if all the $>$ signs are changed to $<$ signs.)

If $w > 0$ and $x > y$, then $wx > wy$ — Statement 3

If $w < 0$ and $x > y$, then $wx < wy$ — Statement 4

If $x > y$ and $y > z$, then $x > z$ — Statement 5

$x > y$ is the same as $y < x$ — Statement 6

$a < x < b$ is the same as both $a < x$ and $x < b$ — Statement 7

If $x > y > 0$ and $w > z > 0$, then $xw > yz$ — Statement 8

If $x > 0$ and $z = x + y$, then $z > y$ — Statement 9

If $x < 0$, then $x^n < 0$ if n is odd — Statement 10

If $x < 0$, then $x^n > 0$ if n is even — Statement 11

If $xy > 0$, then $x > 0$ and $y > 0$ or $x < 0$ and $y < 0$ — Statement 12

If $xy < 0$, then $x > 0$ and $y < 0$ or $x < 0$ and $y > 0$ — Statement 13

EXAMPLE 1

If $0 < x < 1$, then which of the following must be true?

I. $2x < 2$
II. $x - 1 < 0$
III. $x^2 < x$

(A) I only
(B) II only
(C) I and II only
(D) II and III only
(E) I, II, and III

Choice E is correct. We are told that $0 < x < 1$. Using Statement 7, we have

$$0 < x \quad \boxed{1}$$
$$x < 1 \quad \boxed{2}$$

For Item I, we multiply $\boxed{2}$ by 2.

See Statement 3

$$2x < 2$$

Thus, Item I is true.
For Item II, we add -1 to both sides of $\boxed{2}$.

See Statement 1 to get
$$x - 1 < 0$$

Thus, Item II is true.
For Item III, we multiply $\boxed{2}$ by x.

See Statement 3 to get
$$x^2 < x$$

Thus, Item III is true.

All items are true, so Choice E is correct.

EXAMPLE 2

Given that $\frac{a}{b}$ is less than 1, $a > 0$, $b > 0$. Which of the following must be greater than 1?

(A) $\frac{a}{2b}$

(B) $\frac{b}{2a}$

(C) $\frac{\sqrt{b}}{a}$

(D) $\frac{b}{a}$

(E) $\left(\frac{a}{b}\right)^2$

Choice D is correct.

Given: $\frac{a}{b} < 1 \quad \boxed{1}$
$$a > 0 \quad \boxed{2}$$
$$b > 0 \quad \boxed{3}$$

See $\boxed{\text{Statement 3}}$: Multiply $\boxed{1}$ by b. We get

$$b\left(\frac{a}{b}\right) < b\ (1)$$

$$a < b \qquad \boxed{4}$$

Use $\boxed{\text{Statement 3}}$ where $w = \frac{1}{a}$. Divide $\boxed{4}$ by a. We get

$$\frac{a}{a} < \frac{b}{a}$$

$$1 < \frac{b}{a}$$

or

$$\frac{b}{a} > 1$$

EXAMPLE 3

Which combination of the following statements can be used to demonstrate that x is positive?

I. $x > y$
II. $1 < y$

(A) I alone but not II
(B) II alone but not I
(C) I and II taken together but neither taken alone
(D) Both I alone and II alone
(E) Neither I nor II nor both

Choice C is correct. We want to know which of the following

$$x > y \qquad \boxed{1}$$
$$1 < y \qquad \boxed{2}$$

is enough information to conclude that

$$x > 0 \qquad \boxed{3}$$

$\boxed{1}$ alone is not enough to determine $\boxed{3}$ because $0 > x > y$ could be true. (Note: x is greater than y, but they both could be negative.)

$\boxed{2}$ alone is not enough to determine $\boxed{3}$ because we don't know whether x is greater than, less than, or equal to y.

However, if we use $\boxed{1}$ and $\boxed{2}$ together, we can compare the two:

$1 < y$ is the same as $y > 1$.

Therefore, $x > y$ with $y > 1$ yields: $\boxed{\text{Statement 5}}$

$$x > 1. \qquad \boxed{4}$$

Since $1 > 0$ is always true, then from $\boxed{4}$

$x > 0$ is always true.

EXAMPLE 4

What are all values of x such that $(x - 7)(x + 3)$ is positive?

(A) $x > 7$
(B) $-7 < x < 3$
(C) $-3 < x < 7$
(D) $x > 7$ or $x < -3$
(E) $x > 3$ or $x < -7$

Choice D is correct.

$(x - 7)(x + 3) > 0$ when
$x - 7 > 0$ and $x + 3 > 0$ $\boxed{1}$
or $x - 7 < 0$ and $x + 3 < 0$ $\boxed{2}$

$\boxed{\text{Statement 12}}$

From $\boxed{1}$ we have $x > 7$ and $x > -3$ $\boxed{3}$
Thus $x > 7$ $\boxed{4}$

From $\boxed{2}$, we have $x < 7$ and $x < -3$ $\boxed{5}$
Thus $x < -3$ $\boxed{6}$

EXAMPLE 5

If p and q are nonzero real numbers and if $p^2 + q^3 < 0$ and if $p^3 + q^5 > 0$, which of the following number lines shows the relative positions of p, q, and 0?

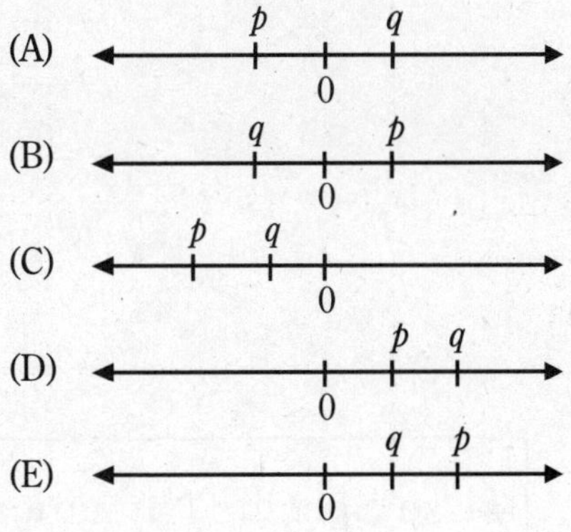

Choice B is correct.

Method 1: Given: $p^2 + q^3 < 0$ $\boxed{1}$
$p^3 + q^5 > 0$ $\boxed{2}$

Subtracting p^2 from $\boxed{1}$ and q^5 from $\boxed{2}$, we have

$$q^3 < -p^2 \qquad \boxed{3}$$
$$p^3 > -q^5 \qquad \boxed{4}$$

Since the square of any real number is greater than 0, $p^2 > 0$ and $-p^2 < 0$. $\boxed{5}$

Using [Statement 5], combining [3] and [5] we get

$q^3 < -p^2 < 0$ [6]
and get $q^3 < 0$. [7]

Thus, $q < 0$. [8]
From [8], we can say $q^5 < 0$ or $-q^5 > 0$. [9]

Using [Statement 5], combining [4] and [9],
$p^3 > -q^5 > 0$ and $p^3 > 0$. Thus $p > 0$. [10]

Using [8] and [10], it is easily seen that Choice B is correct.

Method 2: **Use Strategy 6: Know how to manipulate inequalities.**

Given: $p^2 + q^3 < 0$ [1]
$p^3 + q^5 > 0$ [2]

Since p^2 is always > 0, using this with [1], we know that $q^3 < 0$ and, therefore, $q < 0$. [3]

If $q^3 < 0$ then $q^5 < 0$. [4]

Using [4] and [2], we know that
$p^3 > 0$, and therefore $p > 0$ [5]

Using [3] and [5], only Choice B is correct.

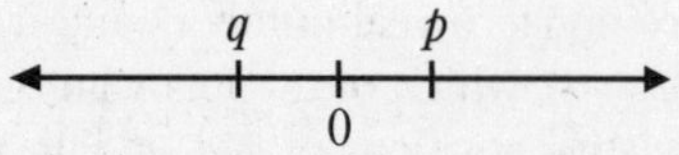

EXAMPLE 6

Janie is older than Tammy, but she is younger than Lori. Let *j*, *t*, and *l* be the ages in years of Janie, Tammy, and Lori, respectively. Which of the following is true?

(A) $j < t < l$
(B) $t < j < l$
(C) $t < l < j$
(D) $l < j < t$
(E) $l < t < j$

Choice B is correct. **(First, use Strategy 2: Translate English words into mathematical expressions.)** "Janie is older than Tammy, but she is younger than Lori" translates to:

Janie's age > Tammy's age [1]
Janie's age < Lori's age [2]
Given: Janie's age $= j$ [3]
Tammy's age $= t$ [4]
Lori's age $= l$ [5]

Substituting [3], [4], and [5] into [1] and [2], we get

$j > t$ [6]
$j < l$ [7]

Use [Statement 5]. Reversing [6], we get

$t < j$ [8]

Combining [8] and [7], we get

$$t < j < l$$

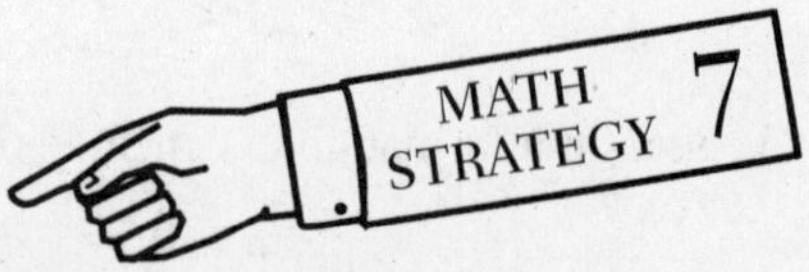

Use Specific Numerical Examples to Prove or Disprove Your Guess

When you do not want to do a lot of algebra, or when you are unable to prove what you think is the answer, you may want to substitute numbers.

EXAMPLE 1

The sum of the cubes of any two consecutive positive integers is always

(A) an odd integer
(B) an even integer
(C) the cube of an integer
(D) the square of an integer
(E) the product of an integer and 3

Choice A is correct. Try specific numbers. Call consecutive positive integers 1 and 2.
Sum of cubes:

$$1^3 + 2^3 = 1 + 8 = 9$$

You have now eliminated choices B and C. You are left with choices A, D, and E.

Now try two other consecutive integers: 2 and 3.

$$2^3 + 3^3 = 8 + 27 = 35$$

Choice A is acceptable. Choice D is false. Choice E is false.

Thus, Choice A is the only choice remaining.

EXAMPLE 2

John is now m years old, and Sally is 4 years older than John. Which represents Sally's age 6 years ago?

(A) $m + 10$
(B) $m - 10$
(C) $m - 2$
(D) $m - 4$
(E) $4m - 6$

Choice C is correct.

Try a specific number.

Let $m = 10$

John is 10 years old.
Sally is 4 years older than John, so Sally is 14 years old.
Sally's age 6 years ago was 8 years.

Now look for the choice that gives you 8 with $m = 10$.

(A) $m + 10 = 10 + 10 = 20$
(B) $m - 10 = 10 - 10 = 0$
(C) $m - 2 = 10 - 2 = 8$—that's the one

See Math Strategy 2, Example 4 (page 75) for an alternate approach to solving this problem, using a different strategy: **Translate English Words into Mathematical Expressions**.

EXAMPLE 3

If $x \neq 0$, then $\frac{(-3x)^3}{-3x^3} =$

(A) -9
(B) -1
(C) 1
(D) 3
(E) 9

Choice E is correct.

Try a specific number.
Let $x = 1$. Then:

$$\frac{(-3x)^3}{-3x^3} = \frac{(-3(1))^3}{-3(1^3)} = \frac{(-3)^3}{-3} = 9$$

EXAMPLE 4

If $a = 4b$, then the average of a and b is

(A) $\frac{1}{2}b$

(B) $\frac{3}{2}b$

(C) $\frac{5}{2}b$

(D) $\frac{7}{2}b$

(E) $\frac{9}{2}b$

Choice C is correct.

Try a specific number.

Let $b = 1$. Then $a = 4b = 4$. So the average =

$$\frac{1+4}{2} = \frac{5}{2}.$$

Look at choices where $b = 1$. The only choice that gives $\frac{5}{2}$ is Choice C.

EXAMPLE 5

The sum of three consecutive even integers is P. Find the sum of the next three consecutive *odd* integers that follow the greatest of the three even integers.

(A) $P + 9$
(B) $P + 15$
(C) $P + 12$
(D) $P + 20$
(E) None of these.

Choice B is correct.

Try specific numbers.
Let the three consecutive even integers be 2, 4, 6.

$$\text{So, } 2 + 4 + 6 = P = 12.$$

The next three consecutive odd integers that follow 6 are:

$$7, 9, 11$$

So the sum of

$$7 + 9 + 11 = 27.$$

Now, where $P = 12$, look for a choice that gives you 27:

(A) $P + 9 = 12 + 9 = 21$—NO
(B) $P + 15 = 12 + 15 = 27$—YES

EXAMPLE 6

If $3 > a$, which of the following is *not* true?

(A) $3 - 3 > a - 3$
(B) $3 + 3 > a + 3$
(C) $3(3) > a(3)$
(D) $3 - 3 > 3 - a$
(E) $\frac{3}{3} > \frac{a}{3}$

Choice D is correct.

<u>Try specific numbers.</u>
Work backward from Choice E if you wish.
Let $a = 1$.
Choice E:

$\frac{3}{3} > \frac{a}{3} = \frac{1}{3}$ TRUE STATEMENT

Choice D:

$3 - 3 > 3 - a = 3 - 1$, or $0 > 2$ FALSE STATEMENT

EXAMPLE 7

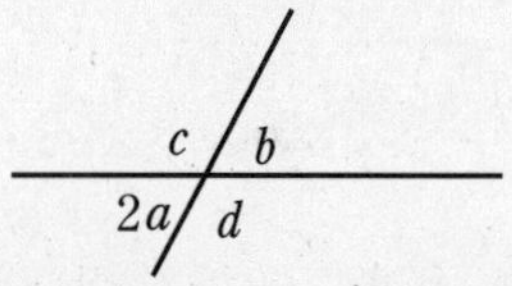

In the figure of intersecting lines above, which of the following is equal to $180 - a$?

(A) $a + d$
(B) $a + 2d$
(C) $c + b$
(D) $b + 2a$
(E) $c + d$

Choice A is correct.

<u>Try a specific number.</u>
Let $\boxed{a = 20°}$
Then $2a = 40°$
Be careful now—all of the other angles are now determined, so don't choose any more.
Because vertical angles are equal, $2a = b$, so

$$\boxed{b = 40°}.$$

Now $c + b = 180°$, so $c + 40 = 180$ and

$$\boxed{c = 140°}.$$

Thus, $\boxed{d = 140°}$ (vertical angles are equal).
Now look at the question:

$$180 - a = 180 - 20 = 160$$

Which is the correct choice?

(A) $a + d = 20 + 140 = 160$—that's the one!

See Math Strategy 17, Example 2 (page 111) for an alternate approach to solving this problem, using a different strategy: **Use the Given Information Effectively (and Ignore Irrelevant Information)**.

MATH STRATEGY 8

When Each Choice Must Be Tested, Start with Choice E and Work Backward

If you must check each choice for the correct answer, start with Choice E and work backward. The reason for this is that the test maker of a question *in which each choice must be tested* often puts the correct answer as Choice D or E. The careless student will start testing with Choice A and work downward to Choice E, wasting time. So if you're trying all the choices, start with the last choice, then the next to last choice, etc. See Example 8 for an example of when this strategy should not be used.

EXAMPLE 1

If p is a positive integer, which *could* be an odd integer?

(A) $2p + 2$
(B) $p^3 - p$
(C) $p^2 + p$
(D) $p^2 - p$
(E) $7p - 3$

Choice E is correct. Start with Choice E first since you have to *test* out the choices.

Method 1: Try a number for p. Let $p = 1$. Then (starting with Choice E),

$7p - 3 = 7(1) - 3 = 4$. 4 is even, so try another number for p to see whether $7p - 3$ is odd. Let $p = 2$.

$7p - 3 = 7(2) - 3 = 11$. 11 is odd. Therefore, Choice E is correct.

Method 2: Look at Choice E. $7p$ could be even or odd, depending on what p is. If p is even, $7p$ is even. If p is odd, $7p$ is odd. Accordingly, $7p - 3$ is either even or odd. Thus, Choice E is correct.

Note: By using either Method 1 or Method 2, it is not necessary to test the other choices.

EXAMPLE 2

If $y = x^2 + 3$, then for which value of x is y divisible by 7?

(A) 10
(B) 8
(C) 7
(D) 6
(E) 5

Choice E is correct. Since you must check all of the choices, start with Choice E:

$$y = 5^2 + 3 = 25 + 3 = 28$$
28 is divisible by 7

If you had started with Choice A, you would have had to test four choices instead of one choice before finding the correct answer.

EXAMPLE 3

Which fraction is greater than $\frac{1}{2}$?

(A) $\frac{4}{9}$

(B) $\frac{17}{35}$

(C) $\frac{6}{13}$

(D) $\frac{12}{25}$

(E) $\frac{8}{15}$

Choice E is correct.

Look at Choice E first.

$$\text{Is } \frac{8}{15} > \frac{1}{2}?$$

Use the cross-multiplication method.

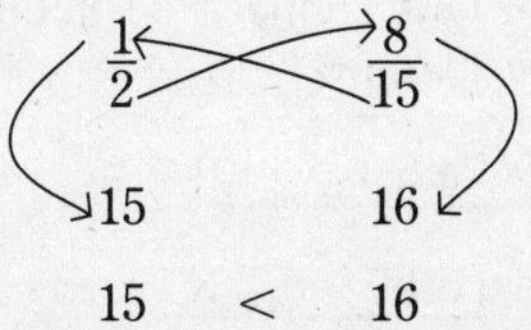

15 < 16

So, $\frac{1}{2} < \frac{8}{15}$.

You also could have looked at Choice E and said $\frac{8}{16} = \frac{1}{2}$ and realized that $\frac{8}{15} > \frac{1}{2}$ because $\frac{8}{15}$ has a smaller denominator than $\frac{8}{16}$.

EXAMPLE 4

If n is an even integer, which of the following is an odd integer?

(A) $n^2 - 2$
(B) $n - 4$
(C) $(n - 4)^2$
(D) n^3
(E) $n^2 - n - 1$

Choice E is correct.

Look at Choice E first.

$n^2 - n - 1$
If n is even
n^2 is even
n is even
1 is odd

So, $n^2 - n - 1 = \text{even} - \text{even} - \text{odd} = \text{odd}$.

EXAMPLE 5

Which of the following is an odd number?

(A) 7×22
(B) $59 - 15$
(C) $55 + 35$
(D) $75 \div 15$
(E) 4^7

Choice D is correct.

Look at Choice E first.

4^7 is even because all positive integral powers of an even number are even.

So now look at Choice D: $\frac{75}{15} = 5$, which is odd.

EXAMPLE 6

$$\begin{array}{r} 3\ \#\ 2 \\ \times\quad 8 \\ \hline 28 \star 6 \end{array}$$

If # and ★ are different digits in the correctly calculated multiplication problem above, then # could be

(A) 1
(B) 2
(C) 3
(D) 4
(E) 6

Choice E is correct.

Try Choice E first.

$$\begin{array}{r} 3\ \#\ 2 \\ \times\quad 8 \\ \hline 28 \star 6 \end{array} \qquad \begin{array}{r} 3\ ⑥\ 2 \\ \times\quad 8 \\ \hline 28\ ⑨\ 6 \end{array}$$

9 and 6 are different numbers, so Choice E is correct.

EXAMPLE 7

Which choice describes a pair of numbers that are *unequal*?

(A) $\frac{1}{6}, \frac{11}{66}$

(B) $3.4, \frac{34}{10}$

(C) $\frac{15}{75}, \frac{1}{5}$

(D) $\frac{3}{8}, 0.375$

(E) $\frac{86}{24}, \frac{42}{10}$

Choice E is correct.

Look at Choice E first.

$$\frac{86}{24} \quad ? \quad \frac{42}{10}$$

Cross multiply:

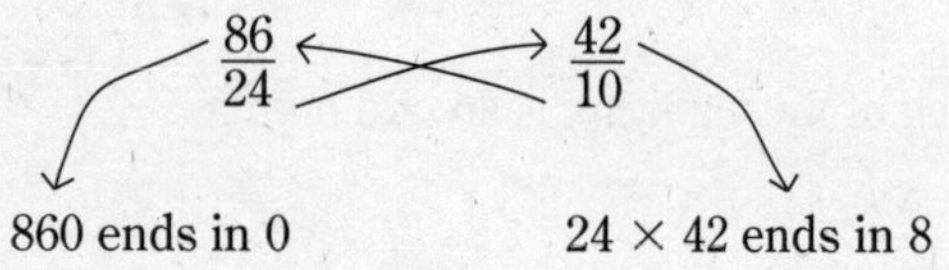

Thus, the numbers must be *different* and *unequal.*

When *Not* to Use This Strategy:

If you can spot something in the question that shows you how to solve the problem readily without having to test each choice, there's no need to go through every answer by working backwards.

EXAMPLE 8

If $|6 - 5y| > 20$, which of the following is a possible value of y?

(A) −3
(B) −1
(C) 1
(D) 3
(E) 5

Choice A is correct.

Instead of plugging in values for y, starting with Choice E, you should realize there will only be one answer listed for which $6 - 5y > 20$. So which choice gives you the largest product for $-5y$? Start by checking the *most negative* choice, or $y = -3$.

This gives you $|6 - 5(-3)| = |6 + 15| = |21|$, which is greater than 20.

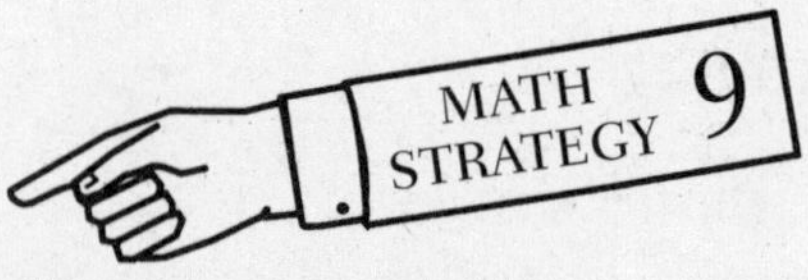

Know How to Solve Problems Using the Formula R × T = D

Almost every problem involving motion can be solved using the formula

$$R \times T = D$$

or

rate × elapsed time = distance

EXAMPLE 1

The diagram below shows two paths: Path 1 is 10 miles long, and Path 2 is 12 miles long. If Person X runs along Path 1 at 5 miles per hour and Person Y runs along Path 2 at y miles per hour, and if it takes exactly the same amount of time for both runners to run their whole path, then what is the value of y?

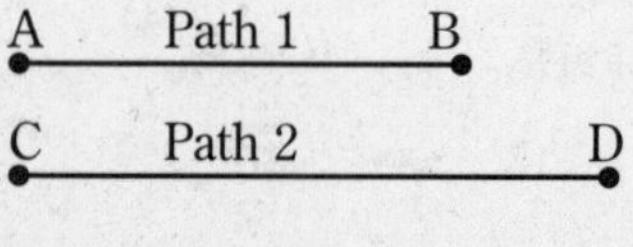

(A) 2
(B) $4\frac{1}{6}$
(C) 6
(D) 20
(E) 24

Choice C is correct. Let T = Time (in hours) for either runner to run the whole path.

Using $R \times T = D$, for Person X, we have
(5 mi/hr) (T hours) = 10 miles

or $\quad 5T = 10$ or $\quad \boxed{1}$
$T = 2$

For Person Y, we have
(y mi/hr) (T hours) = 12 miles
or $yT = 12$
Using $\boxed{1}$ $y(2) = 12$ or $y = 6$.

EXAMPLE 2

A car traveling at 50 miles per hour for two hours travels the same distance as a car traveling at 20 miles per hour for x hours. What is x?

(A) $\frac{4}{5}$
(B) $\frac{5}{4}$
(C) 5
(D) 2
(E) $\frac{1}{2}$

Choice C is correct.

Use $R \times T = D$. Call the distance both cars travel, D (since distance is the same for both cars).

So we get:

$$50 \times 2 = D = 100 \qquad \boxed{1}$$
$$20 \times x = D = 100 \qquad \boxed{2}$$

Solving $\boxed{2}$ you can see that $x = 5$.

EXAMPLE 3

John walks at a rate of 4 miles per hour. Sally walks at a rate of 5 miles per hour. If John and Sally both start at the same starting point, how many miles is one person from the other after t hours of walking? (*Note:* Both are walking on the same road in the same direction.)

(A) $\frac{t}{2}$
(B) t
(C) $2t$
(D) $\frac{4}{5}t$
(E) $\frac{5}{4}t$

Choice B is correct.

Draw a diagram:

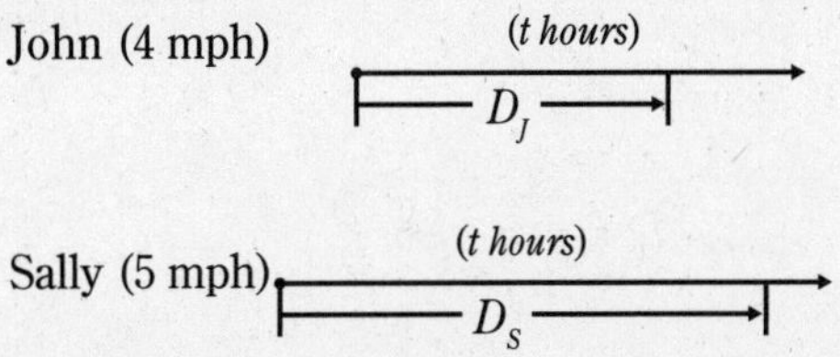

Let D_J be distance that John walks in t hours.
Let D_S be distance that Sally walks in t hours.
Then, using $R \times t = D$,

for John: $4 \times t = D_J$
for Sally: $5 \times t = D_S$

The distance between Sally and John after T hours of walking is:

$$D_S - D_J = 5t - 4t = t$$

EXAMPLE 4

A man rode a bicycle a straight distance at a speed of 10 miles per hour and came back the same distance at a speed of 20 miles per hour. What was the man's total number of miles for the trip back and forth, if his total traveling time was 1 hour?

(A) 15
(B) $7\frac{1}{2}$
(C) $6\frac{1}{3}$
(D) $6\frac{2}{3}$
(E) $13\frac{1}{3}$

Choice E is correct.

Always use $R \times T = D$ (Rate $\times$ Time = Distance) in problems like this. Call the first distance D and the time for the first part T_1. Since he rode at 10 mph:

$$10 \times T_1 = D \qquad \boxed{1}$$

Now for the trip back. He rode at 20 mph. Call the time it took to go back, T_2. Since he came back the *same* distance, we can call that distance D also. So for the trip back using $R \times T = D$, we get:

$$20 \times T_2 = D \qquad \boxed{2}$$

Since it was given that the total traveling time was 1 hour, the total traveling time is:

$$T_1 + T_2 = 1$$

Now here's the trick: Let's make use of the fact that $T_1 + T_2 = 1$. Dividing Equation $\boxed{1}$ by 10, we get:

$$T_1 = \frac{D}{10}$$

Dividing $\boxed{2}$ by 20, we get:

$$T_2 = \frac{D}{20}$$

Now add $T_1 + T_2$ and we get:

$$T_1 + T_2 = 1 = \frac{D}{10} + \frac{D}{20}$$

Factor D:

$$1 = D\left(\frac{1}{10} + \frac{1}{20}\right)$$

Add $\frac{1}{10} + \frac{1}{20}$. Remember the fast way of adding fractions?

$$\frac{1}{10} + \frac{1}{20} = \frac{20+10}{20 \times 10} = \frac{30}{200}$$

So:

$$1 = (D)\frac{30}{200}$$

Multiply by 200 and divide by 30 and we get:

$$\frac{200}{30} = D; D = 6\frac{2}{3}$$

Don't forget, we're looking for $2D$: $2D = 13\frac{1}{3}$

EXAMPLE 5

What is the average rate of a bicycle traveling at 10 mph a distance of 5 miles and at 20 mph the same distance?

(A) 15 mph
(B) 20 mph
(C) $12\frac{1}{2}$mph
(D) $13\frac{1}{3}$mph
(E) 16 mph

Choice D is correct.

Ask yourself, what does *average rate* mean? It *does not* mean the average of the rates! If you thought it did, you would have selected Choice A as the answer (averaging 10 and 20 to get 15)—the "lure" choice.

Average is a word that *modifies* the word *rate* in this case. So you must define the word *rate* first, before you do anything with averaging. Since Rate × Time = Distance,

$$\text{Rate} = \frac{\text{Distance}}{\text{Time}}$$

Then *average* rate must be:

$$\text{Average rate} = \frac{\text{total distance}}{\text{total time}}$$

The *total distance* is the distance covered on the whole trip, which is 5 + 5 = 10 miles.
The *total time* is the time traveled the first 5 miles at 10 mph added to the time the bicycle traveled the next 5 miles at 20 mph.
Let t_1 be the time the bicycle traveled the first 5 miles.
Let t_2 be the time the bicycle traveled the next 5 miles.
Then the *total time* = $t_1 + t_2$.
Since $R \times T = D$,

for the first 5 miles: $10 \times t_1 = 5$
for the next 5 miles: $20 \times t_2 = 5$

Finding t_1: $t_1 = \frac{5}{10}$

Finding t_2: $t_2 = \frac{5}{20}$

So, $t_1 + t_2 = \frac{5}{10} + \frac{5}{20}$

$= \frac{1}{2} + \frac{1}{4}$ (remembering how to quickly add fractions)

$= \frac{4+2}{8}$

$= \frac{6}{8} = \frac{3}{4}$

$$\text{Average rate} = \frac{\text{total distance}}{\text{total time}}$$

$$= \frac{5+5}{\frac{3}{4}}$$

$$= (5+5) \times \frac{4}{3}$$

$$= 10 \times \frac{4}{3} = \frac{40}{3} = 13\frac{1}{3} \text{ (*Answer*)}$$

Here's a formula you can memorize:
If a vehicle travels a certain distance at a mph and travels the same distance at b mph, the *average rate* is

$$\frac{2ab}{a+b}.$$

Try doing the problem using this formula:

$$\frac{2ab}{a+b} = \frac{2 \times (10) \times (20)}{10+20} = \frac{400}{30} = 13\frac{1}{3}$$

Caution: Use this formula only when you are looking for *average rate, and when the distance is the same for both speeds.*

MATH STRATEGY 10

Know How to Use Units of Time, Distance, Area, or Volume to Find or Check Your Answer

By knowing what the units in your answer must be, you will often have an easier time finding or checking your answer. A very helpful thing to do is to treat the units of time or space as variables (like x or y). Thus, you should substitute, multiply, or divide these units as if they were ordinary variables. The following examples illustrate this idea.

EXAMPLE 1

What is the distance in miles covered by a car that traveled at 50 miles per hour for 5 hours?

(A) 10
(B) 45
(C) 55
(D) 200
(E) 250

Choice E is correct. Although this is an easy $R \times T = D$ problem, it illustrates this strategy very well.

Recall that

$$\text{rate} \times \text{time} = \text{distance}$$
$$(50 \text{ mi/hr})(5 \text{ hours}) = \text{distance}$$

Notice that when I substituted into $R \times T = D$, *I kept the units of rate and time* (miles/hour and hours). Now I will *treat these units as if they were ordinary variables.* Thus,

$$\text{distance} = (50 \text{ mi/hr})(5 \text{ hours})$$

I have canceled the variable "hour(s)" from the numerator and denominator of the right side of the equation. Hence,

$$\text{distance} = 250 \text{ miles}$$

The distance has units of "miles," as I would expect. In fact, if the units in my answer had been "miles/hour" or "hours," then I would have been in error.

Thus, *the general procedure* for problems using this strategy is:

Step 1. Keep the units given in the question.
Step 2. Treat the units as ordinary variables.
Step 3. Make sure the answer has units that you would expect.

EXAMPLE 2

How many inches is equivalent to 2 yards, 2 feet, and 7 inches?

(A) 11
(B) 37
(C) 55
(D) 81
(E) 103

Choice E is correct.
Remember that

$$1 \text{ yard} = 3 \text{ feet} \qquad \boxed{1}$$
$$1 \text{ foot} = 12 \text{ inches} \qquad \boxed{2}$$

Treat the units of length as variables! Divide $\boxed{1}$ by 1 yard, and $\boxed{2}$ by 1 foot, to get

$$1 = \frac{3 \text{ feet}}{1 \text{ yard}} \qquad \boxed{3}$$

$$1 = \frac{12 \text{ inches}}{1 \text{ foot}} \qquad \boxed{4}$$

We can multiply any expression by 1 and get the same value. Thus, 2 yards + 2 feet + 7 inches =

$$(2 \text{ yards})(1)(1) + (2 \text{ feet})(1) + 7 \text{ inches} \qquad \boxed{5}$$

Substituting $\boxed{3}$ and $\boxed{4}$ into $\boxed{5}$, 2 yards + 2 feet + 7 inches

$$= 2\,\cancel{\text{yards}}\left(\frac{3\,\cancel{\text{feet}}}{\cancel{\text{yard}}}\right)\left(\frac{12 \text{ inches}}{\cancel{\text{foot}}}\right) + 2\,\cancel{\text{feet}}\left(\frac{12 \text{ inches}}{\cancel{\text{foot}}}\right) + 7 \text{ inches}$$

$$= 72 \text{ inches} + 24 \text{ inches} + 7 \text{ inches}$$

$$= 103 \text{ inches}$$

Notice that the answer is in "inches," as I expected. If the answer had come out in "yards" or "feet," then I would have been in error.

EXAMPLE 3

A car wash cleans x cars per hour, for y hours, at z dollars per car. How much money in *cents* does the car wash receive?

(A) $\frac{xy}{100z}$

(B) $\frac{xyz}{100}$

(C) $100xyz$

(D) $\frac{100x}{yz}$

(E) $\frac{yz}{100x}$

Choice C is correct.

Use units:

$$\left(\frac{x\ \cancel{\text{cars}}}{\cancel{\text{hour}}}\right)(y\ \cancel{\text{hours}})\left(\frac{z\ \text{dollar}}{\cancel{\text{car}}}\right) = xyz \text{ dollars} \qquad \boxed{1}$$

Since there are 100 cents to a dollar, we multiply $\boxed{1}$ by 100. We get $100xyz$ cents.

EXAMPLE 4

There are 3 feet in a yard and 12 inches in a foot. How many yards are there altogether in 1 yard, 1 foot, and 1 inch?

(A) $1\frac{1}{3}$

(B) $1\frac{13}{36}$

(C) $1\frac{11}{18}$

(D) $2\frac{5}{12}$

(E) $4\frac{1}{12}$

Choice B is correct. **Know how to work with units.**

Given: 3 feet = 1 yard
12 inches = 1 foot

Thus,

$$1 \text{ yard} + 1 \text{ foot} + 1 \text{ inch} =$$

$$1\,\text{yard} + 1\,\cancel{\text{foot}}\left(\frac{1\,\text{yard}}{3\,\cancel{\text{feet}}}\right) + 1\,\cancel{\text{inch}}\left(\frac{1\,\cancel{\text{foot}}}{12\,\cancel{\text{inches}}}\right) \times \left(\frac{1\,\text{yard}}{3\,\cancel{\text{feet}}}\right) =$$

$$\left(1 + \frac{1}{3} + \frac{1}{36}\right) \text{yards} =$$

$$\left(1 + \frac{12}{36} + \frac{1}{36}\right) \text{yards} =$$

$$1\frac{13}{36} \text{ yards}$$

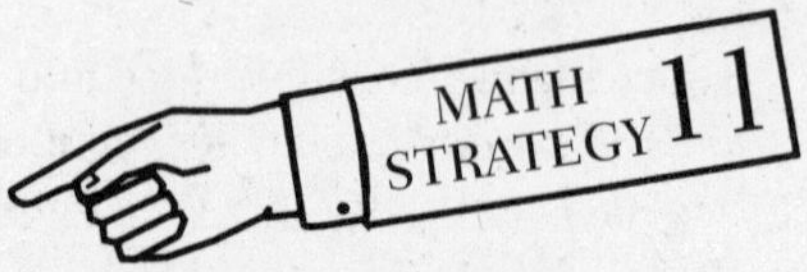

Use New Definitions and Functions Carefully

Some SAT questions use new symbols, functions, or definitions that were created in the question. At first glance, these questions may seem difficult because you are not familiar with the new symbol, function, or definition. *However, most of these questions can be solved through simple substitution or application of a simple definition.*

EXAMPLE 1

If the symbol ϕ is defined by the equation

$$a \,\phi\, b = a - b - ab$$

for all a and b, then $\left(-\frac{1}{3}\right) \phi\ (-3) =$

(A) $\frac{5}{3}$

(B) $\frac{11}{3}$

(C) $-\frac{13}{3}$

(D) -4

(E) -5

Choice A is correct. All that is required is substitution:

$a \phi b = a - b - ab$

$\left(-\frac{1}{3}\right) \phi (-3)$

Substitute $-\frac{1}{3}$ for a and -3 for b in $a - b - ab$:

$$\begin{aligned}\left(-\frac{1}{3}\right) \phi (-3) &= -\frac{1}{3} - (-3) - \left(-\frac{1}{3}\right)(-3)\\ &= -\frac{1}{3} + 3 - 1\\ &= 2 - \frac{1}{3}\\ &= \frac{5}{3} \textit{ (Answer)}\end{aligned}$$

EXAMPLE 2

$$\text{Let } \boxed{x} = \begin{cases}\frac{5}{2}(x+1) & \text{if } x \text{ is an odd integer}\\ \frac{5}{2}x & \text{if } x \text{ is an even integer}\end{cases}$$

Find $\boxed{2y}$, where y is an integer.

(A) $\frac{5}{2}y$
(B) $5y$
(C) $\frac{5}{2}y + 1$
(D) $5y + \frac{5}{2}$
(E) $5y + 5$

Choice B is correct. All we have to do is substitute $2y$ into the definition of $\boxed{x}$. In order to know which definition of $\boxed{x}$ to use, we want to know if $2y$ is even. Since y is an integer, then $2y$ is an even integer. Thus,

$$\boxed{2y} = \frac{5}{2}(2y)$$
$$\text{or } \boxed{2y} = 5y \textit{ (Answer)}$$

EXAMPLE 3

As in the previous Example 1, ϕ is defined as

$$a \phi b = a - b - ab.$$

If $a \phi 3 = 6$, $a =$

(A) $\frac{9}{2}$
(B) $\frac{9}{4}$
(C) $-\frac{9}{4}$
(D) $-\frac{4}{9}$
(E) $-\frac{9}{2}$

Choice E is correct.

$$a \phi b = a - b - ab$$
$$a \phi 3 = 6$$

Substitute a for a, 3 for b:

$$\begin{aligned}a \phi 3 &= a - 3 - a(3) = 6\\ &= a - 3 - 3a = 6\\ &= -2a - 3 = 6\\ 2a &= -9\\ a &= -\frac{9}{2}\end{aligned}$$

EXAMPLE 4

The symbol $\textcircled{x}$ is defined as the greatest integer less than or equal to x.

$\textcircled{-3.4} + \textcircled{21} =$

(A) 16
(B) 16.6
(C) 17
(D) 17.6
(E) 18

Choice C is correct.

$\textcircled{-3.4}$ is defined as the *greatest integer less than or equal to* -3.4. This is -4, since $-4 < -3.4$.

$\textcircled{21}$ is defined as the *greatest integer less than or equal to* 21. That is just 21, since $21 = 21$.

Thus, $-4 + 21 = 17$.

EXAMPLE 5

$\textcircled{\begin{smallmatrix}x & y\\ z & t\end{smallmatrix}}$ is defined as $xz - yt$

$\textcircled{\begin{smallmatrix}2 & 1\\ 1 & 1\end{smallmatrix}} =$

(A) $\textcircled{\begin{smallmatrix}1 & 1\\ 1 & 1\end{smallmatrix}}$
(B) $\textcircled{\begin{smallmatrix}3 & 2\\ 2 & 1\end{smallmatrix}}$
(C) $\textcircled{\begin{smallmatrix}4 & 3\\ 2 & 1\end{smallmatrix}}$
(D) $\textcircled{\begin{smallmatrix}5 & 4\\ 4 & 2\end{smallmatrix}}$
(E) $\textcircled{\begin{smallmatrix}3 & 1\\ 1 & 2\end{smallmatrix}}$

Choice E is correct.

$$\begin{pmatrix} x & y \\ z & t \end{pmatrix} = xz - yt; \quad \begin{pmatrix} 2 & 1 \\ 1 & 1 \end{pmatrix} = ?$$

Substituting 2 for x, 1 for z, 1 for y, and 1 for t,

$$\begin{pmatrix} 2 & 1 \\ 1 & 1 \end{pmatrix} = (2)(1) - (1)(1) = 1$$

Now work from Choice E:

(E) $\begin{pmatrix} 3 & 1 \\ 1 & 2 \end{pmatrix} = xz - yt = (3)(1) - (1)(2) = 3 - 2 = 1$

EXAMPLE 6

If for all numbers a, b, c the operation ● is defined as

$$a \bullet b = ab - a$$

then

$$a \bullet (b \bullet c) =$$

(A) $a(bc - b - 1)$
(B) $a(bc + b + 1)$
(C) $a(bc - c - b - 1)$
(D) $a(bc - b + 1)$
(E) $a(b - a + c)$

Choice A is correct.

$$a \bullet b = ab - a$$

$$a \bullet (b \bullet c) = ?$$

Find $(b \bullet c)$ first. Use substitution:

$a \bullet b = ab - a$
↑ ↑
$b \bullet c$

Substitute b for a and c for b:

$$b \bullet c = b(c) - b$$

Now, $a \bullet (b \bullet c) = a \bullet (bc - b)$
Use definition $a \bullet b = ab - a$
Substitute a for a and $bc - b$ for b:

$a \bullet b = ab - a$
↗ ↗
$a \bullet (bc - b) = a(bc - b) - a$
$= abc - ab - a$
$= a(bc - b - 1)$

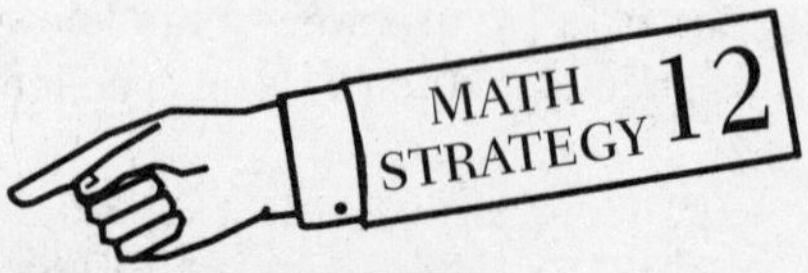

Try Not to Make Tedious Calculations Since There Is Usually an Easier Way

In many of the examples given in these strategies, it has been explicitly stated that one should not calculate complicated quantities. In some of the examples, we have demonstrated a fast and a slow way of solving the same problem. On the actual exam, if you find that your solution to a problem involves a tedious and complicated method, then you are probably doing the problem in a long, hard way.* Almost always, there will be an easier way.

Examples 5 and 6 can also be solved with the aid of a calculator and some with the aid of a calculator allowing for exponential calculations. However, to illustrate the effectiveness of Math Strategy 12, we did not use the calculator method of solving these examples.

* Many times, you can DIVIDE, MULTIPLY, ADD, SUBTRACT, or FACTOR to simplify.

EXAMPLE 1

What is the value of $2^1 + 2^2 + 2^3 + 2^4 + 2^5 + 2^6 + 2^7 + 2^8 + 2^9$?

(A) $2^{11} - 2$
(B) 2^{10}
(C) $2^{10} - 2$
(D) $2^{10} - 4$
(E) $2^{10} - 8$

Choice C is correct.

Let $x = 2^1 + 2^2 + 2^3 + 2^4 + 2^5 + 2^6 + 2^7 + 2^8 + 2^9$. $\boxed{1}$

Now multiply $\boxed{1}$ by 2:

$2x = 2(2^1 + 2^2 + 2^3 + 2^4 + 2^5 + 2^6 + 2^7 + 2^8 + 2^9)$

Thus,

$2x = 2^2 + 2^3 + 2^4 + 2^5 + 2^6 + 2^7 + 2^8 + 2^9 + 2^{10}$ $\boxed{2}$

Subtracting $\boxed{1}$ from $\boxed{2}$, we get

$2x - x = x = 2^{10} - 2^1 = 2^{10} - 2$

EXAMPLE 2

If $16r - 24q = 2$, then $2r - 3q =$

(A) $\frac{1}{8}$
(B) $\frac{1}{4}$
(C) $\frac{1}{2}$
(D) 2
(E) 4

Choice B is correct.

Divide by 8:

$$\frac{16r - 24q}{8} = \frac{2}{8}$$

$$2r - 3q = \frac{1}{4}$$

EXAMPLE 3

If $(a^2 + a)^3 = x(a + 1)^3$, where $a + 1 \neq 0$, then $x =$

(A) a
(B) a^2
(C) a^3
(D) $\frac{a+1}{a}$
(E) $\frac{a}{a+1}$

Choice C is correct.

Isolate x first:

$$x = \frac{(a^2+a)^3}{(a+1)^3}$$

Now use the fact that $\left(\frac{x^3}{y^3}\right) = \left(\frac{x}{y}\right)^3$:

$$\frac{(a^2+a)^3}{(a+1)^3} = \left(\frac{a^2+a}{a+1}\right)^3$$

Now factor $a^2 + a = a(a + 1)$

So:

$$\left(\frac{a^2+a}{a+1}\right)^3 = \left[\frac{a(a+1)}{a+1}\right]^3$$

$$= \left[\frac{a\cancel{(a+1)}}{\cancel{a+1}}\right]^3$$

$$= a^3$$

EXAMPLE 4

If $\frac{p+1}{r+1} = 1$ and p, r are nonzero, and p is not equal to -1, and r is not equal to -1, then

(A) $2 > \frac{p}{r} > 1$ always
(B) $\frac{p}{r} < 1$ always
(C) $\frac{p}{r} = 1$ always
(D) $\frac{p}{r}$ can be greater than 2
(E) $\frac{p}{r} = 2$ always

Choice C is correct.

Get rid of the fraction. Multiply both sides of the equation

$$\frac{p+1}{r+1} = 1 \textit{ by } r+1$$

$$\left(\frac{p+1}{\cancel{r+1}}\right)\cancel{r+1} = r+1$$

$$p+1 = r+1$$

Cancel the 1s:

$$p = r$$

So:

$$\frac{p}{r} = 1$$

EXAMPLE 5

$\frac{4}{250} =$

(A) 0.16
(B) 0.016
(C) 0.0016
(D) 0.00125
(E) 0.000125

Choice B is correct.

Don't divide 4 into 250! Multiply:

$$\frac{4}{250} \times \frac{4}{4} = \frac{16}{1{,}000}$$

$$\text{Now } \frac{16}{100} = .16, \text{ so } \frac{16}{1{,}000} = .016.$$

EXAMPLE 6

$(3 \times 4^{14}) - 4^{13} =$

(A) 4
(B) 12
(C) 2×4^{13}
(D) 3×4^{13}
(E) 11×4^{13}

Choice E is correct.

Factor 4^{13} from
$(3 \times 4^{14}) - 4^{13}$
We get $4^{13}[(3 \times 4^1) - 1]$
or $4^{13}(12 - 1) = 4^{13}(11)$

You will see more of the technique of dividing, multiplying, adding, and subtracting in the next strategy, Math Strategy 13.

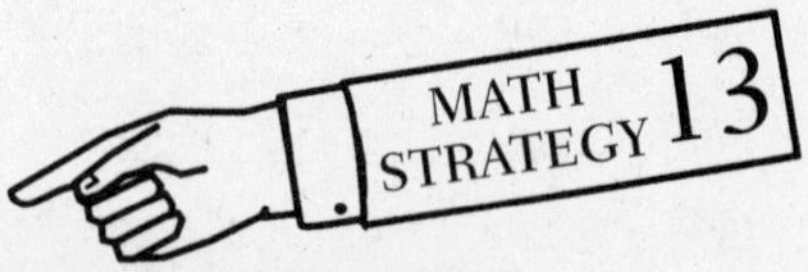

Know How to Find Unknown Expressions by Adding, Subtracting, Multiplying, or Dividing Equations or Expressions

When you want to calculate composite quantities like $x + 3y$ or $m - n$, often you can do it by adding, subtracting, multiplying, or dividing the right equations or expressions.

EXAMPLE 1

If $4x + 5y = 10$ and $x + 3y = 8$, then $\frac{5x + 8y}{3} =$

(A) 18
(B) 15
(C) 12
(D) 9
(E) 6

Choice E is correct. Don't solve for x, then for y.

Try to get the quantity $\frac{5x + 8y}{3}$ by adding or subtracting the equations. In this case, add equations.

$$\begin{array}{r} 4x + 5y = 10 \\ +\ \ x + 3y = 8 \\ \hline 5x + 8y = 18 \end{array}$$

Now divide by 3:

$$\frac{5x + 8y}{3} = \frac{18}{3} = 6 \text{ (Answer)}$$

EXAMPLE 2

If $25x + 8y = 149$ and $16x + 3y = 89$, then $\frac{9x + 5y}{5} =$

(A) 12
(B) 15
(C) 30
(D) 45
(E) 60

Choice A is correct. We are told

$$25x + 8y = 149 \quad \boxed{1}$$
$$16x + 3y = 89 \quad \boxed{2}$$

The long way to do this problem is to solve $\boxed{1}$ and $\boxed{2}$ for x and y, and then substitute these values into $\frac{9x + 5y}{5}$.

The fast way to do this problem is to subtract $\boxed{2}$ from $\boxed{1}$ and get

$$9x + 5y = 60 \quad \boxed{3}$$

Now all we have to do is to divide $\boxed{3}$ by 5:

$$\frac{9x + 5y}{5} = 12 \quad \textit{(Answer)}$$

EXAMPLE 3

If $21x + 39y = 18$, then $7x + 13y =$

(A) 3
(B) 6
(C) 7
(D) 9
(E) It cannot be determined from the information given.

Choice B is correct. We are given

$$21x + 39y = 18 \qquad \boxed{1}$$

Divide $\boxed{1}$ by 3:

$$7x + 13y = 6 \text{ (Answer)}$$

EXAMPLE 4

If $x + 2y = 4$, then $5x + 10y - 8 =$

(A) 10
(B) 12
(C) −10
(D) −12
(E) 0

Choice B is correct.

Multiply $x + 2y = 4$ by 5 to get:

$$5x + 10y = 20$$

Now subtract 8:

$$5x + 10y - 8 = 20 - 8$$
$$= 12$$

EXAMPLE 5

If $6x^5 = y^2$ and $x = \frac{1}{y}$, then $y =$

(A) x^6
(B) $\frac{x^5}{6}$
(C) $6x^6$
(D) $\frac{6x^5}{5}$
(E) $\frac{x^5}{5}$

Choice C is correct.

Multiply $6x^5 = y^2$ by $x = \frac{1}{y}$ to get:

$$6x^6 = y^2 \times \frac{1}{y} = y$$

EXAMPLE 6

If $y^8 = 4$ and $y^7 = \frac{3}{x}$,

what is the value of y in terms of x?

(A) $\frac{4x}{3}$
(B) $\frac{3x}{4}$
(C) $\frac{4}{x}$
(D) $\frac{x}{4}$
(E) $\frac{12}{x}$

Choice A is correct.

Don't solve for the *value* of y first, by finding $y = 4^{\frac{1}{8}}$.

Just divide the two equations:

(Step 1) $y^8 = 4$

(Step 2) $y^7 = \frac{3}{x}$

(Step 3) $\frac{y^8}{y^7} = \frac{4}{\frac{3}{x}}$

(Step 4) $y = 4 \times \frac{x}{3}$

(Step 5) $y = \frac{4x}{3}$ (*Answer*)

EXAMPLE 7

If $x > 0$, $y > 0$ and $x^2 = 27$ and $y^2 = 3$, then $\frac{x^3}{y^3} =$

(A) 9
(B) 27
(C) 36
(D) 48
(E) 54

Choice B is correct.

Divide: $\frac{x^2}{y^2} = \frac{27}{3} = 9$

Take square root: $\frac{x}{y} = 3$

So $\left(\frac{x}{y}\right)^3 = \frac{x^3}{y^3} = 3^3 = 27$

EXAMPLE 8

If $\frac{m}{n} = \frac{3}{8}$ and $\frac{m}{q} = \frac{4}{7}$, then $\frac{n}{q} =$

(A) $\frac{12}{15}$
(B) $\frac{12}{56}$
(C) $\frac{56}{12}$
(D) $\frac{32}{21}$
(E) $\frac{21}{32}$

Choice D is correct.

First get rid of fractions!

Cross-multiply $\frac{m}{n} = \frac{3}{8}$ to get $8m = 3n$. $\boxed{1}$

Now cross-multiply $\frac{m}{q} = \frac{4}{7}$ to get $7m = 4q$. $\boxed{2}$

Now divide Equations $\boxed{1}$ and $\boxed{2}$:

$$\frac{8m}{7m} = \frac{3n}{4q} \qquad \boxed{3}$$

The *m*s cancel and we get:

$$\frac{8}{7} = \frac{3n}{4q} \qquad \boxed{4}$$

Multiply Equation $\boxed{4}$ by 4 and divide by 3 to get

$$\frac{8 \times 4}{7 \times 3} = \frac{n}{q}$$

$$\text{Thus } \frac{n}{q} = \frac{32}{21}.$$

EXAMPLE 9

If $\frac{a+b+c+d}{4} = 20$

And $\frac{b+c+d}{3} = 10$

Then $a =$

(A) 50
(B) 60
(C) 70
(D) 80
(E) 90

Choice A is correct.

We have

$$\frac{a+b+c+d}{4} = 20 \qquad \boxed{1}$$

$$\frac{b+c+d}{3} = 10 \qquad \boxed{2}$$

Multiply Equation $\boxed{1}$ by 4:

We get: $a + b + c + d = 80$ $\boxed{3}$

Now multiply Equation $\boxed{2}$ by 3:

We get: $b + c + d = 30$ $\boxed{4}$

Now subtract Equation $\boxed{4}$ from Equation $\boxed{3}$:

$$\begin{array}{r} a + b + c + d = 80 \quad \boxed{3} \\ -\ (b + c + d = 30) \quad \boxed{4} \\ \hline \text{We get } a = 50. \end{array}$$

EXAMPLE 10

If $y + 2q = 15$, $q + 2p = 5$, and $p + 2y = 7$, then $p + q + y =$

(A) 81
(B) 45
(C) 27
(D) 18
(E) 9

Choice E is correct.

There's no need to solve for each variable. Just *add* the equations and divide by 3! To do this, write one equation below the other. Be sure to line up the common variables.

$$\begin{array}{rcl} y + 2q \qquad\quad &=& 15 \\ q + 2p &=& 5 \\ +\ 2y + \qquad\quad p &=& 7 \\ \hline 3y + 3q + 3p &=& 27 \end{array}$$

$y + 2q + q + 2p + p + 2y = 27$
$3y + 3q + 3p = 27$

Factor by 3:
$3(y + q + p) = 27$

So

$p + q + y = 9$

EXAMPLE 11

If $x > 0$, and $xy = 2$, $yz = 5$, and $xz = 10$, then $xyz =$

(A) 10
(B) 17
(C) 50
(D) 100
(E) 200

Choice A is correct. Since we are dealing with multiplication in all of the equations, *multiply* the expressions *xy*, *yz*, and *xz*.

We get:
$(xy)(yz)(xz) = 2 \times 5 \times 10 = 100$

This becomes
$x^2y^2z^2 = 100$

This is the same as
$(xyz)^2 = 100$

Take the square root of both sides to get
$xyz = 10$

MATH STRATEGY 14

Draw or Extend Lines in a Diagram to Make a Problem Easier; Label Unknown Quantities

EXAMPLE 1

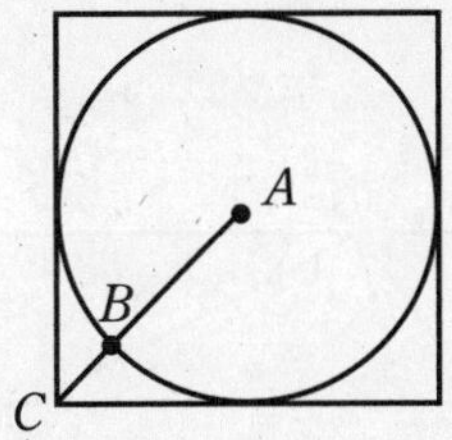

The circle with center A and radius AB is inscribed in the square above. AB is extended to C. What is the ratio of AB to AC?

(A) $\sqrt{2}$

(B) $\frac{\sqrt{2}}{4}$

(C) $\frac{\sqrt{2}-1}{2}$

(D) $\frac{\sqrt{2}}{2}$

(E) None of these.

Choice D is correct. Always draw or extend lines to get more information. Also label unknown lengths, angles, or arcs with letters.

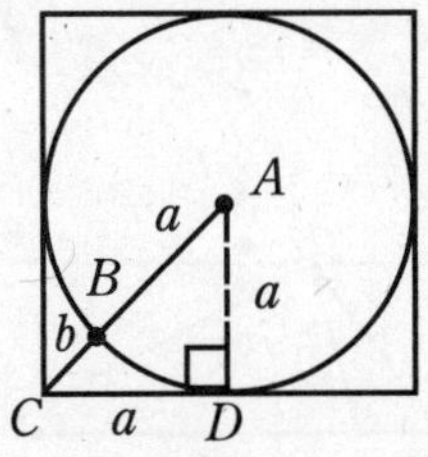

Label $AB = a$ and $BC = b$.
Draw perpendicular AD. Note it is just the radius, a. CD also $= a$, because each side of the square is length $2a$ (the diameter) and CD is $\frac{1}{2}$ the side of the square.

We want to find $\frac{AB}{AC} = \frac{a}{a+b}$

Now ΔADC is an isosceles right triangle so $AD = CD = a$.

By the Pythagorean Theorem,
$a^2 + a^2 = (a + b)^2$ where $a + b$ is the hypotenuse of a right triangle.

We get: $2a^2 = (a + b)^2$
Divide by $(a + b)^2$:

$$\frac{2a^2}{(a+b)^2} = 1$$

Divide by 2:

$$\frac{a^2}{(a+b)^2} = \frac{1}{2}$$

Take square roots of both sides:

$$\frac{a}{(a+b)} = \frac{1}{\sqrt{2}} =$$

$$= \frac{1}{\sqrt{2}}\left(\frac{\sqrt{2}}{\sqrt{2}}\right)$$

$$= \frac{\sqrt{2}}{2} \quad \textit{(Answer)}$$

EXAMPLE 2

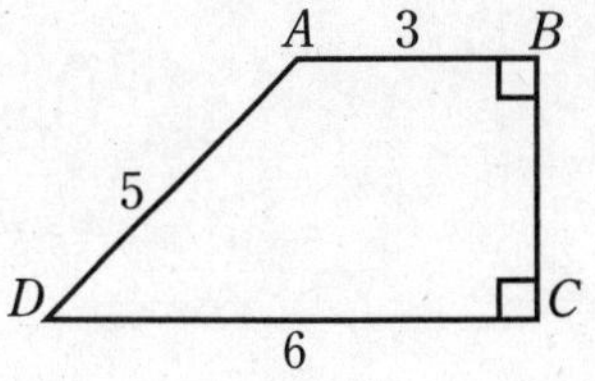

What is the perimeter of the above figure if B and C are right angles?

(A) 14
(B) 16
(C) 18
(D) 20
(E) Cannot be determined.

Choice C is correct.

Draw perpendicular AE. Label side $BC = h$. You can see that $AE = h$.

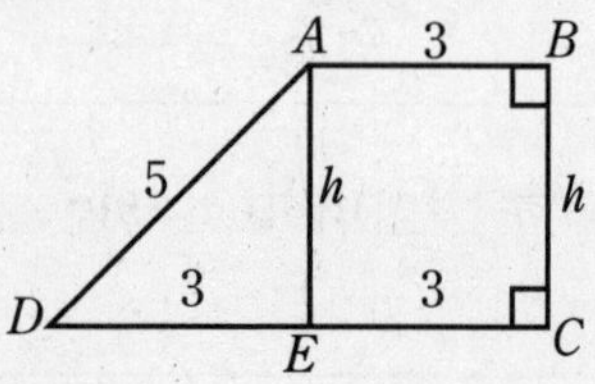

$ABCE$ is a rectangle, so $CE = 3$. This makes $ED = 3$ since the whole $DC = 6$.

Now use the Pythagorean Theorem for triangle AED:

$$h^2 + 3^2 = 5^2$$
$$h^2 = 5^2 - 3^2$$
$$h^2 = 25 - 9$$
$$h^2 = 16$$
$$h = 4$$

So the perimeter is $3 + h + 6 + 5 = 3 + 4 + 6 + 5 = 18$. (*Answer*)

EXAMPLE 3

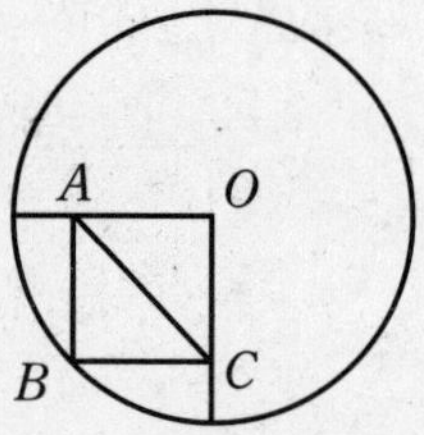

In the figure above, O is the center of a circle with a radius of 6, and $AOCB$ is a square. If point B is on the circumference of the circle, the length of $AC =$

(A) $6\sqrt{2}$
(B) $3\sqrt{2}$
(C) 3
(D) 6
(E) $6\sqrt{3}$

Choice D is correct.

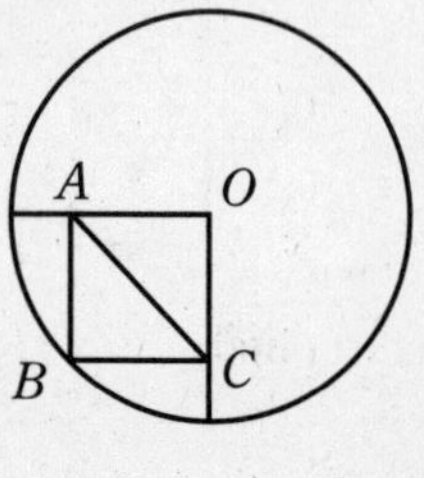

This is tricky if not impossible if you don't draw OB. So draw OB:

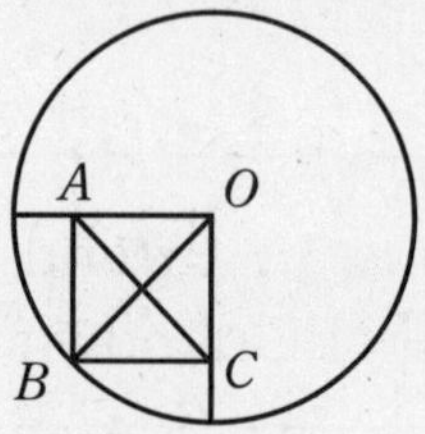

Since $AOCB$ is a square, $OB = AC$; and since $OB = \text{radius} = 6$, $AC = 6$.

EXAMPLE 4

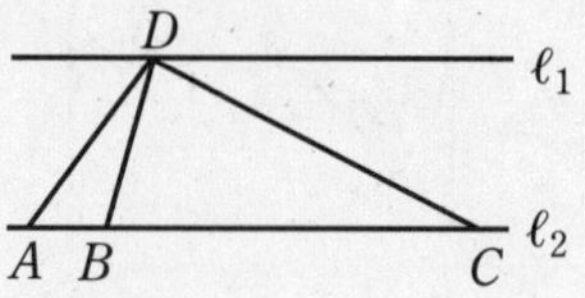

Lines ℓ_1 and ℓ_2 are parallel. $AB = \frac{1}{3}AC$.

$$\frac{\text{The area of triangle } ABD}{\text{The area of triangle } DBC} =$$

(A) $\frac{1}{4}$

(B) $\frac{1}{3}$

(C) $\frac{3}{8}$

(D) $\frac{1}{2}$

(E) Cannot be determined.

Choice D is correct.

$AB = \frac{1}{3}AC$

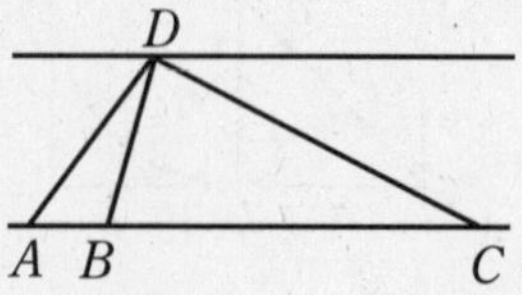

Ask yourself, what is the area of a triangle? It is $\frac{1}{2}$ (height $\times$ base). So let's get the heights and the bases of the triangles ABD and DBC. First draw the altitude (call it h).

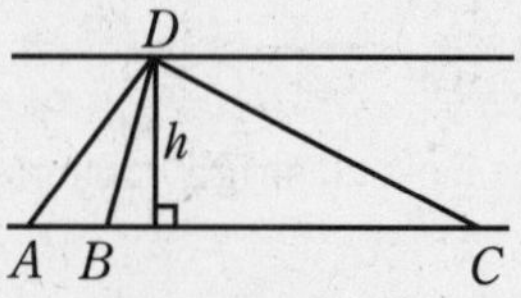

Now label $AB = \frac{1}{3}AC$ (given).

This makes $BC = \frac{2}{3}AC$, since $AB + BC = AC$

Thus the area of $\Delta ABD = \frac{1}{2}h(AB) = \frac{1}{2}h\left(\frac{1}{3}AC\right)$

$$\text{Area of } \Delta DBC = \frac{1}{2}h(BC) = \frac{1}{2}h\left(\frac{2}{3}AC\right)$$

$$\frac{\text{Area of } ABD}{\text{Area of } DBC} = \frac{\frac{1}{2}h\left(\frac{1}{3}AC\right)}{\frac{1}{2}h\left(\frac{2}{3}AC\right)}$$

$$= \frac{\frac{1}{3}}{\frac{2}{3}} = \frac{1}{3} \times \frac{3}{2} = \frac{1}{2}$$

EXAMPLE 5

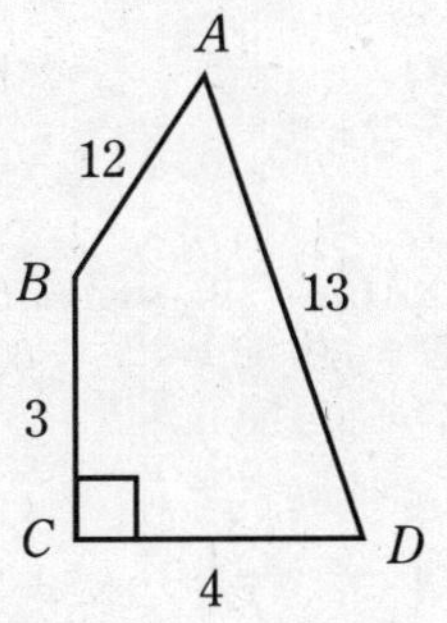

(Note: Figure is not drawn to scale.)

The area of the above figure *ABCD*

(A) is 36
(B) is 108
(C) is 156
(D) is 1,872
(E) Cannot be determined.

Choice A is correct.

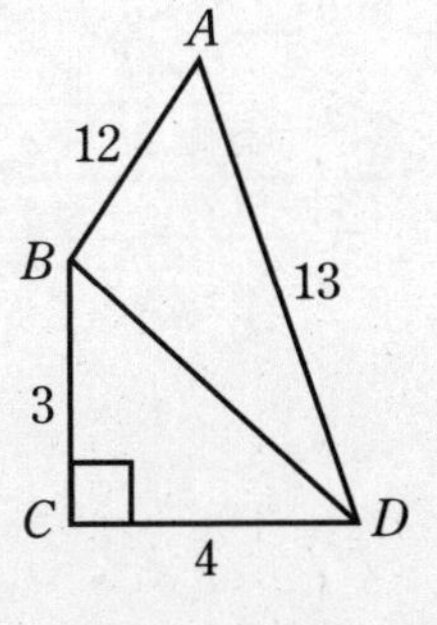

Draw *BD*. *BCD* is a 3–4–5 right triangle, so $BD = 5$. Now remember that a 5–12–13 triangle is also a right triangle, so angle *ABD* is a right angle. The area of triangle *BCD* is $\frac{(3 \times 4)}{2} = 6$ and the area of triangle *BAD* is $\frac{(5 \times 12)}{2} = 30$, so the total area is 36.

EXAMPLE 6

In the above figure, two points, *B* and *C*, are placed to the right of point *A* such that $4AB = 3AC$. The value of $\frac{BC}{AB}$

(A) equals $\frac{1}{3}$

(B) equals $\frac{2}{3}$

(C) equals $\frac{3}{2}$

(D) equals 3

(E) Cannot be determined.

Choice A is correct.

Place *B* and *C* to the right of *A*:

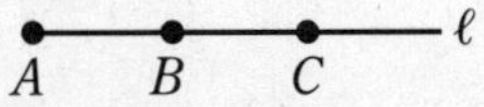

Now label $AB = a$ and $BC = b$:

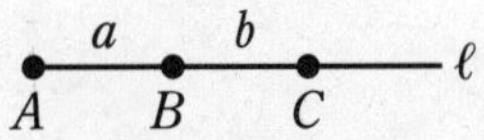

$$\frac{BC}{AB} = \frac{b}{a} \left(\frac{b}{a} \text{ is what we want to find}\right)$$

We are given $4AB = 3AC$.

So, $4a = 3(a + b)$

Expand: $4a = 3a + 3b$

Subtract $3a$: $a = 3b$

Divide by 3 and a: $\frac{1}{3} = \frac{b}{a}$

But remember $\frac{BC}{AB} = \frac{b}{a}$, so $\frac{BC}{AB} = \frac{1}{3}$

EXAMPLE 7

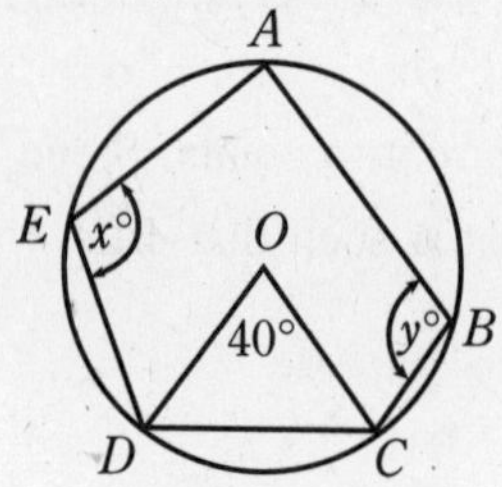

In the figure above, $ABCDE$ is a pentagon inscribed in the circle with center at O. $\angle DOC = 40°$. What is the value of $x + y$?

(A) 80
(B) 100
(C) 180
(D) 200
(E) Cannot be determined.

Choice D is correct.

Label degrees in each arc.

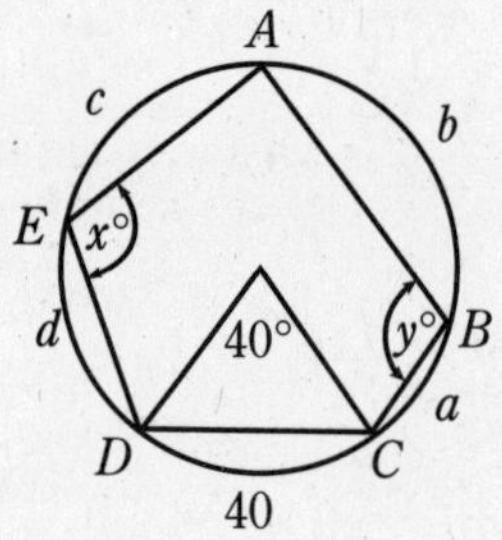

$\angle x$ is measured by $\frac{1}{2}$ the arc it cuts.

$$\text{So, } x = \frac{1}{2}(b + a + 40)$$

$$\text{Likewise, } y = \frac{1}{2}(c + d + 40)$$

You want to find $x + y$, so add:

$$x = \frac{1}{2}(b + a + 40)$$
$$y = \frac{1}{2}(c + d + 40)$$
$$x + y = \frac{1}{2}(b + a + 40 + c + d + 40)$$

But what is $a + b + c + d + 40$? It is the total number of degrees around the circumference, which is 360.

$$\text{So, } x + y = \frac{1}{2}(\underbrace{b + a + c + d + 40} + 40)$$
$$= \frac{1}{2}(360 + 40)$$
$$= \frac{1}{2}(400) = 200$$

EXAMPLE 8

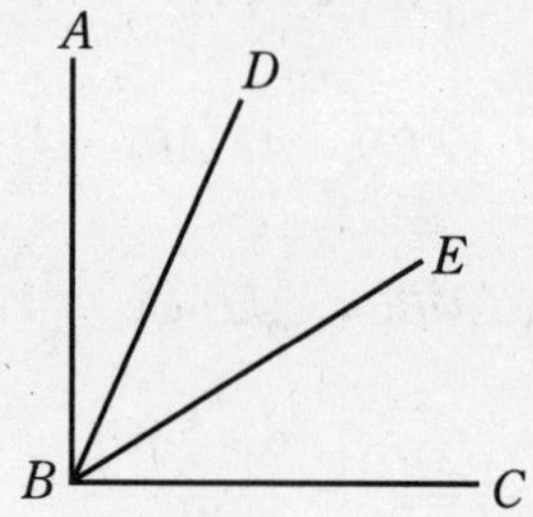

In the above figure, if $\angle ABE = 40°$, $\angle DBC = 60°$, and $\angle ABC = 90°$, what is the measure of $\angle DBE$?

(A) 10°
(B) 20°
(C) 40°
(D) 100°
(E) Cannot be determined.

Choice A is correct.

Label angles first.

Now $\angle ABE = 40$, so $a + b = 40$
$\angle DBC = 60$, so $b + c = 60$
$\angle ABC = 90$, so $a + b + c = 90$

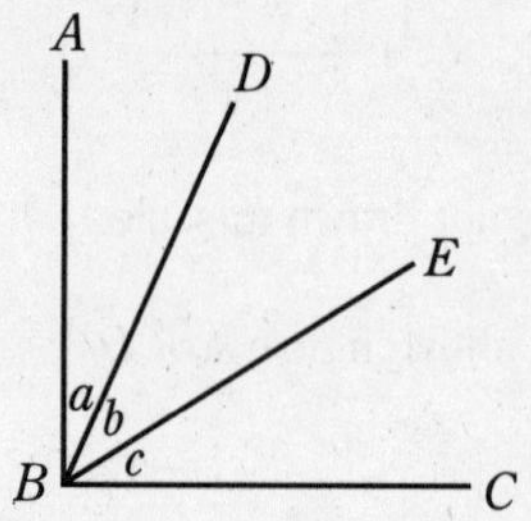

You want to find $\angle DBE$. $\angle DBE = b$, and you want to get the value of b from:

$a + b = 40$ [1]
$b + c = 60$ [2]
$a + b + c = 90$ [3]

Add [1] and [2]: $a + b = 40$
$+ b + c = 60$
$a + 2b + c = 100$
Subtract [3]: $-(a + b + c = 90)$
$b = 10$

EXAMPLE 9

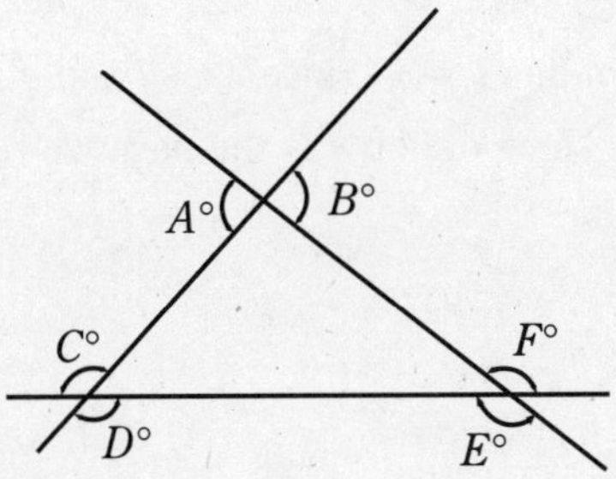

In the figure above, three lines intersect at the points shown. What is the value of $A + B + C + D + E + F$?

(A) 1,080
(B) 720
(C) 540
(D) 360
(E) Cannot be determined.

Choice B is correct.

Relabel, using the fact that *vertical angles are equal.*

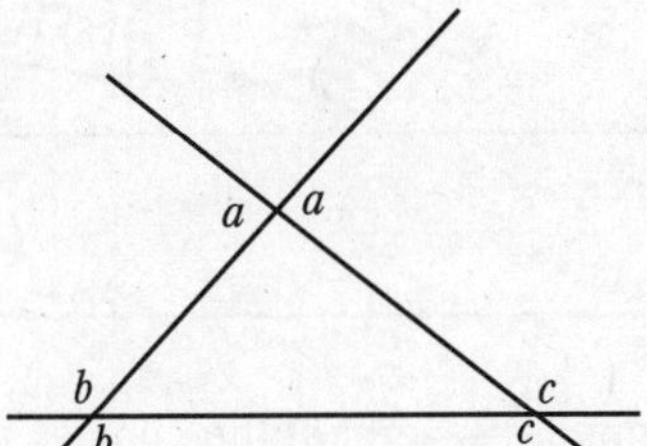

Now use the fact that a straight angle has 180° in it:

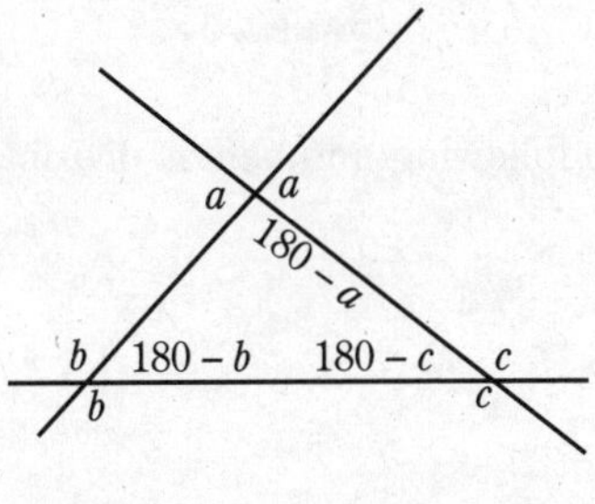

Now use the fact that the sum of the angles of a triangle = 180°:

$$180 - a + 180 - b + 180 - c = 180$$
$$540 - a - b - c = 180$$
$$540 - 180 = a + b + c$$
$$360 = a + b + c$$

Now remember what we are looking to find (the sum):

$$a + a + b + b + c + c = 2a + 2b + 2c$$

But this is just $2(a + b + c) = 2(360) = 720$.

EXAMPLE 10

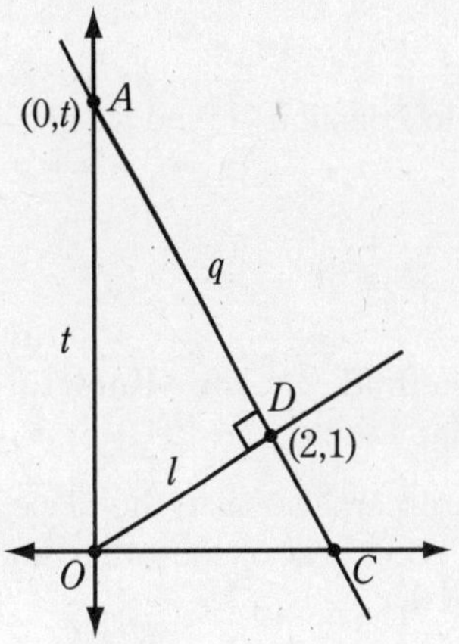

In the figure above, lines l and q are shown to be perpendicular on a coordinate plane. If line l contains the points (0,0) and (2,1), and line q contains the points (2,1) and $(0,t)$, what is the value of t?

(A) −3
(B) −2
(C) 2
(D) 3
(E) 5

Choice E is correct. You want to find the value of t.

Start by drawing line DE, the altitude of ΔDOC. Then label $EC = x$.

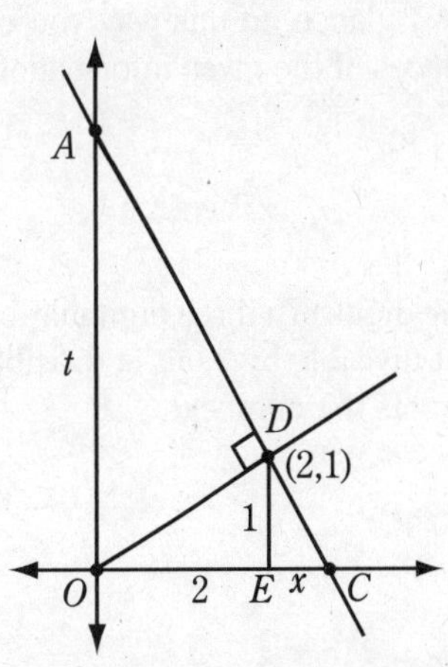

Because the altitude drawn to the hypotenuse of a right triangle forms two similar triangles, $\Delta AOC \sim \Delta DOC \sim \Delta OED$.

This gives $\frac{t}{(2 + x)} = \frac{2}{1}$ [1]

We need to find the value of x in order to find the value of t.

Look at other similar triangles that involve just the variable x:

ΔDEC and ΔOED

This gives: $\frac{2}{1} = \frac{1}{x}$

So, we get: $x = \frac{1}{2}$

Plug $x = \frac{1}{2}$ into Equation $\boxed{1}$ and we get:

$$\frac{t}{\frac{5}{2}} = \frac{2}{1}$$

$t = 5$

Alternate Method If You Knew a Fact about Perpendicular Lines

If the lines are perpendicular, the slope of one line is the negative reciprocal of the other line. **(See Math Refresher 416.)**

Line l contains the points (0,0) and (2,1), so the slope is $\frac{(y_2 - y_1)}{(x_2 - x_1)} = \frac{(1 - 0)}{(2 - 0)} = \frac{1}{2}$.

The slope of line q is $\frac{(y_2 - y_1)}{(x_2 - x_1)} = \frac{(t - 1)}{(0 - 2)} = \frac{(t - 1)}{-2}$.

The slope of line $l = \frac{1}{2}$. Since lines l and q are perpendicular, the slope of line q is the negative reciprocal of line l.

$\frac{t - 1}{-2} = -2$

$t - 1 = -2(-2)$

$t - 1 = 4$

$t = 5$

MATH STRATEGY 15

Know How to Eliminate Certain Choices

Instead of working out a lot of algebra, you may be able to eliminate several of the choices at first glance. In this way you can save yourself a lot of work. The key is to remember to use pieces of the given information to eliminate several of the choices at once.

EXAMPLE 1

The sum of the digits of a three-digit number is 15. If this number is not divisible by 2 but is divisible by 5, which of the following is the number?

(A) 384
(B) 465
(C) 635
(D) 681
(E) 780

Choice B is correct. Use pieces of the given information to eliminate several of the choices.

Which numbers are divisible by 2? Choices A and E are divisible by 2 and, thus, can be eliminated. Of Choices B, C, and D, which are *not* divisible by 5? Choice D can be eliminated. We are left with Choices B and C.

Only Choice B (465) has the sum of its digits equal to 15. Thus, 465 is the only number that satisfies all the pieces of the given information.

If you learn to use this method well, you can save loads of time.

EXAMPLE 2

Which of the following numbers is divisible by 5 and 9, but not by 2?

(A) 625
(B) 639
(C) 650
(D) 655
(E) 675

Choice E is correct. Clearly, a number is divisible by 5 if, and only if, its last digit is either 0 or 5. A number is also divisible by 2 if, and only if, its last digit is divisible by 2. *Certain choices are easily eliminated.* Thus we can *eliminate* Choices B and C.

Method 1: To eliminate some more choices, remember that a number is divisible by 9 if, and only if, the sum of its digits is divisible by 9. Thus, Choice E is the only correct answer.

Method 2: If you did not know the test for divisibility by 9, divide the numbers in Choices A, D, and E by 9 to find the answer.

EXAMPLE 3

If the last digit and the first digit are interchanged in each of the numbers below, which will result in the number with the *largest* value?

(A) 5,243
(B) 4,352
(C) 4,235
(D) 2,534
(E) 2,345

Choice E is correct.
The numbers with the largest last digit will become the largest numbers after interchanging. $\boxed{1}$

Certain choices are easily eliminated.

Using $\boxed{1}$, we see that Choices C and E each end in 5. All others end in digits less than 5 and may be eliminated. Starting with Choice E (see Strategy 8),
Choice E, 2,345, becomes 5,342. $\boxed{2}$
Choice C, 4,235, becomes 5,234. $\boxed{3}$
$\boxed{2}$ is larger than $\boxed{3}$.

EXAMPLE 4

Which of the following could be the value of 3^x where x is an integer?

(A) 339,066
(B) 376,853
(C) 411,282
(D) 422,928
(E) 531,441

Choice E is correct. Let's look at what 3^x looks like for integral values of x:

$3^1 = 3$
$3^2 = 9$
$3^3 = 27$
$3^4 = 81$
$3^5 = 243$
$3^6 = \ldots 9$
$3^7 = \ldots 7$
$3^8 = \ldots 1$

Note that 3^x always has the *units* digit of 3, 9, 7, or 1. So we can eliminate Choices A, C, and D since those choices end in numbers other than 3, 9, 7, or 1. We are left with Choices B and E. The number in the correct choice must be exactly divisible by 3, since it is of the form 3^x (= $3 \times 3 \times 3 \ldots$) where x is an integer. This is a good time to use your calculator. Divide the number in Choice B by 3: You get 125,617.66. That's *not* an integer. So the only remaining choice is Choice E.

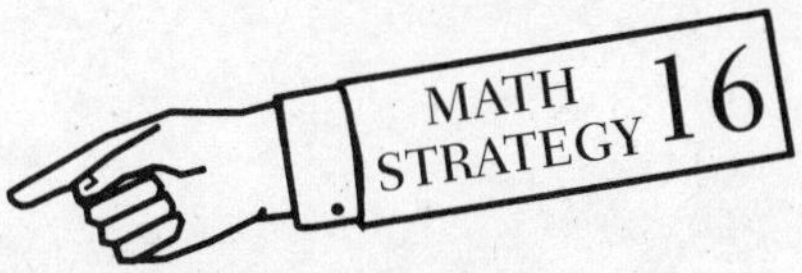

Watch Out for Questions That Seem Very Easy but That Can Be Tricky—Beware of Choice A as a "Lure Choice"

When questions appear to be solved very easily, think again! Watch out especially for the "lure," Choice A.

EXAMPLE 1*

6:06

The diagram above shows a 12-hour digital clock whose hours value is the same as the minutes value. Consider each time when the same number appears for both the hour and the minutes as a "double time" situation. What is the shortest elapsed time period between the appearance of one double time and an immediately succeeding double time?

(A) 61 minutes
(B) 60 minutes
(C) 58 minutes
(D) 50 minutes
(E) 49 minutes

Note: This problem also appears in Strategy 1 of the 5 General Strategies on page 60.

Choice E is correct. Did you think that just by subtracting something like 8:08 from 9:09 you would get the answer (1 hour and 1 minute = 61 minutes)? That's Choice A, which is wrong. So beware, because your answer came too easily for a test like the SAT. You must realize that there is another possibility of "double time" occurrence—12:12 and 1:01, whose difference is 49 minutes. This is Choice E, the correct answer.

EXAMPLE 2

The letters d and m are integral digits in a certain number system. If $0 \leq d \leq m$, how many different possible values are there for d?

(A) m
(B) $m - 1$
(C) $m - 2$
(D) $m + 1$
(E) $m + 2$

Choice D is correct. Did you think that the answer was m? Do not be careless! The list 1,2,3, ..., m contains m elements. If 0 is included in the list, then there are m + 1 elements. Hence, if $0 \leq d \leq m$ where d is integral, then d can have $m + 1$ different values.

EXAMPLE 3

There are some flags hanging in a horizontal row. Starting at one end of the row, the U.S. flag is 25th. Starting at the other end of the row, the U.S. flag is 13th. How many flags are in the row?

(A) 36
(B) 37
(C) 38
(D) 39
(E) 40

Choice B is correct. **The obvious may be tricky!**

Method 1: Given:

The U.S. flag is 25th from one end. [1]
The U.S. flag is 13th from the other end. [2]

At first glance it may appear that adding [1] and [2], 25 + 13 = 38, will be the correct answer. This is WRONG!

The U.S. flag is being counted twice: Once as the 25th and again as the 13th from the other end. The correct answer is

$$25 + 13 - 1 = 37.$$

Method 2:

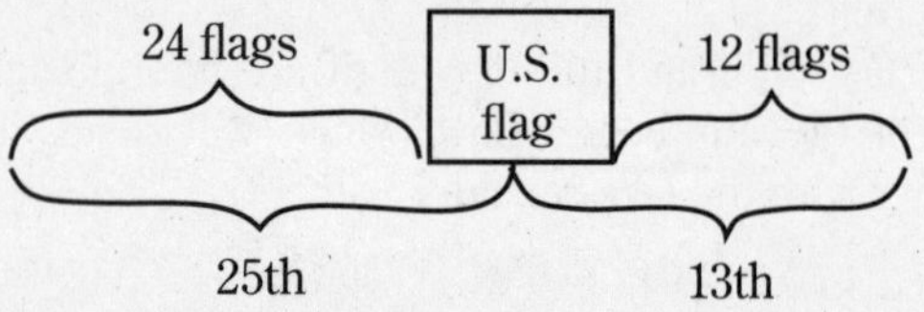

$$24 + 12 + \text{U.S. flag} = 36 + \text{U.S. flag} = 37$$

EXAMPLE 4

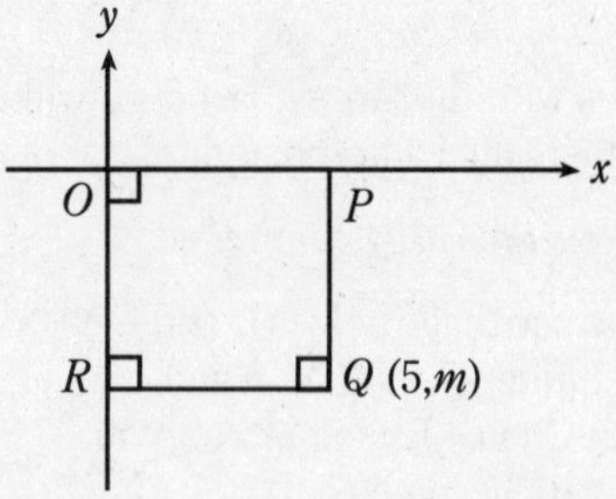

$OR = RQ$ in the figure above. If the coordinates of Q are $(5,m)$, find the value of m.

(A) -5
(B) $-\sqrt{5}$
(C) 0
(D) $\sqrt{5}$
(E) 5

Choice A is correct.

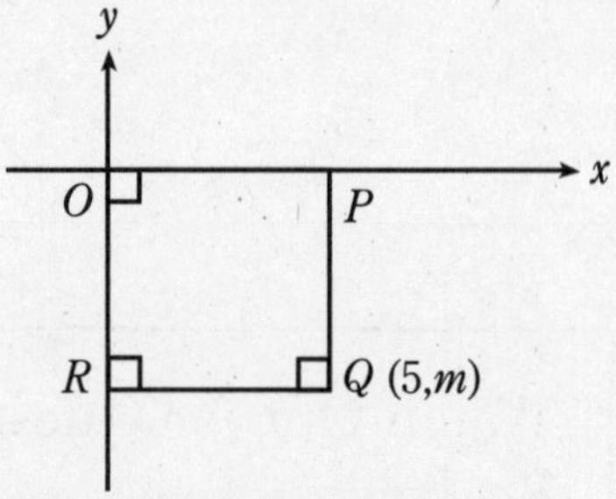

Given: $OR = RQ$ [1]
Coordinates of $Q = (5,m)$ [2]
From [2], we get $RQ = 5$ [3]
Substitute [3] into [1]. We get
$$OR = 5$$

The obvious may be tricky! Since Q is below the x-axis, its y-coordinate is negative. Thus $m = -5$.

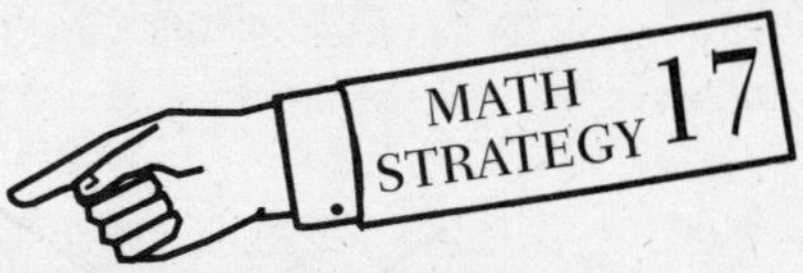

Use the Given Information Effectively (and Ignore Irrelevant Information)

You should always use first the piece of information that tells you the most, gives you a useful idea, or brings you closest to the answer.

EXAMPLE 1

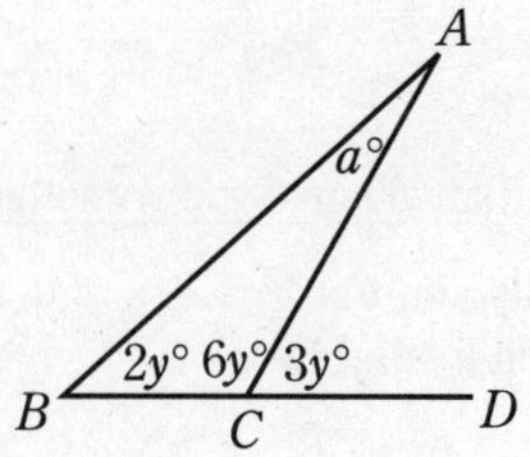

(Note: Figure is not drawn to scale.)

In the figure above, side *BC* of triangle *ABC* is extended to *D*. What is the value of *a*?

(A) 15
(B) 17
(C) 20
(D) 24
(E) 30

Choice C is correct.

Use the piece of information that will give you something definite. You might have first thought of using the fact that the sum of the angles of a triangle = 180°. However, that will give you

$$a + 2y + 6y = 180$$

That's not very useful. However, if you use the fact that the sum of the angles in a straight angle is 180 we get:

$$6y + 3y = 180$$
and we get $9y = 180$
$$y = 20$$

Now we have gotten something useful. At this point, we can use the fact that the sum of the angles in a triangle is 180.

$$a + 2y + 6y = 180$$

Substituting 20 for *y*, we get

$$a + 2(20) + 6(20) = 180$$
$$a = 20 \quad \textit{(Answer)}$$

EXAMPLE 2

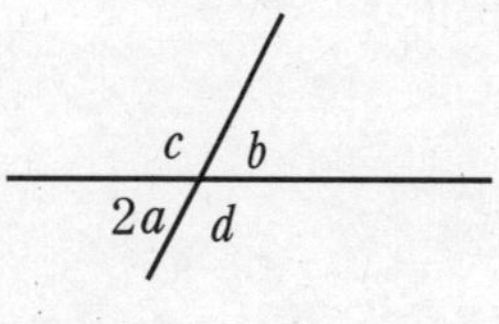

In the figure of intersecting lines above, which of the following is equal to $180 - a$?

(A) $a + d$
(B) $a + 2d$
(C) $c + b$
(D) $b + 2a$
(E) $c + d$

Choice A is correct. Try to get something you can work with. From the diagram,

$$2a + d = 180.$$

So, to find $180 - a$, just subtract *a* from both sides of the above equation.

$$2a + d - a = 180 - a.$$

You get:

$$a + d = 180 - a.$$

See Math Strategy 7, Example 7 (page 90) for an alternate approach to solving this problem, using a different strategy: **Use Specific Numerical Examples to Prove or Disprove Your Guess.**

EXAMPLE 3

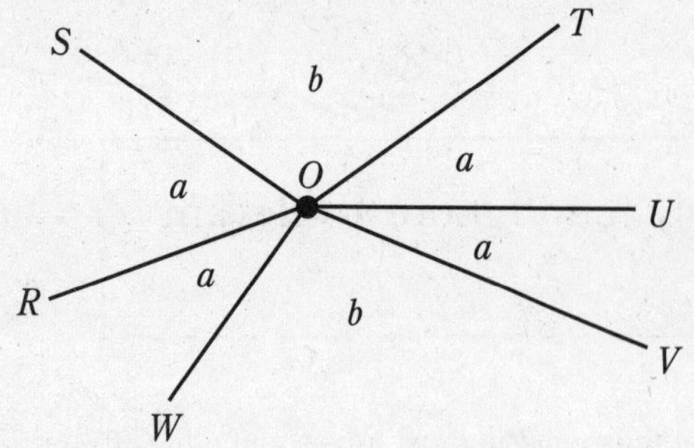

(Note: Figure is not drawn to scale.)

Which of the above angles has a degree measure that can be determined?

(A) $\angle WOS$
(B) $\angle SOU$
(C) $\angle WOT$
(D) $\angle ROV$
(E) $\angle WOV$

Choice C is correct.

Use information that will get you something useful.

$$4a + 2b = 360 \text{ (sum of all angles } = 360°)$$

Divide by 2 to simplify:

$$2a + b = 180$$

Now try all the choices. You could work backward from Choice E, but we'll start with Choice A:

(A) $\angle WOS = 2a$—You know that $2a + b = 180$ but don't know the value of $2a$.
(B) $\angle SOU = b + a$—You know $2a + b = 180$ but don't know the value of $b + a$.
(C) $\angle WOT = b + 2a$—You know that $2a + b = 180$, so you know the value of $b + 2a$.

EXAMPLE 4

If a ranges in value from 0.003 to 0.3 and b ranges in value from 3.0 to 300.0, then the minimum value of $\frac{a}{b}$ is

(A) 0.1
(B) 0.01
(C) 0.001
(D) 0.0001
(E) 0.00001

Choice E is correct.

Start by using the definitions of *minimum* and *maximum*.

The minimum value of $\frac{a}{b}$ is when a is *minimum* and b is *maximum*.

The minimum value of $a = .003$
The maximum value of $b = 300$

So the minimum value of $\frac{a}{b} = \frac{.003}{300} = \frac{.001}{100} = .00001$.

EXAMPLE 5

If $xry = 0$, $yst = 0$, and $rxt = 1$, then which must be 0?

(A) r
(B) s
(C) t
(D) x
(E) y

Choice E is correct.

Use information that will give you something to work with.

$rxt = 1$ tells you that $r \neq 0$, $x \neq 0$, and $t \neq 0$.
So if $xry = 0$ then y must be 0.

EXAMPLE 6*

On a street with 25 houses, 10 houses have *fewer than 6 rooms*, 10 houses have *more than 7 rooms*, and 4 houses have *more than 8 rooms*. What is the total number of houses on the street that are either 6-, 7-, or 8-room houses?

(A) 5
(B) 9
(C) 11
(D) 14
(E) 15

Choice C is correct.

There are three possible situations:

(a) Houses that have *fewer than 6 rooms* (call the number a)
(b) Houses that have *6, 7, or 8 rooms* (call the number b)
(c) Houses that have *more than 8 rooms* (call the number c)

$a + b + c$ must total 25 (given). [1]

a is 10 (given). [2]

c is 4 (given). [3]

Substituting [2] and [3] in [1] we get $10 + b + 4 = 25$.
b must therefore be 11.

*Note: This problem also appears in The World's Shortest Practice Test.

EXAMPLE 7

In a room, there are 5 *blue-eyed blonds.* If altogether there are 14 *blonds* and 8 people with *blue eyes* in the room, how many people are there in the room? (Assume that everyone in the room is blond, has blue eyes, or is a blue-eyed blond.)

(A) 11
(B) 17
(C) 22
(D) 25
(E) 27

Choice B is correct.

Method 1:

Draw two intersecting circles.

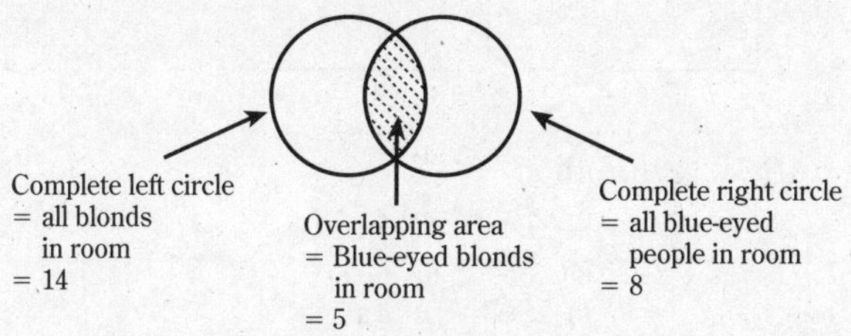

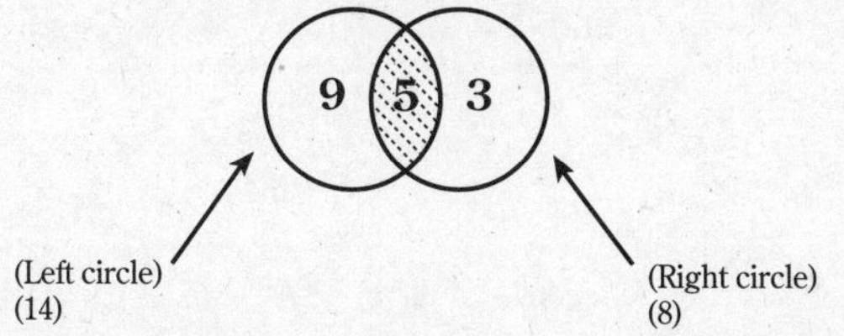

Above, subtracting: all blonds (14) − blue-eyed blonds (5), we get 9.
Above, subtracting: all blue-eyed people (8) − blue-eyed blonds (5), we get 3.
So the number of people in the room is 9 + 5 + 3 = 17.

Method 2:

Total number of people are:

(a) blonds *without* blue eyes
(b) blue-eyed people *who are not* blond
(c) blue-eyed blonds

(a) There are 14 blonds and 5 blue-eyed blonds, so, subtracting, there are 9 blonds *without* blue eyes.
(b) There are 8 people with blue eyes and 5 blue-eyed blonds, so, subtracting, there are 3 blue-eyed people who are *not* blond.
(c) The number of blue-eyed blonds is 5 (given).

Adding the number of people in a, b, and c, we get 9 + 3 + 5 = 17.

EXAMPLE 8

Points *A*, *B*, and *X* do not lie on the same line. Point *X* is 5 units from *A* and 3 units from *B*. How many other points in the same plane as *A*, *B*, and *X* are also 5 units from *A* and 3 units from *B*?

(A) None
(B) One
(C) Two
(D) Four
(E) More than four

Choice B is correct.

First let's draw the points making sure *A*, *B*, and *X* do not lie on the same line.

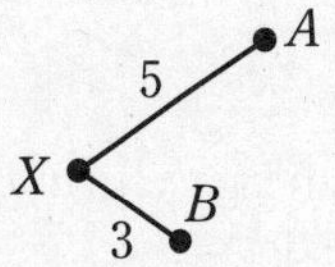

What do we do next? Consider all possibilities. Consider all points that are 5 units from *A*. They would be all points on the circumference of a circle whose radius is 5 units.

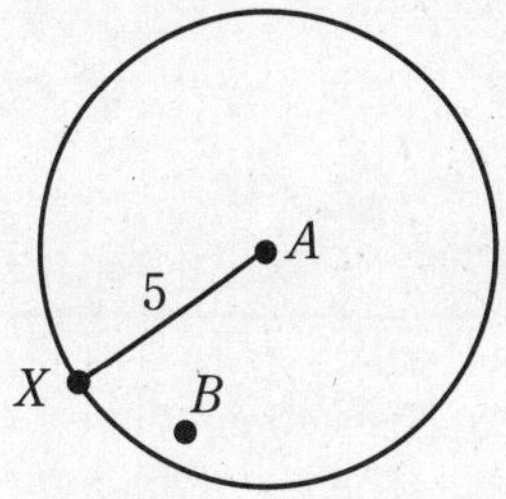

Consider all points that are 3 units from *B*. They would be all points on circumference of a circle whose radius is 5 units.

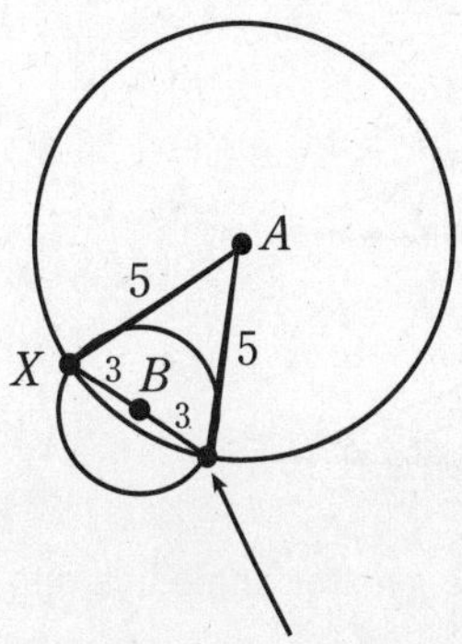

Notice that the two circles intersect at Point *X* and *only one* other point. That point is both 5 units from *A* and 3 units from *B*.

MATH STRATEGY 18

Know and Use Facts about Triangles

By remembering these facts about triangles, you can often save yourself a lot of time and trouble.

I.

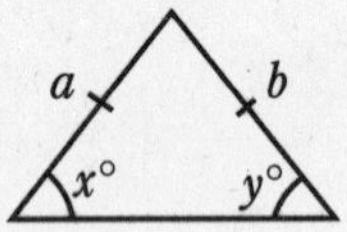

If $a = b$, then $x = y$

The base angles of an isosceles triangle are equal.

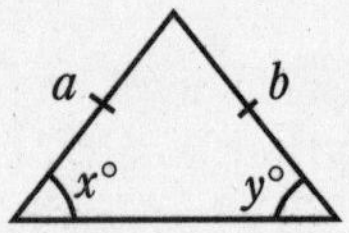

If $x = y$, then $a = b$

If the base angles of a triangle are equal, the triangle is isosceles.

II.

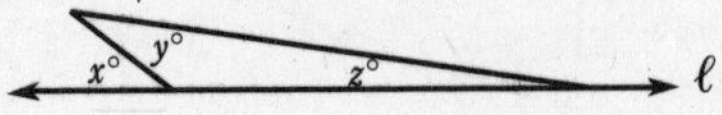

ℓ is a straight line.
Then, $x = y + z$

The measure of an exterior angle is equal to the sum of the measures of the remote interior angles.

III.

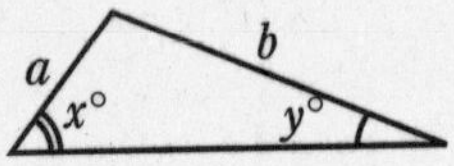

If $a < b$, then $y < x$

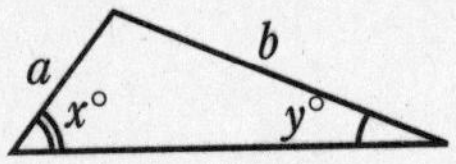

If $y < x$, then $a < b$

In a triangle, the greater angle lies opposite the greater side.

IV.

Similar Triangles

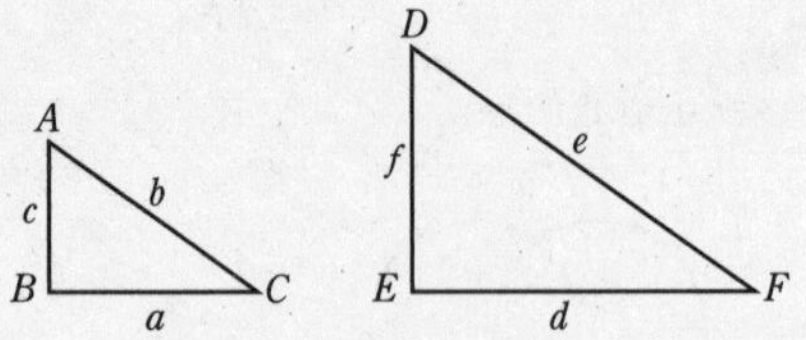

If $\triangle ABC \sim \triangle DEF$, then

$$m\,\angle A = m\,\angle D$$
$$m\,\angle B = m\,\angle E$$
$$m\,\angle C = m\,\angle F$$

and $\frac{a}{d} = \frac{b}{e} = \frac{c}{f}$

V.

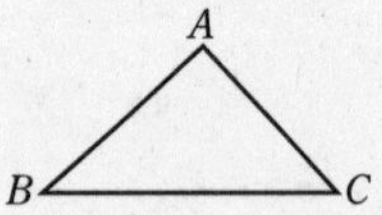

$m\,\angle A + m\,\angle B + m\,\angle C = 180°$

The sum of the interior angles of a triangle is 180 degrees.

VI.

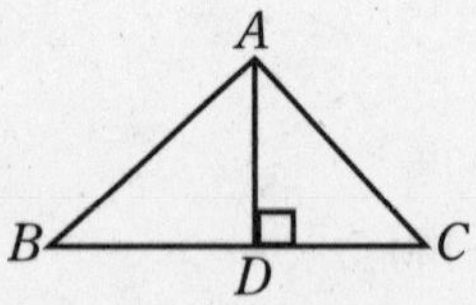

Area of $\triangle ABC = \frac{AD \times BC}{2}$

The area of a triangle is one-half the product of the altitude to a side and the side.

Note: If $m\,\angle A = 90°$,

Area also $= \frac{AD \times BC}{2}$

VII.

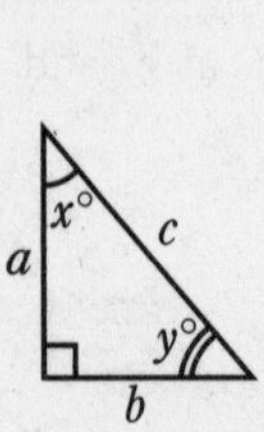

In a right triangle,
$c^2 = a^2 + b^2$
and $x° + y° = 90°$

VIII. Memorize the following standard triangles:

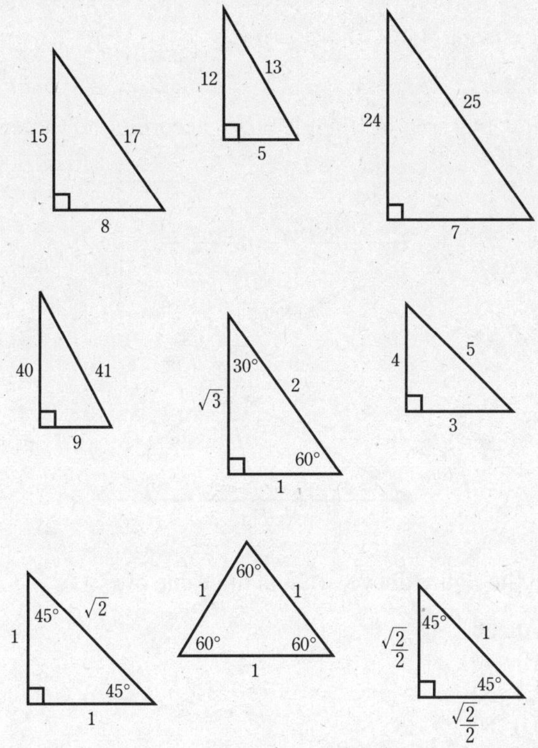

IX.

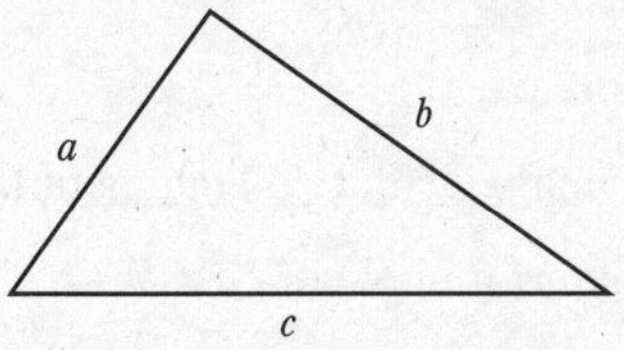

$a + b > c$
$a + c > b$
$b + c > a$

The sum of the lengths of two sides of a triangle is greater than the length of the third side. (This is like saying that the shortest distance between two points is a straight line.)

EXAMPLE 1

In the diagram below, what is the value of x?

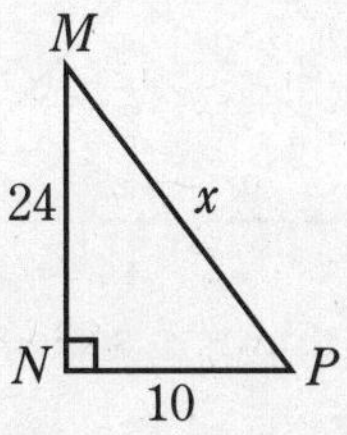

(A) 20
(B) 25
(C) 26
(D) 45
(E) 48

Choice C is correct.

Method 1: Use Statement VII. Then,

$$\begin{aligned} x^2 &= 24^2 + 10^2 \\ &= 576 + 100 \\ &= 676 \end{aligned}$$

Thus, $x = 26$ (*Answer*)

Method 2: Look at Statement VIII. Notice that ΔMNP is similar to one of the standard triangles:

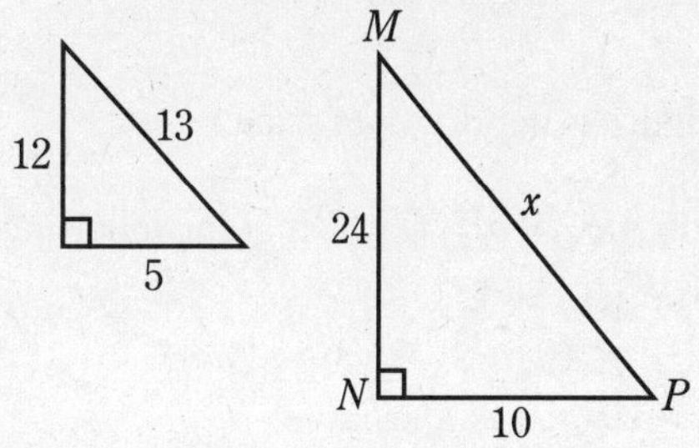

This is true because

$$\frac{12}{24} = \frac{5}{10} \text{ (Look at IV).}$$

$$\text{Hence, } \frac{12}{24} = \frac{13}{x} \text{ or } x = 26 \text{ (Answer)}$$

EXAMPLE 2

If Masonville is 50 kilometers due north of Adamston and Elvira is 120 kilometers due east of Adamston, then the minimum distance between Masonville and Elvira is

(A) 125 kilometers
(B) 130 kilometers
(C) 145 kilometers
(D) 160 kilometers
(E) 170 kilometers

Choice B is correct. *Draw a diagram first.*

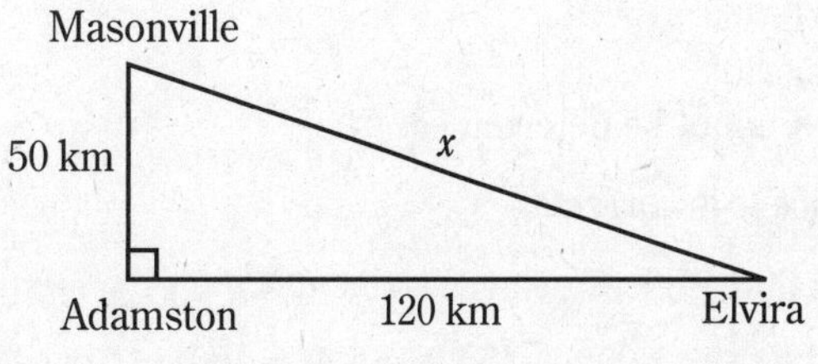

The given information translates into the diagram above. Note Statement VIII. The triangle above is a multiple of the special 5–12–13 right triangle.

$$50 = 10(5)$$
$$120 = 10(12)$$
$$\text{Thus, } x = 10(13) = 130 \text{ kilometers}$$

(*Note:* The Pythagorean Theorem could also have been used: $50^2 + 120^2 = x^2$.)

EXAMPLE 3

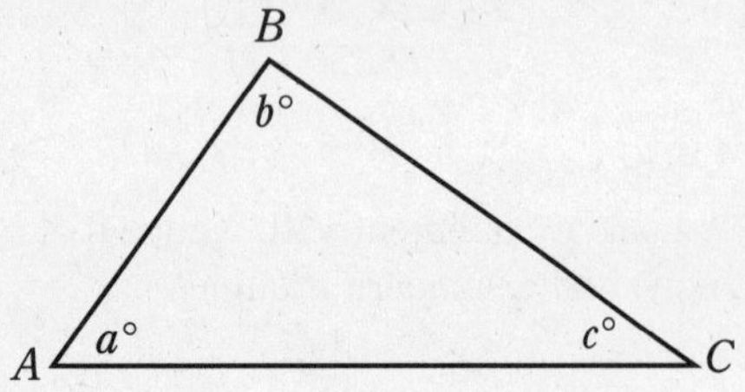

(Note: Figure is not drawn to scale.)

In triangle ABC, if $a > c$, which of the following is true?

(A) $BC = AC$
(B) $AB > BC$
(C) $AC > AB$
(D) $BC > AB$
(E) $BC > AC$

Choice D is correct. <u>(Remember triangle inequality facts.)</u> From basic geometry, Statement III, we know that, since $m\angle BAC > m\angle BCA$, then leg opposite $\angle BAC >$ leg opposite $\angle BCA$, or

$$BC > AB$$

EXAMPLE 4

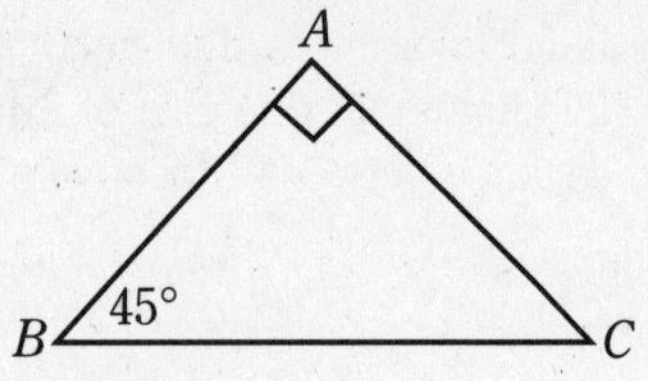

(Note: Figure is not drawn to scale.)

The triangle above has side $BC = 10$, angle $B = 45°$, and angle $A = 90°$. The area of the triangle

(A) is 15
(B) is 20
(C) is 25
(D) is 30
(E) Cannot be determined.

Choice C is correct.

First find angle C using Statement V.

$$90° + 45° + m\angle C = 180°$$

So $m\angle C = 45°$.
Using Statement I, we find $AB = AC$, since $m\angle B = m\angle C = 45°$.
Since our right triangle ABC has $BC = 10$, using Statement VIII (the right triangle $\frac{\sqrt{2}}{2}, \frac{\sqrt{2}}{2}, 1$), multiply by 10 to get a right triangle:

$$\frac{10\sqrt{2}}{2}, \frac{10\sqrt{2}}{2}, 10$$

Thus side $AB = \frac{10\sqrt{2}}{2} = 5\sqrt{2}$

side $AC = \frac{10\sqrt{2}}{2} = 5\sqrt{2}$

Now the area of triangle ABC, according to Statement VI, is

$$\frac{5\sqrt{2} \times 5\sqrt{2}}{2} = \frac{25 \times 2}{2} = 25$$

EXAMPLE 5

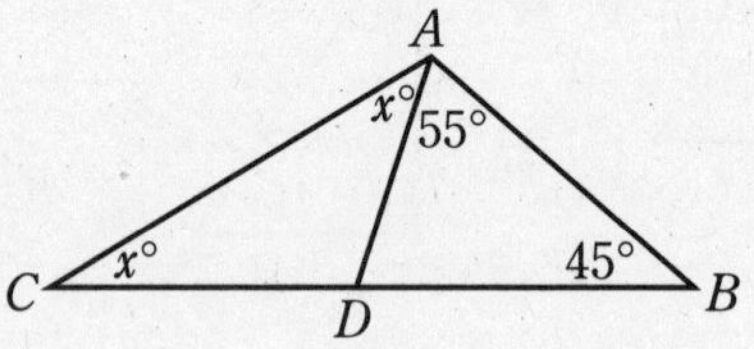

In the figure above, what is the value of x?

(A) 30
(B) 40
(C) 50
(D) 80
(E) 100

Choice B is correct.

<u>Remember triangle facts. Use Statement II.</u>

$\angle ADB$ is an exterior angle of $\triangle ACD$, so

$m\angle ADB = x + x = 2x$ [1]

In $\triangle ADB$, the sum of its angles = 180 (Statement V), so

$$m\angle ADB + 55 + 45 = 180$$
or $$m\angle ADB + 100 = 180$$
or $$m\angle ADB = 80$$ [2]

Equating [1] and [2] we have

$$2x = 80$$
$$x = 40 \text{ (Answer)}$$

EXAMPLE 6

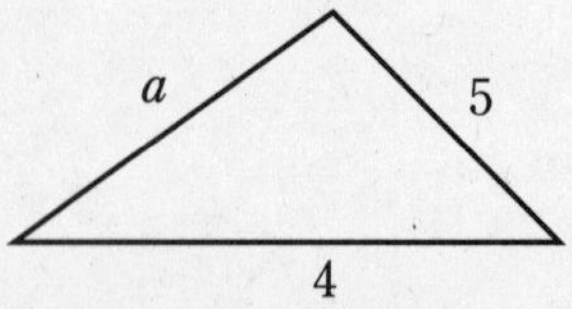

(Note: Figure is not drawn to scale.)

Which of the following represent all of the possibilities for the value of a in the figure above?

(A) $1 < a < 9$
(B) $4 < a < 5$
(C) $0 < a < 9$
(D) $4 < a < 9$
(E) $5 < a < 9$

Choice A is correct. From Statement IX, since the sum of the lengths of two sides of a triangle is greater than the length of the third side, we have:

$a + 5 > 4$ [1]
$a + 4 > 5$ [2]
$5 + 4 > a$ [3]

From [2] we get:

$a > 1.$

From [3] we get:

$9 > a.$

This means that

$9 > a > 1$, or $1 < a < 9$.

MATH STRATEGY 19

When Calculating Answers, Never Multiply and/or Do Long Division If Reducing Can Be Done First

Note: On the SAT exam, because calculators are permitted, you may do the following problems with a calculator also. But it would be wise for you to see the other approach too—how the problem can be solved *without* the use of a calculator.

EXAMPLE 1

If $w = \dfrac{81 \times 150}{45 \times 40}$, then $w =$

(A) 3
(B) $6\frac{3}{4}$
(C) $7\frac{1}{4}$
(D) 9
(E) $20\frac{1}{4}$

Do not multiply in this case. } 81 × 150 and 45 × 40 to get

$$\frac{12{,}150}{1{,}800}$$

Factor first:

$$\frac{\overbrace{9 \times 9}^{81} \times \overbrace{15 \times 10}^{150}}{\underbrace{9 \times 5}_{45} \times \underbrace{4 \times 10}_{40}}$$

Then cancel like factors in numerator and denominator:

$$\frac{\cancel{9} \times 9 \times 15 \times \cancel{10}}{\cancel{9} \times 5 \times 4 \times \cancel{10}}$$

Reduce further:

$$\frac{9 \times \cancel{5} \times 3}{\cancel{5} \times 4}$$

Then simplify: $\frac{27}{4} = 6\frac{3}{4}$ (*Answer*)

Thus, Choice B is correct.

EXAMPLE 2

$$\frac{4^2 + 4^2 + 4^2}{3^3 + 3^3 + 3^3} =$$

(A) $\frac{16}{27}$
(B) $\frac{8}{9}$
(C) $\frac{4}{3}$
(D) $\frac{64}{27}$
(E) $\frac{512}{81}$

Choice A is correct.

$$\frac{4^2 + 4^2 + 4^2}{3^3 + 3^3 + 3^3} =$$

Factor and reduce:

$$\frac{\cancel{3}(4^2)}{\cancel{3}(3^3)} =$$

$$\frac{16}{27}$$

EXAMPLE 3

If $6 \times 7 \times 8 \times 9 = \frac{12 \times 14 \times 18}{x}$, then $x =$

(A) $\frac{1}{2}$
(B) 1
(C) 4
(D) 8
(E) 12

Choice B is correct.

Given: $6 \times 7 \times 8 \times 9 = \frac{12 \times 14 \times 18}{x}$ [1]

so that $x = \frac{12 \times 14 \times 18}{6 \times 7 \times 8 \times 9}$ [2]

Do *not* multiply the numbers out in the numerator and denominator of [2]! It is too much work! Rewrite [2].

Factor and reduce:

$x =$

$$\frac{12 \times 14 \times 18}{6 \times 7 \times 8 \times 9} = \frac{2 \times \cancel{6} \times 2 \times \cancel{7} \times 2 \times \cancel{9}}{\cancel{6} \times \cancel{7} \times 8 \times \cancel{9}}$$

$$= \frac{2 \times 2 \times 2}{8} = \frac{\cancel{8}}{\cancel{8}} = 1 \qquad \textit{(Answer)}$$

EXAMPLE 4

If $\frac{81 \times y}{27} = 21$, then $y =$

(A) $\frac{1}{21}$
(B) $\frac{1}{7}$
(C) 3
(D) 7
(E) 21

Choice D is correct.

Given: $\frac{81 \times y}{27} = 21$

Multiply both sides by 27 to get $81 \times y = 21 \times 27$

$$y = \frac{21 \times 27}{81}$$

Factor and reduce:

$$y = \frac{3 \cdot 7 \times 3 \cdot \cancel{9}}{9 \cdot \cancel{9}}$$

$$= \frac{\cancel{3} \cdot 7 \times \cancel{3}}{\cancel{3} \cdot \cancel{3}}$$

$y = 7$ *(Answer)*

EXAMPLE 5

Find the value of $\frac{y^2 - 7y + 10}{y - 2}$ rounded to the nearest whole number if $y = 8.000001$.

(A) 2
(B) 3
(C) 5
(D) 6
(E) 16

Choice B is correct.

Given: $\frac{y^2 - 7y + 10}{y - 2}$ [1]

Factor and reduce:

Factor the numerator of [1]. We get

$$\frac{(y - 5)\cancel{(y - 2)}}{\cancel{y - 2}} = y - 5$$ [2]

Substitute 8.000001 in [2]. We have

$8.000001 - 5 =$
$3.000001 \approx 3$ *(Answer)*

16 Verbal (Critical Reading) Strategies

Using Critical Thinking Skills in Verbal Questions (Critical Reading Section)

4 Sentence Completion Strategies

For a Sentence with Only One Blank, Fill in the Blank with Each Choice to See the Best Fit*

Before you decide which is the best choice, fill in the blank with each of the five answer choices to see which word will fit best into the sentence as a whole.

EXAMPLE 1

He believed that because there is serious unemployment in our auto industry, we should not _______ foreign cars.

(A) discuss
(B) regulate
(C) research
(D) import
(E) disallow

EXPLANATORY ANSWER

Choice D is correct. The word "import" means to bring in from another country or place. The sentence now makes good sense. The competition resulting from importation of foreign cars reduces the demand for American-made cars. This throws many American auto workers out of jobs.

EXAMPLE 2

His attempt to _______ his guilt was betrayed by the tremor of his hand as he picked up the paper.

(A) extenuate
(B) determine
(C) conceal
(D) intensify
(E) display

EXPLANATORY ANSWER

Choice C is correct. The word "conceal" means to keep secret or to hide. The sentence now makes good sense. The nervousness caused by his guilty conscience is shown by the shaking of his hand. He is thus prevented in his attempt to hide his guilt.

EXAMPLE 3

In large cities, the number of family-owned grocery stores has fallen so sharply that the opportunity to shop in such a place is _______ occasion.

(A) a celebrated
(B) an old
(C) a fanciful
(D) a rare
(E) an avid

EXPLANATORY ANSWER

Choice D is correct. A rare occasion is one that you seldom have the opportunity to participate in. Shopping in a family-owned grocery store in a large city today is, indeed, a rare occasion.

EXAMPLE 4

Legal _______ initiated by the government necessitate that manufacturers use _______ in choosing food additives.

(A) entanglements...knowledge
(B) devices...intensification
(C) talents...discretion
(D) proclivities...moderation
(E) restraints...caution

EXPLANATORY ANSWER

Choice E is correct. Although this is a two-blank question, we should still use Sentence Completion Strategy 1. Try the words in each of the choices in the blanks in the sentence.

Another possibility is Choice A. But the point of the sentence evidently is that government prohibitions of certain food additives necessitate care by manufacturers in choosing food additives that are permitted. Thus Choice A is not as good as Choice E.

*Strategy 1 is considered the Master Strategy for *one-blank* Sentence Completion questions because it can be used effectively to answer every *one-blank* Sentence Completion question. However, it is important that you learn all of the other Sentence Completion Strategies because they can be used to double-check your answers.

EXAMPLE 5

It is unthinkable for a prestigious conductor to agree to include ________ musicians in his orchestra.

(A) capable
(B) seasoned
(C) mediocre
(D) recommended
(E) professional

EXPLANATORY ANSWER

Choice C is correct. The word "mediocre" (meaning average, ordinary) completes the sentence so that it makes good sense. The other choices do *not* do that.

EXAMPLE 6

A desire to be applauded by those in attendance, not his sensitivity to the plight of the underprivileged, was the reason for his ________ at the charity affair.

(A) shyness
(B) discomfort
(C) surprise
(D) arrogance
(E) generosity

Choice E is correct. No other choice makes sense in the sentence. It is clear that the person was primarily interested in being appreciated for his donation.

EXAMPLE 7

The commentator characterized the electorate as ________ because it was unpredictable and given to constantly shifting moods.

(A) mercurial
(B) corrosive
(C) disingenuous
(D) implacable
(E) phlegmatic

EXPLANATORY ANSWER

Choice A is correct. You can see from the sentence that "unpredictable" and "constantly shifting" describe the electorate.

Look for a word in the choices that describes these words in quotations. In order to do this, you need to associate the first choice "mercurial" with the element in chemistry "mercury." You know that mercury (like that in a thermometer) is a liquid metal that moves around very fast and unpredictably. It is also constantly shifting from one place to another. A logical assumption would be that "mercurial" means "shifting" and "unpredictable."

See also **Vocabulary Strategy 3, Sentence Completion Strategy 1**.

For a Sentence with Two Blanks, Begin by Eliminating the Initial Words That Don't Make Sense in the Sentence*

This strategy consists of two steps.

Step 1. Find out which "first words" of the choices make sense in the first blank of the sentence. Don't consider the second word of each pair yet. *Eliminate those choices that contain "first words" that don't make sense in the sentence.*

Step 2. Now consider the *remaining* choices by filling in the pair of words for each choice.

EXAMPLE 1

The salesmen in that clothing store are so ________ that it is impossible to even look at a garment without being ________ by their efforts to convince you to purchase.

(A) offensive...considerate
(B) persistent...harassed
(C) extensive...induced
(D) immune...aided
(E) intriguing...evaluated

*Strategy 2 is considered the Master Strategy for *two-blank* Sentence Completion questions because it can be used effectively to answer every *two-blank* Sentence Completion question. However, it is important to learn all of the other Sentence Completion Strategies because they can be used to double-check your answers.

EXPLANATORY ANSWER

Choice B is correct.

STEP 1 [ELIMINATION]

We have eliminated Choice (C), extensive...induced, because saying salesmen are "extensive" does not make sense here. We have eliminated Choice (D), immune... aided, because salesmen who are "immune" does not make sense here.

STEP 2 [REMAINING CHOICES]

This leaves us with these remaining choices to be considered. With Choice (A), offensive...considerate, the sentence *does not* make sense. With Choice (B), persistent...harassed, the sentence *does* make sense. With Choice (E), intriguing...evaluated, the sentence *does not* make sense.

EXAMPLE 2

Television in our society is watched so _________ that intellectuals who detest the "tube" are _________.

(A) reluctantly...offended
(B) stealthily...ashamed
(C) frequently...revolted
(D) intensely...exultant
(E) noisily...amazed

EXPLANATORY ANSWER

Choice C is correct. We have eliminated Choice A because television is not watched reluctantly in our society. We have eliminated Choice B because television is not watched stealthily in our society. We have eliminated Choice E because it is not common for the viewer to watch television noisily. This leaves us with these remaining choices to be considered. With Choice (D), intensely... exultant, the sentence does *not* make sense. With Choice (C), frequently...revolted, the sentence *does* make sense.

EXAMPLE 3

In view of the company's _________ claims that its scalp treatment would grow hair on bald heads, the newspaper _________ its advertising.

(A) unproved...banned
(B) interesting...canceled
(C) unreasonable...welcomed
(D) innocent...settled
(E) immune...questioned

EXPLANATORY ANSWER

Choice A is correct. The first step is to examine the first word of each choice. We eliminate Choice (D), innocent..., and Choice (E), immune..., because "claims" are not innocent or immune. Now we go on to the remaining choices. When you fill in the two blanks of Choice B and of Choice C, the sentence does *not* make sense. So these two choices are also incorrect. Filling in the two blanks of Choice A makes the sentence meaningful.

EXAMPLE 4

The renowned behaviorist B. F. Skinner believed that those colleges set up to train teachers should _________ change their training philosophy, or else be _________.

(A) inconsistently...supervised
(B) drastically...abolished
(C) haphazardly...refined
(D) secretly...dedicated
(E) doubtlessly...destroyed

EXPLANATORY ANSWER

Choice (B) is correct. We can first eliminate Choice (A), inconsistently, Choice (C), haphazardly, and Choice (D), secretly, because these first blank words do *not* make sense in the sentence. This leaves us with Choice (B), drastically, and Choice (E), doubtlessly. But Choice (E), doubtlessly...destroyed, does *not* make sense. Choice (B), drastically...abolished, *does* make sense.

EXAMPLE 5

The report indicates that the crime rate in the United States remains _________ and that one in every three households _________ some form of major crime in any year.

(A) incredible...visualizes
(B) astronomical...experiences
(C) simultaneous...welcomes
(D) unsuccessful...initiates
(E) constant...anticipates

EXPLANATORY ANSWER

Choice (B) is correct. Examine the first word of each choice. We eliminate Choice (C), simultaneous, and Choice (D), unsuccessful, because it does not make sense to say that the crime rate remains simultaneous or unsuccessful. Now we consider Choice (A), which does *not* make sense in the sentence; Choice B *does* make sense; and Choice E does *not* make sense.

Sometimes you can try the "second word" from each choice and see that only one choice fits in the second blank in the sentence.

EXAMPLE 6

The antithesis of an Olympic athlete, the champion diver was ________ rather than gracious, and unscrupulous rather than ________.

(A) skillful...discerning
(B) rowdy...deceitful
(C) urbane...resolute
(D) surly...honorable
(E) egotistical...artificial

EXPLANATORY ANSWER

Choice D is correct. In the second blank, we're looking for a word that has the opposite tone as "unscrupulous." But is "unscrupulous" negative or positive? Taking the prefix "anti-" from the first part of the sentence, we can deduce that it can be used to mean "not Olympian" (a negative tone), so we're looking for a *positive*-sounding word. "Honorable" is the most logical choice.

Try to Complete the Sentence in Your Own Words Before Looking at the Choices

This strategy often works well, especially with one-blank sentences. You may be able to fill in the blank with a word of your own that makes good sense. Then look at the answer choices to see whether any of the choices has the same meaning as your own word.

EXAMPLE 1

Many buildings with historical significance are now being ________ instead of being torn down.

(A) built
(B) forgotten
(C) destroyed
(D) praised
(E) repaired

EXPLANATORY ANSWER

Choice E is correct. The key words "instead of" constitute an *opposition indicator.* The words give us a good clue—we should fill in the blank with an antonym (opposite) for "torn down." If you used the strategy of trying to complete the sentence *before* looking at the five choices, you might have come up with any of the following appropriate words:

remodeled
reconstructed
remade
renovated

These words all mean the same as the correct Choice E word, "repaired."

EXAMPLE 2

Wishing to ________ the upset passenger who found a nail in his steak, the flight attendant offered him a complimentary can of soda.

(A) appease
(B) berate
(C) disregard
(D) reinstate
(E) acknowledge

EXPLANATORY ANSWER

Choice A is correct. Since the passenger was upset, the flight attendant wished to do something to make him feel better. If you used the strategy of trying to complete the sentence *before* looking at the five choices, you might have come up with the following words that would have the meaning of "to make someone feel better":

pacify
soothe
satisfy
conciliate
relieve

These words all mean the same as the Choice A word, "appease."

EXAMPLE 3

Just as the person who is kind brings happiness to others, so does he bring ________ to himself.

(A) wisdom
(B) guidance
(C) satisfaction
(D) stinginess
(E) insecurity

EXPLANATORY ANSWER

Choice C is correct. You must look for a word that balances with "happiness." Here are some of the words:

joy
goodness
satisfaction
enjoyment

All these words can be linked to Choice C.

EXAMPLE 4

Actors are sometimes very _________ since they must believe strongly in their own worth and talents.

(A) laconic
(B) unequivocal
(C) tedious
(D) egotistic
(E) reticent

EXPLANATORY ANSWER

Choice D is correct. "Since" signifies *result.* So the second clause of the sentence, starting with "since," really tells us that the missing word or words must be one of the following:

boastful
very much interested in one's own self
egotistic
self-centered

Thus, Choice D is correct.

EXAMPLE 5

Hunger has reached epidemic proportions nationwide, leaving up to 20 million people _________ to illness and fear.

(A) agreeable
(B) vulnerable
(C) obvious
(D) acclimated
(E) sensitive

EXPLANATORY ANSWER

Choice B is correct. You might have come up with any of the following words:

susceptible (to)
open (to)
unprotected (from)

These words all mean about the same as the correct one, Choice B: "vulnerable."

Pay Close Attention to the Key Words in the Sentence

A key word may indicate what is happening in the sentence. Here are some examples of key words and what these words may indicate.

Key Word	*Indicating*
although however in spite of rather than nevertheless on the other hand but	OPPOSITION
Key Word	*Indicating*
moreover besides additionally furthermore in fact	SUPPORT

Key Word	*Indicating*
therefore consequently accordingly because when so	RESULT

There are many other words—in addition to these—that can act as key words to help you considerably in getting the right answer. A key word *frequently* appears in the sentence. Watch for it!

EXAMPLE 1

Richard Wagner was frequently intolerant; moreover, his strange behavior caused most of his acquaintances to ________ the composer whenever possible.

(A) contradict
(B) interrogate
(C) shun
(D) revere
(E) tolerate

EXPLANATORY ANSWER

Choice C is correct. The word "moreover" is a *support indicator* in this sentence. As we try each choice word in the blank, we find that "shun" (avoid) is the only logical word that fits. You might have selected Choice A ("contradict"), but very few would seek to contradict an intolerant man with strange behavior.

EXAMPLE 2

Until we are able to improve substantially the ________ status of the underprivileged in our country, a substantial ________ in our crime rate is remote.

(A) burdensome...harmony
(B) beneficial...gloom
(C) financial...reduction
(D) remarkable...puzzle
(E) questionable...disappointment

EXPLANATORY ANSWER

Choice C is correct. The word "Until" is a *result indicator.* As we try the first word of each choice in the first blank, we find that "burdensome," "financial," and "questionable" all make sense up until the second part of the sentence. We therefore eliminate Choices B and D. Now let us try both words in Choices A, C, and E. We then find that we can eliminate Choices A and E as not making sense in the entire sentence. This leaves us with the correct Choice C, which *does* bring out the result of what is stated in the first part of the sentence.

EXAMPLE 3

All of the efforts of the teachers will bring about no ________ changes in the scores of the students because the books and other ________ educational materials are not available.

(A) impartial...worthwhile
(B) unique...reflected
(C) spiritual...inspiring
(D) marked...necessary
(E) effective...interrupted

EXPLANATORY ANSWER

Choice D is correct. First use **Sentence Completion Strategy 2: Eliminate the Words That Don't Make Sense.** Let us first eliminate Choices (A), impartial..., and (C), spiritual..., because we do not speak of "impartial" or "spiritual" changes. Now note that we have a *result* situation here as indicated by the presence of the conjunction "because" in the sentence. Choices B and E do not make sense because "unique" changes have nothing to do with "reflected" educational materials, and "effective" changes have nothing to do with "interrupted" educational materials. Choices B and E certainly do not meet the *result* requirement. Choice D is the only correct choice, because it makes sense to say that there will be no "marked" changes in the scores because the books and other "necessary" educational materials are not available.

EXAMPLE 4

Being ________ person, he insisted at the conference that when he spoke he was not to be interrupted.

(A) a successful
(B) a delightful
(C) a headstrong
(D) an understanding
(E) a solitary

EXPLANATORY ANSWER

Choice C is correct. The main clause of the sentence—"he insisted...not be interrupted"—*supports* the idea expressed in the first three words of the sentence. Accordingly, Choice C, "headstrong" (meaning stubborn), is the only correct choice.

EXAMPLE 5

Although Grete Waitz is a celebrated female marathon runner, she is noted for her ____________________.

(A) vigor
(B) indecision
(C) modesty
(D) speed
(E) endurance

EXPLANATORY ANSWER

Choice C is correct. The beginning word "Although" constitutes an *opposition indicator.* We can then expect the second part of the sentence to indicate an idea that is opposite to what is said in the first part of the sentence. Choice C, "modesty," provides the word that gives us the closest to an opposite idea. Since Waitz is celebrated, we expect her to be immodest. The words in the other choices do *not* give us that opposite idea.

For two-blank sentences, look for contrasts or opposition in the two parts of the sentence—then look for opposite relationships in the choices.

EXAMPLE 6

In spite of the ________ of his presentation, many people were ________ with the speaker's concepts and ideas.

(A) interest...enthralled
(B) power...taken
(C) intensity...shocked
(D) greatness...gratified
(E) strength...bored

EXPLANATORY ANSWER

Choice E is correct. The words *in spite of* at the beginning of the sentence tell you that the two blanks have an *opposite* flavor. Watch for opposites in the choices:

(A) interest...enthralled—NOT OPPOSITE
(B) power...taken—NOT OPPOSITE
(C) intensity...shocked—NOT OPPOSITE
(D) greatness...gratified—NOT OPPOSITE
(E) strength...bored—OPPOSITE

EXAMPLE 7

The instructor displayed extreme stubbornness; although she ________ the logic of the student's argument, she ________ to acknowledge her conclusion as correct.

(A) accepted...refused
(B) concluded...consented
(C) denounced....declined
(D) asserted....acceded
(E) rejected....preferred

EXPLANATORY ANSWER

Choice A is correct. The word *although* signifies a contrast, so the two blanks will have an *opposite* flavor. Watch for opposites in the choices:

(A) accepted...refused—OPPOSITE
(B) concluded...consented—NOT OPPOSITE
(C) denounced....declined—NOT OPPOSITE
(D) asserted....acceded—NOT OPPOSITE
(E) rejected....preferred—NOT OPPOSITE

Critical Reading Strategies

Introduction

Before getting into the detailed strategies, I want to say that the most important way to really understand what you're reading is to **get involved** with the passage—as if a friend of yours was reading the passage to you and you had to be interested so you wouldn't slight your friend. When you see the passage on paper it is also a good idea to **underline** important parts of the passage, which we'll also go over later in one of the strategies.

So many students ask, How do I answer reading comprehension questions? How do I read the passage effectively? Do I look at the questions before reading the passage? Do I underline things in the passage? Do I have to memorize details and dates? How do I get interested and involved in the passage?

All of these are good questions. They will be answered carefully and in the right sequence.

What Reading Comprehension Questions Ask

First of all, it is important to know that most reading comprehension questions ask about one of four things:

1. The MAIN IDEA of the passage
2. INFORMATION SPECIFICALLY MENTIONED in the passage
3. INFORMATION IMPLIED (not directly stated) in the passage
4. The TONE or MOOD of the passage

For example, following are some typical question stems. Each lets you immediately know which of the above is being asked about.

1. It can be inferred from the passage that... (IMPLIED INFORMATION)
2. According to the author... (MAIN IDEA)
3. The passage is primarily concerned with... (MAIN IDEA)
4. The author's statement that... (SPECIFIC INFORMATION)
5. Which of the following describes the mood of the passage? (TONE or MOOD)
6. The author implies that... (IMPLIED INFORMATION)
7. The use of paper is described in lines 14–16... (SPECIFIC INFORMATION)
8. The main purpose of the passage... (MAIN IDEA)
9. The author's tone is best described as... (TONE or MOOD)
10. One could easily see the author as... (IMPLIED INFORMATION)

Getting Involved with the Passage

Now, let's first put aside the burning question: Should I read the questions first before reading the passage? The answer is NO! If you have in mind the four main question types given above, you will not likely be in for any big surprises. Many questions, when you get to them, will be reassuringly familiar in the way they're framed and in their intent. You can best answer them by reading the passage first, allowing yourself to become involved with it.

To give you an idea of what I mean, look over the following passage. When you have finished, I'll show you how you might read it so as to get involved with it and with the author's intent.

Introductory Passage 1

We should also know that "greed" has little to do with the environmental crisis. The two main causes are population pressures, especially the pressures of large metropolitan populations, and the desire—a highly commendable one—to bring a decent living at the lowest possible cost to the largest possible number of people.

The environmental crisis is the result of success—success in cutting down the mortality of infants (which has given us the population explosion), success in raising farm output sufficiently to prevent mass famine (which has given us contamination by pesticides and chemical fertilizers), and success in getting the people out of the tenements of the 19th-century cities and into the greenery and privacy of the single-family home in the suburbs (which has given us urban sprawl and traffic jams). The environmental crisis, in other words, is largely the result of doing too much of the right sort of thing.

To overcome the problems that success always creates, one must build on it. But where to start? Cleaning up the environment requires determined, sustained effort with clear targets and deadlines. It requires, above all, concentration of effort. Up to now we have tried to do a little bit of everything—and tried to do it in the headlines—when what we ought to do first is draw up a list of priorities.

Breakdown and Underlining of the Passage

Before going over the passage with you, I want to suggest some underlining you might want to make and show what different parts of the passage refer to.

We should also know that "greed" has little to do with the environmental crisis. The two main causes are population pressures, especially the pressures of large metropolitan populations, and the desire—a highly commendable one—to bring a decent living at the lowest possible cost to the largest possible number of people.	*Sets stage.*
The environmental crisis is the result of success—success	*This should interest and surprise you.*
in cutting down the mortality of infants (which has given us the population explosion), success in raising farm output sufficiently to prevent mass famine (which has given us contamination by pesticides and chemical fertilizers), and success in getting the people out of the tenements of the 19th-century cities and into the greenery and privacy of the single-family home in the suburbs (which has given us urban sprawl and traffic jams).	*Examples of success.*
The environmental crisis, in other words, is largely the result of doing too much of the right sort of thing.	*Summary of the success examples.*
To overcome the problems that success always creates, one must build on it. But where to start? Cleaning up the environment requires determined, sustained effort with clear targets and deadlines. It requires, above all, concentration of effort. Up to now we have tried to do a little bit of everything—and tried to do it in the headlines—when what we ought to do first is draw up a list of priorities.	*Solutions.*

Now I'll go over the passage with you, showing you what might go through your mind as you read. This will let you see how to get involved with the passage and how this involvement facilitates answering the questions that follow the passage. In many cases, you'll actually be able to anticipate the questions. Of course, when you are preparing for the SAT, you'll have to develop this skill so that you do it rapidly and almost automatically.

Let's look at the first sentence:

We should also know that "greed" has little to do with the environmental crisis.

Immediately you should say to yourself, "So something else must be involved with the environmental crisis." Read on:

The two main causes are population pressures, especially the pressures of large metropolitan populations, and the desire—a highly commendable one—to bring a decent living at the lowest possible cost to the largest possible number of people.

Now you can say to yourself, "Oh, so population pressures and the desire to help the people in the community caused the environmental crisis." You should also get a feeling that the author is not really against these causes of the environmental crisis, and that he or she believes that the crisis is in part a side effect of worthwhile efforts and enterprises. Read on:

The environmental crisis is the result of success—success in cutting down the mortality of infants (which has given us the population explosion), success in raising farm output sufficiently to prevent mass famine (which has given us contamination by pesticides and chemical fertilizers), and success in getting the people out of the tenements of the 19th-century city and into the greenery and privacy of the single-family home in the suburbs (which has given us urban sprawl and traffic jams).

Now you should say to yourself, "It seems that for every positive thing that the author mentions, there is a negative occurrence that leads to the environmental crisis."

Now read the last sentence of this paragraph:

The environmental crisis, in other words, is largely the result of doing too much of the right sort of thing.

Now you can say to yourself, "Gee, we wanted to do the right thing, but we created something bad. It looks like you can't have your cake and eat it too!"

Now you should anticipate that in the next and final paragraph, the author will discuss what may be done to reduce the bad effects that come from the good. Look at the first sentence of the third paragraph:

To overcome the problems that success always creates, one must build on it.

Now you can say to yourself, "Well, how?" In fact, in the next sentence the author asks the very question you just asked: *But where to start?* Read on to find out the author's answer.

Cleaning up the environment requires determined, sustained effort with clear targets and deadlines. It requires, above all, concentration of effort.

So now you can say to yourself, "Oh, so that's what we need—definite goals, deadlines for reaching those goals, and genuine effort to achieve the goals."

The author then discusses what you may have already thought about:

Up to now we have tried to do a little bit of everything...

What the author is saying (and you should realize this) is that up to now, we haven't concentrated on one particular problem at a time. We used "buckshot instead of bullets." Read on:

—and tried to do it in the headlines—when what we ought to do first is draw up a list of priorities.

So you can now see that, in the author's opinion, making a list of priorities and working on them one at a time, with a target in mind, may get us out of the environmental crisis and still preserve our quality of life.

How to Answer Reading Comprehension Questions Most Effectively

Before we start to answer the questions, let me tell you the best and most effective way of answering passage questions. You should read the question and proceed to look at the choices in the order of Choice A, Choice B, etc. If a choice (such as Choice A) doesn't give you the definite feeling that it is correct, don't try to analyze it further. Go on to Choice B. Again, if that choice (Choice B) doesn't make you feel that it's the right one, and you really have to think carefully about the choice, go on to Choice C and the rest of the choices and choose the best one.

Suppose you have gone through all five choices, and you don't know which one is correct, or you don't see any one that stands out as obviously being correct. Then quickly guess or leave the question blank if you wish and go on to the next question. You can go back after you have answered the other questions relating to the passage. But remember, when you return to the questions you weren't sure of, don't spend too much time on them. Try to forge ahead on the test.

Let's proceed to answer the questions now. Look at the first question:

1. This passage assumes the desirability of

(A) using atomic energy to conserve fuel
(B) living in comfortable family lifestyles
(C) settling disputes peacefully
(D) combating cancer and heart disease with energetic research
(E) having greater government involvement in people's daily lives

Look at Choice A. That doesn't seem correct. Now look at Choice B. Do you remember that the author claimed that the environmental crisis is the result of the successful attempt to get people out of their tenements and into a better environment? We can only feel that the author *assumes* this desirability of *living in comfortable family lifestyles* (Choice B) since the author uses the word *success* in describing the transition from living in tenements to living in single-family homes. Therefore, Choice B is correct. You don't need to analyze or even consider the other choices, since we have zeroed in on Choice B.

Let's look at Question 2:

2. According to this passage, one early step in any effort to improve the environment would be to

(A) return to the exclusive use of natural fertilizers
(B) put a high tax on profiteering industries
(C) ban the use of automobiles in the cities
(D) study successful efforts in other countries
(E) set up a timetable for corrective actions

Again, let's go through the choices in the order Choice A, Choice B, etc., until we come up with the right choice. Choices A, B, C, and D seem unlikely to be correct. So look at Choice E. We remember that the author said that we should establish clear targets and deadlines to improve the environment. That makes Choice E look like the correct answer.

Let's look at Question 3:

3. The passage indicates that the conditions that led to overcrowded roads also brought about

(A) more attractive living conditions for many people
(B) a healthier younger generation
(C) greater occupational opportunities
(D) the population explosion
(E) greater concentration of population pressures

Here we would go back to the part of the passage that discussed overcrowded roads. This is where (second paragraph) the author says that urban sprawl and traffic jams are one result of success in getting people out of tenements and into single-family homes. So you can see that Choice A is correct. Again, there is no need to consider other choices, since you should be fairly comfortable with Choice A.

Let's look at Question 4:

4. It could logically be assumed that the author of this passage would support legislation to

(A) ban the use of all pesticides
(B) prevent the use of automobiles in the cities
(C) build additional conventional power plants immediately
(D) organize an agency to coordinate efforts to cope with environmental problems
(E) restrict the press coverage of protests led by environmental groups

This is the type of question that asks you to determine how the author might feel about something else, when you already know something about the author's sentiments on one particular subject.

Choices A, B, and C do not seem correct. But look at Choice D. The author said that the way to get out of the energy crisis is to set targets and deadlines in order to cope with specific problems. The author would therefore probably want to organize an agency to do this. Choice D is correct.

Let's look at another passage, and what I'm going to tell you is what would be going through my mind as I read it. The more you can get involved with the passage in an "active" and not a "passive" way, the faster you'll read it, and the more you'll get out of it.

Introductory Passage 2

Some scraps of evidence bear out those who hold a very high opinion of the average level of culture among the Athenians of the great age. The funeral speech of Pericles is the most famous indication from Athenian literature that its level was indeed high. Pericles was, however, a politician, and he may have been flattering his audience. We know that thousands of Athenians sat hour after hour in the theater listening to the plays of the great Greek dramatists. These plays, especially the tragedies, are at a very high intellectual level throughout. There are no letdowns, no concessions to the lowbrows or to the demands of "realism," such as the scene of the grave-diggers in *Hamlet*. The music and dancing woven into these plays were almost certainly at an equally high level. Our opera—not Italian opera, not even Wagner, but the restrained, difficult opera of the 18th century—is probably the best modern parallel. The comparison is no doubt dangerous, but can you imagine almost the entire population of an American city (in suitable installments, of course) sitting through performances of Mozart's *Don Giovanni* or Gluck's *Orpheus?* Perhaps the Athenian masses went to these plays because of a lack of other amusements. They could at least understand something of what went on, since the subjects were part of their folklore. For the American people, the subjects of grand opera are not part of their folklore.

Let's start reading the passage:

Some scraps of evidence bear out those who hold a very high opinion of the average level of culture among the Athenians of the great age.

Now this tells you that the author is going to talk about the culture of the Athenians. Thus the stage is set. Go on reading now:

The funeral speech of Pericles is the most famous indication from Athenian literature that its level was indeed high.

At this point you should say to yourself, "That's interesting, and there was an example of the high level of culture."

Read on:

Pericles was, however, a politician, and he may have been flattering his audience.

Now you can say, "So that's why those people were so attentive in listening—they were being flattered."

Read on:

We know that thousands of Athenians sat hour after hour in the theater listening to the plays of the great Greek dramatists. These plays, especially the tragedies, are at a very high intellectual level throughout. There are no letdowns, no concessions to the lowbrows or to the demands of "realism"...

At this point you should say to yourself, "That's strange—it could not have been just flattery that kept them listening hour after hour. How did they do it?" You can almost anticipate that the author will now give examples and contrast what he is saying to our plays and our audiences.

Read on:

The music and dancing woven into these plays were almost certainly at an equally high level. Our opera—not Italian opera... is probably the best modern parallel. The comparison is no doubt dangerous, but can you imagine almost the entire population of an American city...sitting through performances of...

Your feeling at this point should be, "No, I cannot imagine that. Why is that so?" So you should certainly be interested to find out.

Read on:

Perhaps the Athenian masses went to these plays because of a lack of other amusements. They could at least understand something of what went on, since the subjects were part of their folklore.

Now you can say, "So that's why those people were able to listen hour after hour—the material was all part of their folklore!"

Read on:

For the American people, the subjects...are not part of their folklore.

Now you can conclude, "So that's why the Americans cannot sit through these plays and perhaps cannot understand them—they were not part of their folklore!"

Here are the questions that follow the passage:

1. The author seems to question the sincerity of

(A) politicians
(B) playwrights
(C) operagoers
(D) lowbrows
(E) gravediggers

2. The author implies that the average American

(A) enjoys *Hamlet*
(B) loves folklore
(C) does not understand grand opera
(D) seeks a high cultural level
(E) lacks entertainment

3. The author's attitude toward Greek plays is one of

(A) qualified approval
(B) grudging admiration
(C) studied indifference
(D) partial hostility
(E) great respect

4. The author suggests that Greek plays

(A) made great demands upon their actors
(B) flattered their audiences
(C) were written for a limited audience
(D) were dominated by music and dancing
(E) stimulated their audiences

Let's try to answer them.

Question 1: Remember the statement about Pericles? This statement was almost unrelated to the passage since it was not discussed or referred to again. And here we have a question about it. Usually, if you see something that you think is irrelevant in a passage you may be pretty sure that a question will be based on that irrelevancy. It is apparent that the author seems to question the sincerity of politicians (*not* playwrights) since Pericles was a politician. Therefore Choice A is correct.

Question 2: We know that it was implied that the average American does not understand grand opera. Therefore Choice C is correct.

Question 3: From the passage, we see that the author is very positive about the Greek plays. Thus the author must have great respect for the plays. Note that the author may not have respect for Pericles, but Pericles was not a playwright; he was a politician. Therefore Choice E (not Choice A) is correct.

Question 4: It is certainly true that the author suggests that the Greek plays stimulated their audiences. They didn't necessarily flatter their audiences—there was only one indication of flattery, and that was by Pericles, who was not a playwright, but a politician. Therefore Choice E (not Choice B) is correct.

Example of Underlinings

Some scraps of evidence bear out those who hold a very high ← *sets stage*
opinion of the average level of culture among the Athenians of
the great age. The funeral speech of Pericles is the most famous
indication from Athenian literature that its level was indeed
high. Pericles was, however, a politician, and he may have been ← *example*
flattering his audience. We know that thousands of Athenians
sat hour after hour in the theater listening to the plays of the
great Greek dramatists. These plays, especially the tragedies,
are at a very high intellectual level throughout. There are no ← *qualification*
letdowns, no concessions to the lowbrows or to the demands
of "realism," such as the scene of the gravediggers in *Hamlet*. ← *further examples*
The music and dancing woven into these plays were almost
certainly at an equally high level. Our opera—not Italian opera,
not even Wagner, but the restrained, difficult opera of the 18th
century—is probably the best modern parallel. The comparison ← *comparison*
is no doubt dangerous, but can you imagine almost the entire
population of an American city (in suitable installments, of
course) sitting through performances of Mozart's *Don Giovanni*
or Gluck's *Orpheus*? Perhaps the Athenian masses went to these
plays because of a lack of other amusements. They could at least
understand something of what went on, since the subjects were ← *explanation of previous statements*
part of their folklore. For the American people, the subjects of
grand opera are not part of their folklore.

Now the whole purpose of analyzing this passage the way I did was to show you that if you get involved and interested in the passage, you will not only anticipate many of the questions, but when you answer them you will be able to zero in on the right question choice without having to necessarily analyze or eliminate the wrong choices first. That's a great time-saver on a standardized test such as the SAT.

Now here's a short passage from which four questions were derived. Let's see if you can answer them after you've read the passage.

Introductory Passage 3*

Sometimes the meaning of glowing water is ominous. Off the Pacific Coast of North America, it may mean that the sea is filled with a minute plant that contains a poison of strange and terrible virulence. About four days after this minute plant comes to alter the coastal plankton, some of the fishes and shellfish in the vicinity become toxic. This is because in their normal feeding, they have strained the poisonous plankton out of the water.

1. Fish and shellfish become toxic when they

   (A) swim in poisonous water
   (B) feed on poisonous plants
   (C) change their feeding habits
   (D) give off a strange glow
   (E) take strychnine into their systems

2. One can most reasonably conclude that plankton are

   (A) minute organisms
   (B) mussels
   (C) poisonous fish
   (D) shellfish
   (E) fluids

3. In the context of the passage, the word "virulence" in line 4 means

   (A) strangeness
   (B) color
   (C) calamity
   (D) potency
   (E) powerful odor

4. The paragraph preceding this one most probably discussed

   (A) phenomena of the Pacific coastline
   (B) poisons that affect man
   (C) the culture of the early Indians
   (D) characteristics of plankton
   (E) phenomena of the sea

EXPLANATORY ANSWERS

1. Choice B is correct. See the last three sentences. Fish become toxic when they feed on poisonous plants. Don't be fooled by using the first sentence, which seemingly leads to Choice A.

**Note:* This example also appears in Part 2, The World's Shortest Practice Test.

2. Choice A is correct. Since we are talking about *minute* plants (second sentence), it is reasonable to assume that plankton are *minute* organisms.

3. Choice D is correct. We understand that the poison is very strong and toxic. Thus it is "potent," virulent.

4. Choice E is correct. Since the second and not the first sentence was about the Pacific Coast, the paragraph preceding this one probably didn't discuss the phenomena of the Pacific coastline. It might have, if the first sentence—the sentence that links the ideas in the preceding paragraph—were about the Pacific coastline. Now, since we are talking about glowing water being ominous (first sentence), the paragraph preceding the passage is probably about the sea or the phenomena of the sea.

Summary

So in summary:

1. Make sure that you get involved with the passage. You may even want to select first the passage that interests you most. For example, if you're interested in science, you may want to choose the science passage first. Just make sure that you make some notation so that you don't mismark your answer sheet by putting the answers in the wrong answer boxes.

2. Pay attention to material that seems unrelated in the passage—there will probably be a question or two based on that material.

3. Pay attention to the mood created in the passage or the tone of the passage. Here again, especially if the mood is striking, there will probably be a question relating to mood.

4. Don't waste valuable time looking at the questions before reading the passage.

5. When attempting to answer the questions (after reading the passage) it is sometimes wise to try to figure out the answer before going through the choices. This will enable you to zero in on the correct answer without wasting time with all of the choices.

6. You may want to underline any information in the passages involving dates, specific names, etc., on your test to have as a ready reference when you come to the questions.

7. Always try to see the overall attempt of the author of the passage or try to get the main gist of why the passage was being written. Try to get involved by asking yourself if you agree or disagree with the author, etc.

The 9 Reading Comprehension Strategies begin on page 135.

About the Double-Reading Passages

On your SAT, you will be given a "double passage" (two separate passages) with about 13 questions. You will also be given a "double paragraph" (two separate paragraphs) with about 4 questions. Some of the questions will be based on *only* the first passage, some will be based on *only* the second passage, and some will be based on *both* passages. Although you may want to read both passages first, then answer all the questions, some of you may find it less anxious to **read the first passage, answer those questions relating to the first passage, then read the second passage and answer those questions relating to the second passage, then finally answer the remaining questions relating to both passages.** By using this approach, since you are reading one passage at a time, the time you would have spent on the second passage could be spent on answering the first set of questions relating to the first passage. This is in case you would have run out of time by reading both passages. The other advantage of this approach is that you do not have to keep both passages in mind at all times when answering the questions. That is, the only time you have to be aware of the content of both passages is when answering only those few questions related to both passages.

9 Reading Comprehension Strategies

This section of Reading Comprehension Strategies includes several passages. These passages, though somewhat shorter than the passages that appear on the actual SAT and in the 5 SAT Practice Tests in this book, illustrate the general nature of the "real" SAT reading passages.

Each of the 9 Reading Comprehension Strategies that follow is accompanied by at least two different passages followed by questions and explanatory answers in order to explain how the strategy is used.

READ. COMP. STRATEGY 1

As You Read Each Question, Determine the Type: Main Idea, Detecting Details, Inference, or Tone/Mood

Here are the four major abilities tested in Reading Comprehension questions:

1. **Main Idea**: The main idea of a passage is the central topic of the passage. As you are reading the passage, try to understand the general point of what the author is trying to convey. Try to ascertain the purpose and feel of the piece. The main idea will summarize the complete passage in a short and succinct way.

2. **Detecting Details**: To detect the details of a passage pay close attention to the specific references and details of the piece. Curious statements such as "Einstein doesn't believe that nature plays dice with the universe" are clues to the details in the passage. When you see a curious statement, underline that statement so you can reference it again easily. Pay close attention when the author describes a specific example.

3. **Inferential Reasoning**: You must able to ascertain what the author is trying to convey through the passage. For example in the quote "Einstein doesn't believe that nature plays dice with the universe," you will have to infer what the author means by this statement. What does the author mean by saying "play dice with the universe"? You'll need to conclude the author's view point via the passage.

4. **Tone or Mood**: The tone or mood of a passage can be found by determining how the author or narrator *feels* in the passage. Is the passage angry or light, happy or melancholy, humorous or frightening? What feeling do you get from the passage? Knowing this will also give you insight as you are reading the passage, and offer psychological insight into the passage.

EXAMPLE 1

The fight crowd is a beast that lurks in the darkness behind the fringe of white light shed over the first six rows by the incandescents atop the ring, and is not to be trusted with pop bottles or other hardware.

People who go to prize fights are sadistic.

When two prominent pugilists are scheduled to pummel one another in public on a summer's evening, men and women file into the stadium in the guise of human beings, and thereafter become a part of a gray thing that squats in the dark until, at the conclusion of the bloodletting, they may be seen leaving the arena in the same guise they wore when they entered.

As a rule, the mob that gathers to see men fight is unjust, vindictive, swept by intense, unreasoning hatreds, and proud of its swift recognition of what it believes to be sportsmanship. It is quick to greet the purely phony move of the boxer who extends his gloves to his rival who has slipped or been pushed to the floor, and to reward this stimulating but still baloney gesture with a pattering of hands that indicates the following: "You are a good sport. We recognize that you are a good sport, and we know a sporting gesture when we see one. Therefore we are all good sports too. Hurrah for us!"

The same crowd doesn't see the same boxer stick his thumb in his opponent's eye or try to cut him with the laces of his glove, butt him or dig him a low one when the referee isn't in a position to see. It roots consistently for the smaller man, and never for a moment considers the desperate psychological dilemma of the larger of the two. It howls with glee at a good finisher making his kill. The Roman hordes were more civilized. Their gladiators asked them whether the final blow should be administered or not. The main attraction at the modern prize fight is the spectacle of a man clubbing a helpless and vanquished opponent into complete insensibility. The referee who stops a bout to save a slugged and punch-drunken man from the final ignominy is hissed by the assembled sportsmen.

QUESTIONS

1. The tone of the passage is chiefly

(A) disgusted
(B) jovial
(C) matter-of-fact
(D) satiric
(E) devil-may-care

2. Which group of words from the passage best indicates the author's opinion?

(A) "referee," "opponent," "finisher"
(B) "gladiators," "slugged," "sporting gesture"
(C) "stimulating," "hissing," "pattering"
(D) "beast," "lurks," "gray thing"
(E) "dilemma," "hordes," "spectacle"

3. Apparently, the author believes that boxing crowds find the referee both

(A) gentlemanly and boring
(B) entertaining and essential
(C) blind and careless
(D) humorous and threatening
(E) necessary and bothersome

EXPLANATORY ANSWERS

1. Choice A is correct. The author is obviously much offended (disgusted) by the inhuman attitude of the crowd watching the boxing match. For example, see these lines:

Line 1: "The fight crowd is a beast."
Line 5: "People who go to prize fights are sadistic."
Lines 13–14: "...the mob that gathers to see men fight is unjust, vindictive, swept by intense...hatreds."
Lines 30–31: "The Roman hordes were more civilized."

To answer this question, you must be able to determine the tone that is dominant in the passage. Accordingly, this is a TONE/MOOD type of question.

2. Choice D is correct. The author's opinion is clearly one of disgust and discouragement because of the behavior of the fight crowd. Accordingly, you would expect the author to use words that were condemnatory, like "beast," and gloom-filled words like "lurks" and "gray thing." To answer this question, you must see relationships between words and feelings. So, we have here an INFERENTIAL REASONING question type.

3. Choice E is correct. Lines 24–27 show that the referee is *necessary:* "The same crowd doesn't see the same boxer stick his thumb into his opponent's eye...when the referee isn't in a position to see." Lines 35–37 show that the referee is *bothersome*: "The referee who stops a bout...is hissed by the assembled sportsmen." To answer this question, you must have the ability to understand the writer's specific statements. Accordingly, this is a DETECTING DETAILS type of question.

EXAMPLE 2*

Mist continues to obscure the horizon, but above us the sky is suddenly awash with lavender light. At once the geese respond. Now, as well as their cries, a beating roar rolls across the water as if five thousand housewives have taken

*Note this example also appears in Part 1, Strategy Diagnostic Test for the SAT.

it into their heads to shake out blankets all at one time. Ten thousand housewives. It keeps up—the invisible rhythmic beating of all those goose wings—for what seems a long time. Even Lonnie is held motionless with suspense.

Then the geese begin to rise. One, two, three hundred—then a thousand at a time—in long horizontal lines that unfurl like pennants across the sky. The horizon actually darkens as they pass. It goes on and on like that, flock after flock, for three or four minutes, each new contingent announcing its ascent with an accelerating roar of cries and wingbeats. Then gradually the intervals between flights become longer. I think the spectacle is over, until yet another flock lifts up, following the others in a gradual turn toward the northeastern quadrant of the refuge.

Finally the sun emerges from the mist; the mist itself thins a little, uncovering the black line of willows on the other side of the wildlife preserve. I remember to close my mouth—which has been open for some time—and inadvertently shut two or three mosquitoes inside. Only a few straggling geese oar their way across the sun's red surface. Lonnie wears an exasperated, proprietary expression, as if he had produced and directed the show himself and had just received a bad review. "It would have been better with more light," he says; "I can't always guarantee just when they'll start moving." I assure him I thought it was a fantastic sight. "Well," he rumbles, "I guess it wasn't too bad."

QUESTIONS

1. In the descriptive phrase "shake out blankets all at one time" (line 5), the author is appealing chiefly to the reader's

(A) background
(B) sight
(C) emotions
(D) thoughts
(E) hearing

2. The mood created by the author is one of

(A) tranquility
(B) excitement
(C) sadness
(D) bewilderment
(E) unconcern

3. The main idea expressed by the author about the geese is that they

(A) are spectacular to watch
(B) are unpredictable
(C) disturb the environment
(D) produce a lot of noise
(E) fly in large flocks

4. Judging from the passage, the reader can conclude that

(A) the speaker dislikes nature's inconveniences
(B) the geese's timing is predictable
(C) Lonnie has had the experience before
(D) both observers are hunters
(E) the author and Lonnie are the same person

EXPLANATORY ANSWERS

1. Choice E is correct. See lines 3–5: "...a beating roar rolls across the water...shake out blankets all at one time." The author, with these words, is no doubt appealing to the reader's hearing. To answer this question, the reader has to identify those words dealing with sound and noise. Therefore, we have here a DETECTING DETAILS type of question. It is also an INFERENTIAL REASONING question type in that the "sound" words such as "beating" and "roar" lead the reader to infer that the author is appealing to the auditory (hearing) sense.

2. Choice B is correct. Excitement courses right through this passage. Here are examples:
Lines 6–7: "...the invisible rhythmic beating of all those goose wings..."
Line 8: "Even Lonnie is held motionless with suspense."
Lines 9–10: "Then the geese begin to rise...a thousand at a time..."
Lines 13–15: "...flock after flock...roar of cries and wingbeats."

To answer this question, you must determine the dominant tone in this passage. Therefore, we have here a TONE/MOOD question type.

3. Choice A is correct. The word "spectacular" means *dramatic, thrilling, impressive.* There is considerable action expressed throughout the passage. Sometimes there is a lull—then the action begins again. See lines 16–17: "I think the spectacle is over, until yet another flock lifts up, following the others..." To answer this question, you must have the ability to judge the general significance of the passage. Accordingly, we have here a MAIN IDEA type of question.

4. Choice C is correct. See lines 25–29: "Lonnie wears an exasperated, proprietary expression...when they'll start moving.'" To answer this question, you must be able to draw a correct inference. Therefore, we have here an INFERENTIAL REASONING type of question.

READ. COMP. STRATEGY 2

Underline the Key Parts of the Reading Passage*

The underlinings will help you to answer questions. Practically every question will ask you to detect the following:

a) the main idea

or

b) information that is specifically mentioned in the passage

or

c) information that is implied (not directly stated) in the passage

or

d) the tone or mood of the passage.

If you find out quickly what the question is aiming for, you will more easily arrive at the correct answer by referring to your underlinings in the passage.

EXAMPLE 1

That one citizen is as good as another is a favorite American axiom, supposed to express the very essence of our Constitution and way of life. But just what do we mean when we utter that platitude? One surgeon is not as good as another. One plumber is not as good as another. We soon become aware of this when we require the attention of either. Yet in political and economic matters we appear to have reached a point where knowledge and specialized training count for very little. A newspaper reporter is sent out on the street to collect the views of various passersby on such a question as "Should the United States defend El Salvador?" The answer of the barfly who doesn't even know where the country is located, or that it is a country, is quoted in the next edition just as solemnly as that of the college teacher of history. With the basic tenets of democracy—that all men are born free and equal and are entitled to life, liberty, and the pursuit of happiness—no decent American can possibly take issue. But that the opinion of one citizen on a technical subject is just as authoritative as that of another is manifestly absurd. And to accept the opinions of all comers as having the same value is surely to encourage a cult of mediocrity.

QUESTIONS

1. Which phrase best expresses the main idea of this passage?

(A) the myth of equality
(B) a distinction about equality
(C) the essence of the Constitution
(D) a technical subject
(E) knowledge and specialized training

2. The author most probably included the example of the question on El Salvador (lines 11–15) in order to

(A) move the reader to rage
(B) show that he is opposed to opinion sampling
(C) show that he has thoroughly researched his project
(D) explain the kind of opinion sampling he objects to
(E) provide a humorous but temporary diversion from his main point

3. The author would be most likely to agree that

(A) some men are born to be masters; others are born to be servants
(B) the Constitution has little relevance for today's world
(C) one should never express an opinion on a specialized subject unless he is an expert in that subject
(D) every opinion should be treated equally
(E) all opinions should not be given equal weight

EXPLANATORY ANSWERS

1. Choice B is correct. See lines 1–7: "That one citizen...attention of either." These lines indicate that there is quite a distinction about equality when we are dealing with all the American people.

2. Choice D is correct. See lines 9–15: "A newspaper reporter...college teacher of history." These lines show that the author probably included the example of the question of El Salvador in order to explain the kind of opinion sampling he objects to.

* Strategy 2 is considered the Master Reading Comprehension Strategy because it can be used effectively in every Reading Comprehension question. However, it is important that you learn the other Reading Comprehension Strategies because they can often be used to double-check your answers.

3. Choice E is correct. See lines 18–22: "But that the opinion…to encourage a cult of mediocrity." Accordingly, the author would be most likely to agree that all opinions should *not* be given equal weight.

EXAMPLE 2

She walked along the river until a policeman stopped her. It was one o'clock, he said. Not the best time to be walking alone by the side of a half-frozen river. He smiled at her, then offered to walk her home. It was the first day of the new year, 1946, eight and a half months after the British tanks had rumbled into Bergen-Belsen.

That February, my mother turned twenty-six. It was difficult for strangers to believe that she had ever been a concentration-camp inmate. Her face was smooth and round. She wore lipstick and applied mascara to her large, dark eyes. She dressed fashionably. But when she looked into the mirror in the mornings before leaving for work, my mother saw a shell, a mannequin who moved and spoke but who bore only a superficial resemblance to her real self. The people closest to her had vanished. She had no proof that they were truly dead. No eyewitnesses had survived to vouch for her husband's death. There was no one living who had seen her parents die. The lack of confirmation haunted her. At night before she went to sleep and during the day as she stood pinning dresses, she wondered if, by some chance, her parents had gotten past the Germans or had crawled out of the mass grave into which they had been shot and were living, old and helpless, somewhere in Poland. What if only one of them had died? What if they had survived and had died of cold or hunger after she had been liberated, while she was in Celle* dancing with British officers?

She did not talk to anyone about these things. No one, she thought, wanted to hear them. She woke up in the mornings, went to work, bought groceries, went to the Jewish Community Center and to the housing office like a robot.

*Celle is a small town in Germany.

QUESTIONS

1. The policeman stopped the author's mother from walking along the river because

(A) the river was dangerous
(B) it was the wrong time of day
(C) it was still wartime
(D) it was so cold
(E) she looked suspicious

2. The author states that his mother thought about her parents when she

(A) walked along the river
(B) thought about death
(C) danced with officers
(D) arose in the morning
(E) was at work

3. When the author mentions his mother's dancing with the British officers, he implies that his mother

(A) compared her dancing to the suffering of her parents
(B) had clearly put her troubles behind her
(C) felt it was her duty to dance with them
(D) felt guilty about dancing
(E) regained the self-confidence she once had

EXPLANATORY ANSWERS

1. Choice B is correct. See lines 1–4: "She walked along…offered to walk her home." The policeman's telling her that it was not the best time to be walking alone indicates clearly that "it was the wrong time of day."

2. Choice E is correct. Refer to lines 19–20: "…and during the day as she stood pinning dresses she wondered…"

3. Choice D is correct. See lines 24–26: "What if they had survived…dancing with British officers?"

READ. COMP. STRATEGY 3

Look Back at the Passage When in Doubt

Sometimes while you are answering a question, you are not quite sure whether you have chosen the correct answer. Often, the underlinings that you have made in the reading passage will help you to determine whether a certain choice is the only correct choice.

EXAMPLE 1

All museum adepts are familiar with examples of *ostrakoi*, the oystershells used in balloting. As a matter of fact, these "oystershells" are usually shards of pottery, conveniently glazed to enable the voter to express his wishes in writing. In the Agora, a great number of these have come to light, bearing the thrilling name Themistocles. Into rival jars were dropped the ballots for or against his banishment. On account of the huge vote taken on that memorable date, it was to be expected that many ostrakoi would be found, but the interest of this collection is that a number of these ballots are inscribed in an *identical* handwriting. There is nothing mysterious about it! The Boss was on the job, then as now. He prepared these ballots and voters cast them—no doubt for the consideration of an obol or two. The *ballot box was stuffed.*

How is the glory of the American boss diminished! A vile imitation, he. His methods as old as Time!

QUESTION

1. The title that best expresses the ideas of this passage is

   (A) An Odd Method of Voting
   (B) Themistocles, an Early Dictator
   (C) Democracy in the Past
   (D) Political Trickery—Past and Present
   (E) The Diminishing American Politician

EXPLANATORY ANSWER

1. Choice D is correct. An important idea that you might have underlined is expressed in lines 12–13: "The Boss was on the job, then as now."

EXAMPLE 2

But the weather predictions that an almanac always contains are, we believe, mostly wasted on the farmer. He can take a squint at the moon before turning in. He can "smell" snow or tell if the wind is shifting dangerously east. He can register forebodingly an extra twinge in a rheumatic shoulder. With any of these to go by, he can be reasonably sure of tomorrow's weather. He can return the almanac to the nail behind the door and put a last stick of wood in the stove. For an almanac, a zero night or a morning's drifted road—none of these has changed much since Poor Richard wrote his stuff and barns were built along the Delaware.

QUESTION

1. The author implies that, in predicting weather, there is considerable value in

   (A) reading the almanac
   (B) placing the last stick of wood in the stove
   (C) sleeping with one eye on the moon
   (D) keeping an almanac behind the door
   (E) noting rheumatic pains

EXPLANATORY ANSWER

1. Choice E is correct. Important ideas that you might have underlined are the following:
   Lines 2–3: "He can take a squint at the moon."
   Lines 3–4: "He can 'smell' snow…"
   Lines 5–6: "He can register forebodingly an extra twinge in a rheumatic shoulder."

   These underlinings will reveal that, in predicting weather, the quote in lines 5–6 gives you the correct answer.

READ. COMP. STRATEGY 4

Before You Start Answering the Questions, Read the Passage *Carefully*

A great advantage of careful reading of the passage is that you will, thereby, get a very good idea of what the passage is about. If a particular sentence is not clear to you as you read, then reread that sentence to get a better idea of what the author is trying to say.

EXAMPLE 1

The American Revolution is the only one in modern history which, rather than devouring the intellectuals who prepared it, carried them to power. Most of the signatories of the Declaration of Independence were intellectuals. This tradition is ingrained in America, whose greatest statesmen have been intellectuals—Jefferson and Lincoln, for example. These statesmen performed their political function, but at the same time they felt a more universal responsibility, and they actively defined this responsibility. Thanks to them there is in America a living school of political science. In fact, it is at the moment the only one perfectly adapted to the emergencies of the contemporary world, and one that can be victoriously opposed to communism. A European who follows American politics will be struck by the constant reference in the press and from the platform to this political philosophy, to the historical events through which it was best expressed, to the great statesmen who were its best representatives.

[Underlining important ideas as you are reading this passage is strongly urged.]

QUESTIONS

1. The title that best expresses the ideas of this passage is

(A) Fathers of the American Revolution
(B) Jefferson and Lincoln—Ideal Statesmen
(C) The Basis of American Political Philosophy
(D) Democracy vs. Communism
(E) The Responsibilities of Statesmen

2. According to the passage, intellectuals who pave the way for revolutions are usually

(A) honored
(B) misunderstood
(C) destroyed
(D) forgotten
(E) elected to office

3. Which statement is true according to the passage?

(A) America is a land of intellectuals.
(B) The signers of the Declaration of Independence were well educated.
(C) Jefferson and Lincoln were revolutionaries.
(D) Adaptability is a characteristic of American political science.
(E) Europeans are confused by American politics.

EXPLANATORY ANSWERS

1. Choice C is correct. Throughout this passage, the author speaks about the basis of American political philosophy. For example, see lines 5–11: "This tradition is ingrained in America,...a living school of political science."

2. Choice C is correct. See lines 1–3: "The American Revolution is the only one...carried them to power." These lines may be interpreted to mean that intellectuals who pave the way for revolutions—other than the American Revolution—are usually destroyed.

3. Choice D is correct. The word "adaptability" means the ability to adapt—to adjust to a specified use or situation. Now see lines 10–14: "...there is in America...opposed to communism."

EXAMPLE 2

The microscopic vegetables of the sea, of which the diatoms are most important, make the mineral wealth of the water available to the animals. Feeding directly on the diatoms and other groups of minute unicellular algae are the marine protozoa, many crustaceans, the young of crabs, barnacles, sea worms, and fishes. Hordes of small carnivores, the first link in the chain of flesh eaters, move among these peaceful grazers. There are fierce little dragons half an inch long, the sharp-jawed arrowworms. There are gooseberry-like comb jellies, armed with grasping tentacles, and there are the shrimplike euphausiids that strain food from the water with their bristly appendages. Since they drift where the currents carry them, with no power or will to oppose that of the sea, this strange community of creatures and the marine plants that sustain them are called *plankton*, a word derived from the Greek, meaning wandering.

[Underlining important ideas as you are reading this passage is strongly urged.]

QUESTIONS

1. According to the passage, diatoms are a kind of

   (A) mineral
   (B) alga
   (C) crustacean
   (D) protozoan
   (E) fish

2. Which characteristic of diatoms does the passage emphasize?

   (A) size
   (B) feeding habits
   (C) activeness
   (D) numerousness
   (E) cellular structure

EXPLANATORY ANSWERS

1. Choice B is correct. See lines 3–5: "Feeding directly on the diatoms...minute unicellular algae are the marine protozoa..." These lines indicate that diatoms are a kind of alga.

2. Choice A is correct. See lines 1–4: "The microscopic vegetables of the sea...minute unicellular algae...." In these lines, the words "microscopic" and "minute" emphasize the small size of the diatoms.

READ. COMP. STRATEGY 5

Get the Meanings of "Tough" Words by Using the Context Method

Suppose you don't know the meaning of a certain word in a passage. Then try to determine the meaning of that word from the context—that is, from the words that are close in position to that word whose meaning you don't know. Knowing the meanings of difficult words in the passage will help you to better understand the passage as a whole.

EXAMPLE 1

Like all insects, it wears its skeleton on the outside—a marvelous chemical compound called *chitin* which sheathes the whole of its body. This flexible armor is tremendously tough, light, shatterproof, and resistant to alkali and acid compounds that would eat the clothing, flesh, and bones of man. To it are attached muscles so arranged around catapult-like hind legs as to enable the hopper to hop, if so diminutive a term can describe so prodigious a leap as ten or twelve feet—about 150 times the length of the one-or-so-inch-long insect. The equivalent feat for a man would be a casual jump, from a standing position, over the Washington Monument.

QUESTIONS

1. The word "sheathes" (line 2) means

   (A) strips
   (B) provides
   (C) exposes
   (D) encases
   (E) excites

2. The word "prodigious" (line 8) means

(A) productive
(B) frightening
(C) criminal
(D) enjoyable
(E) enormous

EXPLANATORY ANSWERS

1. Choice D is correct. The words in line 1: "it wears its skeleton on the outside" give us the idea that "sheathes" probably means "covers" or "encases."

2. Choice E is correct. See the surrounding words in lines 7–10 "enable the hopper to hop...so prodigious a leap as ten or twelve feet—about 150 times the length of the one-or-so-inch-long insect." We may easily infer that the word "prodigious" means "great in size" or "enormous."

EXAMPLE 2

Since the days when the thirteen colonies, each so jealous of its sovereignty, got together to fight the British soldiers, the American people have exhibited a tendency—a genius—to maintain widely divergent viewpoints in normal times, but to unite and agree in times of stress. One reason the federal system has survived is that it has demonstrated this same tendency. Most of the time the three coequal divisions of the general government tend to compete. In crises they tend to cooperate, and not only during war. A singular instance of cooperation took place in the opening days of the first administration of Franklin D. Roosevelt, when the harmonious efforts of the executive and the legislature to arrest the havoc of depression brought the term *rubber-stamp Congress* into the headlines. On the other hand, when in 1937 Roosevelt attempted to bend the judiciary to the will of the executive by "packing" the Supreme Court, Congress rebelled. This frequently proved flexibility—this capacity of both people and government to shift from competition to cooperation and back again as circumstances warrant—suggests that the federal system will be found equal to the very real dangers of the present world situation.

QUESTIONS

1. The word "havoc" (line 13) means

(A) possession
(B) benefit
(C) destruction
(D) symptom
(E) enjoyment

2. The word "divergent" (line 4) means

(A) interesting
(B) discussed
(C) flexible
(D) differing
(E) appreciated

EXPLANATORY ANSWERS

1. Choice C is correct. The prepositional phrase "of depression," which modifies "havoc," should indicate that this word has an unfavorable meaning. The only choice that has an unfavorable meaning is Choice C—"destruction."

2. Choice D is correct. See lines 3–5: "...the American people...widely divergent viewpoints...but to unite and agree in times of stress." The word "but" in this sentence is an *opposition indicator*. We may, therefore, assume that a "divergent viewpoint" is a "differing" one from the idea expressed in the words "to unite and agree in times of stress."

READ. COMP. STRATEGY 6

Circle Transitional Words in the Passage

There are certain transitional words—also called "bridge" or "key" words—that will help you to discover logical connections in a reading passage. *Circling* these transitional words will help you to get a better understanding of the passage.

Here are examples of commonly used transitional words and what these words may indicate.

Transitional Word	*Indicating*
although however in spite of rather than nevertheless on the other hand but	OPPOSITION
Transitional Word	*Indicating*
moreover besides additionally furthermore in fact	SUPPORT
Transitional Word	*Indicating*
therefore consequently accordingly because when so	RESULT

EXAMPLE 1

Somewhere between 1860 and 1890, the dominant emphasis in American literature was radically changed. But it is obvious that this change was not necessarily a matter of conscious concern to all writers. In fact, many writers may seem to have been actually unaware of the shifting emphasis. Moreover, it is not possible to trace the steady march of the realistic emphasis from its first feeble notes to its dominant trumpet-note of unquestioned leadership. The progress of realism is to change the figure to that of a small stream, receiving accessions from its tributaries at unequal points along its course, its progress now and then balked by the sandbars of opposition or the diffusing marshes of error and compromise. Again, it is apparent that any attempt to classify rigidly, as romanticists or realists, the writers of this period is doomed to failure, since it is not by virtue of the writer's conscious espousal of the romantic or realistic creed that he does much of his best work, but by virtue of that writer's sincere surrender to the atmosphere of the subject.

QUESTIONS

1. The title that best expresses the ideas of this passage is

(A) Classifying American Writers
(B) Leaders in American Fiction
(C) The Sincerity of Writers
(D) The Values of Realism
(E) The Rise of Realism

2. Which characteristic of writers does the author praise?

(A) their ability to compromise
(B) their allegiance to a "school"
(C) their opposition to change
(D) their awareness of literary trends
(E) their intellectual honesty

EXPLANATORY ANSWERS

1. Choice E is correct. Note some of the transitional words that help you to interpret the passage and see why a title of "The Rise of Realism" would be warranted. In line 6, "Moreover" is a key word that is connected to "realistic emphasis" in line 7. This idea is also connected to the sentence involving the "progress of realism" in lines 8–9. The word "again" in line 13 is also connected with this rise in realism.

2. Choice E is correct. See lines 15–18: "...since it is not by virtue of...but by virtue of that writer's sincere...of the subject." The transitional word "but" helps us to arrive at the correct answer, which is "their intellectual honesty."

EXAMPLE 2

A humorous remark or situation is, furthermore, always a pleasure. We can go back to it and laugh at it again and again. One does not tire of the *Pickwick Papers,* or of the humor of Mark Twain, any more than the child tires of a nursery tale that he knows by heart. Humor is a feeling, and feelings can be revived. But wit, being an intellectual and not an emotional impression, suffers by repetition. A witticism is really an item of knowledge. Wit, again, is distinctly a gregarious quality, whereas humor may abide in the breast of a hermit. Those who live by themselves almost always have a dry humor. Wit is a city, humor a country, product. Wit is the accomplishment of persons who are busy with ideas; it is the fruit of intellectual cultivation and abounds in coffeehouses, in salons, and in literary clubs. But humor is the gift of those who are concerned with persons rather than ideas, and it flourishes chiefly in the middle and lower classes.

QUESTION

1. It is probable that the paragraph preceding this one discussed the

(A) *Pickwick Papers*
(B) characteristics of literature
(C) characteristics of human nature
(D) characteristics of humor
(E) nature of human feelings

EXPLANATORY ANSWER

1. Choice D is correct. See lines 1–2: "A humorous remark or situation is, furthermore, always a pleasure." The transitional word "furthermore" means "in addition." We may, therefore, assume that something dealing with humor has been discussed in the previous paragraph.

READ. COMP. STRATEGY 7

Don't Answer a Question on the Basis of Your Own Opinion

Answer each question on the basis of the information given or suggested in the passage itself. Your own views or judgments may sometimes conflict with what the author of the passage is expressing. Answer the question according to what the author believes.

EXAMPLE 1

The drama critic, on the other hand, has no such advantages. He cannot be selective; he must cover everything that is offered for public scrutiny in the principal playhouses of the city where he works. The column space that seemed, yesterday, so pitifully inadequate to contain his comments on *Long Day's Journey into Night* is roughly the same as that which yawns today for his verdict on some inane comedy that has chanced to find for itself a numskull backer with five hundred thousand dollars to lose. This state of affairs may help to explain why the New York theater reviewers are so often, and so unjustly, stigmatized as baleful and destructive fiends. They spend most of their professional lives attempting to pronounce intelligent judgments on plays that have no aspiration to intelligence. It is hardly surprising that they lash out occasionally; in fact, what amazes me about them is that they do not lash out more violently and more frequently. As Shaw said of his fellow-critics in the 1890s, they are "a culpably indulgent body of men." Imagine the verbal excoriations that would be inflicted if Lionel Trilling, or someone of comparable eminence, were called on to review five books a month of which three were novelettes composed of criminal confessions. The butchers of Broadway would seem lambs by comparison.

QUESTIONS

1. In writing this passage, the author's purpose seems to have been to

(A) comment on the poor quality of our plays
(B) show why book reviewing is easier than play reviewing
(C) point out the opinions of Shaw
(D) show new trends in literary criticism
(E) defend the work of the play critic

2. The passage suggests that, as a play, *Long Day's Journey into Night* was

(A) inconsequential
(B) worthwhile
(C) poorly written
(D) much too long
(E) pleasant to view

EXPLANATORY ANSWERS

1. Choice E is correct. Throughout the passage, the author is defending the work of the play critic. See, for example, lines 9–14: "This state of affairs...plays that have no aspiration to intelligence." Be sure that you do not answer a question on the basis of your own views. You yourself may believe that the plays presented on the stage today are of poor quality (Choice A) generally. The question, however, asks about the *author's opinion*—not yours.

2. Choice B is correct. See lines 4–9: "The column space...dollars to lose." You yourself may believe that *Long Day's Journey into Night* is a bad play (Choice A or C or D). But remember—the author's opinion, not yours, is asked for.

EXAMPLE 2

History has long made a point of the fact that the magnificent flowering of ancient civilization rested upon the institution of slavery, which released opportunity at the top of the art and literature that became the glory of antiquity. In a way, the mechanization of the present-day world produces the condition of the ancient in that the enormous development of laborsaving devices and of contrivances that amplify the capacities of mankind affords the base for the leisure necessary for widespread cultural pursuits. Mechanization is the present-day slave power, with the difference that in the mechanized society there is no group of the community that does not share in the benefits of its inventions.

QUESTION

1. The author's attitude toward mechanization is one of

(A) awe
(B) acceptance
(C) distrust
(D) fear
(E) devotion

EXPLANATORY ANSWER

1. Choice B is correct. Throughout the passage, the author's attitude toward mechanization is one of acceptance. Such acceptance on the part of the author is indicated particularly in lines 10–13: "Mechanization is...the benefits of its inventions." You yourself may have a feeling of distrust (Choice C) or fear (Choice D) toward mechanization. But the author does not have such feelings.

After Reading the Passage, Read Each Question *Carefully*

Be sure that you read *with care* not only the stem (beginning) of a question, but also *each* of the five choices. Some students select a choice just because it is a true statement—or because it answers part of a question. This can get you into trouble.

EXAMPLE 1

The modern biographer's task becomes one of discovering the "dynamics" of the personality he is studying rather than allowing the reader to deduce that personality from documents. If he achieves a reasonable likeness, he need not fear too much that the unearthing of still more material will alter the picture he has drawn; it should add dimension to it, but not change its lineaments appreciably. After all, he has had more than enough material to permit him to reach conclusions and to paint his portrait. With this abundance of material he can select moments of high drama and find episodes to illustrate character and make for vividness. In any event, biographers, I think, must recognize that the writing of a life may not be as "scientific" or as "definitive" as we have pretended. Biography partakes of a large part of the subjective side of man; and we must remember that those who walked abroad in our time may have one appearance for us—but will seem quite different to posterity.

QUESTION

1. According to the author, which is the real task of the modern biographer?

(A) interpreting the character revealed to him by study of the presently available data
(B) viewing the life of the subject in the biographer's own image
(C) leaving to the reader the task of interpreting the character from contradictory evidence
(D) collecting facts and setting them down in chronological order
(E) being willing to wait until all the facts on his subject have been uncovered

EXPLANATORY ANSWER

1. Choice A is correct. See lines 1–7: "The modern biographer's task...but not change its lineaments appreciably." The word "dynamics" is used here to refer to the physical and moral forces that exerted influence on the main character of the biography. The lines quoted indicate that the author believes that the real task of the biographer is to study the *presently available data.* Choice D may also appear to be a correct choice since a biographer is likely to consider his job to be collecting facts and setting them down in chronological order. But the passage does not directly state that a biographer has such a procedure.

EXAMPLE 2

Although patience is the most important quality a treasure hunter can have, the trade demands a certain amount of courage too. I have my share of guts, but make no boast about ignoring the hazards of diving. As all good divers know, the business of plunging into an alien world with an artificial air supply as your only link to the world above can be as dangerous as stepping into a den of lions. Most of the danger rests within the diver himself.

The devil-may-care diver who shows great bravado underwater is the worst risk of all. He may lose his bearings in the glimmering dim light that penetrates the sea and become separated from his diving companions. He may dive too deep, too long and suffer painful, sometimes fatal, bends.

QUESTION

1. According to the author, an underwater treasure hunter needs above all to be

(A) self-reliant
(B) adventuresome
(C) mentally alert
(D) patient
(E) physically fit

EXPLANATORY ANSWER

1. Choice D is correct. See lines 1–3: "Although patience is the most important...courage too." Choice E ("physically fit") may also appear to be a correct choice, since an underwater diver certainly has to be physically fit. Nevertheless, the passage nowhere states this directly.

Increase Your Vocabulary to Boost Your Reading Comprehension Score

1. You can increase your vocabulary tremendously by learning Latin and Greek roots, prefixes, and suffixes. Knowing the meanings of difficult words will thereby help you to understand a passage better.

   Sixty percent of all the words in our English language are derived from Latin and Greek. By learning certain Latin and Greek roots, prefixes, and suffixes, you will be able to understand the meanings of more than 150,000 additional English words. See "The Gruber Prefix-Root-Suffix List" beginning on page 348.
2. This book also includes an "SAT 3,400-Word List" beginning on page 359. This Word List will prove to be a powerful vocabulary builder for you.

There are other steps—in addition to the two steps explained above—to increase your vocabulary. Here they are:

3. Take vocabulary tests like the 100 SAT-type "tough word" vocabulary tests beginning on page 408.
4. Read as widely as possible—novels, nonfiction, newspapers, magazines.
5. Listen to people who speak well. Many TV programs have very fine speakers. You can pick up many new words listening to such programs.
6. Get into the habit of using a dictionary often. You can get a dictionary app for your phone or look up words online.
7. Play word games—crossword puzzles will really build up your vocabulary.

EXAMPLE 1

Acting, like much writing, is probably a compensation for and release from the strain of some profound maladjustment of the psyche. The actor lives most intensely by proxy. He has to be somebody else to be himself. But it is all done openly and for our delight. The dangerous man, the enemy of nonattachment or any other wise way of life, is the born actor who has never found his way into the Theater, who never uses a stage door, who does not take a call and then wipe the paint off his face. It is the intrusion of this temperament into political life, in which at this day it most emphatically does not belong, that works half the mischief in the world. In every country you may see them rise, the actors who will not use the Theater, and always they bring down disaster from the angry gods who like to see mountebanks in their proper place.

QUESTIONS

1. The meaning of "maladjustment" (lines 2–3) is a

(A) replacement of one thing for another
(B) profitable experience in business
(C) consideration for the feelings of others
(D) disregard of advice offered by others
(E) poor relationship with one's environment

2. The meaning of "psyche" (line 3) is

(A) person
(B) mind
(C) personality
(D) psychology
(E) physique

3. The meaning of "intrusion" (line 9) is

(A) entering without being welcome
(B) acceptance after considering the facts
(C) interest that has developed after a period of time
(D) fear as the result of imagination
(E) refusing to obey a command

4. The meaning of "mountebanks" (line 15) is

(A) mountain climbers
(B) cashiers
(C) high peaks
(D) fakers
(E) mortals

EXPLANATORY ANSWERS

1. Choice E is correct. The prefix "mal" means bad. Obviously a maladjustment is a bad adjustment—that is, a poor relationship with one's environment.

2. Choice B is correct. The root "psyche" means the mind functioning as the center of thought, feeling, and behavior.

3. Choice A is correct. The prefix "in" means "into" in this case. The root "trud, trus" means "pushing into"—or entering without being welcome.

4. Choice D is correct. The root "mont" means "to climb." The root "banc" means a "bench." A mountebank means literally "one who climbs on a bench." The actual meaning of ***mountebank*** is a quack (faker) who sells useless medicines from a platform in a public place.

EXAMPLE 2

The American Museum of Natural History has long portrayed various aspects of man. Primitive cultures have been shown through habitat groups and displays of man's tools, utensils, and art. In more recent years, there has been a tendency to delineate man's place in nature, displaying his destructive and constructive activities on the earth he inhabits. Now, for the first time, the Museum has taken man apart, enlarged the delicate mechanisms that make him run, and examined him as a biological phenomenon.

In the new Hall of the Biology of Man, Museum technicians have created a series of displays that are instructive to a degree never before achieved in an exhibit hall. Using new techniques and new materials, they have been able to produce movement as well as form and color. It is a human belief that beauty is only skin deep. But nature has proved to be a master designer, not only in the matter of man's bilateral symmetry but also in the marvelous packaging job that has arranged all man's organs and systems within his skin-covered case. When these are taken out of the case, greatly enlarged, and given color, they reveal form and design that give the lie to that old saw. Visitors will be surprised to discover that man's insides, too, are beautiful.

QUESTIONS

1. The meaning of "bilateral" (line 17) is

(A) biological
(B) two-sided
(C) natural
(D) harmonious
(E) technical

2. The meaning of "symmetry" (line 17) is

(A) simplicity
(B) obstinacy
(C) sincerity
(D) appearance
(E) proportion

EXPLANATORY ANSWERS

1. Choice B is correct. The prefix "bi" means "two." The root "latus" means "side." Therefore, "bilateral" means "two-sided."

2. Choice E is correct. The prefix "sym" means "together." The root "metr" means "measure." The word "symmetry," therefore, means "proportion," "harmonious relation of parts," "balance."

3 Vocabulary Strategies

Introduction

Although **antonyms** (opposites of words) are not on the SAT, it is still important for you to know vocabulary and the strategies to figure out the meanings of words, since there are many questions involving difficult words in all the sections on the Verbal part of the SAT, that is, the **Sentence Completions** and **Critical Reading Parts.**

VOCABULARY STRATEGY 1

Use Roots, Prefixes, and Suffixes to Get the Meanings of Words

You can increase your vocabulary tremendously by learning Latin and Greek roots, prefixes, and suffixes. Sixty percent of all the words in our English language are derived from Latin and Greek. By learning certain Latin and Greek roots, prefixes, and suffixes, you will be able to understand the meanings of more than 150,000 additional English words. See "The Gruber Prefix-Root-Suffix List" beginning on page 348 and "Hot Prefixes and Roots" in Appendix A beginning on page 1049.

EXAMPLE 1

Opposite of PROFICIENT:

(A) antiseptic
(B) unwilling
(C) inconsiderate
(D) neglectful
(E) awkward

EXPLANATORY ANSWER

Choice E is correct. The prefix PRO means *forward, for the purpose of.* The root FIC means *to make* or *to do.* Therefore, PROFICIENT literally means *doing something in a forward way.* The definition of *proficient* is *skillful, adept, capable.* The antonym of *proficient* is, accordingly, *awkward, incapable.*

EXAMPLE 2

Opposite of DELUDE:

(A) include
(B) guide
(C) reply
(D) upgrade
(E) welcome

EXPLANATORY ANSWER

Choice B is correct. The prefix DE means *downward, against.* The root LUD means *to play* (a game). Therefore, DELUDE literally means *to play a game against.* The definition of *delude* is *to deceive, to mislead.* The antonym of *delude* is, accordingly, *to guide.*

EXAMPLE 3

Opposite of LAUDATORY:

(A) vacating
(B) satisfactory
(C) revoking
(D) faultfinding
(E) silent

EXPLANATORY ANSWER

Choice D is correct. The root LAUD means *praise.* The suffix ORY means a *tendency toward.* Therefore, LAUDATORY means having a *tendency toward praising someone.* The definition of *laudatory* is *praising.* The antonym of laudatory is, accordingly, *faultfinding.*

EXAMPLE 4

Opposite of SUBSTANTIATE:

(A) reveal
(B) intimidate
(C) disprove
(D) integrate
(E) assist

EXPLANATORY ANSWER

Choice C is correct. The prefix SUB means *under.* The root STA means *to stand.* The suffix ATE is a verb form indicating *the act of.* Therefore, SUBSTANTIATE literally means *to perform the act of standing under.* The definition of *substantiate* is *to support* with proof or evidence. The antonym is, accordingly, *disprove.*

EXAMPLE 5

Opposite of TENACIOUS:

(A) changing
(B) stupid
(C) unconscious
(D) poor
(E) antagonistic

EXPLANATORY ANSWER

Choice A is correct.
TEN = to hold; TENACIOUS = holding—OPPOSITE = *changing*

EXAMPLE 6

Opposite of RECEDE:

(A) accede
(B) settle
(C) surrender
(D) advance
(E) reform

EXPLANATORY ANSWER

Choice D is correct.
RE = back; CED = to go; RECEDE = to go back—OPPOSITE = *advance*

EXAMPLE 7

Opposite of CIRCUMSPECT:

(A) suspicious
(B) overbearing
(C) listless
(D) determined
(E) careless

EXPLANATORY ANSWER

Choice E is correct.
CIRCUM = around; SPECT = to look or see; CIRCUMSPECT = to look all around or make sure that you see everything, careful—OPPOSITE = *careless*

EXAMPLE 8

Opposite of MALEDICTION:

(A) sloppiness
(B) praise
(C) health
(D) religiousness
(E) proof

EXPLANATORY ANSWER

Choice B is correct.
MAL = bad; DICT = to speak; MALEDICTION = to speak badly about—OPPOSITE = *praise*

EXAMPLE 9

Opposite of PRECURSORY:

(A) succeeding
(B) flamboyant
(C) cautious
(D) simple
(E) cheap

EXPLANATORY ANSWER

Choice A is correct.
PRE = before; CURS = to run; PRECURSORY = run before—OPPOSITE = *succeeding*

EXAMPLE 10

Opposite of CIRCUMVENT:

(A) to go the straight route
(B) alleviate
(C) to prey on one's emotions
(D) scintillate
(E) perceive correctly

EXPLANATORY ANSWER

Choice A is correct.
CIRCUM = around (like a circle); VENT = to come; CIRCUMVENT = to come around—OPPOSITE = *to go the straight route*

Pay Attention to the Sound or Feeling of the Word—Whether Positive or Negative, Harsh or Mild, Big or Little, Etc.

If the word sounds harsh or terrible, such as "obstreperous," the meaning probably is something harsh or terrible. If you're looking for a word opposite in meaning to "obstreperous," look for a word or words that have a softer sound, such as "pleasantly quiet or docile." The sense of "obstreperous" can also seem to be negative—so if you're looking for a synonym, look for a negative word. If you're looking for an opposite (antonym), look for a positive word.

EXAMPLE 1

Opposite of BELLIGERENCY:

(A) pain
(B) silence
(C) homeliness
(D) elegance
(E) peace

EXPLANATORY ANSWER

Choice E is correct. The word BELLIGERENCY imparts a tone of forcefulness or confusion and means warlike. The opposite would be calmness or peacefulness. The closest choices are B or E, with E a little closer to the opposite in tone for the capitalized word. Of course, if you knew the root BELLI means "war," you could see the opposite as (E) peace.

EXAMPLE 2

Opposite of DEGRADE:

(A) startle
(B) elevate
(C) encircle
(D) replace
(E) assemble

EXPLANATORY ANSWER

Choice B is correct. Here you can think of the DE in DEGRADE as a prefix that is negative (bad) and means *down,* and in fact DEGRADE does mean to debase or lower. So you should look for an opposite that would be a word with a *positive* (good) meaning. The best word from the choices is (B) elevate.

EXAMPLE 3

Opposite of OBFUSCATION:

(A) illumination
(B) irritation
(C) conviction
(D) minor offense
(E) stable environment

EXPLANATORY ANSWER

Choice A is correct. The prefix OB is usually negative, as in obstacle or obliterate, and in fact OBFUSCATE means darken or obscure. So since we are looking for an opposite, you would look for a *positive* word. Choices A and E are positive, and you should go for the more positive of the two, which is Choice A.

EXAMPLE 4

Opposite of MUNIFICENCE:

(A) disloyalty
(B) stinginess
(C) dispersion
(D) simplicity
(E) vehemence

EXPLANATORY ANSWER

Choice B is correct because MUNIFICENCE means generosity. Many of the words ending in ENCE, like OPULENCE, EFFERVESCENCE, LUMINESCENCE, QUINTESSENCE, etc., represent or describe something big or bright. So the opposite of one of these words would denote something small or dark.

You can associate the prefix MUNI with MONEY, as in "municipal bonds," so the word MUNIFICENCE must deal with money and in a big way. The opposite deals with money in a small way. Choice B fits the bill.

EXAMPLE 5

Opposite of DETRIMENT:

(A) recurrence
(B) disclosure
(C) resemblance
(D) enhancement
(E) postponement

EXPLANATORY ANSWER

Choice D is correct. The prefix DE can also mean against and is negative, and DETRIMENT means something that causes damage or loss. So you should look for a positive word. The only one is (D) enhancement.

EXAMPLE 6

Opposite of UNDERSTATE:

(A) embroider
(B) initiate
(C) distort
(D) pacify
(E) violate

EXPLANATORY ANSWER

Choice A is correct. UNDERSTATE means something said in a restrained or downplayed manner. You see "under" in UNDERSTATE, so look for a choice that gives you the impression of something that is "over," as in "overstated." The only choice is (A) embroider, which means to embellish.

EXAMPLE 7

Opposite of DISHEARTEN:

(A) engage
(B) encourage
(C) predict
(D) dismember
(E) misinform

EXPLANATORY ANSWER

Choice B is correct. You see HEART in DISHEARTEN. The DIS is negative and means "not to," or "not to have heart," and DISHEARTEN does mean to discourage. So you want to look for a *positive* word. Choice (B) encourage fits the bill.

EXAMPLE 8

Opposite of FIREBRAND:

(A) an intellect
(B) one who is charitable
(C) one who makes peace
(D) a philanthropist
(E) one who is dishonest

EXPLANATORY ANSWER

Choice C is correct. You see FIRE in FIREBRAND. So think of something fiery or dangerous. The opposite of FIREBRAND must be something that's calm or safe. The best choice is Choice C, whereas a FIREBRAND is someone who causes trouble.

VOCABULARY STRATEGY 3

Use Word Associations to Determine Word Meanings and Their Opposites

Looking at the root or part of any capitalized word may suggest an association with another word that looks similar and whose meaning you know. This new word's meaning may give you a clue as to the meaning of the original word or the opposite in meaning to the original word if you need an opposite. For example, *extricate* reminds us of the word "extract," the opposite of which is "to put together."

EXAMPLE 1

Opposite of STASIS:

(A) stoppage
(B) reduction
(C) depletion
(D) fluctuation
(E) completion

EXPLANATORY ANSWER

Choice D is correct. Think of STATIC or STATIONARY. The opposite would be moving or fluctuating since STASIS means stopping or retarding movement.

EXAMPLE 2

Opposite of APPEASE:

(A) criticize
(B) analyze
(C) correct
(D) incense
(E) develop

EXPLANATORY ANSWER

Choice D is correct. APPEASE means to placate. Think of PEACE in APPEASE. The opposite would be violent or *incense.*

EXAMPLE 3

Opposite of COMMISERATION:

(A) undeserved reward
(B) lack of sympathy
(C) unexpected success
(D) absence of talent
(E) inexplicable danger

EXPLANATORY ANSWER

Choice B is correct. Think of MISERY in the word COMMISERATION. COMMISERATION means the sharing of misery. Choice B is the only appropriate choice.

EXAMPLE 4

Opposite of JOCULAR:

(A) unintentional
(B) exotic
(C) muscular
(D) exaggerated
(E) serious

EXPLANATORY ANSWER

Choice E is correct. Think of JOKE in the word JOCULAR, which means given to joking. The opposite would be *serious.*

EXAMPLE 5

Opposite of ELONGATE:

(A) melt
(B) wind
(C) confuse
(D) smooth
(E) shorten

EXPLANATORY ANSWER

Choice E is correct. Think of the word LONG in ELONGATE, which means to lengthen. The opposite would be short or *shorten.*

EXAMPLE 6

Opposite of SLOTHFUL:

(A) permanent
(B) ambitious
(C) average
(D) truthful
(E) plentiful

EXPLANATORY ANSWER

Choice B is correct. Think of SLOTH, a very, very slow animal. So SLOTHFUL, which means lazy or sluggish, must be slow and unambitious. The opposite would be *ambitious.*

EXAMPLE 7

Opposite of FORTITUDE:

(A) timidity
(B) conservatism
(C) placidity
(D) laxness
(E) ambition

EXPLANATORY ANSWER

Choice A is correct. FORTITUDE means strength in the face of adversity; you should think of FORT or FORTIFY as something strong. The opposite would be weakness or *timidity.*

EXAMPLE 8

Opposite of LUCID:

(A) underlying
(B) abstruse
(C) luxurious
(D) tight
(E) general

EXPLANATORY ANSWER

Choice B is correct. LUCID means easily understood or clear; you should think of LUCITE, a clear plastic. The opposite of clear is hard to see through or abstruse. *Note:* The AB in ABSTRUSE makes Choice B the only *negative* choice, which is the opposite of the positive word LUCID.

EXAMPLE 9

Opposite of POTENT:

(A) imposing
(B) pertinent
(C) feeble
(D) comparable
(E) frantic

EXPLANATORY ANSWER

Choice C is correct. Think of the word POTENTIAL or POWERFUL. To have potential is to have the ability or power to be able to do something. So the opposite would be feeble. You could also have thought of POTENT as a positive word. The opposite would be a negative word. The only two choices that are negative are choices C and E.

PART 5

MINI-MATH REFRESHER

The Most Important Basic Math Rules and Concepts You Need to Know

Make sure that you understand each of the following math rules and concepts. It is a good idea to memorize them all. Refer to the section of the Complete Math Refresher (Part 6 starting on page 167) shown in parentheses, e.g., (409), for a complete explanation of each.

Algebra and Arithmetic

(409) $a(b+c) = ab + ac$

Example:

$$5(4+5) = 5(4) + 5(5) = 20 + 25 = 45$$

(409) $(a+b)(c+d) = ac + ad + bc + bd$

Example:

$$(2+3)(4-6) = (2)(4) + (2)(-6) + (3)(4) + (3)(-6) = 8 - 12 + 12 - 18 = -10$$

(409) $(a+b)^2 = a^2 + 2ab + b^2$

(409) $(a-b)^2 = a^2 - 2ab + b^2$

(409) $(a+b)(a-b) = a^2 - b^2$

(409) $-(a-b) = b - a$

(429) $a^2 = (a)(a)$

Example:

$2^2 = (2)(2) = 4$

$a^3 = (a)(a)(a)$

(429) $\frac{a^x}{a^y} = a^{x-y}$

Examples:

$\frac{a^3}{a^2} = a^{3-2} = a;$

$\frac{2^3}{2^2} = 2^{3-2} = 2$

(429) $a^x a^y = a^{x+y}$

Examples:

$a^2 \times a^3 = a^5;$

$2^2 \times 2^3 = 2^5 = 32$

(429)

$a^0 = 1$

$10^0 = 1$

$10^1 = 10$

$10^2 = 100$

$10^3 = 1{,}000$, etc.

Example:

$$8.6 \times 10^4 = 8.\underbrace{6}_{1}\underbrace{0}_{2}\underbrace{0}_{3}\underbrace{0}_{4}.0$$

(429) $(a^x)^y = a^{xy}$

Examples:

$(a^3)^5 = a^{15}; (2^3)^5 = 2^{15}$

(429) $(ab)^x = a^x b^x$

Examples:

$(2 \times 3)^3 = 2^3 \times 3^3;\ (ab)^2 = a^2 b^2$

(430)

If $y^2 = x$, then $y = \pm\sqrt{x}$.

Example:

If $y^2 = 4$,

then $y = \pm\sqrt{4} = \pm 2$.

(429)

$a^{-y} = \frac{1}{a^y}$

Example: $2^{-3} = \frac{1}{2^3} = \frac{1}{8}$

Percentage Problems

(107)

Percentage

$x\% = \frac{x}{100}$

Example:

$5\% = \frac{5}{100}$

RULE: "What" becomes x

"percent" becomes $\frac{1}{100}$

"of" becomes $\times$ (times)

"is" becomes $=$ (equals)

(107)

Examples:

(1) What percent of 5 is 2?

$\frac{x}{100} \times 5 = 2$

or

$\left(\frac{x}{100}\right)(5) = 2$

$\frac{5x}{100} = 2$

$5x = 200$

$x = 40$

Answer $= 40\%$

(107)

(2) 6 is what percent of 24?

$6 = \frac{x}{100} \times 24$

$6 = \frac{24x}{100}$

$600 = 24x$

$100 = 4x$ (dividing both sides by 6)

$25 = x$

Answer $= 25\%$

Equations

(409)

Example: $x^2 - 2x + 1 = 0$. Solve for x.

Procedure:

Factor: $(x - 1)(x - 1) = 0$

$x - 1 = 0$

$x = 1$

Note that in general:

$(mx + b)(nx + c) = mnx^2 + bnx + mxc + bc$

In the example $x^2 - 2x + 1 = 0$, where $m = 1$, $n = 1$, $b = -1$, $c = -1$,

$$(x - 1)(x - 1) = (1)(1)x^2 + (-1)(1)x + (1)x(-1) + (-1)(-1)$$
$$= x^2 + -x + -x + 1$$
$$= x^2 + -2x + 1$$

(407)

Example: $x + y = 1$; $x - y = 2$. Solve for x and y.

Procedure:

Add equations:

$$\begin{array}{r} x + y = 1 \\ x - y = 2 \\ \hline 2x + 0 = 3 \end{array}$$

Therefore $2x = 3$ and $x = \frac{3}{2}$

Substitute $x = \frac{3}{2}$ back into one of the equations:

$x + y = 1$

$\frac{3}{2} + y = 1$

$y = -\frac{1}{2}$

(402)

Equalities

$$\begin{array}{r} a + b = c \\ + \quad d = d \\ \hline a + b + d = c + d \end{array} \qquad \begin{array}{r} 3 + 4 = 7 \\ + \quad 2 = 2 \\ \hline 3 + 4 + 2 = 7 + 2 \end{array}$$

(419–425)

Inequalities

$>$ means greater than, $<$ means less than, $\geq$ means greater than or equal to, etc.

$$\begin{array}{r} b > c \\ + d > e \\ \hline b + d > c + e \end{array} \qquad \begin{array}{r} 4 > 3 \\ + 7 > 6 \\ \hline 11 > 9 \end{array} \qquad \begin{array}{r} 4 > 3 \\ + -6 > -7 \\ \hline -2 > -4 \end{array}$$

$5 > 4$ $\qquad -5 < -4$

$(6)5 > 4(6)$ $\qquad -(-5) > -(-4)$ (reversing inequality)

Thus

$30 > 24$ $\qquad 5 > 4$

If $-2 < x < +2$ then $+2 > -x > -2$

$a > b > 0$ Thus $a^2 > b^2$

Geometry

(504)

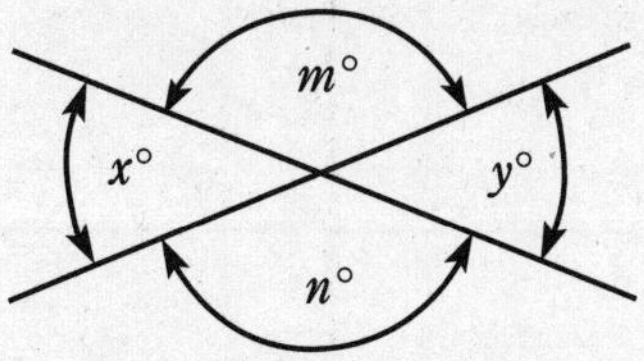

$x° = y°; m° = n°$

(501)

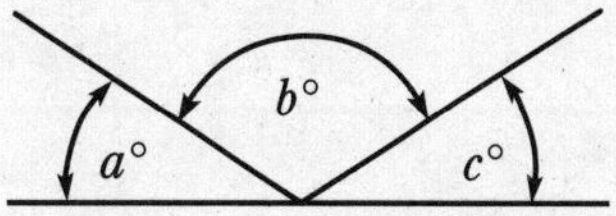

$a° + b° + c° = 180°$

(504)

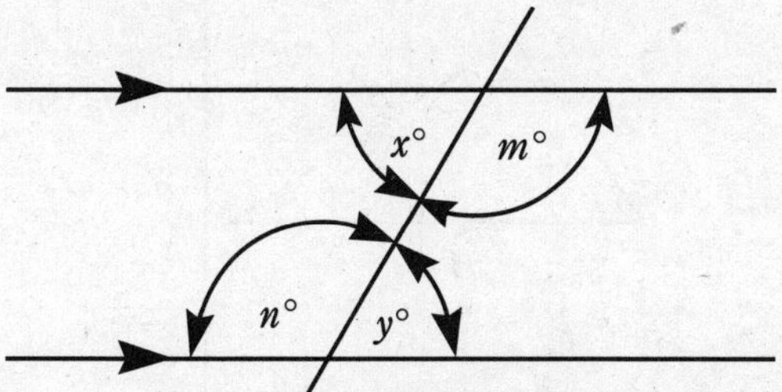

$x° = y°; m° = n°; x° + m° = 180°; n° + y° = 180°; y° + m° = 180°; n° + x° = 180°$

(506)

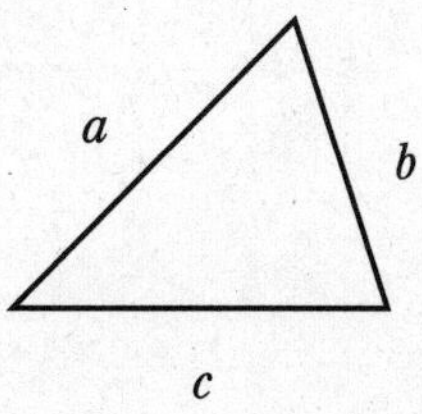

$a + b > c$

(506)

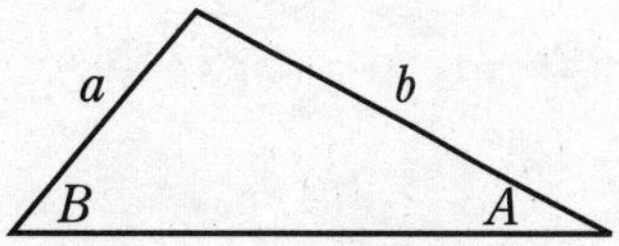

If $\angle B > \angle A$ then $b > a$

(507)

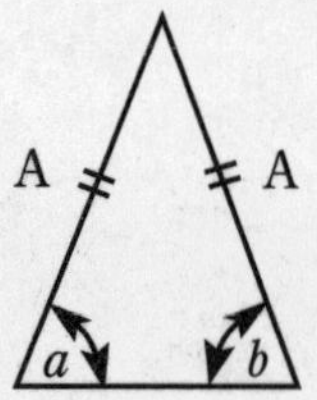

$a = b$

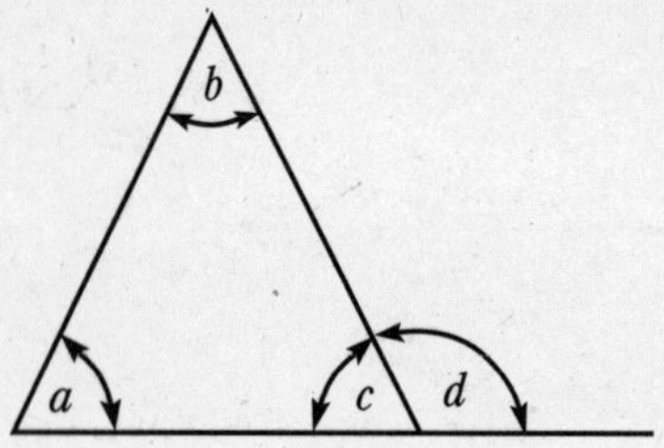

$a + b + c = 180°;$
$c + d = 180°$
Thus $a + b = d$

(501)

Similar Triangles

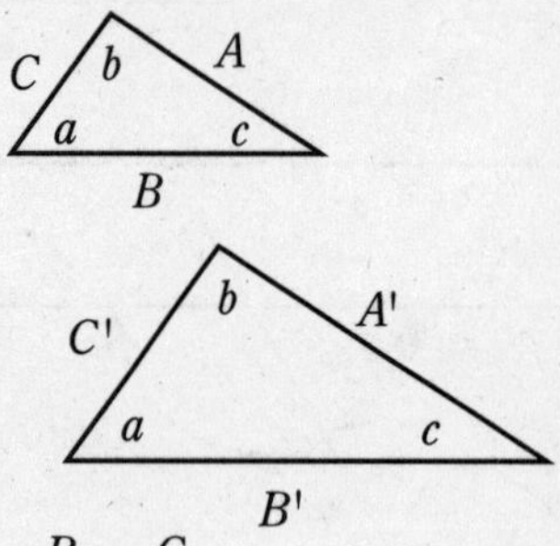

$$\frac{A}{A'} = \frac{B}{B'} = \frac{C}{C'}$$

(510)

Areas & Perimeters

(304)

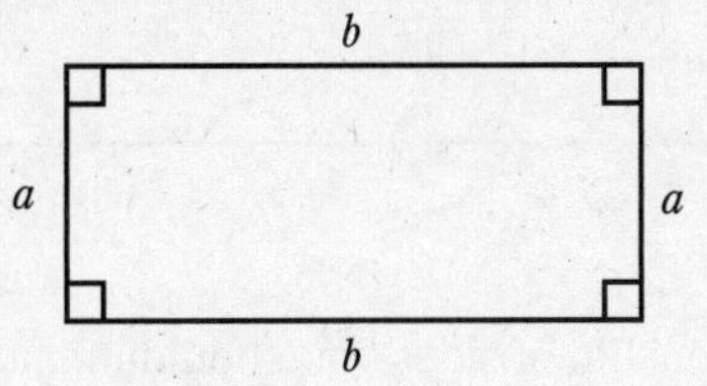

Area = $a \times b$
Perimeter = $2a + 2b$

(306)

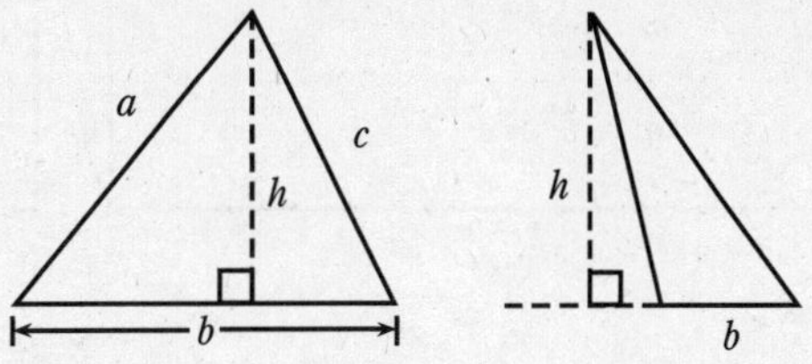

Area = $\frac{1}{2}bh$
Perimeter = $a + b + c$

Area = $\frac{1}{2}bh$

(310)

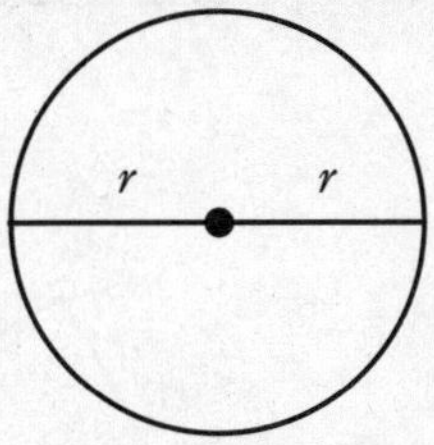

Area = πr^2; π is about 3.14
Circumference (Perimeter) = $2\pi r$

(305)

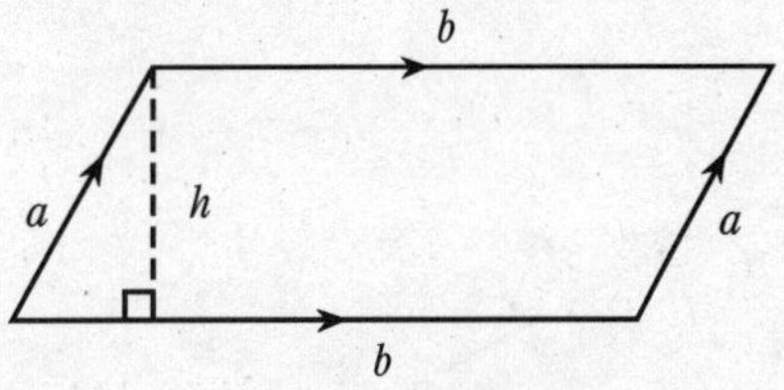

Area = bh;
Perimeter = $2a + 2b$

More on Circles

(526–527)

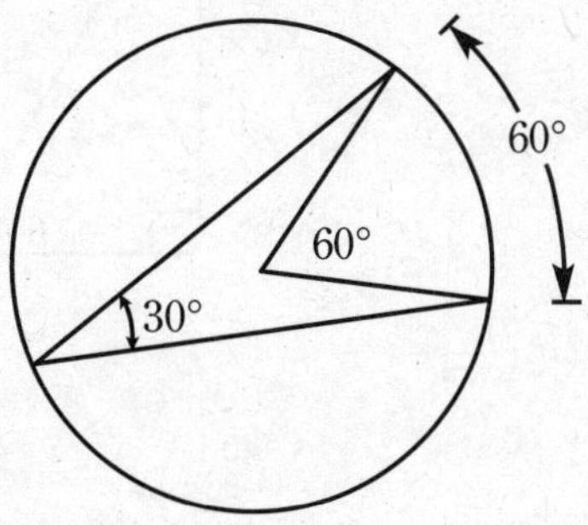

$30° = \frac{1}{2} 60°$

(Angle is $\frac{1}{2}$ intercepted arc)

(527)

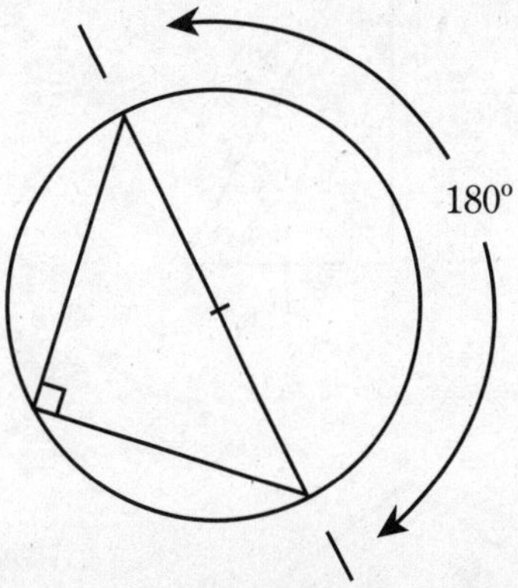

$90° = \frac{1}{2} 180°$

(Inscribed angle = $\frac{1}{2}$ intercepted arc)

(509)

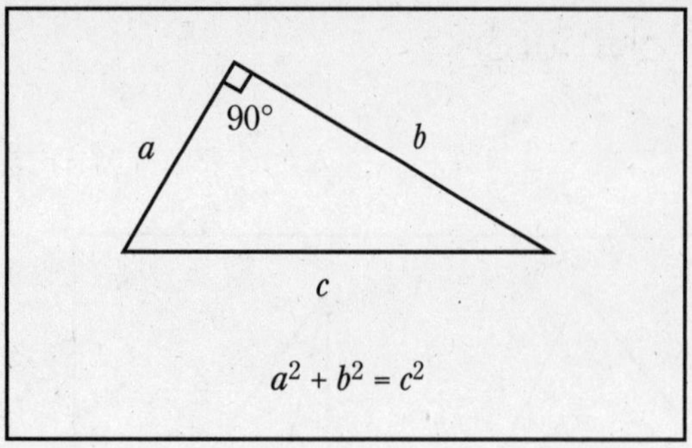

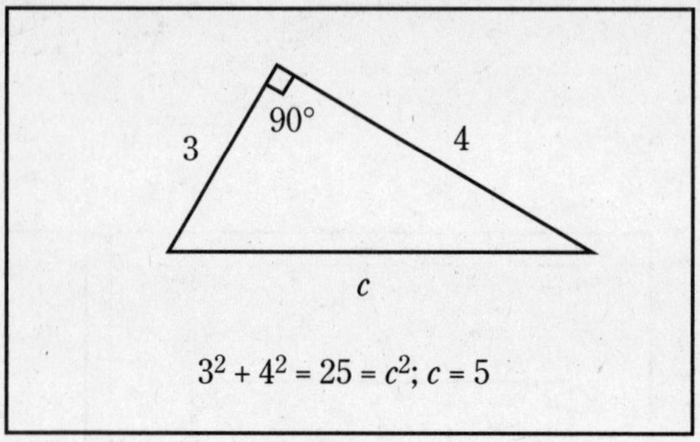

(509)

Here are some right triangles (not drawn to scale) whose relationship of sides you should memorize:

(509)

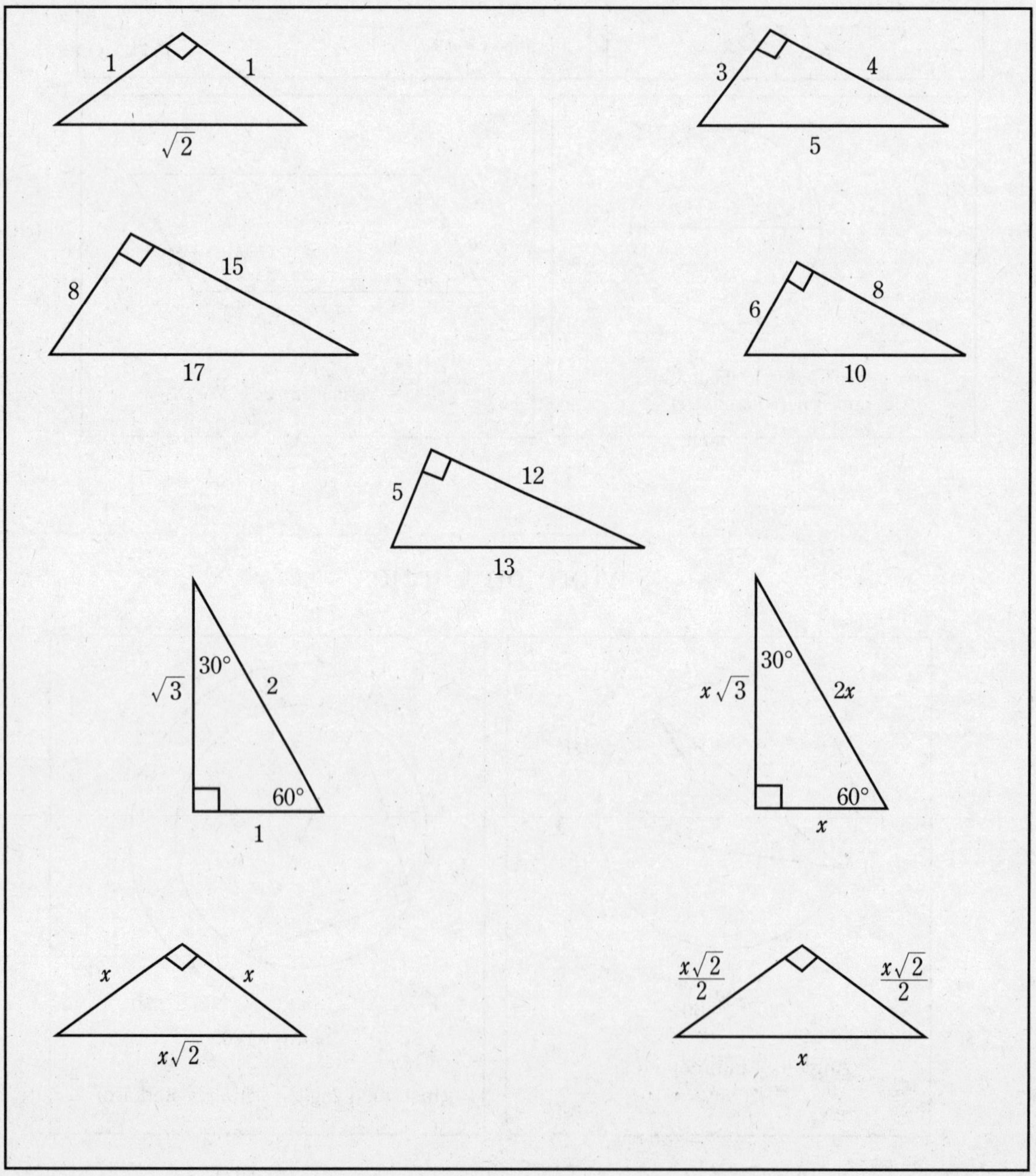

Coordinate Geometry

(410a)

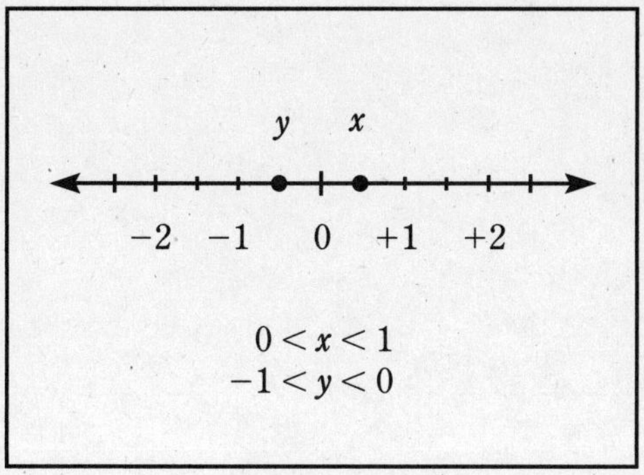

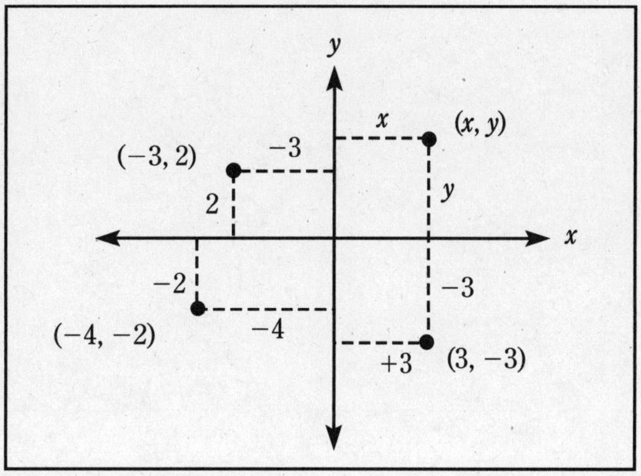

(410b)

(411)

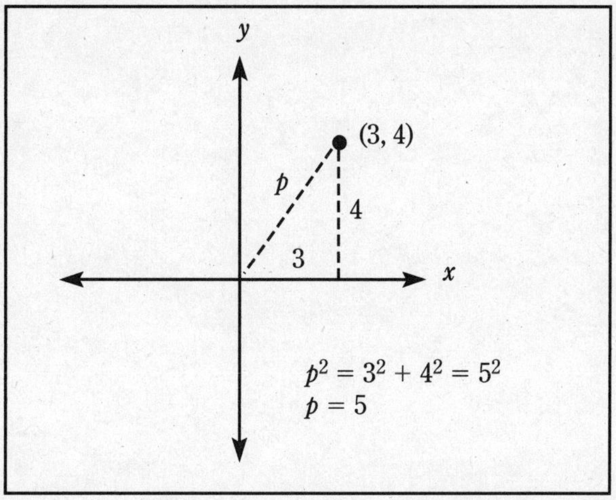

(416)

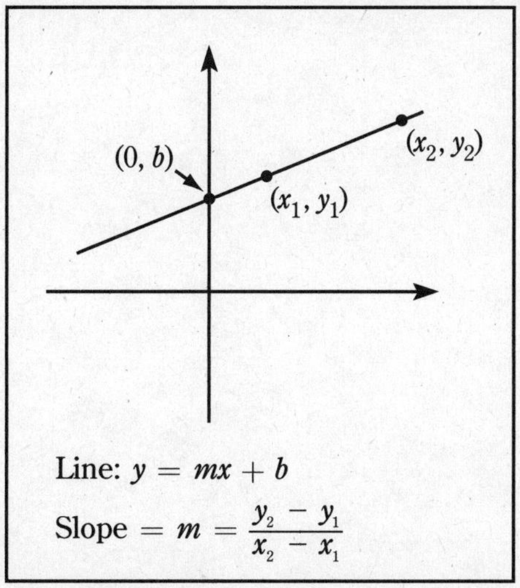

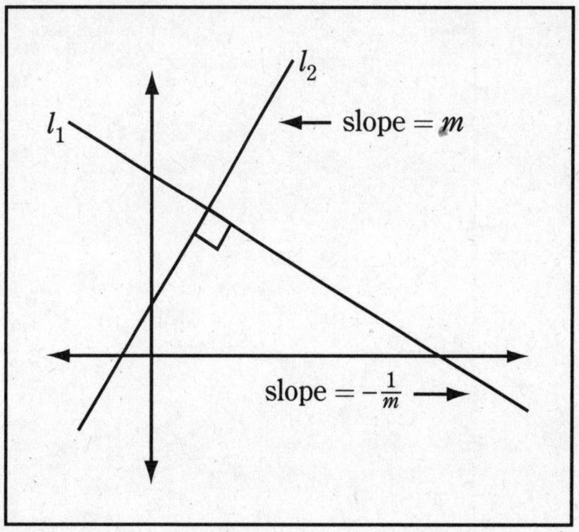

PART 6

COMPLETE SAT MATH REFRESHER

There are many SAT exam takers whose Math background is not quite up to par—probably because their basic Math skills are rusty or because they never did do well in their Math classes. For these Math-troubled students, this Math Refresher section will be "manna from heaven." The pages that follow constitute a complete basic Math course that will help students greatly in preparing for the Math part of the SAT.

This Math Refresher offers the following:

1. a systematic review of every Math area covered by the questions in the Math part of the SAT

and

2. short review tests throughout the Refresher to check whether the student has grasped the Math principles that he or she has just studied.

The review tests will also provide students with valuable reinforcement so that they will remember how to go about solving math problems they would otherwise have difficulty with on the actual SAT.

Each of the 8 "Sessions" in this Math Refresher has a review test ("Practice Test"). Almost every review test has 50 questions followed by 50 detailed solutions. All of the solutions for the 8 review tests include a number (or numbers) in parentheses *after each solution.* The number refers to a specific instructional section where the rules and principles involved in the question are explained simply and clearly.

There is another very important purpose that this Math Refresher serves. You will find, after every solution in the Math sections of the 5 SAT Practice Tests in this book, a key to the mathematical principles of this Math Refresher. For example, a solution may direct you to Math Refresher 202, which deals with Distance and Time problems. If you happen to be weak in this mathematical operation, the 202 Math Refresher explanation will immediately clarify for you how to do Distance and Time problems. In other words, for those who are weak in any phase of Basic Math, this invaluable keying system will help you get the right answer to your SAT Math question—and thereby increase your SAT score.

MATH REFRESHER*
SESSION 1

******Note:* **Many of the examples or methods can be done with a calculator, but it is wise for you to know how to solve problems without a calculator.**

Fractions, Decimals, Percentages, Deviations, Ratios and Proportions, Variations, and Comparison of Fractions

Fractions, Decimals, Percentages

These problems involve the ability to perform numerical operations quickly and correctly. It is essential that you learn the arithmetical procedures outlined in this section.

101. Four different ways to write "*a* divided by *b*" are $a \div b$, $\frac{a}{b}$, $a : b$, $b\overline{)a}$.

Example: 7 divided by 15 is $7 \div 15 = \frac{7}{15} = 7 : 15 = 15\overline{)7}$.

102. The numerator of a fraction is the upper number and the denominator is the lower number.

Example: In the fraction $\frac{8}{13}$, the numerator is 8 and the denominator is 13.

103. Moving a decimal point one place to the right multiplies the value of a number by 10, whereas moving the decimal point one place to the left divides a number by 10. Likewise, moving a decimal point two places to the right multiplies the value of a number by 100, whereas moving the decimal point two places to the left divides a number by 100.

Example: $24.35 \times 10 = 243.5$ (decimal point moved to *right*)
$24.35 \div 10 = 2.435$ (decimal point moved to *left*)

104. To change a fraction to a decimal, divide the numerator of the fraction by its denominator.

Example: Express $\frac{5}{6}$ as a decimal. We divide 5 by 6, obtaining 0.83.

$$\frac{5}{6} = 5 \div 6 = 0.833...$$

105. To convert a decimal to a fraction, delete the decimal point and divide by whatever unit of 10 the number of decimal places represents.

Example: Convert 0.83 to a fraction. First, delete the decimal point. Second, two decimal places represent hundredths, so divide 83 by 100: $\frac{83}{100}$.

$$0.83 = \frac{83}{100}$$

106. To change a fraction to a percent, find its decimal form, multiply by 100, and add a percent sign.

Example: Express $\frac{3}{8}$ as a percent. To convert $\frac{3}{8}$ to a decimal, divide 3 by 8, which gives us 0.375. Multiplying 0.375 by 100 gives us 37.5%.

107. To change a percent to a fraction, drop the percent sign and divide the number by 100.

Example: Express 17% as a fraction. Dropping the % sign gives us 17, and dividing by 100 gives us $\frac{17}{100}$.

108. To *reduce* a fraction, divide the numerator and denominator by the largest number that divides them both evenly.

Example: Reduce $\frac{10}{15}$. Dividing both the numerator and denominator by 5 gives us $\frac{2}{3}$.

Example: Reduce $\frac{12}{36}$. The largest number that divides into both 12 and 36 is 12. Reducing the fraction, we have $\frac{\overset{1}{\cancel{12}}}{\underset{3}{\cancel{36}}} = \frac{1}{3}$.

Note: In both examples, the reduced fraction is exactly equal to the original fraction: $\frac{2}{3} = \frac{10}{15}$ and $\frac{12}{36} = \frac{1}{3}$.

109. To add fractions with like denominators, add the numerators of the fractions, keeping the same denominator.

Example: $\frac{1}{7} + \frac{2}{7} + \frac{3}{7} = \frac{6}{7}$.

110. To add fractions with different denominators, you must first change all of the fractions to *equivalent fractions* with the same denominators.

STEP 1. Find the *lowest (or least) common denominator,* the smallest number divisible by all of the denominators.

Example: If the fractions to be added are $\frac{1}{3}, \frac{1}{4}$, and $\frac{5}{6}$, then the lowest common denominator is 12, because 12 is the smallest number that is divisible by 3, 4, and 6.

STEP 2. Convert all of the fractions to *equivalent fractions,* each having the lowest common denominator as its denominator. To do this, multiply the numerator of each fraction by the number of times that its denominator goes into the lowest common denominator. The product of this multiplication will be the *new numerator.* The denominator of the equivalent fractions will be the lowest common denominator. (See Step 1 above.)

Example: The lowest common denominator of $\frac{1}{3}, \frac{1}{4}$, and $\frac{5}{6}$ is 12. Thus, $\frac{1}{3} = \frac{4}{12}$, because 12 divided by 3 is 4, and 4 times 1= 4. $\frac{1}{4} = \frac{3}{12}$, because 12 divided by 4 is 3, and 3 times 1 = 3. $\frac{5}{6} = \frac{10}{12}$, because 12 divided by 6 is 2, and 2 times 5 = 10.

STEP 3. Now add all of the equivalent fractions by adding the numerators.

Example: $\frac{4}{12} + \frac{3}{12} + \frac{10}{12} = \frac{17}{12}$

STEP 4. Reduce the fraction if possible, as shown in Section 108.

Example: Add $\frac{4}{5}$, $\frac{2}{3}$ and $\frac{8}{15}$. The lowest common denominator is 15, because 15 is the smallest number that is divisible by 5, 3, and 15. Then, $\frac{4}{5}$ is equivalent to $\frac{12}{15}$; $\frac{2}{3}$ is equivalent to $\frac{10}{15}$; and $\frac{8}{15}$ remains as $\frac{8}{15}$. Adding these numbers gives us $\frac{12}{15} + \frac{10}{15} + \frac{8}{15} = \frac{30}{15}$. Both 30 and 15 are divisible by 15, giving us $\frac{2}{1}$, or 2.

111. To *multiply fractions,* follow this procedure:

STEP 1. To find the numerator of the product, multiply all the numerators of the fractions being multiplied.

STEP 2. To find the denominator of the product, multiply all of the denominators of the fractions being multiplied.

STEP 3. Reduce the product.

Example: $\frac{5}{7} \times \frac{2}{15} = \frac{5 \times 2}{7 \times 15} = \frac{10}{105}$. Reduce by dividing both the numerator and denominator by 5, the common factor. $\frac{10}{105} = \frac{2}{21}$.

112. To *divide fractions,* follow this procedure:

STEP 1. Invert the divisor. That is, switch the positions of the numerator and denominator in the fraction you are dividing *by.*

STEP 2. Replace the division sign with a multiplication sign.

STEP 3. Carry out the multiplication indicated.

STEP 4. Reduce the product.

Example: Find $\frac{3}{4} \div \frac{7}{8}$. Inverting $\frac{7}{8}$, the divisor, gives us $\frac{8}{7}$. Replacing the division sign with a multiplication sign gives us $\frac{3}{4} \times \frac{8}{7}$. Carrying out the multiplication gives us $\frac{3}{4} \times \frac{8}{7} = \frac{24}{28}$. The fraction $\frac{24}{28}$ may then be reduced to $\frac{6}{7}$ by dividing both the numerator and the denominator by 4.

113. To *multiply decimals,* follow this procedure:

STEP 1. Disregard the decimal point. Multiply the factors (the numbers being multiplied) as if they were whole numbers.

STEP 2. In each factor, count the number of digits to the *right* of the decimal point. Find the total number of these digits in all the factors. In the product, start at the right and count to the left this (total) number of places. Put the decimal point there.

Example: Multiply 3.8 × 4.01. First, multiply 38 and 401, getting 15,238. There is a total of 3 digits to the right of the decimal points in the factors. Therefore, the decimal point in the product is placed 3 units to the left of the digit farthest to the right (8).

$$3.8 \times 4.01 = 15.238$$

Example: 0.025 × 3.6. First, multiply 25 × 36, getting 900. In the factors, there is a total of 4 digits to the right of the decimal points; therefore, in the product, we place the decimal point 4 units to the left of the digit farthest to the right in 900. However, there are only 3 digits in the product, so we add a 0 to the left of the 9, getting 0900. This makes it possible to place the decimal point correctly, thus: .0900, or .09. From this example, we can derive the rule that in the product we add as many zeros as are needed to provide the proper number of digits to the left of the digit farthest to the right.

114. To find a percent of a given quantity:

STEP 1. Replace the word "of" with a multiplication sign.

STEP 2. Convert the percent to a decimal: drop the percent sign and divide the number by 100. This is done by moving the decimal point two places to the left, adding zeros where necessary.

Examples: 30% = 0.30   2.1% = 0.021   78% = 0.78

STEP 3. Multiply the given quantity by the decimal.

Example: Find 30% of 200.

30% of 200 = 30% × 200 = 0.30 × 200 = 60.00

Deviations

Estimation problems arise when dealing with approximations, that is, numbers that are not mathematically precise. The error, or *deviation*, in an approximation is a measure of the closeness of that approximation.

115. *Absolute error,* or *absolute deviation,* is the difference between the estimated value and the real value (or between the approximate value and the exact value).

Example: If the actual value of a measurement is 60.2 and we estimate it as 60, then the absolute deviation (absolute error) is 60.2 − 60 = 0.2.

116. *Fractional error,* or *fractional deviation,* is the ratio of the absolute error to the exact value of the quantity being measured.

Example: If the exact value is 60.2 and the estimated value is 60, then the fractional error is

$$\frac{60.2-60}{60.2}=\frac{0.2}{60.2}=\frac{0.2\times 5}{60.2\times 5}=\frac{1}{301}.$$

117. *Percent error,* or *percent deviation,* is the fractional error expressed as a percent. (See Section 106 for the method of converting fractions to percents.)

118. Many business problems, including the calculation of loss, profit, interest, and so forth, are treated as deviation problems. Generally, these problems concern the difference between the original value of a quantity and some new value after taxes, after interest, etc. The following chart shows the relationship between business and estimation problems.

Business Problems	*Estimation Problems*
original value	= exact value
new value	= approximate value
net profit net loss net interest	= absolute error
fractional profit fractional loss fractional interest	= fractional error
percent profit percent loss percent interest	= percent error

Example: An item that originally cost \$50 is resold for \$56. Thus the *net profit* is \$56 − \$50 = \$6. The *fractional profit* is $\frac{\$56 - \$50}{\$50} = \frac{\$6}{\$50} = \frac{3}{25}$. The *percent profit* is equal to the percent equivalent of $\frac{3}{25}$, which is 12%. (See Section 106 for converting fractions to percents.)

119. When there are two or more *consecutive changes in value,* remember that the new value of the first change becomes the original value of the second; consequently, successive fractional or percent changes may not be added directly.

Example: Suppose that a \$100 item is reduced by 10% and then by 20%. The first reduction puts the price at \$90 (10% of \$100 = \$10; \$100 − \$10 = \$90). Then, reducing the \$90 (the new original value) by 20% gives us \$72 (20% of \$90 = \$18; \$90 − \$18 = \$72). Therefore, it is *not* correct to simply add 10% and 20% and then take 30% of \$100.

Ratios and Proportions

120. A proportion is an equation stating that two ratios are equal. For example, $3 : 2 = 9 : x$ and $7 : 4 = a : 15$ are proportions. To solve a proportion:

STEP 1. First change the ratios to fractions. To do this, remember that $a : b$ is the same as $\frac{a}{b}$, or $1 : 2$ is equivalent to $\frac{1}{2}$, or $7 : 4 = a : 15$ is the same as $\frac{7}{4} = \frac{a}{15}$.

STEP 2. Now cross-multiply. That is, multiply the numerator of the first fraction by the denominator of the second fraction. Also multiply the denominator of the first fraction by the numerator of the second fraction. Set the first product equal to the second. This rule is sometimes stated as "The product of the means equals the product of the extremes."

Example: When cross-multiplying in the equation $\frac{3}{2} = \frac{9}{y}$, we get $3 \times y = 2 \times 9$, or $3y = 18$.

When we cross-multiply in the equation $\frac{a}{2} = \frac{4}{8}$, we get $8a = 8$, and by dividing each side of the equation by 8 to reduce, $a = 1$.

STEP 3. Solve the resulting equation. This is done algebraically.

Example: Solve for a in the proportion $7 : a = 6 : 18$.

Change the ratios to the fractional relation $\frac{7}{a} = \frac{6}{18}$. Cross-multiply: $7 \times 18 = 6 \times a$, or $126 = 6a$.

Solving for a gives us $a = 21$.

121. In solving proportions that have units of measurement (feet, seconds, miles, etc.), each ratio must have the same units. For example, if we have the ratio 5 inches : 3 feet, we must convert the 3 feet to 36 inches and then set up the ratio 5 inches : 36 inches, or 5 : 36. We might wish to convert inches to feet. Noting that 1 inch = $\frac{1}{12}$ foot, we get 5 inches : 3 feet = $5\left(\frac{1}{12}\right)$ feet: 3 feet = $\frac{5}{12}$ feet : 3 feet.

Example: On a blueprint, a rectangle measures 6 inches in width and 9 inches in length. If the actual width of the rectangle is 16 inches, how many feet are there in the length?

Solution: We set up the proportions, 6 inches : 9 inches = 16 inches : x feet. Since x feet is equal to $12x$ inches, we substitute this value in the proportion. Thus, 6 inches : 9 inches = 16 inches : $12x$ inches. Since all of the units are now the same, we may work with the numbers alone. In fractional terms we have $\frac{6}{9} = \frac{16}{12x}$. Cross-multiplication gives us $72x = 144$, and solving for x gives us $x = 2$. The rectangle is 2 feet long.

Variations

122. In a variation problem, you are given a relationship between certain variables. The problem is to determine the change in one variable when one or more of the other variables changes.

Direct Variation (Direct Proportion)

If x varies directly with y, this means that $x/y = k$ (or $x = ky$) where k is a constant.

> **Example:** If the cost of a piece of glass varies directly with the area of the glass, and a piece of glass of 5 square feet costs \$20, then how much does a piece of glass of 15 square feet cost?

Represent the cost of the glass as c and the area of the piece of glass as A. Then we have $c/A = k$.

Now since we are given that a piece of glass of 5 square feet costs \$20, we can write $20/5 = k$, and we find $k = 4$.

Let's say a piece of glass of 15 square feet costs \$$x$. Then we can write $x/15 = k$. But we found $k = 4$, so $x/15 = 4$ and $x = 60$. \$60 is then the answer.

Inverse Variation (Inverse Proportion)

If x varies inversely with y, this means that $xy = k$ where k is a constant.

> **Example:** If a varies inversely with b and when $a = 5$, $b = 6$, then what is b when $a = 10$?

We have $ab = k$. Since $a = 5$ and $b = 6$, $5 \times 6 = k = 30$. So if $a = 10$, $10 \times b = k = 30$ and $b = 3$.

Other Variations

> **Example:** In the formula $A = bh$, if b doubles and h triples, what happens to the value of A?

STEP 1. Express the new values of the variables in terms of their original values, that is, $b' = 2b$ and $h' = 3h$.

STEP 2. Substitute these values in the formula and solve for the desired variable: $A' = b'h' = (2b)(3h) = 6bh$.

STEP 3. Express this answer in terms of the original value of the variable, that is, since the new value of A is $6bh$, and the old value of A was bh, we can express this as $A_{new} = 6A_{old}$. The new value of the variable is expressed with a prime mark and the old value of the variable is left as it was. In this problem, the new value of A would be expressed as A' and the old value as A. $A' = 6A$.

> **Example:** If $V = e^3$ and e is doubled, what happens to the value of V?
>
> *Solution:* Replace e with $2e$. The new value of V is $(2e)^3$. Since this is a new value, V becomes V'. Thus $V' = (2e)^3$, or $8e^3$. Remember, from the original statement of the problem, that $V = e^3$. Using this, we may substitute V for e^3 found in the equation $V' = 8e^3$. The new equation is $V' = 8V$. Therefore, the new value of V is 8 times the old value.

Comparison of Fractions

In fraction comparison problems, you are given two or more fractions and are asked to arrange them in increasing or decreasing order, or to select the larger or the smaller. The following rules and suggestions will be very helpful in determining which of two fractions is greater.

123. If fractions A and B have the same denominators, and A has a larger numerator, then fraction A is larger. (We are assuming here, and for the rest of this Refresher Session, that numerators and denominators are positive.)

Example: $\frac{56}{271}$ is greater than $\frac{53}{271}$ because the numerator of the first fraction is greater than the numerator of the second.

124. If fractions A and B have the same numerator, and A has a larger denominator, then fraction A is smaller.

Example: $\frac{37}{256}$ is smaller than $\frac{37}{254}$.

125. If fraction A has a larger numerator and a smaller denominator than fraction B, then fraction A is larger than B.

Example: $\frac{6}{11}$ is larger than $\frac{4}{13}$. (If this does not seem obvious, compare both fractions with $\frac{6}{13}$.)

126. Another method is to convert all of the fractions to equivalent fractions. To do this follow these steps:

STEP 1. First find the *lowest common denominator* of the fractions. This is the smallest number that is divisible by all of the denominators of the original fractions. See Section 110 for the method of finding lowest common denominators.

STEP 2. The fraction with the greatest numerator is the largest fraction.

127. Still another method is the *conversion to approximating decimals.*

Example: To compare $\frac{5}{9}$ and $\frac{7}{11}$, we might express both as decimals to a few places of accuracy: $\frac{5}{9}$ is approximately equal to 0.555, while $\frac{7}{11}$ is approximately equal to 0.636, so $\frac{7}{11}$ is obviously greater. To express a fraction as a decimal, divide the numerator by the denominator.

128. If all of the fractions being compared are very close in value to some easy-to-work-with number, such as $\frac{1}{2}$ or 5, you may subtract this number from each of the fractions without changing this order.

Example: To compare $\frac{151}{75}$ with $\frac{328}{163}$ we notice that both of these fractions are approximately equal to 2. If we subtract 2 (that is, $\frac{150}{75}$ and $\frac{326}{163}$, respectively) from each, we get $\frac{1}{75}$ and $\frac{2}{163}$, respectively. Since $\frac{1}{75}$ (or $\frac{2}{150}$) exceeds $\frac{2}{163}$, we see that $\frac{151}{75}$ must also exceed $\frac{328}{163}$.

An alternative method of comparing fractions is to change the fractions to their decimal equivalents and then compare the decimals. (See Sections 104 and 127.) You should weigh the relative amount of work and difficulty involved in each method when you face each problem.

129. The following is a quick way of comparing fractions.

Example: Which is greater, $\frac{3}{8}$ or $\frac{7}{18}$?

Procedure:

Multiply the 18 by the 3. We get 54. Put the 54 on the *left* side.

54

Now *multiply* the 8 by the 7. We get 56. Put the 56 on the *right* side.

54 56

Since 56 > 54 and 56 is on the *right* side, the fraction $\frac{7}{18}$ (which was also originally on the *right* side) is *greater* than the fraction $\frac{3}{8}$ (which was originally on the *left* side).

Example: If $y > x$, which is greater, $\frac{1}{x}$ or $\frac{1}{y}$? (x and y are positive numbers).

Procedure:

Multiply y by 1. We get y. Put y on the left side:

y

Multiply x by 1. We get x. Put x on the right side:

y x

Since $y > x$ (given), $\frac{1}{x}$ (which was originally on the left) is greater than $\frac{1}{y}$ (which was originally on the right).

Example: Which is greater?

$\frac{7}{9}$ or $\frac{3}{4}$

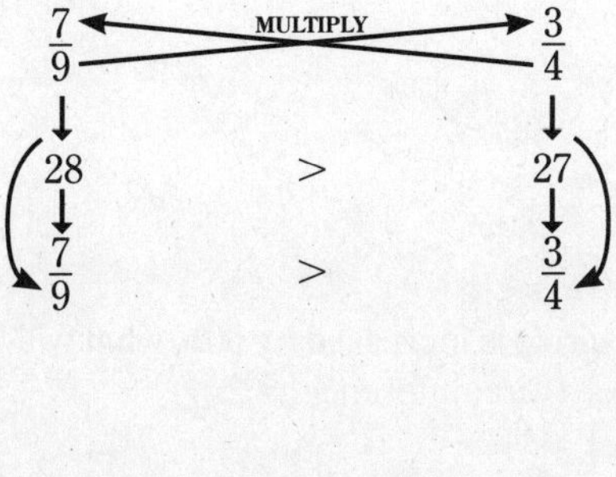

Practice Test 1

Fractions, Decimals, Percentages, Deviations, Ratios and Proportions, Variations, and Comparison of Fractions

Correct answers and solutions follow each test.

1. A B C D E

1. Which of the following answers is the sum of the following numbers:

$2\frac{1}{2}$, $\frac{21}{4}$, 3.350, $\frac{1}{8}$?

(A) 8.225
(B) 9.825
(C) 10.825
(D) 11.225
(E) 12.350

2.500
+ 5.250
+ 3.350
+ 0.125
11.225

2. A B C D E

2. A chemist was preparing a solution that should have included 35 milligrams of a chemical. If she actually used 36.4 milligrams, what was her percentage error (to the nearest 0.01%)?

(A) 0.04%
(B) 0.05%
(C) 1.40%
(D) 3.85%
(E) 4.00%

3. A B C D E

3. A retailer buys a radio from the wholesaler for $75.00. He then marks up the price by $\frac{1}{3}$ and sells it at a discount of 20%. What was his profit on the radio (to the nearest cent)?

(A) $5.00
(B) $6.67
(C) $7.50
(D) $10.00
(E) $13.33

4. A B C D E

4. On a blueprint, $\frac{1}{4}$ inch represents 1 foot. If a window is supposed to be 56 inches wide, how wide would its representation be on the blueprint?

(A) $1\frac{1}{6}$ inches

(B) $4\frac{2}{3}$ inches

(C) $9\frac{1}{3}$ inches

(D) 14 inches

(E) $18\frac{2}{3}$ inches

5. A B C D E

5. If the radius of a circle is increased by 50%, what will be the percent increase in the circumference of the circle? (Circumference $= 2\pi r$)

(A) 25%
(B) 50%
(C) 100%
(D) 150%
(E) 225%

6. A B C D E

6. Which of the following fractions is the greatest?

(A) $\frac{403}{134}$

(B) $\frac{79}{26}$

(C) $\frac{527}{176}$

(D) $\frac{221}{73}$

(E) $\frac{99}{34}$

7. A B C D E

7. A store usually sells a certain item at a 40% profit. One week the store has a sale, during which the item is sold for 10% less than the usual price. During the sale, what is the percent profit the store makes on each of these items?

(A) 4%
(B) 14%
(C) 26%
(D) 30%
(E) 36%

8. A B C D E

8. What is 0.05 percent of 6.5?

(A) 0.00325
(B) 0.013
(C) 0.325
(D) 1.30
(E) 130.0

9. A B C D E

9. What is the value of $\frac{\left(3\frac{1}{2} + 3\frac{1}{4} + 3\frac{1}{4} + 3\frac{1}{2}\right)}{4\frac{1}{2}}$?

(A) $1\frac{1}{2}$

(B) $2\frac{1}{4}$

(C) 3

(D) $3\frac{1}{4}$

(E) $3\frac{3}{8}$

10. A B C D E

10. If 8 men can chop down 28 trees in one day, how many trees can 20 men chop down in one day?

(A) 28 trees
(B) 160 trees
(C) 70 trees
(D) 100 trees
(E) 80 trees

11. A B C D E

11. What is the product of the following fractions: $\frac{3}{100}, \frac{15}{49}, \frac{7}{9}$?

(A) $\frac{215}{44,100}$

(B) $\frac{1}{140}$

(C) $\frac{1}{196}$

(D) $\frac{25}{158}$

(E) $\frac{3}{427}$

12. A B C D E

12. In calculating the height of an object, Mrs. Downs mistakenly observed the height to be 72 cm instead of 77 cm. What was her percentage error (to the nearest hundredth of a percent)?

(A) 6.49%
(B) 6.69%
(C) 6.89%
(D) 7.09%
(E) 7.19%

13. A B C D E

13. A businessman buys 1,440 dozen pens at $2.50 a dozen and then sells them at a price of 25¢ apiece. What is his total profit on the lot of pens?

(A) $60.00
(B) $72.00
(C) $720.00
(D) $874.00
(E) $8,740.00

14. A B C D E

14. On a map, 1 inch represents 1,000 miles. If the area of a country is actually 16 million square miles, what is the area of the country's representation on the map?

(A) 4 square inches
(B) 16 square inches
(C) 4,000 square inches
(D) 16,000 square inches
(E) 4,000,000 square inches

15. A B C D E

15. The formula for the volume of a cone is $V = \frac{1}{3}\pi r^2 h$. If the radius (r) is doubled and the height (h) is divided by 3, what will be the ratio of the new volume to the original volume?

(A) 2 : 3
(B) 3 : 2
(C) 4 : 3
(D) 3 : 4
(E) None of these.

16. A B C D E

16. Which of the following fractions has the smallest value?

(A) $\frac{34.7}{163}$

(B) $\frac{125}{501}$

(C) $\frac{173}{700}$

(D) $\frac{10.9}{42.7}$

(E) $\frac{907}{3,715}$

17. A B C D E

17. Mr. Cutler usually makes a 45% profit on every radio he sells. During a sale, he reduces his margin of profit to 40%, while his sales increase by 10%. What is the ratio of his new total profit to the original profit?

(A) 1 : 1
(B) 9 : 8
(C) 9 : 10
(D) 11 : 10
(E) 44 : 45

18. A B C D E

18. What is 1.3 percent of 0.26?

(A) 0.00338
(B) 0.00500
(C) 0.200
(D) 0.338
(E) 0.500

19. A B C D E

19. What is the average of the following numbers: 3.2, $\frac{47}{12}$, $\frac{10}{3}$?

(A) 3.55

(B) $\frac{10}{3}$

(C) $\frac{103}{30}$

(D) $\frac{209}{60}$

(E) $\frac{1,254}{120}$

20. A B C D E

20. If it takes 16 faucets 10 hours to fill 8 tubs, how long will it take 12 faucets to fill 9 tubs?

(A) 10 hours
(B) 12 hours
(C) 13 hours
(D) 14 hours
(E) 15 hours

21. A B C D E

21. If the 8% tax on a sale amounts to 96¢, what is the final price (tax included) of the item?

(A) $1.20
(B) $2.16
(C) $6.36
(D) $12.00
(E) $12.96

22. A B C D E

22. In a certain class, 40% of the students are girls, and 20% of the girls wear glasses. What percent of the children in the class are girls who wear glasses?

(A) 6%
(B) 8%
(C) 20%
(D) 60%
(E) 80%

23. A B C D E

23. What is 1.2% of 0.5?

(A) 0.0006
(B) 0.006
(C) 0.06
(D) 0.6
(E) 6.0

24. A B C D E

24. Which of the following quantities is the largest?

(A) $\frac{275}{369}$

(B) $\frac{134}{179}$

(C) $\frac{107}{144}$

(D) $\frac{355}{476}$

(E) $\frac{265}{352}$

25. A B C D E

25. If the length of a rectangle is increased by 120%, and its width is decreased by 20%, what happens to the area of the rectangle?

(A) It decreases by 4%.
(B) It remains the same.
(C) It increases by 24%.
(D) It increases by 76%.
(E) It increases by 100%.

26. A B C D E

26. A merchant buys an old carpet for \$25.00. He spends \$15.00 to have it restored to good condition and then sells the rug for \$50.00. What is the percent profit on his total investment?

(A) 20%
(B) 25%
(C) 40%
(D) $66\frac{2}{3}\%$
(E) 100%

27. A B C D E

27. Of the following sets of fractions, which one is arranged in *decreasing* order?

(A) $\frac{5}{9}, \frac{7}{11}, \frac{3}{5}, \frac{2}{3}, \frac{10}{13}$

(B) $\frac{2}{3}, \frac{3}{5}, \frac{7}{11}, \frac{5}{9}, \frac{10}{13}$

(C) $\frac{3}{5}, \frac{5}{9}, \frac{7}{11}, \frac{10}{13}, \frac{2}{3}$

(D) $\frac{10}{13}, \frac{2}{3}, \frac{7}{11}, \frac{3}{5}, \frac{5}{9}$

(E) None of these.

28. A B C D E

28. If the diameter of a circle doubles, the circumference of the larger circle is how many times the circumference of the original circle? (Circumference $= \pi d$)

(A) π
(B) 2π
(C) 1
(D) 2
(E) 4

29. A B C D E

29. The scale on a set of plans is 1 : 8. If a man reads a certain measurement on the plans as 5.6″, instead of 6.0″, what will be the resulting approximate percent error on the full-size model?

(A) 6.7%
(B) 7.1%
(C) 12.5%
(D) 53.6%
(E) 56.8%

30. A B C D E

30. A salesman bought 2 dozen television sets at $300 each. He sold two-thirds of them at a 25% profit but was forced to take a 30% loss on the rest. What was his total profit (or loss) on the television sets?

(A) a loss of $200
(B) a loss of $15
(C) no profit or loss
(D) a gain of $20
(E) a gain of $480

31. A B C D E

31. The sum of $\frac{1}{2}, \frac{1}{3}, \frac{1}{8}$, and $\frac{1}{15}$ is:

(A) $\frac{9}{8}$

(B) $\frac{16}{15}$

(C) $\frac{41}{40}$

(D) $\frac{65}{64}$

(E) $\frac{121}{120}$

32. A B C D E

32. What is $\frac{2}{3}$% of 90?

(A) 0.006
(B) 0.06
(C) 0.6
(D) 6.0
(E) 60

33. A B C D E

33. A man borrows $360. If he pays it back in 12 monthly installments of $31.50, what is his interest rate?

(A) 1.5%
(B) 4.5%
(C) 10%
(D) 5%
(E) 7.5%

34. A B C D E

34. A merchant marks a certain lamp up 30% above original cost. Then he gives a customer a 15% discount. If the final selling price of the lamp was $86.19, what was the original cost?

(A) $66.30
(B) $73.26
(C) $78.00
(D) $99.12
(E) $101.40

35. A B C D E

35. In a certain recipe, $2\frac{1}{4}$ cups of flour are called for to make a cake that serves 6. If Mrs. Jenkins wants to use the same recipe to make a cake for 8, how many cups of flour must she use?

(A) $2\frac{1}{3}$ cups

(B) $2\frac{3}{4}$ cups

(C) 3 cups

(D) $3\frac{3}{8}$ cups

(E) 4 cups

36. A B C D E

36. If 10 men can survive for 24 days on 15 cans of rations, how many cans will be needed for 8 men to survive for 36 days?

(A) 15 cans
(B) 16 cans
(C) 17 cans
(D) 18 cans
(E) 19 cans

37. A B C D E

37. If, on a map, $\frac{1}{2}$ inch represents 1 mile, how long is a border whose representation is $1\frac{1}{15}$ feet long?

(A) $2\frac{1}{30}$ miles

(B) $5\frac{1}{15}$ miles

(C) $12\frac{4}{5}$ miles

(D) $25\frac{3}{5}$ miles

(E) $51\frac{1}{5}$ miles

38. A B C D E

38. In the formula $e = hf$, if e is doubled and f is halved, what happens to the value of h?

(A) h remains the same.
(B) h is doubled.
(C) h is divided by 4.
(D) h is multiplied by 4.
(E) h is halved.

39. A B C D E

39. Which of the following expresses the ratio of 3 inches to 2 yards?

(A) 3 : 2
(B) 3 : 9
(C) 3 : 12
(D) 3 : 24
(E) 3 : 72

40. A B C D E

40. If it takes Mark twice as long to earn $6.00 as it takes Carl to earn $4.00, what is the ratio of Mark's pay per hour to Carl's pay per hour?

(A) 2 : 1
(B) 3 : 1
(C) 3 : 2
(D) 3 : 4
(E) 4 : 3

41. A B C D E

41. What is the lowest common denominator of the following set of fractions:

$\frac{1}{6}, \frac{13}{27}, \frac{4}{5}, \frac{3}{10}, \frac{2}{15}$?

(A) 27
(B) 54
(C) 135
(D) 270
(E) None of these.

42. A B C D E

42. The average grade on a certain examination was 85. Ralph, on the same examination, scored 90. What was Ralph's *percent* deviation from the average score (to the nearest tenth of a percent)?

(A) 5.0%
(B) 5.4%
(C) 5.5%
(D) 5.8%
(E) 5.9%

43. A B C D E

43. Successive discounts of 20% and 12% are equivalent to a single discount of:

(A) 16.0%
(B) 29.6%
(C) 31.4%
(D) 32.0%
(E) 33.7%

44. A B C D E

44. On a blueprint of a park, 1 foot represents $\frac{1}{2}$ mile. If an error of $\frac{1}{2}$ inch is made in reading the blueprint, what will be the corresponding error on the actual park?

(A) 110 feet
(B) 220 feet
(C) 330 feet
(D) 440 feet
(E) None of these.

45. A B C D E

45. If the two sides of a rectangle change in such a manner that the rectangle's area remains constant, and one side increases by 25%, what must happen to the other side?

(A) It decreases by 20%
(B) It decreases by 25%
(C) It decreases by $33\frac{1}{3}$%
(D) It decreases by 50%
(E) None of these.

46. A B C D E

46. Which of the following fractions has the smallest value?

(A) $\frac{6,043}{2,071}$

(B) $\frac{4,290}{1,463}$

(C) $\frac{5,107}{1,772}$

(D) $\frac{8,935}{2,963}$

(E) $\frac{8,016}{2,631}$

47. A B C D E

47. A certain company increased its prices by 30% during 2003. Then, in 2004, it was forced to cut back its prices by 20%. What was the net change in price?

(A) −4%
(B) −2%
(C) +2%
(D) +4%
(E) 0%

48. A B C D E

48. What is 0.04%, expressed as a fraction?

(A) $\frac{2}{5}$

(B) $\frac{1}{25}$

(C) $\frac{4}{25}$

(D) $\frac{1}{250}$

(E) $\frac{1}{2,500}$

49. A B C D E

49. What is the value of the fraction

$$\frac{16 + 12 + 88 + 34 + 66 + 21 + 79 + 11 + 89}{25}?$$

(A) 15.04
(B) 15.44
(C) 16.24
(D) 16.64
(E) None of these.

50. A B C D E

50. If coconuts are twice as expensive as bananas, and bananas are one-third as expensive as grapefruits, what is the ratio of the price of one coconut to one grapefruit?

(A) 2 : 3
(B) 3 : 2
(C) 6 : 1
(D) 1 : 6
(E) None of these.

Answer Key for Practice Test 1

1. D	**14.** B	**27.** D	**39.** E
2. E	**15.** C	**28.** D	**40.** D
3. A	**16.** A	**29.** A	**41.** D
4. A	**17.** E	**30.** E	**42.** E
5. B	**18.** A	**31.** C	**43.** B
6. B	**19.** D	**32.** C	**44.** A
7. C	**20.** E	**33.** D	**45.** A
8. A	**21.** E	**34.** C	**46.** C
9. C	**22.** B	**35.** C	**47.** D
10. C	**23.** B	**36.** D	**48.** E
11. B	**24.** E	**37.** D	**49.** D
12. A	**25.** D	**38.** D	**50.** A
13. C	**26.** B		

Answers and Solutions for Practice Test 1

1. Choice D is correct. First, convert the fractions to decimals, as the final answer must be expressed in decimals: 2.500 + 5.250 + 3.350 + 0.125 = 11.225. (104, 127, 128)

2. Choice E is correct. This is an estimation problem. Note that the correct value was 35, not 36.4. Thus the *real* value is 35 mg and the *estimated* value is 36.4 mg. Thus, percent error is equal to (36.4 − 35) ÷ 35, or 0.04, expressed as a percent, which is 4%. (117)

3. Choice A is correct. This is a business problem. First, the retailer marks up the wholesale price by $\frac{1}{3}$, so the marked-up price equals $\$75(1 + \frac{1}{3})$, or \$100; then it is reduced 20% from the \$100 price, leaving a final price of \$80. Thus, the net profit on the radio is \$5.00. (118)

4. Choice A is correct. Here we have a proportion problem: length on blueprint : actual length = $\frac{1}{4}$ inch : 1 foot. The second ratio is the same as 1 : 48 because 1 foot = 12 inches. In the problem the actual length is 56 inches, so that if the length on the blueprint equals x, we have the proportion $x : 56 = 1 : 48$; $\frac{x}{56} = \frac{1}{48}$. $48x = 56$; so $x = \frac{56}{48}$, or $1\frac{1}{6}$ inches. (120)

5. Choice B is correct. Since $C = 2\pi r$ (where r is the radius of the circle, and C is its circumference), the new value of r, r', is $(1.5)r$ since r is increased by 50%. Using this value of r', we get the new C, $C' = 2\pi r' = 2\pi(1.5)r = (1.5)2\pi r$. Remembering that $C = 2\pi r$, we get that $C' = (1.5)C$. Since the new circumference is 1.5 times the original, there is an increase of 50%. (122)

6. Choice B is correct. In this numerical comparison problem, it is helpful to realize that all of these fractions are approximately equal to 3. If we subtract 3 from each of the fractions, we get $\frac{1}{134}$, $\frac{1}{26}$, $-\frac{1}{176}$, $\frac{2}{73}$, and $-\frac{3}{34}$, respectively. Clearly, the greatest of these is $\frac{1}{26}$, which therefore shows the greatest of the five given fractions. Another method of solving this type of numerical comparison problem is to convert the fractions to decimals by dividing the numerator by the denominator. (127, 128)

7. Choice C is correct. This is another business problem, this time asking for percentage profit. Let the original price be P. A 40% profit means that the store will sell the item for $100\%P + 40\%P$, which is equal to $140\%P$, which in turn is equal to $\left(\frac{140}{100}\right)P = 1.4P$. Then the marked-up price will be $1.4(P)$. Ten percent is taken off this price, to yield a final price of $(0.90)(1.40)(P)$, or $(1.26)(P)$. Thus, the fractional increase was 0.26, so the percent increase was 26%. (118)

8. Choice A is correct. Remember that the phrase "percent of" may be replaced by a multiplication sign. Thus, $0.05\% \times 6.5 = 0.0005 \times 6.5$, so the answer is 0.00325. (114)

9. Choice C is correct. First, add the fractions in the numerator to obtain $13\frac{1}{2}$. Then divide $13\frac{1}{2}$ by $4\frac{1}{2}$. If you cannot see immediately that the answer is 3, you can convert the halves to decimals and divide, or you can express the fractions in terms of their common denominator, thus: $13\frac{1}{2} = \frac{27}{2}$; $4\frac{1}{2} = \frac{9}{2}$; $\frac{27}{2} \div \frac{9}{2} = \frac{27}{2} \times \frac{2}{9} = \frac{54}{18} = 3$. (110, 112)

10. Choice C is correct. This is a proportion problem. If x is the number of men needed to chop down 20 trees, then we form the proportion 8 men : 28 trees = 20 men : x trees, or $\frac{8}{28} = \frac{20}{x}$. Solving for x, we get $x = \frac{(28)(20)}{8}$, or $x = 70$. (120)

11. Choice B is correct. $\frac{3}{100} \times \frac{15}{49} \times \frac{7}{9} = \frac{3 \times 15 \times 7}{100 \times 49 \times 9}$. Canceling 7 out of the numerator and denominator gives us $\frac{3 \times 15}{100 \times 7 \times 9}$. Canceling 5 out of the numerator and denominator gives us $\frac{3 \times 3}{20 \times 7 \times 9}$. Finally, canceling 9 out of both numerator and denominator gives us $\frac{1}{20 \times 7}$, or $\frac{1}{140}$. (111)

12. Choice A is correct. Percent error = (absolute error) ÷ (correct measurement) = 5 ÷ 77 = 0.0649 (approximately) × 100 = 6.49%. (117)

13. Choice C is correct. Profit on each dozen pens = selling price − cost = 12(25¢) − \$2.50 = \$3.00 − \$2.50 = 50¢ profit per dozen. Total profit = profit per dozen × number of dozens = 50¢ × 1440 = \$720.00. (118)

14. Choice B is correct. If 1 inch represents 1,000 miles, then 1 square inch represents 1,000 miles squared, or 1,000,000 square miles. Thus, the area would be represented by 16 squares of this size, or 16 square inches. (120)

15. Choice C is correct. Let V' equal the new volume. Then if $r' = 2r$ is the new radius, and $h' = \frac{h}{3}$ is the new height, $V' = \frac{1}{3}\pi(r')^2(h') = \frac{1}{3}\pi(2r)^2\left(\frac{h}{3}\right) = \frac{4}{9}\pi r^2 h = \frac{4}{3}V$, so the ratio $V' : V$ is equal to 4 : 3. (122)

16. Choice A is correct. Using a calculator, we get: $\frac{34.7}{163} = 0.2128$ for Choice A; $\frac{125}{501} = 0.2495$ for Choice B; $\frac{173}{700} = 0.2471$ for Choice C; $\frac{10.9}{42.7} = 0.2552$ for Choice D; and $\frac{907}{3{,}715} = 0.2441$ for Choice E. Choice A is the smallest value. (104, 127)

17. Choice E is correct. Let N = the original cost of a radio. Then, original profit = 45% × N. New profit = 40% × 110%N = 44% × N. Thus, the ratio of new profit to original profit is 44 : 45. (118)

18. Choice A is correct.
1.3% × 0.26 = 0.013 × 0.26 = 0.00338. (114)

19. Choice D is correct. Average $= \frac{1}{3}\left(3.2 + \frac{47}{12} + \frac{10}{3}\right)$. The decimal $3.2 = \frac{320}{100} = \frac{16}{5}$, and the lowest common denominator of the three fractions is 60, then $\frac{16}{5} = \frac{192}{60}$, $\frac{47}{12} = \frac{235}{60}$ and $\frac{10}{3} = \frac{200}{60}$. Then, $\frac{1}{3}\left(\frac{192}{60} + \frac{235}{60} + \frac{200}{60}\right) = \frac{1}{3}\left(\frac{627}{60}\right) = \frac{209}{60}$. (101, 105, 109)

20. Choice E is correct. This is an inverse proportion. If it takes 16 faucets 10 hours to fill 8 tubs, then it takes 1 faucet 160 hours to fill 8 tubs (16 faucets : 1 faucet = x hours : 10 hours; $\frac{16}{1} = \frac{x}{10}$; $x = 160$). If it takes 1 faucet 160 hours to fill 8 tubs, then (dividing by 8) it takes 1 faucet 20 hours to fill 1 tub. If it takes 1 faucet 20 hours to fill 1 tub, then it takes 1 faucet 180 hours (9 × 20 hours) to fill 9 tubs. If it takes 1 faucet 180 hours to fill 9 tubs, then it takes 12 faucets $\frac{180}{12}$, or 15 hours to fill 9 tubs. (120)

21. Choice E is correct. Let P be the original price. Then $0.08P$ = 96¢, so that $8P$ = \$96, or P = \$12. Adding the tax, which equals 96¢, we obtain our final price of \$12.96. (118)

22. Choice B is correct. The number of girls who wear glasses is 20% of 40% of the children in the class. Thus, the indicated operation is multiplication; 20% × 40% = 0.20 × 0.40 = 0.08 = 8%. (114)

23. Choice B is correct. 1.2% × 0.5 = 0.012 × 0.5 = 0.006. (114)

24. Choice E is correct. Using a calculator to find the answer to three decimal places, we get: $\frac{275}{369} = 0.745$ for Choice A; $\frac{134}{179} = 0.749$ for Choice B; $\frac{107}{144} = 0.743$ for Choice C; $\frac{355}{476} = 0.746$ for Choice D; $\frac{265}{352} = 0.753$ for Choice E. Choice E is the largest value. (104, 127)

25. Choice D is correct. Area = length × width. The new area will be equal to the new length × the new width. The new length = (100% + 120%) × old length = 220% × old length = $\frac{220}{100}$ × old length = 2.2 × old length. The new width = (100% − 20%) × old width = 80% × old width = $\frac{80}{100}$ × old width = .8 × old width. The new area = new width × new length = 2.2 × .8 × old length × old width. So the new area = 1.76 × old area, which is 176% of the old area. This is an increase of 76% from the original area. (122)

26. Choice B is correct. Total cost to merchant = \$25.00 + \$15.00 = \$40.00.
Profit = selling price − cost = \$50 − \$40 = \$10.
Percent profit = profit ÷ cost = \$10 ÷ \$40 = 25%. (118)

27. Choice D is correct. We can convert the fractions to decimals or to fractions with a lowest common denominator. Inspection will show that all sets of fractions contain the same members; therefore, if we convert one set to decimals or find the lowest common denominator for one set, we can use our results for all sets. Converting a fraction to a decimal involves only one operation, a single division, whereas converting to the lowest common denominator involves a multiplication, which must be followed by a division and a multiplication to change each fraction to one with the lowest common denominator. Thus, conversion to decimals is often the simpler method: $\frac{10}{13} = 0.769$; $\frac{2}{3} = 0.666$; $\frac{7}{11} = 0.636$; $\frac{3}{5} = 0.600$; $\frac{5}{9} = 0.555$. (104)

However, in this case there is an even simpler method. Convert two of the fractions to equivalent fractions: $\frac{3}{5} = \frac{6}{10}$ and $\frac{2}{3} = \frac{8}{12}$. We now have $\frac{5}{9}$, $\frac{6}{10}$, $\frac{7}{11}$, $\frac{8}{12}$, and $\frac{10}{13}$. Remember this rule: When the numerator and denominator of a fraction are both positive, adding 1 to both will bring the value of the fraction closer to 1. (For example, $\frac{3}{4} = \frac{2+1}{3+1}$, so $\frac{3}{4}$ is closer to 1 than $\frac{2}{3}$ and is therefore the greater fraction.) Thus we see that $\frac{5}{9}$ is less than $\frac{6}{10}$, which is less than $\frac{7}{11}$, which is less than $\frac{8}{12}$, which is less than $\frac{9}{13}$. $\frac{9}{13}$ is obviously less than $\frac{10}{13}$, so $\frac{10}{13}$ must be the greatest fraction. Thus, in decreasing order the fractions are $\frac{10}{13}$, $\frac{2}{3}$, $\frac{7}{11}$, $\frac{3}{5}$, and $\frac{5}{9}$. This method is a great time-saver once you become accustomed to it.

28. Choice D is correct. The formula governing this situation is $C = \pi d$, where C = circumference and d = diameter. Thus, if the new diameter is $d' = 2d$, then the new circumference is $C' = \pi d' = 2\pi d = 2C$. Thus, the new, larger circle has a circumference twice that of the original circle. (122)

29. Choice A is correct. The most important feature of this problem is recognizing that the scale does not affect percent (or fractional) error, since it simply results in multiplying the numerator and denominator of a fraction by the same factor. Thus, we need only calculate the original percent error. Although it would not be incorrect to calculate the full-scale percent error, it would be time-consuming and might result in unnecessary errors. Absolute error = 0.4″. Actual measurement = 6.0″. Therefore, percent error = (absolute error ÷ actual measurement) × 100% = $\frac{0.4}{6.0}$ × 100%, which equals 6.7% (approximately). (117)

30. Choice E is correct. Total cost = number of sets × cost of each = 24 × \$300 = \$7,200.

Revenue = (number sold at 25% profit × price at 25% profit) + (number sold at 30% loss × price at 30% loss)
= (16 × \$375) + (8 × \$210) = \$6,000 + \$1,680 = \$7,680.

Profit = revenue − cost = \$7,680 − \$7,200 = \$480. (118)

31. Choice C is correct. $\frac{1}{2} + \frac{1}{3} + \frac{1}{8} + \frac{1}{15} = \frac{60}{120} + \frac{40}{120} + \frac{15}{120} + \frac{8}{120} = \frac{123}{120} = \frac{41}{40}$. (110)

32. Choice C is correct. $\frac{2}{3}\% \times 90 = \frac{2}{300} \times 90 = \frac{180}{300} = \frac{6}{10} = 0.6$. (114)

33. Choice D is correct. If the man makes 12 payments of \$31.50, he pays back a total of \$378.00. Since the loan is for \$360.00, his net interest is \$18.00. Therefore, his rate of interest is $\frac{\$18.00}{\$360.00}$, which can be reduced to 0.05, or 5%. (118)

34. Choice C is correct. Final selling price = 85% × 130% × cost = 1.105 × cost. Thus, \$86.19 = 1.105C, where C = cost. C = \$86.19 ÷ 1.105 = \$78.00 (exactly). (118)

35. Choice C is correct. If x is the amount of flour needed for 8 people, then we can set up the proportion $2\frac{1}{4}$ cups : 6 people = x : 8 people. Solving for x gives us $x = \frac{8}{6} \times 2\frac{1}{4}$ or $\frac{8}{6} \times \frac{9}{4} = 3$. (120)

36. Choice D is correct. If 10 men can survive for 24 days on 15 cans, then 1 man can survive for 240 days on 15 cans. If 1 man can survive for 240 days on 15 cans, then 1 man can survive for $\frac{240}{15}$, or 16 days, on 1 can. If 1 man can survive for 16 days on 1 can, then 8 men can survive for $\frac{16}{8}$, or 2 days, on 1 can. If 8 men can survive for 2 days on 1 can, then for 36 days 8 men need $\frac{36}{2}$, or 18 cans, to survive. (120)

37. Choice D is correct. $1\frac{1}{15}$ feet = $1\frac{1}{15}$ × 12 inches = $\frac{16}{15}$ × 12 inches = 12.8 inches. So we have a proportion, $\frac{\frac{1}{2}\text{ inch}}{1\text{ mile}} = \frac{12.8\text{ inches}}{x\text{ miles}}$. Cross-multiplying, we get $\frac{1}{2}x = 12.8$, so $x = 25.6 = 25\frac{3}{5}$. (120)

38. Choice D is correct. If $e = hf$, then $h = \frac{e}{f}$. If e is doubled and f is halved, then the new value of h, $h' = \left(\frac{2e}{\frac{1}{2}f}\right)$. Multiplying the numerator and denominator by 2 gives us $h' = \frac{4e}{f}$. Since $h = \frac{e}{f}$ and $h' = \frac{4e}{f}$ we see that $h' = 4h$. This is the same as saying that h is multiplied by 4. (122)

39. Choice E is correct. 3 inches : 2 yards = 3 inches : 72 inches = 3 : 72. (121)

40. Choice D is correct. If Carl and Mark work for the same length of time, then Carl will earn \$8.00 for every \$6.00 Mark earns (since in the time Mark can earn one \$6.00 wage, Carl can earn *two* \$4.00

wages). Thus, their hourly wage rates are in the ratio \$6.00 (Mark) : \$8.00 (Carl) = 3 : 4. (120)

41. Choice D is correct. The lowest common denominator is the smallest number that is divisible by all of the denominators. Thus we are looking for the smallest number that is divisible by 6, 27, 5, 10, and 15. The smallest number that is divisible by 6 and 27 is 54. The smallest number that is divisible by 54 and 5 is 270. Since 270 is divisible by 10 and 15 also, it is the lowest common denominator. (110, 126)

42. Choice E is correct.

Percent deviation = $\frac{\text{absolute deviation}}{\text{average score}} \times 100\%$.

Absolute deviation = Ralph's score − average score = 90 − 85 = 5.

Percent deviation = $\frac{5}{85} \times 100\% = 500\% \div 85 =$ 5.88% (approximately).

5.88% is closer to 5.9% than to 5.8%, so 5.9% is correct. (117)

43. Choice B is correct. If we discount 20% and then 12%, we are, in effect, taking 88% of 80% of the original price. Since "of" represents multiplication, when we deal with percent we can multiply 88% × 80% = 70.4%. This is a deduction of 29.6% from the original price. (119, 114)

44. Choice A is correct.

This is a simple proportion: $\frac{1 \text{ foot}}{\frac{1}{2} \text{ mile}} = \frac{\frac{1}{2} \text{ inch}}{x}$. Our first step must be to convert all these measurements to one unit. The most logical unit is the one our answer will take—feet. Thus, $\frac{1 \text{ foot}}{2{,}640 \text{ feet}} = \frac{\frac{1}{24} \text{ foot}}{x}$. (1 mile equals 5,280 feet.) Solving for x, we find $x = \frac{2{,}640}{24}$ feet = 110 feet. (120, 121)

45. Choice A is correct. Let the two original sides of the rectangle be a and b and the new sides be a' and b'. Let side a increase by 25%. Then $a' = (100 + 25)\%a = 125\%a = \frac{125}{100}a = 1.25a = \frac{5a}{4}$. We also have that $ab = a'b'$. Substituting $a' = \frac{5a}{4}$, we get $ab = \frac{5a}{4}b'$. The a's cancel and we get $b = \frac{5}{4}b'$. So $b' = \frac{4}{5}b$, a decrease of $\frac{1}{5}$, or 20%.

(122)

46. Choice C is correct. Using a calculator, we get: $\frac{6{,}043}{2{,}071} = 2.9179$ for Choice A; $\frac{4{,}290}{1{,}463} = 2.9323$ for Choice B; $\frac{5{,}107}{1{,}772} = 2.8820$ for Choice C; $\frac{8{,}935}{2{,}963} = 3.0155$ for Choice D; and $\frac{8{,}016}{2{,}631} = 3.0467$ for Choice E. Choice C has the smallest value. (104, 127).

47. Choice D is correct. Let's say that the price was \$100 during 2003. 30% of \$100 = \$30, so the new price in 2003 was \$130. In 2004, the company cut back its prices 20%, so the new price in 2004 =

$\$130 - \left(\frac{20}{100}\right)\$130 =$

$\$130 - \left(\frac{1}{5}\right)\$130 =$

\$130 − \$26 = \$104.
The net change is \$104 − \$100 = \$4.
\$4/\$100 = 4% increase (118)

48. Choice E is correct. $0.04\% = \frac{0.04}{100} = \frac{4}{10{,}000} = \frac{1}{2{,}500}$. (107)

49. Choice D is correct. Before adding you should examine the numbers to be added. They form pairs, like this: 16 + (12 + 88) + (34 + 66) + (21 + 79) + (11 + 89), which equals 16 + 100 + 100 + 100 + 100 = 416. Dividing 416 by 25, we obtain $16\frac{16}{25}$, which equals 16.64. (112)

50. Choice A is correct. We can set up a proportion as follows:

$\frac{1 \text{ coconut}}{1 \text{ banana}} = \frac{2}{1}$, $\frac{1 \text{ banana}}{1 \text{ grapefruit}} = \frac{1}{3}$, so by multiplying the two equations together

$\left(\frac{1 \text{ coconut}}{1 \text{ banana}} \times \frac{1 \text{ banana}}{1 \text{ grapefruit}} = \frac{2}{1} \times \frac{1}{3}\right)$ and canceling the bananas and the 1s in the numerators and denominators, we get: $\frac{1 \text{ coconut}}{1 \text{ grapefruit}} = \frac{2}{3}$, which can be written as 2 : 3. (120)

MATH REFRESHER SESSION 2

Rate Problems: Distance and Time, Work, Mixture, and Cost

Word Problem Setup

200. Some problems require translation of words into algebraic expressions or equations. For example: 8 more than 7 times a number is 22. Find the number. Let n = the number. We have

$$7n + 8 = 22 \qquad 7n = 14 \qquad n = 2$$

Another example: There are 3 times as many boys as girls in a class. What is the ratio of boys to the total number of students? Let n = number of girls. Then

$$3n = \text{number of boys}$$
$$4n = \text{total number of students}$$
$$\frac{\text{number of boys}}{\text{total students}} = \frac{3n}{4n} = \frac{3}{4}$$

201. Rate problems concern a special type of relationship that is very common: rate × input = output. This results from the definition of rate as ***the ratio between output and input***. In these problems, input may represent any type of "investment," but the most frequent quantities used as inputs are time, work, and money. Output is usually distance traveled, work done, or money spent.

Note that the word *per*, as used in rates, signifies a ratio. Thus a rate of 25 miles per hour signifies the ratio between an output of 25 miles and an input of 1 hour.

Frequently, the word *per* will be represented by the fraction sign, thus $\frac{25 \text{ miles}}{1 \text{ hour}}$.

> **Example:** Peter can walk a mile in 10 minutes. He can travel a mile on his bicycle in 2 minutes. How far away is his uncle's house if Peter can walk there and bicycle back in 1 hour exactly?

To solve a rate problem such as the one above, follow these steps:

STEP 1. Determine the names of the quantities that represent input, output, and rate in the problem you are doing. In the example, Peter's input is *time*, and his output is *distance*. His rate will be *distance per unit of time*, which is commonly called *speed.*

STEP 2. Write down the fundamental relationship in terms of the quantities mentioned, making each the heading of a column. In the example, set up the table like this:

$$\text{speed} \times \text{time} = \text{distance}$$

STEP 3. Directly below the name of each quantity, write the unit of measurement in terms of the answer you want. Your choice of unit should be the most convenient one, but remember, once you have chosen a unit, you must convert all quantities to that unit.

We must select a unit of time. Since a ***minute*** was the unit used in the problem, it is the most logical choice. Similarly, we will choose a ***mile*** for our unit of distance. *Speed* (which is the ratio of distance to time) will therefore be expressed in ***miles per minute***, usually abbreviated as mi/min. Thus, our chart now looks like this:

speed × time = distance

mi/min	minutes	miles

STEP 4. The problem will mention various situations in which some quantity of input is used to get a certain quantity of output. Represent each of these situations on a different line of the table, leaving blanks for unknown quantities.

In the sample problem, four situations are mentioned: Peter can walk a mile in 10 minutes; he can bicycle a mile in 2 minutes; he walks to his uncle's house; and he bicycles home. On the diagram, with the appropriate boxes filled, the problem will look like this:

speed × time = distance

	mi/min	minutes	miles
1. walking		10	1
2. bicycling		2	1
3. walking			
4. bicycling			

STEP 5. From the chart and from the relationship at the top of the chart, quantities for filling some of the empty spaces may become obvious. Fill in these values directly.

In the example, on the first line of the chart, we see that the walking speed × 10 equals 1. Thus, the walking *speed* is 0.1 mi/min (mi/min × 10 = 1 mi; mi/min = $\frac{1 \text{ mi}}{10 \text{ min}}$ = 0.1). Similarly, on the second line we see that the bicycle speed equals 0.5 mi/min. Furthermore, his walking speed shown on line 3 will be 0.1, the same speed as on line 1; and his bicycling speed shown on line 4 will equal the speed (0.5) shown on line 2. Adding this information to our table, we get:

speed × time = distance

	mi/min	minutes	miles
1. walking	0.1	10	1
2. bicycling	0.5	2	1
3. walking	0.1		
4. bicycling	0.5		

STEP 6. Next, fill in the blanks with algebraic expressions to represent the quantities indicated, being careful to take advantage of simple relationships stated in the problem or appearing in the chart.

Continuing the example, we represent the time spent traveling shown on line 3 by x. According to the fundamental relationship, the distance traveled on this trip must be $(0.1)x$. Similarly, if y represents the time shown on line 4, the distance traveled is $(0.5)y$. Thus our chart now looks like this:

speed × time = distance

	mi/min	minutes	miles
1. walking	0.1	10	1
2. bicycling	0.5	2	1
3. walking	0.1	x	$(0.1)x$
4. bicycling	0.5	y	$(0.5)y$

STEP 7. Now, from the statement of the problem, you should be able to set up enough equations to solve for all the unknowns. In the example, there are two facts that we have not used yet. First, since Peter is going to his uncle's house and back, it is assumed that the distances covered on the two trips are equal. Thus we get the equation $(0.1)x = (0.5)y$. We are told that the total time to and from his uncle's house is one hour. Since we are using minutes as our unit of time, we convert the one hour to 60 minutes. Thus we get the equation: $x + y = 60$. Solving these two equations ($0.lx = 0.5y$ and $x + y = 60$) algebraically, we find that $x = 50$ and $y = 10$. (See Section 407 for the solution of simultaneous equations.)

STEP 8. Now that you have all the information necessary, you can calculate the answer required. In the sample problem, we are required to determine the distance to the uncle's house, which is $(0.1)x$ or $(0.5)y$. Using $x = 50$ or $y = 10$ gives us the distance as 5 miles.

Now that we have shown the fundamental steps in solving a rate problem, we shall discuss various types of rate problems.

Distance and Time

202. In *distance and time problems* the fundamental relationship that we use is *speed × time = distance*. Speed is the rate, time is the input, and distance is the output. The example in Section 201 was this type of problem.

> **Example:** In a sports car race, David gives Kenny a head start of 10 miles. David's car goes 80 miles per hour and Kenny's car goes 60 miles per hour. How long should it take David to catch up to Kenny if they both leave their starting marks at the same time?

STEP 1. Here the fundamental quantities are *speed, time,* and *distance.*

STEP 2. The fundamental relationship is speed × time = distance. Write this at the top of the chart.

STEP 3. The unit for *distance* in this problem will be a *mile*. The unit for *speed* will be *miles per hour*. Since the speed is in miles per hour, our *time* will be in *hours*. Now our chart looks like this:

speed × time = distance

mi/hr	hours	miles

STEP 4. The problem offers us certain information that we can add to the chart. First we must make two horizontal rows, one for Kenny and one for David. We know that Kenny's speed is 60 miles per hour and that David's speed is 80 miles per hour.

STEP 5. In this case, none of the information in the chart can be used to calculate other information in the chart.

STEP 6. Now we must use algebraic expressions to represent the unknowns. We know that both Kenny and David travel for the same amount of time, but we do not know for how much time, so we will place an x in the space for each boy's time. Now from the relationship of speed $\times$ time $=$ distance, we can calculate Kenny's distance as $60x$ and David's distance as $80x$. Now the chart looks like this:

speed $\times$ **time** $=$ **distance**

	mi/hr	**hours**	**miles**
Kenny	**60**	x	**60x**
David	**80**	x	**80x**

STEP 7. From the statement of the problem we know that David gave Kenny a 10-mile head start. In other words, David's distance is 10 more miles than Kenny's distance. This can be stated algebraically as $60x + 10 = 80x$. That is, Kenny's distance + 10 miles = David's distance.

Solving for x gives us $x = \frac{1}{2}$.

STEP 8. The question asks how much time is required for David to catch up to Kenny. If we look at the chart, we see that this time is x, and x has already been calculated as $\frac{1}{2}$, so the answer is $\frac{1}{2}$ hour.

Work

203. In *work problems* the input is time and the output is the amount of work done. The rate is the work per unit of time.

Example: Jack can chop down 20 trees in 1 hour, whereas it takes Ted $1\frac{1}{2}$ hours to chop down 18 trees. If the two of them work together, how long will it take them to chop down 48 trees?

Solution: By the end of Step 5 your chart should look like this:

rate $\times$ **time** $=$ **work**

	trees/hr	**hours**	**trees**
1. Jack	**20**	**1**	**20**
2. Ted	**12**	**$1\frac{1}{2}$**	**18**
3. Jack	**20**		
4. Ted	**12**		

In Step 6, we represent the time that it takes Jack by x in line 3. Since we have the relationship that rate $\times$ time $=$ work, we see that in line 3 the work is $20x$. Since the two boys work together (therefore, for the same amount of time), the time in line 4 must be x, and the work must be $12x$. Now, in Step 7, we see that the total work is 48 trees. From lines 3 and 4, then, $20x + 12x = 48$. Solving for x gives us $x = 1\frac{1}{2}$. We are asked to find the number of hours needed by the boys to chop down the 48 trees together, and we see that this time is x, or $1\frac{1}{2}$ hours.

Mixture

204. In *mixture problems* you are given a percent or a fractional composition of a substance, and you are asked questions about the weights and compositions of the substance. The basic relationship here is that the percentage of a certain substance in a mixture × the amount of the mixture = the amount of substance.

Note that it is often better to change percents to decimals because it makes it easier to avoid errors.

Example: A chemist has two quarts of 25% acid solution and one quart of 40% acid solution. If he mixes these, what will be the concentration of the mixture?

Solution: Let x = concentration of the mixture. At the end of Step 6, our table will look like this:

concentration × amount of sol = amount of acid

	$\frac{\text{qt (acid)}}{\text{qt (sol)}}$	qts (sol)	qts (acid)
25% solution	0.25	2	0.50
40% solution	0.40	1	0.40
mixture	x	3	$3x$

We now have one additional bit of information: The amount of acid in the mixture must be equal to the total amount of acid in each of the two parts, so $3x = 0.50 + 0.40$. Therefore x is equal to 0.30, which is the same as a 30% concentration of the acid in the mixture.

Cost

205. In *cost problems* the rate is the *price per item*, the input is the *number of items*, and the output is the *value* of the items considered. When you are dealing with dollars and cents, you must be very careful to use the decimal point correctly.

Example: Jim has $3.00 in nickels and dimes in his pocket. If he has twice as many nickels as he has dimes, how many coins does he have altogether?

Solution: After Step 6, our chart should look like this (where c is the number of dimes Jim has):

rate × number = value

	cents/coin	coins	cents
nickels	5	$2c$	$10c$
dimes	10	c	$10c$

Now we recall the additional bit of information that the total value of the nickels and dimes is $3.00, or 300 cents. Thus, $5(2c) + 10c = 300$; $20c = 300$; so $c = 15$, the number of dimes. Jim has twice as many nickels, so $2c = 30$.

The total number of coins is $c + 2c = 3c = 45$.

The following table will serve as review for this Refresher Section.

TYPE OF PROBLEM	FUNDAMENTAL RELATIONSHIP
distance	**speed × time = distance**
work	**rate × time = work done**
mixture	**concentration × amount of solution = amount of ingredient**
cost	**rate × number of items = value**

Practice Test 2

Rate Problems: Distance and Time, Work, Mixture, and Cost

Correct answers and solutions follow each test.

1. A B C D E

1. A man rowed 3 miles upstream (against the current) in 90 minutes. If the river flowed with a current of 2 miles per hour, how long did the man's return trip take?

(A) 20 minutes
(B) 30 minutes
(C) 45 minutes
(D) 60 minutes
(E) 80 minutes

2. A B C D E

2. Charles can do a job in 1 hour, Bill can do the same job in 2 hours, and Bob can do the job in 3 hours. How long does it take them to do the job working together?

(A) $\frac{6}{11}$ hour

(B) $\frac{1}{2}$ hour

(C) 6 hours

(D) $\frac{1}{3}$ hour

(E) $\frac{1}{6}$ hour

3. A B C D E

3. Mr. Smith had $2,000 to invest. He invested part of it at 5% per year and the remainder at 4% per year. After one year, his investment grew to $2,095. How much of the original investment was at the 5% rate?

(A) $500
(B) $750
(C) $1,000
(D) $1,250
(E) $1,500

4. A B C D E

4. A man walks down the road for half an hour at an average speed of 3 miles per hour. He waits 10 minutes for a bus, which brings him back to his starting point at 3:15. If the man began his walk at 2:25 the same afternoon, what was the average speed of the bus?

(A) 1.5 miles per hour
(B) 3 miles per hour
(C) 4.5 miles per hour
(D) 6 miles per hour
(E) 9 miles per hour

5. A B C D E

5. Faucet A lets water flow into a 5-gallon tub at a rate of 1.5 gallons per minute. Faucet B lets water flow into the same tub at a rate of 1.0 gallons per minute. Faucet A runs alone for 100 seconds; then the two of them together finish filling up the tub. How long does the whole operation take?

(A) 120 seconds
(B) 150 seconds
(C) 160 seconds
(D) 180 seconds
(E) 190 seconds

6. A B C D E

6. Coffee A normally costs 75¢ per pound. It is mixed with Coffee B, which normally costs 80¢ per pound, to form a mixture that costs 78¢ per pound. If there are 10 pounds of the mix, how many pounds of Coffee A were used in the mix?

(A) 3
(B) 4
(C) 4.5
(D) 5
(E) 6

7. A B C D E

7. If a man can run p miles in x minutes, how long will it take him to run q miles at the same rate?

(A) $\frac{pq}{x}$ minutes

(B) $\frac{px}{q}$ minutes

(C) $\frac{q}{px}$ minutes

(D) $\frac{qx}{p}$ minutes

(E) $\frac{x}{pq}$ minutes

8. A B C D E

8. A train went 300 miles from City X to City Y at an average rate of 80 mph. At what speed did it travel on the way back if its average speed for the whole trip was 100 mph?

(A) 120 mph

(B) 125 mph

(C) $133\frac{1}{3}$ mph

(D) $137\frac{1}{2}$ mph

(E) 150 mph

9. A B C D E

9. A man spent exactly $2.50 on 3¢, 6¢, and 10¢ stamps. If he bought ten 3¢ stamps and twice as many 6¢ stamps as 10¢ stamps, how many 10¢ stamps did he buy?

(A) 5
(B) 10
(C) 12
(D) 15
(E) 20

10. A B C D E

10. If 6 workers can complete 9 identical jobs in 3 days, how long will it take 4 workers to complete 10 such jobs?

(A) 3 days
(B) 4 days
(C) 5 days
(D) 6 days
(E) more than 6 days

11. A B C D E

11. A barge travels twice as fast when it is empty as when it is full. If it travels 20 miles north with a cargo, spends 20 minutes unloading, and returns to its original port empty, taking 8 hours to complete the entire trip, what is the speed of the barge when it is empty?

(A) less than 3 mph
(B) less than 4 mph but not less than 3 mph
(C) less than 6 mph but not less than 4 mph
(D) less than 8 mph but not less than 6 mph
(E) 8 mph or more

12. A B C D E

12. Bill can hammer 20 nails in 6 minutes. Jeff can do the same job in only 5 minutes. How long will it take them to finish if Bill hammers the first 5 nails, then Jeff hammers for 3 minutes, then Bill finishes the job?

(A) 4.6 minutes
(B) 5.0 minutes
(C) 5.4 minutes
(D) 5.8 minutes
(E) 6.0 minutes

13. A B C D E

13. Jack has two quarts of a 30% acid solution and three pints of a 20% solution. If he mixes them, what will be the concentration (to the nearest percent) of the resulting solution? (1 quart = 2 pints.)

(A) 22%
(B) 23%
(C) 24%
(D) 25%
(E) 26%

14. A B C D E

14. Robert has 12 coins totaling \$1.45. None of his coins is larger than a quarter. Which of the following *cannot* be the number of quarters he has?

(A) 1
(B) 2
(C) 3
(D) 4
(E) 5

15. A B C D E

15. Jim's allowance is \$1.20 per week. Stan's is 25¢ per day. How long will they have to save, if they save both their allowances together, before they can get a model car set that costs \$23.60?

(A) 6 weeks
(B) 8 weeks
(C) 10 weeks
(D) 13 weeks
(E) 16 weeks

16. A B C D E

16. Chuck can earn money at the following schedule: \$2.00 for the first hour, \$2.50 an hour for the next two hours, and \$3.00 an hour after that. He also has the opportunity of taking a different job that pays \$2.75 an hour. He wants to work until he has earned \$15.00. Which of the following is true?

(A) The first job will take him longer by 15 minutes or more.
(B) The first job will take him longer by less than 15 minutes.
(C) The two jobs will take the same length of time.
(D) The second job will take him longer by 30 minutes or more.
(E) The second job will take him longer by less than 10 minutes.

17. A B C D E

17. If Robert can seal 40 envelopes in one minute, and Paul can do the same job in 80 seconds, how many minutes (to the nearest minute) will it take the two of them, working together, to seal 350 envelopes?

(A) 4 minutes
(B) 5 minutes
(C) 6 minutes
(D) 7 minutes
(E) 8 minutes

18. A B C D E

18. Towns A and B are 400 miles apart. If a train leaves A in the direction of B at 50 miles per hour, how long will it take before that train meets another train, going from B to A, at a speed of 30 miles per hour? (Note: The train that leaves B departs at the same time as the train that leaves A.)

(A) 4 hours

(B) $4\frac{1}{3}$ hours

(C) 5 hours

(D) $5\frac{2}{3}$ hours

(E) $6\frac{2}{3}$ hours

19. A B C D E

19. A tub is shaped like a rectangular solid, with internal measurements of 2 feet × 2 feet × 5 feet. If two faucets, each with an output of 2 cubic feet of water per minute, pour water into the tub simultaneously, how many minutes does it take to fill the tub completely?

(A) less than 3 minutes
(B) less than 4 minutes, but not less than 3
(C) less than 5 minutes, but not less than 4
(D) less than 6 minutes, but not less than 5
(E) 6 minutes or more

20. A B C D E

20. A 30% solution of barium chloride is mixed with 10 grams of water to form a 20% solution. How many grams were in the original solution?

(A) 10
(B) 15
(C) 20
(D) 25
(E) 30

21. A B C D E

21. Mr. Adams had a coin collection including only nickels, dimes, and quarters. He had twice as many dimes as he had nickels, and half as many quarters as he had nickels. If the total face value of his collection was $300.00, how many quarters did the collection contain?

(A) 75
(B) 100
(C) 250
(D) 400
(E) 800

22. A B C D E

22. A storekeeper stocks a high-priced pen and a lower-priced model. If he sells the high-priced pens, which yield a profit of $1.20 per pen sold, he can sell 30 in a month. If he sells the lower-priced pens, making a profit of 15¢ per pen sold, he can sell 250 pens in a month. Which type of pen will yield more profit per month, and by how much?

(A) The cheaper pen will yield a greater profit, by $1.50.
(B) The more expensive pen will yield a greater profit, by $1.50.
(C) The cheaper pen will yield a greater profit, by 15¢.
(D) The more expensive pen will yield a greater profit, by 15¢.
(E) Both pens will yield exactly the same profit.

23. A B C D E

23. At a cost of $2.50 per square yard, what would be the price of carpeting a rectangular floor, 18 feet × 24 feet?

(A) $120
(B) $360
(C) $750
(D) $1,000
(E) $1,080

24. A B C D E

24. Tom and Bill agreed to race across a 50-foot pool and back again. They started together, but Tom finished 10 feet ahead of Bill. If their rates were constant, and Tom finished the race in 27 seconds, how long did Bill take to finish it?

(A) 28 seconds
(B) 30 seconds
(C) $33\frac{1}{3}$ seconds
(D) 35 seconds
(E) 37 seconds

25. A B C D E

25. If four men need $24.00 worth of food for a three-day camping trip, how much will two men need for a two-week trip?

(A) $12.00
(B) $24.00
(C) $28.00
(D) $42.00
(E) $56.00

26. A B C D E

26. A man walks 15 blocks to work every morning at a rate of 2 miles per hour. If there are 20 blocks in a mile, how long does it take him to walk to work?

(A) $12\frac{1}{2}$ minutes
(B) 15 minutes
(C) $22\frac{1}{2}$ minutes
(D) $37\frac{1}{2}$ minutes
(E) 45 minutes

27. A B C D E

27. A certain river has a current of 3 miles per hour. A boat takes twice as long to travel upstream between two points as it does to travel downstream between the same two points. What is the speed of the boat in still water?

(A) 3 miles per hour
(B) 6 miles per hour
(C) 9 miles per hour
(D) 12 miles per hour
(E) The speed cannot be determined from the given information.

28. A B C D E

28. Stan can run 10 miles per hour, whereas Jack can run only 8 miles per hour. If they start at the same time from the same point and run in opposite directions, how far apart (to the nearest mile) will they be after 10 minutes?

(A) 1 mile
(B) 2 miles
(C) 3 miles
(D) 4 miles
(E) 5 miles

29. A B C D E

29. Machine A can produce 40 bolts per minute, whereas Machine B can produce only 30 per minute. Machine A begins alone to make bolts, but it breaks down after $1\frac{1}{2}$ minutes, and Machine B must complete the job. If the job requires 300 bolts, how long does the whole operation take?

(A) $7\frac{1}{2}$ minutes
(B) 8 minutes
(C) $8\frac{1}{2}$ minutes
(D) 9 minutes
(E) $9\frac{1}{2}$ minutes

30. A B C D E

30. Ten pints of 15% salt solution are mixed with 15 pints of 10% salt solution. What is the concentration of the resulting solution?

(A) 10%
(B) 12%
(C) 12.5%
(D) 13%
(E) 15%

31. A B C D E

31. Jeff makes \$5.00 every day, from which he must spend \$3.00 for various expenses. Pete makes \$10.00 a day but has to spend \$7.00 each day for expenses. If the two of them save together, how long will it take before they can buy a \$150 car?

(A) 10 days
(B) 15 days
(C) 30 days
(D) 50 days
(E) 75 days

32. A B C D E

32. Two cities are 800 miles apart. At 3:00 P.M., Plane A leaves one city, traveling toward the other city at a speed of 600 miles per hour. At 4:00 the same afternoon, Plane B leaves the first city, traveling in the same direction at a rate of 800 miles per hour. Which of the following answers represents the actual result?

(A) Plane A arrives first, by an hour or more.
(B) Plane A arrives first, by less than an hour.
(C) The two planes arrive at exactly the same time.
(D) Plane A arrives after Plane B, by less than an hour.
(E) Plane A arrives after Plane B, by an hour or more.

33. A B C D E

33. Peter has as many nickels as Charlie has dimes; Charlie has twice as many nickels as Peter has dimes. If together they have \$2.50 in nickels and dimes, how many nickels does Peter have?

(A) 1 nickel
(B) 4 nickels
(C) 7 nickels
(D) 10 nickels
(E) The answer cannot be determined from the given information.

34. A B C D E

34. A man can travel 120 miles in either of two ways. He can travel at a constant rate of 40 miles per hour, or he can travel halfway at 50 miles per hour, then slow down to 30 miles per hour for the second 60 miles. Which way is faster, and by how much?

(A) The constant rate is faster by 10 minutes or more.
(B) The constant rate is faster by less than 10 minutes.
(C) The two ways take exactly the same time.
(D) The constant rate is slower by less than 10 minutes.
(E) The constant rate is slower by 10 minutes or more.

35. A B C D E

35. John walks 10 miles at an average rate of 2 miles per hour and returns on a bicycle at an average rate of 10 miles per hour. How long (to the nearest hour) does the entire trip take him?

(A) 3 hours
(B) 4 hours
(C) 5 hours
(D) 6 hours
(E) 7 hours

36. A B C D E

36. If a plane can travel P miles in Q hours, how long will it take to travel R miles?

(A) $\frac{PQ}{R}$ hours

(B) $\frac{P}{QR}$ hours

(C) $\frac{QR}{P}$ hours

(D) $\frac{Q}{PR}$ hours

(E) $\frac{PR}{Q}$ hours

37. A B C D E

37. A boy can swim 75 feet in 12 seconds. What is his rate to the nearest mile per hour?

(A) 1 mph
(B) 2 mph
(C) 3 mph
(D) 4 mph
(E) 5 mph

38. A B C D E

38. How many pounds of a \$1.20-per-pound nut mixture must be mixed with two pounds of a 90¢-per-pound mixture to produce a mixture that sells for \$1.00 per pound?

(A) 0.5
(B) 1.0
(C) 1.5
(D) 2.0
(E) 2.5

39. A B C D E

39. A broken clock is set correctly at 12:00 noon. However, it registers only 20 minutes for each hour. In how many hours will it again register the correct time?

(A) 12
(B) 18
(C) 24
(D) 30
(E) 36

40. A B C D E

40. If a man travels p hours at an average rate of q miles per hour, and then r hours at an average rate of s miles per hour, what is his overall average rate of speed?

(A) $\frac{pq+rs}{p+r}$

(B) $\frac{q+s}{2}$

(C) $\frac{q+s}{p+r}$

(D) $\frac{p}{q}+\frac{r}{s}$

(E) $\frac{p}{s}+\frac{r}{q}$

41. A B C D E

41. If Walt can paint 25 feet of fence in an hour, and Joe can paint 35 feet in an hour, how many minutes will it take them to paint a 150-foot fence, if they work together?

(A) 150
(B) 200
(C) 240
(D) 480
(E) 500

42. A B C D E

42. If a man travels for a half hour at a rate of 20 miles per hour, and for another half hour at a rate of 30 miles per hour, what is his average speed?

(A) 24 miles per hour
(B) 25 miles per hour
(C) 26 miles per hour
(D) 26.5 miles per hour
(E) The answer cannot be determined from the given information.

43. A B C D E

43. New York is 3,000 miles from Los Angeles. Sol leaves New York aboard a plane heading toward Los Angeles at the same time that Robert leaves Los Angeles aboard a plane heading toward New York. If Sol is moving at 200 miles per hour and Robert is moving at 400 miles per hour, how soon will one plane pass the other?

(A) 2 hours
(B) $22\frac{1}{2}$ hours
(C) 5 hours
(D) 4 hours
(E) 12 hours

44. A B C D E

44. A man exchanged a dollar bill for change and received 7 coins, none of which were half dollars. How many of these coins were dimes?

(A) 0
(B) 1
(C) 4
(D) 5
(E) The answer cannot be determined from the information given.

45. A B C D E

45. A man adds two quarts of pure alcohol to a 30% solution of alcohol in water. If the new concentration is 40%, how many quarts of the original solution were there?

(A) 12
(B) 15
(C) 18
(D) 20
(E) 24

46. A B C D E

46. A certain power company charges 8¢ per kilowatt-hour for the first 1,000 kilowatt-hours, and 6¢ per kilowatt-hour after that. If a man uses a 900-watt toaster for 5 hours, a 100-watt lamp for 25 hours, and a 5-watt clock for 400 hours, how much is he charged for the power he uses? (1 kilowatt = 1,000 watts)

(A) 56¢
(B) 64¢
(C) 72¢
(D) $560.00
(E) $720.00

47. A B C D E

47. At 30¢ per yard, what is the price of 96 inches of ribbon?

(A) 72¢
(B) 75¢
(C) 80¢
(D) 84¢
(E) 90¢

48. A B C D E

48. A man travels for 6 hours at a rate of 50 miles per hour. His return trip takes him $7\frac{1}{2}$ hours. What is his average speed for the whole trip?

(A) 44.4 miles per hour
(B) 45.0 miles per hour
(C) 46.8 miles per hour
(D) 48.2 miles per hour
(E) 50.0 miles per hour

49. A B C D E

49. Stanley puts $100 in the bank for two years at 5% interest compounded annually. At the end of the two years, what is his balance?

(A) $100.00
(B) $105.00
(C) $105.25
(D) $110.00
(E) $110.25

50. A B C D E

50. A 12-gallon tub has a faucet that lets water in at a rate of 3 gallons per minute, and a drain that lets water out at a rate of 1.5 gallons per minute. If you start with 3 gallons of water in the tub, how long will it take to fill the tub completely? (Note that the faucet is on and the drain is open.)

(A) 3 minutes
(B) 4 minutes
(C) 6 minutes
(D) 7.5 minutes
(E) 8 minutes

Answer Key for Practice Test 2

1. B	14. A	27. C	39. B
2. A	15. B	28. C	40. A
3. E	16. B	29. E	41. A
4. E	17. B	30. B	42. B
5. C	18. C	31. C	43. C
6. B	19. D	32. B	44. E
7. D	20. C	33. E	45. A
8. C	21. D	34. A	46. C
9. B	22. A	35. D	47. C
10. C	23. A	36. C	48. A
11. D	24. B	37. D	49. E
12. C	25. E	38. B	50. C
13. E	26. C		

Answers and Solutions for Practice Test 2

1. Choice B is correct. The fundamental relationship here is: rate × time = distance. The easiest units to work with are miles per hour for the rate, hours for time, and miles for distance. Note that the word *per* indicates division, because when calculating a rate, we *divide* the number of miles (distance units) by the number of hours (time units).

We can set up our chart with the information given. We know that the upstream trip took $1\frac{1}{2}$ hours (90 minutes) and that the distance was 3 miles. Thus the upstream rate was 2 miles per hour. The downstream distance was also 3 miles, but we use t for the time, which is unknown. Thus the downstream rate was $\frac{3}{t}$. Our chart looks like this:

rate × time = distance

	mi/hr	**hours**	**miles**
upstream	2	$1\frac{1}{2}$	3
downstream	$\frac{3}{t}$	t	3

We use the rest of the information to solve for t. We know that the speed of the current is 2 miles per hour. We assume the boat to be in still water and assign it a speed, s; then the upstream (against the current) speed of the boat is $s - 2$ miles per hour. Since $s - 2 = 2$, $s = 4$.

Now the speed of the boat downstream (with the current) is $s + 2$, or 6 miles per hour. This is equal to $\frac{3}{t}$, and we get the equation $\frac{3}{t} = 6$, so $t = \frac{1}{2}$ hour.

We must be careful with our units because the answer must be in minutes. We can convert $\frac{1}{2}$ hour to 30 minutes to get the final answer.

(201, 202)

2. Choice A is correct.

rate × time = work

	job/hr	**hours**	**jobs**
Charles	1	1	1
Bill	$\frac{1}{2}$	2	1
Bob	$\frac{1}{3}$	3	1
together	r	t	1

Let r = rate together and t = time together.

Now, $r = 1 + \frac{1}{2} + \frac{1}{3} = \frac{11}{6}$ because *whenever two or more people are working together, their joint rate is the sum of their individual rates.* This is not necessarily true of the time or the work done. In this case, we know that $r \times t = 1$ and $r = \frac{11}{6}$, so $t = \frac{6}{11}$.

(201, 203)

3. Choice E is correct.

rate × principal = interest

	\$/\$	**\$**	**\$**
5%	**0.05**	x	$0.05x$
4%	**0.04**	y	$0.04y$

Let x = part of the \$2,000 invested at 5%. Let y = part of \$2,000 invested at 4%. We know that since the whole \$2,000 was invested, $x + y$ must equal \$2,000. Furthermore, we know that the sum of the interests on both investments equaled \$95, so $0.05x + 0.04y = 95$. Since we have to solve only for x, we can express this as $0.01x + 0.04x + 0.04y = 95$. Then we factor out 0.04. Thus $0.01x + 0.04(x + y) = 95$. Since we know that $x + y = 2{,}000$, we have $0.01x + 0.04(2{,}000) = 95$; $0.01x + 80 = 95$, and $x = 1{,}500$. Thus, \$1,500 was invested at 5%.

(201, 205)

4. Choice E is correct.

rate × time = distance

	mi/min	min	miles
walk	$\frac{1}{20}$	30	a
wait	0	10	0
bus	r	t	a

Let a = distance the man walks. Since the man walks at 3 miles per hour, he walks at $\frac{3 \text{ mi}}{60 \text{ min}}$ or $\frac{1 \text{ mi}}{20 \text{ min}}$. From this we can find $a = \frac{1 \text{ mi}}{20 \text{ min}} \times 30 \text{ min} = 1\frac{1}{2}$ miles. The total time he spent was 50 minutes (the difference between 3:15 and 2:25), and $30 + 10 + t = 50$, so t must be equal to 10 minutes. This reduces our problem to the simple equation $10r = 1\frac{1}{2}$ (where r = rate of the bus), and, on solving, $r = 0.15$ miles per minute. But the required answer is in miles per hour. In one hour, or 60 minutes, the bus can travel 60 times as far as the 0.15 miles it travels in one minute, so that the bus travels $60 \times 0.15 = 9$ miles per hour.

(201, 202)

5. Choice C is correct.

rate × time = water

	gal/min	min	gal
***A* only**	1.5	$\frac{5}{3}$*	2.5
***B* only**	1.0	0	0
A* and *B	2.5	t	x

* ($\frac{5}{3}$ min = 100 sec.)

Let t = time faucets A and B run together.

Let x = amount of water delivered when A and B run together.

We know that the total number of gallons is 5, and A alone delivers 2.5 gallons (1.5 gal/min $\times \frac{5}{3}$ min = 2.5 gal), so x equals 2.5. This leads us to the simple equation $2.5t = 2.5$, so $t = 1$ minute, or 60 seconds. Thus, the whole operation takes $\frac{5}{3} + t$ minutes, or 100 + 60 seconds, totaling 160 seconds.

(201, 203)

6. Choice B is correct.

rate × amount = cost

	¢/lb	lb	¢
Coffee A	75	x	$75x$
Coffee B	80	y	$80y$
mix	78	10	780

Let x = weight of Coffee A in the mix.

Let y = weight of Coffee B in the mix.

We know that the weight of the mix is equal to the sum of the weights of its components. Thus, $x + y = 10$. Similarly, the cost of the mix is equal to the sum of the costs of the components. Thus, $75x + 80y = 780$. So we have $x + y = 10$ and $75x + 80y = 780$. Now $y = 10 - x$, so substituting $y = 10 - x$ in the second equation, we get,

$$75x + 80(10 - x) = 780$$
$$75x + 800 - 80x = 780$$
$$800 - 5x = 780$$
$$20 = 5x$$
$$4 = x$$

Thus 4 pounds of Coffee A were used.

(201, 204, 407)

7. Choice D is correct.

rate × time = distance

	mi/min	min	miles
first run	r	x	p
second run	r	t	q

Let r = rate of the man.

Let t = time it takes him to run q miles.

From the first line, we know that $rx = p$, then $r = \frac{p}{x}$. Substituting this in the second line, we get $\left(\frac{p}{x}\right)t = q$, so $t = q\left(\frac{x}{p}\right)$, or $\frac{qx}{p}$ minutes. (201, 202)

8. Choice C is correct.

rate × **time** = **distance**

	mi/hr	**hrs**	**miles**
X* to *Y	**80**	***t***	**300**
Y* to *X	***r***	***s***	**300**
whole trip	**100**	***s* + *t***	**600**

Let t = time from city X to city Y.

Let s = time from city Y to city X.

Let r = rate of the train from Y to X.

We know that $80t = 300$, so $t = \frac{300}{80}$, or $\frac{15}{4}$. Also, $100(s + t) = 600$, so $s + t = 6$. This and the last equation lead us to the conclusion that $s = 6 - \frac{15}{4}$, or $\frac{9}{4}$. Now, from the middle line, we have $r\left(\frac{9}{4}\right) = 300$, so $r = \frac{400}{3}$, or $133\frac{1}{3}$ miles per hour.
(Note that the reason why we chose the equations in this particular order was that it is easiest to concentrate first on those with the most data already given.) (201, 202)

9. Choice B is correct.

rate × **number** = **cost**

	¢/stamp	**stamps**	**¢**
3¢ stamps	**3**	**10**	**30**
10¢ stamps	**10**	***x***	**10*x***
6¢ stamps	**6**	**2*x***	**12*x***

Let x = the number of 10¢ stamps bought.

We know that the total cost is 250¢, so $30 + 10x + 12x = 250$. This is the same as $22x = 220$, so $x = 10$. Therefore, he bought ten 10¢ stamps. (201, 205)

10. Choice C is correct.

rate × **time** = **work**

	job/day	**days**	**jobs**
6 workers	**6*r***	**3**	**9**
4 workers	**4*r***	***t***	**10**

Let r = rate of one worker.

Let t = time for 4 workers to do 10 jobs.

From the first line, we have $18r = 9$, so $r = \frac{1}{2}$. Substituting this in the second line, $4r = 2$, so $2t = 10$. Therefore $t = 5$. The workers will take 5 days. (201, 203)

11. Choice D is correct.

rate × **time** = **distance**

	mi/hr	**hrs**	**miles**
north	***r***	$\frac{20}{r}$	**20**
unload	**0**	$\frac{1}{3}$	**0**
return	**2*r***	$\frac{10}{r}$	**20**

Let r = loaded rate; then

$2r$ = empty rate

Total time $= \frac{20}{r} + \frac{1}{3} + \frac{10}{r} = 8$ hours.

Multiplying by $3r$ on both sides, we get $90 = 23r$, so $r = 90 \div 23$, or about 3.9 miles per hour. However, the problem asks for the speed *when empty*, which is $2r$, or 7.8. This is less than 8 mph, but not less than 6 mph. (201, 202)

12. Choice C is correct.

rate × **time** = **work**

	nail/min	**min**	**nails**
Bill	***r***	**6**	**20**
Jeff	***s***	**5**	**20**
Bill	***r***	$\frac{5}{r}$	**5**
Jeff	***s***	**3**	**3*s***
Bill	***r***	$\frac{x}{r}$	***x***

Let r = Bill's rate.

Let s = Jeff's rate.

x = number of nails left after Jeff takes his turn.

$6r = 20$, so $r = 3\frac{1}{3}$.

$5s = 20$, so $s = 4$.

Total work $= 5 + 3s + x = 20 = 5 + 12 + x = 20$, so $x = 3$. Thus $\frac{x}{r} = 0.9$.

Total time $= \frac{5}{r} + 3 + \frac{x}{r} = 1.5 + 3 + 0.9 = 5.4$. (201, 203)

13. Choice E is correct.

concentration × volume = amount of acid

	% acid	pts	pts
old sol	30%	4	1.2
	20%	3	0.6
new sol	x%	7	1.8

(2 qts = 4 pts)

Let x% = concentration of new solution.

4 pts of 30% + 3 pts of 20% = 7 pts of x%

1.2 pts + 0.6 pt = 1.8 pts

(x%) (7) = 1.8, so $x = 180 \div 7 = 25.7$ (approximately), which is closest to 26%. (201, 204)

14. Choice A is correct.

coin × number = total value

	¢/coin	coins	¢
pennies	1	p	p
nickels	5	n	$5n$
dimes	10	d	$10d$
quarters	25	q	$25q$

Let p = number of pennies

n = number of nickels

d = number of dimes

q = number of quarters

Total number of coins = $p + n + d + q = 12$.

Total value = $p + 5n + 10d + 25q = 145$.

Now, if $q = 1$, then $p + n + d = 11$, $p + 5n + 10d = 120$. But in this case, the greatest possible value of the other eleven coins would be the value of eleven dimes, or 110 cents, which falls short of the amount necessary to give a total of 145 cents for the twelve coins put together. Therefore, Robert cannot have only one quarter. (201, 205)

15. Choice B is correct.

rate × time = money

	¢/wk	weeks	¢
Jim	120	w	$120w$
Stan	175	w	$175w$
together	295	w	$295w$

(25¢/day = \$1.75/week)

Let w = the number of weeks they save.

Total money = $295w$ = 2,360.

Therefore, $w = 2{,}360 \div 295 = 8$.

So, they must save for 8 weeks. (201, 205)

16. Choice B is correct.

rate × time = pay

	¢/hr	hours	¢
first job	200	1	200
	250	2	500
	300	x	$300x$
second job	275	y	$275y$

Let x = hours at \$3.00.

Let y = hours at \$2.75.

Total pay, first job = $200 + 500 + 300x = 1{,}500$, so $x = 2\frac{2}{3}$.

Total time, first job = $1 + 2 + 2\frac{2}{3} = 5\frac{2}{3}$.

Total pay, second job = $275y = 1{,}500$, so $y = 5\frac{5}{11}$.

Total time, second job = $5\frac{5}{11}$.

$\frac{2}{3}$ hour = 40 minutes

$\frac{5}{11}$ hour = 27.2727 minutes (less than $\frac{2}{3}$ hour). Thus, the first job will take him longer by less than 15 minutes. (201, 203)

17. Choice B is correct.

rate × time = work

	envelopes/min	min	envelopes
Robert	40	t	$40t$
Paul	30	t	$30t$
both	70	t	$70t$

Let t = time to seal 350 envelopes.

Paul's rate is 30 envelopes/minute, as shown by the proportion:

$$\text{rate} = \frac{40 \text{ envelopes}}{80 \text{ seconds}} = \frac{30 \text{ envelopes}}{60 \text{ seconds}}$$

Total work = $70t = 350$, so $t = 5$ minutes. (201, 203)

18. Choice C is correct.

rate × time = distance

	mi/hr	hr	miles
A to B	50	t	$50t$
B to A	30	t	$30t$

Let t = time to meet.

Total distance traveled by two trains together equals $50t + 30t = 80t = 400$ miles, so $t = 5$ hrs. (201, 202)

19. Choice D is correct.

rate × time = amount of water

	cu. ft./min.	min.	cu. ft.
2 faucets	4	t	20

Let t = time to fill the tub.

Volume of tub = 2 ft. × 2 ft. × 5 ft. = 20 cu. ft.

Rate = 2 × rate of each faucet = 2 × 2 cu. ft./min. = 4 cu. ft./min.

Therefore, $t = 5$ minutes. (201, 203)

20. Choice C is correct.

concentration × weight = amount of barium chloride

	%	grams	grams
original	30%	x	$0.30x$
water	0%	10	0
new	20%	$10 + x$	$0.30x$

Let x = number of grams of original solution.

Total weight and amounts of barium chloride may be added by column.

$(20\%) \times (10 + x) = 0.30x$, so $10 + x = 1.50x$, $x = 20$. (201, 204)

21. Choice D is correct.

coin × number = value

	¢/coin	coins	¢
nickels	5	n	$5n$
dimes	10	$2n$	$20n$
quarters	25	$\frac{n}{2}$	$\frac{25n}{2}$

Let n = number of nickels.

Total value $= 5n + 20n + \frac{25n}{2} = \left(37\frac{1}{2}\right)n = 30{,}000$.

Thus, $n = 30{,}000 \div 37\frac{1}{2} = 800$.

The number of quarters is then $\frac{n}{2} = \frac{800}{2} = 400$. (201, 205)

22. Choice A is correct.

rate × number = profit

	¢/pen	pens	¢
high-price	120	30	3,600
low-price	15	250	3,750

Subtracting 3,600¢ from 3,750¢, we get 150¢.

Thus, the cheaper pen yields a profit of 150¢, or \$1.50, more per month than the more expensive one. (201, 205)

23. Choice A is correct.

price ×	area =	cost
$/sq. yd.	**sq. yd.**	**$**
2.50	**48**	**120**

Area must be expressed in square yards; 18 ft. = 6 yds., and 24 ft. = 8 yds., so 18 ft. × 24 ft. = 6 yds. × 8 yds. = 48 sq. yds. The cost would then be $2.50 × 48 = $120.00. (201, 205)

24. Choice B is correct.

	rate ×	time =	distance
	ft/sec	**sec**	**feet**
Tom	r	**27**	**100**
Bill	s	**27**	**90**
Bill	s	t	**100**

Let r = Tom's rate.

Let s = Bill's rate.

Let t = Bill's time to finish the race.

$27s = 90$, so $s = \frac{90}{27} = \frac{10}{3}$;

$st = 100$, and $s = \frac{10}{3}$, so $\frac{10t}{3} = 100$; thus $t = 30$. (201, 202)

25. Choice E is correct. This is a rate problem in which the fundamental relationship is rate × time × number of men = cost. The rate is in dollars/man-days. Thus, our chart looks like this:

	rate ×	time ×	number =	cost
	$/man-days	**days**	**men**	**$**
1st trip	r	**3**	**4**	**12r**
2nd trip	r	**14**	**2**	**28r**

The cost of the first trip is $24, so $12r = 24$ and $r = 2$.

The cost of the second trip is $28r$, or $56. (201, 205)

26. Choice C is correct.

rate ×	time =	distance
blocks/min.	**min**	**blocks**
$\frac{2}{3}$	t	**15**

Let t = time to walk to work.

2 miles/hr = 2(20 blocks)/(60 min) = $\frac{2}{3}$ blocks/minute.

$t = 15 \div \frac{2}{3} = 22\frac{1}{2}$ minutes. (201, 202)

27. Choice C is correct.

	rate ×	time =	distance
	mi/hr	**hrs**	**miles**
down	$r + 3$	h	$h(r + 3)$
up	$r - 3$	$2h$	$2h(r - 3)$

Let h = time to travel downstream.

Let r = speed of the boat in still water.

Since the two trips cover the same distance, we can write the equation: $h(r + 3) = 2h(r - 3)$. Dividing by h, $r + 3 = 2r - 6$, so $r = 9$. (201, 202)

28. Choice C is correct. We could treat this as a regular distance problem and make up a table that would solve it, but there is an easier way here, if we consider the quantity representing the distance between the boys. This distance starts at zero and increases at the rate of 18 miles per hour. Thus, in 10 minutes, or $\frac{1}{6}$ hour, they will be 3 miles apart.

($\frac{1}{6}$ hr × 18 $\frac{\text{mi}}{\text{hr}}$ = 3 mi). (201, 202)

29. Choice E is correct.

	rate ×	time =	work
	bolts/min	**min**	**bolts**
A	**40**	$1\frac{1}{2}$	**60**
B	**30**	t	**240**

Let t = time B works.

Since A produces only 60 out of 300 that must be produced, B must produce 240; then, $30t = 240$, so $t = 8$.

Total time = $t + 1\frac{1}{2} = 8 + 1\frac{1}{2} = 9\frac{1}{2}$. (201, 203)

30. Choice B is correct.

concentration × volume = amount of salt

	%	pints	"pints" of salt
15%	15	10	1.5
10%	10	15	1.5
total	x	25	3.0

Let x = concentration of resulting solution.

(x%) (25) = 3.0, so $x = 300 \div 25 = 12$. (201, 204)

31. Choice C is correct.

rate × time = pay (net)

	$/day	days	$
Jeff	2	d	$2d$
Pete	3	d	$3d$
total	5	d	$5d$

(Net pay = pay − expenses.)

Let d = the number of days it takes to save.

Total net pay = $150.00, so $150 = 5d$, thus $d = 30$.

Do not make the mistake of using 5 and 10 as the rates! (201, 205)

32. Choice B is correct.

rate × time = distance

	mi/hr	hours	miles
plane A	600	h	800
plane B	0	1	0
plane B	800	t	800

Let h = time for trip at 600 mph.

Let t = time for trip at 800 mph.

Plane A: $600h = 800$, so $h = \frac{800}{600} = 1\frac{1}{3}$ hours = 1 hour, 20 minutes.

Plane B: $800t = 800$, so $t = 1$.

Total time for plane A = 1 hour, 20 minutes.

Total time for plane B = 1 hour + 1 hour = 2 hours.

Thus, plane A arrives before plane B by 40 minutes (less than an hour). (201, 202)

33. Choice E is correct.

coin × number = value

	¢/coin	coins	¢
Peter	5	n	$5n$
Peter	10	d	$10d$
Charlie	5	$2d$	$10d$
Charlie	10	n	$10n$

Let n = number of Peter's nickels.

Let d = number of Peter's dimes.

Total value of coins = $5n + 10d + 10d + 10n = 15n + 20d$.

Thus, $15n + 20d = 250$. This has many different solutions, each of which is possible (e.g., $n = 2$, $d = 11$, or $n = 6$, $d = 8$, etc.). (201, 205)

34. Choice A is correct.

rate × time = distance

	mi/hr	hours	miles
constant rate	40	h	120
two rates	50	m	60
	30	n	60

Let h = time to travel 120 miles at the constant rate.

Let m = time to travel 60 miles at 50 mi/hr.

Let n = time to travel 60 miles at 30 mi/hr.

Forming the equations for h, m, and n, and solving, we get:

$$40h = 120;\ h = \frac{120}{40};\ h = 3$$

$$50m = 60;\ m = \frac{60}{50};\ m = 1.2$$

$$30n = 60;\ n = \frac{60}{30};\ n = 2$$

Total time with constant rate = h = 3 hours.

Total time with changing rate = $m + n$ = 3.2 hours.

Thus, the constant rate is faster by 0.2 hours, or 12 minutes. (201, 202)

35. Choice D is correct.

rate × time = distance

	mi/hr	hours	miles
walking	2	h	10
bicycling	10	t	10

Let h = time to walk.

Let t = time to bicycle.

Forming equations: $2h = 10$, so $h = 5$; and $10t = 10$, so $t = 1$.

Total time $= h + t = 5 + 1 = 6$. (201, 202)

36. Choice C is correct.

rate × time = distance

mi/hr	hours	miles
x	Q	P
x	y	R

Let x = rate at which the airplane travels.

Let y = time to travel R miles.

$Qx = P$, so $x = \frac{P}{Q}$.

$xy = \left(\frac{P}{Q}\right)y = R$, so $y = \frac{QR}{P}$ hours = time to travel R miles. (201, 202)

37. Choice D is correct.

rate × time = distance

mi/hr	hours	miles
r	$\frac{1}{300}$	$\frac{75}{5{,}280}$

Let r = rate of swimming.

75 feet $= 75\left(\frac{1}{5{,}280}\text{ mile}\right) = \frac{75}{5{,}280}$ mile

12 seconds $= 12\left(\frac{1}{3{,}600}\text{ hour}\right) = \frac{1}{300}$ hour

$r = \frac{75}{5{,}280} \div \frac{1}{300} = \frac{22{,}500}{5{,}280} = 4.3$ (approximately) = 4 mi/hr (approximately). (201, 202)

38. Choice B is correct.

price × amount = value

	¢/lb	lbs	¢
$1.20 nuts	120	x	$120x$
$0.90	90	2	180
mixture	100	$x + 2$	$180 + 120x$

Let x = pounds of $1.20 mixture.

Total value of mixture $= 100(x + 2) = 180 + 120x$.
$100x + 200 = 180 + 120x$, so $x = 1$ pound. (201, 204)

39. Choice B is correct.

rate × time = loss

hr/hr	hrs	hrs
$\frac{2}{3}$	t	12

(Loss is the amount by which the clock time differs from real time.)

Let t = hours to register the correct time.

If the clock registers only 20 minutes each hour, it loses 40 minutes, or $\frac{2}{3}$ hour each hour. The clock will register the correct time only if it has lost some multiple of 12 hours. The first time this can occur is after it has lost 12 hours. $\left(\frac{2}{3}\right)t = 12$, so $t =$ 18 hours. (201)

40. Choice A is correct.

rate × time = distance

	mi/hr	hrs	miles
	q	p	pq
	s	r	rs
total	x	$p + r$	$pq + rs$

Let x = average speed.

We may add times of travel at the two rates, and also add the distances. Then, $x(p + r) = pq + rs$; thus, $x = \frac{pq + rs}{p + r}$. (201, 202)

41. Choice A is correct.

rate × time = work

	ft/hr	hrs	feet
Joe	35	x	$35x$
Walt	25	x	$25x$
both	60	x	$60x$

Let x = the time the job takes.

Since they are working together, we add their rates and the amount of work they do. Thus, $60x = 150$, so $x = 2.5$ (hours) = 150 minutes. (201, 203)

42. Choice B is correct.

rate × time = distance

	mi/hr	hrs	miles
first $\frac{1}{2}$ hour	20	$\frac{1}{2}$	10
second $\frac{1}{2}$ hour	30	$\frac{1}{2}$	15
total	x	1	25

Let x = average speed.

We add the times and distances; then, using the rate formula, $(x)(1) = 25$, so $x = 25$ mi/hr. (201, 202)

43. Choice C is correct.

rate × time = distance

	mi/hr	hours	miles
Sol	200	t	$200t$
Robert	400	t	$400t$

Let t = time from simultaneous departure to meeting.

Sol's time is equal to Robert's time because they leave at the same time and then they meet. Their combined distance is 3,000 miles, so $200t + 400t = 3{,}000$, or $t = 5$ hours. (201, 202)

44. Choice E is correct.

coin × number = value

	¢/coin	coins	¢
pennies	1	p	p
nickels	5	n	$5n$
dimes	10	d	$10d$
quarters	25	q	$25q$

Let p = number of pennies.
Let n = number of nickels.
Let d = number of dimes.
Let q = number of quarters.

Adding the numbers of coins and their values, we get $p + n + d + q = 7$, and $p + 5n + 10d + 25q = 100$. These equations are satisfied by several values of p, n, d, and q. For example, $p = 0$, $n = 0$, $d = 5$, $q = 2$ satisfies the equation, as does $p = 0$, $n = 3$, $d = 1$, $q = 3$, and other combinations.

Thus, the number of dimes cannot be determined. (201, 205)

45. Choice A is correct.

concentration × amt of solution = amount of alcohol

	%	qts	qts
pure alcohol	100%	2	2
solution	30%	x	$0.30x$
mixture	40%	$2 + x$	$2 + 0.30x$

Let x = quarts of original solution.

Amounts of solution and of alcohol may be added.

$(40\%)(2 + x) = 2 + 0.30x$; so $0.8 + 0.4x = 2.0 + 0.30x$; thus, $x = 12$. (201, 204)

46. Choice C is correct.

rate × time = cost

	¢/kWh	kWh	¢
first 1,000 kWh	**8**	t	**8t**

(time expressed in kilowatt-hours, or kWh)

Let t = number of kWh.

This problem must be broken up into two different parts: (1) finding the total power or the total number of kilowatt-hours (kWh) used, and (2) calculating the charge for that amount. (1) Total power used, $t = (900w)(5\text{ hr}) + (100w)(25\text{ hr}) + (5w)(400\text{ hr}) = (4{,}500 + 2{,}500 + 2{,}000)$ watt-hours = 9,000 watt-hours. (2) One thousand watt-hours equals one kilowatt-hour. Thus, $t = 9$ kilowatt-hours, so that the charge is (8¢)(9) = 72¢. (201, 205)

47. Choice C is correct.

rate × amount = cost

	¢/in	in	¢
1 yard	r	**36**	**30**
96 inches	r	**96**	**96r**

Let r = cost per inch of ribbon.

From the table, $r \times 36$ in = 30¢; $r = \frac{30¢}{36\text{ in.}} = \frac{5¢}{6\text{ in.}}$.

Thus, $96r = 96\left(\frac{5}{6}\right) = 80¢$. (201, 205)

48. Choice A is correct.

rate × time = distance

	mi/hr	hrs	miles
trip	**50**	**6**	**300**
return	r	**$7\frac{1}{2}$**	**300**
total	s	**$13\frac{1}{2}$**	**600**

Let r = rate for return.

Let s = average overall rate.

$(13\frac{1}{2})(s) = 600$; thus, $s = 600 \div 13\frac{1}{2} = 44.4$ (approximately). (201, 202)

49. Choice E is correct.

rate × principal = interest

	%/year	$	$/year
first year	**5**	**100**	**5**
second year	**5**	**105**	**5.25**

Interest first year equals rate × principal = 5% × $100 = $5.

New principal = $105.00.

Interest second year = rate × new principal = 5% × $105 = $5.25.

Final principal = $105.00 + $5.25 = $110.25. (201, 205)

50. Choice C is correct.

rate × time = amount

	gal/min	min	gallons
in	**3**	x	**3x**
out	**$1\frac{1}{2}$**	x	**$1\frac{1}{2}x$**
net	**$1\frac{1}{2}$**	x	**$1\frac{1}{2}x$**

(Net = in − out.)

Let x = time to fill the tub completely.

Since only 9 gallons are needed (there are already 3 in the tub), we have $1\frac{1}{2}x = 9$, so $x = 6$. (201)

MATH REFRESHER SESSION 3

Area, Perimeter, and Volume Problems

Area, Perimeter, and Volume

301. *Formula Problems.* Here, you are given certain data about one or more geometric figures, and you are asked to supply some missing information. To solve this type of problem, follow this procedure:

STEP 1. If you are not given a diagram, draw your own; this may make the answer readily apparent or may suggest the best way to solve the problem. You should try to make your diagram as accurate as possible, but *do not waste time perfecting your diagram.*

STEP 2. Determine the formula that relates to the quantities involved in your problem. In many cases it will be helpful to set up tables containing the various data. (See Sections 303–317.)

STEP 3. Substitute the given information for the unknown quantities in your formulas to get the desired answer.

When doing volume, area, and perimeter problems, keep this hint in mind: Often the solutions to such problems can be expressed as the sum of the areas *or* volumes *or* perimeters of simpler figures. In such cases, do not hesitate to break down your original figure into simpler parts.

In doing problems involving the following figures, these approximations and facts will be useful:

$\sqrt{2}$ is approximately 1.4.

$\sqrt{3}$ is approximately 1.7.

$\sqrt{10}$ is approximately 3.16.

π is approximately $\frac{22}{7}$ or 3.14.

$\sin 30° = \frac{1}{2}$

$\sin 45° = \frac{\sqrt{2}}{2}$ which is approximately 0.71.

$\sin 60° = \frac{\sqrt{3}}{2}$ which is approximately 0.87.

Example: The following figure contains a square, a right triangle, and a semicircle. If $ED = CD$ and the length of CD is 1 unit, find the area of the entire figure.

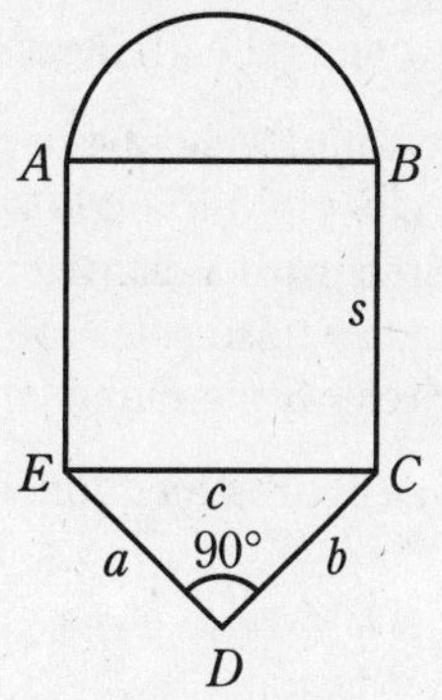

Solution: To calculate the area of the entire figure, we calculate the areas of the triangle, square, and semicircle and then add these together. In a right triangle, the area is $\frac{1}{2}ab$ where a and b are the sides of the triangle. In this case we will call side ED, a, and side CD, b. $ED = CD = 1$, so the area of the triangle is $\frac{1}{2}(1)(1)$, or $\frac{1}{2}$.

The area of a square is s^2, where s is a side. We see that the side EC of the square is the hypotenuse of the right triangle. We can calculate this length by using the formula $c^2 = a^2 + b^2$ where $a = b = 1$; then we can see that $c = \sqrt{2}$. Thus, in this case, $s = \sqrt{2}$ so the area of the square is $(\sqrt{2})^2 = 2$.

AB is the diameter of the semicircle, so $\frac{1}{2}AB$ is the radius. Since all sides of a square are equal, $AB = \sqrt{2}$, and the radius is $\frac{1}{2}\sqrt{2}$. Further, the area of a semicircle is $\frac{1}{2}\pi r^2$, where r is the radius, so the area of this semicircle is $\frac{1}{2}\pi\left(\frac{1}{2}\sqrt{2}\right)^2 = \frac{1}{4}\pi$.

The total area of the whole figure is equal to the area of the triangle plus the area of the square plus the area of the semicircle $= \frac{1}{2} + 2 + \frac{1}{4}\pi = 2\frac{1}{2} + \frac{1}{4}\pi$.

Example: If water flows into a rectangular tank with dimensions of 12 inches, 18 inches, and 30 inches at the rate of 0.25 cubic feet per minute, how long will it take to fill the tank?

Solution: This problem is really a combination of a rate problem and a volume problem. First we must calculate the volume, and then we must substitute in a rate equation to get our final answer. The formula for the volume of a rectangular solid is $V = lwh$, where l, w, and h are the length, width, and height, respectively. We must multiply the three dimensions of the tank to get the volume. However, if we look ahead to the second part of the problem, we see that we want the volume in cubic *feet;* therefore we convert 12 inches, 18 inches, and 30 inches to 1 foot, 1.5 feet, and 2.5 feet, respectively. Multiplying gives us a volume of 3.75 cubic feet. Now substituting in the equation *rate* × *time* = *volume*, we get $0.25 \times \text{time} = 3.75$; $\text{time} = \frac{3.75}{0.25}$; thus, the time is 15 minutes.

302. *Comparison problems.* Here you are asked to identify the largest, or smallest, of a group of figures, or to place them in ascending or descending order of size. The following procedure is the most efficient one:

STEP 1. Always diagram each figure before you come to any conclusions. Whenever possible, try to include two or more of the figures in the same diagram, so that their relative sizes are most readily apparent.

STEP 2. If you have not already determined the correct answer, then (and only then) determine the size of the figures (as you would have done in Section 301) and compare the results.

(Note that even if Step 2 is necessary, Step 1 should eliminate most of the possible choices, leaving only a few formula calculations to be done.)

Example: Which of the following is the greatest in length?

(A) The perimeter of a square with a side of 4 inches.
(B) The perimeter of an isosceles right triangle whose equal sides are 8 inches each.
(C) The circumference of a circle with a diameter of $4\sqrt{2}$ inches.
(D) The perimeter of a pentagon whose sides are all equal to 3 inches.
(E) The perimeter of a semicircle with a radius of 5 inches.

Solution: Diagramming the five figures mentioned, we obtain the following illustration:

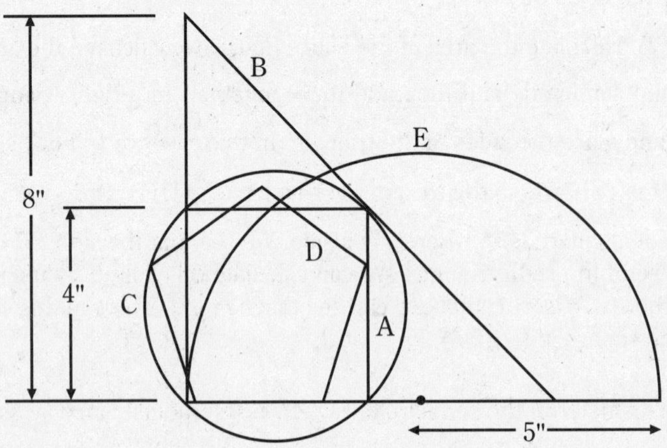

From the diagram, it is apparent that the square and the pentagon are both smaller than the circle. Further observation should show that the circle is smaller than the triangle. Thus we need only to see which is larger—the semicircle or the triangle. The perimeter of the semicircle is found by the formula: $P = 2r + \pi r$ (the sum of the diameter and the semicircular arc, where r is the radius). Since r in this case is 5 inches, the perimeter is approximately $10 + (3.14)5$, or 25.7 inches. The formula for the perimeter of a triangle is the sum of the sides. In this case, two of the sides are 8 inches and the third side can be found by using the relationship $c^2 = a^2 + b^2$, where a and b are the sides of a right triangle, and c is the hypotenuse. Since in our problem $a = b = 8$ inches, $c = \sqrt{8^2 + 8^2} = \sqrt{128} = \sqrt{2(64)} = 8\sqrt{2}$, which is the third side of the triangle. The perimeter is $8 + 8 + 8\sqrt{2}$, which is $16 + 8\sqrt{2}$. This is approximately equal to $16 + 8(1.4)$, or 27.2, so the triangle is the largest of the figures.

FORMULAS USED IN AREA, PERIMETER, AND VOLUME PROBLEMS

It is important that you know as many of these formulas as possible. Problems using these formulas appear frequently on tests of all kinds. You should not need to refer to the tables that follow when you do problems. Learn these formulas before you go any further.

303. *Square.* The area of a square is the square of one of its sides. Thus, if A represents the area, and s represents the length of a side, $A = s^2$. The area of a square is also one-half of the square of its diagonal and may be written as $A = \frac{1}{2}d^2$, where d represents the length of a diagonal. The perimeter of a square is 4 times the length of one of its sides, or $4s$.

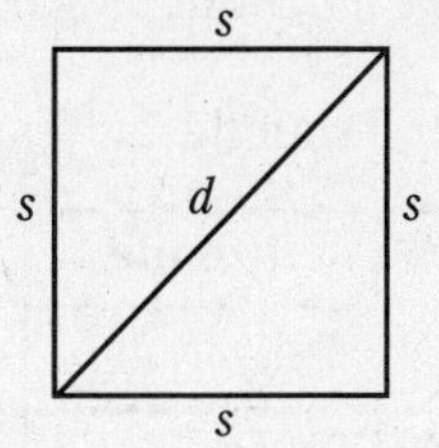

Square

quantity	formula
area	$A = s^2$ $A = \frac{1}{2}d^2$
perimeter	$P = 4s$

304. *Rectangle.* Let a and b represent the length of two adjacent sides of a rectangle, and let A represent the area. Then the area of a rectangle is the product of the two adjacent sides: $A = ab$. The perimeter, P, is the sum of twice one side and twice the adjacent side: $P = 2a + 2b$.

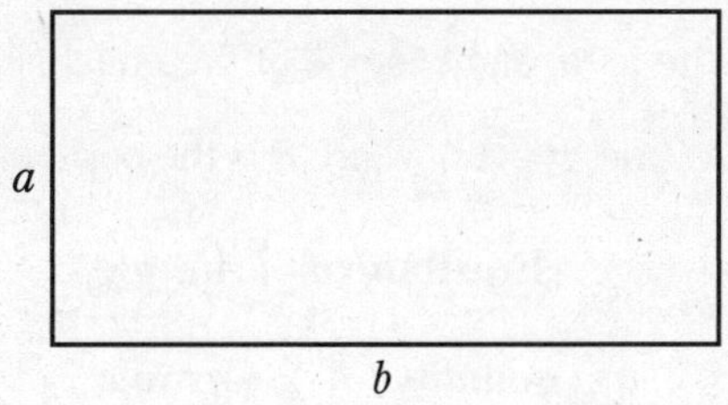

Rectangle

quantity	formula
area	$A = ab$
perimeter	$P = 2a + 2b$

305. *Parallelogram.* The area of a parallelogram is the product of a side and the altitude, h, to that side. $A = bh$ (in this case the altitude to side b). The area can also be expressed as the product of two adjacent sides and the sine of the included angle: $A = ab \sin c$, where c is the angle included between side a and side b. The perimeter is the sum of twice one side and twice the adjacent side. $P = 2a + 2b$. Let a and b represent the length of 2 adjacent sides of a parallelogram. Then, c is the included angle. But A represents its area, P its perimeter, and h the altitude to one of its sides.

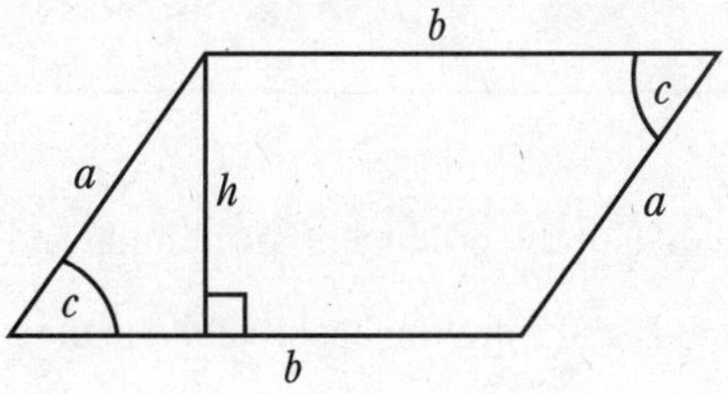

Parallelogram

quantity	formula
area	$A = bh$ $A = ab \sin c$
perimeter	$P = 2a + 2b$

306. *Triangle.* The area of any triangle is one-half of the product of any side and the altitude to that side. $A = \frac{1}{2}bh$, where b is a side, and h the altitude to that side. The area may be written also as one-half of the product of any two adjacent sides and the sine of the included angle. $A = \frac{1}{2}ab \sin c$, where A is the area, a and b are two adjacent sides, and c is the included angle. The perimeter of a triangle is the sum of the sides of the triangle. $P = a + b + c$, where P is the perimeter, and c is the third side.

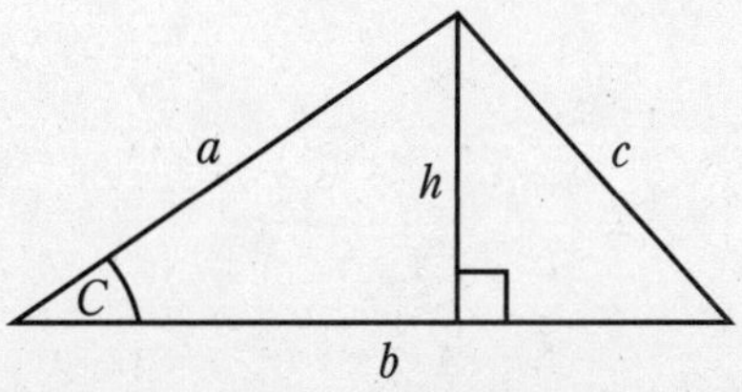

Triangle

quantity	formula
area	$A = \frac{1}{2}bh$ $A = \frac{1}{2}ab \sin c$
perimeter	$P = a + b + c$

307. *Right triangle.* The area of a right triangle is one-half of the product of the two sides adjacent to the right angle. $A = \frac{1}{2}ab$, where A is the area, and a and b are the adjacent sides. The perimeter is the sum of the sides. $P = a + b + c$, where c is the third side, or hypotenuse.

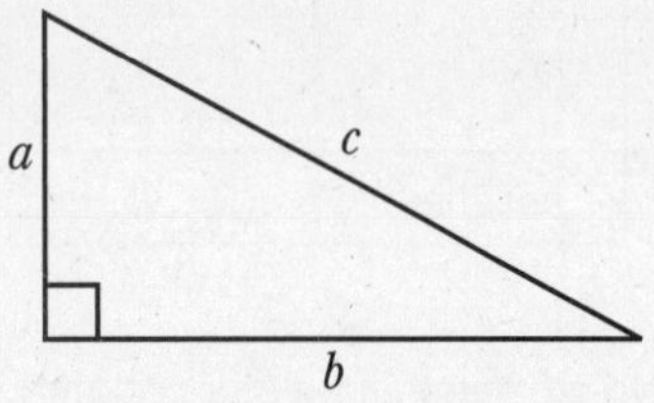

Right Triangle

quantity	formula
area	$A = \frac{1}{2}ab$
perimeter	$P = a + b + c$
hypotenuse	$c^2 = a^2 + b^2$

308. *Equilateral triangle.* The area of an equilateral triangle is one-fourth the product of a side squared and $\sqrt{3}$. $A = \frac{1}{4}s^2\sqrt{3}$, where A is the area, and s is one of the equal sides. The perimeter of an equilateral triangle is 3 times one side. $P = 3s$, where P is the perimeter.

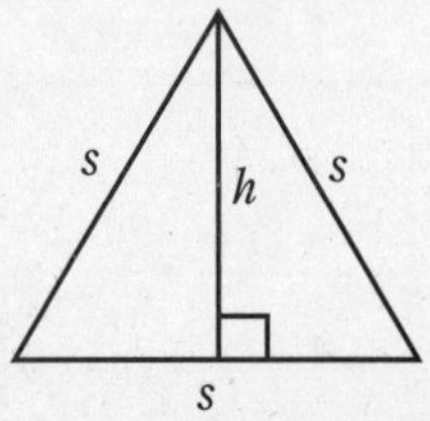

Equilateral Triangle

quantity	formula
area	$A = \frac{1}{4}s^2\sqrt{3}$
perimeter	$P = 3s$
altitude	$h = \frac{1}{2}s\sqrt{3}$

NOTE: The equilateral triangle and the right triangle are special cases of the triangle, and any law that applies to the triangle applies to both the right triangle and the equilateral triangle.

309. *Trapezoid.* The area of a trapezoid is one-half of the product of the altitude and the sum of the bases. $A = \frac{1}{2}h(B + b)$, where A is the area, B and b are the bases, and h is their altitude. The perimeter is the sum of the 4 sides. $P = B + b + c + d$, where P is the perimeter, and c and d are the other 2 sides.

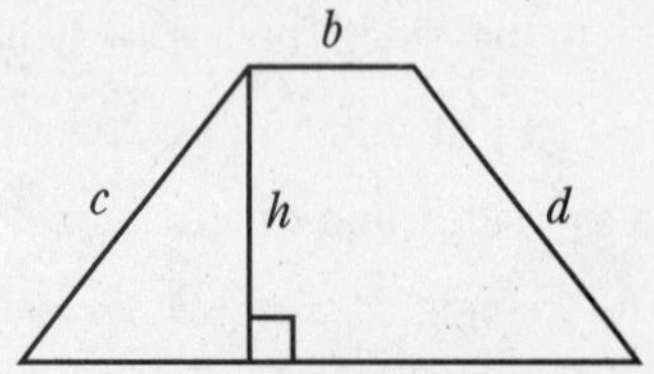

Trapezoid

quantity	formula
area	$A = \frac{1}{2}h(B + b)$
perimeter	$P = B + b + c + d$

310. *Circle.* The area of a circle is π (pi) times the square of the radius. $A = \pi r^2$, where A is the area, and r is the radius. The circumference is pi times the diameter, or pi times twice the radius. $C = \pi d = 2\pi r$, where C is the circumference, d the diameter, and r the radius.

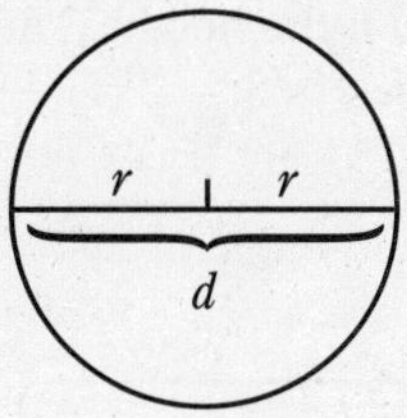

Circle

quantity	formula
area	$A = \pi r^2$
circumference	$C = \pi d = 2\pi r$

311. *Semicircle.* The area of a semicircle is one-half pi times the square of the radius.

$A = \frac{1}{2}\pi r^2$, where A is the area, and r is the radius. The length of the curved portion of the semicircle is one-half pi times the diameter or pi times the radius. $C = \frac{1}{2}\pi d = \pi r$, where C is the circumference, d is the diameter, and r is the radius. The perimeter of a semicircle is equal to the circumference plus the length of the diameter. $P = C + d = \frac{1}{2}\pi d + d$, where P is the perimeter.

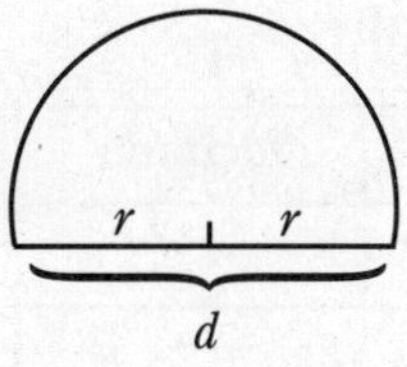

Semicircle

quantity	formula
area	$A = \frac{1}{2}\pi r^2$
circumference	$C = \frac{1}{2}\pi d = \pi r$
perimeter	$P = d\left(\frac{1}{2}\pi + 1\right)$

312. *Rectangular solid.* The volume of a rectangular solid is the product of the length, width, and height. $V = lwh$, where V is the volume, l is the length, w is the width, and h is the height. The volume is also the product of the area of one side and the altitude to that side. $V = Bh$, where B is the area of its base and h the altitude to that side. The surface area is the sum of the area of the six faces. $S = 2wh + 2hl + 2wl$, where S is the surface area.

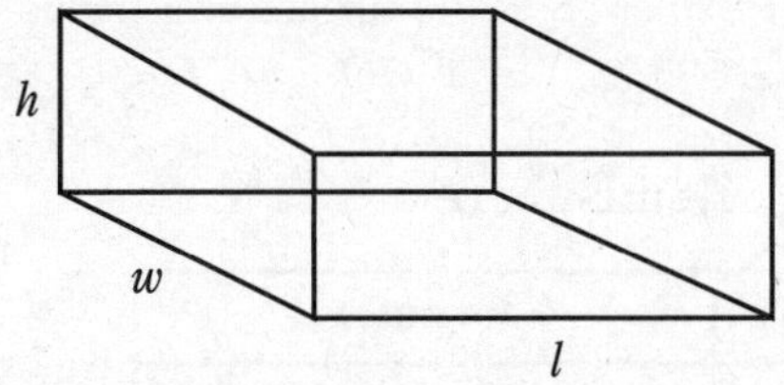

Rectangular Solid

quantity	formula
volume	$V = lwh$ $V = Bh$
surface area	$S = 2wh + 2hl + 2wl$

313. *Cube.* The volume of a cube is its edge cubed. $V = e^3$, where V is the volume and e is an edge. The surface area is the sum of the areas of the six faces. $S = 6e^2$, where S is the surface area.

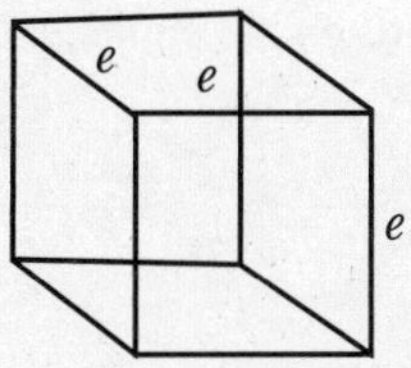

Cube

quantity	formula
volume	$V = e^3$
surface area	$S = 6e^2$

314. *Cylinder.* The volume of a cylinder is the area of the base times the height. $V = Bh$, where V is the volume, B is the area of the base, and h is the height. Note that the area of the base is the area of the circle $= \pi r^2$, where r is the radius of a base. The surface area not including the bases is the circumference of the base times the height. $S_1 = Ch = 2\pi rh$, where S_1 is the surface area without the bases, C the circumference, and h the height. The area of the bases $= 2\pi r^2$. Thus, the area of the cylinder, including the bases, is $S_2 = 2\pi rh + 2\pi r^2 = 2\pi r(h + r)$.

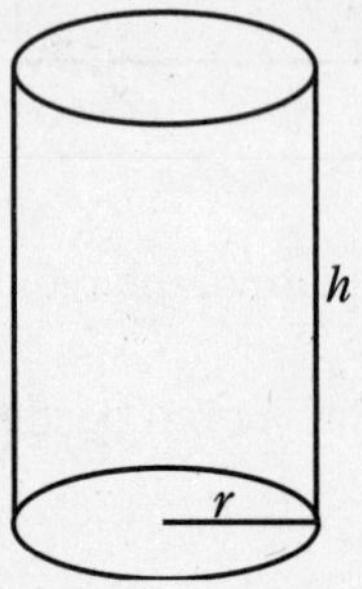

Cylinder

quantity	formula
volume	$V = Bh$ $V = \pi r^2 h$
surface area	$S_1 = 2\pi rh$ (without bases) $S_2 = 2\pi r\,(h + r)$ (with bases)

315. *Sphere.* The volume of a sphere is four-thirds π times the cube of the radius. $V = \frac{4}{3}\pi r^3$, where V is the volume and r is the radius. The surface area is 4π times the square of the radius. $S = 4\pi r^2$, where S is the surface area.

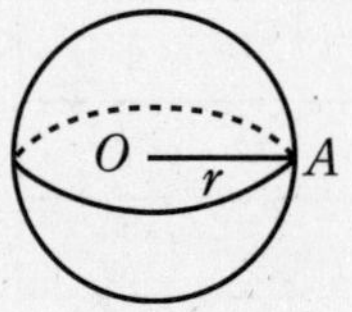

Sphere

quantity	formula
volume	$V = \frac{4}{3}\pi r^3$
surface area	$S = 4\pi r^2$

316. *Hemisphere.* The volume of a hemisphere is two-thirds π times the cube of the radius. $V = \frac{2}{3}\pi r^3$, where V is the volume and r is the radius. The surface area not including the area of the base is 2π times the square of the radius. $S_1 = 2\pi r^2$, where S_1 is the surface area without the base. The total surface area, including the base, is equal to the surface area without the base plus the area of the base. $S_2 = 2\pi r^2 + \pi r^2 = 3\pi r^2$, where S_2 is the surface area including the base.

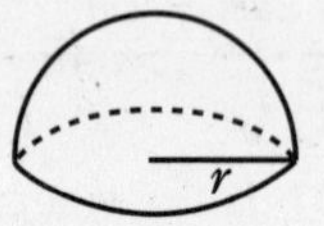

Hemisphere

quantity	formula
volume	$V = \frac{2}{3}\pi r^3$
surface area	$S_1 = 2\pi r^2$ (without base) $S_2 = 3\pi r^2$ (with base)

317. *Pythagorean Theorem.* The Pythagorean Theorem states a very important geometrical relationship. It states that in a right triangle, if c is the hypotenuse (the side opposite the right angle), and a and b are the sides adjacent to the right angle, then $c^2 = a^2 + b^2$.

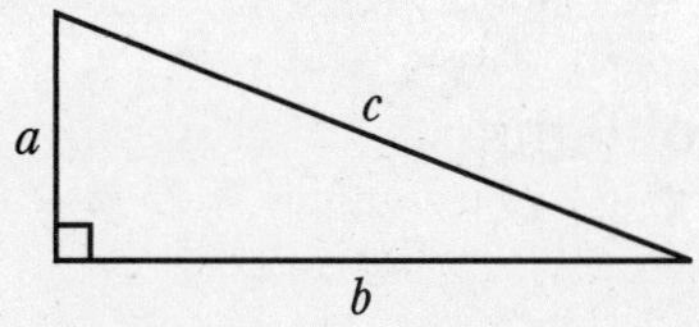

Pythagorean Theorem

quantity	formula
square of hypotenuse	$c^2 = a^2 + b^2$
length of hypotenuse	$c = \sqrt{a^2 + b^2}$

Examples of right triangles are triangles with sides of 3, 4, and 5, or 5, 12, and 13. Any multiples of these numbers also form right triangles—for example, 6, 8, and 10, or 30, 40, and 50.

Using the Pythagorean Theorem to find the diagonal of a square, we get $d^2 = s^2 + s^2$ or $d^2 = 2s^2$, where d is the diagonal and s is a side. Therefore, $d = s\sqrt{2}$, or the diagonal of a square is $\sqrt{2}$ times the side.

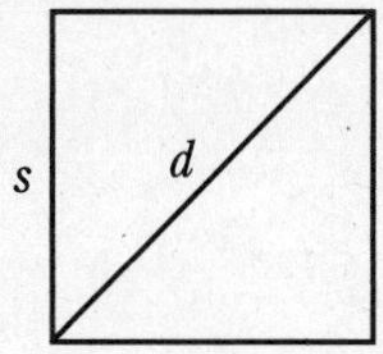

Square

quantity	formula
diagonal	$d = s\sqrt{2}$

318. Another important fact to remember in doing area problems is that areas of two similar (having the same shape) figures are in the same ratio as the squares of corresponding parts of the figures.

Example: Triangles P and Q are similar. Side p of triangle P is 2 inches, the area of triangle P is 3 square inches, and corresponding side q of triangle Q is 4 inches. What is the area of triangle Q?

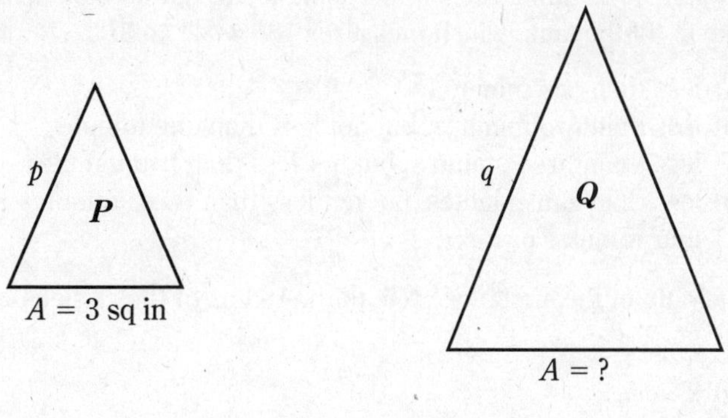

Solution: The square of side p is to the square of side q as the area of P is to the area of Q. If we call x the area of triangle Q, then we get the following relationship: The square of side p is to the square of side q as the area of P is to the area of Q, or

$$\frac{2^2}{4^2} = \frac{3}{x} \text{ or } \frac{4}{16} = \frac{3}{x}$$

Therefore, $x = 12$ square inches.

Practice Test 3

Area, Perimeter, and Volume Problems

Correct answers and solutions follow each test.

1. A B C D E

1. Which of the following figures has the largest area?

(A) a square with a perimeter of 12 inches
(B) a circle with a radius of 3 inches
(C) a right triangle with sides of 3, 4, and 5 inches
(D) a rectangle with a diagonal of 5 inches and sides of 3 and 4 inches
(E) a regular hexagon with a perimeter of 18 inches

2. A B C D E

2. If the area of the base of a rectangular solid is tripled, what is the percent increase in its volume?

(A) 200%
(B) 300%
(C) 600%
(D) 800%
(E) 900%

3. A B C D E

3. How many yards of a carpeting that is 26 inches wide will be needed to cover a floor that is 12 feet by 13 feet?

(A) 22 yards
(B) 24 yards
(C) 27 yards
(D) 36 yards
(E) 46 yards

4. A B C D E

4. If water flows into a rectangular tank at the rate of 6 cubic feet per minute, how long will it take to fill the tank, which measures 18" × 32" × 27"?

(A) less than one minute
(B) less than two minutes, but not less than one minute
(C) less than three minutes, but not less than two minutes
(D) less than four minutes, but not less than three minutes
(E) four minutes or more

5. A B C D E

5. The ratio of the area of a circle to the radius of the circle is

(A) π
(B) 2π
(C) π^2
(D) $4\pi^2$
(E) not determinable

6. A B C D E

6. Which of the following figures has the smallest perimeter or circumference?

(A) a circle with a diameter of 2 feet
(B) a square with a diagonal of 2 feet
(C) a rectangle with sides of 6 inches and 4 feet
(D) a pentagon with each side equal to 16 inches
(E) a hexagon with each side equal to 14 inches

7. A B C D E

7. In the figure shown, DE is parallel to BC. If the area of triangle ADE is half that of trapezoid $DECB$, what is the ratio of AE to AC?

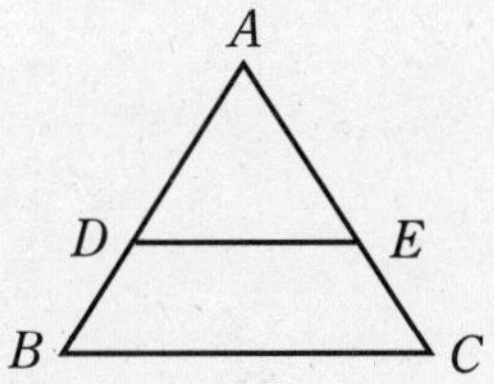

(A) $1:2$
(B) $1:\sqrt{2}$
(C) $1:3$
(D) $1:\sqrt{3}$
(E) $1:\sqrt{3}-1$

8. A B C D E

8. At a speed of 22 revolutions per minute, how long will it take a wheel of radius 10 inches, rolling on its edge, to travel 10 feet? (Assume π equals $\frac{22}{7}$, and express answer to nearest 0.1 second.)

(A) 0.2 seconds
(B) 0.4 seconds
(C) 5.2 seconds
(D) 6.3 seconds
(E) 7.4 seconds

9. A B C D E

9. If the diagonal of a square is 16 inches long, what is the area of the square?

(A) 64 square inches
(B) $64\sqrt{2}$ square inches
(C) 128 square inches
(D) $128\sqrt{2}$ square inches
(E) 256 square inches

10. A B C D E

10. In the diagram shown, $ACDF$ is a rectangle, and $GBHE$ is a circle. If $CD = 4$ inches, and $AC = 6$ inches, what is the number of square inches in the shaded area?

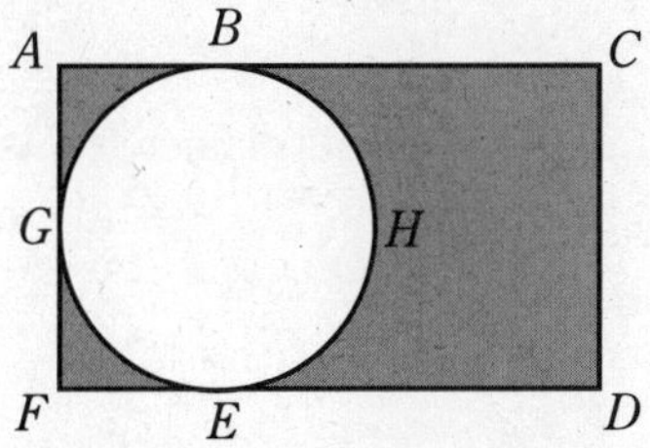

(A) $16 - 4\pi$ square inches
(B) $24 - 4\pi$ square inches
(C) $24 - 16\pi$ square inches
(D) $16 - 2\pi$ square inches
(E) $24 - 2\pi$ square inches

11. A B C D E

11. What is the area of an equilateral triangle with a side of 1 inch?

(A) 1 square inch
(B) $\frac{\sqrt{3}}{2}$ square inch
(C) $\frac{1}{2}$ square inch
(D) $\frac{\sqrt{3}}{4}$ square inch
(E) $\frac{1}{3}$ square inch

12. A B C D E

12. The measurements of a rectangle are 12 feet by 16 feet. What is the area of the smallest *circle* that can cover this rectangle entirely (so that no part of the rectangle is outside the circle)?

(A) 192 square feet
(B) 384 square feet
(C) 100π square feet
(D) 128π square feet
(E) 400π square feet

13. A B C D E

13. A man wishes to cover his floor with tiles, each one measuring $\frac{3}{4}$ inch by 2 inches. If his room is a rectangle, measuring 12 feet by 18 feet, how many such tiles will he need?

(A) 144
(B) 1,152
(C) 1,728
(D) 9,216
(E) 20,736

14. A B C D E

14. The volume of a sphere is equal to the volume of a cylinder. If the radius of the sphere is 4 meters and the radius of the cylinder is 8 meters, what is the height of the cylinder?

(A) 8 meters
(B) $\frac{4}{3}$ meters
(C) 4 meters
(D) $\frac{16}{3}$ meters
(E) 1 meter

15. A B C D E

15. A wheel travels 33 yards in 15 revolutions. What is its diameter? (Assume $\pi = \frac{22}{7}$.)

(A) 0.35 feet
(B) 0.70 feet
(C) 1.05 feet
(D) 1.40 feet
(E) 2.10 feet

16. A B C D E

16. If a rectangle with a perimeter of 48 inches is equal in area to a right triangle with legs of 12 inches and 24 inches, what is the rectangle's diagonal?

(A) 12 inches
(B) $12\sqrt{2}$ inches
(C) $12\sqrt{3}$ inches
(D) 24 inches
(E) The answer cannot be determined from the given information.

17. A B C D E

17. What is the approximate area that remains after a circle $3\frac{1}{2}''$ in diameter is cut from a square piece of cloth with a side of 8″? (Use $\pi = \frac{22}{7}$.)

(A) 25.5 square inches
(B) 54.4 square inches
(C) 56.8 square inches
(D) 142.1 square inches
(E) 284.2 square inches

18. A B C D E

18. A container is shaped like a rectangular solid with sides of 3 inches, 3 inches, and 11 inches. What is its approximate capacity, if 1 gallon equals 231 cubic inches? (1 gallon = 128 fluid ounces.)

(A) 14 ounces
(B) 27 ounces
(C) 55 ounces
(D) 110 ounces
(E) 219 ounces

19. A B C D E

19. The 20-inch-diameter wheels of one car travel at a rate of 24 revolutions per minute, while the 30-inch-diameter wheels of a second car travel at a rate of 18 revolutions per minute. What is the ratio of the speed of the second car to that of the first?

(A) 1 : 1
(B) 3 : 2
(C) 4 : 3
(D) 6 : 5
(E) 9 : 8

20. A B C D E

20. A circular garden twenty feet in diameter is surrounded by a path three feet wide. What is the area of the path?

(A) 9π square feet
(B) 51π square feet
(C) 60π square feet
(D) 69π square feet
(E) 90π square feet

21. A B C D E

21. What is the area of a semicircle with a diameter of 16 inches?

(A) 32π square inches
(B) 64π square inches
(C) 128π square inches
(D) 256π square inches
(E) 512π square inches

22. A B C D E

22. If the edges of a cube add up to 4 feet in length, what is the volume of the cube?

(A) 64 cubic inches
(B) 125 cubic inches
(C) 216 cubic inches
(D) 512 cubic inches
(E) None of these.

23. A B C D E

23. The inside of a trough is shaped like a rectangular solid, 25 feet long, 6 inches wide, and filled with water to a depth of 35 inches. If we wish to raise the depth of the water to 38 inches, how much water must be let into the tank?

(A) $\frac{25}{96}$ cubic feet
(B) $\frac{25}{8}$ cubic feet
(C) $\frac{75}{2}$ cubic feet
(D) 225 cubic feet
(E) 450 cubic feet

24. A B C D E

24. If 1 gallon of water equals 231 cubic inches, approximately how much water will fill a cylindrical vase 7 inches in diameter and 10 inches high? (Assume $\pi = \frac{22}{7}$.)

(A) 1.7 gallons
(B) 2.1 gallons
(C) 3.3 gallons
(D) 5.3 gallons
(E) 6.7 gallons

25. A B C D E

25. Tiles of linoleum, measuring 8 inches × 8 inches, cost 9¢ apiece. At this rate, what will it cost a man to cover a floor with these tiles, if his floor measures 10 feet by 16 feet?

(A) $22.50
(B) $25.00
(C) $28.00
(D) $32.40
(E) $36.00

26. A B C D E

26. Which of the following figures has the largest area?

(A) a 3–4–5 triangle with a hypotenuse of 25 inches
(B) a circle with a diameter of 20 inches
(C) a square with a 20-inch diagonal
(D) a regular hexagon with a side equal to 10 inches
(E) a rectangle with sides of 10 inches and 30 inches

27. A B C D E

27. If the radius of the base of a cylinder is tripled, and its height is divided by three, what is the ratio of the volume of the new cylinder to the volume of the original cylinder?

(A) 1 : 9
(B) 1 : 3
(C) 1 : 1
(D) 3 : 1
(E) 9 : 1

28. A B C D E

28. If 1 cubic foot of water equals 7.5 gallons, how long will it take for a faucet that flows at a rate of 10 gal/min to fill a cube 2 feet on each side (to the nearest minute)?

(A) 4 minutes
(B) 5 minutes
(C) 6 minutes
(D) 7 minutes
(E) 8 minutes

29. A B C D E

29. The ratio of the area of a square to the *square of its diagonal* is which of the following?

(A) 2 : 1
(B) $\sqrt{2} : 1$
(C) 1 : 1
(D) $1 : \sqrt{2}$
(E) 1 : 2

30. A B C D E

30. If $ABCD$ is a square, with side $AB = 4$ inches, and AEB and CED are semicircles, what is the area of the shaded portion of the diagram below?

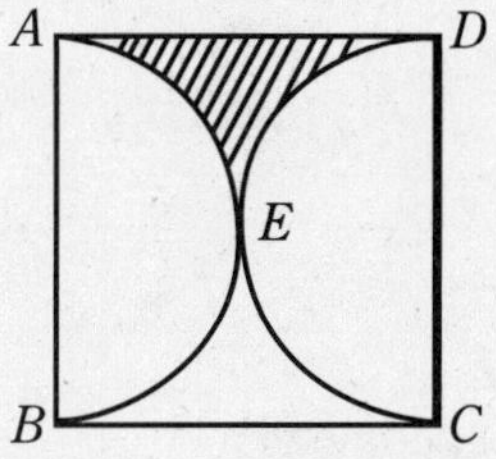

(A) $8 - \pi$ square inches
(B) $8 - 2\pi$ square inches
(C) $16 - 2\pi$ square inches
(D) $16 - 4\pi$ square inches
(E) $16 - 8\pi$ square inches

31. A B C D E

31. If the area of a circle is equal to the area of a rectangle, one of whose sides is equal to π, express the other side of the rectangle, x, in terms of the radius of the circle, r.

(A) $x = r$

(B) $x = \pi r$

(C) $x = r^2$

(D) $x = \sqrt{r}$

(E) $x = \frac{1}{r}$

32. A B C D E

32. If the volume of a cube is 27 cubic meters, find the surface area of the cube.

(A) 9 square meters
(B) 18 square meters
(C) 54 square meters
(D) 3 square meters
(E) 1 square meter

33. A B C D E

33. What is the area of a regular hexagon one of whose sides is 1 inch?

(A) $\frac{3\sqrt{3}}{4}$
(B) $\sqrt{3}$
(C) $\frac{3\sqrt{3}}{2}$
(D) 3
(E) 6

34. A B C D E

34. What is the area of the triangle pictured below?

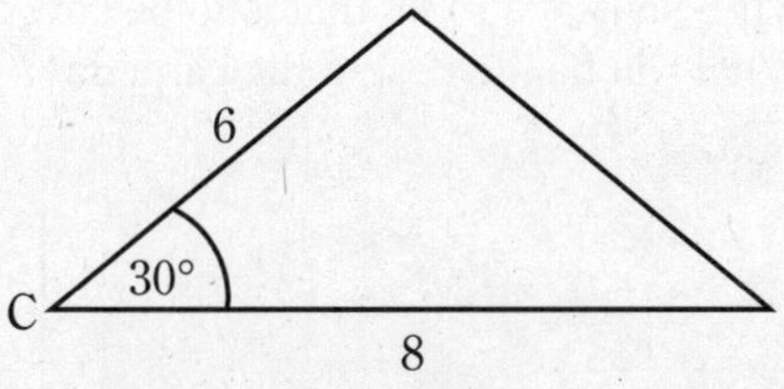

(A) 18 square units
(B) 32 square units
(C) 24 square units
(D) 12 square units
(E) 124 square units

35. A B C D E

35. If a wheel travels 1 mile in 1 minute, at a rate of 600 revolutions per minute, what is the diameter of the wheel, in feet? (Use $\pi = \frac{22}{7}$.)

(A) 2.2 feet
(B) 2.4 feet
(C) 2.6 feet
(D) 2.8 feet
(E) 3.0 feet

36. A B C D E

36. Which of the following figures has the largest perimeter?

(A) a square with a diagonal of 5 feet
(B) a rectangle with sides of 3 feet and 4 feet
(C) an equilateral triangle with a side equal to 48 inches
(D) a regular hexagon whose longest diagonal is 6 feet
(E) a parallelogram with sides of 6 inches and 7 feet

37. A B C D E

37. A man has two containers: The first is a rectangular solid, measuring 3 inches × 4 inches × 10 inches; the second is a cylinder having a base with a radius of 2 inches and a height of 10 inches. If the first container is filled with water, and then this water is poured into the second container, which of the following occurs?

(A) There is room for more water in the second container.
(B) The second container is completely filled, without overflowing.
(C) The second container overflows by less than 1 cubic inch.
(D) The second container overflows by less than 2 (but not less than 1) cubic inches.
(E) The second container overflows by 2 or more cubic inches.

38. A B C D E

38. If, in this diagram, A represents a square with a side of 4″, and B, C, D, and E are semicircles, what is the area of the entire figure?

(A) $16 + 4\pi$ square inches
(B) $16 + 8\pi$ square inches
(C) $16 + 16\pi$ square inches
(D) $16 + 32\pi$ square inches
(E) $16 + 64\pi$ square inches

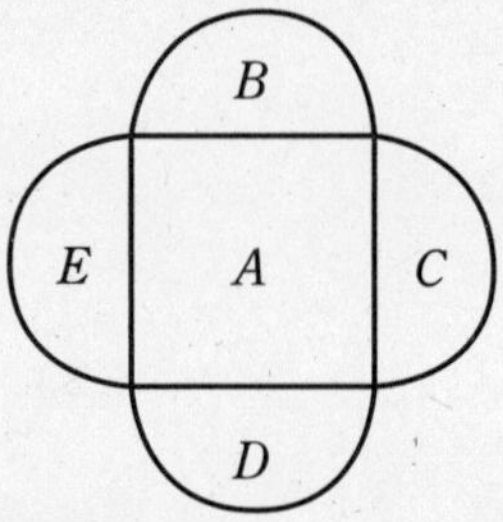

39. A B C D E

39. The area of a square is $81p^2$. What is the length of the square's diagonal?

(A) $9p$
(B) $9p\sqrt{2}$
(C) $18p$
(D) $9p^2$
(E) $18p^2$

40. A B C D E

40. The following diagram represents the floor of a room that is to be covered with carpeting at a price of $2.50 per square yard. What will be the cost of the carpeting?

(A) $70
(B) $125
(C) $480
(D) $630
(E) None of these.

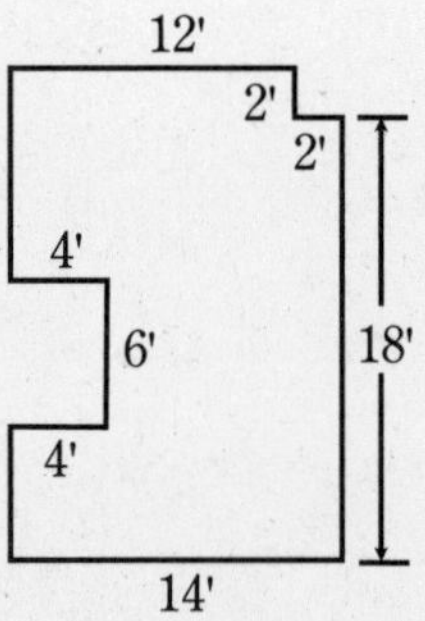

41. A B C D E

41. Which of the following has the largest perimeter?

(A) a square with a diagonal of 10 inches
(B) a 3–4–5 right triangle with a hypotenuse of 15 inches
(C) a pentagon, each of whose sides is 5 inches
(D) a right isosceles triangle with an area of 72 square inches
(E) a regular hexagon with a radius of 5 inches

42. A B C D E

42. If you double the area of the base of a rectangular solid, and also triple the solid's height, what is the ratio of the new volume to the old volume?

(A) 2 : 3
(B) 3 : 2
(C) 1 : 6
(D) 6 : 1
(E) None of these.

43. A B C D E

43. A certain type of linoleum costs $1.50 per square yard. If a room measures 27 feet by 14 feet, what will be the cost of covering it with linoleum?

(A) $44.10
(B) $51.60
(C) $63.00
(D) $132.30
(E) $189.00

44. A B C D E

44. How many circles, each with a 4-inch radius, can be cut from a rectangular sheet of paper, measuring 16 inches $\times$ 24 inches?

(A) 6
(B) 7
(C) 8
(D) 12
(E) 24

45. A B C D E

45. The ratio of the area of an equilateral triangle, in square inches, to its perimeter, in inches, is

(A) 3 : 4
(B) 4 : 3
(C) $\sqrt{3} : 4$
(D) $4 : \sqrt{3}$
(E) The answer cannot be determined from the given information.

46. A B C D E

46. What is the volume of a cylinder whose radius is 4 inches, and whose height is 10 inches? (Assume that $\pi = 3.14$.)

(A) 125.6 cubic inches
(B) 134.4 cubic inches
(C) 144.0 cubic inches
(D) 201.2 cubic inches
(E) 502.4 cubic inches

47. A B C D E

47. The area of a square is $144s^2$. What is the square's diagonal?

(A) $12s$
(B) $12s\sqrt{2}$
(C) $24s$
(D) $144s$
(E) $144s^2$

48. A B C D E

48. A circular pool is ten feet in diameter and five feet deep. What is its volume, in cubic feet?

(A) 50 cubic feet
(B) 50π cubic feet
(C) 125π cubic feet
(D) 250π cubic feet
(E) 500π cubic feet

49. A B C D E

49. A certain type of carpeting is 30 inches wide. How many yards of this carpet will be needed to cover a floor that measures 20 feet by 24 feet?

(A) 48
(B) 64
(C) 144
(D) 192
(E) None of these.

50. A B C D E

50. Two wheels have diameters of 12 inches and 18 inches, respectively. Both wheels roll along parallel straight lines at the same linear speed until the large wheel has revolved 72 times. At this point, how many times has the small wheel revolved?

(A) 32
(B) 48
(C) 72
(D) 108
(E) 162

Answer Key for Practice Test 3

1. B	**14.** B	**27.** D	**39.** B
2. A	**15.** E	**28.** C	**40.** A
3. B	**16.** B	**29.** E	**41.** D
4. B	**17.** B	**30.** B	**42.** D
5. E	**18.** C	**31.** C	**43.** C
6. B	**19.** E	**32.** C	**44.** A
7. D	**20.** D	**33.** C	**45.** E
8. C	**21.** A	**34.** D	**46.** E
9. C	**22.** A	**35.** D	**47.** B
10. B	**23.** B	**36.** D	**48.** C
11. D	**24.** A	**37.** A	**49.** B
12. C	**25.** D	**38.** B	**50.** D
13. E	**26.** B		

Answers and Solutions for Practice Test 3

1. Choice B is correct. This is a fairly difficult comparison problem, but the use of diagrams simplifies it considerably.

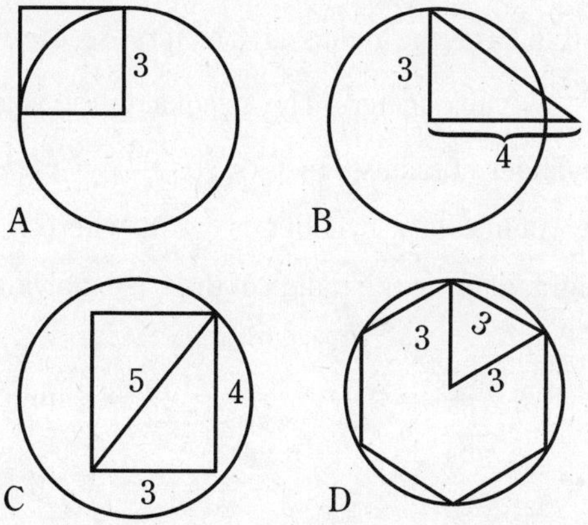

From diagram A it is apparent that the circle is larger than the square. Diagram B shows that the circle is larger than the right triangle. And, since a rectangle with a diagonal of 5 inches is made up of two right triangles, as shown in diagram C, the circle is larger than the rectangle. Finally, as shown in diagram D, the circle is larger than the hexagon. Thus, the circle is the largest of the five figures described. (302)

2. Choice A is correct. This is a formula problem: letting V_o represent the original volume, B_o represent the original area of the base, and h_o represent the original height of the figure, we have the formula $V_o = h_oB_o$. The new volume, V, is equal to $3h_oB_o$. Thus, the new volume is three times the original volume—an *increase* of 200%. (301)

3. Choice B is correct. Here, we must find the length of carpeting needed to cover an area of $12' \times 13'$, or 156 square feet. The formula needed is: $A = lw$, where l = length and w = width, both expressed in *feet.* Now, since we know that A = 156 square feet, and w = 26 inches, or $\frac{26}{12}$ feet, we can calculate l as $156 \div \left(\frac{26}{12}\right)$, or 72 feet. But since the answer must be expressed in yards, we express 72 feet as 24 yards. (304)

4. Choice B is correct. First we must calculate the volume of the tank in cubic feet. Converting the dimensions of the box to feet, we get $1\frac{1}{2}$ feet $\times$ $2\frac{2}{3}$ feet $\times$ $2\frac{1}{4}$ feet, so the total volume is $\frac{3}{2} \times \frac{8}{3} \times \frac{9}{4}$, or 9, cubic feet. Thus, at a rate of 6 cubic feet per minute, it would take $\frac{9}{6}$, or $1\frac{1}{2}$, minutes to fill the tank. (312, 201)

5. Choice E is correct. Here, we use the formula $A = \pi r^2$, where A = area, and r = radius. Thus, the ratio of A to r is just $\frac{A}{r} = \pi r$. Since r is not a constant, the ratio cannot be determined. (310)

6. Choice B is correct. First, we diagram the circle and the square and see that the square has a smaller perimeter. Next, we notice that the circle, which has a larger circumference than the square, has circumference 2π, or about 6.3 feet. But the perimeters of the rectangle (9 feet), of the pentagon (5×16 inches = 80 inches = 6 feet, 8 inches), and of the hexagon (6×14 inches = 84 inches = 7 feet) are all greater than the circumference of the circle, and therefore also greater than the perimeter of the square. Thus, the square has the smallest perimeter. (302)

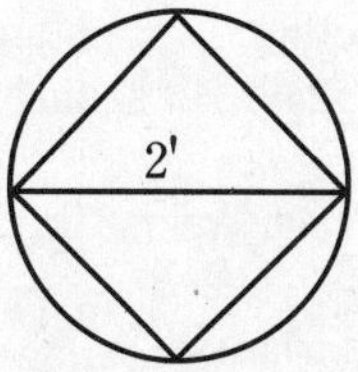

7. Choice D is correct. The formula involved here is $A_1 : A_2 = s_1^{\ 2} : s_2^{\ 2}$, where A_1 represents the area of the triangle with one side of length s_1, and A_2 represents the area of the triangle corresponding to s_2. If we let s_1 represent AE, and s_2 represent AC, so that A_1 is the area of ADE and A_2 is the area of ABC, then we have the resulting formula $\frac{AE}{AC} = \frac{S_1}{S_2} = \sqrt{\frac{A_1}{A_2}}$.

The area of the trapezoid $DECB$ is twice the area of ADE, or $2A_1$, so the area of ABC is equal to the sum of the area of ADE and $DECB$, which equal A_1 and

$2A_1$, respectively; thus, the area of ABC is $3A_1$. So, $A_1 : A_2 = 1 : 3$. Thus, $s_1 : s_2 = \sqrt{\frac{1}{3}} = 1 : \sqrt{3}$. (318)

8. Choice C is correct. Since the radius of the circle is 10 inches, its circumference is $2\pi(10 \text{ inches})$, or $2\left(\frac{22}{7}\right)(10 \text{ inches})$, which equals $\frac{440}{7}$ inches. This is the distance the wheel will travel in one revolution. To travel 10 feet, or 120 inches, it must travel $120 \div \frac{440}{7}$, or $\frac{21}{11}$ revolutions. At a speed of 22 revolutions per minute, or $\frac{11}{30}$ revolutions per second, it will take $\frac{21}{11} \div \frac{11}{30}$, or $\frac{630}{121}$ seconds. Carrying the division to the nearest tenth of a second, we get 5.2 seconds. (310)

9. Choice C is correct. If we let d represent the diagonal of a square, s represent the length of one side, and A represent the area, then we have two formulas: $d = s\sqrt{2}$, and $A = s^2$, relating the three quantities. However, from the first equation, we can see that $s^2 = \frac{d^2}{2}$, so we can derive a third formula, $A = \frac{d^2}{2}$, relating A and d. We are given that d equals 16″, so we can calculate the value of A as $\frac{(16 \text{ inches})^2}{2}$, or 128 square inches. (303)

10. Choice B is correct. The area of the shaded figure is equal to the difference between the areas of the rectangle and the circle. The area of the rectangle is defined by the formula $A = bh$, where b and h are the two adjacent sides of the rectangle. In this case, A is equal to 4 inches × 6 inches, or 24 square inches. The area of the circle is defined by the formula $A = \pi r^2$, where r is the radius. Since BE equals the diameter of the circle and is equal to 4 inches, then the radius must be 2 inches. Thus, the area of the circle is $\pi(2 \text{ inches})^2$, or 4π square inches. Subtracting, we obtain the area of the shaded portion: $24 - 4\pi$ square inches. (304, 310)

11. Choice D is correct. We use the formula for the area of an equilateral triangle, $\frac{\sqrt{3}s^2}{4}$, where s is a side. If $s = 1$, then the area of the triangle is $\frac{\sqrt{3}}{4}$. (308)

12. Choice C is correct. An angle, which is inscribed in a circle, whose sides cut off an arc of 180° (that is, it intersects the ends of a diameter) is a right angle. According to the Pythagorean Theorem, the diameter AC, being the hypotenuse of a triangle with sides of 12 feet and 16 feet, has a length of $\sqrt{12^2 + 16^2} = \sqrt{400} = 20$ feet. Therefore, if we call d the diameter, the area of the circle is $A = \pi\left(\frac{d}{2}\right)^2 = \pi\left(\frac{20}{2}\right)^2 = 100\pi$ square feet.

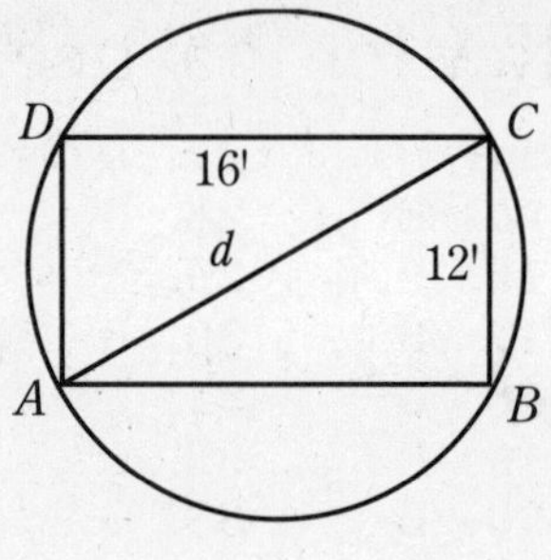

(310)

13. Choice E is correct. The area of the room = 12 feet × 18 feet = 216 square feet. The area of one tile = $\frac{3}{4}$ inches × 2 inches = $\frac{3}{2}$ square inches. The number of tiles = area of the room ÷ area of one tile

$$= \frac{216 \text{ square feet}}{\frac{3}{2} \text{ square inches}} = \frac{216 \times 144 \text{ square inches}}{\frac{3}{2} \text{ square inches}}$$

$$= 216 \times \overset{48}{\cancel{144}} \times \frac{2}{\underset{1}{\cancel{3}}} = 20{,}736 \text{ tiles.}$$ (304)

14. Choice B is correct. The volume of a sphere is found by using the formula $\frac{4}{3}\pi r^3$, where r is the radius. In this case, the radius is 4 meters, so the volume is $\frac{256}{3}\pi$ cubic meters. This is equal to the volume of a cylinder of radius 8 meters, so $\frac{256}{3}\pi = \pi 8^2 h$, since the volume of a cylinder is $\pi r^2 h$, where h is the height, and r is the radius of the base. Solving $\frac{256\pi}{3} = \pi 8^2 h$: $\frac{\frac{256\pi}{3}}{\pi 64} = \frac{\overset{16}{\cancel{256\pi}}}{3} \times \frac{1}{\underset{4}{\cancel{\pi 64}}} = \frac{16}{12} = \frac{4}{3}$ meters.

(314, 315)

15. Choice E is correct. 33 yards = 99 feet = 15 revolutions. Thus, 1 revolution = $\frac{99}{15}$ feet = $\frac{33}{5}$ feet = 6.6 feet. Since 1 revolution = the circumference of the wheel, the wheel's diameter = circumference ÷ π. 6.6 feet ÷ $\frac{22}{7}$ = 2.10 feet. (310)

16. Choice B is correct. The area of the right triangle is equal to $\frac{1}{2}ab$, where a and b are the legs of the triangle. In this case, the area is $\frac{1}{2} \times 12 \times 24$, or 144 square inches. If we call the sides of the rectangle x and y we get $2x + 2y = 48$, or $y = 24 - x$. The area of the rectangle is xy, or $x(24 - x)$. This must be equal to 144, so we get the equation $24x - x^2 = 144$. Adding $x^2 - 24x$ to both sides of this last equation gives us $x^2 - 24x + 144 = 0$, or $(x - 12)^2 = 0$. Thus, $x = 12$. Since $y = 24 - x$, $y = 24 - 12$, or $y = 12$. By the Pythagorean Theorem, the diagonal of the rectangle $= \sqrt{12^2 + 12^2} = \sqrt{144 + 144} = \sqrt{2(144)} = (\sqrt{2})(\sqrt{144}) = 12\sqrt{2}$. (304, 306, 317)

17. Choice B is correct. The area of the square is 64 square inches, since $A = s^2$ where s is the length of a side, and A is the area. The area of the circle is $\pi\left(\frac{7}{4}\right)^2 = \frac{22}{7} \times \frac{49}{16} = \frac{77}{8} = 9.625$. Subtracting, $64 - 9.625 = 54.375 = 54.4$ (approximately). (304, 310)

18. Choice C is correct. The capacity of the volume ($V = lwh$, where l, w, h are the adjacent sides of the solid) of the container = (3 inches) (3 inches) (11 inches) = 99 cubic inches. Since 1 gallon equals 231 cubic inches, 99 cubic inches equal $\frac{99}{231}$ gallons (the fraction reduces to $\frac{3}{7}$). One gallon equals 128 ounces (1 gallon = 4 quarts; 1 quart = 2 pints; 1 pint = 16 ounces), so the container holds $\frac{384}{7}$ ounces = 55 ounces (approximately). (312)

19. Choice E is correct. The speed of the first wheel is equal to its rate of revolution multiplied by its circumference, which equals 24×20 inches $\times\ \pi = 480\pi$ inches per minute. The speed of the second is 18×30 inches $\times\ \pi = 540\pi$ inches per minute. Thus, their ratio is $540\pi : 480\pi = 9 : 8$. (310)

20. Choice D is correct. The area of the path is equal to the area of the ring between two concentric circles of radii 10 feet and 13 feet. This area is obtained by subtracting the area of the smaller circle from the area of the larger circle. The area of the larger circle is equal to $\pi \times$ its radius squared = $\pi(13)^2$ square feet = 169π square feet. By the same process, the area of the smaller circle = 100π square feet. The area of the path = $169\pi - 100\pi = 69\pi$ square feet. (310)

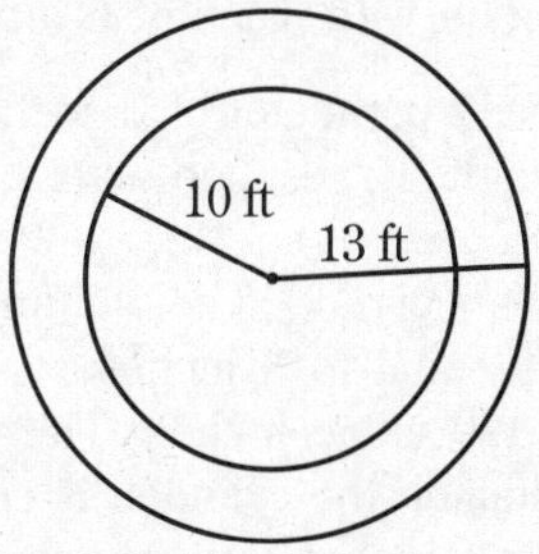

21. Choice A is correct. The diameter = 16 inches, so the radius = 8 inches. Thus, the area of the whole circle = $\pi(8 \text{ inches})^2 = 64\pi$ square inches. The area of the semicircle is one-half of the area of the whole circle, or 32π square inches. (311)

22. Choice A is correct. A cube has 12 equal edges, so the length of one side of the cube is $\frac{1}{12}$ of 4 feet, or 4 inches. Thus, its volume is 4 inches $\times$ 4 inches $\times$ 4 inches = 64 cubic inches. (313)

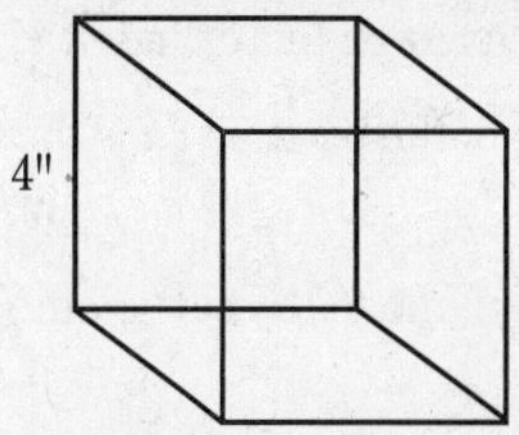

23. Choice B is correct. The additional water will take the shape of a rectangular solid measuring 25 feet $\times$ 6 inches $\times$ 3 inches (3″ = the added depth) = $25 \times \frac{1}{2} \times \frac{1}{4}$ cubic feet = $\frac{25}{8}$ cubic feet. (312)

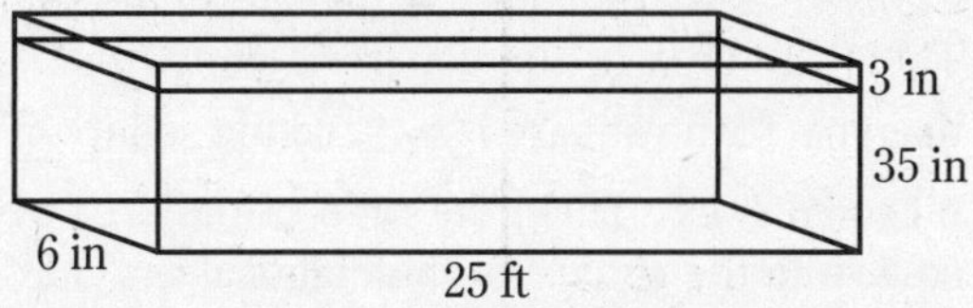

24. Choice A is correct. The volume of the cylinder $= \pi r^2 h = \left(\frac{22}{7}\right)\left(\frac{7}{2}\right)^2(10)$ cubic inches = 385 cubic inches. 231 cubic inches = 1 gallon, so 385 cubic inches = $\frac{385}{231}$ gallons = $\frac{5}{3}$ gallons = 1.7 gallons (approximately). (314)

25. Choice D is correct. The area of floor = 10 feet $\times$ 16 feet = 160 square feet. Area of one tile = 8 inches $\times$ 8 inches = 64 square inches = $\frac{64}{144}$ square feet = $\frac{4}{9}$ square feet. Thus, the number of tiles = area of floor $\div$ area of tile = $160 \div \frac{4}{9} = 360$. At 9¢ apiece, the tiles will cost $32.40. (304)

26. Choice B is correct. Looking at the following three diagrams, we can observe that the triangle, square, and hexagon are all smaller than the circle.

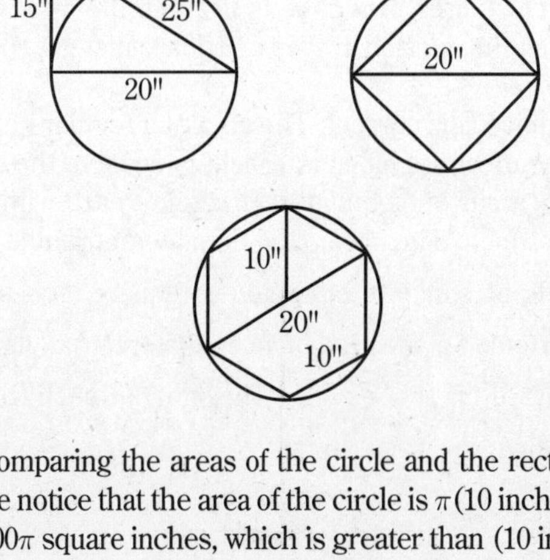

Comparing the areas of the circle and the rectangle, we notice that the area of the circle is $\pi(10 \text{ inches})^2 = 100\pi$ square inches, which is greater than (10 inches) (30 inches) = 300 square inches, the area of the rectangle. (π is approximately 3.14.) (302)

27. Choice D is correct. In a cylinder, $V = \pi r^2 h$, where r is the radius of the base, and h is the height. The new volume, $V' = \pi(3r)^2\left(\frac{h}{3}\right) = 3\pi r^2 h = 3V$. Thus, the ratio of the new volume to the old volume is 3 : 1. (314)

28. Choice C is correct. A cube 2 feet on each side has a volume of $2 \times 2 \times 2 = 8$ cubic feet. Since 1 cubic foot equals 7.5 gallons, 8 cubic feet equals 60 gallons. If the faucet flows at the rate of 10 gallons/minute, it will take 6 minutes to fill the cube. (313)

29. Choice E is correct. Let s = the side of the square. Then, the area of the square is equal to s^2. The diagonal of the square is $s\sqrt{2}$, so the square of the diagonal is $2s^2$. Thus, the ratio of the area of the square to the square of the diagonal is $s^2 : 2s^2$, or 1 : 2. (303)

30. Choice B is correct. The area of the square *ABCD* is equal to 4 inches × 4 inches = 16 square inches. The two semicircles can be placed together diameter-to-diameter to form a circle with a radius of 2 inches, and thus, an area of 4π. Subtracting the area of the circle from the area of the square, we obtain the combined areas of *AED* and *BEC*. But, since the figure is symmetrical, *AED* and *BEC* must be equal. The area of the remainder is $16 - 4\pi$; *AED* is one-half of this remainder, or $8 - 2\pi$ square inches. (303, 310)

31. Choice C is correct. The area of the circle is equal to πr^2, and the area of the rectangle is equal to πx. Since these areas are equal, $\pi r^2 = \pi x$, and $x = r^2$. (304, 310)

32. Choice C is correct. The volume of a cube is e^3 where e is the length of an edge. If the volume is 27 cubic meters, then $e^3 = 27$ and $e = 3$ meters. The surface area of a cube is $6e^2$, and if $e = 3$ meters, then the surface area is 54 square meters. (313)

33. Choice C is correct. The area of a regular hexagon, one of whose sides is 1 inch, is equal to the sum of the areas of 6 equilateral triangles, each with a side of 1 inch. The area of an equilateral triangle with a side of 1 inch is equal to $\frac{\sqrt{3}}{4}$ square inches. (The formula for the area of an equilateral triangle with a side of s is $A = \frac{1}{4}s^2\sqrt{3}$.) The sum of 6 such triangles is $\frac{6\sqrt{3}}{4}$, or $\frac{3\sqrt{3}}{2}$. (308)

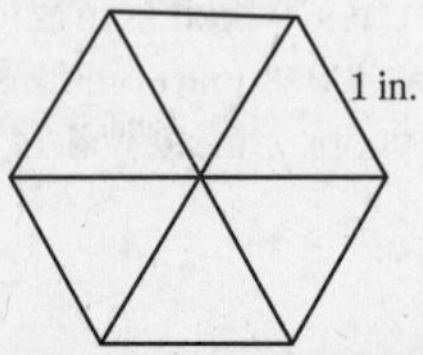

34. Choice D is correct. Draw a perpendicular line from the top of the triangle to the side, which is 8. You have created a 30–60–90 right triangle. The line drawn is $\frac{1}{2}$ of 6 = 3. The area of the whole triangle is the altitude multiplied by the base divided by 2. The altitude is 3 and the base is 8, so the area is $3 \times \frac{8}{2} = 12$. (307)

35. Choice D is correct. Since the wheel takes 1 minute to make 600 revolutions and travels 1 mile in that time, we have the relation 1 mile = 5,280 feet = 600 revolutions. Thus, 1 revolution = $\frac{5{,}280}{600}$ feet = 8.8 feet = circumference = π(diameter) = $\left(\frac{22}{7}\right)$(diameter). Therefore, the diameter = 8.8 feet ÷ $\left(\frac{22}{7}\right)$ = 2.8 feet. (310)

36. Choice D is correct. In this case, it is easiest to calculate the perimeters of the 5 figures. According to the Pythagorean Theorem, a square with a diagonal of 5 feet has a side of $\frac{5}{\sqrt{2}}$, which is equal to $\frac{5\sqrt{2}}{2}$. (This is found by multiplying the numerator and denominator of $\frac{5}{\sqrt{2}}$ by $\sqrt{2}$.) If each side of the square is $\frac{5\sqrt{2}}{2}$, then the perimeter is $\overset{2}{\cancel{4}} \times \frac{5\sqrt{2}}{\cancel{2}} = 10\sqrt{2}$ feet. A rectangle with sides of 3 feet and 4 feet has a perimeter of 2(3) + 2(4), or 14 feet. An equilateral triangle with a side of 48 inches, or 4 feet, has a perimeter of 12 feet. A regular hexagon whose longest diagonal is 6 feet has a side of 3 feet and, therefore, a perimeter of 18 feet. (See the diagram for Solution 41.) Finally, a parallelogram with sides of 6 inches, or $\frac{1}{2}$ foot, and 7 feet has a perimeter of 15 feet. Therefore, the hexagon has the largest perimeter. (302, 317)

37. Choice A is correct. The volume of the first container is equal to 3 inches × 4 inches × 10 inches, or 120 cubic inches. The volume of the second container, the cylinder, is equal to $\pi r^2 h = \pi(2 \text{ inches})^2(10 \text{ inches})$, or 40π cubic inches, which is greater than 120 cubic inches (π is greater than 3). So the second container can hold more than the first. If the first container is filled and the contents poured into the second, there will be room for more water in the second. (312, 314)

38. Choice B is correct. The area of the square is 16 square inches. The four semicircles can be added to form two circles, each of radius 2 inches, so the area of each circle is 4π square inches, and the two circles add up to 8π square inches. Thus, the total area is $16 + 8\pi$ square inches. (303, 311)

39. Choice B is correct. Since the area of the square is $81p^2$, one side of the square will equal $9p$. According to the Pythagorean Theorem, the diagonal will equal $\sqrt{81p^2 + 81p^2} = 9p\sqrt{2}$. (303, 317)

40. Choice A is correct. We can regard the area as a rectangle, 20 ft × 14 ft, with two rectangles, measuring 4 ft × 6 ft and 2 ft × 2 ft, cut out. Thus, the area is equal to 280 sq ft − 24 sq ft − 4 sq ft $= 252$ sq ft $= \frac{252}{9}$ sq yd $= 28$ sq yds. (Remember, 1 square yard equals 9 square feet.) At $2.50 per square yard, 28 square yards will cost $70. (304)

41. Choice D is correct. The perimeter of the square is equal to four times its side; since a side is $\frac{1}{\sqrt{2}}$, or $\frac{\sqrt{2}}{2}$ times the diagonal, the perimeter of the square in question is $4 \times 5\sqrt{2} = 20\sqrt{2}$, which is approximately equal to 28.28 inches. The perimeter of a right triangle with sides that are in a 3–4–5 ratio, i.e., 9 inches, 12 inches, and 15 inches, is $9 + 12 + 15 = 36$ inches. The perimeter of the pentagon is 5×5 inches, or 25 inches. The perimeter of the right isosceles triangle (with sides of 12 inches, 12 inches, and $12\sqrt{2}$ inches) is $24 + 12\sqrt{2}$ inches, which is approximately equal to 40.968 inches. The perimeter of the hexagon is 6×5 inches, or 30 inches. Thus, the isosceles right triangle has the largest perimeter of those figures mentioned. You should become familiar with the approximate value of $\sqrt{2}$, which is 1.414. (302)

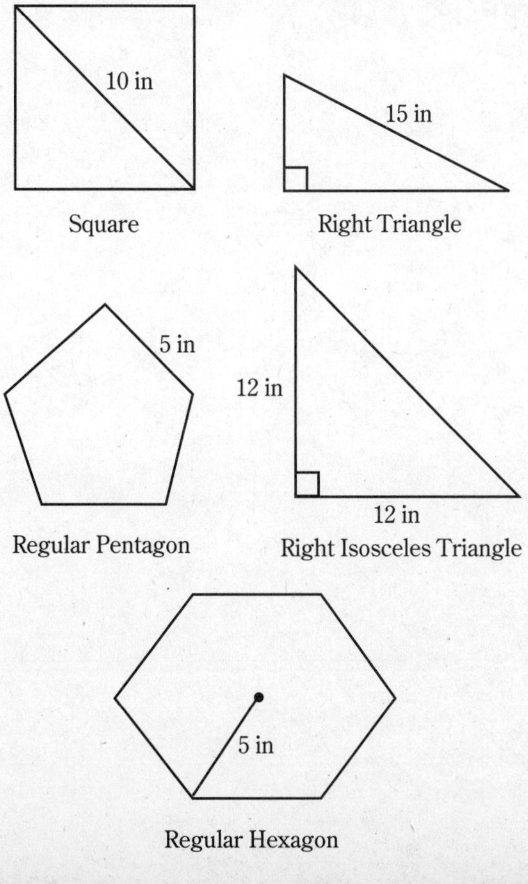

42. Choice D is correct. For rectangular solids, the following formula holds:

$V = Ah$, where A is the area of the base, and h is the height.

If we replace A with $2A$, and h with $3h$, we get $V' = (2A)(3h) = 6V$. Thus, $V' : V = 6 : 1$. (312)

43. Choice C is correct. The area of the room is 27 feet × 14 feet = 378 square feet. 9 square feet = 1 square yard, so the area of the room is 42 square yards. At $1.50 per square yard, the linoleum to cover the floor will cost $63.00. (304)

44. Choice A is correct. A circle with a 4-inch radius has an 8-inch diameter, so there can be only 2 rows of 3 circles each, or 6 circles. (310)

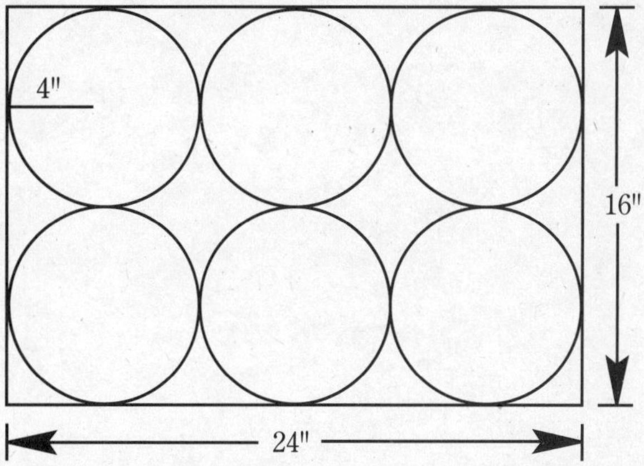

45. Choice E is correct. Let one side of the triangle be s. Then the area of the triangle is $\frac{s^2\sqrt{3}}{4}$. (Either memorize this formula or remember that it is derived by drawing an altitude to divide the triangle into two congruent 30–60–90 right triangles.) The perimeter of the equilateral triangle is $3s$, so the ratio of the area to the perimeter is $\frac{s^2\sqrt{3}}{4} : 3s$, or $s : 4\sqrt{3}$, which cannot be determined unless we know the value of s. (308)

46. Choice E is correct. The formula for volume of a cylinder is $V = \pi r^2 h$, where r is the radius of the base, and h is the height. Here, $r = 4$ inches, and $h = 10$ inches, while $\pi \approx 3.14$. (The symbol $\approx$ means "approximately equal to.") Thus $V \approx (4)^2(10)(3.14) = 160(3.14) = 502.4$ cubic inches. (314)

47. Choice B is correct. If the area of a square is $144s^2$, then one side will equal $12s$, so the diagonal will equal $12s\sqrt{2}$. (The Pythagorean Theorem may be used here to get $d = \sqrt{144s^2 + 144s^2}$, where d is the diagonal.) (303, 317)

48. Choice C is correct. The inside of the pool forms a cylinder of radius 5 feet, and height 5 feet. The volume is $\pi r^2 h$, or $\pi \times 5 \times 5 \times 5 = 125\pi$ cubic feet. (314)

49. Choice B is correct. The area of the floor is 20 feet $\times$ 24 feet $=$ 480 square feet. 30 inches is equal to $2\frac{1}{2}$ feet, and we must find the length that, when multiplied by $2\frac{1}{2}$ feet, will yield 480 square feet. This length is 192 feet, which equals 64 yards (3 feet $=$ 1 yard). (304)

50. Choice D is correct. The circumference of the larger wheel is 18π inches ($C = \pi d$). After 72 revolutions, the larger wheel will have gone a distance of $72(18\pi)$ inches. Since the smaller wheel moves at the same linear speed, it will also have gone $72(18\pi)$ inches. The circumference of the smaller wheel is 12π inches, and if we call the number of revolutions that the smaller wheel makes r, then we know that $12\pi r = 72(18\pi)$. Dividing both sides by 12π gives us $r = 6(18)$ or 108 revolutions. Note that in this problem we have used the relation *distance* $=$ *rate* $\times$ *time*, where the time for both wheels is a fixed quantity. (310)

MATH REFRESHER SESSION 4

Algebra Problems

Algebraic Properties

Algebra is the branch of mathematics that applies the laws of arithmetic to symbols that represent unknown quantities. The most commonly used symbols are the letters of the alphabet such as A, B, C, x, y, z, etc. These symbols can be added, subtracted, multiplied, and divided like numbers. For example, $3a + 2a = 5a$, $2x - x = x$, $3(5b) = 15b$, $\frac{6x}{3x} = 2$. These symbols can be raised to powers like a^3 or y^2. Remember that raising a number to a power means multiplying the number by itself a number of times. For example, $a^3 = a \cdot a \cdot a$. The power is 3, and a is multiplied by itself 3 times.

Generally, in algebra, a variable (an unknown represented by a symbol) appears in an *equation* (a statement that defines the relationship between certain quantities), and values of the variable that *satisfy* the equation must be found. For example, the equation $6a = 12$ is satisfied when the variable, a, is equal to 2. This section is a discussion on how to solve complicated algebraic equations and other related topics.

Fundamental Laws of Our Number System

The following list of laws applies to all numbers, and these laws are necessary to work with when doing arithmetic and algebra problems. Remember these laws and use them in doing problems.

401. If $x = y$ and $y = z$, then $x = z$. This is called *transitivity*. For example, if $a = 3$ and $b = 3$, then $a = b$.

402. If $x = y$, then $x + z = y + z$, and $x - z = y - z$. This means that the same quantity can be added to or subtracted from both sides of an equation. For example, if $a = b$, then add any number to both sides, say 3, and $a + 3 = b + 3$. Or if $a = b$, then $a - 3 = b - 3$.

403. If $x = y$, then $x \cdot z = y \cdot z$ and $x \div z = y \div z$, unless $z = 0$ (see Section 404). This means that both sides of an equation can be multiplied by the same number. For example, if $a = n$, then $5a = 5n$. It also means that both sides of an equation can be divided by the same nonzero number. If $a = b$, then $\frac{a}{3} = \frac{b}{3}$.

404. *Never divide by zero.* This is a very important fact that must be remembered. The quotient of *any* quantity (except zero) divided by zero is infinity.

405. $x + y = y + x$, and $x \cdot y = y \cdot x$. Therefore, $2 + 3 = 3 + 2$, and $2 \cdot 3 = 3 \cdot 2$. Remember that this does not work for division and subtraction. $3 \div 2$ does not equal $2 \div 3$, and $3 - 2$ does not equal $2 - 3$. The property described above is called *commutativity*.

Algebraic Expressions

405a. Since the letters in an algebraic expression stand for numbers, and since we add, subtract, multiply, or divide them to get the algebraic expression, the algebraic expression itself stands for a number. When we are told what value each of the letters in the expression has, we can evaluate the expression. Note that $(+a) \times (+b) = +ab$; $(+a) \times (-b) = -ab$; $(-a) \times (+b) = -ab$; and $-a \times -b = +ab$.

In evaluating algebraic expressions, place the value you are substituting for a letter in parentheses. (This is important when a letter has a negative value.)

> **Example:** What is the value of the expression $a^2 - b^3$ when $a = -2$, and $b = -1$? $a^2 - b^3 = (-2)^2 - (-1)^3 = 4 - (-1) = 5$.

If you can, simplify the algebraic expression before you evaluate it.

> **Example:** Evaluate $\frac{32a^6b^2}{8a^4b^3}$ if $a = 4$, and $b = -2$.

First we divide:

$\frac{32a^6b^2}{8a^4b^3} = \frac{4a^2}{b}$. Then $\frac{4a^2}{b} = \frac{4(+4)^2}{-2} = -32$.

Equations

406. *Linear equations in one unknown.* An equation of this type has only one variable, and that variable is always in the first power, i.e., x or y or a, but never a higher or fractional power, i.e., x^2, y^3, or $a^{\frac{1}{2}}$. Examples of linear equations in one unknown are $x + 5 = 7$, $3a - 2 = 7a + 1$, $2x - 7x = 8 + x$, $8 = -4y$, etc. To solve these equations, follow these steps:

STEP 1. Combine the terms on the left and right sides of the equality. That is, (1) add all of the numerical terms on each side, and (2) add all of the terms with variables on each side. For example, if you have $7 + 2x + 9 = 4x - 3 - 2x + 7 + 6x$, combining terms on the left gives you $16 + 2x$, because $7 + 9 = 16$, and $2x$ is the only variable term on that side. On the right we get $8x + 4$, since $4x - 2x + 6x = 8x$ and $-3 + 7 = 4$. Therefore the new equation is $16 + 2x = 8x + 4$.

STEP 2. Put all of the numerical terms on the right side of the equation and all of the variable terms on the left side. This is done by subtracting the numerical term on the left from both sides of the equation and by subtracting the variable term on the right side from both sides of the equation. In the example $16 + 2x = 8x + 4$, subtract 16 from both sides and obtain $2x = 8x - 12$; then subtracting $8x$ from both sides gives $-6x = -12$.

STEP 3. Divide both sides by the coefficient of the variable. In this case, where $-6x = -12$, dividing by -6 gives $x = 2$. This is the final solution to the problem.

> **Example:** Solve for a in the equation $7a + 4 - 2a = 18 + 17a + 10$.
>
> *Solution:* From Step 1, we combine terms on both sides to get $5a + 4 = 28 + 17a$. As in Step 2, we then subtract 4 and $17a$ from both sides to give $-12a = 24$. By Step 3, we then divide both sides of the equation by the coefficient of a, which is -12, to get $a = -2$.
>
> **Example:** Solve for x in $2x + 6 = 0$.
>
> *Solution:* Here Step 1 is eliminated because there are no terms to combine on either side. Step 2 requires that 6 be subtracted from both sides to get $2x = -6$. Then dividing by 2 gives $x = -3$.

407. *Simultaneous equations in two unknowns.* These are problems in which two equations, each with two unknowns, are given. These equations must be solved together (simultaneously) in order to arrive at the solution.

STEP 1. Rearrange each equation so that both are in the form that has the x term on the left side and the y term and the constant on the right side. In other words, put the equations in the form $Ax = By + C$, where A, B, and C are numerical constants. For example, if one of the equations is $9x - 10y + 30 = 11y + 3x - 6$, then subtract $-10y$ and 30 from both sides to get $9x = 21y + 3x - 36$. Subtracting $3x$ from both sides gives $6x = 21y - 36$, which is in the form of $Ax = By + C$.

The first equation should be in the form $Ax = By + C$, and the second equation should be in the form $Dx = Ey + F$, where A, B, C, D, E, and F are numerical constants.

STEP 2. Multiply the first equation by the coefficient of x in the second equation (D). Multiply the second equation by the coefficient of x in the first equation (A). Now the equations are in the form $ADx = BDy + CD$ and $ADx = AEy + AF$. For example, in the two equations $2x = 7y - 12$ and $3x = y + 1$, multiply the first by 3 and the second by 2 to get $6x = 21y - 36$ and $6x = 2y + 2$.

STEP 3. Equate the right sides of both equations. This can be done because both sides are equal to ADx. (See Section 401 on transitivity.) Thus, $BDy + CD = AEy + AF$. So $21y - 36$ and $2y + 2$ are both equal to $6x$ and are equal to each other: $21y - 36 = 2y + 2$.

STEP 4. Solve for y. This is done in the manner outlined in Section 406. In the equation $21y - 36 = 2y + 2$, $y = 2$. By this method $y = \frac{AF - CD}{BD - AE}$.

STEP 5. Substitute the value of y into either of the original equations and solve for x. In the general equations we would then have either $x = \frac{B}{A}\left[\frac{AF - CD}{BD - AE}\right] + \frac{C}{A}$, or $x = \frac{E}{D}\left[\frac{AF - CD}{BD - AE}\right] + \frac{F}{D}$.

In the example, if $y = 2$ is substituted into either $2x = 7y - 12$ or $3x = y + 1$, then $2x = 14 - 12$ or $3x = 3$ can be solved to get $x = 1$.

Example: Solve for a and b in the equations $3a + 4b = 24$ and $2a + b = 11$.

Solution: First note that it makes no difference in these two equations whether the variables are a and b instead of x and y. Subtract $4b$ from the first equation and b from the second equation to get the equations $3a = 24 - 4b$ and $2a = 11 - b$. Multiply the first by 2 and the second by 3. Thus, $6a = 48 - 8b$ and $6a = 33 - 3b$. Equate $48 - 8b$ and $33 - 3b$ to get $48 - 8b = 33 - 3b$. Solving for b in the usual manner gives us $b = 3$. Substituting the value of $b = 3$ into the equation $3a + 4b = 24$ obtains $3a + 12 = 24$. Solving for a gives $a = 4$. Thus the complete solution is $a = 4$ and $b = 3$.

408.* *Quadratic equations.* Quadratic equations are expressed in the form $ax^2 + bx + c = 0$, where a, b, and c are constant numbers (for example, $\frac{1}{2}$, 4, -2, etc.) and x is a variable. An equation of this form may be satisfied by two values of x, one value of x, or no values of x. Actually, when there are no values of x that satisfy the equation, there are only *imaginary* solutions. On the SAT, you will not have questions where you will have to use these formulas. To determine the number of solutions, find the value of the expression $b^2 - 4ac$ where a, b, and c are the constant coefficients of the equation $ax^2 + bx + c = 0$.

If $b^2 - 4ac$ is *greater* than 0, there are two solutions.

If $b^2 - 4ac$ is *less* than 0, there are no solutions.

If $b^2 - 4ac$ is *equal* to 0, there is one solution.

If solutions exist, they can be found by using the formulas:

$$x = \frac{-b + \sqrt{b^2 - 4ac}}{2a} \text{ and } x = \frac{-b - \sqrt{b^2 - 4ac}}{2a}$$

Note that if $b^2 - 4ac = 0$, the two above solutions will be the same and there will be one solution.

Example: Determine the solutions, if they exist, to the equation $x^2 + 6x + 5 = 0$.

*On the SAT, you will not need to know the quadratic equations formula.

Solution: First, noting $a = 1$, $b = 6$, and $c = 5$, calculate $b^2 - 4ac$, or $6^2 - 4(1)(5)$. Thus, $b^2 - 4ac = 16$. Since this is greater than 0, there are two solutions. They are, from the formulas:

$$x = \frac{-6 + \sqrt{6^2 - 4 \cdot 1 \cdot 5}}{2 \cdot 1} \text{ and } x = \frac{-6 - \sqrt{6^2 - 4 \cdot 1 \cdot 5}}{2 \cdot 1}$$

Simplify these to:

$$x = \frac{-6 + \sqrt{16}}{2} \text{ and } x = \frac{-6 - \sqrt{16}}{2}$$

As $\sqrt{16} = 4$, $x = \frac{-6+4}{2} = \frac{-2}{2}$ and $x = \frac{-6-4}{2} = \frac{-10}{2}$. Thus, the two solutions are $x = -1$ and $x = -5$.

Another method of solving quadratic equations is to *factor* the $ax^2 + bx + c$ into two expressions. This will be explained in the next section.

409. *Factoring.* Factoring is breaking down an expression into two or more expressions, the product of which is the original expression. For example, 6 can be factored into 2 and 3 because $2 \cdot 3 = 6$. $x^2 - x$ can be factored into x and $(x - 1)$ because $x^2 - x = x(x - 1)$. Then, if $x^2 + bx + c$ is factorable, it will be factored into two expressions in the form $(x + d)$ and $(x + e)$. If the expression $(x + d)$ is multiplied by the expression $(x + e)$, their product is $x^2 + (d + e)x + de$. For example, $(x + 3) \cdot (x + 2)$ equals $x^2 + 5x + 6$. To factor an expression such as $x^2 + 6x + 8$, find d and e such that $d + e = 6$ and $de = 8$. Of the various factors of 8, we find that $d = 4$ and $e = 2$. Thus $x^2 + 6x + 8$ can be factored into the expressions $(x + 4)$ and $(x + 2)$. Below are factored expressions.

$x^2 + 2x + 1 = (x + 1)(x + 1)$	$x^2 + 3x + 2 = (x + 2)(x + 1)$
$x^2 + 4x + 4 = (x + 2)(x + 2)$	$x^2 + 5x + 6 = (x + 3)(x + 2)$
$x^2 - 4x + 3 = (x - 3)(x - 1)$	$x^2 - 4x - 5 = (x - 5)(x + 1)$
$x^2 + 10x + 16 = (x + 8)(x + 2)$	$x^2 + 4x - 5 = (x + 5)(x - 1)$
$x^2 - 5x + 6 = (x - 2)(x - 3)$	$x^2 - x - 6 = (x - 3)(x + 2)$

An important rule to remember in factoring is that $a^2 - b^2 = (a + b)(a - b)$. For example, $x^2 - 9 = (x + 3)(x - 3)$. You don't get a middle term in x because the $3x$ cancels with the $-3x$ in the product $(x + 3)(x - 3)$. To apply factoring in solving quadratic equations, factor the quadratic expression into two terms and set each term equal to zero. Then, solve the two resulting equations.

Example: Solve $x^2 - x - 6 = 0$.

Solution: First factor the expression $x^2 - x - 6$ into $x - 3$ and $x + 2$. Setting each of these equal to 0 gives $x - 3 = 0$ and $x + 2 = 0$. Solving these equations gives us $x = 3$ and $x = -2$.

Algebra of Graphs

410a. *Number Lines.* Numbers, positive and negative, can be represented as points on a straight line. Conversely, points on a line can also be represented by numbers. This is done by use of the number line.

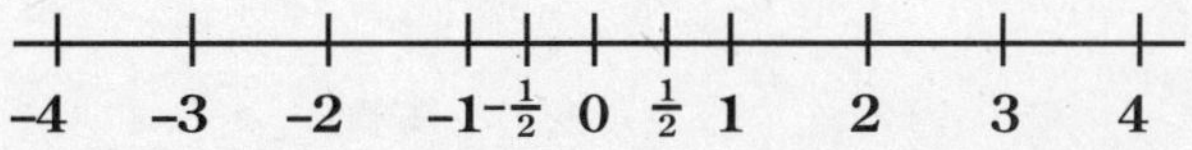

The diagram above is an example of a number line. On a number line, a point is chosen to represent the number zero. Then a point that is 1 unit to the right of 0 represents +1; a point that is $\frac{1}{2}$ unit to the right of 0 is $+\frac{1}{2}$; a point that is 2 units to the right of 0 is +2; and so on. A point that is 1 unit to the left of 0 is −1; a point that is $\frac{1}{2}$ unit to the left of 0 is $-\frac{1}{2}$; a point that is 2 units to the left of 0 is −2; and so on. As you can see, all points to the right of the 0 point represent positive numbers, and all those to the left of the 0 point represent negative numbers.

To find the distance between two points on the line:

1. Find the numbers that represent the points.
2. The distance is the smaller number subtracted from the larger.

For example: Find the distance between point A and point B on the number line.

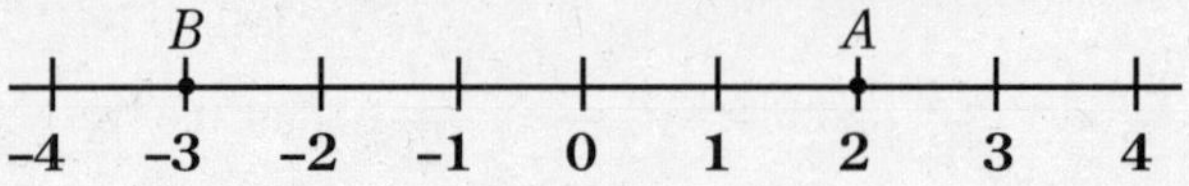

Point A is $+2$ on the number line and point B is -3. $+2$ is larger than -3, so the distance is $+2 - (-3)$ or $+2 + 3 = 5$. By counting the number of units between A and B, the distance is also found to be 5.

410b. *Coordinate geometry.* These problems deal with the algebra of graphs. A graph consists of a set of points whose position is determined with respect to a set of axes usually labeled the x-axis and the y-axis and divided into appropriate units. Locate a point on the graph with an "x-coordinate" of a units and a "y-coordinate" of b units. First move a units along the x-axis (either to the left or right depending on whether a is positive or negative). Then move b units along the y-axis (either up or down depending on the sign of b). A point with an x-coordinate of a, and a y-coordinate of b, is represented by (a,b). The points (2,3), (−1,4), (−2,−3), and (4,−2) are shown on the following graph.

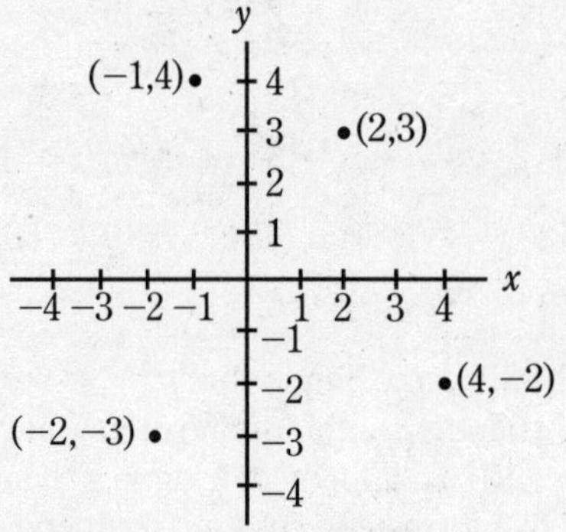

411. *Distance between two points.* If the coordinates of point A are (x_1,y_1) and the coordinates of point B are (x_2,y_2), then the distance on the graph between the two points is $d = \sqrt{(x_2 - x_1)^2 + (y_2 - y_1)^2}$.

Example: Find the distance between the point (2,−3) and the point (5,1).

Solution: In this case $x_1 = 2$, $x_2 = 5$, $y_1 = -3$, and $y_2 = 1$. Substituting into the above formula gives us

$$d = \sqrt{(5-2)^2 + [1-(-3)]^2} = \sqrt{3^2 + 4^2} = \sqrt{25} = 5$$

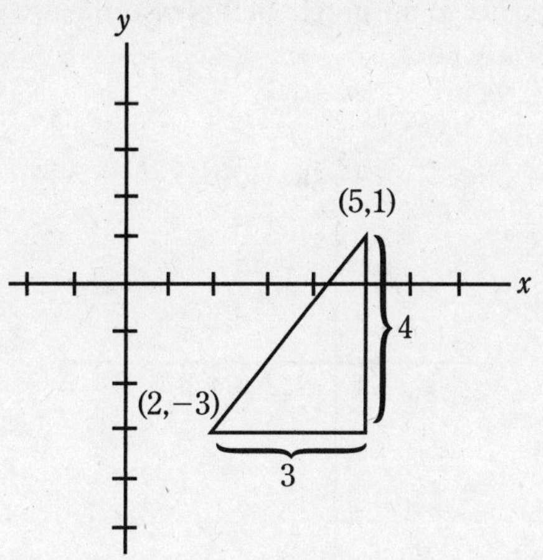

Note: This formula is a consequence of the Pythagorean Theorem. Pythagoras, an ancient Greek mathematician, discovered that the square of the length of the hypotenuse (longest side) of a right triangle is equal to the sum of the square of the lengths of the other two sides. See Sections 317 and 509.

412. *Midpoint of the line segment joining two points.* If the coordinates of the first point are (x_1, y_1) and the coordinates of the second point are (x_2,y_2), then the coordinates of the midpoint will be $\left(\frac{x_1+x_2}{2}, \frac{y_1+y_2}{2}\right)$. In other words, each coordinate of the midpoint is equal to the *average* of the corresponding coordinates of the endpoints.

Example: Find the midpoint of the segment connecting the points (2,4) and (6,2).

Solution: The average of 2 and 6 is 4, so the first coordinate is 4. The average of 4 and 2 is 3; thus the second coordinate is 3. The midpoint is (4,3). $\left[\frac{2+6}{2} = 4, \frac{4+2}{2} = 3\right]$

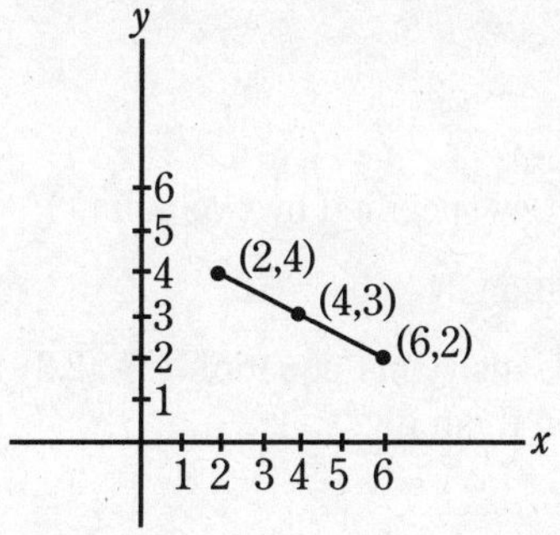

413. *Plotting the graph of a line.* An equation that can be put in the form of $y = mx + b$, where m and b are numerical constants, can be represented as a line on a graph. This means that all of the points on the graph that the line passes through will satisfy the equation. Remember that each point has an x and a y value that can be substituted into the equation. To plot a line, follow the steps below:

STEP 1. Select two values of x and two values of y that will satisfy the equation. For example, in the equation $y = 2x + 4$, the point $(x = 1, y = 6)$ will satisfy the equation, as will the point $(x = -2, y = 0)$. There is an infinite number of such points on a line.

STEP 2. Plot these two points on the graph. In this case, the two points are (1,6) and (−2,0). These points are represented below.

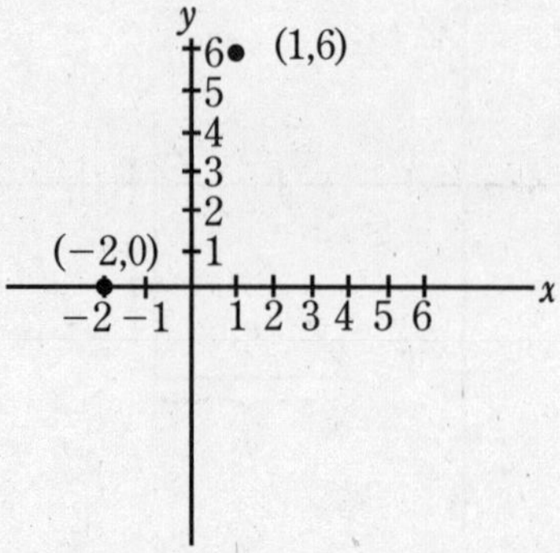

STEP 3. Draw a line connecting the two points. This is the line representing the equation.

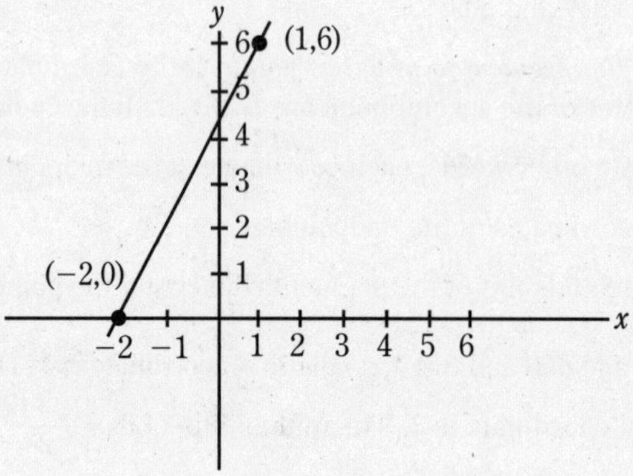

(Note: A straight line is completely specified by two points.)

Example: Graph the equation $2y + 3x = 12$.

Solution: Two points that satisfy this equation are (2,3) and (0,6). Plotting these points and drawing a line between them gives:

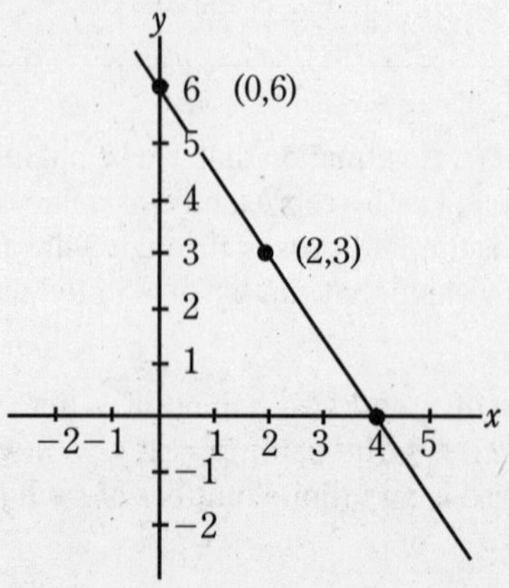

414. *y-intercept.* The *y*-intercept of a line is the point where the line crosses the *y*-axis. At any point where a line crosses the *y*-axis, $x = 0$. To find the *y*-intercept of a line, simply substitute $x = 0$ into the equation of the line, and solve for *y*.

Example: Find the y-intercept of the equation $2x + 3y = 6$.

Solution: If $x = 0$ is substituted into the equation, it simplifies to $3y = 6$. Solving for y gives $y = 2$. Thus, 2 is the y-intercept.

If an equation can be put into the form of $y = mx + b$, then b is the y-intercept.

415. *x-intercept.* The point where a line intersects the x-axis is called the x-intercept. At this point $y = 0$. To find the x-intercept of a line, substitute $y = 0$ into the equation and solve for x.

Example: Given the equation $2x + 3y = 6$, find the x-intercept.

Solution: Substitute $y = 0$ into the equation, getting $2x = 6$. Solving for x, find $x = 3$. Thus the x-intercept is 3.

In the diagram below, the y- and x-intercepts of the equation $2x + 3y = 6$ are illustrated.

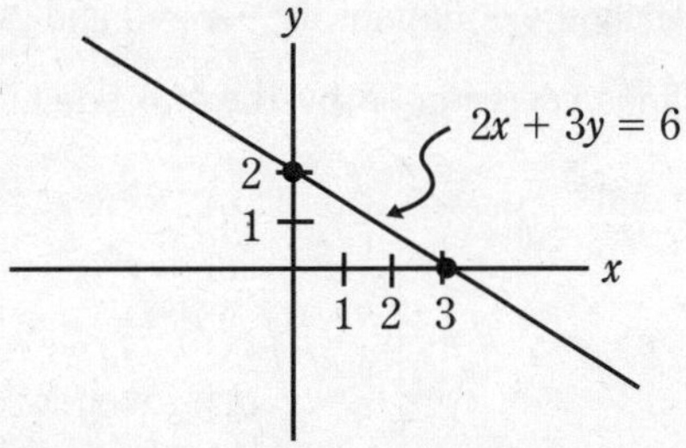

416. *Slope.* The slope of a line is the change in y caused by a 1-unit increase in x. If an equation is in the form of $y = mx + b$, then as x increases 1 unit, y will increase m units. Therefore the slope is m.

Example: Find the slope of the line $2x + 3y = 6$.

Solution: First put the equation into the form of $y = mx + b$. Subtract $2x$ from both sides and divide by 3. The equation becomes $y = -\frac{2}{3}x + 2$. Therefore the slope is $-\frac{2}{3}$.

The slope of the line joining two points, (x_1, y_1) and (x_2, y_2), is given by the expression $m = \frac{y_2 - y_1}{x_2 - x_1}$.

Example: Find the slope of the line joining the points (3,2) and (4,–1).

Solution: Substituting into the above formula gives us $m = \frac{-3}{1} = -3$, where $x_1 = 3$, $x_2 = 4$, $y_1 = 2$, $y_2 = -1$.

If two lines are perpendicular, the slope of one is the negative reciprocal of the other.

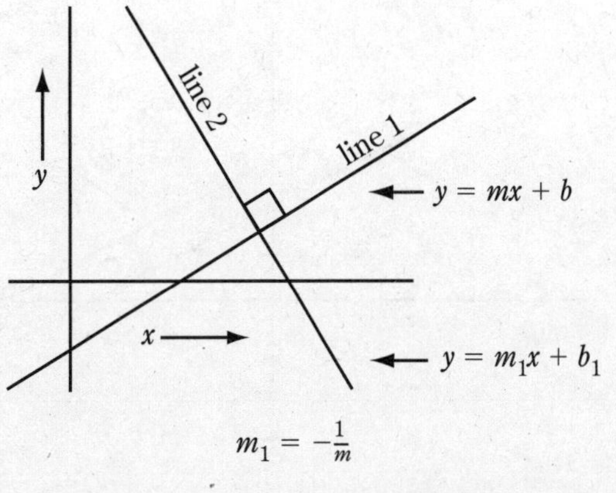

Example: What is the slope of a line perpendicular to the line $y = -3x + 4$?

Solution: Since the slope of the line $y = -3x + 4$ is -3, the slope of the line perpendicular to that line is the negative reciprocal, or $\frac{-1}{-3} = \frac{+1}{3}$.

417. *Graphing simultaneous linear equations.* Recall that simultaneous equations are a pair of equations in two unknowns. Each of these equations is graphed separately, and each is represented by a straight line. The solution of the simultaneous equations (i.e., the pair of values that satisfies *both* at the same time) is represented by the intersection of two lines. Now, for any pair of lines, there are three possible relationships:

1. The lines intersect at one and only one point; in this case, this point represents the unique solution to the pair of equations. This is most often the case. Such lines are called *consistent.*

2. The lines coincide exactly; this represents the case where the two equations are equivalent (just different forms of the same mathematical relation). Any point that satisfies *either* of the two equations automatically satisfies *both.*

3. The lines are parallel and never intersect. In this case the equations are called *inconsistent,* and they have *no* solution at all. Two lines that are parallel will have the same slope.

Example: Solve graphically the equations $4x - y = 5$ and $2x + 4y = 16$.

Solution: Plot the two lines represented by the two equations. (See Section 413.) The graph is shown below.

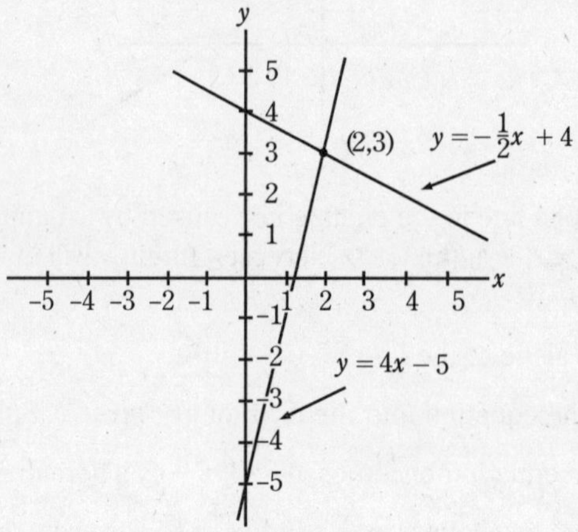

The two lines intersect in the point (2,3), which represents the solution $x = 2$ and $y = 3$. This can be checked by solving the equations as is done in Section 407.

Example: Solve $x + 2y = 6$ and $2x + 4y = 8$.

Solution: Find two points that satisfy each equation. Draw a line connecting these two points. The two graphs will look like this:

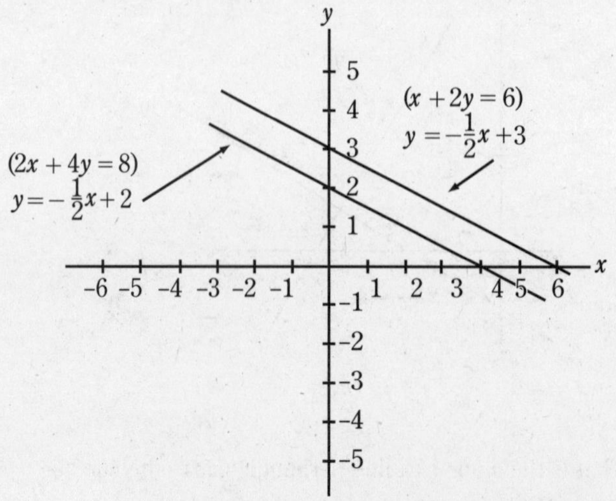

These lines will never intersect, and these equations are termed inconsistent. There is no solution.

Remember that two parallel lines have the same slope. This is an easy way to see whether two lines are consistent or inconsistent.

Example: Find the solution to $2x - 3y = 8$ and $4x = 6y + 16$.

Solution: On the graph these two lines are identical. This means that there is an infinite set of points that satisfy both equations.

Equations of identical lines are multiples of each other and can be reduced to a single equation.

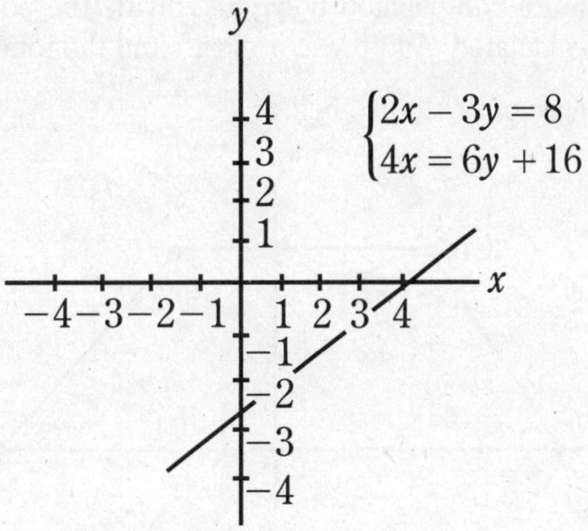

418. *Areas of polygons.* Often, an elementary geometric figure is placed on a graph to calculate its area. This is usually simple for figures such as triangles, rectangles, squares, parallelograms, etc.

Example: Calculate the area of the triangle in the figure below.

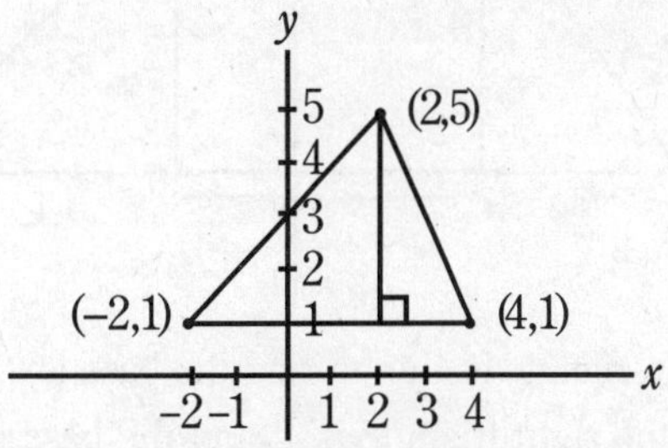

Solution: The area of a triangle is $\frac{1}{2}$(base) (height). On the graph the length of the line joining (−2,1) and (4,1) is 6 units. The height, which goes from point (2,5) to the base, has a length of 4 units. Therefore the area is $\frac{1}{2}(6)(4) = 12$.

Example: Calculate the area of the square pictured below.

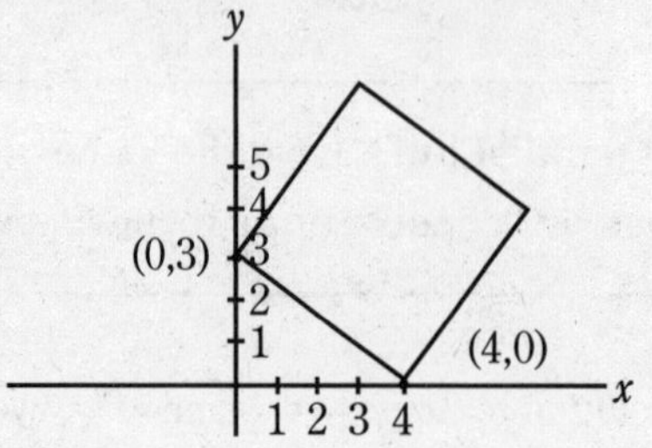

Solution: The area of a square is given by the square of the side. To find this area, first find the length of one side. The length of a segment whose endpoints are (x_1,y_1) and (x_2,y_2) is given by the formula $\sqrt{(x_2 - x_1)^2 + (y_2 - y_1)^2}$. Substituting in (0,3) and (4,0) gives a length of 5 units. Thus the length of one side of the square is 5. Using the formula area $=$ (side)^2 gives an area of 5^2, or 25 square units.

To find the area of more complicated polygons, divide the polygon into simple figures whose areas can be calculated. Add these areas to find the total area.

Example: Find the area of the figure below:

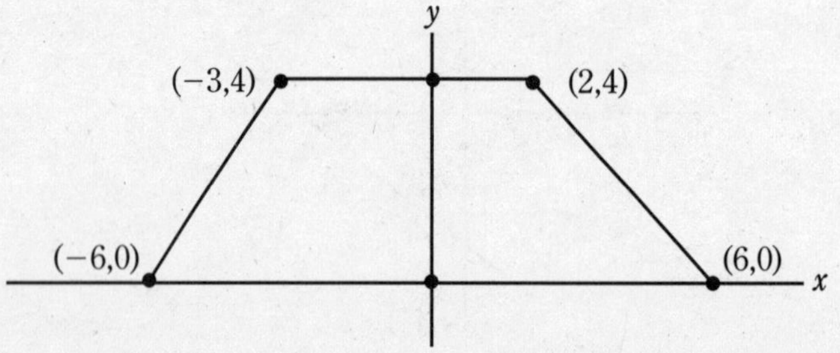

Solution: Divide the figure into two triangles and a rectangle by drawing vertical lines at $(-3,4)$ and $(2,4)$. Thus the polygon is now two triangles and a rectangle.

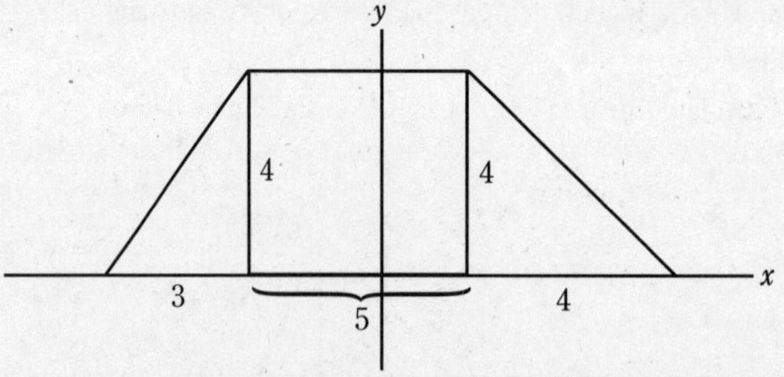

The height of the left triangle is 4 units, and the base is 3. Using $A = \frac{1}{2}bh$ gives the area as 6. The height of the right triangle is 4, and the base is 4. The area is 8. The length of one side of the rectangle is 4, and the other side is 5. Using the formula area $=$ base $\cdot$ height gives the area as 20. Thus the total area is $6 + 8 + 20 = 34$.

Inequalities

419. *Inequalities.* These problems deal with numbers that are less than, greater than, or equal to other numbers. The following laws apply to all inequalities:

$<$ means "less than," thus $3 < 4$
$>$ means "greater than," thus $5 > 2$
$\leq$ means "less than or equal to," thus $x \leq y$ means $x < y$ or $x = y$
$\geq$ means "greater than or equal to," thus $x \geq y$ means $x > y$ or $x = y$

420. If equal quantities are added to or subtracted from both sides of an inequality, the direction of the inequality does *not* change.

$$\text{If } x < y, \text{ then } x + z < y + z \text{ and } x - z < y - z.$$

$$\text{If } x > y, \text{ then } x + z > y + z \text{ and } x - z > y - z.$$

For example, given the inequality $4 > 2$, with 1 added to or subtracted from both sides, the results, $5 > 3$ and $3 > 1$, have the same inequality sign as the original. If the problem is algebraic, e.g., $x + 3 < 6$, it is possible to subtract 3 from both sides to get the simple inequality $x < 3$.

421. Subtracting parts of an inequality from an equation *reverses* the order of the inequality.

$$\text{Given } z = z \text{ and } x < y, \text{ then } z - x > z - y.$$

$$\text{Given } z = z \text{ and } x > y, \text{ then } z - x < z - y.$$

For example, given that $3 < 5$, subtracting 3 from the left-hand and 5 from the right-hand sides of the equation $10 = 10$ results in $7 > 5$. Thus the direction of the inequality is reversed.

Note: Subtracting parts of an equation from an inequality does not reverse the inequality. For example, if $3 < 5$, then $3 - 10 < 5 - 10$.

422. Multiplying or dividing an inequality by a number greater than zero does not change the order of the inequality.

$$\text{If } x > y, \text{ and } a > 0, \text{ then } xa > ya \text{ and } \frac{x}{a} > \frac{y}{a}.$$

$$\text{If } x < y, \text{ and } a > 0, \text{ then } xa < ya \text{ and } \frac{x}{a} < \frac{y}{a}.$$

For example, if $4 > 2$, multiplying both sides by any arbitrary number (for instance, 5) gives $20 > 10$, which is still true. Or, if algebraically $6h < 3$, dividing both sides by 6 gives $h < \frac{1}{2}$, which is true.

423. Multiplying or dividing an inequality by a number less than 0 reverses the order of the inequality.

If $x > y$, and $a < 0$, then $xa < ya$ and $\frac{x}{a} < \frac{y}{a}$.

If $x < y$, and $a < 0$, then $xa > ya$ and $\frac{x}{a} > \frac{y}{a}$.

If $-3 < 2$ is multiplied through by -2 it becomes $6 > -4$, and the order of the inequality is reversed.

Note that negative numbers are always less than positive numbers. Note also that the greater the absolute value of a negative number, the smaller it actually is. Thus, $-10 < -9$, $-8 < -7$, etc.

424. The product of two numbers with like signs is positive.

$$\text{If } x > 0 \text{ and } y > 0, \text{ then } xy > 0.$$

$$\text{If } x < 0 \text{ and } y < 0, \text{ then } xy > 0.$$

For example, -3 times -2 is 6.

425. The product of two numbers with unlike signs is negative.

$$\text{If } x < 0 \text{ and } y > 0, \text{ then } xy < 0.$$

$$\text{If } x > 0 \text{ and } y < 0, \text{ then } xy < 0.$$

For example, -2 times 3 is -6. 8 times -1 is -8, etc.

426. *Linear inequalities in one unknown.* In these problems a first-power variable is given in an inequality, and this variable must be solved for in terms of the inequality. Examples of linear inequalities in one unknown are: $2x + 7 > 4 + x$, $8y - 3 \leq 2y$, etc.

STEP 1. By ordinary algebraic addition and subtraction (as if it were an equality) get all of the constant terms on one side of the inequality and all of the variable terms on the other side. In the inequality $2x + 4 < 8x + 16$ subtract 4 and $8x$ from both sides and get $-6x < 12$.

STEP 2. Divide both sides by the coefficient of the variable. Important: If the coefficient of the variable is negative, you must reverse the inequality sign. For example, in $-6x < 12$, dividing by -6 gives $x > -2$. (The inequality is reversed.) In $3x < 12$, dividing by 3 gives $x < 4$.

Example: Solve for y in the inequality $4y + 7 \geq 9 - 2y$.

Solution: Subtracting $-2y$ and 7 from both sides gives $6y \geq 2$. Dividing both sides by 6 gives $y \geq \frac{1}{3}$.

Example: Solve for a in the inequality $10 - 2a < 0$.

Solution: Subtracting 10 from both sides gives $-2a < -10$. Dividing both sides by -2 gives $a > \frac{-10}{-2}$ or $a > 5$. Note that the inequality sign has been reversed because of the division by a negative number.

427. *Simultaneous linear inequalities in two unknowns.* These are two inequalities, each one in two unknowns. The same two unknowns are to be solved for in each equation. This means the equations must be solved simultaneously.

STEP 1. Plot both inequalities on the same graph. Replace the inequality sign with an equals sign and plot the resulting line. The side of the line that makes the inequality true is then shaded in. For example, graph the inequality $2x - y > 4$. First replace the inequality sign, getting $2x - y = 4$; then, plot the line. The x-intercept is where $y = 0$. The y-intercept is where $x = 0$. So in the equation $2x - y = 4$, the x-intercept is where $2x = 4$, or where $x = 2$. Similarly, in the equation $2x - y = 4$, the y-intercept is where $-y = 4$, or where $y = -4$. (See Sections 414 and 415 for determining x- and y-intercepts.)

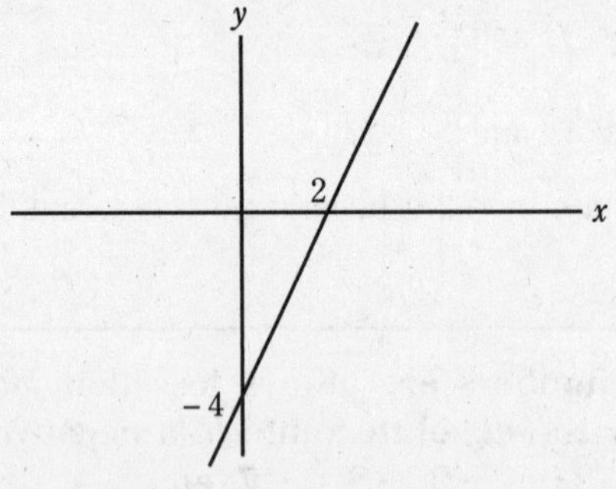

To decide which side of the line satisfies the inequality, choose a convenient point on each side and determine which point satisfies the inequality. Shade in that side of the line. In this case, choose the point (0,0). With this point the equation becomes $2(0) - 0 > 4$, or $0 > 4$. This is not true. Therefore, shade in the other side of the line.

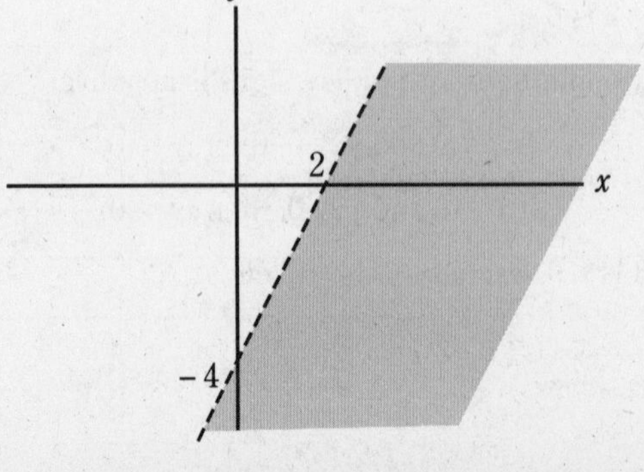

STEP 2. After both inequalities have been solved, the area that is common to both shaded portions is the solution to the problem.

Example: Solve $x + y > 2$ and $3x < 6$.

Solution: First graph $x + y > 2$ by plotting $x + y = 2$ and using the point (4,0) to determine the region where the inequality is satisfied:

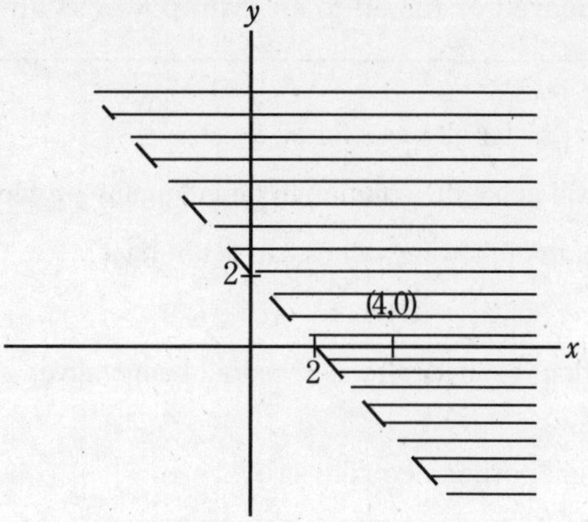

Graph the inequality $3x < 6$ on the same axes and get:

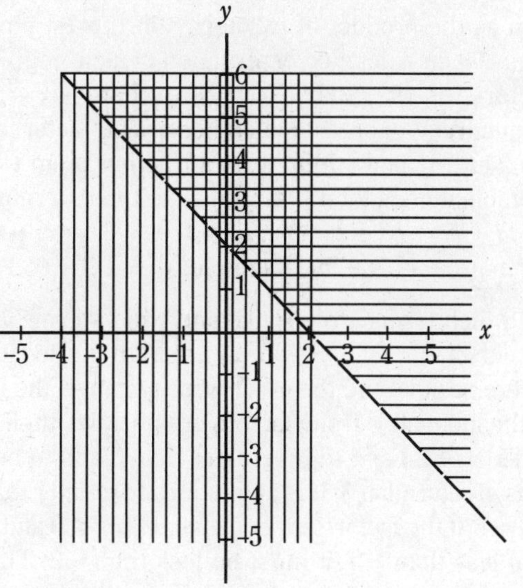

The solution is the double shaded area.

428. *Higher-order inequalities in one unknown.* These are inequalities that deal with variables multiplied by themselves. For example, $x^2 + 3 \geq 0$, $(x - 1)(x + 2) < 4$ and $x^3 - 7x > 0$ are such inequalities. The basic rules to remember in doing such problems are:

1. The product of any number of positive numbers is positive.

For example, $2 \times 3 \times 4 \times 5 = 120$, which is positive, or $\frac{1}{2} \times \frac{1}{2} = \frac{1}{4}$, which is positive.

2. The product of an even number of negative numbers is positive.

For example, $(-3)(-2) = 6$ or $(-3)(-1)(-9)(-2) = 54$, which is positive.

3. The product of an odd number of negative numbers is negative.

For example, $(-1)(-2)(-3) = -6$ or $(-\frac{1}{2})(-2)(-3)(-6)(-1) = -18$.

4. Any number squared or raised to an even power is always positive or zero.

For example, $x^2 \geq 0$ or $a^4 \geq 0$ for all x and for all a.

Often these basic rules will make the solution to an inequality problem obvious.

Example: Which of the following values can x^2 not have?

(A) 5 (B) −2 (C) 0 (D) 144 (E) 9

Solution: We know that $x^2 \geq 0$ for all x so x^2 cannot be negative. −2 is negative, so x^2 cannot equal −2.

The steps in solving a higher-order inequality are:

STEP 1. Bring all of the terms to one side of the inequality, making the other side zero. For example, in the inequality $x^2 > 3x - 2$, subtract $3x - 2$ from both sides to get $x^2 - 3x + 2 > 0$.

STEP 2. Factor the resulting expression. To factor a quadratic expression means to write the original expression as the product of two terms in the 1st power, i.e., $x^2 = x \cdot x$. x is a factor of x^2. (See Section 409 for a detailed explanation of factoring.) The quadratic expression $x^2 - 3x + 2$ when factored is $(x - 2)(x - 1)$. Note that $x \cdot x = x^2$, $-2x - x = -3x$, and $(-1)(-2) = 2$. Most quadratic expressions can easily be factored by taking factors of the last term (in this case 2 and 1) and adding or subtracting them to or from x. Through trial and error, the right combination is found. An important fact to remember when factoring is: $(a + b)(c + d) = ac + ad + bc + bd$. Example: $(x + 4)(x + 2) = x^2 + 4x + 2x + 8 = x^2 + 6x + 8$. Another is that $a^2 - b^2 = (a + b)(a - b)$. Example: $x^2 - 16 = (x + 4)(x - 4)$.

STEP 3. Investigate which terms are positive and which terms are negative. For example, in $(x - 3)(x + 2) > 0$, either $(x - 3)$ and $(x + 2)$ are both positive or $(x - 3)$ and $(x + 2)$ are both negative. If one were positive and the other were negative, the product would be negative and would not satisfy the inequality. If the factors are positive, then $x - 3 > 0$ and $x + 2 > 0$, which yields $x > 3$ and $x > -2$. For x to be greater than 3 and to be greater than −2, it must be greater than 3. If it is greater than 3, it is automatically greater than −2. Thus, with positive factors $x > 3$ is the answer. If the factors are negative, $x - 3 < 0$ and $x + 2 < 0$, or $x < -2$. For x to be less than 3 and less than −2, it must be less than −2. Thus, with negative factors $x < -2$ is the answer. As both answers are possible from the original equation, the solution to the original problem is $x > 3$ or $x < -2$.

Example: For which values of x is $x^2 + 5 < 6x$?

Solution: First subtract $6x$ from both sides to get $x^2 - 6x + 5 < 0$. The left side factors into $(x - 5)(x - 1) < 0$. Now for this to be true, one factor must be positive and one must be negative, that is, their product is less than zero. Thus, $x - 5 > 0$ and $x - 1 < 0$, or $x - 5 < 0$ and $x - 1 > 0$. If $x - 5 < 0$ and $x - 1 > 0$, then $x < 5$ and $x > 1$, or $1 < x < 5$. If $x - 5 > 0$ and $x - 1 < 0$, then $x > 5$ and $x < 1$, which is impossible because x cannot be less than 1 *and* greater than 5. Therefore, the solution is $1 < x < 5$.

Example: For what values of x is $x^2 < 4$?

Solution: Subtract 4 from both sides to get $x^2 - 4 < 0$. Remember that $a^2 - b^2 = (a + b)(a - b)$; thus $x^2 - 4 = (x + 2)(x - 2)$. Hence, $(x + 2)(x - 2) < 0$. For this to be true $x + 2 > 0$, and $x - 2 < 0$ or $x + 2 < 0$ and $x - 2 > 0$. In the first case $x > -2$ and $x < 2$, or $-2 < x < 2$. The second case is $x < -2$ and $x > 2$, which is impossible because x cannot be less than −2 *and* greater than 2. Thus, the solution is $-2 < x < 2$.

Example: When is $(x^2 + 1)(x - 2)^2(x - 3)$ greater than or equal to zero?

Solution: This can be written as $(x^2 + 1)(x - 2)^2(x - 3) \geq 0$. This is already in factors. The individual terms must be investigated. $x^2 + 1$ is always positive because $x^2 \geq 0$, so $x^2 + 1$ must be greater than 0. $(x - 2)^2$ is a number squared, so this is always greater than or equal to zero. Therefore, the product of the first two terms is positive or equal to zero for all values of x. The third term $x - 3$ is positive when $x > 3$, and negative when $x < 3$. For the entire expression to be positive, $x - 3$ must be positive, that is, $x > 3$. For the expression to be equal to zero, $x - 3 = 0$, that is, $x = 3$, or $(x - 2)^2 = 0$, that is, $x = 2$. Thus, the entire expression is positive when $x > 3$ and zero when $x = 2$ or $x = 3$.

Exponents and Roots

429. *Exponents.* An exponent is an easy way to express repeated multiplication. For example, $5 \times 5 \times 5 \times 5 = 5^4$. The 4 is the exponent. In the expression $7^3 = 7 \times 7 \times 7$, 3 is the exponent. 7^3 means 7 is multiplied by itself three times. If the exponent is 0, the expression always has a value of 1. Thus, $6^0 = 15^0 = 1$, etc. If the exponent is 1, the value of the expression is the number base. Thus, $4^1 = 4$ and $9^1 = 9$.

In the problem $5^3 \times 5^4$, we can simplify by counting the factors of 5. Thus $5^3 \times 5^4 = 5^{3+4} = 5^7$. When we multiply and the base number is the same, we keep the base number and add the exponents. For example, $7^4 \times 7^8 = 7^{12}$.

For division, we keep the same base number and subtract exponents. Thus, $8^8 \div 8^2 = 8^{8-2} = 8^6$.

A negative exponent indicates the reciprocal of the expression with a positive exponent, thus $3^{-2} = \frac{1}{3^2}$.

430. *Roots.* The square root of a number is a number whose square is the original number. For example, $\sqrt{16} = 4$, since $4 \times 4 = 16$. (The $\sqrt{\ }$ symbol always means a positive number.)

To simplify a square root, we factor the number.

$$\sqrt{32} = \sqrt{16 \cdot 2} = \sqrt{16} \cdot \sqrt{2} = 4\sqrt{2}$$
$$\sqrt{72} = \sqrt{36 \cdot 2} = \sqrt{36} \cdot \sqrt{2} = 6\sqrt{2}$$
$$\begin{aligned}\sqrt{300} &= \sqrt{25 \cdot 12} = \sqrt{25} \cdot \sqrt{12} \\ &= 5 \cdot \sqrt{12} \\ &= 5 \cdot \sqrt{4 \cdot 3} \\ &= 5 \cdot \sqrt{4} \cdot \sqrt{3} \\ &= 5 \cdot 2\sqrt{3} \\ &= 10\sqrt{3}\end{aligned}$$

We can add expressions with the square roots only if the numbers inside the square root sign are the same. For example,

$$3\sqrt{7} + 2\sqrt{7} = 5\sqrt{7}$$
$$\sqrt{18} + \sqrt{2} = \sqrt{9 \cdot 2} + \sqrt{2} = \sqrt{9} \cdot \sqrt{2} + \sqrt{2} = 3\sqrt{2} + \sqrt{2} = 4\sqrt{2}.$$

431. *Evaluation of expressions.* To evaluate an expression means to substitute a value in place of a letter. For example: Evaluate $3a^2 - c^3$; if $a = -2$, $c = -3$.

$$3a^2 - c^3 = 3(-2)^2 - (-3)^3 = 3(4) - (-27) = 12 + 27 = 39$$

Given: $a \triangledown b = ab + b^2$. Find: $-2 \triangledown 3$.

Using the definition, we get

$$\begin{aligned}-2\triangledown 3 &= (-2)(3) + (3)^2 \\ &= -6 + 9 \\ -2\triangledown 3 &= 3\end{aligned}$$

Practice Test 4

Algebra Problems

Correct answers and solutions follow each test.

1. For what values of x is the following equation satisfied: $3x + 9 = 21 + 7x$?

(A) -3 only
(B) 3 only
(C) 3 or -3 only
(D) no values
(E) an infinite number of values

2. What values may z have if $2z + 4$ is greater than $z - 6$?

(A) any values greater than -10
(B) any values greater than -2
(C) any values less than 2
(D) any values less than 10
(E) None of these.

3. If $ax^2 + 2x - 3 = 0$ when $x = -3$, what value(s) can a have?

(A) -3 only
(B) -1 only
(C) 1 only
(D) -1 and 1 only
(E) -3, -1, and 1 only

4. If the coordinates of point P are (0,8), and the coordinates of point Q are (4,2), which of the following points represents the midpoint of PQ?

(A) (0,2)
(B) (2,4)
(C) (2,5)
(D) (4,8)
(E) (4,10)

5. In the formula $V = \pi r^2 h$, what is the value of r, in terms of V and h?

(A) $\frac{\sqrt{V}}{\pi h}$

(B) $\pi\sqrt{\frac{V}{h}}$

(C) $\sqrt{\pi V h}$

(D) $\frac{\pi h}{\sqrt{V}}$

(E) $\sqrt{\frac{V}{\pi h}}$

6. Solve the inequality $x^2 - 3x < 0$.

(A) $x < -3$
(B) $-3 < x < 0$
(C) $x < 3$
(D) $0 < x < 3$
(E) $3 < x$

7. A B C D E

7. Which of the following lines is parallel to the line represented by $2y = 8x + 32$?

(A) $y = 8x + 32$
(B) $y = 8x + 16$
(C) $y = 16x + 32$
(D) $y = 4x + 32$
(E) $y = 2x + 16$

8. A B C D E

8. In the equation $4.04x + 1.01 = 9.09$, what value of x is necessary to make the equation true?

(A) -1.5
(B) 0
(C) 1
(D) 2
(E) 2.5

9. A B C D E

9. What values of x satisfy the equation $(x + 1)(x - 2) = 0$?

(A) 1 only
(B) -2 only
(C) 1 and -2 only
(D) -1 and 2 only
(E) any values between -1 and 2

10. A B C D E

10. What is the largest possible value of the following expression:
$(x + 2)(3 - x)(2 + x)^2(2x - 6)(2x + 4)$?

(A) -576
(B) -24
(C) 0
(D) 12
(E) Cannot be determined.

11. A B C D E

11. For what value(s) of k is the following equation satisfied:
$2k - 9 - k = 4k + 6 - 3k$?

(A) -5 only
(B) 0
(C) $\frac{5}{2}$ only
(D) no values
(E) more than one value

12. A B C D E

12. In the equation $p = aq^2 + bq + c$, if $a = 1$, $b = -2$, and $c = 1$, which of the following expresses p in terms of q?

(A) $p = (q - 2)^2$
(B) $p = (q - 1)^2$
(C) $p = q^2$
(D) $p = (q + 1)^2$
(E) $p = (q + 2)^2$

13. A B C D E

13. If $A + B + C = 10$, $A + B = 7$, and $A - B = 5$, what is the value of C?

(A) 1
(B) 3
(C) 6
(D) 7
(E) The answer cannot be determined from the given information.

14. A B C D E

14. If $5x + 15$ is greater than 20, which of the following best describes the possible values of x?

(A) x must be greater than 5
(B) x must be greater than 3
(C) x must be greater than 1
(D) x must be less than 5
(E) x must be less than 1

15. A B C D E

15. If $\frac{t^2 - 1}{t - 1} = 2$, then what value(s) may t have?

(A) 1 only
(B) -1 only
(C) 1 or -1
(D) no values
(E) an infinite number of values

16. A B C D E

16. If $4m = 9n$, what is the value of $7m$, in terms of n?

(A) $\frac{63n}{4}$

(B) $\frac{9n}{28}$

(C) $\frac{7n}{9}$

(D) $\frac{28n}{9}$

(E) $\frac{7n}{4}$

17. A B C D E

17. The coordinates of a triangle are (0,2), (2,4), and (1,6). What is the area of the triangle in square units (to the nearest unit)?

(A) 2 square units
(B) 3 square units
(C) 4 square units
(D) 5 square units
(E) 6 square units

18. A B C D E

18. In the formula $s = \frac{1}{2}gt^2$, what is the value of t, in terms of s and g?

(A) $\frac{2s}{g}$

(B) $2\sqrt{\frac{s}{g}}$

(C) $\frac{s}{2g}$

(D) $\sqrt{\frac{s}{2g}}$

(E) $\sqrt{\frac{2s}{g}}$

19. A B C D E

19. In the triangle ABC, angle A is a 30° angle, and angle B is obtuse. If x represents the number of degrees in angle C, which of the following best represents the possible values of x?

(A) $0 < x < 60$
(B) $0 < x < 150$
(C) $60 < x < 180$
(D) $120 < x < 180$
(E) $120 < x < 150$

20. A B C D E

20. Which of the following sets of coordinates does *not* represent the vertices of an isosceles triangle?

(A) (0,2), (0,−2), (2,0)
(B) (1,3), (1,5), (3,4)
(C) (1,3), (1,7), (4,5)
(D) (2,2), (2,0), (1,1)
(E) (2,3), (2,5), (3,3)

21. A B C D E

21. If $2 < a < 5$, and $6 > b > 3$, what are the possible values of $a + b$?

(A) $a + b$ must equal 8.
(B) $a + b$ must be between 2 and 6.
(C) $a + b$ must be between 3 and 5.
(D) $a + b$ must be between 5 and 8.
(E) $a + b$ must be between 5 and 11.

22. A B C D E

22. The area of a square will be doubled if:

(A) the length of the diagonal is divided by 2.
(B) the length of the diagonal is divided by $\sqrt{2}$.
(C) the length of the diagonal is multiplied by 2.
(D) the length of the diagonal is multiplied by $\sqrt{2}$.
(E) None of the above.

23. A B C D E

23. Find the value of y that satisfies the equation $8.8y - 4 = 7.7y + 7$.

(A) 1.1
(B) 7.7
(C) 8.0
(D) 10.0
(E) 11.0

24. A B C D E

24. Which of the following is a factor of the expression $2x^2 + 1$?

(A) $x + 2$
(B) $x - 2$
(C) $x + \sqrt{2}$
(D) $x - \sqrt{2}$
(E) None of these.

25. A B C D E

25. A businessman has ten employees; his salary is equal to six times the *average* of the employees' salaries. If the eleven of them received a total of $640,000 in one year, what was the businessman's salary that year?

(A) $40,000
(B) $60,000
(C) $240,000
(D) $400,000
(E) $440,000

26. A B C D E

26. If $6x + 3 = 15$, what is the value of $12x - 3$?

(A) 21
(B) 24
(C) 28
(D) 33
(E) 36

27. A B C D E

27. If $2p + 7$ is greater than $3p - 5$, which of the following best describes the possible values of p?

(A) p must be greater than 2.
(B) p must be greater than 12.
(C) p must be less than 2.
(D) p must be less than 12.
(E) p must be greater than 2, but less than 12.

28. A B C D E

28. What is the value of q if $x^2 + qx + 1 = 0$, if $x = 1$?

(A) -2
(B) -1
(C) 0
(D) 1
(E) 2

29. A B C D E

29. What is the area (to the nearest unit) of the shaded figure in the diagram below, assuming that each of the squares has an area of 1?

(A) 12
(B) 13
(C) 14
(D) 15
(E) 16

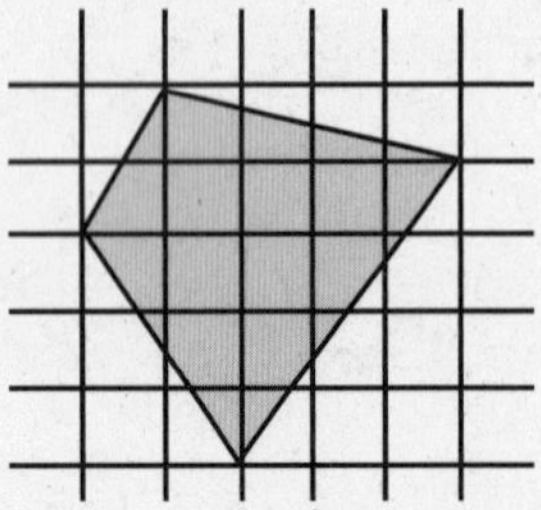

30. A B C D E

30. Which of the following statements is *false*?

(A) Any two numbers, a and b, have a sum equal to $a + b$.
(B) Any two numbers, a and b, have a product equal to $a \cdot b$.
(C) Any two numbers, a and b, have a difference equal to $a - b$.
(D) Any two numbers, a and b, have a quotient equal to $\frac{a}{b}$.
(E) Any two numbers, a and b, have an average equal to $\frac{(a + b)}{2}$.

31. A B C D E

31. If $(x - 1)(x - 2)(x^2 - 4) = 0$, what are the possible values of x?

(A) -2 only
(B) $+2$ only
(C) -1, -2, or -4 only
(D) $+1$, $+2$, or $+4$ only
(E) $+1$, -2, or $+2$ only

32. A B C D E

32. If $P + Q = R$, and $P + R = 2Q$, what is the ratio of P to R?

(A) 1 : 1
(B) 1 : 2
(C) 2 : 1
(D) 1 : 3
(E) 3 : 1

33. A B C D E

33. For what value(s) of r is $\dfrac{r^2+5r+6}{r+2}$ equal to 0?

(A) −2 only
(B) −3 only
(C) +3 only
(D) −2 or −3
(E) +2 or +3

34. A B C D E

34. What is the value of $a^2b + 4ab^2 + 4b^3$, if $a = 15$ and $b = 5$?

(A) 1,625
(B) 2,125
(C) 2,425
(D) 2,725
(E) 3,125

35. A B C D E

35. If $m + 4n = 2n + 8m$, what is the ratio of n to m?

(A) 1 : 4
(B) 1 : −4
(C) −4 : 1
(D) 2 : 7
(E) 7 : 2

36. A B C D E

36. If the value of a lies between −5 and +2, and the value of b lies between −7 and +1, what are the possible values for the product, $a \cdot b$?

(A) between −14 and +2
(B) between −35 and +2
(C) between +2 and +35
(D) between −12 and +3
(E) between −14 and +35

37. A B C D E

37. What is the area, in square units, of a triangle whose vertices lie on points (−5,1), (−5,4), and (2,4)?

(A) 10.5 square units
(B) 12.5 square units
(C) 15.0 square units
(D) 20.0 square units
(E) 21.0 square units

38. A B C D E

38. If $A + B = 12$, and $B + C = 16$, what is the value of $A + C$?

(A) −4
(B) −28
(C) +4
(D) +28
(E) The answer cannot be determined from the given information.

39. A B C D E

39. What is the solution to the equation $x^2 + 2x + 1 = 0$?

(A) $x = 1$
(B) $x = 0$
(C) $x = 1$ and $x = -1$
(D) $x = -1$
(E) no real solutions

40. A B C D E

40. Which of the following equations will have a vertical line as its graph?

(A) $x + y = 1$
(B) $x - y = 1$
(C) $x = 1$
(D) $y = 1$
(E) $xy = 1$

41. A B C D E

41. For what value(s) of x does $x^2 + 3x + 2$ equal zero?

(A) -1 only
(B) $+2$ only
(C) -1 or -2 only
(D) 1 or 2 only
(E) None of these.

42. A B C D E

42. If $a + b$ equals 12, and $a - b$ equals 6, what is the value of b?

(A) 0
(B) 3
(C) 6
(D) 9
(E) The answer cannot be determined from the given information.

43. A B C D E

43. For what value(s) of m is $m^2 + 4$ equal to $4m$?

(A) -2 only
(B) 0 only
(C) $+2$ only
(D) $+4$ only
(E) more than one value

44. A B C D E

44. If $x = 0$, $y = 2$, and $x^2yz + 3xz^2 + y^2z + 3y + 4x = 0$, what is the value of z?

(A) $-\frac{4}{3}$

(B) $-\frac{3}{2}$

(C) $+\frac{3}{4}$

(D) $+\frac{4}{3}$

(E) The answer cannot be determined from the given information.

45. A B C D E

45. If $c + 4d = 3c - 2d$, what is the ratio of c to d?

(A) $1:3$
(B) $1:-3$
(C) $3:1$
(D) $2:3$
(E) $2:-3$

46. A B C D E

46. If $3 < x < 7$, and $6 > x > 2$, which of the following best describes x?

(A) $2 < x < 6$
(B) $2 < x < 7$
(C) $3 < x < 6$
(D) $3 < x < 7$
(E) No value of x can satisfy both of these conditions.

47. A B C D E

47. What are the coordinates of the midpoint of the line segment whose endpoints are (4,9) and (5,15)?

(A) (4,5)
(B) (5,9)
(C) (4,15)
(D) (4.5,12)
(E) (9,24)

48. A B C D E

48. If $\frac{t^2 + 2t}{2t + 4} = \frac{t}{2}$, what does t equal?

(A) -2 only
(B) $+2$ only
(C) any value except $+2$
(D) any value except -2
(E) any value

49. A B C D E

49. If $x + y = 4$, and $x + z = 9$, what is the value of $(y - z)$?

(A) -5
(B) $+5$
(C) -13
(D) $+13$
(E) The answer cannot be determined from the given information.

50. A B C D E

50. Of the following statements, which are equivalent?

I. $-3 < x < 3$
II. $x^2 < 9$
III. $\frac{1}{x} < \frac{1}{3}$

(A) I and II only
(B) I and III only
(C) II and III only
(D) I, II, and III
(E) None of the above.

Answer Key for Practice Test 4

1. A	14. C	27. D	39. D
2. A	15. D	28. A	40. C
3. C	16. A	29. B	41. C
4. C	17. B	30. D	42. B
5. E	18. E	31. E	43. C
6. D	19. A	32. D	44. B
7. D	20. E	33. B	45. C
8. D	21. E	34. E	46. C
9. D	22. D	35. E	47. D
10. C	23. D	36. E	48. D
11. D	24. E	37. A	49. A
12. B	25. C	38. E	50. A
13. B	26. A		

Answers and Solutions for Practice Test 4

1. Choice A is correct. The original equation is $3x + 9 = 21 + 7x$. First subtract 9 and $7x$ from both sides to get $-4x = 12$. Now divide both sides by the coefficient of x, -4, obtaining the solution, $x = -3$. (406)

2. Choice A is correct. Given $2z + 4 > z - 6$. Subtracting equal quantities from both sides of an inequality does not change the order of the inequality. Therefore, subtracting z and 4 from both sides gives a solution of $z > -10$. (419, 420)

3. Choice C is correct. Substitute -3 for x in the original equation to get the following:

$$a(-3)^2 + 2(-3) - 3 = 0$$
$$9a - 6 - 3 = 0$$
$$9a - 9 = 0$$
$$a = 1 \quad (406)$$

4. Choice C is correct. To find the midpoint of the line segment connecting two points, find the point whose x-coordinate is the average of the two given x-coordinates, and whose y-coordinate is the average of the two given y-coordinates. The midpoint here will be $\left(\frac{0+4}{2}, \frac{8+2}{2}\right)$, or (2,5). (412)

5. Choice E is correct. Divide both sides of the equation by πh:

$$\frac{V}{\pi h} = r^2$$

Take the square root of both sides:

$$r = \sqrt{\frac{V}{\pi h}}. \quad (403)$$

6. Choice D is correct. Factor the original expression into $x(x - 3) < 0$. In order for the product of two expressions to be less than 0 (negative), one must be positive and the other must be negative. Thus, $x < 0$ and $x - 3 > 0$; or $x > 0$ and $x - 3 < 0$. In the first case, $x < 0$ and $x > 3$. This is impossible because x cannot be less than 0 *and* greater than 3 at the same time. In the second case $x > 0$ and $x < 3$, which can be rewritten as $0 < x < 3$. (428)

7. Choice D is correct. Divide both sides of the equation $2y = 8x + 32$ by 2 to get $y = 4x + 16$. Now it is in the form of $y = mx + b$, where m is the slope of the line and b is the y-intercept. Thus the slope of the line is 4. Any line parallel to this line must have the same slope. The answer must have a slope of 4. This is the line $y = 4x + 32$. Note that all of the choices are already in the form of $y = mx + b$. (416)

8. Choice D is correct. Subtract 1.01 from both sides to give: $4.04x = 8.08$. Dividing both sides by 4.04 gives a solution of $x = 2$. (406)

9. Choice D is correct. If a product is equal to zero, then one of the factors must equal zero. If $(x + 1)(x - 2) = 0$, either $x + 1 = 0$, or $x - 2 = 0$. Solving these two equations, we see that either $x = -1$ or $x = 2$. (408, 409)

10. Choice C is correct. It is possible, but time-consuming, to examine the various ranges of x, but it will be quicker if you realize that the same factors appear, with numerical multiples, more than once in the expression. Properly factored, the expression becomes:

$$(x + 2)(2 + x)^2(2)(x + 2)(3 - x)(-2)(3 - x) = -4(x + 2)^4(3 - x)^2$$

Since squares of real numbers can never be negative, the whole product has only one negative term and is therefore negative, except when one of the terms is zero, in which case the product is also zero. Thus, the product cannot be larger than zero for any x. (428)

11. Choice D is correct. Combine like terms on both sides of the given equations and obtain the equivalent form: $k - 9 = k + 6$. This is true for no values of k. If k is subtracted from both sides, -9 will equal 6, which is impossible. (406)

12. Choice B is correct. Substitute for the given values of a, b, and c, and obtain $p = q^2 - 2q + 1$; or, rearranging terms, $p = (q - 1)^2$. (409)

13. Choice B is correct. $A + B + C = 10$. Also, $A + B = 7$. Substitute the value 7 for the quantity $(A + B)$ in the first equation and obtain the new equation: $7 + C = 10$ or $C = 3$. $A - B = 5$ could be used with the other two equations to find the values of A and B. (406)

14. Choice C is correct. If $5x + 15 > 20$, then subtract 15 from both sides to get $5x > 5$. Now divide both sides by 5. This does not change the order of the inequality because 5 is a positive number. The solution is $x > 1$. (419, 426)

15. Choice D is correct. Factor $(t^2 - 1)$ to obtain the product $(t + 1)(t - 1)$. For any value of t, except 1, the equation is equivalent to $(t + 1) = 2$, or $t = 1$. One is the only possible value of t. However, this value is not possible as $t - 1$ would equal 0, and the quotient $\frac{t^2 - 1}{t - 1}$ would not be defined. (404, 409)

16. Choice A is correct. If $4m = 9n$, then $m = \frac{9n}{4}$. Multiplying both sides of the equation by 7, we obtain: $7m = \frac{63n}{4}$. (403)

17. Choice B is correct. As the diagram shows, the easiest way to calculate the area of this triangle is to start with the area of the enclosing rectangle and subtract the three shaded triangles.

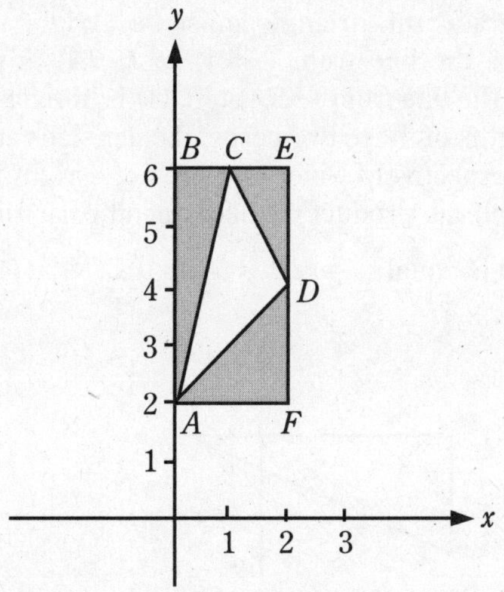

The area of the rectangle $ABEF = (2)(4) = 8$ square units.

The area of the triangle $ABC = \frac{1}{2}(1)(4) = 2$ square units.

The area of the triangle $CDE = \frac{1}{2}(1)(2) = 1$ square unit.

The area of the triangle $ADF = \frac{1}{2}(2)(2) = 2$ square units.

Thus the area of the triangle $ACD = 8 - 5 = 3$ square units. (418)

18. Choice E is correct. Since $s = \frac{1}{2}gt^2$, divide both sides of the equation by $\frac{1}{2}g$ to obtain the form, $\frac{2s}{g} = t^2$. Then, after taking the square roots, $t = \sqrt{\frac{2s}{g}}$. (403)

19. Choice A is correct. The sum of the three angles of a triangle must be 180°. Since angle A is 30°, and angle B is between 90° and 180° (it is obtuse), their sum is greater than 120° and less than 180° (the sum of all three angles is 180°). Their sum subtracted from the total of 180° gives a third angle greater than zero, but less than 60°. (419)

20. Choice E is correct. An isosceles triangle has two equal sides. To find the length of the sides, we use the distance formula, $\sqrt{(x_2 - x_1)^2 + (y_2 - y_1)^2}$. In the first case the lengths of the sides are 4, $2\sqrt{2}$ and $2\sqrt{2}$. Thus two sides have the same length, and it is an isosceles triangle. The only set of points that is not an isosceles triangle is the last one. (411)

21. Choice E is correct. The smallest possible value of a is greater than 2, and the smallest possible value of b is greater than 3, so the smallest possible value of $a + b$ must be greater than $2 + 3 = 5$. Similarly, the largest values of a and b are less than 5 and 6, respectively, so the largest possible value of $a + b$ is less than 11. Therefore, the sum must be between 5 and 11. (419)

22. Choice D is correct. If the sides of the original square are each equal to s, then the area of the square is s^2, and the diagonal is $s\sqrt{2}$. Now, a new square, with an area of $2s^2$, must have a side of $s\sqrt{2}$. Thus, the diagonal is $2s$, which is $\sqrt{2}$ times the original length of the diagonal. (303, 406)

23. Choice D is correct. First place all of the variable terms on one side and all of the numerical terms on the other side. Subtracting $7.7y$ and adding 4 to both sides of the equation gives $1.1y = 11$. Now divide both sides by 1.1 to solve for $y = 10$. (406)

24. Choice E is correct. To determine whether an expression is a factor of another expression, give the variable a specific value in both expressions. An expression divided by its factor will be a whole number. If we give x the value 0, then the expression $2x^2 + 1$ has the value of 1. $x + 2$ then has the value of 2. 1 is not divisible by 2, so the first choice is not a factor. The next choice has the value of -2, also not a factor of 1. Similarly $x + \sqrt{2}$ and $x - \sqrt{2}$ take on the values of $\sqrt{2}$ and $-\sqrt{2}$, respectively, when $x = 0$, and are not factors of $2x^2 + 1$. Therefore, the correct choice is (E). (409)

25. Choice C is correct. Let x equal the average salary of the employees. Then the employees receive a total of $10x$ dollars, and the businessman receives six times the average, or $6x$. Together, the eleven of them receive a total of $10x + 6x = 16x$, which equals \$640,000. Thus, x equals \$40,000, and the businessman's salary is $6x$, or \$240,000. (406)

26. Choice A is correct. $6x + 3 = 15$; therefore $6x = 12$ and $x = 2$. Substituting $x = 2$ into the expression $12x - 3$, gives $24 - 3$, which equals 21. (406)

27. Choice D is correct. $2p + 7 > 3p - 5$. To both sides of the equation add 5 and subtract $2p$, obtaining $12 > p$. Thus, p is less than 12. (419, 426)

28. Choice A is correct. Substituting 1 for x in the given equation obtains $1 + q + 1 = 0$, or $q + 2 = 0$. This is solved only for $q = -2$. (406)

29. Choice B is correct.

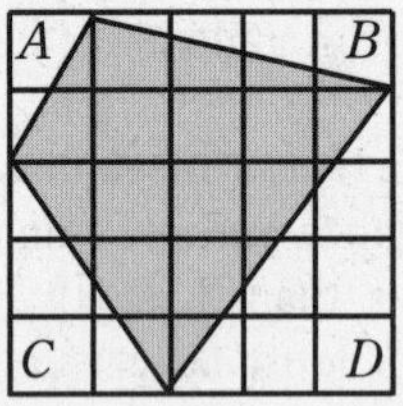

The area of the shaded figure can most easily be found by taking the area of the square surrounding it (25), and subtracting the areas of the four triangles marked A (1), B (2), C (3), and D (6), leaving an area of $25 - (1 + 2 + 3 + 6) = 13$ square units. (418)

30. Choice D is correct. If the number b is equal to zero, the quotient $\frac{a}{b}$ is not defined. For all other pairs, all five statements are true. (401–405)

31. Choice E is correct. If a product equals zero, one of the factors must be equal to zero also. Thus, either $x - 1 = 0$, or $x - 2 = 0$, or $x^2 - 4 = 0$. The possible solutions, therefore, are $x = 1$, $x = 2$, and $x = -2$. (408)

32. Choice D is correct. Solve the equation $P + Q = R$, for Q (the variable we wish to eliminate), to get $Q = R - P$. Substituting this for Q in the second equation yields $P + R = 2(R - P) = 2R - 2P$, or $3P = R$. Therefore, the ratio of P to R is $\frac{P}{R}$, or $\frac{1}{3}$. (406)

33. Choice B is correct. The fraction in question will equal zero if the numerator equals zero, and the denominator is nonzero. The expression $r^2 + 5r + 6$ can be factored into $(r + 2)(r + 3)$. As long as r is not equal to -2 the equation is defined, and $r + 2$ can be canceled in the original equation to yield $r + 3 = 0$, or $r = -3$. For r equals -2, the denominator is equal to zero, and the fraction in the original equation is not defined. (404, 409)

34. Choice E is correct. This problem can be shortened considerably by factoring the expression $a^2b + 4ab^2 + 4b^3$ into the product $(b)(a + 2b)^2$. Now, since $b = 5$, and $(a + 2b) = 25$, our product equals $5 \times 25 \times 25$, or 3,125. (409)

35. Choice E is correct. Subtract $m + 2n$ from both sides of the given equation and obtain the equivalent form, $2n = 7m$. Dividing this equation by $2m$ gives $\frac{n}{m} = \frac{7}{2}$, the ratio of n to m. (406)

36. Choice E is correct. The product will be positive in the case: a positive and b positive, or a negative and b negative; and negative in the case: a positive and b negative, or a negative and b positive. Thus, the positive products must be $(+2)(+1)$ and $(-5)(-7)$. The largest positive value is 35. Similarly, the negative products are $(-5)(+1)$ and $(+2)(-7)$; and the most negative value that can be obtained is -14. Thus, the product falls between -14 and $+35$. (419)

37. Choice A is correct. As can be seen from a diagram, this triangle must be a right triangle, since the line from $(-5,1)$ to $(-5,4)$ is vertical, and the line from $(-5,4)$ to $(2,4)$ is horizontal. The lengths of these two perpendicular sides are 3 and 7, respectively. Since the area of a right triangle is half the product of the perpendicular sides, the area is equal to $\frac{1}{2} \times 3 \times 7$, or 10.5. (410, 418)

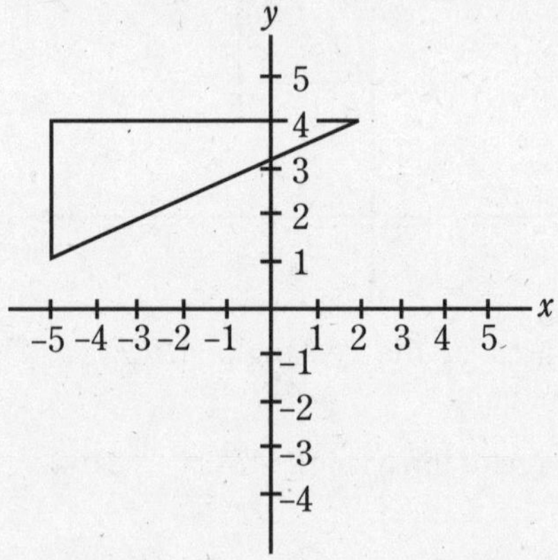

38. Choice E is correct. Solving the first equation for A gives $A = 12 - B$. Solving the second equation for C gives $C = 16 - B$. Thus, the sum $A + C$ is equal to $28 - 2B$. There is nothing to determine the value of B, so the sum of A and C is not determined from the information given. (406)

39. Choice D is correct. Factor $x^2 + 2x + 1$ to get $(x + 1)(x + 1) = 0$. Thus $x + 1 = 0$, so $x = -1$. (409)

40. Choice C is correct. If we graph the five choices we will get:

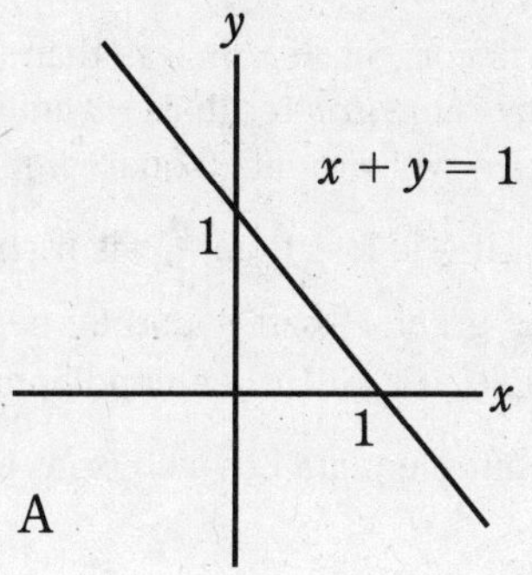

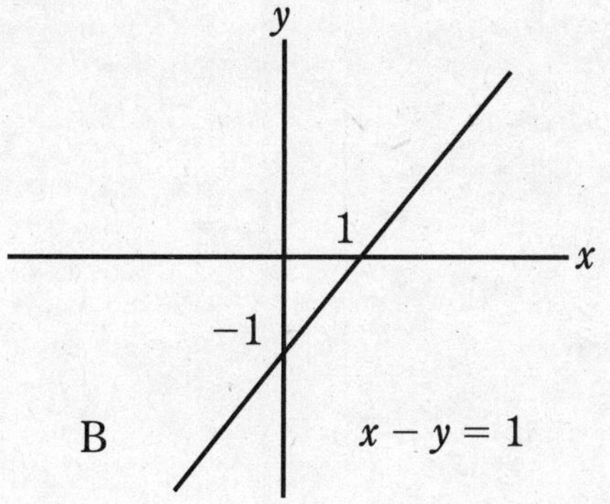

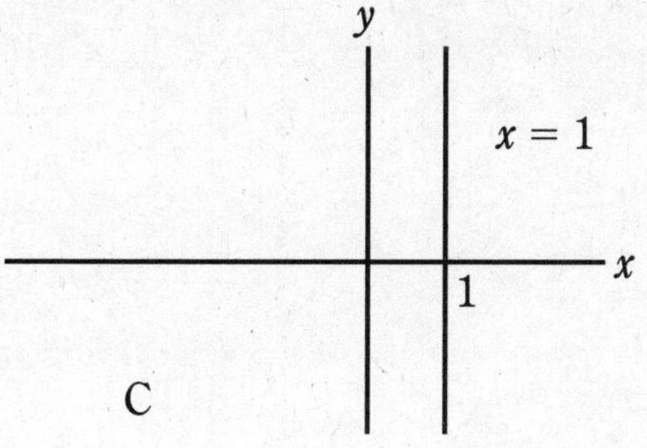

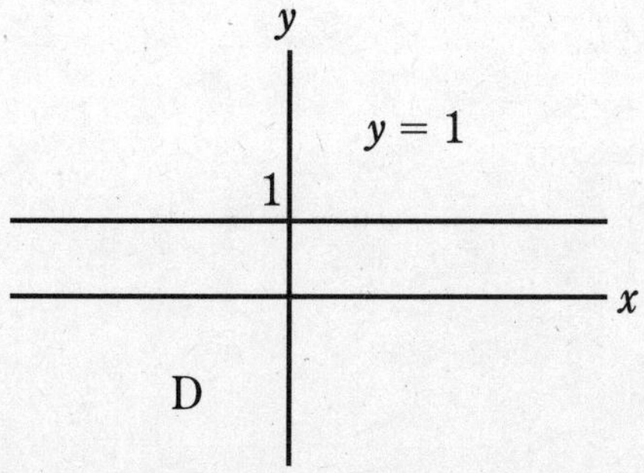

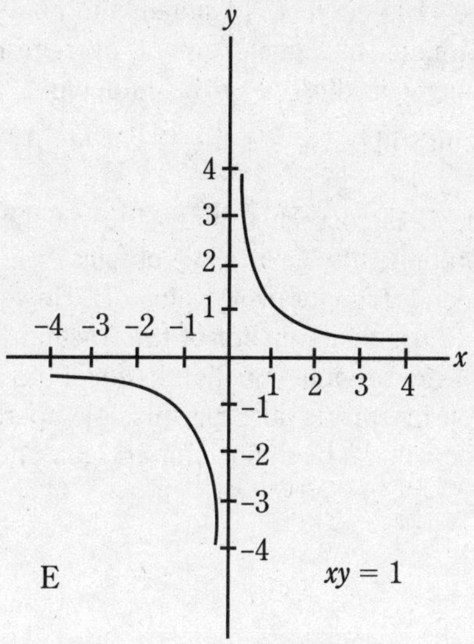

The only choice that is a vertical line is $x = 1$.
(413)

41. Choice C is correct. The factors of $x^2 + 3x + 2$ are $(x + 1)$ and $(x + 2)$. Either $x + 1 = 0$, or $x + 2 = 0$. x may equal either -1 or -2. (408)

42. Choice B is correct. $a + b = 12$ and $a - b = 6$. Rewrite these equations as $a = 12 - b$ and $a = 6 + b$. $12 - b$ and $6 + b$ are both equal to a. Or, $12 - b = 6 + b$. Thus, $6 = 2b$ and $b = 3$. (407)

43. Choice C is correct. Let $m^2 + 4 = 4m$. Subtracting $4m$ from both sides yields $m^2 - 4m + 4 = 0$. Factor to get the following equation: $(m - 2)^2 = 0$. Thus, $m = 2$ is the only solution. (408)

44. Choice B is correct. Substitute for the given values of x and y, obtaining: $(0)^2(2)(z) + (3)(0)(z)^2 + (2)^2(z) + (3)(2) + (4)(0) = 0$. Perform the indicated multiplications, and combine terms. $0(z) + 0(z^2) + 4z + 6 + 0 = 4z + 6 = 0$. This equation has $z = -\frac{3}{2}$ as its only solution. (406)

45. Choice C is correct. $c + 4d = 3c - 2d$. Add $2d - c$ to each side and get $6d = 2c$. (Be especially careful about your signs here.) Dividing by $2d$: $\frac{c}{d} = \frac{6}{2} = \frac{3}{1}$. Thus, $c : d = 3 : 1$. (406)

46. Choice C is correct. x must be greater than 3, less than 7, greater than 2, and less than 6. These conditions can be reduced as follows: If x is less than 6 it is also less than 7. Similarly, x must be greater than 3, which automatically makes it greater than 2. Thus, x must be greater than 3 *and* less than 6.
(419)

47. Choice D is correct. To obtain the coordinates of the midpoint of a line segment, average the corresponding coordinates of the endpoints. Thus, the midpoint will be $\left(\frac{4+5}{2}, \frac{9+15}{2}\right)$ or (4.5,12). (412)

48. Choice D is correct. If both sides of the equation are multiplied by $2t + 4$, we obtain: $t^2 + 2t = t^2 + 2t$, which is true for every value of t. However, when $t = -2$, the denominator of the fraction on the left side of the original equation is equal to zero. Since division by zero is not a permissible operation, this fraction will not be defined for $t = -2$. The equation cannot be satisfied for $t = -2$. (404, 406, 409)

49. Choice A is correct. If we subtract the second of our equations from the first, we will be left with the following: $(x + y) - (x + z) = 4 - 9$, or $y - z = -5$. (402)

50. Choice A is correct. If x^2 is less than 9, then x may take on any value greater than -3 and less than $+3$; other values will produce squares greater than or equal to 9. If $\frac{1}{x}$ is less than $\frac{1}{3}$, x is restricted to positive values greater than 3, and all negative values. For example, if $x = 1$, then conditions I and II are satisfied, but $\frac{1}{x}$ equals 1, which is greater than $\frac{1}{3}$. (419)

MATH REFRESHER SESSION 5

Geometry Problems

Basic Definitions

500. *Plane geometry* deals with points and lines. A point has no dimensions and is generally represented by a dot (·). A line has no thickness, but it does have length. Lines can be straight or curved, but here it will be assumed that a line is straight unless otherwise indicated. All lines have infinite length. Part of a line that has a finite length is called a line segment.

> Remember that the ***distance*** between two lines or from a point to a line always means the perpendicular distance. Thus, the distance between the two lines pictured below in the diagram to the left is line *A*, as this is the only perpendicular line. Also, as shown in the diagram to the right, the distance from a line to a point is the perpendicular from the point to the line. Thus, *AB* is the distance from point *A* to the line segment *CBD*.

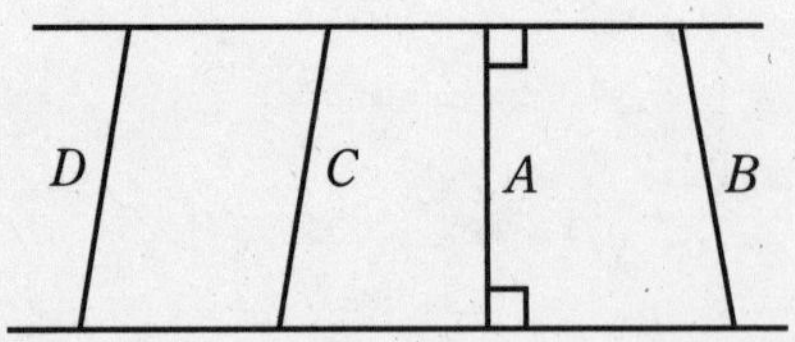

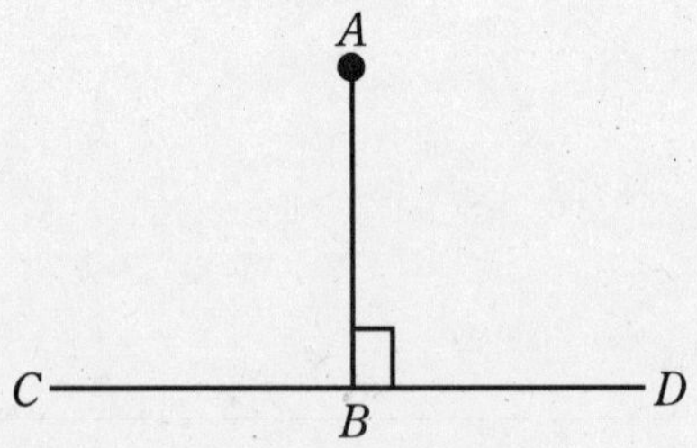

501. *Angles.* An angle is formed when two lines intersect at a point.

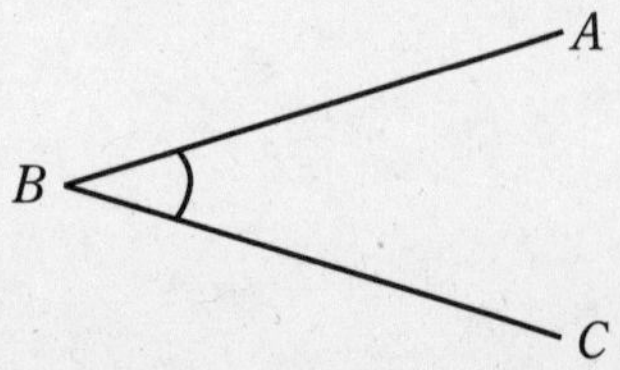

Angle *B*, angle *ABC*, $\angle B$, $\angle ABC$ are all possible names for the angle shown.

The measure of the angle is given in degrees. If the sides of the angle form a straight line, then the angle is said to be a straight angle and has 180°. A circle has 360°, and a straight angle is a turning through a half circle. All other angles are either greater or less than 180°.

Angles are classified in different ways:
An *acute* angle has less than 90°.

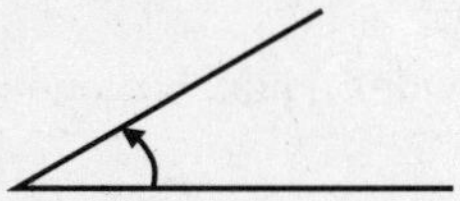

A *right* angle has exactly 90°.

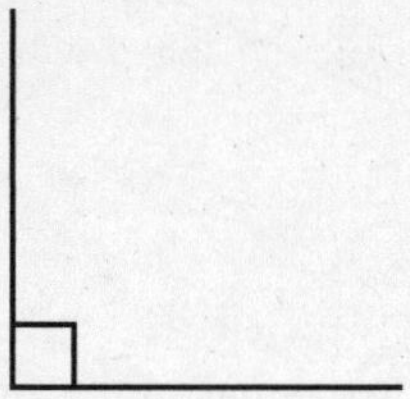

In the diagram, the small square in the corner of the angle indicates a right angle (90°).

An *obtuse* angle has between 90° and 180°.

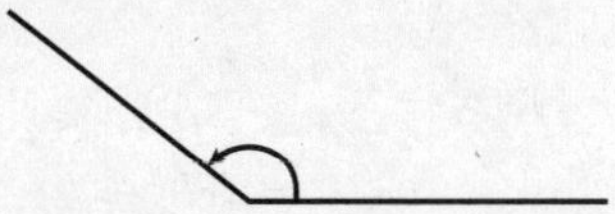

A *straight* angle has exactly 180°.

A *reflex* angle has between 180° and 360°.

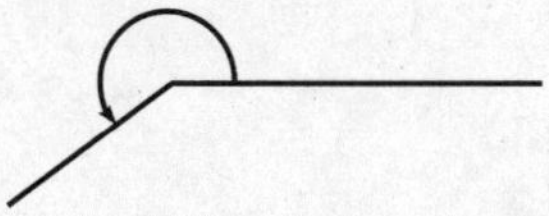

502. Two angles are *complementary* if their sum is 90°. For example, an angle of 30° and an angle of 60° are complementary. Two angles are *supplementary* if their sum is 180°. If one angle is 82°, then its supplement is 98°.

503. *Vertical angles.* These are pairs of opposite angles formed by the intersection of two straight lines. Vertical angles are always equal to each other.

Example: In the diagram shown, angles *AEC* and *BED* are equal because they are vertical angles. For the same reason, angles *AED* and *BEC* are equal.

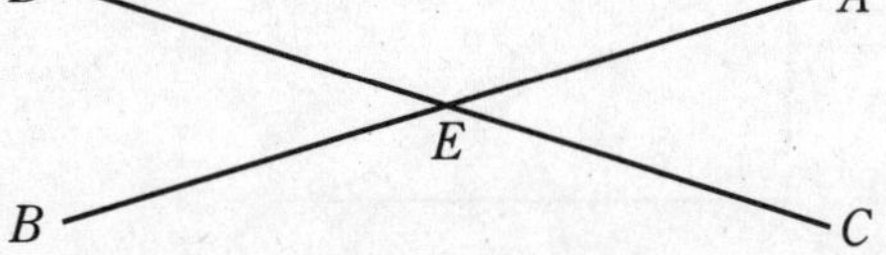

504. When two parallel lines are crossed by a third straight line (called a *transversal*), then all the acute angles formed are equal, and all of the obtuse angles are equal.

Example: In the diagram below, angles 1, 4, 5, and 8 are all equal. Angles 2, 3, 6, and 7 are also equal.

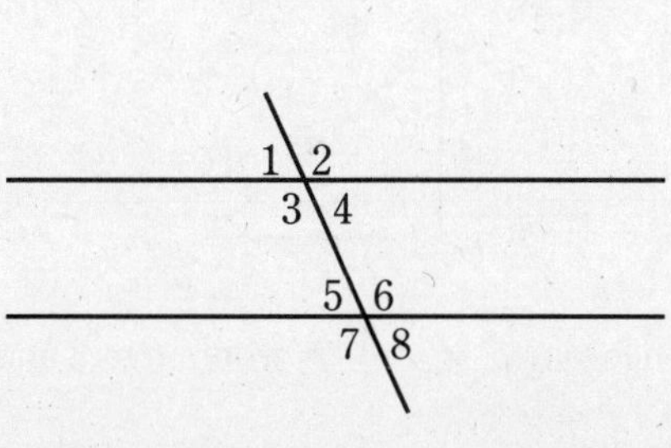

Triangles

505. *Triangles.* A triangle is a closed figure with three sides, each side being a line segment. The sum of the angles of a triangle is *always* 180°.

506. *Scalene triangles* are triangles with no two sides equal. Scalene triangles also have no two angles equal.

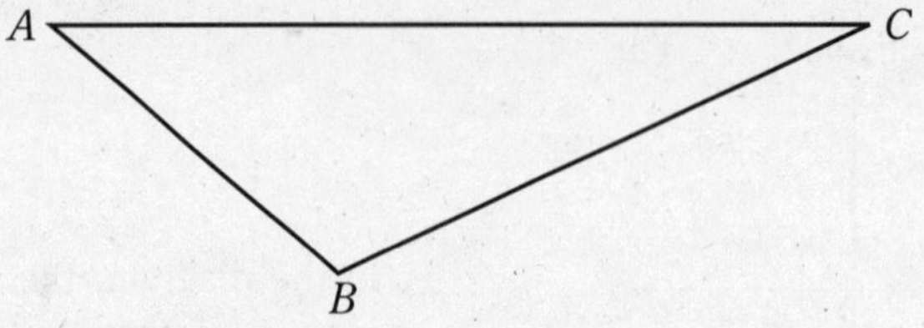

507. *Isosceles triangles* have two equal sides and two equal angles formed by the equal sides and the unequal side. See the figure below.

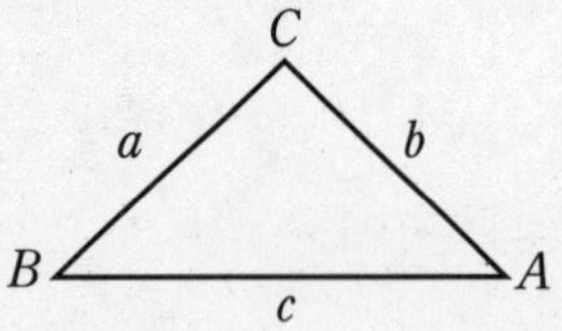

$a = b$
$\angle A = \angle B$
$\angle C = 180° - 2(\angle A)$

508. *Equilateral triangles* have all three sides and all three angles equal. Since the sum of the three angles of a triangle is 180°, each angle of an equilateral triangle is 60°.

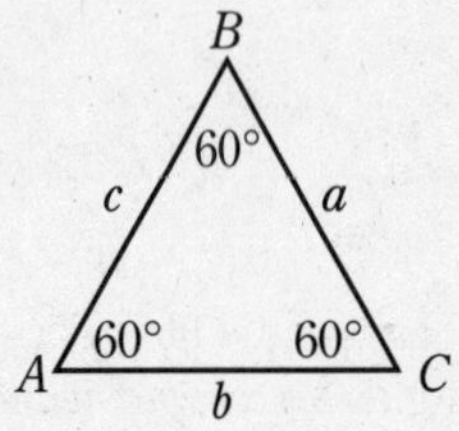

$a = b = c$
$\angle A = \angle B = \angle C = 60°$

509. A *right triangle* has one angle equal to a right angle (90°). The sum of the other two angles of a right triangle is, therefore, 90°. The most important relationship in a right triangle is the Pythagorean Theorem. It states that $c^2 = a^2 + b^2$, where c, the hypotenuse, is the length of the side opposite the right angle, and a and b are the lengths of the other two sides. Recall that this was discussed in Section 317.

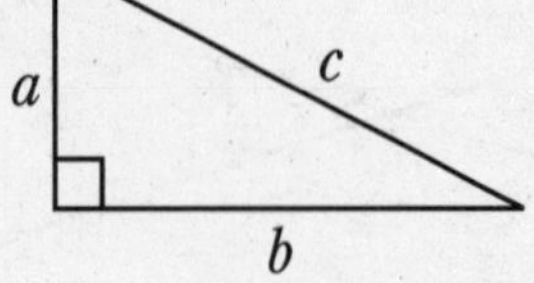

Example: If the two sides of a right triangle adjacent to the right angle are 3 inches and 4 inches respectively, find the length of the side opposite the right angle.

Solution:

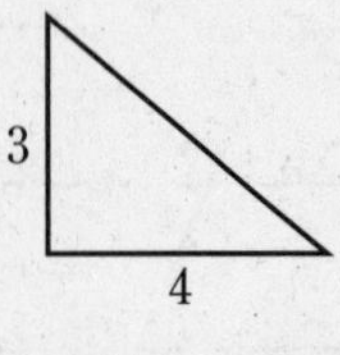

Use the Pythagorean Theorem, $c^2 = a^2 + b^2$, where $a = 3$ and $b = 4$. Then, $c = 3^2 + 4^2$ or $c^2 = 9 + 16 = 25$. Thus $c = 5$.

Certain sets of integers will always fit the formula $c^2 = a^2 + b^2$. These integers can always represent the lengths of the sides of a right triangle. For example, a triangle whose sides are 3, 4, and 5 will always be a right triangle. Further examples are 5, 12, and 13, and 8, 15, and 17. Any multiples of these numbers also satisfy this formula. For example, 6, 8, and 10; 9, 12, and 15; 10, 24, and 26; 24, 45, and 51, etc.

Properties of Triangles

510. Two triangles are said to be *similar* (having the same shape) if their corresponding angles are equal. The sides of similar triangles are in the same proportion. The two triangles below are similar because they have the same corresponding angles.

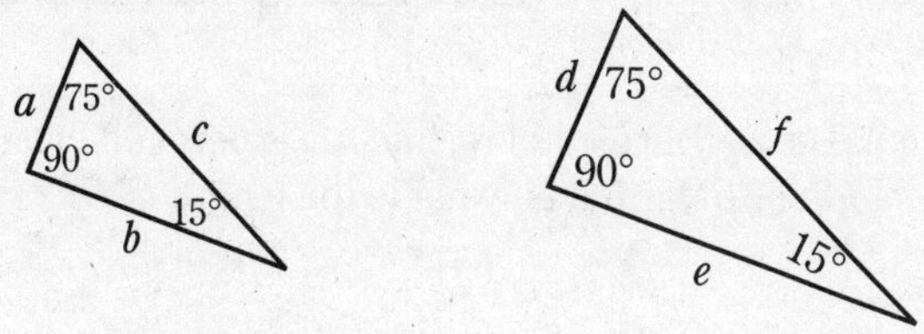

$$a : d = b : e = c : f$$

Example: Two triangles both have angles of 30°, 70°, and 80°. If the sides of the triangles are as indicated below, find the length of side *x*.

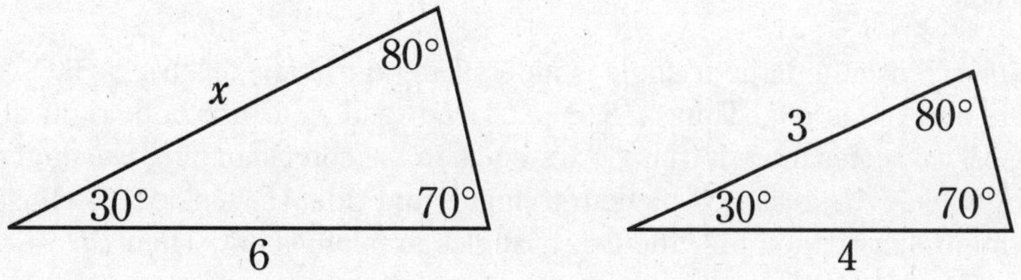

Solution: The two triangles are similar because they have the same corresponding angles. The corresponding sides of similar triangles are in proportion, so $x : 3 = 6 : 4$. This can be rewritten as $\frac{x}{3} = \frac{6}{4}$. Multiplying both sides by 3 gives $x = \frac{18}{4}$, or $x = 4\frac{1}{2}$.

511. Two triangles are *congruent* (*identical* in shape and size) if any one of the following conditions is met:

1. Each side of the first triangle equals the corresponding side of the second triangle.
2. Two sides of the first triangle equal the corresponding sides of the second triangle, and their included angles are equal. The included angle is formed by the two sides of the triangle.
3. Two angles of the first triangle equal the corresponding angles of the second triangle, and any pair of corresponding sides are equal.

Example: Triangles *ABC* and *DEF* in the diagrams below are congruent if any one of the following conditions can be met:

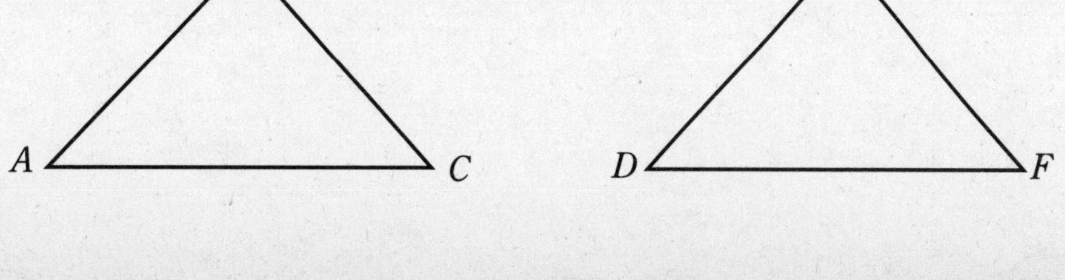

1. The three sides are equal (*sss*) = (*sss*).

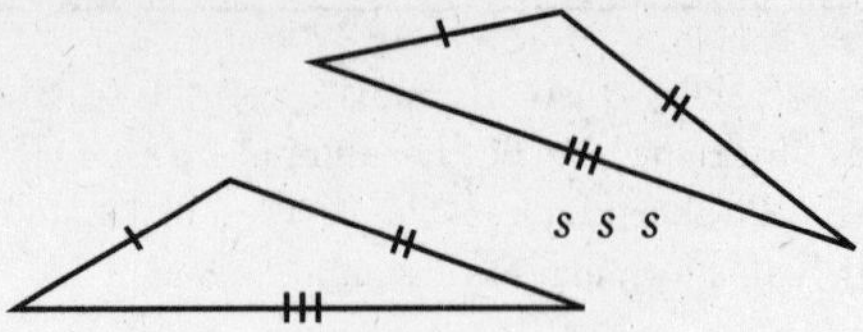

2. Two sides and the included angle are equal (*sas*) = (*sas*).

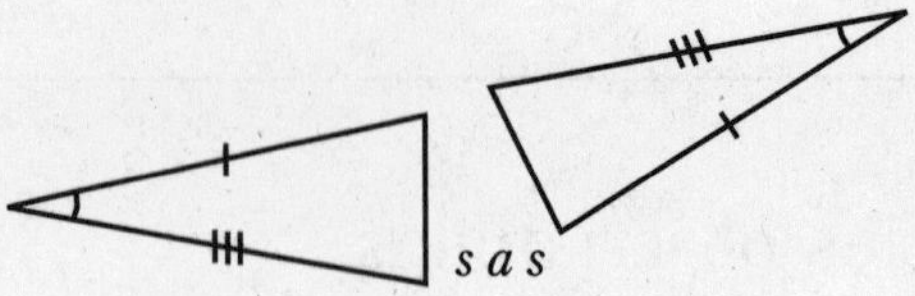

3. Two angles and any one side are equal (*aas*) = (*aas*) or (*asa*) = (*asa*).

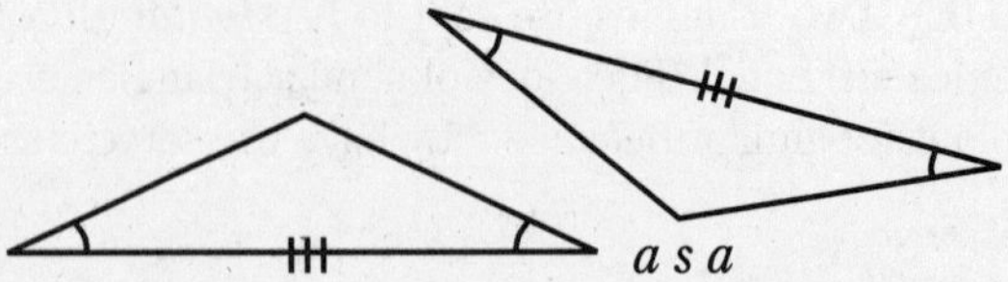

Example: In the equilateral triangle below, line *AD* is perpendicular (forms a right angle) to side *BC*. If the length of *BD* is 5 feet, what is the length of *DC*?

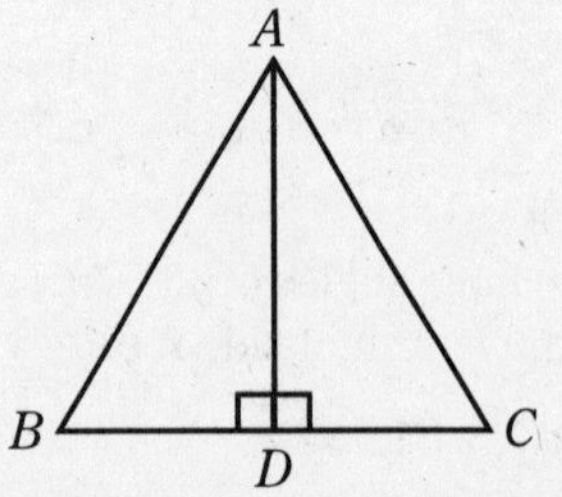

Solution: Since the large triangle is an equilateral triangle, each ∠ is 60°. Therefore ∠*B* is 60° and ∠*C* is 60°. Thus, ∠*B* = ∠*C*. *ADB* and *ADC* are both right angles and are equal. Two angles of each triangle are equal to the corresponding two angles of the other triangle. Side *AD* is shared by both triangles and side *AB* = side *AC*. Thus, according to condition 3 in Section 511, the two triangles are congruent. Then *BD* = *DC* and, since *BD* is 5 feet, *DC* is 5 feet.

512. The *medians* of a triangle are the lines drawn from each vertex to the midpoint of its opposite side. The medians of a triangle cross at a point that divides each median into two parts: one part of one-third the length of the median and the other part of two-thirds the length.

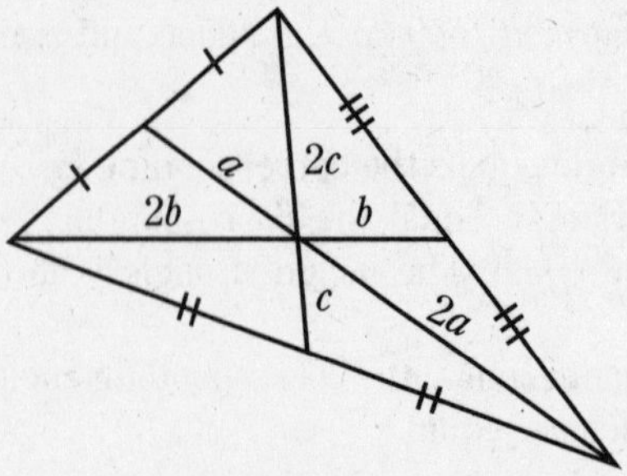

513. The *angle bisectors* of a triangle are the lines that divide each angle of the triangle into two equal parts. These lines meet in a point that is the center of a circle inscribed in the triangle.

514. The *altitudes* of the triangle are lines drawn from the vertices perpendicular to the opposite sides. The lengths of these lines are useful in calculating the area of the triangle, since the area of the triangle is $\frac{1}{2}$(base) (height) and the height is identical to the altitude.

515. The *perpendicular bisectors* of the triangle are the lines that bisect and are perpendicular to each of the three sides. The point where these lines meet is the center of the circumscribed circle.

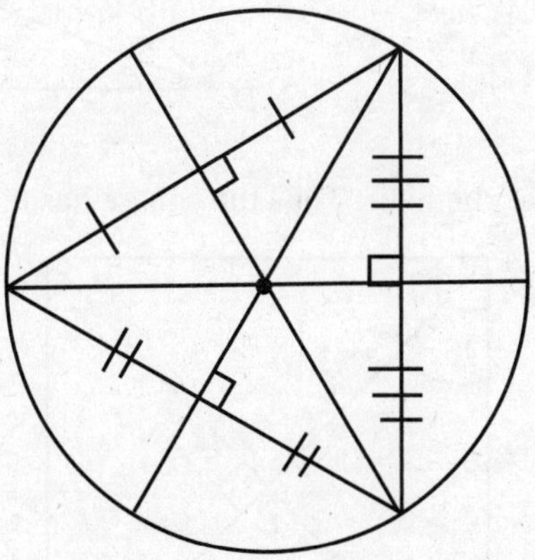

516. The sum of any two sides of a triangle is greater than the third side.

Example: If the three sides of a triangle are 4, 2, and x, then what is known about the value of x?

Solution: Since the sum of two sides of a triangle is always greater than the third side, then $4 + 2 > x$, $4 + x > 2$, and $2 + x > 4$. These three inequalities can be rewritten as $6 > x$, $x > -2$, and $x > 2$. For x to be greater than -2 and 2, it must be greater than 2. Thus, the values of x are $2 < x < 6$.

Four-Sided Figures

517. A *parallelogram* is a four-sided figure with each pair of opposite sides parallel.

A parallelogram has the following properties:

1. Each pair of opposite sides is equal. ($AD = BC$, $AB = DC$)
2. The diagonals bisect each other. ($AE = EC$, $DE = EB$)
3. The opposite angles are equal. ($\angle A = \angle C$, $\angle D = \angle B$)
4. One diagonal divides the parallelogram into two congruent triangles. Two diagonals divide the parallelogram into two pairs of congruent triangles.

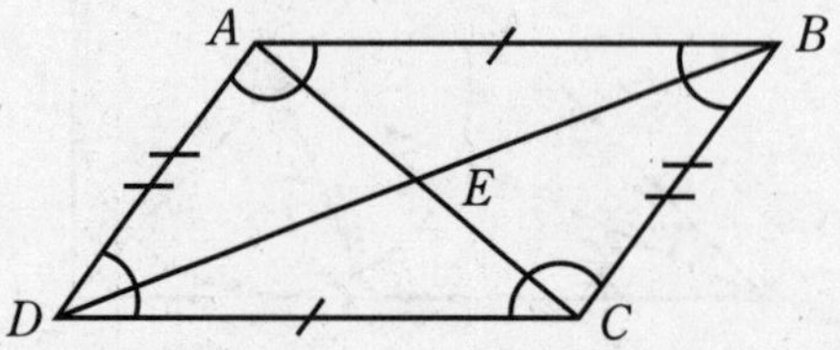

518. A *rectangle* is a parallelogram in which all the angles are right angles. Since a rectangle is a parallelogram, all of the laws that apply to a parallelogram apply to a rectangle. In addition, the diagonals of a rectangle are equal.

$AC = BD$

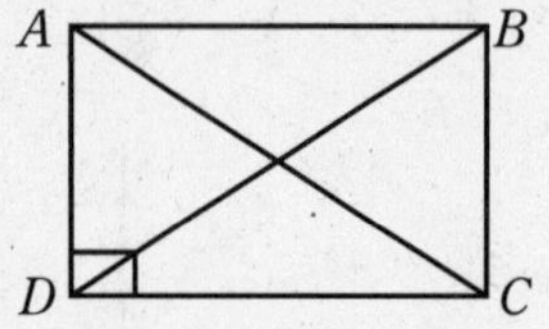

519. A *rhombus* is a parallelogram with four equal sides. Since a rhombus is a parallelogram, all of the laws that apply to a parallelogram apply to a rhombus. In addition, the diagonals of a rhombus are perpendicular to each other and bisect the vertex angles.

$\angle DAC = \angle BAC = \angle DCA = \angle BCA$
$\angle ADB = \angle CDB = \angle ABD = \angle CBD$
AC is perpendicular to DB

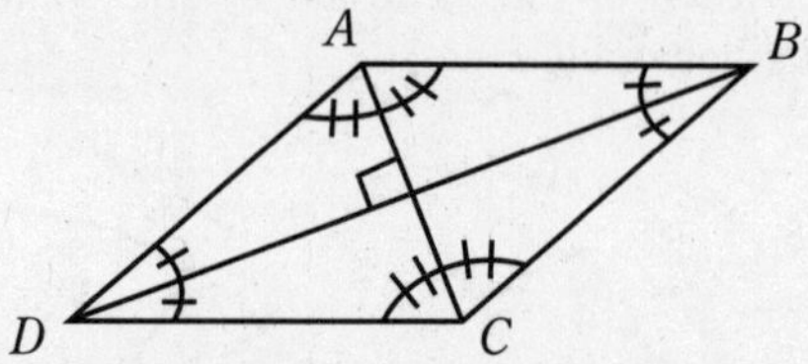

520. A *square* is a rectangular rhombus. Thus the square has the following properties:

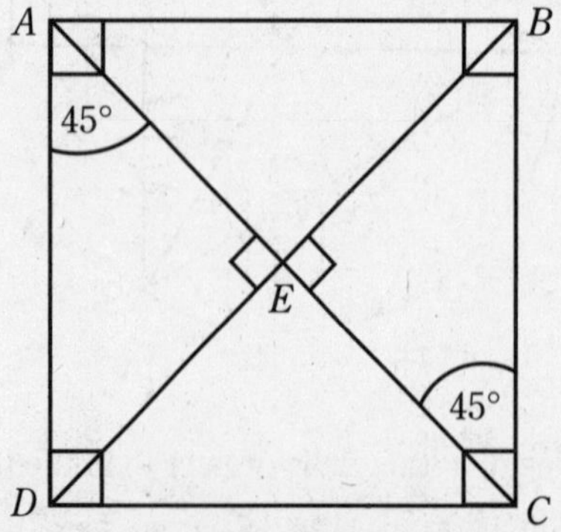

1. All four sides are equal. ($AB = BC = CD = DA$)
2. Opposite pairs of sides are parallel. ($AD \parallel BC$, $AB \parallel DC$)
3. Diagonals are equal, are perpendicular to each other, and bisect each other. ($AC = BD$, $AC \perp BD$, $AE = EC = DE = EB$)
4. All the angles are right angles (90°). ($\angle A = \angle B = \angle C = \angle D = 90°$)
5. Diagonals intersect the vertices at 45°. ($\angle DAC = \angle BCA = 45°$, and similarly for the other 3 vertices.)

Many-Sided Figures

521. A *polygon* is a closed plane figure whose sides are straight lines. The sum of the angles in any polygon is equal to $180(n - 2)°$, where n is the number of sides. Thus, in a polygon of 3 sides (a triangle), the sum of the angles is $180(3 - 2)°$, or $180°$.

522. A *regular polygon* is a polygon all of whose sides are equal and all of whose angles are equal. These polygons have special properties:

1. A regular polygon can be inscribed in a circle and can be circumscribed about another circle. For example, a hexagon is inscribed in a circle in the diagram below.

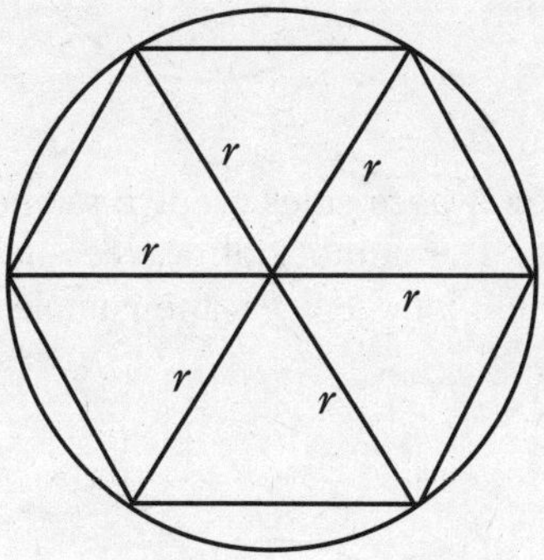

2. Each angle of a regular polygon is equal to the sum of the angles divided by the number of sides, $\frac{180(n-2)°}{n}$. Thus, a square, which is a regular polygon of 4 sides, has each angle equal to $\frac{180(4-2)°}{4}$ or $90°$.

523. An important regular polygon is the *hexagon*. The diagonals of a regular hexagon divide it into 6 equilateral triangles, the sides of which are equal to the sides of the hexagon. If a hexagon is inscribed in a circle, the length of each side is equal to the length of the radius of the circle. (See diagram of hexagon above.)

Circles

524. A *circle* (also see Section 310) is a set of points equidistant from a given point, the *center*. The distance from the center to the circle is the *radius*. Any line that connects two points on the circle is a *chord*. A chord through the center of the circle is a *diameter*. On the circle below, O is the center, line segment OF is a radius, DE is a diameter, and AC is a chord.

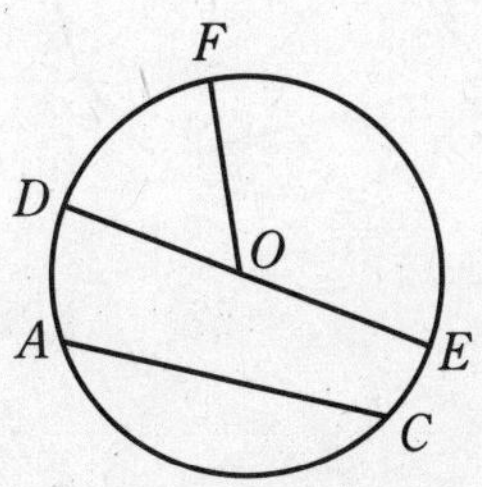

The length of the diameter of a circle is twice the length of the radius. The circumference (distance around the circle) is 2π times the length of the radius. π is a constant approximately equal to $\frac{22}{7}$ or 3.14. The formula for the circumference of a circle is $C = 2\pi r$, where C = circumference and r = radius.

525. A *tangent* to a circle is a line that is perpendicular to a radius and that passes through only one point of the circle. In the diagram below, *AB* is a tangent.

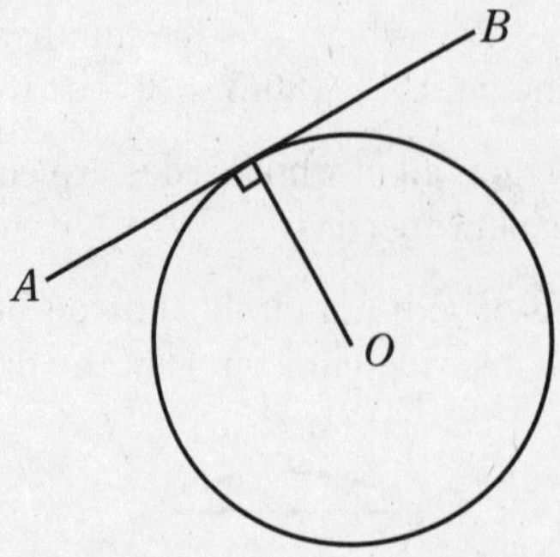

526. A *central angle* is an angle whose sides are two radii of the circle. The vertex of this angle is the center of the circle. The number of degrees in a central angle is equal to the amount of arc length that the radii intercept. As the complete circumference has 360°, any other arc lengths are less than 360°.

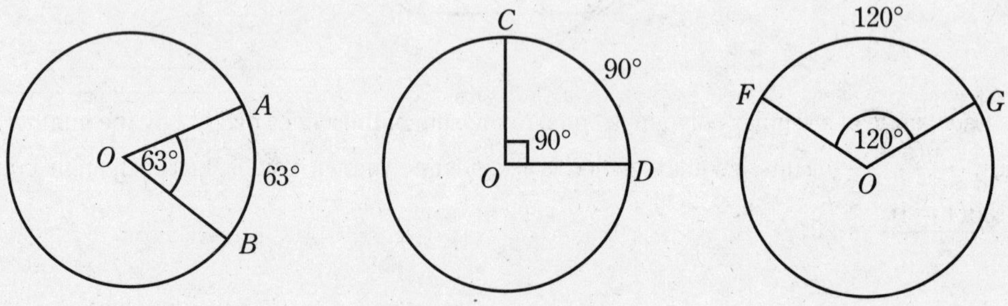

Angles *AOB*, *COD*, and *FOG* are all central angles.

527. An *inscribed angle* of a circle is an angle whose sides are two chords. The vertex of the angle lies on the circumference of the circle. The number of degrees in the inscribed angle is equal to one-half the intercepted arc.

$\angle BAC$ is an inscribed angle.

528. An angle inscribed in a semicircle is always a right angle. $\angle ABC$ and $\angle ADC$ are inscribed in semicircles *AOCB* and *AOCD*, respectively, and are thus right angles.

Note: A semicircle is one-half of a circle.

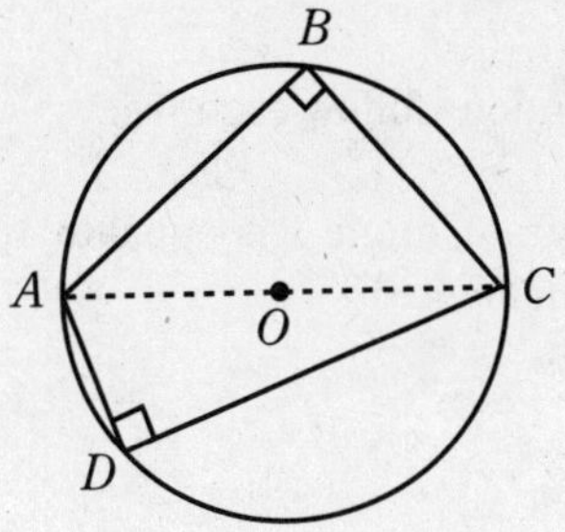

529. Two tangents to a circle from the same point outside of the circle are always equal.

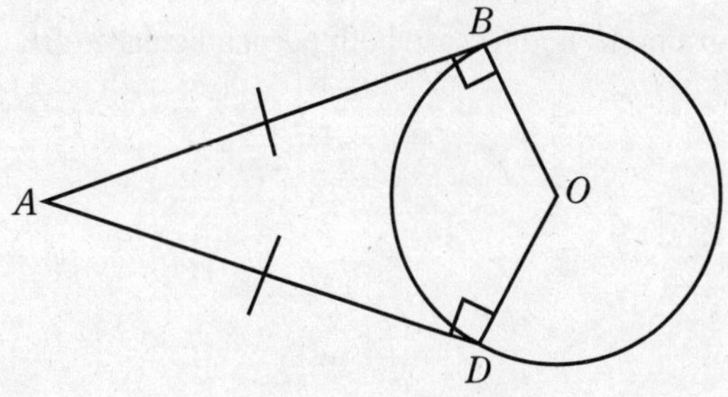

Tangents *AB* and *AD* are equal.

Practice Test 5

Geometry Problems

Correct answers and solutions follow each test.

1. A B C D E

1. In the following diagram, angle 1 is equal to 40°, and angle 2 is equal to 150°. What is the number of degrees in angle 3?

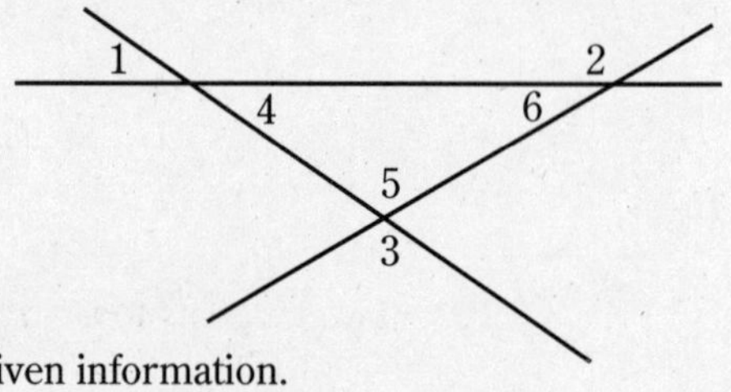

(A) 70°
(B) 90°
(C) 110°
(D) 190°
(E) The answer cannot be determined from the given information.

2. A B C D E

2. In this diagram, *AB* and *CD* are both perpendicular to *BE*. If $EC = 5$, and $CD = 4$, what is the ratio of *AB* to *BE*?

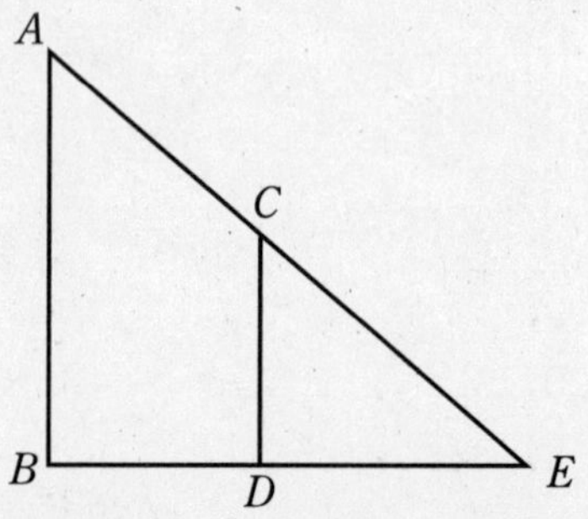

(A) 1 : 1
(B) 4 : 3
(C) 5 : 4
(D) 5 : 3
(E) None of these.

3. A B C D E

3. In triangle *PQR*, $PR = 7.0$, and $PQ = 4.5$. Which of the following cannot possibly represent the length of *QR*?

(A) 2.0
(B) 3.0
(C) 3.5
(D) 4.5
(E) 5.0

4. A B C D E

4. In this diagram, $AB = AC$, and $BD = CD$. Which of the following statements is true?

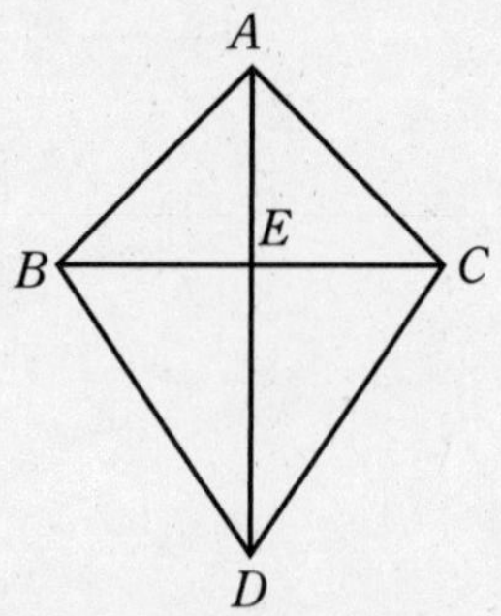

(A) $BE = EC$.
(B) *AD* is perpendicular to *BC*.
(C) Triangles *BDE* and *CDE* are congruent.
(D) Angle *ABD* equals angle *ACD*.
(E) All of these.

5. A B C D E

5. In the following diagram, if $BC = CD = BD = 1$, and angle *ADC* is a right angle, what is the perimeter of triangle *ABD*?

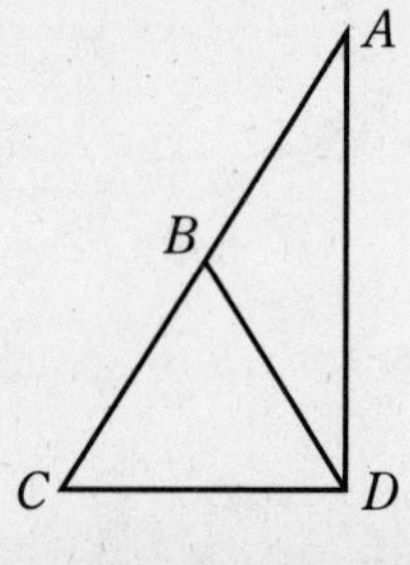

(A) 3
(B) $2 + \sqrt{2}$
(C) $2 + \sqrt{3}$
(D) $3 + \sqrt{3}$
(E) 4

6. A B C D E

6. In this diagram, if *PQRS* is a parallelogram, which of the following can be deduced?

I. $QT + PT = RT + ST$
II. *QS* is perpendicular to *PR*
III. The area of the shaded portion is exactly three times the area of triangle *QRT*.

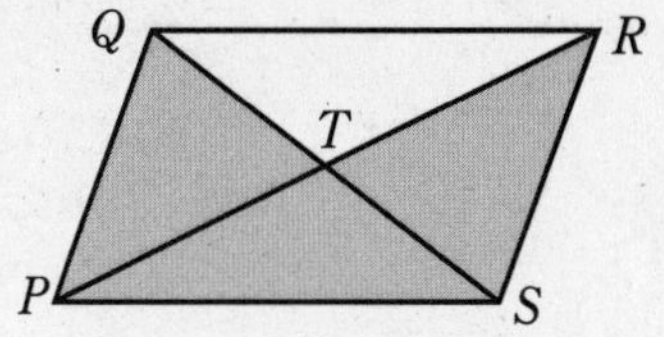

(A) I only
(B) I and II only
(C) II only
(D) I and III only
(E) I, II, and III

7. A B C D E

7. James lives on the corner of a rectangular field that measures 120 yards by 160 yards. If he wants to walk to the opposite corner, he can either travel along the perimeter of the field or cut directly across in a straight line. How many yards does he save by taking the direct route? (Express to the nearest ten yards.)

(A) 40 yards
(B) 60 yards
(C) 80 yards
(D) 100 yards
(E) 110 yards

8. A B C D E

8. In a square, the perimeter is how many times the length of the diagonal?

(A) $\frac{\sqrt{2}}{2}$
(B) $\sqrt{2}$
(C) 2
(D) $2\sqrt{2}$
(E) 4

9. A B C D E

9. How many degrees are there in the angle formed by two adjacent sides of a regular nonagon (nine-sided polygon)?

(A) 40°
(B) 70°
(C) 105°
(D) 120°
(E) 140°

10. A B C D E

10. In the diagram to the right, $AB = CD$. From this we can deduce that:

(A) *AB* is parallel to *CD*.
(B) *AB* is perpendicular to *BD*.
(C) $AC = BD$
(D) Angle *ABD* equals angle *BDC*.
(E) Triangle *ABD* is congruent to triangle *ACD*.

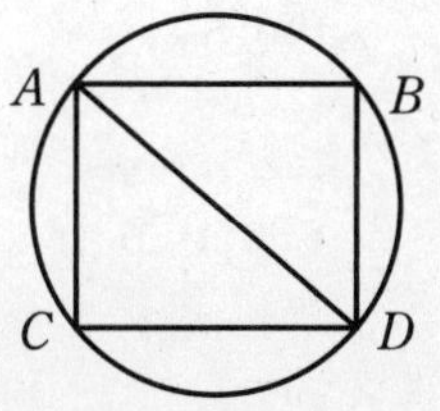

(Note: Figure is not drawn to scale.)

11. A B C D E

11. If two lines, *AB* and *CD*, intersect at a point *E*, which of the following statements is *not* true?

(A) Angle *AEB* equals angle *CED*.
(B) Angles *AEC* and *BEC* are complementary.
(C) Angle *CED* is a straight angle.
(D) Angle *AEC* equals angle *BED*.
(E) Angle *BED* plus angle *AED* equals 180 degrees.

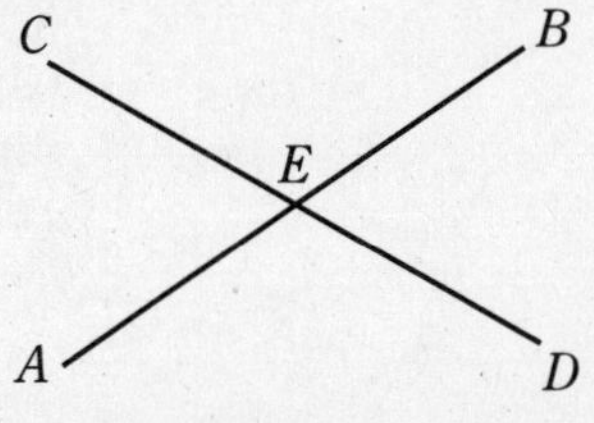

12. A B C D E

12. In the following diagram, $AC = CE$ and $BD = DE$. Which of these statements is (are) true?

I. AB is twice as long as CD.
II. AB is parallel to CD.
III. Triangle AEB is similar to triangle CED.

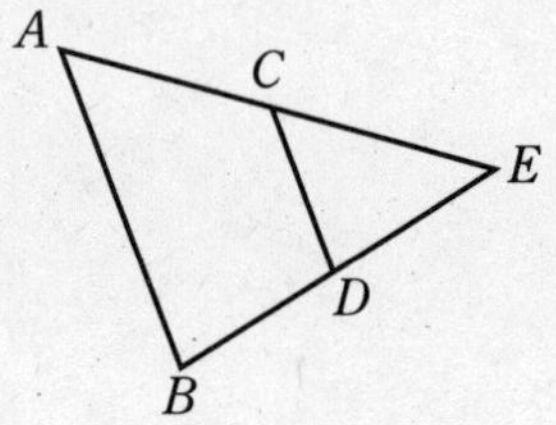

(A) I only
(B) II and III only
(C) I and III only
(D) I, II, and III
(E) None of these.

13. A B C D E

13. In triangle ABC, angle A is obtuse, and angle B equals 30°. Which of the following statements *best* describes angle C?

(A) Angle C must be less than 60°.
(B) Angle C must be less than or equal to 60°.
(C) Angle C must be equal to 60°.
(D) Angle C must be greater than or equal to 60°.
(E) Angle C must be greater than 60°.

14. A B C D E

14. In this diagram, $ABCD$ is a parallelogram, and $BFDE$ is a square. If $AB = 20$ and $CF = 16$, what is the perimeter of the parallelogram $ABCD$?

(A) 72
(B) 78
(C) 86
(D) 92
(E) 96

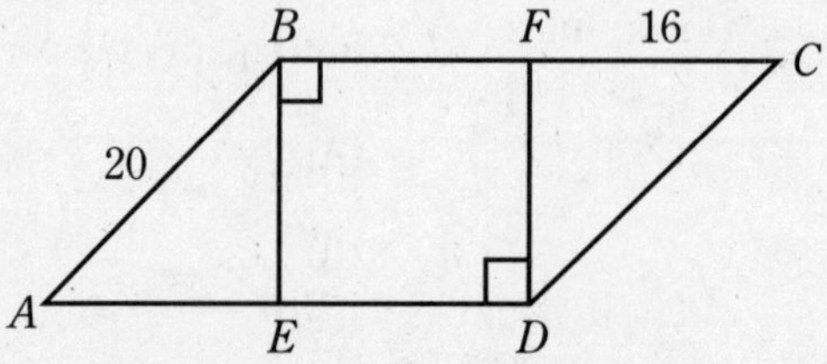

15. A B C D E

15. The hypotenuse of a right triangle is exactly twice as long as the shorter leg. What is the number of degrees in the smallest angle of the triangle?

(A) 30°
(B) 45°
(C) 60°
(D) 90°
(E) The answer cannot be determined from the given information.

16. A B C D E

16. The legs of an isosceles triangle are equal to 17 inches each. If the altitude to the base is 8 inches long, how long is the base of the triangle?

(A) 15 inches
(B) 20 inches
(C) 24 inches
(D) 25 inches
(E) 30 inches

17. A B C D E

17. The perimeter of a right triangle is 18 inches. If the midpoints of the three sides are joined by line segments, they form another triangle. What is the perimeter of this new triangle?

(A) 3 inches
(B) 6 inches
(C) 9 inches
(D) 12 inches
(E) The answer cannot be determined from the given information.

18. A B C D E

18. If the diagonals of a square divide it into four triangles, the triangles *cannot* be

(A) right triangles
(B) isosceles triangles
(C) similar triangles
(D) equilateral triangles
(E) equal in area

19. A B C D E

19. In the diagram below, *ABCDEF* is a regular hexagon. How many degrees are there in angle *ADC*?

(A) 45°
(B) 60°
(C) 75°
(D) 90°
(E) None of these.

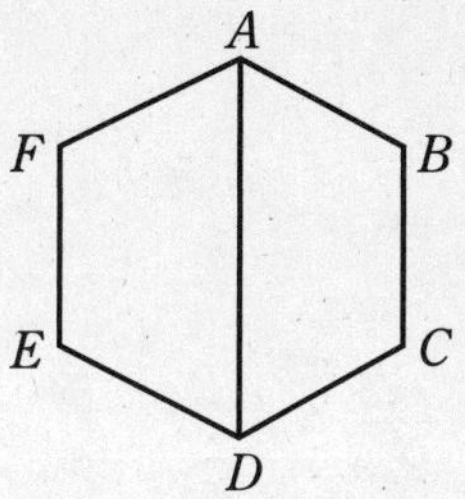

20. A B C D E

20. This diagram depicts a rectangle inscribed in a circle. If the measurements of the rectangle are 10″ × 14″, what is the area of the circle in inches?

(A) 74π
(B) 92π
(C) 144π
(D) 196π
(E) 296π

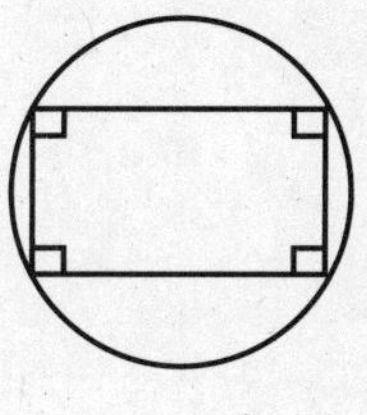

21. A B C D E

21. How many degrees are included between the hands of a clock at 5:00?

(A) 50°
(B) 60°
(C) 75°
(D) 120°
(E) 150°

22. A B C D E

22. *ABCD* is a square. If the midpoints of the four sides are joined to form a new square, the perimeter of the old square is how many times the perimeter of the new square?

(A) 1
(B) $\sqrt{2}$
(C) 2
(D) $2\sqrt{2}$
(E) 4

23. A B C D E

23. Angles *A* and *B* of triangle *ABC* are both acute angles. Which of the following *best* describes angle *C*?

(A) Angle *C* is between 0° and 180°.
(B) Angle *C* is between 0° and 90°.
(C) Angle *C* is between 60° and 180°.
(D) Angle *C* is between 60° and 120°.
(E) Angle *C* is between 60° and 90°.

24. A B C D E

24. The angles of a quadrilateral are in the ratio 1 : 2 : 3 : 4. What is the number of degrees in the largest angle?

(A) 72
(B) 96
(C) 120
(D) 144
(E) 150

25. A B C D E

25. *ABCD* is a rectangle; the diagonals *AC* and *BD* intersect at *E*. Which of the following statements is *not necessarily true*?

(A) *AE* = *BE*
(B) Angle *AEB* equals angle *CED*.
(C) *AE* is perpendicular to *BD*.
(D) Triangles *AED* and *AEB* are equal in area.
(E) Angle *BAC* equals angle *BDC*.

26. A B C D E

26. City A is 200 miles from City B, and City B is 400 miles from City C. Which of the following best describes the distance between City A and City C? (Note: The cities A, B, and C do *not* all lie on a straight line.)

(A) It must be greater than zero.
(B) It must be greater than 200 miles.
(C) It must be less than 600 miles and greater than zero.
(D) It must be less than 600 miles and greater than 200.
(E) It must be exactly 400 miles.

27. A B C D E

27. At 7:30, how many degrees are included between the hands of a clock?

(A) 15°
(B) 30°
(C) 45°
(D) 60°
(E) 75°

28. A B C D E

28. If a ship is sailing in a northerly direction and then turns to the right until it is sailing in a southwesterly direction, it has gone through a rotation of:

(A) 45°
(B) 90°
(C) 135°
(D) 180°
(E) 225°

29. A B C D E

29. x, y, and z are the angles of a triangle. If $x = 2y$, and $y = z + 30°$, how many degrees are there in angle x?

(A) 22.5°
(B) 37.5°
(C) 52.5°
(D) 90.0°
(E) 105.0°

30. A B C D E

30. In the diagram shown, *AB* is parallel to *CD*. Which of the following statements is *not necessarily true*?

(A) $\angle 1 + \angle 2 = 180°$
(B) $\angle 4 = \angle 7$
(C) $\angle 5 + \angle 8 + \angle 2 + \angle 4 = 360°$
(D) $\angle 2 + \angle 3 = 180°$
(E) $\angle 2 = \angle 6$

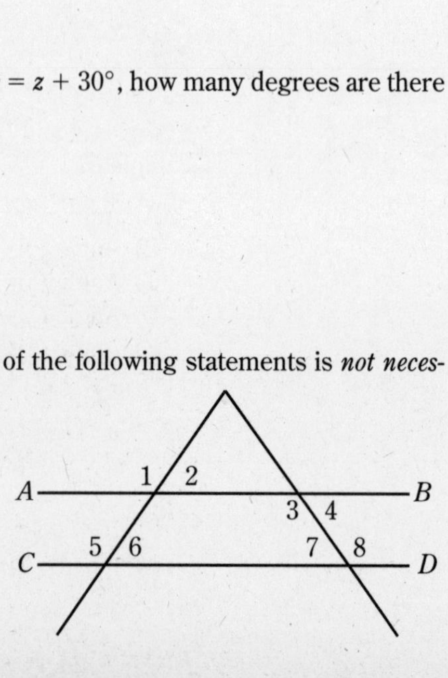

31. A B C D E

31. What is the ratio of the diagonal of a square to the hypotenuse of the isosceles right triangle having the same area?

(A) $1:2$
(B) $1:\sqrt{2}$
(C) $1:1$
(D) $\sqrt{2}:1$
(E) $2:1$

32. A B C D E

32. How many degrees are there between two adjacent sides of a regular ten-sided figure?

(A) 36°
(B) 72°
(C) 120°
(D) 144°
(E) 154°

33. A B C D E

33. Which of the following sets of numbers *cannot* represent the lengths of the sides of a right triangle?

(A) 5, 12, 13
(B) 4.2, 5.6, 7
(C) 9, 28, 35
(D) 16, 30, 34
(E) 7.5, 18, 19.5

34. A B C D E

34. How many degrees are there in the angle that is its own supplement?

(A) 30°
(B) 45°
(C) 60°
(D) 90°
(E) 180°

35. A B C D E

35. If a central angle of 45° intersects an arc 6 inches long on the circumference of a circle, what is the radius of the circle?

(A) $\frac{24}{\pi}$ inches
(B) $\frac{48}{\pi}$ inches
(C) 6π inches
(D) 24 inches
(E) 48 inches

36. A B C D E

36. What is the length of the line segment connecting the two most distant vertices of a 1-inch cube?

(A) 1 inch
(B) $\sqrt{2}$ inches
(C) $\sqrt{3}$ inches
(D) $\sqrt{5}$ inches
(E) $\sqrt{6}$ inches

37. A B C D E

37. Through how many degrees does the hour hand of a clock move in 70 minutes?

(A) 35°
(B) 60°
(C) 80°
(D) 90°
(E) 120°

38. A B C D E

38. In the diagram pictured below, *AB* is tangent to circle *O* at point *A*. *CD* is perpendicular to *OA* at *C*. Which of the following statements is (are) true?

I. Triangles *ODC* and *OBA* are similar.
II. $OA : CD = OB : AB$
III. *AB* is twice as long as *CD*.

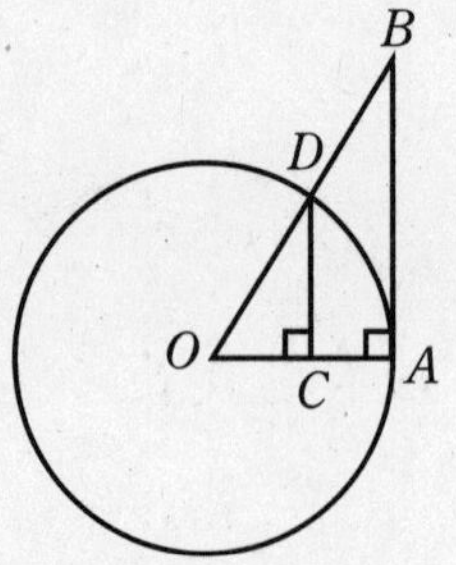

(A) I only
(B) III only
(C) I and II only
(D) II and III only
(E) None of the above combinations.

39. A B C D E

39. The three angles of triangle *ABC* are in the ratio 1 : 2 : 6. How many degrees are in the largest angle?

(A) 45°
(B) 90°
(C) 120°
(D) 135°
(E) 160°

40. A B C D E

40. In this diagram, $AB = AC$, angle $A = 40°$, and *BD* is perpendicular to *AC* at *D*. How many degrees are there in angle *DBC* ?

(A) 20°
(B) 40°
(C) 50°
(D) 70°
(E) None of these.

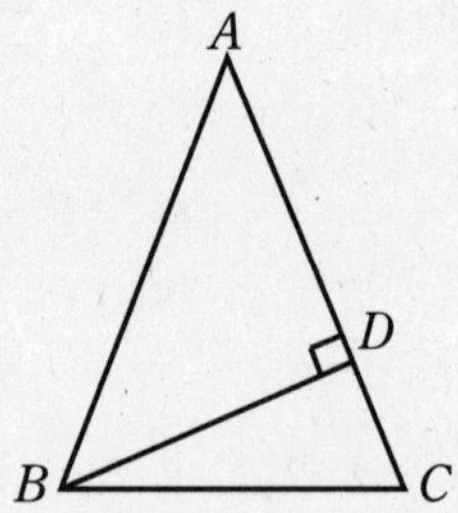

41. A B C D E

41. If the line *AB* intersects the line *CD* at point *E*, which of the following pairs of angles need *not* be equal?

(A) $\angle AEB$ and $\angle CED$
(B) $\angle AEC$ and $\angle BED$
(C) $\angle AED$ and $\angle CEA$
(D) $\angle BEC$ and $\angle DEA$
(E) $\angle DEC$ and $\angle BEA$

42. A B C D E

42. All right isosceles triangles must be

(A) similar
(B) congruent
(C) equilateral
(D) equal in area
(E) None of these.

43. A B C D E

43. What is the area of a triangle whose sides are 10 inches, 13 inches, and 13 inches?

(A) 39 square inches
(B) 52 square inches
(C) 60 square inches
(D) 65 square inches
(E) The answer cannot be determined from the given information.

44. A B C D E

44. If each side of an equilateral triangle is 2 inches long, what is the triangle's altitude?

(A) 1 inch
(B) $\sqrt{2}$ inches
(C) $\sqrt{3}$ inches
(D) 2 inches
(E) $\sqrt{5}$ inches

45. A B C D E

45. In the parallelogram *ABCD*, diagonals *AC* and *BD* intersect at *E*. Which of the following must be true?

(A) $\angle AED = \angle BEC$
(B) $AE = EC$
(C) $\angle BDC = \angle DBA$
(D) Two of the above must be true.
(E) All three of the statements must be true.

46. A B C D E

46. If *ABCD* is a square, and diagonals *AC* and *BD* intersect at point *E*, how many isosceles right triangles are there in the figure?

(A) 4
(B) 5
(C) 6
(D) 7
(E) 8

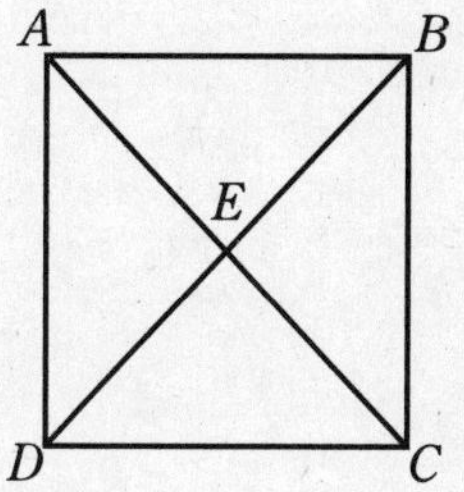

47. A B C D E

47. How many degrees are there in each angle of a regular hexagon?

(A) 60°
(B) 90°
(C) 108°
(D) 120°
(E) 144°

48. A B C D E

48. The radius of a circle is 1 inch. If an equilateral triangle is inscribed in the circle, what will be the length of one of the triangle's sides?

(A) 1 inch
(B) $\frac{\sqrt{2}}{2}$ inches
(C) $\sqrt{2}$ inches
(D) $\frac{\sqrt{3}}{2}$ inches
(E) $\sqrt{3}$ inches

49. A B C D E

49. If the angles of a triangle are in the ratio 2 : 3 : 4, how many degrees are there in the largest angle?

(A) 20°
(B) 40°
(C) 60°
(D) 80°
(E) 120°

50. A B C D E

50. Which of the following combinations may represent the lengths of the sides of a right triangle?

(A) 4, 6, 8
(B) 12, 16, 20
(C) 7, 17, 23
(D) 9, 20, 27
(E) None of these.

Answer Key for Practice Test 5

1. C	**14.** E	**27.** C	**39.** C
2. B	**15.** A	**28.** E	**40.** A
3. A	**16.** E	**29.** E	**41.** C
4. E	**17.** C	**30.** D	**42.** A
5. C	**18.** D	**31.** B	**43.** C
6. D	**19.** B	**32.** D	**44.** C
7. C	**20.** A	**33.** C	**45.** E
8. D	**21.** E	**34.** D	**46.** E
9. E	**22.** B	**35.** A	**47.** D
10. D	**23.** A	**36.** C	**48.** E
11. B	**24.** D	**37.** A	**49.** D
12. D	**25.** C	**38.** C	**50.** B
13. A	**26.** D		

Answers and Solutions for Practice Test 5

1. Choice C is correct. In the problem it is given that $\angle 1 = 40°$ and $\angle 2 = 150°$. The diagram below makes it apparent that: (1) $\angle 1 = \angle 4$ and $\angle 3 = \angle 5$ (vertical angles); (2) $\angle 6 + \angle 2 = 180°$ (straight angle); (3) $\angle 4 + \angle 5 + \angle 6 = 180°$ (sum of angles in a triangle). To solve the problem, $\angle 3$ must be related through the above information to the known quantities in $\angle 1$ and $\angle 2$. Proceed as follows: $\angle 3 = \angle 5$, but $\angle 5 = 180° - \angle 4 - \angle 6$. $\angle 4 = \angle 1 = 40°$ and $\angle 6 = 180° - \angle 2 = 180° - 150° = 30°$. Therefore, $\angle 3 = 180° - 40° - 30° = 110°$. (501, 503, 505)

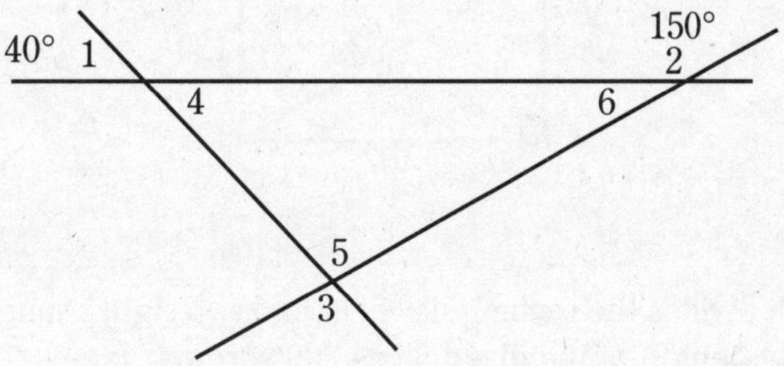

2. Choice B is correct. Since *CD* is perpendicular to *DE*, *CDE* is a right triangle, and using the Pythagorean Theorem yields *DE* = 3. Thus, the ratio of *CD* to *DE* is 4 : 3. But triangle *ABE* is similar to triangle *CDE*. Therefore, *AB* : *BE* = *CD* : *DE* = 4 : 3. (509, 510)

3. Choice A is correct. In a triangle, it is impossible for one side to be longer than the sum of the other two (a straight line is the shortest distance between two points). Thus 2.0, 4.5, and 7.0 cannot be three sides of a triangle. (516)

4. Choice E is correct. *AB* = *AC*, *BD* = *CD*, and *AD* equal to itself is sufficient information (three sides) to prove triangles *ABD* and *ACD* congruent. Also, since *AB* = *AC*, *AE* = *AE*, and $\angle BAE = \angle CAE$ (by the previous congruence), triangles *ABE* and *ACE* are congruent. Since *BD* = *CD*, *ED* = *ED*, and angle *BDE* equals angle *CDE* (by initial congruence), triangles *BDE* and *CDE* are congruent. Through congruence of triangle *ABE* and triangle *ACE*, angles *BEA* and *CEA* are equal, and their sum is a straight angle (180°). They must both be right angles. Thus, from the given information, we can deduce all the properties given as choices. (511)

5. Choice C is correct. The perimeter of triangle ABD is $AB + BD + AD$. The length of BD is 1. Since $BC = CD = BD$, triangle BCD is an equilateral triangle. Therefore, angle $C = 60°$ and angle $BDC = 60°$. Angle A + angle $C = 90°$ (the sum of two acute angles in a right triangle is 90°), and angle BDC + angle $BDA = 90°$ (these two angles form a right angle). Since angle C and angle BDC both equal 60°, angle A = angle $BDA = 30°$. Now two angles of triangle ADB are equal. Therefore, triangle ADB is an isosceles triangle with side BD = side AB. Since $BD = 1$, then $AB = 1$. AD is a leg of the right triangle, with side $CD = 1$ and hypotenuse $AC = 2$. ($AC = AB + BC = 1 + 1$.) Using the relationship $c^2 = a^2 + b^2$ gives us the length of AD as $\sqrt{3}$. Thus the perimeter is $1 + 1 + \sqrt{3}$ or $2 + \sqrt{3}$. (505, 507, 509)

6. Choice D is correct. (I) must be true, since the diagonals of a parallelogram bisect each other, so $QT = ST$, and $PT = RT$. Thus, since the sums of equals are equal, $QT + PT = RT + ST$.

(II) is not necessarily true and, in fact, can be true only if the parallelogram is also a rhombus (all four sides equal).

(III) is true, since the four small triangles each have the same area. The shaded portion contains three such triangles. This can be seen by noting that the altitudes from point P to the bases of triangles PQT and PTS are identical. We have already seen from part (I) that these bases (QT and TS) are also equal. Therefore, only I and III can be deduced from the given information. (514, 517)

7. Choice C is correct.

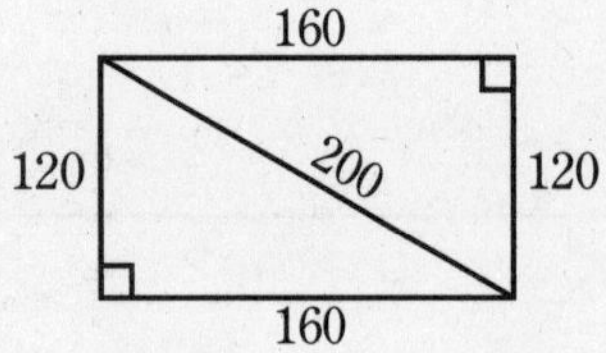

The diagonal path divides the rectangular field into two right triangles. The Pythagorean Theorem gives the length of the diagonal as 200 yards. If James takes the route around the perimeter, he will travel 120 + 160, or 280 yards. Thus, the shorter route saves him 80 yards. (509, 518)

8. Choice D is correct. Let one side of a square be s. Then the perimeter must be $4s$. The diagonal of a square with side s is equal to $s\sqrt{2}$. Dividing the perimeter by the diagonal produces $2\sqrt{2}$. The perimeter is $2\sqrt{2}$ times the diagonal. (509, 520)

9. Choice E is correct. The sum of the angles of any polygon is equal to $180°(n - 2)$, where n is the number of sides. Thus the total number of degrees in a nonagon $= 180°(9 - 2) = 180° \times 7 = 1{,}260°$. The number of degrees in each angle is $\frac{1{,}260°}{n} = \frac{1{,}260°}{9} = 140°$.
(521, 522)

10. Choice D is correct. Since chord *AB* equals chord *CD*, it must be true that arc *AB* equals arc *CD*. By adding arc *AC* to arc *CD* and to arc *AB* it is apparent that arc *ACD* is equal to arc *CAB*. These arcs are intersected by inscribed angles *ABD* and *BDC*. Therefore, the two inscribed angles must be equal. If we redraw the figure as shown below, the falseness of statements (A), (B), (C), and (E) becomes readily apparent. (527)

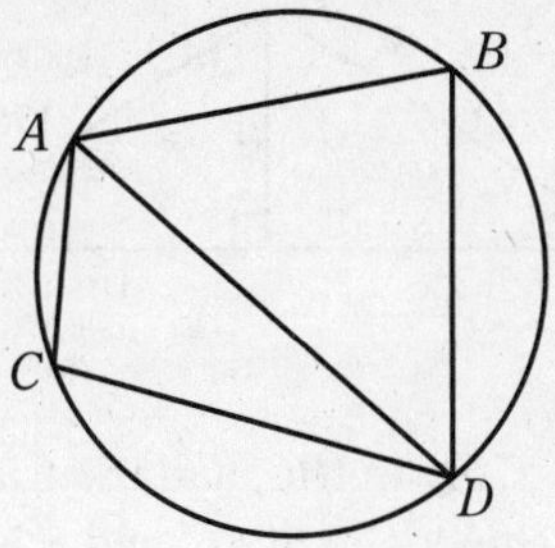

11. Choice B is correct. $\angle AEC + \angle BEC = \angle AEB$, a straight angle (180°). Thus, angles *AEC* and *BEC* are ***supplementary***. (Complementary means that the two angles add up to a ***right*** angle, or 90°.) (501, 502)

12. Choice D is correct. Since $AC = CE$ and $BD = DE$, triangles *AEB* and *CED* are similar, and *AB* is twice as long as *CD*, since by proportionality, $AB : CD = AE : CE = 2 : 1$. From the similarity it is found that angle *ABE* equals angle *CDE*, and, therefore, that *AB* is parallel to *CD*. Thus, all three statements are true. (504, 510)

13. Choice A is correct. Angle *A* must be greater than 90°; angle *B* equals 30°. Thus, the sum of angles *A* and *B* must be greater than 120°. Since the sum of the three angles *A*, *B*, and *C* must be 180°, angle *C* must be ***less than*** 60°. (It cannot equal 60°, because then angle *A* would be a right angle instead of an obtuse angle.) (501, 505)

14. Choice E is correct. *CDF* is a right triangle with one side of 16 and a hypotenuse of 20. Thus, the third side, *DF*, equals 12. Since *BFDE* is a square, *BF* and *ED* are also equal to 12. Thus, $BC = 12 + 16 = 28$, and $CD = 20$. *ABCD* is a parallelogram, so $AB = CD$, $AD = BC$. The perimeter is $28 + 20 + 28 + 20 = 96$. (509, 517, 520)

15. Choice A is correct. Recognize that the sides of a 30°–60°–90° triangle are in the proportion $1 : \sqrt{3} : 2$, and the problem is solved. 30° is the smallest angle. (509)

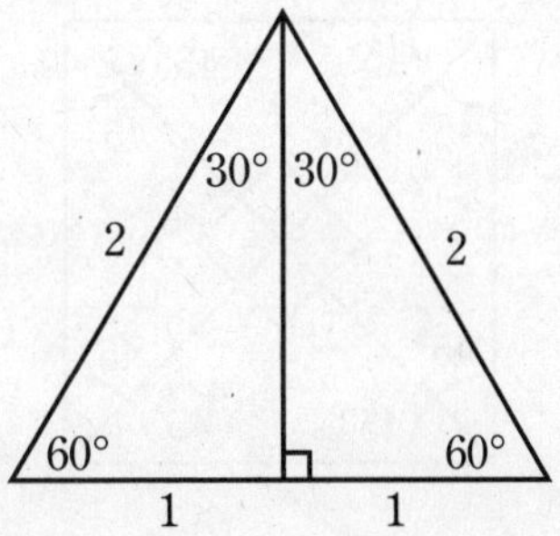

16. Choice E is correct. The altitude to the base of an isosceles triangle divides it into two congruent right triangles, each with one leg of 8 inches, and a hypotenuse of 17 inches. By the Pythagorean Theorem, the third side of each right triangle must be 15 inches long. The base of the isosceles triangle is the sum of two such sides, totaling 30 inches. (507, 509, 514)

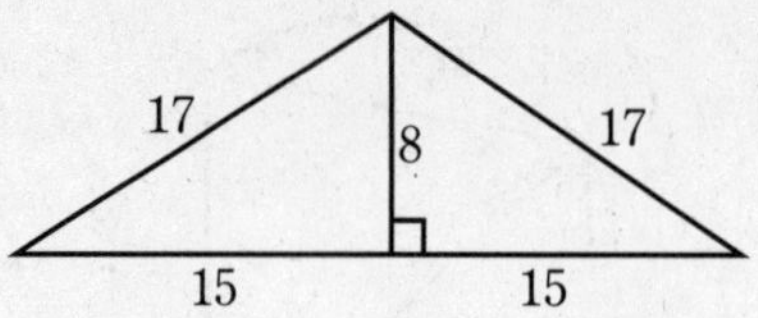

17. Choice C is correct. Call the triangle *ABC*, and the triangle of midpoints *PQR*, where *P* is the midpoint of *BC*, *Q* is the midpoint of *AC*, and *R* is the midpoint of *AB*. Then, *PQ* is equal to half the length of *AB*, $QR = \frac{1}{2}BC$, and $PR = \frac{1}{2}AC$. This has nothing to do with the fact that *ABC* is a right triangle. Thus, the perimeter of the small triangle is equal to $PQ + QR + PR = \frac{1}{2}(AB + BC + AC)$. The new perimeter is half the old perimeter, or 9 inches. (509, 510, 512)

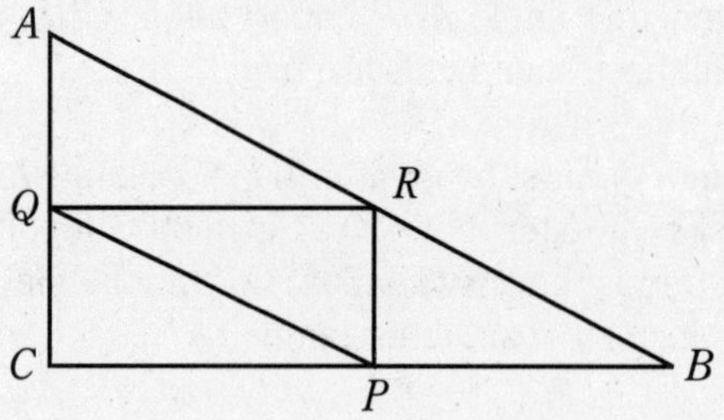

18. Choice D is correct. The diagonals of the square form four right triangles, each of which is isosceles because each has two 45° angles. The triangles are all identical in shape and size, so they all are similar and have the same area. The only choice left is equilateral, which cannot be true, since the sum of the angles at the intersection of the diagonals must be 360°. The sum of four 60° angles would be only 240°. (520)

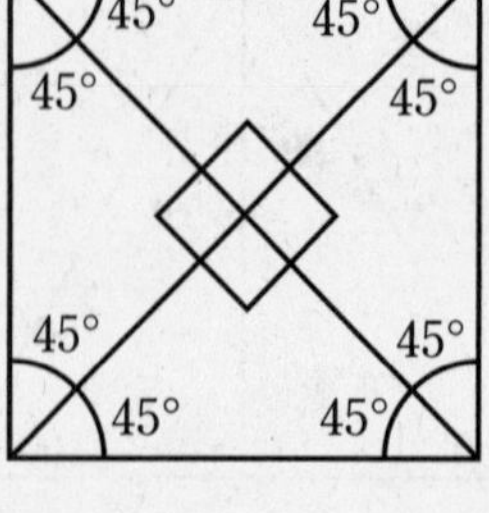

19. Choice B is correct. First, draw in the lines *CF* and *BE*. These intersect *AD* at its midpoint (also the midpoint of *CF* and *BE*) and divide the hexagon into six equilateral triangles. Since *ADC* is an angle of one of these equilateral triangles, it must be equal to 60°. (Another way to do this problem is to calculate the number of degrees in one angle of a regular hexagon and divide this by 2.) (508, 523)

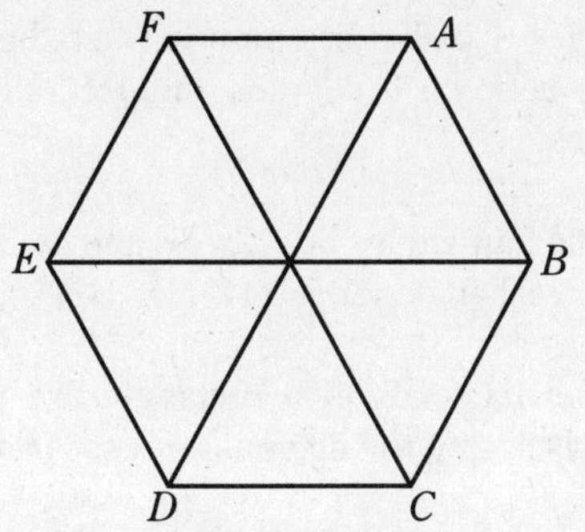

20. Choice A is correct. The diagonal of an inscribed rectangle is equal to the diameter of the circle. To find this length, use the Pythagorean Theorem on one of the two triangles formed by two of the sides of the rectangle and the diagonal. Thus, the square of the diagonal is equal to $10^2 + 14^2 = 100 + 196 = 296$. The area of the circle is equal to π times the square of the radius. The square of the radius of the circle is one-fourth of the diameter squared (since $d = 2r$, $d^2 = 4r^2$), or 74. Thus, the area is 74π. (509, 518, 524)

21. Choice E is correct. Each number (or hour marking) on a clock represents an angle of 30°, as 360° divided by 12 is 30° (a convenient fact to remember for other clock problems). Since the hands of the clock are on the 12 and the 5, there are five hour units between the hands; $5 \times 30° = 150°$. (501, 526)

22. Choice B is correct.

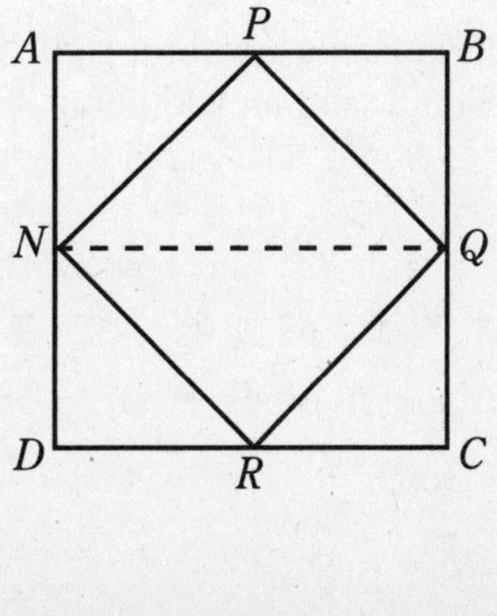

Let S represent the side of the large square. Then the perimeter is $4S$. Let s represent the side of the smaller square. Then the perimeter is $4s$. Line NQ is the diagonal of the smaller square, so the length of NQ is $\sqrt{2}s$. (The diagonal of a square is $\sqrt{2}$ times the side.) Now, NQ is equal to DC, or S, which is the side of the larger square. So now $S = \sqrt{2}s$. The perimeter of the large square equals $4S = 4\sqrt{2}s = \sqrt{2}(4s) = \sqrt{2} \times$ perimeter of the small square. (520)

23. Choice A is correct. Angles A and B are both greater than 0 degrees and less than 90 degrees, so their sum is between 0 degrees and 180 degrees. Then angle C must be between 0 and 180 degrees. (501, 505)

24. Choice D is correct. Let the four angles be x, $2x$, $3x$, and $4x$. The sum, $10x$, must equal $360°$. Thus, $x = 36°$, and the largest angle, $4x$, is $144°$. (505)

25. Choice C is correct. The diagonals of a rectangle are perpendicular only when the rectangle is a square. AE is part of the diagonal AC, so AE will not necessarily be perpendicular to BD. (518)

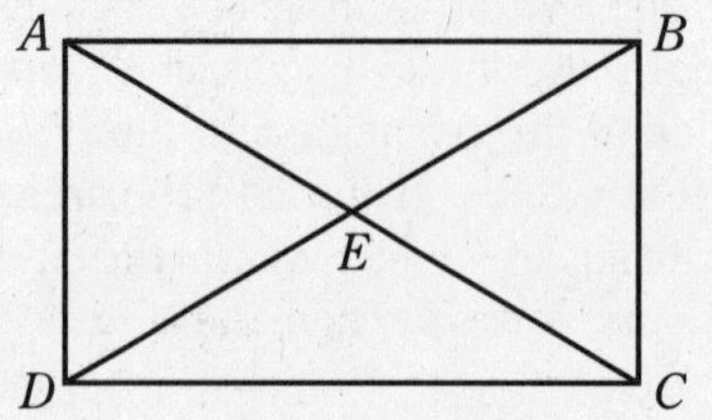

26. Choice D is correct.

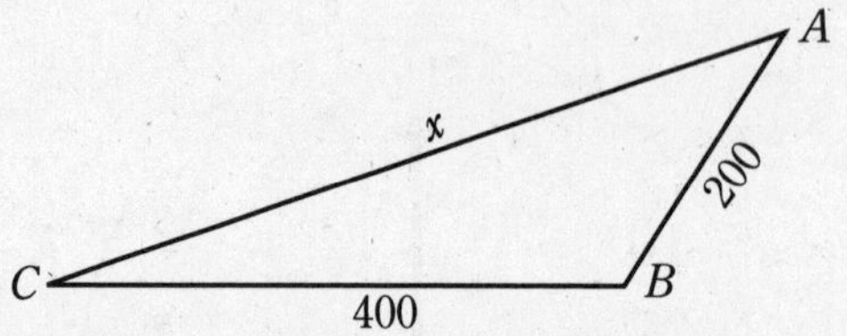

Draw the three cities as the vertices of a triangle. The length of side CB is 400 miles, the length of side AB is 200 miles, and x, the length of side AC, is unknown. The sum of any two sides of a triangle is greater than the third side, or in algebraic terms: $400 + 200 > x$, $400 + x > 200$ and $200 + x > 400$. These simplify to $600 > x$, $x > -200$, and $x > 200$. For x to be greater than 200 and -200, it must be greater than 200. Thus, the values of x are $200 < x < 600$. (506, 516)

27. Choice C is correct. At 7:30, the hour hand is *halfway between the 7 and the 8*, and the minute hand is on the 6. Thus, there are one and one-half "hour units," each equal to $30°$, so the whole angle is $45°$. (501, 526)

28. Choice E is correct. If a ship is facing north, a right turn of $90°$ will face it eastward. Another $90°$ turn will face it south, and an additional $45°$ turn will bring it to southwest. Thus, the total rotation is $90° + 90° + 45° = 225°$. (501)

29. Choice E is correct. Since $y = z + 30°$ and $x = 2y$, then $x = 2(z + 30°) = 2z + 60°$. Thus, $x + y + z$ equals $(2z + 60°) + (z + 30°) + z = 4z + 90°$. This must equal $180°$ (the sum of the angles of a triangle). So $4z + 90° = 180°$, and the solution is $z = 22\frac{1}{2}°$; $x = 2z + 60° = 45° + 60° = 105°$. (505)

30. Choice D is correct. Since AB is parallel to CD, angle 2 = angle 6, and angle 3 + angle 7 = 180°. If angle 2 + angle 3 equals 180°, then angle 2 = angle 7 = angle 6. However, since there is no evidence that angles 6 and 7 are equal, angle 2 + angle 3 does not necessarily equal 180°. Therefore, the answer is (D). (504)

31. Choice B is correct. Call the side of the square s. Then, the diagonal of the square is $\sqrt{2}s$ and the area is s^2. The area of an isosceles right triangle with leg r is $\frac{1}{2}r^2$. Now, the area of the triangle is equal to the area of the square, so $s^2 = \frac{1}{2}r^2$. Solving for r gives $r = \sqrt{2}s$. The hypotenuse of the triangle is $\sqrt{r^2 + r^2}$. Substituting $r = \sqrt{2}s$, the hypotenuse is $\sqrt{2s^2 + 2s^2} = \sqrt{4s^2} = 2s$. Therefore, the ratio of the diagonal to the hypotenuse is $\sqrt{2}s : 2s$. Since $\sqrt{2}s : 2s$ is $\frac{\sqrt{2}s}{2s}$ or $\frac{\sqrt{2}}{2}$, multiply by $\frac{\sqrt{2}}{\sqrt{2}}$, which has a value of 1. $\frac{\sqrt{2}}{2} \cdot \frac{\sqrt{2}}{\sqrt{2}} = \frac{2}{2\sqrt{2}} = \frac{1}{\sqrt{2}}$ or $1 : \sqrt{2}$, which is the final result. (507, 509, 520)

32. Choice D is correct. The formula for the number of degrees in the angles of a polygon is $180(n - 2)$, where n is the number of sides. For a ten-sided figure this is $180°(10 - 2) = 180°(8) = 1440°$. Since the ten angles are equal, they must each equal 144°. (521, 522)

33. Choice C is correct. If three numbers represent the lengths of the sides of a right triangle, they must satisfy the Pythagorean Theorem: The squares of the smaller two must equal the square of the largest one. This condition is met in all the sets given except the set 9, 28, 35. There, $9^2 + 28^2 = 81 + 784 = 865$, but $35^2 = 1{,}225$. (509)

34. Choice D is correct. Let the angle be x. Since x is its own supplement, then $x + x = 180°$, or, since $2x = 180°$, $x = 90°$. (502)

35. Choice A is correct. The length of the arc intersected by a central angle of a circle is proportional to the number of degrees in the angle. Thus, if a 45° angle cuts off a 6-inch arc, a 360° angle intersects an arc eight times as long, or 48 inches. The length of the arc of a 360° angle is equal to the circle's circumference, or 2π times the radius. Thus, to obtain the radius, divide 48 inches by 2π. 48 inches $\div 2\pi = \frac{24}{\pi}$ inches. (524, 526)

36. Choice C is correct. Refer to the diagram pictured below. Calculate the distance from vertex 1 to vertex 2. This is simply the diagonal of a 1-inch square and equal to $\sqrt{2}$ inches. Now, vertices 1, 2, and 3 form a right triangle, with legs of 1 and $\sqrt{2}$. By the Pythagorean Theorem, the hypotenuse is $\sqrt{3}$. This is the distance from vertex 1 to vertex 3, the two most distant vertices. (509, 520)

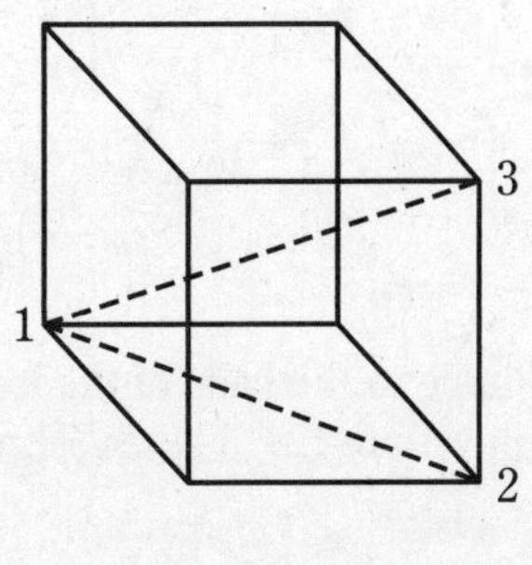

37. Choice A is correct. In one hour, the hour hand of a clock moves through an angle of 30° (one "hour unit"). 70 minutes equals $\frac{7}{6}$ hours, so during that time the hour hand will move through $\frac{7}{6} \times 30°$, or 35°. (501, 526)

38. Choice C is correct. In order to be similar, two triangles must have corresponding angles equal. This is true of triangles *ODC* and *OBA*, since angle *O* equals itself, and angles *OCD* and *OAB* are both right angles. (The third angles of these triangles must be equal, as the sum of the angles of a triangle is always 180°.) Since the triangles are similar, $OD : CD = OB : AB$. But, *OD* and *OA* are radii of the same circle and are equal. Therefore, substitute *OA* for *OD* in the above proportion. Hence, $OA : CD = OB : AB$. There is, however, no information given on the relative sizes of any of the line segments, so statement III may or may not be true. (509, 510, 524)

39. Choice C is correct. Let the three angles equal x, $2x$, and $6x$. Then, $x + 2x + 6x = 9x = 180°$. Therefore, $x = 20°$ and $6x = 120°$. (505)

40. Choice A is correct. Since $AB = AC$, angle *ABC* must equal angle *ACB*. (Base angles of an isosceles triangle are equal.) As the sum of angles *BAC*, *ABC*, and *ACB* is 180°, and angle *BAC* equals 40°, angle *ABC* and angle *ACB* must each equal 70°. Now, *DBC* is a right triangle, with angle $BDC = 90°$ and angle $DCB = 70°$. (The three angles must add up to 180°.) Angle *DBC* must equal 20°. (507, 514)

41. Choice C is correct.

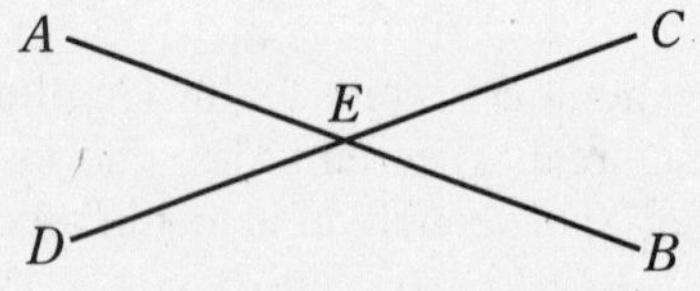

$\angle AEB$ and $\angle CED$ are both straight angles, and are equal; similarly, $\angle DEC$ and $\angle BEA$ are both straight angles. $\angle AEC$ and $\angle BED$ are vertical angles, as are $\angle BEC$ and $\angle DEA$, and are equal. $\angle AED$ and $\angle CEA$ are supplementary and need not be equal. (501, 502, 503)

42. Choice A is correct. All right isosceles triangles have angles of 45°, 45°, and 90°. Since all triangles with the same angles are similar, all right isosceles triangles are similar. (507, 509, 510)

43. Choice C is correct.

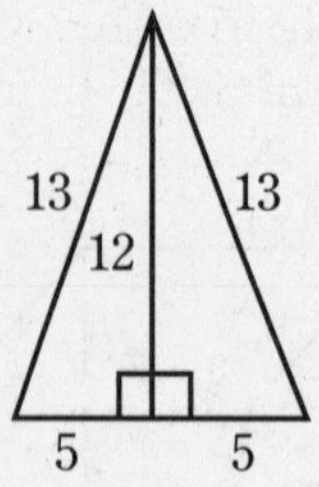

As the diagram shows, the altitude to the base of the isosceles triangle divides it into two congruent right triangles, each with 5–12–13 sides. Thus, the base is 10, the height is 12, and the area is $\frac{1}{2}(10)(12) = 60$. (505, 507, 509)

44. Choice C is correct. The altitude to any side divides the triangle into two congruent $30°–60°–90°$ right triangles, each with a hypotenuse of 2 inches and a leg of 1 inch. The other leg equals the altitude. By the Pythagorean Theorem the altitude is equal to $\sqrt{3}$ inches. (The sides of a $30°–60°–90°$ right triangle are always in the proportion $1 : \sqrt{3} : 2$.) (509, 514)

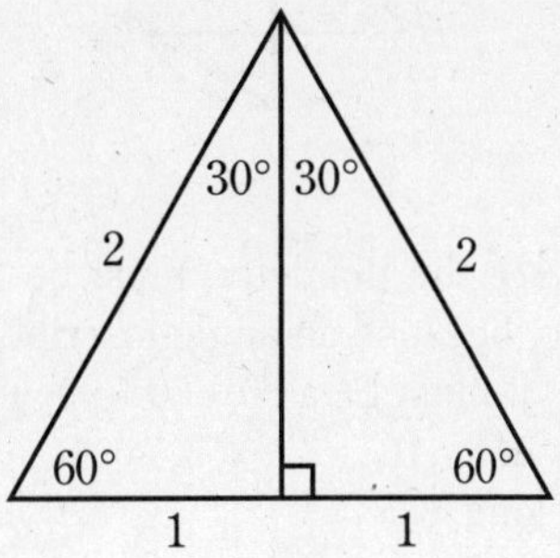

45. Choice E is correct.

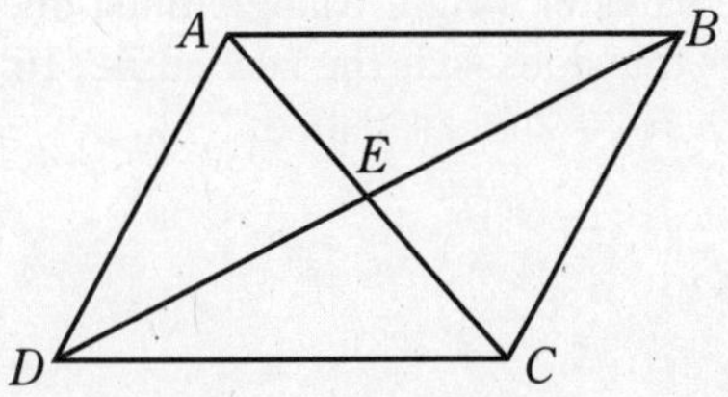

As the diagram illustrates, angles *AED* and *BEC* are vertical and, therefore, equal. $AE = EC$, because the diagonals of a parallelogram bisect each other. Angles *BDC* and *DBA* are equal because they are alternate interior angles of parallel lines ($AB \| CD$). (503, 517)

46. Choice E is correct. There are eight isosceles right triangles: *ABE, BCE, CDE, ADE, ABC, BCD, CDA*, and *ABD.* (520)

47. Choice D is correct. Recall that a regular hexagon may be broken up into six equilateral triangles.

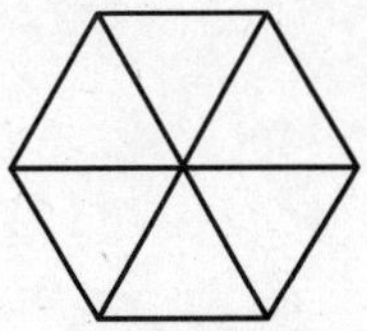

Since the angles of each triangle are $60°$, and two of these angles make up each angle of the hexagon, an angle of the hexagon must be $120°$. (523)

48. Choice E is correct.

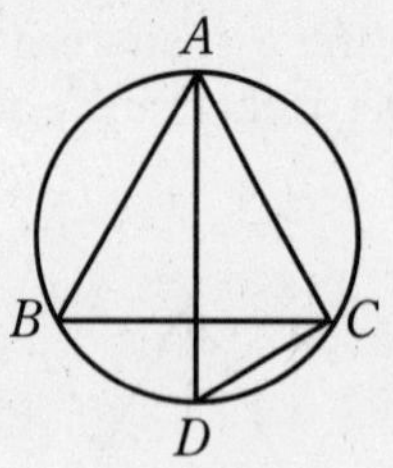

Since the radius equals 1″, AD, the diameter, must be 2″. Now, since AD is a diameter, ACD must be a right triangle, because an angle inscribed in a semicircle is a right angle. Thus, because $\angle DAC = 30°$, it must be a 30°–60°–90° right triangle. The sides will be in the proportion $1 : \sqrt{3} : 2$. As $AD : AC = 2 : \sqrt{3}$, so AC, one of the sides of the equilateral triangle, must be $\sqrt{3}$ inches long. (508, 524)

49. Choice D is correct. Let the angles be $2x$, $3x$, $4x$. Their sum, $9x = 180°$ and $x = 20°$. Thus, the largest angle, $4x$, is 80°. (505)

50. Choice B is correct. The sides of a right triangle must obey the Pythagorean Theorem. The only group of choices that does so is the second: 12, 16, and 20 are in the 3–4–5 ratio, and the relationship $12^2 + 16^2 = 20^2$ is satisfied. (509)

MATH REFRESHER SESSION 6

Miscellaneous Problems: Averages, Standard Deviation, Properties of Integers, Approximations, Combinations, Permutations, Probability, the Absolute Value Sign, and Functions

Averages, Medians, and Modes

601. *Averages.* The average of *n* numbers is merely their sum, divided by *n*.

Example: Find the average of 20, 0, 80, and 12.

Solution: The average is the sum divided by the number of entries, or:

$$\frac{20+0+80+12}{4}=\frac{112}{4}=28$$

A quick way of obtaining an average of a set of numbers that are close together is the following:

STEP 1. Choose any number that will approximately equal the average.

STEP 2. Subtract this approximate average from each of the numbers (this sum will give some positive and negative results). Add the results.

STEP 3. Divide this sum by the number of entries.

STEP 4. Add the result of Step 3 to the approximate average chosen in Step 1. This will be the true average.

Example: Find the average of 92, 93, 93, 96, and 97.

Solution: Choose 95 as an approximate average. Subtracting 95 from 92, 93, 93, 96, and 97 gives −3, −2, −2, 1, and 2. The sum is −4. Divide −4 by 5 (the number of entries) to obtain −0.8. Add −0.8 to the original approximation of 95 to get the true average, 95 − 0.8, or 94.2.

601a. *Medians.* The median of a set of numbers is that number which is in the *middle* of all the numbers.

Example: Find the median of 20, 0, 80, 12, and 30.

Solution: Arrange the numbers in increasing order:

0
12
20
30
80

The *middle* number is 20, so 20 is the *median.*

Note: If there is an *even* number of items, such as

0
12
20
24
30
80

there is no *middle* number.

So in this case we take the average of the two middle numbers, 20 and 24, to get 22, which is the *median.*

In the above set of 6 numbers, if 24 was replaced by 22, the median would be 21 (just the average of 20 and 22).

601b. *Modes.* The mode of a set of numbers is the number that occurs most frequently.

If we have numbers 0, 12, 20, 30, and 80 there is *no* mode, since no one number appears with the greatest frequency. But consider this:

Example: Find the mode of 0, 12, 12, 20, 30, 80.

Solution: 12 appears most frequently, so it is the mode.

Example: Find the mode of 0, 12, 12, 20, 30, 30, 80.

Solution: Here *both* 12 and 30 are modes.

Standard Deviation

602. Let's consider what a standard deviation is with an example:

Consider a population consisting of the following eight values:

2, 4, 4, 4, 5, 5, 7, 9

The eight data points have a mean (or average) value of 5:

$$\frac{2+4+4+4+5+5+7+9}{8}=5$$

To calculate the population standard deviation, first compute the difference of each data point from the mean, and square the result of each:

$(2-5)^2=(-3)^2=9$ $\quad(5-5)^2=0^2=0$
$(4-5)^2=(-1)^2=1$ $\quad(5-5)^2=0^2=0$
$(4-5)^2=(-1)^2=1$ $\quad(7-5)^2=2^2=4$
$(4-5)^2=(-1)^2=1$ $\quad(9-5)^2=4^2=16$

Next divide the sum of these values by the number of values and take the square root to give the standard deviation:

$$\sqrt{\frac{9+1+1+1+0+0+4+16}{8}}=2$$

Therefore, the above has a population standard deviation of 2.

So to calculate the standard deviation of a set of numbers, subtract each number from the average of the numbers, then square what you get for each of the numbers. Add all those results and then divide by how many numbers you originally had. Take the square root of the result. That is your standard deviation.

Properties of Integers

An integer is a whole number; for example, –5, –2, 0, 1, 3, etc.

603. *Even–Odd.* These are problems that deal with even and odd numbers. An even number is divisible by 2, and an odd number is not divisible by 2. All even numbers end in the digits 0, 2, 4, 6, or 8; odd numbers end in the digits 1, 3, 5, 7, or 9. For example, the numbers 358, 90, 18, 9,874, and 46 are even numbers. The numbers 67, 871, 475, and 89 are odd numbers. It is important to remember the following facts:

604. The sum of *two even* numbers is *even*, and the sum of *two odd* numbers is *even*, but the sum of an *odd* number *and* an *even* number is *odd*. For example, $4 + 8 = 12$, $5 + 3 = 8$, and $7 + 2 = 9$.

Example: If m is any integer, is the number $6m + 3$ an even or odd number?

Solution: $6m$ is even, since 6 is a multiple of 2. 3 is odd. Therefore $6m + 3$ is odd since even + odd = odd.

605. The product of *two odd* numbers is *odd*, but the product of an *even* number and *any other* number is an *even* number. For example, $3 \times 5 = 15$ (odd); $4 \times 5 = 20$ (even); $4 \times 6 = 24$ (even).

Example: If m is any integer, is the product $(2m + 3)(4m + 1)$ even or odd?

Solution: Since $2m$ is even and 3 is odd, $2m + 3$ is odd. Likewise, since $4m$ is even and 1 is odd, $4m + 1$ is odd. Thus $(2m + 3)(4m + 1)$ is (odd × odd), which is odd.

606. Even numbers are expressed in the form $2k$, where k may be any integer. Odd numbers are expressed in the form of $2k + 1$ or $2k - 1$, where k may be any integer. For example, if $k = 17$, then $2k = 34$ and $2k + 1 = 35$. If $k = 6$, then we have $2k = 12$ and $2k + 1 = 13$.

Example: Prove that the product of two odd numbers is odd.

Solution: Let one of the odd numbers be represented as $2x + 1$. Let the other number be represented as $2y + 1$. Now multiply $(2x + 1)(2y + 1)$. We get $4xy + 2x + 2y + 1$. Since $4xy + 2x + 2y$ is even because it is a multiple of 2, that quantity is even. Since 1 is odd, we have $4xy + 2x + 2y + 1$ is odd, since even + odd = odd.

607. *Divisibility.* If an integer P is divided by an integer Q, and an integer is obtained as the quotient, then P is said to be divisible by Q. In other words, if P can be expressed as an integral multiple of Q, then P is said to be divisible by Q. For example, dividing 51 by 17 gives 3, an integer. 51 is divisible by 17, or 51 equals 17 times 3. On the other hand, dividing 8 by 3 gives $2\frac{2}{3}$, which is not an integer. 8 is not divisible by 3, and there is no way to express 8 as an integral multiple of 3. There are various tests to see whether an integer is divisible by certain numbers. These tests are listed below:

1. Any integer is divisible *by 2* if the last digit of the number is a 0, 2, 4, 6, or 8.

   Example: The numbers 98, 6,534, 70, and 32 are divisible by 2 because they end in 8, 4, 0, and 2, respectively.

2. Any integer is divisible *by 3* if the sum of its digits is divisible by 3.

   Example: Is the number 34,237,023 divisible by 3?

   Solution: Add the digits of the number. $3 + 4 + 2 + 3 + 7 + 0 + 2 + 3 = 24$. Now, 24 is divisible by 3 $(24 \div 3 = 8)$, so the number 34,237,023 is also divisible by 3.

3. Any integer is divisible *by 4* if the last two digits of the number make a number that is divisible by 4.

Example: Which of the following numbers is divisible by 4?
3,456; 6,787,612; 67,408; 7,877; 345; 98.

Solution: Look at the last two digits of the numbers: 56, 12, 08, 77, 45, 98. Only 56, 12, and 08 are divisible by 4, so only the numbers 3,456; 6,787,612; and 67,408 are divisible by 4.

4. An integer is divisible *by 5* if the last digit is either a 0 or a 5.

Example: The numbers 780, 675, 9,000, and 15 are divisible by 5, while the numbers 786, 5,509, and 87 are not divisible by 5.

5. Any integer is divisible *by 6* if it is divisible by both 2 and 3.

Example: Is the number 12,414 divisible by 6?

Solution: Test whether 12,414 is divisible by 2 and 3. The last digit is a 4, so it is divisible by 2. Adding the digits yields $1 + 2 + 4 + 1 + 4 = 12$. 12 is divisible by 3, so the number 12,414 is divisible by 3. Since it is divisible by both 2 and 3, it is divisible by 6.

6. Any integer is divisible *by 8* if the last three digits are divisible by 8. (Since 1,000 is divisible by 8, you can ignore all multiples of 1,000 in applying this rule.)

Example: Is the number 342,169,424 divisible by 8?

Solution: $424 \div 8 = 53$, so 342,169,424 is divisible by 8.

7. Any integer is divisible *by 9* if the sum of its digits is divisible by 9.

Example: Is the number 243,091,863 divisible by 9?

Solution: Adding the digits yields $2 + 4 + 3 + 0 + 9 + 1 + 8 + 6 + 3 = 36$. 36 is divisible by 9, so the number 243,091,863 is divisible by 9.

8. Any integer is divisible *by 10* if the last digit is a 0.

Example: The numbers 60, 8,900, 5,640, and 34,000 are all divisible by 10 because the last digit in each is a 0.

> Note that if a number P is divisible by a number Q, then P is also divisible by all the factors of Q. For example, 60 is divisible by 12, so 60 is also divisible by 2, 3, 4, and 6, which are all factors of 12.

608. *Prime numbers.* A prime number is one that is divisible only by 1 and itself. The first few prime numbers are 2, 3, 5, 7, 11, 13, 17, 19, 23, 29, 31, 37... Note that the number 1 is not considered a prime number. To determine if a number is prime, follow these steps:

STEP 1. Determine a very rough approximate square root of the number. Remember that the square root of a number is that number which, when multiplied by itself, gives the original number. For example, the square root of 25 is 5 because $5 \times 5 = 25$.

STEP 2. Divide the number by all of the primes that are less than the approximate square root. If the number is not divisible by any of these primes, then it is prime. If it is divisible by one of the primes, then it is not prime.

Example: Is the number 97 prime?

Solution: An approximate square root of 97 is 10. All of the primes less than 10 are 2, 3, 5, and 7. Divide 97 by 2, 3, 5, and 7. No integer results, so 97 is prime.

Example: Is the number 161 prime?

Solution: An approximate square root of 161 is 13. The primes less than 13 are 2, 3, 5, 7, and 11. Divide 161 by 2, 3, 5, 7, and 11. 161 is divisible by 7 ($161 \div 7 = 23$), so 161 is not prime.

Approximations

609. *Rounding off numbers with decimal points.* A number expressed to a certain number of places is rounded off when it is approximated as a number with fewer places of accuracy. For example, the number 8.987 is expressed more accurately than the number rounded off to 8.99. To round off to n places, look at the digit that is to the right of the nth digit. (The nth digit is found by counting n places to the right of the decimal point.) If this digit is less than 5, eliminate all of the digits to the right of the nth digit. If the digit to the right of the nth digit is 5 or more, then add 1 to the nth digit and eliminate all of the digits to the right of the nth digit.

Example: Round off 8.73 to the nearest tenth.

Solution: The digit to the right of the 7 (.7 is seven tenths) is 3. Since this is less than 5, eliminate it, and the rounded off answer is 8.7.

Example: Round off 986 to the nearest tens place.

Solution: The number to the right of the tens place is 6. Since this is 5 or more, add 1 to the 8 and replace the 6 with a 0 to get 990.

610. *Approximating sums with decimal points.* When adding a small (10 or fewer) set of numbers and when the answer must have a given number of places of accuracy, follow the steps below.

STEP 1. Round off each addend (number being added) to one less place than the number of places the answer is to have.

STEP 2. Add the rounded addends.

STEP 3. Round off the sum to the desired number of places of accuracy.

Example: What is the sum of 12.0775, 1.20163, and 121.303, correct to the nearest hundredth?

Solution: Round off the three numbers to the nearest thousandth (one less place than the accuracy of the sum): 12.078, 1.202, and 121.303. The sum of these is 134.583. Rounded off to the nearest hundredth, this is 134.58.

611. *Approximating products.* To multiply certain numbers and have an answer to the desired number of places of accuracy (significant digits), follow the steps below.

STEP 1. Round off the numbers being multiplied to the number of places of accuracy (significant digits) desired in the answer.

STEP 2. Multiply the rounded-off factors (numbers being multiplied).

STEP 3. Round off the product to the desired number of places (significant digits).

Example: Find the product of 3,316 and 1,432 to the nearest thousand.

Solution: First, round off 3,316 to 3 places, to obtain 3,320. Round off 1,432 to 3 places to give 1,430. The product of these two numbers is 4,747,600. Rounded off to 3 places, this is 4,748,000.

612. *Approximating square roots.* The square root of a number is that number which, when multiplied by itself, gives the original number. For example, 6 is the square root of 36. Often on tests a number with different choices for the square root is given. Follow this procedure to determine which is the best choice.

STEP 1. Square all of the choices given.

STEP 2. Select the closest choice that is too large and the closest choice that is too small (assuming that no choice is the exact square root). Find the average of these two *choices* (not of their squares).

STEP 3. Square this average; if the square is greater than the original number, choose the lower of the two choices; if its square is lower than the original number, choose the higher.

Example: Which of the following is closest to the square root of 86: 9.0, 9.2, 9.4, 9.6, or 9.8?

Solution: The squares of the five numbers are 81, 84.64, 88.36, 92.16, and 96.04, respectively. (Actually, it was not necessary to calculate the last two, since they are greater than the third square, which is already greater than 86.) The two closest choices are 9.2 and 9.4; their average is 9.3. The square of 9.3 is 86.49. Therefore, 9.3 is greater than the square root of 86. So, the square root must be closer to 9.2 than to 9.4.

Combinations

613. Suppose that a job has 2 different parts. There are m different ways of doing the first part, and there are n different ways of doing the second part. The problem is to find the number of ways of doing the entire job. For each way of doing the first part of the job, there are n ways of doing the second part. Since there are m ways of doing the first part, the total number of ways of doing the entire job is $m \times n$. The formula that can be used is

$$\text{Number of ways} = m \times n$$

For any problem that involves 2 actions or 2 objects, each with a number of choices, and asks for the number of combinations, this formula can be used. For example: A man wants a sandwich and a drink for lunch. If a restaurant has 4 choices of sandwiches and 3 choices of drinks, how many different ways can he order his lunch?

Since there are 4 choices of sandwiches and 3 choices of drinks, use the formula

$$\begin{aligned}\text{Number of ways} &= 4(3)\\ &= 12\end{aligned}$$

Therefore, the man can order his lunch 12 different ways.

If we have objects a, b, c, and d, and want to arrange them two at a time—that is, like ab, bc, cd, etc.—we have four combinations taken two at a time. This is denoted as ${}_4C_2$. The rule is that ${}_4C_2 = \frac{(4)(3)}{(2)(1)}$. In general, n combinations taken r at a time is represented by the formula:

$${}_nC_r = \frac{(n)(n-1)(n-2)\ldots(n-r+1)}{(r)(r-1)(r-2)\ldots(1)}$$

Examples: ${}_3C_2 = \frac{3 \times 2}{2 \times 1}$; ${}_8C_3 = \frac{8 \times 7 \times 6}{3 \times 2 \times 1}$

Suppose there are 24 people at a party and each person shakes another person's hand (only once). How many handshakes are there?

Solution: Represent the people at the party as *a*, *b*, *c*, *d*, etc.
The combinations of handshakes would be *ab*, *ac*, *bc*, *bd*, etc., or 24 combinations taken 2 at a time:

$${}_{24}C_2. \text{ This is } \frac{24 \times 23}{2 \times 1} = 276.$$

Permutations

613a. Permutations are like combinations, except in permutations the order is important. As an example, if we want to find how many permutations there are of three objects taken 2 at a time, we would have for *a*, *b*, *c*, *ab*, *ba*, *ac*, *ca*, *bc*, *cb*. Thus, as an example, *ba* would be one permutation and *ab* would be another. The permutations of 3 objects taken 2 at a time would be ${}_3P_2 = 3 \times 2$ and not $\frac{(3 \times 2)}{(2 \times 1)}$ as in combinations. The number of permutations of *n* objects taken *r* at a time would be

$${}_nP_r = (n)(n-1)\ldots(n-r+1).$$

Example: How many permutations of the digits 142 are there, where the digits are taken two at a time?

Solution: You have 14, 41, 12, 21, 42, 24. That is, ${}_3P_2 = 3 \times 2 = 6$.

Probability

614. The probability that an event will occur equals the number of favorable ways divided by the total number of ways. If *P* is the probability, *m* is the number of favorable ways, and *n* is the total number of ways, then

$$P = \frac{m}{n}$$

For example: What is the probability that a head will turn up on a single throw of a penny?

The favorable number of ways is 1 (a head).

The total number of ways is 2 (a head and a tail). Thus, the probability is $\frac{1}{2}$.

If *a* and *b* are two mutually exclusive events, then the probability that *a* or *b* will occur is the sum of the individual probabilities.

Suppose P_a is the probability that an event *a* occurs. Suppose that P_b is the probability that a second independent event *b* occurs. Then the probability that the first event *a* occurs *and* the second event *b* occurs subsequently is $P_a \times P_b$.

The Absolute Value Sign

615. The symbol | | denotes absolute value. The absolute value of a number is the numerical value of the number without the plus or minus sign in front of it. Thus all absolute values are positive. For example, $|+3|$ is 3, and $|-2|$ is 2. Here's another example:

If *x* is positive and *y* is negative $|x| + |y| = x - y$. Because *y* is negative, we must have $x - y$ to make the term positive.

Functions

616. Suppose we have a function of x. This is denoted as $f(x)$ (or $g(y)$ or $h(z)$, etc.). As an example, if $f(x) = x$ then $f(3) = 3$.

In this example we substitute the value 3 wherever x appears in the function. Similarly $f(-2) = -2$. Consider another example: If $f(y) = y^2 - y$, then $f(2) = 2^2 - 2 = 2$. $f(-2) = (-2)^2 - (-2) = 6$. $f(z) = z^2 - z$. $f(2z) = (2z)^2 - (2z) = 4z^2 - 2z$.

Let us consider still another example: Let $f(x) = x + 2$ and $g(y) = 2^y$. What is $f[g(-2)]$? Now $g(-2) = 2^{-2} = \frac{1}{4}$. Thus $f[g(-2)] = f\left(\frac{1}{4}\right)$. Since $f(x) = x + 2$, $f\left(\frac{1}{4}\right) = \frac{1}{4} + 2 = 2\frac{1}{4}$.

Practice Test 6

Miscellaneous Problems: Averages, Standard Deviation, Properties of Integers, Approximations, Combinations, Permutations, Probability, the Absolute Value Sign, and Functions

Correct answers and solutions follow each test.

1. A B C D E

1. If n is the first of five consecutive odd numbers, what is their average?

(A) n
(B) $n + 1$
(C) $n + 2$
(D) $n + 3$
(E) $n + 4$

2. A B C D E

2. What is the average of the following numbers: 35.5, 32.5, 34.0, 35.0, 34.5?

(A) 33.0
(B) 33.8
(C) 34.0
(D) 34.3
(E) 34.5

3. A B C D E

3. If P is an even number, and Q and R are both odd, which of the following *must* be true?

(A) $P \cdot Q$ is an odd number.
(B) $Q - R$ is an even number.
(C) $PQ - PR$ is an odd number.
(D) $Q + R$ cannot equal P.
(E) $P + Q$ cannot equal R.

4. A B C D E

4. If a number is divisible by 102, then it is also divisible by:

(A) 23
(B) 11
(C) 103
(D) 5
(E) 2

5. A B C D E

5. Which of the following numbers is divisible by 36?

(A) 35,924
(B) 64,530
(C) 74,098
(D) 152,640
(E) 192,042

6. A B C D E

6. How many prime numbers are there between 45 and 72?

(A) 4
(B) 5
(C) 6
(D) 7
(E) 8

7. A B C D E

7. Which of the following represents the smallest possible value of $(M - \frac{1}{2})^2$, if M is an integer?

(A) 0.00
(B) 0.25
(C) 0.50
(D) 0.75
(E) 1.00

8. A B C D E

8. Which of the following best approximates $\frac{7.40096 \times 10.0342}{.2001355}$?

(A) 0.3700
(B) 3.700
(C) 37.00
(D) 370.0
(E) 3700

9. A B C D E

9. In a class with 6 boys and 4 girls, the students all took the same test. The boys' scores were 74, 82, 84, 84, 88, and 95, while the girls' scores were 80, 82, 86, and 86. Which of the following statements is true?

(A) The boys' average was 0.1 higher than the average for the whole class.
(B) The girls' average was 0.1 lower than the boys' average.
(C) The class average was 1.0 higher than the boys' average.
(D) The boys' average was 1.0 higher than the class average.
(E) The girls' average was 1.0 lower than the boys' average.

10. A B C D E

10. Which of the following numbers *must* be odd?

(A) The sum of an odd number and an odd number.
(B) The product of an odd number and an even number.
(C) The sum of an odd number and an even number.
(D) The product of two even numbers.
(E) The sum of two even numbers.

11. A B C D E

11. Which of the following numbers is the best approximation of the length of one side of a square with an area of 12 square inches?

(A) 3.2 inches
(B) 3.3 inches
(C) 3.4 inches
(D) 3.5 inches
(E) 3.6 inches

12. A B C D E

12. If n is an odd number, then which of the following *best* describes the number represented by $n^2 + 2n + 1$?

(A) It can be odd or even.
(B) It must be odd.
(C) It must be divisible by four.
(D) It must be divisible by six.
(E) The answer cannot be determined from the given information.

13. A B C D E

13. What is the average of the following numbers: $3\frac{1}{2}$, $4\frac{1}{4}$, $2\frac{1}{4}$, $3\frac{1}{4}$, 4?

(A) 3.25
(B) 3.35
(C) 3.45
(D) 3.50
(E) 3.60

14. A B C D E

14. Which of the following numbers is divisible by 24?

(A) 76,300
(B) 78,132
(C) 80,424
(D) 81,234
(E) 83,636

15. A B C D E

15. In order to graduate, a boy needs an average of 65 percent for his five major subjects. His first four grades were 55, 60, 65, and 65. What grade does he need in the fifth subject in order to graduate?

(A) 65
(B) 70
(C) 75
(D) 80
(E) 85

16. A B C D E

16. If t is any integer, which of the following represents an odd number?

(A) $2t$
(B) $2t + 3$
(C) $3t$
(D) $2t + 2$
(E) $t + 1$

17. A B C D E

17. If the average of five whole numbers is an even number, which of the following statements is *not true*?

(A) The sum of the five numbers must be divisible by 2.
(B) The sum of the five numbers must be divisible by 5.
(C) The sum of the five numbers must be divisible by 10.
(D) At least one of the five numbers must be even.
(E) All of the five numbers must be odd.

18. A B C D E

18. What is the product of 23 and 79 to one significant digit?

(A) 1,600
(B) 1,817
(C) 1,000
(D) 1,800
(E) 2,000

19. A B C D E

19. Which of the following is closest to the square root of $\frac{1}{2}$?

(A) 0.25
(B) 0.5
(C) 0.6
(D) 0.7
(E) 0.8

20. A B C D E

20. How many prime numbers are there between 56 and 100?

(A) 8
(B) 9
(C) 10
(D) 11
(E) None of the above.

21. A B C D E

21. If you multiply 1,200,176 by 520,204, and then divide the product by 1,000,000,000, your result will be closest to:

(A) 0.6
(B) 6
(C) 600
(D) 6,000
(E) 6,000,000

22. A B C D E

22. The number 89.999 rounded off to the nearest tenth is equal to which of the following?

(A) 90.0
(B) 89.0
(C) 89.9
(D) 89.99
(E) 89.90

23. A B C D E

23. *a*, *b*, *c*, *d*, and *e* are integers; *M* is their average; and *S* is their sum. What is the ratio of *S* to *M*?

(A) 1 : 5
(B) 5 : 1
(C) 1 : 1
(D) 2 : 1
(E) depends on the values of *a*, *b*, *c*, *d*, and *e*

24. A B C D E

24. The sum of five odd numbers is always:

(A) even
(B) divisible by three
(C) divisible by five
(D) a prime number
(E) None of the above.

25. A B C D E

25. If *E* is an even number, and *F* is divisible by three, then what is the *largest* number by which E^2F^3 *must* be divisible?

(A) 6
(B) 12
(C) 54
(D) 108
(E) 144

26. A B C D E

26. If the average of five consecutive even numbers is 8, which of the following is the smallest of the five numbers?

(A) 4
(B) 5
(C) 6
(D) 8
(E) None of the above.

27. A B C D E

27. If a number is divisible by 23, then it is also divisible by which of the following?

(A) 7
(B) 24
(C) 9
(D) 3
(E) None of the above.

28. A B C D E

28. What is the average (to the nearest tenth) of the following numbers: 91.4, 91.5, 91.6, 91.7, 91.7, 92.0, 92.1, 92.3, 92.3, 92.4?

(A) 91.9
(B) 92.0
(C) 92.1
(D) 92.2
(E) 92.3

29. A B C D E

29. Which of the following numbers is divisible by 11?

(A) 30,217
(B) 44,221
(C) 59,403
(D) 60,411
(E) None of the above.

30. A B C D E

30. Which of the following is the best approximation of the product (1.005) (20.0025) (0.0102)?

(A) 0.02
(B) 0.2
(C) 2.0
(D) 20
(E) 200

31. A B C D E

31. If *a*, *b*, and *c* are all divisible by 8, then their average must be

(A) divisible by 8
(B) divisible by 4
(C) divisible by 2
(D) an integer
(E) None of the above.

32. A B C D E

32. Which of the following numbers is divisible by 24?

(A) 13,944
(B) 15,746
(C) 15,966
(D) 16,012
(E) None of the above.

33. A B C D E

33. Which of the following numbers is a prime?

(A) 147
(B) 149
(C) 153
(D) 155
(E) 161

34. A B C D E

34. The sum of four consecutive odd integers must be:

(A) even, but not necessarily divisible by 4
(B) divisible by 4, but not necessarily by 8
(C) divisible by 8, but not necessarily by 16
(D) divisible by 16
(E) None of the above.

35. A B C D E

35. Which of the following is closest to the square root of $\frac{3}{5}$?

(A) $\frac{1}{2}$

(B) $\frac{2}{3}$

(C) $\frac{3}{4}$

(D) $\frac{4}{5}$

(E) 1

36. A B C D E

36. The sum of an odd and an even number is

(A) a perfect square
(B) negative
(C) even
(D) odd
(E) None of the above.

Answer Key for Practice Test 6

1. E	**10.** C	**19.** D	**28.** A
2. D	**11.** D	**20.** B	**29.** A
3. B	**12.** C	**21.** C	**30.** B
4. E	**13.** C	**22.** A	**31.** E
5. D	**14.** C	**23.** B	**32.** A
6. C	**15.** D	**24.** E	**33.** B
7. B	**16.** B	**25.** D	**34.** C
8. D	**17.** E	**26.** A	**35.** C
9. E	**18.** E	**27.** E	**36.** D

Answers and Solutions for Practice Test 6

1. Choice E is correct. The five consecutive odd numbers must be n, $n + 2$, $n + 4$, $n + 6$, and $n + 8$. Their average is equal to their sum, $5n + 20$, divided by the number of addends, 5, which yields $n + 4$ as the average. (601)

2. Choice D is correct. Choosing 34 as an approximate average results in the following addends: +1.5, −1.5, 0, +1.0, and +0.5. Their sum is +1.5. Now, divide by 5 to get +0.3 and add this to 34 to get 34.3. (To check this, add the five original numbers and divide by 5.) (601)

3. Choice B is correct. Since Q is an odd number, it may be represented by $2m + 1$, where m is an integer. Similarly, call R $2n + 1$, where n is an integer. Thus, $Q - R$ is equal to $(2m + 1) - (2n + 1)$, $2m - 2n$, or $2(m - n)$. Now, since m and n are integers, $m - n$ will be some integer p. Thus, $Q - R = 2p$. Any number in the form of $2p$, where p is any integer, is an even number. Therefore, $Q - R$ *must* be even. (A) and (C) are wrong, because an even number multiplied by an odd is always even. (D) and (E) are only true for specific values of P, Q, and R. (604)

4. Choice E is correct. If a number is divisible by 102, then it must be divisible by all of the factors of 102. The only choice that is a factor of 102 is 2. (607)

5. Choice D is correct. To be divisible by 36, a number must be divisible by both 4 and 9. Only (A) and (D) are divisible by 4. (Recall that only the last two digits must be examined.) Of these, only (D) is divisible by 9. (The sum of the digits of (A) is 23, which is not divisible by 9; the sum of the digits of (D) is 18.) (607)

6. Choice C is correct. The prime numbers between 45 and 72 are 47, 53, 59, 61, 67, and 71. All of the others have factors other than 1 and themselves. (608)

7. Choice B is correct. Since M must be an *integer*, the closest value it can have to $\frac{1}{2}$ is either 1 or 0. In either case, $(M - \frac{1}{2})^2$ is equal to $\frac{1}{4}$, or 0.25. (603)

8. Choice D is correct. Approximate each of the numbers to only one significant digit (this is permissible, because the choices are so far apart; if they had been closer together, two or three significant digits should be used). After this approximation, the expression is: $\frac{7 \times 10}{0.2}$, which is equal to 350. This is closest to 370. (609)

9. Choice E is correct. The average for the boys alone was $\frac{74 + 82 + 84 + 84 + 88 + 95}{6}$, or $507 \div 6 = 84.5$. The girls' average was $\frac{80 + 82 + 86 + 86}{4}$, or $334 \div 4 = 83.5$, which is 1.0 below the boys' average. (601)

10. Choice C is correct. The sum of an odd number and an even number can be expressed as $(2n + 1) + (2m)$, where n and m are integers. ($2n + 1$ must be odd, and $2m$ must be even.) Their sum is equal to $2n + 2m + 1$, or $2(m + n) + 1$. Since $(m + n)$ is an integer, the quantity $2(m + n) + 1$ *must* represent an odd integer. (604, 605)

11. Choice D is correct. The actual length of one of the sides would be the square root of 12. Square each of the five choices to find the square of 3.4 is 11.56, and the square of 3.5 is 12.25. The square root of 12 must lie between 3.4 and 3.5. Squaring 3.45 (halfway between the two choices) yields 11.9025, which is less than 12. Thus the square root of 12 must be greater than 3.45 and therefore closer to 3.5 than to 3.4. (612)

12. Choice C is correct. Factor $n^2 + 2n + 1$ to $(n + 1)(n + 1)$ or $(n + 1)^2$. Now, since n is an odd number, $n + 1$ must be even (the number after every odd number is even). Thus, representing $n + 1$ as $2k$ where k is an integer ($2k$ is the standard representation for an even number) yields the expression: $(n + 1)^2 = (2k)^2$ or $4k^2$. Thus, $(n + 1)^2$ is a multiple of 4, and it must be divisible by 4. A number divisible by 4 must also be even, so (C) is the best choice. (604–607)

13. Choice C is correct. Convert to decimals. Then calculate the value of: $\frac{3.50 + 4.25 + 2.25 + 3.25 + 4.00}{5}$. This equals $17.25 \div 5$, or 3.45. (601)

14. Choice C is correct. If a number is divisible by 24, it must be divisible by 3 and 8. Of the five choices given, only choice (C) is divisible by 8. Add the digits in 80,424 to get 18. As this is divisible by 3, the number is divisible by 3. The number, therefore, is divisible by 24. (607)

15. Choice D is correct. If the boy is to average 65 for five subjects, the total of his five grades must be five times 65, or 325. The sum of the first four grades is $55 + 60 + 65 + 65$, or 245. Therefore, the fifth mark must be $325 - 245$, or 80. (601)

16. Choice B is correct. If t is any integer, then $2t$ is an even number. Adding 3 to an even number always produces an odd number. Thus, $2t + 3$ is always odd. (606)

17. Choice E is correct. Call the five numbers, a, b, c, d, and e. Then the average is $\frac{(a+b+c+d+e)}{5}$. Since this must be even, $\frac{(a+b+c+d+e)}{5} = 2k$, where k is an integer. Thus $a + b + c + d + e = 10k$. Therefore, the sum of the 5 numbers is divisible by 10, 2, and 5. Thus the first three choices are eliminated. If the five numbers were 1, 1, 1, 1, and 6, then the average would be 2. Thus, the average is even, but not all of the numbers are even. Thus, choice (D) can be true. If all the numbers were odd, the sum would have to be odd. This contradicts the statement that the average is even. Thus, choice (E) is the answer. (601, 607)

18. Choice E is correct. First, round off 23 and 79 to one significant digit. The numbers become 20 and 80. The product of these two numbers is 1,600, which rounded off to one significant digit is 2,000. (611)

19. Choice D is correct. 0.7 squared is 0.49. Squaring 0.8 yields 0.64. Thus, the square root of $\frac{1}{2}$ must lie between 0.7 and 0.8. Take the number halfway between these two, 0.75, and square it. This number, 0.5625, is more than $\frac{1}{2}$, so the square root must be closer to 0.7 than to 0.8. An easier way to do problems concerning the square roots of 2 and 3 and their multiples is to memorize the values of these two square roots. The square root of 2 is about 1.414 (remember fourteen-fourteen), and the square root of three is about 1.732 (remember that 1732 was the year of George Washington's birth). Apply these as follows: $\frac{1}{2} = \frac{1}{4} \times 2$. Thus, $\sqrt{\frac{1}{2}} = \sqrt{\frac{1}{4}} \times \sqrt{2} = \frac{1}{2} \times 1.414 = 0.707$, which is very close to 0.7. (612)

20. Choice B is correct. The prime numbers can be found by taking all the odd numbers between 56 and 100 (the even ones cannot be primes) and eliminating all the ones divisible by 3, by 5, or by 7. If a number under 100 is divisible by none of these, it must be prime. Thus, the only primes between 56 and 100 are 59, 61, 67, 71, 73, 79, 83, 89, and 97. (608)

21. Choice C is correct. Since all the answer requires is an order-of-ten approximation, do not calculate the exact answer. Approximate the answer in the following manner: $\frac{1{,}000{,}000 \times 500{,}000}{1{,}000{,}000{,}000} = 500$. The only choice on the same order of magnitude is 600. (609)

22. Choice A is correct. To round off 89.999, look at the number in the hundredths place. 9 is more than 5, so add 1 to the number in the tenths place and eliminate all of the digits to the right. Thus, we get 90.0. (609)

23. Choice B is correct. The average of five numbers is found by dividing their sum by five. Thus, the sum is five times the average, so $S : M = 5 : 1$. (601)

24. Choice E is correct. None of the first four choices is necessarily true. The sum, $5 + 7 + 9 + 13 + 15 = 49$, is not even, divisible by 3, divisible by 5, nor prime. (604, 607, 608)

25. Choice D is correct. Any even number can be written as $2m$, and any number divisible by 3 can be written as $3n$, where m and n are integers. Thus, E^2F^3 equals $(2m)^2(3n)^3 = (4m^2)(27n^3) = 108(m^2n^3)$, and 108 is the largest number by which E^2F^3 must be divisible. (607)

26. Choice A is correct. The five consecutive even numbers can be represented as n, $n + 2$, $n + 4$, $n + 6$, and $n + 8$. Taking the sum and dividing by five yields an average of $n + 4$. Thus, $n + 4 = 8$, the given average, and $n = 4$, the smallest number. (601)

27. Choice E is correct. If a number is divisible by 23, then it is divisible by all of the factors of 23. But 23 is a prime with no factors except 1 and itself. Therefore, the correct choice is (E). (607)

28. Choice A is correct. To find the average, it is convenient to choose 92.0 as an approximate average and then find the average of the differences between the actual numbers and 92.0. Thus, add up: $(-0.6) + (-0.5) + (-0.4) + (-0.3) + (-0.3) + (0.0) + 0.1 + 0.3 + 0.3 + 0.4 = -1.0$; divide this by 10 (the number of quantities to be averaged) to obtain -0.1. Finally, add this to the approximate average, 92.0, to obtain a final average of 91.9. (601)

29. Choice A is correct. To determine if a number is divisible by 11, take each of the digits separately and, beginning with either end, subtract the second from the first, add the following digit, subtract the next one, add the one after that, etc. If this result is divisible by 11, the entire number is. Thus, because $3 - 0 + 2 - 1 + 7 = 11$, we know that 30,217 is divisible by 11. Using the same method, we find that the other four choices are not divisible by 11. (607)

30. Choice B is correct. This is simply an order-of-ten approximation, so round off the numbers and work the following problem. $(1.0)(20.0)(0.01) = 0.20$. The actual answer is closest to 0.2. (611)

31. Choice E is correct. Represent the three numbers as $8p$, $8q$, and $8r$, respectively. Thus, their sum is $8p + 8q + 8r$, and their average is $\frac{(8p + 8q + 8r)}{3}$. This need not even be a whole number. For example, the average of 8, 16, and 32 is $\frac{56}{3}$, or $18\frac{2}{3}$. (601, 607)

32. Choice A is correct. To be divisible by 24, a number must be divisible by both 3 and 8. Only 13,944 and 15,966 are divisible by 3; of these, only 13,944 is divisible by 8 ($13{,}944 = 24 \times 581$). (607)

33. Choice B is correct. The approximate square root of each of these numbers is 13. Merely divide each of these numbers by the primes up to 13, which are 2, 3, 5, 7, and 11. The only number not divisible by any of these primes is 149. (608, 612)

34. Choice C is correct. Call the first odd integer $2k + 1$. (This is the standard representation for a general odd integer.) Thus, the next 3 odd integers are $2k + 3$, $2k + 5$, and $2k + 7$. (Each one is 2 more than the previous one.) The sum of these integers is $(2k + 1) + (2k + 3) + (2k + 5) + (2k + 7) = 8k + 16$. This can be written as $8(k + 2)$, which is divisible by 8, but not necessarily by 16. (606, 607)

35. Choice C is correct. By squaring the five choices, it is evident that the two closest choices are $\left(\frac{3}{4}\right)^2 = 0.5625$ and $\left(\frac{4}{5}\right)^2 = 0.64$. Squaring the number halfway between $\frac{3}{4}$ and $\frac{4}{5}$ gives $(0.775)^2 = 0.600625$. This is greater than $\frac{3}{5}$, so the square root of $\frac{3}{5}$ must be closer to $\frac{3}{4}$ than to $\frac{4}{5}$. (612)

36. Choice D is correct. Let the even number be $2k$, where k is an integer, and let the odd number be $2m + 1$, where m is an integer. Thus, the sum is $2k + (2m + 1)$, $2k + 2m + 1$, or $2(k + m) + 1$. Now $k + m$ is an integer since k and m are integers. Call $k + m$ by another name, p. Thus, $2(k + m) + 1$ is $2p + 1$, which is the representation of an odd number. (604, 606)

MATH REFRESHER SESSION 7

Tables, Charts, and Graphs

Charts and Graphs

701. Graphs and charts show the relationship of numbers and quantities in visual form. By looking at a graph, you can see at a glance the relationship between two or more sets of information. If such information were presented in written form, it would be hard to read and understand.

Here are some things to remember when doing problems based on graphs or charts:

1. Understand what you are being asked to do before you begin figuring.

2. Check the dates and types of information required. Be sure that you are looking in the proper columns, and on the proper lines, for the information you need.

3. Check the units required. Be sure that your answer is in thousands, millions, or whatever the question calls for.

4. In computing averages, be sure that you add the figures you need and no others, and that you divide by the correct number of years or other units.

5. Be careful in computing problems asking for percentages.
   (a) Remember that to convert a decimal into a percent you must multiply it by 100. For example, 0.04 is 4%.
   (b) Be sure that you can distinguish between such quantities as 1% (1 percent) and .01% (one one-hundredth of 1 percent), whether in numerals or in words.
   (c) Remember that if quantity X is greater than quantity Y, and the question asks what percent quantity X is of quantity Y, the answer must be greater than 100 percent.

Tables and Charts

702. A table or chart shows data in the form of a box of numbers or chart of numbers. Each line describes how the numbers are connected.

Example:

Test Score	Number of Students
90	2
85	1
80	1
60	3

Example: How many students took the test?

Solution: To find out the number of students that took the test, just add up the numbers in the column marked "Number of Students." That is, add $2 + 1 + 1 + 3 = 7$.

Example: What was the difference in score between the highest and the lowest score?

Solution: First look at the highest score: 90. Then look at the lowest score: 60. Now calculate the difference: $90 - 60 = 30$.

Example: What was the median score?

Solution: The median score means the score that is in the *middle* of all the scores. That is, there are just as many scores above the median as below it. So in this example, the scores are 90, 90 (there are two 90) 85, 80, and 60, 60, 60 (there are three 60). So we have:

90
90
85
80
60
60
60

80 is right in the middle. That is, there are three scores above it and three scores below it. So 80 is the median.

Example: What was the mean score?

Solution: The mean score is defined as the *average* score. That is, it is the

$$\frac{\text{sum of the scores}}{\text{total number of scores}}$$

The sum of the scores is $90 + 90 + 85 + 80 + 60 + 60 + 60 = 525$. The total number of scores is $2 + 1 + 1 + 3 = 7$, so divide 7 into 525 to get the average: 75.

Graphs

703. To read a graph, you must know what *scale* the graph has been drawn to. Somewhere on the face of the graph will be an explanation of what each division of the graph means. Sometimes the divisions will be labeled. At other times, this information will be given in a small box called a *scale* or *legend.* For instance, a map, which is a specialized kind of graph, will always carry a scale or legend on its face telling you such information as $1'' = 100$ miles or $\frac{1''}{4} = 2$ miles.

Bar Graphs

704. The bar graph shows how information is compared by using broad lines, called bars, of varying lengths. Sometimes single lines are used as well. Bar graphs are good for showing a quick comparison of the information involved; however, the bars are difficult to read accurately unless the end of the bar falls exactly on one of the divisions of the scale. If the end of the bar falls between divisions of the scale, it is not easy to arrive at the precise figure represented by the bar. In bar graphs, the bars can run either vertically or horizontally. The sample bar graph following is a horizontal graph.

EXPENDITURES PER PUPIL—1990

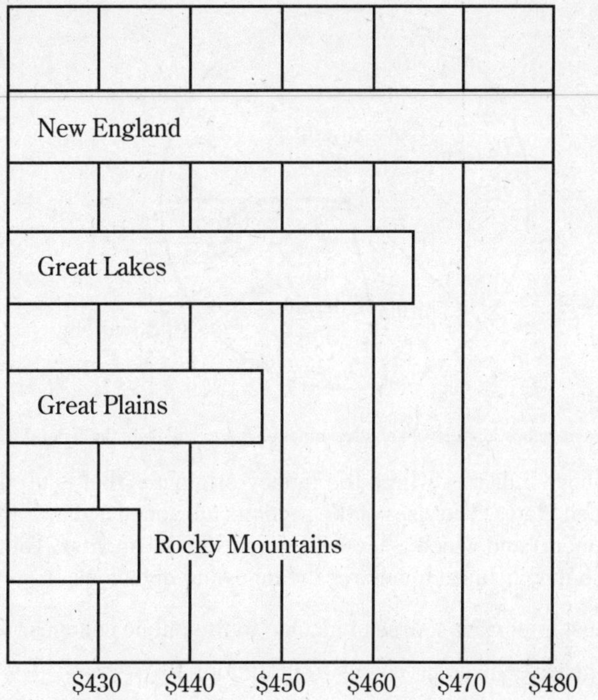

The individual bars in this kind of graph may carry a label within the bar, as in this example. The label may also appear alongside each bar. The scale used on the bars may appear along one axis, as in the example, or it may be noted somewhere on the face of the graph. Each numbered space on the *x*-axis, or horizontal axis, represents an expenditure of $10 per pupil. A wide variety of questions may be answered by a bar graph, such as:

(1) Which area of the country spends least per pupil? Rocky Mountains.

(2) How much does the New England area spend per pupil? $480.

(3) How much less does the Great Plains spend per pupil than the Great Lakes?
$464 – 447 = $17/pupil.

(4) How much more does New England spend on a pupil than the Rocky Mountain area?
$480 – 433 = $47/pupil.

Circle Graphs

705. A circle graph shows how an entire quantity has been divided or apportioned. The circle represents 100 percent of the quantity; the different parts into which the whole has been divided are shown by sections, or wedges, of the circle. Circle graphs are good for showing how money is distributed or collected, and for this reason they are widely used in financial graphing. The information is usually presented on the face of each section, telling you exactly what the section stands for and the value of that section in comparison to the other parts of the graph.

SOURCES OF INCOME—PUBLIC COLLEGES OF THE U.S.

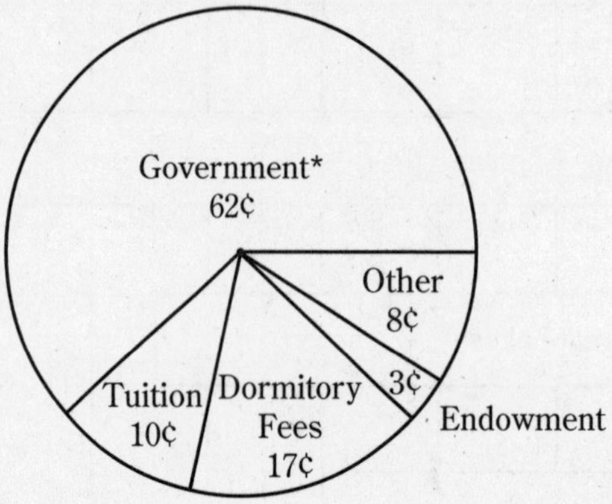

***Government refers to all levels of government—not exclusively the federal government.**

The circle graph above indicates where the money originates that is used to maintain public colleges in the United States. The sizes of the sections tell you at a glance which source is most important (government) and which is least important (endowments). The sections total 100¢, or $1.00. This graph may be used to answer the following questions:

(1) What is the most important source of income to the public colleges? Government.

(2) What part of the revenue dollar comes from tuition? 10¢.

(3) Dormitory fees bring in how many times the money that endowments bring in? $5\frac{2}{3}$ times $\left(\frac{17}{3} = 5\frac{2}{3}\right)$.

(4) What is the least important source of revenue to public colleges? Endowments.

Line Graphs

706. Graphs that have information running both across (horizontally) and up and down (vertically) can be considered to be laid out on a grid having a *y*-axis and an *x*-axis. One of the two quantities being compared will be placed along the *y*-axis, and the other quantity will be placed along the *x*-axis. When we are asked to compare two values, we subtract the smaller from the larger.

SHARES OF STOCK SOLD
NEW YORK STOCK EXCHANGE DURING ONE SIX-MONTH PERIOD

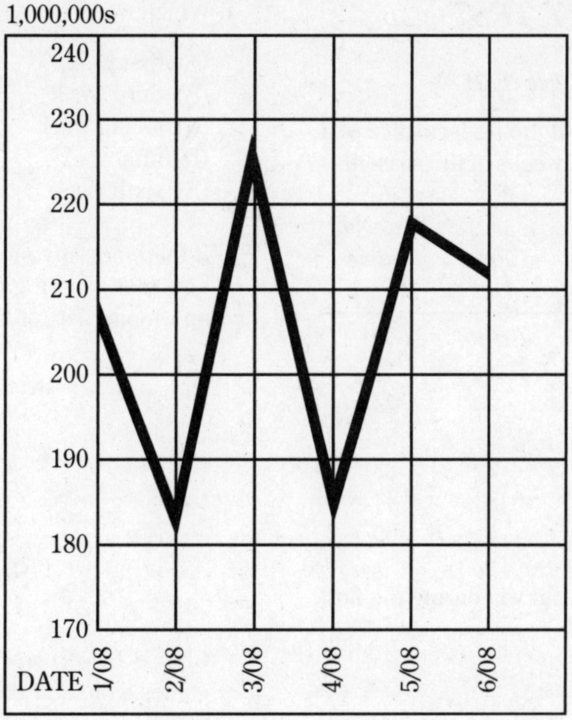

Our sample line graph represents the total shares of stock sold on the New York Stock Exchange between January and June. The months are placed along the *x*-axis, while the sales, in units of 1,000,000 shares, are placed along the *y*-axis.

(1) How many shares were sold in March? 225,000,000.

(2) What is the trend of stock sales between April and May? The volume of sales rose.

(3) Compare the share sales in January and February. 25,000,000 fewer shares were sold in February.

(4) During which months of the period was the increase in sales largest? February to March.

Practice Test 7 and Solutions

Tables, Charts, and Graphs

Correct answers and solutions follow each test.

TABLE CHART TEST

Questions 1–5 are based on this table chart.

The following chart is a record of the performance of a baseball team for the first seven weeks of the season.

	Games Won	*Games Lost*	*Total No. of Games Played*
First Week	5	3	8
Second Week	4	4	16
Third Week	5	2	23
Fourth Week	6	3	32
Fifth Week	4	2	38
Sixth Week	3	3	44
Seventh Week	2	4	50

1. How many games did the team win during the first seven weeks?

(A) 32
(B) 29
(C) 25
(D) 21
(E) 50

2. What percent of the games did the team win?

(A) 75%
(B) 60%
(C) 58%
(D) 29%
(E) 80%

3. According to the chart, which week was the worst for the team?

(A) second week
(B) fourth week
(C) fifth week
(D) sixth week
(E) seventh week

4. Which week was the best week for the team?

(A) first week
(B) third week
(C) fourth week
(D) fifth week
(E) sixth week

5. If there are fifty more games to play in the season, how many more games must the team win to end up winning 70% of the games?

(A) 39
(B) 35
(C) 41
(D) 34
(E) 32

Solutions

1. Choice B is correct. To find the total number of games won, add the number of games won for all the weeks, $5 + 4 + 5 + 6 + 4 + 3 + 2 = 29$. (702)

2. Choice C is correct. The team won 29 out of 50 games, or 58%. (702)

3. Choice E is correct. The seventh week was the only week that the team lost more games than it won. (702)

4. Choice B is correct. During the third week the team won 5 games and lost 2, or it won about 70% of the games that week. Compared with the winning percentages for other weeks, the third week's was the highest. (702)

5. Choice C is correct. To win 70% of all the games, the team must win 70 out of 100. Since it won 29 games out of the first 50 games, it must win $70 - 29$, or 41 games out of the next 50 games. (702)

PIE CHART TEST

Questions 1–5 are based on this pie chart.

POPULATION BY REGION, 1964

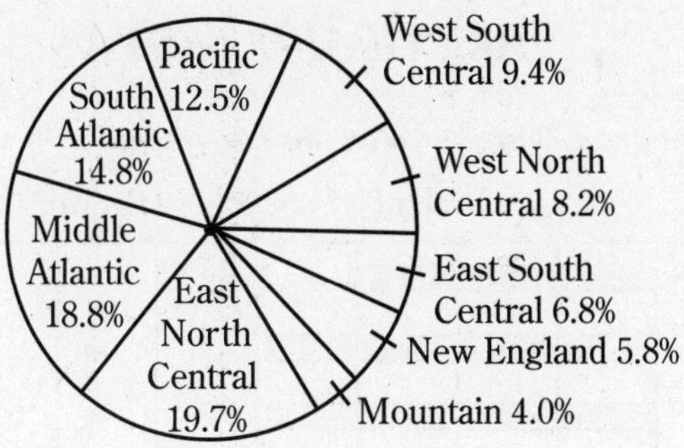

Total U.S. = 191.3 million = 100%

1. Which region was the most populated region in 1964?

(A) East North Central
(B) Middle Atlantic
(C) South Atlantic
(D) Pacific
(E) New England

2. What part of the entire population lived in the Mountain region?

(A) $\frac{1}{10}$

(B) $\frac{1}{30}$

(C) $\frac{1}{50}$

(D) $\frac{1}{25}$

(E) $\frac{1}{8}$

3. What was the approximate population in the Pacific region?

(A) 20 million
(B) 24 million
(C) 30 million
(D) 28 million
(E) 15 million

4. Approximately how many more people lived in the Middle Atlantic region than in the South Atlantic?

(A) 4.0 million
(B) 7.7 million
(C) 5.2 million
(D) 9.3 million
(E) 8.5 million

5. What was the total population in all the regions combined?

(A) 73.3 million
(B) 100.0 million
(C) 191.3 million
(D) 126.8 million
(E) 98.5 million

Solutions

1. Choice A is correct. East North Central, with 19.7% of the total population, had the largest population. (705)

2. Choice D is correct. The Mountain region had 4.0% of the population. 4.0% is $\frac{1}{25}$. (705)

3. Choice B is correct. Pacific had 12.5% of the population. 12.5% of 191.3 million is $.125 \times 191.3$, or about 24 million. (705)

4. Choice B is correct. Middle Atlantic had 18.8% and South Atlantic had 14.8% of the population. So, Middle Atlantic had 4.0% more. 4.0% of 191.3 million is $.04 \times 191.3$, or about 7.7 million. (705)

5. Choice C is correct. All the regions combined had 100% of the population, or 191.3 million. (705)

LINE GRAPH TEST

Questions 1–5 are based on this line graph.

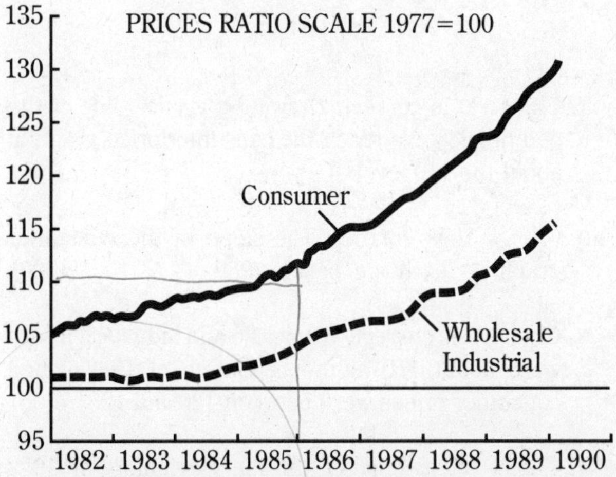

1. On the ratio scale, what were consumer prices recorded as at the end of 1985?

(A) 95
(B) 100
(C) 105
(D) 110
(E) 115

2. During what year did consumer prices rise fastest?

(A) 1983
(B) 1985
(C) 1987
(D) 1988
(E) 1989

3. When wholesale and industrial prices were recorded as 110, consumer prices were recorded as

(A) between 125 and 120
(B) between 120 and 115
(C) between 115 and 110
(D) between 110 and 105
(E) between 105 and 100

4. For the 8 years 1982–1989 inclusive, the average increase in consumer prices was

(A) 1 point
(B) 2 points
(C) 3 points
(D) 4 points
(E) 5 points

5. The percentage increase in wholesale and industrial prices between the beginning of 1982 and the end of 1989 was

(A) 1 percent
(B) 5 percent
(C) 10 percent
(D) 15 percent
(E) less than 1 percent

Solutions

1. Choice D is correct. Drawing a vertical line at the end of 1985, we reach the consumer price graph at about the 110 level. (706)

2. Choice E is correct. The slope of the consumer graph is clearly steepest in 1989. (706)

3. Choice A is correct. Wholesale and industrial prices were about 110 at the beginning of 1989, when consumer prices were between 120 and 125. (706)

4. Choice C is correct. At the beginning of 1982 consumer prices were about 105; at the end of 1989 they were about 130. The average increase is $\frac{130-105}{8} = \frac{25}{8}$ or about 3. (706)

5. Choice D is correct. At the beginning of 1982, wholesale prices were about 100; at the end of 1989, they were about 115. The percent increase is about $\frac{115-100}{100} \times 100\%$, or 15%. (706)

BAR GRAPH TEST

Questions 1–3 are based on this bar graph.

Softwood Plywood Shows Growth

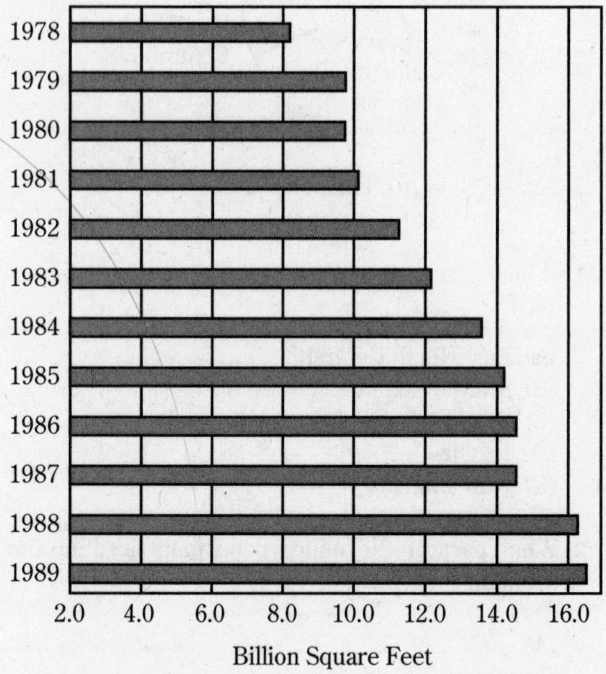

1. What was the approximate ratio of soft plywood produced in 1978 as compared with that produced in 1987?

(A) 1 : 1
(B) 2 : 3
(C) 4 : 7
(D) 3 : 4
(E) 1 : 3

2. For the years 1978 through 1983, excluding 1982, how many billion square feet of plywood were produced altogether?

(A) 23.2
(B) 29.7
(C) 34.1
(D) 49.8
(E) 52.6

3. Between which consecutive odd years and between which consecutive even years was the plywood production jump greatest?

(A) 1985 and 1987; 1978 and 1980
(B) 1983 and 1985; 1984 and 1986
(C) 1979 and 1981; 1980 and 1982
(D) 1981 and 1983; 1980 and 1982
(E) 1983 and 1985; 1982 and 1984

Solutions

1. Choice C is correct. To answer this question, you will have to measure the bars. In 1978, about 8 billion square feet of plywood were produced. In 1987, about 14 billion square feet were produced. The ratio of 8 : 14 is the same as 4 : 7. (704)

2. Choice D is correct. All you have to do is to measure the bar for each year—of course, don't include the 1982 bar—and estimate the length of each bar. Then you add the five lengths. 1978 = 8, 1979 = 10, 1980 = 10, 1981 = 10, 1983 = 12. The total is close to 50. (704)

3. Choice E is correct. The jumps from 1981 to 1983, from 1983 to 1985, and from 1987 to 1989 were all about 2 billion square feet, so you can eliminate answers A and C. The jump from 1982 to 1984 was from 11 to 13.5 = 2.5 billion square feet. None of the other choices shows such broad jumps. (704)

CUMULATIVE GRAPH TEST

Questions 1–5 are based on this cumulative graph.

Spending for Research & Development
by Type of Research, 1987
$164 billion = 100%

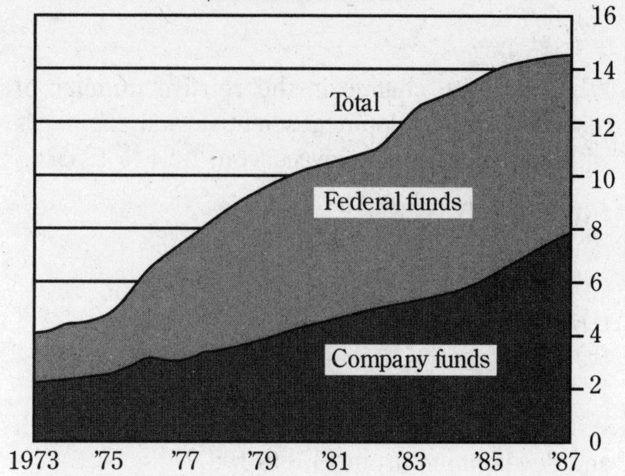

Scientists and engineers engaged full time in R&D and full-time equivalent of those working part time in R&D

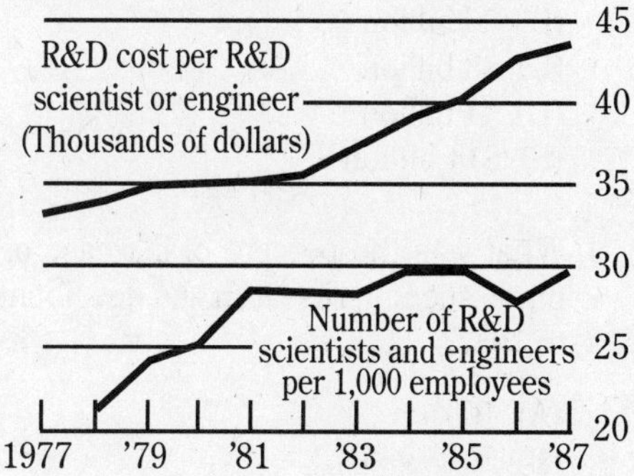

1. About how much in government funds was spent for research and development in 1987?

(A) $4 billion
(B) $6 billion
(C) $12 billion
(D) $16 billion
(E) $24 billion

2. In 1987, about what percent of the total spending in research and development were company funds?

(A) 25%
(B) 35%
(C) 45%
(D) 55%
(E) 65%

3. What was the change in the relative number of research and development scientists and engineers with respect to all employees from 1984 to 1985?

(A) 10%
(B) 5%
(C) 2%
(D) 3%
(E) 0%

4. What was the increase in company funds in research and development from 1973 to 1987?

(A) $12 billion
(B) $6 billion
(C) $8 billion
(D) $4 billion
(E) $14 billion

5. What was the percent of increase of the company funds spent in research and development from 1973 to 1987?

(A) 100%
(B) 50%
(C) 300%
(D) 400%
(E) 1,000%

Solutions

1. Choice B is correct. Total spending was about $14 billion, and company spending was about $8 billion. So, government spending was about $6 billion. (706)

2. Choice D is correct. Company funds totaled about $8 billion, and the total funds were about $14 billion. So, company funds were $\frac{4}{7}$ of total funds, or 57%. (706)

3. Choice E is correct. The graph showing the relative employment of research and development scientists and engineers was horizontal between 1984 and 1985. This means no change. (706)

4. Choice B is correct. Company funds totaled $8 billion in 1987 and $2 billion in 1973. The increase was $6 billion. (706)

5. Choice C is correct. Company funds totaled $2 billion in 1973, and the increase from 1973 to 1987 was $6 billion, or 300% of $2 billion. (706)

MATH REFRESHER
SESSION 8

Modern Math: Sets, Relations, Solution Sets, Axioms, Closed Sets, and Mathematical Symbols

Sets

801. A set is a collection of anything: numbers, letters, objects, etc. The members, or elements, of the set are written between braces like this: {1, 2, 3, 4, 5}. The elements of this set are simply the numbers 1, 2, 3, 4, and 5. Another example of a set is {apples, peaches, pears}. Two sets are equal if they have the same elements. The order in which the elements of the set are listed does not matter. Thus {1, 2, 3, 4, 5} = {5, 4, 3, 2, 1}. We can use one letter to stand for a whole set; for example, $A = \{1, 2, 3, 4, 5\}$.

802. To find the union of two sets:

Write down every member in one or both of the two sets. The union of two sets is a new set. The union of sets A and B is written $A \cup B$.

For example: If $A = \{1, 2, 3, 4\}$ and $B = \{2, 4, 6\}$, find $A \cup B$. All the elements in either A or B or both are 1, 2, 3, 4, and 6. Therefore $A \cup B = \{1, 2, 3, 4, 6\}$.

803. To find the intersection of two sets:

Write down every member that the two sets have in common. The intersection of the sets A and B is a set written $A \cap B$.

Example: If $A = \{1, 2, 3, 4\}$ and $B = \{2, 4, 6\}$, find $A \cap B$. The elements in both A and B are 2 and 4. Therefore $A \cap B = \{2, 4\}$.

> If two sets have no elements in common, then their intersection is the null or empty set, written as $\varnothing$ or { }.

Example: The intersection of {1, 3, 5, 7} with {2, 4, 6, 8} is $\varnothing$ since they have no members in common.

804. To perform several union and intersection operations, first operate on sets within parentheses.

Example: If $A = \{1, 2, 3\}$ and $B = \{2, 3, 4, 5, 6\}$ and $C = \{1, 4, 6\}$ find $A \cup (B \cap C)$.
First we find $B \cap C$ by listing all the elements in both B and C. $B \cap C = \{4, 6\}$.
Then $A \cup (B \cap C)$ is just the set of all members in at least one of the sets A and {4, 6}.
Therefore, $A \cup (B \cap C) = \{1, 2, 3, 4, 6\}$.

805. A subset of a set is a set, all of whose members are in the original set. Thus, {1, 2, 3} is a subset of the set {1, 2, 3, 4, 5}. Note that the null set is a subset of every set, and also that every set is a subset of itself. In general, a set with n elements has 2^n subsets. For example: How many subsets does $\{x, y, z\}$ have? This set has 3 elements and therefore 2^3, or 8 subsets.

Relations

806. When the elements of a set are ordered pairs, then the set is called a relation. An ordered pair is written (x, y). The order of the two components of the ordered pair matters. Therefore the ordered pairs (x, y) and (y, x) are not equal.

> The domain of a relation is the set of the first components of the ordered pairs. The range of a relation is the set of the second components of the ordered pairs. A relation is a function if each element of the domain occurs only once as a first component.

Example: $R = \{(a, b), (a, c), (b, c), (c, d)\}$. Find the domain and range of R. Is the relation R a function?

The domain is the set of first components. These are a, a, b, and c, so that the domain is $\{a, b, c\}$. The range is the set of second components. These are b, c, c, and d. Thus the range is $\{b, c, d\}$. R is not a function since the letter a occurred twice as a first component.

807. The inverse of a relation is the relation with all the ordered pairs reversed. Thus, the inverse of $R = \{(1, 2), (3, 4), (5, 6)\}$ is $\{(2, 1), (4, 3), (6, 5)\}$.

Example: Find the domain of the inverse of $\{(m, n), (p, q), (r, s)\}$.

The domain of the inverse is simply the range of the original relation. So, the domain of the inverse is $\{n, q, s\}$. Similarly, the range of the inverse is the domain of the original relation.

Solution Sets

808. Sets can be used to indicate solutions to equations or inequalities. These sets are called solution sets. A solution set is just the set of the solutions to an equation. We may also demand that the elements of the solution set meet another condition. Thus, the solution set for the equation $10x - 5 = 0$ is simply $\left\{\frac{1}{2}\right\}$, since only $x = \frac{1}{2}$ solves the equation. If we demanded that the solution set consist only of whole numbers, then the solution set would be $\varnothing$ since no whole number solves this equation.

The solution set in the positive integers (whole numbers) for the inequality $x < 4$ is $\{1, 2, 3\}$ since these are the only positive integers less than 4.

> When finding a solution set, first solve the equation or inequality and then use only the solutions that satisfy the condition required.

Example: Find the solution set in the positive integers for the inequality $4x < x + 13$.

First, $4x < x + 13$ means $3x < 13$, or $x < 4\frac{1}{3}$. Since x must be a positive integer, the solution set is the set of positive integers less than $4\frac{1}{3}$, or $\{1, 2, 3, 4\}$. Sometimes we use the following notation:

$$R = \{x : x \geq 10\}$$

This would be read as "the set of all x such that x is greater than or equal to 10."

Axioms

809. On your test, there may be a list of axioms, or rules, about arithmetical operations with numbers. The list will contain examples of the use of the axioms. Problems will then ask you to identify which axiom is used to make a specific statement. An example of these axioms is the distributive law. A problem may ask you: Which axiom is used to justify $3(4 + 1) = 3 \cdot 4 + 3 \cdot 1$? The distributive axiom is used to justify this statement.

Another axiom is the commutative axiom of addition and multiplication. The equations $5 + 3 = 3 + 5$ and $5 \cdot 3 = 3 \cdot 5$ illustrate these rules.

The last two rules are the associative axioms of addition and multiplication. Examples of these operations are the equations $(3 + 5) + 6 = 3 + (5 + 6)$ and $(3 \cdot 5)6 = 3(5 \cdot 6)$.

Closed Sets

810. A set is called "closed" under an operation if, under the operation, any two members of the set constitute an element of the set. Consider, for example, the set {0, 1}. This set is closed under the operation of multiplication because $0 \times 0 = 0$, $1 \times 1 = 1$, and $0 \times 1 = 0$. Note that in order for the set to be closed, the elements multiplied by themselves must also be an element of the set {$0 \times 0 = 0$ and $1 \times 1 = 1$}.

Mathematical Symbols

$\cdot$ multiplication dot; as in $x \cdot y$

( ) parentheses; used to group expressions

% percent

$\div$ division

: ratio

$=$ equals

$\neq$ does not equal

$<$ less than

$>$ greater than

$\leq$ less than or equal to

$\geq$ greater than or equal to

$\sqrt{\ }$ square root

π pi, the ratio between the circumference and diameter of a circle; approximately equal to $\frac{22}{7}$

$\angle$ angle

$\|$ is parallel to

$\perp$ is perpendicular to

$\wedge$ and

$\vee$ or

$\sim$ is similar to, or approximately

$\rightarrow$ implies

$\in$ belongs to

$\subset$ is a subset of

Practice Test 8 and Solutions

Modern Math: Sets, Relations, Solution Sets, Axioms, Closed Sets, and Mathematical Symbols

Correct answers and solutions follow each test.

Sets Test

1. Which set equals {1, 2, 3, 4}?

(A) {a, b, c, d}
(B) {4, 5, 6, 7}
(C) {1, 3, 5, 7, 9}
(D) {4, 3, 2, 1}
(E) None of the above.

2. A = {1, 2, 3, 4, 5}. B = {2, 4, 6, 8}. $A \cap B$ equals

(A) {1, 2, 3, 4, 5, 6, 7, 8}
(B) {2, 4}
(C) {1, 2, 3, 4, 5, 6, 8, 10}
(D) {9}
(E) {1, 2, 6, 8}

3. C = {a, b, c, d}. D = {3, 4, b}. $C \cup D$ equals

(A) {a, b, c, d, 3, 4}
(B) {b}
(C) {3, 4}
(D) {b, d, 4}
(E) {a, c, 3, 4}

4. A = {1, 2, 3}. B = {2, 3, 4}. C = {3, 4, 5}. $(A \cap B) \cap C$ equals

(A) {1, 2, 3, 4, 5}
(B) {1, 3, 5}
(C) {2, 3, 4}
(D) {1}
(E) {3}

5. How many elements are there in the set of even integers between 2 through 10 inclusive?

(A) 3
(B) 5
(C) 7
(D) 9
(E) 10

ASK A PRO

6. How many subsets does {a, b, c} have?

(A) 6
(B) 7
(C) 8
(D) 9
(E) 10

Use the following information to answer Questions 7–10.

A = {1, 3, 2, 5}. B = {2, 4, 6}. C = {1, 3, 5}.

7. $(A \cup B) \cap C$ equals

(A) {1, 2, 3}
(B) {2, 4, 5}
(C) {1, 2, 5}
(D) {1, 3, 5}
(E) {3, 4, 5}

8. $(A \cap B) \cup C$ equals

(A) {1, 2, 3, 5}
(B) {4}
(C) {2, 4}
(D) {1, 3, 5}
(E) {1, 2, 3, 4, 5}

9. How many subsets does $A \cup (B \cup C)$ have?

(A) 2
(B) 4
(C) 16
(D) 32
(E) 64

10. Which set is not a subset of $A \cup C$?

(A) ∅
(B) A
(C) C
(D) {4}
(E) {1, 2, 5}

Answers and Solutions

1. **(D)** {4, 3, 2, 1} contains the same elements as {1, 2, 3, 4}. Since the order does not matter, the sets are equal. (801)

2. **(B)** $A \cap B$ means the set of elements in both A and B, or {2, 4}. (803)

3. **(A)** $C \cup D$ means the set of elements in at least one of C and D, or {a, b, c, d, 3, 4}. (802)

4. **(E)** $(A \cap B) \cap C$ is the set of elements in all three sets. Only 3 is a member of all three sets, so $(A \cap B) \cap C = \{3\}$. (803)

5. **(B)** The set of even integers from 2 through 10 inclusive is {2, 4, 6, 8, 10}, which has 5 elements. (801)

6. **(C)** {a, b, c} has 3 elements and therefore 2^3, or 8 subsets. (805)

7. **(D)** First $(A \cup B) = \{1, 2, 3, 4, 5, 6\}$.
Then $\{1, 2, 3, 4, 5, 6\} \cap \{1, 3, 5\} = \{1, 3, 5\}$. (804)

8. **(A)** First $(A \cap B) = \{2\}$.
Then $\{2\} \cup \{1, 3, 5\} = \{1, 2, 3, 5\}$. (804)

9. **(E)** $A \cup (B \cup C)$ is the set of elements in at least one of the three sets, or {1, 2, 3, 4, 5, 6}, which has 2^6, or 64 subsets. (805)

10. **(D)** $A \cup C = \{1, 2, 3, 5\}$. Since 4 is not an element of this set, {4} is not a subset of $A \cup C$. (802, 805)

Relations Test

1. Which of the following sets are relations?

I. $\{(1, 2), (a, c)\}$
II. $\{(3, 8), (8, 3)\}$
III. $\{(1, a), (2, c)\}$

(A) I only
(B) II only
(C) III only
(D) I and III only
(E) I, II, and III

2. Which of the following relations equals the relation $\{(a, b), (1, 2), (x, y)\}$?

(A) $\{(a, b), (1, x), (2, y)\}$
(B) $\{(x, y), (a, b), (1, 2)\}$
(C) $\{(12, xy), (a, b)\}$
(D) $\{(b, a), (2, 1), (x, y)\}$
(E) None of the above.

3. What is the range of $\{(1, 2), (3, 4), (5, 6)\}$?

(A) $\{1, 2, 3, 4, 5, 6\}$
(B) $\{(1, 2)\}$
(C) $\{(1, 2), (3, 4), (5, 6)\}$
(D) $\{1, 3, 5\}$
(E) None of the above.

4. What is the domain of $\{(1, 2), (2, 1), (1, 5)\}$?

(A) $\{1, 2\}$
(B) $\{(1, 2)\}$
(C) $\{1, 2, 5\}$
(D) $\{8\}$
(E) $\{3\}$

5. Which relation is a function?

(A) $\{(1, 1), (2, 2), (3, 3)\}$
(B) $\{(1, 1), (1, 2), (1, 3)\}$
(C) $\{(a, b), (b, a), (b, b)\}$
(D) $\{(1, 3), (1, 5), (1, 7)\}$
(E) $\{(1, a), (2, b), (2, 1)\}$

6. What is the inverse of $\{(1, 2), (3, 6), (4, 2)\}$?

(A) $\{1, 2, 3, 4, 5, 6\}$
(B) $\{(1, 3), (1, 4), (1, 6)\}$
(C) $\{(2, 1), (6, 3), (2, 4)\}$
(D) $\{(3, 2), (6, 4), (4, 1)\}$
(E) None of the above.

7. Which relation equals its inverse?

(A) $\{(1, 2)\}$
(B) $\{(1, 2), (3, 3)\}$
(C) $\{(1, 2), (3, 3), (2, 1)\}$
(D) $\{(4, 4), (2, 3), (3, 4)\}$
(E) $\{(1, 2), (2, 3), (3, 1)\}$

8. What is the domain of the inverse of $\{(a, 1), (b, 3), (c, 5)\}$?

(A) $\{a, b, c\}$
(B) $\{1, 3, 5\}$
(C) $\{1, a, 2, b, 3, c\}$
(D) $\{a, 5\}$
(E) $\{(a, 5)\}$

9. The inverse of which of the following is a function?

(A) $\{(1, 1), (1, 2), (1, 3)\}$
(B) $\{(a, 0), (b, 0), (c, 0)\}$
(C) $\{(a, j), (r, j), (a, r)\}$
(D) $\{(1, 2), (2, 3), (3, 2)\}$
(E) $\{(u, v), (w, v), (y, x)\}$

10. What is the range of the inverse of $\{(P, Q), (R, S), (T, V)\}$?

(A) $\{1, 2, 3\}$
(B) $\{P, Q, R\}$
(C) $\{Q, S, V\}$
(D) $\{P, R, T\}$
(E) $\{P, Q, R, S, T, V\}$

Answers and Solutions

1. **(E)** A set is a relation if all its elements are ordered pairs; I, II, and III meet this condition. (806)

2. **(B)** Two relations are equal if their elements are equal. Though it doesn't matter in what order the ordered pairs are listed, if the elements of the ordered pairs are switched, the relation is changed. (806)

3. **(E)** The range of a relation is the set of second elements of the ordered pairs. The range of {(1, 2), (3, 4), (5, 6)} is {2, 4, 6}. (806)

4. **(A)** The domain is the set of first elements of the ordered pairs. The domain of {(1, 2), (2, 1), (1, 5)} is {1, 2}. (806)

5. **(A)** To be a function, a relation must not repeat any of the first elements of its ordered pairs. The first elements of {(1, 1), (2, 2), (3, 3)} are all distinct. (806)

6. **(C)** To find the inverse, simply reverse all the ordered pairs. (807)

7. **(C)** Reversing (1, 2) we get (2, 1); reversing (3, 3) we get (3, 3); reversing (2, 1) we get (1, 2). Though they are in a different order, the ordered pairs of the inverse of (C) are the same as the ordered pairs of (C). (807)

8. **(B)** The domain of the inverse is the range of the relation, or {1, 3, 5}. (806, 807)

9. **(A)** If the inverse of the relation is to be a function, the second elements must be all distinct. The second elements of the ordered pairs of (A) are 1, 2, and 3, all distinct. (806, 807)

10. **(D)** The range of the inverse is the domain of the function, or {*P*, *R*, *T*}. (806, 807)

Solution Sets Test

Find the solution sets in Questions 1–3.

1. $2x - 4 = 0$

(A) {2}
(B) {4}
(C) {−4}
(D) {0}
(E) {2, −4}

2. $x + 9 = 3 - x$

(A) {−3}
(B) {9}
(C) {3}
(D) {−3, 9}
(E) ∅

3. $(x + 2)(x - 1) = 0$

(A) {−1}
(B) {−2, −1}
(C) {1}
(D) {−2, 1}
(E) {2, 1}

Find the solution sets in the positive integers for Questions 4–7.

4. $x + 7 = 9$

(A) {7}
(B) {9}
(C) {16}
(D) {2}
(E) {9, 7}

5. $x - 3 = -4$

(A) {−3}
(B) {−4}
(C) {1}
(D) {−1}
(E) ∅

6. $x > 2x - 4$

(A) {1}
(B) {2, 3}
(C) {1, 2, 3}
(D) {1, 2, 3, 4}
(E) ∅

7. $(x + 1)(x - 4) = 0$

(A) {4}
(B) {1, 4}
(C) {−1, 1, 4}
(D) {0}
(E) {−4}

Find the solution set in the negative integers for Questions 8–10.

8. $(x + 3)(x + 6) = 0$

(A) {3, 6}
(B) {−3, −6}
(C) {−3}
(D) {−6}
(E) ∅

9. $(2x + 7)(x - 3) = 0$

(A) {2, 7, −3}
(B) {−3}
(C) $\left\{-3\frac{1}{2}\right\}$
(D) {2}
(E) ∅

10. $10 + 2x > 0$

(A) {−1, −2}
(B) {−10, −8, −6}
(C) {−1, −2, −3, −4, −5}
(D) {−1, −2, −3, −4}
(E) {1, 2, 3, 4}

Answers and Solutions

1. **(A)** $2x - 4 = 0$. $x = 2$, so the solution set is $\{2\}$. (808)

2. **(A)** $x + 9 = 3 - x$. $2x = -6$, or $x = -3$. The solution set is $\{-3\}$. (808)

3. **(D)** $(x + 2)(x - 1) = 0$, so $x = -2$ or 1. The solution set is $\{-2, 1\}$. (808)

4. **(D)** $x + 7 = 9$ or $x = 2$, which is a positive integer. The solution set is $\{2\}$. (808)

5. **(E)** $x - 3 = -4$, or $x = -1$, which is not a positive integer. The solution set is $\varnothing$. (808)

6. **(C)** $x > 2x - 4$, or $x < 4$. The positive integers less than 4 are 1, 2, and 3. (808)

7. **(A)** $(x + 1)(x - 4) = 0$. $x = -1$ or 4. 4 is a positive integer but -1 is not, so the solution set is $\{4\}$. (808)

8. **(B)** $(x + 3)(x + 6) = 0$. $x = -3$ or -6, both of which are negative integers, so the solution set is $\{-3, -6\}$. (808)

9. **(E)** $(2x + 7)(x - 3) = 0$. $x = -3\frac{1}{2}$ or 3, neither of which is a negative integer. The solution set is $\varnothing$. (808)

10. **(D)** $10 + 2x > 0$. $2x > -10$ or $x > -5$. The negative integers greater than -5 are $-1, -2, -3$, and -4. (808)

Axioms Test

Use the following axioms to answer Questions 1–5.

I. Commutative axiom for addition: $a + b = b + a$
II. Associative axiom for addition: $a + (b + c) = (a + b) + c$
III. Commutative axiom for multiplication: $ab = ba$
IV. Associative axiom for multiplication: $(ab)c = a(bc)$
V. Distributive axiom: $a(b + c) = ab + ac$

In Questions 1–4, which axiom can be used to justify the given statements?

1. $3 \cdot 5 = 5 \cdot 3$

(A) I
(B) II
(C) III
(D) IV
(E) V

2. $(3 + 7) + 4 = 3 + (7 + 4)$

(A) I
(B) II
(C) III
(D) IV
(E) V

3. $(2 \cdot 5) \cdot 3 = (5 \cdot 2) \cdot 3$

(A) I
(B) II
(C) III
(D) IV
(E) V

4. $3(6 + 2) = 18 + 6$

(A) I
(B) II
(C) III
(D) IV
(E) V

5. Which two axioms can be used to justify the following:
$5(3 + 4) = 20 + 15$?

(A) I and II
(B) I and III
(C) III and V
(D) IV and V
(E) V and I

Answers and Solutions

1. **(C)** To go from 3 · 5 to 5 · 3, we switch the order of multiplication. The axiom that deals with order of multiplication is the commutative axiom for multiplication, III. (809)

2. **(B)** Switching parentheses in addition involves the associative axiom for addition, II. (809)

3. **(C)** To go from (2 · 5) · 3 to (5 · 2) · 3, we switch the order of multiplying inside the parentheses. This is justified by the commutative axiom for multiplication, III. (809)

4. **(E)** To go from 3(6 + 2) to 3 · 6 + 3 · 2, or 18 + 16, we use the distributive axiom, V. (809)

5. **(E)** To go from 5(3 + 4) to 5 · 3 + 5 · 4, or 15 + 20 we use the distributive axiom, V. To go from 15 + 20 to 20 + 15, we use the commutative axiom of addition, I.

(809)

PART 7

VOCABULARY BUILDING THAT IS GUARANTEED TO RAISE YOUR SAT SCORE

Knowing Word Meanings Is Essential for a Higher SAT Score

Improving your vocabulary is essential if you want to get a high score on the Critical Reading Section of the SAT.

The Critical Reading Section part of the SAT consists of two different question types: Sentence Completions and Reading Comprehension. Almost all SAT exam takers come across many "tough" words in this part, whose meanings they do not know. These students thereby lose many points because if they do not know the meanings of the words in the questions, they aren't able to answer the questions confidently—and so, they are likely to answer incorrectly.

Every correct answer on the SAT gives you approximately 10 points. The 19 Sentence Completion questions contain quite a number of "tough" words whose meanings you will have to know in order to answer these questions correctly.

Several "tough" words show up in the Reading Comprehension passages of every SAT exam. Knowing the meanings of these difficult words will, of course, help you to understand the passages better. It follows that knowing what the passages are all about will help you correctly answer the Reading Comprehension questions that appear in the SAT—*and each correct answer nets you approximately 10 points.*

8 Steps to Word Power

1. Study vocabulary lists. This book has just the list you need for SAT preparation. The SAT 3,400-Word List begins on page 359.

2. Take vocabulary tests. "100 Tests to Strengthen Your Vocabulary" begins on page 408.

3. Learn those Latin and Greek roots, prefixes, and suffixes that make up many English words. It has been estimated that more than half of all English words come from Latin and Greek. "The Gruber Prefix-Root-Suffix List" begins on page 348. Also learn the "Hot Prefixes and Roots" in Appendix A beginning on page 1049.

4. Have a dictionary at home or look up meanings of words online. When you are on the move, you can use a dictionary app on your phone.

5. Read—read—read. By reading a great deal, you will encounter new and valuable words. You will learn the meanings of many of these words by context—that is, you will perceive a clear connection between a new word and the words that surround that word. In this way, you will learn the meaning of that new word.

6. Listen to what is worth listening to. Listen to good radio and TV programs. Listen to people who speak well. Go to selected movies and plays. Just as you will increase your vocabulary by reading widely, you will increase your vocabulary by listening to English that is spoken well.

7. Play word games like crossword puzzles, anagrams, and Scrabble.

8. Make sure you learn the Vocabulary Strategies beginning on page 150.

No One Can Dispute This Fact!

You will pile up SAT points by taking advantage of the valuable Vocabulary Building study and practice materials that are offered to you in the following pages of this chapter.

You Don't Have to Learn the Meaning of Every Word in the SAT 3,400-Word List

Go as far into the alphabetized groups as time permits. Use the Vocabulary Learning Steps listed on page 359. If you cannot learn the meanings of all the words in the 3,400-Word List, don't fret. Whatever words you have added to your vocabulary *before* you take the actual test will raise your SAT Verbal score substantially.

IMPORTANT NOTE: If you cannot spend time memorizing some of the words in the Gruber 3,400-Word List, I strongly suggest that you read through the Vocabulary Strategies in the Strategy Section beginning on page 150. Also make sure you study the roots and prefixes on pages 349 through 352, especially the checked ones. You may also want to study the Hot Prefixes and Roots in Appendix A beginning on page 1049.

The Gruber Prefix-Root-Suffix List That Gives You the Meanings of More Than 150,000 Words

Word Building with Roots, Prefixes, and Suffixes

According to some linguistic studies, approximately 60 percent of our English words are derived from Latin and Greek. One reliable study has shown that a selected list of 20 prefixes and 14 root elements pertain to more than 100,000 words in an unabridged dictionary. Here we have done even better—we've given you a list of prefixes and roots that will give you meanings of more than 150,000 words! The following entries of Latin and Greek roots, prefixes, and suffixes frequently show up in some of the words in the SAT Verbal areas, Sentence Completions and Reading Comprehension. Learn these Latin and Greek word parts to increase your vocabulary immensely—and thus score well in the Verbal part of your SAT.

> The shortest and best way of learning a language is to know the roots of it; that is, those original primitive words from which other words are formed.
>
> —Lord Chesterfield

Lord Chesterfield is, in effect, saying that roots are used as important "building blocks" of many of our English words. As you study the following list of Latin and Greek roots, prefixes, and suffixes, have a dictionary by your side. Look up the meanings of the word examples that are given if you do not know their meanings.

Roots

A ROOT IS THE BASIC ELEMENT—FUNDAMENTAL OR ESSENTIAL PART—OF A WORD.

The checked roots are especially important.

ROOT	MEANING AND EXAMPLE*
✓ **ag, act**	do, act; as *agent, counteract*
agr	field; as *agriculture, agoraphobia*
alt	high; as *altitude, altar*
alter	other; as *altercation, alternative*
✓ **am**	friend, love; as *amity, amorous*
anim	mind, life spirit; as *animate, animal, animosity*
ann, annu, enni	year; as *annuity, annual, anniversary, perennial*
anthrop	man; as *philanthropy, anthropoid*
aper	open; as *aperture, aperient*
apt	fit; as *adapt, aptitude*
aqu	water; as *aqueous, aquacade*
arch	rule, govern; as *anarchy, matriarch*
aster, astr	star; as *asteroid, disaster, astronomy*
aud	hear; as *audible, audition*
aur	gold; as *auriferous*
✓ **bas**	low; as *debase, basement*
bell	war; as *bellicose, antebellum*
ben	good, well; as *benevolent, benefactor*
bibl	book; as *biblical, bibliography*
bio	life; as *biology, biopsy*
brev	short; as *brevity, abbreviation*
cad, cas, cid	fall; as *cadence, casualty, incident*
cand	white, shining; as *candid, candidate*
✓ **cap, capt, cept**	take, hold; as *capable, captive, intercept*
capit	head; as *capital, decapitate*
carn	flesh; as *carnal, carnivorous*
✓ **ced, cess**	yield, go; as *cede, procession*
celer	swift; as *celerity, accelerate*
cent	hundred; as *century, centipede*
chrom	color; as *chromium, chromatic*
chron	time; as *chronology, chronic*

* Refer to a dictionary for word meanings you don't know.

ROOT	MEANING AND EXAMPLE
cid, cis	cut, kill; as *suicide, precision*
clin	lean, bend; as *inclination, recline*
clud, clus	close, shut; as *conclude, recluse*
cogn	know; as *incognito, cognizant*
cord	heart; as *cordial, accord*
corp	body; as *corpulent, corpse*
cosm	world; as *cosmic, cosmopolitan*
✓ **cred**	believe; as *incredible, credentials*
✓ **curr, curs**	run; as *current, cursory*
dec	ten; as *decimal, decade*
dem	people; as *democracy, demographic*
derm	skin; as *epidermis, dermatologist*
di	day; as *diary, sundial*
✓ **dic, dict**	speak, say; as *indicate, contradict*
dign	worthy; as *dignity, indignant*
domin	lord, master; as *dominate, indomitable*
dorm	sleep; as *dormant, dormitory*
✓ **duc, duct**	lead; as *induce, ductile*
ego	I; as *egotism, egomaniac*
equ	equal; as *equity, equanimity*
✓ **fac, fact, fect, fic**	make, do; as *facile, factory, infection, fiction*
✓ **fer**	bear, carry; as *fertile, confer*
fid	faith, trust; as *confide, infidelity*
fin	end; as *infinite, final*
flect, flex	bend; as *reflect, flexible*
form	shape; as *conform, reformation*
✓ **fort**	strong; as *fortitude, fortify*
frag, fract	break; as *fragile, fracture*
fug	flee; as *fugitive, refugee*
fus	pour; as *confuse, fusion*
✓ **gen**	kind, race, birth; as *generate, generic, generation*
gest	carry, bring; as *congestion, gestation*
grad, gress	step, go; as *graduate, digress*

ROOT	MEANING AND EXAMPLE
graph	write; as *autograph, graphic*
grat	pleasing; as *gratitude, congratulate*
hydr	water; as *dehydrated, hydrant*
integr	entire, whole; as *integrate, integral*
✓ **ject**	throw; as *inject, projection*
junct	join; as *conjunction, juncture*
lat	carry; as *translation, dilate*
leg, lig, lect	choose, gather; as *legible, eligible, collect*
liber	free; as *liberate, libertine*
✓ **loc**	place; as *dislocate, local*
log	word, study; as *catalogue, psychology*
loqu, locut	speak, talk; as *loquacious, circumlocution*
luc, lum	light; as *translucent, illuminate*
magn	great; as *magnitude, magnificent*
✓ **man**	hand; as *manufacture, manual*
mar	sea; as *marine, maritime*
mater, matri	mother; as *maternal, matrimony*
mega	large; as *megaton, megaphone*
ment	mind; as *mentality, mentally*
merg	plunge, sink; as *submerge, merger*
meter	measure; as *chronometer, symmetry*
micro	small; as *microscope, microfilm*
migr	wander; as *migrate, immigration*
mir	look; as *admire, mirror*
✓ **mit, miss**	send; as *admit, submission*
mon	advise, remind; as *admonish, monument*
✓ **mort**	death; as *immortality, mortal*
mot, mov	move; as *motor, motility, movable*
✓ **mult**	many; as *multitude, multifarious*
✓ **mut**	change; as *mutation, transmute, immutable*
✓ **nat**	born; as *natal, innate*
nav	ship; as *naval, navigate*
neg	deny; as *negate, renege*
nomen	name; as *nominee, nomenclature, cognomen*
nov	new; as *novelty, novice, innovation*
ocul	eye; as *oculist, binocular*
oper	work; as *cooperation, operate*

ROOT	MEANING AND EXAMPLE
pater, patri	father; as *paternal, patriot*
ped, pod	foot; as *impede, biped, tripod*
ped	child; as *pediatrics, pedagogue*
pel, puls	drive; as *compel, expulsion*
pend, pens	hang; as *pendant, pension*
pet	seek; as *impetus, petition*
petr	stone, rock; as *petrify*
phil	loving; as *philosophy*
phob	fear; as *claustrophobia*
phon	sound; as *phonic, phonetics*
✓ **plic**	fold, bend; as *complicate, implicate*
✓ **pon, pos**	place, put; as *component, compose*
✓ **port**	carry, bring; as *porter, import*
pot	drink; as *potion, potable*
poten	powerful; as *potentate, impotent*
prehend, prehens	take, grasp; as *apprehend, comprehension*
prot	first; as *protagonist, prototype*
psych	mind; as *psychological, psychic*
quer, quir, quis, ques	ask, seek; as *query, inquiry, inquisition, quest*
reg, rig, rect	rule, govern; as *regent, rigid, corrective*
rid, ris	laugh; as *ridiculous, risible*
rupt	break; as *rupture, erupt, interruption*
sacr	holy; as *sacred, sacrificial*
sanct	holy; as *sanction, sanctify*
sci, scio	know; as *science, conscious, omniscient*
scop	watch; as *periscope, horoscope*
✓ **scrib, script**	write; as *describe, prescription*
sec, sect	cut; as *secant, bisect*
sed, sid, sess	sit, seat; as *sedate, reside, session*
sent, sens	feel, think; as *sentiment, sensible*
✓ **sequ, secut**	follow; as *sequel, consecutive*
serv	keep; as *reserve, conservation*
sist	place, stand; as *assist, resistance*
solv, solu	loosen; as *dissolve, absolution*
somn	sleep; as *somnambulist, insomnia*
soph	wisdom; as *sophisticated, philosophy*

ROOT	MEANING AND EXAMPLE
✓ **spec, spect, spic**	look, appear; as *specimen, prospect, conspicuous*
spir	breathe; as *conspire, respiration*
✓ **stat, stab**	stand; as *status, stability*
string, strict	bind; as *stringent, stricture*
stru, struct	build; as *construe, destructive*
sum, sumpt	take; as *assume, presumption*
tang, ting, tact, tig	touch; as *tangent, contingency, contact, contiguous*
teg, tect	cover; as *tegument, detect*
tele	distance; as *telescope, teletype*
tempor	time; as *temporary, extemporaneous*
✓ **ten, tain**	hold, reach; as *tenant, tension, retain*
term	end; as *terminal, terminate*
ter, terr	land, earth; as *inter, terrace*
therm	heat; as *thermometer, thermos*
tort, tors	twist; as *contort, torsion*
✓ **tract**	draw; as *attract, extract*
trit	rub; as *trite, attrition*
trud, trus	thrust; as *intrude, abstruse*
umbra	shade; as *umbrella, umbrage*
urb	city; as *suburb, urban*
vac	empty; as *vacate, evacuation*
vad, vas	go; as *evade, evasive*
val, vail	be strong; as *valid, prevail*
✓ **ven, vent**	come; as *convene, prevention*
✓ **ver**	true; as *veracity, aver*
verb	word; as *verbose, verbatim*
✓ **vert, vers**	turn; as *convert, reverse*
vid, vis	see; as *evident, visible*
vinc, vict	conquer; as *invincible, evict*
viv, vit	live; as *vivacity, vital*
voc, vok	call; as in *vocation, revoke*
volv, volut	roll, turn; as in *involve, revolution*

Prefixes

A PREFIX IS PART OF A WORD THAT MAY BE PLACED BEFORE THE BASIC ELEMENT (ROOT) OF A WORD.

The checked prefixes are especially important.

PREFIX	MEANING AND EXAMPLE
✓ **a, ab, abs**	from, away; as *avert, abjure, absent*
✓ **ad**	to; as *adhere*. By assimilation, *ad* takes the forms of **a, ac, af, al, an, ap, as, at;** as *aspire, accord, affect, allude, annex, appeal, assume, attract*
ambi, amphi	around, both; as *ambidextrous, amphibious*
✓ **ante, anti**	before; as *antedate, anticipate*
✓ **anti**	against; as *antidote, antislavery*
arch	first, chief; as *archangel, archenemy*
auto	self; as *autobiography, automatic*
ben	good, well; as *benediction, benefactor*
✓ **bi**	two; as *bilateral, bisect*
✓ **circum**	around; as *circumnavigate, circumvent*
✓ **com, con, col, cor, co**	together; as *commit, concord, collect, correct, coworker*
✓ **contra, contro, counter**	against; as *contradict, controvert, counteract*
✓ **de**	down, away from, about; as *descend, depart, describe*
demi	half; as *demigod, demitasse*
dia	across, through; as *diameter, diastole*
✓ **dis, di, dif**	apart, not; as *dissension, division, diffident*
✓ **equi**	equal; as *equinox, equivalent*
✓ **ex, e, ef**	out of, from; as *extract, eject, efface*
extra	out of, beyond; as *extraordinary, extraterrestrial*
✓ **hyper**	too much; as *hypercritical, hypersensitive*
hypo	too little, under; as *hypochondriac, hypodermic*

PREFIX	MEANING AND EXAMPLE
✓ **in, il, im, ir**	into, in, on; as *invade, illustrate, immerse, irritate*
✓ **in, il, im, ir**	not; as *indistinct, illegal, impossible, irresponsible*
inter, intro	between, among; as *interpose, introduce*
✓ **mal, mis**	bad; as *malevolent, mistreat*
mono	one, single; as *monotone, monorail*
neo	new; as *neoplasm, neophyte*
✓ **non**	not; as *nonentity, nonconformist*
✓ **ob, of, op**	against; as *obviate, offend, oppose*
✓ **omni**	all; as *omniscient, omnipresent*
ortho	straight; as *orthodox, orthopedic*
pan	all; as *pantheism, Pan-American*
✓ **peri**	around; as *perimeter, periscope*
✓ **poly**	many; as *polygon, polygamy*
✓ **post**	after; as *postpone, postmortem*
✓ **pre**	before; as *predict, precursory*
✓ **pro**	forward, before; as *proceed, provide*
✓ **re**	back, again; as *recur, recede*
retro	backward; as *retrogress, retrospect*
se	apart, away; as *seduce, sedition*
semi	half; as *semicircle, semiconscious*
✓ **sub**	under; as *submarine, subversive*
✓ **super**	above, beyond; as *superpose, supernatural*
syn, sym	with, at the same time; as *synonymous, sympathetic*
✓ **trans**	across; as *transcontinental, transmit*
ultra	beyond; as *ultraliberal, ultramodern*
✓ **un**	not; as *unaware, uninformed*
✓ **uni**	one; as *unanimous, uniform*
vice	instead of; as *vice-chancellor, viceroy*

Suffixes

A SUFFIX IS PART OF A WORD THAT MAY FOLLOW THE BASIC ELEMENT (ROOT) OF A WORD.

The checked suffixes are especially important.

SUFFIX	MEANING AND EXAMPLE
✓ **able, ible**	able; as *pliable, returnable, comestible*
acious, cious	having the quality of; as *capacious, meretricious*
age	act, condition; as *courage, foliage*
al	belonging to; as *legal, regal*
✓ **ance, ence**	state of; as *abundance, indulgence*
✓ **ate, ent, ant, ante**	one who; as *candidate, advocate, resident, tenant, debutante*
ary, eer, er	one who, concerning; as *secretary, engineer, mariner*
✓ **cy**	state, position of; as *adequacy, presidency*
dom	state of; as *freedom, serfdom*
✓ **ence**	state of; as *presence, credence*
er, or	one who; as *player, actor, monitor, employer*
✓ **escent**	becoming; as *adolescent, putrescent*
✓ **fy**	make; as *beautify, sanctify*
hood	state of; as *knighthood, childhood*
ic, id	of, like; as *bucolic, acrid*
✓ **il, ile**	capable of being; as *evil, servile*
✓ **ion**	act of; as *desperation, perspiration*
✓ **ious**	characterized by; as *spacious, illustrious*
✓ **ish**	like; as *boyish, foolish*
ism	belief in or practice of; as *idealism, capitalism*
ist	one who practices or is devoted to; as *anarchist, harpist*
✓ **ive**	relating to; as *abusive, plaintive*
mony	state of; as *harmony, matrimony*
✓ **ness**	quality of; as *willingness, shrewdness*
ory	a place for; as *factory, depository*
✓ **ous, ose**	full of; as *ponderous, verbose*
ship	state of, skill; as *friendship, gamesmanship*
✓ **some**	characteristic of; as *loathsome, fearsome*
tude	state of; as *lassitude, rectitude*
ward	in the direction of; as *windward, backward*
✓ **y**	full of; as *unruly, showy*

A List of SAT Words Appearing More Than Once on Actual SAT Exams

We have made a computerized analysis of frequently occurring words on 47 complete SAT exams. (1,175 questions have been examined.) Following is a list of SAT words or associated words appearing *more than once* on these 47 actual SAT exams.

The definitions of these words have not been included here because we want you to *refer to a dictionary* to learn the meanings of these words, which have been repeated in subsequent SAT question sections.

Note that after each word a numeral indicates the number of times that the word has appeared on the 47 actual SAT exams.

Also note that certain pairs of words have a left-side bracket. The bracket indicates that the words are very closely allied in meaning—so if you learn the meaning of one of the two words in the pair, you will easily arrive at the meaning of the other word of the pair.

Learn the meanings of these words, as they are often repeated in questions of the SAT.

abolish 2
abridge 2
abstemious 2
[**accent 1**
[**accented 1**
accolade 2
acquiesce 2
affirmation 2
amass 2
[**ambivalence 1**
[**ambivalent 1**
ambulatory 2
ameliorate 2
amity 2
anchor 2
antediluvian 2
ascendancy 2
atrophy 2
[**bane 1**
[**baneful 1**
bizarre 2
blunder 2
bungle 2
burgeon 2
[**capitulate 1**
[**capitulation 1**
capricious 4
clemency 2
[**coalesce 2**
[**coalescence 1**
[**cohere 1**
[**coherent 1**
[**compress 1**
[**compression 1**
[**confide 1**
[**confidential 1**
confound 2
congeal 2
[**contaminant 1**
[**contaminate 2**
converge 2
convivial 2
copious 2
corroborate 2
corrugated 2
[**corrupt 1**
[**corruption 1**
cursory 2
[**daunt 3**
[**dauntless 1**
debilitate 2
deplete 2
discrepancy 3
disentangle 2
[**disputatious 1**
[**dispute 2**
[**distend 1**
[**distention 1**
drawback 2
efface 3
[**effervesce 1**
[**effervescent 1**
enhance 2
enigmatic 2
ephemeral 3
equilibrium 3
[**euphonious 1**
[**euphony 1**
evacuate 2
evanescent 2
[**expedite 1**
[**expeditious 1**
[**expendable 1**
[**expenditures 1**
exclude 2
facilitate 2
fallow 2
fertile 2
[**flourish 3**
[**flower 1**
fraudulent 3
[**fruitful 1**
[**fruitless 1**
garner 2
guile 2
hackneyed 2
hefty 2
hideous 2
hilarity 2
humane 2
[**hypocrisy 1**
[**hypocritical 1**
innocuous 2
irascible 2
jettison 2
kindle 2
[**leniency 1**
[**lenient 1**
[**levity 1**
[**levitate 1**
listless 2
maladroit 2
mitigate 2
mobile 2
[**munificent 2**
[**munificence 1**
myriad 2
nefarious 2
[**obscure 1**
[**obscurity 1**
[**opaque 1**
[**opacity 1**
parsimony 2
paucity 2
penury 2
[**peripheral 2**
[**periphery 2**
placate 2
[**precise 1**
[**precision 1**

premature 2
premeditated 2
prevalent 2
proclivity 2
[**prodigal 1**
prodigious 2]
[**profuse 1**
profusion 2]
[**pulverize 1**
pulverized 1]
rant 2
recalcitrant 2
recant 2
replete 2
rescind 2
reserve 2
ruffle 2
rupture 2
saccharine 2
salubrious 2
somber 4
[**specify 1**
specificity 1]
spurn 2
squander 2
stymie 2
subtle 2
summary 2
summon 3
sumptuous 2
[**surreptitious 1**
surreptitiously 1]
tantamount 2
[**tenacious 1**
tenacity 1]
[**transience 1**
transient 1]
turbulence 3
venturesome 3
viable 2
[**vibrancy 1**
vibrant 1]
vilification 2
[**virulence 1**
virulent 1]
whet 2
zany 2

The Most Important/Frequently Used SAT Words and Their Opposites

Following is a list of popular SAT words and their opposites. *Note:* These words fit into specific categories, and it may be a little easier memorizing the meaning of these important words knowing what category they fit into.

POSITIVE	NEGATIVE	POSITIVE	NEGATIVE
TO PRAISE	TO BELITTLE	TO CALM OR MAKE BETTER	TO MAKE WORSE OR RUFFLE
acclaim	admonish	abate	alienate
applaud	assail	accede	antagonize
commend	berate	accommodate	contradict
eulogize	calumniate	allay	dispute
exalt	castigate	ameliorate	embitter
extol	censure	appease	estrange
flatter	chastise	assuage	incense
hail	chide	comply	infuriate
laud	decry	concede	nettle
panegyrize	denigrate	conciliate	oppose
resound	denounce	gratify	oppugn
tout	disparage	mitigate	repulse
	excoriate	mollify	snub
	execrate	pacify	
	flay	palliate	
	lambaste	placate	
	malign	propitiate	
	reprimand	quell	
	reproach	satiate	
	scold		
	upbraid		
	vilify		

POSITIVE	NEGATIVE	POSITIVE	NEGATIVE
PLEASANT	UNPLEASANT	YIELDING	NOT YIELDING
affable	callous	accommodating	adamant
agreeable	cantankerous	amenable	determinate
amiable	captious	compliant	immutable
captivating	churlish	deferential	indomitable
congenial	contentious	docile	inflexible
cordial	gruff	flexible	intractable
courteous	irascible	hospitable	intransigent
decorous	ireful	inclined	recalcitrant
engaging	obstinate	malleable	relentless
gracious	ornery	obliging	resolute
obliging	peevish	pliant	steadfast
sportive	perverse	submissive	tenacious
unblemished	petulant	subservient	
undefiled	querulous	tractable	
	testy		
	vexing		
	wayward		
GENEROUS	CHEAP	COURAGEOUS	TIMID
altruistic	frugal	audacious	diffident
beneficent	miserly	dauntless	indisposed
benevolent	niggardly	gallant	laconic
charitable	paltry	intrepid	reserved
effusive	parsimonious	stalwart	reticent
hospitable	penurious	undaunted	subdued
humanitarian	provident	valiant	timorous
magnanimous	skinflinty	valorous	
munificent	spartan		
philanthropic	tight-fisted		
	thrifty		
ABUNDANT OR RICH	SCARCE OR POOR	LIVELY	BLEAK
affluent	dearth	brisk	dejected
bounteous	deficit	dynamic	dismal
copious	destitute	ebullient	forlorn
luxuriant	exiguous	exhilarating	lackluster
multifarious	impecunious	exuberant	lugubrious
multitudinous	impoverished	inspiring	melancholy
myriad	indigent	provocative	muted
opulent	insolvent	scintillating	prostrate
pecunious	meager	stimulating	somber
plenteous	paltry	titillating	tenebrous
plentiful	paucity		
plethoric	penurious		
profuse	scanty		
prosperous	scarcity		
superabundant	sparse		
teeming			
wealthy			

POSITIVE	NEGATIVE	POSITIVE	NEGATIVE
CAREFUL	CARELESS	HUMBLE	HAUGHTY
chary	culpable	demure	affected
circumspect	felonious	diffident	aristocratic
conscientious	indifferent	indisposed	arrogant
discreet	insouciant	introverted	audacious
exacting	lackadaisical	laconic	authoritarian
fastidious	lax	plebeian	autocratic
gingerly	negligent	reluctant	condescending
heedful	perfunctory	restrained	disdainful
judicious	rash	reticent	egotistical
meticulous	remiss	subdued	flagrant
provident	reprehensible	subservient	flippant
prudent	temerarious	taciturn	imperious
punctilious		timid	impertinent
scrupulous		timorous	impudent
scrutinous		unassuming	insolent
wary		unostentatious	ostentatious
		unpretentious	pompous
			proud
			supercilious
			vainglorious

Note: In many cases you can put the prefix "im" or "un" in front of the word to change its meaning to its opposite.

EXAMPLE: Pecunious. Opposite: Impecunious
Ostentatious. Opposite: Unostentatious

Practice Questions

1. Example: Find the OPPOSITE of EXTOL:

   (A) oppose (B) restrain (C) enter
   (D) deviate (E) denigrate

2. ALLAY (opposite):

   (A) incense (B) drive (C) berate
   (D) signify (E) determine

3. DECOROUS (opposite):

   (A) scanty (B) irascible (C) musty
   (D) pliant (E) rigid

4. AMENABLE (opposite):

   (A) tiresome (B) uncultured (C) intransigent
   (D) soothing (E) careless

5. MUNIFICENT (opposite):

   (A) simple (B) pallid (C) crafty
   (D) penurious (E) stable

6. PLETHORIC (opposite):

   (A) impecunious (B) slothful (C) indifferent
   (D) reticent (E) sly

7. METICULOUS (opposite):

   (A) timid (B) plenteous (C) peevish
   (D) intractable (E) perfunctory

8. IMPERIOUS (opposite):

   (A) unostentatious (B) lackadaisical
   (C) insolvent (D) churlish (E) immutable

9. TIMOROUS (opposite):

   (A) judicious (B) intrepid (C) multifarious
   (D) benevolent (E) tenebrous

10. LUGUBRIOUS (opposite):

    (A) flexible (B) unblemished (C) ebullient
    (D) conciliatory (E) impertinent

Answers to Practice Questions

1. Choice E is correct. EXTOL fits into the category of TO PRAISE. Denigrate fits into the category TO BELITTLE—the opposite category.

2. Choice A is correct. ALLAY fits into the category of TO CALM. Incense fits into the opposite category—TO MAKE WORSE or TO RUFFLE.

3. Choice B is correct. DECOROUS fits into the category of PLEASANT. The opposite category is UNPLEASANT. Irascible fits into this category.

4. Choice C is correct. AMENABLE fits into the category of YIELDING. Intransigent fits into the opposite category—NOT YIELDING.

5. Choice D is correct. MUNIFICENT fits into the category of GENEROUS. Penurious fits into the category of CHEAP, the opposite category.

6. Choice A is correct. PLETHORIC fits into the category of ABUNDANT or RICH. Impecunious fits into the opposite category of SCARCE or POOR.

7. Choice E is correct. METICULOUS fits into the category of CAREFUL. Perfunctory fits into the category of CARELESS (or mechanical).

8. Choice A is correct. IMPERIOUS fits into the category of HAUGHTY (high-brow). Unostentatious fits into the category of HUMBLE, the opposite category.

9. Choice B is correct. TIMOROUS fits into the category of TIMID. Intrepid fits into the opposite category of COURAGEOUS.

10. Choice C is correct. LUGUBRIOUS fits into the category of BLEAK or dismal. Ebullient fits into the opposite category of LIVELY.

The Gruber SAT 3,400-Word List

Every new word that you learn in this SAT word list can help you to add extra points to your SAT verbal score.

Vocabulary Learning Steps

1. Conceal each definition with a card as you go down the column.
2. *Jot down each word whose meaning you do not know.* Then prepare a flash card for each word you did not know. Write the synonym (word with a similar meaning) on the back of the card.
3. Study the flash cards that you have made up.
4. After you have studied the DID-NOT-KNOW flash cards, give yourself a flash card test. Put aside the flash cards for the words you did know.
5. For each word you still do not know, write a sentence that includes the word you still have not learned well.
6. Now test yourself again on the DID-NOT-KNOW flash cards referred to in Step 5. Put aside your flash cards for the words you did know.
7. Study the newly reduced pile of DID-NOT-KNOW flash cards.
8. Give yourself a flash card test on this newly reduced DID-NOT-KNOW pile.
9. Keep reducing your DID-NOT-KNOW flash card pile until you have no DID-NOT-KNOW words.

IMPORTANT

Do not throw your flash cards away. Keep the cards for reinforcement testing in the future.

In past exams, 70 to 80 percent of all test vocabulary words appeared on this list!

ABACK–AZURE

aback (preceded by *taken*) surprised; startled

abandon to leave; to give up; to discontinue

abase to humiliate; to humble; to lower

abash ashamed; embarrassed

abate to lessen; to decrease

abdicate to yield; to give up

abduct to take away; to kidnap

aberration abnormality; deviation

abet to aid; to encourage

abeyance a temporary postponement

abhor to hate; to detest

abide (*two meanings*) to remain; to put up with

abject miserable; wretched

abjure to give up (rights)

ablution a washing; cleansing

abnegate to deny; to reject

abolition doing away with; putting an end to

abominate to detest; to dislike strongly

aborigine original inhabitant

abortive unsuccessful

abound to be large in number

aboveboard honest; frank; open

abrade to wear away

abridge to shorten

abrogate to abolish; to repeal

abscond to leave secretly; to flee

absolve to free from responsibility

abstemious moderate or sparing in eating or drinking

abstinence self-denial; resistance to temptation

abstract (*two meanings*) a summary (*noun*); to remove (*verb*)

abstruse hard to understand

absurd ridiculous; unreasonable

abut to touch; to rest on or against

abysmal wretched; extremely bad

abyss a bottomless pit; anything infinite

academic (*two meanings*) pertaining to school; theoretical or unrealistic

accede to agree to

accelerate to speed up; to move faster

accessible easy to approach; open

access approach; admittance

accessory something additional

acclaim to greet with approval

acclimate to adapt; to get used to

acclivity upward slope

accolade honor; award; approval

accommodate to make fit; to help

accomplice a partner in crime

accord agreement

accost to approach and speak to

accoutrement equipment; outfit

accredit to approve; to certify

accretion an increase; an addition

accrue to gather; to accumulate

acerbic (*two meanings*) sharp or bitter in smell or taste; sharpness of temper or words

Achilles' heel a weakness

acknowledge to admit; to confess

acme highest point; peak

acoustics the branch of physics dealing with sound

acquiesce to agree; to consent

acquit to free of guilt; to clear

acrid bitter to the taste or smell; sarcastic

acrimonious harsh in speech or behavior

acronym word formed from initials

acrophobia fear of heights

actuate to put into motion or action

acumen mental keenness; shrewdness

acute sharp; keen

ad infinitum endlessly; forever

ad lib to act or speak without preparation

adage a familiar saying

adamant stubborn; unyielding

adapt to adjust; to change

addendum something added as a supplement

addled confused

adduce to give an example in proving something

adept highly skilled

adherent (*two meanings*) sticking fast (*adjective*); a follower or a supporter (*noun*)

adipose fatty

adjacent near; close; adjoining

adjudicate to judge

adjunct a subordinate; an assistant

admonish to warn

ado fuss; trouble

Adonis a very handsome man

adorn to dress up; to decorate

adroit skillful; clever

adulation excessive praise or flattery

adulterate to make impure

advent an arrival; a coming

adventitious accidental; nonessential

adversary enemy; opponent

adversity a misfortune; distress

advocate to recommend; to defend

aegis a shield; protection; sponsorship

aesthetic pertaining to beauty

affable friendly; agreeable

affectation a phony attitude; insincerity

affiliate to associate or to unite with

affinity attraction to

affirmation a statement that something is true

affix to attach

affliction great suffering; hardship

affluence wealth

affront an insult

aftermath outcome; result

agape open-mouthed; surprised

agenda a list or program of things to be done

aggrandize to enlarge or to expand

aggravate to worsen an already bad situation; to intensify

aggregate to collect; to gather together

aghast shocked; terrified

agile able to move quickly

agitate to upset; to stir up

agnostic one who doubts the existence of God

agoraphobia fear of open places

agrarian pertaining to farmers and agriculture

ague a fever; plague

alacrity liveliness; willingness

albatross (*two meanings*) a seabird; a constant burden

albeit although

alchemy chemistry of the Middle Ages

alias an assumed name

alien strange; foreign

alienate to make others unfriendly to you

alimentary furnishing food or nourishment

allay to relieve or to calm

alleged so-called; supposed

allegory a symbolic work of literature

allegro rapid; quick

alleviate to lessen; to relieve

allocate to set aside for a specific purpose

allude to hint at; to refer to indirectly

alluring tempting; fascinating; charming

alluvial pertaining to a deposit of sand formed by flowing water

aloft up in the air; high

aloof reserved; cool; indifferent

alter to change

altercation an argument; a disagreement

altruism unselfishness; concern for others

amalgamate to combine; to unite; to blend

amass to accumulate; to collect

amazon a big, strong, masculine woman

ambidextrous equally skillful with either hand

ambient surrounding; on all sides

ambiguous unclear; open to more than one interpretation

ambivalence conflicting feelings toward something or someone

ambrosial pleasing to the taste or smell

ambulatory moving about; capable of walking

ambuscade hidden or secret attack

ameliorate to improve; to make better

amenable agreeable; responsive

amend to change; to alter

amenities courtesies; social graces; pleasantries

amiable friendly; pleasant

amicable friendly; agreeable

amiss wrong; faulty; improper

amity friendship

amnesty official pardon for an offense

amoral lacking a sense of right and wrong

amorous loving

amorphous shapeless

amphibious able to live on both land and water

ample roomy; abundant

amplify to make larger or greater

amulet a charm worn to keep evil away

anachronism something out of place or time

analgesic drug that relieves pain

analogy similarity or comparison

anarchy absence of government

anathema a curse; a person or thing to be avoided

ancillary helping; subordinate

anecdote a short, entertaining story

anent regarding; concerning

anguish great suffering or grief

anhydrous without water

animadversion criticism; comment that opposes

animate to give life to

animosity hatred; hostility

animus hostile feeling

annals historical records

anneal to heat and then cool; to toughen

annihilate to totally destroy

annuity specified income payable at stated intervals

annul to cancel; to do away with

anomalous abnormal; inconsistent

anon soon

anoxia lack of oxygen

antecedent that which goes before something else

antediluvian very old-fashioned; primitive

anterior located in front or forward

anteroom a lobby or waiting room

anthem song of praise

anthology collection of literary works

anthropoid resembling man

anthropomorphic attributing human form to objects, gods, etc.

antic playful or silly act; prank

anticlimax something unimportant coming after something important

antidote a remedy; a counteractive

antipathy intense dislike

antipodes opposite sides (of the earth)

antiquated ancient; extremely old

antithesis an exact opposite

apathy indifference; lack of feeling

ape (*two meanings*) a monkey (*noun*); to imitate or to mimic (*verb*)

aperture an opening; a gap

apex the highest point; summit

aphasia loss of the ability to speak

aphorism brief saying; proverb

apiary place where bees are kept

aplomb self-confidence; poise

apocryphal doubtful; not authentic

apogee farthest point away from the earth

apoplexy sudden loss of consciousness; paralysis

apostate one who gives up his beliefs

apothecary druggist

apothegm brief instructive saying

apotheosis glorification of a person to the rank of God

appall to frighten; to cause loss of courage

apparel clothing; attire

apparition a ghost

appease to soothe; to satisfy

appellation a name

append to attach; to add

apposite appropriate

apprehend (*two meanings*) to seize; to understand

apprehensive fearful; anxious

apprise to inform

approbation approval

appropriate to take possession of (*verb*); suitable (*adjective*)

appurtenance something added to another more important thing

apropos relevant; appropriate; fitting

aptitude ability

aquatic pertaining to water

aquiline like an eagle; curved or hooked

arable good for farming

arbiter a judge; an umpire

arbitrary partial; biased

arbor a shaded area

arcane mysterious

archaic outdated; old-fashioned

archaeology study of remains of past cultures

archetype original; first of its kind

archipelago group of islands

archives public records and documents

ardent intensely enthusiastic

arduous difficult; strenuous

aria a solo in an opera

arid dry

armistice a truce; suspension of hostilities

aromatic pleasant-smelling

arraign to accuse

arrant notorious; downright

array an orderly arrangement

arrears (preceded by *in*) in debt

arrogant proud; haughty

arroyo a deep ditch caused by running water

arson illegal burning of property

artful cunning; tricky; crafty

articulate to speak clearly

artifact a handmade object

artifice trick; deception

artisan one skilled in arts and crafts

ascendant rising

ascertain to find out; to determine

ascetic one who denies his body pleasure and comfort

ascribe to attribute; to credit as to a cause or source

aseptic without bacteria

asinine stupid; silly

askance (preceded by *to look*) sidewise; suspiciously

askew crooked; out of position

asperity harshness; roughness

aspersion a damaging remark

aspire to desire; to have an ambition

assail to attack; to assault

assay to test; to try

assent to agree; to accept

assertive confident; positive

assess to estimate the value of

assiduity diligence; care

assimilate to absorb

assuage to calm; to make less severe

asteroid a very small planet

astral pertaining to the stars

astray in the wrong direction

astringent substance that contracts blood vessels or shrinks tissues

astute shrewd; very smart

asunder into separate parts

asylum a safe place; a refuge

atavistic going back to behavior found in a remote ancestor

atheist one who denies God's existence

atlas book of maps

atone to make up for; to repent

atrocious cruel; brutal

atrophy to waste away; to become useless

attenuated decreased; weakened

attest to confirm; to declare to be correct

attribute (*two meanings*) to credit or assign to (*verb*); a characteristic or trait (*noun*)

attrition a wearing down or away; a decline

atypical abnormal; not usual

au courant up-to-date; fully informed

audacity boldness; daring

audible capable of being heard

audit to examine accounts

augment to increase; to make greater

augur to predict

august majestic; worthy of respect; impressive

aura a radiance; a glow

aural pertaining to the sense of hearing

auroral rosy; pertaining to the dawn

auspices approval; support

auspicious favorable

austere severe; stern; self-disciplined

authenticate to confirm; to make acceptable

authoritative dictatorial; having power

autocratic despotic; unlimited in authority

automaton self-operating machine; robot

autonomy self-rule

autumnal mature; declining

auxiliary giving assistance; subordinate

avarice greed

avenge to get even; to take revenge

aver to declare; to state firmly

averse reluctant; not willing

aversion intense dislike

avert to prevent; to turn away

aviary place where birds are kept

avid enthusiastic

avocation a hobby; not one's regular work

avoirdupois heaviness; weight

avow to declare openly

avuncular like an uncle

awe (*in awe of*) great admiration for or fear of

awry twisted to one side; in the wrong direction

axiom true statement; established principle

azure blue

BACCHANALIAN–BUTTRESS

bacchanalian wild with drunkenness

badger to nag; to annoy

badinage playful, teasing talk

baffle to confuse; to bewilder

bagatelle thing of little value; trifle

bait (*two meanings*) to entrap or to seduce (*verb*); a decoy (*noun*)

baleful harmful; menacing; pernicious

balk to stop short

balm something that calms or soothes

balmy (*two meanings*) mild and refreshing; mentally unstable (*slang*)

banal common; ordinary; trite

bandy to exchange (*as words*)

bane cause of ruin, harm, or distress

banter teasing; good-natured joking

barb a pointed part, as of an arrow or fishhook

barbarous uncultured; crude

bard a poet

bark a boat or sailing vessel

baroque overdecorated; showy

barrage heavy attack

barrister lawyer (*British*)

bask to lie in or be exposed to warmth

bastion a strong defense; a fort

bauble showy but useless thing; trinket

bawdy indecent; humorously obscene

bayou marshy body of water

beacon a light used for warning or guiding

beatitude state of bliss

bedlam (*two meanings*) a madhouse; a noisy uproar

befuddle to confuse; to perplex

beget to produce

begrudge to resent another's success or enjoyment

beguile to deceive; to charm

behemoth huge animal

beholden obligated; indebted

belated delayed or detained

beleaguer to encircle (with an army); to annoy

belittle to put down; to humiliate

belligerent warlike; quarrelsome

bellow to yell loudly

benediction blessing

benefactor one who helps or supports another

beneficiary one who receives benefits or profits

benevolent generous; kindly

benign harmless; gentle

benignant kindly; gentle

bequeath to hand down; to pass on to

berate to scold severely

bereave to leave in a sad or lonely state; to deprive by force

berserk frenzied; violently destructive

beseech to beg; appeal to

beset to attack

besiege to overwhelm; to close in on

besmirch to make dirty

bestial savage; brutal

bestow to give or present

bestride to mount (a horse)

betrothed engaged; pledged to marry

bevy a large group

bewitch to cast a spell on; to charm; to fascinate

bias preference; prejudice

bibliophile lover of books

bibulous absorbent; fond of alcoholic beverages

bicker to quarrel

bide (*one's time*) to wait for a favorable opportunity

biennial occurring every two years

bigot a narrow-minded, prejudiced person

bilious bad-tempered; cross

bilk to cheat; to swindle

binge a spree; wild party

biped two-legged animal

bivouac temporary shelter

bizarre weird; strange

blanch to whiten; to make pale

bland mild; tasteless; dull

blandishment flattery

blasé bored with life; unexcited; indifferent

blasphemy disrespect for holy places, people, or things; irreverence

blatant annoyingly conspicuous; offensively noisy and loud

blazon to display; to proclaim

bleak unsheltered; gloomy

bleary blurred; dimmed

blight destruction; withering; disease

bliss extreme happiness

blithe carefree; lighthearted

bludgeon (*two meanings*) a short, heavy club (*noun*); to bully or coerce (*verb*)

blunt (*two meanings*) abrupt in speech or manner; having a dull edge

blurt (*out*) to utter suddenly or indiscreetly

bluster to speak noisily; to boast

bode to indicate in advance, as an omen does

bog (*two meanings*) a swamp (*noun*); to sink or become stuck in (*verb*)

bogus false; fake

bolster to prop up; to support

bolt to dash out suddenly; to discontinue support of

bombastic using impressive but meaningless language

bon mot witty remark

bona fide genuine; in good faith

bondage slavery

boon a benefit; a blessing; a favor

boor a rude or impolite person

booty stolen money or goods

boreal northern

borne carried; put up with

botch to mess up; to perform clumsily

bountiful plentiful; abundant

bounty reward; generosity

bourgeoisie middle class

bovine pertaining to cows or cattle

bowdlerize to censor; to remove offensive passages of a play, novel, etc.

braggart one who boasts

brandish to shake or wave a weapon aggressively

brash offensively bold; rude

bravado a show of courage; false bravery

brawn muscular strength

brazen shameless or impudent

breach a violation; a gap

breadth width

brethren brothers

brevity briefness

brigand a robber

brine salt water

brisk lively; quick

bristling showing irritation

broach to introduce (a subject)

brochure a pamphlet

bronchial pertaining to the windpipe

browbeat to bully; to intimidate

bruit to spread the news

brunt shock, force, or impact, as of a blow

brusque abrupt in manner, blunt; rough

buccaneer a pirate

bucolic pertaining to the countryside; rural

buffoon clown or fool

bugbear something causing fear

bulbous swollen; shaped like a bulb

bulwark a strong defense

bumptious conceited; arrogant

bungle to do things clumsily or badly

buoy (*two meanings*) a floating object (*noun*); to encourage (*verb*)

buoyant (*two meanings*) able to float; lighthearted and lively

bureaucracy system of government through departments

burgeon to flourish; to grow rapidly

burlesque a speech or action that treats a serious subject with ridicule

burly muscular; husky

burnish to polish

buttress any prop or support

CABAL–CYNOSURE

cabal a small, secret group

cache a hiding place

cacophony harsh or unpleasant sound

cadaverous pale; ghastly; corpselike

cadence rhythm; beat

caesura pause

cajole to coax; to persuade

calamitous causing trouble or misery; disastrous

caliber degree of worth

calligraphy fancy handwriting

callous unyielding; insensitive

callow young and inexperienced

calumny a false accusation; slander

camaraderie loyalty; friendship

canard a false story, report, or rumor

candor honesty; openness; frankness

canine pertaining to dogs

canny shrewd

canon rule; law; standard

cant insincere statements usually made in a singsong tone

cantankerous bad-tempered; quarrelsome

canter smooth, easy pace; gallop

canvass to make a survey

capacious spacious; roomy

capitulate to surrender

capricious erratic; impulsive

captious hard to please; faultfinding

captivate to capture; to charm; to fascinate

carapace shell; hard, protective covering

carcinogenic causing cancer

cardinal principal; chief

careen to swerve; to dip to one side

caricature an exaggerated portrayal

carnage slaughter; massacre

carnal sensual; sexual

carnivorous flesh-eating

carouse to engage in a noisy, drunken party

carp (*two meanings*) a type of fish (*noun*); to complain (*verb*)

carrion decaying flesh

carte blanche freedom to use one's own judgment

cartel association of business firms

cartographer mapmaker

cascade a waterfall

caste social class

castigate to punish

casualty (*two meanings*) an accident; one who is hurt in an accident

cataclysm a violent change

catacomb underground burial place

catalyst person or thing that speeds up a result

cataract (*two meanings*) large waterfall; abnormality of the eye

catastrophe disaster; calamity

cathartic cleansing

catholic universal; wide-ranging

caucus a private meeting

caustic sarcastic; severely critical; corrosive

cauterize to burn

cavalcade a procession; a sequence of events

cavalier a haughty and casually indifferent person

caveat a warning

cavil to quibble; to argue

cavort to leap about; to frolic

celerity speed; swiftness

celestial heavenly

celibate unmarried

censure to criticize sharply

centrifugal moving away from the center

cerebration thinking; using one's brain

certitude sureness; certainty

cessation a stopping; a discontinuance

chafe to irritate; to annoy

chaff worthless matter

chagrin embarrassment; complete loss of courage

chameleon (*two meanings*) a lizard able to change its skin color; a changeable or fickle person

champ (*verb*) to bite impatiently; to show impatience (*to champ at the bit*)

chaos complete disorder

charisma great appeal or attraction

charlatan a fake; a quack

charnel cemetery; tomb

chary (*of*) careful; cautious

chasm a wide gap

chaste pure; virtuous

chastise to punish; to purify

chattel slave

chauvinism fanatical devotion to one's country, sex, religion, etc.

cherub angel; an innocent person

chic stylish; fashionable

chicanery trickery; deception

chide to scold

chimerical imaginary; fantastic; unreal

chirography the art of handwriting

chivalrous courteous; courageous; loyal

choleric easily angered

chronic long-lasting

churlish rude; ill-bred

cipher person or thing of no value; zero

circuitous roundabout; indirect

circumlocution roundabout way of speaking

circumscribe to encircle; to limit or confine

circumspect cautious; careful

circumvent to surround or entrap; to go around or bypass

citadel a fortress

cite to quote a passage, book, author, etc.; to refer to an example

civility politeness

clairvoyant having great insight; keenly perceptive

clamber to climb with effort or difficulty

clamor noise

clandestine secretive; private

clangor harsh ringing sound

clarify to make clear

clarion clear and shrill

claustrophobia fear of enclosed spaces

cleave (*two meanings*) to split something apart; to stick or cling to something

cleft split; divided

clemency mercy; leniency

cliché a trite or worn-out expression

clientele customers

climax highest point

clime climate; region

clique a small, exclusive group

cloistered secluded; confined

clout (*colloquial*) power; influence

cloven divided; split

coadjutor assistant; helper

coalesce to blend; to merge; to fuse

coddle to treat tenderly

coerce to force

coffer a strongbox

cog a gear tooth; a minor part

cogent convincing

cogitate to think; to consider carefully

cognate related; relevant

cognizant aware

cognomen family name; last name

coherent logically connected; consistent

cohesive tending to stick

cohort colleague; associate; partner

coincide to occur simultaneously

collaborate to work together; to cooperate

collage collection of various bits and pieces (*usually artistic*)

collate to put together in order

collateral security for payment of a loan

colloquial informal

colloquy conversation

collusion conspiracy; agreement to commit a wrongful act

colossal huge; enormous

combative eager to fight; argumentative

combustible capable of catching fire easily

comely attractive

commemorative honoring; remembering

commence to begin

commendation praise

commensurate proportionate

commiserate to express pity for

commodious roomy; spacious

communal shared; pertaining to a group of people

compact (*two meanings*) firmly packed (*adjective*); a treaty (*noun*)

compassion pity; sympathy

compatible agreeable; harmonious

compel to force

compendium brief summary

compensatory paying back; making up for

complacent self-satisfied

complement (*note spelling*) to make whole; to complete

compliant yielding; submissive

complicity partnership in a wrongful act

compliment (*note spelling*) to praise

components ingredients; elements

composure calmness of mind or manner

compulsory required

compunction uneasiness; remorse

compute to calculate; to estimate

concave hollow; curved inward

concede to admit; to grant

concentrate (*two meanings*) to think deeply; to increase in strength or degree

concentric having a common center

conception (*two meanings*) a beginning; original idea or plan

concession allowance; the act of yielding

conciliate to soothe the anger of; to win over

concise brief and to the point

conclave secret meeting

concoct to invent; to devise

concomitant accompanying; attending

concord agreement; harmony

concourse a crowd; a wide street

concur to agree

condescend to lower oneself to an inferior's level

condign deserved; suitable

condiment seasoning; spices

condolence expression of sorrow

condone to excuse; to overlook

conducive tending to or leading to

conduit pipe or tube through which fluid or electricity passes

confidant a close, trusted friend

configuration shape; arrangement

confiscate to seize by way of penalty

conflagration a large and destructive fire

confluent merging; flowing together

conformity agreement; doing the same as others

confounded confused; amazed

congeal to freeze solid; to thicken

congenial friendly; agreeable

congenital existing at birth

conglomerate mass; cluster; corporation

congregate to gather; to assemble

congruent in agreement

coniferous bearing cones (*pertaining to trees*)

conjecture to guess

conjugal pertaining to marriage

conjure to call upon or to command a devil or spirit to practice magic; cast a spell on

connivance pretended ignorance of another's wrong-doing; conspiracy

connoisseur an expert

connote to suggest or imply

connubial pertaining to marriage

consanguinity close relationship, usually by blood

consecrate to make holy

consensus general agreement, especially of opinion

console (*two meanings*) a musical panel or unit (*noun*); to comfort (*verb*)

consolidate to combine; to make or become solid

consonant in agreement or harmony

consort (*two meanings*) a husband or wife (*noun*); to associate or join (*verb*)

consternation sudden confusion; panic

constituents voters; supporters

constraints restrictions; limits

constrict to shrink; to bind

construe to analyze; to interpret

consummate to complete (*verb*); perfect (*adjective*)

contagious likely to spread; infectious

contaminant substance that pollutes or infects

contemn to regard with scorn or contempt

contemporary happening in the same time period; current

contemptuous scornful

contentious ready to argue; quarrelsome

contest (*three meanings*) a competitive game (*noun*); to dispute (*verb*); to compete (*verb*)

contiguous nearby; neighboring

contingent possible

contort to twist; to distort

contraband smuggled or stolen goods

contrary opposite

contravene to go against; to oppose

contretemps an embarrassing occurrence

contrite sorrowful; penitent

controversial debatable; questionable

contumacious disobedient; obstinate

contumely rudeness

contusion a bruise

conundrum a riddle

convalesce to recover from an illness

convene to come together; to assemble

conventional ordinary; usual

converge to come together; to meet in a point or line

conversant familiar with

converse (*two meanings*) to talk to someone (*verb*); the opposite (*noun*)

convex curving outward

conveyance a vehicle

convivial sociable; friendly

convoke to call together

convoluted twisted; coiled

cope (*with*) to deal with; to contend with

copious plentiful; abundant

coquetry flirtation

cordial friendly; courteous

cornucopia horn of plenty; abundance

corollary inference; deduction; consequence

corona crown; bright circle

corporeal pertaining to the body

corpulent fat; fleshy

corroborate to strengthen; to confirm

corrosive eating away, as an acid

corrugated wrinkled; ridged; furrowed

cortege funereal procession; group of followers

cosmic pertaining to the universe; vast

cosmopolitan worldly-wise; universal

coterie close circle of friends

countenance (*two meanings*) the face (*noun*); to permit, tolerate, or approve (*verb*)

countermand to cancel an order

counterpart duplicate; copy

coup a brilliant move; a successful and sudden attack

courier messenger

covenant an agreement; a contract

covert hidden; secretive

covet to desire

cower to tremble in fear

coy shy; modest

cozen to trick

crafty sly; tricky

crass stupid; unrefined

crave to desire strongly

craven cowardly

credence belief; trust

credible believable

credulity readiness to believe; gullibility

creed a religious belief

crescendo gradual increase in intensity or loudness

crestfallen dejected; humbled

crevice an opening; a crack

cringe to shrink back, as in fear

criterion measure of value; standard of judging

crone hag; withered old woman

crony close friend

crotchety grouchy; eccentric

crucial extremely important; decisive

crucible a severe test or trial

crux the essential part

cryptic mysterious; secretive

crystallize to settle; to take on a definite form

cubicle small compartment

cudgel club; thick stick

cue a hint; a signal

cuisine style of cooking

culinary pertaining to cooking

cull to select; to pick

culminate to result in; to reach the highest point

culpable blameworthy

cumbersome heavy; hard to handle because of size or weight

cumulative collected; accumulated

cupidity greed

curb to control; to check

curry to try to win favor by flattery

cursive running or flowing

cursory superficial; hasty

curtail to cut short

cynic one who is critical; a fault-finder

cynosure center of attention

DAIS–DYSPHASIA

dais platform; speaker's stand

dale valley

dally to waste time

dank chilly and wet

dappled spotted

dastardly sneaking and cowardly; shameful

daub to smear; to cover over with paint, etc.

daunt to discourage

dawdle to waste time; to idle

de facto in fact; in reality

deadlock a standstill; a tie

dearth a scarcity or lack

debacle a complete failure; total collapse

debase to lower in rank; to humiliate

debauch to corrupt

debilitate to weaken

debonair pleasant; courteous; charming

debris fragments; litter; rubble

debut first public appearance

decadence moral deterioration

decant to pour off (a liquid)

decapitate to behead

decelerate to slow down

deciduous not permanent; passing

decipher decode; figure out the meaning of

declaim to speak dramatically

declivity downward slope

decompose to decay; to break up into parts

decorum appropriate social behavior

decoy a person or thing that entices or lures, as into danger

decrepit broken down by age or disease

decry to speak out against

deduce to reason out; to infer

deem to think; to believe; to judge

defalcate to misuse funds; to embezzle

defamatory damaging another's reputation with false remarks

default to fail to pay a debt or to perform a task

defection desertion

defer to postpone; to put off

deference respect

defile to pollute; to corrupt

definitive comprehensive; complete

deflect to turn aside; to bend

defoliate to strip of leaves

defray to pay the cost of

deft skillful

defunct no longer in existence; extinct

degrade to lower in degree or quality

deify to idolize; to make godlike

deign to lower oneself before an inferior

delectable delicious; very pleasing

delete to leave out; to cross out

deleterious harmful

delineate to describe; to depict

delirium condition of mental disturbance; wild excitement

delude to deceive; to mislead

deluge a flood; a rush

delve to search; to investigate

demagogue a popular leader who appeals to the emotions

demean to degrade; to lower

demeanor behavior

demented deranged; insane

demigod a person who is partly a god and partly human

demise death; ending

demography study of population trends

demolish to tear down

demoralize to discourage; to cause to lose spirit

demur to object; to take exception to

demure shy

denigrate to ruin the reputation of; to blacken

denizen occupant; inhabitant; resident

denomination the name or designation for a class of persons, such as a religious group

denouement outcome; result

denounce to publicly condemn

depict to portray; to represent

depilate to remove hair from

deplete to use up gradually (resources, strength, etc.)

deplore to regret

deploy to place troops in position

depose to remove from office

depraved sinful; immoral

deprecate to disapprove of

depreciate to lessen in value

deranged insane

derelict (*three meanings*) abandoned (*adjective*); negligent (*adjective*); a vagrant or bum (*noun*)

deride to ridicule

derision ridicule

dermatology study of skin diseases

derogatory belittling

descry to discover

desecrate to damage a holy place

desiccate to dry up; to wither

desist to cease or stop

desolate lonely; deserted

despicable contemptible; hateful

despise to scorn; to regard with disgust

despoil to rob; to plunder

despondent depressed; dejected

despot a dictator

destitute poor; lacking

desuetude condition of disuse; extinction

desultory wandering from subject to subject; rambling

détente a lessening of tension or hostility

deter to discourage; to hinder

detergent a cleansing agent

detonate explode

detoxify remove the poison from

detract to take away; to diminish

detriment harm; damage

devastate to destroy; to overwhelm

deviate to turn aside; to digress

devious sly; underhand

devoid completely without

devotee an enthusiastic follower

devout religious; pious; sincere

dexterity skill; cleverness

diabolical devilish; cruel

diadem crown

dialectic logical discussion

diaphanous transparent; very sheer and light

diatribe bitter criticism

dichotomy division into two parts

dicker to bargain; to argue over prices

diction style of speaking

dictum a positive statement

didactic instructive; inclined to lecture others too much

diffident shy; modest

diffuse to spread; to scatter

digress to wander off the subject

dilapidated broken down; falling apart

dilate to expand; to become wider

dilatory slow or late in doing things

dilemma a troubling situation

dilettante a dabbler in the fine arts; one who is not an expert

diligent hard-working; industrious

diminutive small

dint power; force

dipsomaniac drunkard

dire dreadful; causing disaster

dirge a funeral song or hymn

disarray disorder; confusion

disavow to disown; to deny; to repudiate

disburse to pay out

discern to distinguish; to recognize; to perceive

disciple a follower

disclaimer denial; renunciation

disclose to reveal; to make known

discomfiture frustration; confusion

disconcert to upset; to embarrass

disconsolate without hope

discordant disagreeing; harsh-sounding

discount (*two meanings*) reduction (*noun*); to disregard (*verb*)

discountenance to disapprove of

discourse conversation; lecture

discredit to disgrace; to cast doubt on

discreet showing good judgment; cautious

discrepancy inconsistency; difference

discrete separate; not attached

discretion good judgment

discrimination (*two meanings*) prejudice; ability to distinguish

discursive rambling; wandering

disdain to scorn

disgruntled unhappy; discontented

dishearten to discourage; to depress

disheveled untidy

disinter to uncover; to dig up

disinterested impartial; not prejudiced

dismal gloomy; depressing

dismantle to take apart

dismember to cut or pull off limbs

disparage to belittle; to put down

disparity inequality; difference

dispassionate calm; impartial

dispel to drive away

disperse to scatter

disputatious fond of arguing

disreputable having a bad reputation

dissection cutting apart; analysis

dissemble to conceal; to pretend

disseminate to scatter; to spread

dissension disagreement; opposition

dissertation a written essay

dissident disagreeing

dissimulate to hide one's feelings

dissipate to waste; to scatter

dissociate to break ties with; to part company

dissolute immoral; unrestrained

dissonant out of harmony

dissuade to advise or urge against

distend to expand; to swell; to stretch out

distort to twist out of shape

distraught troubled

dither (preceded by *in a*) nervously excited or confused

diurnal daily

divergent varying; different

divers several

diverse different

divest to deprive

divination the act of foretelling the future

divulge to reveal; to make known

docile obedient; submissive

doddering shaky; senile

doff to throw off or away

doggedly stubbornly

dogmatic having a definite opinion; authoritative

doldrums low spirits

dole to distribute; to give out sparingly

doleful sorrowful

dolorous mournful; sad

dolt a dull, stupid person

domicile home; residence

donnybrook rough, rowdy fight

dormant asleep; inactive

dorsal pertaining to the back

dossier a complete group of documents containing detailed information

dotage feeblemindedness of old age

doughty courageous; worthy

dour gloomy

douse to put out (a fire); to extinguish

dowdy shabby; untidy

downtrodden trampled on; suppressed

doyen senior or eldest member

Draconian severe; cruel

dregs leftovers

drivel childish nonsense; stupid talk

droll amusing in an odd way

drone (*three meanings*) a male bee (*noun*); an idle person (*noun*); to talk on and on monotonously (*verb*)

dross waste matter

drudgery hard, tiresome work

dual consisting of two people, items, or parts

dubious doubtful; questionable

ductile capable of being molded or shaped

dudgeon anger, resentment

dulcet pleasing to the ear

dulcimer a type of zither

dupe to trick; to deceive

duplicity deceit; double-dealing; dishonesty

duress force

dutiful obedient

dwindle to shrink; to become smaller

dynamo a powerful person

dyspepsia poor digestion

dysphasia difficulty in speaking

EARNEST–EXULT

earnest sincere; serious

earthy realistic; coarse

ebb to slowly decrease

ebullient enthusiastic

eccentric odd; out of the ordinary

ecclesiastical pertaining to the church

echelon rank of authority; level of power

éclat brilliance; fame

eclectic selecting; choosing from various sources

eclipse to overshadow; to outshine

ecology study of the environment

ecstatic extremely happy

edifice structure; building

edify to improve someone morally; to instruct

educe to draw or bring out

eerie weird; mysterious

efface to erase; to wipe out

effectual effective; adequate

effeminate unmanly; womanly; soft and weak

effervescent bubbly; spirited

effete worn-out; barren

efficacy power to produce an effect

effigy a likeness; an image

efflorescent blossoming; flowering

effluent flowing out

effrontery shameful boldness

effulgent shining forth brilliantly; radiant

effusion a pouring out; an uncontrolled display of emotion

egalitarian pertaining to belief in the equality of all men

ego a feeling of self-importance

egotism selfishness; boasting about oneself

egregious remarkably bad; outrageous

egress exit (*noun and verb*)

ejaculation an exclamation

eject to throw out

elapse to pass; to slip away

elated overjoyed

electrify to thrill

elegy a sad or mournful poem

elicit to draw forth; to cause to be revealed

elite the choice or best of a group of persons

elixir remedy

ellipsis the omission in a sentence of a word or words

eloquent convincing or forceful in speech

elucidate to make clear

elude to avoid; to escape notice

elusive difficult to grasp

elysian blissful; heavenly

emaciated abnormally thin

emanate to come forth; to send forth

emancipate to set free

embark (*on*) to begin a journey or an endeavor

embellish to decorate

embezzle to steal

embroil to involve in trouble; to complicate

embryonic undeveloped; in an early stage

emendation correction

emetic causing vomiting

eminent famous; renowned

emissary one sent on a special mission

emit to send out; to give forth

emollient something that soothes or softens

emolument profit; gain

empathy understanding another's feelings

empirical based on experience rather than theory

emulate to imitate

emulous jealous; envious

enamored (*of*) in love with

enclave a country, or part of a country, surrounded by another country

encomium an expression of high praise

encompass to include; to surround

encore a repeat performance

encroach (*upon*) to trespass; to intrude

encumbrance hindrance; obstruction

encyclopedic filled with knowledge; comprehensive

endearment an expression of affection

endemic confined to a particular country or area

energize to rouse into activity

enervate to weaken

enfranchise to give the right to vote

engender to promote

engrossed completely absorbed in

engulf to overwhelm

enhance to increase in value or beauty; to improve

enigma a puzzling situation; dilemma

enigmatic mysterious; puzzling

enlighten to inform; to reveal truths

enmity hostility; hatred

ennui boredom

enormity an outrageous and immoral act

enrapture to delight beyond measure

ensconce to hide; to conceal; to settle comfortably

ensue to follow; to result from

enthrall to charm; to captivate

entice to attract; to tempt

entity independent being

entomology study of insects

entourage a group of personal attendants

entranced filled with delight or wonder

entreaty a request; a plea

entrenched firmly established; dug in

entrepreneur successful businessman; promoter

enunciate to pronounce words clearly

environs surroundings

envisage to imagine; to form a mental picture

envoy messenger; agent

eon extremely long period of time

ephemeral temporary; short-lived

epic a long poem about heroic occurrences

epicure one who seeks pleasure in fine foods

epigram witty saying

epilogue closing part of a speech or literary work

epiphany appearance of a deity (god); revelation

epistle a letter

epitaph inscription on a tomb

epithet a descriptive word or phrase

epitome a typical example; a summary or condensed account

epoch particular period of history

equanimity calmness; evenness of temperament

equestrian a horseback rider

equilibrium balance; stability

equine pertaining to horses

equinox the time when day and night are of equal length

equipoise balance

equitable fair; just

equity fairness; justice; impartiality

equivocal doubtful; ambiguous

equivocate to confuse by speaking in ambiguous terms

eradicate to erase; to wipe out

ergo therefore

erode to wear away

erotic pertaining to sexual love

err to make a mistake

errant wandering (*in search of adventure*); straying from what is right

erratic irregular; abnormal

erroneous mistaken; wrong

ersatz artificial; inferior substitute

erstwhile formerly; in the past

erudite scholarly; learned

escalate to increase; to grow rapidly; to intensify

escapade a reckless adventure

escarpment steep cliff

eschew to avoid; to keep away from

escrow (preceded by *in*) money deposited with a third person pending fulfillment of a condition

esoteric for a select few; not generally known

espionage spying

espouse to support (*a cause*)

essay (*two meanings*) to try; to attempt (*verb*); a short literary composition dealing with a single subject (*noun*)

estival pertaining to summer

estranged separated; alienated

ethereal spiritual; airy

ethnic pertaining to a particular race or culture

etymology the origin and development of words

eugenics science of improving the human race

eulogy praise for a dead person

euphemism substitution of a pleasant expression for an unpleasant one

euphonious having a pleasant sound; harmonious

euphoria a feeling of well-being

euthanasia mercy killing

evanescent temporary; fleeting

evasive not straightforward; tricky

eventuate to result; to happen finally

evict to expel; to throw out

evince to show clearly

evoke to call forth; to produce

evolve to develop gradually

exacerbate to aggravate; to make more violent

exact (*two meanings*) accurate (*adjective*); to demand or to require (*verb*)

exalt to raise in position; to praise

exasperate to irritate; to annoy extremely

excise (*two meanings*) a tax on liquor, tobacco, etc. (*noun*); to cut out or off (*verb*)

excoriate (*two meanings)* to scrape the skin off; to criticize sharply

excruciating unbearably painful

exculpate to free from blame; to vindicate

execrate to curse

exemplary worthy of imitation

exhilaration liveliness; high spirits

exhort to warn

exhume to bring out of the earth; to reveal

exigent urgent; critical

exiguous scanty; small in quantity

exodus a departure; a going out

exonerate to free from guilt or blame

exorbitant excessive; unreasonable

exorcise to drive out an evil spirit

exotic foreign; excitingly strange

expatiate to enlarge upon; to speak or write at length

expatriate a person who is banished from, or leaves, his native country

expectorate to spit out

expedient practical; advantageous

expedite to speed up; to make easy

expendable replaceable

expiate to atone for

explicate explain in detail; make clear

explicit clear; unambiguous; direct

exploit to use for one's own advantage

expound to explain; to interpret

expressly especially; particularly

expunge to erase

expurgate to remove offensive passages; to cleanse

extant still in existence

extemporaneous offhand; done without preparation

extenuating less serious

extinct no longer in existence

extirpate to destroy; to remove completely

extol to praise

extort to obtain by force

extradite to give up a prisoner to another authority

extraneous unrelated; not essential

extrapolate to estimate; to infer

extricate to set free; to disentangle

extrinsic external; coming from outside

extrovert an outgoing person

exuberant full of enthusiasm

exude to discharge; to ooze

exult to rejoice

FABRICATE–FUTILE

fabricate (*two meanings*) to construct; to lie

fabulous incredible; imaginative

facade outward appearance

facet aspect

facetious joking; sarcastic

facile easy; effortless

facilitate to make easy

facsimile an exact copy; a duplicate

faction a minority within a larger group

factious causing disagreement

factitious artificial

factotum an employee who can do all kinds of work

faculty power; ability; skill

fallacious misleading; deceptive

fallible capable of error

fallow inactive; unproductive

falter to stumble; to hesitate

fanatic a person with uncontrolled enthusiasm

fanciful unreal; imaginative; unpredictable

fanfare noisy or showy display

farcical absurd; ridiculous

fastidious hard to please

fatal causing death

fatalistic believing that all things in life are inevitable

fathom (*two meanings*) nautical measure of 6 feet in depth (*noun*); to comprehend (*verb*)

fatuous foolish

fauna animals of a certain area

fawn (*two meanings*) a young deer (*noun*); to act slavishly submissive (*verb*)

faze to disturb; to discourage

fealty loyalty; devotion

feasible capable of being accomplished; suitable

feat deed or accomplishment

febrile feverish

fecund fertile; productive

feign to pretend

feint a false show; a pretended blow

feisty quick-tempered or quarrelsome

felicity happiness

feline pertaining to cats

fell (*two meanings*) to knock down (*verb*); fierce or cruel (*adjective*)

felon a criminal

felonious treacherous; base; villainous

ferment a state of agitation or excitement

ferret (*two meanings*) a small animal of the weasel family (*noun*); to search or drive out (*verb*)

fervent eager; earnest

fervid very emotional

fester to rot

festive joyous; merry

fete to honor; to entertain

fetid foul-smelling

fetish object with magical power; object that receives respect or devotion

fetter to confine; to put into chains

fiasco a total disaster

fiat an official order

fickle changeable in affections; unfaithful

fictitious false; not genuine

fidelity faithfulness

figment something imagined

filch to steal

filial like a son or daughter

finale the climax; end

finesse diplomacy; tact

finicky extremely particular; fussy

finite limited; measurable

firebrand one who stirs up a revolution

firmament sky; heavens

fiscal pertaining to finances

fissure opening; groove; split

fitful irregular; occurring in spurts

flabbergasted astonished; made speechless

flaccid flabby

flag (*two meanings*) a banner (*noun*); to droop or to slow down (*verb*)

flagellate to whip

flagrant scandalous; shocking

flail to strike freely and wildly

flair a knack; a natural talent

flamboyant showy; conspicuous

flaunt to boast; to show off

flay (*two meanings*) to strip the skin off; to criticize sharply

fledgling a young, inexperienced person

fleece (*two meanings*) wool of a lamb (*noun*); to swindle (*verb*)

flexible bendable

flinch to draw back; to cringe

flippant treating serious matters lightly

flora plant life of a certain area

florid flowery; ornate

flotilla small fleet of ships

flotsam floating cargo or wreckage

flout to mock; to ridicule

fluctuate to move back and forth; to vary

fluent flowing; able to speak and/or write easily and clearly

fluster to upset; to confuse

fluvial pertaining to a river

flux state of continual change

foible a weakness; minor fault

foil (*two meanings*) to prevent the success of a plan (*verb*); a person who, by contrast, makes another person seem better (*noun*)

foist (*on*) to pass off merchandise that is inferior

folderol nonsense

folly a foolish action

foment to stir up; to instigate

foolhardy foolish; reckless

fop an excessively vain man

foray a sudden attack

forbearance patience; restraint

forebear ancestor

foreboding a warning; an omen

foregone (*note spelling, as* forgone *means going or to abstain from something*) long past

forensic pertaining to a formal discussion or debate

forerunner ancestor; predecessor

foreshadow to hint

forestall to prevent by action in advance; to anticipate

forfeit to give up

forgo to do without; to give up

formidable dreadful; discouraging

forte strong point

forthright direct; frank

fortitude strength; courage

fortnight two weeks; fourteen days

fortuitous lucky; by chance

foster to nourish; to encourage

fracas a loud quarrel

fractious irritable; quarrelsome; stubborn

fracture to break or to crack

frailty a weakness; a defect

franchise special right or privilege

fraternal brotherly

fraudulent dishonest; cheating

fraught (*with*) filled

fray (*two meanings*) a noisy quarrel (*noun*); to unravel or to come apart (*verb*)

frenetic frantic; wild

frenzy madness; fury

freshet a fresh water stream

fretful worried; irritated

friction (*two meanings*) a rubbing together (*noun*); conflict or disagreement (*noun*)

frigid extremely cold

frivolous trivial; silly

frowzy dirty; unkempt

frugal economical; thrifty

fruition fulfillment; realization

fruitless barren; yielding no results

frustrate to prevent; to discourage

fugacious pertaining to the passing of time

fulminate to explode; to denounce

fulsome disgusting; sickening; repulsive

furor rage; frenzy; fury

furtive stealthy; secretive

fusion a union; merging

futile useless

GADFLY–GYRATE

---

gadfly a person who annoys others

gaff a hook

gainsay to deny; to contradict

gait manner of walking

gala festive

galaxy a group of stars; any large and brilliant assemblage of persons

gall bitterness

gallant polite; noble

galvanize to stimulate; to startle into sudden activity

gambit strategy; an opening one uses to advantage

gambol to frolic; to romp about

gamut the whole range or extent

gape to stare with open mouth

garble to distort

gargantuan gigantic; huge

garish tastelessly gaudy

garland a wreath of flowers

garner to gather; to acquire

garnish to decorate; to trim

garrulous talkative

gauche awkward; tactless

gaudy flashy; showy

gaunt thin and bony; bleak and barren

gazebo an open structure with an enjoyable view

gazette newspaper

gelid very cold; frozen

genealogy family history

generate to produce; to originate

generic general; not specific; pertaining to a class

genesis origin; beginning

genial warm; friendly

genocide killing of a race of people

genre an art form or class

genteel polite; refined

gentry upper-class people

genuflect to kneel; to bend the knee

germane relevant; fitting

gerontology the study of older people and their problems

gesticulation lively or excited gesture

ghastly horrible; dreadful

ghoul grave robber; ogre

gibberish silly, unintelligible talk

gibbet gallows from which criminals are hanged

gibe to scoff; to ridicule

giddy dizzy; flighty; whirling

gild to cover with gold

gingerly carefully; cautiously

gird to encircle

gist main point; essence

glazed glassy; smooth; shiny

glean to gather patiently and with great effort

glee joy

glib fluent; smooth

glissade a skillful glide over snow or ice in descending a mountain

glitch a malfunction; an error

gloaming twilight; dusk

gloat to look at or think about with great satisfaction

glower to frown; to stare angrily at

glum sad; gloomy

glutinous gluey; sticky

glutton one who eats or drinks too much

gnarled knotty; twisted; roughened

gnome a legendary dwarflike creature

goad to encourage; to spur on

gorge (*two meanings*) a deep valley with steep sides (*noun*); to eat or to swallow greedily (*verb*)

gory bloody

gossamer light; flimsy; fine

Gothic medieval; mysterious

gouge (*two meanings*) to dig out; to swindle or overcharge

gourmand a glutton; a person who eats excessively

gourmet an expert of fine food and drink

gradient a slope; a ramp

granary a storehouse for grain

grandiloquent pretentious; speaking in a pompous style

grandiose impressive; showy

graphic giving a clear and effective picture

grapple to grip and hold; to struggle

grate (*two meanings*) to grind to shreds; to irritate

gratify to please; to satisfy

gratis without payment; free

gratuitous (*two meanings*) free of cost; unnecessary

grave serious; somber

gregarious sociable; friendly

grievous causing grief or sorrow; distressing

grim fierce; stern

grimace a distorted face; an expression of disapproval

grime dirt

gripe complaint

grisly horrible; gruesome; ghastly

grit stubborn courage

gross extreme; vulgar

grotesque absurd; distorted

grotto a cave

grovel to lower oneself to please another

grudging resentful; reluctant

grueling exhausting

gruff rough or harsh in manner

guile deceit; trickery

guileless sincere

guise a false appearance

gull to trick; to deceive

gullible easily deceived; too trusting

gumption courage and initiative

gustatory pertaining to the sense of taste

gusto hearty enjoyment

gusty windy; stormy

guttural pertaining to the throat

gyrate to rotate; to spin

HABITAT–HYPOTHESIS

habitat dwelling

hackneyed trite; commonplace; overused

haggard worn out from sleeplessness, grief, etc.

haggle to bargain over a price

halcyon calm

hale healthy

hallmark a symbol of high quality

hallow to make holy; to bless

hallucination illusion; a false notion

hamper to hinder; to keep someone from acting freely

haphazard dependent upon mere chance

hapless unlucky

harangue long speech

harass to annoy; to bother

harbinger an omen or sign

harbor (*two meanings*) a body of water providing ships with protection from winds, waves, etc. (*noun*); to conceal or hide (*verb*)

hardy courageous; sturdy

harlequin a clown

harpy a greedy, grasping person; a scolding, nagging, bad-tempered woman

harrowing upsetting; distressing

harry to worry; to torment

hart a male deer

haughty snobbish; arrogant

haunt (*three meanings*) to appear as a spirit or ghost; to visit frequently; to disturb or distress

haven a safe place

havoc great destruction

hazard risk; danger

headlong recklessly; impulsively

headstrong stubborn; willful

hearsay rumor; gossip

hearth fireplace

hector to bully

hedonist a pleasure-seeker

heedless careless; unmindful

hefty large and powerful; heavy

hegemony leadership or strong influence

hegira flight; escape

heinous hateful; abominable

hemophilia a blood defect in which the blood does not clot to close a wound

herald to announce; to usher in

herbivorous feeding on vegetation

herculean tremendous in size, strength, or difficulty

heresy rejection of a religious belief

hermetic airtight; tightly sealed

heterodox departing from acceptable beliefs

heterogeneous different; unlike; dissimilar

heyday period of success

hiatus pause or gap

hibernate to be inactive, especially during the winter

hierarchy a ranking, one above the other

hilarity gaiety; joy

hircine goat-like

hirsute hairy; bearded

histrionic theatrical; overly dramatic

hoard to store away; to accumulate

hoary white with age or frost

hoax a practical joke

hobgoblin a frightening apparition; something that causes fear

hodgepodge mixture

hogwash meaningless or insincere talk

hoi polloi common people; the masses

holocaust complete destruction

homage respect; honor

homily a sermon

homogeneous composed of parts all of the same kind

homophonic sounding alike

hone to sharpen

hoodwink to deceive

hoot to shout in disapproval

horde a crowd of people

horticulture the science of gardening

hospice shelter

hovel a dirty, wretched living place

hover to keep lingering about; to wait near at hand

hubris excessive pride or self-confidence

hue a color; a shade

humane kind; compassionate

humbug trick; hoax

humdrum monotonous; routine

humid moist

humility lowliness; meekness

humus black soil for fertilizing

hurtle to dash; speed; run

husbandry the science of raising crops; careful management

hybrid mixed; assorted

hydrophobia fear of water; rabies

hymeneal pertaining to marriage

hyperbole extreme exaggeration

hypercritical overcritical; faultfinding

hypochondriac a person with imaginary ailments

hypocrite one who pretends to be someone or something he is not

hypothesis an assumption; a theory

ICHTHYOLOGY–ITINERANT

ichthyology study of fish

icon a statue or idol

iconoclast a rebel; one who breaks with tradition

idealist one with very high standards

idiosyncrasy a peculiar personality trait

idolatry excessive or blind adoration; worship of idols

idyllic charmingly simple or poetic

igneous pertaining to fire

ignoble dishonorable

ignominious shameful; disgraceful

ignoramus a stupid person

ilk type; sort; kind

illicit unlawful; illegal

illiterate uneducated

illumine to brighten; to inspire

illusion fake impression

illustrious distinguished; bright

imbibe to drink; to absorb

imbroglio a difficult or confusing situation

imbue to fill completely; to penetrate

immaculate spotless; pure

imminent likely to happen; threatening

immolate to kill someone as a sacrificial victim, usually by fire

immortal not subject to death

immunity freedom from disease

immutable unchangeable

impair to weaken; to cause to become worse

impale to pierce with a sharp stake through the body

impalpable vague; not understandable

impartial without prejudice

impasse a dead end; a problem without a solution

impeach to accuse

impeccable flawless; without fault

impecunious without money; penniless

impede to hinder; to obstruct

impediment a barrier; an obstruction

impel push into motion; urge

impending likely to happen soon

imperative extremely necessary

imperious domineering; haughty

impermeable not permitting passage

impertinent rude; disrespectful

imperturbable steady; calm

impervious not capable of being affected; hardened

impetuous acting without thought; impulsive

impetus a stimulus; a moving force

impinge to strike; to collide; to encroach

impious disrespectful toward God

implacable unbending; inflexible; merciless

implausible unbelievable

implement (*two meanings*) a tool (*noun*); to carry out or put into practice (*verb*)

implication an indirect indication; a statement that suggests something

implicit suggested, but not plainly expressed

imply to suggest

import (*two meanings*) significance; meaning (*noun*); to bring in from a foreign country (*verb*)

importune to persistently ask; to beg

impostor a person who goes about under an assumed name or character

impotent powerless; lacking strength

imprecation a curse

impregnable unconquerable

impromptu without preparation; offhand

impropriety pertaining to something that is not proper or suitable

improvident wasteful

improvise to do without preparation

impudent disrespectful; shameless

impugn to attack a person with words; to challenge a person in regard to motives

impunity freedom from punishment

impute to accuse a person of some wrongdoing; to attribute a fault or a crime to a person

inadvertent unintentional

inalienable not able to be transferred to another

inane silly; meaningless

inanimate lifeless; dull; dead

inarticulate pertaining to speech that is not clear or understandable

incandescent very bright; shining

incapacitated disabled; unable to function

incarcerate to imprison

incarnadine blood-red; flesh-colored

incarnate in human form

incendiary causing fire; stirring up trouble

incense to inflame; to enrage

incentive something that incites to action

inception beginning; start

incessant continuous; without pause

inchoate at an early stage; just beginning

incipient beginning to exist or appear

incisive sharp; keen

incite to urge to action; to stir up

inclement (*usually refers to weather*) harsh; unfavorable; severe

incognito disguised

incoherent rambling; not logically connected

incongruous unsuited; inappropriate

inconsequential unimportant

incontrovertible certain; undeniable

incorrigible bad beyond correction or reform

incredulous skeptical; disbelieving

increment an increase; a gain

incriminate to charge with a crime; to connect or relate to a wrongdoing

incubus nightmare

inculcate (*in* or *upon*) to teach earnestly; to influence someone to accept an idea

incumbent (*two meanings*) resting or lying down (*adjective*); one who holds a political office (*noun*)

incur to bring upon oneself; to run into some undesirable consequence

incursion a raid; an invasion

indefatigable incapable of being tired out

indelible incapable of being erased

indemnify to insure; to repay

indicative signifying; implying

indict to charge with a crime; to accuse of a wrongdoing

indigenous native to a particular area; inborn

indigent extremely poor

indignant angry as a result of unjust treatment

indisputable unquestionable; without doubt

indissoluble permanent

indoctrinate to teach someone principles or beliefs

indolent lazy

indomitable unconquerable; unyielding

indubitable unquestionable; certain

induce to cause; to bring about

indulgence gentle treatment; tolerance

inebriated drunk

ineffable not able to be described; unspeakable

ineluctable inevitable; inescapable

inept unfit; bungling; inefficient

inert without power to move; inactive

inevitable unavoidable; sure to happen

inexorable unyielding

infallible certain; without mistakes

infamous having an extremely bad reputation; detestable

infantile childish; immature

infectious passing on a disease with germs; likely to spread; contagious

infer to conclude; to derive by reasoning

infernal hellish; fiendish; diabolical

infidel unbeliever

infinitesimal exceedingly small; minute (pronounced *my-newt*)

infirmity weakness; feebleness

inflated puffed up; swollen

influx a flowing in

infraction the breaking of a law or rule

infringe (*on* or *upon*) to break a law; to violate; to trespass

ingenious clever

ingenuous simple; innocent; naïve

ingrate ungrateful person

ingratiate (*oneself*) to work one's way into another's favor

inherent inborn

inhibition restraint; reserve

inimical harmful; unfriendly

inimitable not able to be imitated or equaled

iniquity wickedness

initiate to begin

injunction a command; an order

inkling a hint

innate inborn; existing from birth

innocuous harmless

innovate to introduce a new idea

innuendo indirect remark; hint

inordinate unusual; excessive

insatiable unable to be satisfied

inscrutable mysterious; difficult to understand

insidious treacherous

insightful having a penetrating understanding of things; mentally alert and sharp

insinuate to hint; to suggest

insipid tasteless; dull

insolent boldly disrespectful

insolvent bankrupt; unable to pay creditors

insomnia sleeplessness

insouciant carefree; happy-go-lucky

instigate to provoke; to stir up

insubordinate disobedient

insular pertaining to an island; detached; isolated

insuperable unconquerable

insurgence rebellion; action against authority

insurrection uprising; rebellion

intact entire; left whole; sound

integral essential; whole

integrate to unify; to bring together into a whole

integrity honesty; sincerity

intellectual intelligent; having mental capacity to a high degree

intelligentsia highly educated, cultured people

inter to bury

interdict to prohibit; to ban

interim meantime; period of time between

interlocutor one who takes part in a conversion

interloper an intruder

interlude a period of time between two events

interminable endless

intermittent starting and stopping; periodic

interpolate to insert between; to estimate

interpose to place between

interregnum pause; interval; any period during which a nation is without a permanent ruler

interrogate to question

interstellar between or among stars

intervene to come between

intimate (*two meanings*) private or personal (*adjective*); to imply (*verb*)

intimidate to make afraid; threaten

intolerant bigoted; narrow-minded

intractable hard to manage

intransigent stubborn; refusing to give in

intrepid fearless; courageous

intricate complex; hard to understand

intrinsic essential; pertaining to a necessary part of something

introspective looking into oneself

introvert a person who is concerned with his own thoughts or feelings

intuitive insightful; knowing by a hidden sense

inundate to fill to overflowing; to flood

inured (*to*) accustomed to

invalidate to deprive of legal value; to make null and void

invariably constantly; uniformly; without changing

invective strong verbal abuse

inveigh (*against*) to make a bitter verbal attack

inveigle to trick; lure; deceive

invert to turn inside out or upside down

inveterate firmly established; deep-rooted

invidious causing resentment; offensive

invigorate to fill with energy

invincible not able to be defeated; unconquerable

invoke to call upon

invulnerable not able to be hurt; immune to attack

iota a small quantity

irascible easily angered

ire anger; wrath

iridescent displaying a wide range of colors like those of the rainbow

irksome annoying; bothersome

ironic contrary to what was expected

irrational senseless; unreasonable

irreconcilable unable to agree

irredeemable hopeless; unable to be brought back

irremediable unable to be corrected or cured

irreparable beyond repair

irrepressible unable to be controlled or restrained

irresolute indecisive; doubtful; undecided

irreverent disrespectful

irrevocable final; unchangeable

itinerant traveling from place to place

JADED–KNUCKLE

jaded tired; worn out; dulled

jargon vocabulary peculiar to a particular trade or group of people; meaningless talk; gibberish

jaundiced (*two meanings*) pertaining to a yellowed skin; prejudiced

jaunt short trip; excursion

jaunty carefree; confident

jeer to sneer; to mock

jeopardy danger

jest to joke; to make light of

jetsam goods cast overboard to lighten a ship

jettison to throw goods overboard

jilt to reject; to cast off

jingoism extreme patriotism

jinx to bring bad luck to

jocose joking; humorous

jocular humorous

jostle to bump; to push

jovial jolly; good-natured

jubilation celebration; rejoicing

judicious wise; showing sound judgment

juggernaut a terrible destructive force

jugular pertaining to the throat or neck

juncture a point of time; a crisis

junket a pleasure trip; an excursion

junta a small group ruling a country

jurisprudence science of law

jut to stick out; to project

juxtapose to place side by side

kaleidoscopic constantly changing

ken range of knowledge

kindle to set on fire; to excite

kindred relative; family, tribe, or race

kinetic pertaining to motion

kismet destiny; fate

kleptomania a compulsion to steal

knave a tricky, deceitful person

knead to work dough, clay, etc., into a uniform mixture

knell the sound made by a bell rung slowly for a death or funeral

knoll a small rounded hill

knuckle (*under*) to yield; (*down*) to apply oneself vigorously

LABYRINTHINE–LUXURIANT

labyrinthine complicated; intricate

lacerate to tear (*flesh*) roughly; to mangle

lachrymose tearful

lackadaisical uninterested; listless

lackey slavish follower

lackluster lacking brilliance or liveliness; dull or vapid

laconic using few words; concise

lactic pertaining to milk

laden burdened; loaded

laggard a slow person; one who falls behind

laity religious worshipers who are not clergy

lambent softly bright or radiant; running or moving lightly over a surface

lament to mourn

laminated covered with thin sheets, often plastic

lampoon a sharp, often harmful satire

languid sluggish; drooping from weakness

languish to become weak or feeble

lank long and slender

lapidary a dealer in precious stones

larceny theft

largess gifts that have been given generously

lascivious lustful or lewd; inciting sexual desire

lassitude a feeling of weakness and weariness

latent present, but hidden

lateral to the side; sideways

latitude freedom; margin

laudable praiseworthy

laureate (*two meanings*) worthy of praise or honor (*adjective*); an honored person (*noun*)

lave to wash or bathe

lavish very generous; extravagant

lax careless or negligent

leeway room for freedom of action; margin

legerdemain sleight of hand; deception

lenient mild; lax; permissive

leonine lionlike; fierce; authoritative

lesion an injury; a wound

lethal deadly; fatal

lethargic dull; slow-moving; sluggish

leviathan anything vast or huge; a sea monster

levity lightness of body or spirit; lack of seriousness

levy to impose and collect taxes

lewd pertaining to lust or sexual desire

lexicon dictionary

liaison a bond; a connection; an illicit relationship between a man and a woman

libation a drink; a beverage

libel a false statement in written form

liberal giving freely; not strict

libertine one who leads an immoral life

libretto the words of an opera

licentious lawless; immoral; lewd

liege lord; master

lieu (*in lieu of*) in place of; instead of

lilliputian tiny; narrow-minded

limber easily bent; flexible

limpid clear, transparent

lineage ancestry; descent

lineaments facial features

linguistic pertaining to language

lionize to treat as a celebrity

liquidate (*two meanings*) to get rid of by killing; to wind up the affairs of a business

lissome moving gracefully; agile or active

listless feeling no interest in anything; indifferent

literal exact; precise; word for word

lithe graceful; flexible

litigation lawsuit

livid darkened or discolored; pale from anger or embarrassment

loath reluctant; unwilling

loathe to hate; to feel disgust for

locus place

lode a rich source of supply such as a mineral deposit

lofty very high; formal; proud

logistics military operations dealing with the supply and maintenance of equipment

loiter to linger; to hang around

loll to lean or lounge about; to droop

longevity a long life

lope to move along with a swinging walk

loquacious talkative

lot fate

lout an awkward, stupid person

lowly humble; ordinary

lucent giving off light; shining

lucid clear; easy to understand; rational or sane

lucrative profitable; producing wealth or riches

ludicrous ridiculous

lugubrious sad; mournful

lull to soothe or calm

luminous bright

lunacy insanity; madness

lunar pertaining to the moon

lupine wolflike; fierce

lurch to move suddenly forward

lurid shocking; glowing; sensational

lurk to lie concealed in waiting; to stay hidden

lush abundant; rich

lustrous shining; bright

luxuriant rich; extravagant

MACABRE–MYTHICAL

macabre horrible; gruesome

Machiavellian deceitful; tricky

machination evil design

macroscopic visible to the naked eye

maelstrom whirlpool

magnanimous generous

magnate important person in any field

magnitude size; extent

maim to cripple; to deprive of the use of some part of the body

maladroit clumsy; unskillful; awkward

malady disease; illness

malaise discomfort; uneasiness

malapropism word humorously misused

malcontent one who is dissatisfied

malediction curse

malefactor wrongdoer; villain

malevolent showing ill will or hatred; very dangerous, harmful

malfeasance wrongdoing

malicious spiteful; vengeful

malign to speak badly of

malignant evil; deadly

malingerer one who pretends to be sick to avoid work

malleable capable of being changed; adaptable

malodorous bad-smelling; stinking

mammoth huge; enormous

manacle handcuff; restraint

mandarin influential person

mandate an order; a command

mandatory required; obligatory

mangle to cut, slash, or crush so as to disfigure

mangy shabby; filthy

manifest evident; obvious

manifold many; varied

manipulate (*two meanings*) to handle or manage with skill; to influence a person in a bad way

manumit to set free

maraud to raid; to plunder

marital pertaining to marriage

maritime pertaining to the sea

marquee a rooflike shelter, such as glass, projecting above an outer door

martial warlike

martinet a strict disciplinarian

martyr one who suffers for a cause

marvel to be amazed; to wonder

masochist one who enjoys his own pain and suffering

massive huge; bulky

masticate to chew

maternal motherly

matriarchy a social organization in which the mother is the head of the family

matrix a place of origin

maudlin excessively sentimental

maul to injure; to handle roughly

mausoleum large tomb for many bodies

maverick a rebel; a nonconformist

mawkish sickeningly sweet; overly sentimental

maxim a proverb or saying

meager inadequate; of poor quality

mean (*three meanings*) nasty or offensive (*adjective*); inferior or low (*adjective*); an average (*noun*)

meander to wander aimlessly

meddlesome interfering; curious

mediate to settle a dispute; to act as a go-between

mediocre ordinary; average; neither good nor bad

meditate to think deeply; to ponder

medley a mixture; a musical selection combining parts from various sources

megalomania false impression of one's own greatness; tendency to exaggerate

melancholy sad; depressed

melee noisy fight

mellifluous smoothly flowing; sweet-sounding

melodramatic overly emotional

memento remembrance; a souvenir

menace a threat; a danger

ménage household; domestic establishment

menagerie collection of wild or strange animals

mendacious lying; false

mendicant a beggar

menial low; degrading

mentor adviser

mercantile pertaining to merchants; commercial

mercenary motivated only by a desire for money

mercurial changeable; fickle; erratic

meretricious gaudy; showy; attractive in a cheap, flashy way

mesa a flat-topped elevation of land with steep rock walls

mesmerize to hypnotize

metamorphosis a change; a transformation

metaphor comparison (without *like* or *as*)

metaphysics pertaining to beyond what is natural

mete (*out*) to distribute in portions

meteoric momentarily dazzling; swift

meteorology study of weather and climate

meticulous excessively careful; finicky

metropolis large city

mettle courage; spirit

miasma pollution; poisonous environment

microcosm a miniature world

mien manner; bearing

migratory wandering; moving from place to place

milieu environment; setting

militant ready and willing to fight

millennium a thousand years

mimic to imitate

minion a devoted follower; a highly regarded person

minuscule very small

minute (*two meanings*) sixtieth part of an hour (pronounced *min-ut*); very small and insignificant (pronounced *my-newt*)

minutiae insignificant details; trivia

mirage an apparition or illusion

mire (*two meanings*) wet, swampy ground (*noun*); to involve in difficulties (*verb*)

mirth joy; amusement; laughter

misanthrope hater of mankind

misapprehension a misunderstanding

miscegenation mixture of races, especially through marriage

mischance unlucky accident; bad luck

misconstrue misinterpret; misjudge

miscreant a vicious person; a villain

misdemeanor a criminal offense less serious than a felony

misgiving doubt; suspicion

misnomer an error in listing the name of a person

misogamy hatred of marriage

misogynist woman-hater

missive letter

mitigate to make less severe; to become milder

mnemonic pertaining to memory

mobile movable; flexible

mock to ridicule; to insult; to lower in esteem

modicum a small amount

modish fashionable; stylish

modulate to soften; to tone down

mogul powerful person

molest to disturb; to bother

mollify to pacify; to calm; to appease

molt to shed, such as feathers and skin

molten melted

momentous very important

monarchy government by one ruler

monastic pertaining to a monk; self-denying

monetary pertaining to money

monitor one who watches or warns

monograph a paper, book, etc., written about a single subject

monolithic unyielding; unified

monologue long speech by one person

monotheism belief in one god

monumental great; important

moot doubtful; debatable

moratorium delay; postponement

morbid depressing; gruesome

mordant sarcastic; biting

mores customs; traditions; morals

moribund dying

morose gloomy; ill-humored

mortal destined to die; causing death

mortify to embarrass; to humiliate

motif theme; central idea

motley diverse; assorted; having different colors

mottled spotted; blotched; streaked

mountebank a phony; a fraud; a charlatan

muddle to confuse; to mix up

mulct to punish with a fine; to obtain money by extortion

mull (*over*) to study or think about

multifarious varied; having many parts

mundane worldly

munificent generous

murky dark; unclear; gloomy

muse to think deeply

muster to gather together

musty stale; moldy

mute silent

mutilate to disfigure; to cripple

mutinous rebellious

muzzle to restrain; to gag

myopic nearsighted; having a limited point of view

myriad infinitely vast in number

myrmidon an unquestioning follower

mythical imaginary; fictitious

NABOB–NUTRIMENT

nabob a very wealthy or powerful person

nadir lowest point

naïve simple; unsophisticated

narcissistic conceited; vain

nascent coming into being; being born

natation the act or art of swimming

nativity birth

naught nothing

nautical pertaining to ships, sailors, navigation

nebulous hazy; vague; uncertain

necromancy magic, especially that practiced by a witch

nefarious wicked

negate to deny; to make ineffective

negligent careless

nemesis something that a person cannot conquer or achieve

neologism new use or coinage of a word

neophyte a beginner; a novice

nepotism favoritism shown toward relatives

nether lower; under

nettle to irritate; to annoy

neutralize to make ineffective; to counteract

nexus connection, tie, or link among the units of a group

nicety delicacy; subtlety

niche recess or hollow in a wall

niggardly stingy; miserly

niggle to spend excessive time on unimportant details

nihilism total rejection of established laws

nimble quick and light in motion

nirvana place of great peace or happiness

nocturnal pertaining to night

nodule a small, rounded mass or lump

noisome foul-smelling; harmful or injurious

nomadic wandering; homeless

nomenclature a set of names or terms

nominal in name only; not in fact

non sequitur something that does not logically follow

nonage a period of immaturity

nonchalant unconcerned; casual

noncommittal having no definite point of view

nonentity person or thing of little importance

nonpareil unequaled; unrivaled

nonplus to confuse; to perplex

nostalgia homesickness; longing for the past

nostrum quack medicine; supposed cure-all

notorious having a bad reputation; infamous

novice a beginner

noxious harmful

nuance delicate variation in meaning, tone, color, etc.

nub a lump or small piece

nubile suitable for marriage, in regard to age and physical development

nugatory worthless; invalid

nullify to make useless or ineffective

numismatist coin collector

nuptial pertaining to marriage

nurture to feed; to sustain

nutriment food; nourishment

OAF–OVOID

oaf a dunce or blockhead

oasis a place that offers a pleasant relief

obdurate stubborn; hard-hearted

obeisance a bow or similar gesture expressing deep respect

obese very fat

obfuscate to confuse; to bewilder; to perplex

oblation an offering for religious or charitable purposes

obligatory required; mandatory

oblique slanted; indirect

obliterate to erase; to do away with

oblivious forgetful; unmindful

obloquy strong disapproval; bad reputation resulting from public criticism

obnoxious objectionable; offensive

obscurant a person who tries to prevent the spread of knowledge

obscure dim; not clear; not easily understood

obsequious excessively submissive; overly attentive

obsequy a funeral rite or ceremony

obsess to control the thoughts or feelings of a person

obsolescent going out of use; becoming extinct

obstinate stubborn

obstreperous boisterous; unruly

obtrude to push something toward or upon a person

obtuse slow to comprehend

obviate to prevent

occidental western; opposite of oriental

occlude to close; to shut; to block out

occult hidden; secret; mysterious

ocular pertaining to sight

odious disgusting; hateful

odoriferous giving off a displeasing or strong smell

odyssey a long journey

offal garbage; waste parts

officious meddling; interfering

ogle to look at with desire

ogre monster; hideous being

olfactory pertaining to smell

oligarchy government in which power is in the hands of only a few individuals

Olympian majestic

omen an event that indicates the future

ominous threatening; indicating evil or harm

omnifarious of all kinds

omnipotent all-powerful

omniscient all-knowing

omnivorous eating any kind of food; absorbing everything

onerous burdensome; heavy

onslaught a furious attack

onus a burden; a responsibility

opaque not transparent; not letting light pass through

opiate narcotic; causing sleep or relief

opportunist one who takes advantage of a situation

oppress to rule harshly; tyrannize

opprobrious shameful; disgraceful

opt (*for*) to choose

optimist one who sees the good side of things

optimum the best; most favorable

opulent rich; luxurious

oracular mysterious; predicting

oration a speech delivered on a special occasion

orbit a curved path, such as a planet takes around the sun

ordain to order; to establish; to arrange

ordeal difficult or painful experience; a primitive form of trial

ordinance law; regulation

organic fundamental; essential; natural, not artificial; carbon-based

Orient, orient (*two meanings*) an area of the Far East, such as Asia (*noun, capitalized*); to adjust or adapt to (*verb, lowercase*)

orifice mouth; opening

ornate showy; highly decorated

ornithology study of birds

orthodox accepting the usual or traditional beliefs

orthography correct spelling

oscillate to swing or move back and forth, like a pendulum

ossify to change into bone; to become rigid

ostensible apparent; conspicuous

ostentatious showing off; boastful

ostracize to banish; to exclude

oust to drive out; to expel

outwit to trick; to get the better of

overt open; aboveboard; not hidden

ovine of or like a sheep

ovoid egg-shaped

PACIFY–PYRRHIC VICTORY

pacify to calm down

pact an agreement

paean song of praise or joy

palatable pleasant to the taste

palatial magnificent

paleontology study of prehistoric life

pall (*two meanings*) something that covers or conceals (*noun*); to become wearisome or unpleasant (*verb*)

palliate to ease; to lessen

pallid pale; dull

palpable obvious; capable of being touched or felt

palpitate to beat rapidly; to tremble

palsy muscle paralysis

paltry trivial; worthless

panacea a cure-all; an answer for all problems

panache self-confidence; a showy manner

pandemic general; widespread

pandemonium wild disorder; confusion

panegyric an expression of praise

pang a sharp pain

panoply suit of armor; any protective covering

panorama unlimited view; comprehensive survey

parable a simple story giving a moral or religious lesson

paradigm a model; an example

paradox a statement that seems contradictory, but probably true

paragon a model of excellence or perfection

parameter boundary; limits

paramount chief; supreme

paranoia mental disorder characterized by a feeling of being persecuted

paraphernalia personal belongings; equipment

paraphrase to reword; to restate

parched dried up; extremely thirsty

pariah an outcast

parity equality; similarity

parley discussion; conference

parlous dangerous

parochial local; narrow; limited

parody a work that imitates another in a ridiculous manner

paroxysm a sudden outburst; a fit

parrot to repeat or imitate without understanding

parry to avoid something such as a thrust or blow

parsimonious stingy; miserly

partisan a strong supporter of a cause

passé old fashioned; out-of-date

passive submissive; unresisting

pastoral pertaining to the country; rural

patent (*two meanings*) a government protection for an inventor (*noun*); evident or obvious (*adjective*)

paternal fatherly

pathogenic causing disease

pathos pity; deep feeling

patriarch an early biblical person regarded as one of the fathers of the human race

patrician aristocratic

patrimony inherited right; heritage

patronage the control of power to make appointments to government jobs

patronize (*two meanings*) to be a customer; to talk down to

paucity scarcity; lack

peccadillo a minor offense

pectoral pertaining to the chest

peculate to steal; to embezzle

pecuniary pertaining to money

pedagogue a schoolteacher

pedantic tending to show off one's learning

pedestrian (*two meanings*) one who walks (*noun*); ordinary or dull (*adjective*)

pedigree a record of ancestors; a line of descent

peer (*two meanings*) an equal (*noun*); to look closely (*verb*)

peerless without equal; unmatched

peevish hard to please; irritable

pejorative having a negative effect; insulting

pellucid transparent; clear

pelt (*two meanings*) skin of a fur-bearing animal (*noun*); to throw things at (*verb*)

penal pertaining to punishment

penchant a strong liking for; an inclination

pendant anything that hangs or is suspended

penitent expressing sorrow for sin or wrongdoing

pensive dreamily thoughtful

penury extreme poverty

peon common worker

perceive to observe

perceptible observable; recognizable

perdition damnation; ruin; hell

peregrinate to travel from place to place

peremptory decisive; final; not open to debate

perennial lasting for a long time; perpetual

perfidious deceitful; treacherous; unfaithful

perforce of necessity

perfunctory done without care; routine

perigee point in an orbit nearest to the earth

perilous dangerous; risky

periphery outside boundary; unimportant aspects of a subject

periphrastic said in a roundabout way

perjury making a false statement while under oath

permeate to spread throughout

pernicious deadly; destructive

peroration the concluding part of a speech

perpetrate to do something evil; to be guilty of

perpetuate to cause to continue

perplexity confusion

perquisite something additional to regular pay

persevere to endure; to continue

personification giving human qualities to a nonhuman being

perspicacity keenness of judgment

perspicuity clearness, as of a statement

pert bold; saucy

pertinent relevant; to the point

perturb to unsettle; to disturb

peruse to read carefully

pervade to spread throughout; to pass through

perverse contrary; cranky

pervert to lead astray; to corrupt

pessimist one who sees the worst in everything

petrify to turn to rock; to paralyze with fear

petrology study of rocks

petty unimportant; minor

petulant irritable; rude

phalanx closely massed body of persons

phenomenon extraordinary person, thing, or event

philander to engage in various love affairs

philanthropy a desire to help mankind; generosity

philately stamp collecting

philippic a bitter verbal attack

philistine uncultured; common (*adjective*); one who is uncultured or common (*noun*)

phlegmatic unemotional; cool; not easily excited

phobia intense fear

phoenix a bird that symbolizes immortality

picaresque pertaining to an adventurous wanderer

piddling trifling; petty

piecemeal bit by bit; gradually

pied many-colored; variegated

piety reverence; devotion

pigment dye; coloring matter

pilgrimage a journey to a holy place

pillage to rob by violence

pillory to expose to public ridicule or abuse

pinnacle peak; highest point

pious religious

piquant stimulating to the taste; exciting interest

pique to irritate or annoy

piscine of or like a fish

pitfall unexpected difficulty; a trap

pithy concise; to the point

pittance small share or amount

pivotal central; crucial

placard small poster

placate to soothe; to calm

placebo harmless, phony medicine; something said or done to soothe

placid calm

plagiarism the claiming of another's work as one's own

plague (*two meanings*) a contagious disease (*noun*); to torment; to trouble (*verb*)

plaintive sorrowful; sad

platitude a dull or trite remark

platonic spiritual; free from sensual desire

plaudit applause; (*in the plural*) any expression of approval

plausible apparently true, fair, or reasonable

plebeian pertaining to a member of the lower classes

plenary full; complete; absolute

plethora abundance

pliant easily bent; adaptable

plight a sad or dangerous situation

ploy a gimmick; a trick

pluck (*two meanings*) to pull at (*verb*); courage (*noun*)

plumb to test; to measure

plunder to rob; to take by force

plutocracy rule by the wealthy class

poach to trespass or steal

podium a platform

poignant keenly distressing; affecting the emotions

polarize to separate into opposing groups

polemic a controversy or argument

politic diplomatic; shrewd

poltroon a coward

polychromatic many-colored

polyglot speaking or writing several languages

polymorphic having many forms

polytheism belief in many gods

pomp brilliant show or display

ponder to think deeply; to consider carefully

ponderous heavy; burdensome

porcine of or like a pig

portable capable of being carried

portal door; gate; entrance

portentous warning; foreshadowing

portly stout; large

posterity future generations

posthumous occurring after death

postulate to assume without proof; to take for granted

potable drinkable

potent powerful; strong

potentate ruler; monarch

potential capacity for being or becoming something

potion a drink

potpourri a mixture

pragmatic practical

prate to talk extensively and pointlessly; to babble

precarious uncertain; dangerous; risky

precede to be, come, or go before

precedent an act that may be used as an example in the future

precept a rule of conduct

precipice cliff

precipitate to bring about an action suddenly

precipitous extremely steep

précis brief summary

preclude to prevent; to shut out

precocious prematurely developed

precursor a forerunner; predecessor

predatory living by plunder, exploitation, etc.

predicate to declare; to assert

predilection a liking; preference; inclination

predispose to make susceptible

preeminent standing out above all others

preen to dress oneself carefully or smartly

prehensile adapted for seizing or grasping something

prelude an introduction

premeditate to plan beforehand

premier first in importance or time

premise statement from which a conclusion is drawn

premonition forewarning; hunch

preponderance superiority in quantity or power; dominance

preposterous absurd; ridiculous

prerogative privilege or right

presage to indicate or warn in advance

prescience knowledge of things before they happen

presentiment anticipation, especially of something evil

prestige influence; importance

presumptuous boldly assuming

pretentious showy; putting on airs

preternatural abnormal; beyond what is natural

pretext a false reason or motive; an excuse

prevail to succeed; to gain the advantage

prevaricate to lie

prim formal; proper

primary first; chief

primeval of the earliest times or ages

primogeniture state of being the firstborn

primordial first; original

primp to dress up in a fussy way

prismatic many-colored

pristine uncorrupted; in its original state

privation loss or lack of something essential

privy (*to*) having knowledge of something private or secret

probe to investigate; to examine

probity honesty; integrity

proclivity inclination; tendency

procrastinate to postpone; to delay

procreate to beget or produce

procrustean designed to get conformity at any cost

procure to obtain; to secure

prod to urge; to poke or jab

prodigal wasteful

prodigious enormous; vast

profane showing disrespect for sacred things

profess to acknowledge; to admit frankly

proffer to offer

proficiency skill; competency

profligate shamelessly immoral; extremely wasteful

profound very deep

profuse abundant

progeny descendants

prognosticate to predict; to foretell

projectile a bullet, shell, grenade, etc., for firing from a gun

proletarian one who belongs to the working class

proliferate to expand; to increase

prolific productive; fertile

prolix tediously long and wordy

prologue introduction

promenade a stroll or a walk; an area used for walking

promiscuous sexually loose

promontory piece of land that juts out

promulgate to announce; to advocate

prone reclining; lying flat; inclined

propagate to spread; to multiply

propensity inclination; tendency

prophetic predicting

propinquity nearness; closeness

propitious favorable

proponent a person who supports a cause or doctrine

propriety conformity; appropriateness

prosaic dull; commonplace; unimaginative

proscribe to denounce; exile

proselyte a person who has changed from one religion to another; a convert

prospectus a report describing a forthcoming project

prostrate lying flat; thrown or fallen to the ground

protagonist main character

protean changeable; variable

protégé one who has been guided or instructed by another

protocol the etiquette observed by diplomats

prototype the original; first of its kind; a model

protract to draw out; to prolong

protrude to stick out; to project

proverbial well-known

provident having foresight

provincial countrified; narrow; limited

provisional temporary

proviso a condition; a stipulation

provoke to anger; to irritate; to annoy

prowess skill; strength; daring

proximity nearness in place or time

proxy one who acts in place of another

prude an overly proper person

prudence caution; good judgment

prune to cut off or lop off, such as twigs, branches, or roots

prurient lustful; obscene; lewd

pseudo false; counterfeit

pseudonym a fake or assumed name

psyche the human soul or spirit

puerile childish; immature

pugilist a boxer

pugnacious eager to fight; quarrelsome

puissant powerful; strong

pulchritude beauty

pulmonary pertaining to the lungs

pulverize to crush or grind into powder; totally destroy

pummel to beat or thrash with the fists

pun the humorous use of a word, or of different words sounding alike, so as to play on their various meanings

punctilious very exact; precise

pundit a learned man; an expert or authority

pungent having a sharp taste or smell; severely critical or sarcastic

punitive pertaining to punishment

puny weak; inferior

purge to cleanse; to purify

puritanical strict; rigid; harsh

purloin to steal

purport to claim to be

purvey to furnish; to supply

pusillanimous cowardly; fearful

putative supposed; believed

putrefy to rot; to decay

pyre a funeral fire in which the corpse is burned

pyretic pertaining to fever

pyromaniac one who likes to start fires; arsonist

Pyrrhic victory success gained at too high a cost

QUACK–QUOTIDIAN

quack an untrained doctor; a pretender to any skill

quadruped a four-footed animal

quaff to gulp; to drink in large quantities

quagmire a swamp; a difficult situation

quail to lose courage; to shrink with fear

quaint strange or unusual in a pleasing or amusing way

qualm a feeling of uneasiness

quandary a puzzling situation; a dilemma

quarry an animal that is being hunted down

quash to cancel; to set aside (as an indictment)

quasi resembling; seeming

quaver to tremble; to shake

quay a wharf

queasy uneasy; nauseated

quell to subdue; to calm down

querulous complaining

query a question

quest a search

queue a line of people waiting their turn

quibble petty objection or argument

quiddity essential quality

quidnunc a gossip or busybody

quiescent at rest; motionless

quietus finishing stroke; anything that ends an activity

quintessence the pure and concentrated essence of something

quip a witty or sarcastic remark

quirk a peculiar characteristic of a person; a sudden twist or turn

quiver to tremble; to shake

quixotic extremely idealistic; romantic; not practical

quizzical odd; questioning; puzzled

quotidian daily

RABBLE–RUTHLESS

rabble mob; disorderly crowd

rabid intense; furious or raging; mad

rack to torment; to torture

raconteur storyteller

radical extreme; complete; violent

rail (*at* or *against*) to complain bitterly

raillery good-humored ridicule

raiment clothing; garments

rakish carefree; lively

rambunctious restless; hard to control

ramification a result; a consequence; a branch

rampant widespread; raging

ramshackle shaky; ready to fall apart

rancid having a bad taste or smell; stale; repulsive

rancor bitter resentment; hatred

rankle to cause irritation; to fester

rant to speak in a loud or violent manner

rapacious taking by force; greedy

rapport a close relationship; harmony

rapt completely absorbed in; overcome with joy, love, etc.

rarefy to make less dense; to refine

rash (*two meanings*) a skin irritation (*noun*); reckless or daring (*adjective*)

raspy harsh; grating

ratify to officially approve of

ratiocinate to reason

ration a fixed portion; a share

rational sensible; reasonable

rationalize to make an excuse for

raucous irritating or harsh in sound

ravage to damage; ruin

ravenous extremely hungry; greedy

raze to destroy; to level to the ground

realm kingdom; region

rebuff to refuse; to snub

rebuke to scold; to blame

rebuttal contradiction; opposing argument

recalcitrant disobedient; hard to manage

recant to withdraw or disavow a statement or opinion

recapitulate to summarize; repeat briefly

recede to go or move back; to withdraw

recess (*two meanings*) a cut or notch in something; a pause or rest

recidivist a person who goes back to crime

recipient one who receives

reciprocal interchangeable; mutual

reciprocate to give in return

recluse hermit; one who shuts himself off from the world

recoil to retreat; to draw back

reconcile to bring into agreement or harmony

recondite difficult to understand; profound

reconnoiter to survey; to check out in advance

recount to tell or relate, as a story

recreant coward; traitor

recrimination countercharge

rectify to correct; to make right

rectitude honesty; moral uprightness

recumbent lying down; reclining

recuperate to get well

recur to happen again

redemption deliverance from sin; a rescue

redolent having a pleasant odor

redoubtable formidable; commanding respect

redress to set right; to remedy

redundant repetitious; unnecessary

reek to give off; emit

refractory stubborn; hard to manage

refulgent shining; glowing

refurbish to make new; to freshen up

refute to prove wrong, such as an opinion

regal pertaining to a king; splendid

regale to entertain

regenerate to re-create; to reform morally; to replace a lost part of the body

regent one who governs

regicide the killing of a king

regime a system of government

regimen a regular system (of exercise, diet, etc.)

regressive moving in a backward direction

regurgitate to rush or surge back, as undigested food

rehabilitate to restore to useful life

reimburse to pay back

reiterate to repeat

rejuvenate to make young again

relegate to banish; to assign to an inferior position

relentless unyielding

relevant significant; pertaining to the subject

relinquish to give up; to let go

relish to enjoy; to take delight in

remediable capable of being corrected

remedial intended to correct

reminisce to remember

remiss negligent

remission a lessening; a forgiveness as of sins or offenses

remonstrate to protest; to complain

remorse regret for wrongdoing

remuneration payment for a service

renaissance rebirth; renewal; revival

renal pertaining to the kidneys

rend to split; to tear apart

rendezvous a meeting; appointment

renegade a deserter; a traitor

renege to go back on one's word

renounce to give up (a belief)

renovate to make new; to repair

reparation compensation; something done to make up for a wrong or injury done

repartee a quick, witty reply

repast a meal

repellent something that drives away or wards off (insects, etc.)

repercussion reaction; aftereffect

repertoire special skills or talents one possesses; collection

repine to complain; to fret

replenish to fill up again

replete well-filled

repose to rest; to sleep (*verb*); rest (*noun*)

reprehensible deserving criticism or blame; shameful

repress to control; to subdue

reprimand to scold

reprisal retaliation; revenge

reproach to blame; to scold

reprobate a wicked person

reproof a rebuke

repudiate to reject; to disown

repugnant distasteful; disgusting

repulse to drive back; to repel

reputed supposed to be

requiem funeral hymn; mass for the dead

requisite required or necessary; indispensable

requite to make a return or repayment

rescind to cancel; to repeal

residue that which remains

resilient recovering quickly; elastic

resolute very determined

resonance fullness of sound

resourceful able to deal effectively with problems

respite a delay; rest

resplendent shining brightly; dazzling

restitution repayment; a giving back

restive restless; uneasy; impatient

restrain to hold back; to control

résumé a summary

resurge to rise again

resurrection revival; rebirth

resuscitate to revive from apparent death or from unconsciousness

retaliation revenge; repayment for an evil act

retentive having a good memory; remembering

reticent silent or reserved in manner

retinue body of attendants or followers

retort a short, witty reply

retract to take back (a statement); to withdraw

retrench to cut down or reduce expenses

retribution deserved punishment

retrieve to get or bring back

retroactive applying to a period before a certain law was passed

retrogressive going backward; becoming worse

retrospect (preceded by *in*) looking back on past events

revelation something made known; a disclosure

revelry noisy merrymaking

reverberate to echo; to resound

revere to honor; to respect

reverie a daydream

revile to abuse; to slander

rhetorical concerned with mere style or effect

ribald vulgar; indecent

rife frequently occurring; widespread

rift a break or split

righteous behaving justly or morally

rigorous strict

risible laughable; funny

risqué daring or indecent; not proper

rite a religious ceremony; a solemn act

robust strong; hearty

rogue a dishonest person; a scoundrel

rollicking jolly; carefree

roster a list

rote (preceded with *by*) from memory, without thought for meaning

rotund round; fat

rout overwhelming defeat

rudimentary elementary; basic

rue to regret; to be sorrowful

ruffian hoodlum; lawless person

ruffle (*two meanings*) a wrinkle or a ripple (*noun*); to irritate or to annoy (*verb*)

ruminate to consider carefully; to meditate on

rupture to break apart; to burst

ruse a skillful trick or deception

rustic pertaining to the country

rustle (*two meanings*) to steal; to make a swishing sound

ruthless cruel; merciless

SACCHARINE–SYNTHETIC

saccharine overly sweet

sacrilege the violation of anything sacred

sacrosanct extremely holy

sadistic deriving pleasure from inflicting pain on others

saga a long story of adventure

sagacious wise

sage a wise person

salacious obscene; lusty

salient significant; conspicuous

saline salty

sallow sickly pale

salubrious healthful

salutary healthful; wholesome

salutatory a welcoming address, as at a graduation

salvage to rescue; to save from destruction

sanctimonious hypocritical in regard to religious belief

sanction to authorize; to give permission

sangfroid calmness; composure

sanguinary bloody

sanguine cheerful; optimistic

sapient wise

sardonic mocking; scornful

sartorial pertaining to clothes or tailoring

satiated satisfied; filled up

satirical sarcastic; ironic

saturate to soak; to fill up

saturnine gloomy; sluggish

saunter to stroll; to walk leisurely

savant a person of extensive learning

savoir faire tact; knowledge of just what to do in any situation

savor to enjoy, as by taste or smell

scant inadequate in size or amount

scapegoat one who takes the blame for others

scathing extremely severe or harsh, such as a remark

schism a split or break

scintilla a tiny amount; a speck

scintillate to sparkle; to twinkle

scion an offspring; a descendant

scoff to ridicule

scope range; extent

scourge a whip or a lash; a person or thing that punishes or destroys

scrupulous honest; ethical; precise

scrutinize to examine closely

scurrilous coarsely abusive; vulgar

scurry run about; to hurry

scuttle to sink (a ship); to abandon

sear to burn; to scorch

sebaceous fatty

seclude to keep apart; to isolate

secrete to hide or conceal

secular worldly; nonreligious

sedate quiet; calm; serious

sedentary sitting most of the time

sediment material that settles on the bottom; residue

sedition rebellion

sedulous hard-working; industrious; diligent

seedy run-down; shabby

seethe to boil; to be violently agitated

seismic pertaining to earthquakes

semblance outward appearance

senile pertaining to mental weakness due to old age

sensate pertaining to feeling

sensual pertaining to enjoyment of food and sex

sensuous pertaining to enjoyment of art, music, etc.

sententious concise; including proverbs and brief remarks

sentient conscious; capable of feeling

sentinel a guard

sepulcher tomb; burial vault

sequel an event or literary work that follows a previous one

sequester to separate; to set aside

seraphic angelic; pure

serendipity a talent for making desirable discoveries by accident

serene calm; peaceful

serpentine winding

serrated having toothlike edges

servile like a slave

servitude slavery; bondage

sever to cut in two; to separate

shackle to keep prisoner; to restrain

sham a pretense

shambles a slaughterhouse; great disorder

shard a fragment

sheepish embarrassed; bashful

shibboleth a slogan; a password

shiftless lazy; inefficient

shoal a shallow place in the water; a reef

shortcomings defects; deficiencies

shrew a nagging, bad-tempered woman

shroud a cloth or sheet in which a corpse is wrapped for burial

sibilant hissing

sibling a brother or sister

simian pertaining to an ape or monkey

simile a comparison using *like* or *as*

simony the sin of buying or selling church benefits

simper to smile in a silly way

simulacrum an image; a likeness

simulate to pretend; to imitate

simultaneous occurring at the same time

sinecure job with no responsibility

sinewy tough; firm; strong

singular extraordinary; remarkable; exceptional

sinister threatening evil; ominous

sinuous curving; winding

siren an attractive but dangerous woman

skeptic one who doubts

skinflint stingy person; miser

skittish restless; excitable; nervous

skulduggery trickery; deception

skulk to sneak around; to lie in hiding

slacken become loose; to relax

slake to lessen (thirst, desire, anger, etc.) by satisfying; to quench

slander to make a false statement against someone

slattern an untidy woman

sleazy cheap; flimsy

sleek smooth and shiny

slither to slide or glide

slothful lazy

slough (*off*) to discard; to shed

slovenly untidy; dirty; careless

smirk to smile in an affected or offensive way

smite to strike forcefully

smolder to burn without flame; to keep feelings concealed

smug self-satisfied

snare to trap

sneer to look at with contempt; to scorn; to deride

snicker to laugh in a half-suppressed way

snippet a small fragment

snivel to whine; to complain

sober not drunk; serious

sobriquet nickname; assumed name

sodden soaked; damp

sojourn a brief stay or visit

solace comfort

solar pertaining to the sun

solecism ungrammatical usage; an error or inconsistency in speech

solicit to ask; to seek; to try to get an order in business

solicitude concern; anxiety

soliloquy act of talking to oneself

solipsistic pertaining to the theory that only oneself exists or can be proved to exist

solitude loneliness

solon a wise man

solvent (*two meanings*) having the ability to pay a debt (*adjective*); a substance that dissolves another (*noun*)

somber dark; gloomy

somnambulate walk in one's sleep

somniferous causing sleep

somnolent drowsy; sleepy

sonorous producing a deep, rich sound

sophistry a deceptive, tricky argument

sophomoric immature; pretentious

soporific causing sleep

sordid dirty; filthy

sot a drunkard

sovereign a monarch or other supreme ruler

spacious roomy; convenient

Spartan warlike; brave; disciplined

spasm a sudden burst of energy

specious not genuine; pleasing to the eye but deceptive

specter a ghost; a phantom

speculate (*two meanings*) to meditate; to participate in a risky business transaction

sphinx person who is difficult to understand

splenetic bad-tempered; irritable

sporadic infrequent; irregular

spry full of life; active

spume foam

spurious deceitful; counterfeit

spurn to reject

squalid filthy; dirty

staccato made up of short, abrupt sounds

stagnant not flowing; stale; sluggish

staid sedate; settled

stalemate a deadlock; a draw

stalwart strong; sturdy

stamina endurance; resistance to fatigue

stance attitude; posture

stark complete; harsh; severe

static inactive; motionless

stationary standing still; not moving

statute law; rule

steadfast firm in purpose; dependable; constant

stench a foul smell

stentorian very loud

stereotyped not original; commonplace

sterling of high quality; excellent

stigma mark of disgrace

stilted artificially formal

stint to be sparing; to conserve

stipend salary

stipulate to specify; to arrange definitely

stoic showing no emotion; indifferent to pleasure or pain

stolid impassive; having little emotion

strait a position of difficulty; a narrow passage of water

stratagem a plan, scheme, or trick

strew to spread about; to scatter

striated striped; marked with lines

stricture negative criticism; a restriction

strident harsh-sounding; loud and shrill

stringent strict; tight

strut to walk in a proud manner; to show off

stultify to make absurd or ridiculous; to render worthless

stupefy to stun; to amaze

stygian dark; gloomy

stymie to hinder; to block

suave polished; sophisticated

sub rosa secretly; confidentially

subaqueous underwater

subjective not objective; personal

subjugate to conquer

sublimate to make a person act noble or moral

sublime majestic; elevated or lofty in thought

subliminal subconscious; unaware

submissive yielding; humbly obedient

subordinate of lower rank

suborn to hire for an unlawful act

subsequent following; occurring later

subservient submissive; helpful, in an inferior capacity

subside to become quiet; to settle down

subsidiary auxiliary; supplementary; serving to assist

substantiate to prove; to confirm; to support

subterfuge trickery; deceit

subterranean underground

subversive tending to overthrow or undermine

succinct concise; brief and to the point

succor assistance; help; relief

succulent juicy

succumb to yield; to give in

suffrage the right to vote

sullen gloomy; showing irritation

sully to soil, stain, or tarnish

sultry hot and moist

sumptuous luxurious; lavish; extravagant

sundry various; assorted

superannuated retired because of old age

supercilious proud; haughty

superficial on the surface; shallow

superfluous excessive; unnecessary

supernal heavenly

supernumerary extra; more than necessary

supersede to take the place of

supervene to take place or occur unexpectedly

supine lying on the back

supplant to replace

supple flexible

suppliant begging; asking humbly

supplicate to pray humbly; to beg

surfeit an excessive amount

surly rude; bad-tempered

surmise to guess

surmount to go beyond; to overcome

surreptitious acting in a sneaky way

surrogate substitute

surveillance supervision; close watch

sustenance nourishment

susurration whispering; murmuring

suture to join together, as with stitches

svelte slender; graceful

swarthy dark-complexioned

swathe to wrap closely or fully

sybarite one who is fond of luxuries and pleasure

sycophant a flatterer; a parasite

sylvan wooded; pertaining to the forest

symbiosis mutual dependence between two different organisms

symmetrical balanced; well-proportioned

synchronize to happen at the same time

synthesis a combination; a fusion

synthetic not genuine; artificial

TABLEAU–TYRO

tableau dramatic scene or picture

taboo forbidden; unacceptable

tabulation a systematic listing by columns or rows

tacit silent; not expressed

taciturn speaking very little

tactics plan; method; strategy

tactile pertaining to sense of touch

taint to infect; to harm a person's reputation

talisman a good luck charm

tally to count; to make a record of

tangent touching

tangible real; capable of being touched

tantalize to tease or torment

tantamount equivalent to

tarn a small lake or pool

tarnish to soil; to discolor; to stain

tarry to linger; to delay

taunt to ridicule; to tease

taurine like a bull

taut tight; tense

tawdry cheap; showy; flashy

tawny yellowish-brown

tedious boring; monotonous

teeming overfilled; pouring out

temerity reckless boldness; rashness

temper (*verb*) to moderate; to soften or tone down

temperate not extreme; moderate

temporal pertaining to time

temporize to be indecisive; to be evasive; to delay an action

tenacious holding on; persistent; stubborn

tendentious biased; favoring a cause

tenet a doctrine; a belief

tensile capable of being stretched; elastic

tentative for the time being; experimental

tenuous slender; flimsy; without substance

tenure the holding or possessing of anything

tepid lukewarm

terminate to put an end to; to conclude

terminus a boundary; a limit

terpsichorean pertaining to dancing

terrestrial earthly; living on land

terse brief; to the point

testy irritable

thanatology the study of death and dying

theocracy government by religious leaders

therapeutic pertaining to the treatment and curing of disease

thermal pertaining to heat

thesaurus a book of synonyms and antonyms; a dictionary

thespian an actor

thrall a slave

threnody a funeral song

throes a violent struggle; pains (*of childbirth*); agony (*of death*)

throng a crowd

thwart to prevent or hinder

timorous fearful; cowardly

tinge a faint color; a trace

tirade a long angry speech; an outburst of bitter denunciation

titanic huge

titillate to tickle; to excite agreeably

titter to laugh in a self-conscious or nervous way

token (*two meanings*) sign or symbol (*noun*); slight or unimportant (*adjective*)

tome large, heavy book

toothsome tasty

topple to overturn; to fall over

torpid inactive; sluggish

torsion twisting; bending

torso the human body excluding the head and limbs

tortuous twisting; winding

torturous causing extreme pain

touchstone standard; a test or criterion for quality

toxic poisonous; harmful

tractable easy to manage

traduce to speak badly of; to slander

trait a characteristic; a quality

tranquil calm; peaceful

transcend to go beyond; to overcome

transcendental supernatural; going beyond ordinary experience or belief

transgression violation of a rule or law

transient temporary; passing

transitory lasting a short time; brief

translucent letting light pass through

transmute to change from one form to another; to transform

transparent easily seen through; clear

transpire to be revealed or become known; to occur

trappings articles of dress; equipment

trauma a shock; an aftereffect

travail very hard work; intense pain

travesty an absurd or inadequate imitation

treacherous dangerous; deceptive; disloyal

treatise a book or writing about some particular subject

treble three times as much

tremulous trembling; quivering

trenchant keen or incisive; vigorous; effective

trepidation fear; alarm

trespass to invade; to enter wrongfully

tribulation trouble

tributary a stream flowing into a river

tribute a gift; an acknowledgment to show admiration

trinity group of three

trite worn out; stale; commonplace

trivia matters or things that are very unimportant; trivialities

truckle (*to*) to submit; to yield

truculent savage; brutal; cruel

truism a self-evident, obvious truth

truncate to shorten; to cut off

truncheon a club

tryst a secret meeting

tumid swollen; bulging

tumult great noise and confusion

turbid muddy; unclear

turbulence wild disorder; violent motion

turgid swollen

turmoil confusion

turpitude baseness; shameful behavior

tussle a struggle; a fight

tutelage instruction

twain two

tycoon a wealthy businessman

tyro a beginner

UBIQUITOUS–UXORIOUS

ubiquitous present everywhere

ulcerous infected

ulterior lying beyond; hidden

ultimatum a final demand or proposal

umbrage a feeling of resentment

unanimity agreement; oneness

unassailable unable to be attacked

uncanny weird; strange

unconscionable unreasonable; excessive

uncouth crude; clumsy

unctuous (*two meanings*) oily; excessively polite

undue inappropriate; unreasonable

undulate to move or sway in wavelike motion

unequivocal clear; definite

unerring accurate; not going astray or missing the mark

unfledged not feathered; immature

unilateral one-sided

unimpeachable above suspicion; unquestionable

uninhibited free; not restricted

unique being the only one of its kind

unison harmony; agreement

universal broad; general; effective everywhere or in all cases

unkempt untidy; sloppy

unmindful unaware

unmitigated absolute; not lessened

unobtrusive inconspicuous; not noticeable

unruly not manageable; disorderly

unsavory unpleasant to taste or smell

unscathed unharmed; uninjured

unseemly not in good taste

untenable unable to be defended or upheld

unwieldy hard to manage because of size or weight

unwitting unintentional; unaware

upbraid to scold; to find fault with

uproarious loud; outrageously funny

urbane refined; suave; citified

urchin a mischievous child

ursine like a bear

usurp to seize illegally

usury excessive amount of money charged as interest

utilitarian useful; practical

utopian perfect; ideal

uxorious overly fond of one's wife

VACILLATE–VULPINE

vacillate to sway back and forth; to hesitate in making a decision

vagabond a wanderer

vagary an odd notion; an unpredictable action

vagrant a homeless person; a wanderer

vain conceited; excessively proud about one's appearance

vainglorious boastfully proud

valedictory saying farewell

valiant courageous; brave

valid true; logical; sound

validate to approve; to confirm

valor courage; bravery

vanguard the front part

vanity excessive pride; conceit

vanquish to defeat

vapid uninteresting; tasteless; tedious

variegated having different colors; diversified

vaunt to brag or boast

veer to change direction

vegetate to lead a dull, inactive life

vehement forceful; furious

velocity speed

venal corrupt; able to be bribed

vendetta bitter quarrel or feud

veneer an outward show that misrepresents

venerable worthy of respect

venerate to regard with respect

venial excusable; minor

venomous poisonous; spiteful; malicious

vent to give release to; to be relieved of a feeling

venturesome daring; adventurous; risky

veracious truthful; honest

verbatim word for word

verbiage overabundance of words

verbose wordy

verdant green; flourishing

verisimilitude the appearance of truth

veritable true; actual; genuine

verity truth

vernacular native language; informal speech

vernal pertaining to spring

versatile good at many things; serving many purposes

vertex top; highest point

vertiginous whirling; dizzy; unstable

verve energy; enthusiasm

vestige a trace; visible evidence of something that is no longer present

veteran an experienced person

vex to irritate; to annoy

viable capable of living; workable; practicable

viaduct a bridge

viands various foods

vicarious taking the place of another person or thing; substituted

viceroy a representative; a deputy appointed by a sovereign to rule a province

vicissitudes unpredictable changes; ups and downs

victimize to make a victim of; to swindle or cheat

victuals food

vie to compete

vigilant watchful

vignette a short literary sketch; a decorative design

vilify to speak evil of; to defame

vindicate to clear of guilt or blame

vindictive spiteful; seeking revenge

vintage representative of the best (*especially of wines*)

viper (*two meanings*) a poisonous snake; a malignant or spiteful person

virago a loud, bad-tempered woman; a shrew

virile masculine; manly

virtuoso an expert; a skilled person

virulent deadly; poisonous; harmful

visage the face; appearance

visceral pertaining to instinctive rather than intellectual motivation

viscous sticky

vista a distant view

vitiate to weaken; to impair

vitreous of or like glass

vitriolic biting; sharp; bitter

vituperate to scold; to criticize

vivify to give life to; to enliven

vixen female fox; ill-tempered woman

vociferous loud; shouting

vogue fashion; style

volant capable of flying

volatile unstable; explosive

volition free will

voluble talkative; fluent

voluminous large; copious

voluptuous sensual; shapely

voracious extremely hungry; greedy

votary loyal follower

vouchsafe to grant; to allow or permit

vulgar showing poor taste or manners

vulnerable defenseless; open to attack

vulpine like a fox; clever

WAIF–ZEST

waif a homeless person

waive to give up (a right)

wallow to indulge oneself; to roll around in

wan pale; weak; tired

wane to gradually decrease in size or intensity

wangle to manipulate; to obtain by scheming or by underhand methods

wanton reckless; immoral

warble to sing melodiously

warp to bend out of shape; to pervert

wary cautious; watchful

wastrel a spendthrift; one who wastes

waver to sway; to be uncertain

wax to grow in size or intensity

weighty of utmost importance

wend to direct one's way

wheedle to coax or to persuade

whet to stimulate; to make sharp

whimsical unpredictable; changeable

wield to handle (*a tool*); to exercise control (*over others*)

willful contrary; stubborn

wily tricky; sly

wince to shrink, as in pain, fear, etc.; to flinch

windfall unexpected good fortune

winsome pleasing; charming

withal in spite of all; nevertheless

wizened withered; shriveled

woe sorrow; grief

wolfish ferocious

wont (*to*) accustomed (*adjective*)

workaday everyday; ordinary

wraith a ghost; an apparition

wrangle to quarrel

wrath anger; rage

wrench to twist; to pull

wrest to take away by force

wroth angry

wrought produced or shaped

wry produced by distorting the face (*a wry grin*); ironic (*wry humor*)

xenophobia fear of foreigners or strangers

xyloid pertaining to wood

yen an intense desire; a longing

yoke to join together; to link

zany comical; clownishly crazy

zeal great enthusiasm

zealot a fanatic

zenith the highest point

zephyr a gentle, mild breeze

zest hearty enjoyment

100 Tests to Strengthen Your Vocabulary

This vocabulary section consists of 100 Vocabulary Tests. Each test consists of 10 multiple-choice questions, including SAT-type words. Practically all the words whose meanings you are tested on in these 100 tests are among the 3,400 words in the SAT Word List beginning on page 359.

These 100 Vocabulary Tests provide you with an opportunity to make sure that you really know the meanings of the hundreds of words you are being tested on. Several of these words are likely to appear on your actual SAT exam.

We suggest that you use the following procedure while you are taking these 100 tests:

1. Take Vocabulary Test 1.
2. Turn to the Answer Keys beginning on page 451.
3. For each word that you got wrong, jot down the word on a "Special List" of your own.
4. Make up a sentence using each word that you got wrong on Vocabulary Test 1.
5. Repeat the above procedure for Vocabulary Tests 2, 3, 4—right on through Vocabulary Test 100.
6. When you have finished taking the 100 Vocabulary Tests, go back to your "Special List." See whether you really know the meanings of these words by having someone else test you on them. For those words you still have trouble with, look up their meanings in a dictionary. Compose three sentences including each of these troublemakers.

Gentle reminder: Knowing the meanings of many of the words in these 100 tests is likely to raise your score in the Verbal (Critical Reading) sections, Sentence Completions, and Reading Comprehension.

Directions for the 100 Vocabulary Tests

Each vocabulary question consists of a word in capital letters, followed by five lettered words or phrases. Choose the word or phrase that is most nearly the *same* in meaning as the word in capital letters. Since some of the questions require you to distinguish fine shades of meaning, consider all choices before deciding which is best.

Vocabulary Test 1

1. FILCH
   (A) hide
   (B) swindle
   (C) drop
   (D) steal
   (E) covet

2. URBANE
   (A) crowded
   (B) polished
   (C) rural
   (D) friendly
   (E) prominent

3. DECANT
   (A) bisect
   (B) speak wildly
   (C) bequeath
   (D) pour off
   (E) abuse verbally

4. ANTITHESIS
   (A) contrast
   (B) conclusion
   (C) resemblance
   (D) examination
   (E) dislike

5. HERETICAL
   (A) heathenish
   (B) impractical
   (C) quaint
   (D) rash
   (E) unorthodox

6. COALESCE
   (A) associate
   (B) combine
   (C) contact
   (D) conspire
   (E) cover

7. CHARLATAN
   (A) clown
   (B) philanthropist
   (C) jester
   (D) dressmaker
   (E) quack

8. GAUCHE
   (A) clumsy
   (B) stupid
   (C) feebleminded
   (D) impudent
   (E) foreign

9. REDUNDANT
   (A) necessary
   (B) plentiful
   (C) sufficient
   (D) diminishing
   (E) superfluous

10. ATROPHY
   (A) lose leaves
   (B) soften
   (C) waste away
   (D) grow
   (E) spread

Vocabulary Test 2

1. RESILIENCE
   (A) submission
   (B) elasticity
   (C) vigor
   (D) determination
   (E) recovery

2. ANALOGY
   (A) similarity
   (B) transposition
   (C) variety
   (D) distinction
   (E) appropriateness

3. FACETIOUS
   (A) obscene
   (B) shrewd
   (C) impolite
   (D) complimentary
   (E) witty

4. DIATRIBE
   (A) debate
   (B) monologue
   (C) oration
   (D) tirade
   (E) conversation

5. MALEDICTION
   (A) curse
   (B) mispronunciation
   (C) grammatical error
   (D) tactless remark
   (E) epitaph

6. AGGREGATE
   (A) result
   (B) difference
   (C) quotient
   (D) product
   (E) sum

7. APLOMB
   (A) caution
   (B) timidity
   (C) self-assurance
   (D) shortsightedness
   (E) self-restraint

8. THERAPEUTIC
   (A) curative
   (B) restful
   (C) warm
   (D) stimulating
   (E) professional

9. TRANSMUTE
   (A) remove
   (B) change
   (C) duplicate
   (D) carry
   (E) explain

10. ATTRITION
   (A) annihilation
   (B) encirclement
   (C) counterattack
   (D) appeasement
   (E) wearing down

Vocabulary Test 3

1. TRUNCATE
   (A) divide equally
   (B) end swiftly
   (C) cut off
   (D) act cruelly
   (E) cancel

2. OSCILLATE
   (A) confuse
   (B) kiss
   (C) turn
   (D) vibrate
   (E) whirl

3. INOCULATE
   (A) make harmless
   (B) infect
   (C) cure
   (D) overcome
   (E) darken

4. PERUSAL
   (A) approval
   (B) estimate
   (C) reading
   (D) translation
   (E) computation

5. QUERULOUS
   (A) peculiar
   (B) fretful
   (C) inquisitive
   (D) shivering
   (E) annoying

6. AUTONOMY
   (A) tyranny
   (B) independence
   (C) plebiscite
   (D) minority
   (E) dictatorship

7. MACHINATIONS
   (A) inventions
   (B) ideas
   (C) mysteries
   (D) plots
   (E) alliances

8. SCHISM
   (A) government
   (B) religion
   (C) division
   (D) combination
   (E) coalition

9. PUSILLANIMOUS
   (A) cowardly
   (B) extraordinary
   (C) ailing
   (D) evil-intentioned
   (E) excitable

10. TERMINOLOGY
   (A) technicality
   (B) finality
   (C) formality
   (D) explanation
   (E) nomenclature

Vocabulary Test 4

1. STIPEND
   (A) increment
   (B) bonus
   (C) commission
   (D) gift
   (E) salary

2. LITIGATION
   (A) publication
   (B) argument
   (C) endeavor
   (D) lawsuit
   (E) ceremony

3. FIASCO
   (A) disappointment
   (B) turning point
   (C) loss
   (D) celebration
   (E) complete failure

4. VAGARY
   (A) caprice
   (B) confusion
   (C) extravagance
   (D) loss of memory
   (E) shiftlessness

5. GRAPHIC
   (A) serious
   (B) concise
   (C) short
   (D) detailed
   (E) vivid

6. CONNOTATION
   (A) implication
   (B) footnote
   (C) derivation
   (D) comment
   (E) definition

7. TORTUOUS
   (A) crooked
   (B) difficult
   (C) painful
   (D) impassable
   (E) slow

8. FULMINATING
   (A) throbbing
   (B) pointed
   (C) wavelike
   (D) thundering
   (E) bubbling

9. CIRCUMVENT
   (A) freshen
   (B) change
   (C) control
   (D) harass
   (E) frustrate

10. CARTEL
   (A) rationing plan
   (B) world government
   (C) industrial pool
   (D) skilled craft
   (E) instrument of credit

Vocabulary Test 5

1. PROLIFIC
   (A) meager
   (B) obedient
   (C) fertile
   (D) hardy
   (E) scanty

2. ASSUAGE
   (A) create
   (B) ease
   (C) enlarge
   (D) prohibit
   (E) rub out

3. DECORUM
   (A) wit
   (B) charm
   (C) adornment
   (D) seemliness
   (E) charity

4. PHLEGMATIC
   (A) tolerant
   (B) careless
   (C) sensitive
   (D) stolid
   (E) sick

5. INTREPID
   (A) quick-witted
   (B) brutal
   (C) fearless
   (D) torrid
   (E) hearty

6. ACTUATE
   (A) frighten
   (B) direct
   (C) isolate
   (D) dismay
   (E) impel

7. MOUNTEBANK
   (A) trickster
   (B) courier
   (C) scholar
   (D) cashier
   (E) pawnbroker

8. LACONIC
   (A) terse
   (B) informal
   (C) convincing
   (D) interesting
   (E) tedious

9. BOORISH
(A) sporting
(B) tiresome
(C) argumentative
(D) monotonous
(E) rude

10. ERUDITE
(A) modest
(B) egotistical
(C) learned
(D) needless
(E) experienced

Vocabulary Test 6

1. ACRIMONIOUS
(A) repulsive
(B) enchanting
(C) stinging
(D) snobbish
(E) disgusting

2. EMBRYONIC
(A) hereditary
(B) arrested
(C) developed
(D) functioning
(E) rudimentary

3. INEXORABLE
(A) unfavorable
(B) permanent
(C) crude
(D) relentless
(E) incomplete

4. PROTRACTED
(A) boring
(B) condensed
(C) prolonged
(D) comprehensive
(E) measured

5. OBSEQUIOUS
(A) courteous
(B) fawning
(C) respectful
(D) overbearing
(E) inexperienced

6. LOQUACIOUS
(A) queer
(B) logical
(C) gracious
(D) rural
(E) voluble

7. PUGNACIOUS
(A) bold
(B) combative
(C) brawny
(D) pug-nosed
(E) valiant

8. ASTRINGENT
(A) bossy
(B) musty
(C) flexible
(D) corrosive
(E) contracting

9. ESCARPMENT
(A) threat
(B) limbo
(C) cliff
(D) behemoth
(E) blight

10. AMENITIES
(A) prayers
(B) ceremonies
(C) pageantries
(D) pleasantries
(E) social functions

Vocabulary Test 7

1. DEPLORE
(A) condone
(B) forget
(C) forgive
(D) deny
(E) regret

2. BANAL
(A) commonplace
(B) flippant
(C) pathetic
(D) new
(E) unexpected

3. ABACUS
(A) casserole
(B) blackboard
(C) slide rule
(D) adding device
(E) long spear

4. SEISMISM
(A) inundation
(B) tide
(C) volcano
(D) earthquake
(E) tornado

5. AMELIORATE
(A) favor
(B) improve
(C) interfere
(D) learn
(E) straddle

6. CHARY
(A) burned
(B) careful
(C) comfortable
(D) fascinating
(E) gay

7. CORPULENT
(A) dead
(B) fat
(C) full
(D) organized
(E) similar

8. ENIGMA
(A) ambition
(B) foreigner
(C) instrument
(D) officer
(E) riddle

9. INEPT
(A) awkward
(B) intelligent
(C) ticklish
(D) tawdry
(E) uninteresting

10. INVETERATE
(A) evil
(B) habitual
(C) inconsiderate
(D) reformed
(E) unintentional

Vocabulary Test 8

1. OBEISANCE
(A) salary
(B) justification
(C) conduct
(D) deference
(E) forethought

2. PEDANTIC
(A) stilted
(B) odd
(C) footworn
(D) selfish
(E) sincere

3. PETULANT
(A) lazy
(B) loving
(C) patient
(D) peevish
(E) wary

4. PROCLIVITY
(A) backwardness
(B) edict
(C) rainfall
(D) slope
(E) tendency

5. TRENCHANT
(A) keen
(B) good
(C) edible
(D) light
(E) subterranean

6. VAPID
(A) carefree
(B) crazy
(C) insipid
(D) spotty
(E) speedy

7. PROGNOSTICATE
(A) forecast
(B) ravish
(C) salute
(D) scoff
(E) succeed

8. PROPRIETY
(A) advancement
(B) atonement
(C) fitness
(D) sobriety
(E) use

9. PULCHRITUDE
(A) beauty
(B) character
(C) generosity
(D) intelligence
(E) wickedness

10. SCRUPULOUS
(A) drunken
(B) ill
(C) masterful
(D) exact
(E) stony

Vocabulary Test 9

1. INVARIABLE
(A) diverse
(B) eternal
(C) fleeting
(D) inescapable
(E) uniform

2. VORACIOUS
(A) excitable
(B) honest
(C) greedy
(D) inclusive
(E) circular

3. CONCENTRATE
(A) agitate
(B) protest
(C) debate
(D) harden
(E) consolidate

4. PLAGIARIZE
(A) annoy
(B) borrow
(C) steal ideas
(D) imitate poorly
(E) impede

5. CORTEGE
(A) advisers
(B) official papers
(C) slaves
(D) retinue
(E) personal effects

6. ANTIPATHY
(A) sympathy
(B) detachment
(C) aversion
(D) amazement
(E) opposition

7. DEMUR
(A) object
(B) agree
(C) murmur
(D) discard
(E) consider

8. PARAGON
(A) dummy
(B) lover
(C) image
(D) model
(E) favorite

9. FINITE
(A) impure
(B) firm
(C) minute
(D) limited
(E) unbounded

10. ANARCHY
(A) laissez-faire
(B) motor-mindedness
(C) pacifism
(D) lawless confusion
(E) self-sufficiency

Vocabulary Test 10

1. DISCRIMINATION
(A) acquittal
(B) insight
(C) caution
(D) indiscretion
(E) distortion

2. INVECTIVE
(A) richness
(B) goal
(C) solemn oath
(D) praise
(E) verbal abuse

3. ADROIT
(A) hostile
(B) serene
(C) pompous
(D) skillful
(E) allergic

4. DISTRESS
(A) injury
(B) contortion
(C) suffering
(D) convulsion
(E) aggravation

5. DILETTANTE
(A) epicure
(B) dabbler
(C) procrastinator
(D) literary genius
(E) playboy

6. PROVISIONAL
(A) military
(B) tentative
(C) absentee
(D) democratic
(E) appointed

7. CONDIMENT
(A) ledger
(B) ore
(C) telegraph device
(D) musical instrument
(E) spice

8. RECALCITRANT
(A) insincere
(B) obstinate
(C) crafty
(D) conservative
(E) reconcilable

9. BON MOT
(A) witticism
(B) pun
(C) praise
(D) last word
(E) exact meaning

10. ACCOUTREMENTS
(A) sealed orders
(B) equipment
(C) cartons
(D) correspondence
(E) financial records

Vocabulary Test 11

1. HYPOTHESIS
(A) assumption
(B) proof
(C) estimate
(D) random guess
(E) established truth

2. ALACRITY
(A) slowness
(B) indecision
(C) caution
(D) promptness
(E) fearlessness

3. JETTISON
(A) throw overboard
(B) dismantle
(C) scuttle
(D) unload cargo
(E) camouflage

4. VACILLATE
(A) glitter
(B) swerve
(C) surrender
(D) soften
(E) waver

5. ASTUTE
(A) shrewd
(B) futile
(C) potent
(D) provocative
(E) ruthless

6. PROVISO
(A) final treaty
(B) condition
(C) demand
(D) official document
(E) proclamation

7. MACABRE
(A) gruesome
(B) meager
(C) sordid
(D) fantastic
(E) cringing

8. AUGMENT
(A) curtail
(B) change
(C) restore
(D) conceal
(E) increase

9. INTEGRAL
(A) useful
(B) powerful
(C) essential
(D) mathematical
(E) indestructible

10. IMPUNITY
(A) shamelessness
(B) power of action
(C) self-reliance
(D) haughtiness
(E) exemption from punishment

Vocabulary Test 12

1. LATENT
(A) inherent
(B) lazy
(C) dormant
(D) crushed
(E) anticipated

2. OBDURATE
(A) patient
(B) stupid
(C) rude
(D) stubborn
(E) tolerant

3. BELLICOSE
(A) boastful
(B) warlike
(C) sluggish
(D) fantastic
(E) oriental

4. ARROYO
(A) cliff
(B) plain
(C) ranch
(D) gully
(E) cactus

5. AUGUR
(A) enrage
(B) foretell
(C) suggest
(D) evaluate
(E) minimize

6. CONTRITE
(A) infectious
(B) worried
(C) penitent
(D) sympathetic
(E) tolerant

7. PETULANT
(A) silly
(B) gay
(C) sarcastic
(D) officious
(E) quarrelsome

8. PAEAN
(A) prize
(B) song of praise
(C) decoration
(D) certificate
(E) story of heroism

9. EXOTIC
(A) romantic
(B) exciting
(C) wealthy
(D) strange
(E) tropical

10. ARCHIPELAGO
(A) slender isthmus
(B) long, narrow land mass
(C) string of lakes
(D) high, flat plain
(E) group of small islands

Vocabulary Test 13

1. PREVARICATE
   (A) hesitate
   (B) lie
   (C) protest
   (D) ramble
   (E) remain silent

2. INCREDULOUS
   (A) argumentative
   (B) imaginative
   (C) indifferent
   (D) irreligious
   (E) skeptical

3. PLACATE
   (A) amuse
   (B) appease
   (C) embroil
   (D) pity
   (E) reject

4. COGNIZANT
   (A) afraid
   (B) aware
   (C) capable
   (D) ignorant
   (E) optimistic

5. DISSONANCE
   (A) disapproval
   (B) disaster
   (C) discord
   (D) disparity
   (E) dissimilarity

6. IMMINENT
   (A) declining
   (B) distinguished
   (C) impending
   (D) terrifying
   (E) unlikely

7. TORSION
   (A) bending
   (B) compressing
   (C) sliding
   (D) stretching
   (E) twisting

8. ACCRUED
   (A) added
   (B) incidental
   (C) miscellaneous
   (D) special
   (E) unearned

9. EFFRONTERY
   (A) bad taste
   (B) conceit
   (C) dishonesty
   (D) impudence
   (E) snobbishness

10. ACQUIESCENCE
   (A) advice
   (B) advocacy
   (C) compliance
   (D) friendliness
   (E) opposition

Vocabulary Test 14

1. RETICENT
   (A) fidgety
   (B) repetitious
   (C) reserved
   (D) restful
   (E) truthful

2. STIPULATE
   (A) bargain
   (B) instigate
   (C) prefer
   (D) request
   (E) specify

3. PSEUDO
   (A) deep
   (B) obvious
   (C) pretended
   (D) provoking
   (E) spiritual

4. FLOTSAM
   (A) dark sand
   (B) fleet
   (C) life preserver
   (D) shoreline
   (E) wreckage

5. AWRY
   (A) askew
   (B) deplorable
   (C) odd
   (D) simple
   (E) striking

6. NEFARIOUS
   (A) clever
   (B) necessary
   (C) negligent
   (D) short-sighted
   (E) wicked

7. GLIB
   (A) cheerful
   (B) delightful
   (C) dull
   (D) fluent
   (E) gloomy

8. PAUCITY
   (A) abundance
   (B) ease
   (C) hardship
   (D) lack
   (E) stoppage

9. LUCRATIVE
   (A) debasing
   (B) fortunate
   (C) influential
   (D) monetary
   (E) profitable

10. INDUBITABLE
   (A) doubtful
   (B) fraudulent
   (C) honorable
   (D) safe
   (E) undeniable

Vocabulary Test 15

1. CONNIVANCE
   (A) approval
   (B) collusion
   (C) conflict
   (D) permission
   (E) theft

2. SAVANT
   (A) diplomat
   (B) inventor
   (C) learned person
   (D) thrifty person
   (E) wiseacre

3. INCIPIENT
   (A) beginning
   (B) dangerous
   (C) hasty
   (D) secret
   (E) widespread

4. VIRILE
   (A) honest
   (B) loyal
   (C) manly
   (D) pugnacious
   (E) virtuous

5. ASSIDUOUS
(A) courteous
(B) diligent
(C) discouraged
(D) frank
(E) slow

6. CATACLYSM
(A) blunder
(B) superstition
(C) treachery
(D) triumph
(E) upheaval

7. AUSPICIOUS
(A) condemnatory
(B) conspicuous
(C) favorable
(D) questionable
(E) spicy

8. SATIRE
(A) conversation
(B) criticism
(C) gossip
(D) irony
(E) jesting

9. VERNACULAR
(A) common speech
(B) correct usage
(C) long words
(D) oratory
(E) poetic style

10. EMOLUMENT
(A) capital
(B) compensation
(C) liabilities
(D) loss
(E) output

Vocabulary Test 16

1. TURGID
(A) dusty
(B) muddy
(C) rolling
(D) swollen
(E) tense

2. EXPUNGE
(A) clarify
(B) copy
(C) delete
(D) investigate
(E) underline

3. ETHNOLOGY
(A) causation
(B) morals
(C) social psychology
(D) study of races
(E) word analysis

4. DEDUCE
(A) diminish
(B) infer
(C) outline
(D) persuade
(E) subtract

5. PANORAMIC
(A) brilliant
(B) comprehensive
(C) pretty
(D) fluorescent
(E) unique

6. IGNOMINY
(A) disgrace
(B) isolation
(C) misfortune
(D) sorrow
(E) stupidity

7. RELEVANT
(A) ingenious
(B) inspiring
(C) obvious
(D) pertinent
(E) tentative

8. GAMUT
(A) game
(B) range
(C) risk
(D) organization
(E) plan

9. APPOSITE
(A) appropriate
(B) contrary
(C) different
(D) spontaneous
(E) tricky

10. AMBULATORY
(A) able to walk
(B) confined to bed
(C) injured
(D) quarantined
(E) suffering from disease

Vocabulary Test 17

1. DISPARAGE
(A) belittle
(B) upgrade
(C) erase
(D) reform
(E) scatter

2. LIMPID
(A) calm
(B) clear
(C) crippled
(D) delightful
(E) opaque

3. DERISIVE
(A) dividing
(B) furnishing
(C) reflecting
(D) expressing ridicule
(E) suggesting

4. DEBILITATE
(A) encourage
(B) insinuate
(C) prepare
(D) turn away
(E) weaken

5. OPULENT
(A) fearful
(B) free
(C) oversized
(D) trustful
(E) wealthy

6. BLANDISHMENT
(A) dislike
(B) flattery
(C) ostentation
(D) praise
(E) rejection

7. CRYPTIC
(A) appealing
(B) arched
(C) deathly
(D) hidden
(E) intricate

8. RAUCOUS
(A) harsh
(B) loud
(C) querulous
(D) rational
(E) violent

9. AVIDITY
(A) friendliness
(B) greediness
(C) resentment
(D) speed
(E) thirst

10. EPITOME
(A) conclusion
(B) effort
(C) letter
(D) summary
(E) summit

Vocabulary Test 18

1. HIATUS
(A) branch
(B) disease
(C) gaiety
(D) insect
(E) break

2. PLENARY
(A) easy
(B) empty
(C) full
(D) rewarding
(E) untrustworthy

3. CAPRICIOUS
(A) active
(B) fickle
(C) opposed
(D) sheeplike
(E) slippery

4. SPECIOUS
(A) frank
(B) particular
(C) deceptive
(D) suspicious
(E) vigorous

5. EXTIRPATE
(A) besmirch
(B) clean
(C) eradicate
(D) favor
(E) subdivide

6. EQUIVOCAL
(A) doubtful
(B) medium
(C) monotonous
(D) musical
(E) well-balanced

7. RECOMPENSE
(A) approval
(B) blessing
(C) gift
(D) prayer
(E) reward

8. BEATIFIC
(A) giving bliss
(B) eager
(C) hesitant
(D) lovely
(E) sad

9. SANGUINE
(A) limp
(B) mechanical
(C) muddy
(D) red
(E) stealthy

10. SURCEASE
(A) end
(B) hope
(C) resignation
(D) sleep
(E) sweetness

Vocabulary Test 19

1. SENTIENT
(A) very emotional
(B) capable of feeling
(C) hostile
(D) sympathetic
(E) wise

2. OBVIATE
(A) grasp
(B) reform
(C) simplify
(D) smooth
(E) make unnecessary

3. PERUSE
(A) endure
(B) perpetuate
(C) read
(D) undertake
(E) urge

4. RANCOR
(A) dignity
(B) fierceness
(C) odor
(D) spite
(E) suspicion

5. TRUNCHEON
(A) baton
(B) canopy
(C) dish
(D) gun
(E) rejected food

6. SEBACEOUS
(A) fatty
(B) fluid
(C) porous
(D) transparent
(E) watery

7. DILATORY
(A) hairy
(B) happy-go-lucky
(C) ruined
(D) tardy
(E) well-to-do

8. EBULLITION
(A) bathing
(B) boiling
(C) refilling
(D) retiring
(E) returning

9. RELEGATE
(A) banish
(B) deprive
(C) designate
(D) report
(E) request

10. RECONDITE
(A) brittle
(B) concealed
(C) explored
(D) exposed
(E) uninformed

Vocabulary Test 20

1. REDOLENT
(A) odorous
(B) quick
(C) refined
(D) repulsive
(E) supple

2. DISSIMULATE
(A) confound
(B) pretend
(C) question
(D) separate
(E) strain

3. SUBLIME
(A) below par
(B) highly praised
(C) extreme
(D) noble
(E) settled

4. VIXEN
(A) fever
(B) quarrelsome woman
(C) sea bird
(D) sedative
(E) squirrel

5. SEDULOUS
(A) deceptive
(B) diligent
(C) grassy
(D) hateful
(E) sweet

6. VITIATE
(A) contaminate
(B) flavor
(C) freshen
(D) illuminate
(E) refer

7. CURVET
(A) come around
(B) follow
(C) leap
(D) restrain
(E) warp

8. ADVENTITIOUS
(A) accidental
(B) courageous
(C) favorable
(D) risk-taking
(E) expected

9. ANIMUS
(A) animosity
(B) breath
(C) faith
(D) light
(E) poison

10. DESCRIED
(A) hailed
(B) rebuffed
(C) recalled
(D) regretted
(E) sighted

Vocabulary Test 21

1. ADULATION
(A) approach
(B) echo
(C) flattery
(D) gift
(E) imitation

2. SUBSEQUENTLY
(A) continually
(B) factually
(C) farther
(D) incidentally
(E) later

3. EXPURGATE
(A) amplify
(B) emphasize
(C) offend
(D) purify
(E) renew

4. LIAISON
(A) derivative
(B) liability
(C) link
(D) malice
(E) officer

5. SEDENTARY
(A) careful
(B) inactive
(C) notched
(D) pleasant
(E) uneventful

6. LASSITUDE
(A) childishness
(B) energy
(C) ignorance
(D) languor
(E) seriousness

7. ALTRUISTICALLY
(A) egotistically
(B) harmfully
(C) harshly
(D) highly
(E) unselfishly

8. PERFIDIOUS
(A) ambiguous
(B) flawless
(C) perforated
(D) treacherous
(E) trusting

9. CONSUMMATE
(A) achieve
(B) devour
(C) effuse
(D) ignite
(E) take

10. MUNIFICENTLY
(A) acutely
(B) awkwardly
(C) cruelly
(D) generously
(E) militarily

Vocabulary Test 22

1. LUGUBRIOUS
(A) calm
(B) doleful
(C) tepid
(D) wan
(E) warm

2. DISCONSOLATE
(A) desolate
(B) emotional
(C) incorrigible
(D) gloomy
(E) sad

3. COTERIE
(A) clique
(B) cure-all
(C) expert judge
(D) forerunner
(E) society girl

4. CONDUIT
(A) doorway
(B) electric generator
(C) power
(D) screen
(E) tube

5. SHIBBOLETH
(A) a friend in need
(B) lonely home
(C) personal complaint
(D) reason for action
(E) watchword

6. EVANESCENT
(A) colorful
(B) consecrated
(C) converted
(D) empty
(E) vanishing

7. PARSIMONIOUS
(A) cautious
(B) ecclesiastical
(C) luxurious
(D) stingy
(E) unique

8. MACHIAVELLIAN
(A) cunning
(B) humble
(C) kingly
(D) machinelike
(E) saintly

9. COMPENDIUM
(A) amplification
(B) appendix
(C) expansion
(D) paraphrase
(E) summary

10. MEGALOMANIA
(A) desire for beauty
(B) mania for sympathy
(C) miserliness
(D) passion for grandeur
(E) pity for the poor

Vocabulary Test 23

1. TORPOR
(A) cyclone
(B) frenzy
(C) sluggishness
(D) strain
(E) twisting

2. ESOTERIC
(A) clear
(B) external
(C) popular
(D) secret
(E) uncertain

3. SUPERCILIOUSLY
(A) critically
(B) haughtily
(C) hypersensitively
(D) naïvely
(E) softly

4. ABSTEMIOUS
(A) blatant
(B) exhilarating
(C) greedy
(D) temperate
(E) wasteful

5. KEN
(A) acceptance
(B) belief
(C) dune
(D) knowledge
(E) woody glen

6. GERMANE
(A) diseased
(B) foreign
(C) infected
(D) pertinent
(E) polished

7. VITUPERATION
(A) abuse
(B) appendectomy
(C) complication
(D) rejuvenation
(E) repeal

8. CHIMERICAL
(A) clever
(B) imaginary
(C) experimental
(D) foreign
(E) provisional

9. DULCIMER
(A) dolly
(B) doublet
(C) duenna
(D) gadget
(E) musical instrument

10. SARTORIAL
(A) disheveled
(B) frozen
(C) satirical
(D) tailored
(E) warm

Vocabulary Test 24

1. VERTIGO
(A) curiosity
(B) dizziness
(C) enlivenment
(D) greenness
(E) invigoration

2. DEBACLE
(A) ceremony
(B) collapse
(C) dance
(D) deficit
(E) dispute

3. CONDIGN
(A) deserved
(B) hidden
(C) perplexed
(D) pretended
(E) unworthy

4. EPHEMERALLY
(A) enduringly
(B) lightly
(C) openly
(D) suspiciously
(E) transiently

5. HISTRIONIC
(A) authentic
(B) hysterical
(C) reportorial
(D) sibilant
(E) theatrical

6. URBANITY
(A) aggressiveness
(B) mercenary
(C) municipality
(D) rustic
(E) suavity

7. TRUCULENT
(A) rambling
(B) relenting
(C) savage
(D) tranquil
(E) weary

8. INVEIGH
(A) allure
(B) entice
(C) guide cautiously
(D) originate
(E) speak bitterly

9. DESULTORY
(A) delaying
(B) disconnected
(C) flagrant
(D) insulting
(E) irritating

10. INGENUOUS
(A) clever
(B) naïve
(C) ignorant
(D) native
(E) unkind

Vocabulary Test 25

1. CUMULATIVE
(A) additive
(B) clumsy
(C) cumbersome
(D) incorrect
(E) secretive

2. EPIGRAM
(A) chemical term
(B) exclamation
(C) outer skin
(D) pithy saying
(E) tombstone

3. GESTICULATE
(A) dance
(B) digest easily
(C) ridicule
(D) travel
(E) use gestures

4. BEGUILE
(A) benefit
(B) bind
(C) deceive
(D) envy
(E) petition

5. AVID
(A) eager
(B) glowing
(C) indifferent
(D) lax
(E) potent

6. LABYRINTH
(A) laboratory
(B) maze
(C) path
(D) portal
(E) room

7. REGURGITATE
(A) make new investments
(B) obliterate
(C) restore to solvency
(D) slacken
(E) surge back

8. PODIUM
(A) chemical element
(B) dais
(C) foot specialist
(D) magistrate
(E) Roman infantryman

9. BEREFT
(A) annoyed
(B) awarded
(C) deprived
(D) enraged
(E) insane

10. ELUCIDATE
(A) condense
(B) escape
(C) evade
(D) explain
(E) shine through

Vocabulary Test 26

1. EMOLLIENT
(A) comical
(B) despicable
(C) enthusiastic
(D) raucous
(E) soothing

2. NOSTALGIC
(A) expressive
(B) forgetful
(C) homesick
(D) inconstant
(E) seasick

3. EXPIATE
(A) atone for
(B) die
(C) hasten
(D) imitate
(E) make holy

4. PARADOX
(A) accepted opinion
(B) axiom
(C) contradiction
(D) enigma
(E) pattern

5. ARCHETYPE
(A) bowman
(B) original model
(C) public records
(D) roguishness
(E) star

6. MUNDANE
(A) deformed
(B) free
(C) rough-shelled
(D) tearful
(E) worldly

7. PALLIATIVE
(A) boring
(B) callous
(C) permanent
(D) softening
(E) unyielding

8. FOMENT
(A) curb
(B) explode
(C) exclude
(D) turn into wine
(E) instigate

9. PREDACIOUS
(A) beautiful
(B) incongruous
(C) peaceful
(D) preying
(E) valuable

10. RESILIENT
(A) thrifty
(B) elastic
(C) timid
(D) fragile
(E) unsociable

Vocabulary Test 27

1. BLATANT
(A) clamorous
(B) conceited
(C) prudish
(D) reticent
(E) unsuited

2. ADVERSITY
(A) advertising
(B) counsel
(C) criticism
(D) misfortune
(E) proficiency

3. CADAVEROUS
(A) cheerful
(B) contemptible
(C) ghastly
(D) hungry
(E) ill-bred

4. WRAITH
(A) anger
(B) apparition
(C) figurine
(D) mannequin
(E) model

5. PERSPICACITY
(A) clearness
(B) dullness
(C) keenness
(D) vastness
(E) wideness

6. EXTRANEOUS
(A) derived
(B) foreign
(C) unsuitable
(D) visible
(E) wasteful

7. PAROXYSM
(A) catastrophe
(B) sudden outburst
(C) illusion
(D) lack of harmony
(E) loss of all bodily movement

8. SAPIENT
(A) discerning
(B) foolish
(C) mocking
(D) soapy
(E) youthful

9. FLACCID
(A) flabby
(B) golden
(C) hard
(D) strong
(E) wiry

10. IMPECUNIOUS
(A) frugal
(B) guiltless
(C) miserly
(D) monied
(E) poor

Vocabulary Test 28

1. ABDUCT
(A) ruin
(B) aid
(C) fight
(D) abolish
(E) kidnap

2. DEMERIT
(A) outcome
(B) fault
(C) prize
(D) notice
(E) belief

3. MUTINOUS
(A) silent
(B) oceangoing
(C) rebellious
(D) miserable
(E) deaf

4. NEGLIGENT
(A) lax
(B) desperate
(C) cowardly
(D) ambitious
(E) informal

5. CONTEST
(A) disturb
(B) dispute
(C) detain
(D) distrust
(E) contain

6. QUERY
(A) wait
(B) lose
(C) show
(D) ask
(E) demand

7. INSIDIOUS
(A) treacherous
(B) excitable
(C) internal
(D) distracting
(E) secretive

8. PALPITATE
(A) mash
(B) stifle
(C) creak
(D) pace
(E) throb

9. ANIMOSITY
(A) hatred
(B) interest
(C) silliness
(D) amusement
(E) power

10. EGOTISM
(A) sociability
(B) aggressiveness
(C) self-confidence
(D) conceit
(E) willingness

Vocabulary Test 29

1. CALLIGRAPHY
(A) weaving
(B) handwriting
(C) drafting
(D) mapmaking
(E) graph making

2. SYNCHRONIZE
(A) happen at the same time
(B) follow immediately in time
(C) alternate between events
(D) postpone to a future time
(E) have difficulty in hearing

3. SEMBLANCE
(A) surface
(B) diplomacy
(C) replacement
(D) appearance
(E) confidence

4. WISTFUL
(A) winding
(B) mutual
(C) exciting
(D) rugged
(E) yearning

5. CURTAIL
(A) threaten
(B) strengthen
(C) lessen
(D) hasten
(E) collide

6. NOXIOUS
(A) spicy
(B) smelly
(C) foreign
(D) noisy
(E) harmful

7. PAUCITY
(A) fatigue
(B) scarcity
(C) nonsense
(D) waste
(E) motion

8. JEOPARDIZE
(A) soothe
(B) cleanse
(C) enjoy
(D) reward
(E) endanger

9. INTREPID
(A) exhausted
(B) moderate
(C) anxious
(D) youthful
(E) fearless

10. TREACHEROUS
(A) ignorant
(B) envious
(C) disloyal
(D) cowardly
(E) inconsiderate

Vocabulary Test 30

1. UNSAVORY
(A) unfriendly
(B) joyless
(C) tactless
(D) colorless
(E) tasteless

2. HEARSAY
(A) testimony
(B) argument
(C) rumor
(D) accusation
(E) similarity

3. HAMPER
(A) restrain
(B) pack
(C) clarify
(D) grip
(E) err

4. BEDLAM
(A) inadequacy
(B) confusion
(C) translation
(D) courtesy
(E) curiosity

5. INFALLIBLE
(A) negative
(B) unfair
(C) essential
(D) certain
(E) weary

6. CONTEND
(A) solve
(B) observe
(C) outwit
(D) encourage
(E) compete

7. AMOROUS
(A) shapeless
(B) helpful
(C) familiar
(D) loving
(E) solemn

8. ALLEVIATE
(A) reject
(B) ease
(C) imitate
(D) consent
(E) elevate

9. NEOPHYTE
(A) participant
(B) officer
(C) beginner
(D) winner
(E) quarrel

10. SOLACE
(A) comfort
(B) weariness
(C) direction
(D) complaint
(E) respect

Vocabulary Test 31

1. ULTIMATUM
(A) shrewd plan
(B) final terms
(C) first defeat
(D) dominant leader
(E) electric motor

2. GIRD
(A) surround
(B) appeal
(C) request
(D) break
(E) glance

3. WANGLE
(A) moan
(B) mutilate
(C) exasperate
(D) manipulate
(E) triumph

4. PROCUREMENT
(A) acquisition
(B) resolution
(C) healing
(D) importance
(E) miracle

5. CULMINATION
(A) rebellion
(B) lighting system
(C) climax
(D) destruction
(E) mystery

6. INSUPERABLE
(A) incomprehensible
(B) elaborate
(C) unusual
(D) indigestible
(E) unconquerable

7. CLICHÉ
(A) summary argument
(B) new information
(C) new hat
(D) trite phrase
(E) lock device

8. CONCESSION
(A) nourishment
(B) plea
(C) restoration
(D) similarity
(E) acknowledgment

9. INSIPID
(A) disrespectful
(B) uninteresting
(C) persistent
(D) whole
(E) stimulating

10. REPRISAL
(A) retaliation
(B) drawing
(C) capture
(D) release
(E) suspicion

Vocabulary Test 32

1. DUBIOUS
(A) economical
(B) well-groomed
(C) boring
(D) discouraged
(E) uncertain

2. ATROCIOUS
(A) brutal
(B) innocent
(C) shrunken
(D) yellowish
(E) unsound

3. PRESTIGE
(A) speed
(B) influence
(C) omen
(D) pride
(E) excuse

4. VINDICATE
(A) outrage
(B) waver
(C) enliven
(D) justify
(E) fuse

5. EXUDE
(A) accuse
(B) discharge
(C) inflect
(D) appropriate
(E) distress

6. FACTION
(A) clique
(B) judgment
(C) truth
(D) type of architecture
(E) health

7. INCLEMENT
(A) merciful
(B) sloping
(C) harsh
(D) disastrous
(E) personal

8. SPURIOUS
(A) concise
(B) false
(C) obstinate
(D) sarcastic
(E) severe

9. SUBSERVIENT
(A) existing
(B) obsequious
(C) related
(D) underlying
(E) useful

10. IMPORTUNE
(A) aggrandize
(B) carry
(C) exaggerate
(D) prolong
(E) urge

Vocabulary Test 33

1. CONTROVERSIAL
(A) faultfinding
(B) pleasant
(C) debatable
(D) ugly
(E) talkative

2. GHASTLY
(A) hasty
(B) furious
(C) breathless
(D) deathlike
(E) spiritual

3. BELLIGERENT
(A) worldly
(B) warlike
(C) loudmouthed
(D) furious
(E) artistic

4. PROFICIENCY
(A) wisdom
(B) oversupply
(C) expertness
(D) advancement
(E) sincerity

5. COMPASSION
(A) rage
(B) strength of character
(C) forcefulness
(D) sympathy
(E) uniformity

6. DISSENSION
(A) treatise
(B) pretense
(C) fear
(D) lineage
(E) discord

7. INTIMATE
(A) charm
(B) hint
(C) disguise
(D) frighten
(E) hum

8. BERATE
(A) classify
(B) scold
(C) underestimate
(D) take one's time
(E) evaluate

9. DEARTH
(A) scarcity
(B) width
(C) affection
(D) wealth
(E) warmth

10. MEDITATE
(A) rest
(B) stare
(C) doze
(D) make peace
(E) reflect

Vocabulary Test 34

1. STAGNANT
(A) inactive
(B) alert
(C) selfish
(D) difficult
(E) scornful

2. MANDATORY
(A) insane
(B) obligatory
(C) evident
(D) strategic
(E) unequaled

3. INFERNAL
(A) immodest
(B) incomplete
(C) domestic
(D) second-rate
(E) fiendish

4. EXONERATE
(A) free from blame
(B) warn
(C) drive out
(D) overcharge
(E) plead

5. ARBITER
(A) friend
(B) judge
(C) drug
(D) tree surgeon
(E) truant

6. ENMITY
(A) boredom
(B) puzzle
(C) offensive language
(D) ill will
(E) entanglement

7. DISCRIMINATE
(A) fail
(B) delay
(C) accuse
(D) distinguish
(E) reject

8. DERISION
(A) disgust
(B) ridicule
(C) fear
(D) anger
(E) heredity

9. EXULTANT
(A) essential
(B) elated
(C) praiseworthy
(D) plentiful
(E) high-priced

10. OSTENSIBLE
(A) vibrating
(B) odd
(C) apparent
(D) standard
(E) ornate

Vocabulary Test 35

1. ABHOR
(A) hate
(B) admire
(C) taste
(D) skip
(E) resign

2. DUTIFUL
(A) lasting
(B) sluggish
(C) required
(D) soothing
(E) obedient

3. ZEALOT
(A) breeze
(B) enthusiast
(C) vault
(D) wild animal
(E) musical instrument

4. MAGNANIMOUS
(A) high-minded
(B) faithful
(C) concerned
(D) individual
(E) small

5. CITE
(A) protest
(B) depart
(C) quote
(D) agitate
(E) perform

6. OBLIVION
(A) hindrance
(B) accident
(C) courtesy
(D) forgetfulness
(E) old age

7. CARDINAL
(A) independent
(B) well-organized
(C) subordinate
(D) dignified
(E) chief

8. DEPLETE
(A) restrain
(B) corrupt
(C) despair
(D) exhaust
(E) spread out

9. SUPERSEDE
(A) retire
(B) replace
(C) overflow
(D) bless
(E) oversee

10. SPORADIC
(A) bad-tempered
(B) infrequent
(C) radical
(D) reckless
(E) humble

Vocabulary Test 36

1. NEUTRALIZE
(A) entangle
(B) strengthen
(C) counteract
(D) combat
(E) converse

2. INSINUATE
(A) destroy
(B) hint
(C) do wrong
(D) accuse
(E) release

3. DIMINUTIVE
(A) proud
(B) slow
(C) small
(D) watery
(E) puzzling

4. PLIGHT
(A) departure
(B) weight
(C) conspiracy
(D) predicament
(E) stamp

5. ILLICIT
(A) unlawful
(B) overpowering
(C) ill-advised
(D) small-scale
(E) unreadable

6. BENIGN
(A) contagious
(B) fatal
(C) ignorant
(D) kindly
(E) decorative

7. REVERIE
(A) abusive language
(B) love song
(C) backward step
(D) daydream
(E) holy man

8. APPREHENSIVE
(A) quiet
(B) firm
(C) curious
(D) sincere
(E) fearful

9. RECOIL
(A) shrink
(B) attract
(C) electrify
(D) adjust
(E) enroll

10. GUISE
(A) trickery
(B) request
(C) innocence
(D) misdeed
(E) appearance

Vocabulary Test 37

1. ACQUIT
   (A) increase
   (B) harden
   (C) clear
   (D) sharpen
   (E) sentence

2. DEXTERITY
   (A) conceit
   (B) skill
   (C) insistence
   (D) embarrassment
   (E) guidance

3. ASSIMILATE
   (A) absorb
   (B) imitate
   (C) maintain
   (D) outrun
   (E) curb

4. DESPONDENCY
   (A) relief
   (B) gratitude
   (C) dejection
   (D) hatred
   (E) poverty

5. BUOYANT
   (A) conceited
   (B) cautioning
   (C) youthful
   (D) musical
   (E) cheerful

6. CULINARY
   (A) having to do with cooking
   (B) pertaining to dressmaking
   (C) fond of eating
   (D) loving money
   (E) tending to be secretive

7. CAPRICE
   (A) wisdom
   (B) ornament
   (C) pillar
   (D) whim
   (E) energy

8. DETERRENT
   (A) restraining
   (B) cleansing
   (C) deciding
   (D) concluding
   (E) crumbling

9. PUGNACIOUS
   (A) sticky
   (B) cowardly
   (C) precise
   (D) vigorous
   (E) quarrelsome

10. ABSCOND
   (A) detest
   (B) reduce
   (C) swallow up
   (D) dismiss
   (E) flee

Vocabulary Test 38

1. BOUNTY
   (A) limit
   (B) boastfulness
   (C) cheerfulness
   (D) reward
   (E) punishment

2. NOVICE
   (A) storyteller
   (B) iceberg
   (C) adolescent
   (D) mythical creature
   (E) beginner

3. BOLSTER
   (A) contradict
   (B) insist
   (C) defy
   (D) sleep
   (E) prop

4. MOBILE
   (A) changeable
   (B) scornful
   (C) mechanical
   (D) stylish
   (E) solid

5. CREDULITY
   (A) prize
   (B) feebleness
   (C) balance
   (D) laziness
   (E) belief

6. DOLDRUMS
   (A) charity
   (B) curing agents
   (C) contagious disease
   (D) low spirits
   (E) places of safety

7. LOATH
   (A) idle
   (B) worried
   (C) unwilling
   (D) ready
   (E) sad

8. INVENTIVE
   (A) aimless
   (B) clever
   (C) moist
   (D) false
   (E) nearby

9. LITHE
   (A) tough
   (B) obstinate
   (C) flexible
   (D) damp
   (E) gay

10. VACILLATE
   (A) waver
   (B) defeat
   (C) favor
   (D) endanger
   (E) humiliate

Vocabulary Test 39

1. OBNOXIOUS
   (A) dreamy
   (B) visible
   (C) angry
   (D) daring
   (E) objectionable

2. VERBATIM
   (A) word for word
   (B) at will
   (C) without fail
   (D) in secret
   (E) in summary

3. ENTICE
   (A) inform
   (B) observe
   (C) permit
   (D) attract
   (E) disobey

4. ACCLAIM
   (A) discharge
   (B) excel
   (C) applaud
   (D) divide
   (E) speed

5. TURBULENCE
(A) treachery
(B) commotion
(C) fear
(D) triumph
(E) overflow

6. DEFER
(A) discourage
(B) postpone
(C) empty
(D) minimize
(E) estimate

7. ADAGE
(A) proverb
(B) supplement
(C) tool
(D) youth
(E) hardness

8. ENSUE
(A) compel
(B) remain
(C) absorb
(D) plead
(E) follow

9. ZENITH
(A) lowest point
(B) compass
(C) summit
(D) middle
(E) wind direction

10. HYPOTHETICAL
(A) magical
(B) visual
(C) two-faced
(D) theoretical
(E) excitable

Vocabulary Test 40

1. IMPROMPTU
(A) offhand
(B) laughable
(C) fascinating
(D) rehearsed
(E) deceptive

2. CHIVALROUS
(A) crude
(B) military
(C) handsome
(D) foreign
(E) courteous

3. HAVOC
(A) festival
(B) disease
(C) ruin
(D) sea battle
(E) luggage

4. REJUVENATE
(A) reply
(B) renew
(C) age
(D) judge
(E) reconsider

5. STILTED
(A) stiffly formal
(B) talking much
(C) secretive
(D) fashionable
(E) senseless

6. SOLILOQUY
(A) figure of speech
(B) historical incident
(C) monologue
(D) isolated position
(E) contradiction

7. AFFABLE
(A) monotonous
(B) affected
(C) wealthy
(D) sociable
(E) selfish

8. NEBULOUS
(A) subdued
(B) eternal
(C) dewy
(D) cloudy
(E) careless

9. STEREOTYPED
(A) lacking originality
(B) illuminating
(C) pictorial
(D) free from disease
(E) sparkling

10. STUPEFY
(A) lie
(B) talk nonsense
(C) bend
(D) make dull
(E) overeat

Vocabulary Test 41

1. SUPERFICIAL
(A) shallow
(B) unusually fine
(C) proud
(D) aged
(E) spiritual

2. DISPARAGE
(A) separate
(B) compare
(C) refuse
(D) belittle
(E) imitate

3. PROTAGONIST
(A) prophet
(B) explorer
(C) talented child
(D) convert
(E) leading character

4. LUDICROUS
(A) profitable
(B) excessive
(C) disordered
(D) ridiculous
(E) undesirable

5. INTREPID
(A) moist
(B) tolerant
(C) fearless
(D) rude
(E) gay

6. SAGE
(A) wise man
(B) tropical tree
(C) tale
(D) era
(E) fool

7. ADMONISH
(A) polish
(B) escape
(C) worship
(D) distribute
(E) caution

8. BESET
(A) plead
(B) perplex
(C) pertain to
(D) deny
(E) harass

9. FIGMENT
(A) ornamental openwork
(B) perfume
(C) undeveloped fruit
(D) statuette
(E) invention

10. GLIB
(A) dull
(B) thin
(C) weak
(D) fluent
(E) sharp

Vocabulary Test 42

1. FORTITUDE
(A) wealth
(B) courage
(C) honesty
(D) loudness
(E) luck

2. ABOLITION
(A) retirement
(B) disgust
(C) enslavement
(D) unrestricted power
(E) complete destruction

3. EPITOME
(A) pool
(B) summary
(C) formula
(D) monster
(E) song

4. MAIM
(A) heal
(B) disable
(C) outwit
(D) murder
(E) bury

5. CRESTFALLEN
(A) haughty
(B) dejected
(C) fatigued
(D) disfigured
(E) impolite

6. CUISINE
(A) headdress
(B) game of chance
(C) leisurely voyage
(D) artistry
(E) style of cooking

7. CENSURE
(A) erase
(B) build up
(C) criticize adversely
(D) charm
(E) help

8. DEVIATE
(A) destroy
(B) lower in value
(C) invent
(D) stray
(E) depress

9. SWARTHY
(A) dark-complexioned
(B) slender
(C) grass-covered
(D) springy
(E) rotating

10. MERCENARY
(A) poisonous
(B) unworthy
(C) serving only for pay
(D) luring by false charms
(E) showing pity

Vocabulary Test 43

1. ACUTE
(A) keen
(B) bitter
(C) brisk
(D) genuine
(E) certain

2. CLIENTELE
(A) legal body
(B) customers
(C) board of directors
(D) servants
(E) tenants

3. SUCCUMB
(A) follow
(B) help
(C) respond
(D) yield
(E) overthrow

4. SLOTH
(A) selfishness
(B) hatred
(C) laziness
(D) misery
(E) slipperiness

5. INFRINGE
(A) enrage
(B) expand
(C) disappoint
(D) weaken
(E) trespass

6. UNCANNY
(A) ill-humored
(B) immature
(C) weird
(D) unrestrained
(E) insincere

7. SUBMISSIVE
(A) unintelligent
(B) underhanded
(C) destructive
(D) enthusiastic
(E) meek

8. PEER
(A) ancestor
(B) teacher
(C) judge
(D) equal
(E) assistant

9. EULOGIZE
(A) kill
(B) apologize
(C) glorify
(D) soften
(E) imitate

10. INNOVATION
(A) change
(B) prayer
(C) hint
(D) restraint
(E) inquiry

Vocabulary Test 44

1. EXHILARATION
(A) animation
(B) withdrawal
(C) payment
(D) suffocation
(E) despair

2. RASPING
(A) irritating
(B) scolding
(C) fastening
(D) sighing
(E) plundering

3. PROPONENT
(A) spendthrift
(B) rival
(C) distributor
(D) advocate
(E) neighbor

4. REDUNDANT
(A) flooded
(B) dreadful
(C) aromatic
(D) excessive
(E) reclining

5. BEGRUDGING
(A) humid
(B) envious
(C) living in seclusion
(D) involving a choice
(E) aimless

6. EMPATHIZE
(A) cheapen
(B) underestimate
(C) charm
(D) sympathize
(E) forgive

7. PRUDENT
(A) lighthearted
(B) eager
(C) cautious
(D) insincere
(E) fast-moving

8. OMNIVOROUS
(A) devouring everything
(B) many-sided
(C) powerful
(D) living on plants
(E) all-knowing

9. APPEND
(A) rely
(B) recognize
(C) arrest
(D) divide
(E) attach

10. STRATAGEM
(A) sneak attack
(B) military command
(C) thin layer
(D) deceptive device
(E) narrow passage

Vocabulary Test 45

1. COLLABORATE
(A) condense
(B) converse
(C) arrange in order
(D) provide proof
(E) act jointly

2. FUTILITY
(A) uselessness
(B) timelessness
(C) stinginess
(D) happiness
(E) indistinctness

3. INTACT
(A) blunt
(B) fashionable
(C) hidden
(D) uninjured
(E) attentive

4. FERVOR
(A) originality
(B) justice
(C) zeal
(D) productivity
(E) corruption

5. UNERRING
(A) modest
(B) illogical
(C) ghostly
(D) matchless
(E) unfailing

6. REFUTE
(A) polish
(B) disprove
(C) throw away
(D) break up
(E) shut out

7. CONSENSUS
(A) steadfastness of purpose
(B) general agreement
(C) lack of harmony
(D) informal vote
(E) impressive amount

8. COMPLIANT
(A) tangled
(B) grumbling
(C) self-satisfied
(D) treacherous
(E) submissive

9. ACCESS
(A) agreement
(B) rapidity
(C) welcome
(D) approach
(E) surplus

10. PRUDENT
(A) wise
(B) overcritical
(C) famous
(D) dull
(E) early

Vocabulary Test 46

1. APPEASE
(A) attack
(B) soothe
(C) pray for
(D) estimate
(E) confess

2. RUTHLESS
(A) senseless
(B) sinful
(C) ruddy
(D) pitiless
(E) degrading

3. MUSTER
(A) rebel
(B) mask
(C) gather
(D) dampen
(E) grumble

4. EXECRATE
(A) embarrass
(B) desert
(C) omit
(D) curse
(E) resign

5. KNOLL
(A) elf
(B) mound
(C) bell
(D) development
(E) technique

6. IRATE
(A) evil
(B) wandering
(C) repetitious
(D) colorful
(E) angry

7. GRIMACE
(A) peril
(B) subtle suggestion
(C) signal
(D) wry face
(E) impurity

8. ACME
(A) layer
(B) summit
(C) edge
(D) pit
(E) interval

9. COVENANT
(A) solemn agreement
(B) formal invitation
(C) religious ceremony
(D) general pardon
(E) hiding place

10. APPALL
(A) honor
(B) decorate
(C) calm
(D) bore
(E) dismay

Vocabulary Test 47

1. INCUR
(A) take to heart
(B) anticipate
(C) bring down on oneself
(D) impress by repetition
(E) attack

2. CAUSTIC
(A) solemn
(B) puzzling
(C) biting
(D) influential
(E) attentive

3. DILATE
(A) retard
(B) fade
(C) wander
(D) expand
(E) startle

4. APATHY
(A) fixed dislike
(B) skill
(C) sorrow
(D) lack of feeling
(E) discontent

5. ELICIT
(A) draw forth
(B) cross out
(C) run away
(D) lengthen
(E) revise

6. JUDICIOUS
(A) wise
(B) dignified
(C) lighthearted
(D) confused
(E) respectful

7. UNSCATHED
(A) unashamed
(B) uninjured
(C) unskilled
(D) unsuccessful
(E) unconscious

8. CHIDE
(A) misbehave
(B) cool
(C) select
(D) conceal
(E) scold

9. CHARLATAN
(A) scholar
(B) acrobat
(C) quack
(D) faithful servant
(E) fast talker

10. DISBURSE
(A) remove forcibly
(B) twist
(C) amuse
(D) vary slightly
(E) pay out

Vocabulary Test 48

1. PARAMOUNT
(A) equal
(B) supreme
(C) well-known
(D) difficult
(E) ready

2. BROCHURE
(A) heavy shoe
(B) weapon
(C) pamphlet
(D) trite remark
(E) ornament

3. FIDELITY
(A) happiness
(B) bravery
(C) prosperity
(D) hardness
(E) loyalty

4. DIFFUSE
(A) explain
(B) scatter
(C) differ
(D) congeal
(E) dart

5. AGGRESSIVE
(A) disgusting
(B) impulsive
(C) shortsighted
(D) coarse-grained
(E) self-assertive

6. AMASS
(A) accumulate
(B) encourage
(C) comprehend
(D) blend
(E) astonish

7. DIABOLIC
(A) puzzling
(B) uneducated
(C) ornamental
(D) fiendish
(E) spinning

8. FORBEARANCE
(A) rejection
(B) forgetfulness
(C) sensitivity
(D) patience
(E) expectation

9. TAINT
(A) snarl
(B) infect
(C) unite
(D) annoy
(E) list

10. DISGRUNTLED
(A) untidy
(B) rambling
(C) disabled
(D) cheating
(E) displeased

Vocabulary Test 49

1. PLACID
(A) apparent
(B) peaceful
(C) wicked
(D) unusual
(E) absent-minded

2. EVASIVE
(A) emotional
(B) effective
(C) destructive
(D) empty
(E) shifty

3. CHAOS
(A) complete disorder
(B) deep gorge
(C) challenge
(D) sudden attack
(E) rejoicing

4. DESPICABLE
(A) insulting
(B) ungrateful
(C) contemptible
(D) unbearable
(E) jealous

5. DERIDE
(A) question
(B) ignore
(C) mock
(D) unseat
(E) produce

6. ELUDE
(A) gladden
(B) fascinate
(C) mention
(D) escape
(E) ignore

7. MUTABLE
(A) colorless
(B) harmful
(C) uniform
(D) changeable
(E) invisible

8. INDICATIVE
(A) suggestive
(B) curious
(C) active
(D) angry
(E) certain

9. LEVITY
(A) cleanness
(B) tastiness
(C) deadliness
(D) sluggishness
(E) lightness

10. EXCRUCIATING
(A) disciplinary
(B) screaming
(C) torturing
(D) offensive
(E) outpouring

Vocabulary Test 50

1. PRECEPT
(A) rule
(B) disguise
(C) refinement
(D) hasty decision
(E) delaying action

2. HOMOGENEOUS
(A) numerous
(B) healthful
(C) similar
(D) assorted
(E) educational

3. ARCHIVES
(A) public records
(B) models
(C) supporting columns
(D) tombs
(E) large ships

4. INFAMY
(A) anger
(B) truth
(C) disgrace
(D) weakness
(E) excitement

5. IMPINGE
(A) swear
(B) involve
(C) erase
(D) encroach
(E) beg

6. DEPOSE
(A) lay bare
(B) deprive of office
(C) empty
(D) behead
(E) blemish

7. OSTENTATIOUS
(A) unruly
(B) showy
(C) varied
(D) scandalous
(E) probable

8. CONCLAVE
(A) private meeting
(B) covered passage
(C) solemn vow
(D) curved surface
(E) ornamental vase

9. FRAY
(A) combat
(B) trickery
(C) unreality
(D) madness
(E) freedom

10. OBSESS
(A) fatten
(B) beset
(C) make dull
(D) exaggerate
(E) interfere

Vocabulary Test 51

1. CHAFE
(A) pretend
(B) joke
(C) drink deeply
(D) irritate
(E) lose courage

2. MISCONSTRUE
(A) hate
(B) destroy
(C) misbehave
(D) misinterpret
(E) misplace

3. PHILANTHROPIST
(A) student of language
(B) collector of stamps
(C) lover of mankind
(D) seeker of truth
(E) enemy of culture

4. CASTE
(A) feudal system
(B) division of society
(C) political theory
(D) method of punishment
(E) monetary system

5. CHASTEN
(A) punish
(B) engrave
(C) attract
(D) trick
(E) laugh at

6. CONDUCIVE
(A) pardonable
(B) identical
(C) incidental
(D) helpful
(E) exceptional

7. SUBORDINATE
(A) hostile
(B) inferior
(C) separate
(D) earlier
(E) adaptable

8. SUPERFLUOUS
(A) inexact
(B) excessive
(C) insincere
(D) excellent
(E) unreal

9. WIELD
(A) protect
(B) handle
(C) postpone
(D) resign
(E) unite

10. GARISH
(A) showy
(B) talkative
(C) sleepy
(D) thin
(E) vine-covered

Vocabulary Test 52

1. MEANDER
(A) grumble
(B) wander aimlessly
(C) come between
(D) weigh carefully
(E) sing

2. DESTITUTION
(A) trickery
(B) fate
(C) lack of practice
(D) recovery
(E) extreme poverty

3. MALIGN
(A) slander
(B) prophesy
(C) entreat
(D) approve
(E) praise

4. IMPOTENT
(A) unwise
(B) lacking strength
(C) free of sin
(D) without shame
(E) commanding

5. SNIVEL
(A) crawl
(B) cut short
(C) whine
(D) doze
(E) giggle

6. SOJOURN
(A) court order
(B) nickname
(C) temporary stay
(D) slip of the tongue
(E) makeshift

7. PLATITUDE
(A) home remedy
(B) trite remark
(C) balance wheel
(D) rare animal
(E) protective film

8. CONCORD
(A) brevity
(B) blame
(C) kindness
(D) worry
(E) agreement

9. ABOMINABLE
(A) hateful
(B) ridiculous
(C) untamed
(D) mysterious
(E) boastful

10. QUALM
(A) sudden misgiving
(B) irritation
(C) cooling drink
(D) deceit
(E) attention to detail

Vocabulary Test 53

1. EQUITABLE
(A) charitable
(B) even-tempered
(C) two-faced
(D) undecided
(E) just

2. AFFRONT
(A) quarrel
(B) fright
(C) denial
(D) boast
(E) insult

3. EPOCH
(A) heroic deed
(B) legend
(C) witty saying
(D) period of time
(E) summary

4. RETRIBUTION
(A) donation
(B) jealousy
(C) intense emotion
(D) slow withdrawal
(E) punishment

5. ABASE
(A) forgive
(B) degrade
(C) attach
(D) take leave
(E) cut off

6. CAREEN
(A) celebrate
(B) mourn
(C) ridicule
(D) lurch
(E) beckon

7. CONVIVIAL
(A) formal
(B) gay
(C) rotating
(D) well-informed
(E) insulting

8. RAMPANT
(A) playful
(B) crumbling
(C) roundabout
(D) unchecked
(E) defensive

9. DOCILE
(A) delicate
(B) positive
(C) dreary
(D) obedient
(E) melodious

10. VESTIGE
(A) bone
(B) test
(C) entrance
(D) cloak
(E) trace

Vocabulary Test 54

1. IMPEDIMENT
(A) foundation
(B) conceit
(C) hindrance
(D) luggage
(E) instrument

2. ADHERE
(A) pursue
(B) control
(C) arrive
(D) cling
(E) attend

3. COMPOSURE
(A) sensitiveness
(B) weariness
(C) stylishness
(D) hopefulness
(E) calmness

4. PROVOCATION
(A) sacred vow
(B) formal announcement
(C) cause of irritation
(D) careful management
(E) expression of disgust

5. SAVORY
(A) thrifty
(B) wise
(C) appetizing
(D) warm
(E) uncivilized

6. CANDID
(A) hidden
(B) shining
(C) straightforward
(D) critical
(E) warmhearted

7. ECLIPSE
(A) stretch
(B) obscure
(C) glow
(D) overlook
(E) insert

8. CORRELATE
(A) punish
(B) wrinkle
(C) conspire openly
(D) give additional proof
(E) connect systematically

9. INFIRMITY
(A) disgrace
(B) unhappiness
(C) rigidity
(D) hesitation
(E) weakness

10. PALPITATE
(A) faint
(B) harden
(C) throb
(D) soothe
(E) taste

Vocabulary Test 55

1. DEBRIS
(A) sadness
(B) decay
(C) ruins
(D) landslide
(E) hindrance

2. CONSOLIDATE
(A) show pity
(B) strengthen
(C) restrain
(D) infect
(E) use up

3. STAMINA
(A) flatness
(B) clearness
(C) hesitation
(D) vigor
(E) reliability

4. FACET
(A) phase
(B) humor
(C) story
(D) discharge
(E) assistance

5. INANIMATE
(A) emotional
(B) thoughtless
(C) lifeless
(D) inexact
(E) silly

6. CALLOUS
(A) frantic
(B) misinformed
(C) youthful
(D) impolite
(E) unfeeling

7. ENHANCE
(A) sympathize
(B) act out
(C) weaken
(D) make greater
(E) fascinate

8. DISREPUTABLE
(A) impolite
(B) bewildered
(C) debatable
(D) unavailable
(E) shameful

9. SEDATE
(A) sober
(B) seated
(C) buried
(D) drugged
(E) timid

10. LUCRATIVE
(A) lazy
(B) coarse
(C) profitable
(D) brilliant
(E) amusing

Vocabulary Test 56

1. IMPRUDENT
(A) reckless
(B) unexcitable
(C) poor
(D) domineering
(E) powerless

2. DISSENSION
(A) friction
(B) analysis
(C) swelling
(D) injury
(E) slyness

3. DISCONCERT
(A) separate
(B) cripple
(C) lessen
(D) upset
(E) dismiss

4. RUDIMENTARY
(A) discourteous
(B) brutal
(C) displeasing
(D) elementary
(E) embarrassing

5. AUTONOMOUS
(A) self-governing
(B) self-important
(C) self-educated
(D) self-explanatory
(E) self-conscious

6. ASCERTAIN
(A) hold fast
(B) long for
(C) declare
(D) find out
(E) avoid

7. LITERAL
(A) flowery
(B) matter-of-fact
(C) sidewise
(D) well-educated
(E) firsthand

8. OSCILLATE
(A) please
(B) swing
(C) purify
(D) saturate
(E) harden

9. CONCISE
(A) accurate
(B) brief
(C) sudden
(D) similar
(E) painful

10. CONSTERNATION
(A) restraint
(B) close attention
(C) dismay
(D) self-importance
(E) acknowledgment

Vocabulary Test 57

1. COLOSSAL
(A) ancient
(B) influential
(C) destructive
(D) dramatic
(E) huge

2. EVICT
(A) summon
(B) excite
(C) force out
(D) prove
(E) draw off

3. MISCHANCE
(A) omission
(B) ill luck
(C) feeling of doubt
(D) unlawful act
(E) distrust

4. FELON
(A) criminal
(B) fugitive
(C) traitor
(D) coward
(E) loafer

5. CENSURE
(A) empty
(B) criticize
(C) spread out
(D) take an oath
(E) omit

6. IMPLICIT
(A) implied
(B) rude
(C) relentless
(D) sinful
(E) daring

7. SLOVENLY
(A) sleepy
(B) tricky
(C) untidy
(D) moody
(E) cowardly

8. EXTRANEOUS
(A) familiar
(B) unprepared
(C) foreign
(D) proper
(E) utmost

9. IMPASSE
(A) command
(B) stubbornness
(C) crisis
(D) deadlock
(E) failure

10. ABSOLVE
(A) forgive
(B) reduce
(C) mix
(D) deprive
(E) detect

Vocabulary Test 58

1. CUMBERSOME
(A) habitual
(B) clumsy
(C) hasty
(D) blameworthy
(E) uneducated

2. CAPTIVATE
(A) charm
(B) dictate terms
(C) overturn
(D) find fault
(E) hesitate

3. ZEALOUS
(A) serious
(B) speedy
(C) flawless
(D) necessary
(E) enthusiastic

4. AROMATIC
(A) shining
(B) precise
(C) ancient
(D) fragrant
(E) dry

5. RETROSPECT
(A) careful inspection
(B) reversal of form
(C) review of the past
(D) respect for authority
(E) special attention

6. WHET
(A) bleach
(B) exhaust
(C) harden
(D) stimulate
(E) question

7. CONTUSION
(A) puzzle
(B) shrinkage
(C) bruise
(D) uncleanness
(E) fraud

8. COMPATIBLE
(A) eloquent
(B) adequate
(C) overfed
(D) comfortable
(E) harmonious

9. CALLOUS
(A) secretive
(B) unruly
(C) gloomy
(D) unfeeling
(E) hotheaded

10. REPUDIATE
(A) reject
(B) revalue
(C) repay
(D) forget
(E) forgive

Vocabulary Test 59

1. PROLETARIAT
(A) revolutionists
(B) intellectuals
(C) slaves
(D) laboring classes
(E) landowners

2. REQUISITE
(A) desirable
(B) ridiculous
(C) liberal
(D) necessary
(E) majestic

3. TENACIOUS
(A) violent
(B) given to arguing
(C) slender
(D) holding fast
(E) menacing

4. SCINTILLATE
(A) whirl
(B) wander
(C) scorch
(D) sharpen
(E) sparkle

5. PROPRIETY
(A) success
(B) cleverness
(C) nearness
(D) security
(E) suitability

6. UNWITTING
(A) undignified
(B) unintentional
(C) slack
(D) obstinate
(E) unaccustomed

7. ATTRIBUTE
(A) quality
(B) tax
(C) desire
(D) law
(E) final sum

8. SCRUPULOUS
(A) scornful
(B) clean
(C) frightening
(D) doubting
(E) conscientious

9. USURP
(A) lend money
(B) replace
(C) murder
(D) surrender
(E) seize by force

10. CESSATION
(A) witnessing
(B) stopping
(C) strain
(D) leave-taking
(E) unwillingness

Vocabulary Test 60

1. RESOLUTE
(A) determined
(B) vibrating
(C) irresistible
(D) elastic
(E) demanding

2. CRYSTALLIZE
(A) glitter
(B) give definite form to
(C) chill
(D) sweeten
(E) polish vigorously

3. REGIME
(A) ruler
(B) military unit
(C) form of government
(D) contagion
(E) guardian

4. LACERATED
(A) unconscious
(B) stitched
(C) slender
(D) raveled
(E) mangled

5. AMISS
(A) friendly
(B) faulty
(C) tardy
(D) central
(E) purposeless

6. INDOLENCE
(A) poverty
(B) laziness
(C) danger
(D) truth
(E) attention

7. PRECARIOUS
(A) trustful
(B) early
(C) previous
(D) cautious
(E) uncertain

8. CONNOISSEUR
(A) investigator
(B) government official
(C) pretender
(D) critical judge
(E) portrait artist

9. HILARITY
(A) wittiness
(B) disobedience
(C) mirth
(D) heedlessness
(E) contentment

10. EMIT
(A) overlook
(B) adorn
(C) discharge
(D) encourage
(E) stress

Vocabulary Test 61

1. DYNAMIC
   (A) specialized
   (B) active
   (C) fragile
   (D) magical
   (E) comparative

2. ACHILLES' HEEL
   (A) source of strength
   (B) critical test
   (C) hereditary curse
   (D) vulnerable point
   (E) base conduct

3. AD LIB
   (A) cheerfully
   (B) freely
   (C) carefully
   (D) literally
   (E) wisely

4. DECRY
   (A) baffle
   (B) weep
   (C) trap
   (D) belittle
   (E) imagine

5. RAVAGE
   (A) ruin
   (B) tangle
   (C) delight
   (D) scold
   (E) crave

6. RENDEZVOUS
   (A) surrender
   (B) appointment
   (C) souvenir
   (D) hiding place
   (E) mutual exchange

7. SKULK
   (A) trail
   (B) shadow
   (C) ambush
   (D) lurk
   (E) race

8. PLETHORA
   (A) formal farewell
   (B) exclusive group
   (C) abundance
   (D) conclusive argument
   (E) good taste

9. NUPTIAL
   (A) moonlike
   (B) blunted
   (C) ritualistic
   (D) matrimonial
   (E) blessed

10. BALKED
   (A) swindled
   (B) thwarted
   (C) enlarged
   (D) waved
   (E) punished

Vocabulary Test 62

1. AD INFINITUM
   (A) to a limit
   (B) from eternity
   (C) occasionally
   (D) endlessly
   (E) periodically

2. EXTRICATE
   (A) disentangle
   (B) die out
   (C) praise
   (D) purify
   (E) argue with

3. SQUALID
   (A) dirty
   (B) unresponsive
   (C) wasteful
   (D) stormy
   (E) congested

4. COERCE
   (A) coincide
   (B) strengthen
   (C) accompany
   (D) compel
   (E) seek out

5. INTER
   (A) bury
   (B) stab
   (C) change
   (D) make peace
   (E) emphasize

6. CRESCENDO
   (A) increasing volume
   (B) decreasing tempo
   (C) abrupt ending
   (D) discordant note
   (E) musical composition

7. INDISCREET
   (A) unpopular
   (B) embarrassing
   (C) disloyal
   (D) unwise
   (E) greatly upset

8. UNWIELDY
   (A) stubborn
   (B) unhealthy
   (C) monotonous
   (D) shameful
   (E) clumsy

9. ENVISAGE
   (A) plot
   (B) conceal
   (C) wrinkle
   (D) contemplate
   (E) sneer

10. INTERIM
   (A) go-between
   (B) meantime
   (C) mixture
   (D) hereafter
   (E) period of rest

Vocabulary Test 63

1. DISHEARTEN
   (A) shame
   (B) discourage
   (C) astound
   (D) disown
   (E) cripple

2. COMPONENT
   (A) memorial
   (B) pledge
   (C) convenience
   (D) ingredient
   (E) similarity

3. LURK
   (A) stagger
   (B) tempt
   (C) sneak
   (D) grin
   (E) rob

4. GRUDGING
   (A) impolite
   (B) dirty
   (C) hoarse
   (D) alarming
   (E) unwilling

5. SEMBLANCE
(A) likeness
(B) noise
(C) foundation
(D) glance
(E) error

6. NETTLE
(A) irritate
(B) catch
(C) accuse
(D) make ill
(E) fade away

7. TREMULOUS
(A) slow
(B) high-pitched
(C) huge
(D) shaking
(E) spirited

8. TERSE
(A) delicate
(B) nervous
(C) mild
(D) numb
(E) concise

9. AFFINITY
(A) solemn declaration
(B) indefinite amount
(C) natural attraction
(D) pain
(E) wealth

10. VOLATILE
(A) disobedient
(B) changeable
(C) forceful
(D) willing
(E) luxurious

Vocabulary Test 64

1. HOMAGE
(A) welcome
(B) honor
(C) coziness
(D) criticism
(E) regret

2. DISPERSE
(A) restore
(B) spread
(C) grumble
(D) soak
(E) spend

3. RATIONAL
(A) resentful
(B) overjoyed
(C) sensible
(D) reckless
(E) apologetic

4. RECLUSE
(A) schemer
(B) criminal
(C) miser
(D) adventurer
(E) hermit

5. COMPLACENCY
(A) tenderness
(B) admiration
(C) dependence
(D) unity
(E) self-satisfaction

6. MENACE
(A) kill
(B) threaten
(C) waste
(D) indicate
(E) tease

7. DUPE
(A) combine
(B) reproduce
(C) fool
(D) grab
(E) follow

8. ABATE
(A) surprise
(B) desert
(C) decrease
(D) humiliate
(E) pay for

9. CONGENITAL
(A) existing at birth
(B) displaying weakness
(C) related by marriage
(D) overcrowded
(E) unintelligent

10. INSURGENT
(A) impractical
(B) unbearable
(C) overhanging
(D) rebellious
(E) patriotic

Vocabulary Test 65

1. CONJECTURE
(A) work
(B) joke
(C) initiate
(D) add
(E) guess

2. DAIS
(A) platform
(B) easy chair
(C) waiting room
(D) ornamental pin
(E) figurehead

3. IMPETUS
(A) deadlock
(B) collision
(C) warning
(D) wickedness
(E) stimulus

4. INTROSPECTIVE
(A) lacking strength
(B) practicing self-examination
(C) highly critical
(D) intrusive
(E) lacking confidence

5. DEIFY
(A) describe
(B) disobey
(C) make presentable
(D) worship as a god
(E) challenge

6. AGGREGATION
(A) method
(B) irritation
(C) prize
(D) collection
(E) blessing

7. EXALTED
(A) honored
(B) underhanded
(C) funny
(D) conceited
(E) secondary

8. POTENTATE
(A) slave
(B) soldier
(C) adviser
(D) informer
(E) ruler

9. INTIMIDATE
 (A) frighten
 (B) suggest
 (C) dare
 (D) border upon
 (E) befriend

10. SARDONIC
 (A) decorative
 (B) polished
 (C) strange
 (D) fashionable
 (E) sarcastic

Vocabulary Test 66

1. ELECTRIFY
 (A) punish
 (B) improve
 (C) thrill
 (D) explain
 (E) investigate

2. DISCRETION
 (A) special privilege
 (B) individual judgment
 (C) unfair treatment
 (D) disagreement
 (E) embarrassment

3. GRAPPLE
 (A) dive
 (B) wrestle
 (C) handle
 (D) fit together
 (E) fondle

4. LAUDABLE
 (A) brave
 (B) comical
 (C) peaceful
 (D) praiseworthy
 (E) conspicuous

5. LONGEVITY
 (A) wisdom
 (B) length of life
 (C) society
 (D) system of measure
 (E) loudness

6. BLANCH
 (A) destroy
 (B) drink
 (C) whiten
 (D) feel
 (E) mend

7. SHREW
 (A) moneylender
 (B) fortune-teller
 (C) chronic invalid
 (D) unruly child
 (E) scolding woman

8. STALWART
 (A) diseased
 (B) feeble
 (C) needy
 (D) sturdy
 (E) truthful

9. APOGEE
 (A) rate of ascent
 (B) force of gravity
 (C) measuring device
 (D) expression of regret
 (E) highest point

10. BANTER
 (A) tease playfully
 (B) strut boldly
 (C) ruin
 (D) bend slightly
 (E) relieve

Vocabulary Test 67

1. REPRESS
 (A) sharpen
 (B) restrain
 (C) repeat
 (D) disgust
 (E) grieve

2. BREACH
 (A) obstruction
 (B) violation
 (C) anticipation
 (D) accusation
 (E) decoration

3. DILIGENT
 (A) hesitant
 (B) prosperous
 (C) offensive
 (D) industrious
 (E) straightforward

4. CONCOCT
 (A) devise
 (B) link together
 (C) harmonize
 (D) meet privately
 (E) sweeten

5. FLAMBOYANT
 (A) scandalous
 (B) showy
 (C) nonsensical
 (D) manly
 (E) temporary

6. ECCENTRICITY
 (A) overabundance
 (B) self-consciousness
 (C) adaptability
 (D) publicity
 (E) oddity

7. VINDICTIVE
 (A) gloomy
 (B) cowardly
 (C) vengeful
 (D) cheerful
 (E) boastful

8. GRAPHIC
 (A) vivid
 (B) harsh-sounding
 (C) free from error
 (D) dignified
 (E) pliable

9. PLACARD
 (A) poster
 (B) souvenir
 (C) soothing medicine
 (D) exact reproduction
 (E) contemptuous remark

10. PUTREFY
 (A) scour
 (B) paralyze
 (C) rot
 (D) neglect
 (E) argue

Vocabulary Test 68

1. GRANDIOSE
 (A) selfish
 (B) thankful
 (C) quarrelsome
 (D) elderly
 (E) impressive

2. INCONGRUOUS
 (A) indistinct
 (B) unsuitable
 (C) unimportant
 (D) illegal
 (E) inconvenient

3. PRONE
(A) disposed
(B) speechless
(C) tardy
(D) two-edged
(E) quick

4. EMISSARY
(A) rival
(B) secret agent
(C) master of ceremonies
(D) refugee
(E) clergyman

5. INVALIDATE
(A) turn inward
(B) deprive of force
(C) mistrust
(D) support with facts
(E) neglect

6. CLEMENCY
(A) purity
(B) timidity
(C) courage
(D) simplicity
(E) mildness

7. UNSCATHED
(A) uninterested
(B) unsettled
(C) unspoken
(D) unharmed
(E) unknown

8. RELINQUISH
(A) shrink from
(B) take pity on
(C) yield
(D) lessen
(E) recall

9. ALLAY
(A) offend
(B) suffer
(C) resemble
(D) assign
(E) calm

10. ANIMOSITY
(A) liveliness
(B) worry
(C) ill will
(D) regret
(E) sarcasm

Vocabulary Test 69

1. SOLICIT
(A) request
(B) worry
(C) command
(D) deny
(E) depend

2. PERTURB
(A) pierce
(B) filter
(C) calculate
(D) agitate
(E) disregard

3. JAUNTY
(A) bored
(B) envious
(C) quarrelsome
(D) chatty
(E) lively

4. DRIVEL
(A) shrill laughter
(B) foolish talk
(C) untidy dress
(D) waste matter
(E) quaint humor

5. FRUGAL
(A) sickly
(B) sparing
(C) slow
(D) chilled
(E) frightened

6. IOTA
(A) first step
(B) sacred picture
(C) ornamental scroll
(D) crystalline substance
(E) very small quantity

7. POACH
(A) squander
(B) trespass
(C) outwit
(D) bully
(E) borrow

8. DEFECTION
(A) delay
(B) slander
(C) respect
(D) desertion
(E) exemption

9. MASTICATE
(A) chew
(B) slaughter
(C) ripen
(D) enroll
(E) tangle

10. ANALOGY
(A) imitation
(B) research
(C) calendar
(D) similarity
(E) disagreement

Vocabulary Test 70

1. DILEMMA
(A) punishment
(B) division in ranks
(C) ability to detect
(D) perplexing choice
(E) word with two meanings

2. CELESTIAL
(A) musical
(B) heavenly
(C) stately
(D) unmarried
(E) aged

3. MILITANT
(A) political
(B) mighty
(C) aggressive
(D) peaceable
(E) illegal

4. EMINENT
(A) noted
(B) moral
(C) future
(D) low
(E) unwise

5. PERCEIVE
(A) resolve
(B) observe
(C) organize
(D) stick in
(E) copy down

6. IDIOSYNCRASY
(A) stupidity
(B) virtue
(C) personal peculiarity
(D) foreign dialect
(E) similarity

7. EDIFICE
(A) tool
(B) large building
(C) garden
(D) mushroom
(E) set of books

8. SEEDY
(A) dishonest
(B) helpless
(C) vague
(D) nervous
(E) shabby

9. SUPPLANT
(A) spend
(B) unite
(C) recall
(D) replace
(E) purpose

10. DESIST
(A) loiter
(B) stand
(C) hurry
(D) stumble
(E) stop

Vocabulary Test 71

1. GIRD
(A) stare
(B) thresh
(C) encircle
(D) complain
(E) perforate

2. BIZARRE
(A) charitable
(B) joyous
(C) flattering
(D) insane
(E) fantastic

3. PERENNIAL
(A) superior
(B) unceasing
(C) notable
(D) short-lived
(E) authoritative

4. PROGENITOR
(A) genius
(B) wastrel
(C) forefather
(D) magician
(E) publisher

5. EMBELLISH
(A) organize
(B) involve
(C) rob
(D) beautify
(E) correct

6. IMPLEMENT
(A) carry out
(B) fall apart
(C) give freely
(D) object strongly
(E) praise highly

7. INSUBORDINATE
(A) unreal
(B) disobedient
(C) inferior
(D) unfaithful
(E) unnecessary

8. ITINERANT
(A) small
(B) intensive
(C) repetitive
(D) wandering
(E) begging

9. ADVERSITY
(A) misfortune
(B) surprise
(C) economy
(D) publicity
(E) warning

10. DISSIPATE
(A) explain
(B) puzzle
(C) rearrange
(D) envy
(E) waste

Vocabulary Test 72

1. VALOR
(A) courage
(B) honesty
(C) beauty
(D) alertness
(E) modesty

2. DISSUADE
(A) offend
(B) lessen
(C) advise against
(D) spread out
(E) separate

3. ERRATIC
(A) unpredictable
(B) upright
(C) well-informed
(D) self-centered
(E) artificial

4. COVET
(A) take for granted
(B) keep secret
(C) disbelieve
(D) steal
(E) long for

5. VERBOSE
(A) forbidden
(B) expanding
(C) talented
(D) wordy
(E) opinionated

6. FLIPPANT
(A) fishlike
(B) anxious
(C) frivolous
(D) savage
(E) shy

7. ACCLAMATION
(A) seasoning
(B) applause
(C) slope
(D) harmony
(E) collection

8. INCITE
(A) include
(B) destroy
(C) withdraw
(D) arouse
(E) perceive

9. FINESSE
(A) end
(B) skill
(C) habit
(D) expense
(E) vanity

10. TANTALIZE
(A) prevent
(B) protect
(C) rob
(D) predict
(E) torment

Vocabulary Test 73

1. INSOMNIA
   (A) boredom
   (B) loss of memory
   (C) seasickness
   (D) sleeplessness
   (E) lonesomeness

2. FEASIBLE
   (A) enjoyable
   (B) juicy
   (C) regrettable
   (D) responsible
   (E) possible

3. BLURT
   (A) brag
   (B) utter impulsively
   (C) challenge
   (D) shout angrily
   (E) weep noisily

4. ALIENATE
   (A) advise
   (B) entertain
   (C) forgive
   (D) sympathize with
   (E) make unfriendly

5. STARK
   (A) barely
   (B) offensively
   (C) uselessly
   (D) completely
   (E) artistically

6. NONCHALANCE
   (A) refinement
   (B) foresight
   (C) air of indifference
   (D) lack of knowledge
   (E) lack of common sense

7. GRIT
   (A) honesty
   (B) reverence
   (C) trustworthiness
   (D) cheerfulness
   (E) bravery

8. MEDIATE
   (A) make changes
   (B) argue earnestly
   (C) consider carefully
   (D) propose hesitantly
   (E) reconcile differences

9. DE FACTO
   (A) commercial
   (B) economic
   (C) in reality
   (D) unnecessary
   (E) the following

10. IRREVOCABLE
   (A) unreliable
   (B) disrespectful
   (C) unforgivable
   (D) unalterable
   (E) heartless

Vocabulary Test 74

1. ABYSMAL
   (A) bottomless
   (B) ill
   (C) forgetful
   (D) unoccupied
   (E) slight

2. PREROGATIVE
   (A) forewarning
   (B) formal investigation
   (C) privilege
   (D) reputation
   (E) opening speech

3. ILLUSTRIOUS
   (A) believable
   (B) unrewarding
   (C) cynical
   (D) decorative
   (E) famous

4. INTERMINABLE
   (A) scanty
   (B) secret
   (C) open-faced
   (D) endless
   (E) stationary

5. FRANCHISE
   (A) secrecy
   (B) right to vote
   (C) imprisonment
   (D) free-for-all
   (E) avoidable tragedy

6. LINEAGE
   (A) brilliance
   (B) ancestry
   (C) narrowness
   (D) straightness
   (E) ceremony

7. RECIPROCATE
   (A) reconsider
   (B) refresh
   (C) repay
   (D) recall
   (E) reclaim

8. REBUFF
   (A) send back
   (B) make over
   (C) snub
   (D) defend
   (E) remind

9. CLANDESTINE
   (A) unfriendly
   (B) fateful
   (C) unified
   (D) secret
   (E) argumentative

10. LETHARGY
   (A) unnatural drowsiness
   (B) excessive caution
   (C) lack of consideration
   (D) vice
   (E) foolishness

Vocabulary Test 75

1. ACCREDITED
   (A) obligated
   (B) approved
   (C) discharged
   (D) quickened
   (E) confessed

2. ADHERENT
   (A) clergyman
   (B) critic
   (C) executive
   (D) supporter
   (E) journalist

3. WHEEDLE
   (A) mourn
   (B) coax
   (C) revolve
   (D) hesitate
   (E) entertain

4. CIRCUITOUS
   (A) electrical
   (B) watery
   (C) roundabout
   (D) forbidding
   (E) tender

5. DESPOT
(A) murderer
(B) impostor
(C) invader
(D) avenger
(E) tyrant

6. DETER
(A) hinder
(B) mistake
(C) neglect
(D) injure
(E) restore

7. UTILITARIAN
(A) practical
(B) widespread
(C) inexpensive
(D) praiseworthy
(E) fortunate

8. INCREDULITY
(A) forgetfulness
(B) faithlessness
(C) immaturity
(D) disbelief
(E) unreality

9. INTERDICT
(A) lessen
(B) separate
(C) fatigue
(D) permit
(E) forbid

10. TIMOROUS
(A) necessary
(B) expected
(C) afraid
(D) wild
(E) brief

Vocabulary Test 76

1. BRAWN
(A) boldness
(B) muscular strength
(C) rustiness
(D) unruliness
(E) protective covering

2. STALEMATE
(A) athletic contest
(B) complete defeat
(C) deadlock
(D) storm
(E) refusal to fight

3. KINDLE
(A) relate
(B) pass on
(C) pretend
(D) arouse
(E) punish

4. POMP
(A) splendor
(B) illness
(C) hopefulness
(D) apple
(E) posture

5. TINGE
(A) mold
(B) draw forth
(C) color slightly
(D) sketch
(E) create

6. RECOIL
(A) steer
(B) link up
(C) put down
(D) scrape
(E) shrink back

7. QUASH
(A) creep
(B) mix thoroughly
(C) repeat
(D) suppress completely
(E) falsify

8. PALTRY
(A) trivial
(B) sacred
(C) metallic
(D) careless
(E) positive

9. IMPETUOUS
(A) controlled
(B) hasty
(C) vigorous
(D) defamatory
(E) vehement

10. HARANGUE
(A) unintelligible prose
(B) ranting speech
(C) poetic imagery
(D) anonymous letter
(E) heavy overcoat

Vocabulary Test 77

1. APROPOS
(A) witty
(B) forceful
(C) nearly correct
(D) richly decorated
(E) to the point

2. INIMICAL
(A) speechless
(B) unfriendly
(C) unnecessarily rude
(D) poor
(E) hopelessly sad

3. SORDID
(A) biting
(B) filthy
(C) mysterious
(D) grief-stricken
(E) sickly

4. CATACLYSM
(A) severe criticism
(B) gorge
(C) launching device
(D) unconsciousness
(E) violent upheaval

5. FETTERED
(A) stricken
(B) scolded
(C) commanded
(D) confined
(E) loosened

6. VERACITY
(A) endurance
(B) selfishness
(C) truthfulness
(D) courtesy
(E) thoughtfulness

7. REPLETE
(A) filled
(B) tarnished
(C) golden
(D) economical
(E) wrecked

8. TREED
(A) met
(B) cornered
(C) followed
(D) searched
(E) scented

9. DERISIVE
(A) hereditary
(B) rebellious
(C) fragmentary
(D) scornful
(E) determined

10. TEMPER
(A) decorate
(B) annoy
(C) blame
(D) postpone
(E) moderate

Vocabulary Test 78

1. RESIDUE
(A) dwelling
(B) remainder
(C) debt
(D) sample
(E) storehouse

2. BUNGLE
(A) complain
(B) approach
(C) live in
(D) handle badly
(E) talk boastfully

3. ADVOCATE
(A) flatter
(B) caution
(C) recommend
(D) take an oath
(E) charge

4. CALAMITOUS
(A) disastrous
(B) inexperienced
(C) hard-hearted
(D) scheming
(E) slanderous

5. JILT
(A) fill in
(B) cast aside
(C) move about
(D) pick up
(E) help forward

6. FUTILE
(A) violent
(B) one-sided
(C) weary
(D) stingy
(E) useless

7. INCESSANT
(A) even
(B) illegal
(C) dirty
(D) continuous
(E) loud

8. PRATTLE
(A) sell
(B) storm
(C) babble
(D) explain
(E) keep

9. PERVERSE
(A) contrary
(B) rhythmic
(C) imaginary
(D) alert
(E) rich

10. QUARRY
(A) dispute
(B) prey
(C) initial
(D) request
(E) output

Vocabulary Test 79

1. PATERNAL
(A) generous
(B) aged
(C) fatherly
(D) thrifty
(E) narrow-minded

2. CALIBER
(A) gaiety
(B) quality
(C) hope
(D) similarity
(E) politeness

3. PARADOX
(A) virtuous man
(B) equal rights
(C) seeming contradiction
(D) complicated design
(E) geometric figure

4. DISPEL
(A) punish
(B) excite
(C) pay out
(D) drive away
(E) misunderstand

5. VERBATIM
(A) out loud
(B) word for word
(C) in set phrases
(D) elegantly expressed
(E) using too many words

6. GRUELING
(A) exhausting
(B) surprising
(C) insulting
(D) embarrassing
(E) boring

7. CREDIBILITY
(A) freedom from prejudice
(B) religious doctrine
(C) capacity for belief
(D) questioning attitude
(E) good judgment

8. APPROPRIATE
(A) betray
(B) compliment
(C) take possession of
(D) give thanks
(E) draw near to

9. EXONERATE
(A) overcharge
(B) lengthen
(C) leave out
(D) free from blame
(E) serve as a model

10. BLAND
(A) flattering
(B) foolish
(C) successful
(D) soothing
(E) sharp

Vocabulary Test 80

1. EFFIGY
(A) representation
(B) shadow
(C) parade
(D) ancestor
(E) present

2. ZEST
(A) operation
(B) mood
(C) great dismay
(D) keen enjoyment
(E) false alarm

3. ASTUTE
(A) shrewd
(B) inflammable
(C) defiant
(D) out of tune
(E) bitter

4. DISCREPANCY
(A) variance
(B) disbelief
(C) feebleness
(D) insult
(E) forcefulness

5. COPIOUS
(A) copyrighted
(B) tricky
(C) abundant
(D) complete
(E) sincere

6. ADVENT
(A) approval
(B) opportunity
(C) welcome
(D) recommendation
(E) arrival

7. IMMINENT
(A) about to occur
(B) never-ending
(C) up-to-date
(D) inconvenient
(E) youthful

8. RANKLE
(A) spread around
(B) seize quickly
(C) crease
(D) search
(E) irritate deeply

9. INJUNCTION
(A) exclamation
(B) rebellion
(C) directive
(D) crisis
(E) illegality

10. DEFT
(A) critical
(B) conceited
(C) lighthearted
(D) skillful
(E) tactful

Vocabulary Test 81

1. HEEDLESS
(A) unfortunate
(B) expensive
(C) careless
(D) happy
(E) weather-beaten

2. IMPEDIMENT
(A) obstacle
(B) base
(C) spice
(D) mechanism
(E) footstool

3. QUAVER
(A) launch
(B) quicken
(C) sharpen
(D) tremble
(E) forget

4. SHACKLE
(A) hide
(B) glide
(C) anger
(D) quiet
(E) hamper

5. LOWLY
(A) idle
(B) silent
(C) humble
(D) sorrowful
(E) solitary

6. CUBICLE
(A) wedge
(B) puzzle
(C) tiny amount
(D) unit of measure
(E) small compartment

7. ARRAIGN
(A) debate
(B) accuse
(C) excite
(D) cancel
(E) protect

8. OBLIVIOUS
(A) unwanted
(B) disorderly
(C) unaware
(D) sickly
(E) evident

9. PROFOUND
(A) plentiful
(B) beneficial
(C) lengthy
(D) religious
(E) deep

10. WAN
(A) pale
(B) humorous
(C) pleasing
(D) watchful
(E) lovesick

Vocabulary Test 82

1. HAUNT
(A) contain
(B) give up
(C) expect
(D) stay around
(E) extend greatly

2. UNMINDFUL
(A) unaware
(B) illogical
(C) unaccustomed
(D) unchanging
(E) inefficient

3. EMANCIPATE
(A) change
(B) overjoy
(C) bring forward
(D) raise up
(E) set free

4. LOLL
(A) find
(B) respect
(C) lounge
(D) steal
(E) trap

5. SUBSEQUENT
(A) later
(B) lower
(C) thick
(D) secret
(E) light

6. CRUCIAL
(A) reverent
(B) decisive
(C) tiresome
(D) dangerous
(E) rude

7. REBUKE
(A) prove
(B) dislike
(C) overwork
(D) swallow
(E) criticize

8. CLOISTERED
(A) uneasy
(B) agreeable
(C) sincere
(D) regretful
(E) confined

9. DRONE
(A) beggar
(B) nightmare
(C) queen bee
(D) humming sound
(E) delaying action

10. PEDESTRIAN
(A) clumsy
(B) senseless
(C) curious
(D) learned
(E) commonplace

Vocabulary Test 83

1. DAWDLE
(A) hang loosely
(B) waste time
(C) fondle
(D) splash
(E) paint

2. ANGUISH
(A) torment
(B) boredom
(C) resentment
(D) stubbornness
(E) clumsiness

3. IMPARTIAL
(A) unlawful
(B) incomplete
(C) unprejudiced
(D) unfaithful
(E) unimportant

4. FORESTALL
(A) press
(B) preserve
(C) prevent
(D) boil
(E) restore

5. EFFRONTERY
(A) boldness
(B) agitation
(C) brilliance
(D) toil
(E) talkativeness

6. EMBROIL
(A) explain
(B) entangle
(C) swindle
(D) greet
(E) imitate

7. INCANDESCENT
(A) insincere
(B) melodious
(C) electrical
(D) magical
(E) glowing

8. STENTORIAN
(A) extremely careful
(B) little known
(C) hardly capable
(D) rarely reliable
(E) very loud

9. RENEGADE
(A) retired soldier
(B) public speaker
(C) complainer
(D) traitor
(E) comedian

10. INTERMITTENT
(A) emphatic
(B) stormy
(C) hopeless
(D) innermost
(E) periodic

Vocabulary Test 84

1. INTERLOPER
(A) thief
(B) intruder
(C) translator
(D) inquirer
(E) representative

2. SCATHING
(A) bitterly severe
(B) hastily spoken
(C) unnecessary
(D) ill-advised
(E) easily misunderstood

3. ACRID
(A) abnormal
(B) gifted
(C) insincere
(D) drying
(E) irritating

4. TALISMAN
(A) peddler
(B) mechanic
(C) charm
(D) juryman
(E) metal key

5. DISPATCH
(A) stir up
(B) leave out
(C) glorify
(D) persuade
(E) send away

6. BOOTY
(A) navy
(B) arson
(C) police
(D) voyage
(E) spoils

7. DEMURE
(A) unforgiving
(B) out-of-date
(C) modest
(D) uncooperative
(E) overemotional

8. CRUX
(A) great disappointment
(B) supporting argument
(C) debatable issue
(D) critical point
(E) criminal act

9. AGGRANDIZE
(A) enlarge
(B) condense
(C) astonish
(D) interpret
(E) attack

10. SUMPTUOUS
(A) dictatorial
(B) topmost
(C) radiant
(D) luxurious
(E) additional

Vocabulary Test 85

1. VERSATILE
   (A) lonesome
   (B) backward
   (C) talkative
   (D) brave
   (E) all-around

2. FORTHRIGHT
   (A) frank
   (B) joyful
   (C) imaginary
   (D) conscious
   (E) preferred

3. TUSSLE
   (A) meet
   (B) struggle
   (C) confuse
   (D) murmur
   (E) practice

4. CLARITY
   (A) loudness
   (B) certainty
   (C) clearness
   (D) glamour
   (E) tenderness

5. ASSESSMENT
   (A) appraisal
   (B) revision
   (C) property
   (D) illness
   (E) warning

6. CLIQUE
   (A) social outcast
   (B) ringing sound
   (C) headdress
   (D) exclusive group
   (E) tangled web

7. NEGATE
   (A) polish to a bright shine
   (B) find quickly
   (C) make ineffective
   (D) file a protest
   (E) take into consideration

8. IMPEL
   (A) accuse
   (B) force
   (C) encourage
   (D) prevent
   (E) pierce

9. CONSTRAINTS
   (A) group processes
   (B) new laws
   (C) doctrines
   (D) current news
   (E) limits

10. ORTHODOX
   (A) accepted
   (B) flawless
   (C) contradictory
   (D) dignified
   (E) extraordinary

Vocabulary Test 86

1. COUNTERPART
   (A) hindrance
   (B) peace offering
   (C) password
   (D) balance of power
   (E) duplicate

2. LOW-KEY
   (A) official
   (B) secret
   (C) restrained
   (D) unheard of
   (E) complicated

3. STIPULATION
   (A) imitation
   (B) signal
   (C) excitement
   (D) agreement
   (E) decoration

4. ANTITHESIS
   (A) fixed dislike
   (B) musical response
   (C) lack of feeling
   (D) direct opposite
   (E) prior knowledge

5. TRANSITORY
   (A) short-lived
   (B) delayed
   (C) idle
   (D) unexpected
   (E) clear

6. ENTRENCHED
   (A) filled up
   (B) bordered by
   (C) followed by
   (D) kept down
   (E) dug in

7. LOT
   (A) name
   (B) right
   (C) folly
   (D) fate
   (E) oath

8. APPREHENSION
   (A) gratitude
   (B) requirement
   (C) apology
   (D) dread
   (E) punishment

9. AMENABLE
   (A) religious
   (B) masculine
   (C) proud
   (D) brave
   (E) agreeable

10. AFFLUENT
   (A) neutral
   (B) sentimental
   (C) wealthy
   (D) handsome
   (E) evil

Vocabulary Test 87

1. VELOCITY
   (A) willingness
   (B) swiftness
   (C) truthfulness
   (D) smoothness
   (E) skillfulness

2. ENVOY
   (A) messenger
   (B) assistant
   (C) planner
   (D) expert
   (E) leader

3. AUXILIARY
   (A) reliable
   (B) mechanical
   (C) sociable
   (D) supporting
   (E) protective

4. PINNACLE
   (A) topmost point
   (B) feather
   (C) fastener
   (D) card game
   (E) small boat

5. BOORISH
(A) shy
(B) rude
(C) thieving
(D) cunning
(E) foreign

6. ENCOMPASS
(A) include
(B) measure
(C) attempt
(D) direct
(E) border on

7. LURCH
(A) trap
(B) brake
(C) stagger
(D) waste time
(E) laugh noisily

8. EFFACE
(A) rub out
(B) paint red
(C) build upon
(D) stay in front
(E) bring about

9. ABOUND
(A) do good
(B) store up
(C) run away
(D) stand firm
(E) be plentiful

10. THWART
(A) avoid
(B) accuse
(C) suffer
(D) block
(E) serve

Vocabulary Test 88

1. PRUNE
(A) cut off
(B) expect
(C) put away
(D) lay waste
(E) remind

2. AMIABLE
(A) active
(B) good-natured
(C) religious
(D) changeable
(E) absentminded

3. IMPROVISE
(A) object loudly
(B) predict
(C) refuse support
(D) prepare offhand
(E) translate

4. CONNIVE
(A) cooperate secretly
(B) enter quickly
(C) pause slightly
(D) push unexpectedly
(E) need greatly

5. GAIT
(A) turning over and over
(B) passing in review
(C) manner of walking
(D) fundamental attitude
(E) crowd of spectators

6. BOTCH
(A) weep
(B) rebel
(C) resent
(D) blunder
(E) complain

7. DEVOID OF
(A) accompanied by
(B) in the care of
(C) without
(D) behind
(E) despite

8. PANG
(A) feeling of indifference
(B) sense of duty
(C) fatal disease
(D) universal remedy
(E) spasm of pain

9. TEDIUM
(A) bad temper
(B) boredom
(C) warmth
(D) abundance
(E) musical form

10. INTIMATE
(A) hospitable
(B) well-behaved
(C) familiar
(D) plainly seen
(E) forgiving

Vocabulary Test 89

1. DELVE
(A) hope for
(B) believe in
(C) set upon
(D) take into account
(E) dig into

2. SHROUDED
(A) found
(B) torn
(C) stoned
(D) wrapped
(E) rewarded

3. EXPLOIT
(A) annoy
(B) join
(C) use
(D) mix up
(E) set free

4. RUT
(A) fixed practice
(B) honest labor
(C) useless regret
(D) happy home
(E) vain hope

5. CONSTITUENTS
(A) tradesmen
(B) students
(C) voters
(D) judges
(E) ministers

6. REPREHENSIBLE
(A) distracting
(B) blameworthy
(C) glowing
(D) frightening
(E) truthful

7. HAZARD
(A) confuse
(B) avoid
(C) resign
(D) chance
(E) overlook

8. ROBUST
(A) bragging
(B) huge
(C) sincere
(D) upright
(E) sturdy

9. PIECEMEAL
   (A) on the spur of the moment
   (B) bit by bit
   (C) over and over
   (D) as a matter of course
   (E) from first to last

10. INSCRUTABLE
   (A) disorderly
   (B) shallow
   (C) unwritten
   (D) painful
   (E) mysterious

Vocabulary Test 90

1. NEEDLE
   (A) join
   (B) prod
   (C) discuss
   (D) give
   (E) command

2. TENTATIVE
   (A) forgotten
   (B) fabricated
   (C) sunny
   (D) temporary
   (E) absentee

3. HUMDRUM
   (A) false
   (B) ugly
   (C) uninteresting
   (D) mournful
   (E) disappointing

4. RATIFY
   (A) create
   (B) revive
   (C) deny
   (D) confirm
   (E) displease

5. HORDE
   (A) crowd
   (B) framework
   (C) nonbeliever
   (D) choir
   (E) warrior

6. RELENTLESS
   (A) unwise
   (B) fearless
   (C) straightforward
   (D) unappetizing
   (E) unyielding

7. MUDDLE
   (A) saucy remark
   (B) confused mess
   (C) delaying tactics
   (D) simple truth
   (E) great outcry

8. ADULTERATE
   (A) grow up
   (B) push ahead
   (C) make impure
   (D) send away
   (E) die off

9. CONCEDE
   (A) gain
   (B) join
   (C) force
   (D) struggle
   (E) admit

10. PLIGHT
   (A) final decision
   (B) spy system
   (C) plant disease
   (D) bad situation
   (E) listening post

Vocabulary Test 91

1. BURLY
   (A) useless
   (B) wild
   (C) strong
   (D) easy
   (E) medical

2. DEBASE
   (A) call to mind
   (B) send from home
   (C) rely upon
   (D) take part in
   (E) reduce the value of

3. STANCE
   (A) performance
   (B) defense
   (C) length
   (D) posture
   (E) concentration

4. EXACT
   (A) fall
   (B) appeal
   (C) strain
   (D) loosen
   (E) demand

5. DANK
   (A) moist
   (B) unhealthy
   (C) smoky
   (D) frozen
   (E) cloudy

6. EXPRESSLY
   (A) definitely
   (B) regularly
   (C) quickly
   (D) safely
   (E) loudly

7. DISCOUNT
   (A) discover
   (B) disgrace
   (C) disregard
   (D) dislike
   (E) display

8. TOKEN
   (A) timely
   (B) minimal
   (C) stiff
   (D) imaginary
   (E) enforced

9. DECADENCE
   (A) false reasoning
   (B) hasty retreat
   (C) self-assurance
   (D) period of decline
   (E) fraud

10. ALACRITY
   (A) eagerness
   (B) joy
   (C) criticism
   (D) milkiness
   (E) fullness

Vocabulary Test 92

1. CLAMOR
   (A) magic spell
   (B) loose garment
   (C) poisoned arrow
   (D) loud noise
   (E) deep-sea fisherman

2. CONVENTIONAL
   (A) inexperienced
   (B) close
   (C) foolish
   (D) kindly
   (E) usual

3. INDISPUTABLE
(A) unjust
(B) undeniable
(C) indelicate
(D) indescribable
(E) unconcerned

4. PUNY
(A) weak
(B) humorous
(C) quarrelsome
(D) studious
(E) innocent

5. FACILITATE
(A) make angry
(B) copy
(C) make easier
(D) joke about
(E) decorate

6. REPULSE
(A) force
(B) disown
(C) restore
(D) repel
(E) indicate

7. CHARISMA
(A) happy feeling
(B) quality of leadership
(C) Greek letter
(D) deep hole
(E) contrary view

8. RIGOR
(A) padding
(B) mold
(C) liner
(D) building
(E) strictness

9. NOXIOUS
(A) harmful
(B) lively
(C) uncertain
(D) unprepared
(E) calming

10. ENLIGHTEN
(A) please
(B) put away
(C) instruct
(D) reduce
(E) criticize

Vocabulary Test 93

1. INTANGIBLE
(A) incomplete
(B) individual
(C) vagile
(D) uninjured
(E) careless

2. COMPLIANT
(A) yielding
(B) standing
(C) admiring
(D) trusting
(E) grabbing

3. ERADICATE
(A) exclaim
(B) heat up
(C) break out
(D) plant
(E) eliminate

4. ABYSS
(A) great ignorance
(B) evil man
(C) bottomless pit
(D) wide sea
(E) religious sign

5. CRITERION
(A) standard
(B) award
(C) achievement
(D) objection
(E) claim

6. IRREVERENT
(A) illogical
(B) unimportant
(C) violent
(D) disrespectful
(E) unafraid

7. SALLOW
(A) temporary
(B) animal-like
(C) stupid
(D) clean
(E) yellowish

8. RENOUNCE
(A) proclaim
(B) approve
(C) give up
(D) guarantee
(E) speak plainly

9. ASSIMILATE
(A) pretend
(B) absorb
(C) poke
(D) copy
(E) expect

10. EXHORT
(A) annoy
(B) deduct
(C) enlarge quickly
(D) urge strongly
(E) stick out

Vocabulary Test 94

1. JEST
(A) spout
(B) trot
(C) joke
(D) judge
(E) leap

2. MOLEST
(A) disturb
(B) reduce
(C) submit
(D) delight
(E) urge

3. TURMOIL
(A) conclusion
(B) reversal
(C) meanness
(D) confusion
(E) mistake

4. ORDINANCE
(A) trial
(B) law
(C) right
(D) fault
(E) property

5. LATERAL
(A) financial
(B) lingering
(C) of the past
(D) from the beginning
(E) to the side

6. PIGMENT
(A) light
(B) pillar
(C) dye
(D) weed
(E) book

7. CONCEPT
(A) desire
(B) thought
(C) solution
(D) method
(E) experiment

8. ORNATE
(A) elaborate
(B) original
(C) systematic
(D) unbecoming
(E) obsolete

9. BEGRUDGE
(A) roar mightily
(B) walk swiftly
(C) give reluctantly
(D) await eagerly
(E) seek desperately

10. REPOSE
(A) task
(B) calm
(C) strain
(D) fact
(E) surprise

Vocabulary Test 95

1. BOLSTER
(A) reinforce
(B) thicken
(C) uncover
(D) quote
(E) bother

2. INFRINGEMENT
(A) old age
(B) added benefit
(C) protection
(D) violation
(E) fireproofing

3. AGILE
(A) colored
(B) healthy
(C) dull
(D) false
(E) nimble

4. DIVERSIFY
(A) fix
(B) vary
(C) correct
(D) relieve
(E) explain

5. RUSTLE
(A) steal
(B) instruct
(C) strive
(D) bend
(E) tax

6. HAPLESS
(A) optimistic
(B) uncounted
(C) unfortunate
(D) simple
(E) unyielding

7. UNPRETENTIOUS
(A) loyal
(B) virtuous
(C) modest
(D) fair
(E) extravagant

8. BUOY
(A) wet
(B) dry up
(C) rescue
(D) sustain
(E) direct

9. PARAGON
(A) weak pun
(B) even distribution
(C) geometric figure
(D) moralistic story
(E) model of excellence

10. INDIGENOUS
(A) confused
(B) native
(C) poor
(D) unconcerned
(E) wrathful

Vocabulary Test 96

1. PROLOGUE
(A) stairway
(B) introduction
(C) conversation
(D) reading
(E) extension

2. ACKNOWLEDGE
(A) propose
(B) strangle
(C) convict
(D) advance
(E) admit

3. INDICTMENT
(A) accusation
(B) publisher
(C) announcer
(D) conviction
(E) trial

4. LACKLUSTER
(A) sparkling
(B) tender
(C) misty
(D) uninspired
(E) disobedient

5. CONDOMINIUM
(A) new type of metal
(B) noisy celebration
(C) individually owned apartment
(D) important decision
(E) group meeting

6. INCUMBENT
(A) office holder
(B) lawyer
(C) politician
(D) green vegetable
(E) sacred honor

7. POLARIZATION
(A) performance in cold weather
(B) point of view
(C) change in opinion
(D) division into opposites
(E) cultural bias

8. GENESIS
(A) wisdom
(B) origin
(C) classification
(D) humor
(E) night

9. DIMINUTION
(A) devotion
(B) difference
(C) difficulty
(D) decision
(E) decrease

10. WARY
(A) sorrowful
(B) lazy
(C) unfriendly
(D) cautious
(E) hopeful

Vocabulary Test 97

1. SLEEK
   (A) smooth
   (B) moldy
   (C) loose
   (D) small
   (E) delicate

2. SUCCULENT
   (A) literal
   (B) tardy
   (C) yielding
   (D) sportsmanlike
   (E) juicy

3. LACERATED
   (A) bright
   (B) gaunt
   (C) punishable
   (D) torn
   (E) tied

4. SUBSIDE
   (A) pay in full
   (B) become quiet
   (C) return soon
   (D) rush around
   (E) send forth

5. ACQUITTAL
   (A) setting free
   (B) agreeing with
   (C) holding forth
   (D) getting up steam
   (E) appealing to higher authority

6. APPREHEND
   (A) inform
   (B) resound
   (C) frighten
   (D) squeeze
   (E) seize

7. IMPERATIVE
   (A) unbiased
   (B) obscure
   (C) repetitious
   (D) compulsory
   (E) unworthy

8. SUBSTANTIATE
   (A) verify
   (B) replace
   (C) influence
   (D) condemn
   (E) accept

9. RANCID
   (A) illegal
   (B) rotten
   (C) ashen
   (D) flimsy
   (E) mean

10. OUST
   (A) nag
   (B) evict
   (C) excel
   (D) defy
   (E) emerge

Vocabulary Test 98

1. TOPPLE
   (A) drink
   (B) choose
   (C) stray
   (D) stumble
   (E) overturn

2. PREVAIL
   (A) preview
   (B) question
   (C) relax
   (D) triumph
   (E) restore

3. CREDENCE
   (A) cowardice
   (B) size
   (C) belief
   (D) variety
   (E) nobility

4. DIVULGE
   (A) send
   (B) shrink
   (C) despair
   (D) separate
   (E) reveal

5. MISGIVINGS
   (A) cheap gifts
   (B) feelings of doubt
   (C) added treats
   (D) false promises
   (E) slips of the tongue

6. ACCLAIM
   (A) find
   (B) restore
   (C) praise
   (D) judge
   (E) demand

7. HALLOWED
   (A) sacred
   (B) noisy
   (C) deep
   (D) permitted
   (E) costumed

8. GUISE
   (A) ability
   (B) direction
   (C) guilt
   (D) appearance
   (E) mistake

9. TUMULT
   (A) vacation
   (B) reversal
   (C) swelling
   (D) suffering
   (E) commotion

10. REMINISCENT
   (A) amazed by
   (B) obligated to
   (C) suggestive of
   (D) under the control of
   (E) careless with

Vocabulary Test 99

1. REMIT
   (A) promise
   (B) injure
   (C) send
   (D) profit
   (E) menace

2. PANDEMONIUM
   (A) wild uproar
   (B) diseased state
   (C) contempt
   (D) luxury
   (E) gloom

3. EJECT
   (A) expose
   (B) exceed
   (C) extend
   (D) expel
   (E) excite

4. TALLY
   (A) load
   (B) record
   (C) hunt
   (D) play
   (E) move

5. DEVASTATE
(A) cough
(B) ruin
(C) chop
(D) point
(E) swell

6. MAUL
(A) trap
(B) cuddle
(C) carve
(D) throw
(E) beat

7. ANIMATION
(A) liveliness
(B) automation
(C) carelessness
(D) dispute
(E) exchange

8. SMOLDER
(A) show suppressed anger
(B) grow up quickly
(C) find easily
(D) report back
(E) become weary

9. PROTRUDE
(A) make a fool of
(B) fall into
(C) put down
(D) thrust out
(E) steer clear of

10. BENEVOLENT
(A) profitable
(B) sociable
(C) wealthy
(D) receptive
(E) charitable

Vocabulary Test 100

1. UNOBTRUSIVE
(A) annoying
(B) unquestionable
(C) inconspicuous
(D) united
(E) healthy

2. SCRUTINY
(A) signal
(B) plot
(C) delay
(D) investigation
(E) announcement

3. HEINOUS
(A) evil
(B) permanent
(C) unreasonable
(D) open
(E) timid

4. GARRULOUS
(A) confused
(B) eager
(C) panting
(D) talkative
(E) informal

5. CONVERSE
(A) junction
(B) poetry
(C) ancestor
(D) follower
(E) opposite

6. MALEFACTOR
(A) fugitive
(B) joker
(C) show-off
(D) evildoer
(E) daydreamer

7. MARTIAL
(A) heavenly
(B) keen
(C) warlike
(D) tremendous
(E) masculine

8. RETORT
(A) answer
(B) jot
(C) retire
(D) recall
(E) decay

9. VIGILANCE
(A) lawlessness
(B) funeral
(C) watchfulness
(D) processional
(E) strength

10. LESION
(A) dream
(B) group
(C) justice
(D) style
(E) injury

Answers to Vocabulary Tests

Test 1

1. **D**
2. **B**
3. **D**
4. **A**
5. **E**
6. **B**
7. **E**
8. **A**
9. **E**
10. **C**

Test 2

1. **B**
2. **A**
3. **E**
4. **D**
5. **A**
6. **E**
7. **C**
8. **A**
9. **B**
10. **E**

Test 3

1. **C**
2. **D**
3. **B**
4. **C**
5. **B**
6. **B**
7. **D**
8. **C**
9. **A**
10. **E**

Test 4

1. **E**
2. **D**
3. **E**
4. **A**
5. **E**
6. **A**
7. **A**
8. **D**
9. **E**
10. **C**

Test 5

1. **C**
2. **B**
3. **D**
4. **D**
5. **C**
6. **E**
7. **A**
8. **A**
9. **E**
10. **C**

Test 6

1. **C**
2. **E**
3. **D**
4. **C**
5. **B**
6. **E**
7. **B**
8. **E**
9. **C**
10. **D**

Test 7

1. **E**
2. **A**
3. **D**
4. **D**
5. **B**
6. **B**
7. **B**
8. **E**
9. **A**
10. **B**

Test 8

1. **D**
2. **A**
3. **D**
4. **E**
5. **A**
6. **C**
7. **A**
8. **C**
9. **A**
10. **D**

Test 9

1. **E**
2. **C**
3. **E**
4. **C**
5. **D**
6. **C**
7. **A**
8. **D**
9. **D**
10. **D**

Test 10

1. **B**
2. **E**
3. **D**
4. **C**
5. **B**
6. **B**
7. **E**
8. **B**
9. **A**
10. **B**

Test 11

1. **A**
2. **D**
3. **A**
4. **E**
5. **A**
6. **B**
7. **A**
8. **E**
9. **C**
10. **E**

Test 12

1. **C**
2. **D**
3. **B**
4. **D**
5. **B**
6. **C**
7. **E**
8. **B**
9. **D**
10. **E**

Test 13

1. **B**
2. **E**
3. **B**
4. **B**
5. **C**
6. **C**
7. **E**
8. **A**
9. **D**
10. **C**

Test 14

1. **C**
2. **E**
3. **C**
4. **E**
5. **A**
6. **E**
7. **D**
8. **D**
9. **E**
10. **E**

Test 15

1. **B**
2. **C**
3. **A**
4. **C**
5. **B**
6. **E**
7. **C**
8. **D**
9. **A**
10. **B**

Test 16

1. **D**
2. **C**
3. **D**
4. **B**
5. **B**
6. **A**
7. **D**
8. **B**
9. **A**
10. **A**

Test 17

1. **A**
2. **B**
3. **D**
4. **E**
5. **E**
6. **B**
7. **D**
8. **A**
9. **B**
10. **D**

Test 18

1. **E**
2. **C**
3. **B**
4. **C**
5. **C**
6. **A**
7. **E**
8. **A**
9. **D**
10. **A**

Test 19

1. **B**
2. **E**
3. **C**
4. **D**
5. **A**
6. **A**
7. **D**
8. **B**
9. **A**
10. **B**

Test 20

1. **A**
2. **B**
3. **D**
4. **B**
5. **B**
6. **A**
7. **C**
8. **A**
9. **A**
10. **E**

Test 21

1. **C**
2. **E**
3. **D**
4. **C**
5. **B**
6. **D**
7. **E**
8. **D**
9. **A**
10. **D**

Test 22

1. **B**
2. **D**
3. **A**
4. **E**
5. **E**
6. **E**
7. **D**
8. **A**
9. **E**
10. **D**

Test 23

1. **C**
2. **D**
3. **B**
4. **D**
5. **D**
6. **D**
7. **A**
8. **B**
9. **E**
10. **D**

Test 24

1. **B**
2. **B**
3. **A**
4. **E**
5. **E**
6. **E**
7. **C**
8. **E**
9. **B**
10. **B**

Test 25

1. **A**
2. **D**
3. **E**
4. **C**
5. **A**
6. **B**
7. **E**
8. **B**
9. **C**
10. **D**

Test 26

1. **E**
2. **C**
3. **A**
4. **C**
5. **B**
6. **E**
7. **D**
8. **E**
9. **D**
10. **B**

Test 27

1. **A**
2. **D**
3. **C**
4. **B**
5. **C**
6. **B**
7. **B**
8. **A**
9. **A**
10. **E**

Test 28

1. **E**
2. **B**
3. **C**
4. **A**
5. **B**
6. **D**
7. **A**
8. **E**
9. **A**
10. **D**

Test 29

1. **B**
2. **A**
3. **D**
4. **E**
5. **C**
6. **E**
7. **B**
8. **E**
9. **E**
10. **C**

Test 30

1. **E**
2. **C**
3. **A**
4. **B**
5. **D**
6. **E**
7. **D**
8. **B**
9. **C**
10. **A**

Test 31

1. **B**
2. **A**
3. **D**
4. **A**
5. **C**
6. **E**
7. **D**
8. **E**
9. **B**
10. **A**

Test 32

1. **E**
2. **A**
3. **B**
4. **D**
5. **B**
6. **A**
7. **C**
8. **B**
9. **B**
10. **E**

Test 33	Test 37	Test 41	Test 45	Test 49	Test 53	Test 57	Test 61
1. **C**	1. **C**	1. **A**	1. **E**	1. **B**	1. **E**	1. **E**	1. **B**
2. **D**	2. **B**	2. **D**	2. **A**	2. **E**	2. **E**	2. **C**	2. **D**
3. **B**	3. **A**	3. **E**	3. **D**	3. **A**	3. **D**	3. **B**	3. **B**
4. **C**	4. **C**	4. **D**	4. **C**	4. **C**	4. **E**	4. **A**	4. **D**
5. **D**	5. **E**	5. **C**	5. **E**	5. **C**	5. **B**	5. **B**	5. **A**
6. **E**	6. **A**	6. **A**	6. **B**	6. **D**	6. **D**	6. **A**	6. **B**
7. **B**	7. **D**	7. **E**	7. **B**	7. **D**	7. **B**	7. **C**	7. **D**
8. **B**	8. **A**	8. **B**	8. **E**	8. **A**	8. **D**	8. **C**	8. **C**
9. **A**	9. **E**	9. **E**	9. **D**	9. **E**	9. **D**	9. **D**	9. **D**
10. **E**	10. **E**	10. **D**	10. **A**	10. **C**	10. **E**	10. **A**	10. **B**

Test 34	Test 38	Test 42	Test 46	Test 50	Test 54	Test 58	Test 62
1. **A**	1. **D**	1. **B**	1. **B**	1. **A**	1. **C**	1. **B**	1. **D**
2. **B**	2. **E**	2. **E**	2. **D**	2. **C**	2. **D**	2. **A**	2. **A**
3. **E**	3. **E**	3. **B**	3. **C**	3. **A**	3. **E**	3. **E**	3. **A**
4. **A**	4. **A**	4. **B**	4. **D**	4. **C**	4. **C**	4. **D**	4. **D**
5. **B**	5. **E**	5. **B**	5. **B**	5. **D**	5. **C**	5. **C**	5. **A**
6. **D**	6. **D**	6. **E**	6. **E**	6. **B**	6. **C**	6. **D**	6. **A**
7. **D**	7. **C**	7. **C**	7. **D**	7. **B**	7. **B**	7. **C**	7. **D**
8. **B**	8. **B**	8. **D**	8. **B**	8. **A**	8. **E**	8. **E**	8. **E**
9. **B**	9. **C**	9. **A**	9. **A**	9. **A**	9. **E**	9. **D**	9. **D**
10. **C**	10. **A**	10. **C**	10. **E**	10. **B**	10. **C**	10. **A**	10. **B**

Test 35	Test 39	Test 43	Test 47	Test 51	Test 55	Test 59	Test 63
1. **A**	1. **E**	1. **A**	1. **C**	1. **D**	1. **C**	1. **D**	1. **B**
2. **E**	2. **A**	2. **B**	2. **C**	2. **D**	2. **B**	2. **D**	2. **D**
3. **B**	3. **D**	3. **D**	3. **D**	3. **C**	3. **D**	3. **D**	3. **C**
4. **A**	4. **C**	4. **C**	4. **D**	4. **B**	4. **A**	4. **E**	4. **E**
5. **C**	5. **B**	5. **E**	5. **A**	5. **A**	5. **C**	5. **E**	5. **A**
6. **D**	6. **B**	6. **C**	6. **A**	6. **D**	6. **E**	6. **B**	6. **A**
7. **E**	7. **A**	7. **E**	7. **B**	7. **B**	7. **D**	7. **A**	7. **D**
8. **D**	8. **E**	8. **D**	8. **E**	8. **B**	8. **E**	8. **E**	8. **E**
9. **B**	9. **C**	9. **C**	9. **C**	9. **B**	9. **A**	9. **E**	9. **C**
10. **B**	10. **D**	10. **A**	10. **E**	10. **A**	10. **C**	10. **B**	10. **B**

Test 36	Test 40	Test 44	Test 48	Test 52	Test 56	Test 60	Test 64
1. **C**	1. **A**	1. **A**	1. **B**	1. **B**	1. **A**	1. **A**	1. **B**
2. **B**	2. **E**	2. **A**	2. **C**	2. **E**	2. **A**	2. **B**	2. **B**
3. **C**	3. **C**	3. **D**	3. **E**	3. **A**	3. **D**	3. **C**	3. **C**
4. **D**	4. **B**	4. **D**	4. **B**	4. **B**	4. **D**	4. **E**	4. **E**
5. **A**	5. **A**	5. **B**	5. **E**	5. **C**	5. **A**	5. **B**	5. **E**
6. **D**	6. **C**	6. **D**	6. **A**	6. **C**	6. **D**	6. **B**	6. **B**
7. **D**	7. **D**	7. **C**	7. **D**	7. **B**	7. **B**	7. **E**	7. **C**
8. **E**	8. **D**	8. **A**	8. **D**	8. **E**	8. **B**	8. **D**	8. **C**
9. **A**	9. **A**	9. **E**	9. **B**	9. **A**	9. **B**	9. **C**	9. **A**
10. **E**	10. **D**	10. **D**	10. **E**	10. **A**	10. **C**	10. **C**	10. **D**

Test 65	Test 69	Test 73	Test 77	Test 81	Test 85	Test 89	Test 93	Test 97
1. **E**	1. **A**	1. **D**	1. **E**	1. **C**	1. **E**	1. **E**	1. **C**	1. **A**
2. **A**	2. **D**	2. **E**	2. **B**	2. **A**	2. **A**	2. **D**	2. **A**	2. **E**
3. **E**	3. **E**	3. **B**	3. **B**	3. **D**	3. **B**	3. **C**	3. **E**	3. **D**
4. **B**	4. **B**	4. **E**	4. **E**	4. **E**	4. **C**	4. **A**	4. **C**	4. **B**
5. **D**	5. **B**	5. **D**	5. **D**	5. **C**	5. **A**	5. **C**	5. **A**	5. **A**
6. **D**	6. **E**	6. **C**	6. **C**	6. **E**	6. **D**	6. **B**	6. **D**	6. **E**
7. **A**	7. **B**	7. **E**	7. **A**	7. **B**	7. **C**	7. **D**	7. **E**	7. **D**
8. **E**	8. **D**	8. **E**	8. **B**	8. **C**	8. **B**	8. **E**	8. **C**	8. **A**
9. **A**	9. **A**	9. **C**	9. **D**	9. **E**	9. **E**	9. **B**	9. **B**	9. **B**
10. **E**	10. **D**	10. **D**	10. **E**	10. **A**	10. **A**	10. **E**	10. **D**	10. **B**

Test 66	Test 70	Test 74	Test 78	Test 82	Test 86	Test 90	Test 94	Test 98
1. **C**	1. **D**	1. **A**	1. **B**	1. **D**	1. **E**	1. **B**	1. **C**	1. **E**
2. **B**	2. **B**	2. **C**	2. **D**	2. **A**	2. **C**	2. **D**	2. **A**	2. **D**
3. **B**	3. **C**	3. **E**	3. **C**	3. **E**	3. **D**	3. **C**	3. **D**	3. **C**
4. **D**	4. **A**	4. **D**	4. **A**	4. **C**	4. **D**	4. **D**	4. **B**	4. **E**
5. **B**	5. **B**	5. **B**	5. **B**	5. **A**	5. **A**	5. **A**	5. **E**	5. **B**
6. **C**	6. **C**	6. **B**	6. **E**	6. **B**	6. **E**	6. **E**	6. **C**	6. **C**
7. **E**	7. **B**	7. **C**	7. **D**	7. **E**	7. **D**	7. **B**	7. **B**	7. **A**
8. **D**	8. **E**	8. **C**	8. **C**	8. **E**	8. **D**	8. **C**	8. **A**	8. **D**
9. **E**	9. **D**	9. **D**	9. **A**	9. **D**	9. **E**	9. **E**	9. **C**	9. **E**
10. **A**	10. **E**	10. **A**	10. **B**	10. **E**	10. **C**	10. **D**	10. **B**	10. **C**

Test 67	Test 71	Test 75	Test 79	Test 83	Test 87	Test 91	Test 95	Test 99
1. **B**	1. **C**	1. **B**	1. **C**	1. **B**	1. **B**	1. **C**	1. **A**	1. **C**
2. **B**	2. **E**	2. **D**	2. **B**	2. **A**	2. **A**	2. **E**	2. **D**	2. **A**
3. **D**	3. **B**	3. **B**	3. **C**	3. **C**	3. **D**	3. **D**	3. **E**	3. **D**
4. **A**	4. **C**	4. **C**	4. **D**	4. **C**	4. **A**	4. **E**	4. **B**	4. **B**
5. **B**	5. **D**	5. **E**	5. **B**	5. **A**	5. **B**	5. **A**	5. **A**	5. **B**
6. **E**	6. **A**	6. **A**	6. **A**	6. **B**	6. **A**	6. **A**	6. **C**	6. **E**
7. **C**	7. **B**	7. **A**	7. **C**	7. **E**	7. **C**	7. **C**	7. **C**	7. **A**
8. **A**	8. **D**	8. **D**	8. **C**	8. **E**	8. **A**	8. **B**	8. **D**	8. **A**
9. **A**	9. **A**	9. **E**	9. **D**	9. **D**	9. **E**	9. **D**	9. **E**	9. **D**
10. **C**	10. **E**	10. **C**	10. **D**	10. **E**	10. **D**	10. **A**	10. **B**	10. **E**

Test 68	Test 72	Test 76	Test 80	Test 84	Test 88	Test 92	Test 96	Test 100
1. **E**	1. **A**	1. **B**	1. **A**	1. **B**	1. **A**	1. **D**	1. **B**	1. **C**
2. **B**	2. **C**	2. **C**	2. **D**	2. **A**	2. **B**	2. **E**	2. **E**	2. **D**
3. **A**	3. **A**	3. **D**	3. **A**	3. **E**	3. **D**	3. **B**	3. **A**	3. **A**
4. **B**	4. **E**	4. **A**	4. **A**	4. **C**	4. **A**	4. **A**	4. **D**	4. **D**
5. **B**	5. **D**	5. **C**	5. **C**	5. **E**	5. **C**	5. **C**	5. **C**	5. **E**
6. **E**	6. **C**	6. **E**	6. **E**	6. **E**	6. **D**	6. **D**	6. **A**	6. **D**
7. **D**	7. **B**	7. **D**	7. **A**	7. **C**	7. **C**	7. **B**	7. **D**	7. **C**
8. **C**	8. **D**	8. **A**	8. **E**	8. **D**	8. **E**	8. **E**	8. **B**	8. **A**
9. **E**	9. **B**	9. **E**	9. **C**	9. **A**	9. **B**	9. **A**	9. **E**	9. **C**
10. **C**	10. **E**	10. **B**	10. **D**	10. **D**	10. **C**	10. **C**	10. **D**	10. **E**

PART 8

GRAMMAR AND USAGE REFRESHER

The following pages will be very helpful in your preparation for the Writing ability parts of the SAT. You will find in these pages a brief but to-the-point review for just about every type of Writing ability question that appears on the actual SAT.

These are the areas covered in this study section:

The Parts of Speech

Clauses and Phrases

The Sentence and Its Parts

Verbs

Nouns and Pronouns

Subject-Verb Relationship

Tense

Verbals

Mood and Voice

Adjective Modifiers

Adverbial Modifiers

Connectives

Correct Usage—Choosing the Right Word

The Parts of Speech*

1a Noun

A **noun** is a word that names a **person, place, thing,** or **idea**.

Persons	Places	Things	Ideas
nurse	forest	banana	love
Henry	Miami	shoe	democracy
uncle	house	television	hunger
Chicano	airport	notebook	cooperation

A noun that is made up of more than one word is called a **compound noun**.

Persons	Places	Things	Ideas
Martin Luther King	high school	telephone book	energy crisis
cab driver	Puerto Rico	car key	arms race
movie star	dining room	park bench	light year
federal judge	Middle East	pork chop	market value

1b Pronoun

A **pronoun** is a word used **in place of a noun.**

Buy a newspaper and bring **it** home.
(The pronoun "it" stands for the noun "newspaper.")

Marlene went to the party, but **she** didn't stay long.
(The pronoun "she" stands for the noun "Marlene.")

A **pronoun** may be used **in place of a noun or a group of nouns.**

Pedro wanted to see the polar bears, camels, and tropical birds, **which** were at the zoo.
(The pronoun "which" stands for the nouns "polar bears, camels, and tropical birds.")

When Mark, Steven, Teresa, and Barbara became eighteen, **they** registered to vote.
(The pronoun "they" stands for the nouns "Mark, Steven, Teresa, and Barbara.")

The **noun that the pronoun replaces** is called the **antecedent** of the pronoun.

The **plates** broke when **they** fell.
(The noun "plates" is the antecedent of the pronoun "they.")

*An index to this entire Grammar Refresher section begins on page 513.

Avoid confusion by repeating the noun instead of using a pronoun if more than one noun might be considered to be the antecedent.

The lamp hit the table when **the lamp** was knocked over.
(**Not:** The lamp hit the table when **it** was knocked over.)

1c Verb

A **verb** is a word or group of words that **expresses action or being**.

The plane **crashed** in Chicago. (action)
Soccer **is** a popular sport. (being)

1d Adjective

An **adjective** is a word that **modifies a noun or pronoun**.

Note: In grammar, to modify a noun means to describe, talk about, explain, limit, specify, or change the character of a noun.

Susan brought us **red** flowers.
(The adjective "red" describes the noun "flowers.")

Everyone at the party looked **beautiful**.
(The adjective "beautiful" describes the pronoun "everyone.")

Several people watched the parade.
(The adjective "several" does not actually describe the noun "people"; it limits or talks about how many "people" watched the parade.)

Those shoes are her **favorite** ones.
(The adjective "favorite" defines or specifies which "ones.")

They have **two** children.
(The adjective "two" limits or specifies how many "children.")

1e Adverb

An **adverb** is a word that **modifies** the meaning of **a verb, an adjective, or another adverb**.

The librarian spoke **softly**.
(The adverb "softly" describes or explains how the librarian "spoke.")

Jackie Onassis was **extremely** rich.
(The adverb "extremely" talks about or specifies how "rich" Jackie Onassis was.)

The job is **very** nearly completed.
(The adverb "very" limits or specifies how "nearly" the job is completed.)

1f Preposition

A **preposition** is a word that **connects a noun or pronoun to another word** in the sentence.

The mayor campaigned **throughout** the city.
(The preposition "throughout" connects the noun "city" to the verb "campaigned.")

A **preposition connects** a noun or pronoun to another word in the sentence **to show a relationship**.

The wife **of** the oil executive was kidnapped.

A friend **of** mine is a good lawyer.

The strainer **for** the sink is broken.

The floor **under** the sink is wet.

David wants to work **in** the city.

The accident occurred **about** eight o'clock.

1g Conjunction

A **conjunction** is a word that **joins words, phrases, or clauses**.

Alan's father **and** mother are divorced. (two words joined)

phrase phrase

Is your favorite song at the end **or** in the middle of the record? (two phrases joined)

You may swim in the pool, **but** don't stay long. (two clauses joined)

(See "Connectives" for a discussion of how prepositions and conjunctions act as connectives.)

1h Interjection

An **interjection** is a word (or group of words) that **expresses surprise, anger, pleasure, or some other emotion**.

Aha! I've caught you.

Oh no! What have you done now?

An **interjection** has **no grammatical relation** to another word.

Ouch! I've hurt myself.

1i A word may belong to more than one part of speech, depending on its meaning.

Example 1

Everyone **but** Sam was invited to the wedding. (preposition)

The Orioles won the pennant, **but** the Angels came close to winning. (conjunction)

Harry has **but** ten dollars left in his bank account. (adverb)

Example 2

He lives **up** the street. (preposition)

It's time to get **up**. (adverb)

The sun is **up**. (adjective)

Every life has its **ups** and downs. (noun)

I'll **up** you five dollars. (verb)

Note: Just for fun—what is the part of speech of the word "behind" in this sentence?

Attempting to save Annie, the fireman ran for the door, dragging her **behind**.

Our answer is an adverb, meaning "at the rear." If your answer was a noun—oh my! The noun means a certain part of the human body. We won't tell you which part.

Clauses and Phrases

2a Clauses

A **clause** is a **group of words** within a sentence.

From his room, **he could see the park**. (one clause)

The children loved the man who sold ice cream. (two clauses)

A clause contains a subject and a verb.

subject verb

Before the race, **the jockeys inspected their horses**. (one clause)

subject verb subject verb

When the rain stopped, the air was cooler. (two clauses)

2b There are two types of clauses: **main** and **subordinate**.*

main clause

During the riot, several people got hurt.

subordinate clause main clause

When she won the lottery, Mrs. Ya-ching shouted with joy.

A **main clause** makes sense by itself.

We got the day off.

A **main clause** expresses a complete thought.

The fire was put out.
(**Not:** When the fire was put out.)

It rained this morning.
(**Not:** Because it rained this morning.)

A **subordinate clause** does not make sense by itself.

While the washing machine was broken, we couldn't wash anything.
(The subordinate clause does not make sense without the rest of the sentence.)

*A main clause may be called an independent clause. A subordinate clause may be called a dependent clause.

Because a subordinate clause does not make sense by itself, a subordinate clause cannot stand as a complete sentence.

While the washing machine was broken...

A subordinate clause depends on a particular word in a main clause to make the subordinate clause mean something.

main clause — subordinate clause

Jack abandoned the car **that had two flat tires.**
(The subordinate clause depends on the noun "car" in the main clause to describe the car.)

main clause — subordinate clause

The job was offered to Ann **because she was best qualified.**
(The subordinate clause depends on the verb "**was** offered" in the main clause to explain **why** the job was offered.)

main clause — subordinate clause

My new neighbor is the one **who is waving.**
(The subordinate clause depends on the pronoun "one" in the main clause to tell **who** is waving.)

A **subordinate clause** may be used in a sentence as an **adjective**, an **adverb**, or a **noun**.

Woody Allen's new film is the funniest movie **that he has made yet.**
(The subordinate clause acts like an adjective because it modifies—talks about—the noun "movie.")

The child giggled **while he was asleep.**
(The subordinate clause functions like an adverb because it modifies the verb "giggled.")

Please tell me **what this is all about.**
(The subordinate clause acts like a noun because it is the object of the action verb "tell.")

2c Phrases

A phrase is a group of words within a sentence.

Thurmon Munson died **in a plane crash.** (one phrase)

Let's sit **under that apple tree.** (one phrase)

At the top of the hill there were some cows grazing. (two phrases)

The phrase itself does not contain a subject or a verb.

subject ↓ verb ↓

Many streets **in the city** need repairs.

A phrase does not make sense by itself.

Ellen has a collection **of beautiful earrings.**
(The phrase "of beautiful earrings" does not make sense by itself; therefore, the phrase cannot stand alone as a complete sentence.)

A phrase may begin with a preposition, a participle, a gerund, or an infinitive.

preposition ↓

Put the milk **into the refrigerator.** (prepositional phrase) participle ↓

There are several people **waiting in line**. (participial phrase)

gerund ↓

Running ten miles a day is hard work. (gerund phrase)

infinitive ↓

To sing well takes a lot of practice. (infinitive phrase)

A **phrase** may be used as a **noun**, an **adjective**, or an **adverb**.

A doctor's job is **to heal people**.
(The infinitive phrase acts like a noun because it names the doctor's job.)

Raising his hands, the pope blessed the crowd.
(The participial phrase acts like an adjective because it describes the pope.)

Most stores close **at five o'clock**.
(The prepositional phrase acts like an adverb because it tells when most stores close.)

The Sentence and Its Parts

3a A **sentence** is a **group of words** that has a **subject** and a **verb**.

subject ↓ verb ↓

The **concert began** at midnight.

subject ↓ verb ↓

During the storm, the **electricity was knocked out**.

3b A sentence may be **declarative, interrogative**, or **exclamatory**.

A **declarative** sentence **states or asserts**.

Inflation is a serious problem.

An **interrogative** sentence **asks a question**.

How long must we suffer?

An **exclamatory** sentence **expresses emotion.** The sentence ends with an exclamation point (!).

What a fool he is!

An **imperative** sentence **makes a request** or **gives a command**.

Don't be afraid to try something new.

A **sentence** expresses a **complete thought**.

The price of gold has gone up.

Bus service will resume on Friday morning.

Note: Because a sentence expresses a complete thought, a sentence makes sense by itself.

Peter likes to tend his vegetable garden. (complete thought)

Peter likes. (incomplete thought—not a sentence)

The gasoline shortage created serious problems. (complete thought)

The gasoline shortage. (incomplete thought—not a sentence)

3c The four types of sentences according to structure are the following:

(1) **Simple** Everyone likes music.

(2) **Compound** The Simons put their house up for sale on Friday, and it was sold by Monday.

(3) **Complex** If you want good Szechuan cooking, you should go to the Hot Wok Restaurant.

(4) **Compound-Complex** Bob met Sally, who was in town for a few days, and they went to a museum.

3d Simple sentence

A **simple sentence** is made up of only **one main (independent) clause.**

I love you.

A simple sentence may be of any length.

The old man sitting on the park bench is the father of a dozen men and women besides being the grandfather of nearly forty children.

Note: A simple sentence **does not have a subordinate clause** in it.

3e Compound sentence

A **compound sentence** has **two or more main clauses.**

main clause — conjunction

Conrad and Isabel got married, and

main clause

they invited several friends to a party.

main clause — conjunction — main clause

Stuart attended college, but he left after a year.

Each main clause in a compound sentence may stand by itself as a simple sentence—as long as the conjunction is left out.

conjunction

Carlos will arrive by plane tonight, and Maria will go to the airport to meet him. (compound sentence)

Carlos will arrive by plane tonight. (simple sentence)

Maria will go to the airport to meet him. (simple sentence)

Note: A compound sentence does not have any subordinate clauses.

3f Complex sentence

A complex sentence contains only one main clause and one or more subordinate clauses.

subordinate clause — main clause

After he signed the treaty, President Bush asked the Senate to ratify it. (one main clause and one subordinate clause)

subordinate clause — main clause

Although they are expensive to install, solar heating systems save money and energy,

subordinate clause

which are hard to get these days. (one main clause and two subordinate clauses) subordinate clause

Because he came from the planet Krypton,

main clause / subordinate clause

Superman had special powers that no one on Earth could equal,

subordinate clause

though many people have tried.
(one main clause and three subordinate clauses)

3g Compound-complex sentence

A compound-complex sentence is made up of **two or more main clauses and one or more subordinate clauses**.

subordinate clause

After his store burned down,

main clause

Mr. Crossman rented the store across the street,

main clause

and his business continued to do well. (two main clauses and one subordinate clause)

main clause

Eric wanted to go to the new club,

subordinate clause

which he had heard was a great place,

main clause

but he did not want to see his ex-girlfriend,

subordinate clause

who worked there. (two main clauses and two subordinate clauses)

3h The parts of a sentence

The basic parts of a sentence are a **subject**, a **verb**, and a **complement**.*

subject ↓ verb ↓ complement ↓

The waiter brought the soup.

compound subject / verb ↓ / complement ↓

Mason and Lucy sold me their stereo.

*The complement is discussed on page 471.

3i Subject

The **subject** of a sentence is the word (or group of words) that **tells who or what is being talked about.**

Ann Landers gives advice to millions of Americans.
(Because Ann Landers is being talked about, "Ann Landers" is the subject of the sentence.)

High **taxes** caused many businesses to close.
(Because we are told that high taxes caused businesses to close, the noun "taxes" is the subject of the sentence.)

Whoever goes to bed last should shut off the lights.
(Because we are told that whoever goes to bed last should do something, the noun clause "whoever goes to bed last" is the subject of the sentence.)

Brushing one's teeth and getting checkups regularly are two important parts of good dental care.
(Because brushing one's teeth and getting checkups are discussed, the two gerund phrases are the **compound subject** of the sentence.)

3j A **subject** may be a **noun, pronoun, verbal, phrase,** or **clause**.

(1) A subject is usually a **noun.**

Our **wedding** will be held outdoors.

The **White House** is the home of the president.

The **police** arrested the antinuclear energy demonstrators.

(2) A subject may be a **pronoun**.

He always gets his way. (personal pronoun used as the subject)

Hers is the tan raincoat. (possessive pronoun used as the subject)

What did you do? (interrogative pronoun used as the subject)

That is my car. (demonstrative pronoun used as the subject)

Everyone was happy. (indefinite pronoun used as the subject)

(3) A subject may be a **verbal.***

To begin is the hardest part of the job. (infinitive used as the subject)

Jogging is good exercise. (gerund used as a subject)

Note: A participle may not be used as a subject because it is a verb form that only does the work of an adjective.

(4) A subject may be a **phrase**.

Smoking cigarettes is unhealthy. (gerund phrase used as a subject)

To obey the law is everyone's duty. (infinitive phrase used as a subject)

(5) A subject may be a subordinate **clause**.

Whatever you decide is all right.

That Danny had cancer saddened his friends.

What will happen is going to surprise you.

Who will star in the movie will be announced.

*See "Verbals" on page 487.

3k Verb

A verb is a word or group of words that **usually tells what the subject does.**

Annie **skated** down the street.

Your baby **has dropped** his toy.

President Nixon **resigned**.

The telephone **is ringing**.

Two or more verbs may have one subject.

They **defeated** the Cubs but **lost** to the Pirates.

Dick **works** during the day and **goes** to school at night.

A verb may express a state or condition.

Lynn **appears** puzzled. (Or: Lynn **appears to be puzzled**.)

The stew **tastes** delicious.

Jason and Martha **are** good friends.

3l The three kinds of verbs are **transitive, intransitive,** and **linking**.

3m A transitive verb tells what its subject does to someone or to something.

The cat **caught** the mouse.

Phil **washed** the dishes.

Carol's mother **slapped** the boy.

3n An intransitive verb tells what its subject does. The action of the intransitive verb does not affect someone or something else.

The old man **slept** in his chair.

The audience **applauded**.

All of the job applicants **waited** patiently.

Note: Many verbs may be transitive or intransitive.

He **will return** the book tomorrow. (transitive)

The manager **will return** in an hour. (intransitive)

Whether a verb is transitive or intransitive depends on how it is used in the sentence.

Chuck **opened** the package.
(The verb is transitive because the action was carried out on something.)

The door **opened** slowly.
(The verb is intransitive because the action by the subject "door" did not affect anything else.)

3o A linking verb links the subject with a noun or a pronoun or an adjective.

Jaws was a terrifying **film**. (noun)

It's **I**.* (pronoun)

*In spoken English, it is acceptable to say "It's me" or "It's us." It is not acceptable, however, to say "It's him," "It's her," or "It's them." For formal tests such as the SAT, follow the rules for case.

The child in this old photograph is **I**. (pronoun)

The girl who loves Peter is **she**. (pronoun)

The Beatles were **popular** in the 1960s. (adjective)

A linking verb may link the subject with an infinitive, a gerund, or a noun clause.

Stephanie's greatest pleasure is **to sing**. (infinitive)

Herb's mistake was **lying**. (gerund)

David's new job seemed **what he had hoped for**. (noun clause)

Linking verbs are **to be, to appear, to grow, to seem, to remain, to become,** and verbs that involve the senses, such as **to look, to smell, to feel, to sound,** and **to taste**.

Karen and Valerie **are** sisters.

Ben **is** strong.

Eric **appears** healthy.

The situation at the prison **remains** tense.

Gertrude **feels** better.

Jim **sounds** angry.

A verb that appears to be a sense-linking verb may not actually be a sense-linking verb.

The milk **smells** sour. (linking verb)

The dog **smells** the fire hydrant. (transitive verb)

Tony **looked** sad. (linking verb)

Rosie **looked** through the window. (intransitive verb)

Note: The use of a particular verb determines whether that verb is sense-linking **or** transitive **or** intransitive.

3p

Transitive verb	**Intransitive verb**	**Linking verb**
1. Expresses action	1. Expresses action	1. Does not express action
2. Is followed by a direct object that receives the action subject → Keith; trans. verb → shot a; direct object → deer.	2. Is not followed by a direct object subject → Jimmy; intrans. verb → grinned.	2. May be followed by a noun or an adjective subject → Juanita; link. verb → is a; predicate noun → nurse. subject → Lenny; link. verb → looks; predicate adjective → sick.

Verbs

4a Five characteristics of every verb are number, person, tense, mood, and voice.

4b Number shows whether the subject of the verb is singular or plural. A good rule to keep in mind is that nouns ending in *s* are plural, while verbs ending in *s* are singular.

Maggie **drives** well. (singular)

Adam and Peter **drive** dangerously. (plural)

Joan's grandmother **is** in Atlanta. (singular)

Arthur's parents **are** from Texas. (plural)

A verb must always agree in number with its subject.

subject ↓ verb ↓

Emily **lives** alone. (subject and verb both singular)

subject ↓ subject ↓ verb ↓

Dennis and Chuck **live** together. (subject and verb both plural)

4c Person tells whether the subject of the verb is speaking, being spoken to, or being spoken about.

I **am** the person in charge. (first person)

You **are** my best friend. (second person)

Bill **is** not here. (third person)

I **swim** at the YMCA. (first person)

You **come** with me. (second person)

Rosa **speaks** Spanish and French. (third person)

All three persons may be singular or plural in number.

	Singular	**Plural**
First person	I run	we run
Second person	you run	you run
Third person	he runs	
	she runs	they run
	it runs	

Note: The same verb form frequently is used for different persons and different numbers.

I **love** ice cream. (first person singular)

We **love** ice cream. (first person plural)

They **love** ice cream. (third person plural)

4d Tense shows when the action of the verb takes place—whether in the present, the past, or the future.

A plane **is passing** over our house right now. (present)

Our guests **are** here. (present)

Two U.S. astronauts **walked** on the moon in 1969. (past)

The workmen **were** here yesterday. (past)

We'll **pay** you tomorrow. (future)

Many people **will be** at the party tomorrow. (future)

4e Mood indicates how a sentence is used—whether it is a statement or a question, a command or a request, a wish or a condition.

Dinner **is** ready. (statement)

Does Elizabeth **work** in New Jersey? (question)

Go away! (command)

Please **pass** me the bread. (request)

If it **doesn't** rain, we can go. (condition)

The three kinds of moods are indicative, imperative, and subjunctive.

The indicative mood is used to express a statement or a question.

Two firemen were injured in the blaze. (statement)

Are you going out tonight? (question)

The imperative mood expresses a command or a request.

Turn off that radio! (command)

May I have a menu? (request—not question)

Note: The imperative mood is frequently indicated by leaving out the pronoun "you."

(You) Stop that!

The subjunctive mood may be used to show that a wish rather than a fact is being expressed.

I wish I **were** ten years younger.

4f Voice indicates whether the subject acts or is acted upon.

The dog **barked** at the stranger. (acts)

The baby **was kissed** several times. (is acted upon)

A verb in the active voice shows that the subject is doing something.

The thieves **wounded** the bank teller. (active voice)

The curtains **blocked** our view. (active voice)

A verb in the passive voice shows that something is being done to the subject.

The garbage **was picked up** this morning. (passive voice)

Tyrone's car **is being washed**. (passive voice)

4g Complement

A complement may be one or more words that come after either a transitive or a linking verb.

complement ↓

Fire destroyed the **building**. (transitive verb)

complement ↓

The cat seemed **startled**. (linking verb)

complement ↓ complement ↓

Tony bought his **wife** a silver **necklace**. (transitive verb)

complement ↓

Adam will be **president** someday. (linking verb)

A complement completes the meaning of the verb.

The junta took **control of the government**.

A baseball broke the **window**.

4h The four ways that a complement may be used in a sentence are 1) as a direct object of the verb, 2) as an indirect object of the verb, 3) as a predicate noun,* and 4) as a predicate adjective.

Sally waters her **garden** every day. (direct object, receiving the action of the verb)

Vincent gave his **brother** a basketball. (indirect object, telling to whom the action of the verb was directed)

Note: The noun "basketball" is the direct object of the transitive verb "gave"; therefore, "basketball" is also a complement.

Arthur Fiedler was the **conductor** of the Boston Pops. (predicate noun, renaming the subject after the linking verb)

Alaska is **huge**. (predicate adjective, describing the subject after the linking verb)

4i A complement used as a direct object of the verb may be a noun, a pronoun, or a subordinate clause.

Uncle Nate plants **vegetables** each spring. (noun used as direct object)

You should see **her** now. (pronoun used as direct object)

Tell me **what you know about life insurance**. (subordinate clause used as direct object)

4j A complement used as an indirect object of the verb may also be a noun, a pronoun, or a subordinate clause.

The nurse sent the **patient** a bill. (noun used as indirect object)

Will you do **me** a favor? (pronoun used as indirect object)

Give **whoever calls today** this information. (subordinate clause used as indirect object)

Note: From the three examples above, you can see that **an indirect object must always precede a direct object**.

*A predicate noun is also called a predicate nominative.

The three previous sentences—which have indirect objects—may be expressed in a different way.

The nurse sent a bill **to the patient**.

Will you do a favor **for me**?

Give this information **to whoever calls today**.

In these three sentences, the prepositional phrases serve the purpose of indirect objects.

4k A complement that acts as a predicate noun may be a noun, a pronoun, a verbal, a phrase, or a clause.

Juan's uncle is **a bus driver**. (noun)

It is **she**. (pronoun)

Fred's favorite sport is **sailing**. (gerund)

President Sadat's desire was **to make peace**. (infinitive phrase)

Fixing cars is **what Tom does best**. (noun clause)

4l A complement that acts like a predicate adjective may be an adjective or an adjective phrase.

Laverne and Shirley **are funny**. (adjective)

The lecture was **about athletics**. (adjective phrase)

Note: Both predicate nouns and predicate adjectives may be called predicate complements.

Nouns and Pronouns

5a Nouns

The five types of nouns are **1) proper, 2) common, 3) collective, 4) concrete,** and **5) abstract.***

5b A proper noun names a particular person, place, or thing.

César Chávez, San Clemente, Statue of Liberty
(Proper nouns always begin with a capital letter.)

5c A common noun names a general sort of person, place, or thing.

waitress, store, table

5d A collective noun names a group of individuals.

congregation, class, political party
(A collective noun is singular in form, but it refers to many people.)

5e A concrete noun names any material object that is inanimate.

apple, hat, ball, box, desk, book, shirt

5f An abstract noun names a quality, state, or idea.

truth, motion, beauty

5g Pronouns

The six kinds of pronouns are **1) personal, 2) relative, 3) interrogative, 4) indefinite, 5) demonstrative,** and **6) reflexive.**

5h A personal pronoun stands for the speaker, the person spoken to, or the person or thing spoken about.

I am going out.
(The first person "I" is speaking.)

You should see the traffic jam downtown.
(The second person "you" is being spoken to.)

She wants to become a lawyer.
(The third person "she" is being spoken about.)

*A noun may be of more than one type. For example, "table" is both a common noun and a concrete noun.

The **personal pronouns** are the following:

I, you, he, she, it, we, they, me, us, him, her, them

The **possessive** forms of the personal pronouns are the following:

my, mine, yours, his, hers, its, our, ours, their, theirs

A pronoun should be in the same person as the noun or pronoun it refers to.

The tree was damaged when lightning struck **it**. (noun and pronoun in third person)

Everyone knows that **he** should dress well to make a good impression. (both pronouns in third person) (Not: **Everyone** knows that you should...)

5i The **relative pronouns** are the following:

who (whom), which, what, that

A relative pronoun may begin a subordinate clause.

The child, **who** was alone, looked unhappy.

A relative pronoun connects the main clause to the subordinate clause.

The problem was in the gas line, **which** was rusty.
(The relative pronoun "which" joins the main clause to the subordinate clause it begins.)

A relative pronoun stands for a noun in the main clause.

Sharon gave me the money **that** I needed.
(The relative pronoun "that" stands for the noun "money" in the main clause.)

When to use the relative pronoun "whom"

"Whom" is the objective case form of "who." We use "whom" as a **direct object,** an **indirect object,** or an **object of the preposition.**

The men **whom** you see are waiting for work.
(The relative pronoun "whom" is the direct object of the verb "see.")

Hansen is the person to **whom** Wilmot gave the bribe money.
(The relative pronoun "whom" is the indirect object of the verb "gave.")

The typewriter was stolen by the messenger about **whom** the office manager had been suspicious.
(The relative pronoun "whom" is the object of the preposition "about.")

5j An interrogative pronoun asks a question.

Who wants to start first?

What did Richard do then?

Which should I take?

Whose is this jacket?

Whom do you want to speak to?

5k An indefinite pronoun refers to a number of persons, places, or things in a general way.

None of the dishes was broken.

Mark finds **everything** about boats interesting.

I'll bring you **another**.

Some of my friends buy lottery tickets.

Other commonly used indefinite pronouns are the following:

any, both, few, many, most, one, other, several, such

5l A demonstrative pronoun points out a specific person or thing.

This is not my handwriting.

May I have two of **those?**

That is my brother.

These are my best friends.

Note: Interrogative, indefinite, and demonstrative pronouns may be used as adjectives.

Which dessert do you want? (interrogative adjective)

Every time I try to skate I fall down. (indefinite adjective)

That dress costs too much. (demonstrative adjective)

5m A reflexive pronoun refers back to the noun it stands for.

I hurt **myself** while jogging.

Amy considers **herself** an adult.

A reflexive pronoun may be the **direct object of a verb,** the **indirect object of a verb,** the **object of a preposition,** or a **predicate noun**.

Kim pushed **himself** and finished the race. (direct object)

Ray bought **himself** a new watch. (indirect object)

Buffie likes to be by **herself**. (object of a preposition)

Mr. Thompson is just not **himself** lately. (predicate nominative)

Note: Do not use "hisself" for "himself," or **"theirselves" for "themselves." These are always incorrect.**

5n Three characteristics shared by all nouns and pronouns are gender, number, and case.

5o Gender indicates the sex of the person or thing named—whether masculine, feminine, or neuter.

Adam wants some ice cream, but **he** is on a diet.
("Adam" and the pronoun "he" are both masculine in gender.)

Alice said **she** was ready.
("Alice" and the pronoun "she" are both feminine in gender.)

The **movie** was good, but **it** was too long.
("Movie" and the pronoun "it" are neither masculine nor feminine; therefore, they are both neuter in gender.)

A pronoun should be in the same gender as the noun it refers to.

5p Number indicates whether one or more than one person or thing is named.

Here is a **letter** for you.
(The one "letter" is singular in number.)

Many **cars** were involved in the accident.
(Many "cars" are plural in number.)

Note: A collective noun is singular in form but usually plural in meaning.

The audience was upset by the delay.
("Audience" is singular in number, although many people are in the audience.)

A pronoun should be in the same number as the noun it refers to.

The **dishes** are not clean, so don't use **them**.
("Dishes" and the pronoun "them" are both plural in number.)

Hockey is a lot of fun, but **it** is rough.
("Hockey" and the pronoun "it" are both singular in number.)

A pronoun that refers to a collective noun that is considered as a unit should be singular in number.

The home team won **its** final game of the season.

A pronoun that refers to a collective noun that is considered as a group of individuals should be plural.

The visiting team felt **they** deserved to win.

A pronoun that refers to an indefinite pronoun antecedent must be singular.

Almost anyone can earn a good living if **he** or **she** works hard.

A pronoun must be singular if it refers to singular antecedents joined by "or" or "nor."

Neither **Earle** nor **Jeff** could find **his** coat.

5q Case shows how a noun or pronoun is used in a sentence.

They stayed out all night.
("They" is the subject.)

Natalie knew **him**.
("Him" is the object of the transitive verb.)

Craig thinks this hat is **his**.
("His" is a pronoun that shows ownership.)

The three cases are nominative, objective, and possessive.

5r The nominative case names the subject of a verb or the predicate noun of a linking verb.

Susan and **I** will call you tonight. (subjects)

My best friends are **Katherine** and **you**. (predicate nouns)

A noun in the nominative case is usually placed before a verb.

Mr. Garcia opened a dry cleaning business.

Ida answered the telephone.

Personal pronouns in the nominative case have the following forms:

I, you, he, she, it, we, they

The subject of a subordinate clause must be in the nominative case even if the clause itself acts as a direct object or an object of a preposition.

Show me **who** is waiting to see me. (subordinate clause as direct object)

Discuss this form with **whoever** applies for the job. (subordinate clause **as** object of a preposition)

5s The objective case indicates that nouns and pronouns act as direct objects, indirect objects, or objects of prepositions.

The storm forced **them** to stay home. (direct object)

Victor enjoyed meeting **her**. (direct object)

Sally called **us, Mary** and **me, into her office**. (direct objects)

The cab driver gave **me** good directions. (indirect object)

Our supervisor showed **him** and **me** some contracts. (indirect objects)

Annette had trouble teaching **them** how to type. (indirect object)

Several of **us** want more food. (object of the preposition)

Between **you** and **me,** I don't like our boss. (objects of the preposition)

Note: Each noun or pronoun in a compound object must be in the objective case.

A noun is in the objective case if it is placed after a transitive verb or after a preposition.

He saw **Greta Garbo**.

Ernie went into the **store**.

Personal pronouns in the objective case have the following forms:

me, you, him, her, it, us, them

5t Only three personal pronouns—**we**, **us**, and **you**—may also be used as **adjective pronouns**.

We women have responded to the challenge of the 2000s.

They are discriminating against **us** women.

You boys should play more quietly.

Note: The adjective pronoun "we" is in the nominative case when it modifies a subject. The adjective pronoun "us" is in the objective case when it modifies an object of a verb or an object of a preposition.

We Republicans support President Bush's bid for re-election. (nominative case when modifying subject)

Mom sent **us** children to bed. (objective case when modifying direct object of verb)

Won't you give **us** boys a chance to earn some money? (objective case when modifying indirect object of verb)

Many children were on the plane with **us** adults. (objective case when modifying object of a preposition)

5u The objective case is used by nouns and pronouns that are the subject of an infinitive.

Paul's father wants **him** to help paint the house.

Should Fred ask **her** to join the club?

A noun or pronoun following the infinitive **to be** must, like its subject, be in the objective case.

Pat didn't expect my friend to be **him**.

Note: If the infinitive **to be** has no subject, the noun or pronoun that comes after the infinitive is in the nominative case.

My twin brother is often thought to be **I**. (nominative case)

5v The possessive case indicates ownership.

Martha's home is in Ohio.

This book is **mine**.

Possession is generally shown by using an apostrophe and *s*:

Bumbry's error	men's room
child's toy	ship's crew

Ownership may be shown by an "of" phrase.

The handle **of the door** is broken.

The "of" phrase is used in formal English to show possession by inanimate things or to avoid awkward constructions.

The passage **of the bill** now in Congress will mean lower taxes.
(Not: The bill's passage…)

The sister **of my uncle's wife** is eighty years old.
(Not: My uncle's wife's sister…)

Personal and relative pronouns have distinct forms to show the possessive case.

The following are personal pronouns (possessive form):
my, mine, your, yours, his, her, hers, our, ours, their, theirs, its*

That dress is **hers**.

Ours is the house on the left.

"Whose" is a relative pronoun. (possessive form)†

No one knows **whose** it is.

The possessive forms **my, your, his, our, their,‡** and **whose** are called adjective pronouns because they modify nouns.

Your shirt has a button missing.

My family is very large.

Their apartment costs a lot of money.

The woman **whose** typewriter I borrowed, gave it to me.

The possessive case is used by nouns and pronouns that come before a gerund.

Bubba's shouting attracted a large crowd. (noun)

My being sick caused me to miss an important lecture. (pronoun)

The possessive case of a compound noun is indicated by adding *'s* to the **last word of the compound noun.**

A **movie star's** life is glamorous.

The **Governor of California's** speech attacked the president.

Pope John Paul II's visit to the United States pleased millions.

Note: The plural of a compound noun is formed by adding *s* to the principal noun.

chief of police (singular)	chief of police's (singular possessive)
chiefs of police (plural)	chiefs of police's (plural possessive)

5w An **appositive** is a **noun or pronoun** usually placed next to another noun or pronoun to rename it.

Two guys, **Nestar and his cousin**, were already there. (identifies the subject)

Clarinda's dog **Sonya** eats only hamburgers. (renames the subject)

*"Its" is the possessive form of the personal pronoun "it." "It's" is a contraction of "it is."
†"Whose" is the possessive form of the relative pronoun "who"; "who's" is a contraction of "who is."
‡"Their" is the possessive form of the relative pronoun "they"; "they're" is a contraction of "they are."

Note: An appositive must always be in the same case as the noun it renames.

We, **my brother and I,** are going hunting together. (both subject and appositive in nominative case)

Uncle Joe gave us, **Stuart and me,** tickets to the World Series. (both object and appositive in case)

5x Direct address and **nominative absolute** constructions are **always in the nominative case**.

Direct address consists of a noun (or pronoun) that names a particular person when someone else addresses that person.

Willy, please come here immediately.

A nominative absolute consists of a noun plus a participle.

The money having been spent, the boys decided to go home.

Subject-Verb Relationship

6a A verb must agree with its subject in number and in person.

Dr. Shu has office hours from 8 until 4.
(The third person singular form of "to have" agrees with the subject "Dr. Shu.")

Robin and I **play** squash every Tuesday.
(The first person plural form of "to play" agrees with the compound subject "Robin and I.")

6b Collective nouns are followed by singular or plural verbs according to the sense of the sentence.

The jury **has** asked for more time.
(The third person singular is used because the jury is considered to be a unified body.)

The jury **are** unable to agree.
(The third person plural is used because the jury is considered to be a group of twelve persons.)

To summarize, a **collective noun** is **singular** when it refers to a group as a single unit.

A minority in Congress **is** delaying passage of the bill.

A **collective noun** is **plural** when it refers to the individual members of the group.

A minority of Congressmen **want** to defeat the bill.

6c Some indefinite pronouns are always singular in meaning.

Each of the candidates **wants** an opportunity to discuss his beliefs.

Anyone is allowed to use the public beach.

Any one of us **is** willing to help.

Some indefinite pronouns are always plural in meaning.

Many of the drawings **were** beautiful.

A **few** of the windows **were** broken.

Several of Joe's friends **are** sorry that he left.

6d A verb should be **singular** if its subject has **"every"** or **"many a"** just before it.

Many a woman feels entitled to more in life than just housework.

Every man, woman, and child wants to be happy.

Some **indefinite pronouns** may be **singular or plural,** depending on the meaning of the sentence.

Some of the books **have** been lost.

Some of the work **was** completed.

All of the ice cream **is** gone.

All of the men **have** left.

Most of the talk **was** about football.

Most of the people **were** dissatisfied.

6e When singular subjects are joined by "or" or "nor," the subject is considered to be singular.

Neither the mother **nor** her daughter **was** ever seen again.

One or the **other** of us **has** to buy the tickets.

6f When one singular and one plural subject are joined by "or" or "nor," the subject closer to the verb determines the number of the verb.

Neither the plumber nor the painters **have** finished.

Either the branch offices or the main office **closes** at 4.

6g When the subjects joined by "or" or "nor" are of different persons, the subject nearer the verb determines the person.

She or you **are** responsible.

You or she **is** responsible.

To avoid such awkward sentences, place a verb next to each subject.

Either she **is** responsible or you **are.**

Either you **are** responsible or she **is.**

6h Even if the verb comes before the subject, the verb agrees with the true subject in number and person.

Are the cat and the dog fighting? (The cat and the dog are…)

Coming at us from the left **was** an ambulance. (An ambulance was…)

There **are** two things you can do.* (Two things are…)

There **is** only one bottle left.* (Only one bottle is…)

6i Interrogative pronouns and the adverbs "where," "here," and "there" do not affect the number or person of the verb when they introduce a sentence.

subject ↓

What **is** the **name** of your friend?

subject ↓

What **are** the **addresses** of some good restaurants?

subject ↓

Who **is** the **man** standing over there?

subject ↓

Who **are** those **people?**

*In this sentence, *there* is an expletive. An expletive is a word that gets a sentence started, but it is not a subject. Another expletive is *it.*

subject ↓

Here **comes** my **friend**.

subject ↓

Here **come** my **parents**.

6j When a predicate noun (following a linking verb) differs in number from the subject, the verb must agree with the subject.

Our biggest problem **is** angry customers.

More gas guzzlers **aren't** what this country needs.

6k Parenthetical phrases or other modifiers that come between the subject and verb **do not change the number or person of the true subject**—which the verb agrees with.

The amount shown, plus interest, **is** due on Friday.

The president, together with his advisers, **is** at Camp David.

Tense

7a Tense specifies the moment of an action or condition.

We **are walking** to the park. (present moment)

We **will walk** to the park tomorrow. (future moment)

We **walked** to the park yesterday. (past moment)

I **have worked** here for three years. (action begun in the past and continued into the present)

I **had worked** in Chicago for four years before I left. (past action completed **before** another past action)

I **will have worked** here six months next Friday. (action to be completed sometime in the future)

7b The six tenses are present, past, future, present perfect, past perfect, and future perfect.

7c The **present tense** shows that an action is **happening in the present** or that a condition exists now.

I **live** here. (action)

He **is** busy now. (condition)

The **present-tense** forms of **to work, to have,** and **to be** follow:

<u>**to work**</u>	<u>**to have**</u>	<u>**to be**</u>
I work	I have	I am
you work	you have	you are
he / she / it } works	he / she / it } has	he / she / it } is
we work	we have	we are
you work	you have	you are
they work	they have	they are

The present tense may indicate **habitual action** or **habitual condition,** or **a general truth**.

Judy **leaves** her office every day at 5 o'clock. (habitual action)

Dana **is** allergic to chocolate. (habitual condition)

Two and two **are** four. (general truth)

The present tense may express **future time with the help of an adverb.**

adverb
↓
Gary flies to Washington **tomorrow**.

adverb
↓
We are going to see a movie **tonight**.

7d The **present perfect tense** shows that an action that **began in the past** is **still going on in the present**.

Betsy and I **have been** in New York for two years. (and are still in New York)

The Johnson family **has owned** a plumbing supply company for sixty years. (and still owns it)

The **present perfect tense** may show that an action **begun in the past was just completed at the present time**.

Our men **have worked** on your car until now.

Charlayne **has** just **walked** in.

The **present perfect tense** is formed with **have or has and a past participle**.

I **have eaten** too much.

Nina **has** always **loved** music.

7e The **past tense** shows that an action **occurred some time in the past** but has **not continued into the present**.

Laura's doctor **advised** her to lose weight.

The plane **landed** on time.

Susan **was living** in Philadelphia then. (progressive form)

We **went** along for the ride.

If the verb in the main clause is in the past tense, the verb in the subordinate clause must also be in the past tense.

The surgeon told his patient that an operation **was** necessary.
(Not: The surgeon told his patient that an operation **is** necessary.)

Lenny said that he **would meet** Frank at 7:30.
(Not: Lenny said that he **will meet** Frank at 7:30.)

The past tense (first, second, and third person—singular and plural) is often formed by adding "ed" to the infinitive (without "to.")

Jim **helped** us many times.

We **called** you last night.

7f The **past perfect tense** indicates that an **action was completed before another action began**.

I remembered the answer after **I had handed in** my exam.

Kenny **had bought** the tickets before he met Ruth.

Margaret **had worked** very hard, so she took a vacation.

Note: The **past tense** shows that an event happened at any time in the past, but the **past perfect tense** indicates that an event happened before another event in the past.

Paula **had finished** dressing before I woke up.
(Not: Paula **finished** dressing before I woke up.)

Jake **had** already **left** by the time I arrived.
(Not: Jake already **left** by the time I arrived.)

The past perfect tense is formed with "had" and a past participle.

Peter **had said** he would call before twelve.

7g The **future tense** indicates that an **action is going to take place sometime in the future.**

All of us **will pay** more for heat this winter.

The weatherman says it **will rain** tomorrow.

Will you **join** us for lunch, Eric?

I'll go away this weekend.

The future tense is formed with "will" and the infinitive (without "to").

Don **will take** you to the airport.

7h The **future perfect tense** is used to express a **future action that will be completed before another future action.**

By the time we get home,* my parents **will have gone** to bed.

We'll start eating after you **(will) have washed** your hands.

Helena **will have finished** her work when we meet her at the office.

The future perfect tense is formed with "will have" and a past participle.

Patty **will have quit** her job by Christmas.

7i All six tenses may be expressed in a progressive form by adding the present participle of a verb to the appropriate form of "to be."

The Cosmos **are winning**. (present progressive)

The Cosmos **were winning**. (past progressive)

The Cosmos **have been winning**. (present perfect progressive)

The Cosmos **had been winning**. (past perfect progressive)

The Cosmos **will be winning**. (future progressive)

The Cosmos **will have been winning**. (future perfect progressive)

7j Principal parts of irregular verbs

We call a verb like "eat" an irregular verb. Any verb that changes internally to form the past participle is an irregular verb.

*See page 484, which discusses how a present tense may express future time.

Present Tense	Past Tense	Past Participle	Present Participle
begin	began	begun	beginning
blow	blew	blown	blowing
break	broke	broken	breaking
burst	burst	burst	bursting
catch	caught	caught	catching
choose	chose	chosen	choosing
come	came	come	coming
do	did	done	doing
drink	drank	drunk	drinking
drive	drove	driven	driving
eat	ate	eaten	eating
fall	fell	fallen	falling
find	found	found	finding
fly	flew	flown	flying
freeze	froze	frozen	freezing
give	gave	given	giving
go	went	gone	going
grow	grew	grown	growing
know	knew	known	knowing
lay (place)	laid	laid	laying
lie (rest)	lay	lain	lying
raise	raised	raised	raising
ring	rang	rung	ringing
rise	rose	risen	rising
run	ran	run	running
set	set	set	setting
sit	sat	sat	sitting
speak	spoke	spoken	speaking
steal	stole	stolen	stealing
swim	swam	swum	swimming
take	took	taken	taking
throw	threw	thrown	throwing
wear	wore	worn	wearing
write	wrote	written	writing

Verbals

8a A verbal is a word formed from a verb.

Skiing can be dangerous.

We could hear our neighbors **arguing**.

Bonnie and Clyde worked hard **to succeed**.

8b The **three kinds of verbals** are **gerunds, participles,** and **infinitives**.

8c A gerund acts like a noun.

Smoking is not allowed in many stores.

Traveling by train can be fun.

Mark's favorite sport is **boating**.

A gerund ends in "ing."

Nureyev's **dancing** is terrific.

Flying is the fastest way to get there.

A phrase that begins with a gerund is called a gerund phrase.

Paying bills on time is a good habit.

Leaving my friends made me sad.

8d A participle acts like an adjective.

The police stopped the **speeding** car.

The **tired** children were sent to bed.

A present participle ends in "ing."

A priest comforted the **dying** woman.

Running, the girl caught up with her friends.

Note: A present participle looks like a gerund because they both end in "ing." A present participle, however, is used as an adjective, not as a noun.

A past participle usually ends in "d," "ed," "t," "n," or "en."

Used clothing is cheaper than new clothes.

Woody left **written** instructions for his assistant.

A phrase that begins with a participle is called a participial phrase.

Getting off the elevator, I met a friend.

Questioned by the police, several witnesses described the robbery.

8e An infinitive is used as a noun or an adjective or an adverb.

Franz loves **to dance**. (noun)

Our candidate has the ability **to win**. (adjective)

Lisa practices every day **to improve**. (adverb)

An infinitive usually begins with "to," but not always.

Sally wants **to know** if you need a ride.

Help me wash my car. (Or: Help me **to wash** my car.)

A phrase introduced by an infinitive is called an infinitive phrase.

His only desire **was to save money**. (infinitive phrase used as a noun)

There must be **a way to solve this problem**. (infinitive phrase used as an adjective)

The doctor is too busy **to see you now**. (infinitive phrase used as an adverb)

8f Gerunds may be present or perfect.

Good **cooking** is her specialty. (present)

Your **having arrived** on time saved me. (perfect)

A gerund in the present form refers to an **action happening at the same time as the action of the main verb.**

Swimming is fun.

Running a mile tired him out.

Taking driving lessons will help you drive better.

A gerund in the perfect form refers to an **action that was completed before the time of the main verb.**

He believes his recovery is a result of his **having prayed**.

Our **having read** the book made the movie boring.

8g Participles may be present, past, or perfect.

The woman **sitting** on the couch is my mother. (present)

Warned by his doctor, Jack began to exercise. (past)

Having been recognized, Elton John was mobbed by his fans. (perfect)

A present participle refers to **action happening at the same time as the action of the main verb.**

present ↓

Smiling broadly, the president **answers** questions from the audience.

past ↓

Smiling broadly, the president **answered** questions from the audience.

present ↓

Holding up his hands, the teacher **is asking** for silence.

past ↓

Holding up his hands, the teacher **asked** for silence.

A past participle sometimes refers to action happening at the same time as the action of the main verb.

Irritated by his sister, Raphael yelled at her.

Dressed up, Tom looks like a new man.

A past participle sometimes refers to action that happened before the action of the main verb.

Burned by the sun, Mary is suffering.

Awakened by the noise, we looked outside.

The perfect participle always refers to action occurring before the action of the main verb.

Having finished work, we can leave.

Having seen that movie, we went somewhere else.

Having left home in a hurry, Michael forgot his raincoat.

8h Infinitives may be present or perfect.

Albert likes **to read** all day. (present)

Tina was supposed **to have brought** the money. (perfect)

The present infinitive shows an action occurring at the same time as the action of the main verb.

I **am trying to finish** this puzzle. (both present)

Jerry **looked** around **to see** who **was** there. (both past)

Dana **will call to ask** you for some advice. (both future)

The present infinitive may indicate action or a state of being at some future time.

I hope **to see** you again.

I expect **to be** there in an hour.

He intended **to write** to us.

An infinitive is never used in a subordinate clause that begins with "that."

I expect everyone to remain seated.

I expect that everyone will remain seated.
(**Not:** I expect that everyone to remain seated.)

The perfect infinitive expresses action occurring before that of the main verb.

I am sorry not **to have met** you before.

He claims **to have seen** a flying saucer.

Avoid using the perfect infinitive after main verbs in the past or past perfect tense.

I had expected **to receive** my mail today.
(**Not:** I had expected **to have received**...)

They hoped **to join** us for dinner.
(**Not:** They hoped **to have joined** us...)

Mike would have liked to **ask** Alice for a date, but he **was** too shy.
(**Not:** Mike would have liked **to have asked** Alice...)

Mood and Voice

9a Mood

The **three moods** that a verb may express are **indicative, imperative,** and **subjunctive**.

9b The indicative mood indicates that the action or state is something believed to be true.

I **am** the greatest.

She **sings** beautifully.

The **indicative** mood is **used in asking a question.**

Are you Mr. Feldman?

Does Tom **want** to watch *Saturday Night Live*?

9c The imperative mood expresses a command or a request or a suggestion.

Answer the telephone. (command)

Give me a napkin, please. (request)

Try turning the handle the other way. (suggestion)

The imperative mood is not only more emphatic than the indicative mood—it is more quickly and easily understood.

Give me that letter. (imperative)

I **would appreciate** it if you would give me that letter. (indicative)

9d The subjunctive mood is often used to express a wish or a condition that is not real—that is, contrary to fact.

I wish the weather **were** nicer.

If this paint **were** dry, we could sit on the bench.

Debbie suggested that Carol **stay** at her apartment.

Carl asked that Stan **agree** to pay for the damage.

The subjunctive mood is also used to express purpose or intention.

Connie said that she **would visit** her mother at Easter.
(**Not:** Connie said that she **will visit** her mother at Easter.)

We made box lunches so that we **would have** food for the trip.
(**Not:** We made box lunches so that we **had** food for the trip.)

The subjunctive mood is mainly indicated by **two forms of the verb "to be."** The forms are **"be"** and **"were."**

Be good.

If I **were** president, I'd nationalize the oil industry.

The present subjunctive uses "be" for all three persons, both singular and plural.

I be, you be, he be, we be, they be

I have one wish—that I **be** president some day.

Mrs. Diggs insists that you **be** given a bonus.

I asked that the child not **be** punished.

The judge ordered that the tenants **be** allowed to stay.

The more common form of the subjunctive is the past subjunctive form "were" for all three persons, both singular and plural.

If {I / you / he / we / they} **were** here, everything would be all right.

The subjunctive mood for verbs other than "to be" is formed by using the present tense first person singular form for all persons.

Mary suggested that Ronald **keep** an extra pair of eyeglasses.

The umpire insisted that the manager **leave** the field.

9e Choosing between the subjunctive and indicative mood.

One should show how he sees a situation: **contrary to fact or within the realm of possibility**. He does this by choosing either the subjunctive mood or the indicative mood.

If his statement **be** true, this is a case of fraud. (subjunctive)
(The writer thinks it is highly improbable that the statement is true.)

If his statement **is** true, this may be a case of fraud. (indicative)
(The writer indicates that it is quite possible that the statement may be true.)

If he **were** at the meeting, he would... (subjunctive)
(The speaker tells the listener that the man is not at the meeting.)

If he **was** at the meeting, he would have been able to speak to the point. (indicative)
(Perhaps the man **was** at the meeting; one doesn't know.)

Had the first payment been made in April, the second would be due in September. (subjunctive)
(The speaker indicates that the payment was **not** made in April.)

If the first payment **was** made in April, the second will be due in September. (indicative)
(Perhaps it was made; perhaps not—the speaker doesn't know.)

Do not use "would have" instead of "had" in "if" clauses to express the past perfect tense of the subjunctive.

If he **had worked** harder, he would have a better job.
(**Not:** If he **would have worked** harder...)

9f Voice

A verb is either in the active voice or in the passive voice.

9g A verb in the active voice indicates that the subject performs an action.

Maggie **reads** every night before going to sleep.

The fire **burned** the entire house.

A verb in the active voice stresses the subject or actor rather than the action.

9h A verb in the passive voice indicates that something is being done to the subject.

The children **were given** lunches to take to school.

The television **was turned** off by my dad.

A verb in the passive voice stresses the action rather than the actor.

9i All transitive verbs—verbs whose action affects something or someone—**can be used in the passive voice.**

Johnny Bench **caught** the ball. (active)

The ball **was caught** by Johnny Bench. (passive)

9j To form the passive, the object of the transitive verb in the active voice is moved ahead of the verb, thus becoming the subject. A form of "to be" is added to the main verb. The subject of the active sentence is either left out or expressed in a prepositional phrase.

subject ↓ | active verb ↓ | direct object ↓

The **tow truck pulled** the **car** out of the ditch. (active voice)

subject ↓ | passive verb ↓ | prepositional phrase

The **car was pulled** out of the ditch **by the tow truck**. (passive voice)

9k If the active sentence has an indirect object as well as a direct object, either the indirect object or the direct object may be the subject of the passive sentence.

active verb ↓ | indirect object ↓ | direct object ↓

Tom **gave** his **sister a kitten**. (active)

subject ↓ | passive verb ↓

A **kitten was given** by Tom to his sister. (passive)

subject ↓ | passive verb ↓

Tom's **sister was given** a kitten by Tom. (passive)

9l The **passive voice is appropriate** to express an action **when the actor is unknown.**

The door **had been locked** before we arrived.

Note: In general, avoid the passive voice for clearer, more forceful sentences.

Modifiers—Adjectives, Adjective Phrases, and Clauses

10a Modifiers

A modifier adds information to another word in the sentence.

Blue flowers were growing in the field.
(The adjective "blue" adds color to the noun "flowers.")

Vera paints **beautifully**.
(The adverb "beautifully" tells how Vera paints.)

10b Modifiers may be a word, a phrase, or a clause.

Billy put on a **clean** shirt. (word)

The wristband of **her watch** was broken. (phrase)

Andy liked the painting **that was done by his friend**. (clause)

There are **various types** of modifiers.

Jill brought us **fresh** fruit. (adjective as modifier)

Bob's friends greeted him **warmly**. (adverb as modifier)

Rudy enjoyed the ride **from Birmingham to Atlanta**. (adjective phrase as modifier)

The rent will increase **after this month**. (adverb phrase as modifier)

Louise holds two jobs **because she supports her sons in college**. (subordinate clause as adverbial modifier)

The houses **where American presidents were born** are museums. (subordinate clause as adjectival modifier)

10c Adjectives modify nouns.

The six kinds of adjectives are the following:

Limiting: Many children are bused to school.

Numerical: Four days have passed since I saw her.

Descriptive: Striped wallpaper hung in the hall.

Proper: American and **Russian** flags lined the parade route.

Pronoun: My book has a torn cover.

Article: A letter has arrived.

10d Articles

The **articles "a"** and **"an"** (indefinite articles) indicate that the **noun they modify is an example of a general type**.

A dove symbolizes peace. (any dove)

A doctor saves lives. (any doctor)

An ambulance brings people to hospitals. (any ambulance)

Note: Do not use the articles "a" or "an" after "kind of," "type of," or "sort of."

A mango is **a kind of fruit**.
(Not: ...**a kind of a fruit**.)

The hybrid is **a new type of car**.
(Not: ...**a new type of a car**.)

That sound gives me **a sort of weird feeling**.
(Not: ...**a sort of a weird feeling**.)

The article "the" (definite article) indicates that the noun it modifies is a particular noun.

The winner received ten thousand dollars. (specific person)

The lamp over there is sold. (specific thing)

10e Single adjectives and compound adjectives

A single adjective usually comes immediately before the word it modifies.

Help me carry this **heavy** package.

A compound adjective consists of **two or more words serving as a single adjective**.

The drought made the earth **bone dry**.

My dictionary is **up to date**.

When a **compound adjective** comes **before a noun,** the words are **joined by a hyphen**.

Woody Allen was my **next-door** neighbor.

A **large-scale** map is hanging on the wall.

When the modifying words follow a noun, they are not hyphenated, unless they are normally hyphenated compounds.

This book is **well written**.

My new watch is **self-winding**. (normally hyphenated)

When two or more adjectives come before a noun but do not act jointly, they are not hyphenated.

Jim was wearing a **white silk** shirt.

I've had a **long, hard** day.

Note: If the word "and" can be inserted between two adjectives that come before a noun without destroying the meaning of the sentence, put a comma in between the two adjectives; otherwise, do not.

Miss Cameron is a **kind, generous** person. (kind **and** generous)

Show us your **new suit**.
(Not: ...your, new suit.)

10f Two or more adjectives may follow the word they modify to make the sentence read more smoothly.

The children, **tired and hungry,** were difficult to control.

10g Most adjectives may show greater or lesser degrees of their characteristic quality.

Today was **cold**. (characteristic quality)

Tomorrow will be **colder** than today. (greater)

The day after will be the **coldest**. (still greater)

Yesterday was **less cold** than today. (lesser)

The day before was the **least cold** this week. (lesser still)

Some adjectives do not show comparison.

Jennifer is **pregnant**.
(She cannot be **more** or **less** pregnant.)

This salad dressing is **perfect**.
(**Not:** ...is **more** or **less** perfect.)

10h The three degrees of comparison are positive, comparative, and superlative.

Tania is **happy**. (positive degree)

Lenny is **happier** than Frank. (comparative degree)

Wayne is the **happiest** of all. (superlative degree)

The positive degree simply names the quality expressed by an adjective.

I like **spicy** food.

The **comparative degree** indicates that the quality described by an adjective exists in one person to a **greater or lesser degree** than in another person or thing.

Susan looks **older** than Liz. (greater)

Marlo was **more excited** than her brother. (greater)

This street is **less clean** than the one where I live. (lesser)

The greater form of the comparative degree is formed by adding "er" to the positive degree or by inserting "more" before the positive form.

rich + er = richer

rich + more = more rich

The lesser form of the comparative degree is formed by inserting "less" before the positive form.

rich + less = less rich

Note: Use the comparative degree when comparing only two things.

The **superlative degree** indicates that the quality described by an adjective exists in the **greatest or least degree** in one person or thing.

Rufus is the **friendliest** dog I know. (greatest)

Florence seems the **least nervous** of us all. (least)

Note: Use the superlative degree when comparing more than two things.

10i Some adjectives do not follow the regular methods of forming their comparative and superlative degrees.

Positive degree	Comparative degree	Superlative degree
good	better	best
bad	worse	worst
little	less, lesser	least

(A dictionary will provide the irregular comparisons of such adjectives.)

Most adjectives of three syllables or more are compared by the use of "more" and "most," rather than by the endings "er" and "est."

Tim is **more capable** of managing a business than Jon.

Alma is the **most wonderful** girl I know.

10j Avoid double comparisons, which are formed by adding both "more" or "most" and "er" or "est."

Alan is the **brightest** little boy.
(**Not:** ...the **most brightest**...)

Eric is a **better** eater than his brother.
(**Not:** ...a **more better** eater...)

10k When two things are compared, both things should be clearly accounted for.

These clothes look cleaner than **those (clothes)**.

George looks older than **he** used to.

An **ellipsis** is the leaving out of one or more words that are grammatically important but that are understood by the reader.

Harvey plays soccer better than I (do).

While (he was) waiting for the pitch, Al Bumbry clenched the bat tightly.

Incomplete subordinate clauses that cause confusion, similar to the confusion caused by **dangling modifiers,** may be corrected by supplying the missing words.

Margaret's dress was torn while **she was** climbing over the fence.
(**Not:** Margaret's dress was torn while climbing over the fence.)

Use the word "other" or "else" to separate the thing being compared from the rest of the group of which the word is a part.

This car gets better mileage than all the **other** cars.

Mary Beth is more beautiful than anyone **else** around.

10l Infinitives, infinitive phrases, participles, and participial phrases may act as adjectives.

Mr. Garcia is the man **to know** if you want a bank loan. (infinitive as adjective)

This is a day **to remember always**. (infinitive phrase as adjective)

Screaming, Nancy woke up from her nightmare. (present participle as adjective)

Covering his face, the defendant walked past the reporters. (participial phrase as adjective)

10m Infinitive and participial phrases that begin a sentence must be able to refer, both logically and grammatically, to the subject of the main clause.

To qualify for the job, you need a high school diploma.
(**Not:** To qualify for the job, a high school diploma is needed. A "high school diploma" cannot apply for the job.)

Rushing to finish, Tina made some errors.
(**Not:** Rushing to finish, some errors were made by Tina. "Errors" cannot rush to finish.)

10n Infinitive and participial phrases are called dangling modifiers if they cannot logically and grammatically attach to the subject of the main clause.

To apply for a credit card, an application form must be filled out. (infinitive phrase as dangling modifier)

Being an only child, my parents spoiled me. (participial phrase as dangling modifier)

Sentences with dangling modifiers may be corrected either by supplying the subject that the phrase can sensibly modify or by changing the phrase to an introductory adverbial clause.

To apply for a credit card, **one** must fill out an application. (Or: **When one applies for a credit card,** an application form must be filled out.)

Being an only child, **I** was spoiled by my parents. (Or: **Because I am an only child,** I was spoiled by my parents.)

10o A prepositional phrase may act as an adjective.

The violent storm damaged the roof **of our house**.

Her leaving **without saying a word** irritated me.
(also considered a **gerund phrase**)

10p A subordinate clause may act as an adjective.

Thanks for the present **that you gave me**.

The woman **who can help you** is not at her desk.

This ring, **which belonged to my grandmother,** is valuable.

The building **where they used to live** is being torn down.

There is never a time **when Ed isn't busy**.

Subordinate clauses that act as adjectives may state essential information or nonessential information.

The train **that you need to take** is leaving from Track 12. (information essential to describe which train)

Peter loves his car, **which he hasn't finished paying for**. (information that is nonessential to describe which car)

10q Restrictive and nonrestrictive clauses

Restrictive clauses, which contain essential information, are not set apart by commas.

The secondhand radio **that I bought for five dollars** works beautifully. (restrictive clause)

Nonrestrictive clauses, which contain secondary information that is not essential to the sentence, are set off by commas.

My friend Dina, **whom I've known for years,** wants me to visit her. (nonrestrictive clause)

10r "Whose" is the possessive form for the relative pronouns "who," "which," and "that."

The boy **whose** father died had to get a job.

The dog **whose** leg was broken runs well now.

Mr. Temple, **whose** wife is a ballerina, teaches French.

The book **whose** cover is damaged is half price.

10s A word, phrase, or clause should be placed as close as possible to the word it modifies.

Give me a glass of **cold** water.
(**Not:** Give me a cold glass…)

We need someone **with experience** to cook breakfast.
(**Not:** We need someone to cook breakfast with experience.)

Grant wore a felt hat **that was obviously too small on his head**.
(**Not:** Grant wore a felt hat on his head that was obviously too small.)

10t A misplaced modifier is a word, phrase, or clause that is misplaced in the sentence so that it modifies the wrong word.

Wrong: Mrs. Kent was injured while preparing her husband's dinner **in a horrible manner**.

Right: Mrs. Kent was injured **in a horrible manner** while preparing her husband's dinner.

Wrong: The old farmer went to the barn to milk the cow **with a cane**.

Right: The old farmer **with a cane** went to the barn to milk the cow.

Wrong: The flames were extinguished before any damage was done **by the Fire Department**.

Right: The flames were extinguished **by the Fire Department** before any damage was done.

10u Squinting modifiers are modifiers that are misplaced so that the reader cannot tell if the word, phrase, or clause modifies the words immediately before the modifier or immediately after.

Wrong: Henry said **today** he would wash his car.

Right: **Today** Henry said he would wash his car. (Or: Henry said he would wash his car **today**.)

Wrong: The dentist told him **frequently** to use dental floss.

Right: The dentist **frequently** told him to use dental floss. (**Or:** The dentist told him to use dental floss **frequently**.)

Modifiers (Continued)—Adverbs, Adverbial Phrases, and Clauses

11a Adverbs modify verbs, adjectives, and adverbs.

Don runs **slowly**. (modifies verb)

Emily is an **extremely** gifted pianist. (modifies adjective)

Eric Heiden skates **incredibly** well. (modifies adverb)

11b The five kinds of adverbs are classified by the questions they answer.

How? Adverbs of manner.

She sings **well**. He speaks **clearly**.

Where? Adverbs of place or direction.

Take me **home**. She was just **here**. He went **out**.

When? Adverbs of time.

Bring it **immediately**. I'll see you **tomorrow**.

How much? Adverbs of degree or measure.

That's **enough**. A little **more,** please.

Why? Adverbs of cause, reason, or purpose.

He left **because** he was afraid.

I have ten dollars, **so** we can go out.

11c The following words can be either adjectives or adverbs, depending on their use.

above	fast	only
better	first	slow
cheap	hard	well
deep	long	
early	much	

The sign said to drive **slow**. (adverb)

Slow drivers can be dangerous. (adjective)

Mark Spitz can swim **better** than I can. (adverb)

Lucy feels **better** now. (adjective)

11d Distinguish carefully **when an adverb should follow a linking verb** and **when a predicate adjective should be used** to follow the linking verb.

Sharon looks **bad**. (predicate adjective meaning that Sharon doesn't look healthy)

Miguel looks **badly**. (adverb meaning that Miguel is doing a poor job looking for something)

Carmen smells **sweet**. (predicate adjective meaning that Carmen has a sweet scent)

Roses smell **sweetly**. (adverb **incorrectly** meaning that roses sniff the air sweetly!)

11e While speaking, one may incorrectly drop the "ly" ending from common adverbs.

I'm **real** glad you called.
(**Correct:** I'm **really** glad you called.)

He **sure** is lucky.
(**Correct:** He **surely** is lucky.)

Do not drop the "ly" ending unless a shorter form is correct.

I bought it **cheaply**. (Or: I bought it **cheap**.)

Come **quickly!** (Or: Come **quick!**)

The adverbs "hardly," "scarcely," "only," and "barely" should not be used with a negative verb construction.

Ernie has hardly any free time.
(**Not:** Ernie **hasn't** hardly any free time.)

Rose and I have scarcely worked this week.
(**Not:** Rose and I **haven't** scarcely worked this week.)

11f An adverb may show greater or lesser degrees of its characteristic quality.

Peter arrived **early**.

Adam came **earlier** than Peter.

Amy came **earliest** of all.

The positive degree simply names the quality expressed by an adverb.

Stephanie runs **quickly**.

The **comparative degree** indicates that the quality described by an adverb exists for one person or thing to **a greater or lesser degree** than for another person or thing.

New air conditioners run **more efficiently** than old ones.

Nat draws **less well** than Monica.

The **comparative degree** of adverbs is formed by inserting **"more" or "less" before the positive degree form,** unless there is an irregular form for the comparative degree.

Charles works **more diligently** than Mark.

Barbara gets angry **less often** than Steven.

This stereo sounds **better** than mine. (irregular form)

The **superlative degree** indicates the quality described by the adverb exists in the **greatest or least degree** for one person or thing.

Ben works **most carefully** when someone is watching.

Elaine explained the problem the **most clearly**.

His was the **least carefully** written report.

The **superlative degree** of adverbs is formed by inserting **"most" or "least" before the positive degree form**.

Who was voted "most likely to succeed"?

Tracy Austin played **least skillfully** during the first set.

When two persons or things are being compared, the comparison should be clear.

I love chocolate more than **Umberto** does.
(**Not:** I love chocolate more than Umberto. Such an incomplete comparison might be interpreted to mean that I love chocolate more than I love Umberto.)

11g An infinitive or an infinitive phrase may be used as an adverb.

Robert was willing **to go**. (infinitive used as adverb)

I am writing **to explain my behavior last night**. (infinitive phrase used as adverb)

11h A prepositional phrase may be used as an adverb.

We left **for the weekend**.

The old man sat **on the park bench**.

The coach supported his team **in every way**.

11i A subordinate clause may be used as an adverb.

Mrs. Maurillo forgot her umbrella **when she left**.

Because they cooperated with him, the president thanked several members of Congress.

11j An adverb or an adverbial phrase should be placed as close as possible to the word it modifies.

Joanne worked **without complaining** while her husband went to school.
(**Not:** Joanne worked while her husband went to school **without complaining**.)

Note how an adverbial misplacement may change the meaning of a sentence.

The room can be painted **only** by me.
(not by anyone else)

The room can **only** be painted by me.
(not wallpapered)

Only the room can be painted by me.
(not the outside of the house)

11k An adverbial clause may be placed either at the beginning of a sentence or, in its natural order, after the main clause.

After you have read this letter, you will understand my reasons.

You will understand my reasons **after you have read this letter**.

Note: An adverbial clause is followed by a comma when it is used to introduce a sentence.

111 Adverbial phrases and clauses should be placed so that only one meaning is possible.

After the movie we all agreed to go for some ice cream. (Or: We all agreed to go for some ice cream **after the movie**.)

(**Not:** We all agreed **after the movie** to go for some ice cream.)

Ask Kay to call me **when she gets in**. (Or: **When she gets in,** ask Kay to call me.)

(**Not:** Ask Kay **when she gets in** to call me.)

Connectives

12a A connective joins one part of a sentence to another part.

Phillip **and** Dennis are giving a concert tonight.
(The connective "and" joins the two parts of the compound subject.)

Did you go out, **or** did you stay home last night?
(The connective "or" joins the two independent clauses.)

The banks are closed **because** today is a holiday.
(The connective "because" joins the main clause to the subordinate clause.)

The investigation **of** the robbery has been completed.
(The connective "of" joins the noun "robbery" to the noun "investigation.")

12b A connective may be a preposition, a conjunction, an adverb, or a pronoun.

Josie left her scarf **on** the bus. (preposition)

Mr. Fernandez campaigned for the presidency, **but** he lost. (conjunction)

Kevin looked back **because** someone was shouting. (conjunction)

Ernie left his home an hour ago; **therefore,** he should be here any minute. (adverb)

The letter **that** was mailed this morning should arrive tomorrow. (pronoun)

12c Prepositions as connectives

A preposition may be **a word or a compound**. A compound consists of two or more words that function as one word.

Come **over** here. (word)

Women live longer than men, **according to** statistics. (compound)

12d A preposition joins a noun or pronoun to the rest of the sentence.

prep.
↓
One of the **windows** is broken. (noun)

prep.
↓
Josh is worried about his **health**. (noun)

prep.
↓
These bags have nothing in **them**. (pronoun)

Choosing the correct preposition is often based on **idiomatic usage**—that is, the way English is used, whether or not it contradicts strict grammatical rules.

12e Some commonly used prepositional idioms are the following:

absolve	from	[blame]
abstain	from	[drinking]
accede	to	[a request]
accommodate	to	[a situation]
accompanied	by	[a lady (**a person**)]
accompanied	with	[applause (**a thing**)]
account	for	[one's actions]
account	to	[one's superior]
acquit	of	[a crime]
adapted	to	[his requirements]
adapted	from	[a novel]
adept	in	[selling a product]
adequate	to	[the demand]
adequate	for	[her needs]
agree	to	[a proposal (**an idea**)]
agree	with	[the teacher (**a person**)]
amenable	to	[an offer]
angry	with	[my cousin (**a person**)]
angry	at	[a remark (**a thing**)]
annoyed	by	[the noise (**a thing**)]
annoyed	with	[the child (**a person**)]
appreciative	of	[their efforts]
averse	to	[hard work (**an idea**)]
basis	for	[agreement]
capable	of	[getting high marks]
concur	with	[the mayor (**a person**)]
concur	in	[the decision (**an idea**)]
confer	with	[someone (**a person**)]
confer	about	[something (**a thing**)]
conform	to	[the rules]
correspond	to	[what I said (**a thing**)]
correspond	with	[his lawyer (**a person**)]
differs	from	[her sister (**a person**)]
differs	with	[what was done (**a thing**)]
disappointed	in	[you (**a person**)]
disappointed	with	[the result (**a thing**)]
enter	into	[an agreement]
enter	upon	[a career]
excepted	from	[further responsibility]
exempt	from	[taxes]
expect	from	[your investment (**a thing**)]
expect	of	[his assistant (**a person**)]
familiar	to	[me (**a person**)]
familiar	with	[the proceedings (**a thing**)]
free	of	[his wife (**a person**)]
free	from	[her nagging (**a thing**)]
identical	with	[something else]
ignorant	of	[his rights]
incompatible	with	[fellow workers]
independent	of	[his relative]
infer	from	[a statement]

involved	in	[a project (**a thing**)]
involved	with	[a friend (**a person**)]
liable	to	[damages (**a thing**)]
necessity	for	[food (**a thing**)]
necessity	of	[avoiding trouble (**doing something**)]
proficient	in	[a skill]
profit	by	[knowledge]
responsible	to	[the owner (**a person**)]
responsible	for	[paying a debt (**a thing**)]
talk	to	[the group (**one person talks**)]
talk	with	[my friends (**all talk**)]
variance	with	[another]
wait	at	[the church (**a place**)]
wait	for	[your uncle (**a person**)]
worthy	of	[consideration]

12f Prepositions should not be used needlessly.

Where is your brother?
(**Not:** Where is your brother **at?**)

Where are you going?
(**Not:** Where are you going **to?**)

Pete started on another project.
(**Not:** Pete started **in** on another project.)

We agreed to divide the housework.
(**Not:** We agreed to divide **up** the housework.)

Prepositions are sometimes left out by mistake.

Irene talked to me **about** her new job and **about** why she left her old one.
(**Not:** Irene talked to me about her new job and why…)

Dr. Rosen was puzzled **by** and concerned **about** Ellen's nightmares.
(**Not:** Dr. Rosen was puzzled and concerned about…)

Note: Two different prepositions are needed for this last sentence.

12g Conjunctions as connectives

A conjunction is a word that joins words, phrases, clauses, or sentences.

Nixon **and** Agnew ended their political careers by resigning. (words joined)

The mouse ran out of the kitchen **and** into the living room. (phrases joined)

Casino gambling in Atlantic City has helped some, **but** it has hurt others. (clauses joined)

Sally has the ability to do the job; **however,** she has too many personal problems. (clauses joined)

12h Conjunctions are coordinate, correlative, or subordinate.

A **coordinate conjunction** and a **correlative conjunction** connect grammatical elements of equal rank. A **subordinate conjunction** connects grammatical elements of unequal rank.

12i Coordinate conjunctions connect two equal elements. They include the following words:

and, but, or, nor, so, yet, for

On our vacation we will go to Boston **or** to Cape Cod. (two phrases)

My two favorite colors are blue **and** green. (two words)

I told Stanley that I couldn't leave my house, **so** he should come over tonight. (two subordinate clauses)

Phil was eager to try the new restaurant, **but** he moved away before trying it. (two independent clauses)

12j Correlative conjunctions include the following **word pairs** in order to connect two equal elements.

either…or, neither…nor, not only…but also, both…and, if…then, since…therefore

Take **either** the dark meat **or** the light meat. (two words)

Not only has Rick quit school, **but** he has **also** left town. (two independent clauses)

Both the Baltimore Orioles **and** the Pittsburgh Pirates won the pennant in 1979. (two words)

I have seen her **neither** in the movies **nor** on television. (two phrases)

Note: The correlative conjunctions "neither…nor" should never be written "neither…or."

Each member of the pair of correlative conjunctions must be followed by the same grammatical construction.

same construction

Woody Allen is **not only** a good **comedian but also** a good film **director**.

different construction

(**Not:** Woody Allen **not only** is a good comedian but **also** a good film director.)

same construction

Either we should spend the night here **or** we should leave right now.

different construction

(**Not: Either** we should spend the night here **or** leave right now.)

12k Conjunctive adverbs

A **conjunctive adverb** may be considered a **type of coordinate conjunction**.

Conjunctive adverbs include the following words, which **serve to connect two equal elements**.

therefore, however, consequently, accordingly, furthermore, besides, moreover, nevertheless, still

Although the clause introduced by a conjunctive adverb is grammatically independent, it is logically dependent on the preceding clause for complete meaning.

A storm knocked down our electric wires; **therefore,** we had to eat by candlelight.

A bad traffic accident ahead of us caused us to be delayed; **nevertheless,** we made the party on time.

You have not paid your rent for six months; **accordingly,** I am going to see a lawyer.

Independent clauses joined by a conjunctive adverb should be separated by a semicolon (;) or a period.

Frank and Marty delayed their vacation one week; **consequently,** I was able to join them.

The judge awarded custody of the child to his mother. **Moreover,** the judge set strict guidelines for visiting privileges.

Certain phrases may act as conjunctive adverbs.

Eunice wanted to buy a fur coat; **on the other hand,** she was trying to save money for a car.

We saw many interesting towns and cities on our tour. **In addition,** we met several nice people.

12l Join only the **same parts of speech** with coordinate conjunctions or with correlative conjunctions. **Faulty parallelism will result if different parts of speech are combined.**

Correct: Jim's day consisted of waking up early, working all day, **and** going back to bed. (three gerund phrases)

Faulty: Jim's day consisted of waking up early, working all day, **and** then to go back to bed. (two gerund phrases combined with an infinitive phrase)

Correct: The president's plan was a disappointment **not only** to the leaders of big business, **but also** to the leaders of organized labor. (two prepositional phrases)

Faulty: The president's plan was a disappointment **not only** to the leaders of big business, but also the leaders of organized labor. (one prepositional phrase and one noun phrase)

12m Connecting elements of unequal rank

A less important idea should be put into a subordinate clause; the more important idea should be expressed in the main or independent clause.

main idea: Bill is going to work for his father, — subordinate idea: although he was offered other jobs.

Bill is going to work for his father, although he was offered other jobs.

12n Subordination may be introduced by a subordinate conjunction, by a relative pronoun, or by a relative adverb.

Eva will want to go straight to bed **after** she comes back from her exercise class. (subordinate conjunction)

I bought the sneakers **that** you wanted. (relative pronoun)

We saw the house **where** they filmed *Gone with the Wind.* (relative adverb)

A subordinate conjunction introduces an adverbial clause.

My mother can knit a sweater **while** she watches television. (adverbial clause tells **when**)

Tell me what he looks like **so that** I'll recognize him. (adverbial clause tells **why**)

12o Some relative pronouns introduce adjective clauses.

Everyone wants a job **that** he likes.

The woman **who** walked across the United States has written a book about her experience.

Bobby gave Connie a new tennis racket, **which** she needed.

Other relative pronouns introduce noun clauses.

Tell me **what** you did.

This book has **whatever** you want to know about scuba diving.

Invite **whomever** you like.

12p A relative adverb introduces an adjective clause.

Do you remember the night **when** we locked ourselves out of the house?

Chris will be at the place **where** we met him last time.

Correct Usage—Choosing the Right Word

The difference between the right word and the almost-right word is the difference between lightning and the lightning bug (firefly).

—Mark Twain

A, an. The indefinite article *a* is used before a consonant sound; the indefinite article *an* is used before a vowel sound. Say *a plan, an idea.*

Accept, except. *Accept* means *to receive; except* when used as a verb means *to leave out.* (We *accepted* the gift. Pedro's name was *excepted* from the honor roll.) The word *except* is used most often as a preposition. *Everyone went except me.*

Affect, effect. *Affect* is a verb that means to *influence.* (Winning the sweepstakes will *affect* his attitude.) *Effect,* as a noun, means *an influence.* (Smoking has an *effect* on one's health.) *Effect,* as a verb, means to *bring about.* (The teacher's praise *effected* a change in the student.)

Affected, as an adjective, has the meaning of *false.* (She had an *affected* way of speaking.)

Aggravate, irritate. *Aggravate* means to make worse. (Drinking iced water will *aggravate* your cold.) *Irritate* means to *annoy* or *exasperate.* (Mary's continuous chattering *irritated* me.)

Ain't. Do not use this expression.

Already, all ready. *Already* means *before* or *by a certain time.* (Mike said that he had *already* done the job.) *All ready* means *completely ready.* (When the buzzer sounded, the horses were *all ready* to start running.)

All right, alright. The only correct spelling is *all right.*

Altogether, all together. *Altogether* means *entirely, wholly.* (Jane is *altogether* too conceited to get along with people.) *All together* means *as a group.* (After the explosion, the boss was relieved to find his workers *all together* in front of the building.)

Among, between. *Among* is used with more than two persons or things. (The manager distributed the gifts *among* all of the employees.) *Between* is used only with two persons or things. (The steak was divided *between* the two children.)

Amount, number. *Amount* is used to refer to things in bulk. (The war costs a great *amount* of money.) *Number* is used to refer to things that can be counted. (A large *number* of pupils attend this school.)

And etc. This is incorrect. The abbreviation *etc.* stands for the Latin *et cetera.* The *et* means *and;* the *cetera* means *other things.* It is wrong to say *and etc.* because the idea of *and* is already included in the *etc.*

Anyways, anywheres, everywheres, somewheres. These expressions are not correct. Omit the final *s* after each.

As, like. *As,* used as a conjunction, is followed by a clause. (Please do it *as* I told you to.) *Like* may not be used as a conjunction. If it is used as a preposition, it is not followed by a verb. (This ice cream looks *like* custard.)

Awful. See **Terrific, terrible.**

Being that. *Being that* is incorrect for *since* or *because.* (*Since* you are tired, you ought to rest.)

Beside, besides. *Beside* means *alongside of; besides* means *in addition to.* (Nixon sat *beside* Autry at the baseball game.) (There is nobody *besides* her husband who understands Ann.)

Between. See **Among.**

Bring, take. Consider the speaker as a starting point. *Bring* is used for something carried in the direction of the speaker. (When you return from lunch, please *bring* me a ham sandwich.) *Take* is used for something carried away from the speaker. (If you are going downtown, please *take* this letter to the post office.)

Bunch. *Bunch* means cluster. Do not use *bunch* for group or crowd. (This is a large *bunch* of grapes.) (A *crowd* of people were at the scene of the accident.)

But that, but what. Do not use these expressions in place of *that* in structures like the following: I do not question *that* (not *but that*) you are richer than I am.

Can't hardly. Don't use this double negative. Say *can hardly.*

Continual, continuous. *Continual* means happening at intervals. (Salesmen are *continually* walking into this office.) *Continuous* means going on without interruption. (Without a moment of dry weather, it rained *continuously* for forty days and forty nights.)

Could of. Do not use for *could have.*

Data. Although *data* is the plural of *datum,* idiom permits the use of this word as a singular. Some authorities still insist on *Data are gathered* rather than *Data is gathered* or *these data* rather than *this data.* Most persons in computer programming now say *Data is gathered* or *this data.*

Deal. Do not use this colloquial term for *arrangement* or *transaction* in formal expression. (He has an *excellent arrangement* [not *deal*] *with the manager.*)

Different from, different than. *Different from* is correct. *Different than* is incorrect. (His method of doing this is *different from* mine.)

Discover, invent. *Discover* means to see or learn something that has not been previously known. (They say the Vikings, not Columbus, *discovered* America.) *Invent* means to create for the first time. (William S. Burroughs *invented* the adding machine.)

Disinterested, uninterested. *Disinterested* means without bias. (An umpire must be *disinterested* to judge fairly in a baseball game.) *Uninterested* means not caring about a situation. (I am totally *uninterested* in your plan.)

Doesn't, don't. *Doesn't* means *does not; don't* means *do not.* Do not say *He don't* (*do not*) when you mean *He doesn't* (*does not*).

Due to. At the beginning of a sentence, *due to* is always incorrect. Use, instead, *on account of, because of,* or a similar expression. (*On account of* bad weather, the contest was postponed.) As a predicate adjective construction, *due to* is correct. His weakness was *due to* his hunger.

Each other, one another. *Each other* is used for two persons. (The executive and his secretary antagonize *each other.*) *One another* is used for more than two persons. (The members of the large family love *one another.*)

Effect. See **Affect.**

Enthuse. Do not use this word. Say *enthusiastic.* (The art critic was *enthusiastic* about the painting.)

Equally as good. This expression is incorrect. Say, instead, *just as good.* (This car is *just as good* as that.)

Farther, further. *Farther* is used for a distance that is measurable. (The farmer's house is about 100 yards *farther* down the road.) *Further* is used to express the extension of an idea. (A *further* explanation may be necessary.)

Fewer, less. *Fewer* applies to what may be counted. (Greenwich Village has *fewer* conservatives than liberals.) *Less* refers to degree or amount. (*Less* rain fell this month than the month before.)

Flout, flaunt. *Flout* means to mock or insult. (The king *flouted* the wise man when the latter offered advice.) *Flaunt* means to make a pretentious display of. (The upstart *flaunted* his diamond ring.)

Further. See **Farther.**

Get. *Get* means *to obtain* or *receive. Get* should not be used in the sense of *to excite, to interest,* or *to understand.* Say: His guitar playing *fascinates* (not *gets*) me. Say: When you talk about lifestyles, I just don't *understand* (not *get*) *you.*

Good, well. Do not use the adjective *good* in place of the adverb *well* in structures like the following: John works *well* (not *good*) in the kitchen. Jim Palmer pitched *well* (not *good*) in last night's game.

Graduate. One *graduates from,* or *is graduated from,* a school. One does not *graduate a school.* (The student *graduated* [or *was graduated*] from high school.)

Had of. Avoid this for *had.* Say: My father always said that he wished he *had* (not *had of*) gone to college.

Hanged, hung. When a person is *executed,* he is *hanged.* When anything is *suspended* in space, it is *hung.*

Hardly. See **Can't hardly**.

Healthful, healthy. *Healthful* applies to *conditions that promote health. Healthy* applies to *a state of health.* Say: Stevenson found the climate of Saranac Lake very *healthful.* Say: Mary is a very *healthy* girl.

If, whether. Use *whether*—not *if*—in structures that follow verbs like *ask, doubt, know, learn, say.* Say: Hank Aaron didn't know *whether* (not *if*) he was going to break Babe Ruth's home run record.

Imply, infer. The speaker *implies* when he suggests or hints at. (The owner of the store *implied* that the patron stole a box of toothpicks.) The listener *infers* when he draws a conclusion from facts or evidence. (From what you say, I *infer* that I am about to be discharged.)

In, into. *In* is used to express a location, without the involvement of motion. (The sugar is *in* the cupboard.) *Into* is used to express motion from one place to another. (The housekeeper put the sugar *into* the cupboard.)

In regards to. This is incorrect. Say *in regard to* or *with regard to.*

Invent. See **Discover**.

Irregardless. Do not use *irregardless.* It is incorrect for *regardless.* (You will not be able to go out tonight *regardless* of the fact that you have done all of your homework.)

Its, it's. *Its* is the possessive of *it; it's* is the contraction for *it is.*

Kind of, sort of. Do not use these expressions as adverbs. Say: Ali was *quite* (not *kind of* or *sort of*) witty in his postfight interview.

Kind of a, sort of a. Omit the *a.* Say: What *kind of* (not *kind of a* or *sort of a*) game is lacrosse?

Lay, lie. See "Principal Parts of Irregular Verbs"—page 485.

Learn, teach. *Learn* means *to gain knowledge. Teach* means *to impart knowledge.* Say: He *taught* (not *learned*) his brother how to swim.

Leave, let. The word *leave* means *to depart.* (I *leave* today for San Francisco.) The word *let* means to allow. (*Let* me take your place.)

Less, fewer. See **Fewer, less**.

Liable, likely. *Liable* means subject to something unpleasant. (If you speed, you are *liable* to get a summons.) *Likely* means probable, with reference to either a pleasant or unpleasant happening. (It is *likely* to snow tomorrow.)

Locate. Do not use *locate* to mean *settle* or *move to.* Say: We will *move to* (not *locate in*) Florida next year.

Might of, must of. Omit the *of.*

Myself, himself, yourself. These pronouns are to be used as intensives. (The Chairman *himself* will open the meeting.) Do not use these pronouns when *me, him,* or *you* will serve. Say: We shall be happy if Joe and *you* (not *yourself*) join us for lunch at the Plaza.

Nice. See **Terrific, terrible**.

Number, amount. See **Amount, number**.

Of, have. Do not use *of* for *have* in structures like *could have.*

Off of. Omit the *of.* Say: The book fell *off* (not *off of*) the shelf.

Pour, spill. When one *pours,* he does it deliberately. (He carefully *poured* the water into her glass.) When one *spills,* he does it accidentally. (I carelessly *spilled* some water on her dress.)

Practical, practicable. *Practical* means *fitted for actual work. Practicable* means *feasible* or *possible.* Say: My business partner is a *practical man.* Say: The boss did not consider the plan *practicable* for this coming year.

Principal, principle. *Principal* applies to a *chief* or the *chief part* of something. *Principle* applies to a *basic law.* Say: Mr. Jones is the *principal* of the school. Professor White was the *principal* speaker. Honesty is a good *principle* to follow.

Raise, rise. See "Principal Parts of Irregular Verbs"—page 485.

Reason is because. Do not use the expression *reason is because*—it is always incorrect. Say the *reason is that.* (The *reason* Jack failed the course *is that* he didn't study.)

Regardless. See **Irregardless.**

Respectfully, respectively. *Respectfully* means *with respect* as in the complimentary close of a letter, *respectfully yours. Respectively* means that each item will be considered *in the order given.* Say: This paper is *respectfully* submitted. Say: The hero, the heroine, and the villain will be played by Albert, Joan, and Harry *respectively.*

Rise, raise. See "Principal Parts of Irregular Verbs"—page 485.

Said. Avoid the legalistic use of *said* like *said letter, said plan, said program* except in legal writing.

Should of. Do not use for *should have.*

Sit, set. See "Principal Parts of Irregular Verbs"—page 485.

Some. Do not use *some* when you mean *somewhat.* Say: I'm confused *somewhat* (not *some*).

Spill, pour. See **Pour, spill.**

Suspicion. Do not use *suspicion* as a verb when you mean *suspect.*

Take, bring. See **Bring, take.**

Teach, learn. See **Learn, teach.**

Terrific, terrible. Avoid "lazy words." Many people don't want to take the trouble to use the exact word. They will use words like *terrific, swell, great, beautiful,* etc., to describe anything and everything that is favorable. And they will use words like *terrible, awful, lousy, miserable,* etc., for whatever is unfavorable. Use the exact word. Say: We had a *delicious* (not terrific) meal. Say: We had a *boring* (not *terrible*) weekend.

This kind, these kind. *This kind* is correct—as is *that kind, these kinds,* and *those kinds.* (My little brother likes *this kind* of pears.) *These kind* and *those kind* are incorrect.

Try and. Do not say *try and.* Say *try to.* (*Try to* visit me while I am in Florida.)

Uninterested. See **Disinterested.**

Wait for, wait on. *Wait for* means *to await; wait on* means *to serve.* Say: I am waiting *for* (not *on*) Carter to call me on the telephone.

Way, ways. Do not use *ways* for *way.* Say: It is a long *way* (not *ways*) to Japan.

Where. Do not use *where* in place of *that* in expressions like the following: I see in the newspaper *that* (not *where*) a nuclear reactor may be built a mile away from our house.

Would of. Do not use for *would have.*

Grammar and Usage Index*

Abstract noun, 5f
Active voice, 9f–g
Adjective, 1d, 10a–s; article, 10d; clause 2b, 10p; comparison, 10g–h; compound, 10e; dangling modifier, 10k; infinitive, 8e, 10l; kinds, 10c; linking verb, 3o; modifier, 10c; or adverb, 11c; participial, 8d; phrase, 2c, 10o; predicate, 4h; pronoun, 5l
Adjective pronoun, 5t
Adverb, 1e, 11a; clause, 2b, 11i; comparison, 11f; connective, 12b; dropping "ly," 11e; infinitive, 8e, 11g; kinds, 11b; linking verb, 11d; or adjective, 11c; phrase, 2c, 11h; placement, 11j–l; relative, 12p; with negative verb, 11e
Antecedent, 1b; of pronoun, 5p; with *or* or *nor,* 5p
Appear, 3o
Appositive, 5w
Article, 10d
Be, 3o
Begin, 7j
Become, 3o
Blow, 7j
Break, 7j
Burst, 7j
Case, 5q; nominative, 5r; objective, 5s; possessive, 5v
Catch, 7j
Choose, 7j
Clause, 2a; main, 2b; nonrestrictive, 10q; restrictive, 10q; subject, 3j; subordinate, 2b
Collective noun, 5d; number, 5p
Come, 7j
Common noun, 5c
Comparative degree, adjectives, 10h–i; adverbs, 11f
Comparison, adjectives, 10g; adverbs, 11f; double comparisons, 10j
Complement, 3h, 4g; adjective, 4h, 4l; direct object, 4h, 4i; indirect object, 4h; noun, 4i–k; phrase, 4k–l; predicate adjective, 4h, 4l; predicate noun, 4h, 4k; pronoun, 4i–k; verb, 4c; verbal, 4k
Complex sentence, 3c, 3f
Compound adjective, 10e
Compound noun, 1a; plural, 5v
Compound preposition, 12c
Compound sentence, 3c, 3e
Compound–complex sentence, 3c, 3g
Concrete noun, 5e
Condition, 4e, 9d
Conjunction, 1g; connective, 12b; 12g–n
Conjunctive adverb, 12k
Connective, 12a–n
Contrary to fact, 9d
Coordinate conjunction, 12i
Correlative conjunction, 12j
Dangling participle, 10n
Declarative sentence, 3b
Definite article, 10d
Demonstrative pronoun, 5l
Dependent clause, 2b
Direct address, 5x
Direct object, 4h; clause, 4i; noun, 4i; pronoun, 4i; passive voice, 9k
Do, 7j
Double comparison, 10j
Drink, 7j
Drive, 7j
Ellipsis, 10k
Every, 6d
Exclamatory sentence, 3b
Expletive, 6h

* This Index does not include items listed in the Correct Usage—Choosing the Right Word chapter. Since these Correct Usage items are in alphabetical order, it will be easy for you to locate any Correct Usage explanation whatsoever.

Fall, 7j
Feel, 3o
Find, 7j
Fly, 7j
Freeze, 7j
Future perfect tense, 7h
Future tense, 7g
Gender, 5o
Gerund, 8c; with linking verb, 3o; noun preceding, 5v; perfect form, 8f; phrase, 2c, 8c; present form, 8f
Give, 7j
Go, 7j
Grow, 3o, 7j
Had, 9e
Hardly, 11e
I, 5u
Idioms, 12d–e
Imperative mood, 4e, 9c
Imperative sentence, 3b
Indefinite article, 10d
Indefinite pronoun, 5k; singular and plural, 6c–d
Independent clause, 2b
Indicative mood, 4e, 9b; and subjunctive, 9e
Indirect object, 4h; noun, 4j; pronoun, 4j; clause, 4j; with passive, 9k
Infinitive, 2c; adjective, 8e, 10l; adverb, 8e; noun, 8e; perfect, 8h; phrase, 8e; 10l–n; present, 8h; subject of, 5u; with linking verb, 3o; with *that,* 8h
Interjection, 1h
Interrogative pronoun, 5j, 6i
Interrogative sentence 3b
Intransitive verb, 3n, 3p
It, 6h
Its, it's, 5v
Know, 7j
Lay, 7j
Lie, 7j
Linking verb, 3p, 3o
Look, 3o
Main clause, 2b
Many, 6c, 6d
Misplaced modifier, 10t
Modifiers, 10a–s, 11a–l; adjective, 1d, 10c; adverb, 1e, 11a; dangling, 10k, 10n; misplaced, 10t; placement, 10s, 11j; squinting, 10u, 11l
Mood, 4e; imperative, 4e, 9c; indicative, 4e, 9b; subjunctive, 4e, 9d; verb, 4e, 9a
Negative construction, 11e
Nominative absolute, 5x
Nominative case, 5r; direct address, 5x; *I,* 5u; nominative absolute, 5x; *we,* 5t
Nonrestrictive clause, 10q
Nor, or, 6e–g
Noun, 1a; abstract, 5f; appositive, 5w; case, 5q; clause, 2b; collective, 5d; common, 5c; concrete, 5e; direct object, 4i; gender, 5o; indirect object, 4j; infinitive, 8e; with linking verb, 3n; number, 5p; phrase, 2c; predicate, 4h; with preposition, 1f; proper, 5b; subject, 3i
Number, 6a–k; indefinite pronouns, 6c–d; noun and pronouns, 5p; subject-verb agreement, 6a; verb, 4b
Objective case, 5s–u
Of, 5v
Or or *nor,* 6e–g
Ownership, 5v
Parenthetical phrase, 6k
Participle, 8d, 8g, 101–n; adjective, 8d, 10l; past, 8g; phrase, 2c, 8d, 101–n; perfect, 8g; present, 8g
Parts of speech, 1a–i
Passive voice, 9h; to form, 9j; with direct and indirect object, 9k; with transitive verb, 9j
Past participle, 8d
Past perfect tense, 7f
Past subjunctive, 9d
Past tense, 7e
Person, 6g–k; of pronoun, 5h; relating to verb, 4c
Personal pronoun, 5h; object case, 5s
Phrases, 2c; gerund, 8c; infinitive, 8e; participial, 8d; subject, 3j
Positive degree, 10h, 11f
Possessive case, 5v
Possessive pronoun, 5h
Predicate adjective, 4h; with linking verb, 11d
Predicate noun, 4h, 6j
Preposition, 1f; connective, 1g, 12b–f; with noun or pronoun, 1f; phrase, 2c
Present participle, 8d
Present perfect tense, 7d
Present tense, 7c
Present subjunctive, 9d
Principal parts of verb, 7j
Progressive form, 7i
Pronoun, 1a; appositive, 5w; case, 5q–v; connective, 12b, 12o; demonstrative, 5l; direct object, 4i; gender, 5o; indefinite, 5k; indirect object, 4j; interrogative, 5j, 6i; with linking verb, 3o; number, 5p; person, 5h; personal, 5h; with preposition, 1f; reflexive, 5m; relative, 5i, 12o; subject, 3i
Proper noun, 5b
Raise, 7j
Reflexive pronoun, 5m
Relative adverb, 12p
Relative pronoun, 5i, 12o
Remain, 3o
Restrictive clause, 10q
Ring, 7j
Rise, 7j
Run, 7j
Scarcely, 11e
Seem, 3o
Sentence, 3a–p
Set, 7j
Simple sentence, 3c–d
Sit, 7j
Smell, 3o
Sound, 3o
Speak, 7j
Squinting modifier, 10u, 11l

Steal, 7j
Subject, 3a, 3h–j, 6a–k; agreement with verb, 6a; collective noun, 6b; of infinitive, 5u
Subjunctive mood, 4e, 9d; and indicative, 9e; past, 9d; present, 9d; *were,* 9d; *would have* and *had,* 9e
Subordinate clause, 2b; adjective, 2b, 10p; adverb, 2b; noun, 2b
Subordinate conjunction, 12n
Superlative degree, 10h–i; 11f
Swim, 7j
Take, 7j
Taste, 3o
Tense, 7a–j, 4d
Their, they're, 5v
There, 6h
Throw, 7j
To be, 5u
Transitive verb, 3m, 3p; 9j
Us, 5t
Verb, 4a–1; active voice, 4f; with collective noun, 6b; with interrogative pronoun, 6i; with predicate noun, 6j; passive voice, 4f; principal parts, 7j; progressive form, 7i; of sentence, 3a; and subject, 3k
Verbal, 3i, 8a–h
Voice, 4f, 9f–l
We, 5t
Wear, 7j
Were, 9d
What, 5i–j
Which, 5i–j
Who, 5i–j
Whom, 5i–j
Who's, 5v
Whose, 5v; interrogative pronoun, 5v; possessive pronoun, 10r; relative pronoun, 5j
Would have, 9e
Write, 7j
You, 5t

PART 9

THE SAT WRITING TEST

The Writing test will include a direct writing sample and multiple-choice questions that require recognition of the conventions of standard written English, appropriate diction, and effective and logical expression.

The SAT Writing test will include

- an essay that will provide a direct measure of writing ability;
- essay topics that will not assume any specific subject-matter knowledge;
- revision-in-context passages that will present a context larger than an individually distinct sentence and therefore permit questions on logic, coherence, and organization;
- revision-in-context tasks that are similar to common in-class exercises in which students revise their own essays; and
- usage questions that will require students to recognize errors. Sentence-correction questions will require recognition of errors and selection of the correct rephrasing.

The SAT Writing Section

The SAT Writing section will measure a student's mastery of the effective development and expression of ideas. It will include both multiple-choice items and an essay. The multiple-choice component of the writing section will measure the student's understanding of how to use language in a clear, consistent manner and how to improve a piece of writing through revision and editing. Students will be asked to recognize sentence errors, to choose the best version of a piece of writing, and to improve paragraphs within a writing context. However, they will not be asked to define or to use grammatical terms, and spelling or capitalization will not be tested.

For the essay, students will have 25 minutes to write a first draft of an original essay. This will be a direct measure of their abilities, under timed conditions, to do the kind of writing required in most college courses—writing that emphasizes precise use of language, logical presentation of ideas, development of a point of view, and clarity of expression.

The combination of the multiple-choice items and the essay will provide an assessment of writing that takes into account both the student's understanding of the conventions of language and his or her ability to develop ideas in a thoughtful, coherent, and convincing essay.

The scores for the SAT Writing section will range from 200 to 800. Two subscores will be given for the writing section: a multiple-choice subscore that will range from 20 to 80 and an essay subscore that will range from 2 to 12. Essays not written on the essay assignment will be given a score of zero. The essay component will count toward roughly one-third of the total writing score, and the multiple-choice component will count toward two-thirds of the total writing score.

Content of the Writing Test

Multiple-Choice Questions: 35 Minutes, 49 Questions*

- Usage—Identifying Sentence Errors: 18 questions
- Sentence Correction—Improving Sentences: 25 questions
- Revision-in-Context—Improving Paragraphs: 6 questions

Essay (Writing Exercise): 25 Minutes

Scoring the Writing Test

All essays will be scored holistically. Two readers will independently read each essay and score according to agreed-upon criteria.

Essay Reporting Service

Students may request that copies of essays be sent to high schools and/or colleges.

*The PSAT will include items in this multiple-choice writing section.

The Essay on the SAT Writing Test

On the SAT, you will be required to write an essay. Here's an example of the directions to the Essay:

SECTION 2	Time—25 minutes 1 Question	ESSAY

Directions: Consider carefully the following excerpt and the assignment below it. Then plan and write an essay that explains your ideas as persuasively as possible. Keep in mind that the support you provide—both reasons and examples—will help make your view convincing to the reader.

Please note the essays are considered "first drafts" and are scored holistically. This means readers will award a score according to the overall quality of the essay. They will take into account aspects of writing such as the development of ideas, supporting examples, organization, word choice, and sentence structure.

> The principle is this: each failure leads us closer to deeper knowledge, to greater creativity in understanding old data, to new lines of inquiry. Thomas Edison experienced 10,000 failures before he succeeded in perfecting the light bulb. When a friend of his remarked that 10,000 failures was a lot, Edison replied, "I didn't fail 10,000 times, I successfully eliminated 10,000 materials and combinations that didn't work."
>
> *Myles Brand, "Taking the Measure of Your Success"*
>
> **Assignment:** What is your view on the idea that it takes failure to achieve success? In an essay, support your position using an example (or examples) from literature, the arts, history, current events, politics, science and technology, or your experience or observation.

WHEN THE SUPERVISOR ANNOUNCES THAT 25 MINUTES HAVE PASSED, YOU MUST STOP WRITING THE ESSAY. DO NOT GO ON TO ANY OTHER SECTION IN THE TEST.

YOU MAY MAKE NOTES ON THIS PAGE, BUT YOU MUST WRITE YOUR ESSAY ON THE ANSWER SHEET.

Here are some more sample Essay topics:

Consider carefully the following statement and the assignment below it. Then plan and write your essay as directed.

> **"Outrageous behavior is instructive. It reveals to us the limits of our tolerance."**

Assignment: The quotation implies that those who go beyond accepted standards help us to clarify our own standards. Do you agree or disagree with the quotation? Discuss, supporting your position with examples from current affairs, literature, history, or your own experience.

Consider carefully the following quotation and the assignment following it. Then plan and write your essay as directed.

> **"People seldom stand up for what they truly believe; instead they merely go along with the popular view."**

Assignment: Do you agree or disagree with this statement? Write an essay in which you support your opinion with specific examples from history, contemporary affairs, literature, or personal observation.

Consider carefully the following statement and the assignment below it. Then plan and write your essay as directed.

> **"Everything has its cost."**

Assignment: Choose an example from literature, current affairs, history, or from personal observation in which a cause, an ideal, or an object had to be paid for at some cost. What was that cost? Was what was gained worth it, or was the cost too high? Give reasons for your position.

A Few Words About Scoring the Essay. Even with some errors in spelling, punctuation, and grammar, a student can get a top score on the essay. The highly trained high school and college composition teachers who score the essays will follow a rubric that focuses upon content, organization, and language usage and sentence structure. Each essay will be scored independently by two such readers on a 1–6 scale. If the readers' scores differ by more than two points, the test will be evaluated by a third reader. We know from our experience with the SAT II: Writing Test that fewer than 2 percent of all scored essays require a third reader.

What Makes a Great Essay

The key aim is to engross the reader. Make the reader want to read what you've written and to be involved with your ideas.

Make sure you provide examples and references to support your ideas or theories. For example, if you are arguing against the idea that ignorance is bliss, you could cite how technology is good for people and contrast that with what happens when one does not use that technology. If you are taking the stance that movies made based on books are never as good as the actual books, you should reference a particular book that will support your point. You may want to give an interesting example that the reader can identify with (e.g., in a movie, you get what you see, whereas in a book, you have room to interpret the characters and you may be able to identify with them more, which allows you to enjoy the book more than the movie).

You should also try to get the reader to sympathize or identify with what you have to say by noting a personal experience that is relevant to the essay topic. A student of mine, while writing an essay about a father-son relationship, noted that one of the most significant moments in his life was when he went fishing with his father. He mentioned that while he learned the sport of fishing, he bonded with his father through the common activity.

Sometimes it is wise to challenge the reader by describing an example that would make the reader think. For example, if you are writing about music and how it affects and calms people, you might mention and try to explain something controversial, such as Hitler's loving Wagner's operatic music. The reader will become more involved with what you are writing and perhaps look forward to the rest of your essay.

To get the reader interested in what you are writing, show examples so that the reader will say, "That's a good example," or "I never thought about that." Better yet, if you can say something that the reader may not be aware of or does not know about, the reader will in fact appreciate having learned something new. That is the ultimate goal of creativity in writing.

The SAT Essay Scoring Guide

Score of 6	Score of 5	Score of 4
An essay in this category is *outstanding,* demonstrating *clear and consistent mastery,* although it may have a few minor errors. A typical essay	An essay in this category is *effective,* demonstrating *reasonably consistent mastery,* although it will have occasional errors or lapses in quality. A typical essay	An essay in this category is *competent,* demonstrating *adequate mastery,* although it will have lapses in quality. A typical essay
• effectively and insightfully develops a point of view on the issue and demonstrates outstanding critical thinking, using clearly appropriate examples, reasons, and other evidence to support its position	• effectively develops a point of view on the issue and demonstrates strong critical thinking, generally using appropriate examples, reasons, and other evidence to support its position	• develops a point of view on the issue and demonstrates competent critical thinking, using adequate examples, reasons, and other evidence to support its position
• is well organized and clearly focused, demonstrating clear coherence and smooth progression of ideas	• is well organized and focused, demonstrating coherence and progression of ideas	• is generally organized and focused, demonstrating some coherence and progression of ideas
• exhibits skillful use of language, using a varied, accurate, and apt vocabulary	• exhibits facility in the use of language, using appropriate vocabulary	• exhibits adequate but inconsistent facility in the use of language, using generally appropriate vocabulary
• demonstrates meaningful variety in sentence structure	• demonstrates variety in sentence structure	• demonstrates some variety in sentence structure
• is free of most errors in grammar, usage, and mechanics	• is generally free of most errors in grammar, usage, and mechanics	• has some errors in grammar, usage, and mechanics
Score of 3	**Score of 2**	**Score of 1**
An essay in this category is *inadequate,* but demonstrates *developing mastery,* and is marked by ONE OR MORE of the following weaknesses:	An essay in this category is *seriously limited,* demonstrating *little mastery,* and is flawed by ONE OR MORE of the following weaknesses:	An essay in this category is *fundamentally lacking,* demonstrating *very little* or *no mastery,* and is severely flawed by ONE OR MORE of the following weaknesses:
• develops a point of view on the issue, demonstrating some critical thinking, but may do so inconsistently or use inadequate examples, reasons, or other evidence to support its position	• develops a point of view on the issue that is vague or seriously limited, demonstrating weak critical thinking, providing inappropriate or insufficient examples, reasons, or other evidence to support its position	• develops no viable point of view on the issue, or provides little or no evidence to support its position
• is limited in its organization or focus, or may demonstrate some lapses in coherence or progression of ideas	• is poorly organized and/or focused, or demonstrates serious problems with coherence or progression of ideas	• is disorganized or unfocused, resulting in a disjointed or incoherent essay
• displays developing facility in the use of language, but sometimes uses weak vocabulary or inappropriate word choice	• displays very little facility in the use of language, using very limited vocabulary or incorrect word choice	• displays fundamental errors in vocabulary
• lacks variety or demonstrates problems in sentence structure	• demonstrates frequent problems in sentence structure	• demonstrates severe flaws in sentence structure
• contains an accumulation of errors in grammar, usage, and mechanics	• contains errors in grammar, usage, and mechanics so serious that meaning is somewhat obscured	• contains pervasive errors in grammar, usage, or mechanics that persistently interfere with meaning

Essays not written on the essay assignment will receive a score of zero.

The Writing Sample

Writing sample essays are read and scored by "readers," high school and college teachers who have experience with the writing demonstrated by students at the end of high school. They do not expect polished compositions. Two readers score each essay on a 6-point scale, with 6 as the highest score and 1 as the lowest. The total writing sample score is the sum of the two readers' scores. It is weighted to equal one-third of the total SAT Writing Test score. If the two readers' scores are more than two points apart, a third reader resolves the discrepancy.

Sample Essays

Reproduced below is a topic used on an SAT Writing Test. You will also see the Scoring Guide for Readers of Student Responses to the Writing Subject Test and actual students' essays. The Scoring Guide, shown on page 522, is used to instruct essay readers. The directions that follow reflect those given in the test.

You have twenty-five minutes to write an essay on the topic assigned below. DO NOT WRITE ON ANOTHER TOPIC. AN ESSAY ON ANOTHER TOPIC IS NOT ACCEPTABLE.

The essay is assigned to give you an opportunity to show how well you can write. You should, therefore, take care to express your thoughts on the topic clearly and effectively. How well you write is much more important than how much you write, but to cover the topic adequately, you will probably need to write more than one paragraph. Be specific.

Your essay must be written on the lines provided on your answer sheet. You will receive no other paper on which to write. You will find that you have enough space if you write on every line, avoid wide margins, and keep your handwriting to a reasonable size. It is important to remember that what you write will be read by someone who is not familiar with your handwriting. Try to write or print so that what you are writing is legible to the reader.

Consider carefully the following statement. Then plan and write your essay as directed.

Nothing requires more discipline than freedom.

Assignment: In an essay, discuss your view of the statement above. Support your view with an example or examples from literature, the arts, history, politics, science and technology, current events, or your experience or observation.

Essays with a Total Score of 12

(Each reader gave the essay a score of 6.)

Although essays in this category differ in approach, style, and opinion, and have slight differences in quality, they all demonstrate the *clear and consistent competence* specified in the scoring guide. These essays are characterized by good organization, good command of the language, pertinent support for the ideas being developed, and an effective presentation. These essays are not perfect, nor are they expected to be, for each is only a first draft written in the twenty-five minutes allotted. The essay below is representative of essays in this category.

The ultimate freedom does not require discipline because to be entirely free, one must have no restrictions created by them or the world around them. But ultimate freedom exists only as a concept and while humans can strive to be free, in reality it can never be achieved. Discipline is therefore inescapable.

In William Shakespeare's *King Lear,* the theme of madness plays a major role in Lear's life. Lear's madness becomes his freedom from the rules around him. In the first scene, Lear gives up his land and therefore, power to his daughters, supposedly freeing himself from obligations in his old age. Yet Lear soon finds that his life and the people in his life are not as he once thought them to be. His daughters Regan and Goneril each display cruelty towards him and place restrictions of Lear. By giving up his power, Lear was in fact giving away his freedom. He can no longer do as he pleases, for example, he must beg each daughter to let him live with them. If discipline is taken to mean restrictions and rules placed upon oneself, then Lear in fact has more as a free man than a powerful man. Lear's freedom, or rather his lack of power, ends up promoting his madness. This madness removes him from obligations, but at the same time creates a different kind of restriction on him. Lear in his mad state may not have restrictions and discipline in the sence generally thought of, but he does in a new sence. The discipline of madness consumes him.

Lear, in both his powerful state and his weakened yet free state has freedom and discipline. And while the concept of ultimate freedom is without discipline, Lear's freedom in both cases is an example of how imperfect freedom does involve discipline. When Lear had power, he was free to make decisions, but these decisions were disciplined choices. When Lear had madness instead of power, he had freedom to do what he wanted, without concern of the consequences, but he had discipline forced upon him by his situation. Because ultimate freedom cannot be attained, freedom as we see it and refer to daily does involve discipline. Only the unachievable, ultimate freedom does not require discipline.

Essays with a Total Score of 10

(Each reader gave the essay a score of 5.)

Essays in this category demonstrate the *reasonably consistent competence* described in the scoring guide. They present pertinent examples and a developed argument. These essays, however, do contain lapses that keep them out of the top category. These lapses range from an awkward sentence or two to a failure to maintain a consistent tone. Still, whatever the flaws, they do not detract from the overall impression that the writing is well done.

In society today, as well as histories past, we have seen that "nothing requires more discipline than freedom". Freedom was a principle that people fought and died for. It was an undisputable right that was sometimes put to the test. However, Adeline Yen Mah and Martin Luther King Jr. prove that nothing isn't worth fighting for.

In "Falling Leaves" by Adeline Yen Mah, we can easily sympathize with her struggle for freedom and rights of passage. Ever since she was a young Chinese girl growing up in a male-dominated world, Adeline had to prove to herself and others that she deserved the praise, affection, and education that her three brothers easily attained. With much determination and introspective spirit, she soon learned the power of her will. By speaking out for her wanting to be rid of her provincial education and moving on to higher learning through attending England's Universities did she recognize that "nothing requires more discipline than freedom."

In addition to Adeline's opposition, Martin Luther King Jr. was a prominent figure in America's history that proved that his efforts were not wasted. He was a firm believer of equal rights for his fellow African American people. Without Martin's unerring attempts at breaking the barriers, there would not have been such a great uproar to stop the injustices.

From time to time, people have felt the restraint and oppression, but Adeline and Martin proved that their voices could not go on unheard. They attacked all obstacles and grew strong enough to realize the importance of their cause. The attainment of freedom have bonded these figures into our nation.

Essays with a Total Score of 8

(Each reader gave the essay a score of 4.)

As the scoring guide describes, essays in this category demonstrate *adequate competence* with occasional errors and lapses in quality. Although the papers show that the writers have adequate command of the skills needed for good writing, the papers have the kinds of flaws that keep them out of the top ranges.

In today's world almost all people are granted certain freedoms in relation to behavior or emotions. In the United States of America this priviledge is especially prevelant through it's democratic government and the constitution it provides to protect the people's rights. Because too much unrestricted freedom can hurt a nation, the freedoms granted to the people must be regulated by each person's self-discipline. As with most things in life, freedom can be taken for granted if responsibility is not taken for one's own actions.

One major freedom given to most teenagers is the priviledge to go away from home for college. This is a major commitment and responsibility because in many cases a student will be living away from his/her parents for the first time. His/her mother and father are no longer around to hassle the youth about homework, going to sleep, or other decisions. It is a beginning college student's own discipline or practicality that must aid the teen in making such lifestyle choices. In order to succeed and keep the new freedom of living away from home, the student must prove that he or she is mature enough to handle it. The student must organize his/her time appropriately, take care of himself/herself, and act like an adult.

Many personal freedoms and liberties are granted to people in life. In exchange for these rights, human beings must show they are worthy of receiving them by showing discipline and maturity in their actions and decision. If people were to live carelessly without regard for the preciousness of their freedom, the world would be full of chaos and injustice.

Important Tips on How to Write the Best Essay

Making Your Sentences Effective

What Is Style?

Many good ideas are lost because they are expressed in a dull, wordy, involved way. We often have difficulty following—we may even ignore—instructions that are hard to read. Yet we find other instructions written in such a clear and simple way that a child could easily follow them. This way of writing—the words we choose and the way we use them—is called style.

No two people write exactly alike. Even when writing about the same thing, they probably will express ideas differently. Some will say what they think more effectively than others; what they say will be more easily read and understood. But there is seldom any one best way to say something. Rather, there are usually several equally good ways. This flexibility is what makes English such a rich language.

Style can't be taught; each person's style is like personality—it is unique to him or her. But we can each improve our styles. Let us consider how we can improve our writing styles by improving our sentences.

How to Write Effective Sentences

We speak in sentences; we write in sentences. A single word or phrase sometimes carries a complete thought, but sentences are more often the real units of thought communication.

Writing good sentences takes concentration, patience, and practice. It involves much more than just stringing words together, one after another, as they tumble from our minds. If writers aren't careful, their sentences may not mean to the reader what they want them to mean; they may mean what they ***didn't*** want them to—or they may mean nothing at all.

This section discusses five things writers can do to write better sentences—or improve sentences already written:

1. Create interest
2. Make your meaning clear
3. Keep your sentences brief
4. Make every word count
5. Vary your sentence patterns

Let's consider interest first.

1. *Create Interest*

We can make our writing more interesting by writing in an informal, conversational style. This style also makes our writing easier to understand and our readers more receptive to our thoughts.

Listen to two men meeting in the coffee shop. One tells the other, "Let me know when you need more paper clips." But how would he have written it? Probably as follows:

Request this office be notified when your activity's supply of paper clips, wire, steel gem pattern, large type 1, stock No. 7510-634-6516, falls below 30-day level prescribed in AFR 67-1, Vol. II, Section IV, subject: Office Supplies. Requisition will be submitted as expeditiously as possible to preclude noncompliance with appropriate directives.

Judging from the formal, academic style of much of our writing, we want to *impress* rather than *express.* There seems to be something about writing that brings out our biggest words, our most complex sentences, and our most formal style. Obviously this is not effective writing. We wouldn't dare say it aloud this formally for fear someone would laugh at us, but we will write it.

WRITE TO EXPRESS

One of the best ways to make our writing more interesting to the reader and, hence, more effective is to write as we talk. Of course we can't write *exactly* as we talk, and we shouldn't want to. We usually straighten out the sentence structure, make our sentences complete rather than fragmentary or run-on, substitute for obvious slang words, and so on. But we can come close to our conversational style without being folksy, ungrammatical, or wordy. This informal style is far more appropriate for the kind of writing we do and for the kind of readers we have than the old formal style. And it certainly makes better reading.

BE DEFINITE, SPECIFIC, AND CONCRETE

Another way—and one of the surest ways—to arouse and hold the interest and attention of readers is to be definite, specific, and concrete.

2. *Make Your Meaning Clear*

You do not need to be a grammarian to recognize a good sentence. After all, the first requirement of grammar is that you focus your reader's attention on the meaning you wish to convey. If you take care to make your meaning clear, your grammar will usually take care of itself. You can, however, do three things to make your meaning clearer to your reader: (1) emphasize your main ideas, (2) avoid wandering sentences, and (3) avoid ambiguity.

EMPHASIZE THE MAIN IDEAS

When we talk, we use gestures, voice changes, pauses, smiles, frowns, and so on to emphasize our main ideas. In writing, we have to use different methods for emphasis. Some are purely mechanical; others are structural.

Mechanical devices include capital letters, underlining or italics, punctuation, and headings. Printers used to capitalize the first letter of a word they wanted to emphasize. We still occasionally capitalize or use a heavier type to emphasize words, phrases, or whole sentences. Sometimes we underline or italicize words that we want to stand out. Often we label or head main sections or subdivisions, as we have done in this book. This effectively separates main ideas and makes them stand out so that the reader doesn't have to search for them.

But mechanical devices for emphasizing an idea—capitalization, particularly—are often overused. The best way to emphasize an idea is to place it effectively in the sentence. The most emphatic position is at the end of the sentence. The next most emphatic position is at the beginning of the sentence. The place of least importance is anywhere in the middle. Remember, therefore, to put the important clause, phrase, name, or idea at the beginning or at the end of your sentences, and never hide the main idea in a subordinate clause or have it so buried in the middle of the sentence that the reader has to dig it out or miss it altogether.

Unemphatic: People drive on the left side instead of the right side in England.
Better: Instead of driving on the right side, people in England drive on the left.

AVOID WANDERING SENTENCES

All parts of a sentence should contribute to one clear idea or impression. Long, straggling sentences usually contain a hodgepodge of unrelated ideas. You should either break long sentences up into shorter sentences or put the subordinate thoughts into subordinate form. Look at this sentence:

The sergeant, an irritable fellow who had been a truck driver, born and brought up in the corn belt of Iowa, strong as an ox and six feet tall, fixed an angry eye on the recruit.

You can see that the main idea is "The sergeant fixed an angry eye on the recruit." That he was an irritable fellow, strong as an ox, and six feet tall adds to the main idea. But the facts that he had been a truck driver and had been born in Iowa add nothing to the main thought, and the sentence is better without them.

The sergeant, an irritable fellow who was strong as an ox and six feet tall, fixed an angry eye on the recruit.

AVOID AMBIGUITY

If a sentence can be misunderstood, it will be misunderstood. A sentence that says, "The truck followed the Jeep until its tire blew out," may be perfectly clear to the writer, but it will mean nothing to the reader until the pronoun *its* is identified.

MAKE SURE THAT YOUR MODIFIERS SAY WHAT YOU MEAN

"While eating oats, the farmer took the horse out of the stable." This sentence provides little more than a laugh until you add to the first part of the sentence a logical subject ("the horse"): "While the horse was eating oats, the farmer took him out of the stable." Sometimes simple misplacement of modifiers in sentences leads to misunderstanding: "The young lady went to the dance with her boyfriend wearing a low-cut gown." You can clarify this sentence by simply rearranging it: "Wearing a low-cut gown, the young lady went to the dance with her boyfriend."

3. *Keep Your Sentences Brief*

Sentences written like ten-word advertisements are hard to read. You cannot get the kind of brevity you want by leaving out the articles (*a, an,* and *the*). You can get brevity by dividing complex ideas into bite-size sentences and by avoiding unnecessary words and phrases and needless repetition and elaboration. Here are some suggestions that will help you to write short, straightforward sentences.

USE VERBS THAT WORK

The verb—the action word—is the most important word in a sentence. It is the power plant that supplies the energy, vitality, and motion in the sentence. So use strong verbs, verbs that really *work* in your sentences.

USE THE ACTIVE VOICE

Sentences written in the basic subject-verb-object pattern are said to be written in the *active voice.* In such sentences, someone or something *does* something to the object—there is a forward movement of the idea. In sentences written in the *passive voice,* the subject merely receives the action—it has something done to it by someone or something, and there is no feeling of forward movement of the idea.

The active voice, in general, is preferable to the passive voice because it helps to give writing a sense of energy, vitality, and motion. When we use the passive voice predominantly, our writing doesn't seem to have much life, the actor in the sentences is not allowed to act, and verbs become weak. So don't rob your writing of its power by using the passive voice when you can use the active voice. Nine out of ten sentences will be both shorter (up to 25 percent shorter) and stronger in the active voice.

Let's compare the two voices:

Active: The pilot (*Actor*) flew (*action*) the aircraft. (*acted upon*)

Passive: The aircraft was flown by the pilot.
(*Acted upon*) (*action*) (*actor*)

Now let's see some typical passive examples:

The committee will be appointed by the principal.
Reports have been received...
Provisions will be made by the manager in case of a subway strike.

Aren't these familiar? In most of these, we should be emphasizing the actor rather than leaving out or subordinating him or her.

See how much more effective those sentences are when they are written in the active voice.

The principal will appoint the committee.
We have received reports...
The manager will make provisions in case of a subway strike.

AVOID USING THE PASSIVE VOICE

The passive voice always takes more words to say what could be said just as well (and probably better) in the active voice. In the passive voice, the subject also becomes less personal and may seem less important, and the motion of the sentence grinds to a halt.

There are times, of course, when the passive voice is useful and justified—as when the person or thing doing the action is unknown or unimportant.

When we use the lifeless passive voice indiscriminately, we make our writing weak, ineffective, and dull. Remember that the normal English word order is subject-verb-object. There may be occasions in your writing when you feel that the passive voice is preferable. But should such an occasion arise, think twice before you write; the passive voice rarely improves your style. Before using a passive construction, make certain that you have a specific reason. After using it, check to see that your sentence is not misleading.

TAKE A DIRECT APPROACH

Closely related to passive voice construction is indirect phrasing.

It is requested...
It is recommended...
It has been brought to the attention of...
It is the opinion of...

Again this is so familiar to us that we don't even question it. But who requested? Who recommended? Who knows? Who believes? No one knows from reading such sentences!

This indirect way of writing, this use of the passive voice and the indirect phrase, is perhaps the most characteristic feature of the formal style of the past. There are many explanations for it. A psychiatrist might say the writer was afraid to take the responsibility for what he or she is writing or merely passing the buck. The writer may unjustifiably believe this style makes him or her anonymous or makes him or her sound less dogmatic and authoritarian.

Express your ideas immediately and directly. Unnecessary expressions like *it is, there is,* and *there are* weaken sentences and delay comprehension. They also tend to place part of the sentence in the passive voice. *It is the recommendation of the sales manager that the report be forwarded immediately* is more directly expressed as *The sales manager recommends that we send the report immediately.*

Change Long Modifiers	*to Shorter Ones*
Mr. Barnes, who is president of the board, will preside.	Mr. Barnes, the board president, will preside.
Vehicles that are defective are…	Defective vehicles are…
They gave us a month for accomplishment of the task.	They gave us a month to do the job.

Break Up Long Sentences

There is not enough time available for the average executive to do everything that might be done and so it is necessary for him to determine wisely the essentials and do them first, then spend the remaining time on things that are "nice to do."

The average executive lacks time to do everything that might be done. Consequently, he must decide what is essential and do it first. Then he can spend the remaining time on things that are "nice to do."

4. Make Every Word Count

Don't cheat your readers. They are looking for ideas—for meaning—when they read your letter, report, or directive. If they have to read several words that have little to do with the real meaning of a sentence or if they have to read a number of sentences to get just a little meaning, you are cheating them. Much of their time and effort is wasted because they aren't getting full benefit. They expected something that you didn't deliver.

MAKE EACH WORD ADVANCE YOUR THOUGHT

Each word in a sentence should advance the thought of that sentence. To leave a word out would destroy the meaning you are trying to convey.

"Naturally," you say. "Of course!" But reread the last letter you wrote. Aren't some of your sentences rather wordy? Couldn't you have said the same thing in fewer words? And finally, how many times did you use a whole phrase to say what could have been said in one word, or a whole clause for what could have been expressed in a short phrase? In short, try tightening up a sentence like this:

The reason that prices rose was that the demand was increasing at the same time that the production was decreasing.

Rewritten:
Prices rose because the demand increased while production decreased.

Doesn't our rewrite say the same thing as the original? Yet we have saved the reader some effort by squeezing the unnecessary words out of a wordy sentence.

Now try this one:

Wordy: The following statistics serve to give a good idea of the cost of production.
Improved: The following statistics give a good idea of the production costs.
or
These statistics show production costs.

And this one:

Wordy: I have a production supervisor who likes to talk a great deal.
Improved: I have a talkative production supervisor.

In all of those rewritten sentences we have saved our reader some time. The same thing has been said in fewer words.

Of course you can be *too* concise. If your writing is too brief or terse, it may "sound" rude and abrupt, and you may lose more than you gain. You need, then, to be politely concise. What you are writing, what you are writing about, and whom you are writing for will help you decide just where to draw the line. However, the general rule, make every word count, still stands. Say what you have to say in as few words as clarity *and tact* will allow.

CONSOLIDATE IDEAS

A second way to save the reader's effort is to consolidate ideas whenever possible. Pack as much meaning as possible into each sentence *without making the sentence structure too complicated.*

Each sentence is by definition an idea, a unit of thought. Each time the readers read one of these units, they should get as much meaning as possible. It takes just about as much effort to read a sentence with a simple thought as it does to read one with a strong idea or with two or three strong ideas.

There are several things we can do to pack meaning into a sentence. In general, they all have to do with summarizing, combining, and consolidating ideas.

Some people write sentences that are weak and insignificant, both in structure and thought. Ordinarily several such sentences can be summarized and the thought put into one good, mature sentence. For example:

We left Wisconsin the next morning. I remember watching three aircraft. They were F-4s. They were flying very low. I felt sure they were going to crash over a half a dozen times. The F-4 is new to me. I hadn't seen one before.

Rewritten:

When we left Wisconsin the next morning, I remember watching three F-4s, a type of aircraft I had never seen before. They were flying so low that over a half-dozen times I felt sure they were going to crash.

When summarizing like this, be sure to emphasize the main action. Notice in the next example how we have kept the main action as our verb and made the other actions subordinate by changing them to verbals.

Poor: It was in 1959 that he *retired* from teaching and he *devoted* his time to *writing* his autobiography. (three verbs, one verbal)

Improved: In 1959 he *retired* from teaching to *devote* his time to *writing* his autobiography. (one verb, two verbals)

Here is an example similar to ones we might find in a directive:

Poor: The evaluation forms will be picked up from your respective personnel office. You should have these completed by 1700 hours, 18 May. They will be delivered immediately to the security section.

Notice that in the above instructions all of the actions are to be performed by the reader or "you." Now let's put these into one sentence, placing the things to be done in a series and using a single subject.

Improved: Pick up the evaluation forms from your personnel office; complete and deliver them to the security section by 1700 hours, 18 May. (The subject [you] is understood.)

The same thing can be done with subjects or predicates:

Poor: Horror stories shown on television appear to contribute to juvenile delinquency. Comic books with their horror stories seem to have the same effect. Even the reports of criminal activities which appear in our newspapers seem to contribute to juvenile delinquency.

Improved: Television, comic books, and newspapers seem to contribute to juvenile delinquency by emphasizing stories of horror and crime.

There is one more thing we can do to make our sentences better. We can vary their length and complexity. The following paragraphs suggest ways to do this.

5. *Vary Your Sentence Patterns*

We should, as a general rule, write predominantly short sentences. Similarly, we should keep our sentences simple enough for our readers to understand them easily and quickly.

But most people soon get tired of nothing but simple, straightforward sentences. So, give your reader an occasional change of pace. Vary both the length and the construction of your sentences.

VARY SENTENCE LENGTH

Some writers use nothing but short, choppy sentences ("The road ended in a wrecked village. The lines were up beyond. There was much artillery around."). In the hands of Hemingway, from whom this example is taken, short sentences can give an effect of purity and simplicity; in the hands of a less skillful writer, choppy sentences are usually only monotonous.

The other extreme, of course, is just as bad. The writer who always writes heavy sentences of 20 to 30 words soon loses the reader. Some great writers use long sentences effectively, but most writers do not.

The readability experts suggest that, for the most effective *communication*, a sentence should rarely exceed 20 words. Their suggestion is a good rule of thumb, but sentence length should vary. And an occasional long sentence is not hard to read if it is followed by shorter ones. A fair goal for most letter writers is an average of 21 words per sentence or fewer. For longer types of writing, such as regulations and manuals, sentences should average 15 words or fewer. The sentences in opening paragraphs and in short letters may run a little longer than the average.

VARY SENTENCE CONSTRUCTION

Just as important as varied sentence length is variety of construction. Four common sentence categories are simple, compound, complex, and compound-complex.

A *simple sentence* consists of only one main (independent) clause:

Rain came down in torrents.
Rain and hail started falling. (Simple sentence with compound subject)
The storm began and soon grew in intensity. (Simple sentence with compound predicate)

A *compound sentence* has two or more main clauses:

Rain started falling, and all work stopped.
The storm began; all work stopped.
The storm began, the workers found shelter, and all work stopped.

A *complex sentence* has one main clause and at least one subordinate (dependent) clause. (Subordinate clauses are underlined in the following sentences.)

They were just starting their work when the rain started.
Before they had made any progress, the rain started falling.
The storm, which grew rapidly in intensity, stopped all work.

A *compound-complex sentence* has two or more main clauses and at least one subordinate clause. (Subordinate clauses are underlined in the following sentences.)

Rain started falling, and all work stopped before they had made any progress.
Although the workers were eager to finish the job, the storm forced them to stop, and they quickly found shelter.
They had made some progress before the storm began, but when it started, all work stopped.

The names of the categories are really not important except to remind you to vary your sentence construction when you write. But remember that sentence variety is not just a mechanical chore to perform after your draft is complete. Good sentence variety comes naturally as the result of proper coordination and subordination when you write.

For example:

If two or more short sentences have the same subject, combine them into one simple sentence with a compound verb:

The men were hot. They were tired, too. They were also angry.
The men were hot and tired and angry.

If you have two ideas of equal weight or parallel thought, write them as two clauses in a compound sentence:

The day was hot and humid. The men had worked hard.
The men had worked hard, and the day was hot and humid.
The day was hot and humid, but the men had worked hard.

If one idea is more important than others, put it in the main clause of a complex sentence:

Poor: The men were tired, and they had worked hard, and the day was hot.

Better: The men were tired because they had worked hard on a hot day.

or

Although the day was hot and the men were tired, they worked hard.

If the adverbial modifier is the least important part of a complex sentence, put it first and keep the end position for the more important main clause:

Instead of: The men finished the job in record time, even though the day was hot and humid and they were tired.

Better: Even though the day was hot and humid and the men were tired, they finished the job in record time.

But be careful about having long, involved subordinate clauses come before the main clause. The reader may get lost or confused before getting to your main point or give up before getting to it. Also beware of letting too many modifying words, phrases, or clauses come between the subject and the verb. This is torture for the reader. The subject and the verb are usually the most important elements of a sentence; keep them close together whenever possible.

Other Types of Questions on the SAT Writing Test

Following are directions and sample question types from the SAT Writing Test.

IDENTIFYING ERRORS

Directions: **The following sentences test your knowledge of grammar, usage, diction (choice of words), and idiom.**

Some sentences are correct.
No sentence contains more than one error.

You will find that the error, if there is one, is underlined and lettered. Elements of the sentence that are not underlined will not be changed. In choosing answers, follow the requirements of standard written English.

If there is an error, select the one underlined part that must be changed to make the sentence correct and fill in the corresponding oval on your answer sheet.

If there is no error, fill in answer oval E.

EXAMPLE:

The other (A) delegates and him (B) immediately (C) accepted the resolution drafted by (D) the neutral states. No error. (E)

SAMPLE ANSWER

Ⓐ ● Ⓒ Ⓓ Ⓔ

Sample Questions with Answers

1. Even before (A) he became the youngest player to win the Wimbledon men's singles (B) championship, Boris Becker had sensed (C) that his life would no longer (D) be the same. No error. (E)

2. If any signer of the Constitution was (A) to return to life for a day, (B) his opinion of (C) our amendments would be (D) interesting. No error. (E)

3. The dean of the college (A), together with (B) some other faculty members, are (C) planning a conference for the purpose of laying (D) down certain regulations. No error. (E)

4. If one lives (A) in Florida one day (B) and in Iceland the next, (C) he is certain (D) to feel the change in temperature. No error. (E)

5. Now (A) that the stress of examinations and interviews are (B) over, we can all (C) relax (D) for a while. No error. (E)

6. The industrial trend (A) is (B) in the direction of more (C) machines and less (D) people. No error. (E)

7. The American standard of living is (A) still higher (B) than most (C) of the other countries of (D) the world. No error. (E)

8. At last, (A) late (B) in the afternoon, a long line of flags and colored umbrellas were (C) seen moving toward (D) the gate of the palace. No error. (E)

9. Due to (A) the failure of the air-cooling system, many in the audience had left (B) the meeting before (C) the principal speaker arrived. (D) No error. (E)

10. Psychologists and psychiatrists will tell (A) us that it is of the utmost importance that a disturbed (B) child receive (C) professional attention as soon as (D) possible. No error. (E)

11. After we waited (A) in line for three hours, (B) much to our disgust, the tickets had been (C) sold out when (D) we reached the window. No error. (E)

12. That angry outburst of Father's (A) last night was so annoying that it resulted in our guests (B) packing up (C) and leaving this (D) morning. No error. (E)

13. Sharp (A) advances last week in the wholesale price of beef is (B) a strong indication of higher meat costs (C) to come, but so far retail prices remain favorable. (D) No error. (E)

14. An acquaintance with the memoirs of Elizabeth Barrett Browning and Robert Browning enable (A) us to appreciate the depth of influence (B) that two people of talent can have on (C) each other. (D) No error. (E)

15. The supervisor was advised (A) to give the assignment to whomever (B) he believed (C) had a strong sense of responsibility, and the courage of (D) his conviction. No error. (E)

16. If he would have (A) lain (B) quietly as instructed by the doctor, he might not (C) have had (D) a second heart attack. No error. (E)

17. The guiding spirit (A) of (B) the *Kenyon Review* is John Crowe Ranson, who (C) you must know as (D) an outstanding American critic. No error. (E)

18. Though (A) you may not agree with (B) the philosophy of Malcolm X, you must admit that he had (C) tremendous influence over (D) a great many followers. No error. (E)

19. There is no objection to him (A) joining the party provided (B) he is willing to fit in with (C) the plans of the group and is ready and (D) able to do his share of the work. No error. (E)

20. Ceremonies (A) were opened (B) by a drum and bugle corps of Chinese children parading up (C) Mott Street in colorful uniforms (D). No error. (E)

21. The reason most (A) Americans don't (B) pay much attention to rising (C) African nationalism is because (D) they really do not know modern Africa. No error. (E)

22. There remains (A) many reasons for the animosity (B) that exists (C) between (D) the Arab countries and Israel. No error. (E)

23. The Federal Aviation Administration ordered (A) an emergency inspection of several (B) Pan American planes on account of (C) a Pan American Boeing 707 had crashed (D) on Bali, in Indonesia. No error. (E)

24. A gang of armed thieves (A), directed by a young woman, has raided (B) the mansion of a gold-mining (C) millionaire near Dublin (D) late last night. No error. (E)

25. I had (A) a male chauvinist pig dream (B) that the women of the world rose up (C) and denounced the women's (D) liberation movement. No error. (E)

IMPROVING SENTENCES

Directions: The following sentences test correctness and effectiveness of expression. In choosing answers, follow the requirements of standard written English; that is, pay attention to grammar, choice of words, sentence construction, and punctuation.

In each of the following sentences, part of the sentence or the entire sentence is underlined. Beneath each sentence you will find five ways of phrasing the underlined part. Choice A repeats the original; the other four are different.

Choose the answer that best expresses the meaning of the original sentence. If you think the original is better than any of the alternatives, choose it; otherwise choose one of the others. Your choice should produce the most effective sentence—clear and precise, without awkwardness or ambiguity.

EXAMPLE:

SAMPLE ANSWER

Ⓐ ● Ⓒ Ⓓ Ⓔ

Laura Ingalls Wilder published her first book and she was sixty-five years old then.

(A) and she was sixty-five years old then
(B) when she was sixty-five
(C) being age sixty-five years old
(D) upon the reaching of sixty-five years
(E) at the time when she was sixty-five

Sample Questions with Answers

26. Such of his novels as was humorous were successful.

(A) Such of his novels as was humorous were successful.
(B) Such of his novels as were humorous were successful.
(C) His novels such as were humorous were successful.
(D) His novels were successful and humorous.
(E) Novels such as his humorous ones were successful.

27. Being that the plane was grounded, we stayed over until the next morning so that we could get the first flight out.

(A) Being that the plane was grounded, we stayed over
(B) In view of the fact that the plane was grounded, we stayed over
(C) Since the plane was grounded, we stayed over
(D) Because the plane was grounded, we stood over
(E) On account of the plane being grounded, we stayed over

28. He never has and he never will keep his word.

(A) He never has and he never will
(B) He has never yet and never will
(C) He has not ever and he will not
(D) He never has or will
(E) He never has kept and he never will

29. The teacher felt badly because she had scolded the bright child who was restless for want of something to do.

(A) felt badly because she had scolded the bright child
(B) felt badly why she had scolded the bright child
(C) felt bad because she had scolded the bright child
(D) felt bad by scolding the bright child
(E) had felt badly because she scolded the bright child

30. This book does not describe the struggle of the blacks to win their voting rights that I bought.

(A) does not describe the struggle of the blacks to win their voting rights that I bought
(B) does not describe the black struggle to win their voting rights that I bought
(C) does not, although I bought it, describe the struggle of the blacks to win their voting rights
(D) which I bought does not describe the struggle to win for blacks their voting rights
(E) that I bought does not describe the struggle of the blacks to win their voting rights

31. Barbara cannot help but think that she will win a college scholarship.

(A) Barbara cannot help but think
(B) Barbara cannot help but to think
(C) Barbara cannot help not to think
(D) Barbara can help but think
(E) Barbara cannot but help thinking

32. In spite of Tom wanting to study, his sister made him wash the dishes.

(A) Tom wanting to study
(B) the fact that Tom wanted to study
(C) Tom's need to study
(D) Tom's wanting to study
(E) Tom studying

33. The old sea captain told my wife and me many interesting yarns about his many voyages.

(A) my wife and me
(B) me and my wife
(C) my wife and I
(D) I and my wife
(E) my wife along with me

34. A great many students from several universities are planning to, if the weather is favorable, attend next Saturday's mass rally in Washington.

(A) are planning to, if the weather is favorable, attend next Saturday's mass rally in Washington
(B) are planning, if the weather is favorable, to attend next Saturday's mass rally in Washington
(C) are planning to attend, if the weather is favorable, next Saturday's mass rally in Washington
(D) are planning to attend next Saturday's mass rally in Washington, if the weather is favorable
(E) are, if the weather is favorable, planning to attend next Saturday's mass rally in Washington

35. Jane's body movements are like those of a dancer.

(A) like those of a dancer
(B) the same as a dancer
(C) like a dancer
(D) a dancer's
(E) like those of a dancer's

Explanatory Answers

1. Choice E is correct. All underlined parts are correct.

2. Choice A is correct. "If any signer of the Constitution *were* to return to life..." The verb in the "if clause" of a present contrary-to-fact conditional statement must have a past subjunctive form (*were*).

3. Choice C is correct. "The dean of the college...*is* planning..." The subject of the sentence (*dean*) is singular. Therefore, the verb must be singular (*is planning*).

4. Choice E is correct. All underlined parts are correct.

5. Choice B is correct. "Now that the stress...*is* over..." The subject of the subordinate clause is singular (*stress*). Accordingly, the verb of the clause must be singular (*is*—not *are*). Incidentally, *examinations* and *interviews* are not subjects—they are objects of the preposition *of.*

6. Choice D is correct. "...of more machines and *fewer* people." We use *fewer* for persons and things that may be counted. We use *less* for bulk or mass.

7. Choice C is correct. "...than *that of most* of the other countries of the world." We must have parallelism so that the word *standard* in the main clause of the sentence acts as an antecedent for the pronoun *that* in the subordinate clause. As the original sentence reads, the American standard of living is still higher than the countries themselves.

8. Choice C is correct. "...a long line of flags...*was* seen..." The subject of the sentence is singular (*line*). Therefore, the verb must be singular (*was seen*).

9. Choice A is correct. "*Because of* the failure..." The rule is that you never start a sentence with *Due to*. As a predicate adjective, *due to* is correct when used in a sentence such as: "His weakness was *due to* his hunger."

10. Choice E is correct. All underlined parts are correct. Note that we would consider "receive" to be correct because it would fall into the category of a subjunctive verb form; the sentence is presenting a situation that isn't yet reality. The subjunctive is used following verbs like *insist*, *request*, *suggest*, and so on. None of those are used directly here, but "psychiatrists will tell us that it is of the utmost importance that" creates a very similar situation.

11. Choice C is correct. "After we waited in line for three hours, the tickets had, *much to our disgust*, been sold out when we reached the window." Avoid squinting constructions—that is, modifiers that are so placed that the reader cannot tell whether they are modifying the words immediately preceding the construction or the words immediately following the construction. As the sentence initially reads, we don't know whether *much to our disgust* modifies *after we waited in line for three hours* or *the tickets had been sold out when we reached the window*.

12. Choice B is correct. "...resulted in our *guests'* packing up..." A noun or pronoun immediately preceding a gerund is in the possessive case. Note that the noun *guests* followed by an apostrophe is possessive.

13. Choice B is correct. "Sharp advances...*are*..." Since the subject of the sentence is plural (*advances*), the verb must be plural (*are*).

14. Choice A is correct. "An acquaintance with the memoirs...*enables* us..." Since the subject of the sentence is singular (*acquaintance*), the verb must be singular (*enables*).

15. Choice B is correct. "...to *whoever*...had a strong sense..." The subject of the subordinate clause is *whoever*, and it takes a nominative form (*whoever*—not *whomever*) since it is a subject. Incidentally, the expression *he believed* is parenthetical, so it has no grammatical relationship with the rest of the sentence.

16. Choice A is correct. "If he *had lain*..." The verb in the "if clause" of a past contrary-to-fact conditional statement must take the *had lain* form—not the *would have lain* form.

17. Choice C is correct. "...John Crowe Ransom, *whom* you must know as an outstanding American critic." The direct object of the subordinate clause—or of any clause or sentence—must be in the objective case and, accordingly, must take the objective form (*whom*—not *who*).

18. Choice E is correct. All underlined parts are correct.

19. Choice A is correct. "There is no objection to *his* joining..." We have here a pronoun that is acting as the subject of the gerund *joining*. As a subject of the gerund, the pronoun must be in the possessive case (*his*).

20. Choice D is correct. "...of Chinese children parading *in colorful uniforms* up Mott Street." In the original sentence, *in colorful uniforms* was a misplaced modifier.

21. Choice D is correct. "The reason...is *that*..." We must say *the reason is that*—not *the reason is because.*

22. Choice A is correct. "There *remain* many reasons..." The word "There" in this sentence is an expletive or introductory adverb. The subject of the sentence ("reasons") must agree with the verb ("remain") in number.

23. Choice C is correct. "...*because* a Pan American Boeing 707 had crashed..." The word group *on account of* has the function of a preposition. We need a subordinate conjunction (*because*) here in order to introduce the clause.

24. Choice B is correct. "...*raided* the mansion..." The past tense (*raided*)—not the present perfect tense (*has raided*)—is necessary because the sentence has a specific past time reference (*last night*).

25. Choice E is correct. All underlined parts are correct.

26. Choice B is correct. Choice A is incorrect because the plural verb ("were") is necessary. The reason for the plural verb is that the subject "as" acts as a relative pronoun whose antecedent is the plural noun "novels." Choice B is correct. Choice C is awkward. Choice D changes the meaning of the original sentence, and so does Choice E.

27. Choice C is correct. Choice A is incorrect—never start a sentence with "being that." Choice B is too wordy. Choice D is incorrect because we "stayed"—not "stood." Choice E is incorrect because "on account of" may never be used as a subordinate conjunction.

28. Choice E is correct. Avoid improper ellipsis. Choices A, B, C, and D are incorrect for this reason. The word "kept" must be included since the second part of the sentence uses another form of the verb ("keep").

29. Choice C is correct. Choice A is incorrect because the copulative verb "felt" takes a predicate adjective ("bad")—not an adverb ("badly"). Choice B is incorrect for the same reason. Moreover, we don't say "felt bad why." Choice D is incorrect because the verbal phrase "by scolding" is awkward in this context. Choice E is incorrect because of the use of "badly" and because the past perfect form of the verb ("had felt") is wrong in this time sequence.

30. Choice E is correct. Choices A, B, and C are incorrect because the part of the sentence that deals with the buying of the book is in the wrong position. Choice D is incorrect because the meaning of the original sentence has been changed. According to this choice, others besides blacks have been struggling.

31. Choice A is correct. The other choices are unidiomatic.

32. Choice D is correct. Choice A is incorrect because the possessive form of the noun ("Tom's") must be used to modify the gerund ("wanting"). Choice B is too wordy. Choice C changes the meaning of the original sentence. Choice E is incorrect for the same reason that Choice A is incorrect. Also, Choice E changes the meaning of the original sentence.

33. Choice A is correct. Choice B is incorrect because "wife" should precede "me." Choice C is incorrect because the object form "me" (not the nominative form "I") should be used as the indirect object. Choice D is incorrect for the reasons given above for Choices B and C. Choice E is too roundabout.

34. Choice D is correct. Choices A, B, C, and E are incorrect because of the misplacement of the subordinate clause ("if the weather is favorable").

35. Choice A is correct. Choices B and C are incorrect because of improper ellipsis. The words "those of" are necessary in these choices. Choice D is incorrect because the sentence should read, for clarity, "Jane's body movements are a dancer's body movements," not "Jane's body movements are a dancer's." In Choice E, the possessive use of "dancer's" is incorrect.

Improving Paragraphs
Revision-in-Context
Passage with Questions

Directions: The following passage is an early draft of an essay. Some parts of the passage need to be rewritten. Read the passage and select the best answers for the questions that follow. Some questions are about particular sentences or parts of sentences and ask you to improve sentence structure and word choice. Other questions refer to parts of the essay or the entire essay and ask you to consider organization and development. In making your decisions, follow the conventions of standard written English.

[1]In more and more families, both husbands and wives work nowadays and with this there are new problems that result. [2]One reason there are so many two-career couples is that the cost of living is very high. [3]Another is because women are now more independent.

[4]An example of a two-career couple is Mr. and Mrs. Long. [5]Mrs. Long is a university professor. [6]Her husband works for a large corporation as a personnel counselor. [7]They have two children. [8]The Longs believe that the number of two-career couples is likely to increase. [9]However, society generally still expects a married woman to continue to fulfill the traditional roles of companion, housekeeper, mother, hostess. [10]Thus, as the Longs have experienced, conflicts arise in many ways. [11]When career opportunities clash, it is difficult for them to decide which career is more important.

[12]There are some basic things that can be done to try to solve a couple's problems. [13]Partners should discuss issues with each other openly. [14]Keep a realistic estimate on how much can be done. [15]Each partner must set priorities, make choices, and agree to trade-offs. [16]Men and women have to understand each other's feelings and be aware of this problem before they get involved.

(SENTENCE STRUCTURE)

1. Which of the following is the best revision of the underlined portion of sentence 1 below?

In more and more families, both husbands and wives work <u>nowadays and with this there are new problems that result.</u>

(A) nowadays, a situation that is causing new problems
(B) nowadays and this is what is causing new problems
(C) nowadays and this makes them have new problems as a result
(D) nowadays and with it are new problems
(E) nowadays, they are having new problems

(USAGE)

2. Which of the following is the best revision of the underlined portion of sentence 3 below?

Another <u>is because women are</u> now more independent.

(A) is women which are
(B) reason is that women are
(C) comes from women being
(D) reason is due to the fact that women are
(E) is caused by the women's being

(SENTENCE COMBINING)

3. Which of the following is the best way to combine sentences 5, 6, and 7?

(A) Mrs. Long, a university professor, and her husband, a personnel counselor for a large corporation, have two children.
(B) As a personnel counselor for a large corporation and as a university professor, Mr. and Mrs. Long have two children.
(C) Having two children are Mr. and Mrs. Long, a personnel counselor for a large corporation and a university professor.
(D) Mrs. Long is a university professor and her husband is a personnel counselor for a large corporation and they have two children.
(E) Mr. and Mrs. Long have two children—he is a personnel counselor for a large corporation and she is a university professor.

(PASSAGE ORGANIZATION)

4. In relation to the passage as a whole, which of the following best describes the writer's intention in the second paragraph?

(A) To summarize contradictory evidence
(B) To propose a solution to a problem
(C) To provide an example
(D) To evaluate opinions set forth in the first paragraph
(E) To convince the reader to alter his or her opinion

(SENTENCE STRUCTURE)

5. In the context of the sentences preceding and following sentence 14, which of the following is the best revision of sentence 14?

(A) You should keep a realistic estimate of how much you can do.
(B) Estimate realistically how much can be done.
(C) Keep estimating realistically about how much can be done.
(D) They should be estimating realistically about how much it is possible for them to do.
(E) They should estimate realistically how much they can do.

Answer Key:

1. A **2.** B **3.** A **4.** C **5.** E

Sample Test with Answers

[1]To enter the perceptual world of whales and dolphins, you would have to change your primary sense from sight to sound. [2]Your brain would process and store sound pictures rather than visual images. [3]Individuals and other creatures would be recognized either by the sounds they made or by the echoes they returned from the sounds you made. [4]Your sense of neighborhood, of where you are, and whom you are with, would be a sound sense. [5]Sound is the primary sense in the life of whales and dolphins. [6]Vision is often difficult or impossible in the dark and murky seas. [7]Many whales and dolphins navigate and hunt at night or below the zone of illuminated water. [8]Vision depends on the presence of light, sounds can be made and used at any time of the day or night, and at all depths. [9]Sounds are infinitely variable: loud to soft, high notes to low notes, short silences to long silences, and many other combinations. [10]Sounds can be stopped abruptly in order to listen to a neighbor in the silence. [11]They can be finitely directed and pinpointed by the listener. [12]And communicating and locating by sound does not require a disruption of daily routines. [13]Whales and dolphins can keep in sound contact simply by blowing bubbles as they exhale.

1. If the passage were split into two paragraphs, the second paragraph should begin with the sentence:

(A) Many whales and dolphins navigate and hunt at night or below the zone of illuminated water.
(B) Sounds are infinitely variable…
(C) Sound is the primary sense in the life of whales and dolphins.
(D) Your sense of neighborhood, of where you are, and whom you are with, would be a sound sense.
(E) Vision is often difficult or impossible in the dark and murky seas.

2. What should be done with sentence 8?

(A) The comma after the word *light* should be omitted and the word *and* inserted.
(B) A semicolon should be substituted for the comma after *light.*
(C) After the word *sounds* there should be a comma, then the word *however,* and then another comma.
(D) The sentence should begin with the words *For instance.*
(E) The sentence should begin with the word *Whereas.*

3. Sentence 11 would be more clear if

(A) the words *by the speaker* were added after the word *directed*
(B) the sentence began with *Sounds* rather than *They*
(C) the word *finitely* were used again before *pinpointed*
(D) the words *by whales or dolphins* were inserted after *directed*
(E) the word *always* followed the word *can*

4. The last sentence, sentence 13, should be

(A) omitted
(B) left as it is
(C) placed before sentence 12
(D) expanded to explain that whales and dolphins are mammals and therefore exhale through lungs
(E) changed to read: *Whales and dolphins can keep in contact with each other through sound simply by blowing bubbles as they exhale.*

Explanatory Answers

1. Choice C is correct. Choice A is incorrect because the sentence is dealing with the limitations in the use of vision in whales and dolphins, and the subject of vision has already been introduced in the previous sentence, sentence 6. Choice B is incorrect for similar reasons: The subject of sound has just been discussed in the previous sentence, and it is logical that this discussion continue. All the sentences before this address themselves to the reader and explain what changes would have to occur in order for us to perceive the world as whales and dolphins do. Sentence 5 turns the discussion to whales and dolphins themselves and their use of sound. (Notice that sentence 1 says "...*you* would have to change *your primary sense*...," and sentence 5 says "Sound is the *primary sense* in the life of *whales and dolphins.*") This is the only logical place to begin a second paragraph. Choice D is incorrect because, as it has been stated, sentences 1 through 4 address the reader and therefore belong in one paragraph. Choice E is wrong because, although it is introducing the subject of vision in whales and dolphins for the first time, it is necessary that it follow directly after sentence 5 in order to show that sound is the primary sense *because* vision is restricted in the dark and murky seas.

2. Choice E is correct. As it stands, sentence 8 contains two complete thoughts—one about vision and one about sound, separated only by a comma, which is grammatically incorrect. Although Choice A remedies this situation, it does not make clear that a *comparison* is being made between the uses of vision and hearing. This is also true of Choice B. Choice C makes the comparison clear by the use of the word *however*, but leaves the two thoughts separated only by a comma, and is therefore wrong. Choice D is wrong for two reasons: The sentence is not really giving an example of something that was stated previously, and therefore the words *for instance* do not make sense here; furthermore, the words *for instance* do not make the comparison clear, and so the sentence remains as two separate thoughts with only a comma between them. Choice E remedies the situation completely: The word *whereas* tells us immediately that a comparison is about to be made, and the first part of the sentence ("Whereas vision depends on the presence of light") is now an *incomplete* thought that must be followed by a comma and then the rest of the sentence.

3. Choice A is correct. The sentence as it stands is unclear because it would make it seem that the listener directs as well as pinpoints the sounds, whereas it is the *speaker* who directs them. Therefore Choice A is correct. There is no need for the sentence to begin with the word *sounds;* since sentence 10 began with it, the word *they* in sentence 11 clearly refers to *sounds.* Therefore Choice B does nothing to improve the sentence. Choice C is incorrect because to pinpoint means to locate precisely or exactly, and therefore it would be redundant to insert the word *finitely.* Although Choice D improves the sentence by telling us *who* directs the sounds, Choice A is better because it is the *speaker* who directs the sounds and the listener who pinpoints them, whether whale or dolphin. Choice E is wrong because it would be assumed by the reader that if sounds *can* be finitely directed and pinpointed, they would be in most cases; to say *always can* would be too extreme.

4. Choice B is correct. Sentence 13 is necessary to show that emitting and listening to sounds do not disrupt the routines of whales and dolphins, stated in sentence 12. To omit the sentence, as Choice A suggests, is incorrect. Choice B is correct; it should be left as it is. Choice C is wrong; sentence 13 explains sentence 12, and therefore needs to follow it, not precede it. Choice D is incorrect because the passage is about the use of sound by whales and dolphins, not about the fact that they are mammals. To go into an explanation of this would be to go into disproportionate detail on this one topic. Choice E is wrong for two reasons: (1) The *with each other* is understood (one has contact *with* something; otherwise it is not *contact*). (2) It also implies that whales keep in contact with dolphins and dolphins with whales, whereas what the author means is that whales and dolphins keep in contact with their own kind. To insert *with each other,* therefore, makes the sentence quite confusing.

The Writing Questions Most Students Get Wrong

With Complete Explanations, Tips, and Comments for All the Students' Wrong Answers

Improving Sentences

The following sentences test correctness and effectiveness of expression. Part of each sentence or the entire sentence is underlined; beneath each sentence are five ways of phrasing the underlined material. Choice A repeats the original phrasing; the other four choices are different. If you think the original phrasing produces a better sentence than any of the alternatives, select Choice A; if not, select one of the other choices.

In making your selection, follow the requirements of standard written English; that is, pay attention to grammar, choice of words, sentence construction, and punctuation. Your selection should result in the most effective sentence—clear and precise, without awkwardness or ambiguity.

EXAMPLE:

Laura Ingalls Wilder published her first book and she was sixty-five years old then.

(A) and she was sixty-five years old then
(B) when she was sixty-five
(C) at age sixty-five years old
(D) upon the reaching of sixty-five years
(E) at the time when she was sixty-five

Ⓐ ● Ⓒ Ⓓ Ⓔ

1. In 1926 historian Carter G. Woodson proposed that the achievements of African Americans being celebrated every February, the month when both Frederick Douglass and President Abraham Lincoln were born.

   (A) being celebrated every February, the month when
   (B) be celebrated every February, the month in which
   (C) ought to be celebrated every February for when
   (D) should be celebrated in every February when
   (E) have a February celebration, which is the month

2. Seeking both protection from predators and opportunities to hunt cooperatively, many fish congregate in schools.

   (A) Seeking both protection from predators and opportunities to hunt cooperatively,
   (B) Seeking protection from predators and to hunt with cooperation;
   (C) Protection from predators and opportunities to hunt cooperatively are sought by
   (D) To seek protection from predators and cooperative hunting opportunities is why
   (E) While seeking both protection from predators and opportunities to hunt, then

3. Crickets produce their characteristic chirp by scraping its right forewing across a series of ridges on its left forewing.

   (A) Crickets produce their characteristic chirp
   (B) A cricket produces their characteristic chirp
   (C) The characteristic chirp of crickets are produced
   (D) The cricket's characteristic chirp, produced
   (E) The cricket produces its characteristic chirp

4. Clara Barton, who founded the American Red Cross, and became the first woman to be paid a salary equal to that of a man by the United States government.

(A) and became the first woman to be paid a salary equal to that of a man
(B) became the first woman to be paid a salary equal to that paid a man
(C) became the first woman receiving equal pay with a man
(D) would become the first woman who was paid equal to a man
(E) and would become the first woman paid equal to a man

5. Since he is hungry and having no money, Jean Valjean steals a loaf of bread early in Victor Hugo's novel.

(A) Since he is hungry and having no money
(B) Hungry and with the lack of money
(C) Being hungry and he has no money
(D) Because he is hungry and has no money
(E) Motivated by being hungry and no money

6. Increasingly aware of the mosquito's role in transmitting certain diseases, and fearing of an epidemic, the mayor finally decided to drain the town pond.

(A) diseases, and fearing of an epidemic
(B) diseases and because of being fearful about an epidemic
(C) diseases and fearful of an epidemic
(D) diseases, while fearing an epidemic
(E) diseases, the fear of an epidemic

7. By failing to resolve the city's fiscal crisis is why the mayor lost his bid for reelection.

(A) By failing to resolve the city's fiscal crisis is why
(B) Because he failed to resolve the city's fiscal crisis,
(C) Due to his failure at resolving the city's fiscal crisis,
(D) He failed to resolve the city's fiscal crisis is the reason that
(E) His failure to resolve the city's fiscal crisis resulted in that

8. The prices of either of the cars seem to be well worth it.

(A) The prices of either of the cars seem to be well worth it.
(B) The price of either of the cars seems to be well worth it.
(C) Either of the cars seems to be well worth its price.
(D) Either of the cars seems to be well worth their prices.
(E) Either of the cars seem to be well worth the price.

Identifying Errors

The following sentences test your ability to recognize grammar and usage errors. Each sentence contains either a single error or no error at all. No sentence contains more than one error. The error, if there is one, is underlined and lettered. If the sentence contains an error, select the one underlined part that must be changed to make the sentence correct. If the sentence is correct, select Choice E. In choosing answers, follow the requirements of standard written English.

EXAMPLE:

The other (A) delegates and him (B) immediately (C) accepted the resolution drafted by (D) the neutral states. No error. (E)

Ⓐ ● Ⓒ Ⓓ Ⓔ

9. If one spends (A) much (B) time with children, you should realize that a promise made to (C) a child is a serious matter because the child will never (D) forget it. No error. (E)

10. Unlike Roman art, which depicted (A) human beings as naturalistically as possible, (B) the Egyptians (C) depicted them in a deliberately (D) stylized manner. No error. (E)

11. Either (A) Caroline or her twin sister Catherine were (B) outdoors shoveling snow for a neighbor yesterday afternoon and would have (C) seen anyone who (D) passed by. No error. (E)

12. The illuminated manuscripts in the rare-books collection, all more than (A) five hundred years old, are (B) the products of (C) a scribal art long since lost. (D) No error. (E)

13. In the middle of the eighteenth century, American surveyors such as (A) George Washington created maps that were much more accurate (B) than previous mapmakers (C) because of (D) dramatic improvements in surveying techniques. No error. (E)

14. Before he found his current job, Edward had spent (A) several miserable years working in a large commercial bakery where the expression of outrageously (B) offensive opinions were (C) as common as saying (D) "hello." No error. (E)

Improving Paragraphs

Directions: The following passage is an early draft of an essay. Some parts of the passage need to be rewritten.

Read the passage and select the best answers for the questions that follow. Some questions are about particular sentences or parts of sentences and ask you to improve sentence structure or word choice. Other questions ask you to consider organization and development. In choosing answers, follow the requirements of standard written English.

Questions 15–16 refer to the following passage.

[1]Have you ever been to a poetry slam? [2]I saw the event listed on the schedule of the Downtown Summer Festival, and I decided to go just to satisfy my curiosity. [3]Even before sitting down, the decision was to stay only for a few minutes. [4]I have always loved poetry, but even good poems can sound dull when people read them aloud in a flat, singsong voice.

15. Which of the following sentences is best to insert between sentences 1 and 2?

    (A) Sometimes people who don't like to read poetry find out that they enjoy listening to it when it is read aloud.
    (B) The first one I attended was in my own hometown.
    (C) People from all around the state come to the Downtown Summer Festival.
    (D) Students, in particular, are attracted to poetry readings.
    (E) The range of events offered this year at the Downtown Summer Festival was more impressive than ever.

16. Which of the following revisions is most needed in sentence 3 (reproduced below)?

    Even before sitting down, the decision was to stay only for a few minutes.

    (A) Delete "down."
    (B) Insert "Furthermore" at the beginning.
    (C) Change "only" to "merely."
    (D) Change "the decision was" to "I had decided."
    (E) Insert "at the poetry slam" after "stay."

Explanatory Answers with Comments for All Wrong Answers

Improving Sentences

1.

(A) You propose that something be done—that is, be celebrated, not being celebrated.

(B) This is correct. You propose that something be done—that is, be celebrated, not being celebrated.

(C) The word "ought" changes the tone and meaning of the sentence by weakening the proposal.

(D) "Should be" is not as direct as "be" and changes the meaning of the sentence.

(E) This is too roundabout—it should be "be celebrated."

2.

(A) This is correct.

(B) The parts of the sentence do not connect properly. "Seeking…to hunt should be of parallel construction: "Seeking…hunting." Also, the semicolon is incorrect here.

(C) "…are sought by many fish congregate in schools." does not make sense.

(D) "To seek…is why" is awkward.

(E) This is not an "if" and "then" type sentence. The word "then" does not connect properly with "while."

3.

(A) "Crickets" is plural and does not agree with "its," which is singular.

(B) "A cricket produces its characteristic chirp" not their characteristic chirp, since cricket is singular.

(C) "The characteristic chirp of crickets is produced…" not are produced since chirp is singular.

(D) "The cricket's characteristic chirp is produced…" The comma should be omitted, and the word is must be included.

(E) This is correct. "The cricket produces its characteristic chirp by scraping its…"; its is singular and so is cricket.

4.

(A) The clause "who founded the American Red Cross" can be left out for this grammar evaluation. The sentence would then read: "Clara Barton and became the first woman…" This is not a complete sentence. It should read: "Clara Barton became the first woman…" Also, the clause "that of a man" should be "that paid a man."

(B) This is correct. The clause "who founded the American Red Cross" can be left out for this grammar evaluation. The sentence should then read: "Clara Barton became the first woman…" Also, the clause "that of a man" should be "that paid a man."

(C) It should be "became the first woman to receive…" not "receiving."

(D) It should be "paid a salary equal to that paid a man."

(E) The "and" is redundant and "paid equal to a man" should be "paid a salary equal to that paid a man."

5.

(A) You say, "he is hungry and has no money," not "he is hungry and having no money."

(B) If we leave out the "and with the lack of money," this will read: "Hungry, Jean Valjean..." It should read, "Because he is hungry, Jean Valjean..."

(C) You should be able to make two sentences with the word "and." "Being hungry, Jean Valjean..." "He has no money, Jean Valjean..." This second sentence does not make sense. This should read: "Having no money, Jean Valjean..."

(D) This is correct. "Because he is hungry and [because he] has no money..."

(E) This is like having two sentences: "Motivated by being hungry, Jean Valjean..." This is okay, but the second sentence, "No money, Jean Valjean..." should read: "Having no money, Jean Valjean..."

6.

(A) You don't say, "fearing of an epidemic"; you say, "fearful of an epidemic."

(B) You don't need the "because of being" part.

(C) This is correct. You say, "fearful of an epidemic."

(D) You don't need "while fearing an epidemic." You can just say, "fearful of an epidemic."

(E) The clause, "the fear of an epidemic" does not connect with "the mayor finally decided..."

7.

(A) You don't say, "By failing...is why..." It should be, "Because he failed..."

(B) This is correct: "Because...the mayor..." (cause and effect).

(C) At the beginning of a sentence, "due to" is always incorrect. Use instead "on account of," "because of," or a similar expression.

(D) You don't say, "He failed to resolve...is the reason..." You say, "His failure to resolve...is the reason that..."

(E) In Choice E, the word "his" does not necessarily refer to "mayor." The word "that" should be omitted. You also have to use the word "losing" instead of "lost" here. "The mayor's failure to resolve the city's fiscal crisis resulted in the mayor's losing his bid for reelection."

8.

(A) The clause "of either of the cars" can be taken out to analyze the grammar. Look at the statement: "The prices seem to be well worth it." That doesn't make sense. It's not the prices that are well worth it; it's the cars that are worth the prices. Also, you wouldn't say, "the prices of either of the cars," you would say, "the price of either of the cars," since you are talking about one or the other car (singular).

(B) The clause "of either of the cars" can be taken out to analyze the grammar. Look at the statement: "The price seems to be well worth it." That doesn't make sense. It's not the price that is well worth it; it's the car that is worth the price.

(C) It's the car that is worth the price, so this choice is correct. "Either" refers to one or the other car, so you are dealing with a singular situation. You should say, "Either of the cars [it] seems to be well worth its price." Notice that it's not "the price" but "its price" because you are talking about the price of one or the other car.

(D) "Either" refers to one or the other car, so you are dealing with a singular situation. You should say, "Either of the cars seems to be well worth its price."

(E) "Either" refers to one or the other car, so you are dealing with a singular situation. You would say, "Either of the cars (it) seems to be well worth its price." Notice that it's not "the price" but "its price" because you are talking about the price of one or the other car.

Identifying Errors

9.

(A) Correct. One spends should be you spend to link to "you should realize…"

(B) Much is okay. Did you think it was more?

(C) Made to is okay. Did you think it should have been made for?

(D) Will never is okay. Did you think it was never will or would never?

(E) No. See Choice A.

10.

(A) Which depicted is okay. Note that it could have also been that depicted. Did you think it should be depicted?

(B) As possible is okay.

(C) Correct. The Egyptians should be Egyptian art since the sentence is discussing art, not people.

(D) Deliberately is okay.

(E) No. See Choice C.

11.

(A) This is okay.

(B) Correct. Either…or refers to one. So were should be was. (Caroline was, her sister was.)

(C) Would have is okay. Did you think it should have been will have or had?

(D) Anyone who is okay. Did you think it was anyone whom?

(E) No. See Choice B.

12.

(A) This is okay. Did you think it was more than?

(B) This is okay. Did you think it was is?

(C) This is okay.

(D) This is okay.

(E) No error is correct.

13.

(A) This is okay.

(B) This is okay.

(C) This is correct. George Washington created maps that were much more accurate than the maps of previous mapmakers—not the previous mapmakers.

(D) No. See Choice C.

(E) No. See Choice C.

14.

(A) This is okay. Did you think it was have spent or spent?

(B) This is okay. Did you think it was outrageous? It's outrageously offensive, not outrageously opinions. The word outrageously modifies the word offensive, not the word opinions.

(C) This is correct. The clause "of outrageously offensive opinions" can be left out of the grammar analysis here. So the sentence would read, "…where the expression…were as common…" But expression is singular, so it should read "…the expression…was."

(D) This is okay. Did you think it was to say? It is the act of saying, not to say.

(E) No. See Choice C.

Improving Paragraphs

15.

(A) This doesn't link to sentence 2.

(B) Choice B is correct. This sentence links sentence 1 and sentence 2. It connects the narrator's question about attending a poetry slam with his description of the first time he attended one.

(C) This doesn't make sense after sentence 1.

(D) This doesn't link to sentence 2.

(E) This doesn't make sense after sentence 1.

16.

(A) This is not a necessary change.

(B) This is not a necessary change.

(C) This is not a necessary change.

(D) This is correct. Since the narrator is talking in first person, you would not use the language the decision. You would keep it consistent and say, "I had decided."

(E) This is not a necessary change.

PART 10

FIVE SAT PRACTICE TESTS

5 Important Reasons for Taking These Practice Tests

Each of the five Practice SATs in the final part of this book is modeled very closely after the actual SAT. You will find that each of these Practice Tests has

a) the same level of difficulty as the actual SAT

and

b) the same question formats as the actual SAT questions.

Accordingly, *taking each of the following tests is like taking the actual SAT*. There are five important reasons for taking each of these Practice SATs:

1. To find out which areas of the SAT you still need to work on.

2. To know just where to concentrate your efforts to eliminate weaknesses.

3. To reinforce the Critical Thinking Skills—19 Math Strategies and 16 Verbal Strategies—that you learned in Part 4 of this book, the Strategy Section. As we advised you at the beginning of Part 4, diligent study of these strategies will result in a sharp rise in your SAT Math and Verbal scores.

4. To strengthen your basic Math skills that might still be a bit rusty. We hope that Part 6, the Complete SAT Math Refresher, helped you to polish your skills.

5. To strengthen your grammar and writing skills. Look at Part 9, the SAT Writing Test and Part 8, the Grammar and Usage Refresher.

These five reasons for taking the five Practice Tests in this section of the book tie in closely with a very important educational principle:

WE LEARN BY DOING!

10 Tips for Taking the Practice Tests

1. Observe the time limits exactly as given.

2. Allow no interruptions.

3. Permit no talking by anyone in the "test area."

4. Use the Answer Sheets provided at the beginning of each Practice Test. Don't make extra marks. Two answers for one question constitute an omitted question.

5. Use scratch paper to figure things out. (On your actual SAT, you are permitted to use the test book for scratchwork.)

6. Omit a question when you start "struggling" with it. Go back to that question later if you have time to do so.

7. Don't get upset if you can't answer several of the questions. You can still get a high score on the test. Even if only 40 to 60 percent of the questions you answer are correct, you will get an average or above-average score.

8. You get the same credit for answering an easy question correctly as you do for answering a tough question correctly.

9. It is advisable to guess if you are sure that at least one of the answer choices is wrong. If you are not sure whether one or more of the answer choices are wrong, statistically it will not make a difference to your total score if you guess or leave the answer blank.

10. *Your SAT score increases by approximately 10 points for every answer you get correct.*

SAT Practice Test 1 Introduction

To See How You Would Do on an SAT and What You Should Do to Improve

This SAT Test is very much like the actual SAT. It follows the genuine SAT very closely. Taking this test is like taking the actual SAT. Following is the purpose of taking this test:

1. To find out what you are *weak* in and what you are *strong* in

2. To know where to concentrate your efforts in order to be fully prepared for the actual test

Taking this test will prove to be a very valuable TIMESAVER for you. Why waste time studying what you already know? Spend your time profitably by studying what you *don't* know. That is what this test will tell you.

In this book, we do not waste precious pages. We get right down to the business of helping you to increase your SAT scores.

Other SAT preparation books place their emphasis on drill, drill, drill. We do not believe that drill work is of primary importance in preparing for the SAT exam. Drill work has its place. In fact, this book contains a great variety of drill material—2,500 SAT-type multiple-choice questions (Critical Reading and Math and Writing), practically all of which have explanatory answers. But drill work must be coordinated with learning Critical Thinking Skills. These skills will help you to think clearly and critically so that you will be able to answer many more SAT questions correctly.

Ready? Start taking the test. It's just like the real thing.

Answer Sheet for Practice Test 1

SECTION 1

Begin your essay on this page. If you need more space, continue on the next page. Do not write outside of the essay box.

Continue on the next page if necessary.

Continuation of ESSAY Section 1 from previous page. Write below only if you need more space.

Start with number 1 for each new section. If a section has fewer questions than answer spaces, leave the extra answer spaces blank. Be sure to erase any errors or stray marks completely.

SECTION 2 –1

1 Ⓐ Ⓑ Ⓒ Ⓓ Ⓔ	11 Ⓐ Ⓑ Ⓒ Ⓓ Ⓔ	21 Ⓐ Ⓑ Ⓒ Ⓓ Ⓔ	31 Ⓐ Ⓑ Ⓒ Ⓓ Ⓔ
2 Ⓐ Ⓑ Ⓒ Ⓓ Ⓔ	12 Ⓐ Ⓑ Ⓒ Ⓓ Ⓔ	22 Ⓐ Ⓑ Ⓒ Ⓓ Ⓔ	32 Ⓐ Ⓑ Ⓒ Ⓓ Ⓔ
3 Ⓐ Ⓑ Ⓒ Ⓓ Ⓔ	13 Ⓐ Ⓑ Ⓒ Ⓓ Ⓔ	23 Ⓐ Ⓑ Ⓒ Ⓓ Ⓔ	33 Ⓐ Ⓑ Ⓒ Ⓓ Ⓔ
4 Ⓐ Ⓑ Ⓒ Ⓓ Ⓔ	14 Ⓐ Ⓑ Ⓒ Ⓓ Ⓔ	24 Ⓐ Ⓑ Ⓒ Ⓓ Ⓔ	34 Ⓐ Ⓑ Ⓒ Ⓓ Ⓔ
5 Ⓐ Ⓑ Ⓒ Ⓓ Ⓔ	15 Ⓐ Ⓑ Ⓒ Ⓓ Ⓔ	25 Ⓐ Ⓑ Ⓒ Ⓓ Ⓔ	35 Ⓐ Ⓑ Ⓒ Ⓓ Ⓔ
6 Ⓐ Ⓑ Ⓒ Ⓓ Ⓔ	16 Ⓐ Ⓑ Ⓒ Ⓓ Ⓔ	26 Ⓐ Ⓑ Ⓒ Ⓓ Ⓔ	36 Ⓐ Ⓑ Ⓒ Ⓓ Ⓔ
7 Ⓐ Ⓑ Ⓒ Ⓓ Ⓔ	17 Ⓐ Ⓑ Ⓒ Ⓓ Ⓔ	27 Ⓐ Ⓑ Ⓒ Ⓓ Ⓔ	37 Ⓐ Ⓑ Ⓒ Ⓓ Ⓔ
8 Ⓐ Ⓑ Ⓒ Ⓓ Ⓔ	18 Ⓐ Ⓑ Ⓒ Ⓓ Ⓔ	28 Ⓐ Ⓑ Ⓒ Ⓓ Ⓔ	38 Ⓐ Ⓑ Ⓒ Ⓓ Ⓔ
9 Ⓐ Ⓑ Ⓒ Ⓓ Ⓔ	19 Ⓐ Ⓑ Ⓒ Ⓓ Ⓔ	29 Ⓐ Ⓑ Ⓒ Ⓓ Ⓔ	39 Ⓐ Ⓑ Ⓒ Ⓓ Ⓔ
10 Ⓐ Ⓑ Ⓒ Ⓓ Ⓔ	20 Ⓐ Ⓑ Ⓒ Ⓓ Ⓔ	30 Ⓐ Ⓑ Ⓒ Ⓓ Ⓔ	40 Ⓐ Ⓑ Ⓒ Ⓓ Ⓔ

SECTION 3 –0

1 Ⓐ Ⓑ Ⓒ Ⓓ Ⓔ	11 Ⓐ Ⓑ Ⓒ Ⓓ Ⓔ	21 Ⓐ Ⓑ Ⓒ Ⓓ Ⓔ	31 Ⓐ Ⓑ Ⓒ Ⓓ Ⓔ
2 Ⓐ Ⓑ Ⓒ Ⓓ Ⓔ	12 Ⓐ Ⓑ Ⓒ Ⓓ Ⓔ	22 Ⓐ Ⓑ Ⓒ Ⓓ Ⓔ	32 Ⓐ Ⓑ Ⓒ Ⓓ Ⓔ
3 Ⓐ Ⓑ Ⓒ Ⓓ Ⓔ	13 Ⓐ Ⓑ Ⓒ Ⓓ Ⓔ	23 Ⓐ Ⓑ Ⓒ Ⓓ Ⓔ	33 Ⓐ Ⓑ Ⓒ Ⓓ Ⓔ
4 Ⓐ Ⓑ Ⓒ Ⓓ Ⓔ	14 Ⓐ Ⓑ Ⓒ Ⓓ Ⓔ	24 Ⓐ Ⓑ Ⓒ Ⓓ Ⓔ	34 Ⓐ Ⓑ Ⓒ Ⓓ Ⓔ
5 Ⓐ Ⓑ Ⓒ Ⓓ Ⓔ	15 Ⓐ Ⓑ Ⓒ Ⓓ Ⓔ	25 Ⓐ Ⓑ Ⓒ Ⓓ Ⓔ	35 Ⓐ Ⓑ Ⓒ Ⓓ Ⓔ
6 Ⓐ Ⓑ Ⓒ Ⓓ Ⓔ	16 Ⓐ Ⓑ Ⓒ Ⓓ Ⓔ	26 Ⓐ Ⓑ Ⓒ Ⓓ Ⓔ	36 Ⓐ Ⓑ Ⓒ Ⓓ Ⓔ
7 Ⓐ Ⓑ Ⓒ Ⓓ Ⓔ	17 Ⓐ Ⓑ Ⓒ Ⓓ Ⓔ	27 Ⓐ Ⓑ Ⓒ Ⓓ Ⓔ	37 Ⓐ Ⓑ Ⓒ Ⓓ Ⓔ
8 Ⓐ Ⓑ Ⓒ Ⓓ Ⓔ	18 Ⓐ Ⓑ Ⓒ Ⓓ Ⓔ	28 Ⓐ Ⓑ Ⓒ Ⓓ Ⓔ	38 Ⓐ Ⓑ Ⓒ Ⓓ Ⓔ
9 Ⓐ Ⓑ Ⓒ Ⓓ Ⓔ	19 Ⓐ Ⓑ Ⓒ Ⓓ Ⓔ	29 Ⓐ Ⓑ Ⓒ Ⓓ Ⓔ	39 Ⓐ Ⓑ Ⓒ Ⓓ Ⓔ
10 Ⓐ Ⓑ Ⓒ Ⓓ Ⓔ	20 Ⓐ Ⓑ Ⓒ Ⓓ Ⓔ	30 Ⓐ Ⓑ Ⓒ Ⓓ Ⓔ	40 Ⓐ Ⓑ Ⓒ Ⓓ Ⓔ

CAUTION Use the answer spaces in the grids below for Section 2 or Section 3 only if you are told to do so in your test book.

Student-Produced Responses ONLY ANSWERS ENTERED IN THE CIRCLES IN EACH GRID WILL BE SCORED. YOU WILL NOT RECEIVE CREDIT FOR ANYTHING WRITTEN IN THE BOXES ABOVE THE CIRCLES.

9	10	11	12	13
/ /	/ /	/ /	/ /	/ /
. . . .	. . . .	. . . .	. . . .	. . . .
0 0 0	0 0 0	0 0 0	0 0 0	0 0 0
1 1 1 1	1 1 1 1	1 1 1 1	1 1 1 1	1 1 1 1
2 2 2 2	2 2 2 2	2 2 2 2	2 2 2 2	2 2 2 2
3 3 3 3	3 3 3 3	3 3 3 3	3 3 3 3	3 3 3 3
4 4 4 4	4 4 4 4	4 4 4 4	4 4 4 4	4 4 4 4
5 5 5 5	5 5 5 5	5 5 5 5	5 5 5 5	5 5 5 5
6 6 6 6	6 6 6 6	6 6 6 6	6 6 6 6	6 6 6 6
7 7 7 7	7 7 7 7	7 7 7 7	7 7 7 7	7 7 7 7
8 8 8 8	8 8 8 8	8 8 8 8	8 8 8 8	8 8 8 8
9 9 9 9	9 9 9 9	9 9 9 9	9 9 9 9	9 9 9 9

14	15	16	17	18
/ /	/ /	/ /	/ /	/ /
. . . .	. . . .	. . . .	. . . .	. . . .
0 0 0	0 0 0	0 0 0	0 0 0	0 0 0
1 1 1 1	1 1 1 1	1 1 1 1	1 1 1 1	1 1 1 1
2 2 2 2	2 2 2 2	2 2 2 2	2 2 2 2	2 2 2 2
3 3 3 3	3 3 3 3	3 3 3 3	3 3 3 3	3 3 3 3
4 4 4 4	4 4 4 4	4 4 4 4	4 4 4 4	4 4 4 4
5 5 5 5	5 5 5 5	5 5 5 5	5 5 5 5	5 5 5 5
6 6 6 6	6 6 6 6	6 6 6 6	6 6 6 6	6 6 6 6
7 7 7 7	7 7 7 7	7 7 7 7	7 7 7 7	7 7 7 7
8 8 8 8	8 8 8 8	8 8 8 8	8 8 8 8	8 8 8 8
9 9 9 9	9 9 9 9	9 9 9 9	9 9 9 9	9 9 9 9

Start with number 1 for each new section. If a section has fewer questions than answer spaces, leave the extra answer spaces blank. Be sure to erase any errors or stray marks completely.

SECTION 4 -0

1 A B C D E	11 A B C D E	21 A B C D E	31 A B C D E
2 A B C D E	12 A B C D E	22 A B C D E	32 A B C D E
3 A B C D E	13 A B C D E	23 A B C D E	33 A B C D E
4 A B C D E	14 A B C D E	24 A B C D E	34 A B C D E
5 A B C D E	15 A B C D E	25 A B C D E	35 A B C D E
6 A B C D E	16 A B C D E	26 A B C D E	36 A B C D E
7 A B C D E	17 A B C D E	27 A B C D E	37 A B C D E
8 A B C D E	18 A B C D E	28 A B C D E	38 A B C D E
9 A B C D E	19 A B C D E	29 A B C D E	39 A B C D E
10 A B C D E	20 A B C D E	30 A B C D E	40 A B C D E

SECTION 5 -2

1 A B C D E	11 A B C D E	21 A B C D E	31 A B C D E
2 A B C D E	12 A B C D E	22 A B C D E	32 A B C D E
3 A B C D E	13 A B C D E	23 A B C D E	33 A B C D E
4 A B C D E	14 A B C D E	24 A B C D E	34 A B C D E
5 A B C D E	15 A B C D E	25 A B C D E	35 A B C D E
6 A B C D E	16 A B C D E	26 A B C D E	36 A B C D E
7 A B C D E	17 A B C D E	27 A B C D E	37 A B C D E
8 A B C D E	18 A B C D E	28 A B C D E	38 A B C D E
9 A B C D E	19 A B C D E	29 A B C D E	39 A B C D E
10 A B C D E	20 A B C D E	30 A B C D E	40 A B C D E

CAUTION Use the answer spaces in the grids below for Section 4 or Section 5 only if you are told to do so in your test book.

Student-Produced Responses ONLY ANSWERS ENTERED IN THE CIRCLES IN EACH GRID WILL BE SCORED. YOU WILL NOT RECEIVE CREDIT FOR ANYTHING WRITTEN IN THE BOXES ABOVE THE CIRCLES.

9	10	11	12	13
/ /	/ /	/ /	/ /	/ /
. . . .	. . . .	. . . .	. . . .	. . . .
0 0 0	0 0 0	0 0 0	0 0 0	0 0 0
1 1 1 1	1 1 1 1	1 1 1 1	1 1 1 1	1 1 1 1
2 2 2 2	2 2 2 2	2 2 2 2	2 2 2 2	2 2 2 2
3 3 3 3	3 3 3 3	3 3 3 3	3 3 3 3	3 3 3 3
4 4 4 4	4 4 4 4	4 4 4 4	4 4 4 4	4 4 4 4
5 5 5 5	5 5 5 5	5 5 5 5	5 5 5 5	5 5 5 5
6 6 6 6	6 6 6 6	6 6 6 6	6 6 6 6	6 6 6 6
7 7 7 7	7 7 7 7	7 7 7 7	7 7 7 7	7 7 7 7
8 8 8 8	8 8 8 8	8 8 8 8	8 8 8 8	8 8 8 8
9 9 9 9	9 9 9 9	9 9 9 9	9 9 9 9	9 9 9 9

14	15	16	17	18
/ /	/ /	/ /	/ /	/ /
. . . .	. . . .	. . . .	. . . .	. . . .
0 0 0	0 0 0	0 0 0	0 0 0	0 0 0
1 1 1 1	1 1 1 1	1 1 1 1	1 1 1 1	1 1 1 1
2 2 2 2	2 2 2 2	2 2 2 2	2 2 2 2	2 2 2 2
3 3 3 3	3 3 3 3	3 3 3 3	3 3 3 3	3 3 3 3
4 4 4 4	4 4 4 4	4 4 4 4	4 4 4 4	4 4 4 4
5 5 5 5	5 5 5 5	5 5 5 5	5 5 5 5	5 5 5 5
6 6 6 6	6 6 6 6	6 6 6 6	6 6 6 6	6 6 6 6
7 7 7 7	7 7 7 7	7 7 7 7	7 7 7 7	7 7 7 7
8 8 8 8	8 8 8 8	8 8 8 8	8 8 8 8	8 8 8 8
9 9 9 9	9 9 9 9	9 9 9 9	9 9 9 9	9 9 9 9

Start with number 1 for each new section. If a section has fewer questions than answer spaces, leave the extra answer spaces blank. Be sure to erase any errors or stray marks completely.

SECTION 6

1 Ⓐ Ⓑ Ⓒ Ⓓ Ⓔ	11 Ⓐ Ⓑ Ⓒ Ⓓ Ⓔ	21 Ⓐ Ⓑ Ⓒ Ⓓ Ⓔ	31 Ⓐ Ⓑ Ⓒ Ⓓ Ⓔ
2 Ⓐ Ⓑ Ⓒ Ⓓ Ⓔ	12 Ⓐ Ⓑ Ⓒ Ⓓ Ⓔ	22 Ⓐ Ⓑ Ⓒ Ⓓ Ⓔ	32 Ⓐ Ⓑ Ⓒ Ⓓ Ⓔ
3 Ⓐ Ⓑ Ⓒ Ⓓ Ⓔ	13 Ⓐ Ⓑ Ⓒ Ⓓ Ⓔ	23 Ⓐ Ⓑ Ⓒ Ⓓ Ⓔ	33 Ⓐ Ⓑ Ⓒ Ⓓ Ⓔ
4 Ⓐ Ⓑ Ⓒ Ⓓ Ⓔ	14 Ⓐ Ⓑ Ⓒ Ⓓ Ⓔ	24 Ⓐ Ⓑ Ⓒ Ⓓ Ⓔ	34 Ⓐ Ⓑ Ⓒ Ⓓ Ⓔ
5 Ⓐ Ⓑ Ⓒ Ⓓ Ⓔ	15 Ⓐ Ⓑ Ⓒ Ⓓ Ⓔ	25 Ⓐ Ⓑ Ⓒ Ⓓ Ⓔ	35 Ⓐ Ⓑ Ⓒ Ⓓ Ⓔ
6 Ⓐ Ⓑ Ⓒ Ⓓ Ⓔ	16 Ⓐ Ⓑ Ⓒ Ⓓ Ⓔ	26 Ⓐ Ⓑ Ⓒ Ⓓ Ⓔ	36 Ⓐ Ⓑ Ⓒ Ⓓ Ⓔ
7 Ⓐ Ⓑ Ⓒ Ⓓ Ⓔ	17 Ⓐ Ⓑ Ⓒ Ⓓ Ⓔ	27 Ⓐ Ⓑ Ⓒ Ⓓ Ⓔ	37 Ⓐ Ⓑ Ⓒ Ⓓ Ⓔ
8 Ⓐ Ⓑ Ⓒ Ⓓ Ⓔ	18 Ⓐ Ⓑ Ⓒ Ⓓ Ⓔ	28 Ⓐ Ⓑ Ⓒ Ⓓ Ⓔ	38 Ⓐ Ⓑ Ⓒ Ⓓ Ⓔ
9 Ⓐ Ⓑ Ⓒ Ⓓ Ⓔ	19 Ⓐ Ⓑ Ⓒ Ⓓ Ⓔ	29 Ⓐ Ⓑ Ⓒ Ⓓ Ⓔ	39 Ⓐ Ⓑ Ⓒ Ⓓ Ⓔ
10 Ⓐ Ⓑ Ⓒ Ⓓ Ⓔ	20 Ⓐ Ⓑ Ⓒ Ⓓ Ⓔ	30 Ⓐ Ⓑ Ⓒ Ⓓ Ⓔ	40 Ⓐ Ⓑ Ⓒ Ⓓ Ⓔ

SECTION 7

1 Ⓐ Ⓑ Ⓒ Ⓓ Ⓔ	11 Ⓐ Ⓑ Ⓒ Ⓓ Ⓔ	21 Ⓐ Ⓑ Ⓒ Ⓓ Ⓔ	31 Ⓐ Ⓑ Ⓒ Ⓓ Ⓔ
2 Ⓐ Ⓑ Ⓒ Ⓓ Ⓔ	12 Ⓐ Ⓑ Ⓒ Ⓓ Ⓔ	22 Ⓐ Ⓑ Ⓒ Ⓓ Ⓔ	32 Ⓐ Ⓑ Ⓒ Ⓓ Ⓔ
3 Ⓐ Ⓑ Ⓒ Ⓓ Ⓔ	13 Ⓐ Ⓑ Ⓒ Ⓓ Ⓔ	23 Ⓐ Ⓑ Ⓒ Ⓓ Ⓔ	33 Ⓐ Ⓑ Ⓒ Ⓓ Ⓔ
4 Ⓐ Ⓑ Ⓒ Ⓓ Ⓔ	14 Ⓐ Ⓑ Ⓒ Ⓓ Ⓔ	24 Ⓐ Ⓑ Ⓒ Ⓓ Ⓔ	34 Ⓐ Ⓑ Ⓒ Ⓓ Ⓔ
5 Ⓐ Ⓑ Ⓒ Ⓓ Ⓔ	15 Ⓐ Ⓑ Ⓒ Ⓓ Ⓔ	25 Ⓐ Ⓑ Ⓒ Ⓓ Ⓔ	35 Ⓐ Ⓑ Ⓒ Ⓓ Ⓔ
6 Ⓐ Ⓑ Ⓒ Ⓓ Ⓔ	16 Ⓐ Ⓑ Ⓒ Ⓓ Ⓔ	26 Ⓐ Ⓑ Ⓒ Ⓓ Ⓔ	36 Ⓐ Ⓑ Ⓒ Ⓓ Ⓔ
7 Ⓐ Ⓑ Ⓒ Ⓓ Ⓔ	17 Ⓐ Ⓑ Ⓒ Ⓓ Ⓔ	27 Ⓐ Ⓑ Ⓒ Ⓓ Ⓔ	37 Ⓐ Ⓑ Ⓒ Ⓓ Ⓔ
8 Ⓐ Ⓑ Ⓒ Ⓓ Ⓔ	18 Ⓐ Ⓑ Ⓒ Ⓓ Ⓔ	28 Ⓐ Ⓑ Ⓒ Ⓓ Ⓔ	38 Ⓐ Ⓑ Ⓒ Ⓓ Ⓔ
9 Ⓐ Ⓑ Ⓒ Ⓓ Ⓔ	19 Ⓐ Ⓑ Ⓒ Ⓓ Ⓔ	29 Ⓐ Ⓑ Ⓒ Ⓓ Ⓔ	39 Ⓐ Ⓑ Ⓒ Ⓓ Ⓔ
10 Ⓐ Ⓑ Ⓒ Ⓓ Ⓔ	20 Ⓐ Ⓑ Ⓒ Ⓓ Ⓔ	30 Ⓐ Ⓑ Ⓒ Ⓓ Ⓔ	40 Ⓐ Ⓑ Ⓒ Ⓓ Ⓔ

CAUTION Use the answer spaces in the grids below for Section 6 or Section 7 only if you are told to do so in your test book.

Student-Produced Responses ONLY ANSWERS ENTERED IN THE CIRCLES IN EACH GRID WILL BE SCORED. YOU WILL NOT RECEIVE CREDIT FOR ANYTHING WRITTEN IN THE BOXES ABOVE THE CIRCLES.

Grids 9, 10, 11, 12, 13, 14, 15, 16, 17, 18 (each: four answer boxes; / / ; . . . . ; 0–9 in each column)

Start with number 1 for each new section. If a section has fewer questions than answer spaces, leave the extra answer spaces blank. Be sure to erase any errors or stray marks completely.

SECTION 8 −0

1 A B C D E	11 A B C D E	21 A B C D E	31 A B C D E
2 A B C D E	12 A B C D E	22 A B C D E	32 A B C D E
3 A B C D E	13 A B C D E	23 A B C D E	33 A B C D E
4 A B C D E	14 A B C D E	24 A B C D E	34 A B C D E
5 A B C D E	15 A B C D E	25 A B C D E	35 A B C D E
6 A B C D E	16 A B C D E	26 A B C D E	36 A B C D E
7 A B C D E	17 A B C D E	27 A B C D E	37 A B C D E
8 A B C D E	18 A B C D E	28 A B C D E	38 A B C D E
9 A B C D E	19 A B C D E	29 A B C D E	39 A B C D E
10 A B C D E	20 A B C D E	30 A B C D E	40 A B C D E

SECTION 9 −0

1 A B C D E	11 A B C D E	21 A B C D E	31 A B C D E
2 A B C D E	12 A B C D E	22 A B C D E	32 A B C D E
3 A B C D E	13 A B C D E	23 A B C D E	33 A B C D E
4 A B C D E	14 A B C D E	24 A B C D E	34 A B C D E
5 A B C D E	15 A B C D E	25 A B C D E	35 A B C D E
6 A B C D E	16 A B C D E	26 A B C D E	36 A B C D E
7 A B C D E	17 A B C D E	27 A B C D E	37 A B C D E
8 A B C D E	18 A B C D E	28 A B C D E	38 A B C D E
9 A B C D E	19 A B C D E	29 A B C D E	39 A B C D E
10 A B C D E	20 A B C D E	30 A B C D E	40 A B C D E

SECTION 10 −1

1 A B C D E	11 A B C D E	21 A B C D E	31 A B C D E
2 A B C D E	12 A B C D E	22 A B C D E	32 A B C D E
3 A B C D E	13 A B C D E	23 A B C D E	33 A B C D E
4 A B C D E	14 A B C D E	24 A B C D E	34 A B C D E
5 A B C D E	15 A B C D E	25 A B C D E	35 A B C D E
6 A B C D E	16 A B C D E	26 A B C D E	36 A B C D E
7 A B C D E	17 A B C D E	27 A B C D E	37 A B C D E
8 A B C D E	18 A B C D E	28 A B C D E	38 A B C D E
9 A B C D E	19 A B C D E	29 A B C D E	39 A B C D E
10 A B C D E	20 A B C D E	30 A B C D E	40 A B C D E

SAT PRACTICE TEST 1

SECTION 1

Time: 25 Minutes—Turn to page 557 of your answer sheet to write your ESSAY.

The purpose of the essay is to have you show how well you can express and develop your ideas. You should develop your point of view, logically and clearly present your ideas, and use language accurately.

You should write your essay on the lines provided on your answer sheet. You should not write on any other paper. You will have enough space if you write on every line and if you keep your handwriting to a reasonable size. Make sure that your handwriting is legible to other readers.

You will have 25 minutes to write an essay on the assignment below. *Do not write on any other topic. If you do so, you will receive a score of 0.*

Think carefully about the issue presented in the following excerpt and the assignment below.

> The well-known proverb "Ignorance is bliss" suggests that people with knowledge of the world's complexities and its limitations are often unhappy, while their less-knowledgeable counterparts remain contented. But how accurate is this folk wisdom? A recent study showed that well-informed people were more likely to report feelings of well-being. In fact, more knowledge leads people to feel better about themselves and more satisfied with their lives.
>
> —Adapted from Lee Sigelman, "Is Ignorance Bliss? A Reconsideration of the Folk Wisdom"

Assignment: What is your belief on the notion that more knowledge makes one happier? Support your position by citing an example or examples from history, science and technology, literature, the arts, politics, current events, sports, or your observation or experience.

DO NOT WRITE YOUR ESSAY IN YOUR TEST BOOK. You will receive credit only for what you write on your answer sheet.

BEGIN WRITING YOUR ESSAY ON PAGE 557 OF THE ANSWER SHEET.

If you finish before time is called, you may check your work on this section only.
Do not turn to any other section in the test.

SECTION 2

Time: 25 Minutes—Turn to Section 2 (page 559) of your answer sheet to answer the questions in this section. 20 Questions

Directions: For this section, solve each problem and decide which is the best of the choices given. Fill in the corresponding circle on the answer sheet. You may use any available space for scratchwork.

Notes:

1. The use of a calculator is permitted.
2. All numbers used are real numbers.
3. Figures that accompany problems in this test are intended to provide information useful in solving the problems. They are drawn as accurately as possible EXCEPT when it is stated in a specific problem that the figure is not drawn to scale. All figures lie in a plane unless otherwise indicated.
4. Unless otherwise specified, the domain of any function *f* is assumed to be the set of all real numbers *x* for which *f*(*x*) is a real number.

REFERENCE INFORMATION

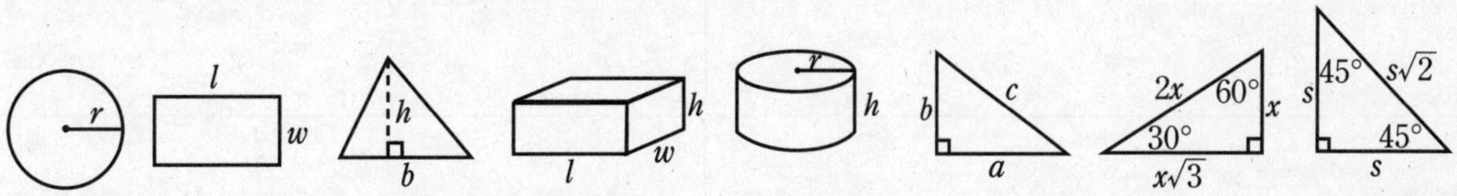

$A = \pi r^2$ $C = 2\pi r$ $A = lw$ $A = \frac{1}{2}bh$ $V = lwh$ $V = \pi r^2 h$ $c^2 = a^2 + b^2$ *Special Right Triangles*

The number of degrees of arc in a circle is 360.
The sum of the measures in degrees of the angles of a triangle is 180.

1. If a and b are positive integers and $ab = 64$, what is the smallest possible value of $a + b$?

(A) 65
(B) 34
(C) 20
(D) 16
(E) 8

8·8

2. Find the value of $x + x^3 + x^5 + x^6$ if $x = -1$.

(A) −4
(B) −2
(C) 1
(D) 2
(E) 4

−1+(−1)+(−1)+1=
−2+(−1)+1=
−3+1=
−2

GO ON TO THE NEXT PAGE

3.
$$\begin{array}{r} AB \\ +\ BA \\ \hline 66 \end{array}$$

If $0 < A < 6$ and $0 < B < 6$ in the addition problem above, how many different integer values of A are possible? (AB and BA both represent two-digit integers.)

(A) Two
(B) Three
(C) Four
(D) Five
(E) Six

4. At 8:00 A.M. the outside temperature was −15°F. At 11:00 A.M. the temperature was 0°F. If the temperature continues to rise at the same uniform rate, what will the temperature be at 5:00 P.M. on the same day?

(A) −15°F
(B) −5°F
(C) 0°F
(D) 15°F
(E) 30°F

Question 5 refers to the following chart.

Number of Shirts	Total Price
1	$12.00
Box of 3	$22.50
Box of 6	$43.40

5. Which of the following is the closest approximation of the lowest cost per shirt, when a box of shirts is purchased?

(A) $7.10
(B) $7.20
(C) $7.30
(D) $7.40
(E) $7.50

6. If $5x^2 - 15x = 0$ and $x \neq 0$, find the value of x.

(A) −10
(B) −3
(C) 10
(D) 5
(E) 3

GO ON TO THE NEXT PAGE

7. The chickens on a certain farm consumed 600 pounds of feed in half a year. During that time the total number of eggs laid was 5,000. If the feed cost \$1.25 per pound, then the feed cost per egg was

(A) \$0.0750
(B) \$0.1250
(C) \$0.15
(D) \$0.25
(E) \$0.3333

8. If X is the set of negative numbers and Y is the set of positive numbers, then the union of X and Y and 0 is the set of

(A) all real numbers
(B) all integers
(C) all rational numbers
(D) all irrational numbers
(E) all odd integers

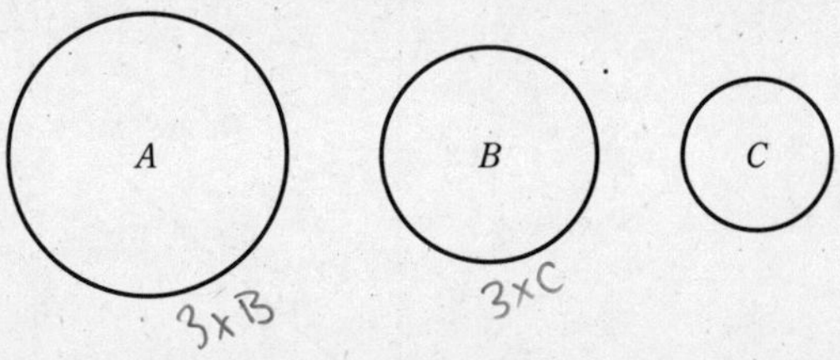

9. In the figure above, there are three circles, *A, B,* and *C.* The area of *A* is three times that of *B,* and the area of *B* is three times that of *C.* If the area of *B* is 1, find the sum of the areas of *A, B,* and *C.*

(A) 3
(B) $3\frac{1}{3}$
(C) $4\frac{1}{3}$
(D) 5
(E) $6\frac{1}{3}$

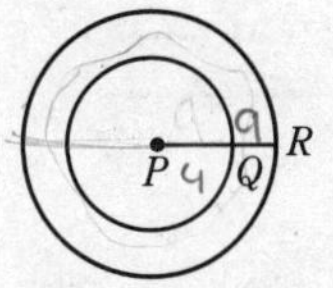

Note: Figure not drawn to scale.

10. In the figure above, two concentric circles with center *P* are shown. *PQR,* a radius of the larger circle, equals 9. *PQ,* a radius of the smaller circle, equals 4. If a circle *L* (not shown) is drawn with center at *R* and *Q* on its circumference, find the radius of circle *L.*

(A) 13
(B) 5
(C) 4
(D) 2
(E) It cannot be determined from the information given.

GO ON TO THE NEXT PAGE

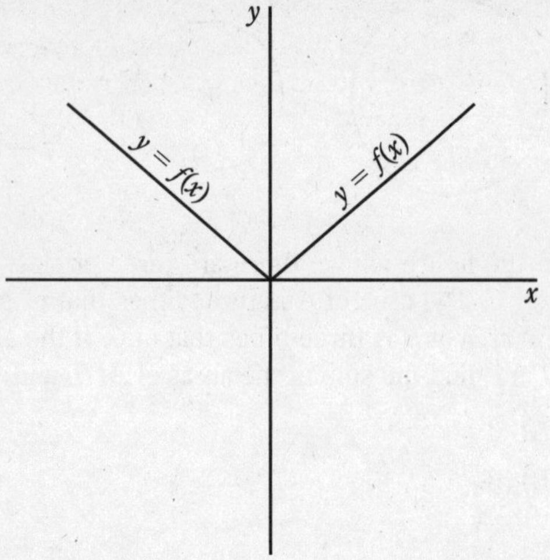

11. The above graph could represent the equation

(A) $y = x$
(B) $y = |x|$
(C) $y = x^2$
(D) $y = x, x > 0$
$y = 0, x = 0$
$y = -|x|, x < 0$
(E) $y = -x$

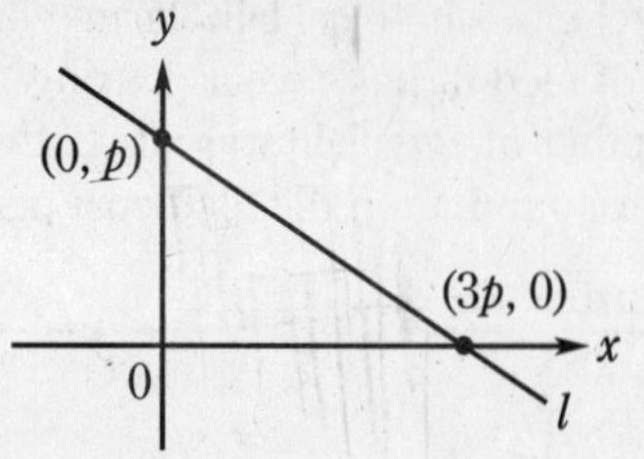

Note: Figure not drawn to scale.

13. What is the slope of line l in the above figure?

(A) -3
(B) $-\frac{1}{3}$
(C) 0
(D) $\frac{1}{3}$
(E) 3

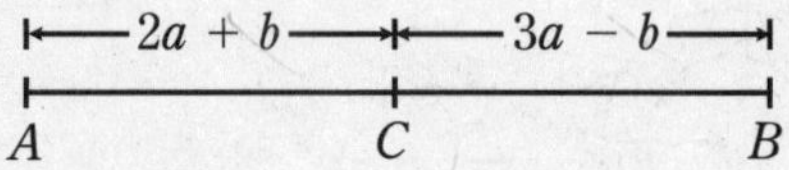

12. Given ACB is a straight line segment, and C is the midpoint of AB, if the two segments have the lengths shown above, then

(A) $a = -2b$
(B) $a = -\frac{2}{5}b$
(C) $a = \frac{2}{5}b$
(D) $a = b$
(E) $a = 2b$

14. Bus A averages 40 kilometers per gallon of fuel. Bus B averages 50 kilometers per gallon of fuel. If the price of fuel is \$3 per gallon, how much less would an 800-kilometer trip cost for Bus B than for Bus A?

(A) \$18
(B) \$16
(C) \$14
(D) \$12
(E) \$10

GO ON TO THE NEXT PAGE

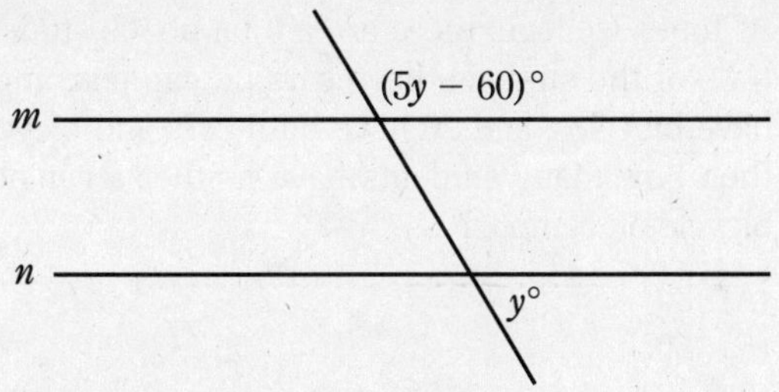

15. $m \| n$ in the figure above. Find y.

(A) 10
(B) 20
(C) 40
(D) 65
(E) 175

16. Given 4 percent of $(2a + b)$ is 18 and a is a positive integer, what is the *greatest* possible value of b?

(A) 450
(B) 449
(C) 448
(D) 43
(E) 8

17. If an ant runs randomly through an enclosed circular field of radius 2 feet with an inner circle of radius 1 foot, what is the probability that the ant will be in the inner circle at any one time?

(A) $\frac{1}{8}$
(B) $\frac{1}{6}$
(C) $\frac{1}{4}$
(D) $\frac{1}{2}$
(E) 1

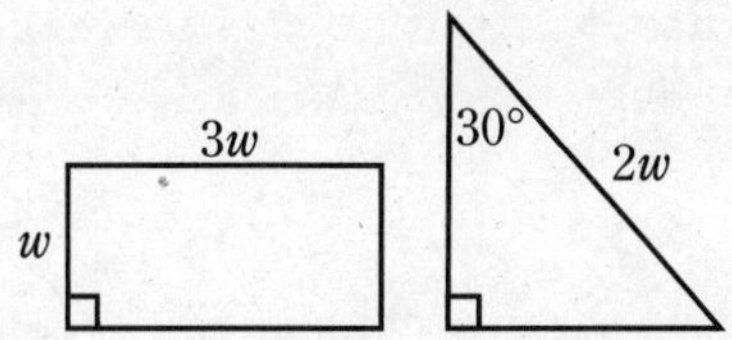

18. The length and width of a rectangle are $3w$ and w, respectively. The length of the hypotenuse of a right triangle, one of whose acute angles is 30°, is $2w$. What is the ratio of the area of the rectangle to that of the triangle?

(A) $2\sqrt{3} : 1$
(B) $\sqrt{3} : 1$
(C) $1 : \sqrt{3}$
(D) $1 : 2\sqrt{3}$
(E) $1 : 6$

GO ON TO THE NEXT PAGE

19. At a certain college, the number of freshmen is three times the number of seniors. If $\frac{1}{4}$ of the freshmen and $\frac{1}{3}$ of the seniors attend a football game, what fraction of the total number of freshmen and seniors attends the game?

(A) $\frac{5}{24}$
(B) $\frac{13}{48}$
(C) $\frac{17}{48}$
(D) $\frac{11}{24}$
(E) $\frac{23}{48}$

20. At Jones College, there are a total of 100 students. If 30 of the students have cars on campus, and 50 have bicycles, and 20 have both cars and bicycles, then how many students have neither a car nor a bicycle on campus?

(A) 80
(B) 60
(C) 40
(D) 20
(E) 0

STOP

If you finish before time is called, you may check your work on this section only.
Do not turn to any other section in the test.

Take a 5 minute break

before starting section 3

SECTION 3

Time: 25 Minutes—Turn to Section 3 (page 559) of your answer sheet to answer the questions in this section.
20 Questions

Directions: For this section, solve each problem and decide which is the best of the choices given. Fill in the corresponding circle on the answer sheet. You may use any available space for scratchwork.

Notes:

1. The use of a calculator is permitted.
2. All numbers used are real numbers.
3. Figures that accompany problems in this test are intended to provide information useful in solving the problems. They are drawn as accurately as possible EXCEPT when it is stated in a specific problem that the figure is not drawn to scale. All figures lie in a plane unless otherwise indicated.
4. Unless otherwise specified, the domain of any function f is assumed to be the set of all real numbers x for which $f(x)$ is a real number.

REFERENCE INFORMATION

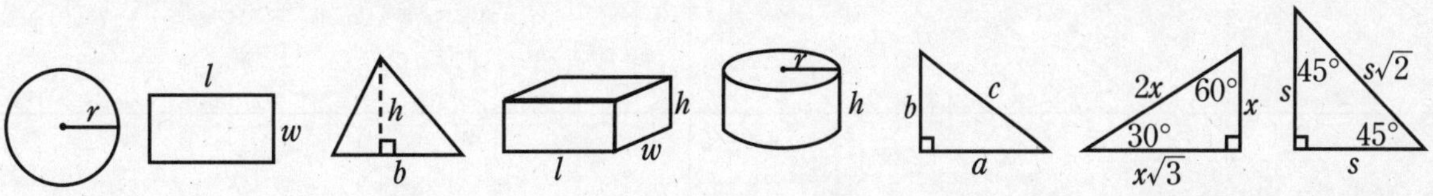

$A = \pi r^2$, $C = 2\pi r$ $A = lw$ $A = \frac{1}{2}bh$ $V = lwh$ $V = \pi r^2 h$ $c^2 = a^2 + b^2$ *Special Right Triangles*

The number of degrees of arc in a circle is 360.
The sum of the measures in degrees of the angles of a triangle is 180.

1. If $55{,}555 = y + 50{,}505$, find the value of $50{,}505 - 10y$.

(A) -5.05
(B) 0
(C) 5
(D) 5.05
(E) 50.5

2. $3x(4x + 2y) =$

(A) $7x + 5xy$
(B) $12x + 6xy$
(C) $12x^2 + 2y$
(D) $12x^2 + 6xy$
(E) $12x^2 + 6x$

GO ON TO THE NEXT PAGE

Box Number	Height of Box (in millimeters)
A	1,700
B	2,450
C	2,735
D	1,928
E	2,130

3. Exactly how many of the boxes listed in the table above are more than 20 decimeters high? (1 decimeter = 100 millimeters)

(A) Zero
(B) One
(C) Two
(D) Three
(E) Four

4. If $a - 3 = 7$, then $2a - 14 =$

(A) −6
(B) −4
(C) 2
(D) 4
(E) 6

5. $\frac{7}{10} + \frac{7}{100} + \frac{77}{1,000} =$

(A) 0.0091
(B) 0.7777
(C) 0.784
(D) 0.847
(E) 0.854

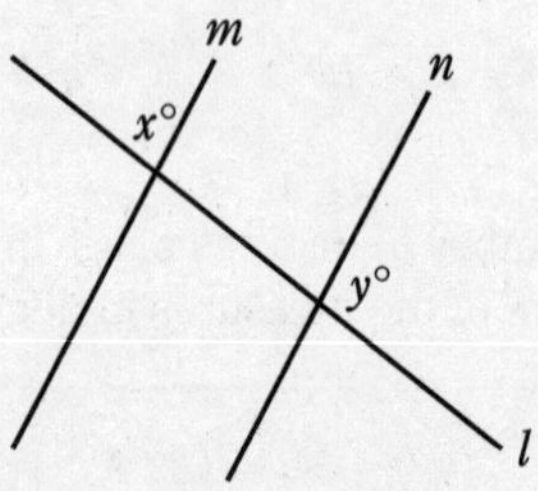

6. Parallel lines m and n are intersected by line l as shown. Find the value of $x + y$.

(A) 180
(B) 150
(C) 120
(D) 90
(E) It cannot be determined from the information given.

GO ON TO THE NEXT PAGE

Item	Value
1	P
2	$P \times 3$
3	$(P \times 3) \div 2$
4	$[(P \times 3) \div 2] + 12$
5	$[(P \times 3) \div 2] + 12 - 1$

7. According to the table above, which item has the greatest value when $P = 12$?

(A) 1
(B) 2
(C) 3
(D) 4
(E) 5

8. If $\frac{3x}{4} = 9$, find $6x$.

(A) 12
(B) 18
(C) 27
(D) 36
(E) 72

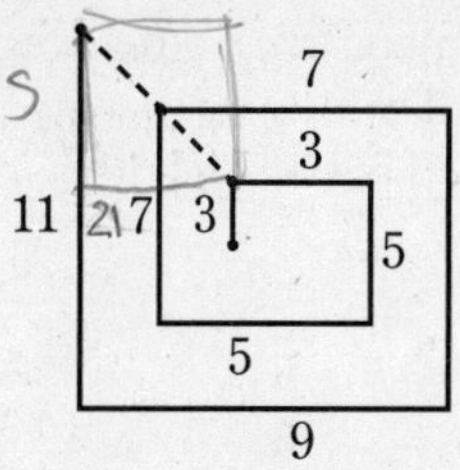

Note: Figure not drawn to scale.

9. In the figure above, each pair of intersecting segments is perpendicular with lengths as shown. Find the length of the dashed line segment.

(A) 7
(B) $6\sqrt{3}$
(C) $4\sqrt{2}$
(D) $\sqrt{46}$
(E) $\sqrt{59}$

10. For how many two-digit positive numbers will tripling the tens digit give us a two-digit number that is triple the original number?

(A) None
(B) One
(C) Two
(D) Three
(E) Four

GO ON TO THE NEXT PAGE

11. If A is the least positive 5-digit integer with *nonzero* digits, none of which is repeated, and B is the greatest of such positive integers, then $B - A =$

(A) 41,976
(B) 66,666
(C) 86,420
(D) 86,424
(E) 89,999

12345
98765

12. At one instant, two meteors are 2,500 kilometers apart and traveling toward each other in straight paths along the imaginary line joining them. One meteor has a velocity of 300 meters per second while the other travels at 700 meters per second. Assuming that their velocities are constant and that they continue along the same paths, how many seconds elapse from the first instant to the time of their collision? (1 kilometer = 1,000 meters)

(A) 250
(B) 500
(C) 1,250
(D) 2,500
(E) 5,000

13. Given the volume of a cube is 8 cubic meters, find the distance from any vertex to the center point inside the cube.

(A) 1 m
(B) $\sqrt{2}$ m
(C) $2\sqrt{2}$ m
(D) $2\sqrt{3}$ m
(E) $\sqrt{3}$ m

14. The sum of a number of consecutive positive integers will always be divisible by 2 if the number of integers is a multiple of

(A) 6
(B) 5
(C) 4
(D) 3
(E) 2

GO ON TO THE NEXT PAGE

15. Find the circumference of a circle that has the same area as a square that has perimeter 2π.

(A) $2\sqrt{2}$
(B) $\pi\sqrt{\pi}$
(C) $\frac{\pi}{2}$
(D) $\frac{\sqrt{2}}{\pi}$
(E) 2

16. If $\frac{a}{b} = \frac{1}{4}$, where a is a positive integer, which of the following is a possible value of $\frac{a^2}{b}$?

I. $\frac{1}{4}$
II. $\frac{1}{2}$
III. 1

(A) None
(B) I only
(C) I and II only
(D) I and III only
(E) I, II, and III

17. A plane left airport A and has traveled x kilometers per hour for y hours. In terms of x and y, how many kilometers from airport A had the plane traveled $\frac{2}{3}y$ hours ago?

(A) $\frac{xy}{6}$
(B) $\frac{xy}{3}$
(C) xy
(D) $\frac{3xy}{2}$
(E) $\frac{xy}{12}$

18. The average (arithmetic mean) of k scores is 20. The average of 10 of these scores is 15. Find the average of the remaining scores in terms of k.

(A) $\frac{20k + 150}{10}$
(B) $\frac{20k - 150}{10}$
(C) $\frac{150 - 20k}{10}$
(D) $\frac{150 - 20k}{k - 10}$
(E) $\frac{20k - 150}{k - 10}$

GO ON TO THE NEXT PAGE

19. A square has an area of R^2. An equilateral triangle has a perimeter of E. If r is the perimeter of the square and e is a side of the equilateral triangle, then, in terms of R and E, $e + r =$

(A) $\frac{E+R}{7}$

(B) $\frac{4R+3E}{3}$

(C) $\frac{3E+4R}{12}$

(D) $\frac{12E+R}{3}$

(E) $\frac{E+12R}{3}$

20. Using the formula $C = \frac{5}{9}(F - 32)$, if the Celsius (C) temperature increased 35°, by how many degrees would the Fahrenheit (F) temperature be increased?

(A) $19\frac{4}{9}°$

(B) 31°

(C) 51°

(D) 63°

(E) 82°

$\frac{9}{5}\,35 = \frac{5}{9}(F-32)$

$63 = F - 32$

$+32 \quad +32$

$95 = F$

STOP

If you finish before time is called, you may check your work on this section only.
Do not turn to any other section in the test.

SECTION 4

Time: 25 Minutes—Turn to Section 4 (page 560) of your answer sheet to answer the questions in this section.
24 Questions

Directions: For each question in this section, select the best answer from among the choices given and fill in the corresponding circle on the answer sheet.

Each sentence below has one or two blanks, each blank indicating that something has been omitted. Beneath the sentence are five words or sets of words labeled A through E. Choose the word or set of words that, when inserted in the sentence, best fits the meaning of the sentence as a whole.

Example:

Hoping to ________ the dispute, negotiators proposed a compromise that they felt would be ________ to both labor and management.

(A) enforce...useful
(B) end...divisive
(C) overcome...unattractive
(D) extend...satisfactory
(E) resolve...acceptable

Ⓐ Ⓑ Ⓒ Ⓓ ●

1. Because the majority of the evening cable TV programs available dealt with violence and sex, the parents decided that the programs were ________ for the children to watch.

(A) exclusive
(B) acceptable
(C) instructive
(D) inappropriate
(E) unnecessary

2. The novel *Uncle Tom's Cabin*, which effectively ________ the unfairness toward black people, was a major influence in ________ the antislavery movement.

(A) portrayed...strengthening
(B) attacked...pacifying
(C) glamorized...launching
(D) viewed...appraising
(E) exposed...condemning

3. Having written 140 books to date, he may well be considered one of the most ________ novelists of the century.

(A) eccentric
(B) controversial
(C) easygoing
(D) unheralded
(E) prolific

4. The articles that he wrote ran the gamut from the serious to the lighthearted, from objective to the ________, from the innocuous to the ________.

(A) constant...evil
(B) casual...realistic
(C) ridiculous...remote
(D) argumentative...hostile
(E) incapacitated...conditioned

5. Because auto repair places have such ________ rates, many community colleges have ________ courses in automotive mechanics.

(A) shattering...planned
(B) exorbitant...instituted
(C) impertinent...discussed
(D) reasonable...introduced
(E) intolerable...discontinued

6. Though Socrates was ________ by his students who found truth in his teachings, his philosophy constituted ________ to the existent government.

(A) accepted...a benefit
(B) denied...an innovation
(C) appraised...an exception
(D) slighted...a challenge
(E) revered...a threat

GO ON TO THE NEXT PAGE

7. The quotation was erroneously _______ to a British poet.

(A) resolved
(B) attributed
(C) activated
(D) relegated
(E) vitiated

8. Mindful that his hardworking parents _______ to give him an education, Lopez, now wealthy, contributes _______ to scholarship funds for the needy.

(A) planned...needlessly
(B) skimped...profitably
(C) squandered...sparingly
(D) struggled...generously
(E) regaled...regretfully

GO ON TO THE NEXT PAGE

Each passage below is followed by questions based on its content. Answer the questions on the basis of what is stated or implied in each passage and in any introductory material that may be provided.

Questions 9–10 are based on the following passage.

Plutarch admired those who could use life for grand purposes and depart from it as grandly, but he would not pass over weaknesses and vices that marred the grandeur. His hero of heroes was Alexander the Great; he admired him above all other men, while his abomination of abominations was bad faith, dishonorable action. Nevertheless he tells with no attempt to extenuate how Alexander promised a safe conduct to a brave Persian army if they surrendered, but then, "even as they were marching away he fell upon them and put them all to the sword," "a breach of his word," Plutarch says sadly, "which is a lasting blemish to his achievements." He adds piteously, "but the only one." He hated to tell that story.

9. Which of the following conclusions is *least* justified by the passage?

(A) Plutarch considered Alexander basically a great man.
(B) The Persians believed that Alexander was acting in good faith.
(C) The Persians withdrew from the battlefield in orderly array.
(D) The author is familiar with Plutarch's writing.
(E) The author considers Plutarch unfair to Alexander.

10. As used in this passage, the word "extenuate" (line 7) means

(A) interpret
(B) exaggerate
(C) emphasize
(D) excuse
(E) condemn

Questions 11–12 are based on the following passage.

It is no longer needful to labor Dickens' power as a portrayer of modern society nor the seriousness of his "criticism of life." But we are still learning to appreciate his supreme attainment as an artist. Richness of poetic imagery, modulations of emotional tone, subtleties of implication, complex unities of structure, intensities of psychological insight, a panoply of achievement, mount up to overwhelming triumph. Though contemporary readers perhaps still feel somewhat queasy about Dickens' sentiment, his comedy and his drama sweep all before them. Even his elaborate and multistranded plots are now seen as great symphonic compositions driving forward through theme and variation to the resolving chords on which they close.

11. According to the passage, readers most recently have begun to appreciate Dickens'

(A) feeling for culture
(B) criticisms of life
(C) rhythms
(D) literary references
(E) literary craftsmanship

12. According to the passage, the endings of Dickens' works are most probably characterized by

(A) frequent use of comic relief
(B) unexpected developments
(C) visually effective symbols
(D) a lack of sense of completion
(E) dramatic power

GO ON TO THE NEXT PAGE

Questions 13–24 are based on the following passage.

The passage describes the author's attitude toward transportation.

Many people who are willing to concede that the railroad must be brought back to life are chiefly thinking of bringing this about on the very terms that have robbed us of a balanced transportation network—that is, by treating speed as the only important factor, forgetting reliability, comfort and safety, and seeking some mechanical dodge for increasing the speed and automation of surface vehicles.

My desk is littered with such technocratic fantasies, hopefully offered as "solutions." They range from old-fashioned monorails and jet-propelled hovercraft (now extinct) to a more scientific mode of propulsion at 2,000 miles an hour, from completely automated highway travel in private cars to automated vehicles a government department is now toying with for "facilitating" urban traffic.

What is the function of transportation? What place does locomotion occupy in the whole spectrum of human needs? Perhaps the first step in developing an adequate transportation policy would be to clear our minds of technocratic cant. Those who believe that transportation is the chief end of life should be put in orbit at a safe lunar distance from the earth.

The prime purpose of passenger transportation is not to increase the amount of physical movement but to increase the possibilities for human association, cooperation, personal intercourse, and choice.

A balanced transportation system, accordingly, calls for a balance of resources and facilities and opportunities in every other part of the economy. Neither speed nor mass demand offers a criterion of social efficiency. Hence such limited technocratic proposals as that for high-speed trains between already overcrowded and overextended urban centers would only add to the present lack of functional balance and purposeful organization viewed in terms of human need. Variety of choices, facilities and destinations, not speed alone, is the mark of an organic transportation system. And, incidentally, this is an important factor of safety when any part of the system breaks down. Even confirmed air travelers appreciate the railroad in foul weather.

If we took human needs seriously in recasting the whole transportation system, we should begin with the human body and make the fullest use of pedestrian movement, not only for health but for efficiency in moving large crowds over short distances. The current introduction of shopping malls, free from wheeled traffic, is both a far simpler and far better *technical* solution than the many costly proposals for introducing moving sidewalks or other rigidly automated modes of locomotion. At every stage we should provide for the right type of locomotion, at the right speed, within the right radius, to meet human needs. Neither maximum speed nor maximum traffic nor maximum distance has by itself any human significance.

With the over-exploitation of the particular car comes an increased demand for engineering equipment, to roll ever-wider carpets of concrete over the bulldozed landscape and to endow the petroleum magnates of some places with fabulous capacities for personal luxury and political corruption. Finally, the purpose of this system, abetted by similar concentration on planes and rockets, is to keep an increasing volume of motorists and tourists in motion, at the highest possible speed, in a sufficiently comatose state not to mind the fact that their distant destination has become the exact counterpart of the very place they have left. The end product everywhere is environmental desolation.

If this is the best our technological civilization can do to satisfy genuine human needs and nurture man's further development, it's plainly time to close up shop. If indeed we go farther and faster along this route, there is plenty of evidence to show that the shop will close up without our help. Behind our power blackouts, our polluted environments, our transportation breakdowns, our nuclear threats, is a failure of mind. Technocratic anesthesia has put us to sleep. Results that were predictable—and predicted!—three-quarters of a century ago without awakening any response still find us unready to cope with them—or even to admit their existence.

13. The author criticizes most railroad advocates because their emphasis is primarily on

(A) monetary costs
(B) speed
(C) traffic flow
(D) reliability
(E) pollution

14. The author states that the purpose(s) of transportation is (are)

I. to move people from place to place efficiently
II. to increase social contact
III. to open up opportunities

(A) I only
(B) II only
(C) III only
(D) I and II only
(E) I, II, and III

15. A solution advocated by the author for transporting masses of people over short distances involves

(A) jet-propelled hovercraft
(B) automated vehicles
(C) conveyor belts
(D) moving sidewalks
(E) pedestrian malls

GO ON TO THE NEXT PAGE

16. Excessive reliance on the automobile, according to the author, is associated with

(A) the enrichment of the oil industry
(B) monopoly power
(C) our transportation breakdown
(D) inefficiency in transportation
(E) a policy of comfort and convenience at all costs

17. It can be inferred that the author would oppose

(A) a balanced transportation system
(B) shopping malls
(C) an expansion of the interstate highway system
(D) less emphasis on technological solutions
(E) sacrificing speed for comfort

18. The author predicts that if we continue our present transportation policy

(A) we will succumb to a technocratic dictatorship
(B) our society may die
(C) we will attain a balanced transportation system
(D) rockets and planes will predominate
(E) human needs will be surrendered

19. The word "radius" in line 49 refers to

(A) the distance from the center of a train wheel to the circumference
(B) the distance of places
(C) the latitude in connection with human needs
(D) the traffic in connection with travel
(E) the time it takes to go from one place to another

20. The author believes that "technocratic" thinking is not consistent with

(A) technological advances
(B) the labor relations groups
(C) faster-moving vehicles
(D) human interests
(E) the scientific mode

21. According to the article, the fulfillment of human needs will require

(A) far greater use of walking
(B) more resources devoted to transportation
(C) abandoning the profit system
(D) a better legislative policy
(E) automated travel

22. The author believes that the nation has placed too great an emphasis on all of the following *except*

(A) speed
(B) traffic flow
(C) diversity
(D) maximizing distance
(E) technological needs

23. It may be inferred that the author is a(n)

(A) highway engineer
(B) historian
(C) railroad industry spokesperson
(D) lawyer
(E) oil baron

24. It is stated in the article that safety in transportation is aided by the existence of

(A) remote air-to-ground control for airplanes
(B) technological sophistication
(C) a variety of transport modes
(D) fail-safe systems
(E) a combination of surface and subsurface systems

STOP

If you finish before time is called, you may check your work on this section only. Do not turn to any other section in the test.

Take a 1 minute break

before starting section 5

SECTION 5

Time: 25 Minutes—Turn to Section 5 (page 560) of your answer sheet to answer the questions in this section.
35 Questions

Directions: For each question in this section, select the best answer from among the choices given and fill in the corresponding circle on the answer sheet.

The following sentences test correctness and effectiveness of expression. Part of each sentence or the entire sentence is underlined; beneath each sentence are five ways of phrasing the underlined material. Choice A repeats the original phrasing; the other four choices are different. If you think the original phrasing produces a better sentence than any of the alternatives, select Choice A; if not, select one of the other choices.

In making your selection, follow the requirements of standard written English; that is, pay attention to grammar, choice of words, sentence construction, and punctuation. Your selection should result in the most effective sentence—clear and precise, without awkwardness or ambiguity.

EXAMPLE:

Laura Ingalls Wilder published her first book and she was sixty-five years old then.

(A) and she was sixty-five years old then
(B) when she was sixty-five
(C) at age sixty-five years old
(D) upon the reaching of sixty-five years
(E) at the time when she was sixty-five

(A) ● (C) (D) (E)

1. At the top of the hill to the left of the tall oak is where they live.

(A) to the left of the tall oak
(B) where the tall oak is to the left of it
(C) and the tall oak is to the left
(D) left of the tall oak
(E) to the tall oak's left

2. Martin pretended to be asleep whenever she came into the room.

(A) whenever she came
(B) at the time she comes
(C) although she came
(D) since she came
(E) by the time she came

3. Once a person starts taking addictive drugs, it is most likely he will be led to take more.

(A) it is most likely he will be led to take more
(B) he will probably take them over and over again
(C) it is hard to stop him from taking more
(D) he is likely to continue taking them
(E) he will have a tendency to continue taking them

4. We have not yet been informed concerning the one who broke the window.

(A) concerning the one who broke the window
(B) about the identity of the individual who is responsible for breaking the window
(C) of the window-breaker
(D) as to who broke the window
(E) who broke the window

5. Having the highest marks in his class, the college offered him a scholarship.

(A) the college offered him a scholarship
(B) the college offered a scholarship to him
(C) he was offered a scholarship by the college
(D) a scholarship was offered him by the college
(E) a college scholarship was offered to him

6. The government's failing to keep it's pledges will mean disaster.

(A) The government's failing to keep it's pledges
(B) The governments failing to keep it's pledges
(C) The government's failing to keep its pledges
(D) The government failing to keep it's pledges
(E) The governments failing to keep their pledges

GO ON TO THE NEXT PAGE

7. Her father along with her mother and sister insist that she stop smoking.

(A) along with her mother and sister insist
(B) along with her mother and sister insists
(C) along with her mother and sister are insisting
(D) along with her mother and sister were insisting
(E) as well as her mother and sister insist

8. Most gardeners like to cultivate these kind of flowers in the early spring.

(A) these kind of flowers
(B) these kind of flower
(C) them kinds of flowers
(D) those kind of flower
(E) this kind of flower

9. The doctor informs us that my aunt has not and never will recover from the fall.

(A) has not and never will recover
(B) has not recovered and never will
(C) has not and never would recover
(D) has not recovered and never will recover
(E) had not and never will recover

10. The senator was neither in favor of or opposed to the proposed legislation.

(A) or opposed to the proposed legislation
(B) and was not opposed to the proposed legislation
(C) the proposed legislation or opposed to it
(D) nor opposed to the proposed legislation
(E) the proposed legislation or opposed to the proposed legislation

11. Glory as well as gain is to be his reward.

(A) Glory as well as gain is to be his reward
(B) As his reward, glory as well as gain is to be his
(C) He will be rewarded by glory as well as gain
(D) Glory also gain are to be his reward
(E) First glory, then gain, will be his reward

GO ON TO THE NEXT PAGE

The following sentences test your ability to recognize grammar and usage errors. Each sentence contains either a single error or no error at all. No sentence contains more than one error. The error, if there is one, is underlined and lettered. If the sentence contains an error, select the one underlined part that must be changed to make the sentence correct. If the sentence is correct, select Choice E. In choosing answers, follow the requirements of standard written English.

EXAMPLE:

The other delegates and him immediately
A B C
accepted the resolution drafted by
D
the neutral states. No error.
E

Ⓐ ● Ⓒ Ⓓ Ⓔ

12. The long lines of cars at gasoline stations have
A
disappeared like as if there were never an
B C
energy crisis. No error.
D E

13. The man told his son to take the car to the
A B
service station because it needed gasoline.
C D
No error.
E

14. The man who's temper is under control at
A B
all times is likely to think clearly and to accomplish
C D
more in his business and social relations. No error.
E

15. Whether nineteenth-century classics should be
taught in school today has become a matter
A B C
of controversy for students and teachers alike.
D
No error.
E

16. Bob wanted to finish his homework completely
A
before his mother had come home from her
B C
sister's house. No error.
D E

17. Inflation together with the high interest rates and
soaring oil prices are hurting the nation's
A B C
economy very seriously. No error.
D E

18. When one leaves his car to be repaired, he
A B
assumes that the mechanic will repair the car
C
good. No error.
D E

19. Bob could easily have gotten a higher score on
A B
his college entrance test if he would have read
C
more in his school career. No error.
D E

20. Any modern novelist would be thrilled to have
A B
his stories compared with Dickens. No error.
C D E

21. The automobile industry is experimenting with a
A
new type of a motor that will consume less
B C
gasoline and cause much less pollution. No error.
D E

22. Sharon planned to pay around a hundred dollars
A
for a new spring coat, but when she saw a
B
gorgeous coat that sold for two hundred
C
dollars, she decided to buy it. No error.
D E

GO ON TO THE NEXT PAGE

23. Had Lincoln have been (A) alive during World War II, he would have regarded (B) the racial situation in (C) the armed forces as a throwback (D) to pre-Civil War days. No error. (E)

24. Members of the staff of the District Attorney (A) made more than $100,000 from a get-rich-quick (B) scheme in which investors were bilked (C) of about $1 million (D). No error. (E)

25. Since oxygen is indispensable (A) to human life, scientists are exploring (B) the possibility of providing (C) oxygen for future inhabitants of space (D) stations. No error. (E)

26. Its (A) my opinion that learning (B) the correct pronunciation should precede (C) any attempt to learn (D) the correct spelling of a word. No error. (E)

27. If I would have known (A) more about (B) the person whom (C) I was writing to, I would have written a better (D) answer. No error. (E)

28. If you compare (A) Bill and Joe as far as (B) scholarship goes, you will have to conclude that Bill is, without (C) any question, the brightest (D). No error. (E)

29. In spite of (A) how very poor (B) Ellen had done (C) in the art competition, she was far (D) from discouraged. No error. (E)

GO ON TO THE NEXT PAGE

Directions: The following passage is an early draft of an essay. Some parts of the passage need to be rewritten.

Read the passage and select the best answers for the questions that follow. Some questions are about particular sentences or parts of sentences and ask you to improve sentence structure or word choice. Other questions ask you to consider organization and development. In choosing answers, follow the requirements of standard written English.

Questions 30–35 refer to the following passage.

[1]In fact the Egyptians pushed their cult of cat worship to the point of aberration. [2]Their devotion cost them the loss of a city in 500 BC when the Persians laid siege to Pelusium, a city near the present location of Port Said. [3]All the tactics of the Persian army had been blocked by the fierce resistance of the Egyptians; moreover, Cambyses, the Persian leader, had a brilliant idea. [4]When the moment for the attack came, the Egyptians were appalled to see hundreds of panic-stricken cats surging ahead of the Persian army. [5]To make matters worse, each advancing Persian soldier carried a live cat in his arms. [6]He ordered his soldiers to search out and seize the greatest possible number of cats in the surrounding countryside and to keep them unharmed without hurting them. [7]The Egyptian defenders would not risk harming one cat and the city of Pelusium capitulated without a drop of blood. [8]Animal worship was prevalent during Egyptian times.

30. What should be done with sentence 3?

(A) Moreover and its surrounding punctuation should be replaced with a comma.
(B) Moreover and its surrounding punctuation should be replaced with *when.*
(C) The Persian leader and surrounding commas should be omitted.
(D) The words *fierce resistance* should be changed to bullheadedness.
(E) The sentence should be left as it is except for changing the semicolon in front of moreover to a comma.

31. In sentence 5 To make matters worse should be

(A) changed to It was made worse by
(B) omitted
(C) changed to Plus
(D) left as it is
(E) placed at the end of the sentence

32. The end of sentence 6 would be

(A) improved by adding in the least little way
(B) best if left as it is
(C) clearer if it ended after cats
(D) best if it ended after unharmed
(E) improved if it said unhurt without harming them

33. Sentence 6 should be

(A) placed after sentence 3
(B) omitted
(C) placed after sentence 8, with ordered changed to had ordered
(D) made into two sentences, the first to stop after countryside
(E) joined to sentence 5 with which was because

34. Sentence 7 would be more accurate if

(A) capitulated were changed to crumbled
(B) a drop of blood were changed to further battle
(C) surrendered without fighting at all were substituted for capitulated without a drop of blood
(D) having resisted were substituted for a drop of blood
(E) because of bloodshed were substituted for without a drop of blood

35. Sentence 8 should be

(A) left where it is
(B) placed right after sentence 1
(C) placed before sentence 1
(D) omitted
(E) placed after sentence 5

STOP

If you finish before time is called, you may check your work on this section only.
Do not turn to any other section in the test.

SECTION 6

Time: 25 Minutes—Turn to Section 6 (page 561) of your answer sheet to answer the questions in this section.
18 Questions

Directions: This section contains two types of questions. You have 25 minutes to complete both types. For questions 1–8, solve each problem and decide which is the best of the choices given. Fill in the corresponding circle on the answer sheet. You may use any available space for scratchwork.

Notes:

1. The use of a calculator is permitted.
2. All numbers used are real numbers.
3. Figures that accompany problems in this test are intended to provide information useful in solving the problems. They are drawn as accurately as possible EXCEPT when it is stated in a specific problem that the figure is not drawn to scale. All figures lie in a plane unless otherwise indicated.
4. Unless otherwise specified, the domain of any function f is assumed to be the set of all real numbers x for which $f(x)$ is a real number.

REFERENCE INFORMATION

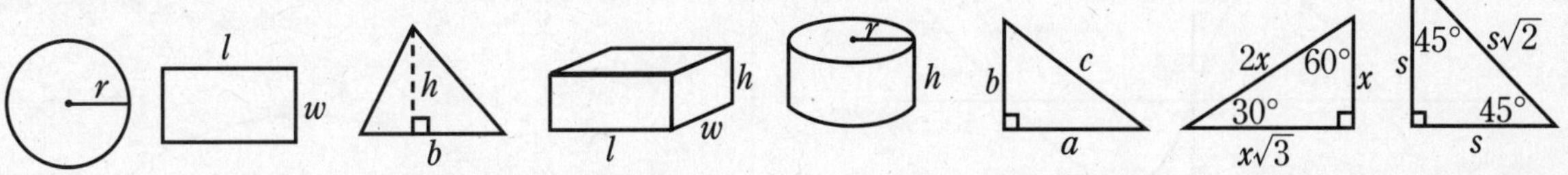

$A = \pi r^2$ $C = 2\pi r$ $A = lw$ $A = \frac{1}{2}bh$ $V = lwh$ $V = \pi r^2 h$ $c^2 = a^2 + b^2$ *Special Right Triangles*

The number of degrees of arc in a circle is 360.
The sum of the measures in degrees of the angles of a triangle is 180.

1. If $\sqrt{x}$ is an odd integer, which of the following *MUST* be even?

(A) x
(B) $3\sqrt{x}$
(C) $\sqrt{2x}$
(D) $2\sqrt{x}$
(E) x^2

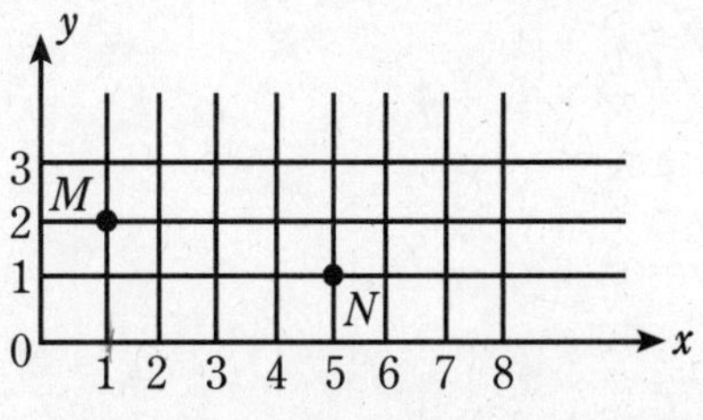

2. If a rectangle is drawn on the grid above with $\overline{MN}$ as one of its diagonals, which of the following could be the coordinates of another vertex of the rectangle?

(A) (1,0)
(B) (2,0)
(C) (3,3)
(D) (4,3)
(E) (5,2)

GO ON TO THE NEXT PAGE

x	$f(x)$
0	3
1	4
2	2
3	5
4	8

3. According to the table above, for what value of x does $f(x) = x + 2$?

(A) 0
(B) 1
(C) 2
(D) 3
(E) 4

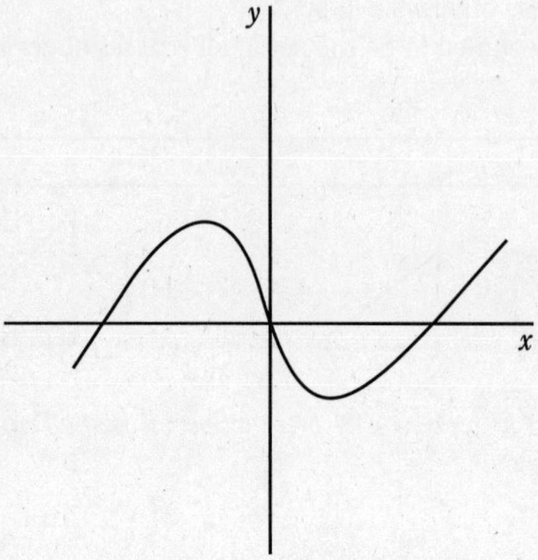

4. Which equation could represent the graph above?

(A) $y = x^3 + 2$
(B) $y = x^3 + 2x + 4$
(C) $y = x^2$
(D) $y = x^3 - x$
(E) $y = x^3 + x^2 - x - 1$

5. The degree measures of the four angles of a quadrilateral are w, x, y, and z, respectively. If w is the average (arithmetic mean) of x, y, and z, then $x + y + z =$

(A) 45°
(B) 90°
(C) 120°
(D) 180°
(E) 270°

6. A certain mixture contains carbon, oxygen, hydrogen, and other elements in the percentages shown in the graph below. If the total mixture weighs 24 pounds, which number represents the closest number of pounds of carbon that is contained in the mixture?

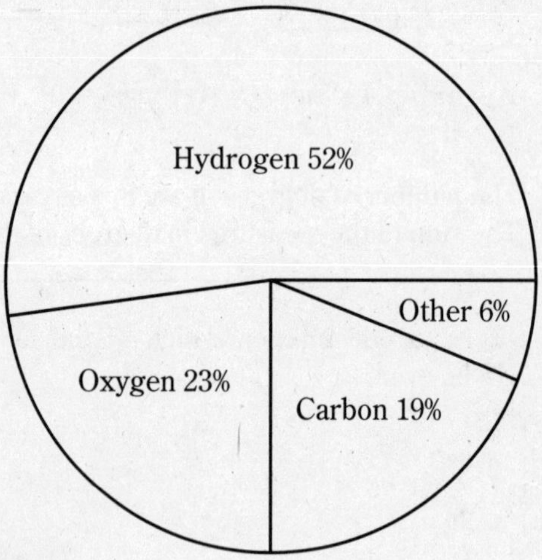

(A) 5.2
(B) 4.6
(C) 2.1
(D) 1.2
(E) 0.5

GO ON TO THE NEXT PAGE

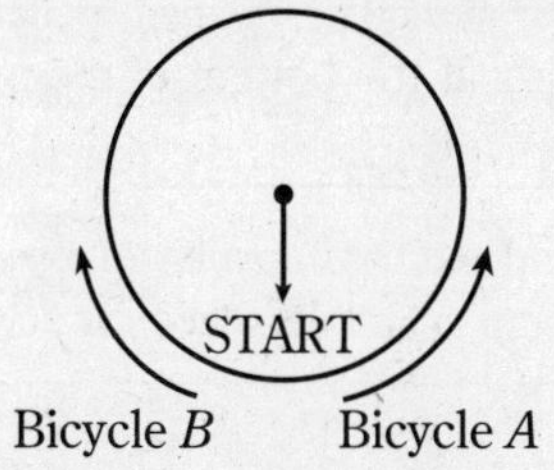

7. In the figure above, two bicycles are being pedaled in opposite directions around a circular racetrack of circumference = 120 feet. Bicycle A is traveling at 5 feet/second in the counterclockwise direction, and Bicycle B is traveling at 8 feet/second in the clockwise direction. When Bicycle B has completed exactly 600 revolutions, how many complete revolutions will Bicycle A have made?

(A) 180
(B) 375
(C) 475
(D) 960
(E) It cannot be determined from the given information.

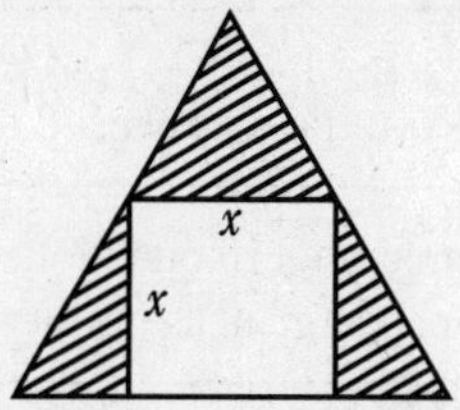

8. A square of side x is inscribed inside an equilateral triangle of area $x^2\sqrt{3}$. If a rectangle with width x has the same area as the shaded region shown in the figure above, what is the length of the rectangle in terms of x?

(A) $\sqrt{3}x - 1$
(B) $x\sqrt{3}$
(C) $\sqrt{3} - x$
(D) $x(\sqrt{3} - 1)$
(E) $x^2\sqrt{3} - x^2$

GO ON TO THE NEXT PAGE

Directions: For Student-Produced Response questions 9–18, use the grids at the bottom of the answer sheet page on which you have answered questions 1–8.

Each of the remaining 10 questions requires you to solve the problem and enter your answer by marking the circles in the special grid, as shown in the examples below. You may use any available space for scratchwork.

Answer: $\frac{7}{12}$ or 7/12

Write answer in boxes. →

Grid in result. →

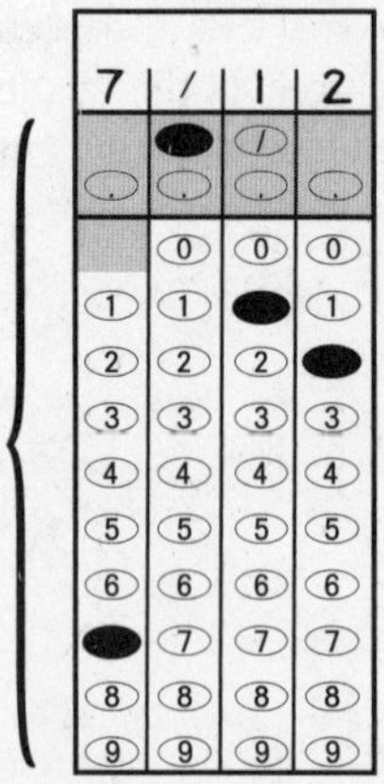

← Fraction line

Answer: 2.5

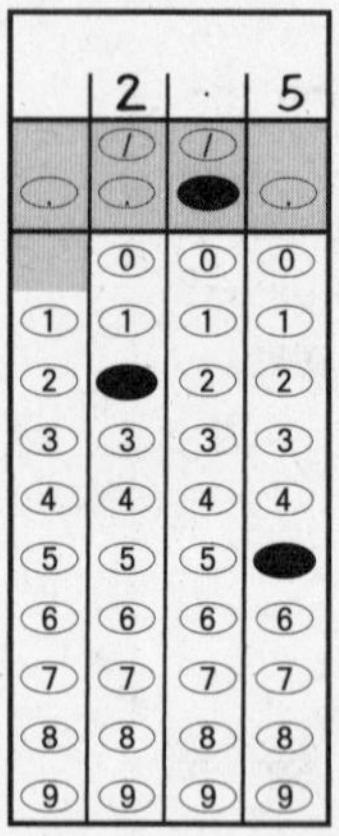

← Decimal point

Answer: 201
Either position is correct.

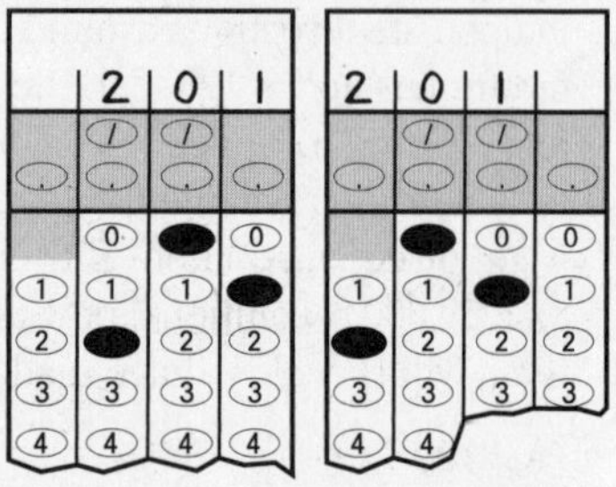

Note: You may start your answers in any column, space permitting. Columns not needed should be left blank.

- Mark no more than one oval in any column.
- Because the answer sheet will be machine-scored, **you will receive credit only if the ovals are filled in correctly.**
- Although not required, it is suggested that you write your answer in the boxes at the top of the columns to help you fill in the ovals accurately.
- Some problems may have more than one correct answer. In such cases, grid only one answer.
- No question has a negative answer.
- **Mixed numbers** such as $2\frac{1}{2}$ must be gridded as 2.5 or 5/2. (If  is gridded, it will be interpreted as $\frac{21}{2}$, not $2\frac{1}{2}$.)

- Decimal Accuracy: If you obtain a decimal answer, **enter the most accurate value the grid will accommodate.** For example, if you obtain an answer such as 0.6666..., you should record the result as .666 or .667. **Less accurate values such as .66 or .67 are not acceptable.**

Acceptable ways to grid $\frac{2}{3} = .6666\ldots$

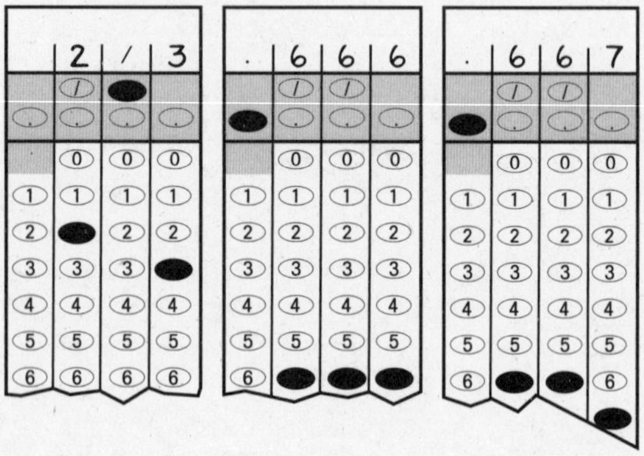

9. If $\frac{1}{4} < x < \frac{1}{3}$, find one value of x.

x=.2

10. Given $3x + y = 17$ and $x + 3y = -1$, find the value of $3x + 3y$.

GO ON TO THE NEXT PAGE

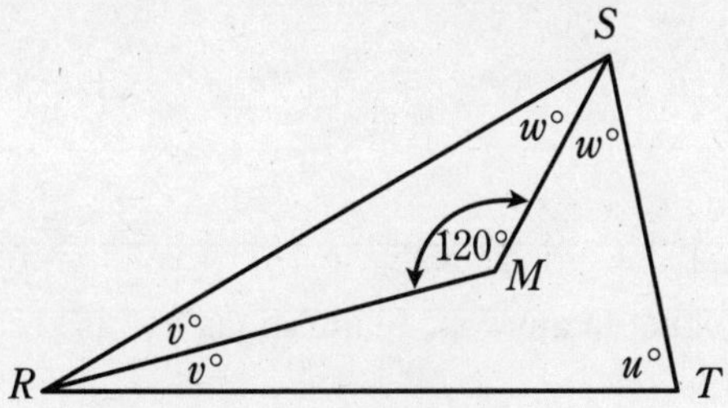

Note: Figure not drawn to scale.

11. If $\angle RST = 80°$, find u.

80´

12. There are 22 people on an island. A tram can carry at most 4 people at a time. What is the least number of trips that the tram must make to the mainland to get all the people to the mainland?

88

13. Let us define the operation ⊙ as

$a \odot b = (a + b)^2 - (a - b)^2$

Find the value of $\sqrt{18} \odot \sqrt{2}$.

√2.02

14. How many ordered pairs of *integers* (x,y) satisfy $x^2 + y^2 < 9$?

1 2 3 4 5

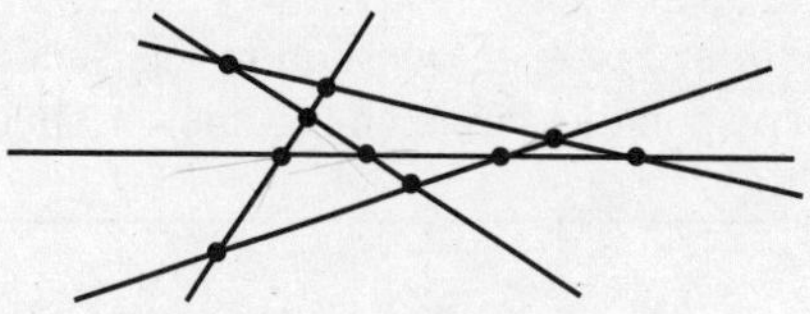

15. The figure above demonstrates that 5 straight lines can have 10 points of intersection. What is the maximum number of points of intersection of 4 straight lines?

2

16. A boy planned to buy some chocolate bars at 50 cents each but instead decided to purchase 30-cent chocolate bars. If he originally had enough money to buy 21 of the 50-cent bars, how many of the less expensive ones did he buy?

35

17. Let d be the least integer greater than 96,666 such that four of d's digits are identical. Find the value of $d - 96{,}666$.

800

18. Find 25 percent of 25 percent of 2.

0.32

STOP

If you finish before time is called, you may check your work on this section only. Do not turn to any other section in the test.

Take a 5 minute break

before starting section 7

SECTION 7

Time: 25 Minutes—Turn to Section 7 (page 561) of your answer sheet to answer the questions in this section.
24 Questions

Directions: For each question in this section, select the best answer from among the choices given and fill in the corresponding circle on the answer sheet.

Each sentence below has one or two blanks, each blank indicating that something has been omitted. Beneath the sentence are five words or sets of words labeled A through E. Choose the word or set of words that, when inserted in the sentence, best fits the meaning of the sentence as a whole.

Example:

Hoping to _______ the dispute, negotiators proposed a compromise that they felt would be _______ to both labor and management.

(A) enforce...useful
(B) end...divisive
(C) overcome...unattractive
(D) extend...satisfactory
(E) resolve...acceptable

Ⓐ Ⓑ Ⓒ Ⓓ ●

1. He tried his hardest to maintain his _______ in the face of the threatening mob.

(A) synthesis
(B) analogy
(C) fraternity
(D) umbrage
(E) composure

2. The low-cost apartment buildings, new and well managed, are _______ to those accustomed to living in tenements _______ by shady characters.

(A) a boon...haunted
(B) a specter...inhabited
(C) an exodus...frequented
(D) an example...viewed
(E) a surprise...approached

3. Before the inflation _______, one could have had a complete meal in a restaurant for five dollars, including the tip, whereas today a hot dog, coffee, and dessert would _______ add up to two or three times that much.

(A) spiral...indubitably
(B) cancellation...rapidly
(C) problem...improbably
(D) abundance...consequently
(E) incidence...radically

4. Although the death of his dog had saddened him markedly, his computer designing skills remained completely _______.

(A) twisted
(B) unaffected
(C) incapable
(D) repaired
(E) demolished

5. The guerrillas were so _______ that the general had to develop various strategies to trap them.

(A) distant
(B) wild
(C) unreasonable
(D) elusive
(E) cruel

GO ON TO THE NEXT PAGE

The two passages below are followed by questions based on their content and on the relationship between the two passages. Answer the questions on the basis of what is stated or implied in the passages and in any introductory material that may be provided.

Questions 6–9 are based on the following passages.

Passage 1

Classical physics is the physics of the macroscopic world (our world which we can see, touch, and hear). It is very appealing to the purist in that there are no uncertainties in measurement of physical quantities. When we set up an apparatus to measure something, the apparatus does not interfere with the measurement. For example, if we want to figure out how fast something is traveling, we can also find out exactly where it is at the time of measurement of its speed. There is certainty in classical physics, the "exact" physics. Thus when a bridge is built, we know exactly what stress the bridge may withstand. When a car is constructed, we know what specifications the engine must have to have the car do what we want.

Passage 2

Modern physics, or physics of the sub-microscopic world (the world of electrons, protons, and neutrons), is very perplexing since there seems to be an apparent violation of cause and effect. There exists only a probability and not certainty in measurement of important physical quantities because the measurement device affects the measurement. For example, if we know exactly in what position an electron is, we cannot determine its speed. Thus the more we know the value of one physical quantity, the less certain we are of a corresponding physical quantity. To paraphrase Albert Einstein, "the universe does not play dice with nature." Ironically, modern physics really controls and determines the outcome of the physics of the macroscopic physics (since the macroscopic world is really made up of constituents in the sub-microscopic realm). Thus modern physics is the foundation of all physics since it contains the basic and fundamental elements used to create all physics.

6. It can be assumed that Albert Einstein believed that

(A) only classical physics existed in nature
(B) there was certainty in all aspects of physics theories
(C) classical physics violates cause and effect
(D) speed and position are not the fundamental characteristics of particles
(E) when a new car is constructed, in order for it to be most efficient, a new physics must be employed

7. Modern physics differs from classical physics chiefly in that

(A) the measurement device does not affect the measurement in classical physics
(B) no quantity in modern physics can be determined
(C) modern physics is not as fundamental as classical physics
(D) classical physics does not deal primarily with measurement
(E) speed is always constant in classical physics

8. Which of the following would resolve the seeming paradox between modern and classical physics?

(A) There could be a third type of physics which would incorporate the phenomena of both classical and modern physics.
(B) One could consider that physics is either macroscopic or microscopic in nature.
(C) One would not consider speed and position as a fundamental set of physical quantity.
(D) Exactness of measurement would not be a requirement in physics.
(E) One could assume that electrons, protons, and neutrons do not exist in nature.

9. Which key elements exist in either classical physics or modern physics but not in both?

(I) existence of cause and effect
(II) probability and not certainty of two quantities
(III) the structure of a bridge

(A) (I) only
(B) (II) only
(C) (III) only
(D) (I) and (II) only
(E) (I), (II), and (III)

GO ON TO THE NEXT PAGE

Questions 10–15 are based on the following passage.

The following passage tracks the career of the famous artist Vincent van Gogh, and his encounter with another famous artist, Paul Gauguin.

It was at Arles, the small city in the south of France where he stayed from early in 1888 to the spring of 1889, that Vincent van Gogh had his first real bout with madness. After a quarrel with Paul Gauguin, he cut off part of his own ear. Yet Arles was also the scene of an astonishing burst of creativity. Over the short span of 15 months, van Gogh produced some 200 paintings and more than 100 drawings and watercolors, a record that only Picasso has matched in the modern era. Orchards and wheatfields under the glowing sun, neighbors and townspeople, interiors of the Yellow House where he lived, were all subjects of his frenetic brush. The Arles canvases, alive with color—vermilion, emerald green, Prussian blue, and a particularly brilliant yellow—have intensity of feeling that mark the high point of his career, and deeply affected the work of artists to follow, notably the Fauves and the German Expressionists.

Van Gogh went to Arles after two years in Paris, where his beloved younger brother Theo, who supported him psychologically and financially for most of his adult life, was an art dealer. In Paris, Vincent had met Gauguin and other important artists—Lautrec, Degas, Pissarro, and Seurat. Like the last two, he worked in the Neo-Impressionist, or Pointillist, style—applying color in tiny dots or strokes that "mixed" in the viewer's eye to create effects of considerable intensity. But he wanted "gayer" colors than Paris provided, the kind of atmosphere evoked by the Japanese prints he so admired. Then, too, the French capital had exhausted him, mentally and physically. He felt that in Arles, not exactly a bustling arts center, he might find serenity, and even establish an artistic tradition.

It was van Gogh's hope of founding a new artists' colony in the south that made him eager to have Gauguin, whose talent van Gogh readily recognized, join him at Arles. The plan, on Vincent's part, was for Gauguin to stay in Arles for maybe a year, working and sharing with him the small living quarters and studio he had found for himself and dubbed the Yellow House. At first, the two men got along well. But they did not at all agree on judgments of other artists. Still, Gauguin had an influence on van Gogh. Gauguin began pushing the younger artist to paint from memory rather than actuality.

Before the year was up, whether because of Gauguin's attempts to change van Gogh's style, or what, the two men had apparently begun to get on each other's nerves. Gauguin wrote to Theo that he felt he had to return to Paris, citing his and Vincent's "temperamental incompatibility." A letter from Vincent to Theo followed, noting that Gauguin was "a little out of sorts with the good town of Arles, and especially with me."

But then, the two apparently made up—but not for long. Gauguin returned to Paris and never saw van Gogh again, although they later had friendly correspondence.

Despite any problem with his relationship with Gauguin, van Gogh maintained his enormous creativity and prolific nature in those months in Arles.

10. Which of the following is the best title for the passage?

(A) Where van Gogh's Art Reached Its Zenith
(B) An Unfortunate Mismatch Between Two Great Artists
(C) Another Tale of a Genius Unable to Adjust to Society
(D) A Prolific Painter Whose Art Will Live On
(E) Van Gogh's Frustration in His Hope to Found a New Artists' Colony

11. According to the passage, which of the following statements is not true?

(A) Fauvism is a movement in painting typified by vivid colors.
(B) Gauguin was an older man than Theo.
(C) Pissarro was a painter associated with the Neo-Impressionist school.
(D) Van Gogh's work began to deteriorate after Gauguin's departure from Arles.
(E) Van Gogh's behavior was, at times, quite abnormal.

12. For which of the following reasons did van Gogh decide to leave Paris and go to Arles?

I. He sought a different environment for the kind of painting he wished to do.
II. He had hopes of forming a new artists' colony.
III. He wanted a more peaceful location where there was less stress.

(A) II only
(B) III only
(C) I and II only
(D) I and III only
(E) I, II, and III

13. The word "frenetic" in line 12 most nearly means

(A) colorful
(B) smooth
(C) bright
(D) rapid
(E) frantic

14. Gauguin's attitude toward van Gogh is best described in the passage as one of

(A) gentle ridicule
(B) unallayed suspicion
(C) tolerant acceptance
(D) open condescension
(E) resentful admiration

GO ON TO THE NEXT PAGE

15. Aside from his quarrel with Gauguin, we may infer that a major contributory reason for van Gogh's going to the extreme of cutting off part of his ear was his

(A) concern about being able to support himself financially
(B) inability to get along with Gauguin
(C) failure to form an artists' colony in Arles
(D) mental and emotional instability
(E) being upset by Gauguin's attempts to change his style

GO ON TO THE NEXT PAGE

Questions 16–24 are based on the following passage.

The following passage is excerpted from the essay Self-Reliance *by the American writer Ralph Waldo Emerson.*

Infancy conforms to nobody: all conform to it, so that one babe commonly makes four or five out of the adults who prattle and play to it. So God has armed youth and puberty and manhood no less with its own piquancy and charm, and made it enviable and gracious and its claims not to be put by, if it will stand by itself. Do not think the youth has no force, because he cannot speak to you and me. Hark! in the next room his voice is sufficiently clear and emphatic. It seems he knows how to speak to his contemporaries. Bashful or bold, then, he will know how to make us seniors very unnecessary.

The nonchalance of boys who are sure of a dinner, and would disdain as much as a lord to do or say aught to conciliate one, is the healthy attitude of human nature. A boy is in the parlor what the pit is in the playhouse; independent, irresponsible, looking out from his corner on such people and facts as pass by, he tries and sentences them on their merits, in the swift, summary way of boys, as good, bad, interesting, silly, eloquent, troublesome. He lumbers himself never about consequences, about interests; he gives an independent, genuine verdict. You must court him: he does not court you. But the man is, as it were, clapped into jail by his consciousness. As soon as he has once acted or spoken with eclat, he is a committed person, watched by the sympathy or the hatred of hundreds, whose affections must now enter into his account. There is no Lethe for this. Ah, that he could pass again into his neutrality.

These are the voices which we hear in solitude, but they grow faint and inaudible as we enter into the world. Society everywhere is in conspiracy against the manhood of every one of its members. Society is a joint-stock company, in which the members agree, for the better securing of his bread to each shareholder, to surrender the liberty and culture of the eater. The virtue in most request is conformity. Self-reliance is its aversion. It loves not realities and creators, but names and customs.

Whoso would be a man must be a nonconformist. He who would gather immortal palms must not be hindered by the name of goodness, but must explore if it be goodness. Nothing is at last sacred but the integrity of your own mind.

No law can be sacred to me but that of my nature. Good and bad are but names very readily transferable to that or this; the only right is what is after my constitution, the only wrong what is against it. A man is to carry himself in the presence of all opposition as if every thing were titular and ephemeral but he. I am ashamed to think how easily we capitulate to badges and names, to large societies and dead institutions. Every decent and well-spoken individual affects and sways me more than is right. I ought to go upright and vital, and speak the rude truth in all ways.

I shun father and mother and wife and brother, when my genius calls me. I would write on the lintels of the doorpost, *Whim.* I hope it is somewhat better than whim at last, but we cannot spend the day in explanation. Expect me not to show cause why I seek or why I exclude company. Then, again, do not tell me, as a good man did to-day, of my obligation to put all poor men in good situations. Are they *my* poor? I tell thee, thou foolish philanthropist, that I grudge the dollar, the dime, the cent, I give to such men as do not belong to me and to whom I do not belong. There is a class of persons to whom by all spiritual affinity I am bought and sold; for them I will go to prison, if need be; but your miscellaneous popular charities; the education at college of fools; the building of meeting-houses to the vain end to which many now stand; alms to sots; and the thousandfold Relief Societies;—though I confess with shame I sometimes succumb and give the dollar, it is a wicked dollar which by and by I shall have the manhood to withhold.

For nonconformity the world whips you with its displeasure. And therefore a man must know how to estimate a sour face. The by-standers look askance on him in the public street or in the friend's parlor. If this aversion had its origin in contempt and resistance like his own, he might well go home with a sad countenance; but the sour faces of the multitude, like their sweet faces, have no deep cause, but are put on and off as the wind blows and a newspaper directs. Yet is the discontent of the multitude more formidable than that of the senate and the college.

The other terror that scares us from self-trust is our consistency; a reverence for our past act or word, because the eyes of others have no other data for computing our orbit than our past acts, and we are loath to disappoint them.

But why should you keep your head over your shoulder? Why drag about this corpse of your memory, lest you contradict somewhat you have stated in this or that public place? Suppose you should contradict yourself; what then?

A foolish consistency is the hobgoblin of little minds, adored by little statesmen and philosophers and divines. With consistency a great soul has simply nothing to do. He may as well concern himself with his shadow on the wall. Speak what you think now in hard words, and to-morrow speak what to-morrow thinks in hard words again, though it contradict everything you said to-day.—"Ah, so you shall be sure to be misunderstood."—Is it so bad, then, to be misunderstood? Pythagoras was misunderstood, and Socrates, and Jesus, and Luther, and Copernicus, and Galileo, and Newton, and every pure and wise spirit that ever took flesh. To be great is to be misunderstood.

16. The main theme of the selection is best expressed as follows:

(A) "A foolish consistency is the hobgoblin of little minds."
(B) "Eternal youth means eternal independence."
(C) "Whoso would be a man must be a nonconformist."
(D) "Colleges are designed to educate fools."
(E) "Infancy conforms to nobody."

GO ON TO THE NEXT PAGE

17. We are most nonconformist during our period of

(A) infancy
(B) puberty
(C) youth
(D) manhood
(E) old age

18. According to the author, "To be great is to be misunderstood" means that

(A) one should never say exactly what one means
(B) to be misunderstood is to be great
(C) all great men have always been misunderstood
(D) a man should not hesitate to change his mind if he sees the need to, even at the risk of being considered inconsistent
(E) nice people seldom succeed

19. The refusal of young people to cater to accepted public opinion is, according to the author,

(A) characteristic of the rebelliousness of youth
(B) a healthy attitude of human nature
(C) a manifestation of deep-seated immaturity
(D) simply bad manners
(E) part of growing up

20. From the selection, one may infer that the "pit in the playhouse" was

(A) a section containing the best seats in the theater
(B) favored by independent, outspoken, unselfconscious playgoers
(C) an underground theater
(D) a generally staid, quiet section of the theater, favored by young people only
(E) the actors' dressing rooms

21. "Society is a joint-stock company," etc., is one way in which the author shows

(A) that the public is anticulture
(B) society is highly organized and structured
(C) how society rejects self-reliance
(D) that there is no room for solitude in our world
(E) the public's interest in the stock market

22. The word "eclat" (line 23), as used in this selection, means

(A) fun-loving and luxury
(B) violence and force
(C) disrespect and resistance
(D) reason and logic
(E) spirit and enthusiasm

23. "I would write on the lintels of the doorpost, *Whim.*" By this, the author means

(A) that one should renounce his immediate family
(B) that signposts have an important educational function in our society
(C) that an impulsive action may have a subsequent rational explanation
(D) that one must never be held responsible for what one says and does
(E) that everyone should do foolish things occasionally

24. The statement that best sums up the spirit and sense of this selection is

(A) "Nothing is at last sacred but the integrity of your own mind."
(B) "With consistency a great soul has simply nothing to do."
(C) "Do not think the youth has no force, because he cannot speak to you and me."
(D) "The virtue in most request is conformity."
(E) "A man must know how to estimate a sour face."

STOP

If you finish before time is called, you may check your work on this section only. Do not turn to any other section in the test.

SECTION 8

Time: 20 Minutes—Turn to Section 8 (page 562) of your answer sheet to answer the questions in this section.
16 Questions

Directions: For this section, solve each problem and decide which is the best of the choices given. Fill in the corresponding circle on the answer sheet. You may use any available space for scratchwork.

Notes:

1. The use of a calculator is permitted.
2. All numbers used are real numbers.
3. Figures that accompany problems in this test are intended to provide information useful in solving the problems. They are drawn as accurately as possible EXCEPT when it is stated in a specific problem that the figure is not drawn to scale. All figures lie in a plane unless otherwise indicated.
4. Unless otherwise specified, the domain of any function f is assumed to be the set of all real numbers x for which $f(x)$ is a real number.

REFERENCE INFORMATION

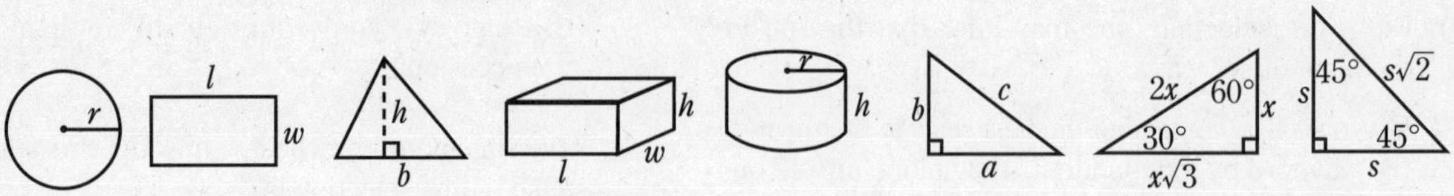

$A = \pi r^2$ $C = 2\pi r$ | $A = lw$ | $A = \frac{1}{2}bh$ | $V = lwh$ | $V = \pi r^2 h$ | $c^2 = a^2 + b^2$ | *Special Right Triangles*

The number of degrees of arc in a circle is 360.
The sum of the measures in degrees of the angles of a triangle is 180.

1. Tommy and Bobby like to watch their school's baseball team play. Tommy watched $\frac{2}{3}$ of all the games the team played last season. Bobby watched 28 games. If Tommy watched more games than Bobby did last season, which of the following could be the number of games the team played last season?

(A) 33
(B) 36
(C) 39
(D) 42
(E) 45

2. If 8 people share a winning lottery ticket and divide the cash prize equally, what percent of the prize do 2 of them together receive?

(A) 8%
(B) 10%
(C) 20%
(D) 25%
(E) 40%

GO ON TO THE NEXT PAGE

3. An athlete runs 90 laps in 6 hours. This is the same as how many laps per minute?

(A) $\frac{1}{15}$

(B) $\frac{1}{9}$

(C) $\frac{1}{4}$

(D) $\frac{1}{2}$

(E) 1

4. If $x = 16$, $x^{-\frac{3}{4}} =$

(A) $\frac{1}{2}$

(B) $\frac{1}{4}$

(C) $\frac{1}{8}$

(D) $\frac{1}{16}$

(E) $\frac{1}{32}$

5. Which of the following is a graph of $y = 2x - 4$?

(A)

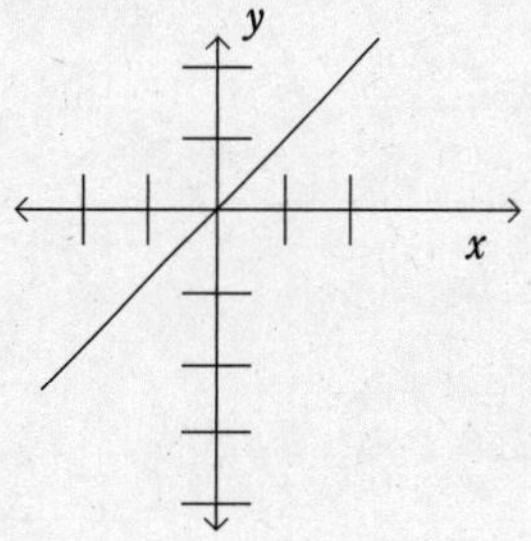

(B)

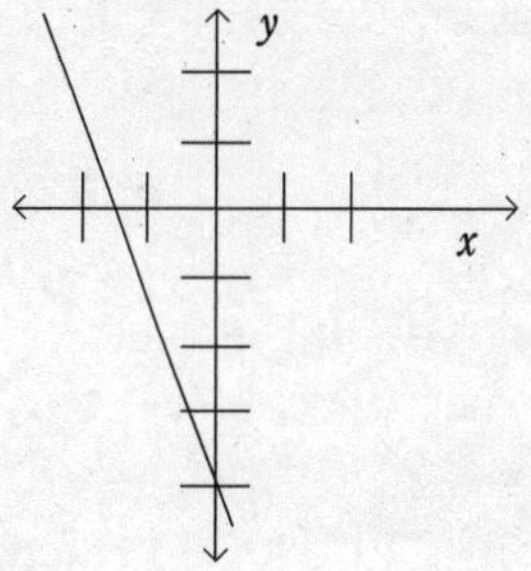

(C)

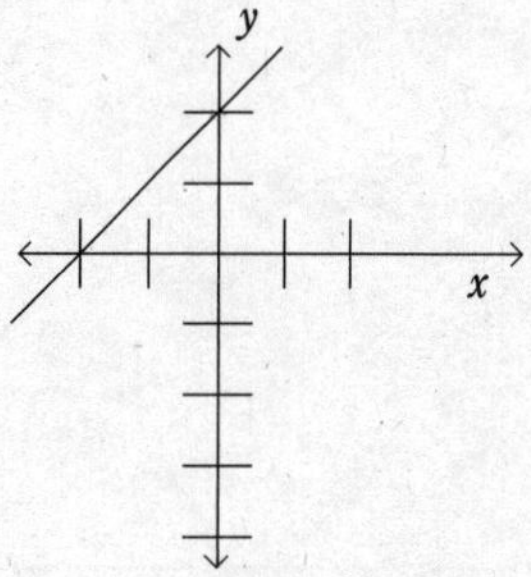

(D)

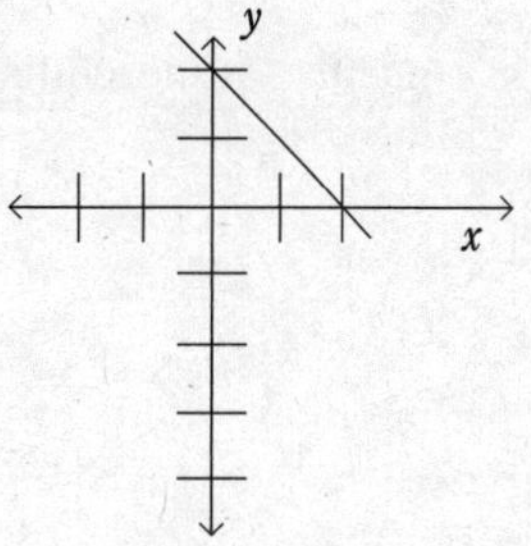

(E)

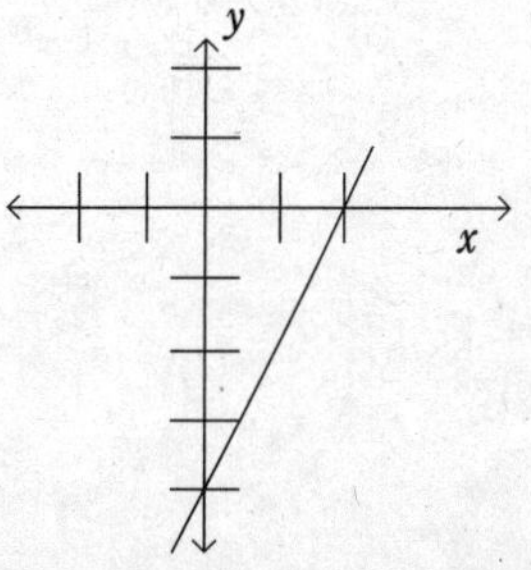

GO ON TO THE NEXT PAGE

6. $[(3a^3b^2)^3]^2 =$

(A) $27a^9b^6$
(B) $54a^9b^6$
(C) $729a^9b^6$
(D) $729a^{18}b^{12}$
(E) $729a^{54}b^{16}$

7. Given that $\left(\frac{3}{10}\right)^2$ is equal to p hundredths, find the value p.

(A) 5
(B) 6
(C) 9
(D) 12
(E) 32

8. Paul's average (arithmetic mean) for 3 tests was 85. The average of his scores for the first 2 tests was also 85. What was his score for the third test?

(A) 80
(B) 85
(C) 90
(D) 95
(E) It cannot be determined from the information given.

9. The operation ⊡ is defined for all numbers x and y by the following: $x \boxdot y = 3 + xy$. For example, $2 \boxdot 7 = 3 + 2(7) = 17$. If $y \neq 0$ and x is a number such that $x \boxdot y = 3$, then find x.

(A) 0
(B) $-\frac{3}{y}$
(C) $-y + 3$
(D) $\frac{3}{y}$
(E) $y + 3$

GO ON TO THE NEXT PAGE

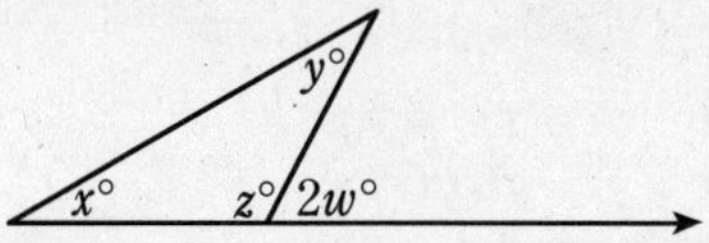

10. In the figure above, one side of a triangle has been extended. What is the value of $w + x + y$?

(A) $3w$
(B) $3z$
(C) $2x + y$
(D) $2x + 2y$
(E) $2w + z$

Questions 11–12 refer to the following game.

A computer generates numbers. Points are assigned as described in the following table each time any of the four number pairs given appears in a number.

Number Pair	Number of Points
"33"	11
"34"	6
"43"	4
"44"	3

11. As an example, the number 4,347 is assigned 4 points for "43" and 6 points more for "34," giving a total of 10 points. Which of the following numbers would be assigned the most points?

(A) 934,432
(B) 464,457
(C) 834,415
(D) 437,934
(E) 336,283

12. If a certain number has 13 points assigned to it, which of the following statements must be true?

I. 33 is not in the number.
II. 34 is in the number.
III. 43 is in the number.

(A) I only
(B) II only
(C) III only
(D) I and III only
(E) I, II, and III

13. The ratio of Sue's age to Bob's age is 3 to 7. The ratio of Sue's age to Joe's age is 4 to 9. The ratio of Bob's age to Joe's age is

(A) 28 to 27
(B) 7 to 9
(C) 27 to 28
(D) 10 to 13
(E) 13 to 10

GO ON TO THE NEXT PAGE

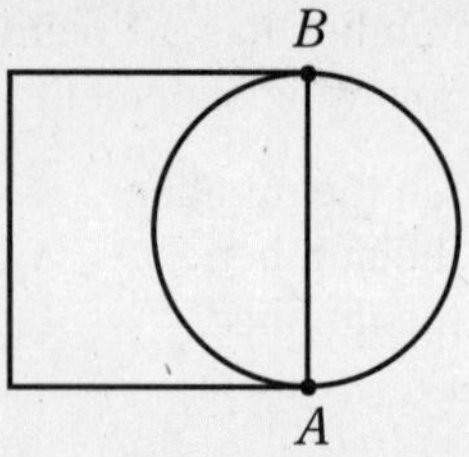

14. The square in the figure above has two sides tangent to the circle. If the area of the circle is $9a^2\pi^2$, find the area of the square in terms of a and π.

(A) $12a^2\pi^2$
(B) $36a^2\pi$
(C) $36a^2\pi^2$
(D) $18a^4\pi^2$
(E) $9a^4\pi^2$

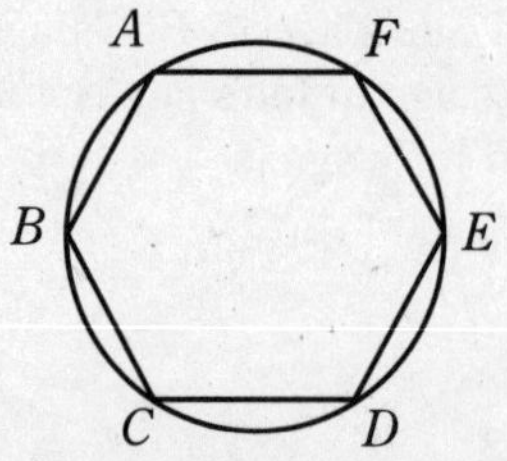

15. Equilateral polygon *ABCDEF* is inscribed in the circle. If the length of arc *BAF* is 14π, find the length of the diameter of the circle.

(A) 7
(B) 14
(C) 7π
(D) 21
(E) 42

16. If $f(x) = a^x$ then

(A) $f(x + y) = f(x) + f(y)$
(B) $f(x + y) = f(x)f(y)$
(C) $f(x - y) = f(x) - f(y)$
(D) $f(xy) = f(x)f(y)$
(E) $f\left(\frac{x}{y}\right) = \frac{f(x)}{f(y)}$

STOP

If you finish before time is called, you may check your work on this section only. Do not turn to any other section in the test.

SECTION 9

Time: 20 Minutes—Turn to Section 9 (page 562) of your answer sheet to answer the questions in this section.
19 Questions

Directions: For each question in this section, select the best answer from among the choices given and fill in the corresponding circle on the answer sheet.

Each sentence below has one or two blanks, each blank indicating that something has been omitted. Beneath the sentence are five words or sets of words labeled A through E. Choose the word or set of words that, when inserted in the sentence, best fits the meaning of the sentence as a whole.

Example:

Hoping to ______ the dispute, negotiators proposed a compromise that they felt would be ______ to both labor and management.

(A) enforce...useful
(B) end...divisive
(C) overcome...unattractive
(D) extend...satisfactory
(E) resolve...acceptable

Ⓐ Ⓑ Ⓒ Ⓓ ●

1. A sense of fairness ______ that the punishment should fit the crime; yet, in actual practice, judicial decisions ______ greatly for the same type of criminal offense.

(A) assumes...coincide
(B) relegates...deviate
(C) accumulates...simplify
(D) insists...compromise
(E) dictates...vary

2. The typist made no effort to be ______; she double-spaced the first and third letters, then single-spaced the second, fourth, and fifth letters.

(A) consistent
(B) prompt
(C) amicable
(D) courteous
(E) considerate

3. As an outstanding publisher, Alfred Knopf was able to make occasional ______, but his bad judgment was tolerated in view of his tremendous ______.

(A) appearances...energy
(B) mistakes...success
(C) remarks...connections
(D) enemies...audacity
(E) conferences...patience

4. Their married life was not ______ since it was fraught with bitter fighting and arguments.

(A) nubile
(B) tranquil
(C) obvious
(D) cogent
(E) imminent

5. Because of his ______ driving, the other car was forced to turn off the road or be hit.

(A) perceptive
(B) negligent
(C) resourceful
(D) placid
(E) exemplary

6. The ______ in the Bible are both entertaining and instructive.

(A) syllables
(B) abatements
(C) milestones
(D) parables
(E) utilities

GO ON TO THE NEXT PAGE

The two passages below are followed by questions based on their content and on the relationship between the two passages. Answer the questions on the basis of what is stated or implied in the passages and in any introductory material that may be provided.

Questions 7–19 are based on the following passages.

The following two passages describe different time periods. Passage 1 discusses the medieval time period; Passage 2 describes the present and speculates on the future.

Passage 1

To the world when it was half a thousand years younger, the outlines of all things seemed more clearly marked than to us. The contrast between suffering and joy, between adversity and happiness, appeared more striking. All experience had yet to the minds of men the directness and absoluteness of the pleasure and pain of child-life. Every event, every action, was still embodied in expressive and solemn forms, which raised them to the dignity of a ritual.

Misfortunes and poverty were more afflicting than at present; it was more difficult to guard against them, and to find solace. Illness and health presented a more striking contrast; the cold and darkness of winter were more real evils. Honors and riches were relished with greater avidity and contrasted more vividly with surrounding misery. We, at the present day, can hardly understand the keenness with which a fur coat, a good fire on the hearth, a soft bed, a glass of wine, were formerly enjoyed.

Then, again, all things in life were of a proud or cruel publicity. Lepers sounded their rattles and went about in processions, beggars exhibited their deformity and their misery in churches. Every order and estate, every rank and profession, was distinguished by its costume. The great lords never moved about without a glorious display of arms and liveries, exciting fear and envy. Executions and other public acts of justice, hawking, marriages and funerals, were all announced by cries and processions, songs and music. The lover wore the colors of his lady; companions the emblem of their brotherhood; parties and servants the badges of their lords. Between town and country, too, the contrast was very marked. A medieval town did not lose itself in extensive suburbs of factories and villas; girded by its walls, it stood forth as a compact whole, bristling with innumerable turrets. However tall and threatening the houses of noblemen or merchants might be, in the aspect of the town, the lofty mass of the churches always remained dominant.

The contrast between silence and sound, darkness and light, like that between summer and winter, was more strongly marked than it is in our lives. The modern town hardly knows silence or darkness in their purity, nor the effect of a solitary light or a single distant cry.

All things presenting themselves to the mind in violent contrasts and impressive forms lent a tone of excitement and passion to everyday life and tended to produce that perpetual oscillation between despair and distracted joy, between cruelty and pious tenderness which characterize life in the Middle Ages.

Passage 2

In 1575—over 400 years ago!—the French scholar Louis Le Roy published a learned book in which he voiced despair over the upheavals caused by the social and technological innovations of his time, what we now call the Renaissance. "All is pell-mell, confounded, nothing goes as it should." We, also, feel that our times are out of joint; we even have reason to believe that our descendants will be worse off than we are.

The earth will soon be overcrowded and its resources exhausted. Pollution will ruin the environment, upset the climate, damage human health. The gap in living standards between the rich and the poor will widen and lead the angry, hungry people of the world to acts of desperation including the use of nuclear weapons as blackmail. Such are the inevitable consequences of population and technological growth *if* present trends continue. But what a big *if* this is!

The future is never a projection of the past. Animals probably have no chance to escape from the tyranny of biological evolution, but human beings are blessed with the freedom of social evolution. For us, trend is not destiny. The escape from existing trends is now facilitated by the fact that societies anticipate future dangers and take preventive steps against expected upheavals.

Despite the widespread belief that the world has become too complex for comprehension by the human brain, modern societies have often responded effectively to critical situations.

The decrease in birthrates, the partial banning of pesticides, the rethinking of technologies for the production and use of energy are but a few examples illustrating a sudden reversal of trends caused not by political upsets or scientific breakthroughs, but by public awareness of consequences.

Even more striking are the situations in which social attitudes concerning future difficulties undergo rapid changes before the problems have come to pass—witness the heated controversies about the ethics of behavior control and of genetic engineering even though there is as yet no proof that effective methods can be developed to manipulate behavior and genes on a population scale.

One of the characteristics of our times is thus the rapidity with which steps can be taken to change the orientation of certain trends and even to reverse them. Such changes usually emerge from grassroots movements rather than from official directives.

GO ON TO THE NEXT PAGE

7. Conditions like those described in Passage 1 would most likely have occurred about

(A) A.D. 55
(B) A.D. 755
(C) A.D. 1055
(D) A.D. 1455
(E) A.D. 1755

8. The phrase "with greater avidity" in line 13 is best interpreted to mean with greater

(A) desire
(B) sadness
(C) terror
(D) silence
(E) disappointment

9. In Passage 1, all of the following are stated or implied about towns in the Middle Ages *except*

(A) Towns had no suburbs.
(B) Towns were always quite noisy.
(C) Towns served as places of defense.
(D) Towns always had large churches.
(E) Merchants lived in the towns.

10. The author's main purpose in Passage 1 is to

(A) describe the miseries of the period
(B) show how life was centered on the town
(C) emphasize the uncontrolled and violent course of life at the time
(D) point out how the upper classes mistreated the lower classes
(E) indicate how religious people were in those days

11. According to Passage 1, people at that time, as compared with people today, were

(A) worse off
(B) better off
(C) less intelligent
(D) more subdued
(E) more sensitive to certain events

12. In the first paragraph of Passage 2, the mood expressed is one of

(A) blatant despair
(B) guarded optimism
(C) poignant nostalgia
(D) muted pessimism
(E) unbridled idealism

13. According to Passage 2, if present trends continue, which one of the following situations will *not* occur?

(A) New sources of energy from vast coal deposits will be substituted for the soon-to-be-exhausted resources of oil and natural gas.
(B) The rich will become richer and the poor will become poorer.
(C) An overpopulated earth will be unable to sustain its inhabitants.
(D) Nuclear weapons will play a more prominent role in dealings among peoples.
(E) The ravages of pollution will render the earth and its atmosphere a menace to mankind.

14. Which of the following is the best illustration of the meaning of "trend is not destiny" in line 68?

(A) Urban agglomerations are in a state of crisis.
(B) Human beings are blessed with the freedom of social evolution.
(C) The world has become too complex for comprehension by the human brain.
(D) Critical processes can overshoot and cause catastrophes.
(E) The earth will soon be overcrowded and its resources exhausted.

15. According to Passage 2, evidences of the insight of the public into the dangers that surround us can be found in all of the following *except*

(A) an increase in the military budget by the president
(B) a declining birthrate
(C) picketing against expansion of nuclear plants
(D) opposition to the use of pesticides
(E) public meetings to complain about dumping chemicals

16. The author's attitude in Passage 2 is one of

(A) willing resignation
(B) definite optimism
(C) thinly veiled cynicism
(D) carefree abandon
(E) angry impatience

17. If there is a continuity in history, which of the following situations in Passage 1 is thought to lead to violence in the future of Passage 2?

(A) the overcrowding of the population
(B) the executions in public
(C) the contrast between the social classes
(D) the contrast between illness and health
(E) the contrast between religion and politics

GO ON TO THE NEXT PAGE

18. One can conclude from reading both passages that the difference between the people in Passage 1 and the people in Passage 2 is that

(A) the people in Passage 2 act on their awareness in contrast to the people in Passage 1
(B) the people in Passage 2 are more intense and colorful than the people in Passage 1
(C) there was no controversy between sociology and science in the society in Passage 2 in contrast to the society mentioned in Passage 1
(D) the people in Passage 1 are far more religious
(E) sociological changes were faster and more abrupt with the people of Passage 1

19. From a reading of both passages, one may conclude that

(A) people in both passages are equally subservient to authority
(B) the future is a mirror to the past
(C) the topic of biological evolution is of great importance to the scientists of both periods
(D) the evolution of science has created great differences in the social classes
(E) the people in Passage 1 are more involved in everyday living, whereas the people in Passage 2 are usually seeking change

STOP

If you finish before time is called, you may check your work on this section only. Do not turn to any other section in the test.

SECTION 10

Time: 10 Minutes—Turn to Section 10 (page 562) of your answer sheet to answer the questions in this section.
14 Questions

Directions: For each question in this section, select the best answer from among the choices given and fill in the corresponding circle on the answer sheet.

The following sentences test correctness and effectiveness of expression. Part of each sentence or the entire sentence is underlined; beneath each sentence are five ways of phrasing the underlined material. Choice A repeats the original phrasing; the other four choices are different. If you think the original phrasing produces a better sentence than any of the alternatives, select Choice A; if not, select one of the other choices.

In making your selection, follow the requirements of standard written English; that is, pay attention to grammar, choice of words, sentence construction, and punctuation. Your selection should result in the most effective sentence—clear and precise, without awkwardness or ambiguity.

EXAMPLE:

Laura Ingalls Wilder published her first book and she was sixty-five years old then.

(A) and she was sixty-five years old then
(B) when she was sixty-five
(C) at age sixty-five years old
(D) upon the reaching of sixty-five years
(E) at the time when she was sixty-five

Ⓐ ● Ⓒ Ⓓ Ⓔ

1. She prefers to write poems that describe the slums and study the habits of the underprivileged.

(A) study the habits of the underprivileged
(B) study the underprivileged's habits
(C) studying the habits of the underprivileged
(D) to study the habits of the underprivileged
(E) she prefers to study the habits of the underprivileged

2. By studying during weekends, her grades improved surprisingly.

(A) By studying during weekends, her grades improved surprisingly.
(B) By studying during weekends, she improved her grades surprisingly.
(C) She was surprised to find her grades improved after studying during weekends.
(D) Her grades, by studying during weekends, improved surprisingly.
(E) Surprisingly, by studying during weekends, her grades improved.

3. The streets here are as dirty as any other city, according to recent research studies.

(A) as dirty as any other city
(B) so dirty as any other city
(C) dirty like any other city
(D) as dirty as those of any other city
(E) as those of any city

4. Betty is good looking, with blue eyes, and has a pleasant manner.

(A) with blue eyes, and has a pleasant manner
(B) with eyes of blue, and a pleasant manner
(C) blue-eyed and pleasant
(D) blue eyes as well as pleasant
(E) and has blue eyes as well as a pleasant manner

5. Further acquaintance with the memoirs of Elizabeth Barrett Browning and Robert Browning enables us to appreciate the depth of influence that two people of talent can have on one another.

(A) of talent can have on one another
(B) of talent can exert on one another
(C) with talent can have one for the other
(D) of talent can have on each other
(E) who are talented can have

GO ON TO THE NEXT PAGE

6. If you saw the amount of pancakes he consumed at breakfast this morning, you would understand why he is so overweight.

(A) If you saw the amount of pancakes he consumed
(B) If you would see the amount of pancakes he consumed
(C) When you see the amount of pancakes he consumed
(D) If you saw the number of pancakes he consumed
(E) If you had seen the number of pancakes he consumed

7. The debutante went to the concert with her fiancé wearing a sheer blouse.

(A) The debutante went to the concert with her fiancé wearing a sheer blouse
(B) The debutante went to the concert, wearing a sheer blouse, with her fiancé
(C) The debutante, wearing a sheer blouse, went to the concert with her fiancé
(D) With her fiancé, wearing a sheer blouse, the debutante went to the concert
(E) To the concert, wearing a sheer blouse, went the debutante with her fiancé

8. Briefly the functions of a military staff are to advise the commander, transmit his instructions, and the supervision of the execution of his decisions.

(A) and the supervision of the execution of his decisions
(B) also the supervision of the execution of his decisions
(C) and supervising the execution of his decisions
(D) and supervise the execution of his decisions
(E) and have supervision of the execution of his decisions

9. The 15-round decision that Frazier was given over Ali was not popular with all of the boxing fans.

(A) The 15-round decision that Frazier was given over Ali
(B) Frazier's 15-round decision over Ali
(C) The Frazier 15-round decision over Ali
(D) The decision of 15 rounds that Frazier was given over Ali
(E) Ali's 15-round decision that Frazier was given over him

10. This test was as hard, if not harder than, the one I took last week.

(A) This test was as hard
(B) This test was so hard
(C) This test was as hard as
(D) This test was so hard as
(E) This was a test as hard

11. We took a plane from JFK Airport that carried few passengers.

(A) We took a plane from JFK Airport that carried few passengers
(B) The plane that was taken by us from JFK Airport carries few passengers
(C) The plane we took carried few passengers
(D) We took a plane that carried few passengers from JFK Airport
(E) The plane that we took from JFK Airport carried few passengers

12. I wanted to and would have gone to the play if I had the money.

(A) I wanted to and would have gone
(B) Having wanted to, I would have gone
(C) I wanted to go and would have gone
(D) Although I wanted to go and would have gone
(E) I wanted and would have gone

13. Either I'll go to the store today or tomorrow morning.

(A) Either I'll go to the store today or tomorrow morning
(B) Either I'll go to the store today or I'll go tomorrow morning
(C) I'll go to the store today, or if not today, then tomorrow morning
(D) I'll go to the store either today or tomorrow morning
(E) I'll go either today or tomorrow morning to the store

14. For a while he had a job after school, which caused his grades to suffer.

(A) which caused his grades to suffer
(B) and for this reason his grades were suffering
(C) and this condition caused his grades to suffer
(D) so his grades suffered as a result of this
(E) this was the reason his grades suffered

STOP

If you finish before time is called, you may check your work on this section only.
Do not turn to any other section in the test.

How Did You Do on This Test?

Step 1. Go to the Answer Key on pages 610–612.

Step 2. For your "raw score," calculate it using the directions on pages 613–614.

Step 3. Get your "scaled score" for the test by referring to the Raw Score/Scaled Score Conversion Tables on pages 615–617.

THERE'S ALWAYS ROOM FOR IMPROVEMENT!

Answer Key for Practice Test 1

Math

Section 2

	Correct Answer
1	D
2	B
3	D
4	E
5	B
6	E
7	C
8	A
9	C
10	B
11	B
12	E
13	B
14	D
15	C
16	C
17	C
18	A
19	B
20	C

20
Number correct

0
Number incorrect

Section 3

	Correct Answer
1	C
2	D
3	D
4	E
5	D
6	A
7	B
8	E
9	C
10	D
11	C
12	D
13	E
14	C
15	B
16	E
17	B
18	E
19	E
20	D

19
Number correct

1
Number incorrect

Section 6

	Correct Answer
1	D
2	E
3	D
4	D
5	E
6	B
7	B
8	D

8
Number correct

0
Number incorrect

Student-Produced Response Questions

9	7/24 or x where $.25 < x < .3333$
10	12
11	60
12	6
13	24
14	25
15	6
16	35
17	333
18	1/8 or .125

9
Number correct

1
Number incorrect

Section 8

	Correct Answer
1	E
2	D
3	C
4	C
5	E
6	D
7	C
8	B
9	A
10	A
11	A
12	D
13	A
14	B
15	E
16	B

14
Number correct

2
Number incorrect

Critical Reading and Writing

Critical Reading

Section 4

	Correct Answer
1	D
2	A
3	E
4	D
5	B
6	E
7	B
8	D
9	E
10	D
11	E
12	E
13	B
14	E
15	E
16	A
17	C
18	B
19	B
20	D
21	A
22	C
23	B
24	C

24
Number correct

0
Number incorrect

Section 7

	Correct Answer
1	E
2	A
3	A
4	B
5	D
6	B
7	A
8	A
9	D
10	A
11	D
12	E
13	E
14	C
15	D
16	C
17	A
18	D
19	B
20	B
21	C
22	E
23	C
24	A

24
Number correct

0
Number incorrect

Section 9

	Correct Answer
1	E
2	A
3	B
4	B
5	B
6	D
7	D
8	A
9	B
10	C
11	E
12	D
13	A
14	B
15	A
16	B
17	C
18	A
19	E

17
Number correct

2
Number incorrect

Writing

Section 1

____

Essay score

Section 5

	Correct Answer
1	A
2	A
3	D
4	D
5	C
6	C
7	B
8	E
9	D
10	D
11	A
12	B
13	D
14	A
15	E
16	C
17	B
18	D
19	C
20	D
21	B
22	A
23	A
24	E
25	E
26	A
27	A
28	D
29	B
30	B
31	D
32	D
33	A
34	B
35	C

32
____

Number correct

3
____

Number incorrect

Section 10

	Correct Answer
1	D
2	B
3	D
4	C
5	D
6	E
7	C
8	D
9	A
10	C
11	E
12	C
13	D
14	C

10
____

Number correct

4
____

Number incorrect

Scoring the SAT Practice Test

Check your responses with the correct answers on the previous pages. Fill in the blanks below and do the calculations to get your Math, Critical Reading, and Writing raw scores. Use the table to find your Math, Critical Reading, and Writing scaled scores.

Get Your Math Score

How many Math questions did you get **right**?

Section 2: Questions 1–20 ________

Section 6: Questions 1–18 + ________

Section 8: Questions 1–16 + ________

Total = ________ **(A)**

How many Math questions did you get **wrong**?

Section 2: Questions 1–20 ________

Section 6: Questions 1–8 + ________

Section 8: Questions 1–16 + ________

Total = ________

× 0.25 = ________ **(B)**

A – B = ________

Math Raw Score

Round Math raw score to the nearest whole number.

____

Use the Score Conversion Table to find your Math scaled score.

____

Get Your Critical Reading Score

How many Critical Reading questions did you get **right**?

Section 4: Questions 1–24 ________

Section 7: Questions 1–24 + ________

Section 9: Questions 1–19 + ________

Total = ________ **(A)**

How many Critical Reading questions did you get **wrong**?

Section 4: Questions 1–24 ________

Section 7: Questions 1–24 + ________

Section 9: Questions 1–19 + ________

Total = ________

× 0.25 = ________ **(B)**

A – B = ________

Critical Reading Raw Score

Round Critical Reading raw score to the nearest whole number.

____

Use the Score Conversion Table to find your Critical Reading scaled score.

____

Get Your Writing Score

How many multiple-choice Writing questions did you get **right**?

Section 5: Questions 1–35 ________

Section 10: Questions 1–14 + ________

Total = ________ **(A)**

How many multiple-choice Writing questions did you get **wrong**?

Section 5: Questions 1–35 ________

Section 10: Questions 1–14 + ________

Total = ________

× 0.25 = ________ **(B)**

A – B = ________

Writing Raw Score

Round Writing raw score to the nearest whole number.

____

Use the Score Conversion Table to find your Writing multiple-choice scaled score.

____

Estimate your Essay score using the Essay Scoring Guide.

____

Use the SAT Score Conversion Table for Writing Composite to find your Writing scaled score. You will need your Writing raw score and your Essay score to use this table.

____

SAT Score Conversion Table

Raw Score	Critical Reading Scaled Score	Math Scaled Score	Writing Multiple-Choice Scaled Score*	Raw Score	Critical Reading Scaled Score	Math Scaled Score	Writing Multiple-Choice Scaled Score*
67	800			31	510	550	60
66	800			30	510	540	58
65	790			29	500	530	57
64	770			28	490	520	56
63	750			27	490	520	55
62	740			26	480	510	54
61	730			25	480	500	53
60	720			24	470	490	52
59	700			23	460	480	51
58	690			22	460	480	50
57	690			21	450	470	49
56	680			20	440	460	48
55	670			19	440	450	47
54	660	800		18	430	450	46
53	650	790		17	420	440	45
52	650	760		16	420	430	44
51	640	740		15	410	420	44
50	630	720		14	400	410	43
49	620	710	80	13	400	410	42
48	620	700	80	12	390	400	41
47	610	680	80	11	380	390	40
46	600	670	79	10	370	380	39
45	600	660	78	9	360	370	38
44	590	650	76	8	350	360	38
43	590	640	74	7	340	350	37
42	580	630	73	6	330	340	36
41	570	630	71	5	320	330	35
40	570	620	70	4	310	320	34
39	560	610	69	3	300	310	32
38	550	600	67	2	280	290	31
37	550	590	66	1	270	280	30
36	540	580	65	0	250	260	28
35	540	580	64	–1	230	240	27
34	530	570	63	–2	210	220	25
33	520	560	62	–3	200	200	23
32	520	550	61	–4	200	200	20
				and below			

This table is for use only with the test in this book.

* The Writing multiple-choice score is reported on a 20–80 scale. Use the SAT Score Conversion Table for Writing Composite for the total writing scaled score.

SAT Score Conversion Table for Writing Composite

Writing Multiple-Choice Raw Score	Essay Raw Score 0	1	2	3	4	5	6
–12	200	200	200	210	240	270	300
–11	200	200	200	210	240	270	300
–10	200	200	200	210	240	270	300
–9	200	200	200	210	240	270	300
–8	200	200	200	210	240	270	300
–7	200	200	200	210	240	270	300
–6	200	200	200	210	240	270	300
–5	200	200	200	210	240	270	300
–4	200	200	200	230	270	300	330
–3	200	210	230	250	290	320	350
–2	200	230	250	280	310	340	370
–1	210	240	260	290	320	360	380
0	230	260	280	300	340	370	400
1	240	270	290	320	350	380	410
2	250	280	300	330	360	390	420
3	260	290	310	340	370	400	430
4	270	300	320	350	380	410	440
5	280	310	330	360	390	420	450
6	290	320	340	360	400	430	460
7	290	330	340	370	410	440	470
8	300	330	350	380	410	450	470
9	310	340	360	390	420	450	480
10	320	350	370	390	430	460	490
11	320	360	370	400	440	470	500
12	330	360	380	410	440	470	500
13	340	370	390	420	450	480	510
14	350	380	390	420	460	490	520
15	350	380	400	430	460	500	530
16	360	390	410	440	470	500	530
17	370	400	420	440	480	510	540
18	380	410	420	450	490	520	550
19	380	410	430	460	490	530	560
20	390	420	440	470	500	530	560
21	400	430	450	480	510	540	570
22	410	440	460	480	520	550	580
23	420	450	470	490	530	560	590
24	420	460	470	500	540	570	600
25	430	460	480	510	540	580	610

Writing Multiple-Choice Raw Score	Essay Raw Score						
	0	1	2	3	4	5	6
26	440	470	490	520	550	590	610
27	450	480	500	530	560	590	620
28	460	490	510	540	570	600	630
29	470	500	520	550	580	610	640
30	480	510	530	560	590	620	650
31	490	520	540	560	600	630	660
32	500	530	550	570	610	640	670
33	510	540	550	580	620	650	680
34	510	550	560	590	630	660	690
35	520	560	570	600	640	670	700
36	530	560	580	610	650	680	710
37	540	570	590	620	660	690	720
38	550	580	600	630	670	700	730
39	560	600	610	640	680	710	740
40	580	610	620	650	690	720	750
41	590	620	640	660	700	730	760
42	600	630	650	680	710	740	770
43	610	640	660	690	720	750	780
44	620	660	670	700	740	770	800
45	640	670	690	720	750	780	800
46	650	690	700	730	770	800	800
47	670	700	720	750	780	800	800
48	680	720	730	760	800	800	800
49	680	720	730	760	800	800	800

Chart for Self-Appraisal Based on the Practice Test You Have Just Taken

The Chart for Self-Appraisal below tells you quickly where your SAT strengths and weaknesses lie. Check or circle the appropriate box in accordance with the number of your correct answers for each area of the Practice Test you have just taken.

	Writing (Multiple-Choice)	*Sentence Completions*	*Reading Comprehension*	*Math Questions**
EXCELLENT	42–49	16–19	40–48	44–54
GOOD	37–41	13–15	35–39	32–43
FAIR	31–36	9–12	26–34	27–31
POOR	20–30	5–8	17–25	16–26
VERY POOR	0–19	0–4	0–16	0–15

* Sections 2, 6, 8 only.

Note: In our tests, we have chosen to have Section 3 as the experimental section. We have also chosen it to be a math section since we felt that students may need more practice in the math area than in the verbal area. Note that on the actual SAT you will take, the order of the sections can vary and you will not know which one is experimental, so it is wise to answer all sections and not to leave any section out.

SAT-I VERBAL AND MATH SCORE/PERCENTILE CONVERSION TABLE

Critical Reading and Writing

SAT scaled verbal score	Percentile rank
800	99.7+
790	99.5
740–780	99
700–730	97
670–690	95
640–660	91
610–630	85
580–600	77
550–570	68
510–540	57
480–500	46
440–470	32
410–430	21
380–400	13
340–370	6
300–330	2
230–290	1
200–220	0–0.5

Math

SAT scaled math score	Percentile rank
800	99.5+
770–790	99.5
720–760	99
670–710	97
640–660	94
610–630	89
590–600	84
560–580	77
530–550	68
510–520	59
480–500	48
450–470	37
430–440	26
390–420	16
350–380	8
310–340	2
210–300	0.5
200	0

Section 1—Essay

The following are guidelines for scoring the essay.

The SAT Scoring Guide

Score of 6	**Score of 5**	**Score of 4**
An essay in this category is *outstanding,* demonstrating *clear and consistent mastery,* although it may have a few minor errors. A typical essay	An essay in this category is *effective,* demonstrating *reasonably consistent mastery,* although it will have occasional errors or lapses in quality. A typical essay	An essay in this category is *competent,* demonstrating *adequate mastery,* although it will have lapses in quality. A typical essay
• effectively and insightfully develops a point of view on the issue and demonstrates outstanding critical thinking, using clearly appropriate examples, reasons, and other evidence to support its position	• effectively develops a point of view on the issue and demonstrates strong critical thinking, generally using appropriate examples, reasons, and other evidence to support its position	• develops a point of view on the issue and demonstrates competent critical thinking, using adequate examples, reasons, and other evidence to support its position
• is well organized and clearly focused, demonstrating clear coherence and smooth progression of ideas	• is well organized and focused, demonstrating coherence and progression of ideas	• is generally organized and focused, demonstrating some coherence and progression of ideas
• exhibits skillful use of language, using a varied, accurate, and apt vocabulary	• exhibits facility in the use of language, using appropriate vocabulary	• exhibits adequate but inconsistent facility in the use of language, using generally appropriate vocabulary
• demonstrates meaningful variety in sentence structure	• demonstrates variety in sentence structure	• demonstrates some variety in sentence structure
• is free of most errors in grammar, usage, and mechanics	• is generally free of most errors in grammar, usage, and mechanics	• has some errors in grammar, usage, and mechanics
Score of 3	**Score of 2**	**Score of 1**
An essay in this category is *inadequate,* but demonstrates *developing mastery,* and is marked by ONE OR MORE of the following weaknesses:	An essay in this category is *seriously limited,* demonstrating *little mastery,* and is flawed by ONE OR MORE of the following weaknesses:	An essay in this category is *fundamentally lacking,* demonstrating *very little* or *no mastery,* and is severely flawed by ONE OR MORE of the following weaknesses:
• develops a point of view on the issue, demonstrating some critical thinking, but may do so inconsistently or use inadequate examples, reasons, or other evidence to support its position	• develops a point of view on the issue that is vague or seriously limited, demonstrating weak critical thinking, providing inappropriate or insufficient examples, reasons, or other evidence to support its position	• develops no viable point of view on the issue, or provides little or no evidence to support its position
• is limited in its organization or focus, or may demonstrate some lapses in coherence or progression of ideas	• is poorly organized and/or focused, or demonstrates serious problems with coherence or progression of ideas	• is disorganized or unfocused, resulting in a disjointed or incoherent essay
• displays developing facility in the use of language, but sometimes uses weak vocabulary or inappropriate word choice	• displays very little facility in the use of language, using very limited vocabulary or incorrect word choice	• displays fundamental errors in vocabulary
• lacks variety or demonstrates problems in sentence structure	• demonstrates frequent problems in sentence structure	• demonstrates severe flaws in sentence structure
• contains an accumulation of errors in grammar, usage, and mechanics	• contains errors in grammar, usage, and mechanics so serious that meaning is somewhat obscured	• contains pervasive errors in grammar, usage, or mechanics that persistently interfere with meaning

Essays not written on the essay assignment will receive a score of zero.

Explanatory Answers for Practice Test 1

Section 2: Math

As you read these solutions, you are advised to do two things if you answered the Math question incorrectly:

1. When a specific Math Strategy is referred to in the solution, study that strategy, which you will find in "19 Math Strategies" (beginning on page 69).
2. When the solution directs you to the "Complete Math Refresher" (beginning on page 167)—for example, Math Refresher 305—study the 305 Math principle to get a clear idea of the Math operation that was necessary for you to know in order to answer the question correctly.

1. Choice D is correct.

Given: $ab = 64$ and a and b are positive integers [1]

(Use Strategy 7: Use numerics to help find the answer.)

If $a = 64$, $b = 1$, then [1] is satisfied and $a + b = 65$ [2]

If $a = 32$, $b = 2$, then [1] is satisfied and $a + b = 34$ [3]

If $a = 16$, $b = 4$, then [1] is satisfied and $a + b = 20$ [4]

If $a = 8$, $b = 8$, then [1] is satisfied and $a + b = 16$ [5]

The only other pairs of values that satisfy [1] are each of the above pairs of values reversed for a and b. Thus [5], $a + b = 16$, is the smallest value of $a + b$.

(Math Refresher #406)

2. Choice B is correct.

Given: $x + x^3 + x^5 + x^6$ [1]

$x = -1$ [2]

Substitute [2] into [1]. We get

$$-1 + (-1)^3 + (-1)^5 + (-1)^6 = -1 - 1 - 1 + 1 = -2$$

(Math Refresher #431 and #429)

3. Choice D is correct.

Given:

$$\begin{array}{r} AB \\ +\ BA \\ \hline 66 \end{array}$$

$0 < A < 6$ [1]

$0 < B < 6$ [2]

[3]

(Use Strategy 17: Use the given information effectively.) From [3] we see that

$B + A = 6$ [4]

(Use Strategy 7: Use numerics to help find the answer.) Conditions [1], [2], and [4] can be satisfied when:

$A = 1, B = 5$
$A = 2, B = 4$
$A = 3, B = 3$
$A = 4, B = 2$
$A = 5, B = 1$

Thus, there are five possible values of A.

(Math Refresher #431)

4. Choice E is correct.

Given: Temperature at 11:00 A.M. = 0°F [1]
Temperature at 8:00 A.M. = −15°F [2]
Let x = Temperature at 5:00 P.M. [3]
y = Temperature rise [4]

(Use Strategy 13: Find unknowns by subtracting.) Subtract [2] from [1]. We get

Temperature rise in 3 hours = 15°F [5]

Subtract the times in [1] and [3]. We get

Time change = 6 hours [6]

Use [4], [5], and [6] to find temperature rise from 11:00 A.M. to 5:00 P.M. We get

$$\frac{3 \text{ hours}}{6 \text{ hours}} = \frac{15°\text{F}}{y}$$
$$3y = 6 \times 15°\text{F}$$
$$y = 30°\text{F}$$

Use [1], [3], and [7] to find the final temperature.

$$x = 0°\text{F} + 30°\text{F}$$
$$x = 30°\text{F}$$

(Math Refresher #120)

5. Choice B is correct

Number of Shirts	Total Price
1	$12.00
Box of 3	$22.50
Box of 6	$43.40

From the chart above, we know

6 shirts = $43.40 [1]

(Use Strategy 13: Find unknowns by division.) Dividing [1] by 6, we get

$$\frac{6 \text{ shirts}}{6} = \frac{\$43.40}{6}$$
$$1 \text{ shirt} = \$7.23\bar{3}$$
$$\text{Cost per shirt} \approx \$7.20$$

(Math Refresher #406)

6. Choice E is correct.

Given: $5x^2 - 15x = 0$ [1]
$x \neq 0$ [2]

(Use Strategy 12: Try not to make tedious calculations.)

Factoring [1], we get

$$5x(x - 3) = 0$$
$$5x = 0 \text{ or } x - 3 = 0$$
$$x = 0 \text{ or } x = 3$$ [3]

Applying [2] to [3], we get

$$x = 3$$

(Math Refresher #409)

7. Choice C is correct. **(Use Strategy 2: Translate words to algebra.)** In $\frac{1}{2}$ year, 600 pounds of feed were used at a rate of $1.25 per pound. Thus (600 pounds) × ($1.25 per pound), or $750, was spent. Hence,

$$\text{Feed cost per egg} = \frac{\text{Total cost for feed}}{\text{number of eggs}}$$
$$= \frac{\$750}{5{,}000 \text{ eggs}}$$

(Use Strategy 19: Factor and reduce.)

$$= \frac{\$75 \times 10}{500 \times 10 \text{ eggs}}$$
$$= \frac{\$25 \times 3}{25 \times 20 \text{ eggs}}$$
$$= \frac{\$3}{20} \text{ per egg}$$
$$= \$0.15 \text{ per egg}$$

(Math Refresher #200)

8. Choice A is correct. The union of X and Y and 0 is the set of all the elements of X and Y and 0. The elements of all *negative*, *0*, and *positive* numbers is the set of all *real* numbers.

(Math Refresher #802)

9. Choice C is correct. **(Use Strategy 2: Translate from words to algebra.)**

Given: Area B = 1 [1]
Area A = 3(Area B) [2]
Area B = 3(Area C) [3]

Substitute [1] into [2]. We get

Area A = 3(1) = 3 [4]

Substitute [1] into [3]. We get

$$1 = 3(\text{Area C})$$
$$\frac{1}{3} = \text{Area C}$$ [5]

Using [1], [4], and [5], we have

Sum of areas A, B, and C = $3 + 1 + \frac{1}{3}$

Sum of areas A, B, and C = $4\frac{1}{3}$

(Math Refresher #200)

10. Choice B is correct.

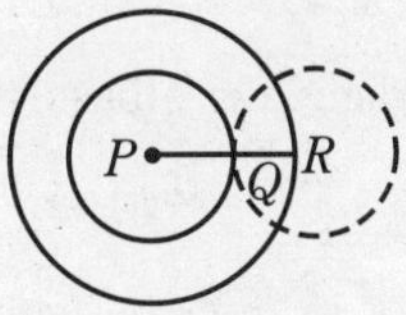

Given: $PQR = 9$ [1]
$PQ = 4$ [2]

(Use Strategy 3: The whole equals the sum of its parts.) From the diagram, we see that

$$PQR = PQ + QR \quad [3]$$

Substitute [1] and [2] into [3]. We get

$$9 = 4 + QR$$
$$5 = QR$$

QR is the radius of a circle with center R and Q on its circumference. (See dotted circle in diagram.)

(Math Refresher #524)

11. Choice B is correct. $y = f(x)$ is positive or 0 for all x, so only Choices B and C are appropriate. Since $y = f(x)$ represents straight lines, then Choice B is appropriate, while Choice C is eliminated.

(Math Refresher #616 and #615)

12. Choice E is correct.

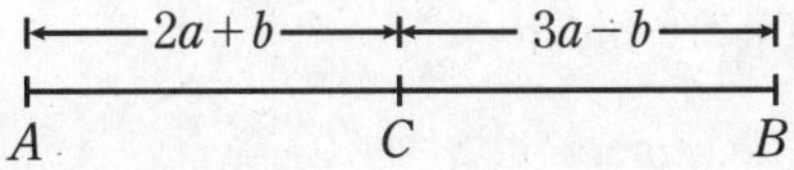

Given: C is the midpoint of AB
Thus, $AC = CB$ [1]
Substituting the lengths from the diagram into [1], we have

$$2a + b = 3a - b$$
$$b = a - b$$
$$2b = a$$

(Math Refresher #406)

13. Choice B is correct. **(Use Strategy 17: Use the given information effectively.)** Slope is defined as $\frac{y_2 - y_1}{x_2 - x_1}$ where (x_1, y_1) is a point on the line and (x_2, y_2) is another point on the line. We are given that one point is $(0, p)$ and the other point is $(3p, 0)$ so,

$$\frac{y_2 - y_1}{x_2 - x_1} = \frac{p - 0}{0 - 3p} = \frac{p}{-3p} = -\frac{1}{3}$$

(Math Refresher #416)

14. Choice D is correct.

Given: Bus A averages $\frac{40 \text{ km}}{\text{gallon}}$ [1]

Bus B averages $\frac{50 \text{ km}}{\text{gallon}}$ [2]

Trip distance = 800 km [3]

Fuel cost = $\frac{\$3}{\text{gallon}}$ [4]

(Use strategy 10: Know how to use units.)

Divide [3] by [1]. We get

$$\frac{800 \text{ km}}{40 \text{ km/gallon}} = \frac{800}{40} \text{ gallons} = \text{20 gallons used by Bus A} \quad [5]$$

Divide [3] by [2]. We get

$$\frac{800 \text{ km}}{50 \text{ km/gallon}} = \frac{800 \text{ gallons}}{50} = \text{16 gallons used by Bus B} \quad [6]$$

Multiply [5] by [4]. We get

$$\text{20 gallons} \times \frac{\$3}{\text{gallon}} = \text{\$60 cost for fuel for Bus A} \quad [7]$$

Multiply [6] by [4]. We get

$$\text{16 gallons} \times \frac{\$3}{\text{gallon}} = \text{\$48 cost for fuel for Bus B} \quad [8]$$

(Use Strategy 13: Find unknowns by subtracting.)

Subtract [8] from [7]. We get $60 − $48 = $12 difference in the fuel costs between Bus A and Bus B for an 800 km trip.

(Math Refresher #202)

15. Choice C is correct.

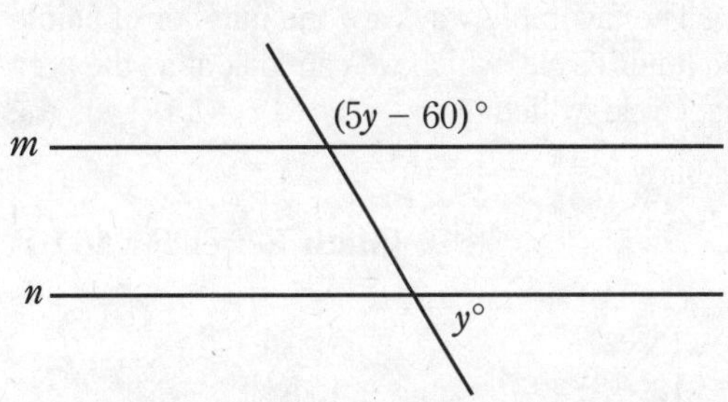

(Use Strategy 17: Use the given information effectively.)

Given: $m \| n$ [1]

From [1] we know that the two angles are supplementary. Thus,

$$(5y - 60)° + y° = 180°$$
$$6y - 60 = 180°$$
$$6y = 240°$$
$$y = 40°$$

(Math Refresher #504)

16. Choice C is correct. **(Use Strategy 2: Translate from words to algebra.)**

We have: $\frac{4}{100} \times (2a + b) = 18$ $\boxed{1}$

(Use Strategy 13: Find unknowns by multiplication.) Multiply $\boxed{1}$ by $\frac{100}{4}$. We get

$$\frac{100}{4}\left(\frac{4}{100} \times (2a+b)\right) = \frac{100}{4}(18)$$

(Use Strategy 19: Factor and reduce.)

$$2a + b = \frac{\cancel{4} \times 25}{\cancel{4}}(18)$$

$$2a + b = 450$$

$$b = 450 - 2a \qquad \boxed{2}$$

(Use Strategy 17: Use the given information effectively.)

b will be greatest when a is smallest. $\boxed{3}$
Given: a is a positive integer $\boxed{4}$

Applying $\boxed{4}$ to $\boxed{3}$, we get

$$a = 1 \qquad \boxed{5}$$

Substituting $\boxed{5}$ into $\boxed{2}$, we have

$$b = 450 - 2(1)$$
$$= 450 - 2$$
$$b = 448$$

(Math Refresher #406)

17. Choice C is correct. **(Use Strategy 17: Use the given information effectively.)** The probability is the number of favorable ways divided by the number of total ways. The total ways is the number of points in the large circle of radius 2 feet. We can look at that as the area of the large circle, which is $\pi r^2 = 2 \times 2\pi = 4\pi$. The favorable ways are the number of points in the inner circle, which we can look at as the area of that circle, which is $\pi r^2 = 1 \times 1\pi = 1\pi$. Thus the probability is $\frac{1\pi}{4\pi} = \frac{1}{4}$.

(Math Refresher #614)

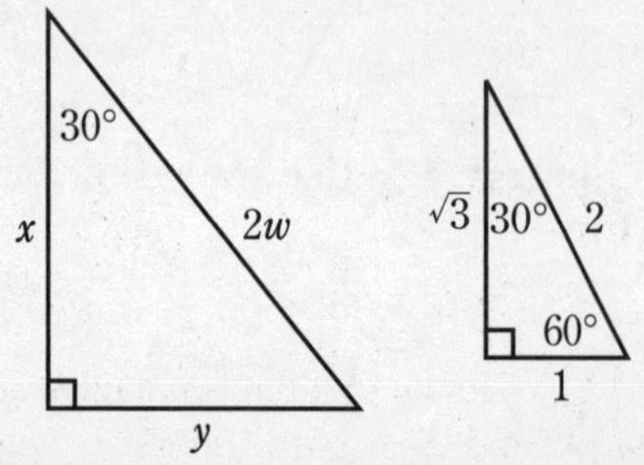

18. Choice A is correct. **(Use Strategy 18: Remember special right triangles.)** The triangle at left (given) is similar to the triangle at right, which is one of the standard triangles.

Corresponding sides of similar triangles are proportional. Thus,

$$\frac{\cancel{2}w}{\cancel{2}} = \frac{y}{1} \text{ and } \frac{\cancel{2}w}{\cancel{2}} = \frac{x}{\sqrt{3}}$$

or $\quad y = w$ and $x = w\sqrt{3}$

$$\text{Area of triangle} = \frac{1}{2}(\text{base})(\text{height})$$
$$= \frac{1}{2}(y)(x)$$
$$= \frac{1}{2}(w)(w\sqrt{3})$$
$$\text{Area of triangle} = \frac{\sqrt{3}}{2}w^2 \qquad \boxed{1}$$
$$\text{Area of rectangle} = (3w)(w) = 3w^2 \qquad \boxed{2}$$

Using $\boxed{1}$ and $\boxed{2}$, we have

$$\frac{\text{area of rectangle}}{\text{area of triangle}} = \frac{3\cancel{w^2}}{\frac{\sqrt{3}}{2}\cancel{w^2}}$$
$$= \frac{3}{\frac{\sqrt{3}}{2}} = 3 \times \frac{2}{\sqrt{3}}$$
$$= \frac{6}{\sqrt{3}} = \frac{6\sqrt{3}}{3} = 2\sqrt{3}$$

or $2\sqrt{3} : 1$ (*Answer*)

(Math Refresher #510, #509, #306, and #304)

19. Choice B is correct.
(Use Strategy 2: Translate from words to algebra.)

Let f = Number of freshmen
s = Number of seniors

We are given $f = 3s$ $\boxed{1}$
$\frac{1}{4}$ of the freshmen $= \frac{1}{4}f$ $\boxed{2}$
$\frac{1}{3}$ of the seniors $= \frac{1}{3}s$ $\boxed{3}$
Total number of freshmen and seniors $= f + s$ $\boxed{4}$

(Use Strategy 17: Use the given information effectively.)

The desired fraction uses $\boxed{2}$, $\boxed{3}$, and $\boxed{4}$ as follows:

$$\frac{\frac{1}{4}f + \frac{1}{3}s}{f+s} \qquad \boxed{5}$$

Substituting $\boxed{1}$ in $\boxed{5}$, we get

$$\frac{\left(\frac{1}{4}(3s) + \frac{1}{3}s\right)}{3s + s} = \frac{\left(\frac{3}{4}s + \frac{1}{3}s\right)}{4s} \qquad \boxed{6}$$

Multiplying $\boxed{6}$, numerator and denominator, by 12, we get:

$$\left(\frac{12}{12}\right)\frac{\frac{3}{4}s+\frac{1}{3}s}{4s} =$$

$$\frac{9s+4s}{48s} =$$

$$\frac{13\not{s}}{48\not{s}} =$$

$$\frac{13}{48} \qquad \textit{(Answer)}$$

(Math Refresher #200 and #402)

20. Choice C is correct.
(Use Strategy 2: Translate from words to algebra.) Set up a Venn diagram:

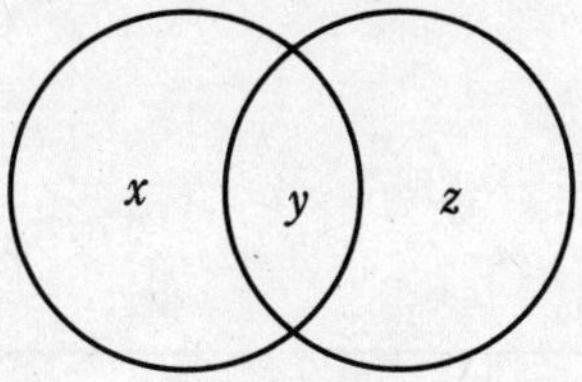

x = number of students with *only* a car
z = number of students with *only* a bicycle
y = number of students having a car and a bicycle

Total students $= 100$ $\boxed{1}$
We are given: $x + y = 30$ $\boxed{2}$
$z + y = 50$ $\boxed{3}$
$y = 20$ $\boxed{4}$

Substituting $\boxed{4}$ into $\boxed{2}$ and into $\boxed{3}$, we get

$x = 10, z = 30$ $\boxed{5}$

Using $\boxed{4}$ and $\boxed{5}$, we have:

The sum of $x + y + z =$
$10 + 20 + 30 = 60$ $\boxed{6}$

This is the number of students who have either a car, a bicycle, or both.

Using $\boxed{1}$ and $\boxed{6}$, we get $100 - 60 = 40$ as the number who have neither a car nor a bicycle.

(Math Refresher #200 and #406)

Explanatory Answers for Practice Test 1 (continued)

Section 3: Math

As you read these solutions, you are advised to do two things if you answered the Math question incorrectly:

1. When a specific Math Strategy is referred to in the solution, study that strategy, which you will find in "19 Math Strategies" (beginning on page 69).
2. When the solution directs you to the "Complete Math Refresher" (beginning on page 167)—for example, Math Refresher 305—study the 305 Math principle to get a clear idea of the Math operation that was necessary for you to know in order to answer the question correctly.

1. Choice C is correct. **(Use Strategy 17: Use the given information effectively.)**

Given: $55{,}555 = y + 50{,}505$
$5{,}050 = y$ [1]

We need: $50{,}505 - 10y$ [2]

Substitute [1] into [2]. We get
$50{,}505 - 10(5{,}050) =$
$50{,}505 - 50{,}500 =$
5

(Math Refresher #406)

2. Choice D is correct. Using the distributive property, we get $3x(4x + 2y) = 12x^2 + 6xy$

(Math Refresher #409)

3. Choice D is correct. **(Use Strategy 17: Use the given information effectively.)**

We are told that 1 decimeter = 100 millimeters. Therefore, 20 decimeters = 2,000 millimeters. E, C, and B are greater than 2,000 millimeters.

(Math Refresher #121)

4. Choice E is correct.

Given: $a - 3 = 7$ [1]

(Use Strategy 13: Find unknowns by addition, subtraction, and multiplication.)

Fast Method: From [1], we can subtract 7 from both sides, and then add 3 to both sides to get

$$a - 7 = 3$$ [2]

Multiplying [2] by 2, we get

$$2a - 14 = 6$$ *(Answer)*

Slow Method: Solve [1] to get

$$a = 10$$ [3]

Now substitute [3]:

$$2a - 14 = 2(10) - 14 = 6$$ *(Answer)*

(Math Refresher #406 and #431)

5. Choice D is correct.

(Use Strategy 17: Use the given information effectively.)

Change all fractions to decimal form:

$$\frac{7}{10} = 0.7$$

$$\frac{7}{100} = 0.07$$

$$\frac{77}{1{,}000} = 0.077$$

Adding these, we get 0.847 *(Answer)*

(Math Refresher #104)

6. Choice A is correct.

(Use Strategy 14: Label unknown quantities to help solve the problem.)

Know the properties of parallel lines. If 2 parallel lines are crossed by a transversal, the pairs of corresponding angles are equal. Thus,

$$x = a$$ [1]

From the diagram, $a + y = 180$ [2]

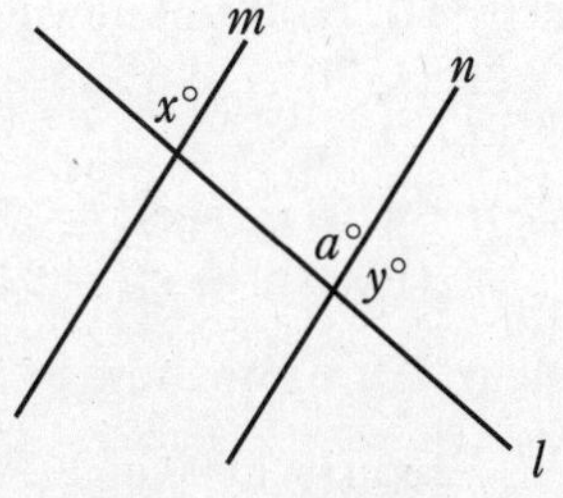

Substituting [1] into [2], we get

$$x + y = 180$$ *(Answer)*

(Math Refresher #504)

7. Choice B is correct.

(Use Strategy 7: Use numerics to help find the answer.)

12 must be substituted for P in each of the five expressions and the results evaluated.

Item 1:	$P = 12$	12
Item 2:	$P \times 3 = 12 \times 3 =$	36
Item 3:	$(P \times 3) \div 2 = (12 \times 3) \div 2 =$	18
Item 4:	$[(P \times 3) \div 2] + 12 =$	
	$[(12 \times 3) \div 2] + 12 =$	30
Item 5:	$[(P \times 3) \div 2] + 12 - 1 =$	
	$[(12 \times 3) \div 2] + 12 - 1 =$	29

Item 2 is greatest in value.

(Math Refresher #431)

8. Choice E is correct.

Given: $\frac{3x}{4} = 9$ [1]

(Use Strategy 13: Find unknowns by multiplication.)

Multiplying [1] by 4, we get

$$\cancel{4}\left(\frac{3x}{\cancel{4}}\right) = (9)4$$

$$3x = 36$$ [2]

Multiply [2] by 2. We have

$$2(3x) = 2(36)$$
$$6x = 72$$

(Math Refresher #406)

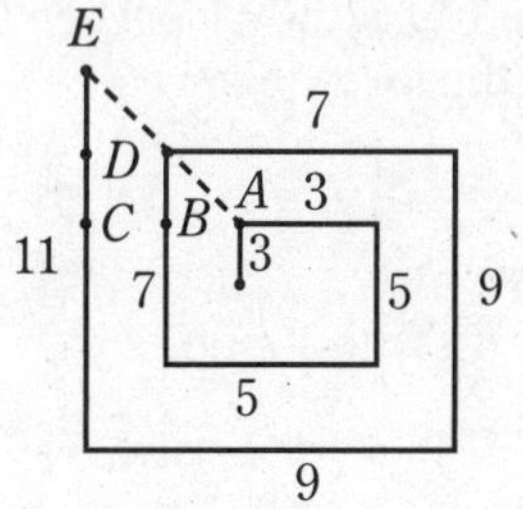

9. Choice C is correct.

From the diagram we find that

$$AB = 2$$ [1]
$$BC = 2$$ [2]
$$CD = 2$$ [3]
$$DE = 2$$ [4]

(Use Strategy 3: The whole equals the sum of its parts.)

We know $AB + BC = AC$ [5]

Substituting [1] and [2] into [5], we get

$$2 + 2 = AC$$
$$4 = AC$$ [6]

We know $CD + DE = CE$. [7]

Substituting [3] and [4] into [7], we get

$$2 + 2 = CE$$
$$4 = CE \qquad [8]$$

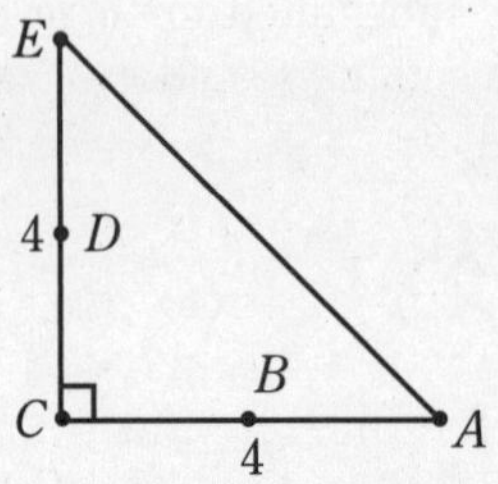

Filling [6] and [8] into the diagram and using the fact that all the segments drawn were perpendicular, we have ΔECA is an isosceles right triangle.

(Use Strategy 18: Know and use facts about triangles.)

In the isosceles right triangle, the

$$\text{hypotenuse} = \text{leg}(\sqrt{2}) \qquad [9]$$

Substituting [6] or [8] into [9], we get

$$EA = 4\sqrt{2} \qquad [6]$$

(Math Refresher #507 and #509)

10. Choice D is correct.

(Use Strategy 11: Use new definitions carefully.)

Two-digit numbers which have a units digit = 0 that can be tripled in value when the tens digit is tripled are the following:

Original number	*Tripled tens digit number*
10	30
20	60
30	90

The above numbers are the only numbers that result in a two-digit number as defined in the problem. Thus, 3 is the correct answer.

This problem can also be solved using a more sophisticated method.

Call the number $10t + u$ (where t is the tens digit and u is the units digit).

(Use Strategy 2: Translate Words to Math)

In the number $10t + u$, tripling the tens digit gives us the number $10(3t) + u$.

A two-digit number that is triple the original number translates to $3(10t + u)$.

Setting these quantities equal, we get:

$$10(3t) + u = 3(10t + u) \qquad [1]$$
$$30t + u = 30t + 3u$$
$$u = 3u$$

Therefore $u = 0$.

So the number $10t + u = 10t$, where $t = 1, 2,$ or 3 (three numbers). t can't be more than 3 because [1] would not give us a two-digit number.

(Math Refresher #406)

11. Choice C is correct.

(Use Strategy 11: Use new definitions carefully.)

By definition, $A = 12{,}345$ [1]
$B = 98{,}765$ [2]

(Use Strategy 13: Find unknowns by subtracting.)

Subtracting [1] from [2], we get

$$B - A = 98{,}765 - 12{,}345$$
$$B - A = 86{,}420$$

(Math Refresher #405a)

12. Choice D is correct.

Given:

Meteor 1 travels at 300 meters/second [1]
Meteor 2 travels at 700 meters/second [2]

Draw a diagram:

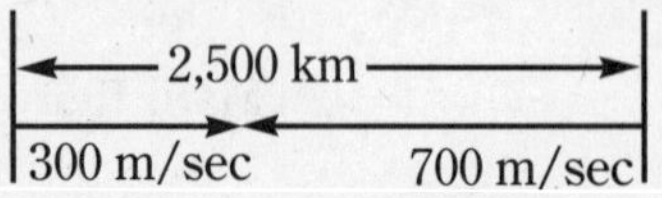

Let t be the time it takes meteors to meet. Call x the distance Meteor 1 travels. Then $2{,}500 - x$ is the distance Meteor 2 travels.

(Use Strategy 9: Know Rate, Time, and Distance relationships.)

$$\text{Rate} \times \text{Time} = \text{Distance}$$
$$300 \text{ m/sec} \times t = x \qquad [3]$$
$$700 \text{ m/sec} \times t = 2500 - x \qquad [4]$$

(Use Strategy 13: Find unknowns by addition.)

Add [3] and [4]

$$(300 \text{ m/sec})t + (700 \text{ m/sec})t = 2{,}500 \text{ km}$$
$$(1{,}000 \text{ m/sec})t = 2{,}500 \text{ km} \qquad [5]$$

(Use Strategy 10: Know how to use units.)

$$1 \text{ km} = 1{,}000 \text{ m} \qquad [6]$$

Substitute [6] in [5]:

$$(1{,}000 \text{ m/sec})t = 2{,}500(1{,}000) \text{ m} \qquad [7]$$

Divide [7] by 1,000 m:

$$t/\text{sec} = 2{,}500$$
$$t = 2{,}500 \text{ sec}$$

(Math Refresher #121, #201, and #202)

13. Choice E is correct.

(Use Strategy 17: Use the given information effectively.)

The center point inside a cube is the midpoint of an inner diagonal of the cube. Thus, the distance from any vertex to this center point is $\frac{1}{2}$ the length of the inner diagonal.
We know length of inner diagonal of a cube

$$= \sqrt{(edge)^2 + (edge)^2 + (edge)^2}$$

inner diagonal $= \sqrt{3(\text{edge})^2}$ [1]

inner diagonal $= \text{edge}\sqrt{3}$ [2]

Given: Volume = 8 cubic meters [3]

We know volume of a cube $= (\text{edge})^3$ [4]

Substituting [3] into [4], we get

$$8 \text{ cubic meters} = (\text{edge})^3$$
$$\sqrt[3]{8 \text{ cubic meters}} = \sqrt[3]{(\text{edge})^3}$$
$$2 \text{ meters} = \text{edge} \quad [5]$$

Substituting [5] into [2], we get
inner diagonal $= 2\sqrt{3}$ meters [6]

Using [1] and [6], we find

$$\text{distance we need} = \frac{1}{2}(\text{inner diagonal})$$
$$= \frac{1}{\not 2}(\not 2\sqrt{3} \text{ meters})$$
$$= \sqrt{3} \text{ meters}$$

Distance we need $= \sqrt{3}$ m

(Math Refresher #313, #429, #430, and #406)

14. Choice C is correct.

(Use Strategy 2: Translate from words to algebra.)

Let a = a positive integer
Then $a + 1$, $a + 2$, $a + 3$, $a + 4$, etc., are the next positive integers.

(Use Strategy 13: Find unknowns by addition.)

Add the first 2 positive integers. We get
Sum of first 2 positive integers =

$$a + a + 1 = 2a + 1 \quad [1]$$

[1] is not divisible by 2.

Now add the third positive integer, $a + 2$, to [1].

We get

Sum of first 3 positive integers =

$$2a + 1 + a + 2 = 3a + 3 \quad [2]$$

[2] is not divisible by 2.

Now add the fourth positive integer, $a + 3$, to [2].

We have

Sum of first 4 positive integers
$$= 3a + 3 + a + 3$$
$$= 4a + 6 \quad [3]$$

Since [3] can be written as $2(2a + 3)$, it is divisible by 2.

Thus, if the number of integers is a multiple of 4, the sum of the consecutive positive integers will be divisible by 2.

(Math Refresher #200 and #607)

15. Choice B is correct. **(Use Strategy 2: Translate from words to algebra.)**

Given: Square has perimeter 2π [1]
Let S = side of square.
We know perimeter of a square $= 4S$ [2]

Substitute [1] into [2]. We get

$$\text{Perimeter of square} = 4S$$
$$2\pi = 4S$$
$$\frac{2\pi}{4} = S$$
$$\frac{\pi}{2} = S \quad [3]$$

We are given that:
area of circle = area of square [4]
We know that:
area of circle $= \pi r^2$ [5]
area of square $= S^2$ [6]

Substituting [5] and [6] into [4], we get

$$\pi r^2 = S^2 \quad [7]$$

Substitute [3] into [7]. We get

$$\pi r^2 = \left(\frac{\pi}{2}\right)^2$$
$$\pi r^2 = \frac{\pi^2}{4}$$
$$r^2 = \frac{\pi^2}{4\pi}$$
$$r^2 = \frac{\pi}{4}$$
$$r = \sqrt{\frac{\pi}{4}} = \frac{\sqrt{\pi}}{2} \quad [8]$$

We know the circumference of a circle $= 2\pi r$ [9]

Substitute [8] into [9]. We have

$$\text{Circumference} = \not 2\pi\left(\frac{\sqrt{\pi}}{\not 2}\right)$$

$$\text{Circumference} = \pi\sqrt{\pi}$$

(Math Refresher #303 and #310)

16. Choice E is correct.

$$Given: \frac{a}{b} = \frac{1}{4} \quad \boxed{1}$$

(Use Strategy 13: Find unknowns by multiplying.) Cross-multiply $\boxed{1}$. We have

$$4a = b \quad \boxed{2}$$

Substituting $4a = b$ in the given $\frac{a^2}{b}$, we get

$$\frac{a^2}{b} = \frac{a^2}{4a} = \frac{a}{4} \quad \boxed{3}$$

(Use Strategy 7: Use numerics to help find the answer.) If $a = 1$ is substituted into $\boxed{3}$, we have

$$\frac{a^2}{b} = \frac{a}{4} = \frac{1}{4}$$

Thus, Choice I is satisfied. If $a = 2$ is substituted into $\boxed{3}$, we get

$$\frac{a^2}{b} = \frac{a}{4} = \frac{2}{4} = \frac{1}{2}$$

Thus, Choice II is satisfied. If $a = 4$ is substituted into $\boxed{3}$, we have

$$\frac{a^2}{b} = \frac{a}{4} = \frac{4}{4} = 1$$

Thus Choice III is satisfied.

(Math Refresher #111 and #112)

17. Choice B is correct. **(Use Strategy 2: Translate from words to algebra.)**

$$Given: \text{Rate of plane } = x\,\frac{\text{km}}{\text{hour}} \quad \boxed{1}$$

$$\text{Time of flight } = y \text{ hours} \quad \boxed{2}$$

Need: Distance plane had flown $\frac{2}{3}y$ hours ago $\boxed{3}$

Subtracting $\boxed{3}$ from $\boxed{2}$, we get

Time plane had flown $\frac{2}{3}y$ hours ago $= y - \frac{2}{3}y$

Time plane had flown $\frac{2}{3}y$ hours ago $= \frac{1}{3}y$ hours $\boxed{4}$

(Use Strategy 9: Know the rate, time, and distance relationship.)

We know: Rate $\times$ Time $=$ Distance $\boxed{5}$

Substitute $\boxed{1}$ and $\boxed{4}$ into $\boxed{5}$. We get

$$x\,\frac{\text{km}}{\text{hour}} \times \frac{1}{3}y \text{ hours} = \text{Distance}$$

$\frac{xy}{3}$ = Distance plane had flown $\frac{2}{3}y$ hours ago.

(Math Refresher #201 and #202)

18. Choice E is correct.

(Use Strategy 5:

$$\textbf{Average} = \frac{\textbf{sum of values}}{\textbf{total number of values}}\textbf{)}$$

We know that

$$\text{Average} = \frac{\text{sum of values}}{\text{total number of values}} \quad \boxed{1}$$

Given: Average of k scores is 20 $\boxed{2}$

Substitute $\boxed{2}$ into $\boxed{1}$. We get

$$20 = \frac{\text{sum of } k \text{ values}}{k}$$

$$20k = \text{Sum of } k \text{ values} \quad \boxed{3}$$

Given: Average of 10 of these scores is 15. $\boxed{4}$

Substitute $\boxed{4}$ into $\boxed{1}$. We have

$$15 = \frac{\text{sum of 10 scores}}{10}$$

$$150 = \text{Sum of 10 scores} \quad \boxed{5}$$

There are $k - 10$ scores remaining. $\boxed{6}$

(Use Strategy 3: The whole equals the sum of its parts.)

We know: Sum of 10 scores + Sum of remaining scores = Sum of k scores $\boxed{7}$

Substituting $\boxed{3}$ and $\boxed{5}$ into $\boxed{7}$, we get

150 + Sum of remaining scores = $20k$

Sum of remaining scores = $20k - 150$ $\boxed{8}$

Substituting $\boxed{6}$ and $\boxed{8}$ into $\boxed{1}$, we get

$$\text{Average of remaining scores} = \frac{20k - 150}{k - 10}$$

(Math Refresher #601)

19. Choice E is correct.

Given: Area of square $= R^2$ $\boxed{1}$

Perimeter of equilateral triangle $= E$ $\boxed{2}$

Perimeter of square $= r$ $\boxed{3}$

Side of equilateral triangle $= e$ $\boxed{4}$

(Use Strategy 17: Use the given information effectively.)

We know perimeter of a square = 4(side) $\boxed{5}$

We know area of a square = $(\text{side})^2$ $\boxed{6}$

Substituting $\boxed{1}$ into $\boxed{6}$, we get

$$R^2 = (\text{side})^2$$

$$R = \text{side} \quad \boxed{7}$$

Substituting $\boxed{7}$ and $\boxed{3}$ into $\boxed{5}$, we have

$$r = 4(R)$$

$$r = 4R \quad \boxed{8}$$

We know perimeter of an equilateral triangle = 3(side) $\boxed{9}$

Substituting [2] and [4] into [9], we get

$$E = 3(e)$$
$$E = 3e \quad [10]$$
$$\frac{E}{3} = e$$

We need $e + r$. [11]

(Use Strategy 13: Find unknowns by addition.) Add [8] and [10] to get [11]. We have

$$e + r = \frac{E}{3} + 4R$$
$$= \frac{E}{3} + 4R\left(\frac{3}{3}\right)$$
$$= \frac{E}{3} + \frac{12R}{3}$$
$$e + r = \frac{E + 12R}{3}$$

(Math Refresher #303 and #308)

20. Choice D is correct.

Given: $C = \frac{5}{9}(F - 32)$ [1]

Call the number of degrees that the Fahrenheit temperature (F°) increases, x.

(Now use Strategy 17: Use the given information effectively.)

The Centigrade temperature (C°) is given as

$$C = \frac{5}{9}(F - 32)$$

This can be rewritten as:

$$C = \frac{5}{9}F - \frac{5}{9}(32) \quad [1]$$

When the Centigrade temperature increases by 35°, the Fahrenheit temperature increases by x°, so we get:

$$C + 35 = \frac{5}{9}[(F + x) - 32]$$
$$C + 35 = \frac{5}{9}F + \frac{5}{9}x - \frac{5}{9}(32) \quad [2]$$

(Now use Strategy 13: Find unknowns by subtraction.)

Subtract [1] from [2]:

$$C + 35 = \frac{5}{9}F + \frac{5}{9}x - \frac{5}{9}(32) \quad [2]$$
$$- \quad C = \frac{5}{9}F - \frac{5}{9}(32) \quad [1]$$
$$35 = \frac{5}{9}x \quad [3]$$

Multiply [3] by 9:

$$35 \times 9 = 5x \quad [4]$$

(Use Strategy 19: Don't multiply when reducing can be done first.)

Divide [4] by 5:

$$\frac{35 \times 9}{5} = x \quad [5]$$

Now reduce $\frac{35}{5}$ to get 7 and we get for [5]

$$7 \times 9 = x$$
$$63 = x$$

(Math Refresher #406)

Explanatory Answers for SAT Practice Test 1 (continued)

Section 4: Critical Reading

As you read these Explanatory Answers, you are advised to refer to "16 Verbal (Critical Reading) Strategies" (beginning on page 119) whenever a specific strategy is referred to in the answer. Of particular importance are the following Master Verbal Strategies:

Sentence Completion Master Strategy 1—page 120.
Sentence Completion Master Strategy 2—page 121.
Reading Comprehension Master Strategy 2—page 138.

Note: All Reading questions use Reading Comprehension Strategies 1, 2, and 3 (pages 135–140) as well as other strategies indicated.

1. Choice D is correct. **See Sentence Completion Strategy 4.** The first word, "Because," is a *result indicator.* We can then expect some action to take place after the information about what the evening cable TV programs deal with. The expected action is that parents will consider such programs "inappropriate." Accordingly, only Choice D is correct.

2. Choice A is correct. See **Sentence Completion Strategy 2.** Examine the first word of each choice. Choice (C), glamorized..., and Choice (D) viewed..., do *not* make good sense because a word does not effectively glamorize or effectively view unfairness. Now consider the other choices. Choice (A), portrayed...strengthening, is the only choice which has a word pair that makes sense in the sentence.

3. Choice E is correct. See **Sentence Completion Strategy 1.** The word "prolific" (meaning "producing abundant works or results") completes the sentence so that it makes good sense. The other choices do *not* do that.

4. Choice D is correct. Although this is a two-blank question, we should use **Sentence Completion Strategy 1** (primarily used for one-blank questions). Note that we have a set of three opposites: from the "serious" to the "lighthearted," from the "objective" to the "argumentative," and from the "innocuous" (meaning *harmless, innocent*) to the "hostile." The other choices do *not* have this opposite pattern.

5. Choice B is correct. See **Sentence Completion Strategy 2.** Examine the first word of each choice. Choice (A), shattering..., and Choice (C), impertinent..., do *not* make sense because rates at a repair place are not aptly called shattering or impertinent. Now consider the other choices. Choices D and

E do *not* make sense in the sentence. Choice (B), exorbitant...instituted, *does* make sense.

6. Choice E is correct. See **Sentence Completion Strategy 2.** Examine the first word of each choice. Choice (B), denied..., and Choice (D), slighted..., do *not* make sense because students who found truth in Socrates' teachings would not deny or slight him. Now consider the other choices. Choice (A), accepted..., a benefit and Choice (C), appraised... an exception, do not make sense in the sentence. Choice (E), revered...a threat, *does* make sense in the sentence.

7. Choice B is correct. See **Sentence Completion Strategy 1.** Try each of the choices. The only one that fits is Choice B: The quotation was erroneously *ascribed,* or *credited to,* a British poet.

8. Choice D is correct. See **Sentence Completion Strategy 2.** Examine the first word of each choice. We eliminate Choice (C), squandered, and Choice (E), regaled, because hardworking parents do *not* squander (spend money recklessly) or regale (entertain) to give their son an education. Now consider the other choices. The word pairs of Choice A and Choice B do *not* make sense in the sentence. Choice (D), struggled...generously, *does* make good sense.

9. (E) See lines 5–6 and lines 10–12.

10. (D) In the context, you can see that "extenuate" means to excuse. See **Reading Comprehension Strategy 5**.

11. (E) See lines 4–8: "Richness of poetic imagery..." and lines 10–13: "Even his elaborate and multi-stranded plots..."

12. (E) See lines 10–13, which describe the forcefulness and power up to the closing.

13. Choice B is correct. See the first paragraph: "Many people who are willing to concede that the railroad must be brought back to life are chiefly thinking of bringing this about...by treating speed as the only important factor..."

14. Choice E is correct. See the fourth paragraph: "The prime purpose of passenger transportation is not to increase the amount of physical movement but to increase the possibilities for human association, cooperation, personal intercourse, and choice." Also see the fifth paragraph, sentences 1 and 4. Note that although I is not a prime purpose, it is still a purpose.

15. Choice E is correct. See paragraph 6: "The current introduction of shopping malls...is...a...far better *technical* solution than the many costly proposals for introducing moving sidewalks or other rigidly automated modes of locomotion."

16. Choice A is correct. See the next-to-last paragraph: "With the over-exploitation of the particular car comes an increased demand...to endow the petroleum magnates...with fabulous capacities for personal luxury..."

17. Choice C is correct. See the next-to-last paragraph: "With the over-exploitation of the particular car comes an increased demand...to roll ever-wider carpets of concrete over the bulldozed landscape..."

18. Choice B is correct. See the last paragraph: "If indeed we go farther and faster along this route, there is plenty of evidence to show that the shop will close up without our help."

19. Choice B is correct. From the context of the paragraph, we are talking about distances. Don't get lured into Choice C because you read about "human needs" in the paragraph or Choice D just because you see "traffic" mentioned. See also **Reading Comprehension Strategy 5.**

20. Choice D is correct. From lines 28–32 and other sections of the passage, we can see that the author believes that "technocratic" thinking neither addresses nor is concerned with real human needs.

21. Choice A is correct. See paragraph 6: "If we took human needs seriously...we should...make the fullest use of pedestrian movement..."

22. Choice C is correct. See paragraph 5: "Variety of choices, facilities and destinations, not speed alone, is the mark of an organic transportation system."

23. Choice B is correct. Judging from the time-perspective of the author, and the more general nature of the article, Choice B would be the best answer.

24. Choice C is correct. See paragraph 5: "And... [variety] is an important factor of safety when any part of the system breaks down."

Explanatory Answers for Practice Test 1 (continued)

Section 5: Writing

For further practice and information, please refer to Grammar and Usage Refresher starting on page 455.

1. **(A)** Choice A is correct. Choice B is awkward. The parenthetical effect of Choice C gives the sentence an ungrammatical structure. The ellipsis of "to the" before the beginning of Choice D, is improper. The possessive use ("oak's") in Choice E results in a bad-sounding sentence.

2. **(A)** Choice A is correct. The present tense in Choice B is incorrect. Choices C, D, and E change the meaning of the original sentence.

3. **(D)** Choices A, B, and E are too wordy. Choice C changes the meaning of the original sentence. Choice D is correct.

4. **(D)** Choice A does not come to the point immediately with the use of the expression "concerning the one." Choice B is too wordy. Choice C is not clear. Choice D is correct. Choice E requires an introductory prepositional compound such as "as to."

5. **(C)** Choices A, B, D, and E are incorrect because of a dangling participle error. In these four choices, the participle "Having" must refer to the subject of the sentence. This subject must follow directly after the participial construction ("Having...in his class"). Accordingly, Choice C is the only correct choice.

6. **(C)** Choice A is incorrect because "its" as a possessive pronoun does not take an apostrophe. Choice B is incorrect because the possessive of "government" ("government's") must be used to modify the gerund "failing." Choice C is correct. Choice D is incorrect for the same reason that Choice B is incorrect. Choice E is incorrect for two reasons: (1) it changes the meaning of the original sentence; (2) even if we change the meaning from singularity to plurality, "governments" must correctly be the possessive form "governments'" to modify the gerund "failing."

7. **(B)** The key to getting the correct answer in this question is knowing this grammatical rule: *When explanatory words intervene between the subject and the verb, the number or person of the real subject is not changed.* Note that the subject "father" of the original sentence is singular. Accordingly, Choices A, C, D, and E (each of which has a singular subject, "father") are incorrect with a plural verb. Moreover, Choice D changes the present time of the original sentence to past time. Choice B is correct.

8. **(E)** The demonstrative adjective ("this," "that," "these," "those,") must agree in number with the noun ("kind") it modifies. Accordingly, Choices A, B, and D are incorrect. Choice C is incorrect because the personal pronoun "them" may not be used as an adjective. Choice E is correct.

9. **(D)** Choices A, B, C, and E are incorrect because they suffer from incomplete verb comparison. This is a form of improper ellipsis. The corrections would be as follows: Choice A—"has not recovered"; Choice B—"never will recover"; Choice C—(two corrections necessary) "has not recovered" and "never will recover" (the subjunctive "would" should not be used here); Choice E—"has not recovered." Note that in Choice E, the past perfect tense should not be used. Choice D is correct.

10. **(D)** It is important to know that "neither-nor" go together as correlative conjunctions. The pairing of "neither" with "or" is incorrect. Therefore, Choices A, C, and E are incorrect. Choice B is awkward. Choice D is correct.

11. **(A)** Choice A is correct. Note that "Glory" is the singular subject that takes the singular verb "is." "Reward" is the predicate nominative after the copulative verb "is." The other four choices are incorrect because they are indirect and awkward.

12. **(B)** "...disappeared *as if*..." The correct expression is "as if"—not "like as if." Incidentally, Choice C (*were*) is correct because it is the correct form of the contrary-to-fact conditional.

13. **(D)** "...because *the car* needed gasoline." The pronoun *it* has an indefinite antecedent. We cannot tell whether *it* refers to the car or the service station. Accordingly, we must be specific by using *car* instead of *it.*

14. **(A)** "The man *whose* temper is under control..." The contraction (*who's* meaning *who is*) is obviously incorrect here. We need the possessive adjective *whose* to modify the noun (*temper*).

15. **(E)** All underlined parts are correct.

16. **(C)** "...before his mother *came* home..." The past perfect tense (*had come*) is used for a past action that occurs before another past action. The mother's coming home did not occur before Bob wanted to finish his homework. Therefore, the past tense (*came*) should be used—not the past perfect tense (*had come*).

17. **(B)** "Inflation together with the high interest rates and soaring oil prices *is hurting*..." The subject of the sentence is *Inflation.* This is a singular subject so the verb must be singular—*is hurting* (not *are hurting*). The words *rates* and *prices* are not parts of the subject.

18. **(D)** "...will repair the car *well.*" The adverb (*well*)—not the adjective (*good*)—is used to modify the verb (*will repair*).

19. **(C)** "...if he *had read* more..." The "if" clause of a contrary-to-fact past tense requires the verb *had read*—not *would have read.*

20. (D) "...to have his stories compared with *those of* Dickens." We have an improper ellipsis in the original sentence. The additional words (*those of*) are necessary to complete the meaning of the sentence.

21. **(B)** "...with a new *type* of motor..." Do not use the article *a* or *an* after *kind of, type of, sort of,* etc.

22. **(A)** "Sharon planned to pay *about*..." *About* means *approximately; around* means *on all sides.*

23. **(A)** "Had Lincoln *been* alive..." In a past contrary-to-fact situation, the "if" clause verb should take the form *had been*—not *had have been.*

24. **(E)** All underlined parts are correct.

25. **(E)** All underlined parts are correct.

26. **(A)** "*It's* my opinion..." We need the contraction here (*It's* meaning *It is*).

27. **(A)** "If I *had known* more..." The "if" clause of the past contrary-to-fact conditional statement requires the *had known* form—not the *would have known* form.

28. **(D)** "If you compare Bill and Joe...Bill is, without any question, the *brighter.*" In comparing two individuals, we use the comparative form (*brighter*)—not the superlative form (*brightest*).

29. **(B)** "In spite of how *poorly* Ellen had done..." The adverb (*poorly*)—not the adjective (*poor*)—must be used to modify the verb (*had done*).

30. **(B)** Choice A is incorrect: The removal of the conjunction and replacement with a comma would leave two independent clauses incorrectly joined with only a comma. Choice B is correct: Replacing "moreover" and surrounding punctuation with "when" would correctly make the second clause subordinate to the first and also establish a time sequence for the two pieces of information. Choice C is incorrect because omitting "the Persian leader" would result in an information gap about who Cambyses was. Choice D is incorrect in that "bullheadedness" indicates irrational stubbornness and is, therefore, not an accurate description of the motives of people defending their own city in battle; "fierce resistance" is more appropriate. Choice E is incorrect because "moreover" (meaning "beyond what has been stated, further, or besides") does not furnish an adequate transition between the idea of the first sentence and the idea of the second sentence which need to be related to each other in a time sequence. The comma—instead of the semicolon—would be incorrect punctuation preceding the conjunctive adverb.

31. **(D)** Choice A is incorrect because the introduction of "It was made worse" would create a run-on sentence. Choice B is incorrect in that omitting the phrase would remove a needed transition to carry the action from sentence 4 to sentence 5 by indicating that a second tactic was used. The phrase also furnishes some dramatic reinforcement of the idea that the Egyptians were "appalled." Choice C is incorrect because "plus" can be used as an adjective or a preposition but not, as in this sentence, as a conjunction. Neither the meaning "in addition to" nor "added" fits the structure of the sentence. Choice D is correct because the phrase is useful as a transition and for emphasis. (See explanation for Choice B.) Choice E is incorrect in that placing the phrase at the end of the sentence deprives the phrase of its use as a transition between sentences 5 and 6.

32. **(D)** Choice A is incorrect: "unharmed without hurting them" is redundant; adding "in the least little way" would only compound the repetition. Choice B is incorrect since the redundancy would remain. Choice C is incorrect: The sentence would lose clarity without the information that the soldiers were to keep the cats safely. Choice D is correct because omitting "without hurting them" would cure the redundancy. Choice E is incorrect because the base words "hurt" and "harm" would be merely reversed without eliminating the repetition weakness.

33. **(A)** Choice A is correct: The proper place for sentence 6 is after sentence three. In that position, sentence 6 would show the chronological order of events correctly and the tense of "ordered" would be accurate. Choice B is incorrect since the omission of the sentence would leave a puzzling information gap about where the cats came from. Choice C is incorrect: Placed at the end of the paragraph, even with an appropriate change in the verb to "had ordered," the sentence would furnish anticlimactic information, well after the time the data was needed. Choice D is incorrect because beginning a new sentence after "countryside" would leave the remaining words as a sentence fragment. Choice E is incorrect not only because it would leave sentence 6 in a position in which chronology is not clearly indicated, but also because inserting "which was because" creates unnecessary wordiness and a pronoun with an ambiguous reference while leaving "ordered" in the wrong tense.

34. **(B)** Choice A is incorrect: "capitulated" is an accurate synonym for "surrendered," while "crumbled" would suggest the physical decay of the city walls or buildings. Choice B is correct: Since previous battle has been suggested in sentence 3 ("the Persian army...blocked by the fierce resistance"), sentence 8 would be more accurate if it ended with "further battle." Choice C is incorrect because, as noted, the Egyptians had previously fought the Persians. Choice D is incorrect: Even though "having resisted" is a complete idea and far preferable to the incomplete idea of "a drop of blood," the substitution is still inaccurate because the Egyptians had previously resisted. Choice E is incorrect because it conveys a totally inaccurate idea of the reason for the surrender of Pelusium.

35. **(C)** Since sentence 8 describes animal worship generally (not specifically), this would lead directly to sentence 1, which is more specific, especially because of the words "In fact" at the beginning of sentence 1.

Explanatory Answers for Practice Test 1 (continued)

Section 6: Math

As you read these solutions, you are advised to do two things if you answered the Math question incorrectly:

1. When a specific Math Strategy is referred to in the solution, study that strategy, which you will find in "19 Math Strategies" (beginning on page 69).
2. When the solution directs you to the "Complete Math Refresher" (beginning on page 167)—for example, Math Refresher 305—study the 305 Math principle to get a clear idea of the Math operation that was necessary for you to know in order to answer the question correctly.

1. Choice D is correct.
Method 1: **(Use Strategy 8: When all choices must be tested, start with Choice E.)**

Since $\sqrt{x}$ is odd, then x is odd. $\boxed{1}$
Let us start with solution E.

Choice E: If x is odd (from $\boxed{1}$ above), then x^2 is odd. Choice D: If $\sqrt{x}$ is odd, $2\sqrt{x}$ is *even*, and the solution is found.

(Use Strategy 7: Use numerics to help you get the answer.)

Method 2: Choose an odd number for $\sqrt{x}$—for example,

$$\sqrt{x} = 3$$
$$\text{Then } x = 9$$
$$\text{Choice E:} \quad x^2 = 81 \text{ (odd)}$$
$$\text{Choice D:} \quad 2\sqrt{x} = 2(3) = 6 \text{ (even)}$$

The answer is clearly Choice D.

(Math Refresher #430, #431, and #603)

2. Choice E is correct. **(Use Strategy 8: When all choices must be tested, start with Choice E.)** Since we must check all the choices, we should start with Choice E. Clearly, if x is the point whose coordinates are (5,2), then $m\angle MXN = 90°$ and Choice E must be correct.

(Math Refresher #410b)

3. Choice D is correct. You want to find a value of x such that $f(x) = x + 2$, so you look for a value of x in the x-column that makes $f(x)$ in the $f(x)$ column, $x + 2$. You can see that $x = 3$ corresponds to $f(x) = 5$, which is just $x + 2$ (or $3 + 2$).

(Math Refresher #616, #702)

4. Choice D is correct. **(Use Strategy 15: Certain choices may be easily eliminated.)** Since (according to the graph), $y = 0$ when $x = 0$, Choices A, B, and E are incorrect. Choice C is incorrect since the graph is not a parabola. The only feasible choice is Choice D.

(Math Refresher #410b)

5. Choice E is correct. **(Use Strategy 2: Translate from words to algebra.)** The sum of the degree measures of the 4 angles of any quadrilateral is always 360. Therefore,

$$w + x + y + z = 360° \quad \boxed{1}$$

(Use Strategy 5: Average = $\left(\frac{\text{sum of values}}{\text{total number of values}}\right)$

If w is the average (arithmetic mean) of x, y, and z, then

$$w = \frac{x+y+z}{3}$$

Multiplying both sides of the above equation by 3, we have

$$3w = x + y + z \quad \boxed{2}$$

Substituting equation $\boxed{2}$ into equation $\boxed{1}$, we get

$$w + 3w = 360°$$

or $$4w = 360°$$

or $$w = 90°$$

From equation $\boxed{2}$, we conclude that $x + y + z = 3w = 3(90) = 270°$

(Math Refresher #521, #601, and #406)

6. Choice B is correct. **(Use Strategy 17: Use the given information effectively.)** The circle graph tells you that 19% of this mixture is carbon. Since the total mixture weighs 24 pounds, 19% of that will be the amount of carbon in the mixture (in pounds). We would multiply 24 lbs × .19. But since the choices are not that close and since we are looking for the *closest* number of pounds, make the problem simpler by multiplying 24 × .20 = 4.8, which is close to 4.6.

(Math Refresher #705)

7. Choice B is correct. **(Use Strategy 10: Use units of Time, Distance, etc.)** Since the track circumference is 120 feet:

# of feet/120 = # of revolutions

(Use Strategy 9: Use the Rate × Time = Distance formula.)

Rate × Time = Distance

$$\frac{1}{120}\text{Rate} \times \text{Time} = \frac{1}{120}\text{Distance} = \text{Revolutions}$$

For Bicycle B:

$$\left(\frac{1}{120}\right)8 \times t = 600$$

For Bicycle A:

$$\left(\frac{1}{120}\right)5 \times t = a$$

The key is to realize that the time, t, is identical for both bicycles.

(Use Strategy 13: Find unknowns by dividing equations.)

$$\frac{\left(\frac{1}{120}\right)8 \times t}{\left(\frac{1}{120}\right)5 \times t} = \frac{600}{a}$$

$$\frac{8}{5} = \frac{600}{a}$$

$$8a = 3000$$

$$a = 375$$

(Math Refresher #202, #403)

8. Choice D is correct. The key to this problem is to find the area of the shaded region in terms of known quantities. **(Use Strategy 3: The whole equals the sum of its parts.)** Area of shaded region and also the area of the rectangle

$$= \text{Area of triangle} - \text{Area of square}$$
$$= x^2\sqrt{3} - x^2$$
$$= x^2(\sqrt{3} - 1)$$

We are given that an unknown rectangle has width $= x$ $\boxed{1}$
and area $= x^2(\sqrt{3} - 1)$ $\boxed{2}$

Since length × width = area,
length = area ÷ width $\boxed{3}$

Substituting $\boxed{1}$ and $\boxed{2}$ into $\boxed{3}$, we have

$$\text{length of rectangle} = \frac{x^2(\sqrt{3} - 1)}{x}$$

$$\text{length of rectangle} = x(\sqrt{3} - 1)$$

(Math Refresher #303, #304, and #306)

9. 7/24, 2/7, 3/10, 3/11, or any number between 0.25 and .3333. (Use Strategy 17: Use the given information effectively.)

Without a calculator:

Get a common denominator 12. Then write $\frac{1}{4} = \frac{3}{12}$ and $\frac{1}{3} = \frac{4}{12}$ to get a quantity *in between* $\frac{3}{12}$ and $\frac{4}{12}$.

Write $\frac{3}{12} = \frac{6}{24}$ and $\frac{4}{12} = \frac{8}{24}$

Thus $\frac{6}{24} < x < \frac{8}{24}$ and x can be $\frac{7}{24}$.

Or write $\frac{1}{4} = \frac{2}{8}$ and $\frac{1}{3} = \frac{2}{6}$. $\frac{2}{8} < \frac{2}{7} < \frac{2}{6}$, so $\frac{2}{7}$ is an answer. $\frac{3}{10}$ and $\frac{3}{11}$ are also acceptable.

With a calculator:

Calculate $\frac{1}{4} = 0.25$; Calculate $\frac{1}{3} = 0.3333\ldots$

"Grid" any number between 0.25 and 0.3333, like 0.26, 0.27… .332, .333.

(Math Refresher #419)

10. 12

$$\textit{Given: } 3x + y = 17 \quad \boxed{1}$$
$$x + 3y = -1 \quad \boxed{2}$$

(Use Strategy 13: Find unknowns by adding.)

Adding $\boxed{1}$ and $\boxed{2}$, we get

$$4x + 4y = 16 \quad \boxed{3}$$

(Use Strategy 13: Find unknowns by division.) Dividing $\boxed{3}$ by 4, we have

$$x + y = 4 \quad \boxed{4}$$

(Use Strategy 13: Find unknowns by multiplying.) Multiply $\boxed{4}$ by 3. We get

$$3x + 3y = 12$$

(Math Refresher #407)

11. 60

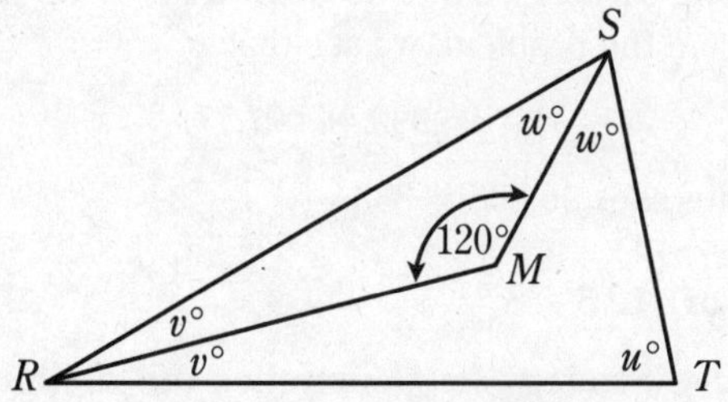

$$\textit{Given: } \angle M = 120° \quad \boxed{1}$$
$$\angle RST = 80° \quad \boxed{2}$$

(Use Strategy 3: The whole equals the sum of its parts.) From the diagram we see that

$$\angle RST = w + w \quad \boxed{3}$$

Substitute $\boxed{2}$ into $\boxed{3}$. We get

$$80° = w + w$$
$$80° = 2w$$
$$40° = w \quad \boxed{4}$$

We know that in triangle *RMS*

$$v + w + 120° = 180° \quad \boxed{5}$$

Substituting $\boxed{4}$ into $\boxed{5}$, we get

$$v + 40° + 120° = 180°$$
$$v + 160° = 180°$$
$$v = 20° \quad \boxed{6}$$

From the diagram we see that

$$\angle SRT = v + v \quad \boxed{7}$$

Substitute $\boxed{6}$ into $\boxed{7}$. We get

$$\angle SRT = 20° + 20°$$
$$\angle SRT = 40° \quad \boxed{8}$$

We know that in triangle *RST*

$$\angle RST + \angle SRT + u = 180° \quad \boxed{9}$$

Substitute $\boxed{2}$ and $\boxed{8}$ into $\boxed{9}$. We get

$$80° + 40° + u = 180°$$
$$120° + u = 180°$$
$$u = 60°$$

(Math Refresher #505)

12. 6 (Use Strategy 17: Use the given information effectively.) If the tram carries its maximum of 4 people then

$$\frac{22 \text{ people}}{\frac{4 \text{ people}}{\text{trip}}} = 5\tfrac{1}{2} \text{ trips}$$

(Use Strategy 16: The obvious may be tricky!) There is no such thing as $\frac{1}{2}$ a trip. The $\frac{1}{2}$ arises because the last trip, the *6th* trip only, takes 2 people. So there are 6 trips.

(Math Refresher #101)

13. 24 *Method 1:* **(Use Strategy 4: Remember classic expressions.)**

$$(a + b)^2 = a^2 + 2ab + b^2 \quad \boxed{1}$$
$$(a - b)^2 = a^2 - 2ab + b^2 \quad \boxed{2}$$

(Use Strategy 11: Use new definitions carefully. These problems are generally easy.)

Using $\boxed{1}$ and $\boxed{2}$, we have

$$a \odot b = (a + b)^2 - (a - b)^2$$
$$= a^2 + 2ab + b^2 - (a^2 - 2ab + b^2)$$
$$= 4ab \quad \boxed{3}$$

When we use $\boxed{3}$ with $a = \sqrt{18}$ and $b = \sqrt{2}$, we get

$$\sqrt{18} \odot \sqrt{2} = 4(\sqrt{18})(\sqrt{2})$$
$$= 4(\sqrt{36})$$
$$= 4(6)$$
$$= 24$$

Method 2: $a \odot b = (a + b)^2 - (a - b)^2$

$$2\sqrt{18} \odot \sqrt{2}$$
$$= (\sqrt{18} + \sqrt{2})^2 - (\sqrt{18} - \sqrt{2})^2$$
$$= 18 + 2\sqrt{36} + 2 - (18 - 2\sqrt{36} + 2)$$
$$= 18 + 12 + 2 - 18 + 12 - 2$$
$$= 24$$

The calculations in Method 2 are much more complex!

(Math Refresher #409 and #431)

14. 25 If you have patience, it is not too hard to list all ordered pairs of integers (x, y) such that

$$x^2 + y^2 < 9$$

(Use Strategy 17: Use the given information effectively.)

However, to save time, try listing the possible values of each variable.

$x = -2, -1, 0, 1, 2$

$y = -2, -1, 0, 1, 2$

Since each variable has 5 possible values, the total number of ordered pairs for which $x^2 + y^2 < 9$ is:

(# of values for x) (# of values for y) $= 5 \times 5 = 25$

Another way to do this problem is to note that $x^2 + y^2 = 9$ is the equation of a circle of radius 3 whose center is at (0, 0).

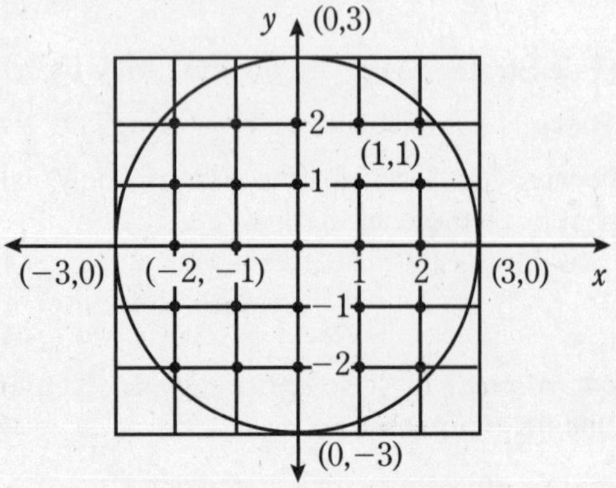

Thus, $x^2 + y^2 < 9$ is the region inside the circle. We want to find the number of ordered pairs of integers (x, y) inside the circle. As we can count from the picture above, there are 25 such ordered pairs.

(Math Refresher #410 and #431)

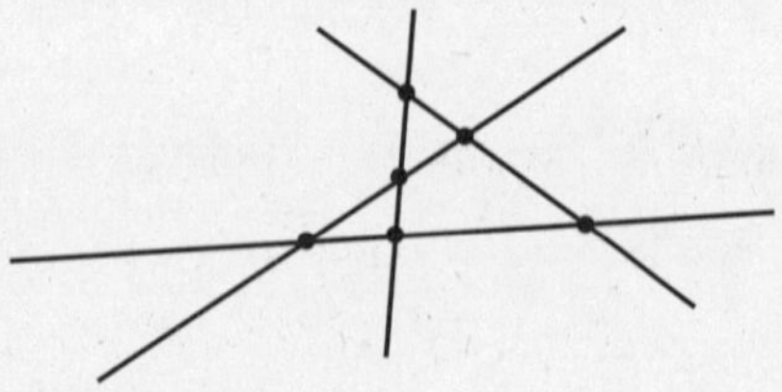

15. 6 (Use Strategy 17: Use the given information effectively.)

Method 1: You can just take out one line and you will have 6 points (see above).

Method 2: There is a formula for finding the maximum number of points of intersection of n straight line segments.

It is $\frac{n(n-1)}{2}$ [1]

Substituting 4 into [1], we get

$$\frac{4(4-1)}{2} = \frac{4(3)}{2} = \frac{12}{2} = 6$$

(Math Refresher #405a)

16. 35 (Use Strategy 2: Translate from words to algebra.) The boy originally had enough money to buy 21 bars at 50¢ per bar. Thus, he had $21 \times 50 =$ 1,050 cents = \$10.50. Therefore,

Number of 30¢ bars he bought

$$= \frac{\text{total amount he had}}{\text{price of each bar}}$$

$$= \frac{\$10.50}{\$.30}$$

= 35 bars

(Math Refresher #200 and #406)

17. 333

(Use Strategy 16: The obvious may be tricky!) From the problem, we see that

$$d = 96{,}999;\ \textit{not}\ 97{,}777$$

Thus, $d - 96{,}666 = 333$

18. $\frac{1}{8}$ or .125

(Use Strategy 2: Remember the definition of percent.) 25 percent of 2 is

$$\frac{25}{100} \times 2$$

Thus, 25 percent of 25 percent of 2 is

$$\frac{25}{100} \times \frac{25}{100} \times 2 = \frac{1}{4} \times \frac{1}{4} \times 2$$

$$= \frac{2}{16}$$

$$= \frac{1}{8}$$

(Math Refresher #114)

Explanatory Answers for SAT Practice Test 1 (continued)

Section 7: Critical Reading

As you read these Explanatory Answers, you are advised to refer to "16 Verbal (Critical Reading) Strategies" (beginning on page 119) whenever a specific strategy is referred to in the answer. Of particular importance are the following Master Verbal Strategies:

Sentence Completion Master Strategy 1—page 120.
Sentence Completion Master Strategy 2—page 121.
Reading Comprehension Master Strategy 2—page 138.

Note: All Reading questions use Reading Comprehension Strategies 1, 2, and 3 (pages 135–140) as well as other strategies indicated.

1. Choice E is correct. See **Sentence Completion Strategy 1.** Try each choice. He tried his hardest to maintain his *calm*, or *poise.*

2. Choice A is correct. See **Sentence Completion Strategy 2.** Examine the first word of each choice. Choice (B), a specter…, and Choice (C), an exodus…, do *not* make sense because a nice apartment building is not a specter (ghost) or an exodus (a departure). Now consider the other choices. Choice (A), a boon…haunted, is the only choice that makes sense in the sentence. The word "haunted" here means "visited frequently."

3. Choice A is correct. See **Sentence Completion Strategy 2.** Examine the first word of each choice. Choice (B), cancellation…, and Choice (D), abundance…, do *not* make sense because we do not refer to an inflation cancellation or an inflation abundance. Now consider the other choices. Choice (A), spiral…indubitably (meaning "unquestionably, certainly"), is the only choice which has a word pair that makes sense in the sentence.

4. Choice B is correct. See **Sentence Completion Strategy 4.** The first word, "although," is an *opposition indicator.* After the subordinate clause "although…markedly," we can expect an opposing idea in the main clause that follows and completes the sentence. Choice (B), unaffected, gives us the word that brings out the opposition thought that we expect in the sentence. Choices A, C, D, and E do not give us a sentence that makes sense.

5. Choice D is correct. See **Sentence Completion Strategy 1.** The word "elusive" means "cleverly or skillfully; able to avoid being caught." Therefore, Choice (D) elusive is the only correct choice. Don't assume that *guerrillas* are *gorillas.* A general (of an army) would not be involved with trapping gorillas!

6. Choice B is correct. In line 24, the statement "the universe does not play dice with nature" illustrates that Einstein believes that there is certainty and not mere probability in all aspects of physics.

7. Choice A is correct. See lines 4–6 and lines 17–19 about measurement devices. Choice B is incorrect because in lines 20–21, we may know the exact position of an electron but not its exact speed. Choice C is incorrect: See lines 28–30. Choice D is incorrect because in lines 4–6, it just explains that the apparatus does not interfere with measurement, not that we don't deal with measurement.

8. Choice A is correct. Since classical and modern physics seem to be somewhat contradictory, there could exist a "unified" physics that would incorporate both without retaining the paradoxes inherent in classical and modern physics. The other choices do not resolve the issue.

9. Choice D is correct. For (I), it is seen that cause and effect exist in classical physics but not in modern physics; for (II), probability exists in modern physics whereas certainty exists in classical physics; for (III), the structure of a bridge is apparent in both modern and classical physics since the subatomic make-up of the bridge and the macroscopic structure of the supports, etc. also exists. Thus only (I) and (II) are true and Choice D is correct.

10. Choice A is correct. The passage deals mainly with van Gogh's 15-month stay in Arles. It was in this small French town that his art, in fact, did reach its zenith. See lines 5–9: "Yet Arles…in the modern era." Although Choices B, C, D, and E have some association with the passage, none of these choices represents the best title for the passage as a whole. Therefore, these choices are incorrect.

11. Choice D is correct. Answer Choice D is neither stated nor implied in the passage; therefore, it is the correct choice. First see lines 42–45: "Before the year was up…had to return to Paris." Note that Gauguin had stayed in Arles *less* than a year. Now see lines 5–9: "Yet Arles was also the scene…in the modern era." Choice A is true—therefore an incorrect choice. See lines 12–16: "The Arles canvases, alive with color…notably the Fauves." Choice B is true—therefore an incorrect choice. First see lines 17–20: "Van Gogh went to Arles…beloved younger brother Theo…an art dealer." Now see lines 39–41: "…Gauguin had an influence on van Gogh… pushing the younger artist…than actuality." Choice C is true—therefore an incorrect choice. See lines 20–23: "In Paris…Neo-Impressionist…style." Choice E is true—therefore incorrect. See lines 1–5: "It was at Arles…cut off part of his own ear."

12. Choice E is correct. Let us consider each of the three Roman numeral items. Item I is true. See lines 25–27: "But he wanted 'gayer' colors… Japanese prints he so admired."

Item II is true. First see lines 28–30: "He felt that in Arles…establish an artistic tradition." Now see lines 31–34: "It was van Gogh's hope…join him at Arles."

Item III is true. See lines 27–30: "Then, too, the French capital…an artistic tradition."

Accordingly, Choice E is the only correct choice.

13. Choice E is correct. In the context in the sentence "…under the glowing sun…," it would appear that the word "frenetic" should mean "frantic." Choice A is incorrect because the author would not be likely to repeat the word "colorful" in the next sentence.

14. Choice C is correct. Gauguin's attitude of tolerant acceptance of van Gogh is indicated in the following lines of the passage. Lines 37–41: "At first…rather than actuality." Lines 45–49: "Gauguin wrote to Theo…especially with me." Lines 50–52: "But then…they later had friendly correspondence." Choices A, B, D, and E are incorrect because the passage does not give evidence of the attitudes mentioned in these choices.

15. Choice D is correct. The passage indicates that there was a buildup of stresses and strains on van Gogh that he was eventually unable to cope with because of his mental and emotional instability. This condition led him to such acts as cutting off a piece of his ear. Finally—though the passage does not include this fact—van Gogh committed suicide in Paris on July 29, 1890, by shooting himself in the chest. The following lines in the passage are related to van Gogh's mental and emotional instability. Lines 1–3: "It was at Arles…had his first real bout with madness." Lines 17–20: "Van Gogh went to Arles…supported him psychologically and financially…art dealer." Lines 45–46: "Gauguin wrote to Theo…'temperamental incompatibility.'"

Choices B and E are incorrect because these were not the basic reasons for van Gogh's extreme action. The basic reason was van Gogh's mental and emotional instability (Choice D). Choice C is incorrect because the passage mentions nothing about van Gogh's failure to form an artists' colony in Arles.

16. Choice C is correct. The theme of this essay, *Self-Reliance,* by the American writer Ralph Waldo Emerson (1803–1882), is expressed in various other ways throughout the essay. For example: in referring to the independence of opinion that one loses with one's loss of early youth; in condemning our surrender of the freedom of solitude to the group actions of society at large; and in encouraging us not to fear the consequences of being inconsistent and misunderstood.

17. Choice A is correct. The infant can be, and is expected to be, completely irresponsible. "Infancy conforms to nobody: all conform to it, so that one babe commonly makes four or five out of the adults who prattle and play to it."

18. Choice D is correct. "Speak what you think now in hard words, and to-morrow speak what to-morrow thinks in hard words again, though it contradict everything you said to-day." The misunderstanding will occur because what you say may be the opposite of conventional opinion, or may be ahead of its time. But the risk is worth it.

19. Choice B is correct. It is a natural prerogative of youth to give "an independent, genuine verdict." He naturally cares very little about what older people may think because "It seems he knows how to speak to his contemporaries. Bashful or bold, then, he will know how to make us seniors very unnecessary."

20. Choice B is correct. The "pit" or gallery in a theater usually contains the least expensive seats. Consequently, it is favored by those less economically endowed, and, according to the author, less committed to conventional manners and highly dignified behavior. In effect, these are the people who go to the theater to see, rather than to be seen.

21. Choice C is correct. When people desert solitude (or individual action) to join society (group action), they surrender a large part of individual freedom in exchange for a livelihood. They thus become more reliant and dependent on others than on themselves. The metaphor of the joint-stock company is a good one because such a company is faceless and without identity. No one member stands out above any other member.

22. Choice E is correct. "Spirit and enthusiasm" are something individualistic and definite. To be spirited and enthusiastic is to be spontaneous, natural, and uninhibited. One must (according to the author) be committed and courageous "As soon as he has once acted or spoken with eclat...." See also **Reading Comprehension Strategy 5.**

23. Choice C is correct. To act out of whim is to act impulsively and in an unpremeditated, spontaneous (and generally sincere) manner. The author, however, is not endorsing ***whimsical*** action simply because it is uninhibited ("I hope it is somewhat better than whim at last, but we cannot spend the day in explanation"), but because it is a way of speaking freely, and usually with complete honesty.

24. Choice A is correct. The essence of true self-reliance and genuine nonconformity is, as Shakespeare put it, "To thine own self be true." If one is dishonest with oneself, one will be dishonest with others; if one is honest with oneself, one will be honest with others.

Explanatory Answers for Practice Test 1 (continued)

Section 8: Math

As you read these solutions, you are advised to do two things if you answered the Math question incorrectly:

1. When a specific Math Strategy is referred to in the solution, study that strategy, which you will find in "19 Math Strategies" (beginning on page 69).
2. When the solution directs you to the "Complete Math Refresher" (beginning on page 167)—for example, Math Refresher 305—study the 305 Math principle to get a clear idea of the Math operation that was necessary for you to know in order to answer the question correctly.

1. Choice E is correct.

(Use Strategy 2: Translate from words to algebra.)

Let g = number of games the team played
28 = number of games Bobby watched
$\frac{2}{3}g$ = number of games Tommy watched

We are given

$$\frac{2}{3}g > 28 \qquad \boxed{1}$$

Multiplying $\boxed{1}$ by $\frac{3}{2}$, we get

$$\left(\frac{3}{2}\right)\frac{2}{3}g > 28\left(\frac{3}{2}\right)$$
$$g > 42$$

Only Choice E satisfies this relationship.

(Math Refresher #200, #422, and #426)

2. Choice D is correct.

Given: 8 people divide a cash prize equally $\boxed{1}$

(Use Strategy 2: Translate from words to algebra.)

From $\boxed{1}$ we get:

Each person receives $\frac{1}{8}$ of the total prize $\boxed{2}$

2 people receive $\frac{2}{8} = \frac{1}{4}$ of the prize $\boxed{3}$

To change $\boxed{3}$ to a percent we multiply by 100.

$$100\left(\frac{1}{4}\right) = \frac{100}{4}$$
$$= 25\%$$

(Math Refresher #200 and #106)

3. Choice C is correct.

(Use Strategy 10: Know how to use units.)

We are given his rate is $\frac{90 \text{ laps}}{6 \text{ hours}}$

$$\frac{90 \text{ laps}}{6 \cancel{\text{hours}}} \times \frac{1 \cancel{\text{hour}}}{60 \text{ minutes}} = \frac{90 \text{ laps}}{360 \text{ minutes}}$$

$\frac{1}{4}$ lap per minute (*Answer*)

(Math Refresher #121)

4. Choice C is correct. $x^{-\frac{3}{4}} = \frac{1}{x^{\frac{3}{4}}} = \frac{1}{(\sqrt[4]{x})^3}$

$$x^{-\frac{3}{4}} = \frac{1}{(\sqrt[4]{16})^3} = \frac{1}{(2)^3} = \frac{1}{8}$$

(Math Refresher #429)

5. Choice E is correct. **(Use Strategy 15: Know how to eliminate certain choices.)** The graph $y = 2x - 4$ is a straight line such that when $x = 0$, $y = -4$ and when $y = 0$, $2x - 4 = 0$ and thus $x = 2$. So we look for a line that cuts the y-axis (vertical axis where $x = 0$) at $y = -4$, and cuts the x-axis (horizontal axis where $y = 0$) at $x = 2$.

(Math Refresher #413, #414, and #415)

6. Choice D is correct. **(Use Strategy 17: Use the given information effectively.)**

$$[(3a^3b^2)^3]^2 = (3a^3b^2)^6 = 3^6a^{18}b^{12}$$

Checking the choices, we find only Choice D has $a^{18}b^{12}$ and must be correct.

Note: We did not have to calculate 3^6!

(Math Refresher #429)

7. Choice C is correct. **(Use Strategy 17: Use the given information effectively.)**

$$\left(\frac{3}{10}\right)^2 = \frac{9}{100} = \frac{p}{100}$$

Thus $p = 9$.

(Math Refresher #429)

8. Choice B is correct.

Given: Paul's average on 3 tests = 85 [1]
Paul's average on first 2 tests = 85 [2]

(Use Strategy 5:

$$\textbf{Average} = \frac{\textbf{sum of values}}{\textbf{total number of values}}\textbf{)}$$

We know Average = $\frac{\text{sum of values}}{\text{total number of values}}$ [3]

Let x be the first test score [4]
y be the second test score [5]
z be the third test score [6]

Substituting [1], [4], [5], and [6] into [3], we have

$$85 = \frac{x+y+z}{3} \quad [7]$$

(Use Strategy 13: Find unknowns by multi-plication.)

Multiply [7] by 3. We get

$$3(85) = \left(\frac{x+y+z}{\cancel{3}}\right)\cancel{3} \quad [8]$$

$$255 = x + y + z$$

Substituting [2], [4], and [5] into [3], we have

$$85 = \frac{x+y}{2} \quad [9]$$

Multiplying [9] by 2, we get

$$2(85) = \left(\frac{x+y}{\cancel{2}}\right)\cancel{2}$$

$$170 = x + y \quad [10]$$

Substituting [10] into [8], we get

$$225 = 170 + z$$
$$85 = z$$

(Math Refresher #601, #431, and #406)

9. Choice A is correct.

(Use Strategy 11: Use new definitions carefully.)

Given: $x \boxdot y = 3 + xy$ [1]
$y \neq 0$ [2]
$x \boxdot y = 3$ [3]

Substituting [3] into [1], we get

$$3 = 3 + xy$$
$$0 = xy \quad [4]$$

Noting [2], we divide [4] by y

$$\frac{0}{y} = \frac{xy}{y}$$
$$0 = x$$

(Math Refresher #431 and #406)

10. Choice A is correct.

(Use Strategy 3: The whole equals the sum of its parts.)

From the given diagram, it is clear that

$$z + 2w = 180 \quad [1]$$

Since the sum of the measures of the angles of a triangle is 180, then

$$x + y + z = 180 \quad [2]$$

(Use Strategy 13: Find unknowns by subtracting equations.)

Subtracting [2] from [1],

$$2w - (x + y) = 0$$

or $2w = x + y$ [3]

Using [3], we calculate the unknown expression,

$$w + x + y = w + 2w$$
$$= 3w$$

(Math Refresher #501, #505, and #406)

11. Choice A is correct.

(Use Strategy 11: Use new definitions carefully.)

All choices must be evaluated using the definition.

Choice A, 934,432, would be assigned 6 + 3 + 4 = 13 points, while the other choices all receive fewer than 13 points.

(Math Refresher #702)

Number Pair	Number of Points
"33"	11
"34"	6
"43"	4
"44"	3

12. Choice D is correct.

Given: A certain number has 13 points.

(Use Strategy 11: Use new definitions carefully.)

From the chart, the only ways to accumulate 13 points are:

$6 + 4 + 3$ [1]
$3 + 3 + 3 + 4$ [2]

I. 33 is not in the number is always true.
II. 34 is in the number is *not* always true.
III. 43 is in the number is always true.

Thus, I and III are always true.

(Math Refresher #702)

13. Choice A is correct.

(Use Strategy 2: Translate from words to algebra.)

"The ratio of Sue's age to Bob's age is 3 to 7" becomes

$$\frac{\text{Sue's age } (S)}{\text{Bob's age } (B)} = \frac{3}{7}$$

or $\frac{S}{B} = \frac{3}{7}$ [1]

"The ratio of Sue's age to Joe's age is 4 to 9" becomes

$\frac{S}{J} = \frac{4}{9}$ [2]

Cross multiplying [1], we have $7S = 3B$

or $\frac{7S}{3} = B$ [3]

Cross multiplying [2], we have $9S = 4J$

or $\frac{9S}{4} = J$ [4]

We need the ratio of Bob's age to Joe's age. [5]

Substituting [3] and [4] into [5], we get

$$\frac{\text{Bob's age}}{\text{Joe's age}} = \frac{\frac{7S}{3}}{\frac{9S}{4}}$$
$$= \frac{7S}{3} \div \frac{9S}{4}$$
$$= \frac{7S}{3} \times \frac{4}{9S}$$
$$\frac{\text{Bob's age}}{\text{Joe's age}} = \frac{28}{27}$$

(Math Refresher #200, #120, and #112)

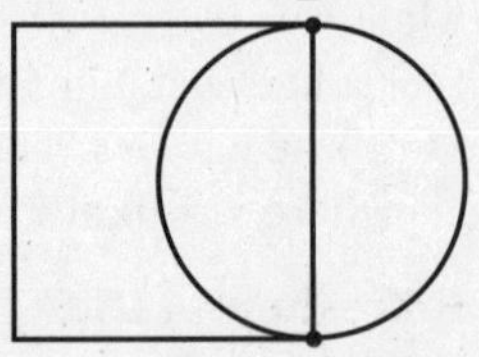

14. Choice B is correct.

(Use Strategy 17: Use the given information effectively.)

Given: Area of circle $= 9a^2\pi^2$ [1]
Two sides of square are tangent to the circle [2]

We know that the area of a circle $= \pi r^2$ where r is the radius. [3]

Substituting [1] into [3], we have

$9a^2\pi^2 = \pi r^2$ [4]

Dividing by π, we get

$9a^2\pi = r^2$ [5]

Since $2r$ is the side of the square, the area of the square is

$$(2r)^2 = 4r^2$$

From [5], multiplying both sides of the equation by 4, we get

$$4(9a^2\pi) = 4r^2$$

Thus $36a^2\pi = 4r^2 =$ area of square

(Math Refresher #303, #310, and #406)

15. Choice E is correct.

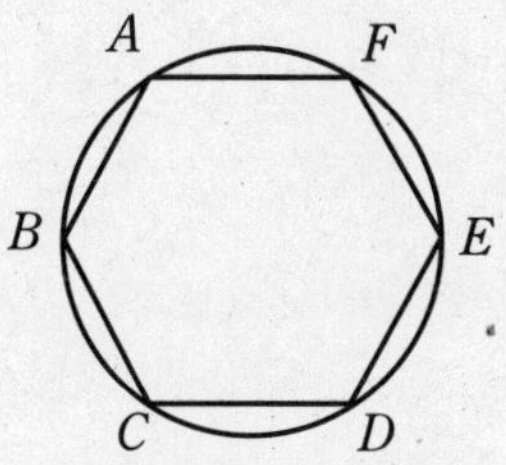

Given: $\widehat{BAF} = 14\pi$ [1]

ABCDEF is equilateral [2]

From [2] we know that all 6 sides are equal. [3]
From [3] we know that all 6 arcs are equal. [4]

From [1] and [4] and noting that $\widehat{AB}$ equals $\frac{1}{2}\widehat{BAF}$, we find

$\widehat{AB} = \widehat{BC} = \widehat{CD} = \widehat{DE} = \widehat{EF} = \widehat{FA} = 7\pi$ [5]

(Use Strategy 3: The whole equals the sum of its parts.)

Circumference of circle =

$6 \times 7\pi$ (since there are 6 arcs) [6]

We know circumference $= 2\pi r$ [7]

Using [6] and [7], we get

$$2\pi r = 6 \times 7\pi$$
$$2\pi r = 42\pi$$
$$2r = 42$$ [8]

We know diameter $= 2 \times$ radius [9]
So diameter $= 42$

(Math Refresher #310 and #524)

16. Choice B is correct.

(Use Strategy 13: Know how to find unknown expressions.)

$f(x) = a^x$

so $f(x + y) = a^{x+y}$

$a^{x+y} = a^x a^y = f(x)f(y)$

(Math Refresher #616 and #429)

Explanatory Answers for Practice Test 1 (continued)

Section 9: Critical Reading

As you read these Explanatory Answers, you are advised to refer to "16 Verbal (Critical Reading) Strategies" (beginning on page 119) whenever a specific strategy is referred to in the answer. Of particular importance are the following Master Verbal Strategies:

Sentence Completion Master Strategy 1—page 120.
Sentence Completion Master Strategy 2—page 121.
Reading Comprehension Master Strategy 2—page 138.

Note: All Reading questions use Reading Comprehension Strategies 1, 2, and 3 (pages 135–140) as well as other strategies indicated.

1. Choice E is correct. See **Sentence Completion Strategy 2.** Examine the first word of each choice. Choice (B) relegates...(meaning to banish or to assign to a lower position), and Choice (C), accumulates..., do *not* make sense since we do not say that a sense of fairness relegates or accumulates. Now consider the other choices. Choice (E), dictates...vary, is the only choice that makes sense in the sentence. This is because if you say *a sense of fairness dictates that the punishment should fit the crime*, the opposite (because of the word *yet*) would indicate that there are different punishments for the same crime. That is, the *punishments* (or judgments) *vary* greatly.

2. Choice A is correct. See **Sentence Completion Strategy 1.** The typist's inconsistency is obvious in the manner in which she typed the five letters. Choices B, C, D, and E are incorrect because they do not make good sense in the sentence.

3. Choice B is correct. See **Sentence Completion Strategy 2.** Let us first examine the first word of each choice. We can then eliminate Choice (C), remarks..., and Choice (E), conferences..., because an outstanding publisher's being able to make occasional remarks or occasional conferences does not make good sense. Now we go on to the three remaining choices. When you fill in the two blanks of Choice A and of Choice D, the sentence does not make sense. So these two choices are also incorrect. Filling in the two blanks of Choice B makes the sentence meaningful.

4. Choice B is correct. See **Sentence Completion Strategies 1 and 4.** Try each choice being aware that "since" is a *result indicator.* Their married life was not *smooth and content.*

5. Choice B is correct. See **Sentence Completion Strategies 1 and 4.** Try each choice, being aware that "because" is a *result indicator.* This happened because of his *careless, indifferent* driving.

6. Choice D is correct. See **Sentence Completion Strategy 1.** Try each choice. Parables are *stories* or fables that illustrate a moral or ethical point while relating a simple incident.

7. Choice D is correct. Line 1 ("To the world when it was half a thousand years younger...") indicates that the author is describing the world roughly five hundred years ago. Choice D—A.D. 1455—is therefore the closest date. Although Choice C is also in the Middle Ages, it is almost a thousand years ago. So it is an incorrect choice. Choices A, B, and E are obviously incorrect choices.

8. Choice A is correct. We can see that "with greater avidity" is an adverbial phrase telling the reader how "honors and riches" were enjoyed and desired. See lines 14–17: "We, at the present day...formerly enjoyed." The reader thus learns that even simple pleasures such as a glass of wine were more keenly enjoyed then. Choices B, C, D, and E are incorrect because the passage does *not* state or imply that "with greater avidity" means "with greater sadness *or* terror *or* silence *or* disappointment." See also **Reading Comprehension Strategy 5**.

9. Choice B is not true—therefore it is the correct choice. See lines 37–39: "The contrast between silence and sound...than it is in our lives." The next sentence states that the modern town hardly knows silence. These two sentences together imply that the typical town of the Middle Ages did have periods of silence.

   Choice A is true—therefore an incorrect choice. See lines 30–32: "A medieval town...in extensive suburbs of factories and villas." Choice C is true—therefore an incorrect choice. See lines 32–33: "...it [a medieval town] stood forth...with innumerable turrets."

   Choice D is true—therefore an incorrect choice. See lines 35–36: "...the lofty mass of the churches always remained dominant."

   Choice E is true—therefore an incorrect choice. See lines 33–35: "However tall...in the aspect of the town."

10. Choice C is correct. Throughout Passage 1, the author is indicating the strong, rough, uncontrolled forces that pervaded the period. See, for example, the following references. Lines 9–10: "Misfortunes and poverty were more afflicting than at present." Lines 18–19: "Then, again, all things in life...cruel publicity." Lines 24–27: "Executions...songs and music." Therefore, Choice C is correct. Choice A is incorrect because the passage speaks of joys as well as miseries. See lines 14–17: "We, at the present day...formerly enjoyed." Choice B is incorrect for this reason: Although the author contrasts town and country, he gives no indication as to which was dominant in that society. Therefore, Choice B is incorrect. Choice D is incorrect. The author contrasts how it felt to be rich or poor, but he does not indicate that the rich mistreated the poor. Choice E is incorrect because the pious nature of the people in the Middle Ages is only one of the many elements discussed in the passage.

11. Choice E is correct. See lines 4–6: "All experience...pain of child-life." Throughout the passage, this theme is illustrated with specific examples. Choices A and B are incorrect because they are one-sided. In the passage, many conditions that may make the Middle Ages seem worse than today are matched with conditions that may make the Middle Ages seem better than today. Choice C is incorrect because nowhere in the passage is intelligence mentioned or implied. Choice D is incorrect because the third paragraph indicates that, far from being subdued, people went about their lives with a great deal of show and pageantry.

12. Choice A is incorrect because the author stops short of outright despair in the last sentence of the first paragraph by tempering the outbursts of the Renaissance scholar with the milder "our times are out of joint." Choices B and E are incorrect because there is no positive feeling expressed in the first paragraph. Choice C is incorrect because there is no feeling of attraction toward an earlier age. Choice D is correct because the negative feeling is not quite full-bodied.

13. Choice A is correct. There is no mention of energy sources at any point in the selection. Therefore this answer is correct. Choices B, C, D, and E are mentioned in paragraph 2.

14. Choice B is correct. The positive outlook of the words "trend is not destiny" is best exemplified by Choice B, which implies that man can improve his situation. The other statements are negative or pessimistic pronouncements.

15. Choice A is correct. The author cites Choices B, C, D, and E in paragraph 5 as examples of renewed public awareness. The reference to the president's increase in the military budget does not indicate evidence of the public's insight regarding a danger.

16. Choice B is correct. Choices A and C are incorrect because the author is consistently expressing optimism in man's ability to learn from past mistakes. Choice B is the correct answer. Accordingly, Choice D contradicts the realistic tone of the essay. Choice E is not at all characteristic of the writer's attitude.

17. Choice C is correct. See lines 13–14 and lines 56–59. Note that the author of Passage 2 states that *if* present trends continue, the gap in living standards between the rich and the poor will lead to acts of desperation, including the use of nuclear weapons.

18. Choice A is correct. See lines 73–78. Note that Choice B is incorrect; see lines 41–46 and the descriptions in the rest of Passage 1. Choice C is incorrect; see lines 82–84. Choice E is incorrect; see lines 86–88.

19. Choice E is correct. See lines 73–90 and lines 41–46 and throughout Passage 1. Note that Choice A is incorrect; see lines 88–90.

Explanatory Answers for Practice Test 1 (continued)

Section 10: Writing

For further practice and information, please refer to Grammar and Usage Refresher starting on page 455.

1. Choice D is correct. Choices A, B, and C are incorrect because they lack parallelism. Note that the infinitive phrase "to write poems" should balance with the infinitive phrase "to study the habits." Choice D, which does have the parallelism required, is correct. Choice E is too wordy.

2. Choice B is correct. This question is concerned with the correct position of the gerund phrase "By studying." Choice A is incorrect because "grades" have been doing the "studying" with such sentence structure. Choices C, D, and E are incorrect for the same reason. Choice B is correct since "she" is obviously the one who is doing the "studying."

3. Choice D is correct. Choice A is incorrect because of the improper omission of the demonstrative pronoun "those." Choices B and C are incorrect for the same reason. Choice D is correct. Choice E is incorrect because we must bring out the comparison with *another* city.

4. Choice C is correct. Parallelism is the important consideration here. Choice C is correct as the only choice that fulfills the requirements of parallel structure.

5. Choice D is correct. The expression "one another" refers to three or more; "each other" refers to two only. Therefore, Choices A and B are incorrect and Choice D is correct. Choice C is awkward. Choice E changes the meaning of the original sentence.

6. Choice E is correct. The past contrary-to-fact conditional form is "had seen." Therefore, Choices A, B, C, and D are all incorrect. Choice E is correct. Moreover, Choice C has the wrong tense and the wrong tense sequence. It should also be seen that when you speak of *pancakes* you speak of *number* of *pancakes*. If you speak of *flour*, you speak of *amount* of *flour*.

7. Choice C is correct. A misplaced modifier may create a very embarrassing situation—so we can observe in the original sentence. We certainly don't want the fiancé wearing a sheer blouse. Such a blouse clearly belongs on the female. Choices A and D are, therefore, incorrect. Choice B is incorrect because it may appear that the concert is wearing the sheer blouse. Choice C is, of course, correct. Choice E is not acceptable because (1) the phrase "wearing a sheer blouse" is a "squinting" modifier, and (2) the sentence would be inappropriately poetic.

8. Choice D is correct. We are looking for *balanced construction* in this question. Note that the correct Choice D gives us a balanced infinitive construction: "to advise," "(to) transmit," and "(to) supervise." None of the other choices offers this balanced construction.

9. Choice A is correct. Choices B and C are incorrect because Frazier did not "own" the decision—it was rendered by the judges and the referee. Choice D is too roundabout. Choice E changes the meaning of the original sentence—and it is too roundabout.

10. Choice C is correct. Choices A, B, and E suffer from incomplete comparison. The conjunction (a second "as") is required to complete the comparison: "This test was as hard...*as* the one I took last week." Choice D is incorrect because the conjunction "so" should be used in a negative construction: "This test was *not* so hard..." Choice C is correct because it completes the comparison.

11. Choice E is correct. Choice A is incorrect because the plane and *not* JFK Airport carried few passengers. Choice B is incorrect because there is a lack of agreement in the verb tenses. Also the active voice should be used. See correct Choice E. Choice C does not include a reference to JFK Airport, which is necessary to the meaning of the original sentence. Choice D is ambiguous. Choice E is correct.

12. Choice C is correct. Choice A is incorrect because the word "go" is needed after the word "to" (otherwise the sentence means "I wanted to gone"). Choice B also requires the word "go" after "to." Choice C is correct. In Choice D, the word "although" changes the original sentence to a fragment. Choice E requires the words "to go" after "wanted."

13. Choice D is correct. Choices A and B are incorrect because "Either" should be placed before "today." Choice C is too wordy. Choice D is correct. Choice E is awkward.

14. Choice C is correct. Choice A is incorrect because "which" should be used to refer to a noun or pronoun and *not* a clause, as it is used here. In Choice B, there is a lack of agreement in the verb tenses. Choice C is correct. Choice D is awkward. Choice E is a complete sentence, making the original a run-on sentence.

What You Must Do Now to Raise Your SAT Score

1. a) Follow the directions on page 613 to determine your scaled score for the SAT Test you've just taken. These results will give you a good idea about how hard you'll need to study in order to achieve a certain score on the actual SAT.

   b) Using your correct answer count as a basis, indicate for yourself your areas of strength and weakness as revealed by the "Chart for Self-Appraisal" on page 618.

2. Eliminate your weaknesses in each of the SAT test areas (as revealed in the "Chart for Self-Appraisal") by taking the following Giant Steps toward SAT success:

Critical Reading Part

Giant Step 1

Take advantage of the Critical Reading Strategies that begin on page 119. Read again the Explanatory Answer for each of the Critical Reading questions that you got wrong. Refer to the Critical Reading Strategy that applies to each of your incorrect answers. Learn each of these Critical Reading Strategies thoroughly. These strategies are crucial if you want to raise your SAT Verbal score substantially.

Giant Step 2

You can improve your vocabulary by doing the following:

1) Study the SAT 3,400-Word List beginning on page 359.

2) Take the 100 SAT-type "tough word" Vocabulary Tests beginning on page 408.

3) Study the Gruber Prefix-Root-Suffix List beginning on page 348.

4) Learn the Hot Prefixes and Roots beginning on page 1049.

5) Read through A List of SAT Words Appearing More Than Once beginning on page 353.

6) Look through the Most Important Words and Their Opposites beginning on page 355.

7) Learn the 3 Vocabulary Strategies beginning on page 150.

8) Read as widely as possible—not only novels. Nonfiction is important too...and don't forget to read newspapers and magazines.

9) Listen to people who speak well. Tune in to worthwhile TV programs.

10) Use the dictionary frequently and extensively—at home, on the bus, at work, etc.

11) Play word games—for example, crossword puzzles, anagrams, and Scrabble. Another game is to compose your own Sentence Completion questions. Try them on your friends.

Math Part

Giant Step 3

Make good use of the 19 Math Strategies that begin on page 69. Read again the solutions for each Math question that you answered incorrectly. Refer to the Math Strategy that applies to each of your incorrect answers. Learn each of these Math Strategies thoroughly. We repeat that these strategies are crucial if you want to raise your SAT Math score substantially.

Giant Step 4

You may want to take the **101 Most Important Math Questions You Need to Know How to Solve** test beginning on page 31 and follow the directions after the test for a basic Math skills diagnosis.

For each Math question that you got wrong in the test, note the reference to the Complete Math Refresher section beginning on page 167. This reference will explain clearly the mathematical principle involved in the solution of the question you answered incorrectly. Learn that particular mathematical principle thoroughly.

For Both the Math and Critical Reading Parts

Giant Step 5

You may want to take the **Strategy Diagnostic Test** beginning on page 1 to assess whether you're using the best strategies for the questions.

For the Writing Part

Giant Step 6

Take a look at Part 9, the SAT Writing Test, which describes the various item types in the Writing Section and sample questions with answers and explanations. Also make use of the Grammar Refresher—Part 8.

3. After you have done some of the tasks you have been advised to do in the suggestions, proceed to Practice Test 2, beginning on page 661.

   After taking Practice Test 2, concentrate on the weaknesses that still remain.

4. Continue the foregoing procedures for Practice Tests 3, 4, and 5.

   If you do the job *right* and follow the steps listed earlier, you are likely to raise your SAT score on each of the Verbal, Math, and Writing parts substantially.

I am the master of my fate:
I am the captain of my soul.

—From the poem "Invictus"
by William Ernest Henley

Answer Sheet for Practice Test 2

SECTION 1

Begin your essay on this page. If you need more space, continue on the next page. Do not write outside of the essay box.

Continue on the next page if necessary.

Continuation of ESSAY Section 1 from previous page. Write below only if you need more space.

Start with number 1 for each new section. If a section has fewer questions than answer spaces, leave the extra answer spaces blank. Be sure to erase any errors or stray marks completely.

SECTION 2

1 Ⓐ Ⓑ Ⓒ Ⓓ Ⓔ	11 Ⓐ Ⓑ Ⓒ Ⓓ Ⓔ	21 Ⓐ Ⓑ Ⓒ Ⓓ Ⓔ	31 Ⓐ Ⓑ Ⓒ Ⓓ Ⓔ
2 Ⓐ Ⓑ Ⓒ Ⓓ Ⓔ	12 Ⓐ Ⓑ Ⓒ Ⓓ Ⓔ	22 Ⓐ Ⓑ Ⓒ Ⓓ Ⓔ	32 Ⓐ Ⓑ Ⓒ Ⓓ Ⓔ
3 Ⓐ Ⓑ Ⓒ Ⓓ Ⓔ	13 Ⓐ Ⓑ Ⓒ Ⓓ Ⓔ	23 Ⓐ Ⓑ Ⓒ Ⓓ Ⓔ	33 Ⓐ Ⓑ Ⓒ Ⓓ Ⓔ
4 Ⓐ Ⓑ Ⓒ Ⓓ Ⓔ	14 Ⓐ Ⓑ Ⓒ Ⓓ Ⓔ	24 Ⓐ Ⓑ Ⓒ Ⓓ Ⓔ	34 Ⓐ Ⓑ Ⓒ Ⓓ Ⓔ
5 Ⓐ Ⓑ Ⓒ Ⓓ Ⓔ	15 Ⓐ Ⓑ Ⓒ Ⓓ Ⓔ	25 Ⓐ Ⓑ Ⓒ Ⓓ Ⓔ	35 Ⓐ Ⓑ Ⓒ Ⓓ Ⓔ
6 Ⓐ Ⓑ Ⓒ Ⓓ Ⓔ	16 Ⓐ Ⓑ Ⓒ Ⓓ Ⓔ	26 Ⓐ Ⓑ Ⓒ Ⓓ Ⓔ	36 Ⓐ Ⓑ Ⓒ Ⓓ Ⓔ
7 Ⓐ Ⓑ Ⓒ Ⓓ Ⓔ	17 Ⓐ Ⓑ Ⓒ Ⓓ Ⓔ	27 Ⓐ Ⓑ Ⓒ Ⓓ Ⓔ	37 Ⓐ Ⓑ Ⓒ Ⓓ Ⓔ
8 Ⓐ Ⓑ Ⓒ Ⓓ Ⓔ	18 Ⓐ Ⓑ Ⓒ Ⓓ Ⓔ	28 Ⓐ Ⓑ Ⓒ Ⓓ Ⓔ	38 Ⓐ Ⓑ Ⓒ Ⓓ Ⓔ
9 Ⓐ Ⓑ Ⓒ Ⓓ Ⓔ	19 Ⓐ Ⓑ Ⓒ Ⓓ Ⓔ	29 Ⓐ Ⓑ Ⓒ Ⓓ Ⓔ	39 Ⓐ Ⓑ Ⓒ Ⓓ Ⓔ
10 Ⓐ Ⓑ Ⓒ Ⓓ Ⓔ	20 Ⓐ Ⓑ Ⓒ Ⓓ Ⓔ	30 Ⓐ Ⓑ Ⓒ Ⓓ Ⓔ	40 Ⓐ Ⓑ Ⓒ Ⓓ Ⓔ

SECTION 3

1 Ⓐ Ⓑ Ⓒ Ⓓ Ⓔ	11 Ⓐ Ⓑ Ⓒ Ⓓ Ⓔ	21 Ⓐ Ⓑ Ⓒ Ⓓ Ⓔ	31 Ⓐ Ⓑ Ⓒ Ⓓ Ⓔ
2 Ⓐ Ⓑ Ⓒ Ⓓ Ⓔ	12 Ⓐ Ⓑ Ⓒ Ⓓ Ⓔ	22 Ⓐ Ⓑ Ⓒ Ⓓ Ⓔ	32 Ⓐ Ⓑ Ⓒ Ⓓ Ⓔ
3 Ⓐ Ⓑ Ⓒ Ⓓ Ⓔ	13 Ⓐ Ⓑ Ⓒ Ⓓ Ⓔ	23 Ⓐ Ⓑ Ⓒ Ⓓ Ⓔ	33 Ⓐ Ⓑ Ⓒ Ⓓ Ⓔ
4 Ⓐ Ⓑ Ⓒ Ⓓ Ⓔ	14 Ⓐ Ⓑ Ⓒ Ⓓ Ⓔ	24 Ⓐ Ⓑ Ⓒ Ⓓ Ⓔ	34 Ⓐ Ⓑ Ⓒ Ⓓ Ⓔ
5 Ⓐ Ⓑ Ⓒ Ⓓ Ⓔ	15 Ⓐ Ⓑ Ⓒ Ⓓ Ⓔ	25 Ⓐ Ⓑ Ⓒ Ⓓ Ⓔ	35 Ⓐ Ⓑ Ⓒ Ⓓ Ⓔ
6 Ⓐ Ⓑ Ⓒ Ⓓ Ⓔ	16 Ⓐ Ⓑ Ⓒ Ⓓ Ⓔ	26 Ⓐ Ⓑ Ⓒ Ⓓ Ⓔ	36 Ⓐ Ⓑ Ⓒ Ⓓ Ⓔ
7 Ⓐ Ⓑ Ⓒ Ⓓ Ⓔ	17 Ⓐ Ⓑ Ⓒ Ⓓ Ⓔ	27 Ⓐ Ⓑ Ⓒ Ⓓ Ⓔ	37 Ⓐ Ⓑ Ⓒ Ⓓ Ⓔ
8 Ⓐ Ⓑ Ⓒ Ⓓ Ⓔ	18 Ⓐ Ⓑ Ⓒ Ⓓ Ⓔ	28 Ⓐ Ⓑ Ⓒ Ⓓ Ⓔ	38 Ⓐ Ⓑ Ⓒ Ⓓ Ⓔ
9 Ⓐ Ⓑ Ⓒ Ⓓ Ⓔ	19 Ⓐ Ⓑ Ⓒ Ⓓ Ⓔ	29 Ⓐ Ⓑ Ⓒ Ⓓ Ⓔ	39 Ⓐ Ⓑ Ⓒ Ⓓ Ⓔ
10 Ⓐ Ⓑ Ⓒ Ⓓ Ⓔ	20 Ⓐ Ⓑ Ⓒ Ⓓ Ⓔ	30 Ⓐ Ⓑ Ⓒ Ⓓ Ⓔ	40 Ⓐ Ⓑ Ⓒ Ⓓ Ⓔ

CAUTION Use the answer spaces in the grids below for Section 2 or Section 3 only if you are told to do so in your test book.

Student-Produced Responses ONLY ANSWERS ENTERED IN THE CIRCLES IN EACH GRID WILL BE SCORED. YOU WILL NOT RECEIVE CREDIT FOR ANYTHING WRITTEN IN THE BOXES ABOVE THE CIRCLES.

Grids for questions 9, 10, 11, 12, 13, 14, 15, 16, 17, 18 — each grid has four columns:

	/	/	
.	.	.	.
	0	0	0
1	1	1	1
2	2	2	2
3	3	3	3
4	4	4	4
5	5	5	5
6	6	6	6
7	7	7	7
8	8	8	8
9	9	9	9

Start with number 1 for each new section. If a section has fewer questions than answer spaces, leave the extra answer spaces blank. Be sure to erase any errors or stray marks completely.

SECTION 4

1 A B C D E	11 A B C D E	21 A B C D E	31 A B C D E
2 A B C D E	12 A B C D E	22 A B C D E	32 A B C D E
3 A B C D E	13 A B C D E	23 A B C D E	33 A B C D E
4 A B C D E	14 A B C D E	24 A B C D E	34 A B C D E
5 A B C D E	15 A B C D E	25 A B C D E	35 A B C D E
6 A B C D E	16 A B C D E	26 A B C D E	36 A B C D E
7 A B C D E	17 A B C D E	27 A B C D E	37 A B C D E
8 A B C D E	18 A B C D E	28 A B C D E	38 A B C D E
9 A B C D E	19 A B C D E	29 A B C D E	39 A B C D E
10 A B C D E	20 A B C D E	30 A B C D E	40 A B C D E

SECTION 5

1 A B C D E	11 A B C D E	21 A B C D E	31 A B C D E
2 A B C D E	12 A B C D E	22 A B C D E	32 A B C D E
3 A B C D E	13 A B C D E	23 A B C D E	33 A B C D E
4 A B C D E	14 A B C D E	24 A B C D E	34 A B C D E
5 A B C D E	15 A B C D E	25 A B C D E	35 A B C D E
6 A B C D E	16 A B C D E	26 A B C D E	36 A B C D E
7 A B C D E	17 A B C D E	27 A B C D E	37 A B C D E
8 A B C D E	18 A B C D E	28 A B C D E	38 A B C D E
9 A B C D E	19 A B C D E	29 A B C D E	39 A B C D E
10 A B C D E	20 A B C D E	30 A B C D E	40 A B C D E

CAUTION Use the answer spaces in the grids below for Section 4 or Section 5 only if you are told to do so in your test book.

Student-Produced Responses ONLY ANSWERS ENTERED IN THE CIRCLES IN EACH GRID WILL BE SCORED. YOU WILL NOT RECEIVE CREDIT FOR ANYTHING WRITTEN IN THE BOXES ABOVE THE CIRCLES.

9 10 11 12 13

14 15 16 17 18

Start with number 1 for each new section. If a section has fewer questions than answer spaces, leave the extra answer spaces blank. Be sure to erase any errors or stray marks completely.

SECTION 6

1 A B C D E	11 A B C D E	21 A B C D E	31 A B C D E
2 A B C D E	12 A B C D E	22 A B C D E	32 A B C D E
3 A B C D E	13 A B C D E	23 A B C D E	33 A B C D E
4 A B C D E	14 A B C D E	24 A B C D E	34 A B C D E
5 A B C D E	15 A B C D E	25 A B C D E	35 A B C D E
6 A B C D E	16 A B C D E	26 A B C D E	36 A B C D E
7 A B C D E	17 A B C D E	27 A B C D E	37 A B C D E
8 A B C D E	18 A B C D E	28 A B C D E	38 A B C D E
9 A B C D E	19 A B C D E	29 A B C D E	39 A B C D E
10 A B C D E	20 A B C D E	30 A B C D E	40 A B C D E

SECTION 7

1 A B C D E	11 A B C D E	21 A B C D E	31 A B C D E
2 A B C D E	12 A B C D E	22 A B C D E	32 A B C D E
3 A B C D E	13 A B C D E	23 A B C D E	33 A B C D E
4 A B C D E	14 A B C D E	24 A B C D E	34 A B C D E
5 A B C D E	15 A B C D E	25 A B C D E	35 A B C D E
6 A B C D E	16 A B C D E	26 A B C D E	36 A B C D E
7 A B C D E	17 A B C D E	27 A B C D E	37 A B C D E
8 A B C D E	18 A B C D E	28 A B C D E	38 A B C D E
9 A B C D E	19 A B C D E	29 A B C D E	39 A B C D E
10 A B C D E	20 A B C D E	30 A B C D E	40 A B C D E

CAUTION Use the answer spaces in the grids below for Section 6 or Section 7 only if you are told to do so in your test book.

Student-Produced Responses ONLY ANSWERS ENTERED IN THE CIRCLES IN EACH GRID WILL BE SCORED. YOU WILL NOT RECEIVE CREDIT FOR ANYTHING WRITTEN IN THE BOXES ABOVE THE CIRCLES.

Grids 9, 10, 11, 12, 13, 14, 15, 16, 17, 18 (each: / / ; . . . . ; 0–9 in each column)

Start with number 1 for each new section. If a section has fewer questions than answer spaces, leave the extra answer spaces blank. Be sure to erase any errors or stray marks completely.

SECTION 8

-3

1 A B C D E	11 A B C D E	21 A B C D E	31 A B C D E
2 A B C D E	12 A B C D E	22 A B C D E	32 A B C D E
3 A B C D E	13 A B C D E	23 A B C D E	33 A B C D E
4 A B C D E	14 A B C D E	24 A B C D E	34 A B C D E
5 A B C D E	15 A B C D E	25 A B C D E	35 A B C D E
6 A B C D E	16 A B C D E	26 A B C D E	36 A B C D E
7 A B C D E	17 A B C D E	27 A B C D E	37 A B C D E
8 A B C D E	18 A B C D E	28 A B C D E	38 A B C D E
9 A B C D E	19 A B C D E	29 A B C D E	39 A B C D E
10 A B C D E	20 A B C D E	30 A B C D E	40 A B C D E

SECTION 9

-2

1 A B C D E	11 A B C D E	21 A B C D E	31 A B C D E
2 A B C D E	12 A B C D E	22 A B C D E	32 A B C D E
3 A B C D E	13 A B C D E	23 A B C D E	33 A B C D E
4 A B C D E	14 A B C D E	24 A B C D E	34 A B C D E
5 A B C D E	15 A B C D E	25 A B C D E	35 A B C D E
6 A B C D E	16 A B C D E	26 A B C D E	36 A B C D E
7 A B C D E	17 A B C D E	27 A B C D E	37 A B C D E
8 A B C D E	18 A B C D E	28 A B C D E	38 A B C D E
9 A B C D E	19 A B C D E	29 A B C D E	39 A B C D E
10 A B C D E	20 A B C D E	30 A B C D E	40 A B C D E

SECTION 10

-0

1 A B C D E	11 A B C D E	21 A B C D E	31 A B C D E
2 A B C D E	12 A B C D E	22 A B C D E	32 A B C D E
3 A B C D E	13 A B C D E	23 A B C D E	33 A B C D E
4 A B C D E	14 A B C D E	24 A B C D E	34 A B C D E
5 A B C D E	15 A B C D E	25 A B C D E	35 A B C D E
6 A B C D E	16 A B C D E	26 A B C D E	36 A B C D E
7 A B C D E	17 A B C D E	27 A B C D E	37 A B C D E
8 A B C D E	18 A B C D E	28 A B C D E	38 A B C D E
9 A B C D E	19 A B C D E	29 A B C D E	39 A B C D E
10 A B C D E	20 A B C D E	30 A B C D E	40 A B C D E

SAT PRACTICE TEST 2

SECTION 1

Time: 25 Minutes—Turn to page 655 of your answer sheet to write your ESSAY.

The purpose of the essay is to have you show how well you can express and develop your ideas. You should develop your point of view, logically and clearly present your ideas, and use language accurately.

You should write your essay on the lines provided on your answer sheet. You should not write on any other paper. You will have enough space if you write on every line and if you keep your handwriting to a reasonable size. Make sure that your handwriting is legible to other readers.

You will have 25 minutes to write an essay on the assignment below. *Do not write on any other topic. If you do so, you will receive a score of 0.*

Think carefully about the issue presented in the following excerpt and the assignment below.

"It has been often said that rapid technological change requires us to change our morals, customs, and institutions. This observation is believable only if we assume that humanity was made for the machine, not the machine for humanity. If anything, technological progress makes our sense of tradition more necessary than ever.

"Maintaining traditions is not (or need not be) merely a resistance to change, but a positive attachment to some particular way of life and the community that embodies it."

—Adapted from Karl Jahn, "Tradition and Progress"

Assignment: In the above excerpt, Jahn argues that we do not have to change our traditions to keep pace with technological changes. To what extent do you agree or disagree with his position? Support your position with reasons and examples from your own experience, reading, and observations.

DO NOT WRITE YOUR ESSAY IN YOUR TEST BOOK. You will receive credit only for what you write on your answer sheet.

BEGIN WRITING YOUR ESSAY ON PAGE 655 OF THE ANSWER SHEET.

If you finish before time is called, you may check your work on this section only.
Do not turn to any other section in the test.

SECTION 2

Time: 25 Minutes—Turn to Section 2 (page 657) of your answer sheet to answer the questions in this section.
20 Questions

Directions: For this section, solve each problem and decide which is the best of the choices given. Fill in the corresponding circle on the answer sheet. You may use any available space for scratchwork.

Notes:

1. The use of a calculator is permitted.
2. All numbers used are real numbers.
3. Figures that accompany problems in this test are intended to provide information useful in solving the problems. They are drawn as accurately as possible EXCEPT when it is stated in a specific problem that the figure is not drawn to scale. All figures lie in a plane unless otherwise indicated.
4. Unless otherwise specified, the domain of any function f is assumed to be the set of all real numbers x for which $f(x)$ is a real number.

REFERENCE INFORMATION

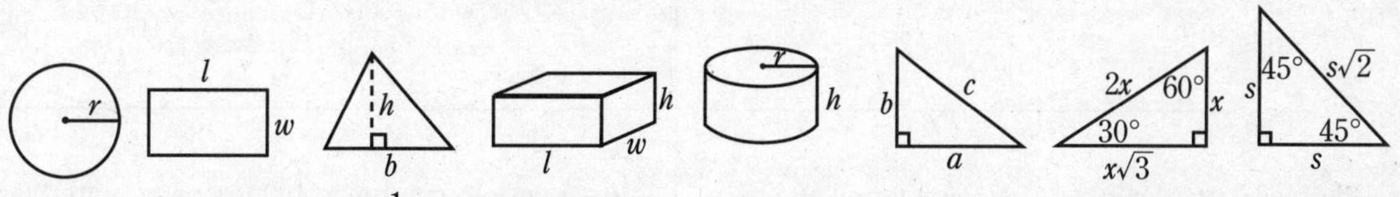

$A = \pi r^2$ $C = 2\pi r$ $A = lw$ $A = \frac{1}{2}bh$ $V = lwh$ $V = \pi r^2 h$ $c^2 = a^2 + b^2$ *Special Right Triangles*

The number of degrees of arc in a circle is 360.
The sum of the measures in degrees of the angles of a triangle is 180.

1. Given that $500w = 3 \times 700$, find the value of w.

(A) $\frac{5}{21}$
(B) 2
(C) $\frac{11}{5}$
(D) $\frac{21}{5}$
(E) 7

2. If $\frac{3+y}{y} = 7$, then $y =$

(A) 4
(B) 3
(C) 2
(D) 1
(E) $\frac{1}{2}$

GO ON TO THE NEXT PAGE

3. The positive integer x is a multiple of 9 and also a multiple of 12. The smallest possible value of x is

(A) 3
(B) 12
(C) 21
(D) 36
(E) 72

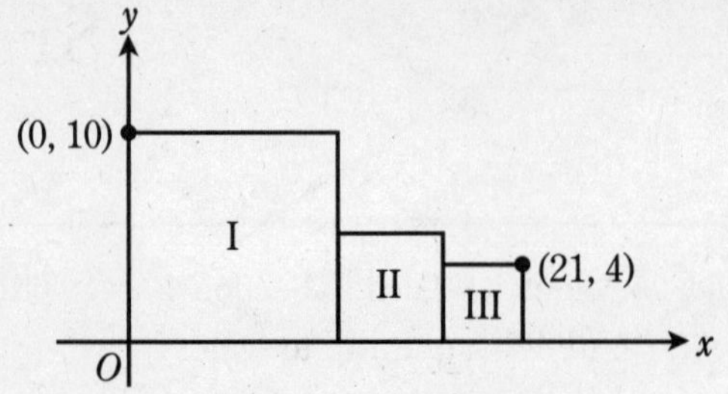

Note: Figure is not drawn to scale.

5. In the figure above, squares I, II, and III are situated along the x-axis as shown. Find the area of square II.

(A) 16
(B) 25
(C) 49
(D) 100
(E) 121

4. Find $(r - s)(t - s) + (s - r)(s - t)$ for all numbers $r, s,$ and t.

(A) 0
(B) 2
(C) $2rt$
(D) $2(s - r)(t - s)$
(E) $2(r - s)(t - s)$

6. A certain cup holds 100 grams of butter. If a cake requires 75 grams of butter and a pie requires 225 grams of butter, then 4 cups of butter is *not* enough for any of the following *except*

(A) 6 cakes
(B) 2 pies
(C) 3 cakes and 1 pie
(D) 2 cakes and 2 pies
(E) 2 cakes and 1 pie

GO ON TO THE NEXT PAGE

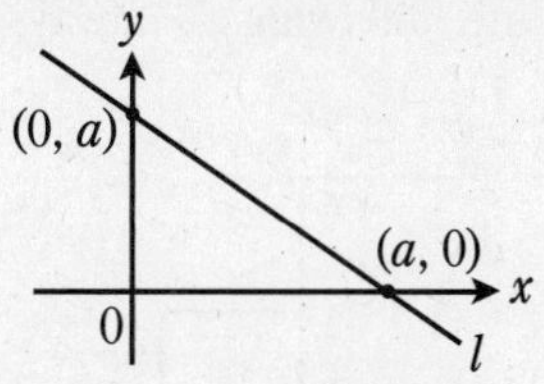

Note: Figure is not drawn to scale.

7. In the rectangular coordinate system above, which of the following is true about line ℓ?

I. the slope is -1
II. the distance of point $(0,a)$ to point $(a,0)$ is equal to $a\sqrt{2}$
III. the acute angle that line ℓ makes with the x-axis is 45°

(A) I only
(B) II only
(C) III only
(D) II and III only
(E) I, II, and III

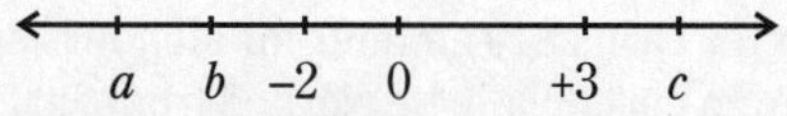

8. In the above number line, a, b, and c are real numbers. Which is true?

(A) $b > -1$
(B) $|b| < 2$
(C) $-|c| = c$
(D) $|b| > |a|$
(E) $|a| > |b|$

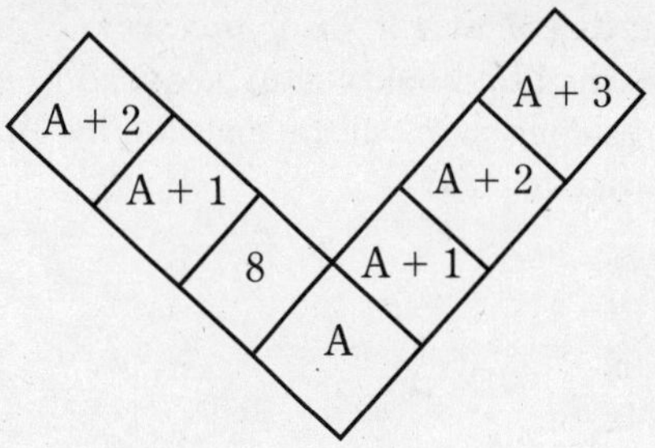

9. If the sum of the four terms in each of the diagonal rows is the same, then $A =$

(A) 4
(B) 5
(C) 6
(D) 7
(E) 8

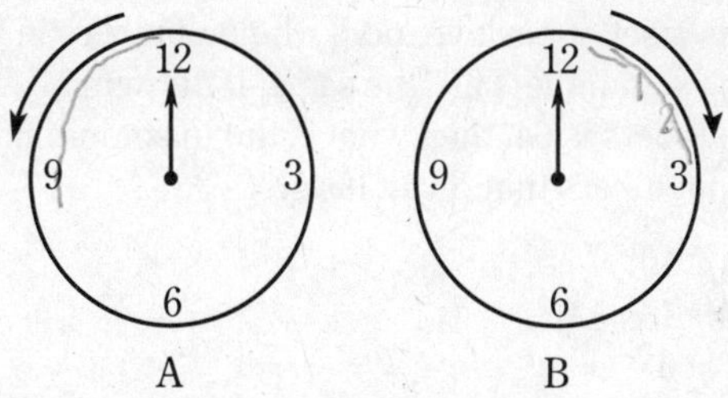

10. The two dials shown above operate simultaneously in the following manner. The hand in A turns *counterclockwise* while the hand in B turns *clockwise.* The hand of A moves to 9 at exactly the same moment that the hand of B moves to 3. Then the hand of A moves to 6 at exactly the same moment that the hand of B moves to 6, and so on. If each hand starts at 12, where will each hand be at the end of 17 moves?

(A) Both at 12
(B) Both at 9
(C) A at 3 and B at 12
(D) A at 3 and B at 9
(E) A at 9 and B at 3

GO ON TO THE NEXT PAGE

11. Given that $w = 7r + 6r + 5r + 4r + 3r$, which of the terms listed below may be added to w so that the resulting sum will be divisible by 7 for every positive integer r?

(A) $7r$
(B) $6r$
(C) $5r$
(D) $4r$
(E) $3r$

12. S is a set of positive, odd, whole numbers in which no two numbers are the same. If the sum of all of its members is 64, then what is the maximum number of members that S can have?

(A) 10
(B) 13
(C) 6
(D) 8
(E) 7

13. Which of the following is always true for real numbers a, b, x, y?

I. $(a^x)^y = a^{xy}$
II. $a^{x+y} = a^x a^y$
III. $(ab)^x = a^x b^x$

(A) I only
(B) II only
(C) III only
(D) I and II only
(E) I, II, and III

14. A painter earns $10 an hour for all hours spent on a job. For a certain job, he worked from 7:00 A.M. until 5:00 P.M. on Monday, Tuesday, and Thursday and from 1:00 P.M. until 7:00 P.M. on Wednesday, Friday, and Saturday. How much did he earn for the entire job?

(A) $420
(B) $450
(C) $480
(D) $510
(E) $540

GO ON TO THE NEXT PAGE

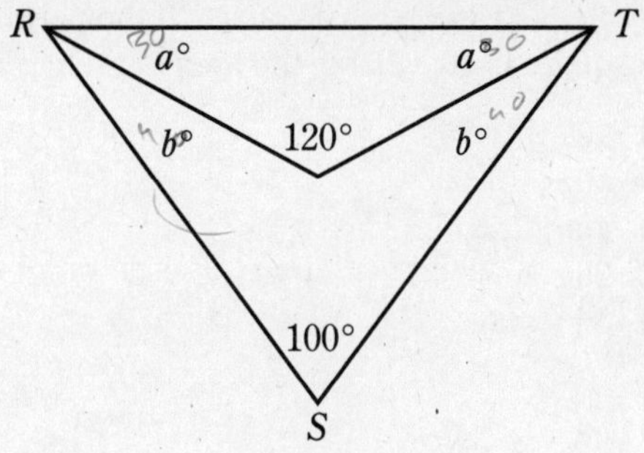

Note: Figure is not drawn to scale.

15. Given ΔRST above, what is the value of b?

(A) 50°
(B) 40°
(C) 30°
(D) 20°
(E) 10°

Question 16

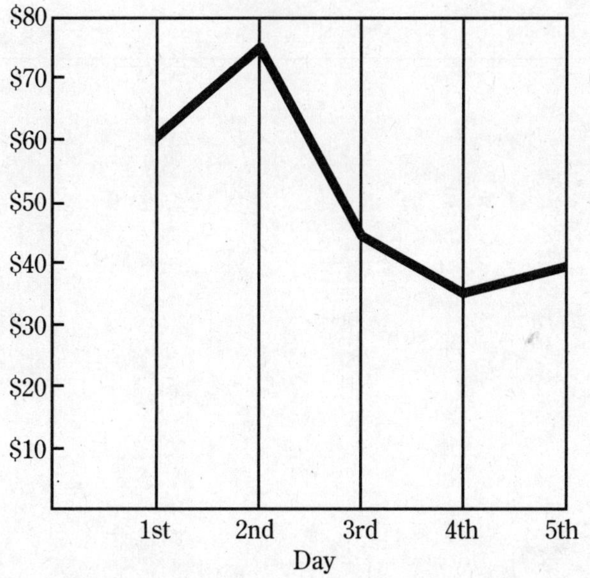

16. John works for 5 days. His daily earnings are displayed on the above graph. If John earned \$35 on the sixth day, what would be the difference between the median and the mode of the wages for the six days?

(A) \$5.50
(B) \$6.50
(C) \$7.50
(D) \$8.50
(E) \$9.50

17. If ⓐ ⓑ $= \dfrac{a+1}{b-1}$ where a and b are positive integers and $b > 1$, which of the following is largest?

(A) ②③
(B) ③③
(C) ③⑤
(D) ④⑤
(E) ⑤③

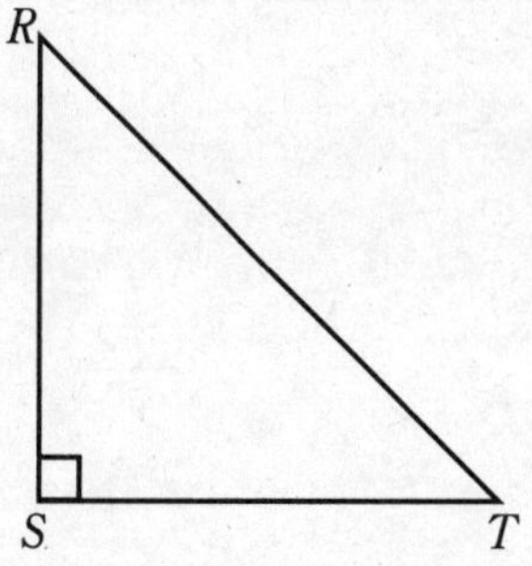

18. In ΔRST above, RS and ST have lengths equal to the same integer. All of the following could be the area of triangle RST *except*

(A) $\frac{1}{2}$
(B) 2
(C) $4\frac{1}{2}$
(D) $12\frac{1}{2}$
(E) 20

GO ON TO THE NEXT PAGE

19. A rectangular solid has dimensions of 2 feet × 2 feet × 1 foot. If it is sliced in small cubes, each of edge 0.1 foot, what is the maximum number of such cubes that can be formed?

(A) 40
(B) 500
(C) 1,000
(D) 2,000
(E) 4,000

20. A circle is inscribed in a square. If the perimeter of the square is 40, what is the area of the circle?

(A) 100π
(B) 50π
(C) 40π
(D) 25π
(E) 5π

STOP

If you finish before time is called, you may check your work on this section only.
Do not turn to any other section in the test.

Take a 5 minute break

before starting section 3

SECTION 3

Time: 25 Minutes—Turn to Section 3 (page 657) of your answer sheet to answer the questions in this section.
18 Questions

Directions: For this section, solve each problem and decide which is the best of the choices given. Fill in the corresponding circle on the answer sheet. You may use any available space for scratchwork.

Notes:

1. The use of a calculator is permitted.
2. All numbers used are real numbers.
3. Figures that accompany problems in this test are intended to provide information useful in solving the problems. They are drawn as accurately as possible EXCEPT when it is stated in a specific problem that the figure is not drawn to scale. All figures lie in a plane unless otherwise indicated.
4. Unless otherwise specified, the domain of any function f is assumed to be the set of all real numbers x for which $f(x)$ is a real number.

REFERENCE INFORMATION

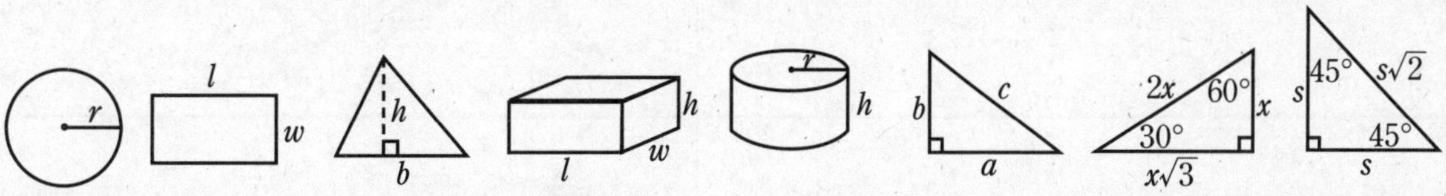

$A = \pi r^2$ $C = 2\pi r$ $A = lw$ $A = \frac{1}{2}bh$ $V = lwh$ $V = \pi r^2 h$ $c^2 = a^2 + b^2$ *Special Right Triangles*

The number of degrees of arc in a circle is 360.
The sum of the measures in degrees of the angles of a triangle is 180.

1. If 3 is added to a number and this sum is divided by 4, the result is 6. What is the number?

(A) 5
(B) 7
(C) 12
(D) 21
(E) 27

2. Given that $\frac{3}{4} < x < \frac{4}{5}$, which of the following is a possible value of x?

(A) $\frac{7}{16}$
(B) $\frac{13}{20}$
(C) $\frac{31}{40}$
(D) $\frac{16}{20}$
(E) $\frac{6}{7}$

GO ON TO THE NEXT PAGE

3. If the perimeter of a square is 20 meters, how many square meters are contained in its area?

(A) 100
(B) 25
(C) 20
(D) 10
(E) 5

4. Given that $80 + a = -32 + b$, find the value of $b - a$.

(A) −112
(B) −48
(C) 2.5
(D) 48
(E) 112

5. If x is a positive integer, which of the following must be an even integer?

(A) $x + 2$
(B) $2x + 1$
(C) $3x + 1$
(D) $x^2 + x + 1$
(E) $x^2 + x + 2$

6. If $ax = r$ and $by = r - 1$, then which of the following is a correct expression for x?

(A) $\frac{by + 1}{a}$
(B) $\frac{by - 1}{a}$
(C) $\frac{by + r}{a}$
(D) $by + ar$
(E) $ab + ry$

GO ON TO THE NEXT PAGE

7. Container A holds twice as much as container B, and container C holds as much as A and B put together. If we start with A and B full, and C empty, and pour half the contents of A and a third of the contents of B into container C, what fraction of C's capacity will be filled?

(A) $\frac{5}{6}$

(B) $\frac{4}{9}$

(C) $\frac{5}{12}$

(D) $\frac{7}{12}$

(E) $\frac{7}{18}$

8. What is the diameter of a wheel which, when rotating at a speed of 10 revolutions per minute, takes 12 seconds to travel 16 feet?

(A) 4π feet

(B) $\frac{4}{\pi}$ feet

(C) 8π feet

(D) $\frac{8}{\pi}$ feet

(E) $\frac{16}{\pi}$ feet

GO ON TO THE NEXT PAGE

Directions: For Student-Produced Response questions 9–18, use the grids at the bottom of the answer sheet page on which you have answered questions 1–8.

Each of the remaining 10 questions requires you to solve the problem and enter your answer by marking the circles in the special grid, as shown in the examples below. You may use any available space for scratchwork.

Answer: $\frac{7}{12}$ or 7/12

Write answer in boxes. →

Grid in result. →

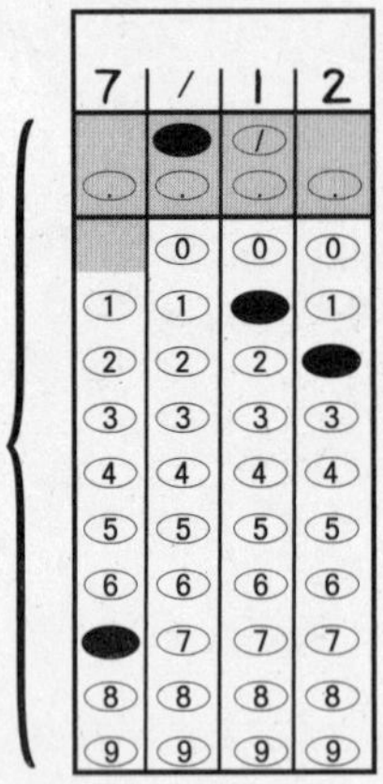

← Fraction line

Answer: 2.5

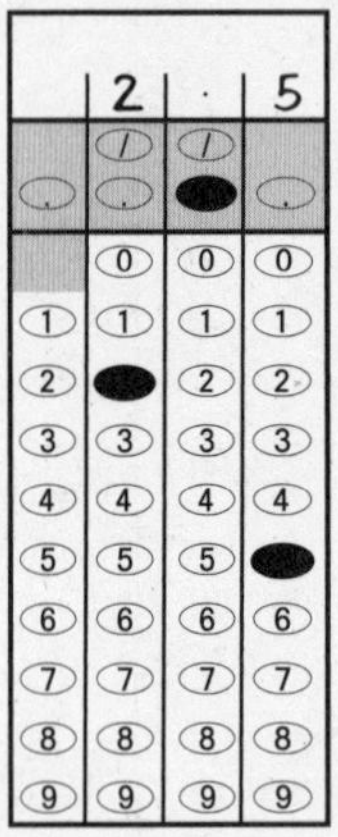

← Decimal point

Answer: 201
Either position is correct.

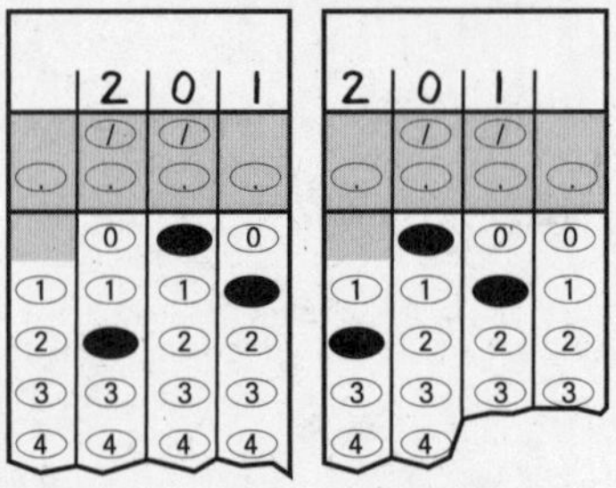

Note: You may start your answers in any column, space permitting. Columns not needed should be left blank.

- Mark no more than one oval in any column.
- Because the answer sheet will be machine-scored, **you will receive credit only if the ovals are filled in correctly.**
- Although not required, it is suggested that you write your answer in the boxes at the top of the columns to help you fill in the ovals accurately.
- Some problems may have more than one correct answer. In such cases, grid only one answer.
- No question has a negative answer.
- **Mixed numbers** such as $2\frac{1}{2}$ must be gridded as 2.5 or 5/2. (If  is gridded, it will be interpreted as $\frac{21}{2}$, not $2\frac{1}{2}$.)
- Decimal Accuracy: If you obtain a decimal answer, **enter the most accurate value the grid will accommodate.** For example, if you obtain an answer such as 0.6666..., you should record the result as .666 or .667. **Less accurate values such as .66 or .67 are not acceptable.**

Acceptable ways to grid $\frac{2}{3}$ = .6666...

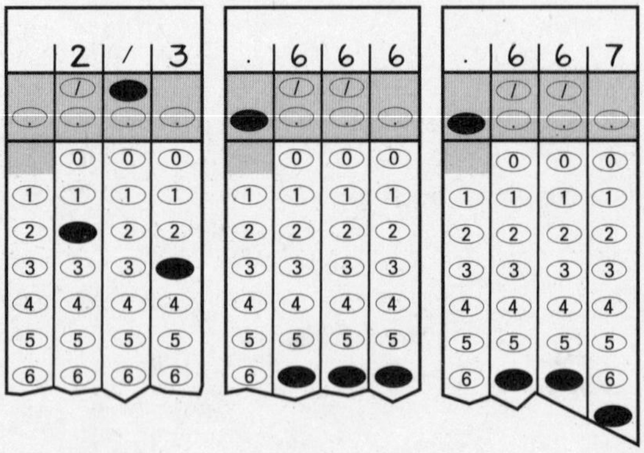

9. If $\frac{5}{8}$ of a number is 3 less than $\frac{3}{4}$ of the number, what is the number?

10. Let 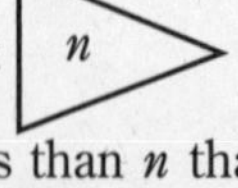 represent the greatest even integer less than n that divides n, for any positive integer n. For example, 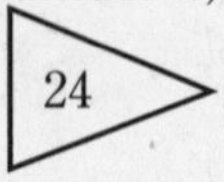 = 12. Find the value of 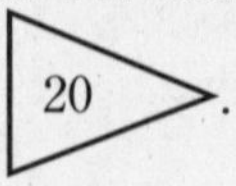.

GO ON TO THE NEXT PAGE

11. If $m = 94$ and $n = 6$, then find the value of $23m + 23n$.

2300

12. A horizontal line has a length of 100 yards. A vertical line is drawn at one of its ends. If lines are drawn every ten yards thereafter, until the other end is reached, how many vertical lines are finally drawn?

10

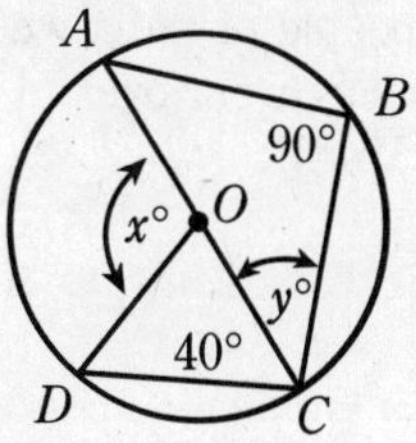

Note: Figure not drawn to scale

13. In the circle above with center O, diameter AC, and $AB = BC$, find the value of $x + y$.

108°

14. In a certain class containing 60 students, the average (arithmetic mean) age is 20. In another class containing 20 students, the average age is 40. Find the average age of all 80 students.

30

15. In the addition problem shown below, if □ is a constant, what must □ equal in order for the answer to be correct?

```
   □1
   6□
 + □9
 ----
  15□
```

□ = 4

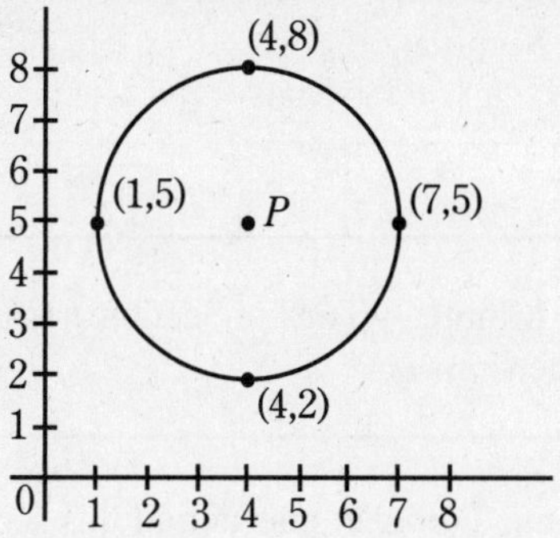

16. Given the circle above, with center P, what is the length of its radius?

17. A lawn covers 108.6 square feet. Russ mowed all of the lawn in three evenings. He mowed $\frac{2}{9}$ of the lawn during the first evening. He mowed twice that amount on the second evening. On the third and final evening he mowed the remaining lawn. How many square feet were mowed the third evening?

18. If 9 people are standing in a straight line in a circle, what is the *smallest* number of people who must move so that all 9 will be standing on the circumference of another circle?

STOP

If you finish before time is called, you may check your work on this section only.
Do not turn to any other section in the test.

SECTION 4

Time: 25 Minutes—Turn to Section 4 (page 658) of your answer sheet to answer the questions in this section.
24 Questions

Directions: For each question in this section, select the best answer from among the choices given and fill in the corresponding circle on the answer sheet.

Each sentence below has one or two blanks, each blank indicating that something has been omitted. Beneath the sentence are five words or sets of words labeled A through E. Choose the word or set of words that, when inserted in the sentence, best fits the meaning of the sentence as a whole.

Example:

Hoping to _______ the dispute, negotiators proposed a compromise that they felt would be _______ to both labor and management.

(A) enforce...useful
(B) end...divisive
(C) overcome...unattractive
(D) extend...satisfactory
(E) resolve...acceptable

Ⓐ Ⓑ Ⓒ Ⓓ ●

1. Though he was a highly skilled computer programmer, he had little or no _______ in designing educational software.

(A) emotion
(B) opportunity
(C) structure
(D) competition
(E) creativity

2. He is one of the most _______ professors that I have ever had, with a _______ knowledge of his subject and a thoroughness in his teaching.

(A) capable...limited
(B) tantamount...tremendous
(C) collegiate...remarkable
(D) scholarly...profound
(E) active...carefree

3. Because the people of India were _______ under British rule, many went over to the Japanese side during World War II.

(A) employed
(B) deported
(C) educated
(D) abused
(E) satisfied

4. The author told the publisher that the royalty payment specified in the contract was _______ because the research costs, including traveling for writing the book, were far more than the royalties projected for a year.

(A) rational
(B) precarious
(C) payable
(D) insufficient
(E) incomprehensible

5. Maggie was quite _______ about having her husband remove his shoes before he stepped into the living room; yet the rest of the apartment was very _______ whenever I visited them.

(A) indifferent...comfortable
(B) perplexed...weird
(C) firm...disorderly
(D) considerate...modern
(E) humorous...attractive

6. Those who were invited to Peter's party had to come dressed in _______ clothes, thus convincing all the guests of his _______ inclination.

(A) sonorous...imaginative
(B) tawdry...humble
(C) raucous...peace-loving
(D) tattered...nightmarish
(E) old-fashioned...nostalgic

GO ON TO THE NEXT PAGE

7. Her devotion to music ______ his own interest in an art he had once loved as a child.

(A) belied
(B) revived
(C) defiled
(D) reviled
(E) exiled

8. President Anwar el-Sadat of Egypt, disregarding ______ criticism in the Arab world and in his own government, ______ accepted Prime Minister Menachem Begin's invitation to visit Israel in order to address the Israeli Knesset.

(A) categorical…previously
(B) blemished…stiffly
(C) charismatic…meticulously
(D) acrimonious…formally
(E) malignant…plaintively

GO ON TO THE NEXT PAGE

Each passage below is followed by questions based on its content. Answer the questions on the basis of what is stated or implied in each passage and in any introductory material that may be provided.

Questions 9–10 are based on the following passage.

A legendary island in the Atlantic Ocean beyond the Pillars of Hercules was first mentioned by Plato in the *Timaeus*. Atlantis was a fabulously beautiful and prosperous land, the seat of an empire nine thousand years before Solon. Its inhabitants overran parts of Europe and Africa, Athens alone being able to defy them. Because of the impiety of its people, the island was destroyed by an earthquake and inundation. The legend may have existed before Plato and may have sprung from the concept of Homer's Elysium. The possibility that such an island once existed has caused much speculation, resulting in a theory that pre-Columbian civilizations in America were established by colonists from the lost island.

9. According to the passage, we may most safely conclude that the inhabitants of Atlantis

(A) were known personally to Homer
(B) were ruled by Plato
(C) were a religious and superstitious people
(D) used the name Columbia for America
(E) left no recorded evidence of their existence

10. According to the legend, Atlantis was destroyed because the inhabitants

(A) failed to obtain an adequate food supply
(B) failed to conquer Greece
(C) failed to respect their gods
(D) believed in Homer's Elysium
(E) had become too prosperous

Questions 11–12 are based on the following passage.

Lithography is the art of drawing with a greasy substance, usually crayon, on a stone, metal, or paper surface, and then printing. It is based on the fact that grease attracts grease and is repelled by water. It is the most direct of all the graphic arts, for in practicing it the artist first sees the exact value of each line that he draws and then has his drawing reproduced so accurately that it may truly be said to have been multiplied. In making either an etching, a process in which a drawing is engraved on a metal plate through a thin film of wax, or a woodblock, in which the drawing is carved in wood, the artist must wait for a print to estimate his work fairly. When a lithograph is made, the artist's drawing grows in definite values under his eyes and he can make changes in it as he works.

11. A great advantage of lithography as a means of reproducing drawings is that it

(A) is quicker and neater than other methods
(B) gives faithful reproductions
(C) requires a metal plate
(D) requires no special materials
(E) is less expensive than other methods

12. Many artists like to use lithography to reproduce their drawings because they

(A) know in advance the value of each picture
(B) often get unexpected results
(C) get higher prices for lithographs than for etchings
(D) can get clearer enlargements
(E) can make alterations and corrections

GO ON TO THE NEXT PAGE

Questions 13–24 are based on the following passage.

The following passage discusses advanced technological institutions and their relation to the workforce, with social implications.

A second major hypothesis would argue that the most important dimension of advanced technological institutions is the social one; that is, the institutions are agencies of highly centralized and intensive social control. Technology conquers nature, as the saying goes. But to do so it must first conquer man. More precisely, it demands a very high degree of control over the training, mobility, and skills of the workforce. The absence (or decline) of direct controls or of coercion should not serve to obscure from our view the reality and intensity of the social controls which are employed (such as the internalized belief in inequality of opportunity, indebtedness through credit, advertising, selective service channeling, and so on).

Advanced technology has created a vast increase in occupational specialties, many of them requiring many, many years of highly specialized training. It must motivate this training. It has made ever more complex and "rational" the ways in which these occupational specialties are combined in our economic and social life. It must win passivity and obedience to this complex activity. Formerly, technical rationality had been employed only to organize the production of rather simple physical objects, for example, aerial bombs. Now technical rationality is increasingly employed to organize all of the processes necessary to the utilization of physical objects, such as bombing systems, maintenance, intelligence and supply systems. For this reason it seems a mistake to argue that we are in a "post-industrial" age, a concept favored by the *laissez innover* school. On the contrary, the rapid spread of technical rationality into organizational and economic life and, hence, into social life is more aptly described as a second and much more intensive phase of the industrial revolution. One might reasonably suspect that it will create analogous social problems.

Accordingly, a third major hypothesis would argue that there are very profound social antagonisms or contradictions not less sharp or fundamental than those ascribed by Marx to the development of nineteenth-century industrial society. The general form of the contradictions might be described as follows: a society characterized by the employment of advanced technology requires an ever more socially disciplined population, yet retains an ever declining capacity to enforce the required discipline.

One may readily describe four specific forms of the same general contradiction. Occupationally, the workforce must be over-trained and under-utilized. Here, again, an analogy to classical industrial practice serves to shorten and simplify the explanation. I have in mind the assembly line. As a device in the organization of the work process, the assembly line is valuable mainly in that it gives management a high degree of control over the pace of the work and, more to the point in the present case, it divides the work process into units so simple that the quality of the work performed is readily predictable. That is, since each operation uses only a small fraction of a worker's skill, there is a very great likelihood that the operation will be performed in a minimally acceptable way. Alternately, if each operation taxed the worker's skill, there would be frequent errors in the operation, frequent disturbance of the work flow, and a thoroughly unpredictable quality to the end product. The assembly line also introduces standardization in work skills and thus makes for a high degree of interchangeability among the workforce.

For analogous reasons the workforce in advanced technological systems must be relatively over-trained or, what is the same thing, its skills relatively under-used. My impression is that this is no less true now of sociologists than of welders, of engineers than of assemblers. The contradiction emerges when we recognize that technological progress requires a continuous increase in the skill levels of its workforce, skill levels which frequently embody a fairly rich scientific and technical training, while at the same time the advance of technical rationality in work organization means that those skills will be less and less fully used.

Economically, there is a parallel process at work. It is commonly observed that the workforce within technologically advanced organizations is asked to work not less hard but more so. This is particularly true for those with advanced training and skills. Brzezinski's conjecture that technical specialists undergo continuous retraining is off the mark only in that it assumes such retraining only for a managing elite. To get people to work harder requires growing incentives. Yet the prosperity which is assumed in a technologically advanced society erodes the value of economic incentives (while of course, the values of craftsmanship are "irrational"). Salary and wage increases and the goods they purchase lose their overriding importance once necessities, creature comforts, and an ample supply of luxuries are assured. As if in confirmation of this point, it has been pointed out that among young people, one can already observe a radical weakening in the power of such incentives as money, status, and authority.

GO ON TO THE NEXT PAGE

13. The term "technical rationality" in line 20 is used in conjunction with

(A) a 20th-century euphemism for the industrial revolution
(B) giving credibility to products of simple technology
(C) the incorporation of unnecessary skills into economic social living
(D) effective organization of production processes
(E) safeguarding against technological over-acceleration

14. The author states that advanced technological institutions exercise control by means of

(A) assembly-line work process
(B) advertising, selective service channeling, etc.
(C) direct and coercive pressures
(D) salary incentives
(E) authoritarian managerial staffs

15. The word "taxed" in line 56 means

(A) a burdensome or excessive demand on the worker
(B) a financial obstacle the worker must endure
(C) the speed at which the worker must complete the job
(D) the efficiency of the worker's performance on the job
(E) the standardization in work skills of the work-force

16. The passage indicates that technologically advanced institutions

(A) fully utilize worker skills
(B) fare best under a democratic system
(C) necessarily overtrain workers
(D) find it unnecessary to enforce discipline
(E) are operated by individuals motivated by traditional work incentives

17. The value of the assembly line is that it

I. minimizes the frequency of error
II. allows for interchangeability among the work-force
III. allows for full utilization of workers' skills

(A) I and III only
(B) I and II only
(C) II and III only
(D) I, II, and III
(E) I only

18. Technologies cannot conquer nature unless

(A) there is unwavering worker allegiance to the goals of the institutions
(B) there is strict adherence to a *laissez innover* policy
(C) worker and management are in concurrence
(D) there is another more intense, industrial revolution
(E) the institutions have control over the training, mobility, and skills of the workforce

19. The article states that the workforce within the framework of a technologically advanced organization is

(A) expected to work less hard
(B) segregated into levels defined by the degree of technical training
(C) familiarized with every process of production
(D) expected to work harder
(E) isolated by the fact of its specialization

20. From the tone of the article, it can be inferred that the author is

(A) an eloquent spokesman for technological advancement
(B) in favor of increased employee control of industry
(C) a social scientist objectively reviewing an industrial trend
(D) vehemently opposed to the increase of technology
(E) skeptical of the workings of advanced technological institutions

21. According to the author, economic incentives

(A) are necessary for all but the managerial elite
(B) are bigger and better in a society made prosperous by technology
(C) cease to have importance beyond a certain level of luxury
(D) are impressive only to new members of the workforce
(E) are impressive to all but the radical young

22. The "managing elite" in line 80 refers to

(A) all the "blue" collar workers
(B) the assembly-line workers only
(C) the craftsman only
(D) the owners of the organizations
(E) the top technical specialists

GO ON TO THE NEXT PAGE

23. According to the article, technological progress requires

I. increasing skill levels of workforce
II. less utilization of work skills
III. rich scientific and technical training

(A) I and II only
(B) II and III only
(C) I and III only
(D) III only
(E) I, II, and III

24. The article states that money, status, and authority

(A) will always be powerful work incentives
(B) are not powerful incentives for the young
(C) are unacceptable to radical workers
(D) are incentives that are a throwback to 19th-century industrial society
(E) are incentives evolving out of human nature

STOP

If you finish before time is called, you may check your work on this section only. Do not turn to any other section in the test.

Take a 1 minute break

before starting section 5

SECTION 5

Time: 25 Minutes—Turn to Section 5 (page 658) of your answer sheet to answer the questions in this section.
35 Questions

Directions: For each question in this section, select the best answer from among the choices given and fill in the corresponding circle on the answer sheet.

The following sentences test correctness and effectiveness of expression. Part of each sentence or the entire sentence is underlined; beneath each sentence are five ways of phrasing the underlined material. Choice A repeats the original phrasing; the other four choices are different. If you think the original phrasing produces a better sentence than any of the alternatives, select Choice A; if not, select one of the other choices.

In making your selection, follow the requirements of standard written English; that is, pay attention to grammar, choice of words, sentence construction, and punctuation. Your selection should result in the most effective sentence—clear and precise, without awkwardness or ambiguity.

EXAMPLE:

Laura Ingalls Wilder published her first book and she was sixty-five years old then.

(A) and she was sixty-five years old then
(B) when she was sixty-five
(C) at age sixty-five years old
(D) upon the reaching of sixty-five years
(E) at the time when she was sixty-five

Ⓐ ● Ⓒ Ⓓ Ⓔ

1. Although I know this house and this neighborhood as well as I know myself, and although my friend here seems not hardly to know them at all, nevertheless he has lived here longer than I.

(A) and although my friend here seems not hardly to know them at all
(B) and even though my friend here seems hardly to know them at all
(C) and in spite of the fact that my friend doesn't hardly seem to know them at all
(D) and because my friend here hardly seems to know them at all
(E) my friend here seems hardly to know them at all

2. So I leave it with all of you: Which came out of the open door—the lady or the tiger.

(A) the lady or the tiger.
(B) the lady or the Tiger!
(C) the Tiger or the lady.
(D) the Lady or the tiger.
(E) the lady or the tiger?

3. The machine is not easy to fool, it isn't altogether foolproof either.

(A) it isn't altogether foolproof either
(B) or is it foolproof
(C) and it isn't completely fooled by anyone
(D) nor is it entirely foolproof
(E) so it isn't altogether foolproof

4. The police and agents of the F.B.I. arrested the owner of a Madison Avenue art gallery yesterday and charged him with receiving paintings stolen last November.

(A) arrested the owner of a Madison Avenue art gallery yesterday
(B) yesterday arrested the owner of a Madison Avenue art gallery
(C) arrested the owner yesterday of a Madison Avenue art gallery
(D) had the owner of a Madison Avenue art gallery yesterday arrested
(E) arranged the arrest yesterday of a Madison Avenue art gallery owner

GO ON TO THE NEXT PAGE

5. Deciding whether Shakespeare's plays or his sonnets are better poetry, that is a task only for those prepared to examine the texts closely and able to distinguish subtle differences in the use of poetic devices.

(A) Deciding whether Shakespeare's plays or his sonnets are better poetry, that is a task
(B) In deciding whether Shakespeare's plays or his sonnets are better poetry is a task
(C) In order to decide whether Shakespeare's plays or his sonnets are better poetry is a task
(D) Deciding whether Shakespeare's plays or his sonnets are the best poetry is a task
(E) Deciding whether Shakespeare's plays or his sonnets are better poetry is a task

6. Go where he may, he is the life of the party.

(A) Go where he may,
(B) Where he may go,
(C) Wherever he goes,
(D) Wherever he may happen to go,
(E) Whatever he does,

7. At first we were willing to support him, afterwards it occurred to us that he ought to provide for himself.

(A) afterwards it occurred to us that
(B) that wasn't the thing to do since
(C) but we came to realize that
(D) we came to the conclusion, however, that
(E) then we decided that

8. The statistics were checked and the report was filed.

(A) The statistics were checked and the report was filed.
(B) The statistics and the report were checked and filed.
(C) The statistics were checked and the report filed.
(D) The statistics and the report were checked and filed respectively.
(E) Only after the statistics were checked was the report filed.

9. Dick was awarded a medal for bravery on account he risked his life to save the drowning child.

(A) on account he risked his life
(B) being that he risked his life
(C) when he risked his life
(D) the reason being on account of his risking his life
(E) since he had risked his life

10. The teacher asked the newly admitted student which was the country that she came from.

(A) which was the country that she came from.
(B) from which country she had come from.
(C) the origin of the country she had come from.
(D) which country have you come from?
(E) which country she was from.

11. If Jack would have listened to his wife, he would not have bought those worthless stocks.

(A) would have listened to his wife
(B) would listen to his wife
(C) had listened to his wife
(D) listened to what his wife had said
(E) would have listened to his wife's advice

GO ON TO THE NEXT PAGE

The following sentences test your ability to recognize grammar and usage errors. Each sentence contains either a single error or no error at all. No sentence contains more than one error. The error, if there is one, is underlined and lettered. If the sentence contains an error, select the one underlined part that must be changed to make the sentence correct. If the sentence is correct, select Choice E. In choosing answers, follow the requirements of standard written English.

Example:

The other (A) delegates and him (B) immediately (C) accepted the resolution drafted by (D) the neutral states. No error. (E)

Ⓐ ● Ⓒ Ⓓ Ⓔ

12. The girl who won (A) the beauty contest is nowhere near (B) as beautiful as (C) my mother was (D) when she was a bride. No error. (E)

13. Sitting opposite (A) my sister and me (B) in the subway were them (C) same men who walked alongside (D) us and tried to speak to us on Fifth Avenue. No error. (E)

14. Even if (A) Detroit could provide nonpolluting (B) cars by the original deadline to meet prescribed (C) federal standards for clean air, the effect in big cities would be slight because only (D) new cars would be properly equipped. No error. (E)

15. Of the two cars that the Smiths have, (A) the Plymouth is, without any question, (B) the cheapest (C) to run. (D) No error. (E)

16. Man cannot (A) live by bread (B) alone, or (C) can he live (D) without bread. No error. (E)

17. Having swam (A) two-thirds (B) of the distance across (C) the English Channel, Dixon could not give up (D) now. No error. (E)

18. In the discussion, one speaker held (A) that, since we live in a money-oriented (B) society, the average individual cares little (C) about solving anyone's else (D) problems. No error. (E)

19. Due to (A) the meat boycott, the butchers were doing (B) about half of (C) the business that they were doing previous (D) to the boycott. No error. (E)

20. We requested the superintendent of the building to clean (A) up the storage room in (B) the basement so that (C) the children had (D) enough space for their bicycles. No error. (E)

21. Lidocaine's (A) usefulness as (B) a local anesthetic was discovered by two Swedish chemists who repeatedly tested (C) the drug's (D) effects on their bodies. No error. (E)

22. After he won (A) the marathon relatively easily, (B) he decided to continue his training program and even to enter (D) more races. No error. (E)

GO ON TO THE NEXT PAGE

23. Learning by doing, long a guiding principal of
A B C
many educators, has been somewhat neglected
D
during the current back-to-basics boom. No error.
E

24. The Watergate scandal may be a thing of the past,
A B
but the Republicans will feel it's effects for a long
C D
time to come. No error.
E

25. If we had began our vacation a day earlier, we
A B
wouldn't have had so much trouble getting a plane
C D
reservation. No error.
E

26. All of the class presidents but Jerry, Alice, and
A
I were at the meeting to select the delegates for next
B C
month's convention. No error.
D E

27. Everyone who attends a concert at the sports
A B
arena knows that they will be searched for drugs
C
before entering. No error.
D E

28. Our professor assigned us to write a short story,
A B
but I found I could not write one quick. No error.
C D E

29. One of the key suspects in the killing of a
A B
United States drug agent were captured early
C D
today by the police. No error.
E

GO ON TO THE NEXT PAGE

Directions: The following passage is an early draft of an essay. Some parts of the passage need to be rewritten.

Read the passage and select the best answers for the questions that follow. Some questions are about particular sentences or parts of sentences and ask you to improve sentence structure or word choice. Other questions ask you to consider organization and development. In choosing answers, follow the requirements of standard written English.

Questions 30–35 refer to the following passage.

[1]The typical Miwok Indian village was compromised of both private family dwellings and communal dwellings. [2]One was a men's sweathouse. [3]In the sweathouse, grown men and adolescent boys who were learning to be hunters sat around a small, open fire. [4]Sometimes exchanging information and anecdotes and sometimes preparing themselves for the hunt to come by fasting, sweating and silent contemplation. [5]Occasionally a woman past childbearing age would be admitted to the sweathouse. [6]Adolescent girls learned to weave baskets and cook. [7]When one of these older women was accepted into the membership of the Miwok men's "clubhouse," her acceptance was by popular acclaim and was based on her ability to tell entertaining or enlightening stories. [8]As far as anthropologists know, no equal accommodations were made for males to enter the communal women's house, which was set aside for menstruating or pregnant women.

30. What should be done with sentence 1?

(A) It should be omitted.
(B) Was compromised of should be changed to included.
(C) It should be joined to sentence 2 with a semicolon.
(D) It should not be changed.
(E) The words was and of should be omitted.

31. Sentence 2 should

(A) be left as it is
(B) begin with there instead of one
(C) be joined to sentence 1 with and, omitting one was
(D) omitted
(E) begin with among the latter instead of one

32. Sentence 3 would be most improved by

(A) connecting it to sentence 2 with *where* and omitting in the sweat house
(B) omitting adolescent
(C) placing learning to be hunters before grown men and omitting who were
(D) connecting it to sentence 2 with a semicolon
(E) beginning with It was there

33. Sentence 4 ought to

(A) be made into two sentences, the first to end with anecdotes
(B) begin with Sometimes they exchanged
(C) be improved by substituting once in a while for the second sometimes
(D) be connected to sentence 3 with a comma
(E) have or substituted for and sometimes after anecdotes

34. What is the best thing to do with sentence 6?

(A) Place it in parentheses in sentence 3, after adolescent boys.
(B) Place it before sentence 5.
(C) Omit it.
(D) Place it after sentence 7.
(E) Leave it as it is.

35. Sentence 8 should

(A) stop after house
(B) be placed after sentence 5
(C) be made into two sentences, the first to end after house
(D) begin a new paragraph
(E) have ladies substituted for women

STOP

If you finish before time is called, you may check your work on this section only.
Do not turn to any other section in the test.

SECTION 6

Time: 25 Minutes—Turn to Section 6 (page 659) of your answer sheet to answer the questions in this section.
18 Questions

Directions: This section contains two types of questions. You have 25 minutes to complete both types. For questions 1–8, solve each problem and decide which is the best of the choices given. Fill in the corresponding circle on the answer sheet. You may use any available space for scratchwork.

Notes:

1. The use of a calculator is permitted.
2. All numbers used are real numbers.
3. Figures that accompany problems in this test are intended to provide information useful in solving the problems. They are drawn as accurately as possible EXCEPT when it is stated in a specific problem that the figure is not drawn to scale. All figures lie in a plane unless otherwise indicated.
4. Unless otherwise specified, the domain of any function *f* is assumed to be the set of all real numbers *x* for which *f*(*x*) is a real number.

REFERENCE INFORMATION

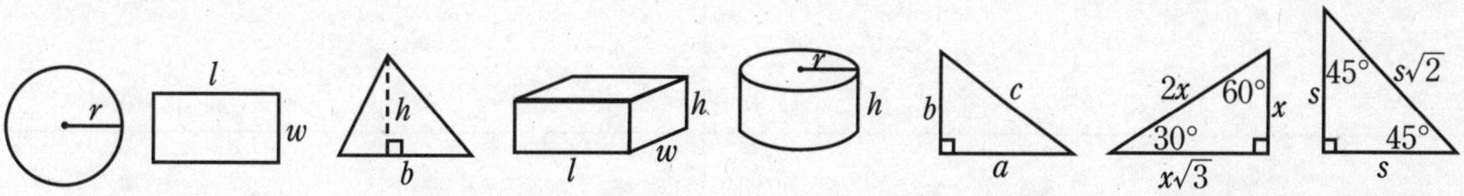

$A = \pi r^2$ $A = lw$ $A = \frac{1}{2}bh$ $V = lwh$ $V = \pi r^2 h$ $c^2 = a^2 + b^2$ *Special Right Triangles*

$C = 2\pi r$

The number of degrees of arc in a circle is 360.
The sum of the measures in degrees of the angles of a triangle is 180.

1. If *a*, *b* are odd numbers, and *c* is even, which of the following is an even number?

(A) $ab + c$
(B) $a(b + c)$
(C) $(a + b) + (b + c)$
(D) $(a + b) - c$
(E) $a + bc$

2. Distribution of Stamps in Harry's Collection

English	22%
French	18%
South American	25%
U.S.	35%

Distribution of U.S. Stamps in Harry's Collection

Commemoratives	52%
Special Delivery	10%
Postage Due	15%
Air Mail	23%

According to the table above, of Harry's collection, U.S. Air Mail stamps make up

(A) 4.00%
(B) 8.05%
(C) 15.50%
(D) 16.00%
(E) 21.35%

GO ON TO THE NEXT PAGE

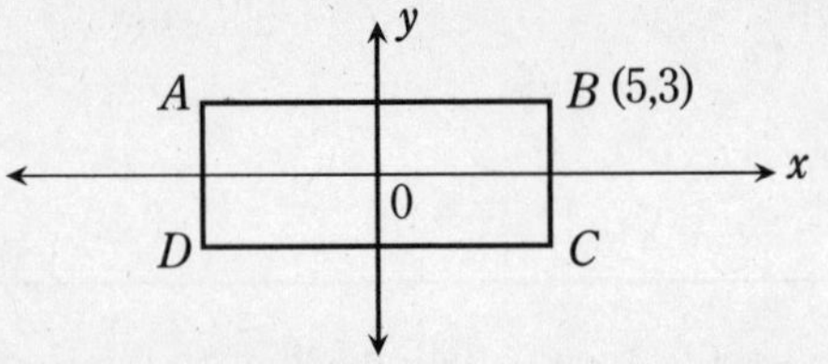

3. In the figure above, the sides of rectangle *ABCD* are parallel to the *y*-axis and *x*-axis as shown. If the rectangle is rotated clockwise about the origin through 90°, what are the new coordinates of *B*?

(A) (3, −5)
(B) (−3, 5)
(C) (−3, −5)
(D) (5, −3)
(E) (−5, 3)

4. The half-life of a certain radioactive substance is 6 hours. In other words, if you start with 8 grams of the substance, 6 hours later you will have 4 grams. If a sample of this substance contains *x* grams, how many grams remain after 24 hours?

(A) $\frac{x}{32}$
(B) $\frac{x}{16}$
(C) $\frac{x}{8}$
(D) $2x$
(E) $4x$

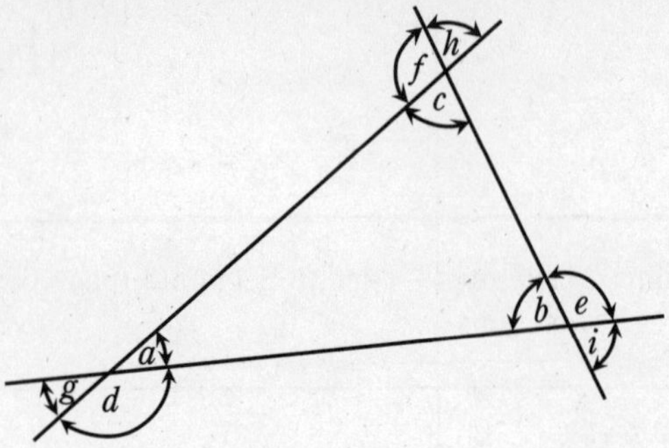

5. In the figure above, what is the sum of the degree measures of the marked angles?

(A) 360°
(B) 720°
(C) 900°
(D) 1080°
(E) The answer cannot be determined from the information given.

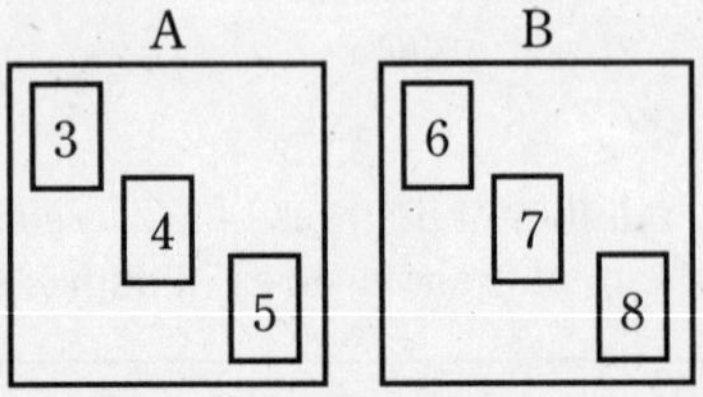

6. Box A contains 3 cards, numbered 3, 4, and 5. Box B contains 3 cards, numbered 6, 7, and 8. If one card is drawn from each box and their sum is calculated, how many different numerical results are possible?

(A) eight
(B) seven
(C) six
(D) five
(E) four

GO ON TO THE NEXT PAGE

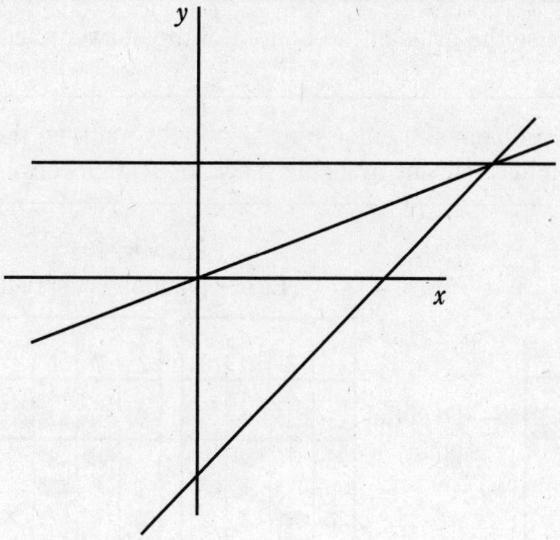

7. Which of the following equations could *not* represent any of the above graphs?

(A) $2y = x$
(B) $y = 2$
(C) $y = 2x - 6$
(D) $y = 2x + 4$
(E) $y = 4$

8. If $f(x) = |x| - x$, which of the following is true?

(A) $f(x) = f(-x)$
(B) $f(2x) = 2f(x)$
(C) $f(x + y) = f(x) + f(y)$
(D) $f(x) = -f(-x)$
(E) $f(x - y) = 0$

GO ON TO THE NEXT PAGE

Directions: For Student-Produced Response questions 9–18, use the grids at the bottom of the answer sheet page on which you have answered questions 1–8.

Each of the remaining 10 questions requires you to solve the problem and enter your answer by marking the circles in the special grid, as shown in the examples below. You may use any available space for scratchwork.

Answer: $\frac{7}{12}$ or 7/12

Answer: 2.5

Answer: 201
Either position is correct.

Write answer in boxes. →

Grid in result. →

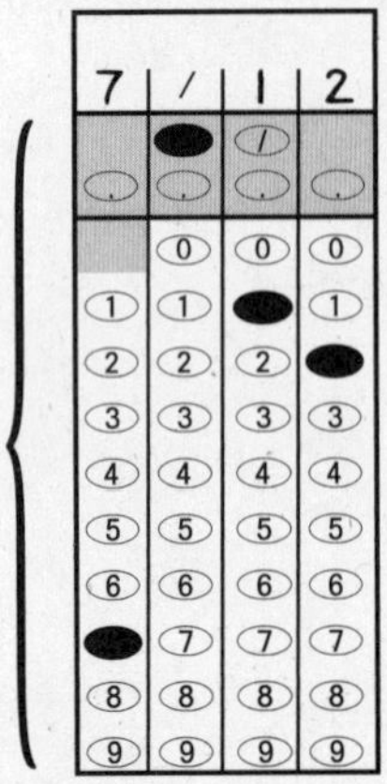

← Fraction line

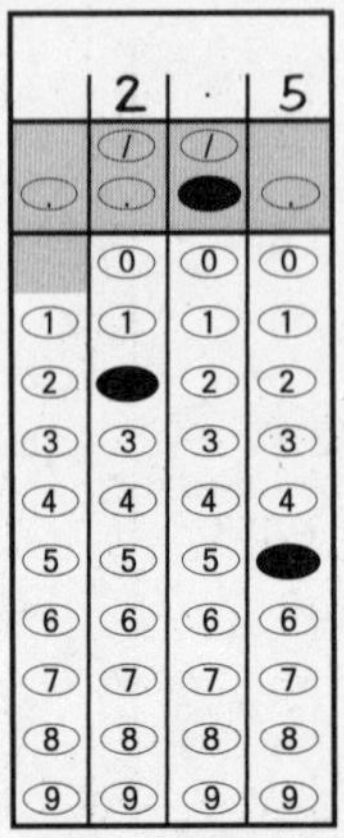

← Decimal point

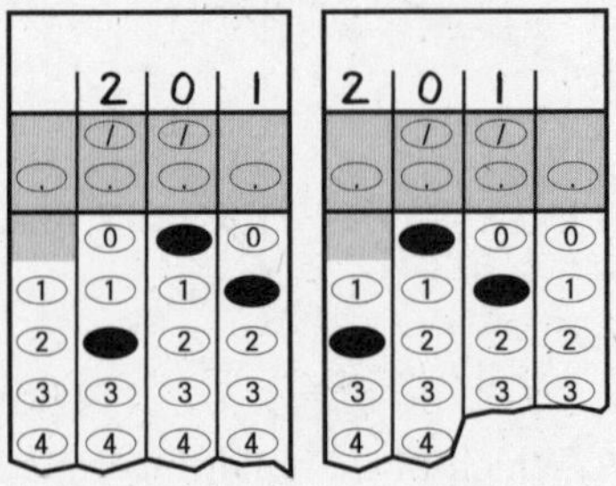

Note: You may start your answers in any column, space permitting. Columns not needed should be left blank.

- Mark no more than one oval in any column.
- Because the answer sheet will be machine-scored, **you will receive credit only if the ovals are filled in correctly.**
- Although not required, it is suggested that you write your answer in the boxes at the top of the columns to help you fill in the ovals accurately.
- Some problems may have more than one correct answer. In such cases, grid only one answer.
- No question has a negative answer.
- **Mixed numbers** such as $2\frac{1}{2}$ must be gridded as 2.5 or 5/2. (If 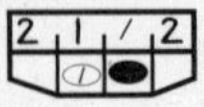 is gridded, it will be interpreted as $\frac{21}{2}$, not $2\frac{1}{2}$.)
- Decimal Accuracy: If you obtain a decimal answer, **enter the most accurate value the grid will accommodate.** For example, if you obtain an answer such as 0.6666..., you should record the result as .666 or .667. **Less accurate values such as .66 or .67 are not acceptable.**

Acceptable ways to grid $\frac{2}{3}$ = .6666...

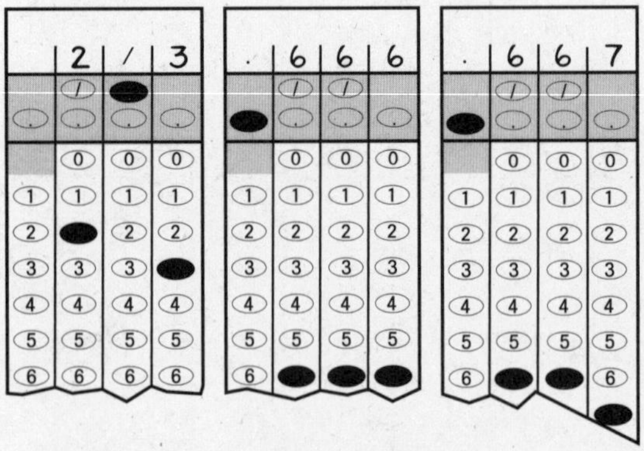

9. If f is a linear function and $f(5) = 6$ and $f(7) = 8$ what is the slope of the graph of f in the xy plane?

10. A bag contains exactly 4 blue marbles, 7 green marbles, and 8 yellow marbles. Fred draws marbles at random from the bag without replacement, one by one. If he does not look at the marbles he draws out, what is the smallest number of marbles he will have to draw out before he knows for sure that on his *next* draw he will have marbles in every color?

GO ON TO THE NEXT PAGE

11. If 12 is the average (arithmetic mean) of 5 different integers, each integer > 0, then what is the greatest that any one of the integers could be?

12. A classroom has 12 seated students, 5 students at the board, and 7 empty seats. If 3 students leave the room, 2 enter, and all now in the room are seated, how many empty seats will there be?

13. How many different *pairs* of parallel edges are there on a rectangular solid?

14. If the sum of $2r$ and $2r + 3$ is less than 11, find a positive value of r.

GO ON TO THE NEXT PAGE

15. Given the sum of two angles of a quadrilateral is 90°, find the average (arithmetic mean) of the measures of the other two angles. (Disregard the degree sign when gridding in your answer.)

17. If $x^2 + 2xy + y^2 = 25$, $x + y > 0$ and $x - y = 1$, then find the value of x.

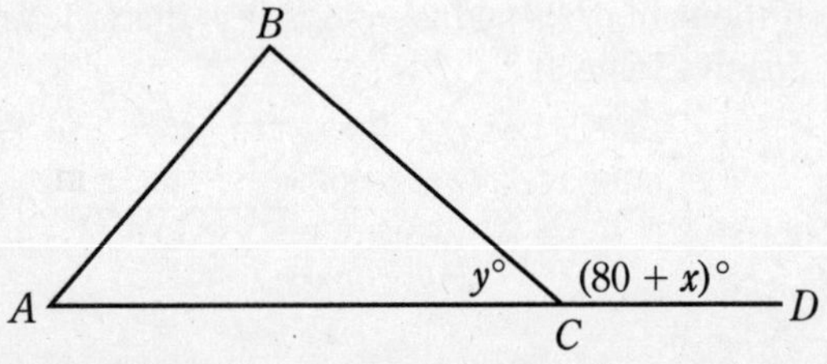

Note: Figure is not drawn to scale.

16. If AD is a straight line segment in the figure above, find the value of $x + y$.

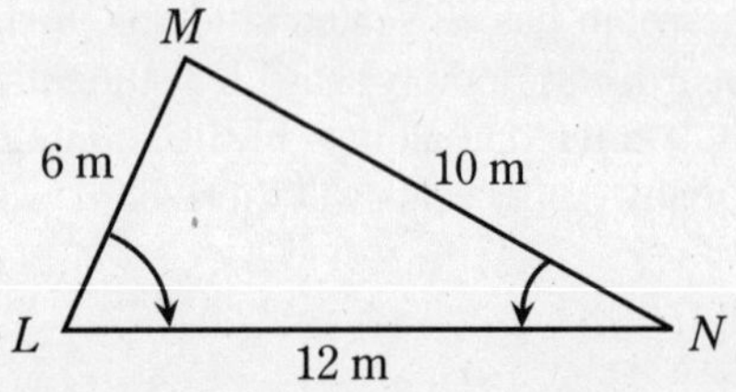

18. In the figure above, if sides LM and NM are cut apart from each other at point M creating 2 free-swinging segments and each is folded down to LN in the directions shown by the arrows, what will be the length, in meters, of the overlap of the 2 segments? (Disregard the thickness of the segments.)

STOP

If you finish before time is called, you may check your work on this section only.
Do not turn to any other section in the test.

Take a 5 minute break

before starting section 7

SECTION 7

Time: 25 Minutes—Turn to Section 7 (page 659) of your answer sheet to answer the questions in this section.
24 Questions

Directions: For each question in this section, select the best answer from among the choices given and fill in the corresponding circle on the answer sheet.

Each sentence below has one or two blanks, each blank indicating that something has been omitted. Beneath the sentence are five words or sets of words labeled A through E. Choose the word or set of words that, when inserted in the sentence, best fits the meaning of the sentence as a whole.

Example:

Hoping to ________ the dispute, negotiators proposed a compromise that they felt would be ________ to both labor and management.

(A) enforce...useful
(B) end...divisive
(C) overcome...unattractive
(D) extend...satisfactory
(E) resolve...acceptable

Ⓐ Ⓑ Ⓒ Ⓓ ●

1. The foreman's leniency, especially in being over-friendly, had its ________, one of which was ________ workmanship.

(A) compensations...unacceptable
(B) innuendoes...superior
(C) drawbacks...shoddy
(D) frequencies...attractive
(E) cancellations...mediocre

2. Although the physical setup of the high school's lunchroom seems rundown in many respects, it was enlarged and ________ quite recently.

(A) visited
(B) examined
(C) occupied
(D) renovated
(E) criticized

3. The activities that interested Jack were those that provided him with ________ pleasure, like dancing, feasting, and partying.

(A) questionable
(B) distant
(C) immediate
(D) limited
(E) delayed

4. His current inability to complete his assignments in a timely and efficient manner has resulted in a feeling of ________ even in his most ________ backers.

(A) urgency...lackadaisical
(B) flexibility...hostile
(C) expectancy...cautious
(D) dizziness...visible
(E) disappointment...fervent

5. The two performers taking the parts of shy, romantic teenagers were quite ________ in their roles even though they were in their forties.

(A) convincing
(B) flippant
(C) amateurish
(D) personable
(E) boring

GO ON TO THE NEXT PAGE

The two passages below are followed by questions based on their content and on the relationship between the two passages. Answer the questions on the basis of what is stated or implied in the passages and in any introductory material that may be provided.

Questions 6–9 are based on the following passages.

Passage 1

To keep clear of concealment, to keep clear of the need of concealment, to do nothing which one might not do out in a crowded street of onlookers in the heart of a city at the middle of the day—I cannot say to me how more and more it seems to me to be the glory of a young man's life. It is an awful hour when the first necessity of hiding anything comes. The whole life is different thereafter. When there are questions to be feared and eyes to be avoided and subjects which must not be touched, then the bloom of life is gone. Put off that day as long as possible. Put it off forever if you can.

Passage 2

Keeping things to yourself is an art. It is indeed a virtue to be able to hold back and not share what you would otherwise be tempted to convey. We must protect ourselves from invaders that will use what we tell them and make us vulnerable to the slings and arrows of life. Who knows how what we tell them they will use for our detriment and what consequences will occur in all lives which touch us. There is no better time for concealment than today.

6. The title below that best expresses the ideas of both passages is:

(A) A Time for Concealment
(B) Fear and Vulnerability
(C) A Code for Living
(D) Penalties for Procrastination
(E) Youth vs. Age

7. A description of the two paragraphs would be best noted as

(A) Pro and con
(B) Contrasting and authoritarian
(C) Procrastinating and tenacious
(D) Optimistic and cautious
(E) Encouraging and dangerous

8. Which aspects do the authors of both paragraphs *not* discuss?

(A) How the authors show the reader to accomplish what they advocate
(B) The consequences of not conforming to the author's caution
(C) When to abide by the author's admonition
(D) The dangers of not conforming to the author's warnings
(E) The element of fear and timing

9. Which lines describe analogies?

(A) lines 1 and 12
(B) lines 2, 3, and 15
(C) lines 6 and 18
(D) lines 8 and 19
(E) lines 9 and 16

GO ON TO THE NEXT PAGE

Questions 10–15 are based on the following passage.

The following passage describes the development of tumors, differentiating between the process of formation of malignant and benign ones.

Neoplasia, or the development of tumors, is the abnormal biological process in which some intrinsic cellular change within a group of normal cells produces a group of cells which no longer respond to the mechanisms which regulate normal cells. As a result, this group of cells increases in number but fails to achieve the specialized characteristics associated with normal cells. The degree to which neoplastic cells resemble their normal counterpart cells, both in appearance and behavior, allows us to classify tumors as either benign or malignant. Benign tumors look and behave like their normal tissue of origin, are usually slow-growing, are rarely fatal and remain localized. Malignant tumors, on the other hand, look very little like their tissue of origin and behave in such a manner that the animal which bears the tumor frequently succumbs.

The characteristic which most strikingly separates malignant tumors from benign tumors is the ability of malignant cells to become widely disseminated and to establish secondary sites of tumor far distant from the original tumor. This process of widespread dissemination, which is called metastasis, is not well understood; however, some of the features of the process have been ascertained. Before metastasis can occur, the malignant cells must invade the surrounding normal tissue. Initial attempts to invade are inhibited by the normal tissue. With time, the neoplastic cells undergo changes which allow them to overcome this inhibition, and tumor cells leave the primary mass of tumor. The entire process of inhibition by normal tissue and the eventual breakdown of inhibition is undoubtedly complex.

Malignant cells are characteristically less adhesive, one to another, than are normal cells. The outer membrane of the malignant cells contains less calcium than the membrane of normal cells. The malignant cell also acquires a greater negative electrical charge. After malignant cells have invaded the surrounding normal tissue, they ultimately enter the bloodstream where most of the cells die. Those cells which survive will form a metastasis at a distant site only if they can adhere to the wall of a small blood vessel. The factors which govern this adherence include the size of the malignant cell or a clump of these cells, the diameter of the blood vessel and the stickiness of the blood vessel wall. Stickiness of the blood vessel wall is at least partially due to the status of blood clotting components in the blood. In addition to these mechanical considerations, some patterns of metastasis are explicable only on the basis of a receptive chemical environment or "soil" in which the malignant cell can grow. Finally, although a number of the characteristics of malignant neoplastic cells have been elucidated as described above, it still must be stated that many aspects of their behavior remain a mystery.

10. The main topic of this passage is

(A) the meaning of neoplasia
(B) the inhibition of tumor metastasis by normal tissue
(C) the transformation of benign tumors into malignant tumors
(D) the manner in which malignant tumors behave in the body
(E) the fate of malignant cells after they enter the bloodstream

11. Before malignant cells can be disseminated to widespread parts of the body, they must first

(A) acquire new outer membrane characteristics
(B) inhibit the lethal effects of components of the blood
(C) penetrate the surrounding normal tissue
(D) locate the proper chemical environment in which to grow
(E) achieve sufficient size to become lodged in a blood vessel

12. According to the passage, the property of a malignant cell that most greatly enhances its metastatic potential is

(A) its ability to choose the proper "soil"
(B) its ability to invade the surrounding tissue
(C) the amount of calcium in the outer membrane of the cell
(D) the extent of deviation from the appearance of a normal cell
(E) its ability to attach itself to the wall of a small blood vessel

13. It can be concluded from the passage that

(A) benign tumors usually progress to malignant tumors
(B) malignant cells reach distant tissues by routes yet to be ascertained
(C) if the wall of a blood vessel is "sticky," a tumor metastasis has a better chance to develop
(D) the outer membrane of malignant cells is the same as that of normal cells
(E) the pattern of metastasis of a particular tumor is predictable with considerable accuracy

GO ON TO THE NEXT PAGE

14. According to this passage, characteristics that distinguish malignant neoplastic cells from normal cells include all of the following *except*

(A) their growth rate
(B) their physical appearance
(C) their outer membrane characteristics
(D) their normal tissue of origin
(E) their ability to invade surrounding tissue and metastasize

15. The word "explicable" in line 45 means

(A) withdrawn
(B) with exception
(C) created
(D) explainable
(E) malignant

GO ON TO THE NEXT PAGE

Questions 16–24 are based on the following passage.

The following passage is about the old Middle West and its influence on modern society.

The old Middle West is gone. However, it still lives in song and story. Give most children the choice of visiting Valley Forge or Dodge City…Dodge City wins. It is more glamorous in their imagination than Valley Forge.

The old Middle West developed a strong, compassionate people out of the hardships and suffering of the destructive blizzards of earlier generations—"northern" that swept over it with white clouds of blinding snow and ice—and southern winds that brought the black blizzards of dust storms.

The Middle West is realistic about the nation's domestic and international affairs. It views both with intense interest and anxiety, for it knows that—although stubborn resistance to change can lead to catastrophe—change often does have unforeseen ramifications.

This caution is still—especially on political major questions—present in the modern Middle West and is its particular contribution to our national relationships.

I think the Middle West's strength is in its customary cautious approach to the day of reckoning in our complex industrial structure and what should be put forward for its solution. That solution will take time, for slapdash approaches never work.

It took thirty years for our great country to recover from the upheaval of the Civil War. It took thirty years for our country to discard the Democrat policy that the way to settle economic troubles was with fiat money. It made inflation the prime issue in 1936. It still is.

Our era has seen some fifty years of war and international tension piled on top of World War I, and enormous industrial development.

The new West is more worldly minded than the old Middle West was, and, in general, is a balance between the East Coast—with alignment toward Europe and the Atlantic countries—and the West Coast—with its interests in Asian affairs.

There is still a noticeable difference between the atmosphere in the Middle West and that of the Eastern states. It is more free and easy. There are not as many old families with local supremacy. The East's "money power"—as the old Middle West called it—is now the "Establishment."

The parallel factor is the desire on the part of many heads of families in many lines of activity to change from the tensions and insecurity of life in the big cities to the pleasure and comfort that come from the security of living in smaller towns. In the Middle West, it has increasingly taken the form of people remaining in the smaller cities and giving them new life and intelligence. This has strengthened smaller communities and offset the flow of Middle Westerners to the big cities. There are, however, signs that cities in general are no longer content to be corrupt. There is pragmatic awakening that can mean a new leadership—with a growing understanding of their problems and responsibilities. This newly awakened urban leadership, joining the Midwest and small city leadership in the quest for stability, may just possibly be the salvation of the big cities.

That is a reversal of the trend that started some years ago that seemed to threaten the stagnation of the Middle West by the tide of migration to the big metropolitan areas.

The Jews are almost the only people in America today—or, in the world, for that matter—that, during Passover, recall to the memory of the present generation their tremendous racial achievements, their leadership and their heroes of long ago.

On the other hand, the freedom of communications—the easy movement of Americans around their great country—and the ease of changing occupations are remarkable in the United States. All contribute to breaking down ethnic and religious group prejudices.

Possibly one reason we have so much difficulty in resolving our problems of a complex society is that we have tended to lose not only a sense of national identity, but a sense of pride in and a strong feeling for the special qualities of our local area.

What Americans must find is a way to square their diversification, and the freedom upon which it is based, with the older sense of identity and of stability. Perhaps the contemporary Middle West offers the answer in its freer acceptance of people as they are, and as they are capable of becoming—a surviving characteristic of mutual helpfulness, willingness to accept change—not for change's sake, but on its merits.

16. The author would agree that the "old Middle West" remains

(A) intact in only a few areas
(B) only in tales that are told
(C) unchanged in many small towns
(D) in spirit but is lost in practice
(E) a reality only to children who view it on television

17. The author feels that the strength of the Middle West lies in its

(A) tolerance of differences of opinion
(B) worldliness
(C) cautiousness
(D) free and easy atmosphere
(E) ability to recover from strife

18. A current trend that the author finds encouraging is

(A) a gradual reduction in inflation
(B) the increasing complexity of the national industrial structure
(C) realism in domestic and international affairs
(D) people staying in the smaller towns and cities
(E) a growing sense of national identity

GO ON TO THE NEXT PAGE

19. The character of the old Middle West was formed by

I. weather hardships
II. the Gold Rush of 1849
III. the Civil War

(A) I only
(B) II only
(C) III only
(D) I and II only
(E) I and III only

20. The word "pragmatic" in line 51 means

(A) lethargic
(B) anticipatory
(C) flippant
(D) practical
(E) governmental

21. The author feels that we have had trouble in solving the problems of a complex society because

(A) of fiat money
(B) city governments are corrupt
(C) our cities are too large to be managed
(D) we have lost our attachment to local areas
(E) of the breakdown of ethnic and religious groups

22. It can be inferred that the author is

(A) a wealthy Middle West businessman
(B) a radical reformer
(C) a former political candidate
(D) a Middle West farmer
(E) a suburbanite

23. The word "diversification" in line 76 most likely refers to

(A) jobs
(B) income
(C) social stature
(D) intelligence
(E) race or religion

24. The author states that the following have been factors leading to the breakdown of ethnic and religious prejudices:

I. Ease of communications
II. Increased education at school and on the job
III. Ease of changing occupations

(A) I only
(B) II only
(C) III only
(D) I and II only
(E) I and III only

STOP

If you finish before time is called, you may check your work on this section only.
Do not turn to any other section in the test.

SECTION 8

Time: 20 Minutes—Turn to Section 8 (page 660) of your answer sheet to answer the questions in this section.
16 Questions

Directions: For this section, solve each problem and decide which is the best of the choices given. Fill in the corresponding circle on the answer sheet. You may use any available space for scratchwork.

Notes:

1. The use of a calculator is permitted.
2. All numbers used are real numbers.
3. Figures that accompany problems in this test are intended to provide information useful in solving the problems. They are drawn as accurately as possible EXCEPT when it is stated in a specific problem that the figure is not drawn to scale. All figures lie in a plane unless otherwise indicated.
4. Unless otherwise specified, the domain of any function f is assumed to be the set of all real numbers x for which $f(x)$ is a real number.

REFERENCE INFORMATION

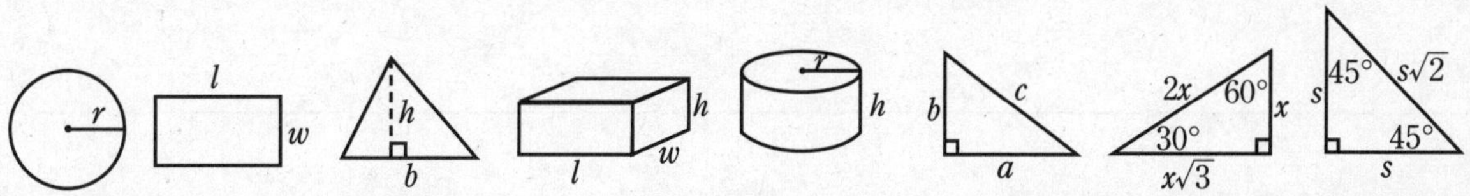

$A = \pi r^2$ $C = 2\pi r$ $A = lw$ $A = \frac{1}{2}bh$ $V = lwh$ $V = \pi r^2 h$ $c^2 = a^2 + b^2$ *Special Right Triangles*

The number of degrees of arc in a circle is 360.
The sum of the measures in degrees of the angles of a triangle is 180.

1. If x inversely varies with y and when $x = 5$, $y = 4$, find x when $y = 10$.

(A) 2
(B) 3
(C) 4
(D) 5
(E) The answer cannot be determined from the information given.

2. The projected sales of a music book per month is 4,000 at \$1; 1,000 at \$2; 250 at \$4; and 160 at \$5. If x is the price of the book, what are the expected sales per month in terms of x?

(A) $\frac{1{,}000}{x^2}$

(B) $\frac{1{,}000}{x}$

(C) $\frac{2{,}000}{x^2}$

(D) $\frac{4{,}000}{x^2}$

(E) $\frac{4{,}000}{x}$

GO ON TO THE NEXT PAGE

3. If $x^{-3} = 27$, what is the value of $x^{\frac{1}{2}}$?

(A) $\frac{1}{3}$

(B) $\sqrt{2}$

(C) $\sqrt{3}$

(D) $\frac{\sqrt{3}}{3}$

(E) $\frac{\sqrt{3}}{4}$

4. If $f(x) = 2x + 3^x$, what is the value of $f(2)$?

(A) 9
(B) 10
(C) 11
(D) 12
(E) 13

5. The graphs of $y = x + 2$ and $y = x^2 + 4x + 4$ intersect at

(A) $x = 2, x = -1$
(B) $x = -2$ only
(C) $x = -1$ only
(D) $x = -1, x = -2$
(E) $x = 2, x = 1$

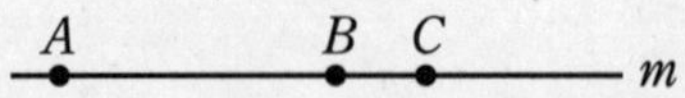

6. Points *A*, *B*, and *C* are on line *m*, as shown above, such that $AC = \frac{4}{3}AB$. What is the ratio of *BC* to *AB*?

(A) $\frac{1}{4}$

(B) $\frac{1}{3}$

(C) $\frac{1}{2}$

(D) $\frac{2}{3}$

(E) The answer cannot be determined from the given information.

GO ON TO THE NEXT PAGE

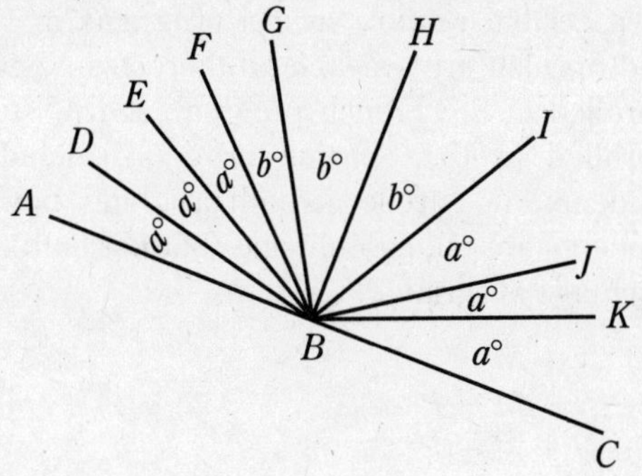

Note: Figure is not drawn to scale.

7. In the figure above, AC is a straight line segment. Line segments are drawn from B to D, E, F, G, H, I, J, and K, respectively. Which of the following angles has a degree measure that can be found?

(A) $\angle FBG$
(B) $\angle EBG$
(C) $\angle DBG$
(D) $\angle GBI$
(E) $\angle GBJ$

8. Given $8r + 3s = 12$ and $7r + 2s = 9$, find the value of $5(r + s)$.

(A) 5
(B) 10
(C) 15
(D) 20
(E) 25

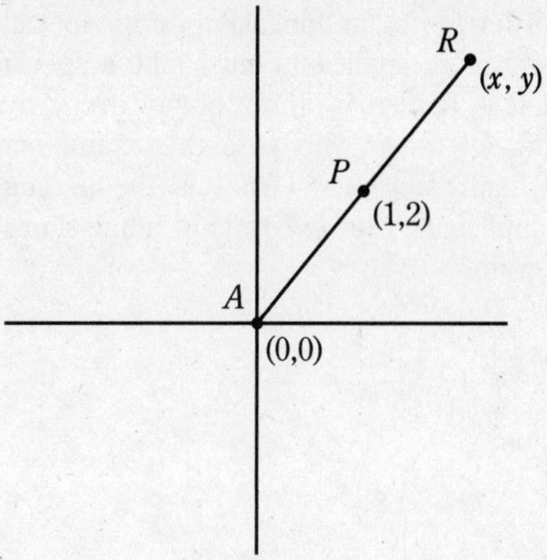

9. If points (1, 2) and (x, y) are on the line represented in the above diagram, which of the following could represent the value of x and y?

(A) $x = 3, y = 5$
(B) $x = 4, y = 8$
(C) $x = 5, y = 11$
(D) $x = 6, y = 15$
(E) $x = 7, y = 17$

10. If p is the average of x and y, and if q is the average of y and z, and if r is the average of x and z, then what is the average of x, y, and z?

(A) $\frac{p+q+r}{3}$
(B) $\frac{p+q+r}{2}$
(C) $\frac{2}{3}(p + q + r)$
(D) $p + q + r$
(E) $\frac{3}{2}(p + q + r)$

GO ON TO THE NEXT PAGE

11. In order to obtain admission into a special school program, all applicants must take a special exam, which is passed by three out of every five applicants. Of those who pass the exam, one-fourth are finally accepted. What is the percentage of all applicants who *fail* to gain admission into the program?

(A) 55
(B) 60
(C) 75
(D) 85
(E) 90

12. Which of the following represents a possible length of the hypotenuse of a triangle whose perpendicular sides are both integers?

(A) $\sqrt{44}$
(B) $\sqrt{45}$
(C) $\sqrt{46}$
(D) $\sqrt{47}$
(E) $\sqrt{48}$

13. In a certain school, special programs in French and Spanish are available. If there are N students enrolled in the French program, and M students enrolled in the Spanish program, including P students who enrolled in both programs, how many students are taking only one (but not both) of the language programs?

(A) $N + M$
(B) $N + M - P$
(C) $N + M + P$
(D) $N + M - 2P$
(E) $N + M + 2P$

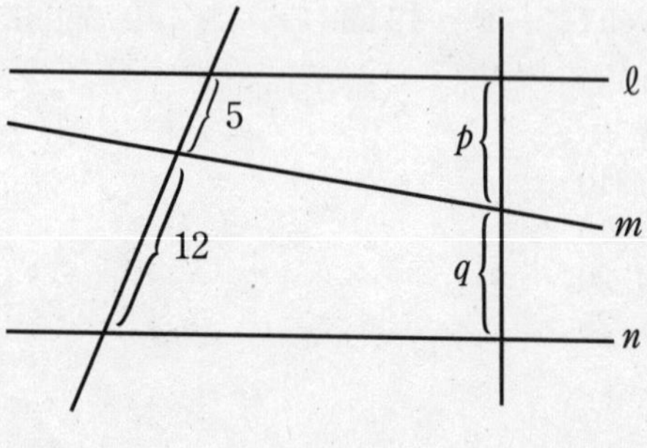

14. Lines ℓ and n are parallel to each other, but line m is parallel to neither of the other two. Find $\frac{p}{q}$ if $p + q = 13$.

(A) $\frac{13}{5}$
(B) $\frac{12}{5}$
(C) $\frac{7}{6}$
(D) $\frac{1}{5}$
(E) The answer cannot be determined from the information given.

GO ON TO THE NEXT PAGE

15. Ross wants to make up 3 letter combinations. He wants each combination to have exactly 3 of the following letters: *A, B, C,* and *D*. No letter can be used more than once. For example, "*AAB*" is not acceptable. What is the maximum number of such triplets that Ross can make up? (The order of the letters must be considered. Example: "*ABC*" and "*CBA*" are acceptable triplets.)

(A) 6
(B) 9
(C) 24
(D) 27
(E) 64

16. The tables below show the number of uniforms ordered at two schools and the cost of the types of uniforms ordered in child and adult sizes. Find the total cost of all the uniforms in child sizes ordered at School B.

Number of Child Uniforms Ordered

	Type A	Type B	Type C
School A	20	50	40
School B	30	60	50

Cost of Uniforms

	Child	Adult
Type A	$9	$12
Type B	$10	$14
Type C	$11	$16

(A) $30
(B) $140
(C) $1,420
(D) $1,480
(E) $1,490

STOP

If you finish before time is called, you may check your work on this section only. Do not turn to any other section in the test.

SECTION 9

Time: 20 Minutes—Turn to Section 9 (page 660) of your answer sheet to answer the questions in this section.
19 Questions

Directions: For each question in this section, select the best answer from among the choices given and fill in the corresponding circle on the answer sheet.

Each sentence below has one or two blanks, each blank indicating that something has been omitted. Beneath the sentence are five words or sets of words labeled A through E. Choose the word or set of words that, when inserted in the sentence, best fits the meaning of the sentence as a whole.

Example:

Hoping to ________ the dispute, negotiators proposed a compromise that they felt would be ________ to both labor and management.

(A) enforce...useful
(B) end...divisive
(C) overcome...unattractive
(D) extend...satisfactory
(E) resolve...acceptable

Ⓐ Ⓑ Ⓒ Ⓓ ●

1. He was ______ about a rise in the value of the stocks he had recently purchased and was eager to make a change in his investment portfolio.

(A) fearful
(B) unconcerned
(C) hesitant
(D) amused
(E) dubious

2. Nature's brute strength is never more ______ than during a major earthquake, when the earth shifts with a sickening sway.

(A) frightening
(B) effective
(C) replaceable
(D) placating
(E) complete

3. Instead of providing available funds to education and thus ______ the incidence of crime, the mayor is ______ the funds to the building of more prisons.

(A) disdain...denying
(B) revoke...assigning
(C) abolish...confining
(D) reduce...diverting
(E) nourish...planning

4. The dancer excelled neither in grace nor technique, but the ______ musical accompaniment gives the performance a(n) ______ of excellence.

(A) gradual...sensation
(B) soothing...mandate
(C) well-rehearsed...diction
(D) superb...aura
(E) chronic...effervescence

5. Her fine reputation as a celebrated actress was ______ by her appearance in a TV soap opera.

(A) enhanced
(B) blemished
(C) appreciated
(D) concluded
(E) intensified

6. The dictator's slow, easy manner and his air of gentility ______ his firm intention to ensure no opposition to his planned ______ policies.

(A) revealed...eager
(B) accepted...professional
(C) belied...drastic
(D) disregarded...inane
(E) animated...crude

GO ON TO THE NEXT PAGE

The two passages below are followed by questions based on their content and on the relationship between the two passages. Answer the questions on the basis of what is stated or implied in the passages and in any introductory material that may be provided.

Questions 7–19 are based on the following passages.

The following passages represent two different views of living—the views of living in the country and of living in the city.

Passage 1

The snow falls gently on our quiet meadow sloping down to Penobscot Bay, with spruce trees back against the gray of the water. A raven croaks from a nearby treetop. Two gulls sail over the house and squawk unintelligibly together. The only other sounds are the wood fire snapping, the kettle steaming on the stove and Pusso purring.

There is no phone to ring, no radio to turn on, no television to watch. We need don no city disguise and ride subways, catch trains, attend cocktail parties or dinners. We can choose and make our own music, reread our favorite books, wear our old clothes, eat when and what we like from a well-stocked root cellar, or happily abstain from food, if we wish, the whole day. There is wood to cut, snow to shovel, mail to answer, but all in our own good time. No one is pushing, no one shoving, no one ordering about. There is no job to lose; we make our own jobs. Free men? Almost.

A neighbor may amble in on snowshoes and bring us word of his horse's health or wife's pregnancy. Over a glass of cider we may talk of snowmobile incursions or hunters' depredations. He may bring us a huge cabbage he has grown and we send him back with a bottle of our rose hips juice and a knitted doll for his little daughter. In our chat beside the fire we will probably not touch on the outside world, though we are not unaware of what stirs the nation.

The newspaper, reaching us by mail, brings us echoes of an inconsequential election between two shadow-boxing candidates for an office no one should covet. We read that two high officials, the Episcopal Bishop of New York and the chief of the Soviet delegation to the United Nations, have separately been held up in daylight and robbed by armed men in Central Park. We learn that invaders are entering classrooms in Manhattan's public schools and at knife or gunpoint relieving teachers of their cash and trinkets before their open-mouthed pupils.

We thank our lucky stars that we live out in the wilderness, that we are not on congested streets and highways or clustered in high-rise city rookeries, with jangling noise and turmoil all about, that we are not in smog, that we can drink clean clear water, not fluoridized or chlorinated, from our bubbling spring, that our homegrown food is not stale, preserved or embalmed and bought from the supermarket.

We are thankful for what the wilderness makes possible. Peace, progress, prosperity? We prefer peace, quiet, and frugality.

Passage 2

You look out the window of your one-bedroom apartment and see swarms of people in the streets as if the day never ends. You live with the interminable sounds of the cars, trucks, and repair services and hassles encountered. But there is an excitement that makes you alive. You can leave your apartment at three in the morning and go to a coffee shop which remains open. You can lose your identity and forget about your problems by mingling during the day with the thousands of people roaming the streets. You may be walking right next to a famous celebrity or a lowly degenerate. But it doesn't matter. It is the excitement that counts, the fact that you can call anybody anytime by phone, get up-to-the-minute news through radio or TV. You can choose from hundreds of international restaurants, and although the food may not be homegrown, you certainly have the exciting ambience of a packed restaurant with constant movement. You can choose from the best of hospitals and doctors, although it may take you some time to get an appointment with a doctor or get to the hospital because of traffic. But the noise, the inconveniences, the muggings, all this goes with the territory—with the excitement. You can always escape to the country by train, car, bus, or even plane if you need to. However, city living is certainly not for everyone. And your ability to live or even survive in a city depends on your temperament, your principles, your occupation and your interests. But for many, the trade-off for a vibrant life, a pulse which never ends, and access to almost every cultural event almost at any time is certainly a lure to live in the city environment.

7. The general feeling running through Passage 1 is one of

(A) guarded resentment
(B) tolerable boredom
(C) restless indecision
(D) peaceful satisfaction
(E) marked indifference

8. Which of the following is the most appropriate title for Passage 1?

(A) Winter in the Country
(B) The Frills Aren't Needed
(C) Peace, Progress, and Prosperity
(D) Life Goes On
(E) A Lack of Conveniences

GO ON TO THE NEXT PAGE

9. The author's reference to "an inconsequential election between two shadow-boxing candidates" (lines 26–27) indicates that the author

(A) has no faith in politicians
(B) is opposed to professional prizefighting
(C) does not believe in having any elections
(D) prefers that people govern themselves
(E) is of the opinion that all elections are fixed

10. The author of Passage 1 states or implies that

(A) there is no work to be done
(B) he is a completely free man
(C) his wife is pregnant
(D) he reads no newspapers
(E) he has a farm

11. Of the states below, the location of the author's home in Passage 1 is most likely in the state of

(A) Arizona
(B) Florida
(C) Maine
(D) Louisiana
(E) Georgia

12. It can be inferred from Passage 2 that the author believes that in the city

(A) many people live in one-bedroom apartments
(B) when eating out, you'll never get homegrown food
(C) you can meet rich and poor at the most expensive restaurants
(D) losing one's identity is considered a "plus"
(E) friendliness is a "way of life"

13. The word "interminable" in line 47 means

(A) loud
(B) harsh
(C) ongoing
(D) bright
(E) close

14. The passages differ in that

(A) in Passage 2, there is more of a tendency to qualify the good with the bad
(B) in Passage 1 there are no hospitals in the village, whereas there are many in Passage 2
(C) the author of Passage 1 believes that everyone should live in the country, whereas in Passage 2 the author believes that everyone would do well in the city
(D) in Passage 1 there are no post offices to deliver mail
(E) in Passage 1 the author never reads newspapers, whereas the author in Passage 2 is interested in up-to-the-minute news

15. Which is more likely to be surprising to the respective author?

(A) Passage 1 author: reading a headline in a news paper: "Scientists Find Cancer Cure"
(B) Passage 2 author: speaking with a famous movie celebrity in the street
(C) Passage 2 author: finding a movie at two in the morning
(D) Passage 1 author: seeing some people skip a few meals
(E) Passage 2 author: hearing someone complain about city living

16. The word "frugality" in line 44 means

(A) progress
(B) stinginess
(C) wastefulness
(D) poverty
(E) quiet

17. The word "don" in line 8 is related to

(A) motion
(B) purchasing goods
(C) clothing
(D) eating
(E) fishing

18. We can infer from the authors of each passage that

(A) the author of Passage 1 believes most news is bad whereas the author of Passage 2 believes most news is good
(B) the author of Passage 1 believes politics and elections are useless whereas the author in Passage 2 believes they are necessary
(C) the author of Passage 1 believes that city schools are dangerous and prefers not to have his or her children attend them whereas the author of Passage 2 may agree but accepts the situation
(D) the author of Passage 1 believes only the parks in the cities are safe whereas the author of Passage 2 believes that crime "goes with the territory"
(E) one author likes home-grown food, whereas the other does not

GO ON TO THE NEXT PAGE

19. Which situation or condition is described or mentioned in one passage but not in the other?

(I) The sociable and friendly nature of the people
(II) The positive effects of the environment
(III) The impossibility of attaining any news from outside locations or sources

(A) I only
(B) II only
(C) III only
(D) I and II only
(E) I, II, and III

STOP

If you finish before time is called, you may check your work on this section only. Do not turn to any other section in the test.

SECTION 10

Time: 10 Minutes—Turn to Section 10 (page 660) of your answer sheet to answer the questions in this section.
14 Questions

Directions: For each question in this section, select the best answer from among the choices given and fill in the corresponding circle on the answer sheet.

The following sentences test correctness and effectiveness of expression. Part of each sentence or the entire sentence is underlined; beneath each sentence are five ways of phrasing the underlined material. Choice A repeats the original phrasing; the other four choices are different. If you think the original phrasing produces a better sentence than any of the alternatives, select Choice A; if not, select one of the other choices.

In making your selection, follow the requirements of standard written English; that is, pay attention to grammar, choice of words, sentence construction, and punctuation. Your selection should result in the most effective sentence—clear and precise, without awkwardness or ambiguity.

EXAMPLE:

Laura Ingalls Wilder published her first book and she was sixty-five years old then.

(A) and she was sixty-five years old then
(B) when she was sixty-five
(C) at age sixty-five years old
(D) upon the reaching of sixty-five years
(E) at the time when she was sixty-five

Ⓐ ● Ⓒ Ⓓ Ⓔ

1. The bank robber approached the teller quietly, cautiously, and in an unpretentious manner.

(A) and in an unpretentious manner
(B) and with no pretense
(C) and by acting unpretentious
(D) and by acting unpretentiously
(E) and unpretentiously

2. The conduct of the judge with the accused seemed very unfair to the jury.

(A) with the accused
(B) toward the accused
(C) as to the man who was accused
(D) and the accused
(E) as far as the accused was concerned

3. Every typist in the office except she was out sick at least one day during the past month.

(A) except she
(B) except her
(C) excepting she
(D) but not her
(E) outside of her

4. Sam is a professor of theoretical physics, while his brothers are architects with outstanding reputations.

(A) while his brothers are architects
(B) also his brothers are architects
(C) his brothers architects
(D) as his brothers are architects
(E) and his brothers are architects

5. A reward was offered to whoever would return the dog to its owner.

(A) to whoever would return the dog to its owner
(B) to whomever would return the dog to its owner
(C) to whosoever would return the dog to its owner
(D) to whomsoever would return the dog to its owner
(E) to whichever person would return the dog to its owner

6. Irregardless of the outcome of the battle, neither side will be able to claim a decisive victory.

(A) Irregardless of the outcome of the battle
(B) Irregardless of how the battle ends
(C) Regardless of the outcome of the battle
(D) Despite the outcome of the battle
(E) Irregardless of the battle

GO ON TO THE NEXT PAGE

7. One of the finest examples of early Greek sculpture are to be found in the British Museum in London.

(A) are to be found in the British Museum
(B) were to be found in the British Museum
(C) are found in the British Museum
(D) is to be found in the British Museum
(E) are in the British Museum

8. We were surprised at him canceling the order without giving any previous indication of his intentions.

(A) We were surprised at him canceling the order without giving any previous indication of his intentions.
(B) We were surprised that he canceled the order and didn't tell anyone.
(C) His canceling the order surprised us all.
(D) We were surprised at his canceling the order without giving any previous indication of his intentions.
(E) We were surprised at him canceling the order and not letting anyone know about it.

9. When going for an interview, a high school graduate should be prepared to answer the questions that will be asked of him without hesitation.

(A) a high school graduate should be prepared to answer the questions that will be asked of him without hesitation
(B) a high school graduate should without hesitation be prepared to answer the questions that will be asked of him
(C) a high school graduate should be prepared without hesitation to answer the questions that will be asked of him
(D) a high school graduate should be prepared to answer without hesitation the questions that will be asked of him
(E) a high school graduate should be prepared to answer the questions without hesitation that will be asked of him

10. When a student learns a foreign language, he must not only learn to speak and write it, but understand the culture of those who speak it.

(A) but understand the culture of those who speak it
(B) and he must understand the culture of those who speak it
(C) he must understand the culture of those who speak it
(D) but must also understand the culture of those who speak it
(E) but in addition he must also understand the culture of those who speak it

11. The paintings of Dali, like many artists, have been both applauded as great masterpieces and dismissed as rubbish.

(A) like many artists
(B) like most other artists
(C) like the paintings of many artists
(D) like many other paintings
(E) like those of many other artists

12. Because the sick man laid in bed for several months, he developed pneumonia.

(A) Because the sick man laid in bed
(B) Because the sick man had laid in bed
(C) Because the sick man had lain in bed
(D) Because the sick man is laying in bed
(E) Because the sick man lies in bed

13. The pollution bills recently passed by the House are different than those that were vetoed earlier.

(A) different than those
(B) different from those
(C) different to those
(D) different from the earlier ones
(E) different to the ones

14. Neither you nor I are going to agree with the speaker; sometimes, however, it is a good idea to listen to someone whom one may disagree with.

(A) Neither you nor I are going to agree
(B) Neither of us are going to agree
(C) Neither you nor me is going to agree
(D) Neither you nor I am going to agree
(E) Neither I nor you am going to agree

STOP

If you finish before time is called, you may check your work on this section only.
Do not turn to any other section in the test.

How Did You Do on This Test?

Step 1. Go to the Answer Key on pages 710–712.

Step 2. For your "raw score," calculate it using the directions on pages 713–714.

Step 3. Get your "scaled score" for the test by referring to the Raw Score/Scaled Score Conversion Tables on pages 715–717.

THERE'S ALWAYS ROOM FOR IMPROVEMENT!

Answer Key for Practice Test 2

Math

Section 2

	Correct Answer
1	D
2	E
3	D
4	E
5	C
6	E
7	E
8	E
9	B
10	E
11	E
12	D
13	E
14	C
15	E
16	C
17	E
18	E
19	E
20	D

Number correct

Number incorrect

Section 3

	Correct Answer
1	D
2	C
3	B
4	E
5	E
6	A
7	B
8	D

Number correct

Number incorrect

Student-Produced Response Questions

9	24
10	10
11	2300
12	11
13	125
14	25
15	4
16	3
17	36.2
18	7

Number correct

Number incorrect

Section 6

	Correct Answer
1	D
2	B
3	A
4	B
5	B
6	D
7	D
8	B

Number correct

Number incorrect

Student-Produced Response Questions

9	1/1, 1, 1.0, etc.
10	15
11	50
12	3
13	18
14	1.999 1.998… .001, or any number r such that $0 < r < 2$. like 1/2, 1/4, etc.
15	135
16	100
17	3
18	4

Number correct

Number incorrect

Section 8

	Correct Answer
1	A
2	D
3	D
4	E
5	D
6	B
7	C
8	C
9	B
10	A
11	D
12	B
13	D
14	E
15	C
16	C

Number correct

Number incorrect

Critical Reading and Writing

Critical Reading

Section 4

	Correct Answer
1	E
2	D
3	D
4	D
5	C
6	E
7	B
8	D
9	E
10	C
11	B
12	E
13	D
14	B
15	A
16	C
17	B
18	E
19	D
20	E
21	C
22	E
23	E
24	B

Number correct

Number incorrect

Section 7

	Correct Answer
1	C
2	D
3	C
4	E
5	A
6	C
7	B
8	A
9	E
10	D
11	C
12	E
13	C
14	D
15	D
16	B
17	C
18	D
19	A
20	D
21	D
22	C
23	E
24	E

Number correct

Number incorrect

Section 9

	Correct Answer
1	E
2	A
3	D
4	D
5	B
6	C
7	D
8	B
9	A
10	E
11	C
12	D
13	C
14	A
15	A
16	B
17	C
18	C
19	A

Number correct

Number incorrect

Writing

Section 1

____

Essay score

Section 5

	Correct Answer
1	B
2	E
3	D
4	B
5	E
6	C
7	C
8	A
9	E
10	E
11	C
12	B
13	C
14	E
15	C
16	C
17	A
18	D
19	A
20	D
21	E
22	A
23	C
24	C
25	A
26	B
27	C
28	D
29	D
30	B
31	E
32	A
33	D
34	C
35	D

____

Number correct

____

Number incorrect

Section 10

	Correct Answer
1	E
2	B
3	B
4	E
5	A
6	C
7	D
8	D
9	D
10	D
11	E
12	C
13	B
14	D

____

Number correct

____

Number incorrect

Scoring the SAT Practice Test 2

Check your responses with the correct answers on the previous pages. Fill in the blanks below and do the calculations to get your Math, Critical Reading, and Writing raw scores. Use the table to find your Math, Critical Reading, and Writing scaled scores.

Get Your Math Score

How many Math questions did you get **right**?

Section 2: Questions 1–20 ________

Section 6: Questions 1–18 + ________

Section 8: Questions 1–16 + ________

Total = ________ **(A)**

How many Math questions did you get **wrong**?

Section 2: Questions 1–20 ________

Section 6: Questions 1–8 + ________

Section 8: Questions 1–16 + ________

Total = ________

× 0.25 = ________ **(B)**

A – B = ________

Math Raw Score

Round Math raw score to the nearest whole number.

____

Use the Score Conversion Table to find your Math scaled score.

____

Get Your Critical Reading Score

How many Critical Reading questions did you get **right**?

Section 4: Questions 1–24 ________

Section 7: Questions 1–24 + ________

Section 9: Questions 1–19 + ________

Total = ________ **(A)**

How many Critical Reading questions did you get **wrong**?

Section 4: Questions 1–24 ________

Section 7: Questions 1–24 + ________

Section 9: Questions 1–19 + ________

Total = ________

× 0.25 = ________ **(B)**

A – B = ________

Critical Reading Raw Score

Round Critical Reading raw score to the nearest whole number.

____

Use the Score Conversion Table to find your Critical Reading scaled score.

____

Get Your Writing Score

How many multiple-choice Writing questions did you get **right**?

Section 5: Questions 1–35 ________

Section 10: Questions 1–14 + ________

Total = ________ **(A)**

How many multiple-choice Writing questions did you get **wrong**?

Section 5: Questions 1–35 ________

Section 10: Questions 1–14 + ________

Total = ________

× 0.25 = ________ **(B)**

A – B = ________

Writing Raw Score

Round Writing raw score to the nearest whole number.

____

Use the Score Conversion Table to find your Writing multiple-choice scaled score.

____

Estimate your Essay score using the Essay Scoring Guide.

____

Use the SAT Score Conversion Table for Writing Composite to find your Writing scaled score. You will need your Writing raw score and your Essay score to use this table.

____

SAT Score Conversion Table

Raw Score	Critical Reading Scaled Score	Math Scaled Score	Writing Multiple-Choice Scaled Score*	Raw Score	Critical Reading Scaled Score	Math Scaled Score	Writing Multiple-Choice Scaled Score*
67	800			31	510	550	60
66	800			30	510	540	58
65	790			29	500	530	57
64	770			28	490	520	56
63	750			27	490	520	55
62	740			26	480	510	54
61	730			25	480	500	53
60	720			24	470	490	52
59	700			23	460	480	51
58	690			22	460	480	50
57	690			21	450	470	49
56	680			20	440	460	48
55	670			19	440	450	47
54	660	800		18	430	450	46
53	650	790		17	420	440	45
52	650	760		16	420	430	44
51	640	740		15	410	420	44
50	630	720		14	400	410	43
49	620	710	80	13	400	410	42
48	620	700	80	12	390	400	41
47	610	680	80	11	380	390	40
46	600	670	79	10	370	380	39
45	600	660	78	9	360	370	38
44	590	650	76	8	350	360	38
43	590	640	74	7	340	350	37
42	580	630	73	6	330	340	36
41	570	630	71	5	320	330	35
40	570	620	70	4	310	320	34
39	560	610	69	3	300	310	32
38	550	600	67	2	280	290	31
37	550	590	66	1	270	280	30
36	540	580	65	0	250	260	28
35	540	580	64	–1	230	240	27
34	530	570	63	–2	210	220	25
33	520	560	62	–3	200	200	23
32	520	550	61	–4	200	200	20
				and below			

This table is for use only with the test in this book.

* The Writing multiple-choice score is reported on a 20–80 scale. Use the SAT Score Conversion Table for Writing Composite for the total writing scaled score.

SAT Score Conversion Table for Writing Composite

Writing Multiple-Choice Raw Score	Essay Raw Score						
	0	1	2	3	4	5	6
–12	200	200	200	210	240	270	300
–11	200	200	200	210	240	270	300
–10	200	200	200	210	240	270	300
–9	200	200	200	210	240	270	300
–8	200	200	200	210	240	270	300
–7	200	200	200	210	240	270	300
–6	200	200	200	210	240	270	300
–5	200	200	200	210	240	270	300
–4	200	200	200	230	270	300	330
–3	200	210	230	250	290	320	350
–2	200	230	250	280	310	340	370
–1	210	240	260	290	320	360	380
0	230	260	280	300	340	370	400
1	240	270	290	320	350	380	410
2	250	280	300	330	360	390	420
3	260	290	310	340	370	400	430
4	270	300	320	350	380	410	440
5	280	310	330	360	390	420	450
6	290	320	340	360	400	430	460
7	290	330	340	370	410	440	470
8	300	330	350	380	410	450	470
9	310	340	360	390	420	450	480
10	320	350	370	390	430	460	490
11	320	360	370	400	440	470	500
12	330	360	380	410	440	470	500
13	340	370	390	420	450	480	510
14	350	380	390	420	460	490	520
15	350	380	400	430	460	500	530
16	360	390	410	440	470	500	530
17	370	400	420	440	480	510	540
18	380	410	420	450	490	520	550
19	380	410	430	460	490	530	560
20	390	420	440	470	500	530	560
21	400	430	450	480	510	540	570
22	410	440	460	480	520	550	580
23	420	450	470	490	530	560	590
24	420	460	470	500	540	570	600
25	430	460	480	510	540	580	610

Writing Multiple-Choice Raw Score	Essay Raw Score 0	1	2	3	4	5	6
26	440	470	490	520	550	590	610
27	450	480	500	530	560	590	620
28	460	490	510	540	570	600	630
29	470	500	520	550	580	610	640
30	480	510	530	560	590	620	650
31	490	520	540	560	600	630	660
32	500	530	550	570	610	640	670
33	510	540	550	580	620	650	680
34	510	550	560	590	630	660	690
35	520	560	570	600	640	670	700
36	530	560	580	610	650	680	710
37	540	570	590	620	660	690	720
38	550	580	600	630	670	700	730
39	560	600	610	640	680	710	740
40	580	610	620	650	690	720	750
41	590	620	640	660	700	730	760
42	600	630	650	680	710	740	770
43	610	640	660	690	720	750	780
44	620	660	670	700	740	770	800
45	640	670	690	720	750	780	800
46	650	690	700	730	770	800	800
47	670	700	720	750	780	800	800
48	680	720	730	760	800	800	800
49	680	720	730	760	800	800	800

Chart for Self-Appraisal Based on the Practice Test You Have Just Taken

The Chart for Self-Appraisal below tells you quickly where your SAT strengths and weaknesses lie. Check or circle the appropriate box in accordance with the number of your correct answers for each area of the Practice Test 2 you have just taken.

	Writing (Multiple-Choice)	*Sentence Completions*	*Reading Comprehension*	*Math Questions**
EXCELLENT	42–49	16–19	40–48	44–54
GOOD	37–41	13–15	35–39	32–43
FAIR	31–36	9–12	26–34	27–31
POOR	20–30	5–8	17–25	16–26
VERY POOR	0–19	0–4	0–16	0–15

* Sections 2, 6, and 8 only

Note: In our tests, we have chosen to have Section 3 as the experimental section. We have also chosen it to be a math section since we felt that students may need more practice in the math area than in the verbal area. Note that on the actual SAT you will take, the order of the sections can vary and you will not know which one is experimental, so it is wise to answer all sections and not to leave any section out.

SAT VERBAL AND MATH SCORE/PERCENTILE CONVERSION TABLE

Critical Reading and Writing

SAT scaled verbal score	Percentile rank
800	99.7+
790	99.5
740–780	99
700–730	97
670–690	95
640–660	91
610–630	85
580–600	77
550–570	68
510–540	57
480–500	46
440–470	32
410–430	21
380–400	13
340–370	6
300–330	2
230–290	1
200–220	0–0.5

Math

SAT scaled math score	Percentile rank
800	99.5+
770–790	99.5
720–760	99
670–710	97
640–660	94
610–630	89
590–600	84
560–580	77
530–550	68
510–520	59
480–500	48
450–470	37
430–440	26
390–420	16
350–380	8
310–340	2
210–300	0.5
200	0

Section 1—Essay

The following are guidelines for scoring the essay.

The SAT Scoring Guide

Score of 6	**Score of 5**	**Score of 4**
An essay in this category is *outstanding,* demonstrating *clear and consistent mastery,* although it may have a few minor errors. A typical essay	An essay in this category is *effective,* demonstrating *reasonably consistent mastery,* although it will have occasional errors or lapses in quality. A typical essay	An essay in this category is *competent,* demonstrating *adequate mastery,* although it will have lapses in quality. A typical essay
• effectively and insightfully develops a point of view on the issue and demonstrates outstanding critical thinking, using clearly appropriate examples, reasons, and other evidence to support its position	• effectively develops a point of view on the issue and demonstrates strong critical thinking, generally using appropriate examples, reasons, and other evidence to support its position	• develops a point of view on the issue and demonstrates competent critical thinking, using adequate examples, reasons, and other evidence to support its position
• is well organized and clearly focused, demonstrating clear coherence and smooth progression of ideas	• is well organized and focused, demonstrating coherence and progression of ideas	• is generally organized and focused, demonstrating some coherence and progression of ideas
• exhibits skillful use of language, using a varied, accurate, and apt vocabulary	• exhibits facility in the use of language, using appropriate vocabulary	• exhibits adequate but inconsistent facility in the use of language, using generally appropriate vocabulary
• demonstrates meaningful variety in sentence structure	• demonstrates variety in sentence structure	• demonstrates some variety in sentence structure
• is free of most errors in grammar, usage, and mechanics	• is generally free of most errors in grammar, usage, and mechanics	• has some errors in grammar, usage, and mechanics

Score of 3	**Score of 2**	**Score of 1**
An essay in this category is *inadequate,* but demonstrates *developing mastery,* and is marked by ONE OR MORE of the following weaknesses:	An essay in this category is *seriously limited,* demonstrating *little mastery,* and is flawed by ONE OR MORE of the following weaknesses:	An essay in this category is *fundamentally lacking,* demonstrating *very little* or *no mastery,* and is severely flawed by ONE OR MORE of the following weaknesses:
• develops a point of view on the issue, demonstrating some critical thinking, but may do so inconsistently or use inadequate examples, reasons, or other evidence to support its position	• develops a point of view on the issue that is vague or seriously limited, demonstrating weak critical thinking, providing inappropriate or insufficient examples, reasons, or other evidence to support its position	• develops no viable point of view on the issue, or provides little or no evidence to support its position
• is limited in its organization or focus, or may demonstrate some lapses in coherence or progression of ideas	• is poorly organized and/or focused, or demonstrates serious problems with coherence or progression of ideas	• is disorganized or unfocused, resulting in a disjointed or incoherent essay
• displays developing facility in the use of language, but sometimes uses weak vocabulary or inappropriate word choice	• displays very little facility in the use of language, using very limited vocabulary or incorrect word choice	• displays fundamental errors in vocabulary
• lacks variety or demonstrates problems in sentence structure	• demonstrates frequent problems in sentence structure	• demonstrates severe flaws in sentence structure
• contains an accumulation of errors in grammar, usage, and mechanics	• contains errors in grammar, usage, and mechanics so serious that meaning is somewhat obscured	• contains pervasive errors in grammar, usage, or mechanics that persistently interfere with meaning

Essays not written on the essay assignment will receive a score of zero.

Explanatory Answers for Practice Test 2

Section 2: Math

As you read these solutions, you are advised to do two things if you answered the Math question incorrectly:

1. When a specific Math Strategy is referred to in the solution, study that strategy, which you will find in "19 Math Strategies" (beginning on page 69).
2. When the solution directs you to the "Complete Math Refresher" (beginning on page 167)—for example, Math Refresher 305—study the 305 Math principle to get a clear idea of the Math operation that was necessary for you to know in order to answer the question correctly.

1. Choice D is correct.

Given: $500w = 3 \times 700$ $\boxed{1}$

(Use Strategy 13: Find an unknown by dividing.)

Divide $\boxed{1}$ by 500, giving

$$\frac{500w}{500} = \frac{3 \times 700}{500}$$

(Use Strategy 19: Factor and reduce first. Then multiply.)

$$w = \frac{3 \times 7 \times \cancel{100}}{5 \times \cancel{100}}$$

$$w = \frac{21}{5}$$

(Math Refresher #406)

2. Choice E is correct.

Given: $\frac{3+y}{y} = 7$ $\boxed{1}$

(Use Strategy 13: Find an unknown by multiplying.)

Multiply $\boxed{1}$ by y, to get

$$\cancel{y}\left(\frac{3+y}{\cancel{y}}\right) = (7)y$$

$$3 + y = 7y$$

$$3 = 6y$$

$$\frac{3}{6} = y$$

$$\frac{1}{2} = y$$

(Math Refresher #406)

3. Choice D is correct. **(Use Strategy 2: Translate from words to algebra.)**

x is a multiple of 9, gives

$$x \in \{9, 18, 27, 36, 45, 54, \ldots\ldots\} \quad \boxed{1}$$

x is a multiple of 12, gives

$$x \in \{12, 24, 36, 48, 60, 72, \ldots\ldots\} \quad \boxed{2}$$

The smallest value that appears in both sets $\boxed{1}$ and $\boxed{2}$ is 36.

(Math Refresher #801 and #803)

4. Choice E is correct.

Method 1:

Given: $(r - s)(t - s) + (s - r)(s - t)$ $\boxed{1}$

(Use Strategy 17: Use the given information effectively.)

Recognizing that $(s - r) = -1(r - s)$ $\boxed{2}$

$(s - t) = -1(t - s)$ $\boxed{3}$

Substituting $\boxed{2}$ and $\boxed{3}$ into $\boxed{1}$, we get

$$(r - s)(t - s) + [-1(r - s)][-1(t - s)] =$$
$$(r - s)(t - s) + (-1)(-1)(r - s)(t - s) =$$
$$2(r - s)(t - s)$$

Method 2:

Given: $(r - s)(t - s) + (s - r)(s - t)$ $\boxed{1}$

Multiply both pairs of quantities from $\boxed{1}$, giving

$$rt - rs - st + s^2 + s^2 - st - rs + rt =$$
$$2rt - 2rs - 2st + 2s^2 =$$
$$2(rt - rs - st + s^2) =$$
$$2[r(t - s) - s(t - s)] =$$
$$2(r - s)(t - s)$$

(Math Refresher #409)

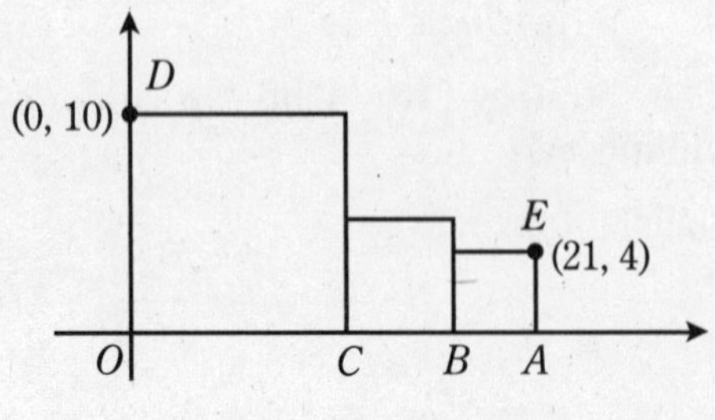

5. Choice C is correct.

We want to find the area of the middle square, which is $(CB)^2$. **(Use Strategy 3: The whole equals the sum of its parts.)**

$$OA = OC + CB + BA \quad \boxed{1}$$

From the diagram, we get

$$OA = 21 \quad \boxed{2}$$
$$AE = 4 \quad \boxed{3}$$
$$OD = 10 \quad \boxed{4}$$

Since each figure is a square, we get

$$BA = AE \quad \boxed{5}$$
$$OC = OD \quad \boxed{6}$$

Substituting $\boxed{5}$ into $\boxed{3}$, we get

$$AE = BA = 4 \quad \boxed{7}$$

Substituting $\boxed{6}$ into $\boxed{4}$, we get

$$OD = OC = 10 \quad \boxed{8}$$

Substituting $\boxed{2}$, $\boxed{7}$, and $\boxed{8}$ into $\boxed{1}$, we get

$$21 = 10 + CB + 4$$
$$21 = 14 + CB$$
$$7 = CB \quad \boxed{9}$$

Area of square II = $(CB)^2$
Area of square II = 7^2 (From $\boxed{9}$)
Area of square II = 49

(Math Refresher #410 and #303)

6. Choice E is correct.

Given: 1 cup = 100 grams $\boxed{1}$
1 cake = 75 grams $\boxed{2}$
1 pie = 225 grams $\boxed{3}$

Using $\boxed{1}$, we get

4 cups = 4(100 grams)
4 cups = 400 grams $\boxed{4}$

(Using Strategy 8: When all choices must be tested, start with E and work backward.)

2 cakes and 1 pie is Choice E. $\boxed{5}$
Substituting $\boxed{2}$ and $\boxed{3}$ in $\boxed{5}$, we get

2(75 grams) + 225 grams =
150 grams + 225 grams =
375 grams $\boxed{6}$

Since $\boxed{6}$ is less than $\boxed{4}$, there *is enough* in 4 cups. So Choice E is correct.

(Math Refresher #121 and #431)

7. Choice E is correct.

I: Slope is defined as $\frac{y_2 - y_1}{x_2 - x_1}$ where (x_1, y_1) and (x_2, y_2) are points on the line. Thus here $0 = x_1$, $a = y_1$, $a = x_2$, and $0 = y_2$.

Thus $\frac{y_2 - y_1}{x_2 - x_1} = \frac{0 - a}{a - 0} = -1$: I is therefore true.

(Use Strategy 18: Know and use facts about triangles.)

II: The triangle created is an isosceles right triangle with sides a, a, $a\sqrt{2}$. Thus II is true.
III: In an isosceles right triangle, the interior angles of the triangle are 90-45-45 degrees. Thus III is true.

(Math Refresher #416, #411, #509)

8. Choice E is correct. **(Use Strategy 8: When all choices must be tested, start with E and work backward.)** Choice A is incorrect: On the number line b is to the left of -2, so this implies that b is less than -2 (written as $b < -2$). Since $b < -2$, b is certainly less than -1 (written as $b < -1$). Thus Choice A is incorrect. Choice B is false because if $b < -2$, the absolute value of b (denoted as $|b|$) must be greater than 2. Choice C is false: c is positive ($c > +3 > 0$) so $c \neq -|c|$, since $-|c|$ is negative. Choice D is false: Since a and b are negative numbers and since $a < b$, $|a| > |b|$. Choice E is correct and Choice D is incorrect.

(Math Refresher #419, #615, and #410)

9. Choice B is correct. **(Use Strategy 2: Translate from words to algebra.)** We are told:

$$A + 8 + A + 1 + A + 2$$
$$= A + A + 1 + A + 2 + A + 3 \quad \boxed{1}$$

(Use Strategy 1: Cancel expressions that appear on both sides of an equation.)

Each side contains an A, $A + 1$, and $A + 2$. Canceling each of these from each side, we get $\cancel{A} + 8 + \cancel{A} + \cancel{1} + \cancel{A} + \cancel{2} = \cancel{A} + \cancel{A} + \cancel{1} + \cancel{A} + \cancel{2} + A + 3$.

$$\text{Thus, } 8 = A + 3$$
$$5 = A$$

(Math Refresher #406)

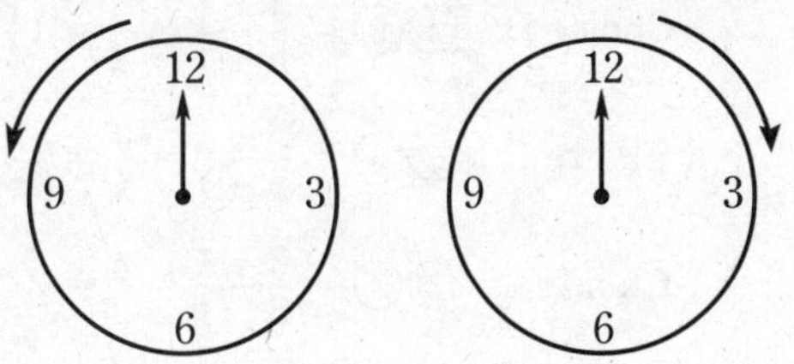

A B

10. Choice E is correct. **(Use Strategy 11: New definitions lead to easy questions.)**

By the definition of a move, every 4 moves brings each hand back to 12.

Thus, after 4, 8, 12, and 16 moves, respectively, each hand is at 12.

Hand A, moving counterclockwise, moves to 9 on its 17th move.

Hand B, moving clockwise, moves to 3 on its 17th move.

11. Choice E is correct. **(Use Strategy 17: Use the given information effectively.)**

Given: $w = 7r + 6r + 5r + 4r + 3r$
Then, $w = 25r$ $\boxed{1}$

We are told we must add something to w so that the resulting sum will be divisible by 7 for every positive integer r.

Check the choices. **(Use Strategy 8: Start with Choice E.)** Add $3r$ to $\boxed{1}$

$$25r + 3r = 28r = 7(4r)$$

will always be divisible by 7. Thus, Choice E is correct.

(Math Refresher #431)

12. Choice D is correct. **(Use Strategy 7: Use numerics to help find the answer.)** To obtain the maximum number of members of S, choose the numbers as small as possible; hence $1 + 3 + 5 + 7 + 9 + 11 + 13 + 15 = 64$.

Hence, the maximum is 8.

(Math Refresher #801)

13. Choice E is correct. **(Use Strategy 7: Use numerics to help find the answer.)** I, II, and III are correct.

Examples: $(2^3)^2 = 2^6 = 64$,

$2^{3+2} = 2^3\,2^2 = 32$, $(2 \times 3)^2 = 2^2\,3^2 = 36$.

(Math Refresher #429)

14. Choice C is correct. **(Use Strategy 2: Translate from words to algebra.)**

The number of hours from 7:00 A.M. to 5:00 P.M. is 10.

The number of hours from 1:00 P.M. to 7:00 P.M. is 6.

He worked 10 hours for 3 days and 6 hours for 3 days. Thus,

$$\text{Total hours} = 3(10) + 3(6)$$
$$= 30 + 18$$
$$\text{Total hours} = 48 \quad \boxed{1}$$
$$\text{Total earnings} = \text{Hours worked} \times \text{Hourly rate} \quad \boxed{2}$$

Given: He earns \$10 per hour $\boxed{3}$

Substituting $\boxed{1}$ and $\boxed{3}$ into $\boxed{2}$, we get

Total earnings = 48 × \$10
Total earnings = \$480

(Math Refresher #200 and #406)

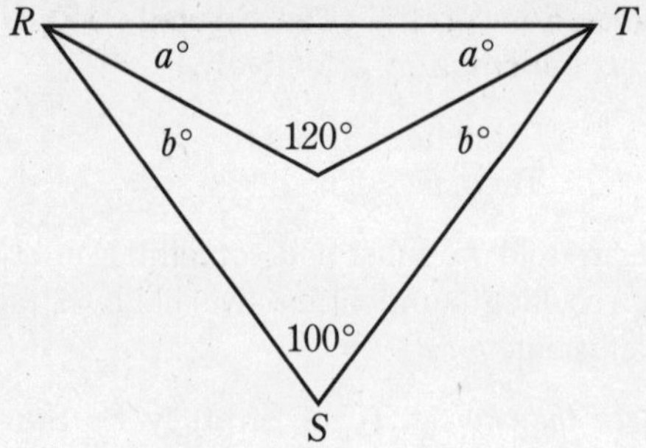

15. Choice E is correct. **(Use Strategy 3: The whole equals the sum of its parts.)**

The sum of the angles in a $\triangle = 180$. For the small triangle we have

$$\begin{aligned} 120 + a + a &= 180 \\ 120 + 2a &= 180 \\ 2a &= 60 \\ a &= 30 \quad \boxed{1} \end{aligned}$$

For $\triangle$ *RST*, we have

$$100 + m\angle SRT + m\angle STR = 180 \quad \boxed{2}$$

From the diagram, we get

$$\begin{aligned} m\angle SRT &= a + b \quad \boxed{3} \\ m\angle STR &= a + b \quad \boxed{4} \end{aligned}$$

Substituting $\boxed{3}$ and $\boxed{4}$ into $\boxed{2}$, we get

$$100 + a + b + a + b = 180$$
$$100 + 2a + 2b = 180$$

$$2a + 2b = 80 \quad \boxed{5}$$

Substituting $\boxed{1}$ into $\boxed{5}$, we get

$$\begin{aligned} 2(30) + 2b &= 80 \\ 60 + 2b &= 80 \\ 2b &= 20 \\ b &= 10 \end{aligned}$$

(Math Refresher #505 and #406)

Question 16

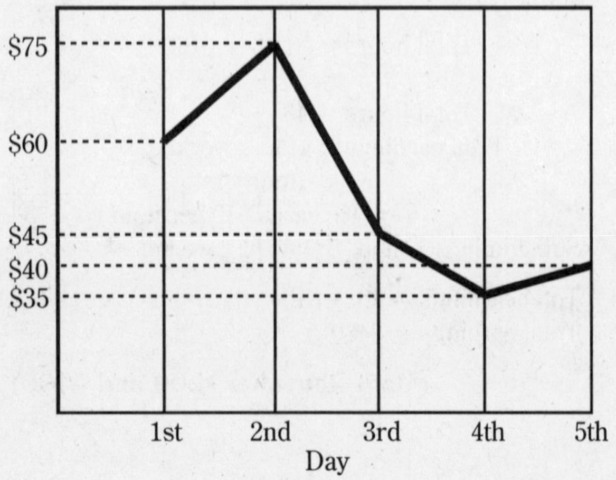

16. Choice C is correct. In ascending order, the wages for the six days are:

$35
$35
$40
$45
$60
$75

The median is the middle number. But wait! There is no middle number. So we average the two middle numbers, 40 and 45, to get 42.5.

The mode is the number appearing most frequently, that is, 35. So $42.50 - 35 = 7.50 = \$7.50$.

(Math Refresher #601a, #601b)

17. Choice E is correct. **(Use Strategy 11: Use new definitions carefully. Use Strategy 8: When all choices must be tested, start with E and work backward.)**

Given: $\textcircled{a}\textcircled{b} = \dfrac{a+1}{b-1}$

Choice E: $\textcircled{5}\textcircled{3} = \dfrac{5+1}{3-1} = \dfrac{6}{2} = 3$

Note that the other choices have b as either 3 or 5, which makes the denominator $b - 1$ as either 2 or 4. Since all the other choices (D, C, B, A) have a less than 5, the fraction in Choice E is greatest.

The remaining choices are shown below.

Choice D: $\textcircled{4}\textcircled{5} = \dfrac{4+1}{5-1} = \dfrac{5}{4} = 1\frac{1}{4}$

Choice C: $\textcircled{3}\textcircled{5} = \dfrac{3+1}{5-1} = \dfrac{4}{4} = 1$

Choice B: $\textcircled{3}\textcircled{3} = \dfrac{3+1}{3-1} = \dfrac{4}{2} = 2$

Choice A: $\textcircled{2}\textcircled{3} = \dfrac{2+1}{3-1} = \dfrac{3}{2} = 1\frac{1}{2}$

(Math Refresher #431)

18. Choice E is correct. **(Use Strategy 17: Use the given information effectively.)**

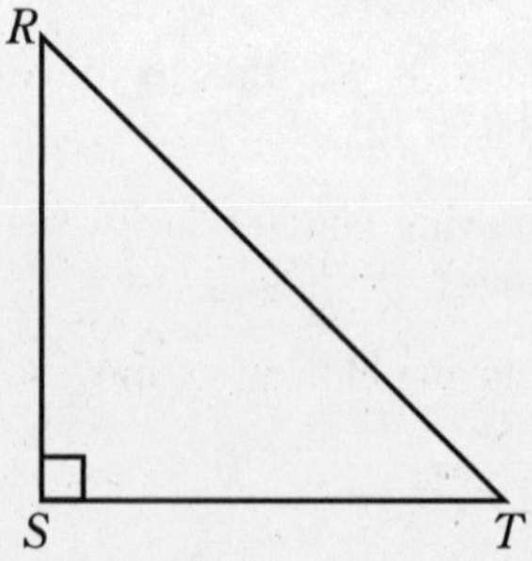

We know that area of $\triangle = \frac{1}{2} \times$ base $\times$ height [1]

We are given that $RS = ST =$ an integer [2]
Substituting [2] into [1], we get

Area $\triangle RST = \frac{1}{2} \times$ (An integer) $\times$ (same integer)

Area $\triangle RST = \frac{1}{2} \times$ (An integer)^2 [3]

Multiplying [3] by 2, we have

2(Area $\triangle RST$) = (An integer)^2 [4]

(Use Strategy 8: When all choices must be tested, start with E and work backward.)

Substituting Choice E, 20, into [4], we get

2(20) = (An integer)^2
40 = (An integer)^2 [5]
[5] is *not* possible, since 40 isn't the square of an integer.

(Math Refresher #307, #406, and #431)

19. Choice E is correct. **(Use Strategy 17: Use the given information effectively.)**

Volume of rectangular solid = $l \times w \times h$ [1]

Substituting the given dimensions into [1], we get

Volume of solid = 2 feet × 2 feet × 1 foot
Volume of solid = 4 cubic feet [2]
Volume of cube = (edge)^3 [3]
Substituting edge = 0.1 foot into [3], we get
Volume of cube = (0.1 foot)^3
Volume of cube = 0.001 cubic feet [4]

(Use Strategy 3: The whole equals the sum of its parts.) Since the volume of the rectangular solid must equal the sum of the small cubes, we need to know

$\frac{\text{volume of rectangular solid}}{\text{volume of cube}}$ = Number of cubes [5]

Substituting [2] and [4] into [5], we get

$\frac{\text{4 cubic feet}}{\text{0.001 cubic feet}}$ = Number of cubes

$\frac{4}{0.001}$ = Number of cubes

Multiplying numerator and denominator by 1,000, we get

$\frac{4}{0.001} \times \frac{1{,}000}{1{,}000}$ = Number of cubes

$\frac{4{,}000}{1}$ = Number of cubes

4,000 = Number of cubes

(Math Refresher #312 and #313)

20. Choice D is correct. **(Use Strategy 2: Translate from words to algebra. Use Strategy 17: Use the given information effectively.)**

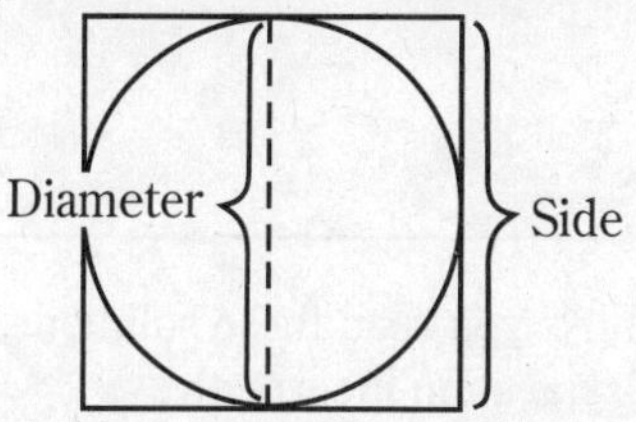

Given the perimeter of the square = 40

Thus, 4(side) = 40
side = 10 [1]

A side of the square = length of diameter of circle.

Thus, diameter = 10 from [1]
Since diameter = 2(radius)
10 = 2(radius)
5 = radius [2]
Area of a circle = πr^2 [3]

Substituting [2] into [3], we have
Area of circle = $\pi 5^2$
Area of circle = 25π

(Math Refresher #303 and #310)

Explanatory Answers for Practice Test 2 (continued)

Section 3: Math

As you read these solutions, you are advised to do two things if you answered the Math question incorrectly:

1. When a specific Math Strategy is referred to in the solution, study that strategy, which you will find in "19 Math Strategies" (beginning on page 69).
2. When the solution directs you to the "Complete Math Refresher" (beginning on page 167)—for example, Math Refresher 305—study the 305 Math principle to get a clear idea of the Math operation that was necessary for you to know in order to answer the question correctly.

1. Choice D is correct. **(Use Strategy 2: Translate from words to algebra.)**

Let n = the number.

Then $\frac{n+3}{4} = 6$

Multiplying both sides by 4, we have

$$4\left(\frac{n+3}{4}\right) = (6)4$$

$$n + 3 = 24$$

$$n = 21$$

(Math Refresher #200)

2. Choice C is correct. **(Use Strategy 17: Use the given information effectively.)**

Given: $\frac{3}{4} < x < \frac{4}{5}$

Change both fractions to fractions with the same denominator. Thus,

$$\frac{3}{4} < x < \frac{4}{5}$$

becomes

$$\frac{15}{20} < x < \frac{16}{20}$$

(Use Strategy 15: Certain choices may be easily eliminated.)

Choice B = $\frac{13}{20}$ can be instantly eliminated.

Choice D = $\frac{16}{20}$ can be instantly eliminated.

Change both fractions to 40ths to compare Choice C. Thus,

$$\frac{30}{40} < x < \frac{32}{40}$$

Choice C = $\frac{31}{40}$ is a possible value of x.

(Math Refresher #108 and #419)

3. Choice B is correct. **(Use Strategy 2: Translate from words to algebra.)**

Perimeter of a square = 4 × side. [1]
We are given that perimeter = 20 meters [2]

Substituting [2] into [1], we get

20 meters = 4 × side
5 meters = side [3]
Area of square = $(\text{side})^2$ [4]

Substituting [3] into [4], we get

Area of square = $(5 \text{ meters})^2$
Area of square = 25 square meters

(Math Refresher #303)

4. Choice E is correct. **(Use Strategy 17: Use the given information effectively.)**

Given: $80 + a = -32 + b$

Subtract a from both sides, getting

$$\begin{array}{rcl} 80 + a & = & -32 + b \\ -a & & -a \\ \hline 80 & = & -32 + b - a \end{array}$$

Add 32 to both sides, giving

$$\begin{array}{rcl} 80 & = & -32 + b - a \\ +32 & & +32 \\ \hline 112 & = & b - a \end{array}$$

(Math Refresher #406)

5. Choice E is correct. **(Use Strategy 8: When all choices must be tested, start with E and work backward.)**

Choice E is $x^2 + x + 2$

(Use Strategy 7: Use specific number examples.)

Let $x = 3$ (an odd positive integer)

Then $x^2 + x + 2 =$
$3^2 + 3 + 2 =$
$9 + 3 + 2 =$
$14 =$ (an even result)

Now let $x = 2$ (an even positive integer)

Then $x^2 + x + 2 =$
$2^2 + 2 + 2 =$
$4 + 2 + 2 =$
$8 =$ (an even result)

Whether x is odd or even, Choice E is even.

(Math Refresher #431)

The more sophisticated way of doing this is to use **Strategy 8: When all choices must be tested, start with Choice E and work backward.**

Choice E is $x^2 + x + 2$.

(Use Strategy 4: Factor quantities.)

$x^2 + x + 2 = x(x + 1) + 2$.

Note that since x is an integer, $x(x + 1)$ is always the product of an even integer multiplied by an odd integer. So $x(x + 1)$ is even and thus 2 times an integer. 2 is even, so $x(x + 1) + 2$ is even. And since $x(x + 1) + 2 = x^2 + x + 2$, $x^2 + x + 2$ is even.

(Math Refresher #409)

6. Choice A is correct. **(Use Strategy 17: Use the given information effectively.)**

Given: $ax = r$ [1]
$by = r - 1$ [2]

The quick method is to substitute [1] into [2], giving

$$by = ax - 1$$
$$by + 1 = ax$$
$$\frac{by + 1}{a} = x$$

(Math Refresher #431 and #406)

7. Choice B is correct. **(Use Strategy 2: Translate from words to algebra.)** Let the capacity of container B be x. Then the capacity of container A will be $2x$, and that of container C will be $3x$. The amount poured into container C is equal to half of $2x$ plus one-third of x, or $\frac{2x}{2} + \frac{x}{3} = x + \frac{x}{3} = \frac{4x}{3}$. Dividing this amount by the total capacity of container C, we find the fraction that was filled: $\frac{\left(\frac{4x}{3}\right)}{3x} = \frac{4}{9}$.

(Math Refresher #406)

8. Choice D is correct. **(Use Strategy 17: Use the given information effectively.)** In 12 seconds, the wheel travels through 2 revolutions (since 12 seconds is $\frac{1}{5}$ of the minute it would take for ten revolutions). Since this distance is equal to 16 feet, the wheel travels 8 feet per revolution; thus, 8 feet must be the circumference of the wheel. To find the diameter, we divide this figure by π (because the circumference of a circle is π times its diameter). Thus, the diameter is $\frac{8}{\pi}$ feet.

(Math Refresher #310)

9. 24 (Use Strategy 2: Translate from words to algebra.)

Let n = the number

We are given:

$$\frac{5}{8}n = \frac{3}{4}n - 3 \qquad \boxed{1}$$

(Use Strategy 13: Find unknowns by multiplication.) Multiply $\boxed{1}$ by 8. We get

$$8\left(\frac{5}{8}n\right) = 8\left(\frac{3}{4}n - 3\right)$$

$$5n = \frac{24}{4}n - 24$$

$$5n = 6n - 24$$

$$24 = n \qquad \textit{(Answer)}$$

(Math Refresher #200 and #406)

10. 10 (Use Strategy 11: Use new definitions carefully.)

By definition

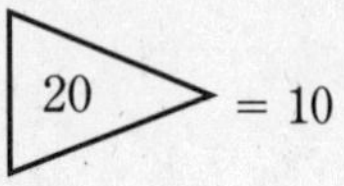

(Math Refresher #603 and #607)

11. 2300 (Use Strategy 12: Try not to make tedious calculations.)

$$23m + 23n = 23(m + n)$$
$$= 23(94 + 6)$$
$$= 23(100)$$
$$= 2300$$

Multiplying 23(94) and 23(6) and adding would be time-consuming and therefore tedious.

(Math Refresher #431)

12. 11 Since lines are drawn every 10 yards after the first one, $\frac{100}{10}$ lines, or 10 additional lines, are drawn.

(Use Strategy 2: Translate from words to algebra.) The total number of lines on the field = the original line + the number of additional lines

$$= 1 + 10 = 11$$

(Math Refresher #200)

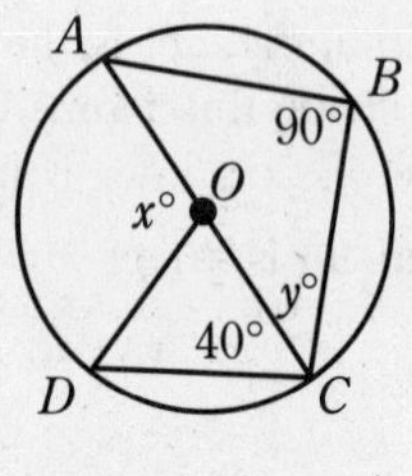

13. 125 (Use Strategy 18: Know and use facts about triangles.) Since $AB = BC$ in ΔABC, it is isosceles, and the opposite angles are equal. So

$$m\angle A = y \qquad \boxed{1}$$

(Use Strategy 3: The whole equals the sum of its parts.) The sum of the angles in a triangle is 180°, so

$$m\angle A + y + 90 = 180$$

Subtracting 90 from both sides gives

$$m\angle A + y = 90 \qquad \boxed{2}$$

From $\boxed{1}$, the angles are equal, so substituting y for $m\angle A$ in $\boxed{2}$ gives

$$y + y = 90$$
$$\frac{2y}{2} = \frac{90}{2}$$
$$y = 45 \qquad \boxed{3}$$

$x°$ is a central angle, so it is measured by the intercepted arc AD. $\angle DCA = 40°$ is an inscribed angle and measures $\frac{1}{2}$ its intercepted arc AD. Therefore, the intercepted arc $AD = 80°$. So $x = 80$; therefore $x + y = 80 + 45 = 125$.

(Math Refresher #507, #505, #406, and #527)

14. 25

(Use Strategy 5:

$$\textbf{Average} = \frac{\textbf{sum of values}}{\textbf{total number of values}}\textbf{)}$$

Average age of students in a class

$$= \frac{\text{sum of the ages of students in the class}}{\text{number of students in the class}} \qquad \boxed{1}$$

Thus,

Average age of all 80 students

$$= \frac{\text{sum of the ages of the 80 students}}{80} \qquad \boxed{2}$$

Using $\boxed{1}$, we know that

$$20 = \frac{\text{sum of the ages of the 60 students}}{60}$$

$$\text{and } 40 = \frac{\text{sum of the ages of the 20 students}}{20}$$

Thus,

the sum of the ages of the 60 students

$$= (60)(20) = 1{,}200$$

and the sum of the ages of the 20 students

$$= (40)(20) = 800$$

Hence, the sum of the ages of the 80 students

= sum of the ages of the 60 students
+ sum of the ages of the 20 students
= 1,200 + 800 = 2,000 [3]

Substituting [3] into [2], we get

$$\frac{2{,}000}{80} = 25$$

Average age of all 80 students = 25 (*Answer*)

(Math Refresher #601 and #406)

15. **4** By trial and error, it can be seen that 4 is the answer. A second way of approaching this problem is as follows:

Let □ = x. Then we have

$$\begin{array}{r} x\,1 \\ 6\,x \\ x\,9 \\ \hline 15\,x \end{array}$$

We get $1 + x + 9 = 10 + x$. So we carry the 1 and get $1 + x + 6 + x = 15$. So $7 + 2x = 15$, $2x = 8$, $x = 4$.

A third way to approach this problem (and the most sophisticated way) is: Let □ = x. Then □1 is x 1, which is $10x + 1$ since □ is in the tens column. (Any number XY is $10X + Y$; any number XYZ is $100X + 10Y + Z$.) 6 □ = 6 x = $60 + x$. □9 = x 9 = $10x + 9$. So adding, we get

$10x + 1 + 60 + x + 10x + 9 = 21x + 70$.

This must equal 15□ = 15 x =

$$100 + 50 + x = 150 + x.$$

So $21x + 70 = 150 + x$ and $20x = 80$; $x = 4$. **(Use Strategy 17: Use the given information effectively.)**

(Math Refresher #406)

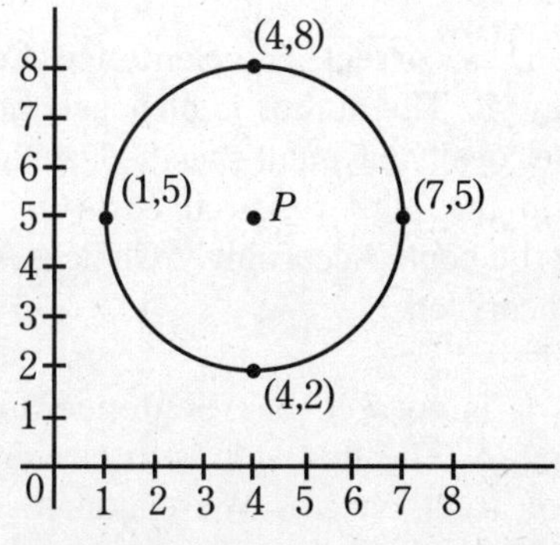

16. **3 (Use Strategy 17: Use the given information effectively.)** The coordinates of the center P are (4,5). By definition, the length of a radius is the distance from the center to any point on the circle. Therefore,

radius = distance from (7,5) to (4,5)
= 7 − 4
radius = 3

(Math Refresher #410 and #524)

17. **36.2 (Use Strategy 2: Translate from words to algebra.)**

Fraction mowed during evening 1 = $\frac{2}{9}$ [1]

Fraction mowed during evening 2 = $2\left(\frac{2}{9}\right) = \frac{4}{9}$ [2]

Adding [1] and [2], we get

Total fraction mowed during first two evenings = $\frac{2}{9} + \frac{4}{9}$
= $\frac{6}{9}$

Total fraction mowed during first two evenings = $\frac{2}{3}$

(Use Strategy 3: The whole equals the sum of its parts.)

Amount left for evening 3 =
1 whole lawn − $\frac{2}{3}$ already mowed

Amount left for evening 3 = $\frac{1}{3}$ [3]

Given: Lawn area = 108.6 square feet [4]

Multiplying [3] by [4], we get

Amount left for evening 3 = $\frac{1}{3} \times 108.6$ square feet

Amount left for evening 3 = 36.2 square feet

(Math Refresher #200 and #109)

18. **7** All nine people are on a straight line in a circle, and we want to have the least number of people move so that all nine are on the circumference of *another* circle. **(Use Strategy 17: Use the given information effectively.)** Draw the situation:

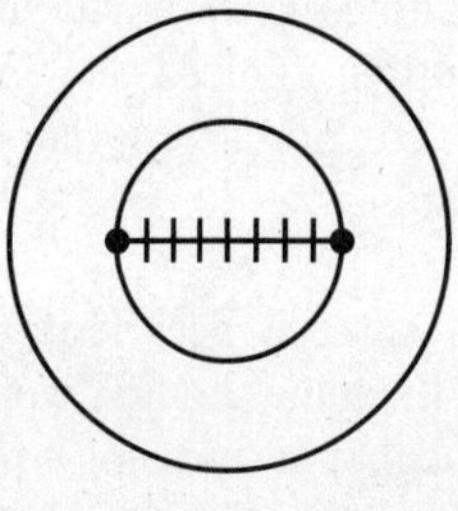

You can see that since two people are already on the circumference of the inner circle, you need to move the other seven to be on the circumference of the inner circle, so all nine will be on the circumference of the *same* circle.

(Math Refresher #524)

Explanatory Answers for Practice Test 2 (continued)

Section 4: Critical Reading

As you read these Explanatory Answers, refer to "16 Verbal (Critical Reading) Strategies" (beginning on page 119) whenever a specific strategy is referred to in the answer. Of particular importance are the following Master Verbal Strategies:

Sentence Completion Master Strategy 1—page 120.
Sentence Completion Master Strategy 2—page 121.
Reading Comprehension Master Strategy 2—page 138.

Note: All Reading questions use Reading Comprehension Strategies 1, 2, and 3 (pages 135–140) as well as other strategies indicated.

1. Choice E is correct. See **Sentence Completion Strategy 4.** The first word, "Though," is an *opposition indicator.* The beginning of the sentence speaks positively about the computer programmer. We must find a word that gives us a negative idea about him. Choice E, creativity, is the appropriate word. The other choices are incorrect because their words are not appropriate to give us that opposite feeling.

2. Choice D is correct. See **Sentence Completion Strategy 2.** Examine the first word of each choice. Choice B, tantamount (meaning equivalent to)..., and Choice C, collegiate..., do *not* make sense because we do not speak of a tantamount professor or a collegiate professor. Now consider the other choices. Choice D, scholarly...profound, is the only choice which has a word pair that makes sense in the sentence.

3. Choice D is correct. See **Sentence Completion Strategy 1.** The beginning word "Because" is a *result indicator.* We may expect, then, a reason in the first part of the sentence for the Indian people to escape from British rule and join the Japanese. The word "abused" (Choice D) provides the reason. The words in the other choices do not make sense in the sentence.

4. Choice D is correct. See **Sentence Completion Strategy 1.** The author is obviously not satisfied with the royalty payment specified, as the sentence refers to the high research costs necessary for writing the book. Accordingly, Choices A, B, C, and E are incorrect.

5. Choice C is correct. See **Sentence Completion Strategy 2.** The first step is to examine the first word of each choice. We eliminate Choice B, perplexed, and Choice D, considerate, because the first part of the sentence makes no sense with these choices. Now we go to the remaining choices. Choice A and Choice E do *not* make sense in the sentence and are therefore incorrect. Choice C *does* make sense in the sentence.

6. Choice E is correct. See **Sentence Completion Strategy 2.** The first step is to examine the first word of each choice. We eliminate Choice A and Choice C because there are no such things as "sonorous clothes" or "raucous clothes." Now we go to the remaining choices. Choice B, tawdry...humble, and Choice D, tattered...nightmarish, do *not* make sense in the sentence. Choice E, old-fashioned... nostalgic, *does* make sense in the sentence.

7. Choice B is correct. See **Sentence Completion Strategy 1.** Try each choice: Her devotion to music *brought back* or *reawakened* his former interest in it.

8. Choice D is correct. See **Sentence Completion Strategy 2.** Look at the first word of each choice. The first words in Choices C and E do not quite sound right in the sentence. So eliminate Choices C and E. Now try both words in each of the remaining choices in the sentence. You can see that Choice D fits best: Sadat disregarded sharp or bitter criticism—that is, *acrimonious* criticism. He accepted Israel's invitation in accordance with conventional requirements—that is, *formally.*

9. Choice E is correct. Throughout the passage there was no evidence for the existence of the inhabitants of Atlantis. There was only a theory that was discussed in lines 11–13.

10. Choice C is correct. See lines 6–7. "because of the impiety of its people...."

11. Choice B is correct. See lines 6–8 describing the accuracy of reproduction.

12. Choice E is correct. See lines 13–14 where it describes that changes can be made.

13. Choice D is correct. See paragraph 2: "Formerly, technical rationality had been employed only to organize the production of rather simple physical objects.... Now technical rationality is increasingly employed to organize all of the processes necessary to the utilization of physical objects...."

14. Choice B is correct. See paragraph 1: "The absence of direct controls or of coercion should not serve to obscure from our view the...social controls which are employed (such as...advertising, selective service channeling, and so on)."

15. Choice A is correct. It can be seen from the context of the sentence: "...there would be frequent errors...." Choice A is correct. See also **Reading Comprehension Strategy 5.**

16. Choice C is correct. See paragraph 5: "...the workforce must be relatively over-trained...."

17. Choice B is correct. See paragraph 4: "The assembly line also introduced standardization in work skills and thus makes for a high degree of interchangeability among the workforce....If each operation taxed the workers still there would be frequent errors...."

18. Choice E is correct. See paragraph 1: "Technology conquers nature...to do so it must first conquer man...it demands a very high degree of control over the training, mobility, and skills of the workforce."

19. Choice D is correct. See paragraph 6: "...the workforce within technologically advanced organizations is asked to work not less hard but more so."

20. Choice E is correct. See paragraph 3: "...there are very profound social antagonisms or contradictions...." This article is one of skepticism. It frequently points out the contradictions, irrationality, and coercive tactics exhibited by advanced technological institutions.

21. Choice C is correct. See paragraph 6: "Salary and wage increases...lose their...importance...once... an ample supply of luxuries are assured."

22. Choice E is correct. We link "technical specialists" with "such retraining only for a managing elite." Therefore Choice E is correct. See also **Reading Comprehension Strategy 5.**

23. Choice E is correct. See paragraph 5: "...technological progress requires a continuous increase in the skill levels of its workforce, skill levels which frequently embody a fairly rich scientific and technical training...those skills will be less and less fully used."

24. Choice B is correct. See paragraph 6: "...among young people one can already observe a radical weakening in the power of such incentives as money, status, and authority."

Explanatory Answers for Practice Test 2 (continued)

Section 5: Writing

For further practice and information, please refer to Grammar and Usage Refresher starting on page 455.

1. **(B)** Avoid the double negative. Choices A and C suffer from the double-negative fault. Choice B is correct. Choice D changes the meaning of the original sentence. Choice E creates a run-on sentence.

2. **(E)** The original sentence is interrogative. Accordingly, the sentence must end with a question mark. Choice E is correct.

3. **(D)** Choice A is incorrect because it creates a run-on sentence. Choice B fails to include the all-inclusive ("altogether," "completely," "entirely") idea of the original sentence. Choice C changes the meaning of the original sentence. Choice D is correct. Choice E changes the meaning of the original sentence.

4. **(B)** The adverb "yesterday" should, in this sentence, be placed before the modified verb ("arrested"). The time should be placed close to the event, so "yesterday" should not be next to "gallery." Therefore, Choices A and C are incorrect and Choice B is correct. Choices D and E are too roundabout.

5. **(E)** Choice A is incorrect because "that" is redundant; "deciding" is the subject and "that" merely repeats it. Choices B and C are incorrect because they have no subject. Prepositional phrases cannot act as subjects of sentences. Choice D is incorrect because only two items are being compared, so the comparative ("better"), not the superlative ("best"), is needed. Choice E is correct because a gerund ("deciding") can act as the subject of a sentence.

6. **(C)** Choice A is out-of-date. Choice B does not give the meaning intended in the original sentence. Choice C is correct. Choice D is too wordy. Choice E changes the meaning of the original sentence.

7. **(C)** Choices A, B, D, and E are incorrect because each choice begins its own new sentence. Each of these choices, therefore, creates a run-on sentence. Choice C is correct.

8. **(A)** Choice A is correct. Choices B and E change the meaning of the original sentence. Choice C is incorrect grammatically because the verb ellipsis is improper—"the report *was* filed." Choice D is too involved.

9. **(E)** The expression "on account" in Choice A cannot be used as a subordinate conjunction. The expression "being that" in Choice B is always incorrect. Choice C changes the meaning of the original sentence. Choice D is too wordy. Choice E is correct.

10. **(E)** Choice A is too wordy. The double use of the preposition "from" in Choice B is incorrect. Choice

C is too wordy. Choice D, as direct discourse, would be correct with the proper punctuation: "... student, 'Which country have you come from?'" Choice E is correct.

11. (C) Sequence of tenses in contrary-to-fact past situations requires the "had listened" form of the verb. Choice C is therefore correct and all the other choices are incorrect. Moreover, in Choice E, there is no need to use the word "advice" since the rest of the choice implies that advice has been given.

12. (B) "...is not *nearly* as beautiful...." Do not use the expression *nowhere near* for *not nearly.*

13. (C) "...where *those* same men...." The demonstrative pronoun-adjective form (*those*)—not the personal pronoun form (*them*)—must be used to modify the noun *men.*

14. (E) All underlined parts are correct.

15. (C) "...the *cheaper* to run." Since we are comparing two things, we must use the comparative degree—not the superlative degree (*cheapest*).

16. (C) "...*nor* can he live without bread." The coordinate conjunction *nor* is used when the alternative statement is negative.

17. (A) "*Having swum* two-thirds of the distance...." The past participle of *swim* is *swum.*

18. (D) "...about solving *anyone else's* problems." Say *anyone else's, somebody else's,* etc. Do *not* say *anyone's else, somebody's else.*

19. (A) "*Because of* the meat boycott...." Do not begin a sentence with the words *due to. Due* is an adjective. As an adjective, it must have a noun to modify.

20. (D) "...so that the children *would have* enough space...." In a clause expressing purpose, the subjunctive form of the verb (*would have*)—not the indicative form (*had*)—should be used.

21. (E) All underlined parts are correct.

22. (A) "After he *had won* the marathon...he decided...." The past perfect tense (*had won*)—not the past tense (*won*)—is necessary when an action in the past has taken place *before* another action in the past.

23. (C) "...long a guiding *principle* of many educators...." *Principal* applies to a chief or the chief part of something. *Principle* applies to a basic law.

24. (C) "...the Republicans will feel *its* effects...." The possessive adjective *its* does not have an apostrophe. (There is another word, *it's,* that means *it is.*)

25. (A) "If we *had begun* our vacation...." The past perfect tense of *to begin* is *had begun*—not *had began.*

26. (B) "All of the class presidents but Jerry, Alice, and *me*...." The preposition (*but*) must take an object form (*me*)—not a subject form (*I*).

27. (C) "Everyone who attends...knows that *he* or *she* will be searched...." A pronoun must agree with its antecedent in number. Therefore, the singular pronoun *he* or *she*—not *they*—must be used because the antecedent of the pronoun is singular (*everyone*).

28. (D) "...write one *quickly.*" The adverb form is needed to modify the verb *could write.*

29. (D) "One of the key suspects...*was captured*...." *One* is the singular subject of the sentence. The verb, therefore, must be singular (*was captured*). The plural verb (*were captured*) is incorrect.

30. (B) Choice A is incorrect because the sentence is needed to communicate information vital to understanding the paragraph. Choice B is correct, since "compromised" is not the same as "comprised." Choice C is incorrect: Joining the two sentences with a semicolon would be all right, but the faulty diction of "compromised" would remain. Choices D and E are incorrect because the misused word is not changed.

31. (E) Choice A is incorrect: The pronoun "one" is ambiguous in its reference, failing to make the fact perfectly clear that the men's sweathouse was one of the communal dwellings. Choice B is incorrect in that beginning the sentence with "there" makes no transition at all between sentence 1 and sentence 2, failing completely to indicate the communal nature of the sweathouse. Choice C is incorrect because joining "a men's sweathouse" to "family dwellings and communal dwellings" with "and" makes the sense appear to be that there are three classes of buildings, rather than indicating that the sweathouse belongs in the second group of buildings. Choice D is incorrect: The sentence cannot be omitted since it furnishes a necessary piece of information for understanding sentence 3. Choice E is correct because substituting "among the latter" for "one" makes the reference entirely clear that the sweathouse is one of the communal buildings.

32. **(A)** Choice A is correct: Changing sentence 3 into a dependent clause beginning with "where" improves the sentence by doing away with the awkward repetition of "sweathouse" at the end of sentence 2 and the beginning of sentence 3. Choice B is incorrect in that omitting the adjective "adolescent" serves only to reduce the accuracy and clarity of the information about how old the boys were. Choice C is incorrect: Placing the modifier before "grown men" indicates that both the men and boys were learning, a meaning that common sense dictates as improbable. Choice D is incorrect: The sentence would not be improved by being joined to sentence 2 with a semicolon since the awkward repetition of "sweathouse" would remain. Choice E is incorrect: While "it was there" would eliminate the repetition of "sweathouse," almost no sentence is improved by adding an unnecessary "it was" or "there was"; in this case, since "where" is available as a transition in Choice A, this is the choice that offers the greatest improvement.

33. **(D)** Choice A is incorrect: Since "sentence" 4 is already a fragment, breaking it into two portions would only compound the present error. Choice B is incorrect: Beginning with "sometimes they exchanged" would furnish a subject and verb predicate for the sentence but would result in a lack of parallel structure when followed by "sometimes preparing themselves." Choice C is incorrect because the substitution would not correct the sentence fragment. Choice D is correct in that connecting the fragment to sentence 3 with a comma would make the words function properly as modifying phrases. Choice E is incorrect in that the suggested substitution does not correct the sentence fragment.

34. **(C)** Choice A is incorrect: Placing the sentence after "boys" in sentence 3 merely interrupts the sequence of ideas in that sentence with extraneous information which does not belong in that context. Choice B is incorrect since introducing the information in sentence 6 between sentences 4 and 5 is distracting and serves no purpose. Choice C is correct because the information in sentence 6 does not belong in the paragraph at all since it has no relevance to the topic of the men's sweathouse. Choice D is incorrect because placement after sentence 7 would not make the information any more relevant to the paragraph than the present placement does. Choice E is incorrect because the sentence does not belong in the paragraph.

35. **(D)** Choice A is incorrect: It would be merely prudish to stop the sentence before naming the uses of the women's house since the uses of the men's house have been named. Choice B is incorrect: Placing sentence 8 after sentence 5 would interrupt the sequence of information about the admission of women to the sweathouse. Choice C is incorrect because if the first sentence ended with "house," the remaining words would constitute a sentence fragment. Choice D is correct: The sentence introduces a new topic, that of the women's communal house, and should, therefore, start a new paragraph. Choice E is incorrect: The word "lady" connotes a woman of breeding and refinement and may even suggest a distinction in a social hierarchy. Because of these connotations, the word should not be used to denote a female person generically.

Explanatory Answers for Practice Test 2 (continued)

Section 6: Math

As you read these solutions, you are advised to do two things if you answered the Math question incorrectly:

1. When a specific Math Strategy is referred to in the solution, study that strategy, which you will find in "19 Math Strategies" (beginning on page 69).
2. When the solution directs you to the "Complete Math Refresher" (beginning on page 167)—for example, Math Refresher 305—study the 305 Math principle to get a clear idea of the Math operation that was necessary for you to know in order to answer the question correctly.

1. Choice D is correct.
Method 1: Remember that

1. The sum of two odd numbers is even.
2. The sum, difference, and product of two even numbers is even.
3. The product of two odd numbers is odd.

Given: a is odd, b is odd, c is even. Therefore, $a + b$ is even.

$$(a + b) - c \text{ is even.}$$

Method 2: Choose a numerical example.
(Use Strategy 7: Use number examples.)
Let $a = 3$, $b = 5$, and $c = 4$
(Use Strategy 8: When all choices must be tested, start with Choice E and work backward.)
Then Choice E $(a + bc) = 23$
Therefore, Choice E is odd.
Choice D $(a + b) - c = 4$
Therefore, Choice D is even.

(Math Refresher #603, #604, #605, and #431)

2. Choice B is correct. **(Use Strategy 2: Translate words to numbers.)** 35% of all of Harry's stamps are American, and 23% of these are Air Mail. 23% of 35% equals

$$\frac{23}{100} \times \frac{35}{100} = \frac{805}{10{,}000} = \frac{8.05}{100}$$

which equals 8.05%.

(Math Refresher #702)

3. Choice A is correct. **(Use Strategy 14: Draw lines to help solve the problem.)** Before the rotation, we have

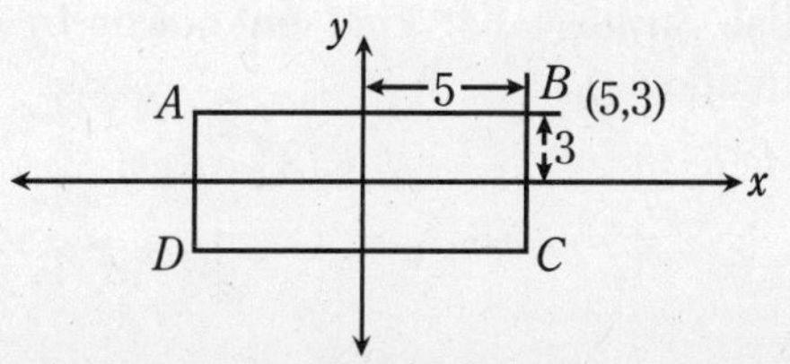

After the rotation, we have

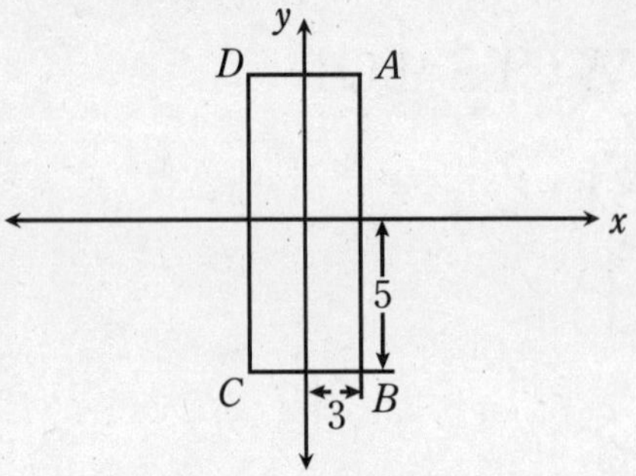

Note that the new y-coordinate of B is negative because B is below the x-axis. Since B is to the right of the y-axis, its x-coordinate is positive. By looking at the second diagram, we see that the coordinates of B are:

$$(3, -5).$$

(Math Refresher #410b)

4. Choice B is correct. **(Use Strategy 11: Use new definitions carefully.)**

After 6 hours $\frac{x}{2}$ grams remain.

After 12 hours, $\frac{1}{2}\left(\frac{x}{2}\right)$ grams remain.

After 18 hours, $\frac{1}{2}\left(\frac{1}{2}\right)\left(\frac{x}{2}\right)$ grams remain.

After 24 hours, $\frac{1}{2}\left(\frac{1}{2}\right)\left(\frac{1}{2}\right)\left(\frac{x}{2}\right) = \frac{x}{16}$ grams remain.

(Math Refresher #431)

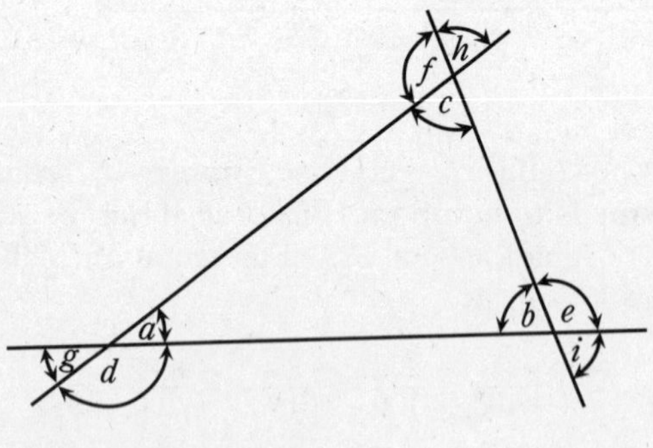

5. Choice B is correct.

Method I: Shortest method:

$$a + b + c = 180 \quad \boxed{1}$$
$$g + d = 180 \quad \boxed{2}$$
$$e + i = 180 \quad \boxed{3}$$
$$f + h = 180 \quad \boxed{4}$$

(Use Strategy 13: Find unknowns by adding equations.)

Adding $\boxed{1} + \boxed{2} + \boxed{3} + \boxed{4}$, we get

$$a + b + c + g + d + e + i + f + h = 720$$

Method II:

From the diagram, we get

$$a + d = 180 \quad \boxed{1}$$
$$b + e = 180 \quad \boxed{2}$$
$$c + f = 180 \quad \boxed{3}$$

(Use Strategy 13: Find unknowns by adding equations.)

Adding $\boxed{1} + \boxed{2} + \boxed{3}$, we get

$$a + b + c + d + e + f = 540 \quad \boxed{4}$$

(Use Strategy 3: The whole equals the sum of its parts.)

The sum of the angles of a $\triangle = 180$

$$\text{Thus, } a + b + c = 180 \quad \boxed{5}$$

From the diagram (vertical angles), we have

$$a = g, b = i, c = h \quad \boxed{6}$$

Substituting $\boxed{6}$ into $\boxed{5}$, we get

$$g + i + h = 180 \quad \boxed{7}$$

Adding $\boxed{4} + \boxed{7}$, we get

$$a + b + c + d + e + f + g + i + h = 720$$

Method III:

Let X be the value of $a + b + c + d + e + f + g + h + i$.

Label the unmarked angles j, k, and l.

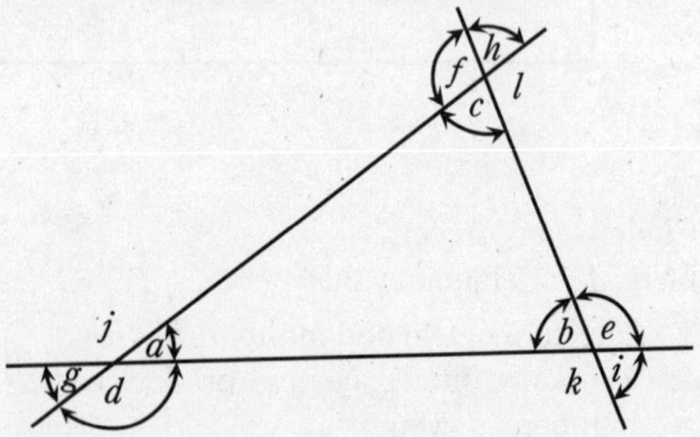

We know that the sum of the angles in a circle is 360°. So we get:

$$a + d + g + j = 360 \quad \boxed{8}$$
$$b + e + i + k = 360 \quad \boxed{9}$$
$$c + f + h + l = 360 \quad \boxed{10}$$

(Use Strategy 13: Add equations.)

$$X + j + k + l = 3(360) \quad \boxed{11}$$

We know that the sum of angles in a straight line is 180°. So we get:

$$j + a = 180 \quad \boxed{12}$$
$$k + b = 180 \quad \boxed{13}$$
$$l + c = 180 \quad \boxed{14}$$

By adding equations [12], [13], and [14] together, we get:

$$j + k + l + a + b + c = 3(180) \quad [15]$$

And since the angles of a triangle = 180°

$$a + b + c = 180 \quad [16]$$

Substituting [16] into [15], we get:

$$j + k + l + 180 = 3(180)$$

$$j + k + l = 3(180) - 180 = 2(180) = 360 \quad [17]$$

Substituting [17] into [11], we get:

$$X + 360 = 3(360)$$

$$X = 3(360) - 360 = 2(360) = 720$$

(Math Refresher #501, #505, and #406)

6. Choice D is correct. **(Use Strategy 11: Use new definitions carefully.)** The smallest sum occurs when we choose 3 from A and 6 from B.

Therefore, the minimum sum = 3 + 6 = 9

The largest sum occurs when we choose 5 from A and 8 from B.

Therefore, the maximum sum = 5 + 8 = 13

All numbers from 9 to 13 inclusive can be sums.

Thus, there are 5 different sums possible.

(Math Refresher #431)

7. Choice D is correct. **(Use Strategy 8: When all choices must be tested, start with Choice E and work backward.)** The equation that does not represent any of the illustrated graphs is $y = 2x + 4$ because none of the illustrated graphs has a slope of 2 and crosses the y-axis ($x = 0$) at $y = 4$.

(Math Refresher #416 and #414)

8. Choice B is correct. $f(2x) = |2x| - 2x = 2|x| - 2x = 2f(x)$.

(Math Refresher #616 and #615)

9. **1/1, 1, 1.0, etc. (Use Strategy 17: Use the given information effectively.)** This means that when $x = 5, y = 6$ and when $x = 7, y = 8$.

The slope is $(y_2-y_1)/(x_2-x_1)$. Thus $(y_2-y_1)/(x_2-x_1) = (8-6)/(7-5) = 1/1$.
See diagram below:

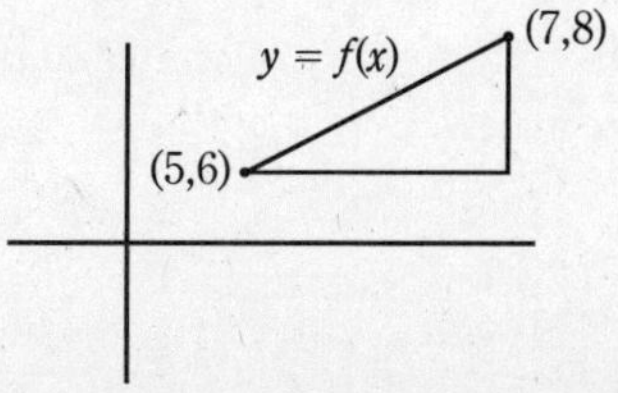

(Math Refresher #616 and #416)

10. **15 (Use Strategy 17: Use the given information effectively.)**

Given: a bag with 4 blue, 7 green, and 8 yellow marbles.

Fred could draw 15 marbles and have only green and yellow marbles (8 + 7). On his next pick, however, he would be sure of having one of each color.

(Use Strategy 16: The obvious may be tricky!)

It is his sixteenth draw that gets Fred one of each color, but the question asks how many Fred would have drawn, so that on his *next* draw he will have 1 marble of every color.

He would have drawn *15*. The sixteenth is the next draw, but not the answer to the question.

The correct answer is 15.

11. **50 (Use Strategy 5: Remember $\text{average} = \left(\frac{\text{sum of values}}{\text{total number of values}}\right)$)**

We are told that the average of 5 different integers is 12. Thus,

$$\frac{x+y+z+w+v}{5} = 12 \quad [1]$$

Multiplying [1] by 5, we get

$$5\left(\frac{x+y+z+w+v}{5}\right) = 5(12)$$

$$x + y + z + w + v = 60 \quad [2]$$

(Use Strategy 17: Use the given information effectively.)

For one of the integers to be the greatest, the other four must be as small as possible. Thus,

let $x = 1$ [3]
let $y = 2$ [4]
let $z = 3$ [5]
let $w = 4$ [6]

The four smallest possible different integers > 0.

Substituting [3], [4], [5], and [6] into [2], we get

$$1 + 2 + 3 + 4 + v = 60$$
$$10 + v = 60$$
$$v = 50$$

Thus, the greatest possible value for any of the integers is 50.

(Math Refresher #601 and #406)

12. 3 (Use Strategy 2: Translate from words to algebra.)

Given: 12 seated students, 5 students at board

This translates to $12 + 5 = 17$ students in all. [1]

Given: 12 seated students, 7 empty seats

This translates to $12 + 7 = 19$ seats in all. [2]

Subtracting [1] from [2] gives

$19 - 17 = 2$ vacant seats when all are seated [3]

Given: 3 leave and 2 enter

This translates to $-3 + 2$

$= -1$, or a net loss of 1 student. [4]

Combining [4] and [3], we have
$2 + 1 = 3$ vacant seats.

(Math Refresher #200)

13. 18

Method I:

(Use Strategy 14: Draw lines to help solve the problem.)

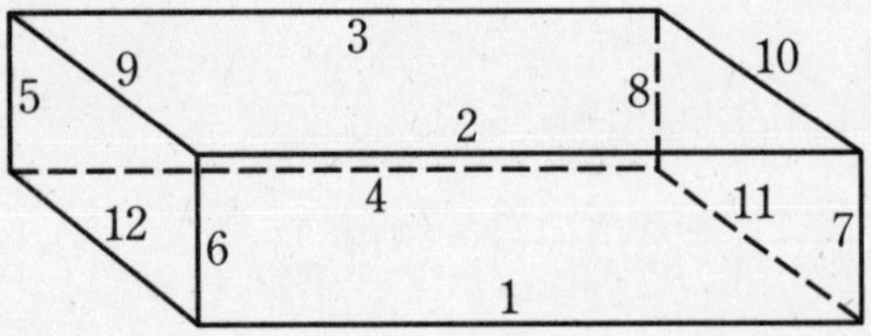

Above is a rectangular solid with each of its edges numbered 1 through 12, respectively. There are 3 groups of 4 parallel edges each.

1, 2, 3, and 4 are parallel.
5, 6, 7, and 8 are parallel.
9, 10, 11, and 12 are parallel.

Within each group of 4 parallel edges, there are 6 pairs of parallel edges. For example, within the first group listed above, 1 and 2 are parallel, 1 and 3 are parallel, etc. Because there are 3 groups and each group has 6 pairs of parallel edges, there are $3 \times 6 = 18$ different pairs of parallel edges in all. Below is a listing of all the pairs:

1–2	2–3	5–6	6–7
1–3	2–4	5–7	6–8
1–4	3–4	5–8	7–8

9–10	10–11
9–11	10–12
9–12	11–12

Method II:

A rectangular solid exists in three dimensions; within each dimension, there are four edges that run parallel to each other. Therefore the combinations of parallel edges for *one* dimension, taken two at a time, is:

$${}_4C_2 = \frac{(4 \times 3)}{(2 \times 1)} = 6$$

Since there are three dimensions, the total number of combinations is:

$$3({}_4C_2) = 3(6) = 18$$

(Math Refresher #613)

14. 1.999, 1.998... .001, or any number $0 < r < 2$, like $\frac{1}{2}, \frac{1}{4}$, etc. (Use Strategy 2: Translate from words to algebra.)

$$\begin{aligned} 2r + 2r + 3 &< 11 \\ 4r + 3 &< 11 \\ 4r &< 8 \\ r &< 2 \end{aligned}$$ [1]

(Math Refresher #422)

15. 135 (Use Strategy 3: The whole equals the sum of its parts.)

The sum of the four angles in a quadrilateral $= 360°$ [1]

Given: the sum of two angles $= 90°$ [2]

Let a and b represent the two remaining angles. [3]

Substituting [2] and [3] into 1, we get

$$90° + a + b = 360°$$
$$a + b = 270°$$ [4]

(Use Strategy 5:

$$\textbf{Average} = \frac{\textbf{sum of values}}{\textbf{total number of values}}\Big)$$

Average of a and $b = \frac{a+b}{2}$ [5]

Applying [5] to [4], we get

$$\frac{a+b}{2} = \frac{270°}{2}$$

Average of $a + b = 135°$

(Math Refresher #521)

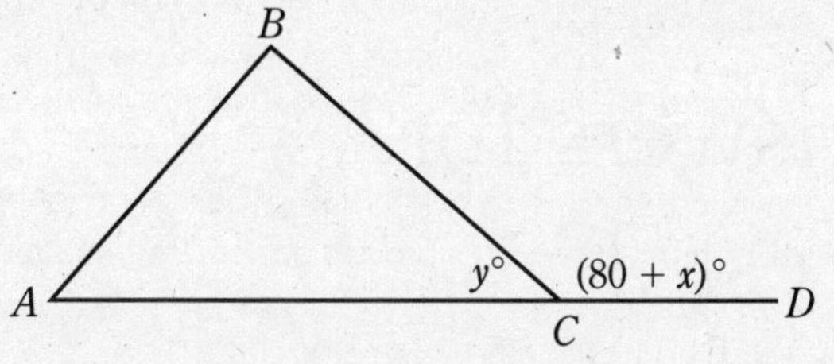

16. 100 (Use Strategy 3: The whole equals the sum of its parts.)

$$m\angle ACB + m\angle BCD = m\angle ACD \qquad \boxed{1}$$

We are given that AD is a straight line segment. We know that

$$m\angle ACD = 180 \qquad \boxed{2}$$
$$\text{Given: } m\angle ACB = y \qquad \boxed{3}$$
$$m\angle BCD = 80 + x \qquad \boxed{4}$$

We substitute $\boxed{2}$, $\boxed{3}$, and $\boxed{4}$ into $\boxed{1}$

Thus, $y + 80 + x = 180$
Subtract 80: $y + x = 100$

(Math Refresher #501 and #406)

17. 3 (Use Strategy 4: Remember classic expressions.)

$$x^2 + 2xy + y^2 = (x + y)^2 \qquad \boxed{1}$$
$$\text{Given: } x^2 + 2xy + y^2 = 25 \qquad \boxed{2}$$

Substitute $\boxed{1}$ into $\boxed{2}$, giving

$$(x + y)^2 = 25$$
$$x + y = \pm 5 \qquad \boxed{3}$$
$$\text{Given: } x + y > 0 \qquad \boxed{4}$$

Using $\boxed{3}$ and $\boxed{4}$ together, we conclude that

$$x + y = +5 \qquad \boxed{5}$$
$$\text{Given: } x - y = 1 \qquad \boxed{6}$$

(Use Strategy 13: Find an unknown by adding equations.)

Adding $\boxed{5}$ and $\boxed{6}$, we have

$$2x = 6$$
$$x = 3$$

(Math Refresher #409 and #407)

18. 4 (Use Strategy 17: Use the given information effectively.)

Method I:

Remembering that the sum of 2 sides of a triangle is greater than the third side, we know that

$$LM + MN > LN$$
or
$$6 + 10 > 12$$
$$16 > 12$$

The difference between 16 and 12: $16 - 12 = 4$ is the amount of overlap.

Method 2: **(Use Strategy 14: Draw lines when appropriate.)**

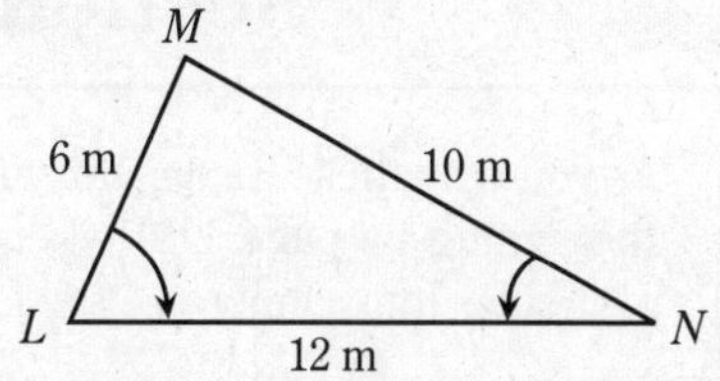

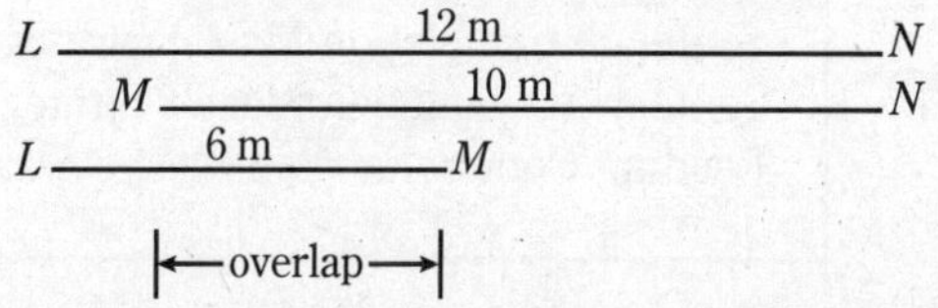

$\boxed{2}$

$\boxed{3}$

In the figure above, the segments have been redrawn so that the result can be easily discovered.

In $\boxed{2}$, the distance $LM = 12\text{ m} - 10\text{ m} = 2\text{ m} \qquad \boxed{4}$

Subtracting $\boxed{4}$ from the distance LM in $\boxed{3}$, we get $6\text{ m} - 2\text{ m} = 4\text{ m}$ overlap.

(Math Refresher #419)

Explanatory Answers for Practice Test 2 (continued)

Section 7: Critical Reading

As you read these Explanatory Answers, refer to "16 Verbal (Critical Reading) Strategies" (beginning on page 119) whenever a specific strategy is referred to in the answer. Of particular importance are the following Master Verbal Strategies:

Sentence Completion Master Strategy 1—page 120.
Sentence Completion Master Strategy 2—page 121.
Reading Comprehension Master Strategy 2—page 138.

Note: All Reading questions use Reading Comprehension Strategies 1, 2, and 3 (pages 135–140) as well as other strategies indicated.

1. Choice C is correct. See **Sentence Completion Strategy 2.** The first step is to examine the first word of each choice. We eliminate Choice B, innuendoes, Choice D, frequencies, and Choice E, cancellations, because the foreman's leniency did not have innuendoes or frequencies or cancellations. Now we go to the remaining choices. Choice A, compensations...unacceptable, does *not* make sense in the sentence. Choice C, drawbacks...shoddy, makes the sentence meaningful.

2. Choice D is correct. See **Sentence Completion Strategy 4.** The word "Although" at the beginning of the sentence is an *opposition indicator.* As a contrast to the rundown condition of the school, the word "renovated" is the acceptable choice.

3. Choice C is correct. The word "immediate" is the only one that makes sense in the blank. See **Sentence Completion Strategy 1.**

4. Choice E is correct. See **Sentence Completion Strategy 2.** The first words of Choice B (flexibility) and Choice D (dizziness) do not make sense in the first part of the sentence. Therefore, we eliminate these two choices. When we try the two words in each of the remaining choices, only Choice E (disappointment...fervent) makes good sense in the sentence as a whole.

5. Choice A is correct. See **Sentence Completion Strategy 4.** The *opposition indicator* "even though" should lead us to the correct Choice A with the fill-in word "convincing."

6. Choice C is correct. Although what is mentioned in (A), (B), and (D) is mentioned in both passages, the passages describe essentially a code for living life and dealing with people.

7. Choice B is correct. The passages are contrasting in that one proposes concealing and the other openness, and the tone is didactic and authoritarian.

Although you may have thought that Choice A was correct, the passages are not really pro and con to something.

8. Choice A is correct. The authors do not show the reader *how* to conceal or not conceal. For Choices B and D: The authors do show the consequences and danger of not conforming to the authors' advice: In passage 1, lines 9–10: "bloom of life is gone." In passage 2, lines 15–16: "make us vulnerable to the slings and arrows of life." For Choice C, both passages really say that one should abide by the authors' admonition as soon as possible; see line 10: "Put off that day as long as possible" and lines 18–19: "There is no better time for concealment than today." For Choice E: In both passages the fear is addressed and, as in Choice C, timing is addressed.

9. Choice E is correct. In Passage 1: Note line 9—"*bloom of life* is gone." In Passage 2: Note lines 15–16, "make us vulnerable to the *slings and arrows of life.*" The phrases in italics describe analogies: *bloom,* as in a flower, and *slings and arrows,* as in weapons.

10. Choice D is correct. Beginning with lines 12–13 ("Malignant tumors, on the other hand...") the passage is primarily concerned with the manner in which malignant tumors behave in the body. Choice A is incorrect because the definition of neoplasia is confined only to the first sentence: "Neoplasia...normal cells." Choice B is incorrect because the inhibition of tumor metastasis is discussed only in lines 22–29. Choice C does not occur and is not discussed in the passage. Therefore, Choice C is incorrect. Choice E is not discussed until lines 34–36. "After malignant cells...most of the cells die." Therefore, Choice E is not correct.

11. Choice C is correct. See lines 22–24: "Before metastasis can occur...surrounding normal tissue." Choice A is incorrect because the passage does not indicate that malignant cells shed their original membrane in order to acquire a new membrane. The passage simply states in lines 31–33: "The outer membrane...of normal cells." Choice B is incorrect because the passage nowhere states that malignant cells "inhibit the lethal effects of the components of the blood." Choices D and E are incorrect because the passage does not indicate in any way what these two choices state.

12. Choice E is correct. See lines 37–39: "Those cells which survive...small blood vessel." Although the passage does refer to Choices A, B, C, and D, none of these choices represents a characteristic of a malignant cell that most greatly enhances its metastatic potential. Therefore, these four choices are all incorrect.

13. Choice C is correct. See lines 37–42: "Those cells which survive...stickiness of the blood vessel wall." Choice A is incorrect because the passage does not indicate that benign tumors become malignant tumors. Choice B is incorrect. See lines 20–22: "This process...have been ascertained." Choice D is incorrect. See lines 31–33: "The outer membrane... of normal cells." Choice E is incorrect. See lines 49–50: "...it still must be stated...a mystery."

14. Choice D is correct. First see lines 10–11: "Benign tumors...tissue of origin." Now see lines 12–13: "Malignant tumors...tissue of origin." Choice A is incorrect. See lines 10–11: "Benign tumors...are usually slow-growing." We infer, therefore, that malignant cells are fast growing. Choice B is incorrect. See lines 12–13: "Malignant tumors...tissue of origin..." Choice C is incorrect. See lines 31–33: "The outer membrane...of normal cells." Choice E is incorrect. See lines 16–20: "The characteristic... the original tumor."

15. Choice D is correct. From the context of the rest of the sentence, it can be seen that the word "explicable" means "explainable." See also **Reading Comprehension Strategy 5**.

16. Choice B is correct. See lines 1–2: "The old Middle West is gone. However, it still lives in song and story." Choices A, C, D, and E are incorrect because the passage makes no reference to what these choices state.

17. Choice C is correct. See lines 19–20: "I think the Middle West's strength is in its customary cautious approach...." Choice D (line 39) is incorrect because it is not cited as the strength of the Middle West. Choices A, B, and E may be true, but they are not indicated in the passage.

18. Choice D is correct. See lines 46–49: "In the Middle West it has...taken the form of people remaining in the smaller cities and giving them new life and intelligence. This has strengthened smaller communities...." Choices A, B, C, and E are incorrect because the passage does not indicate these choices as current trends.

19. Choice A is correct. See lines 5–10: "The old Middle West developed...out of...destructive blizzards...and...dust storms." Therefore, Item I is true. Items II and III cannot be accepted because the passage says nothing about the Gold Rush of 1849 and the Civil War as factors in the formation of the Middle West. Accordingly, Choices B, C, D, and E are incorrect.

20. Choice D is correct. From the context of the sentence—"...with a growing understanding of their problems and responsibilities"—the best meaning of "pragmatic" would be "practical." See also **Reading Comprehension Strategy 5**.

21. Choice D is correct. See the next-to-last paragraph: "...so much difficulty in resolving our problems of a complex society is that we have tended to lose...a strong feeling for the special qualities of our local area."

22. Choice C is correct. See paragraph 6: "It made inflation the prime issue in 1936...." Also see paragraph 4: "especially on political major questions" and the flavor and content of the rest of the passage.

23. Choice E is correct. Given the context of the sentence with the ideas expressed throughout the passage, "diversification" refers to race or religion. See also **Reading Comprehension Strategy 5**.

24. Choice E is correct. See the second-from-last paragraph: "...freedom of communications...and the ease of changing occupations...contribute to breaking down ethnic and religious group prejudices."

Explanatory Answers for Practice Test 2 (continued)

Section 8: Math

As you read these solutions, you are advised to do two things if you answered the Math question incorrectly:

1. When a specific Math Strategy is referred to in the solution, study that strategy, which you will find in "19 Math Strategies" (beginning on page 69).
2. When the solution directs you to the "Complete Math Refresher" (beginning on page 167)—for example, Math Refresher 305—study the 305 Math principle to get a clear idea of the Math operation that was necessary for you to know in order to answer the question correctly.

1. Choice A is correct. **(Use Strategy 2: Translate from words to algebra.)** "x varies inversely with y" means that xy = constant. We are given that $x = 5$ and $y = 4$ so $5 \times 4 = 20$ and 20 is therefore the *constant.* Thus $xy = 20$. So when $y = 10$, $x(10) = 20$ and thus $x = 2$.

(Math Refresher #122)

2. Choice D is correct. We write a table:

Sales	*Cost per book*
(1) 4,000	\$1
(2) 1,000	\$2
(3) 250	\$4
(4) 160	\$5

(Use Strategy 8: When all choices must be tested, start with Choice E and work backward.)

For Choice E:

For (1): $\frac{4{,}000}{1} = 4{,}000$; for (2): $\frac{4{,}000}{2} = 2{,}000$—doesn't check with sales of (2), which is 1,000. So try Choice D:

For (1): $\frac{4{,}000}{1^2} = 4{,}000$

For (2): $\frac{4{,}000}{2^2} = 1{,}000$ (checks with (2))

For (3): $\frac{4{,}000}{4^2} = 250$ (checks with (3))

For (4): $\frac{4{,}000}{5^2} = 160$ (checks with (4))

Choice D is correct.

(Math Refresher #122)

3. Choice D is correct. **(Use Strategy 16: The obvious may be tricky.)** If $x^{-3} = 27$, then $\frac{1}{x^3} = 27$ so $\frac{1}{27} = x^3$ and $\frac{1}{3^3} = x^3$. Thus $x = \frac{1}{3}$. $x^{\frac{1}{2}} = \left(\frac{1}{3}\right)^{\frac{1}{2}} = \frac{1}{\sqrt{3}}$. Multiply numerator and denominator by $\sqrt{3}$ (rationalizing the denominator) and we get $x^{\frac{1}{2}} = \frac{1}{\sqrt{3}} = \frac{\sqrt{3}}{\sqrt{3}(\sqrt{3})} = \frac{\sqrt{3}}{3}$.

(Math Refresher #429 and #430)

4. Choice E is correct. We substitute $x = 2$. So $f(2) = 2(2) + 3^2 = 4 + 9 = 13$

(Math Refresher #616)

5. Choice D is correct. **(Use Strategy 17: Use the given information effectively.)**

We set $x + 2 = x^2 + 4x + 4$.
Since $x^2 + 4x + 4 = (x + 2)(x + 2)$,
we have $x + 2 = (x + 2)(x + 2)$
Thus $x = -2$ or $1 = x + 2$
Therefore $x = -2$ or $x = -1$

Or, for a more straightforward approach:

$$x + 2 = x^2 + 4x + 4$$
$$0 = x^2 + 3x + 2$$

Factoring, we get:

$$0 = (x + 1)(x + 2)$$

We get:

$$x + 1 = 0 \text{ or } x + 2 = 0.$$

Thus $x = -1$ or $x = -2$

(Math Refresher #417)

6. Choice B is correct.

Given: $AC = \frac{4}{3}(AB)$ [1]

(Use Strategy 13: Find unknowns by multiplication.)

Multiply [1] by 3. We get

$3(AC) = 4(AB)$ [2]

(Use Strategy 3: The whole equals the sum of its parts.)

From the diagram, we see that

$AC = AB + BC$ [3]

Substituting [3] into [2], we have

$$3(AB + BC) = 4(AB)$$
$$3AB + 3BC = 4AB$$

$3BC = 1AB$ [4]

(Use Strategy 13: Find unknowns by division.)

Dividing [4] by $3AB$, we get

$$\frac{3BC}{3AB} = \frac{1AB}{3AB}$$
$$\frac{BC}{AB} = \frac{1}{3}$$

(Math Refresher #406 and #403)

7. Choice C is correct.

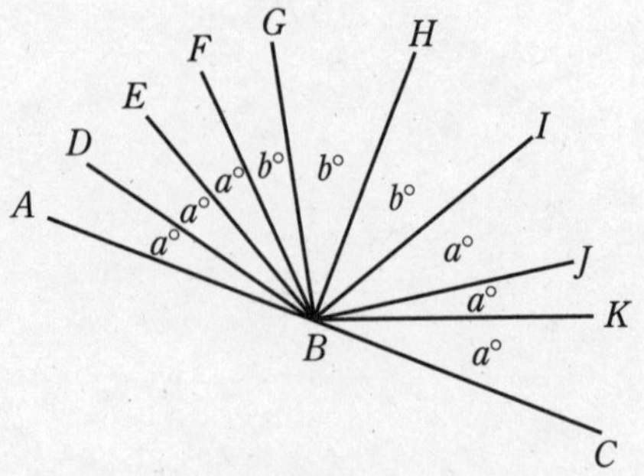

(Use Strategy 3: The whole equals the sum of its parts.) The whole straight angle ABC is equal to the sum of the individual angles.

Thus, $m\angle ABC = a + a + a + b + b + b + a + a + a$

$m\angle ABC = 6a + 3b$ [1]

We know $m\angle ABC = 180°$ [2]

Substituting [2] into [1], we get

$180° = 6a + 3b$ [3]

(Use Strategy 13: Find an unknown expression by dividing.) Dividing both sides of [3] by 3, we have

$60° = 2a + b$ [4]

Choice C, $m\angle DBG = 2a + b$, so its measure can be determined. It is 60° (from [4]).

(Math Refresher #501 and #406)

8. Choice C is correct.

Given: $8r + 3s = 12$ [1]
$7r + 2s = 9$ [2]

(Use Strategy 13: Find unknowns by subtracting.)

Subtracting [2] from [1], we get

$r + s = 3$ [3]

Multiplying [3] by 5, we get

$$5(r + s) = (3)5$$
$$5(r + s) = 15$$

(Math Refresher #406 and #407)

9. Choice B is correct. **(Use Strategy 17: Use the given information effectively.)** Since the slope of the line is constant, the *ratio* of the *difference* in *y*-coordinates to the *difference* in *x*-coordinates must be constant for any two points on the line. For points *P* and *A*, this ratio is

$$\frac{2-0}{1-0} = 2$$

The only choice of *x* and *y* which gives the ratio 2 for point *R* and point *A* is Choice B, since if $x = 4$ and $y = 8$,

$$\frac{8-0}{4-0} = 2.$$

All the other choices give a different ratio from 2.

(Math Refresher #416)

10. Choice A is correct.
(Use Strategy 5: Average $= \dfrac{\text{sum of values}}{\text{total number of values}}$)

$$p = \frac{x+y}{2} \quad \boxed{1}$$

$$q = \frac{y+z}{2} \quad \boxed{2}$$

$$r = \frac{x+z}{2} \quad \boxed{3}$$

(Use Strategy 13: Find unknown expressions by adding equations.) Adding $\boxed{1}$, $\boxed{2}$, and $\boxed{3}$, we get

$$p+q+r = \frac{x+y}{2} + \frac{y+z}{2} + \frac{x+z}{2}$$

$$= \frac{2x+2y+2z}{2}$$

$$p+q+r = x+y+z \quad \boxed{4}$$

The average of *x*, *y*, and $z = \dfrac{x+y+z}{3}$ $\boxed{5}$

Substitute $\boxed{4}$ into $\boxed{5}$. We have

The average of *x*, *y*, and $z = \dfrac{p+q+r}{3}$ *(Answer)*

(Math Refresher #601 and #109)

11. Choice D is correct. **(Use Strategy 17: Use the given information effectively.)** Two-fifths, or 40%, of the applicants fail on the examination. Of the 60% remaining, three-fourths fail to get into the program. $\frac{3}{4} \times 60\% = 45\%$. Thus, the total number of failures is equal to 40% + 45%, or 85%.

Or, to solve it algebraically:

Let *x* be the number of applicants.

$\frac{3}{5}x$ = applicants who passed the exam

$\dfrac{\frac{3}{5}x}{4} = \frac{3}{20}x$ = applicants who passed the exam and were accepted

$\dfrac{\frac{3}{20}x}{x} = \frac{3}{20}$ = % of all applicants who gain admission

$1 - \frac{3}{20} = \frac{17}{20} = 85\%$ = % who *fail* to gain admission

(Math Refresher #106)

12. Choice B is correct. **(Use Strategy 18: Know and use facts about triangles.)** Let the two perpendicular sides equal *a* and *b*, and the hypotenuse be *c*. By the Pythagorean theorem, $a^2 + b^2 = c^2$. Thus, c^2 must be the sum of two square numbers; but our only possible choices for c^2 are 44, 45, 46, 47, and 48. Listing the square numbers which do not exceed these, we find 1, 4, 9, 16, 25, and 36. The only choice which can be broken down into the sum of two of these squares is 45, which equals 36 + 9. (To show that we cannot so break down the others, we need only notice that 36 + 16 = 52 is too large, 36 + 4 = 40 is too small; 25 + 25 = 50 is too large, 25 + 16 = 41 is too small; and there are no other values in between, so 36 + 9 = 45 is the only choice). Since $c^2 = 45$, *c* must equal $\sqrt{45}$.

(Math Refresher #509, #307, and #430)

13. Choice D is correct. **(Use Strategy 17: Use the given information effectively.)** Of the *N* French students, *P* are in both programs, so only $(N - P)$ are in the French program *alone*; similarly, $(M - P)$ students are in the Spanish program *only*. Thus, the number of students in only one language program is equal to $(N - P) + (M - P)$, which equals $N + M - 2P$. (*Note*: The following diagram may help you to visualize the answer better.)

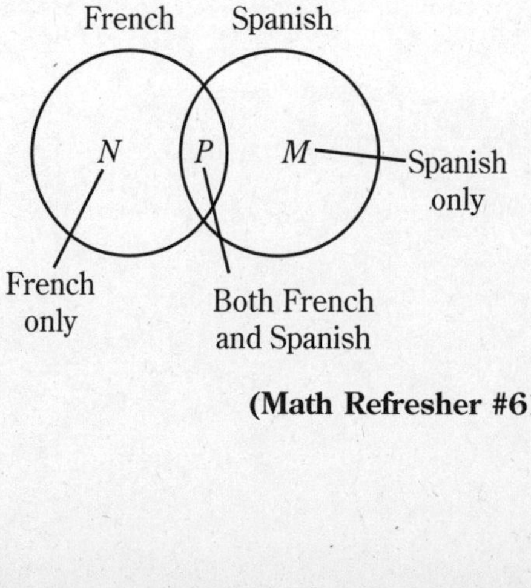

(Math Refresher #613)

14. Choice E is correct. Since we know only that $\overleftrightarrow{m}$ is not parallel to either $\overleftrightarrow{\ell}$ or $\overleftrightarrow{n}$, both of the following situations could be true. **(Use Strategy 17: Use the given information effectively.)**

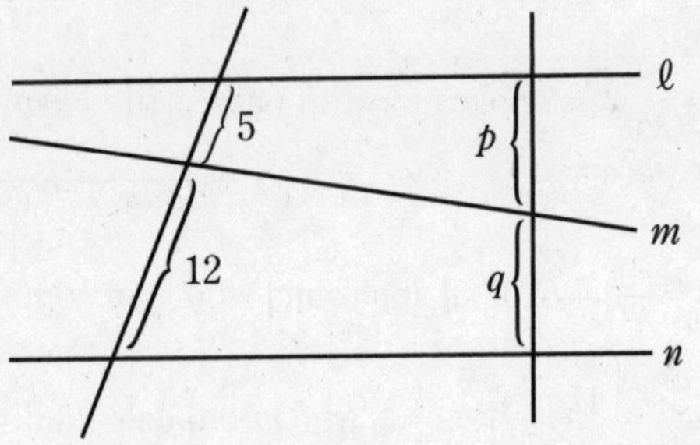

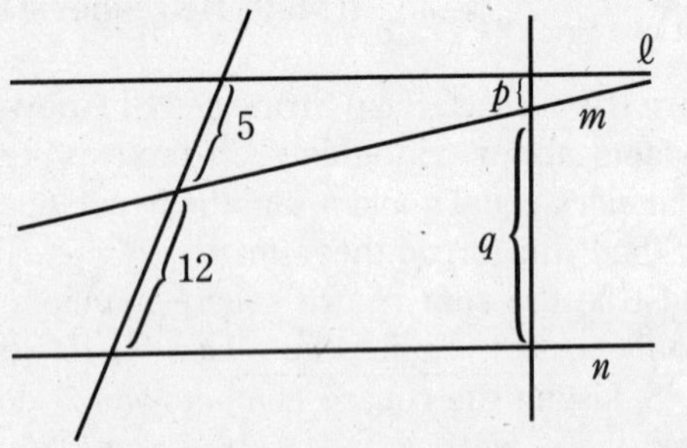

(Note: $p + q = 13$ is still true in both cases in the drawings above.) Clearly, the value of $\frac{p}{q}$ is different for each case. Hence, $\frac{p}{q}$ cannot be determined unless we know more about $\overleftrightarrow{m}$.

15. Choice C is correct. **(Use Strategy 17: Use the given information effectively.)** There are 4 choices for the first letter of the 3-letter combinations. Since each letter cannot be used more than once in a combination, there are only 3 choices for the second letter and only 2 choices for the third letter. Thus, the maximum number of 3-letter combinations that Ross can make up is

$$= 4 \cdot 3 \cdot 2$$
$$= 24$$

(Math Refresher #613a)

16. Choice C is correct. **(Use Strategy 17: Use the given information effectively (and ignore irrelevant information).)** To find the total cost of all uniforms in *child* sizes at *School B*, we would multiply the number of uniforms at School B of Type A with the Child's Type A cost, multiply the number of uniforms at School B of Type B with the Child's Type B cost, and multiply the number of uniforms at School B of Type C with the Child's Type C cost, and add those three quantities. That is: $30 \times \$9 + 60 \times \$10 + 50 \times \$11 = \$1,420$.

(Math Refresher #702)

Explanatory Answers for Practice Test 2 (continued)

Section 9: Critical Reading

As you read these Explanatory Answers, refer to "16 Verbal (Critical Reading) Strategies" (beginning on page 119) whenever a specific strategy is referred to in the answer. Of particular importance are the following Master Verbal Strategies:

Sentence Completion Master Strategy 1—page 120.
Sentence Completion Master Strategy 2—page 121.
Reading Comprehension Master Strategy 2—page 138.

Note: All Reading questions use Reading Comprehension Strategies 1, 2, and 3 (pages 135–140) as well as other strategies indicated.

1. Choice E is correct. The fact that the investor was eager to make an investment change points to his being "dubious" about his current investment—the stocks he had recently purchased. See **Sentence Completion Strategy 1.**

2. Choice A is correct. See **Sentence Completion Strategy 4.** The word "when" is a *support indicator* in this sentence. As we try each choice, we find that "frightening" is the only word that fits in this sentence. The fact that "the earth shifts with a sickening sway" reinforces the initial idea that "nature's brute strength is never more frightening."

3. Choice D is correct. See **Sentence Completion Strategy 2.** Consider the first word of each choice. We can thus eliminate Choice A, disdain, because one doesn't "disdain" the incidence of crime, and we can eliminate Choice B, revoke, because one doesn't "revoke" the incidence of crime. Now consider the other three choices. Choice D, with its two fill-in words "reduce" and "diverting," is the only choice that makes sense in the sentence.

4. Choice D is correct. See **Sentence Completion Strategy 2.** Consider the first word of each choice. We can first eliminate Choice A, gradual, because "gradual" musical accompaniment does not make sense, and we can eliminate Choice E, chronic, because the "chronic" musical accompaniment does not make sense. Now consider the other three choices. Choice D, with its two fill-in words "superb" and "aura," is the only choice that makes sense in the sentence.

5. Choice B is correct. See **Sentence Completion Strategy 4.** The first part of the sentence about her fine reputation as a celebrated actress is obviously in opposition to her appearance in a TV soap opera. Accordingly, the word "blemished" is the only possible choice.

6. Choice C is correct. See **Sentence Completion Strategy 2.** First, let us examine the first words in each choice. We eliminate Choice B because one's manner does not "accept" his intention. We eliminate Choice D because one's manner does not "disregard" his intention. We eliminate Choice E because one's manner does not "animate" his intention. This leaves us with Choice A (revealed...eager), which does *not* make good sense, and Choice C (belied...drastic), which *does* make good sense.

7. Choice D is correct. The author is definitely satisfied and happy with the simple life he and his partner are leading. See lines such as the following: "We thank our lucky stars that we live out in the wilderness" (lines 35–36) and "We are thankful for what the wilderness makes possible" (lines 42–43). Choices A, B, C, and E are incorrect because the author gives no indication that the lifestyle, as he describes it, is marked by resentment, boredom, indecision, or indifference.

8. Choice B is correct. Throughout the passage, the author is showing that frills are not necessary for a happy life. Example: "There is no phone to ring, no radio to turn on, no television to watch" (lines 7–8). Choices A and D are incorrect because they are much too general. Choice C is an inappropriate title because progress and prosperity are not of interest to the author. Choice E is an inappropriate title because the author is not concerned about conveniences such as a phone, radio, or television. He has what he needs—"peace, quiet, and frugality" (lines 43–44).

9. Choice A is correct. The author indicates that the typical election is inconsequential—that is, unproductive, of no use. One may conclude, then, that the author has no faith in the typical candidates who run for office. Choices B, C, D, and E are incorrect because the author does not express these sentiments in the passage—although he may agree with those choices.

10. Choice E is correct. The author must have a farm because he says: "...our homegrown food is not stale, preserved or embalmed and bought from the supermarket" (lines 40–41). Choice A is incorrect because the author states: "There is wood to cut, snow to shovel..." (lines 13–14). Choice B is incorrect. See lines 14–16: "No one is pushing, no one shoving...we make our own jobs. Free men? Almost." Therefore, the author is not *completely* a free man. Choice C is incorrect because it is his neighbor's wife who may be pregnant (line 18). Choice D is incorrect. See line 25: "The newspaper, reaching us by mail..."

11. Choice C is correct. Maine is the only one of the five states listed that would likely have snow (line 1) and spruce (evergreen) trees (line 2). Therefore, Choices A, B, D, and E are incorrect.

12. Choice D is correct. Choice A is incorrect. From line 45, you cannot conclude that the author believes that even though he or she lives in a one-bedroom apartment, much of the population in the city lives in one-bedroom apartments. Choice B is incorrect. Although the author says in line 59 that food may not be home-grown, the author doesn't say that you'll never get home-grown food. Choice C is incorrect. Although the author states that you may bump into rich and poor on a street, the author doesn't claim that both eat at the most expensive restaurants. Choice D is correct. In lines 51–52 the author links losing one's identity with forgetting about problems. Thus it can be assumed that losing one's identity is a plus. Choice E is incorrect. There is no reference to friendliness as a way of life.

13. Choice C is correct. The word "interminable" (line 47) refers to *sounds of cars, trucks, repair, services,* and *hassles encountered.* Thus the word cannot be "loud" (Choice A), "bright" (Choice D), "harsh" (Choice B), or "close" (Choice E). It makes sense that *interminable* relates to *time* (Choice C). Note that "term" has to do with a specific length of time, and the prefix "in" here means "not," so *interminable* must mean "not having a specific term or length of time," that is, *ongoing.* See also **Reading Comprehension Strategy 5**.

14. Choice A is correct. Note that in Passage 2, the author mentions in many instances the good with the bad: "Excitement, hassles, services, traffic," and so on.

15. Choice A is correct. The author of Passage 1 seems to feel (lines 25–34) that all or most news is bad, so the author would be surprised at seeing a headline as described in Choice A. Choice B is incorrect. The author of Passage 2 (line 54) may bump into a celebrity in the street and indeed talk with the celebrity. Choice C is incorrect. The author believes that he or she can go to a coffee shop at three in the morning, so a movie theater is also probably open at two in the morning. Choice D is incorrect. See line 12. Choice E is incorrect. The author of Passage 2 acknowledges that certain types of people may not enjoy living in the city (lines 67–70), and the author admits that there are negative aspects about city living.

16. Choice B is correct. Note the comparison in lines 43–44. "Peace, progress, prosperity? We prefer peace, quiet, and frugality." Thus "frugality" must relate to "prosperity" with a somewhat *opposite* meaning and obviously not have too negative a connotation since the author is striving for this. The

only word that makes sense is "stinginess." See also **Reading Comprehension Strategy 5**.

17. Choice C is correct. In lines 8–9 the author links "don" with "city disguise, cocktail parties, dinners." It is logical to assume that "don" relates to "clothing." See also **Reading Comprehension Strategy 5**.

18. Choice C is correct. See lines 31–34. Choice A is incorrect: Although the author of Passage 1 may believe that most news is bad, there is no reference to the author of Passage 2's believing that most news is good. Choice B is incorrect: Although it is true that the author of Passage 1 may believe that most elections are useless, there is no reference to the author of Passage 2's believing that they are necessary. Choice D is incorrect: We cannot infer that the author of Passage 1 believes that the parks in cities are safe (see lines 27–31 about Central Park). The author of Passage 2 may agree that crime "goes with the territory." However, Choice D in its entirety is incorrect. Choice E is incorrect. We cannot assume that one author does not like home-grown food (even though, for example, the author of Passage 2 may not get to eat it).

19. Choice A is correct. For (I), see lines 17–23. This type of friendly socialization is not mentioned in Passage 2. For (II), see lines 35–43 and lines 70–74. Positive effects are mentioned in both passages. For (III), see line 25: "The newspaper, reaching us by mail..." and lines 56–57: "get up-to-the-minute news through radio or TV..." Thus this condition is described in both passages.

Explanatory Answers for Practice Test 2 (continued)

Section 10: Writing

For further practice and information, please refer to Grammar and Usage Refresher starting on page 455.

1. **(E)** Choice E is the only correct choice since the other choices lack parallelism. Choice D is incorrect for an additional reason—the predicate adjective "unpretentious" (not the adverb "unpretentiously") should be used after the copulative verbal "acting."

2. **(B)** Choice A is incorrect because it is unidiomatic. Choice B is correct. Choices C and E are incorrect because they are too wordy. Choice D improperly omits "conduct of the (accused)."

3. **(B)** The object form of the pronoun must be used for the object of any preposition. Therefore, Choices A and C are incorrect and Choice B is correct. Choice D is incorrect because we need the nominative form of the personal pronoun ("she") as the subject ("but not she"). Choice E is incorrect because it is too informal for the context.

4. **(E)** Choice A is incorrect because "while" pertains to time and should not be substituted loosely for "and." Choice B is incorrect because it does not tie up grammatically with the rest of the sentence. Choice C is incorrect for the same reason. Choice D is incorrect because the subordinate conjunction "as" does not make sense here. Choice E is correct.

5. **(A)** Choice A is correct. Choice B wrongly substitutes the objective case "whomever" for the nominative "whoever," the subject of the verb "would return." Choice C uses the form "whoso-ever," which, while correct, is legalistic and not needed here. Choice D again uses the objective case. Choice E is awkward.

6. **(C)** There is no such word as "irregardless." Therefore Choices A, B, and E cannot be right. "Despite" in Choice D does not give the same meaning as "regardless." Choice C is the correct one.

7. **(D)** Choice A wrongly uses the plural verb "are to be found" after the subject of the sentence, "One." (The plural word "examples" is not the subject of the prepositional phrase "of the finest examples.") Choice B simply uses the same plural verb in the past tense instead of the present. Choice C does not correct the error. Choice D does, by using the singular verb "is." Choice E is incorrect because of the use of the plural verb "are."

8. **(D)** Choice A fails to use the possessive case of the pronoun that governs a gerund. Choice B changes the meaning of the sentence. Choice C corrects the error but omits a necessary part of the meaning. Choice D is correct. Choice E retains the error of Choice A and, in addition, distorts the meaning of the sentence.

9. **(D)** Choices A, B, C, and E should place the adverbial phrase "without hesitation" after the infinitive it modifies, "to answer." Since the meaning is to "answer without hesitation," the phrase "without hesitation" should be placed right after the infinitive "to answer." This is done in Choice D.

10. **(D)** Choice A is incorrect because the expression "not only" must be accompanied by "but also." B is also incorrect for this reason. C is a complete sentence, making the original a run-on sentence. Choice D is correct. In Choice E, the words "in addition" are unnecessary.

11. **(E)** Choices A and B are incorrect because there is improper ellipsis of "like those." Choice C is too wordy. Choice D changes the meaning of the original sentence. Choice E is correct.

12. **(C)** Choice A is incorrect because "laid" is the past tense of the verb "to lay," and the verb required is "to lie." Choice B is incorrect because "had laid" is the past perfect tense of the verb "to lay." Choice C is correct; Choice D is incorrect because it is in the present tense and it also is a form of the verb "to lay." Choice E is in the present tense—it should be in the past perfect tense.

13. **(B)** In making a comparison, the word "different" is followed by the word "from" rather than by the word "than." For this reason, Choices A, C, and E are incorrect. Choice D uses the word "from" correctly but the choice includes the unnecessary repetition of "earlier." Choice B is, of course, correct.

14. **(D)** Choices A and E are incorrect because in a "neither-nor" construction, the verb agrees with the noun or pronoun that follows "nor." Choice B is incorrect because "neither" must be followed by a singular verb. Choice C is incorrect because the nominative form of the pronoun ("Neither you nor *I*") should be used, since "I" is a subject in the sentence. Choice D is correct.

What You Must Do Now to Raise Your SAT Score

1. a) Follow the directions on page 713 to determine your scaled score for the SAT Test you've just taken. These results will give you a good idea about how hard you'll need to study in order to achieve a certain score on the actual SAT.

   b) Using your Test correct answer count as a basis, indicate for yourself your areas of strength and weakness as revealed by the "Chart for Self-Appraisal" on page 718.

2. Eliminate your weaknesses in each of the SAT Test areas (as revealed in the "Chart for Self-Appraisal") by taking the following Giant Steps toward SAT success:

Critical Reading Part

Giant Step 1

Take advantage of the Critical Reading Strategies that begin on page 119. Read again the Explanatory Answer for each of the Critical Reading questions that you got wrong. Refer to the Critical Reading Strategy that applies to each of your incorrect answers. Learn each of these Critical Reading Strategies thoroughly. These strategies are crucial if you want to raise your SAT Verbal score substantially.

Giant Step 2

You can improve your vocabulary by doing the following:

1) Study the SAT 3,400-Word List beginning on page 359.

2) Take the 100 SAT-type "tough word" Vocabulary Tests beginning on page 408.

3) Study the Gruber Prefix-Root-Suffix List beginning on page 348.

4) Learn the Hot Prefixes and Roots beginning on page 1049.

5) Read through A List of SAT Words Appearing More Than Once beginning on page 353.

6) Look through the Most Important Words and Their Opposites beginning on page 355.

7) Learn the 3 Vocabulary Strategies beginning on page 150.

8) Read as widely as possible—not only novels. Nonfiction is important too…and don't forget to read newspapers and magazines.

9) Listen to people who speak well. Tune in to worthwhile TV programs.

10) Use the dictionary frequently and extensively—at home, on the bus, at work, etc.

11) Play word games—for example, crossword puzzles, anagrams, and Scrabble. Another game is to compose your own Sentence Completion questions. Try them on your friends.

Math Part

Giant Step 3

Make good use of the 19 Math Strategies that begin on page 69. Read again the solutions for each Math question that you answered incorrectly. Refer to the Math Strategy that applies to each of your incorrect answers. Learn each of these Math Strategies thoroughly. We repeat that these strategies are crucial if you want to raise your SAT Math score substantially.

Giant Step 4

You may want to take the **101 Most Important Math Questions You Need to Know How to Solve** test beginning on page 31 and follow the directions after the test for a basic Math skills diagnosis.

For each Math question that you got wrong in the Test, note the reference to the Complete Math Refresher section beginning on page 167. This reference will explain clearly the mathematical principle involved in the solution of the question you answered incorrectly. Learn that particular mathematical principle thoroughly.

For Both the Math and Critical Reading Parts

Giant Step 5

You may want to take the **Strategy Diagnostic Test** beginning on page 1 to assess whether you're using the best strategies for the questions.

For the Writing Part

Giant Step 6

Take a look at Part 9, the SAT Writing Test, which describes the various item types in the Writing Section and sample questions with answers and explanations. Also make use of the Grammar Refresher—Part 8.

3. After you have done some of the tasks you have been advised to do in the suggestions, proceed to Practice Test 3, beginning on page 760.

   After taking Practice Test 3, concentrate on the weaknesses that still remain.

4. Continue the foregoing procedures for Practice Tests 4 and 5.

   If you do the job *right* and follow the steps listed earlier, you are likely to raise your SAT score on each of the Verbal, Math, and Writing parts of the test substantially.

> I am the master of my fate:
> I am the captain of my soul.
>
> —From the poem "Invictus"
> by William Ernest Henley

Answer Sheet for Practice Test 3

SECTION 1

Begin your essay on this page. If you need more space, continue on the next page. Do not write outside of the essay box.

Continue on the next page if necessary.

Continuation of ESSAY Section 1 from previous page. Write below only if you need more space.

Start with number 1 for each new section. If a section has fewer questions than answer spaces, leave the extra answer spaces blank. Be sure to erase any errors or stray marks completely.

SECTION 2

1 A B C D E	11 A B C D E	21 A B C D E	31 A B C D E
2 A B C D E	12 A B C D E	22 A B C D E	32 A B C D E
3 A B C D E	13 A B C D E	23 A B C D E	33 A B C D E
4 A B C D E	14 A B C D E	24 A B C D E	34 A B C D E
5 A B C D E	15 A B C D E	25 A B C D E	35 A B C D E
6 A B C D E	16 A B C D E	26 A B C D E	36 A B C D E
7 A B C D E	17 A B C D E	27 A B C D E	37 A B C D E
8 A B C D E	18 A B C D E	28 A B C D E	38 A B C D E
9 A B C D E	19 A B C D E	29 A B C D E	39 A B C D E
10 A B C D E	20 A B C D E	30 A B C D E	40 A B C D E

SECTION 3

1 A B C D E	11 A B C D E	21 A B C D E	31 A B C D E
2 A B C D E	12 A B C D E	22 A B C D E	32 A B C D E
3 A B C D E	13 A B C D E	23 A B C D E	33 A B C D E
4 A B C D E	14 A B C D E	24 A B C D E	34 A B C D E
5 A B C D E	15 A B C D E	25 A B C D E	35 A B C D E
6 A B C D E	16 A B C D E	26 A B C D E	36 A B C D E
7 A B C D E	17 A B C D E	27 A B C D E	37 A B C D E
8 A B C D E	18 A B C D E	28 A B C D E	38 A B C D E
9 A B C D E	19 A B C D E	29 A B C D E	39 A B C D E
10 A B C D E	20 A B C D E	30 A B C D E	40 A B C D E

CAUTION Use the answer spaces in the grids below for Section 2 or Section 3 only if you are told to do so in your test book.

Student-Produced Responses ONLY ANSWERS ENTERED IN THE CIRCLES IN EACH GRID WILL BE SCORED. YOU WILL NOT RECEIVE CREDIT FOR ANYTHING WRITTEN IN THE BOXES ABOVE THE CIRCLES.

9 10 11 12 13

14 15 16 17 18

	/	/	
.	.	.	.
	0	0	0
1	1	1	1
2	2	2	2
3	3	3	3
4	4	4	4
5	5	5	5
6	6	6	6
7	7	7	7
8	8	8	8
9	9	9	9

Start with number 1 for each new section. If a section has fewer questions than answer spaces, leave the extra answer spaces blank. Be sure to erase any errors or stray marks completely.

SECTION 4

1 Ⓐ Ⓑ Ⓒ Ⓓ Ⓔ	11 Ⓐ Ⓑ Ⓒ Ⓓ Ⓔ	21 Ⓐ Ⓑ Ⓒ Ⓓ Ⓔ	31 Ⓐ Ⓑ Ⓒ Ⓓ Ⓔ
2 Ⓐ Ⓑ Ⓒ Ⓓ Ⓔ	12 Ⓐ Ⓑ Ⓒ Ⓓ Ⓔ	22 Ⓐ Ⓑ Ⓒ Ⓓ Ⓔ	32 Ⓐ Ⓑ Ⓒ Ⓓ Ⓔ
3 Ⓐ Ⓑ Ⓒ Ⓓ Ⓔ	13 Ⓐ Ⓑ Ⓒ Ⓓ Ⓔ	23 Ⓐ Ⓑ Ⓒ Ⓓ Ⓔ	33 Ⓐ Ⓑ Ⓒ Ⓓ Ⓔ
4 Ⓐ Ⓑ Ⓒ Ⓓ Ⓔ	14 Ⓐ Ⓑ Ⓒ Ⓓ Ⓔ	24 Ⓐ Ⓑ Ⓒ Ⓓ Ⓔ	34 Ⓐ Ⓑ Ⓒ Ⓓ Ⓔ
5 Ⓐ Ⓑ Ⓒ Ⓓ Ⓔ	15 Ⓐ Ⓑ Ⓒ Ⓓ Ⓔ	25 Ⓐ Ⓑ Ⓒ Ⓓ Ⓔ	35 Ⓐ Ⓑ Ⓒ Ⓓ Ⓔ
6 Ⓐ Ⓑ Ⓒ Ⓓ Ⓔ	16 Ⓐ Ⓑ Ⓒ Ⓓ Ⓔ	26 Ⓐ Ⓑ Ⓒ Ⓓ Ⓔ	36 Ⓐ Ⓑ Ⓒ Ⓓ Ⓔ
7 Ⓐ Ⓑ Ⓒ Ⓓ Ⓔ	17 Ⓐ Ⓑ Ⓒ Ⓓ Ⓔ	27 Ⓐ Ⓑ Ⓒ Ⓓ Ⓔ	37 Ⓐ Ⓑ Ⓒ Ⓓ Ⓔ
8 Ⓐ Ⓑ Ⓒ Ⓓ Ⓔ	18 Ⓐ Ⓑ Ⓒ Ⓓ Ⓔ	28 Ⓐ Ⓑ Ⓒ Ⓓ Ⓔ	38 Ⓐ Ⓑ Ⓒ Ⓓ Ⓔ
9 Ⓐ Ⓑ Ⓒ Ⓓ Ⓔ	19 Ⓐ Ⓑ Ⓒ Ⓓ Ⓔ	29 Ⓐ Ⓑ Ⓒ Ⓓ Ⓔ	39 Ⓐ Ⓑ Ⓒ Ⓓ Ⓔ
10 Ⓐ Ⓑ Ⓒ Ⓓ Ⓔ	20 Ⓐ Ⓑ Ⓒ Ⓓ Ⓔ	30 Ⓐ Ⓑ Ⓒ Ⓓ Ⓔ	40 Ⓐ Ⓑ Ⓒ Ⓓ Ⓔ

SECTION 5

1 Ⓐ Ⓑ Ⓒ Ⓓ Ⓔ	11 Ⓐ Ⓑ Ⓒ Ⓓ Ⓔ	21 Ⓐ Ⓑ Ⓒ Ⓓ Ⓔ	31 Ⓐ Ⓑ Ⓒ Ⓓ Ⓔ
2 Ⓐ Ⓑ Ⓒ Ⓓ Ⓔ	12 Ⓐ Ⓑ Ⓒ Ⓓ Ⓔ	22 Ⓐ Ⓑ Ⓒ Ⓓ Ⓔ	32 Ⓐ Ⓑ Ⓒ Ⓓ Ⓔ
3 Ⓐ Ⓑ Ⓒ Ⓓ Ⓔ	13 Ⓐ Ⓑ Ⓒ Ⓓ Ⓔ	23 Ⓐ Ⓑ Ⓒ Ⓓ Ⓔ	33 Ⓐ Ⓑ Ⓒ Ⓓ Ⓔ
4 Ⓐ Ⓑ Ⓒ Ⓓ Ⓔ	14 Ⓐ Ⓑ Ⓒ Ⓓ Ⓔ	24 Ⓐ Ⓑ Ⓒ Ⓓ Ⓔ	34 Ⓐ Ⓑ Ⓒ Ⓓ Ⓔ
5 Ⓐ Ⓑ Ⓒ Ⓓ Ⓔ	15 Ⓐ Ⓑ Ⓒ Ⓓ Ⓔ	25 Ⓐ Ⓑ Ⓒ Ⓓ Ⓔ	35 Ⓐ Ⓑ Ⓒ Ⓓ Ⓔ
6 Ⓐ Ⓑ Ⓒ Ⓓ Ⓔ	16 Ⓐ Ⓑ Ⓒ Ⓓ Ⓔ	26 Ⓐ Ⓑ Ⓒ Ⓓ Ⓔ	36 Ⓐ Ⓑ Ⓒ Ⓓ Ⓔ
7 Ⓐ Ⓑ Ⓒ Ⓓ Ⓔ	17 Ⓐ Ⓑ Ⓒ Ⓓ Ⓔ	27 Ⓐ Ⓑ Ⓒ Ⓓ Ⓔ	37 Ⓐ Ⓑ Ⓒ Ⓓ Ⓔ
8 Ⓐ Ⓑ Ⓒ Ⓓ Ⓔ	18 Ⓐ Ⓑ Ⓒ Ⓓ Ⓔ	28 Ⓐ Ⓑ Ⓒ Ⓓ Ⓔ	38 Ⓐ Ⓑ Ⓒ Ⓓ Ⓔ
9 Ⓐ Ⓑ Ⓒ Ⓓ Ⓔ	19 Ⓐ Ⓑ Ⓒ Ⓓ Ⓔ	29 Ⓐ Ⓑ Ⓒ Ⓓ Ⓔ	39 Ⓐ Ⓑ Ⓒ Ⓓ Ⓔ
10 Ⓐ Ⓑ Ⓒ Ⓓ Ⓔ	20 Ⓐ Ⓑ Ⓒ Ⓓ Ⓔ	30 Ⓐ Ⓑ Ⓒ Ⓓ Ⓔ	40 Ⓐ Ⓑ Ⓒ Ⓓ Ⓔ

CAUTION Use the answer spaces in the grids below for Section 4 or Section 5 only if you are told to do so in your test book.

Student-Produced Responses ONLY ANSWERS ENTERED IN THE CIRCLES IN EACH GRID WILL BE SCORED. YOU WILL NOT RECEIVE CREDIT FOR ANYTHING WRITTEN IN THE BOXES ABOVE THE CIRCLES.

Grids 9, 10, 11, 12, 13, 14, 15, 16, 17, 18 (each grid identical):

	/	/	
.	.	.	.
	0	0	0
1	1	1	1
2	2	2	2
3	3	3	3
4	4	4	4
5	5	5	5
6	6	6	6
7	7	7	7
8	8	8	8
9	9	9	9

Start with number 1 for each new section. If a section has fewer questions than answer spaces, leave the extra answer spaces blank. Be sure to erase any errors or stray marks completely.

SECTION 6

1 A B C D E	11 A B C D E	21 A B C D E	31 A B C D E
2 A B C D E	12 A B C D E	22 A B C D E	32 A B C D E
3 A B C D E	13 A B C D E	23 A B C D E	33 A B C D E
4 A B C D E	14 A B C D E	24 A B C D E	34 A B C D E
5 A B C D E	15 A B C D E	25 A B C D E	35 A B C D E
6 A B C D E	16 A B C D E	26 A B C D E	36 A B C D E
7 A B C D E	17 A B C D E	27 A B C D E	37 A B C D E
8 A B C D E	18 A B C D E	28 A B C D E	38 A B C D E
9 A B C D E	19 A B C D E	29 A B C D E	39 A B C D E
10 A B C D E	20 A B C D E	30 A B C D E	40 A B C D E

SECTION 7

1 A B C D E	11 A B C D E	21 A B C D E	31 A B C D E
2 A B C D E	12 A B C D E	22 A B C D E	32 A B C D E
3 A B C D E	13 A B C D E	23 A B C D E	33 A B C D E
4 A B C D E	14 A B C D E	24 A B C D E	34 A B C D E
5 A B C D E	15 A B C D E	25 A B C D E	35 A B C D E
6 A B C D E	16 A B C D E	26 A B C D E	36 A B C D E
7 A B C D E	17 A B C D E	27 A B C D E	37 A B C D E
8 A B C D E	18 A B C D E	28 A B C D E	38 A B C D E
9 A B C D E	19 A B C D E	29 A B C D E	39 A B C D E
10 A B C D E	20 A B C D E	30 A B C D E	40 A B C D E

CAUTION Use the answer spaces in the grids below for Section 6 or Section 7 only if you are told to do so in your test book.

Student-Produced Responses ONLY ANSWERS ENTERED IN THE CIRCLES IN EACH GRID WILL BE SCORED. YOU WILL NOT RECEIVE CREDIT FOR ANYTHING WRITTEN IN THE BOXES ABOVE THE CIRCLES.

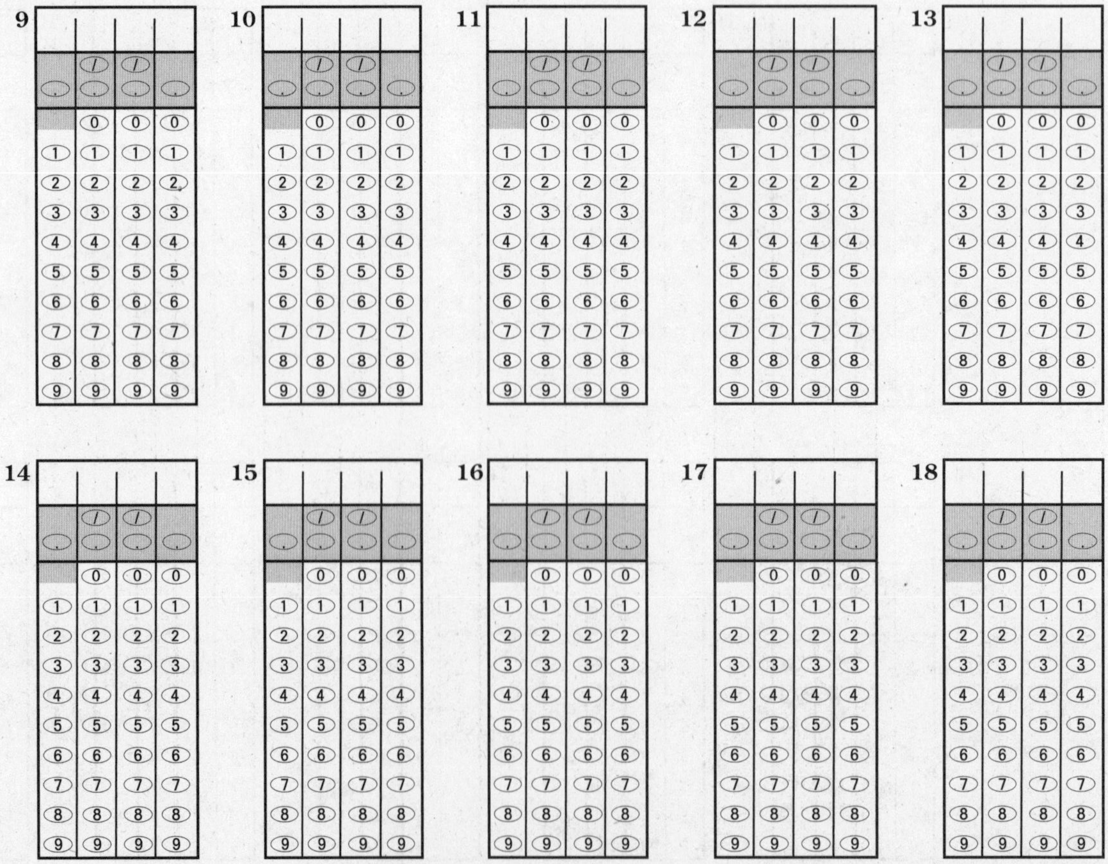

Start with number 1 for each new section. If a section has fewer questions than answer spaces, leave the extra answer spaces blank. Be sure to erase any errors or stray marks completely.

SECTION 8

1 A B C D E	11 A B C D E	21 A B C D E	31 A B C D E
2 A B C D E	12 A B C D E	22 A B C D E	32 A B C D E
3 A B C D E	13 A B C D E	23 A B C D E	33 A B C D E
4 A B C D E	14 A B C D E	24 A B C D E	34 A B C D E
5 A B C D E	15 A B C D E	25 A B C D E	35 A B C D E
6 A B C D E	16 A B C D E	26 A B C D E	36 A B C D E
7 A B C D E	17 A B C D E	27 A B C D E	37 A B C D E
8 A B C D E	18 A B C D E	28 A B C D E	38 A B C D E
9 A B C D E	19 A B C D E	29 A B C D E	39 A B C D E
10 A B C D E	20 A B C D E	30 A B C D E	40 A B C D E

SECTION 9

1 A B C D E	11 A B C D E	21 A B C D E	31 A B C D E
2 A B C D E	12 A B C D E	22 A B C D E	32 A B C D E
3 A B C D E	13 A B C D E	23 A B C D E	33 A B C D E
4 A B C D E	14 A B C D E	24 A B C D E	34 A B C D E
5 A B C D E	15 A B C D E	25 A B C D E	35 A B C D E
6 A B C D E	16 A B C D E	26 A B C D E	36 A B C D E
7 A B C D E	17 A B C D E	27 A B C D E	37 A B C D E
8 A B C D E	18 A B C D E	28 A B C D E	38 A B C D E
9 A B C D E	19 A B C D E	29 A B C D E	39 A B C D E
10 A B C D E	20 A B C D E	30 A B C D E	40 A B C D E

SECTION 10

1 A B C D E	11 A B C D E	21 A B C D E	31 A B C D E
2 A B C D E	12 A B C D E	22 A B C D E	32 A B C D E
3 A B C D E	13 A B C D E	23 A B C D E	33 A B C D E
4 A B C D E	14 A B C D E	24 A B C D E	34 A B C D E
5 A B C D E	15 A B C D E	25 A B C D E	35 A B C D E
6 A B C D E	16 A B C D E	26 A B C D E	36 A B C D E
7 A B C D E	17 A B C D E	27 A B C D E	37 A B C D E
8 A B C D E	18 A B C D E	28 A B C D E	38 A B C D E
9 A B C D E	19 A B C D E	29 A B C D E	39 A B C D E
10 A B C D E	20 A B C D E	30 A B C D E	40 A B C D E

SAT PRACTICE TEST 3

SECTION 1

Time: 25 Minutes—Turn to page 754 of your answer sheet to write your ESSAY.

The purpose of the essay is to have you show how well you can express and develop your ideas. You should develop your point of view, logically and clearly present your ideas, and use language accurately.

You should write your essay on the lines provided on your answer sheet. You should not write on any other paper. You will have enough space if you write on every line and if you keep your handwriting to a reasonable size. Make sure that your handwriting is legible to other readers.

You will have 25 minutes to write an essay on the assignment below. *Do not write on any other topic. If you do so, you will receive a score of 0.*

Think carefully about the issue presented in the following quotations and the assignment below.

1. *While secrecy can be destructive, some of it is indispensable in human lives. Some control over secrecy and openness is needed in order to protect identity. Such control may be needed to guard privacy, intimacy, and friendship.*

   Adapted from Sissela Bok, "The Need for Secrecy"

2. *Secrecy and a free, democratic government, President Harry Truman once said, don't mix. An open exchange of information is vital to the kind of informed citizenry essential to healthy democracy.*

   Editorial, "Overzealous Secrecy Threatens Democracy"

Assignment: Do you believe that people need to keep secrets, or do you believe that secrecy is harmful? Write an essay in which you develop your point of view on this issue. Support your position with reasoning and examples based on your own reading, observations, and experiences.

DO NOT WRITE YOUR ESSAY IN YOUR TEST BOOK. You will receive credit only for what you write on your answer sheet.

BEGIN WRITING YOUR ESSAY ON PAGE 754 OF THE ANSWER SHEET.

If you finish before time is called, you may check your work on this section only.
Do not turn to any other section in the test.

SECTION 2

Time: 25 Minutes—Turn to Section 2 (page 756) of your answer sheet to answer the questions in this section.
20 Questions

Directions: For this section, solve each problem and decide which is the best of the choices given. Fill in the corresponding circle on the answer sheet. You may use any available space for scratchwork.

Notes:

1. The use of a calculator is permitted.
2. All numbers used are real numbers.
3. Figures that accompany problems in this test are intended to provide information useful in solving the problems. They are drawn as accurately as possible EXCEPT when it is stated in a specific problem that the figure is not drawn to scale. All figures lie in a plane unless otherwise indicated.
4. Unless otherwise specified, the domain of any function f is assumed to be the set of all real numbers x for which $f(x)$ is a real number.

REFERENCE INFORMATION

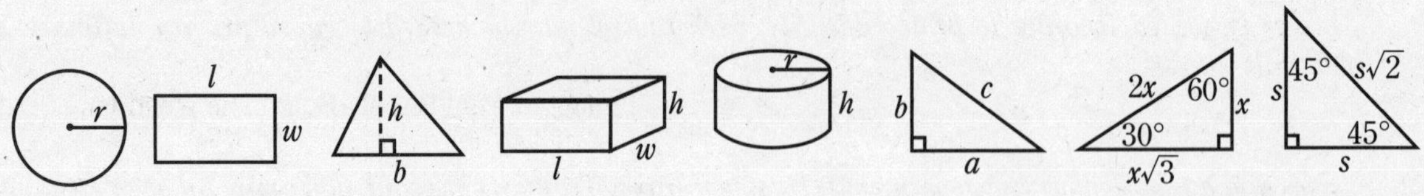

$A = \pi r^2$ $C = 2\pi r$ | $A = lw$ | $A = \frac{1}{2}bh$ | $V = lwh$ | $V = \pi r^2 h$ | $c^2 = a^2 + b^2$ | *Special Right Triangles*

The number of degrees of arc in a circle is 360.
The sum of the measures in degrees of the angles of a triangle is 180.

1. A certain number is divided by 3, but its value remains the same. What is this number?

(A) -1
(B) $-\frac{1}{2}$
(C) 0
(D) $\frac{1}{2}$
(E) 1

2. A man walks a certain distance in the direction 30° south of west, stops, and then turns 35° to his right. In what new direction is he facing?

(A) 65° north of west
(B) 35° north of west
(C) $32\frac{1}{2}°$ north of west
(D) 30° north of west
(E) 5° north of west

GO ON TO THE NEXT PAGE

3. What is the value of $\frac{1}{5}K$ if $\frac{9}{5}K = 18$?

(A) $\frac{1}{9}$
(B) $\frac{1}{5}$
(C) 2
(D) 5
(E) 10

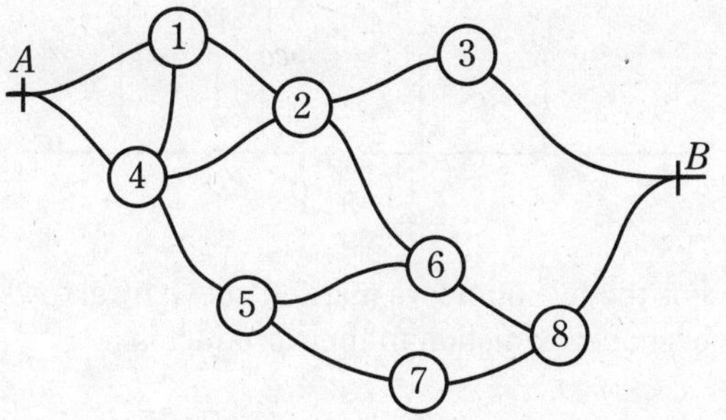

4. The figure above is a piece of fishnet. Which of the following statements must be true about an ant crawling on the net from Point A to Point B?

(A) If it goes through 2, it must go through 7.
(B) If it goes through 3, it must go through 1.
(C) Its route must go through either 2 or 7.
(D) If it goes through 4, it must go through 3 or 5.
(E) If it goes through 8, it must go through 2 or 5.

5. Let x, y, and z be negative numbers such that $x < y < z$. Which expression is the smallest?

(A) $(z)(z)$
(B) $(y)(z)$
(C) $(x)(z)$
(D) $(y)(x)$
(E) $(x)(x)$

6. A sequence of integers is defined as follows: The first term is 2, and every additional term is obtained by subtracting 2 from the previous term and tripling the resulting difference. For example, the second term would be 0. Which of the following is a true statement about this sequence?

(A) The terms behave as follows: even, even, odd, odd, even, even, odd, odd,...
(B) The terms behave as follows: even, odd, even, odd, even, odd,...
(C) The terms behave as follows: even, even, even, odd, odd, odd, even, even, even,...
(D) All of the terms, except for the first one, are odd.
(E) All of the terms are even.

GO ON TO THE NEXT PAGE

$$A = \left\{\frac{3}{8}, 2, \frac{3}{2}, 6, \frac{13}{2}, 8\right\}$$

$$B = \left\{\frac{3}{8}, \frac{8}{3}, 6, 8\right\}$$

7. If n is a member of both the sets A and B above, which of the following must be true?

I. n is an integer
II. $8n$ is an integer
III. $n = 6$

(A) None
(B) I only
(C) II only
(D) III only
(E) I and II only

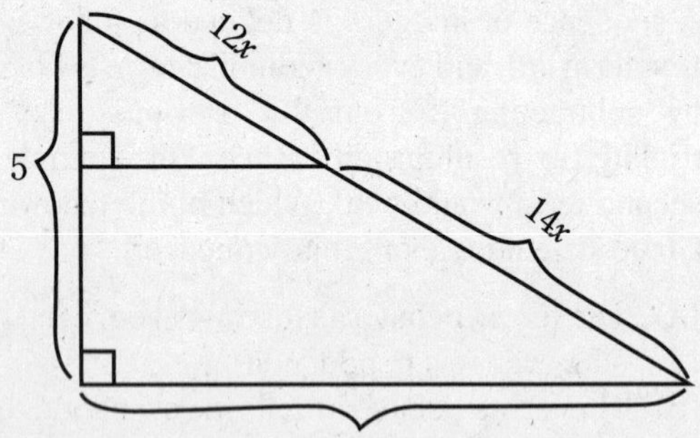

8. If the segments shown in the diagram have the indicated lengths, find the value of x.

(A) 13
(B) 12
(C) 5
(D) 2
(E) $\frac{1}{2}$

9. If x and y are integers such that $1 < |x| < 5$ and $2 < |y| < 7$, what is the least possible value of $x + y$?

(A) -10
(B) -8
(C) -5
(D) 5
(E) 10

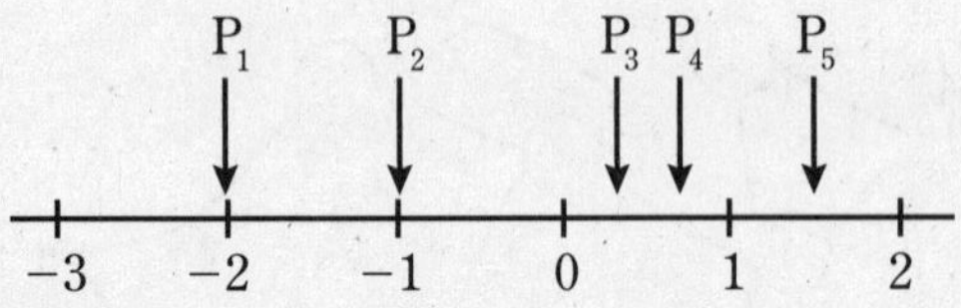

10. For the five numbers marked above by arrows, the best approximation to their product is

(A) $\frac{1}{3}$
(B) $\frac{2}{3}$
(C) $\frac{3}{2}$
(D) 3
(E) -3

GO ON TO THE NEXT PAGE

11. If K is the sum of three consecutive even integers and y is the sum of the greatest three consecutive *odd* integers that precede the least of the three even integers, express y in terms of K.

(A) $y = K - 5$
(B) $y = K - 10$
(C) $y = K - 15$
(D) $y = K - 20$
(E) The answer cannot be determined from the information given.

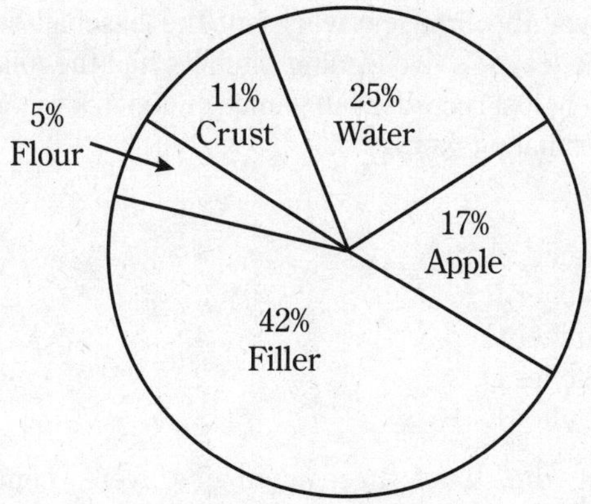

Apple Pie Ingredients

12. If John buys a 2 lb apple pie with ingredients distributed as shown, how much of his pie is water?

(A) $\frac{1}{4}$ lb
(B) $\frac{1}{2}$ lb
(C) $\frac{3}{4}$ lb
(D) 1 lb
(E) $1\frac{1}{4}$ lb

13. The number of subsets of the set {1,2,3} is

(A) 4
(B) 5
(C) 6
(D) 7
(E) 8

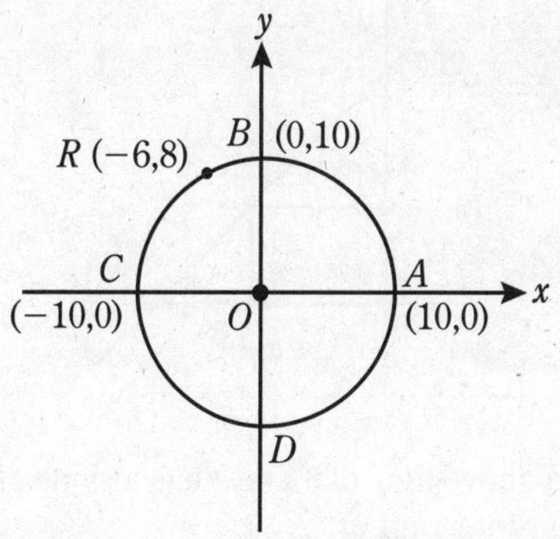

14. In the figure above, S is a point (not shown) such that segment RS divides the area of circle O into two equal parts. What are the coordinates of S?

(A) (6,−8)
(B) (6,8)
(C) (8,−6)
(D) (−6,−8)
(E) (8,6)

GO ON TO THE NEXT PAGE

	First Place (6 points)	Second Place (4 points)	Third Place (2 points)
Game 1			
Game 2		Bob	
Game 3			Bob

15. The figure above is a partially filled-in score card for a video game contest. Alan, Bob, and Carl each played in all of the three games. There were no ties. What is the *minimum* possible score for Carl in this tournament?

(A) 2
(B) 6
(C) 8
(D) 12
(E) The answer cannot be determined from the information given.

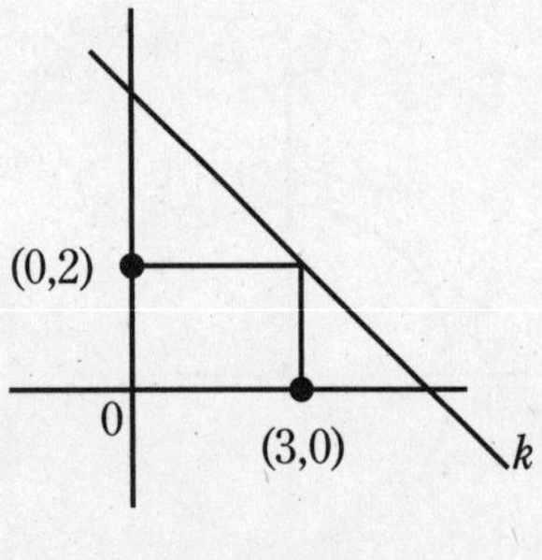

16. In the above figure, if line k has a slope of -1, what is the y-intercept of k?

(A) 4
(B) 5
(C) 6
(D) 7
(E) 8

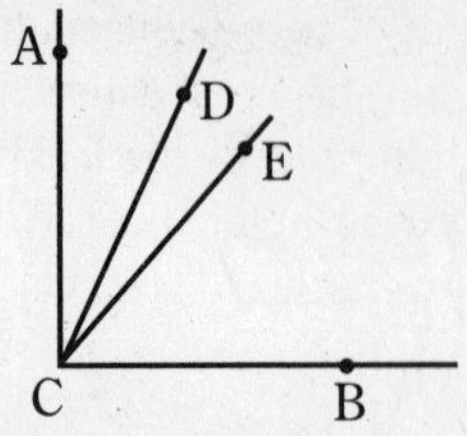

Note: Figure is not drawn to scale.

17. Given that $AC \perp BC$, $\angle DCB = 62°$, and $\angle ACE = 37°$, find $\angle DCE$ in degrees.

(A) 5°
(B) 9°
(C) 13°
(D) 25°
(E) 27°

18. Over the first few weeks of the baseball season, the league's five leading pitchers had the following won–lost records. (All games ended in a win or loss for that pitcher.)

	Won	Lost
Pitcher A	4	2
Pitcher B	3	2
Pitcher C	4	1
Pitcher D	2	2
Pitcher E	3	1

At the time these statistics were compiled, which pitcher was leading the league in winning percentage? (That is, which pitcher had won the greatest percentage of his games?)

(A) Pitcher A
(B) Pitcher B
(C) Pitcher C
(D) Pitcher D
(E) Pitcher E

GO ON TO THE NEXT PAGE

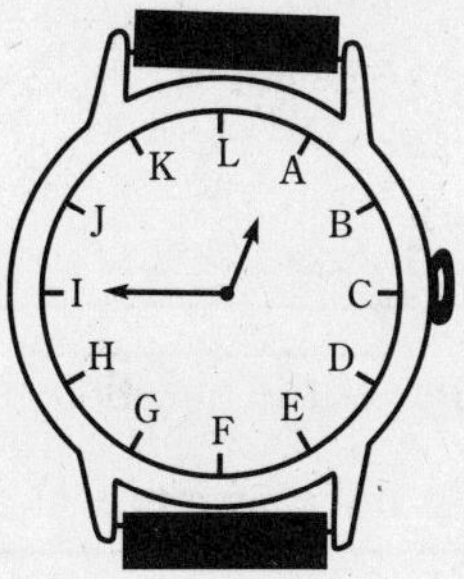

19. In the watch shown above, the normal numbers 1, 2, 3,..., 12 have been replaced by the letters A, B, C,..., L. In terms of these letters, a correct reading of the time shown would be

(A) I minutes after L
(B) 3E minutes before A
(C) 5C minutes after L
(D) I minutes before A
(E) None of the above

20. 27 equal cubes, each with a side of length r, are arranged so as to form a single larger cube with a volume of 81. If the larger cube has a side of length s, then r divided by s equals

(A) $\frac{1}{3}$

(B) $\frac{1}{\sqrt{3}}$

(C) $\frac{1}{2}$

(D) $\frac{1}{8}$

(E) $\frac{1}{27}$

STOP

If you finish before time is called, you may check your work on this section only.
Do not turn to any other section in the test.

Take a 5 minute break

before starting section 3

SECTION 3

Time: 25 Minutes—Turn to Section 3 (page 756) of your answer sheet to answer the questions in this section.
20 Questions

Directions: For this section, solve each problem and decide which is the best of the choices given. Fill in the corresponding circle on the answer sheet. You may use any available space for scratchwork.

Notes:

1. The use of a calculator is permitted.
2. All numbers used are real numbers.
3. Figures that accompany problems in this test are intended to provide information useful in solving the problems. They are drawn as accurately as possible EXCEPT when it is stated in a specific problem that the figure is not drawn to scale. All figures lie in a plane unless otherwise indicated.
4. Unless otherwise specified, the domain of any function f is assumed to be the set of all real numbers x for which $f(x)$ is a real number.

REFERENCE INFORMATION

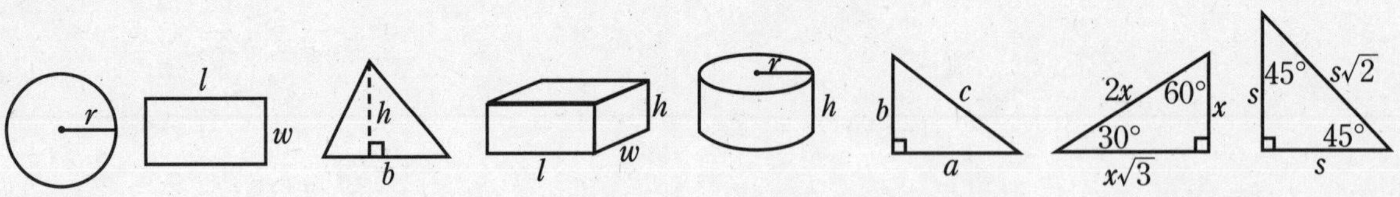

$A = \pi r^2$ $A = lw$ $A = \frac{1}{2}bh$ $V = lwh$ $V = \pi r^2 h$ $c^2 = a^2 + b^2$ *Special Right Triangles*

$C = 2\pi r$

The number of degrees of arc in a circle is 360.
The sum of the measures in degrees of the angles of a triangle is 180.

1. A piece of rope is lying on a number line. One of its ends is at coordinate −4, and the other is at coordinate 7. What is the length of the rope?

(A) 3
(B) 5
(C) 7
(D) 9
(E) 11

2. A long jumper has jumps of 8.4 meters, 8.1 meters, and 9.3 meters. What is the average (arithmetic mean) of these jumps?

(A) 8.5
(B) 8.6
(C) 8.7
(D) 8.8
(E) 8.9

GO ON TO THE NEXT PAGE

3. If $x + 9 = -11 - x$, then $x =$

(A) -10
(B) -2
(C) 2
(D) 10
(E) 20

4. If $3y = 12$ and $\frac{10}{x} = 5$, then $\frac{y+11}{x+15} =$

(A) $\frac{7}{10}$
(B) $\frac{3}{4}$
(C) $\frac{15}{17}$
(D) 1
(E) $\frac{17}{15}$

5. Johnny deposited \$50 in a savings bank at the beginning of the year. Johnny's money earns him interest at the rate of 8 percent of the amount deposited, for each year that Johnny leaves his money in the bank. If Johnny leaves his \$50 in the bank for exactly one year and then decides to withdraw all of his money, how much money (including interest) can he withdraw? (The interest is not compounded.)

(A) \$50.04
(B) \$50.08
(C) \$54.00
(D) \$54.08
(E) \$58.00

6. If $(x + 6)^2 = 12x + 72$, then $x =$

(A) 0
(B) ±1
(C) ±3
(D) ±6
(E) ±12

GO ON TO THE NEXT PAGE

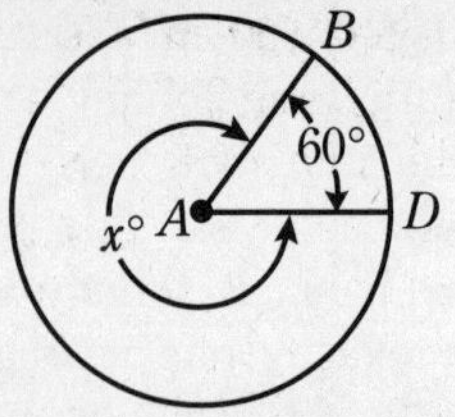

Note: Figure is not drawn to scale.

7. In the circle above, A is the center of the circle. Find the value of $x - 60$.

(A) 60
(B) 120
(C) 240
(D) 300
(E) 360

8. To the nearest hundred, how many minutes are there in a week?

(A) 1,000
(B) 1,100
(C) 10,000
(D) 10,100
(E) 11,000

9. If $\overset{x}{\bigtriangledown}$ is defined by the equation $\overset{x}{\bigtriangledown} = \frac{x^3}{4}$ for real numbers x, which of the following equals 16?

(A) $\overset{2}{\bigtriangledown}$
(B) $\overset{4}{\bigtriangledown}$
(C) $\overset{8}{\bigtriangledown}$
(D) $\overset{16}{\bigtriangledown}$
(E) $\overset{64}{\bigtriangledown}$

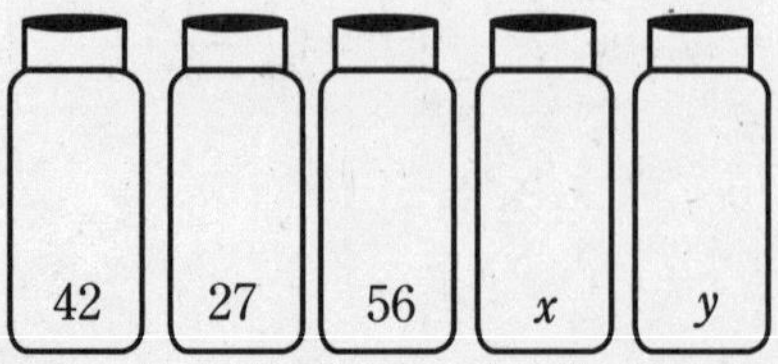

10. 200 pieces of candy have been randomly put into five jars. The number of pieces of candy in three of the five jars is shown in the figure above. What is the maximum possible value of x? (x is the number of pieces of candy in the fourth jar.)

(A) 69
(B) 75
(C) 102
(D) 144
(E) 200

GO ON TO THE NEXT PAGE

11. There are 16 pages in a booklet. Last night, Ron read $\frac{1}{4}$ of the booklet. This morning, Ron read $\frac{1}{4}$ of the remaining pages. How many pages does Ron still have left to read?

(A) 7
(B) 8
(C) 9
(D) 10
(E) 11

12. A different candle was lit at noon each day between December 9 and December 21, inclusive. How many candles were lit during this period?

(A) 10
(B) 11
(C) 12
(D) 13
(E) 14

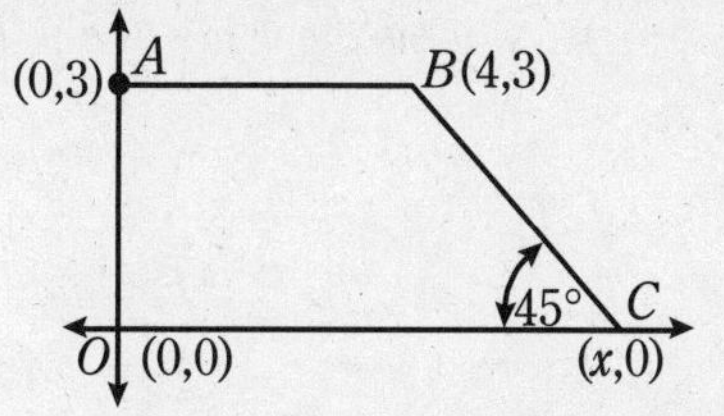

13. What is the area of quadrilateral *ABCO* in the figure above?

(A) 10.5
(B) 14.5
(C) 16.5
(D) 21.0
(E) The answer cannot be determined from the information given.

14. The difference between the sum of two numbers and the difference of the two numbers is 6. Find the larger of the two numbers if their product is 15.

(A) 3
(B) 5
(C) 17
(D) 20
(E) 23

GO ON TO THE NEXT PAGE

15. If $\frac{1}{a} + \frac{1}{b} = 10$, what is the value of $a + b$?

(A) $\frac{1}{10}$
(B) $\frac{2}{5}$
(C) 1
(D) 10
(E) The answer cannot be determined from the information given.

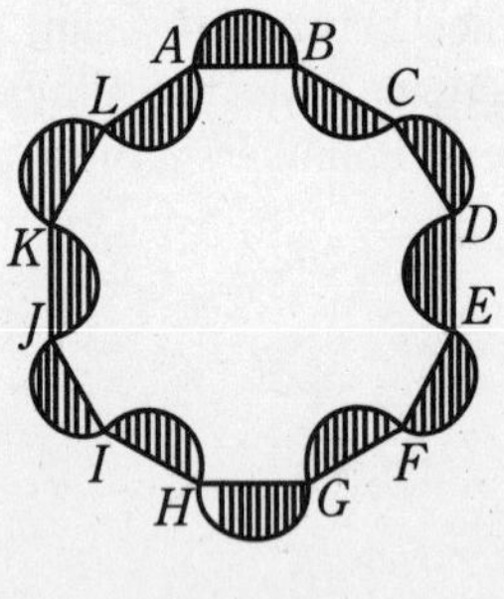

16. In the figure above, *ABCDEFGHIJKL* is a regular dodecagon (a regular twelve-sided polygon). The curved path is made up of 12 semicircles, each of whose diameters is a side of the dodecagon. If the perimeter of the dodecagon is 24, find the area of the shaded region.

(A) 6π
(B) 12π
(C) 24π
(D) 36π
(E) 48π

17. Bobby had b marbles and Charlie had c marbles. After Bobby gave 6 marbles to Charlie, Bobby still had 18 more marbles than Charlie. Find $c - b$.

(A) 30
(B) 12
(C) 3
(D) −12
(E) −30

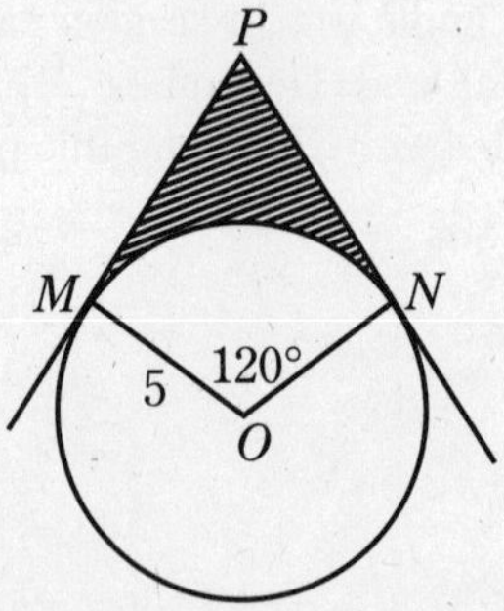

18. $\overline{PM}$ and $\overline{PN}$ are tangent to circle O at M and N, respectively; $m\ \angle MON = 120°$ and $OM = ON = 5$. Find the perimeter of the shaded region.

(A) $10 + 10\pi$
(B) $5\sqrt{3} + 10\pi$
(C) $5\sqrt{3} + \frac{10}{3}\pi$
(D) $10\sqrt{3} + \frac{10\pi}{3}$
(E) $10\sqrt{3} + 10\pi$

GO ON TO THE NEXT PAGE

19. If $x + y + z = 3(a + b)$, which of the following is the average (arithmetic mean) of x, y, z, a, and b in terms of a and b?

(A) $\frac{a+b}{5}$

(B) $\frac{4(a+b)}{15}$

(C) $\frac{a+b}{2}$

(D) $\frac{4(a+b)}{5}$

(E) $a + b$

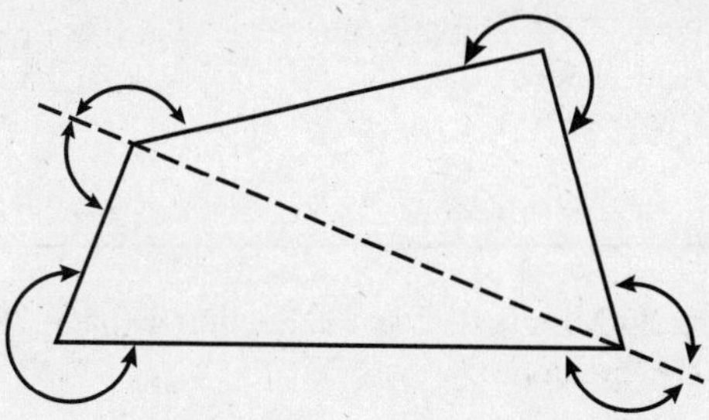

20. The arrows in the diagram above represent all of the exterior angles of the figure. The sum of the degree measures of these angles is

(A) 720
(B) 1,080
(C) 1,440
(D) 1,800
(E) The answer cannot be determined from the information given.

STOP

If you finish before time is called, you may check your work on this section only.
Do not turn to any other section in the test.

SECTION 4

Time: 25 Minutes—Turn to Section 4 (page 757) of your answer sheet to answer the questions in this section.
24 Questions

Directions: For each question in this section, select the best answer from among the choices given and fill in the corresponding circle on the answer sheet.

Each sentence below has one or two blanks, each blank indicating that something has been omitted. Beneath the sentence are five words or sets of words labeled A through E. Choose the word or set of words that, when inserted in the sentence, best fits the meaning of the sentence as a whole.

Example:

Hoping to _______ the dispute, negotiators proposed a compromise that they felt would be _______ to both labor and management.

(A) enforce...useful
(B) end...divisive
(C) overcome...unattractive
(D) extend...satisfactory
(E) resolve...acceptable

Ⓐ Ⓑ Ⓒ Ⓓ ●

1. As a general dealing with subordinates, he was like two sides of a coin: _______ yet known for his severity, _______ yet a man of few words.

(A) agreeable...talkative
(B) brilliant...handsome
(C) fair...outgoing
(D) understanding...candid
(E) harsh...pleasant

2. The profession of a major-league baseball player involves more than _______ in these times when astronomical salaries and _______ contract bargaining are commonplace.

(A) skill...astute
(B) agitation...traditional
(C) practice...minimal
(D) enthusiasm...whimsical
(E) intellect...mystical

3. Internal dissension in this congressional committee can _______ affirmative action for months and increase the chances of racial _______.

(A) encourage...regard
(B) complicate...agreement
(C) induce...movement
(D) apply...validity
(E) delay...upheaval

4. Although there was considerable _______ among the members of the panel as to the qualities essential for a champion, Sugar Ray Robinson was _______ voted the greatest fighter of all time.

(A) suspicion...quietly
(B) disagreement...overwhelmingly
(C) discussion...incidentally
(D) sacrifice...happily
(E) research...irrelevantly

5. The police commissioner insisted on severity in dealing with the demonstrators rather than the _______ approach that his advisers suggested.

(A) arrogant
(B) defeatist
(C) violent
(D) conciliatory
(E) retaliatory

6. Feeling no particular affection for either of his two acquaintances, he was able to judge their dispute very _______.

(A) impartially
(B) accurately
(C) immaculately
(D) heatedly
(E) judiciously

GO ON TO THE NEXT PAGE

7. His choice for the new judge won the immediate _______ of city officials, even though some of them had _______ about him.

(A) acclaim…reservations
(B) disdain…information
(C) apprehension…dilemmas
(D) vituperation…repercussions
(E) enmity…preconceptions

8. There are some individuals who thrive on action and, accordingly, cannot tolerate a _______ lifestyle.

(A) passive
(B) chaotic
(C) brazen
(D) grandiose
(E) vibrant

GO ON TO THE NEXT PAGE

Each passage below is followed by questions based on its content. Answer the questions on the basis of what is stated or implied in each passage and in any introductory material that may be provided.

Questions 9–10 are based on the following passage.

A cliché is made, not born. The process begins when someone hits upon a bright new way of stating a common experience. At that point, the remark is an epigram. But if it is particularly apt as well as catchy, the saying receives wide circulation as verbal coin. Soon it is likely to be suffering from overwork. It has then arrived at cliché-hood. The dictionary records the doom of the successful epigram in defining a cliché: "A trite phrase; a hackneyed expression." For the epigrammatist, the only cheer in this process is that it proves his expression was good. Even this situation is covered by a cliché: "Imitation is the sincerest form of flattery."

9. The writer suggests that an epigram is

(A) fresh
(B) trite
(C) ordinary
(D) cheerful
(E) noble

10. According to the author, the chief difference between an epigram and a cliché is in their

(A) origin
(B) length
(C) meaning
(D) use
(E) purpose

Questions 11–12 are based on the following passage.

In the ordinary course of nature, the great beneficent changes come slowly and silently. The noisy changes, for the most part, mean violence and disruption. The roar of storms and tornadoes, the explosions of volcanoes, the crash of thunder, are the result of a sudden break in the equipoise of the elements; from a condition of comparative repose and silence they become fearfully swift and audible. The still small voice is the voice of life and growth and perpetuity. In the history of a nation it is the same.

11. As used in the passage, the word "equipoise" (line 6) most nearly means

(A) stress
(B) balance
(C) course
(D) slowness
(E) condition

12. The author implies that growth and perpetuity in nature and in history are the result of

(A) quiet changes
(B) a period of silence
(C) undiscovered action
(D) storms and tornadoes
(E) violence and disruptions

GO ON TO THE NEXT PAGE

Questions 13–24 are based on the following passage.

The following passage is about the Depression, which was caused by the stock market crash of 1929, whose effect lasted into the subsequent decade.

The American people were dismayed by the sudden proof that something had gone wrong with their economic system, that it lacked stability and was subject to crises of unpredictable magnitude. They had encountered hard times and temporary depressions before, and such reverses had tended for over a century to broaden out and to become international misfortunes. But the depression that began in 1929 proved so severe, so general, and so difficult to arrest, that it caused a "loss of nerve."

Students of economics pointed out that periods of inflation and deflation, of "boom and bust," had alternated for generations. Any strong stimulus such as a war might force the economy of the Western world into high gear; when the fighting ceased, reconstruction and a "backlog" of consumers' orders unfilled in wartime might for a time keep the machines running at full speed; but within a decade the market was likely to become satiated and a fall in demand would then cause a recession. Adjustment and recovery were certain to come in time, and come the sooner if a new stimulus developed. The threat of another war, or war itself, that put millions of men in uniform and created a demand for munitions, was one such stimulus. War provided a limitless market for expendable goods, the type of goods the machines were best fitted to supply, and solved unemployment by creating more military and civilian jobs. Such reasoning as this brought no comfort, however, for it implied a choice between war and depression, and the cure was worse than the disease. "Is modern industry a sick giant that can rouse itself only to kill?" one critic asked. There was no clear answer. But the American people were not willing to accept such a grim diagnosis and insisted that there must be some method of coordinating a supply and demand within the framework of a peacetime economy.

The problem appeared to be as much psychological as economic. In prosperous times business expanded, prices rose, wages increased, and the expectation that the boom would continue indefinitely tempted people to live beyond their means. They purchased goods on credit, confident that they could meet the payments later. The increasing prosperity, in part genuine but overstimulated by optimism and artificial elements, encouraged farmers and manufacturers to overproduce until the supply exceeded the capacity of the market to absorb it. Then when business confidence began to falter, and stock quotations began to drop, panic set in. Speculators who saw their "paper profits" vanishing began to unload their securities with a disastrous effect on prices. Dealers with overloaded shelves slashed their prices to keep their goods moving, and canceled outstanding orders. Manufacturers, seeing orders shrink, reduced output. All down the line the contraction of business left employees without jobs, and lacking wages they could not meet their debts. Once started, this spiral of deflation seemed to have no limit.

It is natural for people to blame others when misfortune strikes, and after 1929 the American people became suddenly critical of their business leaders, who had failed to foresee or avert the swift transition from prosperity to privation. The conviction spread that the heads of great banks and corporations, the promoters and financiers and stockbrokers, had misled the public. Demands raised earlier in American history were revived, demands for "cheap" money with which to pay off debts, demands that the great trusts and monopolies be investigated, demands that the federal government intervene to correct business abuses and aid the destitute. More and more people began to feel that the system of free business enterprise, of unregulated economic competition, so highly praised in the 1920s, must be wrong if it could lead to crises that brought such widespread misery and unemployment.

But President Hoover was firm in his conviction that the American economic system was fundamentally sound and that it would be a mistake for the government to interfere unduly. Government supervision and regulation of business, he felt, would stifle freedom and lead to government control of activities that should be left to private initiative. "You cannot extend the mastery of the government over the daily life of a people," he warned, "without somewhere making it master of people's souls and thoughts." He believed that the government's role should be limited to helping business help itself, and to this end he supported an act (1932) which created the Reconstruction Finance Corporation to aid ailing businesses, as well as hard-pressed states, with government loans. Hoover also inaugurated a public works program which he hoped would effectively relieve unemployment. But beyond such indirect measures as these he did not believe the federal government should go. Meanwhile the burden of providing direct relief for the millions of unemployed and their families was exhausting the resources of state and local governments and private agencies—and still the breadlines formed as jobs and savings went.

GO ON TO THE NEXT PAGE

13. According to the passage, President Hoover

(A) urged more and more government regulation
(B) did little or nothing to aid ailing business
(C) made efforts to relieve unemployment
(D) had sincere doubts about the soundness of the American economic system
(E) expressed the belief that we should convert gradually to a socialistic form of government

14. The author indicates that recovery from a recession most likely comes about

(A) during wartime
(B) during peacetime
(C) by decreasing manufacturing
(D) by lowering wages
(E) by raising the interest rate

15. Which of the following was *not* a cause of the 1929 Depression?

(A) too much buying on credit
(B) rising prices
(C) overproduction of goods
(D) lack of economic stability
(E) political unrest throughout the world

16. According to the passage, when the stock quotations began to drop,

(A) manufacturers immediately increased output
(B) unemployment decreased
(C) there was a reduction of business
(D) dealers increased their prices
(E) speculators held on to their securities

17. As used in line 56, the word "privation" means

(A) solitude
(B) lack of basic necessities
(C) strictness
(D) a smooth transition
(E) a reduction in the usual business sales rate

18. The word "inaugurated" in line 81 means

(A) stifled
(B) amalgamated
(C) began
(D) commemorated
(E) oversaw

19. According to the passage, the Reconstruction Finance Corporation

(A) remodeled old private and government buildings
(B) served as a price-regulating organization
(C) helped the unemployed to find jobs during the Depression
(D) gave government loans to certain businesses
(E) supported the unemployed by public relief programs

20. Which statement would the author *not* agree to?

(A) There will continue to be economic crises.
(B) The end of the spiral of deflation was usually in sight.
(C) War tends to reduce unemployment.
(D) War is not the answer to avoiding economic depression.
(E) The Depression of 1929 had psychological roots.

21. As seen from the passage, as a result of the Depression

(A) the value of the free enterprise system was questioned
(B) more people demanded that the government stay out of business
(C) people put more trust in business leaders
(D) a third of the population was unemployed
(E) the government was forced to increase taxes

22. The author would agree that war is economically advantageous in that

(A) it implies a choice between war and depression
(B) it increases unemployment
(C) the market becomes satiated
(D) it solves bouts of inflation
(E) it increases aggregate demand

23. After 1929, the following demands were raised *except*

(A) abolition of the great financial cartels
(B) cheap money
(C) investigation of trusts and monopolies
(D) intervention of the federal government to correct business abuses
(E) intervention of the federal government to aid the poor

GO ON TO THE NEXT PAGE

24. As seen by the passage, the contraction of business in 1929 led to

(A) war fever
(B) increased unemployment
(C) payment of debts
(D) demand exceeding supply
(E) skyrocketing prices

STOP

If you finish before time is called, you may check your work on this section only. Do not turn to any other section in the test.

Take a 1 minute break

before starting section 5

SECTION 5

Time: 25 Minutes—Turn to Section 5 (page 757) of your answer sheet to answer the questions in this section. 35 Questions

Directions: For each question in this section, select the best answer from among the choices given and fill in the corresponding circle on the answer sheet.

The following sentences test correctness and effectiveness of expression. Part of each sentence or the entire sentence is underlined; beneath each sentence are five ways of phrasing the underlined material. Choice A repeats the original phrasing; the other four choices are different. If you think the original phrasing produces a better sentence than any of the alternatives, select Choice A; if not, select one of the other choices.

In making your selection, follow the requirements of standard written English; that is, pay attention to grammar, choice of words, sentence construction, and punctuation. Your selection should result in the most effective sentence—clear and precise, without awkwardness or ambiguity.

EXAMPLE:

Laura Ingalls Wilder published her first book and she was sixty-five years old then.

(A) and she was sixty-five years old then
(B) when she was sixty-five
(C) at age sixty-five years old
(D) upon the reaching of sixty-five years
(E) at the time when she was sixty-five

Ⓐ ● Ⓒ Ⓓ Ⓔ

1. The most primitive boat of all is the dugout canoe, being carved from a tree trunk.

(A) being carved from a tree trunk
(B) carving from a tree trunk
(C) carved from a tree trunk
(D) having been carved from a tree trunk
(E) its being carved from a tree trunk

2. Whether you can find a place to park your car is probably the hardest part of the day's outing.

(A) Whether you can find a place to park your car
(B) Finding a place to park your car
(C) To park your car in a place
(D) Taking your car to a place where you can park it
(E) Finding a car parking place near you

3. The trustee resigned in protest from the town board against its approval of the rent control law.

(A) in protest from the town board against its approval
(B) protesting against the approval by the town board
(C) from the town board in protest against its approval
(D) against the town board, protesting its approval
(E) in protest from the town board, protesting its approval

4. In the summer, the number of injuries from ladder falls soars.

(A) from ladder falls
(B) coming from people falling off their ladders
(C) because of falls from ladders
(D) caused by falls from ladders
(E) which come from the result of falls from ladders

5. Thousands of people are blind because their glaucoma has reached an advanced stage.

(A) because their glaucoma
(B) due to their glaucoma
(C) since they have their glaucoma and it
(D) having their glaucoma
(E) from their glaucoma

GO ON TO THE NEXT PAGE

6. Driving a racing car on a speedway is in some ways like when you are riding a horse on a bridle path.

(A) is in some ways like when you are riding
(B) in some ways is in the same class as riding
(C) is in some ways similar to when you are riding
(D) is in some ways similar to riding
(E) is like a ride in some ways of

7. Seeing their father, the cigarettes were immediately concealed by the children.

(A) Seeing their father, the cigarettes were immediately concealed by the children
(B) Their father being seen by them, the children immediately concealed the cigarettes
(C) The children having seen their father, the cigarettes were concealed immediately
(D) When the children saw their father, they immediately concealed the cigarettes
(E) When their father was seen, the children immediately concealed the cigarettes

8. Henry VIII had many wives, Henry VI one, but each is remembered not for his women but for his talent.

(A) Henry VIII had many wives, Henry VI one
(B) Henry VIII had many wives, Henry VI having one
(C) Henry VIII having many wives, Henry VI just one
(D) Henry VIII has had many wives, but Henry VI only one
(E) Henry VIII had many wives, Henry VI had only one wife

9. Biologists often say that it is not chemists or physicists but that they have the answer to the improvement of life on earth.

(A) it is not chemists or physicists but that they have
(B) it is not chemists or physicists but they have
(C) they, and not chemists or physicists have
(D) it is not chemists or physicists but it is they who have
(E) it is they, not chemists or physicists, who have

10. The underprivileged student is getting a better education, there are better teachers for them and better facilities.

(A) education, there are better teachers for them
(B) education; he has better teachers
(C) education; they have better teachers
(D) education, he has better teachers
(E) education; because he has better teachers

11. When the university administration changed its role from that of a judge and prosecutor to that of an adviser and friend, not only did the students stop their demonstrations but they also sided with the administration against the outsiders.

(A) When the university administration changed its role from that of a judge and prosecutor to that of an adviser and friend
(B) When the university administration changed its role from that of a judge and prosecutor to an adviser and friend
(C) When the university administration changed its role from that of a judge and prosecutor to one of an adviser and friend
(D) As a result of the administration's changing its role from judge and prosecutor to that of adviser and friend
(E) As to the university administration, in changing its role from that of a judge and prosecutor to that of an adviser and friend

GO ON TO THE NEXT PAGE

The following sentences test your ability to recognize grammar and usage errors. Each sentence contains either a single error or no error at all. No sentence contains more than one error. The error, if there is one, is underlined and lettered. If the sentence contains an error, select the one underlined part that must be changed to make the sentence correct. If the sentence is correct, select Choice E. In choosing answers, follow the requirements of standard written English.

EXAMPLE:

The other delegates and him immediately
A B C
accepted the resolution drafted by
D
the neutral states. No error.
E

Ⓐ ● Ⓒ Ⓓ Ⓔ

12. You may not realize it but the weather in
A B
Barbados during Christmas is like New York in
C D
June. No error.
E

13. Stores were jammed with last-minute Christmas
A B
shoppers, and the festive spirit was greatly
C
disrupted by homemade bombs that exploded at
D
two department stores. No error.
E

14. The teacher did not encourage the student any
A
even though the boy began to weep when he
B
was told that his poor marks would likely hold up
C D
his graduation. No error.
E

15. Allen has stated that he has always had a great
A B
interest and admiration for the work of the British
C D
economist Keynes. No errors.
E

16. Besides my job as a legal secretary, I also have a job
A
as a condominium manager that requires me to
B C
solve a large amount of problems. No error.
D E

17. Who's to decide that certain terminally-ill patients
A B
should be taken off life-support systems while others
C D
should remain dependent upon machines? No error.
E

18. When the results of the polls were published in the
A
paper, my brother, who was a candidate for mayor,
B
was not discouraged any because he was among
C D
the top four candidates. No error.
E

19. A mother along with her five children were rescued
A B
from the burning apartment building by a postal
worker who was making his daily deliveries earlier
C
than usual. No error.
D E

20. My partner in the computer class worked on the
A
same programs as I, but his method of solving the
B
problems was quite different than mine. No error.
C D E

21. The school board members did like they were
A B C
expected to do when they decided to increase the
length of the school day rather than the length of
D
the school year. No error.
E

GO ON TO THE NEXT PAGE

22. A woman (A) perished on Sunday when the hot air balloon in which she had rode (B) caught (C) fire as it touched (D) down. No error. (E)

23. From every community comes (A) reports that (B) there has been (C) an increase in vandalism by teenagers. (D) No error. (E)

24. When the hurricane struck, (A) the people who had gone (B) to the shelter found that there wasn't (C) scarcely enough food for everyone. (D) No error. (E)

25. By the time I graduate (A) from (B) law school, my sister will have been practicing (C) law for three years. (D) No error. (E)

26. I had to borrow a book off of (A) my English instructor since (B) the campus bookstore had sold (C) all (D) the copies of the required text. No error. (E)

27. Neither the school board members or (A) the city council (B) wanted to change (C) the school boundaries in order (D) to reduce the over-enrollment. No error. (E)

28. When my neighbor, who (A) cannot swim, (B) was a teenager, he had rescued (C) a drowning (D) swimmer by pulling him into his rowboat. No error. (E)

29. As (A) an incentive to attend (B) the local college, our father told my brother and I (C) that we could use his company car for (D) transportation. No error. (E)

GO ON TO THE NEXT PAGE

Directions: The following passage is an early draft of an essay. Some parts of the passage need to be rewritten.

Read the passage and select the best answers for the questions that follow. Some questions are about particular sentences or parts of sentences and ask you to improve sentence structure or word choice. Other questions ask you to consider organization and development. In choosing answers, follow the requirements of standard written English.

Questions 30–35 refer to the following passage.

[1]We know that a proportion of our sleeping time is spent dreaming. [2]This is true for everyone, whether you are the kind of person who ordinarily remembers your dreams or not. [3]Often our dreams show us "the other side of the picture," making us aware of things we have failed to take conscious note of during the day. [4]Moreover, if you dream that your new boss, who seems gruff and unfriendly during waking hours, is smiling at you and praising you for your work, perhaps you have subliminally picked up signals that day that his bark is worse than his bite.

[5]All of us need our dreams, and the younger we are, the more necessary they appear to be. [6]Babies spend nearly half their sleep in the dreaming phase. [7]When adult subjects in an experiment were given drugs that eliminated their dreaming for several nights, they became increasingly irritable and anxious, and often began having difficulty concentrating. [8]Too much dreaming appears to have its drawbacks too. [9]If you doze late on Sunday morning, you often wake up feeling tired. [10]The reason is that the longer you sleep, the longer your dreams become. [11](Dreaming periods are short during the first part of the night and lengthen as your sleep progresses.)

30. The word Moreover, in sentence 4 should be

(A) left as it is
(B) changed to However,
(C) changed to For instance,
(D) changed to In short,
(E) changed to Some people believe

31. Sentence 8 would be improved if

(A) it were joined to sentence 7 with a semicolon
(B) it were joined to sentence 7 with and
(C) it began with Although
(D) it began with Yet
(E) it were placed after sentence 9

32. Sentence 10 should be

(A) eliminated
(B) joined to sentence 9 with a semicolon
(C) joined to sentence 9 with a comma
(D) placed at the end of the paragraph
(E) shortened to read The longer you sleep, the longer your dreams become

33. Which of the following sentences would make the best introductory sentence to the passage?

(A) Dreams have fascinated man since ancient times.
(B) Many people dismiss dreams as unimportant.
(C) You do not need a psychoanalyst to learn something from your dreams.
(D) Socrates said dreams represented the voice of our consciences; Freud called them "the royal road to the unconscious."
(E) New research indicates that, night and day, dreams play an important part in all of our lives.

34. In sentence 7, the word When should be

(A) left as it is
(B) changed to If
(C) changed to Only
(D) changed to Before
(E) changed to Nevertheless

35. What should be done with sentence 11?

(A) The parentheses should be eliminated.
(B) An exclamation point should be used instead of a period.
(C) The sentence should be italicized.
(D) The sentence should be made into two sentences without the parentheses.
(E) It should be left as it is.

STOP

If you finish before time is called, you may check your work on this section only.
Do not turn to any other section in the test.

SECTION 6

Time: 25 Minutes—Turn to Section 6 (page 758) of your answer sheet to answer the questions in this section.
18 Questions

Directions: This section contains two types of questions. You have 25 minutes to complete both types. For questions 1–8, solve each problem and decide which is the best of the choices given. Fill in the corresponding circle on the answer sheet. You may use any available space for scratchwork.

Notes:

1. The use of a calculator is permitted.
2. All numbers used are real numbers.
3. Figures that accompany problems in this test are intended to provide information useful in solving the problems. They are drawn as accurately as possible EXCEPT when it is stated in a specific problem that the figure is not drawn to scale. All figures lie in a plane unless otherwise indicated.
4. Unless otherwise specified, the domain of any function f is assumed to be the set of all real numbers x for which $f(x)$ is a real number.

REFERENCE INFORMATION

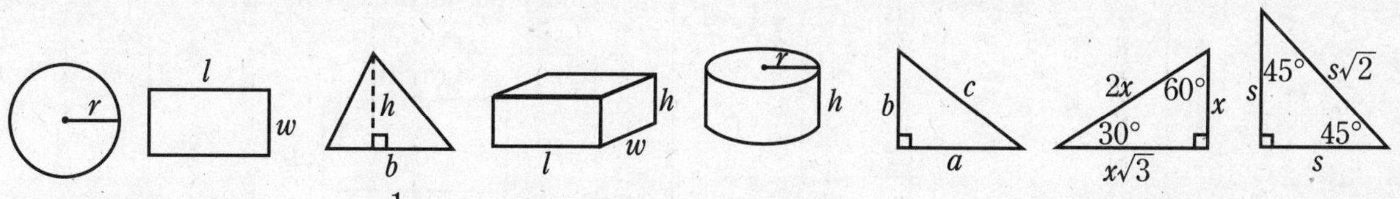

$A = \pi r^2$ $C = 2\pi r$ | $A = lw$ | $A = \frac{1}{2}bh$ | $V = lwh$ | $V = \pi r^2 h$ | $c^2 = a^2 + b^2$ | *Special Right Triangles*

The number of degrees of arc in a circle is 360.
The sum of the measures in degrees of the angles of a triangle is 180.

1. From the equations $7a = 4$ and $7a + 4b = 12$, one can conclude that b is

(A) −1
(B) 0
(C) 1
(D) 2
(E) any integer

2. How many values of x satisfy $-\frac{1}{2} < \frac{x}{3} < -\frac{1}{4}$ where x is an integer?

(A) none
(B) one
(C) two
(D) three
(E) infinitely many

GO ON TO THE NEXT PAGE

3. If r and s are negative numbers, then all of the following must be positive *except*

(A) $\frac{r}{s}$
(B) rs
(C) $(rs)^2$
(D) $r + s$
(E) $-r - s$

4. If $f(x) = x^2 + 2x + 1$, $f(x - 1) =$

(A) $x^2 + 2x$
(B) 0
(C) 1
(D) x^2
(E) $2x + 1$

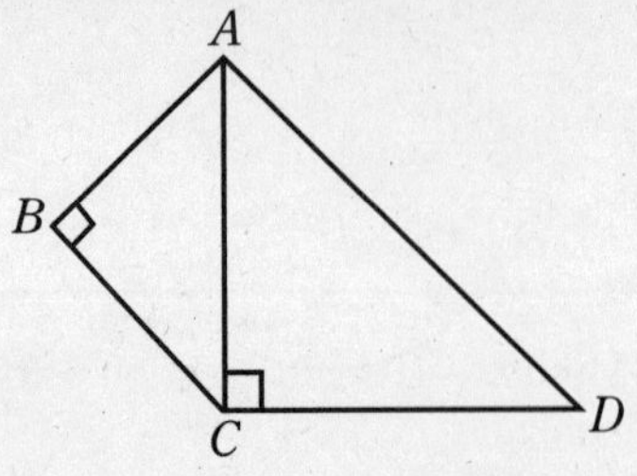

5. In the figure above, $AB = BC$ and $AC = CD$. How many of the angles have a measure of 45 degrees?

(A) none
(B) two
(C) three
(D) four
(E) five

6. Which of the rectangles below has a length of $\frac{4}{3}$, if each has an area of 4?

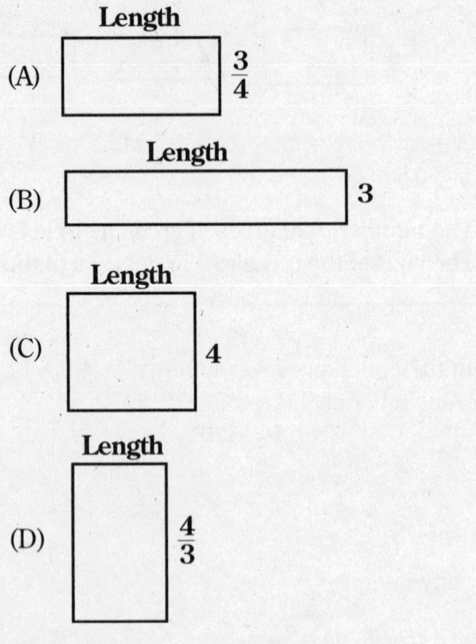

Note: Figures are not drawn to scale.

GO ON TO THE NEXT PAGE

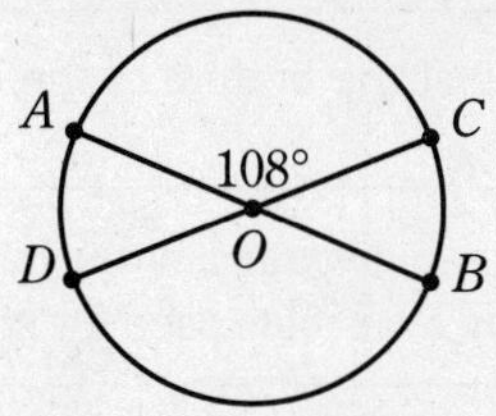

7. O is the center of a circle of diameter 20 and $\angle AOC = 108°$. Find the sum of the lengths of minor arcs $\overset{\frown}{AC}$ and $\overset{\frown}{DB}$.

(A) 5π
(B) 8π
(C) 10π
(D) 12π
(E) 15π

8. Which is true of the graphs $y = 2x^2$ and $y = -2x^2$?

I. They have only one point in common.
II. The shapes of both are the same but one is right side up and the other is upside down.
III. They both represent linear functions.

(A) I only
(B) II only
(C) III only
(D) I and II only
(E) I, II, and III

GO ON TO THE NEXT PAGE

Directions: For Student-Produced Response questions 9–18, use the grids at the bottom of the answer sheet page on which you have answered questions 1–8.

Each of the remaining 10 questions requires you to solve the problem and enter your answer by marking the circles in the special grid, as shown in the examples below. You may use any available space for scratchwork.

Answer: $\frac{7}{12}$ or 7/12 | Answer: 2.5 | Answer: 201
Either position is correct.

Write answer in boxes. →

Grid in result. →

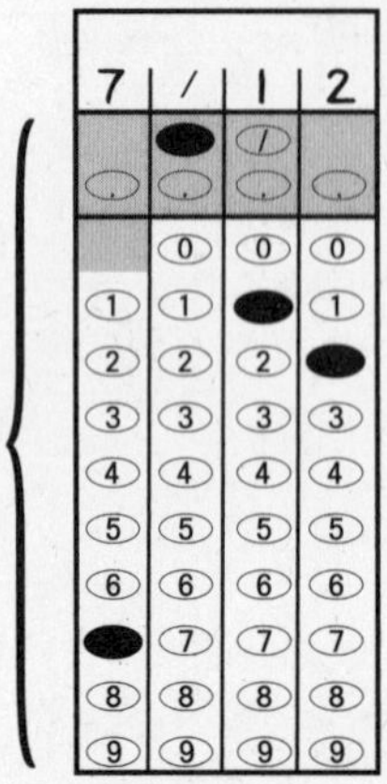

← Fraction line

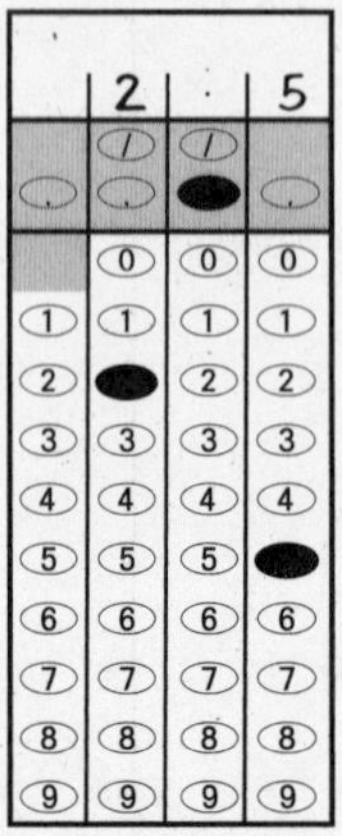

← Decimal point

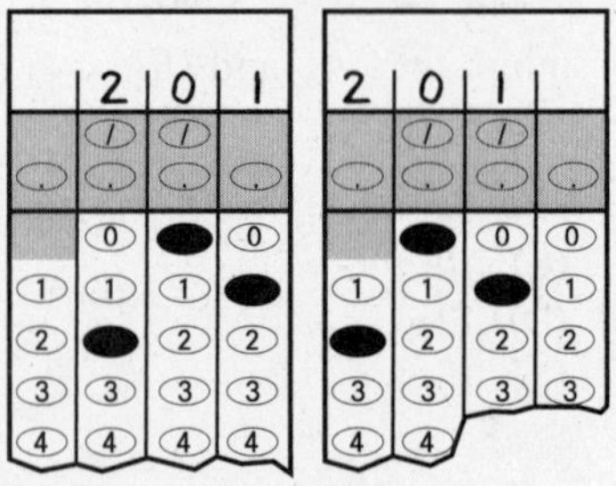

Note: You may start your answers in any column, space permitting. Columns not needed should be left blank.

- Mark no more than one oval in any column.
- Because the answer sheet will be machine-scored, **you will receive credit only if the ovals are filled in correctly.**
- Although not required, it is suggested that you write your answer in the boxes at the top of the columns to help you fill in the ovals accurately.
- Some problems may have more than one correct answer. In such cases, grid only one answer.
- No question has a negative answer.
- **Mixed numbers** such as $2\frac{1}{2}$ must be gridded as 2.5 or 5/2. (If  is gridded, it will be interpreted as $\frac{21}{2}$, not $2\frac{1}{2}$.)
- Decimal Accuracy: If you obtain a decimal answer, **enter the most accurate value the grid will accommodate.** For example, if you obtain an answer such as 0.6666..., you should record the result as .666 or .667. **Less accurate values such as .66 or .67 are not acceptable.**

Acceptable ways to grid $\frac{2}{3}$ = .6666...

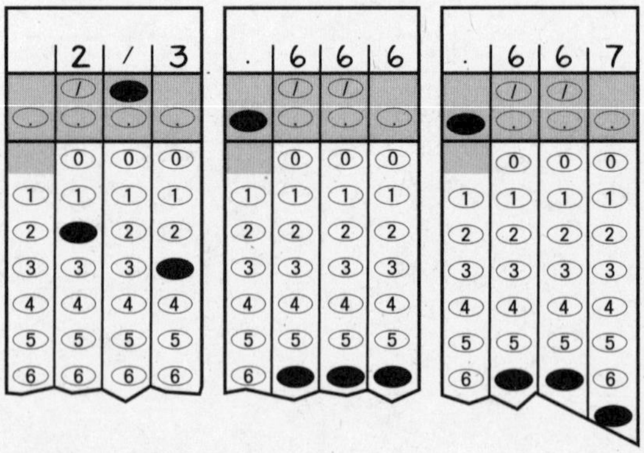

9. Susan has 3 times as many jelly beans as Mary, and Rose has 18 times as many jelly beans as Mary. What is the ratio

$$\frac{\text{Rose's jelly beans}}{\text{Susan's jelly beans}}?$$

10. If two cubes have edges of 1 and 2, what is the sum of their volumes?

GO ON TO THE NEXT PAGE

11. If the numerical value of the binomial coefficient $\binom{n}{2}$ is given by the formula $\frac{n(n-1)}{2}$, then what is the numerical value of $\binom{15}{2}$?

---

12. The letters r and s represent numbers satisfying $r^2 = 9$ and $s^2 = 25$. What is the difference between the greatest possible values of $s - r$ and $r - s$?

---

13. According to the graph, what percent of the people in the group had brown eyes?

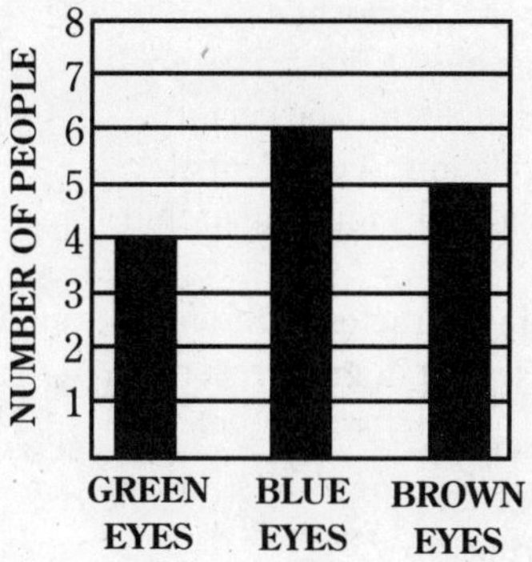

$$\begin{array}{r} N\,5 \\ \times\ LM \\ \hline 3\,8\,5 \\ 3\,8\,5 \\ \hline 4{,}2\,3\,5 \end{array}$$

14. In the multiplication problem above, L, M, and N each represent one of the digits 0 through 9. If the problem is computed correctly, find N.

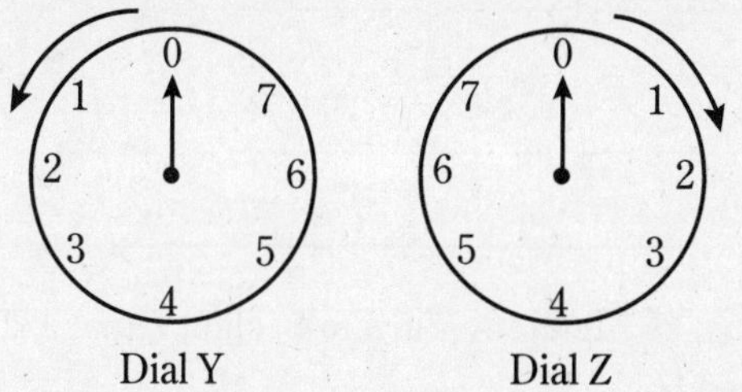

15. In the figure above, the hand of dial Z moves in a clockwise direction. When its hand makes one complete revolution, it causes the hand of dial Y to move 1 number in the counterclockwise direction. How many complete revolutions of the hand of dial Z are needed to move the hand of dial Y 3 complete revolutions?

---

16. To make enough paste to hang 6 rolls of wallpaper, a $\frac{1}{4}$ pound package of powder is mixed with $2\frac{1}{2}$ quarts of water. How many pounds of powder are needed to make enough of the same mixture of paste to hang 21 rolls of paper?

---

17. On a mathematics test, the average score for a certain class was 90. If 40 percent of the class scored 100 and 10 percent scored 80, what was the average score for the remainder of the class?

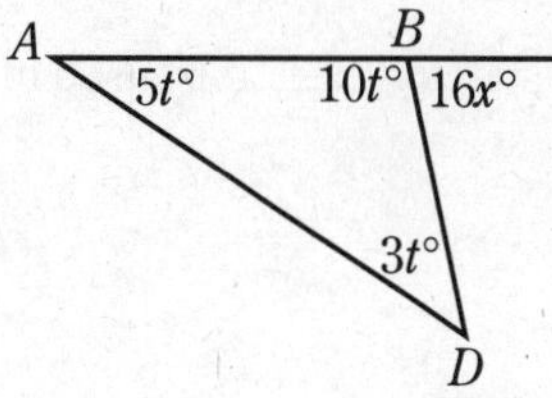

18. In the figure above, ABC is a line segment. What is the value of x?

STOP

If you finish before time is called, you may check your work on this section only.
Do not turn to any other section in the test.

Take a 5 minute break
before starting section 7

SECTION 7

Time: 25 Minutes—Turn to Section 7 (page 758) of your answer sheet to answer the questions in this section.
24 Questions

Directions: For each question in this section, select the best answer from among the choices given and fill in the corresponding circle on the answer sheet.

Each sentence below has one or two blanks, each blank indicating that something has been omitted. Beneath the sentence are five words or sets of words labeled A through E. Choose the word or set of words that, when inserted in the sentence, best fits the meaning of the sentence as a whole.

Example:

Hoping to ________ the dispute, negotiators proposed a compromise that they felt would be ________ to both labor and management.

(A) enforce...useful
(B) end...divisive
(C) overcome...unattractive
(D) extend...satisfactory
(E) resolve...acceptable

Ⓐ Ⓑ Ⓒ Ⓓ ●

1. The girl's extreme state of ______ aroused in him a feeling of pity.

(A) disapproval
(B) exultation
(C) enthusiasm
(D) degradation
(E) jubilation

2. Although our team was aware that the Raiders' attack power was ______ as compared with that of our players, we were stupid to be so ______.

(A) calculated...alert
(B) sluggish...easygoing
(C) acceptable...serious
(D) determined...detailed
(E) premeditated...willing

3. The ______ prime minister caused the downfall of the once ______ country.

(A) heroic...important
(B) respected...rich
(C) incompetent...powerful
(D) vacillating...confidential
(E) insightful...unconquerable

4. The main character in the novel was dignified and ______, a man of great reserve.

(A) garrulous
(B) aloof
(C) boring
(D) hypocritical
(E) interesting

5. The nonsmoker's blood contains ______ amounts of carbon monoxide; on the other hand, the smoker's blood contains ______ amounts.

(A) frequent...extensive
(B) heavy...adequate
(C) minute...excessive
(D) definite...puzzling
(E) bland...moderate

GO ON TO THE NEXT PAGE

The two passages below are followed by questions based on their content and on the relationship between the two passages. Answer the questions on the basis of what is stated or implied in the passages and in any introductory material that may be provided.

Questions 6–9 are based on the following passages.

Passage 1

Classical music is termed "classical" because it can be heard over and over again without the listener tiring of the music. A symphony of Brahms can be heard and heard again with the same or even heightened enjoyment a few months later. It is unfortunate that the sales of classical music are dismal compared to other types of music. Perhaps this is because many people in our generation were not exposed to classical music at an early age and therefore did not get to know the music.

Passage 2

Contemporary nonclassical music has a high impact on the listener but unfortunately is not evergreen. Its enjoyment lasts only as long as there is current interest in the topic or emotion that the music portrays, and that only lasts for three months or so until other music replaces it, especially when another bestselling song comes out. The reason why the impact of this type of music is not as great when it first comes out is thought to be because technically the intricacy of the music is not high and not sophisticated, although many critics believe it is because the music elicits a particular emotional feeling that gradually becomes worn out in time.

6. According to the passage, it can be assumed that the majority of younger people do not like classical music because they

(A) buy only the bestselling songs
(B) do not have the sophistication of a true music lover
(C) grow tired of classical music
(D) did not hear that type of music in their youth
(E) are more restless than the older generation

7. The reason that the enjoyment of a particular piece of contemporary music may not last as long as a piece of classical music is due to the

(A) emotion of a person, which is thought to change in time
(B) high sophistication of the classical music and its technical intricacy
(C) fact that there is always another piece of contemporary music that replaces the one before it
(D) youth desiring something new
(E) economy and marketing of the songs

8. The term "evergreen" in line 11 most nearly means

(A) colorful
(B) lasting
(C) current
(D) likeable
(E) encompassing

9. Which of the following is addressed in one passage but not the other?

(A) The time period of enjoyment of the music
(B) The type of music
(C) A specific example illustrating a point
(D) The instruments used in the music
(E) The musicians playing the music

GO ON TO THE NEXT PAGE

Questions 10–15 are based on the following passage.

The following passage is excerpted from the Brahmin's life, Siddhartha.

Siddhartha was now pleased with himself. He could have dwelt for a long time yet in that soft, well-upholstered hell, if this had not happened, this moment of complete hopelessness and despair and the tense moment when he was ready to commit suicide. Was it not his Self, his small, fearful and proud Self, with which he had wrestled for many years, which had always conquered him again and again, which robbed him of happiness and filled him with fear?

Siddhartha now realized why he had struggled in vain with this Self when he was a Brahmin and an ascetic. Too much knowledge had hindered him; too many holy verses, too many sacrificial rites, too much mortification of the flesh, too much doing and striving. He had been full of arrogance; he had always been the cleverest, the most eager—always a step ahead of the others, always the learned and intellectual one, always the priest or the sage. His Self had crawled into his priesthood, into this arrogance, into this intellectuality. It sat there tightly and grew, while he thought he was destroying it by fasting and penitence. Now he understood it and realized that the inward voice had been right, that no teacher could have brought him salvation. That was why he had to go into the world, to lose himself in power, women and money; that was why he had to be a merchant, a dice player, a drinker and a man of property, until the priest and Samana in him were dead. That was why he had to undergo those horrible years, suffer nausea, learn the lesson of the madness of an empty, futile life till the end, till he reached bitter despair, so that Siddhartha the pleasure-monger and Siddhartha the man of property could die. He had died and a new Siddhartha had awakened from his sleep. He also would grow old and die. Siddhartha was transitory, all forms were transitory, but today he was young, he was a child—the new Siddhartha—and he was very happy.

These thoughts passed through his mind. Smiling, he listened thankfully to a humming bee. Happily he looked into the flowing river. Never had a river attracted him as much as this one. Never had he found the voice and appearance of flowing water so beautiful. It seemed to him as if the river had something special to tell him, something which he did not know, something which still awaited him. The new Siddhartha felt a deep love for this flowing water and decided that he would not leave it again so quickly.

10. The "soft, well-upholstered hell" (line 2) is a reference to

(A) an attractive yet uncomfortable dwelling where Siddhartha resided
(B) Siddhartha's lifestyle, which made him an unhappy person
(C) a place to which Siddhartha went when he wished to be completely by himself
(D) Siddhartha's abode in a previous life not referred to in the passage
(E) a figment of Siddhartha's imagination that used to haunt him

11. Which of the following best describes the relation between the second and third paragraphs?

(A) Paragraph 3 shows how much happier one can be by living alone than in living with others, as brought out in paragraph 2.
(B) Paragraph 3 discusses the advantages of a simple life as opposed to the more complicated lifestyle discussed in paragraph 2.
(C) Paragraph 3 contrasts the life of a person without wealth and a formal religion with a person who has wealth and a formal religion, as in paragraph 2.
(D) Paragraph 3 demonstrates the happiness that can come as a result of giving up the power and the worldly pleasures referred to in paragraph 2.
(E) Paragraph 3 generalizes about the specific points made in paragraph 2.

12. Which of the following questions does the passage answer?

(A) What is the meaning of a Brahmin?
(B) Why did Siddhartha decide to commit suicide?
(C) Where did Siddhartha own property?
(D) For how many years was Siddhartha a member of the priesthood?
(E) Where did Siddhartha go to school?

13. The word "transitory" in line 31 most likely means

(A) quick on one's feet
(B) invisible
(C) short-lived
(D) going from one place to another
(E) frozen

GO ON TO THE NEXT PAGE

14. Which statement best expresses the main idea of this passage?

(A) Arrogance constitutes a great hindrance for one who seeks to lead a peaceful life.
(B) One has to discipline himself so that he will refrain from seeking pleasures that will prove harmful later.
(C) The quest for knowledge is commendable provided that search has its limitations.
(D) There is a voice within a person that can advise him how to attain contentment.
(E) Peace and quiet are more important than wealth and power in bringing happiness.

15. What is the meaning of "Self," as it is referred to in the passage?

(A) one's love of nature
(B) one's own lifestyle
(C) one's inner voice
(D) one's remembrances
(E) one's own interests

GO ON TO THE NEXT PAGE

Questions 16–24 are based on the following passage.

The following passage explores how brilliant people think, how they may come up with their theories, and what motivates their thinking and creativity.

The discoveries made by scientific geniuses, from Archimedes through Einstein, have repeatedly revolutionized both our world and the way we see it. Yet no one really knows how the mind of a genius works. Most people think that a very high IQ sets the great scientist apart. They assume that flashes of profound insight like Einstein's are the product of mental processes so arcane that they must be inaccessible to more ordinary minds.

But a growing number of researchers in psychology, psychiatry, and the history of science are investigating the way geniuses think. The researchers are beginning to give us tantalizing glimpses of the mental universe that can produce the discoveries of an Einstein, an Edison, a Da Vinci—or any Nobel Prize winner.

Surprisingly, most researchers agree that the important variable in genius is not the IQ but creativity. Testers start with 135 as the beginning of the "genius" category, but the researchers seem to feel that, while an IQ above a certain point—about 120—is very helpful for a scientist, having an IQ that goes much higher is not crucial for producing a work of genius. All human beings have at least four types of intelligence. The great scientist possesses the ability to move back and forth among them—the logical-mathematical, the spatial, which includes visual perception, the linguistic, and the bodily-kinesthetic.

Some corroboration of these categories comes from the reports of scientists who describe thought processes centered around images, sensations, or words. Einstein reported a special "feeling at the tips of the fingers" that told him which path to take through a problem. The idea for a self-starting electric motor came to Nikola Tesla one evening as he was reciting a poem by Goethe and watching a sunset. Suddenly he imagined a magnetic field rapidly rotating inside a circle of electromagnets.

Some IQ tests predict fairly accurately how well a person will do in school and how quickly he or she will master knowledge, but genius involves more than knowledge. The genius has the capacity to leap significantly beyond his present knowledge and produce something new. To do this, he sees the relationship between facts or pieces of information in a new or unusual way.

The scientist solves a problem by shifting from one intelligence to another, although the logical-mathematical intelligence is dominant. Creative individuals seem to be marked by a special fluidity of mind. They may be able to think of a problem verbally, logically, and also spatially.

Paradoxically, fluid thinking may be connected to another generally agreed-upon trait of the scientific genius—persistence, or unusually strong motivation to work on a problem. Persistence kept Einstein looking for the solution to the question of the relationship between the law of gravity and his special theory of relativity. Yet surely creative fluidity enabled him to come up with a whole new field that included both special relativity and gravitation.

Many scientists have the ability to stick with a problem even when they appear not to be working on it. Werner Heisenberg discovered quantum mechanics one night during a vacation he had taken to recuperate from the mental jumble he had fallen into trying to solve the atomic-spectra problem.

16. Which statement is true, according to the passage?

(A) The law of gravity followed the publication of Einstein's theory of relativity.
(B) Nikola Tesla learned about magnets from his research of the works of Goethe.
(C) Archimedes and Einstein lived in the same century.
(D) Most scientists have IQ scores above 120.
(E) We ought to refer to intelligences rather than to intelligence.

17. The author believes that, among the four intelligences he cites, the most important one for the scientist is

(A) spatial
(B) bodily-kinesthetic
(C) linguistic
(D) logical-mathematical
(E) not singled out

18. The author focuses on the circumstances surrounding the work of great scientists in order to show that

(A) scientific geniuses are usually eccentric in their behavior
(B) the various types of intelligence have come into play during their work
(C) scientists often give the impression that they are relaxing when they are really working on a problem
(D) scientists must be happy to do their best work
(E) great scientific discoveries are almost always accidental

19. The passage can best be described as

(A) a comparison of how the average individual and the great scientist think
(B) an account of the unexpected things that led to great discoveries by scientists
(C) an explanation of the way scientific geniuses really think
(D) a criticism of intelligence tests as they are given today
(E) a lesson clarifying scientific concepts such as quantum mechanics and relativity

GO ON TO THE NEXT PAGE

20. The passage suggests that a college football star who is majoring in literature is quite likely to have which intelligences to a high degree?

I. logical-mathematical
II. spatial
III. linguistic
IV. bodily-kinesthetic

(A) I only
(B) II only
(C) III only
(D) I, II, and III only
(E) II, III, and IV only

21. Which statement would the author most likely *not* agree with?

(A) Most people believe that IQ is what makes the scientist brilliant.
(B) Some scientists may come up with a solution to a problem when they are working on something else.
(C) Creativity is much more important than basic intelligence in scientific discovery.
(D) Scientists and artists may think alike in their creative mode.
(E) Scientists usually get the answer to a problem fairly quickly, and if they get stuck they usually go on to another problem.

22. "Fluidity" as described in lines 52–54 can best be defined as

(A) persistence when faced with a problem
(B) having a flighty attitude in dealing with scientific problems
(C) being able to move from one scientific area to another
(D) having an open mind in dealing with scientific phenomena
(E) being able to generate enormous excitement in the scientist's work

23. The word "paradoxically" in line 47 means

(A) ironically
(B) seemingly contradictorily
(C) in a manner of speaking
(D) experimentally
(E) conditionally

24. The author's attitude toward scientists in this passage can be seen as one of

(A) objective intrigue
(B) grudging admiration
(C) subtle jealousy
(D) growing impatience
(E) boundless enthusiasm

STOP

If you finish before time is called, you may check your work on this section only.
Do not turn to any other section in the test.

SECTION 8

Time: 20 Minutes—Turn to Section 8 (page 759) of your answer sheet to answer the questions in this section.
16 Questions

Directions: For this section, solve each problem and decide which is the best of the choices given. Fill in the corresponding circle on the answer sheet. You may use any available space for scratchwork.

Notes:

1. The use of a calculator is permitted.
2. All numbers used are real numbers.
3. Figures that accompany problems in this test are intended to provide information useful in solving the problems. They are drawn as accurately as possible EXCEPT when it is stated in a specific problem that the figure is not drawn to scale. All figures lie in a plane unless otherwise indicated.
4. Unless otherwise specified, the domain of any function f is assumed to be the set of all real numbers x for which $f(x)$ is a real number.

REFERENCE INFORMATION

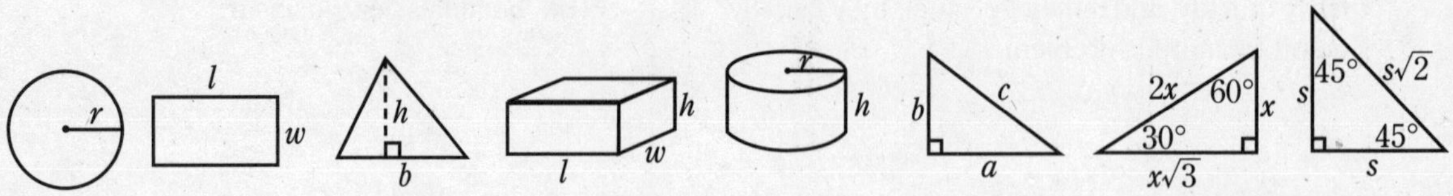

$A = \pi r^2$ $C = 2\pi r$ $A = lw$ $A = \frac{1}{2}bh$ $V = lwh$ $V = \pi r^2 h$ $c^2 = a^2 + b^2$ *Special Right Triangles*

The number of degrees of arc in a circle is 360.
The sum of the measures in degrees of the angles of a triangle is 180.

1. A box of candy contains 0.6 of a pound of caramels and 3.6 pounds of coconut. What percent of the contents of the box, by weight, consists of caramels?

(A) 6%
(B) $14\frac{2}{7}\%$
(C) $16\frac{2}{3}\%$
(D) 25%
(E) $33\frac{1}{3}\%$

GO ON TO THE NEXT PAGE

Distribution of $100,000 Land Improvement Funds to Five High Schools

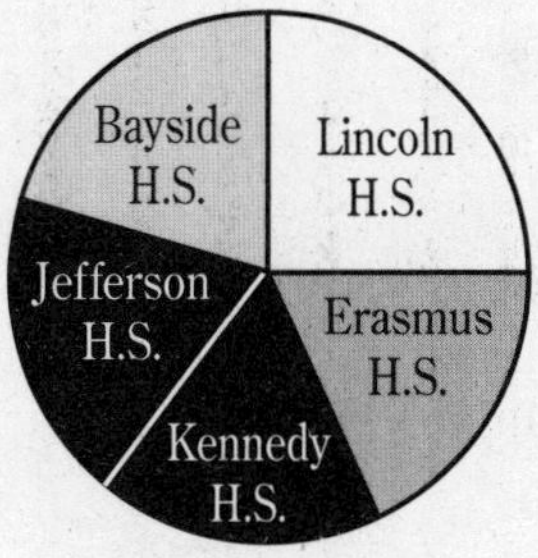

2. The circle graph above describes the distribution of $100,000 to five high schools for land improvement. Which high school received an amount closest to $25,000?

(A) Bayside H.S.
(B) Lincoln H.S.
(C) Erasmus H.S.
(D) Kennedy H.S.
(E) Jefferson H.S.

3. If $y = r - 6$ and $z = r + 5$, which of the following is an expression representing r in terms of y and z?

(A) $\frac{y+z+1}{2}$
(B) $\frac{y+z-1}{2}$
(C) $y + z - 1$
(D) $y + z$
(E) $y + z + 1$

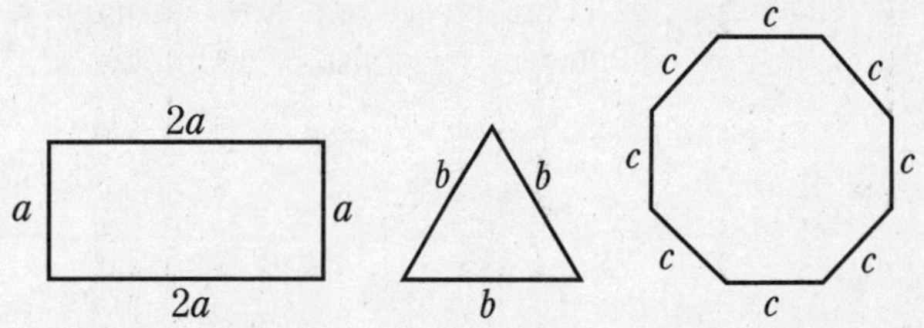

Note: Figures are not drawn to scale.

4. Which of the following is true if the three polygons above have equal perimeters?

(A) $b < a < c$
(B) $a < c < b$
(C) $a < b < c$
(D) $c < b < a$
(E) $c < a < b$

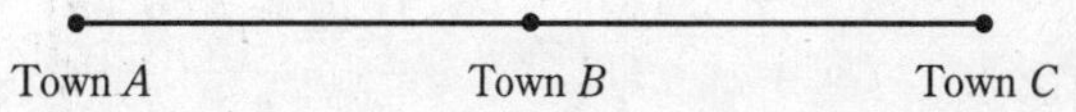

5. A car travels from Town A to Town B in 3 hours. It travels from Town B to Town C in 5 hours. If the distance AB is equal to the distance BC, what is the ratio of the car's average speed between A and B to its average speed for the whole distance AC?

(A) 5 : 3
(B) 4 : 3
(C) 1 : 1
(D) 1 : 3
(E) 1 : 5

GO ON TO THE NEXT PAGE

6. Given that ax is an integer and bx is an integer, which of the following must also be an integer?

I. a and b
II. x
III. $(a + b)x$

(A) None
(B) I only
(C) III only
(D) II and III only
(E) I, II, and III

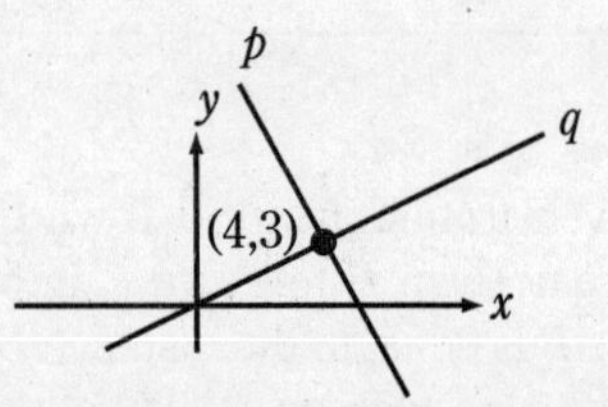

7. In the xy-coordinate system above, the lines q and p are perpendicular. The point $(3,a)$ is on line p. What is the value of a?

(A) 3
(B) 4
(C) $4\frac{1}{3}$
(D) $4\frac{2}{3}$
(E) $5\frac{1}{3}$

8. The function $f(x) = \frac{x-3}{2x+4}$ is not defined at

I. $x = 3$
II. $x = 2$
III. $x = -2$

(A) I only
(B) II only
(C) III only
(D) I and II only
(E) I and III only

9. A sphere is inscribed in a cube whose volume is 64. What is the diameter of the sphere?

(A) 2
(B) $2\sqrt{2}$
(C) 8
(D) $4\sqrt{2}$
(E) 4

GO ON TO THE NEXT PAGE

10. If $\frac{m}{n} = \frac{x}{m}$, then $x =$

(A) $\frac{m^2}{n}$
(B) $\frac{m}{n}$
(C) $\frac{n}{m^2}$
(D) $\frac{1}{n}$
(E) n

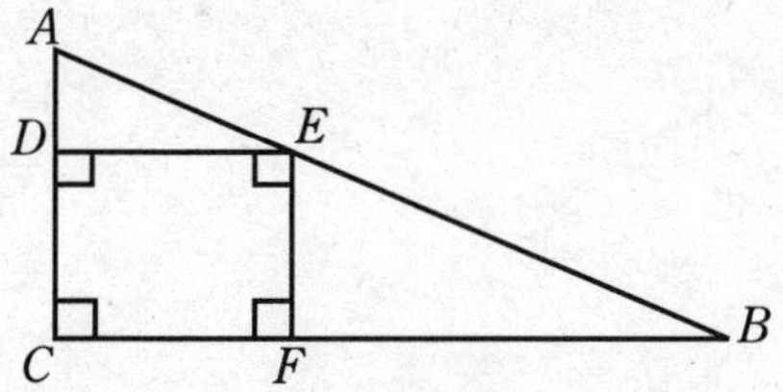

11. The rectangle $CDEF$ has been inscribed in the right triangle ABC, as shown in the figure above. If $CD = \frac{3}{4}AC$ and $CF = \frac{2}{7}BC$, what is the ratio of the area of $\triangle ABC$ to the area of $\square CDEF$?

(A) $\frac{14}{3}$
(B) $\frac{7}{3}$
(C) $\frac{7}{6}$
(D) $\frac{1}{6}$
(E) The answer cannot be determined from the information given.

12. The number of boys in a certain class exceeds the number of girls by 7. If the number of boys is $\frac{5}{4}$ of the number of girls, how many boys are there in the class?

(A) 21
(B) 28
(C) 35
(D) 42
(E) 63

13. In 1999, the population of Smithdale was 900. Every year, the population of Smithdale had a net increase of 100. For example, in 2000, the population of Smithdale was 1,000. In which of the following periods was the percent increase in population of Smithdale the greatest?

(A) 1999–2000
(B) 2000–2001
(C) 2001–2002
(D) 2002–2003
(E) The answer cannot be determined from the information given.

GO ON TO THE NEXT PAGE

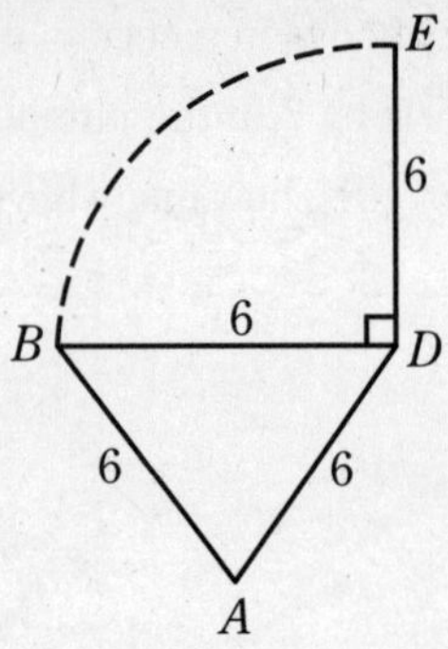

14. Arc BE is a quarter circle with radius 6, and C, which is not shown, is an arbitrary point on arc BE. If $AB = BD = AD = 6$, then all of the possible values of the perimeter P of the quadrilateral $ABCD$ are

(A) $P = 18$
(B) $12 < P \leq 18$
(C) $18 < P \leq 24$
(D) $18 < P \leq 18 + 6\sqrt{2}$
(E) $18 < P \leq 30$

15. If $x > 0$ and $y > 0$ and $x^9 = 4$ and $x^7 = \frac{9}{y^2}$, which of the following is an expression for the value of x in terms of y?

(A) $\frac{4}{9}y$
(B) $\frac{2}{3}y$
(C) $\frac{3}{2}y^2$
(D) $6y$
(E) $36y^2$

16. When Stanley received $10x$ DVDs, he then had $5y + 1$ times as many DVDs as he had originally. In terms of x and y, how many DVDs did Stanley have originally?

(A) $10x(5y + 1)$
(B) $\frac{5y+1}{10x}$
(C) $\frac{2x}{y}$
(D) $\frac{10}{5y+1}$
(E) None of the above

STOP

If you finish before time is called, you may check your work on this section only.
Do not turn to any other section in the test.

SECTION 9

Time: 20 Minutes—Turn to Section 9 (page 759) of your answer sheet to answer the questions in this section.
19 Questions

Directions: For each question in this section, select the best answer from among the choices given and fill in the corresponding circle on the answer sheet.

Each sentence below has one or two blanks, each blank indicating that something has been omitted. Beneath the sentence are five words or sets of words labeled A through E. Choose the word or set of words that, when inserted in the sentence, best fits the meaning of the sentence as a whole.

Example:

Hoping to ______ the dispute, negotiators proposed a compromise that they felt would be ______ to both labor and management.

(A) enforce...useful
(B) end...divisive
(C) overcome...unattractive
(D) extend...satisfactory
(E) resolve...acceptable

Ⓐ Ⓑ Ⓒ Ⓓ ●

1. As a truly objective person, Mr. Jones allows neither ______ attempts to please him nor open ______ on the part of his students to influence his marks.

(A) unearned...respect
(B) condescending...humor
(C) sincere...reliance
(D) backward...offense
(E) hypocritical...defiance

2. Because the subject matter was so technical, the instructor made every effort to use ______ terms to describe it.

(A) candid
(B) simplified
(C) discreet
(D) specialized
(E) involved

3. Violent crime has become so ______ in our cities that hardly a day goes by when we are not made aware of some ______ act on our local news broadcasts.

(A) scarce...momentous
(B) pervasive...benign
(C) conclusive...serious
(D) common...heinous
(E) ridiculous...unacceptable

4. Although they are ______ by intense police patrols, burglars ______ to prowl the subways.

(A) incited...decline
(B) enlivened...attempt
(C) hindered...cease
(D) persuaded...refuse
(E) impeded...continue

5. Britain's seizure of American ships and ______ of our sailors to serve in the British Navy were two major causes of the War of 1812.

(A) compelling
(B) recruiting
(C) bribing
(D) enlisting
(E) deriding

6. Since he had not worked very hard on his project, the student was quite ______ upon learning that he had won the contest.

(A) annoyed
(B) apathetic
(C) rebuffed
(D) dismayed
(E) elated

GO ON TO THE NEXT PAGE

The two passages below are followed by questions based on their content and on the relationship between the two passages. Answer the questions on the basis of what is stated or implied in the passages and in any introductory material that may be provided.

Questions 7–19 are based on the following passages.

The following two passages are about science. The first describes science in general, and the second focuses on the subject of physics, one of the disciplines of science.

Passage 1

Science, like everything else that man has created, exists, of course, to gratify certain human needs and desires. The fact that it has been steadily pursued for so many centuries, that it has attracted an ever-wider extent of attention, and that it is now the dominant intellectual interest of mankind, shows that it appeals to a very powerful and persistent group of appetites. It is not difficult to say what these appetites are, at least in their main divisions. Science is valued for its practical advantages, it is valued because it gratifies curiosity, and it is valued because it provides the imagination with objects of great aesthetic charm. This last consideration is of the least importance, so far as the layman is concerned, although it is probably the most important consideration of all to scientific men. It is quite obvious, on the other hand, that the bulk of mankind value science chiefly for the practical advantages it brings with it.

This conclusion is borne out by everything we know about the origin of science. Science seems to have come into existence merely for its bearings on practical life.

More than two thousand years before the beginning of the Christian era, both the Babylonians and the Egyptians were in possession of systematic methods of measuring space and time. They had a rudimentary geometry and a rudimentary astronomy. This rudimentary science arose to meet the practical needs of an agricultural population. Their geometry resulted from the measurements made necessary by the problems of land surveying. The cultivation of crops, dependent on the seasons, made a calendar almost a necessity. The day, as a unit of time, was, of course, imposed by nature. The movement of the moon conveniently provided another unit, the month, which was reckoned from one new moon to the next. Twelve of these months were taken to constitute a year, and the necessary adjustments were made from time to time by putting in extra months.

Passage 2

Let's be honest right at the start. Physics is neither particularly easy to comprehend nor easy to love, but then again, *what*—or for that matter, *who*—is? For most of us it is a new vision, a different way of understanding with its own scales, rhythms, and forms. And yet, as with *Macbeth*, *Mona Lisa*, or *La Traviata*, physics has its rewards. Surely you have already somehow prejudged this science. It's all too easy to compartmentalize our human experience: science in one box; and music, art, and literature in other boxes.

The Western mind delights in little boxes—life is easier to analyze when it's presented in small pieces in small compartments (we call it specialization). It is our traditional way of seeing the trees and missing the forest. The label on the box for physics too often reads "Caution: Not for Common Consumption" or "Free from Sentiment." If you can, please tear off that label and discard the box or we will certainly, sooner or later, bore each other to death. There is nothing more tedious than the endless debate between humanist and scientist on whose vision is truer; each of us is less for what we lack of the other.

It is pointless and even worse to separate physics from the body of all creative work, to pluck it out from history, to shear it from philosophy, and then to present it pristine, pure, all-knowing, and infallible. We know nothing of what will be with absolute certainty. There is no scientific tome of unassailable, immutable truth. Yet what little we do know about physics reveals an inspiring grandeur and intricate beauty.

7. The main idea of Passage 1 is that

(A) science originated and developed because of the practical advantages it offers
(B) the Egyptians and the Babylonians used scientific methods to meet the practical needs of feeding their people
(C) the use of geometry and astronomy are very important for agricultural development
(D) science has a different value for scientists than it does for the rest of the population
(E) science is valued not only for its practical contributions to mankind but also for its potential to stir the imagination

8. According to Passage 1,

(A) the Babylonians and the Egyptians were the first to use scientific methods
(B) the Christians were the first to have a calendar
(C) a 12-month calendar was first used by the Egyptians and Babylonians
(D) the Christians preceded the Babylonians and Egyptians
(E) scientists are probably more attracted to the charm of science than to its practical benefits

GO ON TO THE NEXT PAGE

9. The author of Passage 1 implies that scientists are generally

(A) sociable
(B) imaginative
(C) practical
(D) philosophical
(E) arrogant

10. The word "rudimentary" in line 23 means

(A) sophisticated
(B) flawed
(C) unworkable
(D) basic
(E) coarse

11. According to the author of Passage 2, what does the label on the box for physics suggest about physics?

(A) It is a dangerous area of study.
(B) It is a cause for great excitement.
(C) It is uninteresting to the ordinary person.
(D) It is difficult to understand because it is completely subjective.
(E) It is a subject that should be elective but not required.

12. What statement does the author of Passage 2 make about physics?

(A) It should be recognized for its unique beauty.
(B) It is a boring course of study.
(C) It appeals only to the Western mind.
(D) It is superior to music, art, and literature.
(E) It is unpopular with people who are romantic.

13. What is the main idea of Passage 2?

(A) Scientists contribute more to mankind than do humanists.
(B) The Western mind is more precise than other minds.
(C) Complete vision needs both the scientist and the humanist.
(D) Humanists and scientists share no common ground.
(E) Physics is as important as other science.

14. In which manner does the author of Passage 2 address his audience?

(A) affectionately
(B) arrogantly
(C) humorously
(D) cynically
(E) frankly

15. In line 47, the phrase "seeing the trees and missing the forest" means

(A) putting experiences into categories
(B) viewing the world too narrowly
(C) analyzing scientific discoveries
(D) making judgments too hastily
(E) ignoring the beauty of natural surroundings

16. The author of Passage 2 leaves out an important aspect of the subject that is addressed in Passage 1. This aspect is the

(A) reaction of laymen to physics
(B) the specialization in science
(C) the purity of physics
(D) the practical applications of physics
(E) the arguments between humanists and scientists

17. Which device or method does the author of Passage 2 use that is not used by the author of Passage 1?

(A) analogy through objects
(B) critique
(C) contrast with respect to perceived values
(D) historical referencing
(E) examples to support a claim

18. Which subject is not directly mentioned in either passage?

(A) agriculture
(B) astronomy
(C) art
(D) philosophy
(E) chemistry

19. The word "intricate" in line 61 means

(A) eloquent
(B) complicated
(C) devastating
(D) uninteresting
(E) pointless

STOP

If you finish before time is called, you may check your work on this section only. Do not turn to any other section in the test.

SECTION 10

Time: 10 Minutes—Turn to Section 10 (page 759) of your answer sheet to answer the questions in this section.
14 Questions

Directions: For each question in this section, select the best answer from among the choices given and fill in the corresponding circle on the answer sheet.

The following sentences test correctness and effectiveness of expression. Part of each sentence or the entire sentence is underlined; beneath each sentence are five ways of phrasing the underlined material. Choice A repeats the original phrasing; the other four choices are different. If you think the original phrasing produces a better sentence than any of the alternatives, select Choice A; if not, select one of the other choices.

In making your selection, follow the requirements of standard written English; that is, pay attention to grammar, choice of words, sentence construction, and punctuation. Your selection should result in the most effective sentence—clear and precise, without awkwardness or ambiguity.

EXAMPLE:

Laura Ingalls Wilder published her first book and she was sixty-five years old then.

(A) and she was sixty-five years old then
(B) when she was sixty-five
(C) at age sixty-five years old
(D) upon the reaching of sixty-five years
(E) at the time when she was sixty-five

Ⓐ ● Ⓒ Ⓓ Ⓔ

1. In the next booklet, the sales manager and personnel director will tell you something about his work.

(A) the sales manager and personnel director will tell you something about his work
(B) the sales manager who is also director of personnel will tell you something about their work
(C) the sales manager who is also personnel director will tell you something
(D) the sales manager and personnel director will tell you something as it applies to his work
(E) the sales manager and the personnel director will tell you something about what his work is

2. I have enjoyed the study of the Spanish language not only because of its beauty but also to make use of it in business.

(A) to make use of it in business
(B) because of its use in business
(C) on account it is useful in business
(D) one needs it in business
(E) since all business people use it

3. Known to every man, woman, and child in the town, friends were never lacking to my grandfather.

(A) friends were never lacking to my grandfather
(B) my grandfather was not lacking to his friends
(C) friends never lacked my grandfather
(D) my grandfather never lacked no friends
(E) my grandfather never lacked friends

4. No sooner had he entered the room when the lights went out and everyone began to scream.

(A) when the lights went out
(B) than the lights went out
(C) and the lights went out
(D) but the lights went out
(E) the lights went out

5. John, whose mother is a teacher, is not so good a student as many other friends I have with no academic background in their families.

(A) is not so good a student as many other friends
(B) is not as good a student like many other friends
(C) is not quite the student as are other friends
(D) as a student is not as good as many other friends
(E) does not have the studious qualities of many other friends

GO ON TO THE NEXT PAGE

6. After our waiting in line for three hours, much to our disgust, the tickets had been sold out when we reached the window.

(A) much to our disgust, the tickets had been sold out
(B) the tickets had been, much to our disgust, sold out
(C) the tickets had been sold out, much to our disgust,
(D) the sold-out tickets had, much to our disgust, been disposed of
(E) and much to our disgust, the tickets had been sold out

7. When the members of the committee are at odds, and when also, in addition, they are in the process of offering their resignations, problems become indissoluble.

(A) and when also, in addition, they are in the process
(B) and also when they are in the process
(C) and when, in addition, they are in the process
(D) they are in the process
(E) and when the members of the committee are in the process

8. There is no objection to him joining the party if he is willing to fit in with the plans of the group.

(A) There is no objection to him joining the party
(B) There is no objection on him joining the party
(C) There is no objection to his joining the party
(D) No objection will be raised upon him joining the party
(E) If he decides to join the party, there will be no objection

9. As no one knows the truth as fully as him, no one but him can provide the testimony needed to clear the accused of the very serious charges.

(A) as fully as him, no one but him
(B) as fully as he, no one but him
(C) as fully as he, no one but he
(D) as fully as he does, no one but he
(E) as fully as he does, no one but he alone

10. After having completed his experiments on cancer, the scientist tried to determine if his findings could be used to help prevent this dreaded disease.

(A) After having completed his experiments on cancer
(B) As soon as he completed his experiments on cancer
(C) Having completed his experiments on cancer
(D) After the experiments of the scientist on cancer were completed
(E) When his experiments on cancer are completed

11. The principal, as well as the students and faculty, is trying to affect constructive changes in the school curriculum.

(A) is trying to affect
(B) try to affect
(C) are trying to effect
(D) is trying to effect
(E) does try to encourage

12. Because of the recent General Motors strike, less workers will be hired in the coming year.

(A) less workers will be hired in the coming year
(B) not as many workers will be hired in the coming year as before
(C) in the coming year less workers will be hired
(D) few workers will be hired in the coming year
(E) fewer workers will be hired in the coming year

13. If the director would have changed some of the dialogue in the script, the scene would have worked better.

(A) If the director would have changed
(B) If changes had been made in
(C) If the director had changed
(D) Had there been changes made in
(E) If there would have been changes in

14. Neither Bill nor Jack had their money with them.

(A) Neither Bill nor Jack had their money with them.
(B) Neither of the boys had their money with them.
(C) Neither Bill or Jack had his money with him.
(D) Neither boy had his money with him.
(E) Neither Bill nor Jack had his money with him.

STOP

If you finish before time is called, you may check your work on this section only. Do not turn to any other section in the test.

How Did You Do on This Test?

Step 1. Go to the Answer Key on pages 808–810.

Step 2. For your "raw score," calculate it using the directions on pages 811–812.

Step 3. Get your "scaled score" for the test by referring to the Raw Score/Scaled Score Conversion Tables on pages 813–815.

THERE'S ALWAYS ROOM FOR IMPROVEMENT!

Answer Key for Practice Test 3

Math

Section 2

	Correct Answer
1	C
2	E
3	C
4	E
5	A
6	E
7	C
8	E
9	A
10	B
11	C
12	B
13	E
14	A
15	C
16	B
17	B
18	C
19	B
20	A

Number correct

Number incorrect

Section 3

	Correct Answer
1	E
2	B
3	A
4	C
5	C
6	D
7	C
8	D
9	B
10	B
11	C
12	D
13	C
14	B
15	E
16	A
17	E
18	D
19	D
20	B

Number correct

Number incorrect

Section 6

	Correct Answer
1	D
2	B
3	D
4	D
5	D
6	B
7	D
8	D

Number correct

Number incorrect

Student-Produced Response Questions

9	6/1, 6, or 12/2
10	9
11	105
12	0
13	33 1/3 or 33.3
14	5
15	24
16	7/8 or .875
17	84
18	5

Number correct

Number incorrect

Section 8

	Correct Answer
1	B
2	B
3	A
4	E
5	B
6	C
7	C
8	C
9	E
10	A
11	B
12	C
13	A
14	D
15	B
16	C

Number correct

Number incorrect

Critical Reading and Writing

Critical Reading

Section 4

	Correct Answer
1	C
2	A
3	E
4	B
5	D
6	A
7	A
8	A
9	A
10	D
11	B
12	A
13	C
14	A
15	E
16	C
17	B
18	C
19	D
20	B
21	A
22	E
23	A
24	B

Number correct

Number incorrect

Section 7

	Correct Answer
1	D
2	B
3	C
4	B
5	C
6	D
7	A
8	B
9	C
10	B
11	D
12	B
13	C
14	E
15	E
16	E
17	D
18	B
19	C
20	E
21	E
22	C
23	B
24	A

Number correct

Number incorrect

Section 9

	Correct Answer
1	E
2	B
3	D
4	E
5	A
6	E
7	A
8	E
9	B
10	D
11	C
12	A
13	C
14	E
15	B
16	D
17	A
18	E
19	B

Number correct

Number incorrect

Writing

Section 1

____

Essay score

Section 5

	Correct Answer
1	C
2	B
3	C
4	D
5	A
6	D
7	D
8	A
9	E
10	B
11	A
12	D
13	E
14	A
15	C
16	D
17	E
18	C
19	B
20	D
21	A
22	B
23	A
24	C
25	E
26	A
27	A
28	C
29	C
30	C
31	D
32	B
33	E
34	A
35	E

____

Number correct

____

Number incorrect

Section 10

	Correct Answer
1	A
2	B
3	E
4	B
5	A
6	C
7	C
8	C
9	B
10	C
11	D
12	E
13	C
14	E

____

Number correct

____

Number incorrect

Scoring the SAT Practice Test 3

Check your responses with the correct answers on the previous pages. Fill in the blanks below and do the calculations to get your Math, Critical Reading, and Writing raw scores. Use the table to find your Math, Critical Reading, and Writing scaled scores.

Get Your Math Score

How many Math questions did you get **right**?

Section 2: Questions 1–20 ________

Section 6: Questions 1–18 + ________

Section 8: Questions 1–16 + ________

Total = ________ **(A)**

How many Math questions did you get **wrong**?

Section 2: Questions 1–20 ________

Section 6: Questions 1–8 + ________

Section 8: Questions 1–16 + ________

Total = ________

× 0.25 = ________ **(B)**

A – B = ________

Math Raw Score

Round Math raw score to the nearest whole number.

____

Use the Score Conversion Table to find your Math scaled score.

____

Get Your Critical Reading Score

How many Critical Reading questions did you get **right**?

Section 4: Questions 1–24 ________

Section 7: Questions 1–24 + ________

Section 9: Questions 1–19 + ________

Total = ________ **(A)**

How many Critical Reading questions did you get **wrong**?

Section 4: Questions 1–24 ________

Section 7: Questions 1–24 + ________

Section 9: Questions 1–19 + ________

Total = ________

× 0.25 = ________ **(B)**

A – B = ________

Critical Reading Raw Score

Round Critical Reading raw score to the nearest whole number.

____

Use the Score Conversion Table to find your Critical Reading scaled score.

____

Get Your Writing Score

How many multiple-choice Writing questions did you get **right**?

Section 5: Questions 1–35 ________

Section 10: Questions 1–14 + ________

Total = ________ **(A)**

How many multiple-choice Writing questions did you get **wrong**?

Section 5: Questions 1–35 ________

Section 10: Questions 1–14 + ________

Total = ________

× 0.25 = ________ **(B)**

A – B = ________

Writing Raw Score

Round Writing raw score to the nearest whole number.

____

Use the Score Conversion Table to find your Writing multiple-choice scaled score.

____

Estimate your Essay score using the Essay Scoring Guide and the sample Essays.

____

Use the SAT Score Conversion Table for Writing Composite to find your Writing scaled score. You will need your Writing raw score and your Essay score to use this table.

____

SAT Score Conversion Table

Raw Score	Critical Reading Scaled Score	Math Scaled Score	Writing Multiple-Choice Scaled Score*	Raw Score	Critical Reading Scaled Score	Math Scaled Score	Writing Multiple-Choice Scaled Score*
67	800			31	510	550	60
66	800			30	510	540	58
65	790			29	500	530	57
64	770			28	490	520	56
63	750			27	490	520	55
62	740			26	480	510	54
61	730			25	480	500	53
60	720			24	470	490	52
59	700			23	460	480	51
58	690			22	460	480	50
57	690			21	450	470	49
56	680			20	440	460	48
55	670			19	440	450	47
54	660	800		18	430	450	46
53	650	790		17	420	440	45
52	650	760		16	420	430	44
51	640	740		15	410	420	44
50	630	720		14	400	410	43
49	620	710	80	13	400	410	42
48	620	700	80	12	390	400	41
47	610	680	80	11	380	390	40
46	600	670	79	10	370	380	39
45	600	660	78	9	360	370	38
44	590	650	76	8	350	360	38
43	590	640	74	7	340	350	37
42	580	630	73	6	330	340	36
41	570	630	71	5	320	330	35
40	570	620	70	4	310	320	34
39	560	610	69	3	300	310	32
38	550	600	67	2	280	290	31
37	550	590	66	1	270	280	30
36	540	580	65	0	250	260	28
35	540	580	64	–1	230	240	27
34	530	570	63	–2	210	220	25
33	520	560	62	–3	200	200	23
32	520	550	61	–4	200	200	20
				and below			

This table is for use only with the test in this book.

* The Writing multiple-choice score is reported on a 20–80 scale. Use the SAT Score Conversion Table for Writing Composite for the total writing scaled score.

SAT Score Conversion Table for Writing Composite

Writing Multiple-Choice Raw Score	Essay Raw Score						
	0	1	2	3	4	5	6
–12	200	200	200	210	240	270	300
–11	200	200	200	210	240	270	300
–10	200	200	200	210	240	270	300
–9	200	200	200	210	240	270	300
–8	200	200	200	210	240	270	300
–7	200	200	200	210	240	270	300
–6	200	200	200	210	240	270	300
–5	200	200	200	210	240	270	300
–4	200	200	200	230	270	300	330
–3	200	210	230	250	290	320	350
–2	200	230	250	280	310	340	370
–1	210	240	260	290	320	360	380
0	230	260	280	300	340	370	400
1	240	270	290	320	350	380	410
2	250	280	300	330	360	390	420
3	260	290	310	340	370	400	430
4	270	300	320	350	380	410	440
5	280	310	330	360	390	420	450
6	290	320	340	360	400	430	460
7	290	330	340	370	410	440	470
8	300	330	350	380	410	450	470
9	310	340	360	390	420	450	480
10	320	350	370	390	430	460	490
11	320	360	370	400	440	470	500
12	330	360	380	410	440	470	500
13	340	370	390	420	450	480	510
14	350	380	390	420	460	490	520
15	350	380	400	430	460	500	530
16	360	390	410	440	470	500	530
17	370	400	420	440	480	510	540
18	380	410	420	450	490	520	550
19	380	410	430	460	490	530	560
20	390	420	440	470	500	530	560
21	400	430	450	480	510	540	570
22	410	440	460	480	520	550	580
23	420	450	470	490	530	560	590
24	420	460	470	500	540	570	600
25	430	460	480	510	540	580	610

Writing Multiple-Choice Raw Score	Essay Raw Score						
	0	1	2	3	4	5	6
26	440	470	490	520	550	590	610
27	450	480	500	530	560	590	620
28	460	490	510	540	570	600	630
29	470	500	520	550	580	610	640
30	480	510	530	560	590	620	650
31	490	520	540	560	600	630	660
32	500	530	550	570	610	640	670
33	510	540	550	580	620	650	680
34	510	550	560	590	630	660	690
35	520	560	570	600	640	670	700
36	530	560	580	610	650	680	710
37	540	570	590	620	660	690	720
38	550	580	600	630	670	700	730
39	560	600	610	640	680	710	740
40	580	610	620	650	690	720	750
41	590	620	640	660	700	730	760
42	600	630	650	680	710	740	770
43	610	640	660	690	720	750	780
44	620	660	670	700	740	770	800
45	640	670	690	720	750	780	800
46	650	690	700	730	770	800	800
47	670	700	720	750	780	800	800
48	680	720	730	760	800	800	800
49	680	720	730	760	800	800	800

This table is for use only with the test in this book.

Chart for Self-Appraisal Based on the Practice Test You Have Just Taken

The Chart for Self-Appraisal below tells you quickly where your SAT strengths and weaknesses lie. Check or circle the appropriate box in accordance with the number of your correct answers for each area of the Practice Test you have just taken.

	Writing (Multiple-choice)	*Sentence Completions*	*Reading Comprehension*	*Math Questions**
EXCELLENT	42–49	16–19	40–48	44–54
GOOD	37–41	13–15	35–39	32–43
FAIR	31–36	9–12	26–34	27–31
POOR	20–30	5–8	17–25	16–26
VERY POOR	0–19	0–4	0–16	0–15

* Sections 2, 6, 8 only.

Note: In our tests, we have chosen to have Section 3 as the experimental section. We have also chosen it to be a math section since we felt that students may need more practice in the math area than in the verbal area. Note that on the actual SAT you will take, the order of the sections can vary and you will not know which one is experimental, so it is wise to answer all sections and not to leave any section out.

SAT-I VERBAL AND MATH SCORE/PERCENTILE CONVERSION TABLE

Critical Reading and Writing

SAT scaled verbal score	Percentile rank
800	99.7+
790	99.5
740–780	99
700–730	97
670–690	95
640–660	91
610–630	85
580–600	77
550–570	68
510–540	57
480–500	46
440–470	32
410–430	21
380–400	13
340–370	6
300–330	2
230–290	1
200–220	0–0.5

Math

SAT scaled math score	Percentile rank
800	99.5+
770–790	99.5
720–760	99
670–710	97
640–660	94
610–630	89
590–600	84
560–580	77
530–550	68
510–520	59
480–500	48
450–470	37
430–440	26
390–420	16
350–380	8
310–340	2
210–300	0.5
200	0

Section 1—Essay

The following are guidelines for scoring the essay.

The SAT Scoring Guide

Score of 6	Score of 5	Score of 4
An essay in this category is *outstanding,* demonstrating *clear and consistent mastery,* although it may have a few minor errors. A typical essay	An essay in this category is *effective,* demonstrating *reasonably consistent mastery,* although it will have occasional errors or lapses in quality. A typical essay	An essay in this category is *competent,* demonstrating *adequate mastery,* although it will have lapses in quality. A typical essay
• effectively and insightfully develops a point of view on the issue and demonstrates outstanding critical thinking, using clearly appropriate examples, reasons, and other evidence to support its position	• effectively develops a point of view on the issue and demonstrates strong critical thinking, generally using appropriate examples, reasons, and other evidence to support its position	• develops a point of view on the issue and demonstrates competent critical thinking, using adequate examples, reasons, and other evidence to support its position
• is well organized and clearly focused, demonstrating clear coherence and smooth progression of ideas	• is well organized and focused, demonstrating coherence and progression of ideas	• is generally organized and focused, demonstrating some coherence and progression of ideas
• exhibits skillful use of language, using a varied, accurate, and apt vocabulary	• exhibits facility in the use of language, using appropriate vocabulary	• exhibits adequate but inconsistent facility in the use of language, using generally appropriate vocabulary
• demonstrates meaningful variety in sentence structure	• demonstrates variety in sentence structure	• demonstrates some variety in sentence structure
• is free of most errors in grammar, usage, and mechanics	• is generally free of most errors in grammar, usage, and mechanics	• has some errors in grammar, usage, and mechanics
Score of 3	**Score of 2**	**Score of 1**
An essay in this category is *inadequate,* but demonstrates *developing mastery,* and is marked by ONE OR MORE of the following weaknesses:	An essay in this category is *seriously limited,* demonstrating *little mastery,* and is flawed by ONE OR MORE of the following weaknesses:	An essay in this category is *fundamentally lacking,* demonstrating *very little* or *no mastery,* and is severely flawed by ONE OR MORE of the following weaknesses:
• develops a point of view on the issue, demonstrating some critical thinking, but may do so inconsistently or use inadequate examples, reasons, or other evidence to support its position	• develops a point of view on the issue that is vague or seriously limited, demonstrating weak critical thinking, providing inappropriate or insufficient examples, reasons, or other evidence to support its position	• develops no viable point of view on the issue, or provides little or no evidence to support its position
• is limited in its organization or focus, or may demonstrate some lapses in coherence or progression of ideas	• is poorly organized and/or focused, or demonstrates serious problems with coherence or progression of ideas	• is disorganized or unfocused, resulting in a disjointed or incoherent essay
• displays developing facility in the use of language, but sometimes uses weak vocabulary or inappropriate word choice	• displays very little facility in the use of language, using very limited vocabulary or incorrect word choice	• displays fundamental errors in vocabulary
• lacks variety or demonstrates problems in sentence structure	• demonstrates frequent problems in sentence structure	• demonstrates severe flaws in sentence structure
• contains an accumulation of errors in grammar, usage, and mechanics	• contains errors in grammar, usage, and mechanics so serious that meaning is somewhat obscured	• contains pervasive errors in grammar, usage, or mechanics that persistently interfere with meaning

Essays not written on the essay assignment will receive a score of zero.

Explanatory Answers for Practice Test 3

Section 2: Math

As you read these solutions, you are advised to do two things if you answered the Math question incorrectly:

1. When a specific Math Strategy is referred to in the solution, study that strategy, which you will find in "19 Math Strategies" (beginning on page 69).
2. When the solution directs you to the "Complete Math Refresher" (beginning on page 167)—for example, Math Refresher 305—study the 305 Math principle to get a clear idea of the Math operation that was necessary for you to know in order to answer the question correctly.

1. Choice C is correct. **(Use Strategy 2: Translate from words to algebra.)** Let n = the number. We are told

$$\frac{n}{3} = n \quad \boxed{1}$$

Subtracting $\frac{n}{3}$ from both sides of $\boxed{1}$,

$$n - \frac{n}{3} = 0 \quad \boxed{2}$$

Multiplying $\boxed{2}$ by 3, we get

$$3\left(n - \frac{n}{3}\right) = 0$$
$$3n - n = 0$$
$$2n = 0$$
$$n = 0$$

(Math Refresher #200 and #406)

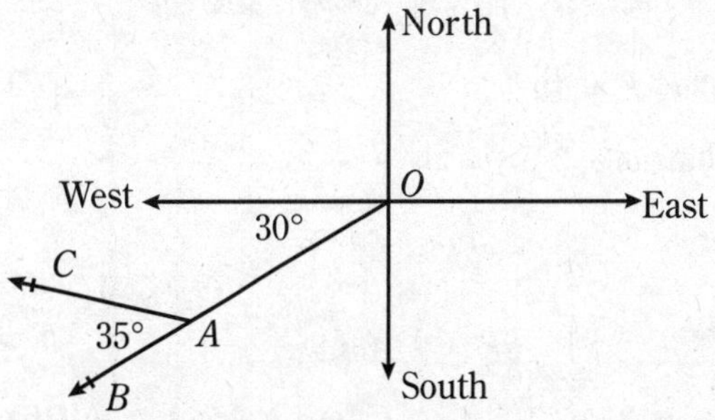

2. Choice E is correct. **(Use Strategy 14: Draw lines to help solve the problem.)**

Originally, the man is facing in the direction of OA. After he turns, he is facing in the direction of $\overrightarrow{AC}$, where $m\angle CAB = 35$. We want to find out the direction of $\overrightarrow{AC}$ with respect to the North–South–East–West axes. In other words, when we redraw the above diagram with $\ell \parallel W\text{-}E$ axis, and $m \parallel N\text{-}S$ axis, then $\overrightarrow{AC}$ is $x°$ north of west. $\boxed{1}$

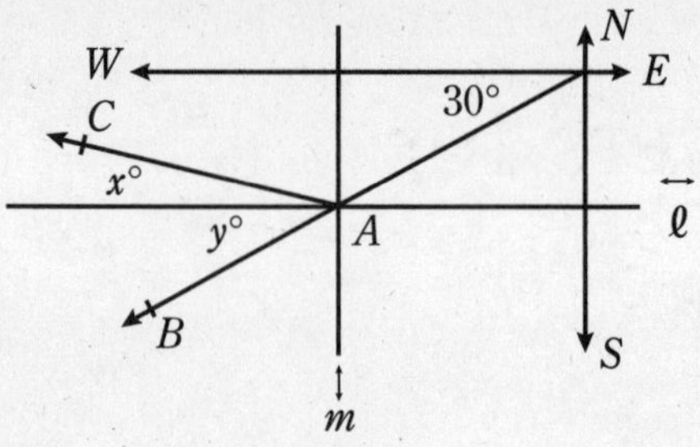

Since $m\angle CAB = 35$, then

$$x + y = 35 \qquad \boxed{2}$$

Since $\ell \parallel W\text{-}E$ axis, then

$$y = 30° \qquad \boxed{3}$$

Subtracting $\boxed{3}$ from $\boxed{2}$,

$$x = 5° \qquad \boxed{4}$$

Thus, using $\boxed{4}$ and $\boxed{1}$, $\overrightarrow{AC}$ is 5° north of west.

(Math Refresher #504 and #501)

3. Choice C is correct.

Short Method: Given $\frac{9}{5}K = 18 \qquad \boxed{1}$

(Use Strategy 13: Find unknowns by division.)

Dividing $\boxed{1}$ by 9, we have

$$\left(\frac{1}{\cancel{9}}\right)\frac{\cancel{9}}{5}K = \overset{2}{\cancel{18}}\left(\frac{1}{\cancel{9}}\right)$$

$$\frac{1}{5}K = 2 \text{ (Answer)}$$

Long Method: Given $\frac{9}{5}K = 18 \qquad \boxed{1}$

Multiply $\boxed{1}$ by $\frac{5}{9}$, getting

$$\left(\frac{\cancel{5}}{\cancel{9}}\right)\frac{\cancel{9}}{\cancel{5}}K = \overset{2}{\cancel{18}}\left(\frac{5}{\cancel{9}}\right)$$

Finding $K = 10 \qquad \boxed{2}$

Multiplying $\boxed{2}$ by $\frac{1}{5}$ gives

$$\frac{1}{5}K = \overset{2}{\cancel{10}}\left(\frac{1}{\cancel{5}}\right)$$

$$\frac{1}{5}K = 2 \text{ (Answer)}$$

(Math Refresher #406)

4. Choice E is correct. **(Use Strategy 8: When all choices must be tested, start with E and work backward.)** The only way to solve this question is to test the choices one by one. We start with Choice E, and it is correct.

5. Choice A is correct.

Given: $x, y, z < 0 \qquad \boxed{1}$
$x < y \qquad \boxed{2}$
$y < z \qquad \boxed{3}$

(Use Strategy 6: Know how to manipulate inequalities.)

Method 1: When you multiply an inequality by a negative number, you must reverse the inequality. For example, multiplying $\boxed{2}$ and $\boxed{3}$ by x, we get

$$x^2 > xy \qquad \boxed{4}$$
$$xy > xz \qquad \boxed{5}$$

multiplying $\boxed{2}$ and $\boxed{3}$ by z, we get

$$xz > yz \qquad \boxed{6}$$
$$yz > z^2 \qquad \boxed{7}$$

Comparing $\boxed{4}$, $\boxed{5}$, $\boxed{6}$, and $\boxed{7}$, we have

$$x^2 > xy > xz > yz > z^2$$

Thus, Choice A is correct.

(Use Strategy 7: Use numerics to help.)

Method 2: Choose specific numeric values for x, y, z satisfying $\boxed{1}$, $\boxed{2}$, and $\boxed{3}$.

For example, let $x = -3$, $y = -2$, $z = -1$
The choices become

(A) 1
(B) 2
(C) 3
(D) 6
(E) 9

Choice A is correct.

(Math Refresher #419, #423, and #431)

6. Choice E is the correct answer. **(Use Strategy 11: Use new definitions carefully. These problems are generally easy.)** The first few terms of the sequence are found as follows:

Given: Term 1 = 2

By definition, Term 2 = (Term 1 − 2)3
= (2 − 2)3
= (0)3
Term 2 = 0

Term 3 = (Term 2 − 2)3
= (0 − 2)3
= (−2)3
= −6

Term 4 = (Term 3 − 2)3
= (−6 − 2)3
= (−8)3
= −24

and so on.
2, 0, −6, −24 are all even, so Choices A, B, C, and D can be eliminated.

(Math Refresher #431)

7. Choice C is correct. **(Use Strategy 17: Use the given information effectively.)** $n = \frac{3}{8}$ is a member of both sets. Note that n is not an integer in this case, and certainly in this case n is not equal to 6. Thus I and III are not true for this case. Members of both sets are $\frac{3}{8}$, 6, and 8. So for any of these members, $8n$ is an integer. Thus II is always true.

(Math Refresher #801)

8. Choice E is correct.

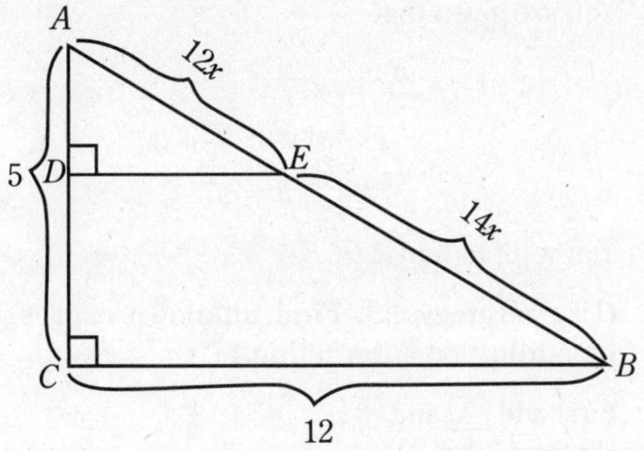

Method 1: **(Use Strategy 18: Remember right triangle facts.)** Triangle BCA is a right triangle, so we can use the Pythagorean Theorem:

$$(AB)^2 = (AC)^2 + (BC)^2$$
$$(12x + 14x)^2 = 5^2 + 12^2$$
$$(26x)^2 = 25 + 144$$
$$676x^2 = 169$$
$$x^2 = \frac{169}{676}$$

(Use Strategy 19: Factor and reduce.)

$$x^2 = \frac{\cancel{13} \times \cancel{13}}{\cancel{13} \times \cancel{13} \times 4} = \frac{1}{4}$$
$$x = \frac{1}{2}$$

Method 2: **(Use Strategy 18: Remember special right triangles.)** Triangle BCA is a right triangle with legs 5 and 12. 5–12–13 is a special right triangle. Thus, AB must = 13

Therefore $12x + 14x = 13$
$$26x = 13$$
$$x = \frac{13}{26}$$
$$x = \frac{1}{2}$$

(Math Refresher #509 and #406)

9. Choice A is correct. **(Use Strategy 6: Know how to manipulate inequalities.)** The least possible value of $x + y$ is when x is least and y is least. You can see that the smallest value of x is -4 (not 2 or -2) in the inequality $1 < |x| < 5$. The smallest value of y is -6 (not 3 or -3) in the inequality $2 < |y| < 7$. Thus the smallest value of $x + y = -10$.

(Math Refresher #615 and #419)

10. Choice B is correct. **(Use Strategy 17: Use the given information effectively.)** By looking at the diagram, we have

$$P_1 = -2$$
$$P_2 = -1$$

We can approximate the other numbers by looking at their positions on the number line:

$$P_3 \approx \frac{1}{3}$$
$$P_4 \approx \frac{2}{3}$$
$$P_5 \approx \frac{3}{2}$$

Thus,

$$P_1 P_2 P_3 P_4 P_5 \approx (-2)(-1)\left(\frac{1}{3}\right)\left(\frac{2}{\cancel{3}}\right)\left(\frac{\cancel{3}}{2}\right)$$
$$P_1 P_2 P_3 P_4 P_5 \approx \frac{2}{3}$$

(Math Refresher #410)

11. Choice C is correct. **(Use Strategy 2: Translate from words to algebra.)** Let the 3 consecutive even integers be

$$x, x + 2, x + 4 \qquad \boxed{1}$$

where x is even. We are told that

$$x + x + 2 + x + 4 = K$$
or $$3x + 6 = K \qquad \boxed{2}$$

From $\boxed{1}$, we know that

$$x - 5, x - 3, x - 1$$

must be the 3 consecutive odd integers immediately preceding x. We are told that

$$x - 5 + x - 3 + x - 1 = y$$
or $$3x - 9 = y \qquad \boxed{3}$$

(Use Strategy 13: Find unknown expressions by subtraction.) Subtracting $\boxed{3}$ from $\boxed{2}$, we get

$$15 = K - y$$
or $$y = K - 15$$

(Math Refresher #200 and #406)

12. Choice B is correct. **(Use Strategy 2: Translate from words to math.)** From the diagram we can see that 25% is water, so $0.25 \times 2 \text{ lb} = \frac{1}{2}$ lb is water.

(Math Refresher #705)

13. Choice E is correct. **(Use Strategy 16: Watch out for questions that can be tricky.)** The subsets of {1,2,3} are {1}, {2}, {3}, {1,2}, {1,3}, {2,3}, {1,2,3}, and { }.

(Math Refresher #805)

14. Choice A is correct. **(Use Strategy 17: Use the given information effectively.)** A segment that divides the area of a circle into two equal parts must be a diameter. Thus, segment *RS* must go through point *O*.

Since *ROS* is a diameter, then *RO* = *OS*, each segment being a radius.

Since *R* is in the 2nd quadrant, *S* must be in the 4th quadrant.

You can see that the *x*-coordinate of *S* must be positive and the *y*-coordinate of S must be negative.

$$S = (-1(-6), -1(8))$$
$$S = (6, -8)$$

(Math Refresher #524 and #410b)

	First Place (6 points)	Second Place (4 points)	Third Place (2 points)
Game 1			
Game 2		Bob	
Game 3			Bob

15. Choice C is correct. **(Use Strategy 17: Use the given information effectively.)** Carl can attain the *minimum* possible score by placing third in Game 1 and Game 2 and second in Game 3.

From the chart he would have 2, 2, and 4 points for each of these finishes.
Thus, minimum score = 2 + 2 + 4
minimum score = 8 points

(Math Refresher #701 and #702)

16. Choice B is correct. **(Use Strategy 17: Use the given information effectively.)** Use $y = mx + b$ for representation of line *k*. *m* is the slope of the line and *b* is the *y*-intercept (that is, the value of *y* when $x = 0$). You can see that a point on the graph is at $x = 3$ and $y = 2$ from the points (0,2) and (3,0). Thus, substituting $x = 3$ and $y = 2$ into $y = mx + b$, we get $2 = m(3) + b$. Since *m* is the slope of the graph and is equal to -1, we get

$$2 = (-1)(3) + b.$$
$$2 = -3 + b$$

and so $5 = b$.

(Math Refresher #415 and #416)

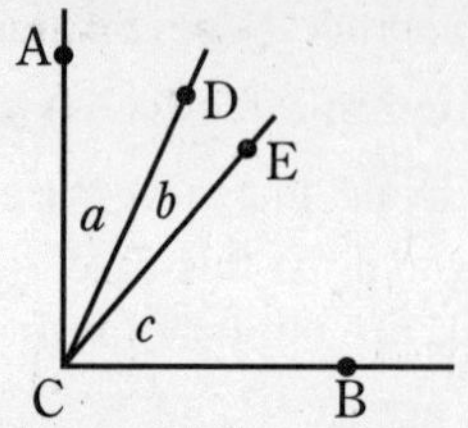

17. Choice B is correct. **(Use Strategy 14: Label unknown quantities.)**

Label angles as above with *a, b, c*.

You are given that

$$a + b + c = 90 \quad \boxed{1}$$
$$b + c = 62 \quad \boxed{2}$$
$$a + b = 37 \quad \boxed{3}$$

You want to find $\angle DCE = b$

(Use Strategy 13: Find unknown expressions by adding or subtracting.)

First add $\boxed{2}$ and $\boxed{3}$:
We get:

$$a + 2b + c = 62 + 37 = 99 \quad \boxed{4}$$

Now subtract $\boxed{1}$ from $\boxed{4}$:

$$\begin{array}{r} a + 2b + c = 99 \\ a + b + c = 90 \\ \hline b \quad\quad = 9 \end{array}$$

(Math Refresher #509)

18. Choice C is correct. **(Use Strategy 2: Remember how to calculate percent.)**

Winning percentage =

$$\frac{\text{\# of games won}}{\text{total \# of games played}} \times 100$$

For example,

Winning % for pitcher A

$$= \frac{4}{4+2} \times 100 = \frac{4}{6} \times 100$$
$$= \frac{\not{2} \times 2}{\not{2} \times 3} \times 100$$
$$= \frac{200}{3} = 66\frac{2}{3}\%$$

For each pitcher, we have

Pitcher	Winning Percentage
A	$66\frac{2}{3}\%$
B	60%
C	80%
D	50%
E	75%

Pitcher C has the highest winning percentage.

(Math Refresher #106)

19. Choice B is correct. **(Use Strategy 11: Use new definitions carefully.)**

Given: A, B, C, ..., L =

1, 2, 3, ..., 12 (respectively) [1]

The time on the watch is 15 minutes before 1. [2]

From [1], we know that

E = 5 and A = 1 [3]

Substituting [3] into [2], we have

3E minutes before A.

(Math Refresher #431)

20. Choice A is correct.

Volume of cube = $(\text{side})^3$

Thus, volume of each small cube = r^3 [1]

Volume of larger cube = s^3 [2]

and sum of the volumes of the 27 cubes = $27r^3$ [3]

(Use Strategy 3: The whole equals the sum of its parts.) We are told that the sum of the volumes of the 27 cubes = the volume of the larger cube

= 81 [4]

From [2], [3], and [4] together, we have

$27r^3 = 81$ [5]

$s^3 = 81$ [6]

(Use Strategy 13: Find unknown expressions by division.) Dividing [5] by [6], we get

$27\frac{r^3}{s^3} = 1$ [7]

Multiplying [7] by $\frac{1}{27}$, we get

$\frac{r^3}{s^3} = \frac{1}{27}$

or $\frac{r}{s} = \frac{1}{3}$

(Math Refresher #313 and #429)

Explanatory Answers for Practice Test 3 (continued)

Section 3: Math

As you read these solutions, you are advised to do two things if you answered the Math question incorrectly:

1. When a specific Math Strategy is referred to in the solution, study that strategy, which you will find in "19 Math Strategies" (beginning on page 69).
2. When the solution directs you to the "Complete Math Refresher" (beginning on page 167)—for example, Math Refresher 305—study the 305 Math principle to get a clear idea of the Math operation that was necessary for you to know in order to answer the question correctly.

1. Choice E is correct.

The distance between points on a number line is found by:

$$|a - b| = |-4 - (7)| =$$

$$|-4 - 7| = |-11| = 11$$

(Math Refresher #410a)

2. Choice B is correct.

(Use Strategy 5:

$$\textbf{Average} = \frac{\textbf{sum of values}}{\textbf{total number of values}}\Bigg)$$

The average is found by $\frac{8.4 + 8.1 + 9.3}{3} =$

$$\frac{25.8}{3} =$$

$$8.6$$

(Math Refresher #601)

3. Choice A is correct. **(Use Strategy 13: Find unknowns by addition.)**

Given: $x + 9 = -11 - x$ $\boxed{1}$

Adding $x - 9$ to both sides of $\boxed{1}$,

$$2x = -20$$

$$\text{or } x = -10$$

(Math Refresher #406)

4. Choice C is correct. **(Use Strategy 17: Use the given information effectively.)**

Given: $3y = 12$ and $\frac{10}{x} = 5$ $\boxed{1}$

Solving $\boxed{1}$ for x and y:

$$y = 4 \text{ and } x = 2 \quad \boxed{2}$$

Substitute equation $\boxed{2}$ into unknown expression.

$$\frac{y+11}{x+15}=\frac{4+11}{2+15}$$
$$=\frac{15}{17}$$

(Math Refresher #406 and #431)

5. Choice C is correct. **(Use Strategy 10: Know how to use units.)**

Interest = rate × time × amount deposited

$$= \frac{8\%}{\text{year}} \times 1 \text{ year} \times \$50$$
$$= .08 \times 1 \times \$50$$
$$= \$4$$

(Use Strategy 3: The whole equals the sum of its parts.)

$$\text{Total amount} = \text{Deposit} + \text{Interest}$$
$$= \$50 + \$4$$
$$= \$54$$

(Math Refresher #113, #114, and #121)

6. Choice D is correct.

Given: $(x + 6)^2 = 12x + 72$ $\boxed{1}$

(Use Strategy 17: Use the given information effectively.)

Complete the squaring operation on the left side of the equation:

$$(x + 6)^2 = x^2 + 12x + 36$$

Continue the equation with $\boxed{1}$

$$x^2 + 12x + 36 = 12x + 72 \qquad \boxed{2}$$

(Use Strategy 1: Cancel numbers and expressions that appear on both sides of an equation.)

We get: $x^2 + 36 = 72$
Therefore, $x^2 = 36$
$x = \pm 6$

(Math Refresher #409)

7. Choice C is correct. **(Use Strategy 3: The whole equals the sum of its parts.)**

From the diagram, we see that

$$x + 60 = 360 \qquad \boxed{1}$$

Subtracting 60 from both sides of $\boxed{1}$, we get

$$x = 300 \qquad \boxed{2}$$

Subtracting 60 from both sides of $\boxed{2}$, we get

$$x - 60 = 240$$

(Math Refresher #526 and #406)

8. Choice D is correct. **(Use Strategy 10: Know how to use units.)**

Since 60 min = 1 hour, 24 hours = 1 day, and 7 days = 1 week, we have

$$\left(\frac{60 \text{ min}}{\cancel{\text{hour}}}\right)\left(\frac{24 \cancel{\text{ hours}}}{\cancel{\text{day}}}\right)\left(\frac{7 \cancel{\text{ days}}}{\text{week}}\right) = 10{,}080$$

or 1 week = 10,080 minutes. To the nearest hundred, 1 week ≈ 10,100 minutes.

(Math Refresher #121)

9. Choice B is correct. **(Use Strategy 11: Use new definitions carefully.)**

Method 1: By definition, $\bigtriangledown\!\!\!\!\!\!{\scriptstyle x}\;\; = \frac{x^3}{4}$

We are looking for

$$\frac{x^3}{4} = 16 \qquad \boxed{1}$$

(Use Strategy 13: Find unknowns by multiplication.)

Multiplying $\boxed{1}$ by 4, we have

$$x^3 = 64$$
$$x = 4$$

Method 2: Calculate each of the choices, A through E, until you find the one whose value is 16.

(Math Refresher #429 and #431)

10. Choice B is correct. **(Use Strategy 2: Translate from words to algebra.)**

We are given:

$42 + 27 + 56 + x + y = 200$
or $125 + x + y = 200$
or $x + y = 75$
or $x = 75 - y$ $\boxed{1}$

(Use Strategy 17: Use the given information effectively.)

From $\boxed{1}$, it is clear that x is a maximum when y is a minimum. Since y is the number of pieces of candy in a jar, its minimum value is

$$y = 0 \qquad \boxed{2}$$

Substituting $\boxed{2}$ into $\boxed{1}$,

$$x = 75$$

(Math Refresher #200, #426, and #431)

11. Choice C is correct. **(Use Strategy 2: Translate from words to algebra.)**

Number of pages Ron read last night

$$= \frac{1}{4} \times 16 = 4$$

(Use Strategy 3: The whole equals the sum of its parts.)

Number of pages remaining immediately after Ron finished reading last night = 16 − 4 = 12

Number of pages read this morning = $\frac{1}{4} \times 12 = 3$

Pages still not read

= Remaining pages − pages read this morning
= 12 − 3

Pages still not read = 9

(Math Refresher #200)

12. Choice D is correct. **(Use Strategy 16: Watch out for questions that can be tricky.)**

Number of candles lit = Number of days between December 9 and 21, *inclusive* = 13

Not 21 − 9 = 12, which is just the difference.

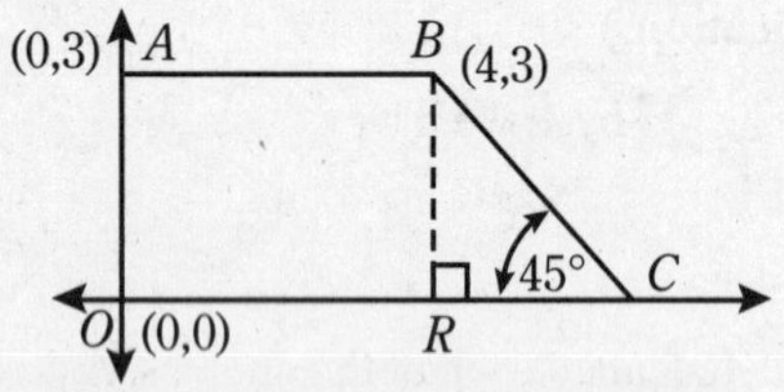

13. Choice C is correct.

Method 1: **(Use Strategy 17: Use the given information effectively.)**

The above figure has *AB* parallel to the *x*-axis. (Both *A* and *B* have *y*-coordinates of 3.) Thus, the figure is a trapezoid.

Its height (*OA*) is 3 [1]
Its top base is 4 [2]

(Use Strategy 14: Draw lines when appropriate.)

Draw *BR* perpendicular to the *x*-axis.
$BR = OA = 3$ and $AB = OR = 4$

(Use Strategy 18: Remember isosceles triangle facts.)

Triangle *BRC* is an isosceles right triangle.
Thus, $BR = RC = 3$

The bottom base of the trapezoid

$= OC = OR + RC = 4 + 3 = 7$ [3]

The area of a trapezoid

$= \frac{1}{2}h(\text{base } 1 + \text{base } 2)$ [4]

Substituting [1], [2], and [3] into [4], we have

Area of trapezoid = $\frac{1}{2}(3)(4 + 7) = \frac{1}{2}(3)(11)$
$= 16.5$

Method 2: **(Use Strategy 14: Draw lines when appropriate.)**

Draw *BR* perpendicular to the *x*-axis.

ABRO is a rectangle and *BRC* is an isosceles triangle.

Area $ABRO$ = (base) × (height)
$= 4 \times 3$
$= 12$ [1]

Area $BRC = \frac{1}{2} \times$ (base) × (height)
$= \frac{1}{2} \times 3 \times 3$
$= 4.5$ [2]

(Use Strategy 3: The whole equals the sum of its parts.)

Using [1] and [2], the total area of figure *ABCO*

= Area of *ABRO* + Area of *BRC*
= 12 + 4.5
= 16.5

(Math Refresher #410, #304, #306, #309, and #431)

14. Choice B is correct. **(Use Strategy 2: Translate from words to algebra.)**

Let $x + y$ = sum of the 2 numbers [1]

$x - y$ = difference of the 2 numbers [2]

xy = product of the 2 numbers [3]

We are told that the difference between their sum and their difference is 6. [4]

Substituting [1] and [2] into [4], we have

$x + y - (x - y) = 6$
$x + y - x + y = 6$
$2y = 6$
$y = 3$ [5]

Substituting [5] into [3], we get

$x(3) = 15$
$x = 5$

Clearly, 5 is the larger number.

(Math Refresher #200 and #406)

15. Choice E is correct.

Given:

$\frac{1}{a} + \frac{1}{b} = 10$ [1]

Method 1: You should suspect that $a + b$ does not have a unique value because [1] is one equation in two variables, and thus a and b are not uniquely determined. To prove that $a + b$ is not uniquely determined, you can use the next method.

(Use Strategy 7: Use numerics to help find the answer.)

Method 2: Choose values of a and b satisfying $\boxed{1}$, and calculate $a + b$.

EXAMPLE 1

$$a = \frac{1}{4} \qquad b = \frac{1}{6}$$

$$a + b = \frac{5}{12}$$

EXAMPLE 2

$$a = \frac{1}{5} \qquad b = \frac{1}{5}$$

$$a + b = \frac{2}{5}$$

Thus, $a + b$ has at least two different values.

(Math Refresher #431 and #110)

16. Choice A is correct. **(Use Strategy 3: The whole equals the sum of its parts.)**

The area between the curved path and the dodecagon is simply the sum of the areas of the 12 semicircles.

Since $\qquad$ area of circle $= \pi r^2$

then $\qquad$ area of semicircle $= \frac{1}{2}\pi r^2$

where r is the radius of the circle.

Thus, area of shaded region $= 12\left(\frac{1}{2}\pi r^2\right)$

$$= 6\pi r^2 \qquad \boxed{1}$$

We are told diameter of semicircle = side of dodecagon. $\boxed{2}$

Since each side of a regular dodecagon has the same length, then

length of a side of dodecagon =

$$\frac{\text{perimeter of dodecagon}}{12} =$$

$$\frac{24}{12} = 2$$

From $\boxed{2}$, we know that

diameter of semicircle = 2

Thus, radius of semicircle = 1 $\boxed{3}$

Substituting $\boxed{3}$ into $\boxed{1}$,

area of shaded region $= 6\pi$

(Math Refresher #310, #311, and #522)

17. Choice E is correct. **(Use Strategy 2: Translate from words to algebra.)** From what we are told in the problem, notice that

$b - 6$ = the number of Bobby's marbles after Bobby gave 6 away

$c + 6$ = the number of Charlie's marbles after Bobby gave 6 away

We are told

$$b - 6 = c + 6 + 18$$

$$\text{or } b - 6 = c + 24 \qquad \boxed{1}$$

(Use Strategy 13: Find unknowns by adding equations or expressions.) Adding $-b - 24$ to both sides of $\boxed{1}$, we get

$$c - b = -30$$

(Math Refresher #200 and #406)

18. Choice D is correct. **(Use Strategy 3: The whole equals the sum of its parts.)** The perimeter of the shaded region

$$= PM + PN + \text{length of } \widehat{MN} \qquad \boxed{1}$$

From basic geometry, we know that if two tangents to a circle meet at a point, the lengths of the tangents from that point to where they touch the circle are equal. If a radius is drawn from the center of a circle to the point where the tangent touches the circle, the angle of the radius line is perpendicular to the tangent. Thus,

$$PM = PN \qquad m\angle PMO = 90 \qquad \boxed{2}$$

and that OP bisects $\angle MON$. **(Use Strategy 14: Draw additional lines.)** Thus, we can redraw the diagram. **(Use Strategy 18: Remember standard right triangles.)**

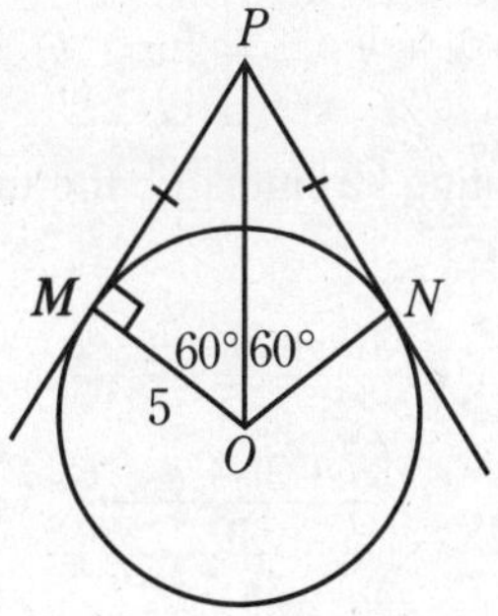

ΔPMO is similar to one of the standard triangles previously discussed.

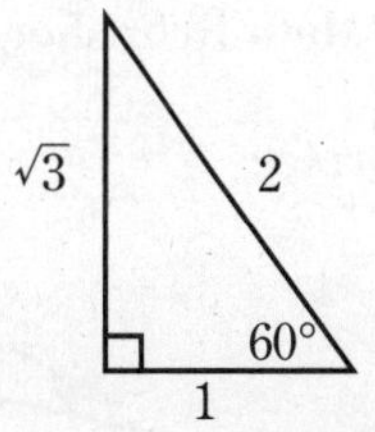

Corresponding sides of similar triangles are *in proportion*, so that

$$\frac{\sqrt{3}}{1} = \frac{PM}{5}$$

$$\text{or } PM = 5\sqrt{3} = PN \qquad \boxed{3}$$

It is always true that the length of $\widehat{MN}$

$$= \frac{m\angle MON}{360} \times \text{circumference of the circle}$$

$$= \frac{m\angle MON}{360} \times 2\pi(5)$$

$$= \frac{120}{360} \times 2\pi(5)$$

(Use Strategy 19: Factor and reduce.)

$$= \frac{12 \times \cancel{10}}{36 \times \cancel{10}} \times 2\pi(5)$$

$$= \frac{\cancel{12}}{\cancel{12} \times 3} \times 2\pi(5)$$

$$= \frac{10\pi}{3} \qquad \boxed{4}$$

Substituting $\boxed{4}$ and $\boxed{3}$ into $\boxed{1}$, we get the perimeter of shaded region $= 10\sqrt{3} + \frac{10\pi}{3}$

(Math Refresher #310, #509, #510, and #529)

19. Choice D is correct.

(Use Strategy 5:

$$\textbf{Average} = \frac{\textbf{sum of values}}{\textbf{total number of values}}\Big)$$

We want to find

$$\frac{x+y+z+a+b}{5} \qquad \boxed{1}$$

We are given

$$x+y+z = 3(a+b) \qquad \boxed{2}$$

By substituting $\boxed{2}$ into $\boxed{1}$, the unknown expression becomes

$$\frac{3(a+b)+a+b}{5}$$

$$= \frac{3a+3b+a+b}{5}$$

$$= \frac{4a+4b}{5}$$

$$= \frac{4(a+b)}{5}$$

(Math Refresher #601 and #431)

20. Choice B is correct.

Method I:

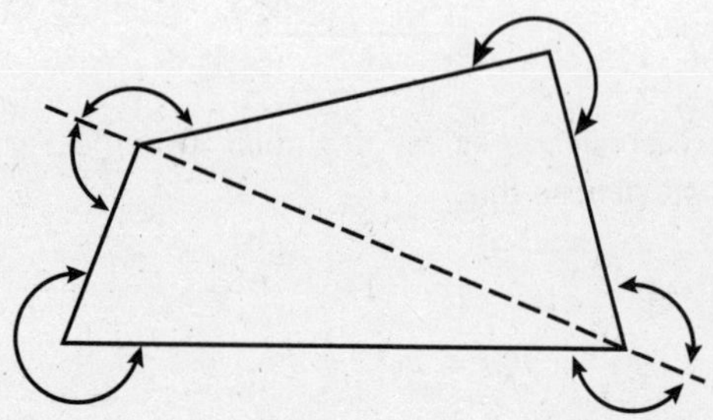

(Use Strategy 3: The whole equals the sum of its parts).

What we really have here is $4 \times 360°$ (four circles) minus the sum of the internal angles in the quadrilateral.

That is: $4 \times 360 - 360$

This is equal to $3 \times 360 = 1{,}080$

Method II:

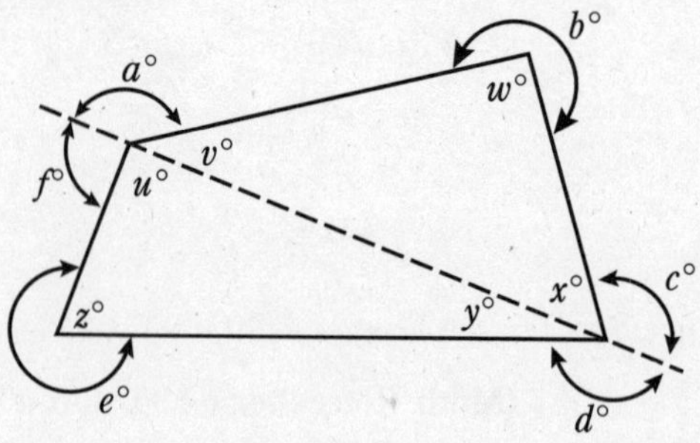

(Use Strategy 14: Label unknown quantities.) With the diagram labeled as above, we want to find

$$a+b+c+d+e+f \qquad \boxed{1}$$

(Use Strategy 3: The whole equals the sum of its parts.) Looking at the diagram, we see

$$a+f+u+v = 360 \qquad \boxed{2}$$

$$b+w = 360 \qquad \boxed{3}$$

$$c+d+x+y = 360 \qquad \boxed{4}$$

$$e+z = 360 \qquad \boxed{5}$$

(Use Strategy 13: Find unknown quantities by addition.) Adding equations $\boxed{2}$ through $\boxed{5}$,

$$a+b+c+d+e+f$$
$$+u+v+w+x+y+z$$
$$= 1{,}440 \qquad \boxed{6}$$

Since the sum of the measures of the angles of a triangle is 180, then

$$v+w+x = 180 \qquad \boxed{7}$$

$$u+y+z = 180 \qquad \boxed{8}$$

Substituting $\boxed{7}$ and $\boxed{8}$ into $\boxed{6}$

$$a+b+c+d+e+f+180+180 = 1{,}440$$
$$\text{or } a+b+c+d+e+f = 1{,}080$$

(Math Refresher #526, #505, and #406)

Explanatory Answers for Practice Test 3 (continued)

Section 4: Critical Reading

As you read these Explanatory Answers, refer to "16 Verbal (Critical Reading) Strategies" (beginning on page 119), whenever a specific strategy is referred to in the answer. Of particular importance are the following Master Verbal Strategies:

Sentence Completion Master Strategy 1—page 120.
Sentence Completion Master Strategy 2—page 121.
Reading Comprehension Master Strategy 2—page 138.

Note: All Reading questions use Reading Comprehension Strategies 1, 2, and 3 (pages 135–140) as well as other strategies indicated.

1. Choice C is correct. See **Sentence Completion Strategy 4.** Since the general "was like two sides of a coin," we have an *opposition indicator* to guide us. It is not ordinary for a man who is fair to be a man of severity. Nor is it ordinary for a man who is outgoing to be a man of few words.

2. Choice A is correct. See **Sentence Completion Strategy 2.**

STEP 1 [ELIMINATION]

We have eliminated Choices B and E because "agitation" and "intellect" do not make sense in the first blank.

STEP 2 [REMAINING CHOICES]

This leaves us with the remaining choices to be considered. The sentence *does not* make sense with the second word "minimal" of Choice C and the second word "whimsical" of Choice D. The sentence *does* make sense with the words "skill" and "astute" (meaning "cunning") of Choice A.

3. Choice E is correct. See **Sentence Completion Strategy 4.** "Internal dissension" is likely to have a negative effect on "affirmative action." We, accordingly, have an *opposition indicator.* Therefore, we eliminate Choice A, encourage, Choice C, induce, and Choice D, apply. This leaves us with Choice B, complicate, and Choice E, delay. Choice (B) complicate...agreement, *does not* make sense. Choice E, delay...upheaval, *does* make sense.

4. Choice B is correct. See **Sentence Completion Strategy 2.** We can first eliminate Choice A, suspicion..., and Choice D, sacrifice..., because these first blank words do not make sense in the sentence. This leaves us with Choice B, disagreement, Choice C, discussion, and Choice E, research. However, Choice C, discussion...incidentally, and Choice E, research...irrelevantly, *do not* make sense. Choice B, disagreement...overwhelmingly, *does* make sense.

5. Choice D is correct. See **Sentence Completion Strategies 3 and 4.** The key words "rather than"

tell us that a word *opposite* to "severity" is needed to fill in the blank space. If you used the strategy of trying to complete the sentence *before* looking at the five choices, you might have chosen for your blank fill-in one of these appropriate words: easy, friendly, diplomatic, pleasing, soothing. Each of these words has a meaning much like that of the word "conciliatory." The words of the other four choices are *not* appropriate in the sentence. Therefore, these choices are incorrect.

6. Choice A is correct. See **Sentence Completion Strategy 1.** Try each choice. He would be able to be impartial, or unbiased, only as a result of not being emotionally attached to either acquaintance; he would not necessarily be able to be accurate (Choice B) or judicious (Choice E).

7. Choice A is correct. See **Sentence Completion Strategy 4.** This sentence calls for two words of contrasting nature, as shown by the words "even though." The only pair that has this contrast in meaning is Choice A.

8. Choice A is correct. The word "passive" means "submissive, not participating, accepting without objection." See **Sentence Completion Strategy 1.** A person who loves action certainly cannot tolerate a passive lifestyle. Choices B, C, D, and E are incorrect because an action-loving person may, indeed, tolerate a chaotic or brazen or grandiose or vibrant lifestyle.

9. Choice A is correct. See lines 2–3: "hits upon a bright new way…At that point, the remark is an epigram."

10. Choice D is correct. See lines 5–7: "Soon it is likely to be suffering from overwork. It has then arrived at clichéhood." This indicates how the epigram is used.

11. Choice B is correct. From the context in the sentence, "…the crash of thunder, are the result of a sudden break in the equipoise…," you can see that "equipoise" must relate to "status quo" or "balance."

12. Choice A is correct. See lines 8–9: "The still small voice…"

13. Choice C is correct. See paragraph 5, lines 81–82: "Hoover also inaugurated…relieve unemployment."

14. Choice A is correct. See paragraph 2, lines 19–22: "The threat of another war…was one such stimulus."

15. Choice E is correct. According to the passage, political unrest was the result—not the cause—of the 1929 Depression.

16. Choice C is correct. See paragraph 3, lines 48–50: "All down the line…not meet their debts."

17. Choice B is correct. From the context of the sentence, we see that we should look for a word or phrase opposite in meaning or in contrast to the word "prosperity." Choice B is perfect. See also **Reading Comprehension Strategy 5.**

18. Choice C is correct. Given the context of the rest of the sentence, "inaugurated" must have to do with having begun something. Therefore, Choice C is correct. See also **Reading Comprehension Strategy 5.**

19. Choice D is correct. See paragraph 5, lines 79–81: "…Reconstruction Finance Corporation…with government loans."

20. Choice B is correct. See paragraph 3, last sentence: "Once started, this spiral of deflation seemed to have no limit."

21. Choice A is correct. See paragraph 4, lines 63–67: "More and more…brought such widespread misery and unemployment."

22. Choice E is correct. See paragraph 2: "War provided a limitless market for expendable goods."

23. Choice A is correct. See paragraph 4: All are mentioned except A.

24. Choice B is correct. See paragraph 3: "…the contraction of business left employees without jobs…"

Explanatory Answers for Practice Test 3 (continued)

Section 5: Writing

For further practice and information, please refer to Grammar and Usage Refresher starting on page 455.

1. **(C)** Choices A and B are incorrect uses of the present participle form to modify the noun *canoe.* Choice C is the correct use of the past participle. Choice D is incorrect because, in this sentence, it is an awkward use of the past participle. Choice E is an incorrect use of the present participle preceded by the inappropriate possessive pronoun *its.*

2. **(B)** What we are looking for here is a group of words to be used as a subject. Choice A is incorrect because the clause beginning with *whether* conveys an uncertainty, which is not the meaning of the sentence. Choice B is correct as a positive statement. It is a gerund phrase followed by an infinitive phrase. Choices C, D, and E are incorrect because they are awkward and vague.

3. **(C)** Choice A is incorrect because the phrases are misplaced, resulting in an unclear statement. Choices B and D are incorrect. They are awkwardly constructed and omit the fact that the trustee resigned from the town board. Choice C is correct. Choice E is incorrect because it is repetitious and awkward.

4. **(D)** Choice A is incorrect because the meaning of the phrase is unclear. Choice B is incorrect because the use of the participial form *coming* is awkward. Choice C is incorrect because it is too vague. Choice D is correct. Choice E is incorrect because it is too wordy.

5. **(A)** Choice A is correct. Choice B is incorrect. The use of *due to* calls for a participle, *having reached,* while the sentence contains a finite verb *has reached.* Choice E is incorrect also because the structure of the phrase calls for the use of a participle. Choice C is incorrect because it is awkward and wordy. Choice D is incorrect because it makes the sentence ungrammatical.

6. **(D)** Choice A is incorrect because "like when" is ungrammatical. Choice B is incorrect because it is too indirect. Choice C is incorrect because "similar to when" is ungrammatical. Choice D is correct. Choice E is incorrect because it is awkwardly expressed.

7. **(D)** Choice A is incorrect because the present participle "Seeing" is incorrectly modifying "the cigarettes." Choices B, C, and E are too roundabout. Choice D is correct.

8. **(A)** Choice A is correct. Choice B is incorrect because the nominative absolute construction "Henry VI having one" throws the sentence out of balance. Choice C is incorrect because we need a finite verb ("had"), not the participle "having." Choice D is incorrect because the present perfect tense ("has had") should be replaced by the past tense ("had"). Choice E is too wordy.

9. **(E)** Choice A is incorrect because it is awkward and because the pronoun "they" has an indefinite antecedent. Choice B is incorrect for the same reason. Choice C is incorrect—it would be correct if changed to "they, not chemists and physicists, have." Choice D is too wordy. Choice E is correct.

10. **(B)** Choice A is incorrect because we have a run-on sentence. The comma should be replaced by a semicolon or a period. Choice A is incorrect for another reason: the singular pronoun "him" (not "them") should be used because the antecedent ("student") of the pronoun is singular. Choice B is correct. Choice C is incorrect because the pronoun "they" should be singular. Choice D is incorrect because it creates a run-on sentence. Choice E is incorrect—the semicolon should be eliminated.

11. **(A)** Choice A is correct. Choice B is incorrect because of the improper ellipsis of the words "that of" which should precede "an adviser and friend." Choice C is incorrect, because the word "one" should be replaced by the words "that of." Choices D and E are incorrect because they are too indirect. Moreover, in Choice D, right after the words "its role" we should place the words "that of."

12. **(D)** "...is like *that of* New York in June." We have an improper ellipsis here. We must include the words *that of,* meaning *the weather of.*

13. **(E)** All underlined parts are correct.

14. **(A)** "The teacher did not encourage the student *in any way* even though..." We cannot properly use the indefinite pronoun *any* to modify the verb (*did not encourage*). The adverbial phrase *in any way* should be used for this purpose.

15. **(C)** "...a great interest *in* and admiration for the work of..." We are not permitted to omit the preposition *in* since it is necessary to introduce the object of the preposition (*work*).

16. **(D)** "...requires me to solve a large *number* of problems." *Amount* is used to refer to things in bulk. *Number* is used to refer to things or people that can be counted.

17. **(E)** All underlined parts are correct.

18. **(C)** "...my brother...was not discouraged *in any way...*" We cannot properly use the indefinite pronoun *any* to modify the adjective (*discouraged*). The adverbial phrase *in any way* should be used for this purpose.

19. **(B)** "A mother...was rescued..." The singular subject (*mother*) requires a singular subject (*was rescued*—not *were rescued*).

20. **(D)** "...his method...was quite *different from* mine." *Different from* is always the correct form; *different than* is always incorrect.

21. **(A)** "The school board members did *as* they were expected..." The conjunction (*as*) should be used to introduce the dependent clause (*as they were expected to*)—not the preposition (*like*).

22. **(B)** "...in which she *had ridden*..." The past perfect tense of *to ride* is *had ridden*—not *had rode.*

23. **(A)** "From every community *come* reports..." The plural form of the verb (*come*) must be used to agree with the plural subject *reports.* "From every community" is an introductory prepositional phrase.

24. **(C)** "...there *was* scarcely enough food..." The word *scarcely* is considered a negative. Using *scarcely* with the word *not* (a double negative) is to be avoided.

25. **(E)** All underlined parts are correct.

26. **(A)** "...to borrow a book *from*..." One borrows *from* someone. The phrase *off of* is always incorrect.

27. **(A)** "Neither the school board members *nor* the city council..." Correlative conjunctions are always used in pairs. The correlative conjunction pair is *neither...nor*—not *neither...or.*

28. **(C)** We must preserve sequence of tenses. When two different parts of a sentence refer to the same period of time, the same tense must be used in each case. In this sentence, when the neighbor *was* (past tense) a teenager, he *rescued* (past tense) a swimmer.

29. **(C)** "...our father told my brother and *me*..." The indirect object of a clause or sentence must be in the objective case and, accordingly, must take the objective form (*me*—not *I*).

30. **(C)** The word *Moreover* is misused in the sentence as it stands; it means "besides." Thus Choice A is incorrect. Choice B is wrong since far from showing contrast to sentence 3, sentence 4 gives a specific example to show what the previous sentence means. Therefore, Choice C is correct: It is the only suggestion that shows an example is coming up. Choice D is wrong since *In short* implies that a summary statement is to follow (nor is sentence 4 particularly brief!). Although it is the second best answer, Choice E is inappropriate since it suggests that there is doubt about sentence 4. The writer has stated sentence 3 as a fact (having qualified it with the word *often*); therefore sentence 4 should be stated more definitely. Note too that sentence 4 is already qualified by the word *perhaps;* beginning the sentence *Some people believe* would water down the example to the point that it means almost nothing.

31. **(D)** Since sentence 8 has nothing to do with what has been said in sentence 7, it should not be joined to this sentence with either a semicolon or *and.* Therefore Choices A and B are both incorrect. Choice C is wrong as well, since if the sentence began with *Although,* it would be a fragment. Choice D is correct: *Yet* is a transitional word that sets up the contrast with sentence 7, but, unlike *Although,* leaves it a complete sentence. Choice E is incorrect—if the sentence were moved, sentence 9 would be a complete non sequitur after sentence 7. Nor would the transition *The reason is* in sentence 10 follow logically after sentence 8.

32. **(B)** Choice A is incorrect since, if the sentence were eliminated, no explanation would be given for sentence 9 and the reader would have to guess at it from sentence 11. Choice B is correct—since sentences 8, 9, and 10 are all quite short, it would be good to combine two of them. The semicolon is the correct form of punctuation to join two complete sentences. Choice C is incorrect: If sentence 10 were joined to sentence 9 with a comma, the result would be a run-on sentence. Choice D is incorrect since, if sentence 10 were moved to the end of the paragraph, it would refer not to sentence 9 but to sentence 11. Choice E is wrong because it would leave out the helpful transition *The reason is,* which shows the relationship between sentences 9 and 10.

33. **(E)** Although Choices A, B, C, and D would all make good introductory sentences for a general passage on dreams, Choice E is the only one that applies directly to this particular passage. Note how "New research indicates" leads smoothly into the beginning of the next sentence: "We know that..." The intention of the entire passage is to show us that dreams "play an important part in all of our lives." Choice C is probably the next best choice, but it would apply only to sentences 3 and 4.

34. **(A)** Since we are concerned with timing, that is, adults at a certain time are given drugs, we use the word *When.* None of the other choices serve what the author is trying to get across.

35. **(E)** Sentence 11 further explains and clarifies the previous sentence and should therefore be in parentheses. None of the other choices describe anything that would be useful or better clarify the passage.

Explanatory Answers for Practice Test 3 (continued)

Section 6: Math

As you read these solutions, you are advised to do two things if you answered the Math question incorrectly:

1. When a specific Math Strategy is referred to in the solution, study that strategy, which you will find in "19 Math Strategies" (beginning on page 69).
2. When the solution directs you to the "Complete Math Refresher" (beginning on page 167)—for example, Math Refresher 305—study the 305 Math principle to get a clear idea of the Math operation that was necessary for you to know in order to answer the question correctly.

1. Choice D is correct. **(Use Strategy 17: Use the given information effectively.)**

Given:

$$7a = 4 \quad \boxed{1}$$
$$7a + 4b = 12 \quad \boxed{2}$$

Substituting $\boxed{1}$ into $\boxed{2}$,

$$4 + 4b = 12$$
or $$4b = 8$$
or $$b = 2$$

(Math Refresher #406 and #407)

2. Choice B is correct. **(Use Strategy 6: Know how to manipulate inequalities.)**

Multiply the string of inequalities

$-\frac{1}{2} < \frac{x}{3} < -\frac{1}{4}$ by 3 to get x alone:

$$3\left[-\frac{1}{2} < -\frac{x}{3} < -\frac{1}{4}\right] =$$
$$-\frac{3}{2} < x < -\frac{3}{4} \quad \boxed{1}$$

Only one integer, $x = -1$, will satisfy $\boxed{1}$

(Math Refresher #422 and #426)

3. Choice D is correct.

Method 1: By inspection, Choice D is the sum of two negatives, which must be negative.

Method 2: **(Use Strategy 7: Try numerics to help find the answer.)**

Let $r = -1, s = -2$

(Use Strategy 8: When all choices must be tested, start with E and work backward.)

$$\text{Choice E is } -r - s = -(-1) - (-2)$$
$$= 1 + 2$$
$$= 3$$

Choice D is $r + s = -1 + (-2) = -3$

Thus D is negative and the answer.

(Math Refresher #431)

4. Choice D is correct. $f(x-1)=$

$$(x-1)^2+2(x-1)+1=$$
$$x^2-2x+1+2x-2+1=x^2$$

(Math Refresher #616 and #409)

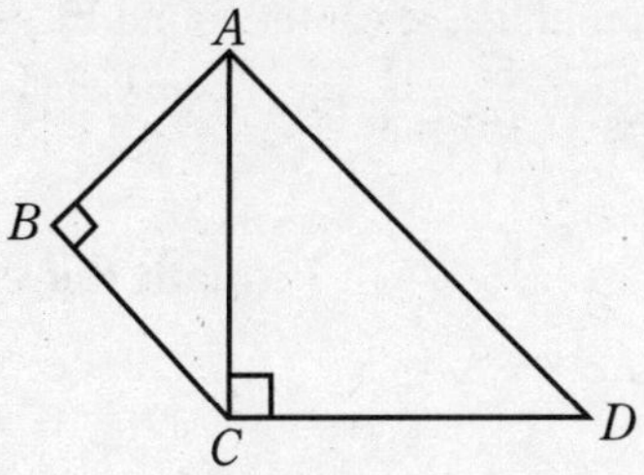

5. Choice D is correct. **(Use Strategy 18: Remember the isosceles right triangle.)**

Given: $AB = BC$ [1]
$AC = CD$ [2]

From [1] we get that $\triangle ABC$ is an isosceles right triangle. Therefore, $\angle BAC$ and $\angle BCA$ are each 45-degree angles.

From [2] we get that $\triangle ACD$ is an isosceles right triangle. Therefore, $\angle CAD$ and $\angle CDA$ are each 45-degree angles.

Thus, there are four 45-degree angles.

(Math Refresher #505 and #509)

6. Choice B is correct. **(Use Strategy 2: Translate from words to algebra.)**

We know that:

Area of rectangle = length × width [1]

We are given: Area = 4 [2]

$\text{length} = \frac{4}{3}$ [3]

Substituting [2] and [3] into [1], we get

$4 = \frac{4}{3} \times \text{width}$ [4]

(Use Strategy 13: Find unknowns by multiplication.)

Multiply [4] by $\frac{3}{4}$. We get

$$\frac{3}{\cancel{4}}(\cancel{4}) = \frac{\cancel{3}}{\cancel{4}}\left(\frac{\cancel{4}}{\cancel{3}} \times \text{width}\right)$$

$3 = \text{width}$

(Math Refresher #304 and #406)

7. Choice D is correct.

Since vertical angles are equal, then

$m\angle AOC = m\angle DOB = 108$ [1]

Thus, from [1], we get length of

minor $\overset{\frown}{AC}$ = length of minor $\overset{\frown}{DB}$ [2]

From geometry we know

$$\text{length of minor } \overset{\frown}{AC} = \frac{108}{360} \times \text{circumference of circle}$$
$$= \frac{108}{360} \times \pi(\text{diameter})$$
$$= \frac{108}{360} \times \pi(20)$$

(Use Strategy 19: Factor and reduce.)

$$\text{length of minor } \overset{\frown}{AC} = \frac{\cancel{18} \times 6}{\cancel{18} \times \cancel{20}} \times \pi(\cancel{20})$$

$\text{length of minor } \overset{\frown}{AC} = 6\pi$ [3]

Length $\overset{\frown}{AC}$ + Length $\overset{\frown}{DB}$ can be found using [2] and [3]

Length $\overset{\frown}{AC}$ + Length $\overset{\frown}{DB}$ = $6\pi + 6\pi$

Length $\overset{\frown}{AC}$ + Length $\overset{\frown}{DB}$ = 12π

(Math Refresher #503 and #310)

8. Choice D is correct. The graphs are represented as follows: Plot $x = 0, y = 0$.

For $y = 2x^2$, when $x = \pm1$, $y = 2$; when $x = \pm2$; $y = 8$

For $y = -2x^2$, when $x = \pm1$, $y = -2$; when $x = \pm2$, $y = -8$
The graphs are represented as follows:

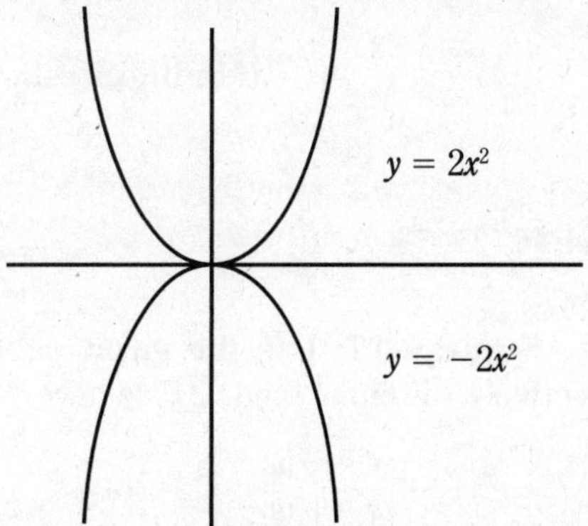

Thus, I and II are true. III is false. A linear function is of the form $y = mx + b$.

(Math Refresher #410)

9. $\frac{6}{1}$ **or 6 or** $\frac{12}{2}$

(Use Strategy 2: Translate from words to algebra.)

Let M = number of Mary's jelly beans [1]

Let S = number of Susan's jelly beans [2]

And R = number of Rose's jelly beans [3]

We are looking for $\frac{\text{Rose's jelly beans}}{\text{Susan's jelly beans}}$ [4]

According to the given, $S = 3M$ [5]
Also given, $R = 18M$ [6]

Dividing [6] by [5], we get

$$\frac{R}{S} = \frac{6}{1}$$

(Math Refresher #200 and #120)

10. 9

$$\text{Volume of cube} = (\text{side})^3$$

Thus, the volume of a cube whose edge has length of $1 = 1^3 = 1$.

The volume of a cube whose edge has the length of $2 = 2^3 = 8$. Thus the sum of the volumes of the two cubes $= 8 + 1 = 9$.

(Math Refresher #313)

11. 105

(Use Strategy 11: Use new definitions carefully. These problems are generally easy.)

$$\text{Given: } \left(\frac{n}{2}\right) = \frac{n(n-1)}{2}$$

$$\text{Thus } \left(\frac{15}{2}\right) = \frac{15(15-1)}{2} = \frac{15(14)}{2} = 105$$

(Math Refresher #431)

12. 0

Given: $r^2 = 9$ [1]
$s^2 = 25$ [2]

(Use Strategy 17: Use the given information effectively.) From [1] and [2], we have

$r = 3 \text{ or } -3$ [3]
$s = 5 \text{ or } -5$ [4]

The greatest possible value of $s - r$ occurs when s is a maximum and r is a minimum or

$5 - (-3) = 8$ [5]

The greatest possible value of $r - s$ occurs when r is a maximum and s is a minimum or

$3 - (-5) = 8$ [6]

The answer to this question is the difference between [5] and [6]:

$$8 - 8 = 0$$

(Math Refresher #430)

13. $33\frac{1}{3}$, which translates to 33.3 in "grid" form.

(Use Strategy 2: Translate from words to algebra.) According to the graph, 4 people had green eyes, 6 people had blue eyes, and 5 had brown eyes, so there were 15 people in the group. The percentage, x, can be found by setting up the ratio $\frac{x}{100} = \frac{5}{15} = \frac{1}{3}$, or $x = 33\frac{1}{3}$. $33\frac{1}{3}$% had brown eyes.

(Math Refresher #704)

14. 5

$$\begin{array}{r} N5 \\ \times\, LM \\ \hline 385 \\ +\,385 \\ \hline 4235 \end{array}$$

(Use Strategy 17: Use the given information effectively.) From the given problem we see that

$$N5 \times M = 385$$

(Use Strategy 7: Use numerical examples.)

Try $N = 1$

$$15 \times M = 385$$

M must be greater than 10, which is incorrect.

Try $N = 2$

$$25 \times M = 385$$

M must be greater than 10, which is incorrect.

Try $N = 3$

$$35 \times M = 385$$

M must be greater than 10, which is incorrect.

Try $N = 4$

$$45 \times M = 385$$

M is not an integer.

Try $N = 5$

$$55 \times M = 385. \text{ Thus, } M = 7$$

Therefore, L can be equal to 7 to give:

$$\begin{array}{r} 55 \\ \times\, 77 \\ \hline 385 \\ +\,385 \\ \hline 4235 \end{array}$$

ALTERNATE METHOD

The number "$N5$" can be written as $10N + 5$. For example, "25" $= 10 \times 2 + 5$. So in the multiplication example given, we have

$$(10N + 5) \times M = 385 \quad \boxed{1}$$

(Use Strategy 12: *Factor* to make problem simpler.)

$$10N + 5 = 5(2N + 1)$$

So from $\boxed{1}$, $5(2N + 1) \times M = 385$

Now divide by 5:

$$(2N + 1)M = 77$$

Because the only two integers that can give us 77 when multiplied are 11 and 7, or 77 and 1, and because N and M are integers, each must be less than 10, $2N + 1 = 11$, $M = 7$.

If $2N + 1 = 11$, then $N = 5$.

15. 24

(Use Strategy 11: Use new definitions carefully.)

By definition, the hand of dial Y moves one number for each complete revolution of the hand of dial Z. $\boxed{1}$

The hand of Dial Y must move 8 numbers to complete one of its own revolutions. Therefore, it must move 24 numbers to complete 3 of its revolutions.

From $\boxed{1}$ above, 24 numbers on dial Y correspond to 24 complete revolutions on dial Z.

(Math Refresher #120)

16. $\frac{7}{8}$ or .875

(Use Strategy 17: Use the given information effectively.)

Given: 6 rolls uses $\frac{1}{4}$ pound of powder $\boxed{1}$

6 rolls uses $2\frac{1}{2}$ quarts of water $\boxed{2}$

Number $\boxed{2}$ is not necessary to solve the problem!

We need to know how much powder is needed for the same mixture for 21 rolls. Let x = number of pounds for 21 rolls. We set up a proportion:

$$\frac{6 \text{ rolls}}{\frac{1}{4} \text{ pound}} = \frac{21 \text{ rolls}}{x}$$

(Use Strategy 10: Know how to use units.)

$$(6 \text{ rolls})x = (21 \text{ rolls}) \times \left(\frac{1}{4} \text{ pound}\right)$$

$$6x = 21 \times \frac{1}{4} \text{ pound} \quad \boxed{3}$$

(Use Strategy 13: Find unknowns by multiplication.) Multiply $\boxed{3}$ by $\frac{1}{6}$. We get

$$\frac{1}{6}(6x) = \frac{1}{6}\left(21 \times \frac{1}{4} \text{ pound}\right)$$

$$x = \frac{1}{6} \times 21 \times \frac{1}{4} \text{ pound}$$

$$x = \frac{21}{24} \text{ pound}$$

$$x = \frac{7}{8} \text{ of a pound}$$

(Math Refresher #200, #120, and #406)

17. 84

(Use Strategy 5:

$$\textbf{Average} = \frac{\textbf{sum of values}}{\textbf{total number of values}}\Big)$$

Method I: The simplest math and the quickest solution:

Suppose there are 10 students in the class.

Since 40% of the class scored 100, 4 students scored 100.

Since 10% of the class scored 80, 1 student scored 80.

That leaves us with 50% of the class, or 5 students, who scored an average of d.

The overall average was 90, so

$$90 = \frac{(4 \times 100) + (1 \times 80) + (5 \times d)}{10}$$

$$90 = \frac{400 + 80 + 5d}{10}$$

$$900 = 400 + 80 + 5d = 480 + 5d$$

$$420 = 5d$$

$$d = 84$$

Method II: How a mathematician would solve this

Let N be the number of students.

Then $0.4N$ = Number of students scoring 100

$0.1N$ = Number of students scoring 80

(Use Strategy 3: The whole equals the sum of its parts.)

We know that 50% of the class has been accounted for, so

$0.5N$ = Number of students remaining

Let d be the average score for the remaining students.

The overall average was 90, so

$$90 = \frac{(0.4N \times 100) + (0.1N \times 80) + (0.5N \times d)}{N}$$

$$= \frac{40N + 8N + (0.5N \times d)}{N}$$

$$= \frac{48N + (0.5N \times d)}{N}$$

$$90 = 48 + (.5 \times d) = 48 + \frac{d}{2}$$

$$42 = \frac{d}{2}$$

$$d = 84$$

(Math Refresher #601, #114, and #406)

18. 5 (Use Strategy 3: The whole equals the sum of its parts.) The sum of the angles in a triangle = 180°.

Therefore $3t° + 5t° + 10t° = 180$

$$18t = 180$$

$$t = 10 \qquad \boxed{1}$$

Since ABC is a line segment, straight angle ABC = 180°. $\boxed{2}$

(Use Strategy 3: The whole equals the sum of its parts.)

$$\angle ABC = \angle ABD + \angle DBC \qquad \boxed{3}$$

Substituting the given and $\boxed{2}$ in $\boxed{3}$ gives

$$180 = 10t + 16x \qquad \boxed{4}$$

Substituting $\boxed{1}$ in $\boxed{4}$, we have

$$180 = 10(10) + 16x$$

$$180 = 100 + 16x$$

$$80 = 16x$$

$$5 = x$$

(Math Refresher #505, #406, and #501)

Explanatory Answers for Practice Test 3 (continued)

Section 7: Critical Reading

As you read these Explanatory Answers, refer to "16 Verbal (Critical Reading) Strategies" (beginning on page 119) whenever a specific strategy is referred to in the answer. Of particular importance are the following Master Verbal Strategies:

Sentence Completion Master Strategy 1—page 120.
Sentence Completion Master Strategy 2—page 121.
Reading Comprehension Master Strategy 2—page 138.

Note: All Reading questions use Reading Comprehension Strategies 1, 2, and 3 (pages 135–140) as well as other strategies indicated.

1. Choice D is correct. See **Sentence Completion Strategy 1.** The word "degradation" means deterioration, a lowering of position. The sight of a person in such a state would generally bring about a feeling of pity. Choices A, B, C, and E do *not* make good sense in the sentence. Therefore, these choices are incorrect.

2. Choice B is correct. See **Sentence Completion Strategy 4.** The key word "although" in this sentence indicates that there is opposition or difference between the first part of the sentence and the last part. Since our team knew that the opponents (the Raiders) were "sluggish," we were stupid—we should have pushed hard instead of being so "easygoing." The other four choices are incorrect because their word pairs do not make sense in the sentence.

3. Choice C is correct. See **Sentence Completion Strategy 2.** We first examine the first word of each choice. We eliminate Choice A, heroic, Choice B, respected, and Choice E, insightful, because a prime minister with any of these positive qualities would hardly be expected to cause a downfall of his country. So Choices A, B, and E are incorrect.

   We now consider the remaining choices. Choice D, vacillating...confidential, does not make sense in the sentence because we cannot refer to a country as confidential. Therefore, Choice D is also incorrect. Choice C, incompetent...powerful, makes sense and is the correct choice.

4. Choice B is correct. See **Sentence Completion Strategy 1.** The word "aloof" means "withdrawn, distant, uninvolved." A character who is dignified and who is a man of reserve is likely to be aloof.

5. Choice C is correct. See **Sentence Completion Strategy 2.** Let us first examine the first word of each choice. We can eliminate Choice A, frequent, Choice B, heavy, and Choice E, bland, because saying that blood contains frequent or heavy or bland amounts does not make sense. So Choices A, B, and E are incorrect.

   We now consider the remaining choices. Choice D, definite...puzzling, does *not* make sense because blood does not contain puzzling amounts. Therefore, Choice D is also incorrect. Choice C, minute (pronounced "mine-yute"—meaning exceptionally small)...excessive, makes sense and *is* the correct choice.

6. Choice D is correct. See lines 7–9 where it states that many people in our generation were not exposed to classical music. Don't be lured into the distractor Choice A, even though there was mention of sales.

7. Choice A is correct. See lines 19–21 where it mentions that the emotional feeling gradually wears out in time.

8. Choice B is correct. Since the next sentence after the word "evergreen" qualifies that enjoyment lasts only for a short time, "lasting" would be an appropriate definition of "evergreen" in this context. Be careful of the distractor choice "colorful."

9. Choice C is correct. Note that only in Passage 1, lines 3–5, is an example of a symphony of Brahms illustrating the point. No specific examples are presented in Passage 2. In Choice A, the time period is addressed in *both* passages. In Choice B the types of music are presented in *both* passages (classical in Passage 1 and contemporary in Passage 2). In Choice D, no instrument is addressed in either passage and in Choice E, specific musicians are not mentioned in either passage.

10. Choice B is correct. See lines 25–29: "That was why...till he reached bitter despair...the man of property could die." The "well-upholstered hell" constituted the lifestyle that almost caused him to commit suicide. The passage shows no justification for Choices A, C, D, or E. Accordingly, these are incorrect choices.

11. Choice D is correct. Throughout paragraph 3 we see the evidence of the speaker's happiness as a result of his renouncing the "power, women and money" (lines 22–23) as well as the arrogance and intellectuality referred to in line 17. Choices A, B, and C are incorrect because, though the passage discusses these choices, they do not really *pinpoint* the relation between the third and fourth paragraphs. Choice E is incorrect because paragraph 3 does not generalize about the specific points made in paragraph 2.

12. Choice B is correct. His "complete hopelessness and despair" (lines 3–4) led to Siddhartha's decision to commit suicide. The passage does not answer the questions expressed in Choices A, C, D, and E. Therefore, these choices are incorrect.

13. Choice C is correct. From the context of the sentence and the one preceding it, we can see that the word "transitory" means short-lived. (We are dealing with time.) See also **Reading Comprehension Strategy 5.**

14. Choice E is correct. The unhappiness that may result from wealth and power is brought out clearly throughout the second paragraph. In contrast, peace and quiet are likely to assure a happy life. The last paragraph demonstrates this conclusively. Although Choices A, B, C, and D are vital points, none of the choices is sufficiently inclusive to be considered the *main* idea of the passage. References to these choices follow. Choice A—lines 13–21: "He had been full of arrogance...brought him salvation." Choice B—lines 5–8: "Was it not his Self...filled him with fear?" Choice C—lines 10–11: "Too much knowledge had hindered him." Choice D—lines 19–21: "Now he understood...brought him salvation."

15. Choice E is correct. The word "Self" as it is used in this passage means one's own interests, welfare, or advantage; self-love. By an extension of these definitions, "Self" may be considered selfishness. See lines 5–8: "Was it not his Self...filled him with fear?" See also lines 16–17. Accordingly, Choices A, B, C, and D are incorrect.

16. Choice E is correct. See lines 21–22: "All human beings have at least four types of intelligence." Choice A is incorrect. See lines 50–52: "Persistence kept Einstein looking for the solution to the question of the relationship between the law of gravity and his special theory of relativity." Isaac Newton (1642–1727) formulated the law of gravitation. Choice B is incorrect. The passage simply states: "The idea for a self-starting electric motor came to Nikola Tesla one evening as he was reciting a poem by Goethe and watching a sunset" (lines 30–33). Choice C is incorrect. The author indicates a span of time when he states: "The discoveries made by scientific geniuses, from Archimedes through Einstein..." (lines 1–2). Archimedes was

an ancient Greek mathematician, physicist, and inventor (287–212 BC), whereas Einstein was, of course, a modern scientist (1879–1955). Choice D is incorrect. The passage states: "...while an IQ above a certain point—about 120—is very helpful for a scientist,...[it] is not crucial for producing a work of genius" (lines 18–21). The passage does not specifically say that most scientists have IQ scores above 120.

17. Choice D is correct. See lines 42–44: "The scientist solves a problem by shifting from one intelligence to another, although the logical-mathematical intelligence is dominant." Accordingly, Choices A, B, C, and E are incorrect.

18. Choice B is correct. When the author describes the work experiences of Einstein and Tesla, he refers to their use of one or more of the four types of intelligence. Moreover, lines 26–28 state: "Some corroboration of these [four intelligence] categories comes from the reports of scientists who describe thought processes centered around images, sensations, or words." Choices A, C, D, and E are incorrect because the author does not refer to these choices in the passage.

19. Choice C is correct. The author indicates that great scientists use to advantage four intelligences—logical-mathematical, spatial, linguistic, and bodily-kinesthetic. See lines 22–25: "The great scientist possesses the ability to move back and forth among them—the logical-mathematical, the spatial, which includes visual perception, the linguistic, and the bodily-kinesthetic." Choices B and D are brought out in the passage but not at any length. Therefore, Choices B and D are incorrect. Choice A is incorrect because the author nowhere compares the thinking of the average individual and that of the great scientist. Choice E is incorrect because though the concepts are mentioned, they are certainly not clarified in the passage.

20. Choice E is correct. As a football star, he would certainly have to have a high level of (a) spatial intelligence [II], which involves space sensitivity as well as visual perception, and (b) bodily-kinesthetic intelligence [IV], which involves the movement of muscles, tendons, and joints. As a literature major, he would certainly have to have a high level of linguistic intelligence [III], which involves the ability to read, write, speak, and listen. Whether he would have logical-mathematical intelligence to a high degree is questionable. It follows that Choices A, B, C, and D are incorrect.

21. Choice E is correct. According to what is stated in lines 50–56, persistence is an important characteristic of the scientist. Thus the author would probably not agree with the statement in Choice E. The author would agree with the statement in Choice A: See lines 4–5. Note that although the author may not agree that IQ is what makes the scientist brilliant, he believes that *most* people feel that way. The author would agree with the statement in Choice B. See lines 30–32 and lines 56–60. The author would agree with the statement in Choice C. See lines 15–16 in the context of the rest of the passage. The author would probably not disagree with the statement in Choice D since the author does not appear to distinguish artists from scientists in their thinking process even though the passage is primarily about the scientists: See lines 9–14.

22. Choice C is correct. See lines 52–54. Note that although "persistence" is mentioned in lines 47–52, the passage states that fluid thinking may be connected to persistence, not defined as persistence. Thus Choice A is incorrect. See also **Reading Comprehension Strategy 5**.

23. Choice B is correct. Given the context in lines 47–54, the word "paradoxically" means seemingly contradictorily. See also **Reading Comprehension Strategy 5**.

24. Choice A is correct. It can be seen in the passage that the author is intrigued by and interested in the way the scientist thinks but at the same time feels that the scientist reports the findings very objectively.

Explanatory Answers for Practice Test 3 (continued)

Section 8: Math

As you read these solutions, you are advised to do two things if you answered the Math question incorrectly:

1. When a specific Math Strategy is referred to in the solution, study that strategy, which you will find in "19 Math Strategies" (beginning on page 69).
2. When the solution directs you to the "Complete Math Refresher" (beginning on page 167)—for example, Math Refresher 305—study the 305 Math principle to get a clear idea of the Math operation that was necessary for you to know in order to answer the question correctly.

1. Choice B is correct. **(Use Strategy 2: Know the definition of percent.)**

Percent of Caramels =

$$\frac{\text{weight of caramels}}{\text{total weight}} \times 100 \quad \boxed{1}$$

Given:

Weight of Caramels = 0.6 pounds $\boxed{2}$
Weight of Coconuts = 3.6 pounds $\boxed{3}$

Adding $\boxed{2}$ and $\boxed{3}$, we get

Total Weight = 0.6 pounds + 3.6 pounds
Total Weight = 4.2 pounds $\boxed{4}$

Substituting $\boxed{2}$ and $\boxed{4}$ into $\boxed{1}$, we have

$$\text{Percent of Caramels} = \frac{0.6 \text{ pounds}}{4.2 \text{ pounds}} \times 100$$

$$= \frac{.6}{4.2} \times 100$$

$$= \frac{6}{42} \times 100$$

$$= \frac{600}{42} = \frac{300}{21} =$$

$$\text{Percent of Caramels} = 14\frac{2}{7}$$

(Math Refresher #106 and #107)

2. Choice B is correct. Notice that \$25,000 is one-fourth of \$100,000 (the total funds). **(Use Strategy 17: Use the given information effectively.)**

That is, $\frac{25{,}000}{100{,}000} = \frac{1}{4}$.

So look for the piece or part of the circle that is closest to $\frac{1}{4}$ of the whole circle. $\frac{1}{4}$ of the whole circle (360°) is 90°. Lincoln H.S. represents about $\frac{1}{4}$ of the whole circle, or 90°.

(Math Refresher #705)

3. Choice A is correct.

Given: $y = r - 6$ [1]
$z = r + 5$ [2]

(Use Strategy 13: Find unknown expressions by addition of equations.)

Adding [1] and [2], we get

$$y + z = 2r - 1$$
$$y + z + 1 = 2r$$
$$\frac{y+z+1}{2} = r$$

(Math Refresher #407)

4. Choice E is correct. **(Use Strategy 2: Translate from words to algebra.)**

Given: The 3 polygons have equal perimeters, which gives us

$6a = 3b$ [1]
$8c = 6a$ [2]

Dividing [1] by 6, we get

$a = \frac{3}{6}b = \frac{1}{2}b$ [3]

Thus, $a < b$

Dividing [2] by 8, we get

$c = \frac{6}{8}a = \frac{3}{4}a$ [4]

Thus, $c < a$

(Use Strategy 6: Know how to use inequalities.)

Using the Transitive Property of Inequalities with [3] and [4], we have $c < a < b$.

(Math Refresher #304, #306, and #406)

5. Choice B is correct. **(Use Strategy 9: Know the formula for rate, time, and distance.)**

Rate × Time = Distance [1]

Given: Time from A to B = 3 hours [2]

Time from B to C = 5 hours [3]

Distance from A to B = Distance from B to C [4]

Using [4], let Distance from A to B = Distance from B to C = D [5]

Substituting [2] and [5] into [1], we get

$\text{Rate}_{AB} \times 3 = D$

$\text{Rate}_{AB} = \frac{D}{3}$ [6]

Substituting [3] and [5] into [1], we get

$\text{Rate}_{BC} \times 5 = D$

$\text{Rate}_{BC} = \frac{D}{5}$ [7]

From [5] we get the whole distance from A to $C = 2D$ [8]

From [2] and [3] we get the time for the whole trip = 3 + 5 = 8 [9]

Substituting [8] and [9] into [1], we get

$\text{Rate}_{AC} \times 8 = 2D$

$\text{Rate}_{AC} = \frac{2D}{8}$

$\text{Rate}_{AC} = \frac{D}{4}$ [10]

We are asked to find the ratio

$$\frac{\text{average speed from } A \text{ to } B}{\text{average speed from } A \text{ to } C}$$ [11]

Substituting [6] and [10] into [11], we have

$$\frac{\text{average speed from } A \text{ to } B}{\text{average speed from } A \text{ to } C} =$$

$$\frac{\frac{D}{3}}{\frac{D}{4}} =$$

$$\frac{D}{3} \div \frac{D}{4} =$$

$$\frac{D}{3} \times \frac{4}{D} =$$

$$\frac{4}{3} = 4:3$$

(Math Refresher #201, #202, and #120)

6. Choice C is correct. **(Use Strategy 7: Use number examples.)**

If $a = \frac{2}{3}$, $b = \frac{4}{3}$, and $x = \frac{3}{2}$ [1]

Then, substituting from [1], we get

$ax = \frac{2}{3}\left(\frac{3}{2}\right)$ $\quad$ $bx = \frac{4}{3}\left(\frac{3}{2}\right) = \frac{4}{2}$

$ax = 1$ $\quad$ $bx = 2$

Neither a nor b nor x is an integer, but both ax and bx are integers.

Thus, Choices B, D, and E are eliminated.

(Use Strategy 13: Find unknown expressions by addition of equations.)

Adding ax to bx, we get

$ax + bx =$
$(a + b)x$ [2]

Since ax and bx are integers, [2] is an integer. Thus, Choice C is correct.

(Math Refresher #431)

7. Choice C is correct. **(Use Strategy 17: Use the given information effectively.)** For line q, $y = mx + b_1$. Since the line q crosses the origin where $x = 0$ and $y = 0$, b_1 must $= 0$. Thus for line q, $y = mx$. Now since (4,3) is on line q, this means when $x = 4$, $y = 3$, so if $y = mx$, $3 = m(4)$ and $m = \frac{3}{4}$. Now let's look at line p. For this line, $y = Mx + b$. Since the lines p and q are perpendicular, the slope of one is the *negative reciprocal* of the other. Thus $m = -1/M$. Since $m = \frac{3}{4}$, $\frac{3}{4} = -1/M$ and so $M = -\frac{4}{3}$. Thus for line p, $y = -\left(\frac{4}{3}\right)x + b$. The point (4,3) is also on line p so substituting $x = 4$ and $y = 3$ in the equation $y = -\left(\frac{4}{3}\right)x + b$, we get: $3 = -\left(\frac{4}{3}\right)(4) + b$. We get $3 = -\frac{16}{3} + b$, and thus $3 + \frac{16}{3} = b$ and $b = \frac{25}{3}$. Thus for line p, $y = -\left(\frac{4}{3}\right)x + \frac{25}{3}$. If $(3,a)$ is on line p, then substituting $x = 3$ and $y = a$, we get $a = -\left(\frac{4}{3}\right)3 + \frac{25}{3} = -4 + \frac{25}{3} = \frac{13}{3} = 4\frac{1}{3}$.

(Math Refresher #414)

8. Choice C is correct. The function $f(x)$ is not defined when the denominator is 0. So if $2x + 4 = 0$, $2x = -4$ and $x = -2$. Thus only III is the case where the function is not defined.

(Math Refresher #616)

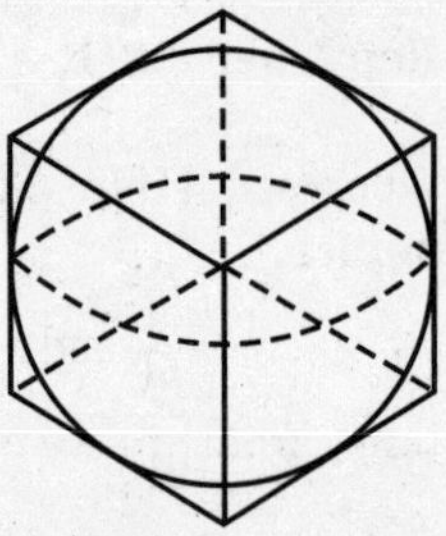

9. Choice E is correct. **(Use Strategy 17: Use the given information effectively.)**

Clearly, we can see from the picture above that the diameter of the sphere has the same length as a side of the cube. We know

Volume of cube = (length of side)^3 [1]

We are given

Volume of cube = 64 [2]

Substituting [2] into [1], 64 = (length of side)^3

Thus,

length of side = 4 = diameter of sphere

(Math Refresher #313 and #315)

10. Choice A is correct.

Given: $\frac{m}{n} = \frac{x}{m}$ [1]

(Use Strategy 13: Find unknowns by multiplication.)

Multiplying [1] by m, we have

$$m\left(\frac{m}{n}\right) = \left(\frac{x}{m}\right)m$$

$$\frac{m^2}{n} = x$$

(Math Refresher #406)

11. Choice B is correct. **(Use Strategy 17: Use the given information effectively.)** We are given

$$CD = \frac{3}{4}AC \quad [1]$$

$$CF = \frac{2}{7}BC \quad [2]$$

We want to find

$$\frac{\text{area of } \triangle ABC}{\text{area of rectangle } CDEF}$$

We know that the area of rectangle $CDEF$

$$= (CD)(CF) \quad [3]$$

and area of $\triangle ABC$

$$= \frac{1}{2}(AC)(BC) \quad [4]$$

Substituting [1] and [2] into [3],
Area of rectangle $CDEF$

$$= \left(\frac{3}{4}AC\right)\left(\frac{2}{7}BC\right) = \frac{3}{14}(AC)(BC) \quad [5]$$

Substituting [4] and [5] into the unknown expression,

$$\frac{\text{area of } \triangle ABC}{\text{area of rectangle } CDEF} = \frac{\frac{1}{2}(\cancel{AC})(\cancel{BC})}{\frac{3}{14}(\cancel{AC})(\cancel{BC})}$$

$$= \frac{1}{2} \times \frac{14}{3} = \frac{14}{6} = \frac{7}{3} \text{ (Answer)}$$

(Math Refresher #304, #306, #431, and #120)

12. Choice C is correct. **(Use Strategy 2: Translate from words to algebra.)**

Let b = number of boys
g = number of girls

We are given

$$b = g + 7 \quad [1]$$

$$b = \frac{5}{4}g \quad [2]$$

(Use Strategy 13: Find unknowns by multiplication.) Multiplying [2] by $\frac{4}{5}$,

$$\frac{4}{5}b = g \quad [3]$$

Substituting [3] into [1],

$$b = \frac{4}{5}b + 7 \quad [4]$$

Multiplying [4] by 5,

$$5b = 4b + 35$$

or $$b = 35$$

(Math Refresher #200 and #406)

13. Choice A is correct. **(Use Strategy 2: Translate words to algebra—see translation table for percent increase.)**

$$\text{Percent increase} = \frac{\text{amount of increase}}{\text{original amount}} \quad [1]$$

Amount of increase is given as 100 per year [2]

Substituting [2] into [1], we get

$$\%\text{ increase} = \frac{100}{\text{original amount}} \quad [3]$$

(Use Strategy 12: Try not to make tedious calculations.) The greatest % increase will occur when the original amount is least.

Since the population is increasing by 100 every year, it is least at the beginning, in 1999.

Thus [3] will be greatest from 1999–2000.

(Math Refresher #114 and #118)

14. Choice D is correct.

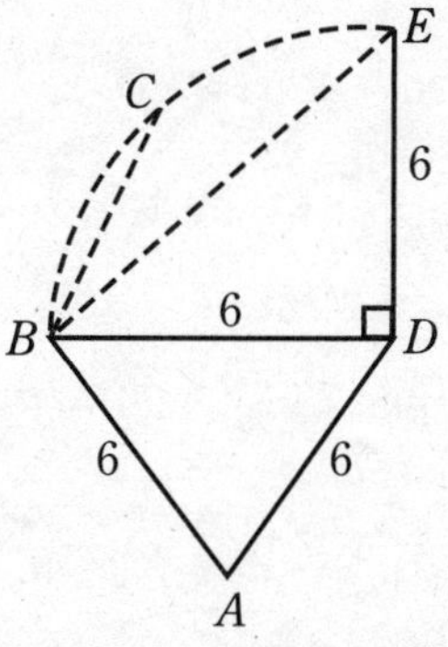

(Use Strategy 14: Draw lines where appropriate.)

Given: $AB = BD = AD = 6$ [1]

C can be any point on arc $\widehat{BE}$, not just where it appears in the drawing above. For any point C on arc $\widehat{BE}$

$$CD = 6 \quad [2]$$

because CD = radius of the circular arc.

(Use Strategy 3: The whole equals the sum of its parts.) We want to find P = perimeter of

$$ABCD = AB + BC + CD + AD \quad [3]$$

Substituting [2] and [1] into [3],

$$P = 18 + BC \quad [4]$$

We cannot find BC, but we can find the highest and lowest possible values for BC. Clearly, since BC is a side of a quadrilateral,

$$BC > 0 \quad [5]$$

By looking at the diagram, we see that the highest possible value of BC occurs when C coincides with E.

$$BC \leq BE \quad [6]$$

must be true. BE can easily be found. $\triangle EDB$ is similar to one of the standard triangles discussed before. **(Use Strategy 18: Remember special right triangles.)**

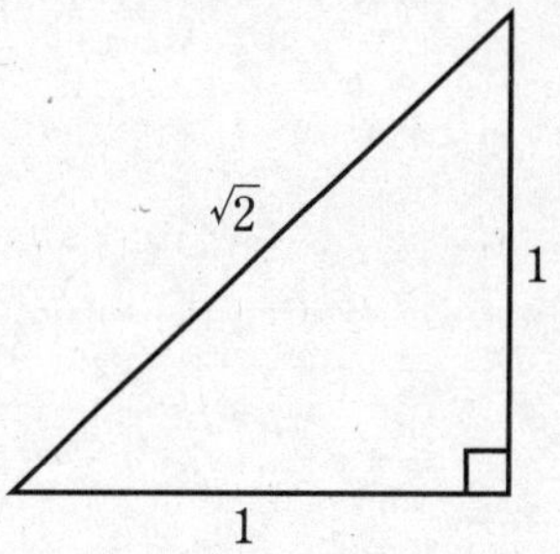

Corresponding sides of similar triangles are proportional, so that

$$\frac{\sqrt{2}}{1} = \frac{BE}{6}$$

or

$$BE = 6\sqrt{2} \quad [7]$$

Substituting [7] into [6],

$$BC \leq 6\sqrt{2} \quad [8]$$

Comparing [4] and [8],

$$P = 18 + BC \leq 18 + 6\sqrt{2} \quad [9]$$

Comparing [4] and [5],

$$P = 18 + BC > 18 \quad [10]$$

From [9] and [10] together,

$$18 < P \leq 18 + 6\sqrt{2}$$

(Math Refresher #431, #507, #509, and #510)

15. Choice B is correct.

Given: $x^9 = 4$ [1]

$$x^7 = \frac{9}{y^2} \quad [2]$$

$x > 0$ and $y > 0$

(Use Strategy 13: Find unknown by division of equations.)

Divide $\boxed{1}$ by $\boxed{2}$. We get

$$\frac{x^9}{x^7} = \frac{4}{\frac{9}{y^2}}$$

$$x^2 = 4 \times \frac{y^2}{9}$$

$$x^2 = \frac{4}{9}y^2$$

$$\sqrt{x^2} = \sqrt{\frac{4}{9}y^2}$$

$$x = \frac{2}{3}y$$

(*Note:* This is the only solution because $x > 0$ and $y > 0$.)

(Math Refresher #431 and #430)

16. Choice C is correct. **(Use Strategy 2: Translate from words to algebra.)** Let s = the number of DVDs Stanley originally had.

Thus, $s + 10x$ = the number of DVDs Stanley had after receiving $10x$ DVDs.

We are told

$$s + 10x = (5y + 1)s$$

or $$s + 10x = 5ys + s$$

or $$10x = 5ys$$

or $$s = \frac{10x}{5y}$$

$$s = \frac{2x}{y}$$

(Math Refresher #200)

Explanatory Answers for Practice Test 3 (continued)

Section 9: Critical Reading

As you read these Explanatory Answers, refer to "16 Verbal (Critical Reading) Strategies" (beginning on page 119) whenever a specific strategy is referred to in the answer. Of particular importance are the following Master Verbal Strategies:

Sentence Completion Master Strategy 1—page 120.
Sentence Completion Master Strategy 2—page 121.
Reading Comprehension Master Strategy 2—page 138.

Note: All Reading questions use Reading Comprehension Strategies 1, 2, and 3 (pages 135–140) as well as other strategies indicated.

1. Choice E is correct. See **Sentence Completion Strategy 2.** Let us first examine the first word of each choice. We can then eliminate Choice A, unearned, and Choice D, backward, because saying unearned attempts to please or backward attempts to please *does not* make sense. So Choices A and D are incorrect.

   Let us now consider the remaining choices. The second words of Choice B, …humor, and Choice C, …reliance, *do not* make sense in the sentence. Choice E, hypocritical…defiance, makes sense and is the correct choice.

2. Choice B is correct. See **Sentence Completion Strategy 3.** If you used this strategy of trying to complete the sentence *before* looking at the five choices, you might have come up with any of the following words:

simple	ordinary
understandable	common
easy-to-understand	

   These words all mean about the same as the correct Choice B, simplified. Therefore, Choices A, C, D, and E are incorrect.

3. Choice D is correct. See **Sentence Completion Strategy 2.** We first examine the first word of each choice. We can then eliminate Choice C, conclusive, and Choice E, ridiculous, because violent crime does not become conclusive or ridiculous. Now we go on to the three remaining choices. When you fill in the two blanks with Choice A and with Choice B, the sentence does not make sense. So these two choices are also incorrect. Filling in the two blanks with Choice D makes the sentence acceptable.

4. Choice E is correct. See **Sentence Completion Strategy 4.** We have an *opposition indicator* here with the first word "Although." We can now assume that the opening clause of the sentence—"Although…patrols"—will contradict the thought expressed in the rest of the sentence. Choice E,

impeded...continue, fills in the blanks so that the sentence makes sense. The other choices are incorrect because their word-pairs do not make sense.

5. Choice A is correct. See **Sentence Completion Strategy 3.** This strategy suggests that you try to complete the sentence *before* looking at the five choices. Doing this, you might have come up with any of the following words that indicate an additional type of force or injury besides "seizure":

coercing forcing pressuring

These words all come close to the meaning of correct Choice A, compelling. Therefore, Choices B, C, D, and E are incorrect.

6. Choice E is correct. See **Sentence Completion Strategy 4.** We have an *opposition indicator* here—the student's not working hard and his winning the contest. We, therefore, look for a definitely positive word as our choice to contrast with the negative thought embodied in his not working hard. That positive word is "elated" (Choice E), which means delighted beyond measure. Accordingly Choices A, B, C, and D are incorrect.

7. Choice A is correct. The main idea of the passage is expressed in lines 18–19: "Science seems to have come into existence merely for its bearings on practical life." This main idea is also expressed in other parts of the passage. For example—lines 1–2: "Science, like everything else...needs and desires." Also lines 15–16: "...the bulk of mankind...advantages it brings with it." Finally, all through the last paragraph of the passage we learn how the Babylonians and the Egyptians reaped practical benefits with the help of science. Choices B, C, D, and E are true, but they are too confining to be considered the main idea of the passage. Therefore, these choices are incorrect.

8. Choice E is correct. See lines 8–14: "Science is valued...most important consideration of all to scientific men." Choice A is incorrect. The passage does not indicate that this choice is true. Furthermore, others *before* the Babylonians and the Egyptians also used scientific methods. Choice B is incorrect. See lines 27–29: "The cultivation of crops...made a calendar almost a necessity [for the Babylonians and Egyptians]." Choice C is incorrect. First see lines 20–23: "More than two thousand years before...measuring space and time." Now see lines 32–34: "Twelve of these months...putting in extra months." Choice D is incorrect. See lines 20–23 again.

9. Choice B is correct. See lines 8–14: "Science is valued...provides the imagination...most important consideration of all to scientific men." Choices A, C, D, and E are incorrect because the author does not imply in any way that scientists are sociable, practical, philosophical, or arrogant people.

10. Choice D is correct. You can see from lines 20–25 that "rudimentary" must be related to something fundamental or basic. In fact in lines 24–25, this rudimentary science met the practical needs of the population, so Choices B, C, and E would have been ruled out anyway. See also **Reading Comprehension Strategy 5.**

11. Choice C is correct. The two labels (lines 48–49) obviously have negative implications about the value of physics and thus indicate that physics is uninteresting and pointless to the ordinary person. Accordingly, Choice C is correct. It follows, then, that Choice B—which states that physics "is a cause for great excitement"—is incorrect. Choices A, D, and E are incorrect because none of these choices is stated or implied in the passage.

12. Choice A is correct. See lines 60–62: "Yet what little we do know...grandeur and intricate beauty." Choices B, C, D, and E are incorrect because none of these Choices is brought up in the passage.

13. Choice C is correct. See lines 52–54: "There is nothing...what we lack of the other." Also see lines 55–58: "It is pointless...all-knowing, and infallible." None of the other choices is indicated in the passage. Accordingly, Choices A, B, D, and E are incorrect.

14. Choice E is correct. See the very first sentence of the passage: "Let's be honest right at the start." This frankness on the part of the author pervades the entire passage. Choices A, B, C, and D are, therefore, incorrect.

15. Choice B is correct. The author is, in effect, saying that one must appreciate the forest as a whole—not merely certain individual trees. He therefore implies that we should not separate physics from the body of all creative work. See lines 55–56: "It is pointless...all creative work..." Choices A, C, D, and E are incorrect because they are not justified by the content of the passage.

16. Choice D is correct. The practical use of science is discussed in lines 20–34 of Passage 1 but not in Passage 2. Choice A is incorrect: lines 44–51 imply the way laymen view physics. Choice B is incorrect: specialization in science is mentioned in lines 44–47 of Passage 2. Choice C is incorrect: purity of physics is mentioned in line 58 of Passage 2. Choice E is incorrect: lines 51–54 address the arguments between humanists and scientists.

17. Choice A is correct. See lines 44–51 of Passage 2: "boxes." Choices B, C, D, and E are incorrect:

critique is certainly used by both authors. The author in Passage 1 contrasts with respect to perceived values in lines 8–16. Historical referencing and examples to support a claim are used in Passage 1 in lines 20–34.

18. Choice E is correct. Choice A, agriculture, is mentioned in line 25. Choice B, astronomy, is mentioned in line 24. Choice C, art, is mentioned in line 43. Choice D, philosophy, is mentioned in line 57. However, Choice A, chemistry, is not directly mentioned.

19. Choice B is correct. Choice A can be immediately ruled out because it repeats the meaning of "grandeur" and would make it redundant (line 61). Since the author described physics as complex, "complicated" would be a good choice. Note that Choices D and E are incorrect because the author believes that although the outside world may view physics as uninteresting or pointless, it is not the real characteristic of physics. It would be unlikely that the noun "beauty" (line 62) would be described by a negative adjective or word (especially because it is also associated with the positive word "grandeur"). Thus it is unlikely that "complicated" is a negative word such as *devastating, uninteresting,* or *pointless,* ruling out Choices C, D, and E. See also **Reading Comprehension Strategy 5**.

Explanatory Answers for Practice Test 3 (continued)

Section 10: Writing

For further practice and information, please refer to Grammar and Usage Refresher starting on page 455.

1. **(A)** Choice A is correct. If you are questioning the singularity of the possessive adjective "his," it is correct. The subject of the sentence consists of a singular compound subject, "the sales manager and personnel director." If we wanted to indicate plurality here, we would have to insert the article "the" before the second member ("personnel director") of the compound subject. Choice B is incorrect because "their" must refer to a plural antecedent. Choice C is incorrect because it changes the meaning of the original sentence. Choice D is awkward. Choice E is too wordy.

2. **(B)** Choice A is incorrect because it does not parallel the structure of "not only because of its beauty." Choice B is correct. Choices C, D, and E are incorrect for the same reason that Choice A is incorrect—the lack of parallel structure. Moreover, Choice C is incorrect because "on account" cannot be used as a subordinate conjunction.

3. **(E)** The past participle "known" must modify the subject of the sentence. Choices A and C are, therefore, incorrect because the subject must be "grandfather"—he is the one (not "friends") that is "known to every man, woman, and child in the town." Choice B changes the meaning of the original sentence. Choice D has a double negative ("never...no..."). Choice E is correct.

4. **(B)** Choice A is incorrect since the correct expression is "no sooner...than..." Choice B is correct. Choices C, D, and E are incorrect because we must have the "no sooner...than" construction.

5. **(A)** Choice A is correct. Choice B is incorrect for two reasons: (1) We use the adverb "so" instead of "as" in a negative comparison; (2) "like" may not be used instead of "as" in this type of comparison. Choice C is awkward. Choice D is roundabout. Choice E changes the meaning of the original sentence.

6. **(C)** The problem in this question is the correct placement of the modifier. The preposition phrase "much to our disgust" is an adverbial phrase showing result. The phrase, therefore, modifies the verb "had been sold out." Accordingly, the phrase should, in this sentence, follow right after the verb it modifies. Choice C, therefore, is correct and the other choices are incorrect. Choice D, incidentally, is incorrect for another reason—it is illogical: the sold-out tickets are obviously disposed of when they are sold out.

7. **(C)** Choice A is incorrect because in this sentence "also" means the same as "in addition." Choice B is awkward. Choice C is correct as a subordinate clause which parallels the preceding subordinate clause. Choice D creates a run-on sentence. Choice E is too wordy.

8. **(C)** Choices A, B, and D are incorrect because of the use of “him joining.” The word “joining” is a gerund in this sentence. Its possessive adjective must be “his”—not “him.” Choice B, moreover, has the unidiomatic expression “objection on.” Choice C is correct. Choice E changes the meaning of the original sentence.

9. **(B)** Choice A is incorrect because the nominative form (“he”) is required: “as fully as him” is wrong. Choice B is correct. Choices C, D, and E are incorrect because the object of the preposition must have an objective case form—the preposition “but” must be followed by the object case form “him.”

10. **(C)** Choice A is incorrect because the verb should be the past perfect form (“had completed”) to indicate an action that took place prior to “tried.” Choice B changes the meaning of the original sentence. Choice C is correct. Choice D is awkward. Choice E changes the tense of the original sentence.

11. **(D)** Choice A uses the word “affect” incorrectly. It means “to influence” and in the original sentence it is incorrectly used to mean “to bring about.” Choice B also uses the word “affect” incorrectly and in addition the verb needed is “is trying” as it refers to the principal *only*. Choice C is incorrect because the singular verb is required. Choice D is correct. Choice E is not correct because it changes the meaning of the original sentence.

12. **(E)** Choice A is incorrect because the word “fewer” should be used instead of “less,” because “less” denotes amount or degree and “fewer” denotes number. Choice B is not correct because “as before” is superfluous. Choice C is incorrect for the same reason as Choice A (above). Choice D changes the meaning of the original sentence. Choice E is correct.

13. **(C)** Choice A is incorrect because in this past contrary-to-fact situation, the verb of the “if” clause should be expressed in the past perfect tense (“had changed”). Choice B does not include a reference to the director, which is necessary to the meaning of the original sentence. Choice C is correct. Choice D is incorrect because it does not include a reference to the director, which, as indicated previously, is necessary to the meaning of the original sentence. Choice E omits a reference to the director and also uses “would have been” incorrectly.

14. **(E)** Choices A and B are incorrect because when two singular antecedents are joined by “nor,” they should be referred to by a singular pronoun. Also, Choice B does not include the names of the boys, which were included in the original sentence. Choice C uses the word “or” incorrectly, rather than “nor.” Choice D does not include the names of the boys and so it changes the meaning of the original sentence. Choice E is correct.

What You Must Do Now to Raise Your SAT Score

1. a) Follow the directions on page 811 to determine your scaled score for the SAT Test you've just taken. These results will give you a good idea about how hard you'll need to study in order to achieve a certain score on the actual SAT.

   b) Using your Test correct answer count as a basis, indicate for yourself your areas of strength and weakness as revealed by the "Chart for Self-Appraisal" on page 816.

2. Eliminate your weaknesses in each of the SAT test areas (as revealed in the "Chart for Self-Appraisal") by taking the following Giant Steps toward SAT success:

Critical Reading Part

Giant Step 1

Take advantage of the Critical Reading Strategies that begin on page 119. Read again the Explanatory Answer for each of the Critical Reading questions that you got wrong. Refer to the Critical Reading Strategy that applies to each of your incorrect answers. Learn each of these Critical Reading Strategies thoroughly. These strategies are crucial if you want to raise your SAT Verbal score substantially.

Giant Step 2

You can improve your vocabulary by doing the following:

1) Study the SAT 3,400-Word List beginning on page 359.

2) Take the 100 SAT-type "tough word" Vocabulary Tests beginning on page 408.

3) Study the Gruber Prefix-Root-Suffix List beginning on page 348.

4) Learn the Hot Prefixes and Roots beginning on page 1049.

5) Read through A List of SAT Words Appearing More Than Once beginning on page 353.

6) Look through the Most Important Words and Their Opposites beginning on page 355.

7) Learn the 3 Vocabulary Strategies beginning on page 150.

8) Read as widely as possible—not only novels. Nonfiction is important too…and don't forget to read newspapers and magazines.

9) Listen to people who speak well. Tune in to worthwhile TV programs.

10) Use the dictionary frequently and extensively—at home, on the bus, at work, etc.

11) Play word games—for example, crossword puzzles, anagrams, and Scrabble. Another game is to compose your own Sentence Completion questions. Try them on your friends.

Math Part

Giant Step 3

Make good use of the 19 Math Strategies that begin on page 69. Read again the solutions for each Math question that you answered incorrectly. Refer to the Math Strategy that applies to each of your incorrect answers. Learn each of these Math Strategies thoroughly. We repeat that these strategies are crucial if you want to raise your SAT Math score substantially.

Giant Step 4

You may want to take the **101 Most Important Math Questions You Need to Know How to Solve** test beginning on page 31 and follow the directions after the test for a basic Math skills diagnosis.

For each Math question that you got wrong in the Test, note the reference to the Complete Math Refresher section beginning on page 167. This reference will explain clearly the mathematical principle involved in the solution of the question you answered incorrectly. Learn that particular mathematical principle thoroughly.

For Both the Math and Critical Reading Parts

Giant Step 5

You may want to take the **Strategy Diagnostic Test** beginning on page 1 to assess whether you're using the best strategies for the questions.

For the Writing Part

Giant Step 6

Take a look at Part 9, the SAT Writing Test, which describes the various item types in the Writing Section and sample questions with answers and explanations. Also make use of the Grammar Refresher—Part 8.

3. After you have done some of the tasks you have been advised to do in the suggestions, proceed to Practice Test 4, beginning on page 860.

After taking Practice Test 4, concentrate on the weaknesses that still remain.

4. Continue the foregoing procedures for Practice Test 5.

If you do the job *right* and follow the steps listed earlier, you are likely to raise your SAT score on each of the Verbal, Math, and Writing parts of the test substantially.

I am the master of my fate:
I am the captain of my soul.

—From the poem "Invictus"
by William Ernest Henley

Answer Sheet for Practice Test 4

SECTION 1

Begin your essay on this page. If you need more space, continue on the next page. Do not write outside of the essay box.

Continue on the next page if necessary.

Continuation of ESSAY Section 1 from previous page. Write below only if you need more space.

Start with number 1 for each new section. If a section has fewer questions than answer spaces, leave the extra answer spaces blank. Be sure to erase any errors or stray marks completely.

SECTION 2

1 Ⓐ Ⓑ Ⓒ Ⓓ Ⓔ	11 Ⓐ Ⓑ Ⓒ Ⓓ Ⓔ	21 Ⓐ Ⓑ Ⓒ Ⓓ Ⓔ	31 Ⓐ Ⓑ Ⓒ Ⓓ Ⓔ
2 Ⓐ Ⓑ Ⓒ Ⓓ Ⓔ	12 Ⓐ Ⓑ Ⓒ Ⓓ Ⓔ	22 Ⓐ Ⓑ Ⓒ Ⓓ Ⓔ	32 Ⓐ Ⓑ Ⓒ Ⓓ Ⓔ
3 Ⓐ Ⓑ Ⓒ Ⓓ Ⓔ	13 Ⓐ Ⓑ Ⓒ Ⓓ Ⓔ	23 Ⓐ Ⓑ Ⓒ Ⓓ Ⓔ	33 Ⓐ Ⓑ Ⓒ Ⓓ Ⓔ
4 Ⓐ Ⓑ Ⓒ Ⓓ Ⓔ	14 Ⓐ Ⓑ Ⓒ Ⓓ Ⓔ	24 Ⓐ Ⓑ Ⓒ Ⓓ Ⓔ	34 Ⓐ Ⓑ Ⓒ Ⓓ Ⓔ
5 Ⓐ Ⓑ Ⓒ Ⓓ Ⓔ	15 Ⓐ Ⓑ Ⓒ Ⓓ Ⓔ	25 Ⓐ Ⓑ Ⓒ Ⓓ Ⓔ	35 Ⓐ Ⓑ Ⓒ Ⓓ Ⓔ
6 Ⓐ Ⓑ Ⓒ Ⓓ Ⓔ	16 Ⓐ Ⓑ Ⓒ Ⓓ Ⓔ	26 Ⓐ Ⓑ Ⓒ Ⓓ Ⓔ	36 Ⓐ Ⓑ Ⓒ Ⓓ Ⓔ
7 Ⓐ Ⓑ Ⓒ Ⓓ Ⓔ	17 Ⓐ Ⓑ Ⓒ Ⓓ Ⓔ	27 Ⓐ Ⓑ Ⓒ Ⓓ Ⓔ	37 Ⓐ Ⓑ Ⓒ Ⓓ Ⓔ
8 Ⓐ Ⓑ Ⓒ Ⓓ Ⓔ	18 Ⓐ Ⓑ Ⓒ Ⓓ Ⓔ	28 Ⓐ Ⓑ Ⓒ Ⓓ Ⓔ	38 Ⓐ Ⓑ Ⓒ Ⓓ Ⓔ
9 Ⓐ Ⓑ Ⓒ Ⓓ Ⓔ	19 Ⓐ Ⓑ Ⓒ Ⓓ Ⓔ	29 Ⓐ Ⓑ Ⓒ Ⓓ Ⓔ	39 Ⓐ Ⓑ Ⓒ Ⓓ Ⓔ
10 Ⓐ Ⓑ Ⓒ Ⓓ Ⓔ	20 Ⓐ Ⓑ Ⓒ Ⓓ Ⓔ	30 Ⓐ Ⓑ Ⓒ Ⓓ Ⓔ	40 Ⓐ Ⓑ Ⓒ Ⓓ Ⓔ

SECTION 3

1 Ⓐ Ⓑ Ⓒ Ⓓ Ⓔ	11 Ⓐ Ⓑ Ⓒ Ⓓ Ⓔ	21 Ⓐ Ⓑ Ⓒ Ⓓ Ⓔ	31 Ⓐ Ⓑ Ⓒ Ⓓ Ⓔ
2 Ⓐ Ⓑ Ⓒ Ⓓ Ⓔ	12 Ⓐ Ⓑ Ⓒ Ⓓ Ⓔ	22 Ⓐ Ⓑ Ⓒ Ⓓ Ⓔ	32 Ⓐ Ⓑ Ⓒ Ⓓ Ⓔ
3 Ⓐ Ⓑ Ⓒ Ⓓ Ⓔ	13 Ⓐ Ⓑ Ⓒ Ⓓ Ⓔ	23 Ⓐ Ⓑ Ⓒ Ⓓ Ⓔ	33 Ⓐ Ⓑ Ⓒ Ⓓ Ⓔ
4 Ⓐ Ⓑ Ⓒ Ⓓ Ⓔ	14 Ⓐ Ⓑ Ⓒ Ⓓ Ⓔ	24 Ⓐ Ⓑ Ⓒ Ⓓ Ⓔ	34 Ⓐ Ⓑ Ⓒ Ⓓ Ⓔ
5 Ⓐ Ⓑ Ⓒ Ⓓ Ⓔ	15 Ⓐ Ⓑ Ⓒ Ⓓ Ⓔ	25 Ⓐ Ⓑ Ⓒ Ⓓ Ⓔ	35 Ⓐ Ⓑ Ⓒ Ⓓ Ⓔ
6 Ⓐ Ⓑ Ⓒ Ⓓ Ⓔ	16 Ⓐ Ⓑ Ⓒ Ⓓ Ⓔ	26 Ⓐ Ⓑ Ⓒ Ⓓ Ⓔ	36 Ⓐ Ⓑ Ⓒ Ⓓ Ⓔ
7 Ⓐ Ⓑ Ⓒ Ⓓ Ⓔ	17 Ⓐ Ⓑ Ⓒ Ⓓ Ⓔ	27 Ⓐ Ⓑ Ⓒ Ⓓ Ⓔ	37 Ⓐ Ⓑ Ⓒ Ⓓ Ⓔ
8 Ⓐ Ⓑ Ⓒ Ⓓ Ⓔ	18 Ⓐ Ⓑ Ⓒ Ⓓ Ⓔ	28 Ⓐ Ⓑ Ⓒ Ⓓ Ⓔ	38 Ⓐ Ⓑ Ⓒ Ⓓ Ⓔ
9 Ⓐ Ⓑ Ⓒ Ⓓ Ⓔ	19 Ⓐ Ⓑ Ⓒ Ⓓ Ⓔ	29 Ⓐ Ⓑ Ⓒ Ⓓ Ⓔ	39 Ⓐ Ⓑ Ⓒ Ⓓ Ⓔ
10 Ⓐ Ⓑ Ⓒ Ⓓ Ⓔ	20 Ⓐ Ⓑ Ⓒ Ⓓ Ⓔ	30 Ⓐ Ⓑ Ⓒ Ⓓ Ⓔ	40 Ⓐ Ⓑ Ⓒ Ⓓ Ⓔ

CAUTION Use the answer spaces in the grids below for Section 2 or Section 3 only if you are told to do so in your test book.

Student-Produced Responses ONLY ANSWERS ENTERED IN THE CIRCLES IN EACH GRID WILL BE SCORED. YOU WILL NOT RECEIVE CREDIT FOR ANYTHING WRITTEN IN THE BOXES ABOVE THE CIRCLES.

Grids 9, 10, 11, 12, 13, 14, 15, 16, 17, 18 (each grid):

	/	/	
.	.	.	.
	0	0	0
1	1	1	1
2	2	2	2
3	3	3	3
4	4	4	4
5	5	5	5
6	6	6	6
7	7	7	7
8	8	8	8
9	9	9	9

Start with number 1 for each new section. If a section has fewer questions than answer spaces, leave the extra answer spaces blank. Be sure to erase any errors or stray marks completely.

SECTION 4

1 A B C D E	11 A B C D E	21 A B C D E	31 A B C D E
2 A B C D E	12 A B C D E	22 A B C D E	32 A B C D E
3 A B C D E	13 A B C D E	23 A B C D E	33 A B C D E
4 A B C D E	14 A B C D E	24 A B C D E	34 A B C D E
5 A B C D E	15 A B C D E	25 A B C D E	35 A B C D E
6 A B C D E	16 A B C D E	26 A B C D E	36 A B C D E
7 A B C D E	17 A B C D E	27 A B C D E	37 A B C D E
8 A B C D E	18 A B C D E	28 A B C D E	38 A B C D E
9 A B C D E	19 A B C D E	29 A B C D E	39 A B C D E
10 A B C D E	20 A B C D E	30 A B C D E	40 A B C D E

SECTION 5

1 A B C D E	11 A B C D E	21 A B C D E	31 A B C D E
2 A B C D E	12 A B C D E	22 A B C D E	32 A B C D E
3 A B C D E	13 A B C D E	23 A B C D E	33 A B C D E
4 A B C D E	14 A B C D E	24 A B C D E	34 A B C D E
5 A B C D E	15 A B C D E	25 A B C D E	35 A B C D E
6 A B C D E	16 A B C D E	26 A B C D E	36 A B C D E
7 A B C D E	17 A B C D E	27 A B C D E	37 A B C D E
8 A B C D E	18 A B C D E	28 A B C D E	38 A B C D E
9 A B C D E	19 A B C D E	29 A B C D E	39 A B C D E
10 A B C D E	20 A B C D E	30 A B C D E	40 A B C D E

CAUTION Use the answer spaces in the grids below for Section 4 or Section 5 only if you are told to do so in your test book.

Student-Produced Responses ONLY ANSWERS ENTERED IN THE CIRCLES IN EACH GRID WILL BE SCORED. YOU WILL NOT RECEIVE CREDIT FOR ANYTHING WRITTEN IN THE BOXES ABOVE THE CIRCLES.

Grids 9, 10, 11, 12, 13, 14, 15, 16, 17, 18 (each with four columns: / / ; . . . . ; 0 0 0 ; 1 1 1 1 ; 2 2 2 2 ; 3 3 3 3 ; 4 4 4 4 ; 5 5 5 5 ; 6 6 6 6 ; 7 7 7 7 ; 8 8 8 8 ; 9 9 9 9)

Start with number 1 for each new section. If a section has fewer questions than answer spaces, leave the extra answer spaces blank. Be sure to erase any errors or stray marks completely.

SECTION 6

1 Ⓐ Ⓑ Ⓒ Ⓓ Ⓔ	11 Ⓐ Ⓑ Ⓒ Ⓓ Ⓔ	21 Ⓐ Ⓑ Ⓒ Ⓓ Ⓔ	31 Ⓐ Ⓑ Ⓒ Ⓓ Ⓔ
2 Ⓐ Ⓑ Ⓒ Ⓓ Ⓔ	12 Ⓐ Ⓑ Ⓒ Ⓓ Ⓔ	22 Ⓐ Ⓑ Ⓒ Ⓓ Ⓔ	32 Ⓐ Ⓑ Ⓒ Ⓓ Ⓔ
3 Ⓐ Ⓑ Ⓒ Ⓓ Ⓔ	13 Ⓐ Ⓑ Ⓒ Ⓓ Ⓔ	23 Ⓐ Ⓑ Ⓒ Ⓓ Ⓔ	33 Ⓐ Ⓑ Ⓒ Ⓓ Ⓔ
4 Ⓐ Ⓑ Ⓒ Ⓓ Ⓔ	14 Ⓐ Ⓑ Ⓒ Ⓓ Ⓔ	24 Ⓐ Ⓑ Ⓒ Ⓓ Ⓔ	34 Ⓐ Ⓑ Ⓒ Ⓓ Ⓔ
5 Ⓐ Ⓑ Ⓒ Ⓓ Ⓔ	15 Ⓐ Ⓑ Ⓒ Ⓓ Ⓔ	25 Ⓐ Ⓑ Ⓒ Ⓓ Ⓔ	35 Ⓐ Ⓑ Ⓒ Ⓓ Ⓔ
6 Ⓐ Ⓑ Ⓒ Ⓓ Ⓔ	16 Ⓐ Ⓑ Ⓒ Ⓓ Ⓔ	26 Ⓐ Ⓑ Ⓒ Ⓓ Ⓔ	36 Ⓐ Ⓑ Ⓒ Ⓓ Ⓔ
7 Ⓐ Ⓑ Ⓒ Ⓓ Ⓔ	17 Ⓐ Ⓑ Ⓒ Ⓓ Ⓔ	27 Ⓐ Ⓑ Ⓒ Ⓓ Ⓔ	37 Ⓐ Ⓑ Ⓒ Ⓓ Ⓔ
8 Ⓐ Ⓑ Ⓒ Ⓓ Ⓔ	18 Ⓐ Ⓑ Ⓒ Ⓓ Ⓔ	28 Ⓐ Ⓑ Ⓒ Ⓓ Ⓔ	38 Ⓐ Ⓑ Ⓒ Ⓓ Ⓔ
9 Ⓐ Ⓑ Ⓒ Ⓓ Ⓔ	19 Ⓐ Ⓑ Ⓒ Ⓓ Ⓔ	29 Ⓐ Ⓑ Ⓒ Ⓓ Ⓔ	39 Ⓐ Ⓑ Ⓒ Ⓓ Ⓔ
10 Ⓐ Ⓑ Ⓒ Ⓓ Ⓔ	20 Ⓐ Ⓑ Ⓒ Ⓓ Ⓔ	30 Ⓐ Ⓑ Ⓒ Ⓓ Ⓔ	40 Ⓐ Ⓑ Ⓒ Ⓓ Ⓔ

SECTION 7

1 Ⓐ Ⓑ Ⓒ Ⓓ Ⓔ	11 Ⓐ Ⓑ Ⓒ Ⓓ Ⓔ	21 Ⓐ Ⓑ Ⓒ Ⓓ Ⓔ	31 Ⓐ Ⓑ Ⓒ Ⓓ Ⓔ
2 Ⓐ Ⓑ Ⓒ Ⓓ Ⓔ	12 Ⓐ Ⓑ Ⓒ Ⓓ Ⓔ	22 Ⓐ Ⓑ Ⓒ Ⓓ Ⓔ	32 Ⓐ Ⓑ Ⓒ Ⓓ Ⓔ
3 Ⓐ Ⓑ Ⓒ Ⓓ Ⓔ	13 Ⓐ Ⓑ Ⓒ Ⓓ Ⓔ	23 Ⓐ Ⓑ Ⓒ Ⓓ Ⓔ	33 Ⓐ Ⓑ Ⓒ Ⓓ Ⓔ
4 Ⓐ Ⓑ Ⓒ Ⓓ Ⓔ	14 Ⓐ Ⓑ Ⓒ Ⓓ Ⓔ	24 Ⓐ Ⓑ Ⓒ Ⓓ Ⓔ	34 Ⓐ Ⓑ Ⓒ Ⓓ Ⓔ
5 Ⓐ Ⓑ Ⓒ Ⓓ Ⓔ	15 Ⓐ Ⓑ Ⓒ Ⓓ Ⓔ	25 Ⓐ Ⓑ Ⓒ Ⓓ Ⓔ	35 Ⓐ Ⓑ Ⓒ Ⓓ Ⓔ
6 Ⓐ Ⓑ Ⓒ Ⓓ Ⓔ	16 Ⓐ Ⓑ Ⓒ Ⓓ Ⓔ	26 Ⓐ Ⓑ Ⓒ Ⓓ Ⓔ	36 Ⓐ Ⓑ Ⓒ Ⓓ Ⓔ
7 Ⓐ Ⓑ Ⓒ Ⓓ Ⓔ	17 Ⓐ Ⓑ Ⓒ Ⓓ Ⓔ	27 Ⓐ Ⓑ Ⓒ Ⓓ Ⓔ	37 Ⓐ Ⓑ Ⓒ Ⓓ Ⓔ
8 Ⓐ Ⓑ Ⓒ Ⓓ Ⓔ	18 Ⓐ Ⓑ Ⓒ Ⓓ Ⓔ	28 Ⓐ Ⓑ Ⓒ Ⓓ Ⓔ	38 Ⓐ Ⓑ Ⓒ Ⓓ Ⓔ
9 Ⓐ Ⓑ Ⓒ Ⓓ Ⓔ	19 Ⓐ Ⓑ Ⓒ Ⓓ Ⓔ	29 Ⓐ Ⓑ Ⓒ Ⓓ Ⓔ	39 Ⓐ Ⓑ Ⓒ Ⓓ Ⓔ
10 Ⓐ Ⓑ Ⓒ Ⓓ Ⓔ	20 Ⓐ Ⓑ Ⓒ Ⓓ Ⓔ	30 Ⓐ Ⓑ Ⓒ Ⓓ Ⓔ	40 Ⓐ Ⓑ Ⓒ Ⓓ Ⓔ

CAUTION Use the answer spaces in the grids below for Section 6 or Section 7 only if you are told to do so in your test book.

Student-Produced Responses ONLY ANSWERS ENTERED IN THE CIRCLES IN EACH GRID WILL BE SCORED. YOU WILL NOT RECEIVE CREDIT FOR ANYTHING WRITTEN IN THE BOXES ABOVE THE CIRCLES.

Grids 9, 10, 11, 12, 13, 14, 15, 16, 17, 18 (each grid identical):

	/	/	
.	.	.	.
	0	0	0
1	1	1	1
2	2	2	2
3	3	3	3
4	4	4	4
5	5	5	5
6	6	6	6
7	7	7	7
8	8	8	8
9	9	9	9

Start with number 1 for each new section. If a section has fewer questions than answer spaces, leave the extra answer spaces blank. Be sure to erase any errors or stray marks completely.

SECTION 8

1 A B C D E	11 A B C D E	21 A B C D E	31 A B C D E
2 A B C D E	12 A B C D E	22 A B C D E	32 A B C D E
3 A B C D E	13 A B C D E	23 A B C D E	33 A B C D E
4 A B C D E	14 A B C D E	24 A B C D E	34 A B C D E
5 A B C D E	15 A B C D E	25 A B C D E	35 A B C D E
6 A B C D E	16 A B C D E	26 A B C D E	36 A B C D E
7 A B C D E	17 A B C D E	27 A B C D E	37 A B C D E
8 A B C D E	18 A B C D E	28 A B C D E	38 A B C D E
9 A B C D E	19 A B C D E	29 A B C D E	39 A B C D E
10 A B C D E	20 A B C D E	30 A B C D E	40 A B C D E

SECTION 9

1 A B C D E	11 A B C D E	21 A B C D E	31 A B C D E
2 A B C D E	12 A B C D E	22 A B C D E	32 A B C D E
3 A B C D E	13 A B C D E	23 A B C D E	33 A B C D E
4 A B C D E	14 A B C D E	24 A B C D E	34 A B C D E
5 A B C D E	15 A B C D E	25 A B C D E	35 A B C D E
6 A B C D E	16 A B C D E	26 A B C D E	36 A B C D E
7 A B C D E	17 A B C D E	27 A B C D E	37 A B C D E
8 A B C D E	18 A B C D E	28 A B C D E	38 A B C D E
9 A B C D E	19 A B C D E	29 A B C D E	39 A B C D E
10 A B C D E	20 A B C D E	30 A B C D E	40 A B C D E

SECTION 10

1 A B C D E	11 A B C D E	21 A B C D E	31 A B C D E
2 A B C D E	12 A B C D E	22 A B C D E	32 A B C D E
3 A B C D E	13 A B C D E	23 A B C D E	33 A B C D E
4 A B C D E	14 A B C D E	24 A B C D E	34 A B C D E
5 A B C D E	15 A B C D E	25 A B C D E	35 A B C D E
6 A B C D E	16 A B C D E	26 A B C D E	36 A B C D E
7 A B C D E	17 A B C D E	27 A B C D E	37 A B C D E
8 A B C D E	18 A B C D E	28 A B C D E	38 A B C D E
9 A B C D E	19 A B C D E	29 A B C D E	39 A B C D E
10 A B C D E	20 A B C D E	30 A B C D E	40 A B C D E

SAT PRACTICE TEST 4

SECTION 1

Time: 25 Minutes—Turn to page 854 of your answer sheet to write your ESSAY.

The purpose of the essay is to have you show how well you can express and develop your ideas. You should develop your point of view, logically and clearly present your ideas, and use language accurately.

You should write your essay on the lines provided on your answer sheet. You should not write on any other paper. You will have enough space if you write on every line and if you keep your handwriting to a reasonable size. Make sure that your handwriting is legible to other readers.

You will have 25 minutes to write an essay on the assignment below. *Do not write on any other topic. If you do so, you will receive a score of 0.*

Think carefully about the issue presented in the following quotation and the assignment below.

> The most exciting thing we can experience is the mysterious. It is the fundamental emotion which stands at the cradle of true art and true science. He who does not know it and can no longer wonder, no longer feel amazement, is as good as dead, a snuffed-out candle.
>
> —Adapted from Albert Einstein, "What I Believe."

Assignment: In which ways have you experienced "the mysterious" and how has that made you feel alive and excited about life? Based on your experience or experiences, discuss how the above quote rings true and how science or art illustrates the "mysterious."

DO NOT WRITE YOUR ESSAY IN YOUR TEST BOOK. You will receive credit only for what you write on your answer sheet.

BEGIN WRITING YOUR ESSAY ON PAGE 854 OF THE ANSWER SHEET.

If you finish before time is called, you may check your work on this section only.
Do not turn to any other section in the test.

SECTION 2

Time: 25 Minutes—Turn to Section 2 (page 856) of your answer sheet to answer the questions in this section. 20 Questions

Directions: For this section, solve each problem and decide which is the best of the choices given. Fill in the corresponding circle on the answer sheet. You may use any available space for scratchwork.

Notes:

1. The use of a calculator is permitted.
2. All numbers used are real numbers.
3. Figures that accompany problems in this test are intended to provide information useful in solving the problems. They are drawn as accurately as possible EXCEPT when it is stated in a specific problem that the figure is not drawn to scale. All figures lie in a plane unless otherwise indicated.
4. Unless otherwise specified, the domain of any function f is assumed to be the set of all real numbers x for which $f(x)$ is a real number.

REFERENCE INFORMATION

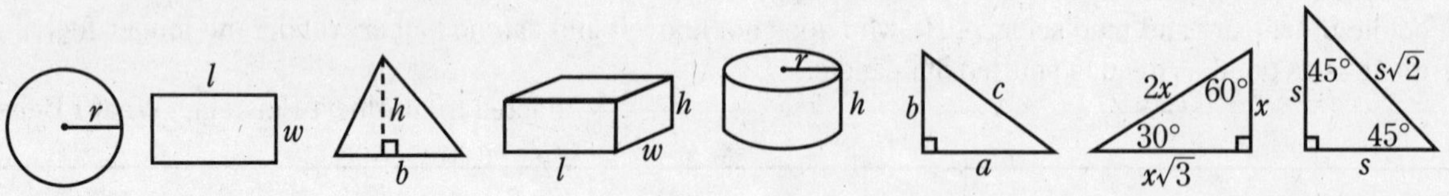

$A = \pi r^2$ $C = 2\pi r$ | $A = lw$ | $A = \frac{1}{2}bh$ | $V = lwh$ | $V = \pi r^2 h$ | $c^2 = a^2 + b^2$ | *Special Right Triangles*

The number of degrees of arc in a circle is 360.
The sum of the measures in degrees of the angles of a triangle is 180.

1. What is another expression for 8 less than the quotient of x and 3?

(A) $\frac{x-8}{3}$
(B) $\frac{x}{3} - 8$
(C) $8 - 3x$
(D) $3x - 8$
(E) $3(8 - x)$

2. Each of Phil's buckets has a capacity of 11 gallons. Each of Mark's buckets can hold 8 gallons. How much more water, in gallons, can 7 of Phil's buckets hold than 7 of Mark's buckets?

(A) 3
(B) 7
(C) 21
(D) 24
(E) 56

GO ON TO THE NEXT PAGE

3. Which of the following is equal to $\frac{|x|}{|y|}$ for all real numbers x and y?

(A) $\frac{x}{y}$

(B) $\frac{|x|}{y}$

(C) $\frac{x}{|y|}$

(D) $\left|\frac{x}{y}\right|$

(E) $-\left|\frac{x}{y}\right|$

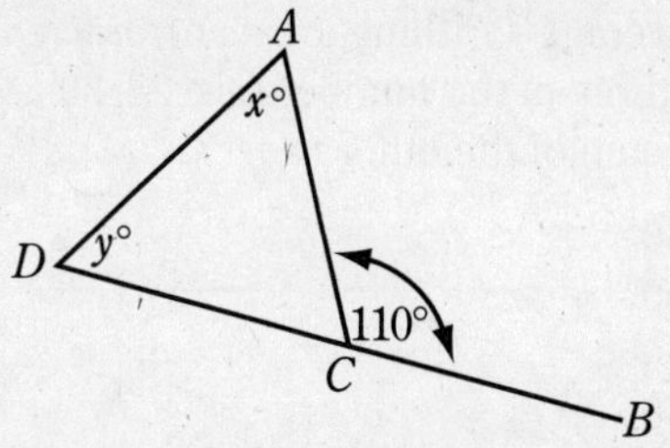

5. In the figure above, $m\angle ACB = 110°$ and $AC = CD$. What is the value of $2y$?

(A) 45
(B) 70
(C) 90
(D) 110
(E) 140

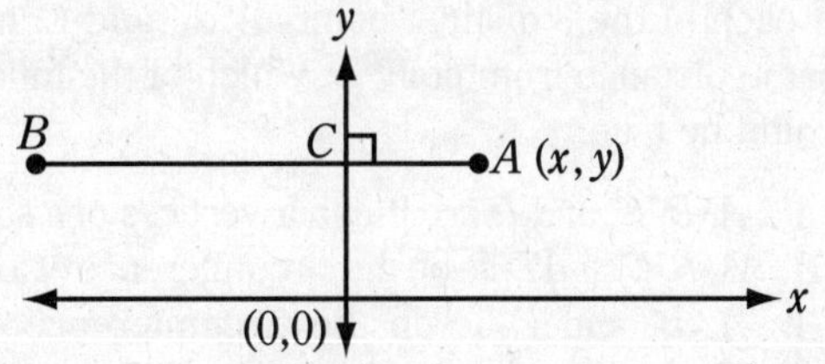

4. If $3AC = BC$ in the figure above, what are the coordinates of B?

(A) $(x, 3y)$
(B) $(-x, 3y)$
(C) $(3x, y)$
(D) $(-3x, y)$
(E) $(-3x, 3y)$

6. If $(x + y)^2 = 9$, what is $x + y$?

(A) 0
(B) 3
(C) 9
(D) 27
(E) The answer cannot be determined from the information given.

GO ON TO THE NEXT PAGE

7. The average (arithmetic mean) of five numbers is 34. If three of the numbers are 28, 30, and 32, what is the sum of the other two?

(A) 40
(B) 50
(C) 60
(D) 70
(E) 80

9. For any positive integer, x, $\textcircled{x} = \frac{x^2}{3}$ and $\boxed{x} = \frac{9}{x}$. What is an expression for $\textcircled{x} \times \boxed{x}$?

(A) $3x$
(B) x
(C) 1
(D) $\frac{x^3}{64}$
(E) $27x^3$

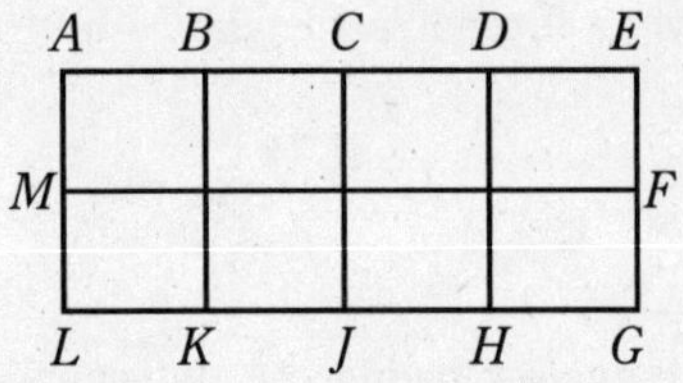

8. In the figure above, rectangle $AEGL$ has been divided into 8 congruent squares. If the perimeter of one of these squares is 16, what is the value of $AE + MF + LG + AL + BK + CJ + DH + EG$?

(A) 32
(B) 44
(C) 88
(D) 128
(E) 176

10. If each of the 3 distinct points A, B, and C are the same distance from point D, which of the following could be true?

I. A, B, C, and D are the four vertices of a square.
II. A, B, C, and D lie on the circumference of a circle.
III. A, B, and C lie on the circumference of the circle whose center is D.

(A) I only
(B) II only
(C) III only
(D) II and III only
(E) I, II, and III

GO ON TO THE NEXT PAGE

11. Of the following five diagrams below, which diagram describes the dark region as the set of elements that belongs to all of the sets A, B, and C?

(A)
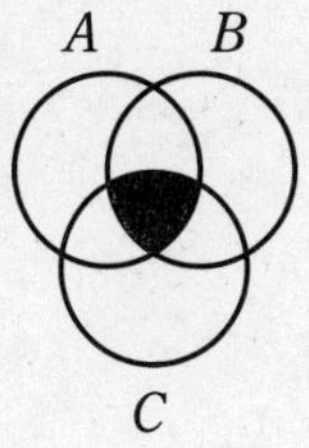

(B)

(C)
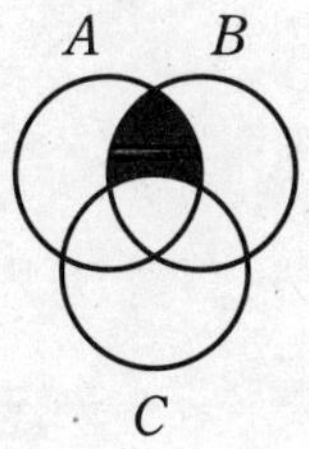

(D)

(E)
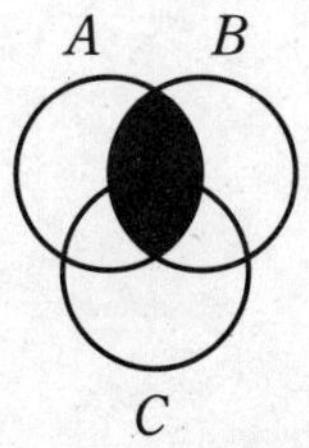

12. If the points (1,3), (3,5), and (6,*y*) all lie on the same line, the value of *y* is

(A) 8
(B) 7
(C) 6
(D) 5
(E) 4

13. In a certain small town, *p* gallons of gasoline are needed per month for each car in town. At this rate, if there are *r* cars in town, how long, in months, will *q* gallons last?

(A) $\frac{pq}{r}$
(B) $\frac{qr}{p}$
(C) $\frac{r}{pq}$
(D) $\frac{q}{pr}$
(E) pqr

GO ON TO THE NEXT PAGE

Questions 14–15

The next two questions refer to the following definition:

The *l*-length of the segment from point A to point B is $B - A$.

14. What is the *l*-length from -3 to 3?

(A) -6
(B) -3
(C) 0
(D) 3
(E) 6

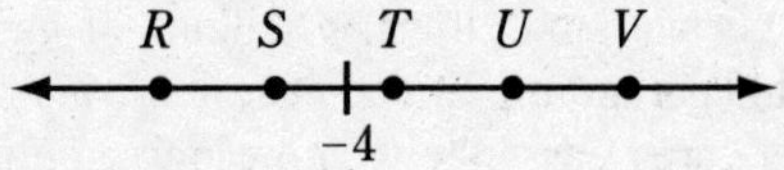

15. Of all segments beginning at -4 and ending at one of the integers indicated above on the number line, which segment has the *least* *l*-length?

(A) From -4 to R
(B) From -4 to S
(C) From -4 to T
(D) From -4 to U
(E) From -4 to V

16. If the sum of 5 consecutive positive integers is w, in terms of w, which of the following represents the sum of the next 5 consecutive positive integers?

(A) $w + 5$
(B) $5w + 5$
(C) $5w + 25$
(D) $w + 25$
(E) $w^2 + 25$

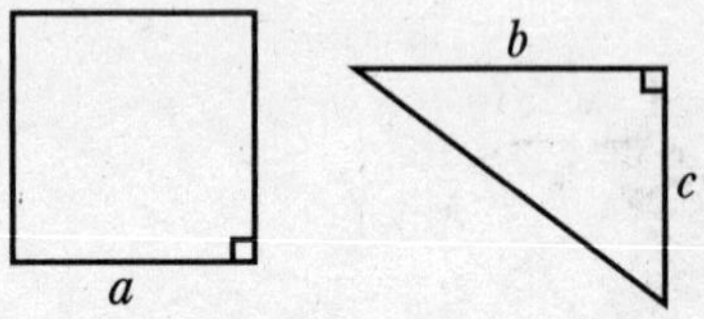

17. If the area of the square is twice the area of the triangle and $bc = 100$, then find a^2.

(A) 400
(B) 200
(C) 100
(D) 50
(E) 25

GO ON TO THE NEXT PAGE

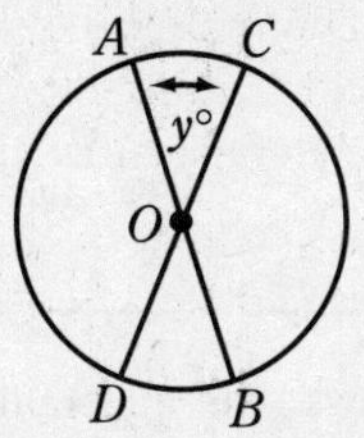

Note: Figure is not drawn to scale

18. In the figure above, $\overline{AB}$ and $\overline{CD}$ are diameters of the circle whose center is O. If the radius of the circle is 2 inches and the sum of the lengths of arcs $\widehat{AD}$ and $\widehat{BC}$ is 3π inches, then $y =$

(A) 45
(B) 60
(C) 75
(D) 90
(E) 120

19. Five years ago, Ross was N times as old as Amanda was. If Amanda is now 19 years old, how old is Ross now in terms of N?

(A) $14N - 5$
(B) $14N + 5$
(C) $19N + 5$
(D) $15N + 5$
(E) $19N - 5$

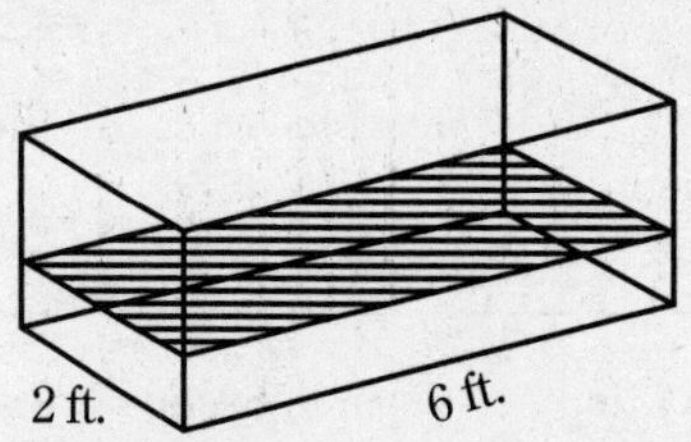

20. The figure above shows water in a tank whose base is 2 feet by 6 feet. If a rectangular solid whose dimensions are 1 foot by 1 foot by 2 feet is totally immersed in the water, how many *inches* will the water rise?

(A) $\frac{1}{6}$
(B) 1
(C) 2
(D) 3
(E) 12

STOP

If you finish before time is called, you may check your work on this section only.
Do not turn to any other section in the test.

Take a 5 minute break

before starting section 3

SECTION 3

Time: 25 Minutes—Turn to Section 3 (page 856) of your answer sheet to answer the questions in this section.
18 Questions

Directions: This section contains two types of question. You have 25 minutes to complete both types. For questions 1–8, solve each problem and decide which is the best of the choices given. Fill in the corresponding circle on the answer sheet. You may use any available space for scratchwork.

Notes:

1. The use of a calculator is permitted.
2. All numbers used are real numbers.
3. Figures that accompany problems in this test are intended to provide information useful in solving the problems. They are drawn as accurately as possible EXCEPT when it is stated in a specific problem that the figure is not drawn to scale. All figures lie in a plane unless otherwise indicated.
4. Unless otherwise specified, the domain of any function f is assumed to be the set of all real numbers x for which $f(x)$ is a real number.

REFERENCE INFORMATION

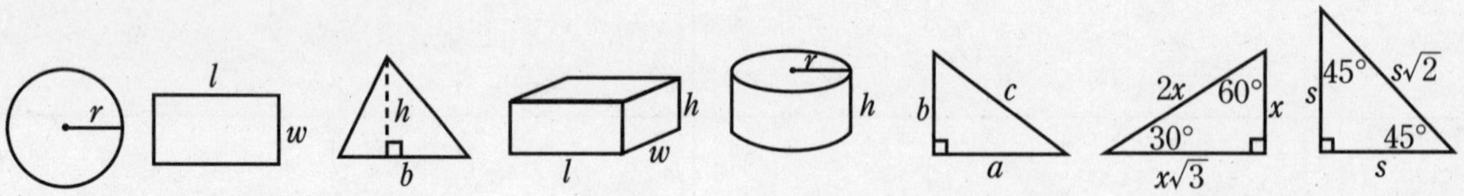

$A = \pi r^2$ $C = 2\pi r$ $A = lw$ $A = \frac{1}{2}bh$ $V = lwh$ $V = \pi r^2 h$ $c^2 = a^2 + b^2$ *Special Right Triangles*

The number of degrees of arc in a circle is 360.
The sum of the measures in degrees of the angles of a triangle is 180.

1. If $x + by = 3x + y = 5$ and $y = 2$, then $b =$

(A) 0
(B) 1
(C) 2
(D) 3
(E) 4

2. There are 2 boys and 3 girls in the class. The ratio of boys to girls in the class is equal to all of the following *except*

(A) 4 : 6
(B) 9 : 12
(C) 6 : 9
(D) 12 : 18
(E) 18 : 27

GO ON TO THE NEXT PAGE

3. What fraction of 1 week is 24 min?

(A) $\frac{1}{60}$
(B) $\frac{1}{168}$
(C) $\frac{1}{420}$
(D) $\frac{1}{1,440}$
(E) $\frac{1}{10,080}$

4. $2 \times 10^{-5} \times 8 \times 10^{2} \times 5 \times 10^{2} =$

(A) .00008
(B) .008
(C) .08
(D) 8
(E) 800

5. Johnny spent $\frac{2}{5}$ of his allowance on candy and $\frac{5}{6}$ of the remainder on ice cream. If his allowance is \$30, how much money did he have left after buying the candy and ice cream?

(A) \$1
(B) \$2
(C) \$3
(D) \$5
(E) \$10

Questions 6–7 refer to the following diagram:

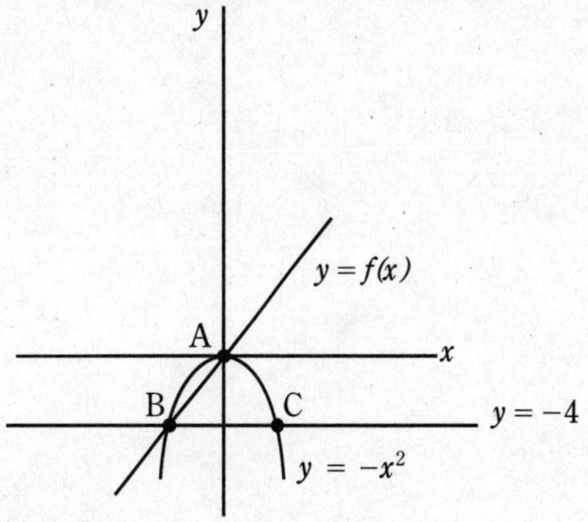

6. The *x*-coordinate of point B is

(A) −2
(B) −3
(C) −4
(D) −5
(E) −6

GO ON TO THE NEXT PAGE

7. The graph of the equation $y = f(x)$ is of the form $y = mx + b$, where b is

(A) 0
(B) 1
(C) 2
(D) 3
(E) 4

8. At how many points does the graph of the equation $y = x^4 + x^3$ intersect the x-axis?

(A) 0
(B) 1
(C) 2
(D) 3
(E) 4

GO ON TO THE NEXT PAGE

Directions: For Student-Produced Response questions 9–18, use the grids at the bottom of the answer sheet page on which you have answered questions 1–8.

Each of the remaining 10 questions requires you to solve the problem and enter your answer by marking the circles in the special grid, as shown in the examples below. You may use any available space for scratchwork.

Answer: $\frac{7}{12}$ or 7/12 Answer: 2.5 Answer: 201
Either position is correct.

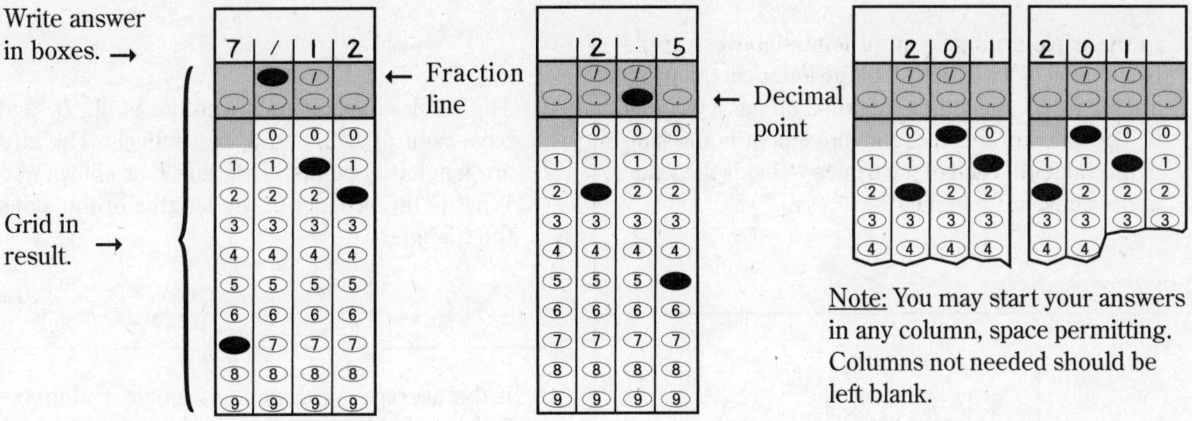

Note: You may start your answers in any column, space permitting. Columns not needed should be left blank.

- Mark no more than one oval in any column.
- Because the answer sheet will be machine-scored, **you will receive credit only if the ovals are filled in correctly.**
- Although not required, it is suggested that you write your answer in the boxes at the top of the columns to help you fill in the ovals accurately.
- Some problems may have more than one correct answer. In such cases, grid only one answer.
- No question has a negative answer.
- **Mixed numbers** such as $2\frac{1}{2}$ must be gridded as 2.5 or 5/2. (If 2 1 / 2 is gridded, it will be interpreted as $\frac{21}{2}$, not $2\frac{1}{2}$.)
- Decimal Accuracy: If you obtain a decimal answer, **enter the most accurate value the grid will accommodate.** For example, if you obtain an answer such as 0.6666..., you should record the result as .666 or .667. **Less accurate values such as .66 or .67 are not acceptable.**

Acceptable ways to grid $\frac{2}{3}$ = .6666...:

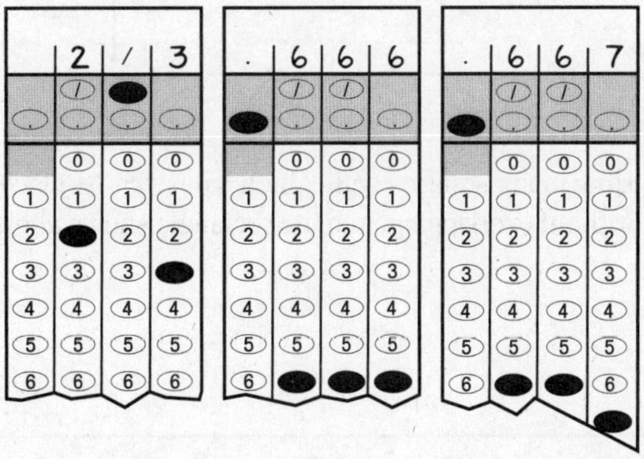

9. If $\frac{5}{8}$ of x is 40, then find the value of $\frac{3}{8}$ of x.

10. A piece of wire is bent to form a circle of radius 3 feet. How many pieces of wire, each 2 feet long, can be made from the wire?

11. Dick spent $7 in order to buy baseballs and tennis balls. If baseballs are 70¢ each and tennis balls are 60¢ each, what is the greatest possible number of tennis balls that Dick could have bought?

GO ON TO THE NEXT PAGE

12. Let $f(x)$ be defined for all x by the equation $f(x) = 12x + 8$. Thus, $f(2) = 32$. If $f(x) \div f(0) = 2x$, then find the value of x.

ABA	*BBB*	*CBA*	*BBA*
ACC	*CBC*	*CCC*	*ACA*
BAC	*ABC*	*BCA*	*CAB*
CBB	*BCA*	*AAB*	*ACC*

13. In the triple arrangement of letters above, a triple has a value of 1 if exactly 2 of the letters in the triple are the same. Any other combination has a value of 0. The value of the entire arrangement is the sum of the values of each of the triples. What is the value of the above arrangement?

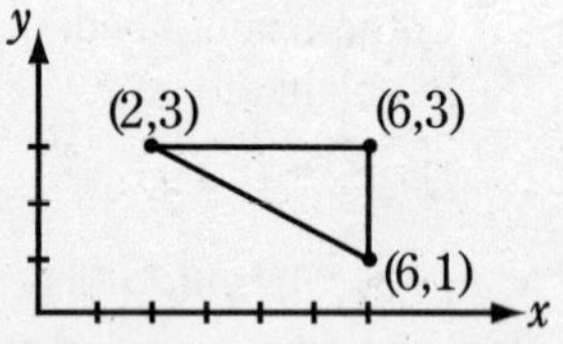

14. In the figure above, what is the area of the triangle?

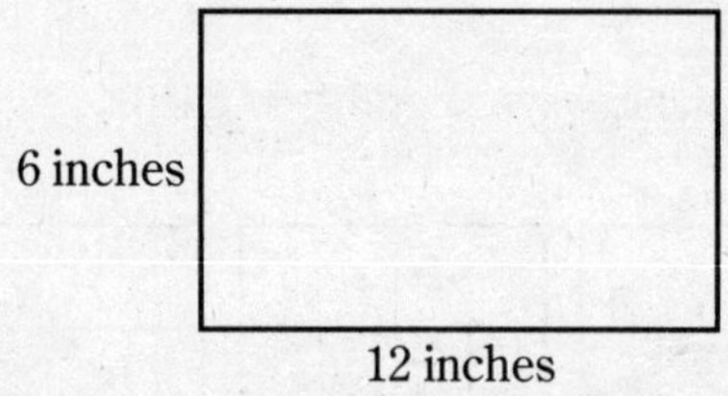

15. How many squares with 2-inch sides can be placed, without overlapping, into the rectangle shown above?

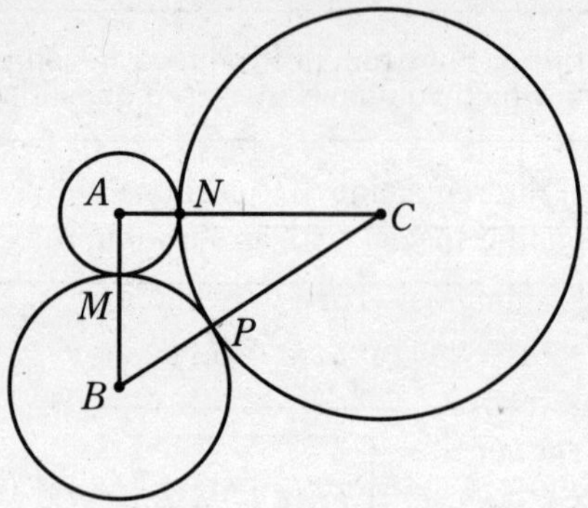

16. The circles having their centers at A, B, and C have radii of 1, 2, and 3, respectively. The circles are tangent at points M, N, and P as shown above. What is the product of the lengths of the sides of the triangle?

17. If the average (arithmetic mean) of 4 numbers is 8,000 and the average (arithmetic mean) of 3 of the 4 numbers is 7,500, then what must the fourth number be?

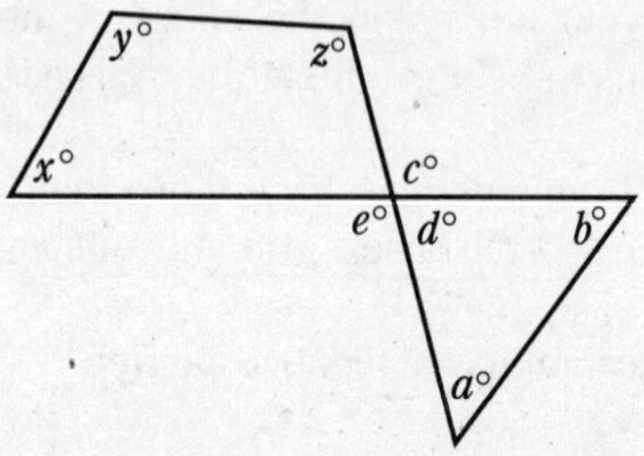

18. Five line segments intersect to form the figure above. What is the value of $x + y + z$ if $c = 100$?

STOP

If you finish before time is called, you may check your work on this section only.
Do not turn to any other section in the test.

SECTION 4

Time: 25 Minutes—Turn to Section 4 (page 857) of your answer sheet to answer the questions in this section.
24 Questions

Directions: For each question in this section, select the best answer from among the choices given and fill in the corresponding circle on the answer sheet.

Each sentence below has one or two blanks, each blank indicating that something has been omitted. Beneath the sentence are five words or sets of words labeled A through E. Choose the word or set of words that, when inserted in the sentence, best fits the meaning of the sentence as a whole.

Example:

Hoping to ______ the dispute, negotiators proposed a compromise that they felt would be ______ to both labor and management.

(A) enforce...useful
(B) end...divisive
(C) overcome...unattractive
(D) extend...satisfactory
(E) resolve...acceptable

Ⓐ Ⓑ Ⓒ Ⓓ ●

1. In a rising tide of ______ in public education, Miss Anderson was an example of an informed and ______ teacher—a blessing to children and an asset to the nation.

(A) compromise...inept
(B) pacifism...inspiring
(C) ambiguity...average
(D) mediocrity...dedicated
(E) oblivion...typical

2. It is ______ that primitive man considered eclipses to be ______ .

(A) foretold...spectacular
(B) impossible...ominous
(C) understandable...magical
(D) true...rational
(E) glaring...desirable

3. By ______ the conversation, the girl had once again proved that she had overcome her shyness.

(A) appreciating
(B) recognizing
(C) hearing
(D) initiating
(E) considering

4. Only an authority in that area would be able to ______ such highly ______ subject matter included in the book.

(A) understand...general
(B) confuse...simple
(C) read...useless
(D) comprehend...complex
(E) misconstrue...sophisticated

5. The professor displayed extreme stubbornness; not only did he ______ the logic of the student's argument, but he ______ to acknowledge that the textbook conclusion was correct.

(A) amplify...hesitated
(B) reject...refused
(C) clarify...consented
(D) justify...expected
(E) ridicule...proposed

6. The ______ of the explorers was reflected in their refusal to give up.

(A) tenacity
(B) degradation
(C) greed
(D) harassment
(E) sociability

GO ON TO THE NEXT PAGE

7. Ironically, the protest held in order to strengthen the labor movement served to ______ it.

(A) justify
(B) coddle
(C) weaken
(D) invigorate
(E) appease

8. In spite of David's tremendous intelligence, he was frequently ______ when confronted with practical matters.

(A) coherent
(B) baffled
(C) cautious
(D) philosophical
(E) pensive

GO ON TO THE NEXT PAGE

Each passage below is followed by questions based on its content. Answer the questions on the basis of what is stated or implied in each passage and in any introductory material that may be provided.

Questions 9–10 are based on the following passage.

In the South American rain forest abide the greatest acrobats on earth. The monkeys of the Old World, agile as they are, cannot hang by their tails. It is only the monkeys of America that possess this skill. They are called ceboids and their unique group includes marmosets, owl monkeys, sakis, spider monkeys, squirrel monkeys and howlers. Among these the star gymnast is the skinny, intelligent spider monkey. Hanging head down like a trapeze artist from the loop of a liana, he may suddenly give a short swing, launch himself into space and, soaring outward and downward across a 50-foot void of air, lightly catch a bough on which he spied a shining berry. Owl monkeys cannot match his leap, for their arms are shorter, their tails untalented. The marmosets, smallest of the tribe, tough noisy hoodlums that travel in gangs, are also capable of leaps into space, but their landings are rough: smack against a tree trunk with arms and legs spread wide.

9. Which of the following titles best expresses the ideas of this selection?
   - (A) The Star Gymnast
   - (B) Monkeys and Trees
   - (C) Travelers in Space
   - (D) The Uniqueness of Monkeys
   - (E) Ceboid Acrobats

10. Compared to monkeys of the Old World, American monkeys are
    - (A) smaller
    - (B) quieter
    - (C) more dexterous
    - (D) more protective of their young
    - (E) less at home in their surroundings

Questions 11–12 are based on the following passage.

A critic of politics finds himself driven to deprecate the power of words while using them copiously in warning against their influence. It is indeed in politics that their influence is most dangerous, so that one is almost tempted to wish that they did not exist, and that society might be managed silently, by instinct, habit, and ocular perception, without this supervening Babel of reports, arguments, and slogans.

11. The author implies that critics of misused language
    - (A) become fanatical on this subject
    - (B) are guilty of what they criticize in others
    - (C) are clever in contriving slogans
    - (D) tell the story of the Tower of Babel
    - (E) rely too strongly on instincts

12. Which statement is true according to the passage?
    - (A) Critics of politics are often driven to take desperate measures.
    - (B) Words, when used by politicians, have the greatest capacity for harm.
    - (C) Politicians talk more than other people.
    - (D) Society would be better managed if mutes were in charge.
    - (E) Reports and slogans are not to be trusted.

GO ON TO THE NEXT PAGE

Questions 13–24 are based on the following passage.

The following passage deals with the importance of castles in medieval Europe and how they affected the society at that time.

Medieval Europe abounded in castles. Germany alone had ten thousand and more, most of them now vanished; all that a summer journey in the Rhineland and the southwest now can show are a handful of ruins and a few nineteenth century restorations. Nevertheless, anyone journeying from Spain to the Dvina, from Calabria to Wales, will find castles rearing up again and again to dominate the open landscape. There they still stand, in desolate and uninhabited districts where the only visible forms of life are herdsmen and their flocks, with hawks circling the battlements, far from the traffic and comfortably distant even from the nearest small town: these were the strongholds of the European aristocracy.

The weight of aristocratic dominance was felt in Europe until well after the French Revolution; political and social structure, the Church, the general tenor of thought and feeling were all influenced by it. Over the centuries, consciously or unconsciously, the other classes of this older European society—the clergy, the bourgeoisie and the "common people"—adopted many of the outward characteristics of the aristocracy, who became their model, their standard, their ideal. Aristocratic values and ambitions were adopted alongside aristocratic manners and fashions of dress. Yet the aristocracy were the object of much contentious criticism and complaint; from the thirteenth century onwards their military value and their political importance were both called in question. Nevertheless, their opponents continued to be their principal imitators. In the eleventh and twelfth centuries, the reforming Papacy and its clerical supporters, although opposed to the excessively aristocratic control of the Church (as is shown by the Investiture Contest), nevertheless themselves first adopted and then strengthened the forms of this control. Noblemen who became bishops or who founded new Orders helped to implant aristocratic principles and forms of government deep within the structure and spiritual life of the Church. Again, in the twelfth and thirteenth centuries the urban bourgeoisie, made prosperous and even rich by trade and industry, were rising to political power as the servants and legal proteges of monarchy. These "patricians" were critical of the aristocracy and hostile towards it. Yet they also imitated the aristocracy, and tried to gain admittance to the closed circle and to achieve equality of status. Even the unarmed peasantry, who usually had to suffer more from the unrelieved weight of aristocratic dominance, long remained tenaciously loyal to their lords, held to their allegiance by that combination of love and fear, *amor et timor*, which was so characteristic of the medieval relationship between lord and servant, between God and man.

The castles and strongholds of the aristocracy remind us of the reality of their power and superiority. Through the long warring centuries when men went defenseless and insecure, the "house," the lord's fortified dwelling, promised protection, security and peace to all whom it sheltered. From the ninth to the eleventh centuries, if not later, Europe was in many ways all too open. Attack came from the sea, in the Mediterranean from Saracens and Vikings, the latter usually in their swift, dragon-prowed, easily manoeuvered longboats, manned by some sixteen pairs of oarsmen and with a full complement of perhaps sixty men. There were periods when the British Isles and the French coasts were being raided every year by Vikings and in the heart of the continent marauding Magyar armies met invading bands of Saracens. The name of Pontresina, near St. Moritz in Switzerland, is a memento of the stormy tenth century; it means *pons Saracenorum*, the "fortified Saracen bridge," the place where plundering expeditions halted on their way up from the Mediterranean.

It was recognized in theory that the Church and the monarchy were the principal powers and that they were bound by the nature of their office to ensure peace and security and to do justice; but at this period they were too weak, too torn by internal conflicts to fulfill their obligations. Thus more and more power passed into the hands of warriors invested by the monarchy and the Church with lands and rights of jurisdiction, who in return undertook to support their overlords and to protect the unarmed peasantry.

Their first concern, however, was self-protection. It is almost impossible for us to realize how primitive the great majority of these early medieval "castles" really were. Until about 1150 the fortified houses of the Anglo-Norman nobility were simple dwellings surrounded by a mound of earth and a wooden stockade. These were the motte and bailey castles: the motte was the mound and its stockade, the bailey an open court lying below and also stockaded. Both were protected, where possible, by yet another ditch filled with water, the moat. In the middle of the motte there was a wooden tower, the keep or *donjon*, which only became a genuine stronghold at a later date and in places where stone was readily available. The stone castles of the French and German nobility usually had only a single communal room in which all activities took place.

In such straitened surroundings, where warmth, light and comfort were lacking, there was no way of creating an air of privacy. It is easy enough to understand why the life of the landed nobility was often so unrestrained, so filled with harshness, cruelty and brutality, even in later, more "chivalrous" periods. The barons' daily life was bare and uneventful, punctuated by war, hunting (a rehearsal for war), and feasting. Boys were trained to fight from the age of seven or eight, and their education in arms continued until they were twenty-one, although in some cases they started to fight as early as fifteen. The peasants of the surrounding countryside, bound to their lords by a great variety of ties, produced the sparse fare which was all that the undeveloped agriculture of the early medieval period could sustain. Hunting was a constant necessity, to make up for the lack of butcher's meat, and in England and Germany in the eleventh and twelfth centuries even the kings had to progress from one crown estate to another, from one bishop's palace to the next, to maintain themselves and their retinue.

GO ON TO THE NEXT PAGE

13. According to the passage, class conflict in the Middle Ages was kept in check by

(A) the fact that most people belonged to the same class
(B) tyrannical suppressions of rebellions by powerful monarchs
(C) the religious teachings of the church
(D) the fact that all other classes admired and attempted to emulate the aristocracy
(E) the fear that a relatively minor conflict would lead to a general revolution

14. According to the author, the urban bourgeoisie was hostile to the aristocracy because

(A) the bourgeoisie was prevented by the aristocracy from seeking an alliance with the kings
(B) aristocrats often confiscated the wealth of the bourgeoisie
(C) the bourgeoisie saw the aristocracy as their rivals
(D) the aristocrats often deliberately antagonized the bourgeoisie
(E) the bourgeoisie felt that the aristocracy was immoral

15. According to the passage, castles were originally built

(A) as status symbols
(B) as strongholds against invaders
(C) as simple places to live in
(D) as luxurious chateaux
(E) as recreation centers for the townspeople

16. One of the groups that invaded central Europe during the Middle Ages from the ninth century on was the

(A) Magyars
(B) Franks
(C) Angles
(D) Celts
(E) Welsh

17. It can be seen from the passage that the aristocracy was originally

(A) the great landowners
(B) members of the clergy
(C) the king's warriors
(D) merchants who became wealthy
(E) slaves who had rebelled

18. The reform popes eventually produced an aristocratic church because

(A) they depended on the aristocracy for money
(B) they themselves were more interested in money than in religion
(C) they were defeated by aristocrats
(D) many aristocrats entered the structure of the church and impressed their values on it
(E) the aristocrats were far more religious than other segments of the population

19. The word "contentious" in line 25 is best interpreted to mean

(A) careful
(B) solid
(C) controversial
(D) grandiose
(E) annoying

20. According to the passage, hunting served the dual purpose of

(A) preparing for war and engaging in sport
(B) preparing for war and getting meat
(C) learning how to ride and learning how to shoot
(D) testing horses and men
(E) getting furs and ridding the land of excess animals

21. The phrase "amor et timor" in line 47 is used to describe

(A) the rivalry between the bourgeoisie and the aristocracy
(B) the Church's view of man and his relationship to God
(C) the peasant's loyalty to the aristocracy
(D) the adaptation of aristocratic manners and dress
(E) the payment of food in exchange for protection

22. The passage indicates that protection of the peasantry was implemented by

(A) the king's warriors
(B) the Magyar mercenaries
(C) the replacement of wood towers by stone donjons
(D) the princes of the Church
(E) the ruling monarchy

GO ON TO THE NEXT PAGE

23. According to the passage, the effectiveness of the Church and king was diminished by

(A) the ambition of the military
(B) conflicts and weaknesses within the Church and Royal house
(C) peasant dissatisfaction
(D) the inherent flaws of feudalism
(E) economic instability

24. "Retinue," the last word in the passage, refers to

(A) food
(B) all material goods
(C) money
(D) attendants
(E) family

STOP

If you finish before time is called, you may check your work on this section only.
Do not turn to any other section in the test.

Take a 1 minute break

before starting section 5

SECTION 5

Time: 25 Minutes—Turn to Section 5 (page 857) of your answer sheet to answer the questions in this section.
35 Questions

Directions: For each question in this section, select the best answer from among the choices given and fill in the corresponding circle on the answer sheet.

The following sentences test correctness and effectiveness of expression. Part of each sentence or the entire sentence is underlined; beneath each sentence are five ways of phrasing the underlined material. Choice A repeats the original phrasing; the other four choices are different. If you think the original phrasing produces a better sentence than any of the alternatives, select Choice A; if not, select one of the other choices.

In making your selection, follow the requirements of standard written English; that is, pay attention to grammar, choice of words, sentence construction, and punctuation. Your selection should result in the most effective sentence—clear and precise, without awkwardness or ambiguity.

EXAMPLE:

Laura Ingalls Wilder published her first book and she was sixty-five years old then.

(A) and she was sixty-five years old then
(B) when she was sixty-five
(C) at age sixty-five years old
(D) upon the reaching of sixty-five years
(E) at the time when she was sixty-five

Ⓐ ● Ⓒ Ⓓ Ⓔ

1. After the defendant charged him with being prejudiced, the judge withdrew from the case.

(A) After the defendant charged him with being prejudiced
(B) On account of the defendant charged him with being prejudiced
(C) Charging the defendant with being prejudiced
(D) Upon the defendant charging him with being prejudiced
(E) The defendant charged him with being prejudiced

2. Although the mourners differed in color and in dress, they all sat silently together for an hour to honor Whitney M. Young Jr.

(A) Although the mourners differed in color and in dress
(B) Because the mourners differed in color and in dress
(C) The mourners having differed in color and in dress
(D) When the mourners differed in color and in dress
(E) The mourners differed in color and in dress

3. To avoid the hot sun, our plans were that we would travel at night.

(A) To avoid the hot sun, our plans were that we would travel at night.
(B) To try to avoid the hot sun, our plans were for travel at night.
(C) Our plans were night travel so that we could avoid the hot sun.
(D) We planned to travel at night, that's how we would avoid the hot sun.
(E) To avoid the hot sun, we made plans to travel at night.

4. Whatever she had any thoughts about, they were interrupted as the hotel lobby door opened.

(A) Whatever she had any thoughts about
(B) Whatever her thoughts
(C) Whatever be her thoughts
(D) What her thoughts were
(E) What thoughts

GO ON TO THE NEXT PAGE

5. The use of radar, as well as the two-way radio, make it possible for state troopers to intercept most speeders.

(A) make it possible
(B) makes it possible
(C) allows the possibility
(D) makes possible
(E) make it a possibility

6. Irregardless what reasons or excuses are offered, there is only one word for his behavior: cowardice.

(A) Irregardless what reasons or excuses are offered
(B) Regardless about what reasons or excuses he may offer
(C) Since he offered reasons and excuses
(D) Nevertheless he offered reasons and excuses
(E) No matter what reasons and excuses are offered

7. What a man cannot state, he does not perfectly know.

(A) What a man cannot state, he does not perfectly know.
(B) A man cannot state if he does not perfectly know.
(C) A man cannot perfectly know if he does not state.
(D) That which a man cannot state is that which he cannot perfectly know.
(E) What a man cannot state is the reason he does not perfectly know.

8. Professional writers realize that they cannot hope to effect the reader precisely as they wish without care and practice in the use of words.

(A) they cannot hope to effect
(B) they cannot hope to have an effect on
(C) they cannot hope to affect
(D) they cannot hope effecting
(E) they cannot try to affect

9. I've met two men whom, I believe, were policemen.

(A) whom, I believe
(B) who, I believe
(C) each, I believe
(D) and I believe they
(E) who

10. Such people never have and never will be trusted.

(A) never have and never will be trusted
(B) never have and will be trusted
(C) never have trusted and never will trust
(D) never have been trusted and never will be trusted
(E) never have had anyone trust them and never will have anyone trust them

11. Your employer would have been inclined to favor your request if you would have waited for an occasion when he was less busy.

(A) if you would have waited for an occasion
(B) if you would only have waited for an occasion
(C) if you were to have waited for an occasion
(D) if you waited for an occasion
(E) if you had waited for an occasion

GO ON TO THE NEXT PAGE

The following sentences test your ability to recognize grammar and usage errors. Each sentence contains either a single error or no error at all. No sentence contains more than one error. The error, if there is one, is underlined and lettered. If the sentence contains an error, select the one underlined part that must be changed to make the sentence correct. If the sentence is correct, select Choice E. In choosing answers, follow the requirements of standard written English.

EXAMPLE:

The other (A) delegates and him (B) immediately (C) accepted the resolution drafted by (D) the neutral states. No error. (E)

(A) ● (C) (D) (E)

12. Because of (A) the bomb threat, everyone was asked (B) to evacuate the bank but (C) a security guard, a fireman, and I. (D) No error. (E)

13. Having drank (A) almost all the lemonade that (B) his wife had made (C) for the picnic, Dick could (D) not face her. No error. (E)

14. The wealthy socialite decided that her fortune would be left (A) to whomever (B) of her relatives could present (C) her with the best plan for dispensing part of the money to deserving (D) charities. No error. (E)

15. Shortly after arriving (A) at the amusement park with the eager third-graders, the parents realized (B) that they had brought nowhere near (C) the number (D) of chaperones required to control the children. No error. (E)

16. The board members along with (A) the chairman were planning (B) a series (C) of speakers to lecture on different dividend plans for their (D) employees. No error. (E)

17. Due to (A) his (B) not studying and not attending review sessions, Paul got (C) a failing mark in his bar exam, resulting in (D) a retraction of the job offer from the law firm. No error. (E)

18. When I was (A) in high school, I worked hard (B) to buy the kind of a (C) car that most of (D) my friends were also driving. No error. (E)

19. The literature professor has complained (A) that many student poets are so conceited (B) that they compare their (C) poems with Robert Frost (D). No error. (E)

20. I appreciate you (A) offering to help (B) me with my research project, but the honor system prevents (C) students from giving and receiving assistance (D). No error. (E)

21. In the final heat of the mile race, only two (A) runners finished the race, but even the slowest (B) of the two was able (C) to break the school record that had been set (D) a decade earlier. No error. (E)

GO ON TO THE NEXT PAGE

22. Passing the written (A) test that (B) is required for a driver's license is usually easier (C) than to pass (D) the driving test. No error. (E)

23. All the aspiring (A) young writers submitted their stories (B), each hoping (C) that they (D) would win first prize. No error. (E)

24. Her answer to (A) the essay question on the test was all together (B) incorrect, but because it was very well written (C) she received partial (D) credit for her work. No error. (E)

25. When I introduced Scott and Wilma, they (A) acted as if (B) they never met (C) before even though (D) they had gone to the same high school. No error. (E)

26. The realtor felt badly (A) about not being able (B) to sell their (C) house because they were in a big hurry to move to (D) their condominium. No error. (E)

27. The president of the newly formed nation took (A) steps to encourage (B) several thousands (C) of people to immigrate into (D) the country. No error. (E)

28. The Governor asked the attorney to head (A) the committee because he (B) was convinced (C) that (D) the committee needed to start work immediately. No error. (E)

29. Both (A) my sisters participate (B) in sports, but my older (C) sister is the better (D) athlete. No error. (E)

GO ON TO THE NEXT PAGE

Directions: The following passage is an early draft of an essay. Some parts of the passage need to be rewritten.

Read the passage and select the best answers for the questions that follow. Some questions are about particular sentences or parts of sentences and ask you to improve sentence structure or word choice. Other questions ask you to consider organization and development. In choosing answers, follow the requirements of standard written English.

Questions 30–35 refer to the following passage.

[1]It has been proven beyond doubt that using seat belts in automobiles and wearing helmets while riding motorcycles can save lives. [2]The federal government has passed laws requiring the installation of seat belts in all new cars. [3]Still, there are people who argue that government has no right to interfere with individual comfort and freedom by mandating the installation and use of these safety devices. [4]In many states, laws prohibit motorcyclists from riding without helmets. [5]What these people fail to realize is that, although wearing a seat belt may be somewhat uncomfortable or confining, it is not as uncomfortable as broken bones nor as confining as a wheelchair or a coffin. [6]Motorcyclists who refuse to wear helmets may enjoy a degree of pleasure in feeling the free wind blow through their hair, but, if thrown in an accident, their heads can be as easily squashed as "free and natural" cantaloupes. [7]These safety devices may limit pleasure and freedom in small ways because they greatly increase the opportunity to live pleasant and free lives in more important ways.

30. What should be done with sentence 4?

(A) It should be placed before sentence 1.
(B) It should be attached to sentence 3 with and.
(C) Nothing should be done with it.
(D) It should be placed after sentence 2.
(E) It should be attached to sentence 5 with a semicolon.

31. In sentence 3, mandating should be

(A) omitted
(B) left as it is
(C) changed to prohibiting
(D) placed before individual
(E) changed to issuing directions that are in favor of

32. In sentence 6, what change is needed?

(A) These riders are should be inserted before thrown.
(B) Cantaloupes should be changed to balloons.
(C) They should be substituted for their heads.
(D) Commas should be placed around who refuse to wear helmets.
(E) Degree should be changed to measure.

33. Sentence 7 would be improved by

(A) turning it into two sentences, the first to end after small ways
(B) putting a comma after devices
(C) beginning the sentence with while
(D) omitting in more important ways
(E) changing because to but

34. Which would get the author's point across more effectively?

(A) Inserting a sentence that would describe statistics about the danger of not wearing seat belts or helmets.
(B) Describing the mechanics of how a seat belt works and how a helmet protects the head.
(C) Describing the governmental agency that enforced the laws.
(D) Pinpointing the states that enforce the helmet law.
(E) Citing the safest cars and motorcycles.

35. To begin the author's paragraph,

(A) sentence 2 should be placed first
(B) sentence 4 should be placed first
(C) sentence 6 should be placed first
(D) sentence 7 should be placed first, deleting the first word, "These," in that sentence
(E) sentence 1 should remain as the introductory sentence

STOP

If you finish before time is called, you may check your work on this section only.
Do not turn to any other section in the test.

SECTION 6

Time: 25 Minutes—Turn to Section 6 (page 858) of your answer sheet to answer the questions in this section.
18 Questions

Directions: This section contains two types of questions. You have 25 minutes to complete both types. For questions 1–8, solve each problem and decide which is the best of the choices given. Fill in the corresponding circle on the answer sheet. You may use any available space for scratchwork.

Notes:

1. The use of a calculator is permitted.
2. All numbers used are real numbers.
3. Figures that accompany problems in this test are intended to provide information useful in solving the problems. They are drawn as accurately as possible EXCEPT when it is stated in a specific problem that the figure is not drawn to scale. All figures lie in a plane unless otherwise indicated.
4. Unless otherwise specified, the domain of any function f is assumed to be the set of all real numbers x for which $f(x)$ is a real number.

REFERENCE INFORMATION

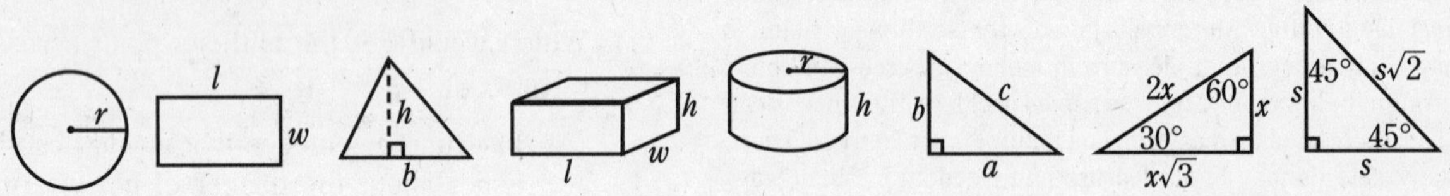

$A = \pi r^2$, $C = 2\pi r$ $\quad A = lw \quad A = \frac{1}{2}bh \quad V = lwh \quad V = \pi r^2 h \quad c^2 = a^2 + b^2$ *Special Right Triangles*

The number of degrees of arc in a circle is 360.
The sum of the measures in degrees of the angles of a triangle is 180.

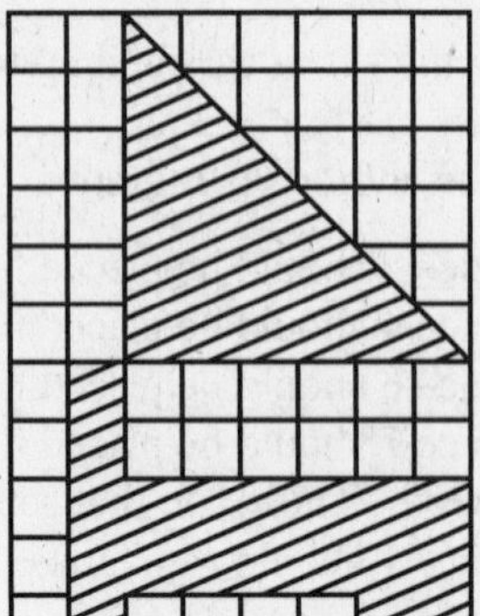

1. If each square in the grid above has a side of length 1, find the sum of the areas of the shaded regions.

(A) 55
(B) 46
(C) 37
(D) 30
(E) 24

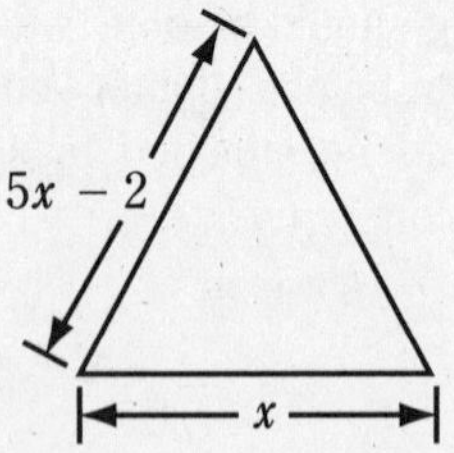

2. The figure above is an equilateral triangle. What is its perimeter?

(A) $\frac{1}{4}$
(B) $\frac{1}{2}$
(C) $1\frac{1}{2}$
(D) $3\frac{1}{2}$
(E) The answer cannot be determined from the information given.

GO ON TO THE NEXT PAGE

3. If w waves pass through a certain point in s seconds, how many waves would pass through that point in t seconds?

(A) wst

(B) $\frac{t}{s}$

(C) $\frac{ws}{t}$

(D) $\frac{ts}{w}$

(E) $\frac{tw}{s}$

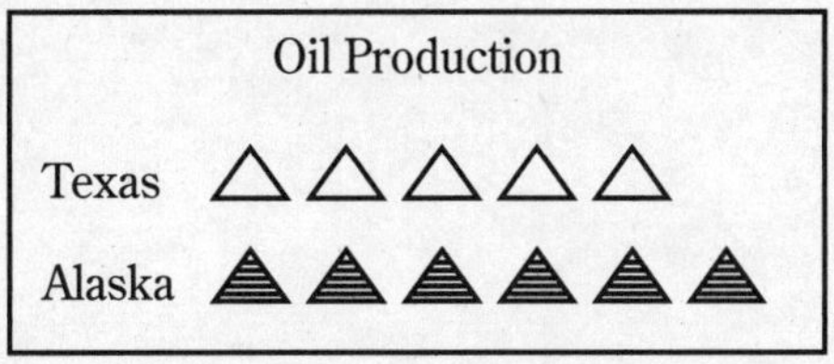

4. In the chart above, the amount represented by each shaded triangle is three times that represented by each unshaded triangle. What fraction of the total production represented by the chart was produced in Alaska?

(A) $\frac{6}{11}$

(B) $\frac{18}{5}$

(C) $\frac{18}{23}$

(D) $\frac{12}{17}$

(E) $\frac{23}{17}$

5. A box contains exactly 24 coins—nickels, dimes, and quarters. The probability of selecting a nickel by reaching into the box without looking is $\frac{3}{8}$. The probability of selecting a dime by reaching into the box without looking is $\frac{1}{8}$. How many quarters are in the box?

(A) 6
(B) 8
(C) 12
(D) 14
(E) 16

6. Which of the following designs *can* be formed by combining rectangles with size and shading the same as that shown above if overlap is not permitted?

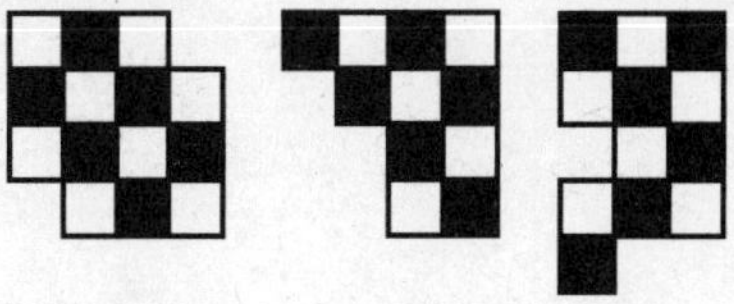

(A) I only
(B) II only
(C) III only
(D) I and II only
(E) II and III only

GO ON TO THE NEXT PAGE

7. If $f(x) = (x - 1)^2 + (x - 2)^2 + (x - 3)^2$, then $f(x + 2) =$

(A) $3x^2 + 4x + 2$
(B) $3x$
(C) $(x + 2)^2 + x^2 + (x - 2)^2$
(D) $3x^2 + 2$
(E) $4x^2 + 4$

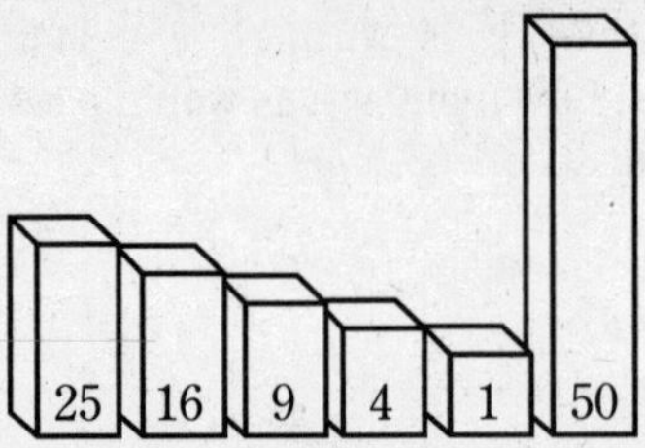

8. Six containers, whose capacities in cubic centimeters are shown, appear in the figure above. The 25-cubic-centimeter container is filled with flour, and the rest are empty. The contents of the 25-cubic-centimeter container are used to fill the 16-cubic-centimeter container, and the excess is dumped into the 50-cubic-centimeter container. Then the 16-cubic-centimeter container is used to fill the 9-cubic-centimeter container, and the excess is dumped into the 50-cubic-centimeter container. The process is repeated until all containers, except the 1-cubic-centimeter and the 50-cubic-centimeter containers, are empty. What percent of the 50-cubic-centimeter container is *empty*?

(A) 24%
(B) 48%
(C) 50%
(D) 52%
(E) 76%

GO ON TO THE NEXT PAGE

Directions: For Student-Produced Response questions 9–18, use the grids at the bottom of the answer sheet page on which you have answered questions 1–8.

Each of the remaining 10 questions requires you to solve the problem and enter your answer by marking the circles in the special grid, as shown in the examples below. You may use any available space for scratchwork.

Answer: $\frac{7}{12}$ or 7/12

Write answer in boxes. →

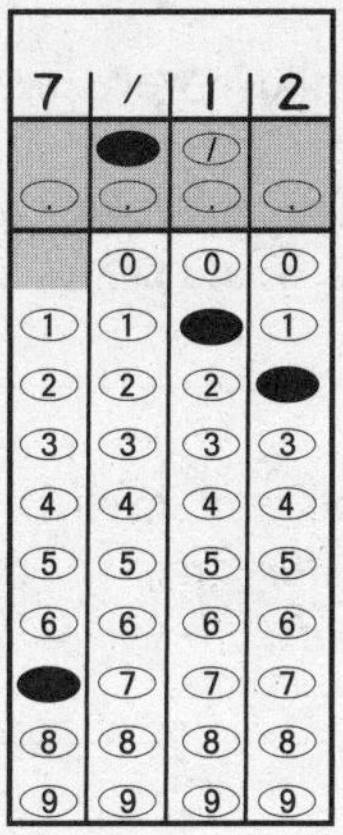

← Fraction line

Grid in result. →

Answer: 2.5

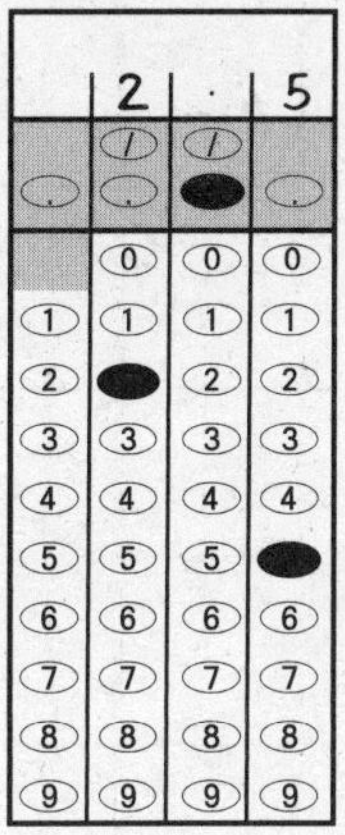

← Decimal point

Answer: 201
Either position is correct.

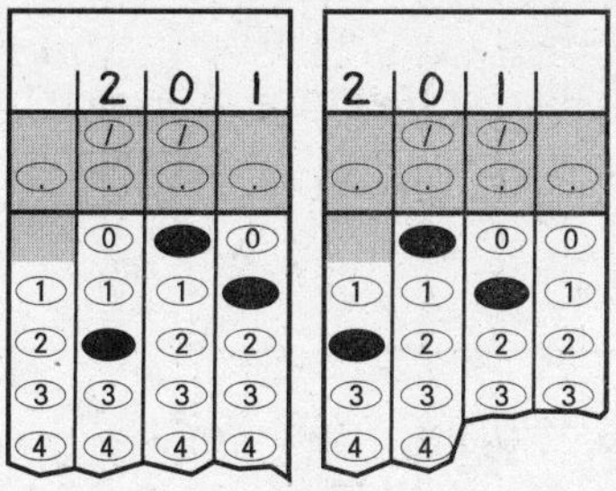

Note: You may start your answers in any column, space permitting. Columns not needed should be left blank.

- Mark no more than one oval in any column.
- Because the answer sheet will be machine-scored, **you will receive credit only if the ovals are filled in correctly.**
- Although not required, it is suggested that you write your answer in the boxes at the top of the columns to help you fill in the ovals accurately.
- Some problems may have more than one correct answer. In such cases, grid only one answer.
- No question has a negative answer.
- **Mixed numbers** such as $2\frac{1}{2}$ must be gridded as 2.5 or 5/2. (If 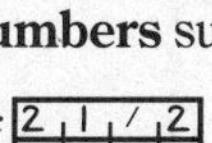 is gridded, it will be interpreted as $\frac{21}{2}$, not $2\frac{1}{2}$.)

- Decimal Accuracy: If you obtain a decimal answer, **enter the most accurate value the grid will accommodate.** For example, if you obtain an answer such as 0.6666..., you should record the result as .666 or .667. **Less accurate values such as .66 or .67 are not acceptable.**

Acceptable ways to grid $\frac{2}{3} = .6666...$:

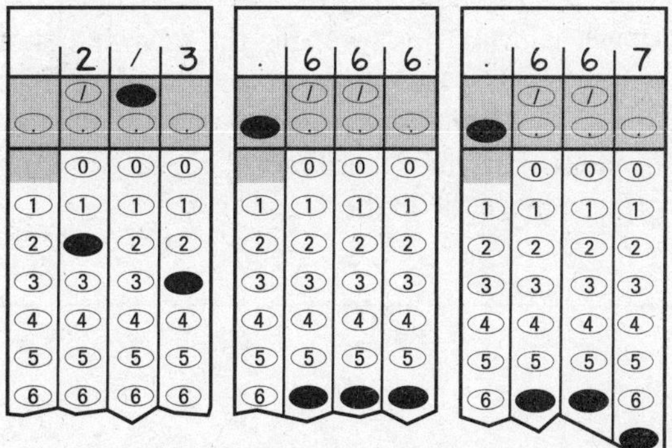

9. If $ab = 40$, $\frac{a}{b} = \frac{5}{2}$, and a and b are positive numbers, find the value of a.

10. Stephanie earned \$$x$ while working 10 hours. Evelyn earned \$$y$ while working 20 hours. If they both earn the same hourly wage and $x + y = 60$, how many dollars did Stephanie earn?

GO ON TO THE NEXT PAGE

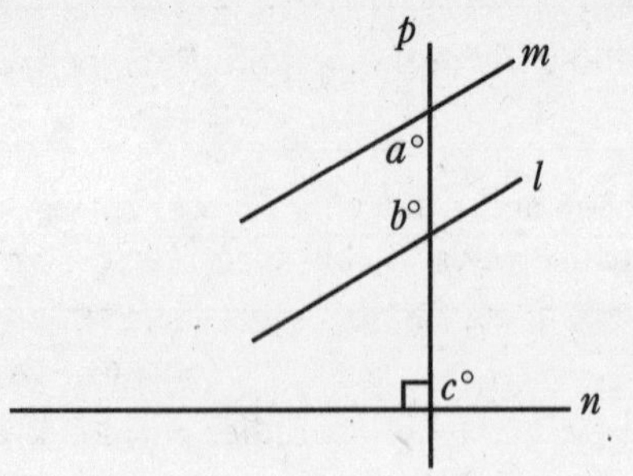

11. In the figure above, m is parallel to l and p is perpendicular to n. Find the value of $a + b + c$.

12. The difference of the areas of two circles is 21π. If their radii are $r + 3$ and r, find the radius of the *larger* circle.

	FIRST PLACE	SECOND PLACE	THIRD PLACE
	(8 points)	(4 points)	(2 points)
EVENT ①	TEAM A	TEAM B	TEAM C
EVENT ②	TEAM B	TEAM A	TEAM C

13. The results of two games involving 3 teams are shown above. Thus, we have the following standings: A and B both have 12 points, and C has 4 points. Assuming no ties, what is the least number of additional games that Team C will have to play in order to have the highest total score?

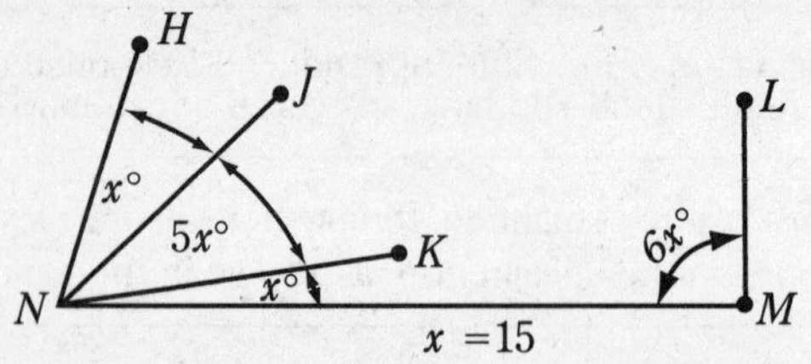

Note: Figure is not drawn to scale.

14. If the figure above were drawn to scale and all line segments were extended indefinitely in *both directions*, how many intersection points would there be in addition to N and M?

15. If a is 10 percent greater than b, and ac is 32 percent greater than bd, then c is what percent greater than d?

16. Since one gross = 12 dozen, what fraction of a gross of eggs is 3 eggs?

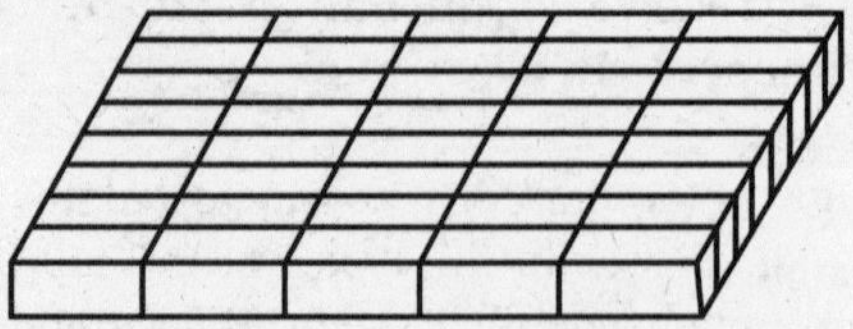

17. The figure above represents a layer of bricks, where each brick has a volume of 40 cubic inches. If all bricks are stacked in layers as shown, and the final pile of bricks occupies 8,000 cubic inches, how many layers are there in the final pile of bricks?

18. Let x be the smallest possible 3-digit number greater than or equal to 100 in which no digit is repeated. If y is the largest positive 3-digit number that can be made using all of the digits of x, what is the value of $y - x$?

STOP

If you finish before time is called, you may check your work on this section only.
Do not turn to any other section in the test.

Take a 5 minute break

before starting section 7

SECTION 7

Time: 25 Minutes—Turn to Section 7 (page 858) of your answer sheet to answer the questions in this section.
24 Questions

Directions: For each question in this section, select the best answer from among the choices given and fill in the corresponding circle on the answer sheet.

Each sentence below has one or two blanks, each blank indicating that something has been omitted. Beneath the sentence are five words or sets of words labeled A through E. Choose the word or set of words that, when inserted in the sentence, best fits the meaning of the sentence as a whole.

Example:

Hoping to ________ the dispute, negotiators proposed a compromise that they felt would be ________ to both labor and management.

(A) enforce...useful
(B) end...divisive
(C) overcome...unattractive
(D) extend...satisfactory
(E) resolve...acceptable

Ⓐ Ⓑ Ⓒ Ⓓ ●

1. Governor Edwards combined ______ politics with administrative skills to dominate the state; in addition to these assets, he was also ______.

(A) corrupt...glum
(B) inept...civil
(C) incriminating...sincere
(D) astute...dapper
(E) trivial...lavish

2. After four years of ______ curbs designed to protect the American auto industry, the president cleared the way for Japan to ______ more cars to the United States.

(A) profitable...drive
(B) flexible...produce
(C) motor...direct
(D) import...ship
(E) reciprocal...sell

3. The photographs of Ethiopia's starving children demonstrate the ______ of drought, poor land use, and overpopulation.

(A) consequences
(B) prejudices
(C) inequities
(D) indications
(E) mortalities

4. There had been a yearning for an end to ______ with the Soviet Union, but little evidence had existed that nuclear-arms agreements had contributed to our ______.

(A) treaties...silence
(B) advantages...relations
(C) differences...amity
(D) tensions...security
(E) commerce...decision

5. The union struck shortly after midnight after its negotiating committee ______ a company offer of a 3% raise.

(A) applauded
(B) rejected
(C) considered
(D) postponed
(E) accepted

GO ON TO THE NEXT PAGE

The two passages below are followed by questions based on their content and on the relationship between the two passages. Answer the questions on the basis of what is stated or implied in the passages and in any introductory material that may be provided.

Questions 6–9 are based on the following passages.

Passage 1

Homeschooling is becoming more and more desirable because children do not have the burden of traveling to school and becoming exposed to other children's sickness and everything else that goes with being in a crowded room. There is also the individual attention that the parent or tutor can give the student, which creates a better and more efficient learning environment. As standards become more and more flexible, homeschooling may in fact be the norm of the future.

Passage 2

In many studies, it was shown that students benefit in a classroom setting since the interaction and dialogue with other students creates a stimulating learning environment. The more students who are in a class, the more diversity within the group and the more varied the feedback. With a good teacher and facilitator, a classroom can be very beneficial for the student's cognitive development.

6. In Passage 1, the author's condition for an effective learning condition is based on

(A) flexible standards
(B) the closeness of a parent and a child
(C) the reduction of travel time
(D) a one-on-one learning experience
(E) the sanitary conditions in the learning environment

7. Which of the following is *not* addressed in Passage 2?

(A) The advantage of classroom learning with the student interacting and sharing ideas with other students
(B) The student exposed to multicultural ways in approaching the learning experience
(C) The teacher's playing an active role in the learning experience
(D) The more students in the classroom leading to the more feedback each student can receive
(E) The positive relationship between the different types of students and learning

8. Which criterion is the same in homeschooling and regular classroom schooling?

(A) the health condition
(B) the burden of traveling
(C) the feedback with other students
(D) the diversity of the students
(E) the learning experience

9. Which of the following adjustments would make an ideal environment for learning, according to what is addressed in both passages?

(A) In homeschooling, the student could travel on weekends to cultural areas.
(B) In school, the teacher could occasionally work with the student on an individual basis.
(C) In homeschooling, the student could be exposed to and interact with other students on a regular basis.
(D) The student could spend one-half of his educational time in school and one-half of his educational time at home.
(E) The student could learn at home and go to school to socialize.

GO ON TO THE NEXT PAGE

Questions 10–15 are based on the following passage.

The following passage is about the literature of the African-American culture and its impact on society.

The literature of an oppressed people is the conscience of man, and nowhere is this seen with more intense clarity than in the literature of African Americans. An essential element of African-American literature is that the literature as a whole—not the work of occasional authors—is a movement against concrete wickedness. In African-American literature, accordingly, there is a grief rarely to be found elsewhere in American literature, and frequently a rage rarely to be found in American letters: a rage different in quality, more profound, more towering, more intense—the rage of the oppressed. Whenever an African-American artist picks up pen or horn, his target is likely to be American racism, his subject the suffering of his people, and the core element his own grief and the grief of his people. Almost all of African-American literature carries the burden of this protest.

The cry for freedom and the protest against injustice indicate a desire for the birth of the New Man, a testament to the New Unknown World to be discovered, to be created by man. African-American literature is, as a body, a declaration that despite the perversion and cruelty that cling like swamproots to the flesh of man's feet, man has options for freedom, for cleanliness, for wholeness, for human harmony, for goodness: for a human world. Like the spirituals that are a part of it, African-American literature is a passionate assertion that man will win freedom. Thus, African-American literature rejects despair and cynicism; it is a literature of realistic hope and life affirmation. This is not to say that no African-American literary work reflects cynicism or despair, but rather that the basic theme of African-American literature is that man's goodness will prevail.

African-American literature is a statement against death, a statement as to what life should be: life should be vivacious, exuberant, wholesomely uninhibited, sensual, sensuous, constructively antirespectable; life should abound and flourish and laugh; life should be passionately lived and man should be loving; life should be not a sedate waltz or foxtrot but a vigorous breakdance. Thus, when the African-American writer criticizes America for its cruelty, the criticism implies that America is drawn to death and repelled by what should be the human style of life, the human way of living.

Black literature in America is, then, a setting forth of man's identity and destiny; an investigation of man's iniquity and a statement of belief in his potential godliness; a prodding of man toward exploring and finding deep joy in his humanity.

10. The author states or implies that

(A) a separate-but-equal doctrine is the answer to American racism
(B) African-American literature is superior to American literature
(C) hopelessness and lack of trust are the keynotes of African-American literature
(D) standing up for one's rights and protesting about unfairness are vital
(E) traditional forms of American-type dancing should be engaged in

11. When the author, in referring to African-American literature, states that "life should be...constructively antirespectable" (lines 32–34), it can be inferred that people ought to

(A) do their own thing provided what they do is worthwhile
(B) show disrespect for others when they have the desire to do so
(C) be passionate in public whenever the urge is there
(D) shun a person because he is of another race or color
(E) be enraged if their ancestors have been unjustly treated

12. With reference to the passage, which of the following statements are true about African-American literature?

I. It expresses the need for nonviolent opposition to antiracism.
II. It urges a person to have respect for himself and for others.
III. It voices the need for an active, productive, and satisfying life.

(A) I only
(B) II only
(C) I and III only
(D) II and III only
(E) I, II, and III

13. The tone of the passage is one of

(A) anger and vindictiveness
(B) hope and affirmation
(C) forgiveness and charity
(D) doubt and despair
(E) grief and cruelty

GO ON TO THE NEXT PAGE

14. Which of the following constitute(s) the author's view of a "human world?"

I. harmony
II. cleanliness
III. wholeness

(A) I only
(B) I and II only
(C) II and III only
(D) I and III only
(E) I, II, and III

15. The word "iniquity" (line 44) means

(A) potential
(B) creation
(C) wickedness
(D) cleverness
(E) greatness

GO ON TO THE NEXT PAGE

Questions 16–24 are based on the following passage.

The following passage is based on B. F. Skinner's book About Behaviorism *and discusses the pros and cons of Skinner's work on behaviorism and the various points made by Skinner.*

In his compact and modestly titled book *About Behaviorism*, Dr. B. F. Skinner, the noted behavioral psychologist, lists the 20 most salient objections to "behaviorism or the science of behavior," and he has gone on to answer them both implicitly and explicitly. He has answers and explanations for everyone.

For instance, to those who object that behaviorists "deny the existence of feelings, sensations, ideas, and other features of mental life," Dr. Skinner concedes that "a good deal of clarification" is in order. What such people are really decrying is "methodological behaviorism," an earlier stage of the science whose goal was precisely to close off mentalistic explanations of behavior, if only to counteract the 2,500-year-old influence of mentalism. But Dr. Skinner is a "radical behaviorist." "Radical behaviorism...takes a different line. It does not deny the possibility of self-observation or self-knowledge or its possible usefulness... It restores introspection...."

For instance, to those who object that behaviorism "neglects innate endowment and argues that all behavior is acquired during the lifetime of the individual," Dr. Skinner expresses puzzlement. Granted, "A few behaviorists...have minimized if not denied a genetic contribution, and in their enthusiasm for what may be done through the environment, others have no doubt acted as if a genetic endowment were unimportant, but few would contend that behavior is 'endlessly malleable.'" And Dr. Skinner himself, sounding as often as not like some latter-day Social Darwinist, gives as much weight to the "contingencies of survival" in the evolution of the human species as to the "contingencies of reinforcement" in the lifetime of the individual.

For instance, to those who claim that behaviorism "cannot explain creative achievements—in art, for example, or in music, literature, science, or mathematics"—Dr. Skinner provides an intriguing ellipsis. "Contingencies of reinforcement also resemble contingencies of survival in the production of novelty....In both natural selection and operant conditioning the appearance of 'mutations' is crucial. Until recently, species evolved because of random changes in genes or chromosomes, but the geneticist may arrange conditions under which mutations are particularly likely to occur. We can also discover some of the sources of new forms of behavior which undergo selection by prevailing contingencies or reinforcement, and fortunately the creative artist or thinker has other ways of introducing novelties."

And so go Dr. Skinner's answers to the 20 questions he poses—questions that range all the way from asking if behaviorism fails "to account for cognitive processes" to wondering if behaviorism "is indifferent to the warmth and richness of human life, and...is incompatible with the... enjoyment of art, music, and literature and with love for one's fellow men."

But will it wash? Will it serve to silence those critics who have characterized B. F. Skinner variously as a mad, manipulative doctor, as a naïve 19th-century positivist, as an unscientific technician, and as an arrogant social engineer? There is no gainsaying that *About Behaviorism* is an unusually compact summary of both the history and "the philosophy of the science of human behavior" (as Dr. Skinner insists on defining behaviorism). It is a veritable artwork of organization. And anyone who reads it will never again be able to think of behaviorism as a simplistic philosophy that reduces human beings to black boxes responding robotlike to external stimuli.

Still, there are certain quandaries that *About Behaviorism* does not quite dispel. For one thing, though Dr. Skinner makes countless references to the advances in experiments with human beings that behaviorism has made since it first began running rats through mazes many decades ago, he fails to provide a single illustration of these advances. And though it may be true, as Dr. Skinner argues, that one can extrapolate from pigeons to people, it would be reassuring to be shown precisely how.

More importantly, he has not satisfactorily rebutted the basic criticism that behaviorism "is scientistic rather than scientific. It merely emulates the sciences." A true science doesn't predict what it will accomplish when it is firmly established as a science, not even when it is posing as "the philosophy of that science." A true science simply advances rules for testing hypotheses.

But Dr. Skinner predicts that behaviorism will produce the means to save human society from impending disaster. Two key concepts that keep accreting to that prediction are "manipulation" and "control." And so, while he reassures us quite persuasively that his science would practice those concepts benignly, one can't shake off the suspicion that he was advancing a science just in order to save society by means of "manipulation" and "control." And that is not so reassuring.

16. According to the passage, Skinner would be most likely to agree that

(A) studies of animal behavior are applicable to human behavior
(B) introspection should be used widely to analyze conscious experience
(C) behaviorism is basically scientistic
(D) behavioristic principles and techniques will be of no use in preventing widespread disaster
(E) an individual can form an infinite number of sentences that he has never heard spoken

GO ON TO THE NEXT PAGE

17. The reader may infer that

(A) Skinner's philosophy is completely democratic in its methodology
(B) behaviorism, in its early form, and mentalism were essentially the same
(C) the book *About Behaviorism* is difficult to understand because it is not well structured
(D) methodological behaviorism preceded both mentalism and radical behaviorism
(E) the author of the article has found glaring weaknesses in Skinner's defense of behaviorism

18. When Skinner speaks of "contingencies of survival" (line 29) and "contingencies of reinforcement" (lines 30–31), the word "contingency" most accurately means

(A) frequency of occurrence
(B) something incidental
(C) a quota
(D) dependence on chance
(E) one of an assemblage

19. The author of the article says that Skinner sounds "like some latter-day Social Darwinist" (line 28) most probably because Skinner

(A) is a radical behaviorist who has differed from methodological behaviorists
(B) has predicted that human society faces disaster
(C) has been characterized as a 19th-century positivist
(D) has studied animal behavior as applicable to human behavior
(E) believes that the geneticist may arrange conditions for mutations to occur

20. It can be inferred from the passage that "extrapolate" (line 72) means

(A) to gather unknown information by extending known information
(B) to determine how one organism may be used to advantage by another organism
(C) to insert or introduce between other things or parts
(D) to change the form or the behavior of one thing to match the form or behavior of another thing
(E) to transfer an organ of a living thing into another living thing

21. One *cannot* conclude from the passage that

(A) Skinner is a radical behaviorist but not a methodological behaviorist
(B) *About Behavior* does not show how behaviorists have improved in experimentation with human beings
(C) only human beings are used in experiments conducted by behaviorists
(D) methodological behaviorism rejects the introspective approach
(E) the book being discussed is to the point and well organized

22. In Skinner's statement that "few would contend that behavior is 'endlessly malleable'" (lines 26–27), he means that

(A) genetic influences are of primary importance in shaping human behavior
(B) environmental influences may be frequently supplemented by genetic influences
(C) self-examination is the most effective way of improving a behavior pattern
(D) the learning process continues throughout life
(E) psychologists will never come to a common conclusion about the best procedure for studying and improving human behavior

23. According to the author, which of the following are true concerning *scientistic* and *scientific* disciplines?

I. The scientific one develops the rules for testing the theory; the scientistic one does not.
II. There is no element of prediction in scientistic disciplines.
III. Science never assumes a philosophical nature.

(A) I only
(B) I and III only
(C) I and II only
(D) II and III only
(E) I, II, and III

24. The word "veritable" (line 60) means

(A) abundant
(B) careful
(C) political
(D) true
(E) believable

STOP

If you finish before time is called, you may check your work on this section only. Do not turn to any other section in the test.

SECTION 8

Time: 20 Minutes—Turn to Section 8 (page 859) of your answer sheet to answer the questions in this section.
16 Questions

Directions: For this section, solve each problem and decide which is the best of the choices given. Fill in the corresponding circle on the answer sheet. You may use any available space for scratchwork.

Notes:

1. The use of a calculator is permitted.
2. All numbers used are real numbers.
3. Figures that accompany problems in this test are intended to provide information useful in solving the problems. They are drawn as accurately as possible EXCEPT when it is stated in a specific problem that the figure is not drawn to scale. All figures lie in a plane unless otherwise indicated.
4. Unless otherwise specified, the domain of any function f is assumed to be the set of all real numbers x for which $f(x)$ is a real number.

REFERENCE INFORMATION

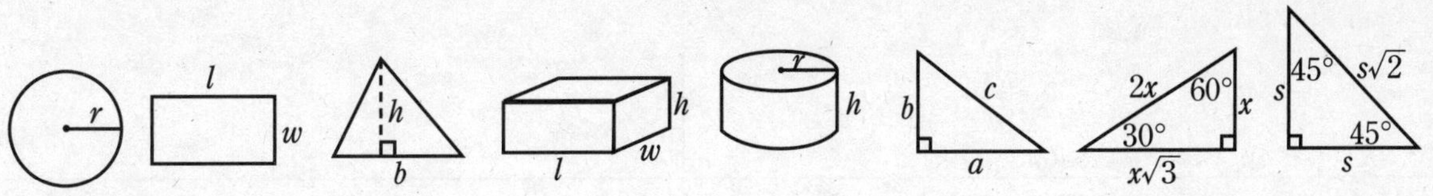

$A = \pi r^2$ $C = 2\pi r$ $A = lw$ $A = \frac{1}{2}bh$ $V = lwh$ $V = \pi r^2 h$ $c^2 = a^2 + b^2$ *Special Right Triangles*

The number of degrees of arc in a circle is 360.
The sum of the measures in degrees of the angles of a triangle is 180.

1. If $5x = 3$, then $(5x + 3)^2 =$

(A) 0
(B) 9
(C) 25
(D) 36
(E) 64

2. The ratio of girls to boys in a class is 8 : 7. The number of students in the class could be any of the following *except*

(A) 15
(B) 45
(C) 50
(D) 60
(E) 90

GO ON TO THE NEXT PAGE

3. The above figure is an equilateral triangle divided into four congruent, smaller, equilateral triangles. If the perimeter of a smaller triangle is 1, then the perimeter of the whole large triangle is

(A) 2
(B) 4
(C) 6
(D) 8
(E) 16

4. Dick has \$15.25 and spent \$7.50 at the sporting goods store. How much money does he have left?

(A) \$0.25
(B) \$1.75
(C) \$6.75
(D) \$7.75
(E) \$8.25

5. Given $\frac{4^3 + 4^3 + 4^3 + 4^3}{4^y} = 4$, find y.

(A) 3
(B) 4
(C) 8
(D) 12
(E) 64

6. If $\frac{2x^2 + x - 5}{x^3 + 4x^2} = \frac{1}{2}$ then which of the following is true?

(A) $x^3 - 2x = 10$
(B) $x^3 + 2x = 10$
(C) $x^3 - 2x = -10$
(D) $x^3 + 2x = -10$
(E) $x^3 + 2x + 2x^2 = 10$

GO ON TO THE NEXT PAGE

7. A population that starts at 100 and doubles after eight years can be expressed as the following, where t stands for the number of years that have elapsed from the start:

(A) 100×2^t
(B) $100 \times 2^{\frac{t}{7}}$
(C) $100 \times 2^{t-8}$
(D) $100 \times 2^{\frac{t}{8}}$
(E) 100×2^{16t}

9. If $a^b = x$ and $x^b = y$, then

(A) $a^{2b} = y$
(B) $a^{b^2} = y$
(C) $b^a = y$
(D) $(ax)^b = y$
(E) $(ax)^b = x$

8. Find the solution set in positive integers of $2x + 5 < 5$.

(A) {1, 2, 3, 4}
(B) {1, 2}
(C) {0}
(D) { }
(E) infinity

10. Two lines in a plane are represented by $y = x - 1$ and $2x + 5y = 9$. The coordinates of the point at which the lines intersect are

(A) (2,1)
(B) (1,2)
(C) (2,5)
(D) (5,2)
(E) (3,3)

GO ON TO THE NEXT PAGE

$$C = md + t$$

11. The cost, C, of a business trip is represented by the equation above, where m is a constant, d is the number of days of the complete trip, and t is the cost of transportation, which does not change. If the business trip was increased by 5 days, how much more did the business trip cost than the original planned trip?

(A) $5d$
(B) $5m$
(C) $5t$
(D) $d(m - 3)$
(E) $m(d - 3)$

12. Which of the following represents x on a number line if $(x - 3) \leq 0$?

(A) 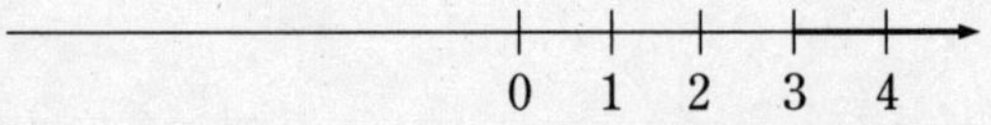

(B) 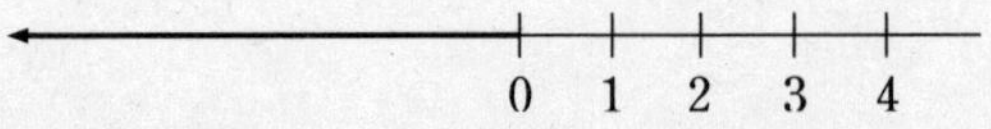

(C) 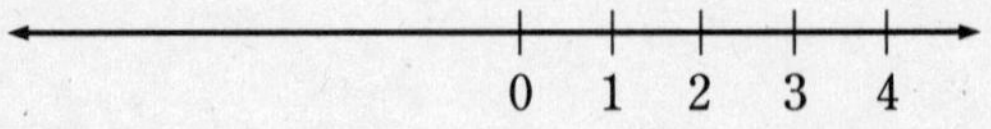

(D) 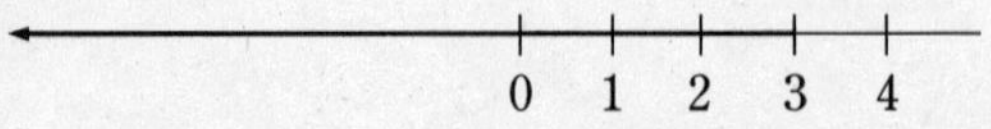

(E) 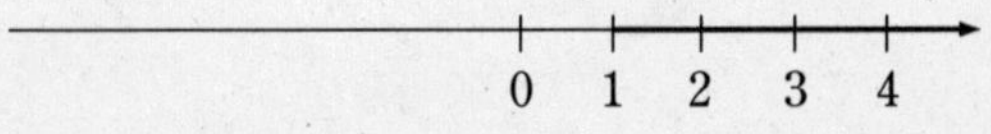

$$4x - 3y = 9$$
$$8x + ky = 19$$

13. For which value of k will the system of equations above have *no* solution?

(A) $+6$
(B) $+3$
(C) 0
(D) -3
(E) -6

14. Given that $r \neq 0$ and $r = 5w = 7a$, find the value of $r - w$ in terms of a.

(A) $\frac{1a}{7}$
(B) $\frac{7a}{5}$
(C) $3a$
(D) $\frac{28a}{5}$
(E) $28a$

GO ON TO THE NEXT PAGE

15. The figure above consists of equal semicircles each touching the other at the ends of their diameters. If the radius of each circle is 2, what is the *total enclosed* area?

(A) $\frac{\sqrt{3}}{4} + \pi$

(B) $\sqrt{3} + 2\pi$

(C) $4\sqrt{3} + 6\pi$

(D) 6π

(E) $\frac{\sqrt{2}}{4} + 4\pi$

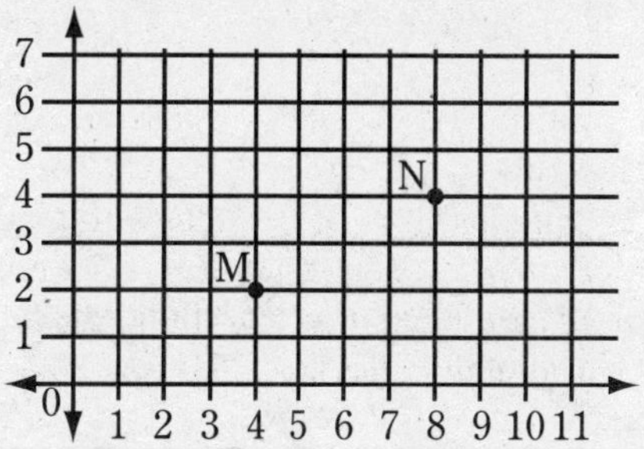

16. Which of the following points, when plotted on the grid above, will be three times as far from $M(4,2)$ as from $N(8,4)$?

(A) (2,1)
(B) (4,4)
(C) (6,3)
(D) (7,1)
(E) (10,5)

STOP

If you finish before time is called, you may check your work on this section only.
Do not turn to any other section in the test.

SECTION 9

Time: 20 Minutes—Turn to Section 9 (page 859) of your answer sheet to answer the questions in this section. 19 Questions

Directions: For each question in this section, select the best answer from among the choices given and fill in the corresponding circle on the answer sheet.

Each sentence below has one or two blanks, each blank indicating that something has been omitted. Beneath the sentence are five words or sets of words labeled A through E. Choose the word or set of words that, when inserted in the sentence, *best* fits the meaning of the sentence as a whole.

Example:

Hoping to _______ the dispute, negotiators proposed a compromise that they felt would be _______ to both labor and management.

(A) enforce...useful
(B) end...divisive
(C) overcome...unattractive
(D) extend...satisfactory
(E) resolve...acceptable

Ⓐ Ⓑ Ⓒ Ⓓ ●

1. Illegally parked vehicles block hydrants and crosswalks, _______ the flow of traffic when double-parked, and _______ the law.

(A) stem...enforce
(B) expedite...violate
(C) reduce...resist
(D) drench...challenge
(E) impede...flout

2. With the film rental business _______, the DVD player is changing the way millions of Americans use their _______ time.

(A) advertising...canceled
(B) suffering...valuable
(C) stabilizing...extra
(D) recording...unused
(E) booming...leisure

3. The fact that the _______ of confrontation is no longer as popular as it once was _______ progress in race relations.

(A) practice...inculcates
(B) reticence...indicates
(C) glimmer...foreshadows
(D) insidiousness...reiterates
(E) technique...presages

4. The _______ of scarcity amidst plenty characterizes even a rich country in a time of inflation.

(A) coherence
(B) tedium
(C) facet
(D) sequence
(E) paradox

5. The scientist averred that a nuclear war could _______ enough smoke and dust to blot out the sun and freeze the earth.

(A) pervert
(B) extinguish
(C) generate
(D) evaluate
(E) perpetrate

6. Until his death he remained _______ in the belief that the world was conspiring against him.

(A) ignominious
(B) taciturn
(C) tantamount
(D) obdurate
(E) spurious

GO ON TO THE NEXT PAGE

The two passages below are followed by questions based on their content and on the relationship between the two passages. Answer the questions on the basis of what is stated or implied in the passages and in any introductory material that may be provided.

Questions 7–19 are based on the following passages.

The following two passages are about violence. The first discusses televised violence; the second attempts to address the history of violence in general.

Passage 1

Violence is alive and well on television. Yet there appears to be a difference in the quality, variety, and pervasiveness of today's televised violence. Some observers believe that, as a result of more than three decades of television, viewers have developed a kind of immunity to the horror of violence. By the age of 16, for example, the average young person will have seen some 18,000 murders on television. One extension of this phenomenon may be an appetite for more varied kinds of violence. On the basis of the amount of exposure, certain things that initially would have been beyond the pale have become more readily accepted.

Violence on TV has been more prevalent in recent years, in large measure because there are fewer situation comedies and more action series, but also because some 25 million of the nation's 85 million homes with television now receive one of the cable services that routinely show uncut feature films containing graphic violence as early as 8:00 in the evening.

The evidence is becoming overwhelming that just as witnessing violence in the home may contribute to children learning and acting out violent behavior, violence on TV and in the movies may lead to the same result. Studies have shown that a steady diet of watching graphic violence or sexually violent films such as those shown on cable TV has caused some men to be more willing to accept violence against women, such as rape and wife-beating. Not only actual violence, but the kind of violence coming through the television screen is causing concern. One of the principal developments is the increasing sophistication of the weaponry. The simple gunfight of the past has been augmented by high-tech crimes like terrorist bombings. A gunfighter shooting down a sheriff is one thing. When you have terrorist bombs, the potential is there for hundreds to die. Programs in the past used the occasional machine gun, but such weapons as the M-60 machine gun and Uzi semiautomatic have become commonplace today on network shows.

Many people are no longer concerned about televised violence because they feel it is the way of the world. It is high time that broadcasters provide public messages on TV screens that would warn viewers about the potentially harmful effects of viewing televised violence.

Passage 2

We have always been a lawless and a violent people. Thus, our almost unbroken record of violence against the Indians and all others who got in our way—the Spaniards in the Floridas, the Mexicans in Texas; the violence of the vigilantes on a hundred frontiers; the pervasive violence of slavery (a "perpetual exercise," Jefferson called it, "of the most boisterous passions"); the lawlessness of the Ku Klux Klan during Reconstruction and after; and of scores of race riots from those of Chicago in 1919 to those of New Orleans in the 1960s. Yet, all this violence, shocking as it doubtless was, no more threatened the fabric of our society or the integrity of the Union than did the lawlessness of Prohibition back in the Twenties. The explanation for this is to be found in the embarrassing fact that most of it was official, quasi-official, or countenanced by public opinion: exterminating the Indian; flogging the slave; lynching the outlaw; exploiting women and children in textile mills and sweatshops; hiring Pinkertons to shoot down strikers; condemning immigrants to fetid ghettos; punishing blacks who tried to exercise their civil or political rights. Most of this was socially acceptable—or at least not wholly unacceptable—just as so much of our current violence is socially acceptable: the many thousands of automobile deaths every year; the mortality rate for black babies at twice that for white; the deaths from cancer induced by cigarettes or by air pollution; the sadism of our penal system and the horrors of our prisons; the violence of some police against the so-called "dangerous classes of society."

What we have now is the emergence of violence that is not acceptable either to the Establishment, which is frightened and alarmed, or to the victims of the Establishment, who are no longer submissive and who are numerous and powerful. This is now familiar "crime in the streets," or it is the revolt of the young against the economy, the politics, and the wars of the established order, or it is the convulsive reaction of the blacks to a century of injustice. But now, too, official violence is no longer acceptable to its victims—or to their ever more numerous sympathizers: the violence of great corporations and of government itself against the natural resources of the nation; the long drawn-out violence of the white majority against blacks and other minorities; the violence of the police and the National Guard against the young; the massive violence of the military against the peoples of other countries. These acts can no longer be absorbed by large segments of our society. It is this new polarization that threatens the body politic and the social fabric much as religious dissent threatened them in the Europe of the sixteenth and seventeenth centuries.

GO ON TO THE NEXT PAGE

7. The title that best summarizes the content of Passage 1 is

(A) TV's Role in the Rising Crime Rate
(B) Violence on TV—Past and Present
(C) TV Won't Let Up on Violence
(D) Violence Raises the TV Ratings
(E) Violence Galore on Cable TV

8. Which of the following types of TV programs would the author of Passage 1 be *least* likely to approve of?

(A) A cowboy Western called "Have Gun, Will Travel"
(B) A talk show dealing with teenage pregnancy caused by rape
(C) A documentary dealing with Vietnam veterans suffering from the aftereffects of herbicide spraying during the war
(D) A movie showing a bomb exploding in a bus carrying civilians on their way to work
(E) A soap opera in which a jealous husband is shown murdering his wife's lover, then his own wife

9. According to Passage 1,

(A) television programs are much different today from what they were a generation ago
(B) a very large percentage of the viewers are presently worried about the showing of violence on television
(C) situation comedy programs are more popular on TV now than ever before
(D) broadcasting stations are considering notifying viewers about possible dangers of watching programs that include violence
(E) violence on the television screen is more extreme than it was about 20 years ago

10. As an illustration of current "socially acceptable" violence, the author of Passage 2 would probably include

(A) National Guard violence at Kent, Ohio, during the Vietnam War
(B) the Vietnam War
(C) the cruelties of our prison system
(D) the police behavior in Chicago at the 1968 Democratic Convention
(E) "crime in the streets"

11. It can be inferred that the author's definition of violence (Passage 2)

(A) includes the social infliction of harm
(B) is limited to nongovernmental acts of force
(C) is confined to governmental acts of illegal force
(D) is synonymous with illegal conduct by either government or citizen
(E) is shared by the FBI

12. The author of Passage 2 describes current violence as

I. acceptable neither to the authorities nor to the victims
II. carried out primarily by corporations
III. increasingly of a vigilante nature

(A) I only
(B) II only
(C) III only
(D) I and II only
(E) II and III only

13. The author of Passage 2 mentions all of the following forms of violence in the nineteenth century *except*

(A) the activities of the Klan during Reconstruction
(B) wiping out the Indians
(C) the New York City draft riots of the 1860s
(D) the Annexation of Texas and Florida
(E) the practice of slavery

14. Which action or activity would the author of Passage 2 be most likely to disapprove of?

(A) trying to prevent a mugging
(B) reading a science fiction story
(C) watching a rock music TV performance
(D) attending a Super Bowl football game
(E) participating in a country square dance

15. The word "pervasiveness" in line 2 of Passage 1 (also note "pervasive" in line 46 of Passage 2) means

(A) variety
(B) televised
(C) seeping through
(D) quality
(E) terribleness

GO ON TO THE NEXT PAGE

16. Which of the following, according to the author of Passage 1, is a contributing factor to the marked increase of violent deaths?

I. cable television
II. present feature films
III. technology

(A) I only
(B) II only
(C) II and III only
(D) I and II only
(E) I, II, and III

17. The author of Passage 2 would probably argue with the author of Passage 1 in the resolution of violence (lines 37–41) that

(A) if violence were curtailed on television, it would pop up elsewhere
(B) television does not show a significant amount of violence to warrant warnings against such programs
(C) television can also influence the public toward nonviolence
(D) there are more dangers to television than the portrayal of violence
(E) violence is inbred in television

18. From the passages, which can we assume to be *false*?

(A) Unlike the author of Passage 1, the author of Passage 2 believes that society is disgusted with violence.
(B) The author of Passage 1 believes that sophisticated weaponry causes increased violence, whereas the author of Passage 2 believes that violence is inherent in society.
(C) The type of violence discussed by the author of Passage 2 is much more encompassing than the type of violence discussed by the author of Passage 1.
(D) Both authors propose a direct resolution for at least a start to the end of violence.
(E) Both authors believe either that violence is a part of daily living or at least that many feel that violence is a part of daily living.

19. The word "polarization" in line 87 means

(A) electrical tendencies
(B) governments in different parts of the world
(C) completely opposing viewpoints
(D) extreme religious differences
(E) cold climatic conditions

STOP

If you finish before time is called, you may check your work on this section only.
Do not turn to any other section in the test.

SECTION 10

Time: 10 Minutes—Turn to Section 10 (page 859) of your answer sheet to answer the questions in this section.
14 Questions

Directions: For each question in this section, select the best answer from among the choices given and fill in the corresponding circle on the answer sheet.

The following sentences test correctness and effectiveness of expression. Part of each sentence or the entire sentence is underlined; beneath each sentence are five ways of phrasing the underlined material. Choice A repeats the original phrasing; the other four choices are different. If you think the original phrasing produces a better sentence than any of the alternatives, select Choice A; if not, select one of the other choices.

In making your selection, follow the requirements of standard written English; that is, pay attention to grammar, choice of words, sentence construction, and punctuation. Your selection should result in the most effective sentence—clear and precise, without awkwardness or ambiguity.

EXAMPLE:

Laura Ingalls Wilder published her first book and she was sixty-five years old then.

(A) and she was sixty-five years old then
(B) when she was sixty-five
(C) at age sixty-five years old
(D) upon the reaching of sixty-five years
(E) at the time when she was sixty-five

Ⓐ ● Ⓒ Ⓓ Ⓔ

1. I find Henry James' prose style more difficult to read than James Joyce.

(A) I find Henry James's prose style more difficult to read than James Joyce.
(B) I find Henry Jame's prose style more difficult to read than James Joyce'.
(C) I find Henry James's prose style more difficult to read than James Joyce's.
(D) I find the prose style of Henry James more difficult to read than James Joyce.
(E) Henry James' prose style I find more difficult to read than I find James Joyce.

2. Neither Dr. Conant nor his followers knows what to do about the problem.

(A) Neither Dr. Conant nor his followers knows what to do about the problem.
(B) Neither Dr. Conant or his followers knows what to do about the problem.
(C) Neither Dr. Conant nor his followers know what to do about the problem.
(D) Neither Dr. Conant nor his followers know what to do as far as the problem goes.
(E) As to the problem, neither Dr. Conant nor his followers know what to do.

3. The students requested a meeting with the chancellor since they desired a greater voice in university policy.

(A) The students requested a meeting with the chancellor
(B) A meeting with the chancellor was requested by the students
(C) It occurred to the students to request a meeting with the chancellor
(D) The chancellor was the one with whom the students requested a meeting
(E) The students insisted upon a meeting with the chancellor

4. Three American scientists were jointly awarded the Nobel Prize in Medicine for their study of viruses which led to discoveries.

(A) for their study of viruses which led to discoveries
(B) for their discoveries concerning viruses
(C) as a prize for their discoveries about viruses
(D) the discovery into viruses being the reason
(E) for their virus discoveries

GO ON TO THE NEXT PAGE

5. You must convince me of promptness in returning the money before I can agree to lend you $100.

(A) You must convince me of promptness in returning the money
(B) The loan of the money must be returned promptly
(C) You must understand that you will have to assure me of a prompt money return
(D) You will have to convince me that you will return the money promptly
(E) You will return the money promptly

6. Because Bob was an outstanding athlete in high school, in addition to a fine scholastic record, he was awarded a scholarship at Harvard.

(A) in addition to a fine scholastic record
(B) also a student of excellence
(C) and had amassed an excellent scholastic record
(D) his scholastic record was also outstanding
(E) as well as a superior student

7. Although pre-season odds against the Mets had been 100 to 1, the Orioles were trounced by them in the World Series.

(A) the Orioles were trounced by them in the World Series
(B) the World Series victors were the Mets who trounced the Orioles
(C) they won the World Series by trouncing the Orioles
(D) which is hard to believe since the Orioles were trounced in the World Series
(E) it was the Mets who trounced the Orioles in the World Series

8. Before you can make a fresh fruit salad, you must buy oranges, bananas, pineapples and peaches are necessary.

(A) you must buy oranges, bananas, pineapples and peaches are necessary
(B) you must buy oranges and bananas and pineapples and peaches
(C) you must buy oranges and bananas. And other fruit such as pineapples and peaches
(D) you must buy oranges and bananas and other fruit. Such as pineapples and peaches
(E) you must buy oranges, bananas, pineapples, and peaches

9. The physical education department of the school offers instruction to learn how to swim, how to play tennis, and how to defend oneself.

(A) to learn how to swim, how to play tennis, and how to defend oneself
(B) in swimming, playing tennis, and defending oneself
(C) in regard to how to swim, how to play tennis, and how to defend oneself
(D) for the purpose of swimming, playing tennis, and defending oneself
(E) in swimming, playing tennis, and to defend oneself

10. He is not only chairman of the Ways and Means Committee, but also of the Finance Committee.

(A) He is not only chairman of the Ways and Means Committee, but also of the Finance Committee.
(B) He is the chairman not only of the Ways and Means Committee, but also of the Finance Committee.
(C) He is the chairman of the Ways and Means Committee and the chairman of the Finance Committee.
(D) Not only is he the chairman of the Ways and Means Committee, but also of the Finance Committee.
(E) Both the Finance Committee and the Ways and Means Committee are committees in which he is the chairman.

11. First the student did research in the library, and then his English composition was written.

(A) and then his English composition was written
(B) and then the English composition was written by the student
(C) and following this he then wrote his English composition
(D) and then he wrote his English composition
(E) then he wrote his English composition

12. Two candidates for the U.S. Senate, Buckley and him, made speeches to the group.

(A) Two candidates for the U.S. Senate, Buckley and him, made speeches to the group.
(B) Two candidates for the U.S. Senate, Buckley and he, made speeches to the group.
(C) Buckley and him, two candidates for the U.S. Senate, made speeches to the group.
(D) Speeches to the group were made by Buckley and he, two candidates for the U.S. Senate.
(E) Buckley and he made speeches to the group.

GO ON TO THE NEXT PAGE

13. A student of American history for many years, Stephen Douglas and his economic policies were thoroughly familiar to him.

(A) A student of American history for many years
(B) After having been a student of American history for many years
(C) He was a student of American history for many years
(D) Being that he was student of American history for many years
(E) Since he was a student of American history for many years

14. Does anyone know to who this book belongs?

(A) to who this book belongs
(B) to whom this book belongs to
(C) to whom this book belongs
(D) who this book belongs to
(E) to whom this belongs

STOP

If you finish before time is called, you may check your work on this section only. Do not turn to any other section in the test.

How Did You Do on This Test?

Step 1. Go to the Answer Key on pages 908–910.

Step 2. For your "raw score," calculate it using the directions on pages 911–912.

Step 3. Get your "scaled score" for the test by referring to the Raw Score/Scaled Score Conversion Tables on pages 913–915.

THERE'S ALWAYS ROOM FOR IMPROVEMENT!

Answer Key for Practice Test 4

Math

Section 2

	Correct Answer
1	B
2	C
3	D
4	D
5	D
6	E
7	E
8	C
9	A
10	C
11	A
12	A
13	D
14	E
15	A
16	D
17	C
18	A
19	B
20	C

Number correct

Number incorrect

Section 3

	Correct Answer
1	C
2	B
3	C
4	D
5	C
6	A
7	A
8	C

Number correct

Number incorrect

Student-Produced Response Questions

9	24
10	9
11	7
12	2
13	8
14	4
15	18
16	60
17	9500
18	280

Number correct

Number incorrect

Section 6

	Correct Answer
1	C
2	C
3	E
4	C
5	C
6	C
7	D
8	D

Number correct

Number incorrect

Student-Produced Response Questions

9	10
10	20
11	270
12	5
13	2
14	2
15	20
16	1/48 or .020 or .021
17	5
18	108

Number correct

Number incorrect

Section 8

	Correct Answer
1	D
2	C
3	A
4	D
5	A
6	C
7	D
8	D
9	B
10	A
11	B
12	D
13	E
14	D
15	C
16	E

Number correct

Number incorrect

Critical Reading and Writing

Critical Reading

Section 4

	Correct Answer
1	D
2	C
3	D
4	D
5	B
6	A
7	C
8	B
9	E
10	C
11	B
12	B
13	D
14	C
15	B
16	A
17	C
18	D
19	C
20	B
21	C
22	A
23	B
24	D

Number correct

Number incorrect

Section 7

	Correct Answer
1	D
2	D
3	A
4	D
5	B
6	D
7	B
8	E
9	C
10	D
11	A
12	D
13	B
14	E
15	C
16	A
17	E
18	D
19	D
20	A
21	C
22	B
23	A
24	D

Number correct

Number incorrect

Section 9

	Correct Answer
1	E
2	E
3	E
4	E
5	C
6	D
7	C
8	D
9	E
10	C
11	A
12	A
13	C
14	D
15	C
16	E
17	A
18	D
19	C

Number correct

Number incorrect

Writing

Section 1

____

Essay score

Section 5

	Correct Answer
1	A
2	A
3	E
4	B
5	B
6	E
7	A
8	C
9	B
10	D
11	E
12	D
13	A
14	B
15	C
16	E
17	A
18	C
19	D
20	A
21	B
22	D
23	D
24	B
25	C
26	A
27	E
28	B
29	E
30	D
31	B
32	A
33	E
34	A
35	E

____

Number correct

____

Number incorrect

Section 10

	Correct Answer
1	C
2	C
3	A
4	B
5	D
6	E
7	E
8	E
9	B
10	B
11	D
12	B
13	E
14	C

____

Number correct

____

Number incorrect

Scoring the SAT Practice Test 4

Check your responses with the correct answers on the previous pages. Fill in the blanks below and do the calculations to get your Math, Critical Reading, and Writing raw scores. Use the table to find your Math, Critical Reading, and Writing scaled scores.

Get Your Math Score

How many Math questions did you get **right**?

Section 2: Questions 1–20 ________

Section 6: Questions 1–18 + ________

Section 8: Questions 1–16 + ________

Total = ________ **(A)**

How many Math questions did you get **wrong**?

Section 2: Questions 1–20 ________

Section 6: Questions 1–18 + ________

Section 8: Questions 1–16 + ________

Total = ________

× 0.25 = ________ **(B)**

A – B = ________

Math Raw Score

Round Math raw score to the nearest whole number.

____

Use the Score Conversion Table to find your Math scaled score.

____

Get Your Critical Reading Score

How many Critical Reading questions did you get **right**?

Section 4: Questions 1–24 ________

Section 7: Questions 1–24 + ________

Section 9: Questions 1–19 + ________

Total = ________ **(A)**

How many Critical Reading questions did you get **wrong**?

Section 4: Questions 1–24 ________

Section 7: Questions 1–24 + ________

Section 9: Questions 1–19 + ________

Total = ________

× 0.25 = ________ **(B)**

A – B = ________

Critical Reading Raw Score

Round Critical Reading raw score to the nearest whole number.

____

Use the Score Conversion Table to find your Critical Reading scaled score.

____

Get Your Writing Score

How many multiple-choice Writing questions did you get **right**?

Section 5: Questions 1–35 ________

Section 10: Questions 1–14 + ________

Total = ________ **(A)**

How many multiple-choice Writing questions did you get **wrong**?

Section 5: Questions 1–35 ________

Section 10: Questions 1–14 + ________

Total = ________

× 0.25 = ________ **(B)**

A – B = ________

Writing Raw Score

Round Writing raw score to the nearest whole number.

____

Use the Score Conversion Table to find your Writing multiple-choice scaled score.

____

Estimate your Essay score using the Essay Scoring Guide.

____

Use the SAT Score Conversion Table for Writing Composite to find your Writing scaled score. You will need your Writing raw score and your Essay score to use this table.

____

SAT Score Conversion Table

Raw Score	Critical Reading Scaled Score	Math Scaled Score	Writing Multiple-Choice Scaled Score*	Raw Score	Critical Reading Scaled Score	Math Scaled Score	Writing Multiple-Choice Scaled Score*
67	800			31	510	550	60
66	800			30	510	540	58
65	790			29	500	530	57
64	770			28	490	520	56
63	750			27	490	520	55
62	740			26	480	510	54
61	730			25	480	500	53
60	720			24	470	490	52
59	700			23	460	480	51
58	690			22	460	480	50
57	690			21	450	470	49
56	680			20	440	460	48
55	670			19	440	450	47
54	660	800		18	430	450	46
53	650	790		17	420	440	45
52	650	760		16	420	430	44
51	640	740		15	410	420	44
50	630	720		14	400	410	43
49	620	710	80	13	400	410	42
48	620	700	80	12	390	400	41
47	610	680	80	11	380	390	40
46	600	670	79	10	370	380	39
45	600	660	78	9	360	370	38
44	590	650	76	8	350	360	38
43	590	640	74	7	340	350	37
42	580	630	73	6	330	340	36
41	570	630	71	5	320	330	35
40	570	620	70	4	310	320	34
39	560	610	69	3	300	310	32
38	550	600	67	2	280	290	31
37	550	590	66	1	270	280	30
36	540	580	65	0	250	260	28
35	540	580	64	–1	230	240	27
34	530	570	63	–2	210	220	25
33	520	560	62	–3	200	200	23
32	520	550	61	–4 and below	200	200	20

This table is for use only with the test in this book.

* The Writing multiple-choice score is reported on a 20–80 scale. Use the SAT Score Conversion Table for Writing Composite for the total writing scaled score.

SAT Score Conversion Table for Writing Composite

Writing Multiple-Choice Raw Score	Essay Raw Score						
	0	1	2	3	4	5	6
–12	200	200	200	210	240	270	300
–11	200	200	200	210	240	270	300
–10	200	200	200	210	240	270	300
–9	200	200	200	210	240	270	300
–8	200	200	200	210	240	270	300
–7	200	200	200	210	240	270	300
–6	200	200	200	210	240	270	300
–5	200	200	200	210	240	270	300
–4	200	200	200	230	270	300	330
–3	200	210	230	250	290	320	350
–2	200	230	250	280	310	340	370
–1	210	240	260	290	320	360	380
0	230	260	280	300	340	370	400
1	240	270	290	320	350	380	410
2	250	280	300	330	360	390	420
3	260	290	310	340	370	400	430
4	270	300	320	350	380	410	440
5	280	310	330	360	390	420	450
6	290	320	340	360	400	430	460
7	290	330	340	370	410	440	470
8	300	330	350	380	410	450	470
9	310	340	360	390	420	450	480
10	320	350	370	390	430	460	490
11	320	360	370	400	440	470	500
12	330	360	380	410	440	470	500
13	340	370	390	420	450	480	510
14	350	380	390	420	460	490	520
15	350	380	400	430	460	500	530
16	360	390	410	440	470	500	530
17	370	400	420	440	480	510	540
18	380	410	420	450	490	520	550
19	380	410	430	460	490	530	560
20	390	420	440	470	500	530	560
21	400	430	450	480	510	540	570
22	410	440	460	480	520	550	580
23	420	450	470	490	530	560	590
24	420	460	470	500	540	570	600
25	430	460	480	510	540	580	610

Writing Multiple-Choice Raw Score	Essay Raw Score						
	0	1	2	3	4	5	6
26	440	470	490	520	550	590	610
27	450	480	500	530	560	590	620
28	460	490	510	540	570	600	630
29	470	500	520	550	580	610	640
30	480	510	530	560	590	620	650
31	490	520	540	560	600	630	660
32	500	530	550	570	610	640	670
33	510	540	550	580	620	650	680
34	510	550	560	590	630	660	690
35	520	560	570	600	640	670	700
36	530	560	580	610	650	680	710
37	540	570	590	620	660	690	720
38	550	580	600	630	670	700	730
39	560	600	610	640	680	710	740
40	580	610	620	650	690	720	750
41	590	620	640	660	700	730	760
42	600	630	650	680	710	740	770
43	610	640	660	690	720	750	780
44	620	660	670	700	740	770	800
45	640	670	690	720	750	780	800
46	650	690	700	730	770	800	800
47	670	700	720	750	780	800	800
48	680	720	730	760	800	800	800
49	680	720	730	760	800	800	800

Chart for Self-Appraisal Based on the Practice Test You Have Just Taken

The Chart for Self-Appraisal below tells you quickly where your SAT strengths and weaknesses lie. Check or circle the appropriate box in accordance with the number of your correct answers for each area of the Practice Test you have just taken.

	Writing (Multiple-choice)	*Sentence Completions*	*Reading Comprehension*	*Math Questions**
EXCELLENT	42–49	16–19	40–48	44–54
GOOD	37–41	13–15	35–39	32–43
FAIR	31–36	9–12	26–34	27–31
POOR	20–30	5–8	17–25	16–26
VERY POOR	0–19	0–4	0–16	0–15

* Sections 2, 6, 8 only.

Note: In our tests, we have chosen to have Section 3 as the experimental section. We have also chosen it to be a math section since we felt that students may need more practice in the math area than in the verbal area. Note that on the actual SAT you will take, the order of the sections can vary and you will not know which one is experimental, so it is wise to answer all sections and not to leave any section out.

SAT-I VERBAL AND MATH SCORE/PERCENTILE CONVERSION TABLE

Critical Reading and Writing

SAT scaled verbal score	Percentile rank
800	99.7+
790	99.5
740–780	99
700–730	97
670–690	95
640–660	91
610–630	85
580–600	77
550–570	68
510–540	57
480–500	46
440–470	32
410–430	21
380–400	13
340–370	6
300–330	2
230–290	1
200–220	0–0.5

Math

SAT scaled math score	Percentile rank
800	99.5+
770–790	99.5
720–760	99
670–710	97
640–660	94
610–630	89
590–600	84
560–580	77
530–550	68
510–520	59
480–500	48
450–470	37
430–440	26
390–420	16
350–380	8
310–340	2
210–300	0.5
200	0

Section 1—Essay

The following are guidelines for scoring the essay.

The SAT Scoring Guide

Score of 6 An essay in this category is *outstanding,* demonstrating *clear and consistent mastery,* although it may have a few minor errors. A typical essay	**Score of 5** An essay in this category is *effective,* demonstrating *reasonably consistent mastery,* although it will have occasional errors or lapses in quality. A typical essay	**Score of 4** An essay in this category is *competent,* demonstrating *adequate mastery,* although it will have lapses in quality. A typical essay
• effectively and insightfully develops a point of view on the issue and demonstrates outstanding critical thinking, using clearly appropriate examples, reasons, and other evidence to support its position	• effectively develops a point of view on the issue and demonstrates strong critical thinking, generally using appropriate examples, reasons, and other evidence to support its position	• develops a point of view on the issue and demonstrates competent critical thinking, using adequate examples, reasons, and other evidence to support its position
• is well organized and clearly focused, demonstrating clear coherence and smooth progression of ideas	• is well organized and focused, demonstrating coherence and progression of ideas	• is generally organized and focused, demonstrating some coherence and progression of ideas
• exhibits skillful use of language, using a varied, accurate, and apt vocabulary	• exhibits facility in the use of language, using appropriate vocabulary	• exhibits adequate but inconsistent facility in the use of language, using generally appropriate vocabulary
• demonstrates meaningful variety in sentence structure	• demonstrates variety in sentence structure	• demonstrates some variety in sentence structure
• is free of most errors in grammar, usage, and mechanics	• is generally free of most errors in grammar, usage, and mechanics	• has some errors in grammar, usage, and mechanics
Score of 3 An essay in this category is *inadequate,* but demonstrates *developing mastery,* and is marked by ONE OR MORE of the following weaknesses:	**Score of 2** An essay in this category is *seriously limited,* demonstrating *little mastery,* and is flawed by ONE OR MORE of the following weaknesses:	**Score of 1** An essay in this category is *fundamentally lacking,* demonstrating *very little* or *no mastery,* and is severely flawed by ONE OR MORE of the following weaknesses:
• develops a point of view on the issue, demonstrating some critical thinking, but may do so inconsistently or use inadequate examples, reasons, or other evidence to support its position	• develops a point of view on the issue that is vague or seriously limited, demonstrating weak critical thinking, providing inappropriate or insufficient examples, reasons, or other evidence to support its position	• develops no viable point of view on the issue, or provides little or no evidence to support its position
• is limited in its organization or focus, or may demonstrate some lapses in coherence or progression of ideas	• is poorly organized and/or focused, or demonstrates serious problems with coherence or progression of ideas	• is disorganized or unfocused, resulting in a disjointed or incoherent essay
• displays developing facility in the use of language, but sometimes uses weak vocabulary or inappropriate word choice	• displays very little facility in the use of language, using very limited vocabulary or incorrect word choice	• displays fundamental errors in vocabulary
• lacks variety or demonstrates problems in sentence structure	• demonstrates frequent problems in sentence structure	• demonstrates severe flaws in sentence structure
• contains an accumulation of errors in grammar, usage, and mechanics	• contains errors in grammar, usage, and mechanics so serious that meaning is somewhat obscured	• contains pervasive errors in grammar, usage, or mechanics that persistently interfere with meaning

Essays not written on the essay assignment will receive a score of zero.

Explanatory Answers for Practice Test 4

Section 2: Math

As you read these solutions, you are advised to do two things if you answered the Math question incorrectly:

1. When a specific Math Strategy is referred to in the solution, study that strategy, which you will find in "19 Math Strategies" (beginning on page 69).
2. When the solution directs you to the "Complete Math Refresher" (beginning on page 167)—for example, Math Refresher 305—study the 305 Math principle to get a clear idea of the Math operation that was necessary for you to know in order to answer the question correctly.

1. Choice B is correct. **(Use Strategy 2: Translate from words to algebra.)**

The quotient of x and 3

$\frac{x}{3}$

$\left.\frac{x}{3} - 8\right\}$ = 8 less than the quotient

and is the required answer.

(Math Refresher #200)

2. Choice C is correct. **(Use Strategy 2: Translate from words to algebra.)**

7 of Phil's buckets − 7 of Mark's buckets =
7 × 11 gallons − 7 × 8 gallons =
77 gallons − 56 gallons =
21 gallons

(Math Refresher #200)

3. Choice D is correct. **(Use Strategy 7: Use number examples.)** You can show that

$$\frac{|x|}{|y|} = \left|\frac{x}{y}\right|$$

For example: $\frac{|-2|}{|4|} = \left|\frac{-2}{4}\right| = \frac{1}{2}; \frac{|-3|}{|-6|} = \left|\frac{-3}{-6}\right| = \frac{1}{2}$

(Math Refresher #615)

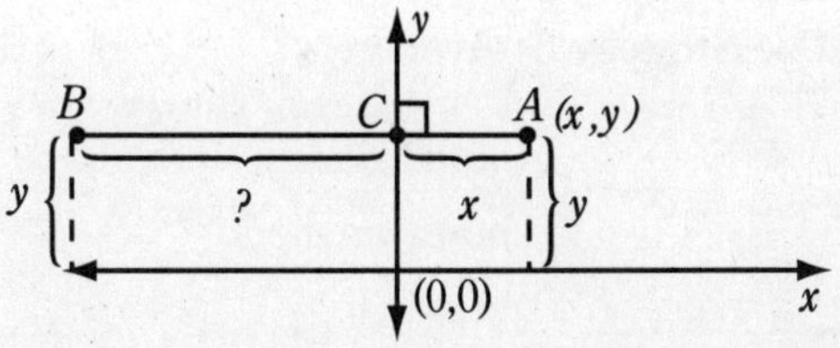

4. Choice D is correct. **(Use Strategy 14: Label unknown quantities.)**

As shown in the diagram above, the y-coordinates of A and B must be the same because they both lie along the same horizontal line. Since B lies to the left of the y-axis, its x-coordinate must be negative. Since $3AC = BC$, then the x-coordinate of B is

$$-3x$$

and we already know that the y-coordinate is y.

Thus, $(-3x, y)$ is the answer.

(Math Refresher #410)

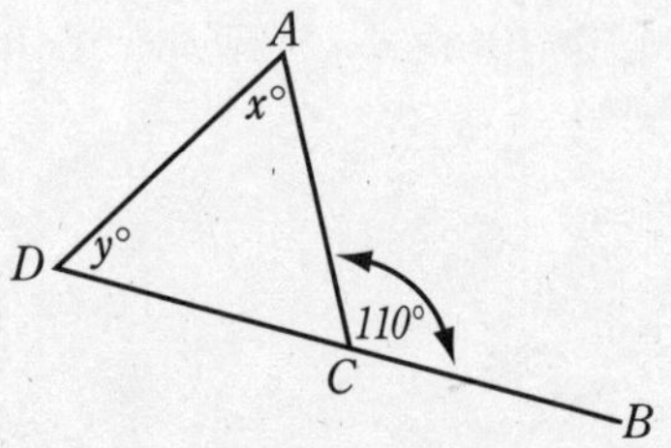

5. Choice D is correct. **(Use Strategy 18: Remember triangle facts.)**

Since $AC = CD$, we know that

$$x = y \qquad \boxed{1}$$

We also know that

$$m\angle ACB = m\angle D + m\angle A \qquad \boxed{2}$$

Substituting the given into $\boxed{2}$, we have

$$110 = y + x \qquad \boxed{3}$$

Substituting $\boxed{1}$ into $\boxed{3}$, we get

$$110 = y + y$$
$$110 = 2y$$

(Math Refresher #507 and #406)

6. Choice E is correct. **(Use Strategy 16: The obvious may be tricky!)**

Given: $(x + y)^2 = 9$
So that $x + y = 3$ or -3

From the information given, we cannot determine whether $x + y$ equals 3 or -3.

(Math Refresher #409)

7. Choice E is correct.

(Use Strategy 5: Average $= \dfrac{\textbf{sum of values}}{\textbf{total number of values}}$**)**

Let x, y = two unknown numbers.

Thus, $\dfrac{28 + 30 + 32 + x + y}{5} = 34 \qquad \boxed{1}$

Multiplying $\boxed{1}$ by 5,

$$28 + 30 + 32 + x + y = 170$$
or $$90 + x + y = 170$$
or $$x + y = 80$$

(Math Refresher #601 and #406)

8. Choice C is correct. **(Use Strategy 2: Translate from words to algebra.)**

Let x = side of one of the eight squares.

Thus, we are given

$$4x = 16$$
$$\text{or } x = 4 \qquad \boxed{1}$$

From what we are told in the problem, we conclude that

$$AE = MF = LG = 4x \qquad \boxed{2}$$
and $$AL = BK = CJ = DH = EG = 2x \qquad \boxed{3}$$

(Use Strategy 3: The whole equals the sum of its parts.)

Thus, using $\boxed{1}$, $\boxed{2}$, and $\boxed{3}$,

$$AE + MF + LG + AL + BK + CJ + DH + EG$$
$$= 4x + 4x + 4x + 2x + 2x + 2x + 2x + 2x$$
$$= 22x = 88$$

(Math Refresher #200, #303, and #304)

9. Choice A is correct. **(Use Strategy 11: Use new definitions carefully.)**

Given: $\textcircled{x} = \dfrac{x^2}{3}$ and $\boxed{x} = \dfrac{9}{x}$

Thus, $\textcircled{x} \times \boxed{x} = \dfrac{x^2}{3} \times \dfrac{9}{x} = 3x$

(Math Refresher #431)

10. Choice C is correct. **(Use Strategy 17: Use the given information effectively.)**

For I, we have:

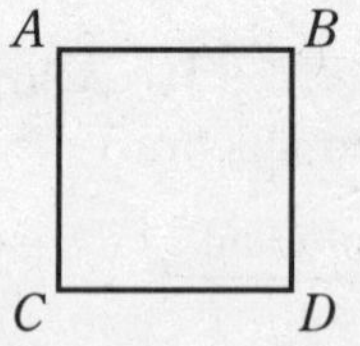

Clearly $DB < DA$, so I could not be true.

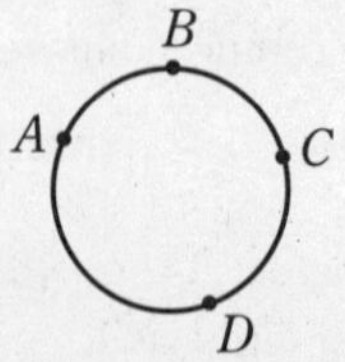

Clearly D can be the same distance from 2 points (A and B), but not from 3, so II does not apply.

Only Choice C, III only, is now possible.

Choice III is demonstrated below, although it was not necessary for us to examine it.

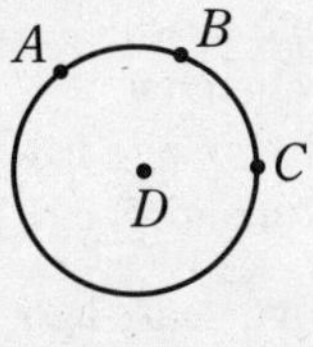

By definition, all points on the circle are the same distance from the center, so $DA = DB = DC$.

(Math Refresher #303 and #310)

11. Choice A is correct. It can be seen that the dark region in Choice A is common to sets A, B, and C. Thus the diagram in Choice A describes the dark region as the set of elements that belongs to all of the sets A, B, and C.

(Math Refresher #803)

12. Choice A is correct. **(Use Strategy 17: Use the given information effectively.)** Since the slope of a line is constant, the *ratio* of the *difference* in *y*-coordinates to the *difference* in *x*-coordinates must be constant for any two points on the line. For points (1,3) and (3,5), this ratio is

$$\frac{5-3}{3-1} = 1$$

Thus, for points (6,*y*) and (3,5) we must have

$$\frac{y-5}{6-3} = 1$$

Therefore,

$$y - 5 = 3$$

and $y = 8$.

(Math Refresher #416)

13. Choice D is correct. **(Use Strategy 10: Know how to use units.)**

$$\left(\frac{p \text{ gallons}}{\cancel{\text{car}}}\right) \times (r\ \cancel{\text{cars}}) = pr \text{ gallons for each month}$$

$$\frac{q\ \cancel{\text{gallons}}}{pr\dfrac{\cancel{\text{gallons}}}{\text{months}}} = \frac{q}{pr} \text{ months}$$

(Math Refresher #121)

14. Choice E is correct. **(Use Strategy 11: Use new definitions carefully.)**

By definition, the *l*-length from -3 to $3 =$

$$3 - (-3) =$$
$$3 + 3 =$$
$$6$$

(Math Refresher #431)

15. Choice A is correct.

By definition, the *l*-length from -4 to each of the other points follows:

$$R - (-4) = R + 4 \qquad \boxed{1}$$
$$S - (-4) = S + 4 \qquad \boxed{2}$$
$$T - (-4) = T + 4 \qquad \boxed{3}$$
$$U - (-4) = U + 4 \qquad \boxed{4}$$
$$V - (-4) = V + 4 \qquad \boxed{5}$$

From their position on the number line we know that

$$R < S < T < U < V \qquad \boxed{6}$$

(Use Strategy 6: Know how to manipulate inequalities.)

Adding 4 to each term of $\boxed{6}$, we get

$$R + 4 < S + 4 < T + 4 < U + 4 < V + 4 \qquad \boxed{7}$$

It is obvious from $\boxed{7}$ that $R + 4$ is smallest.

Thus, $\boxed{1}$ above, point *R*, has the least *l*-length from -4.

(Math Refresher #420)

16. Choice D is correct. **(Use Strategy 2: Translate from words to algebra.)**

Let x, $x + 1$, $x + 2$, $x + 3$, $x + 4$ represent the 5 consecutive integers.

Then, $x + x + 1 + x + 2 + x + 3 + x + 4 = w$

$$5x + 10 = w \qquad \boxed{1}$$

The next 5 consecutive positive integers will be

$$x + 5, x + 6, x + 7, x + 8, x + 9$$

Their sum will be

$$x + 5 + x + 6 + x + 7 + x + 8 + x + 9 =$$
$$5x + 35 \qquad \boxed{2}$$

We can write $\boxed{2}$ as

$$5x + 35 = 5x + 10 + 25 \qquad \boxed{3}$$

Substituting $\boxed{1}$ into $\boxed{3}$, we get

$$5x + 10 + 25 = w + 25$$

(Math Refresher #200 and #406)

17. Choice C is correct. **(Use Strategy 2: Translate from words to algebra.)**

We are told that the area of the square is twice the area of the triangle. This translates to:

$$a^2 = \cancel{2}\left(\frac{1}{\cancel{2}} \times b \times c\right)$$
$$a^2 = bc \qquad \boxed{1}$$

We are given that $bc = 100$ [2]

Substituting [2] into [1], we get

$$a^2 = 100$$

(Math Refresher #200, #303, #306)

18. Choice A is correct.

Given that the radius of the circle equals 2, we have

$$\text{Circumference} = 2\pi(\text{radius}) = 2\pi(2) = 4\pi \text{ inches} \quad [1]$$

We are given that $\widehat{AD} + \widehat{BC} = 3\pi$ inches [2]

(Use Strategy 3: The whole equals the sum of its parts.)

We know that $\widehat{AD} + \widehat{BC} + \widehat{AC} + \widehat{DB}$ = circumference of the circle. [3]

Substituting [1] and [2] into [3], we have

$$3\pi \text{ inches} + \widehat{AC} + \widehat{DB} = 4\pi \text{ inches}$$

$$\widehat{AC} + \widehat{DB} = \pi \text{ inches} \quad [4]$$

Let's figure out how to relate the length of $\widehat{AC} + \widehat{DB} = \pi$ inches with the angle y. We know that the central angle is measured by its arc.

Now get a proportion:

$$\frac{360°}{2\pi r} = \frac{y°}{\widehat{AC}}$$

Since $r = 2$,

$$\frac{360°}{4\pi} = \frac{y°}{\widehat{AC}} \quad [5]$$

But $\widehat{AC} + \widehat{DB} = \pi$ inches, and since $\widehat{AC} = \widehat{DB}$,

$$\widehat{AC} = \frac{1}{2}\pi \quad [6]$$

From [5], using [6], we get:

$$\frac{360°}{4\pi} = \frac{y°}{\frac{1}{2}\pi}$$

and we get

$$\frac{180}{4} = y = 45.$$

(Math Refresher #310, #524, and #120)

19. Choice B is correct. **(Use Strategy 2: Translate from words to algebra.)**

Let r = Ross's age now.
19 = Amanda's age now.
Thus, $r - 5$ = Ross's age five years ago. [1]
$19 - 5 = 14$ = Amanda's age five years ago. [2]

We are given: Five years ago, Ross was N times as old as Amanda was. [3]

Substituting [1] and [2] into [3], we have

$$r - 5 = N(14)$$
$$r = 14N + 5$$

(Math Refresher #406)

20. Choice C is correct.

The volume of the rectangular solid to be immersed is:

$$V = (1 \text{ ft})(1 \text{ ft})(2 \text{ ft}) = 2 \text{ cu ft} \quad [1]$$

When the solid is immersed, the volume of the displaced water will be:

$$(2 \text{ ft})(6 \text{ ft})(x \text{ ft}) = 12x \text{ cu ft} \quad [2]$$

where x represents the height of the displaced water. [1] and [2] must be equal. So

$$2 \text{ cu ft} = 12x \text{ cu ft}$$

$$\frac{1}{6} \text{ ft} = x$$

(Use Strategy 10: Know how to use units.)

$$\left(\frac{1}{6}\cancel{\text{ft}}\right)\left(\frac{12 \text{ inches}}{\cancel{\text{foot}}}\right) =$$

$\frac{12}{6}$ = 2 inches that the displaced water will rise.

(Math Refresher #312 and #121)

Explanatory Answers for Practice Test 4 (continued)

Section 3: Math

As you read these solutions, you are advised to do two things if you answered the Math question incorrectly:

1. When a specific Math Strategy is referred to in the solution, study that strategy, which you will find in "19 Math Strategies" (beginning on page 69).
2. When the solution directs you to the "Complete Math Refresher" (beginning on page 167)—for example, Math Refresher 305—study the 305 Math principle to get a clear idea of the Math operation that was necessary for you to know in order to answer the question correctly.

1. Choice C is correct. **(Use Strategy 17: Use the given information effectively.)**

Given: $x + by = 5$ [1]
$3x + y = 5$ [2]
$y = 2$ [3]

We want to find b.

Substituting [3] into [2], we get

$3x + 2 = 5$
or $x = 1$ [4]

Substituting [3] and [4] into [1], we have

$1 + 2b = 5$
or $2b = 4$
or $b = 2$

(Math Refresher #406 and #431)

2. Choice B is correct.

The ratio of boys to girls in the class is 2 : 3. Choice C is the answer because 9 : 12 = 3 : 4, which does not equal 2 : 3.

(Math Refresher #108)

3. Choice C is correct. **(Use Strategy 10: Know how to use units.)**

Since 7 days = 1 week, 24 hours = 1 day, and 60 minutes = 1 hour, then

$$1 \text{ week} = (1\ \cancel{\text{week}})\left(\frac{7\ \cancel{\text{days}}}{\cancel{\text{week}}}\right)\left(\frac{24\ \cancel{\text{hours}}}{\cancel{\text{day}}}\right)\left(\frac{60 \text{ minutes}}{\cancel{\text{hour}}}\right)$$
$$= (7)(24)(60) \text{ minutes}$$

Thus,

$$\frac{24 \text{ minutes}}{1 \text{ week}} = \frac{\cancel{24}\ \cancel{\text{minutes}}}{(7)(\cancel{24})(60)\ \cancel{\text{minutes}}} = \frac{1}{420}$$

(Math Refresher #121)

4. Choice D is correct. **(Use Strategy 17: Use the given information effectively.)**

$$2 \times 10^{-5} \times 8 \times 10^2 \times 5 \times 10^2$$
$$= 2 \times 8 \times 5 \times 10^{-5} \times 10^2 \times 10^2$$
$$= 8 \times 10^0$$
$$= 8 \times 1$$
$$= 8$$

(Math Refresher #429)

5. Choice C is correct. **(Use Strategy 2: Translate from words to algebra.)**

Allowance = \$30

Amount spent on candy $= \frac{2}{5} \times \$30 = \$12$

Amount left after Johnny bought candy $= \$30 - \$12 = \$18$

Amount spent on ice cream $= \frac{5}{6} \times \$18 = \$15$

Amount left after buying candy and ice cream $= \$18 - \$15 = \$3$

(Math Refresher #200)

6. Choice A is correct. **(Use Strategy 17: Use the given information effectively.)** $y = -x^2 = -4$. $x = 2$ or $x = -2$. Since point B lies on the left side of the y-axis, $x = -2$.

(Math Refresher #410b)

7. Choice A is correct. **(Use Strategy 17: Use the given information effectively.)** It is seen from the graph of $y = f(x)$ that when $x = 0$, $y = 0$. Thus $0 = m(0) + b$ and $b = 0$.

(Math Refresher #414)

8. Choice C is correct. When the graph intersects the x-axis, $y = 0$. Thus we set $y = 0 = x^4 + x^3$.

We can write this as

$$x^3(x + 1) = 0$$

Thus $x = 0$ and $x = -1$

The graph therefore intersects the x-axis at two points.

(Math Refresher #415)

9. 24 **(Use Strategy 2: Translate from words to algebra.)**

Given: $\frac{5}{8}$ of x is 40
↓ ↓ ↓ ↓ ↓
$\frac{5}{8} \times x = 40$ [1]

(Use Strategy 13: Find unknowns by multiplication.)

Fast Method: To get the value of $\frac{3}{8}$ of x, multiply [1] by $\frac{3}{5}$ to get

$$\frac{3}{5}\left(\frac{5}{8}x\right) = \frac{3}{5}(40)$$
$$\frac{3}{8}x = \frac{3}{\not{5}} \times \not{5} \times 8$$
$$\frac{3}{8}x = 24$$

Slow Method: Solve [1] for x by multiplying [1] by $\frac{8}{5}$:

$$x = 64 \qquad [2]$$

Now substitute [2] into the unknown expression:

$$\frac{3}{8}x = \frac{3}{8}(64)$$
$$= \frac{3}{\not{8}} \times \not{8} \times 8$$
$$= 24$$

(Math Refresher #200 and #406)

10. 9 **(Use Strategy 2: Translate from words to algebra.)** We are given that the wire is bent to form a circle of radius 3 feet. This means that its length is equal to the circumference of the circle.

Thus, Length of wire $= 2\pi r = 2\pi(3)$ feet
$= 6\pi$ feet
$\approx 6(3.14)$ feet
Length of wire ≈ 18.84 feet [1]

(Use Strategy 3: Know how to find unknown quantities.)

$$\text{Number of pieces 2 feet long} = \frac{\text{total length}}{2 \text{ feet}} \qquad [2]$$

Substituting [1] into [2], we have

$$\text{Number of pieces 2 feet long} \approx \frac{18.84 \text{ feet}}{2 \text{ feet}}$$
$$\approx 9.42$$
$$= 9 \text{ complete pieces}$$

(Math Refresher #310)

11. 7 **(Use Strategy 2: Translate from words to algebra.)**

Let b = number of baseballs that Dick bought
t = number of tennis balls that Dick bought
$.70b$ = amount spent on baseballs
$.60t$ = amount spent on tennis balls

Thus, we are told

$$.70b + .60t = 7.00 \qquad [1]$$

Multiply [1] by 10:

$$7b + 6t = 70 \qquad [2]$$

Solve $\boxed{2}$ for t:

$$t = \frac{70 - 7b}{6} = \frac{7(10 - b)}{6} \qquad \boxed{3}$$

(Use Strategy 17: Use the given information effectively.) From $\boxed{3}$, we see that the maximum value of t occurs at the minimum value of b. Since b and t are numbers of balls, b and t must be nonnegative integers. Thus, the minimum value of b is 0. When $b = 0$, $t = \frac{70}{6}$, which is not an integer. For t to be an integer, $\boxed{3}$ tells us that $(10 - b)$ is a multiple of 6. The smallest value of b that makes $(10 - b)$ a multiple of 6 is $b = 4$. Thus, $t = 7$ is the maximum value of t, and 7 is the answer.

(Math Refresher #200, #406, and #431)

12. 2 (Use Strategy 11: Use new definitions carefully.)

Given:

$$f(x) = 12x + 8 \qquad \boxed{1}$$

$$\text{and } f(x) \div f(0) = 2x \qquad \boxed{2}$$

Calculate $f(0)$:

$$f(0) = 12(0) + 8 = 8 \qquad \boxed{3}$$

Substitute $\boxed{1}$ and $\boxed{3}$ into $\boxed{2}$:

$$\frac{12x + 8}{8} = 2x \qquad \boxed{4}$$

Multiply both sides of $\boxed{4}$ by 8:

$$12x + 8 = 16x$$

or $$8 = 4x$$

or $$x = 2$$

(Math Refresher #431 and #406)

13. 8 (Use Strategy 11: Use new definitions carefully.)

In the given letter columns, only 8 triples have the property that exactly 2 of the letters in the triple are the same. Thus, 8 triples have a value of 1, and all the other triples have a value of 0. Hence, the value of the entire group of letter columns is 8.

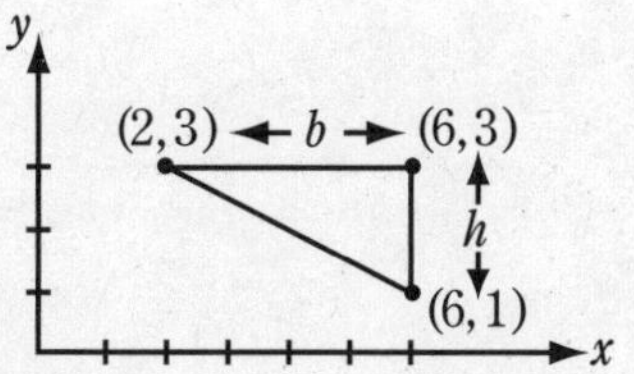

14. 4 (Use Strategy 17: Use the given information effectively.)

It is clear from the diagram above that the triangle is a right triangle whose area is

$$A = \frac{1}{2}bh \qquad \boxed{1}$$

From the given coordinates, we can also say that

$$b = 6 - 2 = 4 \qquad \boxed{2}$$

$$h = 3 - 1 = 2 \qquad \boxed{3}$$

Substituting $\boxed{2}$ and $\boxed{3}$ into $\boxed{1}$,

$$A = \frac{1}{\not{2}}(4)(\not{2})$$

$$A = 4$$

(Math Refresher #306 and #410)

15. 18 (Use Strategy 17: Use the given information effectively.)

The area of a rectangle is length × width. The number of squares that can be packed into the rectangle

$$= \frac{\text{area of entire rectangle}}{\text{area of each square}}$$

$$= \frac{6 \times 12}{2 \times 2}$$

$$= \frac{72}{4}$$

$$= \frac{\not{4} \times 18}{\not{4}}$$

$$= 18$$

(Math Refresher #304 and #431)

16. 60 Since we are given the radii of the circles, we have

$$AN = AM = 1 \qquad \boxed{1}$$

$$BM = BP = 2 \qquad \boxed{2}$$

$$CN = CP = 3 \qquad \boxed{3}$$

We want to find

$$(AB)(BC)(AC) \qquad \boxed{4}$$

(Use Strategy 3: The whole equals the sum of its parts.) From the diagram, we see that

$$AB = AM + BM \qquad \boxed{5}$$

$$BC = BP + CP \qquad \boxed{6}$$

$$AC = AN + CN \qquad \boxed{7}$$

Substituting $\boxed{1}$, $\boxed{2}$, $\boxed{3}$ into $\boxed{5}$, $\boxed{6}$, $\boxed{7}$ we have

$$AB = 3$$

$$BC = 5$$

$$AC = 4$$

Thus,

$$(AB)(BC)(AC) = (3)(5)(4) = 60$$

(Math Refresher #524)

17. 9500

(Use Strategy 5:

$$\textbf{Average} = \frac{\text{sum of values}}{\text{total number of values}}\Big)$$

We are given:

$$\frac{x+y+z+w}{4} = 8{,}000 \qquad \boxed{1}$$

(Use Strategy 13: Find unknowns by multiplication.) Multiplying $\boxed{1}$ by 4, we get

$$x + y + z + w = 32{,}000 \qquad \boxed{2}$$

We are given that any 3 have an average of 7,500, so using x, y, and z as the 3, we get

$$\frac{x+y+z}{3} = 7{,}500 \qquad \boxed{3}$$

Multiplying $\boxed{3}$ by 3, we get

$$x + y + z = 22{,}500 \qquad \boxed{4}$$

Substituting $\boxed{4}$ into $\boxed{2}$, we get

$$22{,}500 + w = 32{,}000$$

or $$w = 9{,}500$$

(Math Refresher #601 and #406)

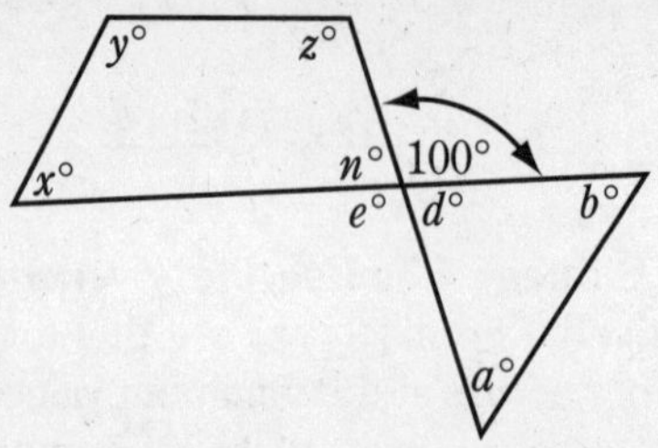

18. 280

(Use Strategy 17: Use the given information effectively.)

From the diagram, $n = d$ (vertical angles). $\boxed{1}$

We know $x + y + z + n = 360$ $\boxed{2}$

Substituting $\boxed{1}$ into $\boxed{2}$, we get

$$x + y + z + d = 360 \qquad \boxed{3}$$

Subtracting d from $\boxed{3}$, we have

$$x + y + z = 360 - d \qquad \boxed{4}$$

We know that $100 + d = 180$ from the diagram.

So, $d = 180 - 100 = 80$ $\boxed{5}$

Substituting $\boxed{5}$ into $\boxed{4}$, we get

$$x + y + z = 360 - 80$$
$$x + y + z = 280$$

(Math Refresher #521, #503, and #406)

Explanatory Answers for Practice Test 4 (continued)

Section 4: Critical Reading

As you read these Explanatory Answers, refer to "16 Verbal (Critical Reading) Strategies" (beginning on page 119) whenever a specific strategy is referred to in the answer. Of particular importance are the following Master Verbal Strategies:

Sentence Completion Master Strategy 1—page 120.
Sentence Completion Master Strategy 2—page 121.
Reading Comprehension Master Strategy 2—page 138.

Note: All Reading questions use Reading Comprehension Strategies 1, 2, and 3 (pages 135–140) as well as other strategies indicated.

1. Choice D is correct. See **Sentence Completion Strategy 2**. Examine the first word of each choice. Choice B, pacifism, and Choice E, oblivion, are incorrect choices because a rising tide of pacifism or oblivion in public education does *not* make good sense. Now consider the other choices. Choice A, compromise...inept, and Choice C, ambiguity...average, do *not* make good sense in the sentence. Choice D, mediocrity...dedicated, *does* make good sense.

2. Choice C is correct. See **Sentence Completion Strategy 2**. First we eliminate Choice A, foretold, Choice B, impossible, and Choice E, glaring. Reason: These choices do not make sense in the sentence up to the word "eclipses." We further eliminate Choice D, true...rational, because it does not make sense for anyone to consider an eclipse rational. Only Choice C, understandable...magical, makes sense.

3. Choice D is correct. The fact that the girl had become more self-confident indicates that she would be more active in participating in a conversation. If you used **Sentence Completion Strategy 3**—trying to complete the sentence *before* looking at the five choices—you might have come up with any of the following appropriate words:

starting	beginning
launching	originating

The other choices are, therefore, incorrect.

4. Choice D is correct. See **Sentence Completion Strategy 2**. Let us first examine the first word of each choice. We can eliminate Choice B, confuse, and Choice E, misconstrue, because it does *not* make sense to say that an authority would be able to "confuse" or "misconstrue" something in a book. So Choices B and E are incorrect.

Let us now consider the remaining choices. Choice A, understand...general, and Choice C, read...useless, do *not* make sense in the sentence. Therefore, these choices are incorrect. Choice D, comprehend...complex, *does* make sense.

5. Choice B is correct. See **Sentence Completion Strategy 4**. The words "not only" constitute a *support indicator.* The second part of the sentence is, therefore, expected to reinforce the first part of the sentence. Choice B, reject...refused, supplies the two words that provide a sentence that makes sense. Choices A, C, D, and E are incorrect because their word pairs do not produce sentences that make sense.

6. Choice A is correct. See **Sentence Completion Strategy 3**. If you used this strategy of trying to complete the sentence *before* looking at the five choices, you might have come up with any of the following appropriate words:

   persistence   perseverance
   steadfastness

   These words all mean the same as Choice A, tenacity. Note that the root "ten" in "tenacity" means "to hold." Accordingly, Choices B, C, D, and E are incorrect.

7. Choice C is correct. See **Sentence Completion Strategy 4**. The adverb "ironically" means "in a manner so that the opposite of what is expected takes place." So we have an *opposition indicator* here. Choice C, weaken, is, of course, the opposite of strengthen. Accordingly, Choices A, B, D, and E are incorrect.

8. Choice B is correct. See **Sentence Completion Strategy 4**. The words "in spite of" constitute an *opposition indicator.* We can then expect an opposing idea to complete the sentence. The word "baffled" means "puzzled" or "unable to comprehend." Choice B, baffled, gives us the word that brings out the opposition thought we expect in the sentence. Choices A, C, D, and E do not give us a sentence that makes sense.

9. Choice E is correct. See the beginning sentence, which states, "the greatest acrobats on earth," introducing the monkeys, which in line 4 are called "ceboids." The whole passage is about the "ceboid acrobats."

10. Choice C is correct. See lines 12–17, where the comparisons are made.

11. Choice B is correct. See lines 1–3. Note that even if you didn't know the meaning of "deprecate," you could figure that the word imparted a negative connotation since the prefix "de" means "away from" and is negative. Also don't get lured into Choice D just because "Babel" was mentioned.

12. Choice B is correct. See line 4: "...influence is most dangerous..."

13. Choice D is correct. The second paragraph states that "the other classes...adopted many of the outward characteristics of the aristocracy."

14. Choice C is correct. The second paragraph implies that the bourgeoisie was "rising to political power" and rivaling the power of the aristocracy.

15. Choice B is correct. The third and fifth paragraphs describe the castles as "strongholds" and "fortified houses."

16. Choice A is correct. This information is given in paragraph 3, where it states that "the Magyar armies" harried central Europe.

17. Choice C is correct. The fourth paragraph relates how "power passed into the hands of warriors invested by the monarchy and the Church with lands."

18. Choice D is correct. Paragraph 2 states, "Noblemen who became bishops or who founded new Orders helped to implant aristocratic principles...deep within...the Church."

19. Choice C is correct. Given the context of the rest of the sentence, it can be seen that Choice C is correct. See also **Reading Comprehension Strategy 5**.

20. Choice B is correct. The last paragraph states that hunting was a rehearsal for war and it made up "for the lack of butcher's meat."

21. Choice C is correct. See paragraph 2: "Even the unarmed peasantry...long remained tenaciously loyal to their lords, held to their allegiance by that combination of love and fear, *amor et timor*..."

22. Choice A is correct. See paragraph 4: "...warriors... undertook...to protect the unarmed peasantry."

23. Choice B is correct. See paragraph 4: "It was recognized in theory that the Church and the monarchy were the principal powers and that they were bound by the nature of their office to ensure peace and security...but...they were too weak, too torn by internal conflicts to fulfill their obligations."

24. Choice D is correct. Given the context of the rest of the sentence, it would appear that because of the word "themselves," "retinue" must refer to humans. It is more likely that it refers to "attendants" than to "family." See also **Reading Comprehension Strategy 5**.

Explanatory Answers for Practice Test 4 (continued)

Section 5: Writing

For further practice and information, please refer to Grammar and Usage Refresher starting on page 455.

1. **(A)** Choice A is correct. Choice B is incorrect because "on account" may not be used as a subordinate conjunction. Choice C is incorrect because it gives the meaning that the judge is doing the charging. Choice D is incorrect because the possessive noun ("defendant") modifying the gerund ("charging") must take the form "defendant's." Choice E creates a run-on sentence.

2. **(A)** Choice A is correct. Choices B, C, and D are incorrect because they change the meaning of the original sentence. Choice E creates a run-on sentence.

3. **(E)** Choices A and B are incorrect because they give the idea that the plans are trying to avoid the hot sun. Choice C is awkward. Choice D is a run-on sentence. Choice E is correct.

4. **(B)** Choice A is too wordy. Choice B is correct. Choice C is incorrect because it changes the tense of the original sentence—"Whatever (may) be her thoughts" is in the present tense. Choice D does not retain the meaning of the original sentence. Choice E makes no sense.

5. **(B)** Choices A and E are incorrect because the subject word "use" requires a singular verb ("makes"). Choice B is correct. Choices C and D are awkward.

6. **(E)** "Irregardless" (Choice A) is incorrect. "Regardless about" (Choice B) is unidiomatic. Choices C and D change the meaning of the original sentence. Moreover, Choice D makes the sentence ungrammatical. Choice E is correct.

7. **(A)** Choice A is correct. Choices B, C, and E change the meaning of the original sentence. Choice D is too wordy.

8. **(C)** The infinitive "to effect" means "to bring about"—this is not the meaning intended in the original sentence. Therefore, Choices A, B, and D are incorrect. Choice C is correct. Choice E changes the meaning of the original sentence.

9. **(B)** In the original sentence, "who" should replace "whom" as the subject of the subordinate clause ("who were policemen"). "I believe" is simply a parenthetical expression. Therefore, Choice A is incorrect and Choice B is correct. Choice C creates a run-on sentence. Choice D improperly changes the sentence from a complex type to a compound type. Choice E does not retain the meaning of the original sentence.

10. **(D)** Choices A and B suffer from improper ellipsis. Choice C changes the meaning of the original sentence. Choice D is correct. Choice E is too wordy.

11. **(E)** Sequence of tenses in a past contrary-to-fact condition requires the "had waited" form in the "if" clause. Therefore Choices A, B, C, and D are incorrect, and Choice E is correct.

12. **(D)** "...but a security guard, a fireman, and *me*." The preposition *but* is understood before *me*. Since *me* is the object of the preposition *but*, it has an objective form (*me*)—not a nominative form (*I*).

13. **(A)** "Having drunk...the lemonade..." The past participle of *drink* is *drunk*.

14. **(B)** "...to *whoever*...could present her..." The subject of the dependent clause must have a nominative case form (*whoever*)—not an objective case form (*whomever*).

15. **(C)** "...they had brought *not nearly* the number..." Do not use the expression *nowhere near* for *not nearly*.

16. **(E)** All underlined parts are correct.

17. **(A)** "*Because of* his not studying..." Do not begin a sentence with the words *due to*. *Due* is an adjective. As an adjective, it must have a noun to modify.

18. **(C)** "...to buy the *kind of* car..." Do not use the article *a* or *an* after *kind of, type of, sort of*, etc.

19. **(D)** "...compare their poems *with those of Robert Frost*." We have an improper ellipsis in the original sentence. The additional words (*those of*) are necessary to complete the meaning of the sentence.

20. **(A)** "I appreciate *your* offering..." Nouns and pronouns that precede gerunds are in the possessive case. We, therefore, say *your offering*—not *you offering*.

21. **(B)** "...the *slower* of the two..." Since we are here comparing two runners, we must use the comparative degree (*slower*)—not the superlative degree (*slowest*).

22. **(D)** "...is usually easier than passing the driving test." This sentence requires parallelism: "*Passing* the driving test" should parallel "*Passing* the written test..."

23. **(D)** "...each hoping that *he* would win..." A pronoun should be in the same number as the noun or pronoun to which it refers. In the sentence, *he* refers to *each*, which is a singular pronoun.

24. **(B)** "Her answer...was *altogether* incorrect..." *Altogether* means *entirely, wholly. All together* means *as a group*.

25. **(C)** "...they acted as if they never *had met* before..." We must use the past perfect tense (*had met*) to indicate an action taking place before another past action (*acted*).

26. **(A)** "The realtor felt *bad*..." After the copulative verb (*felt*), the word referring to the subject should be a predicate adjective (*bad*)—not an adverb (*badly*).

27. **(E)** All underlined parts are correct.

28. **(B)** The pronoun *he* has an indefinite antecedent. We cannot tell whether *he* refers to the Governor or the attorney. Accordingly, we must be specific by using either *the Governor* or *the attorney*.

29. **(E)** All underlined parts are correct.

30. **(D)** Choice A is incorrect because sentence 1 is needed to open the paragraph in order to establish the fact that safety devices have been proven to save lives. If this information does not precede every other idea in the paragraph, the logical reasons for the laws and for obeying them are not clear. Therefore, sentence 4 should not be placed before sentence 1. Choices B and C are incorrect in that sentence 4 is in an illogical position in the paragraph and should be moved rather than attached to sentence 3 (Choice B) or left in its present position (Choice C). Choice D is correct: The logical position for the idea about laws governing the use of motorcycle helmets is directly following the idea about laws governing the installation of seat belts. (The two ideas are so closely related that they might appropriately be joined in a complex sentence.) Additionally, in the present position of sentence 4, "these safety devices" seem to apply only to "seat belts" in sentence 2, whereas the clear intent of the paragraph as a whole is that "safety devices" refer to both seat belts and helmets. Choice E is incorrect because the present position of sentence 4 is not logical and creates the inaccurate reference to only one safety device.

31. **(B)** Choice A is incorrect, since omitting "mandating" creates the illogical sense that government interferes with individuals by using safety devices. Government might possibly be said to interfere with individuals by installing seat belts, but it cannot interfere with individuals by using seat belts, an idea that is awkward in any case since "government" does not constitute an entity capable of using a seat belt. Choice B is correct because "mandating" means "issuing an authoritative command or instruction," a sense that agrees with the idea of passing a law. Choice C is incorrect in that "prohibiting" or "forbidding" the use of safety devices results in a meaning that runs counter to

the whole sense of the paragraph. Choice D is incorrect in that nonsense would result from placing "mandating" before "individual." The government would then be said to interfere with the issuing of commands making individual comfort and freedom obligatory. Choice E is incorrect in that such a wordy substitute is never preferable to one correct word; moreover, the phrase is inaccurate in that the "directions" (or laws) do not express a preference ("in favor of") but an order.

32. (A) Choice A is correct: The insertion of "these riders are" is necessary to correct the existing situation in which the modifier "if thrown in an accident" incorrectly attaches itself to "their heads." Choice B is incorrect not only because the dangling modifier is not corrected but also because a cantaloupe, with its hard rind and juicy interior, is a better figure of speech for a human head than a flexible, partially transparent balloon filled with gas or air. Choice C is incorrect because replacing "their heads" with "they" would create a situation in which "if thrown in an accident" would modify a pronoun which might refer either to motorcyclists or to helmets. The rest of the sentence referring to cantaloupes would make a poor comparison if applied to the bodies of the motor cyclists and would convey no pertinent meaning if applied to helmets. Choice D is incorrect because "who refuse to wear helmets" is a restrictive clause defining particular motorcyclists and should not be made into a nonrestrictive clause by placing commas around it. Choice E is incorrect in that the dangling modifier would not be corrected and nothing would be gained in sense by creating the awkwardly repetitive sounds of "measure of pleasure."

33. (E) Choice A is incorrect: Turning sentence 7 into two sentences with the first ending after "small ways" would leave the second sentence as a dependent clause fragment. Choice B is incorrect because the subject and its verb should not be separated with a comma. Choice C is incorrect: Beginning the sentence with "while" would be a good choice if "because" were removed, but Choice C does not specify this omission, and "because" is not an appropriate conjunction. Choice D is incorrect: While the phrase "in more important ways" could be omitted (even though it adds balance to the sentence in paralleling "in small ways"), the major problem in the sentence would be passed over in making only this deletion. Choice E is correct: The word "because" should be changed to "but." The second idea in the sentence is not "a reason for" or "the result of" the first idea, relationships indicated by "because." The two ideas in the sentence are contrasting (that devices may "limit" but also "greatly increase" comfort and freedom) and should be connected with a conjunction showing this contrast.

34. (A) Statistical backup would qualify the author's position and show the dangers more specifically and in a more documented fashion. Choices B, C, D are weak, and Choice E is irrelevant.

35. (E) Since the paragraph supports wearing seat belts and helmets, the author must have a strong first introductory statement for why seat belts and helmets are warranted. Sentence 1 serves that purpose and should be kept as the first sentence.

Explanatory Answers for Practice Test 4 (continued)

Section 6: Math

As you read these solutions, you are advised to do two things if you answered the Math question incorrectly:

1. When a specific Math Strategy is referred to in the solution, study that strategy, which you will find in "19 Math Strategies" (beginning on page 69).
2. When the solution directs you to the "Complete Math Refresher" (beginning on page 167)—for example, Math Refresher 305—study the 305 Math principle to get a clear idea of the Math operation that was necessary for you to know in order to answer the question correctly.

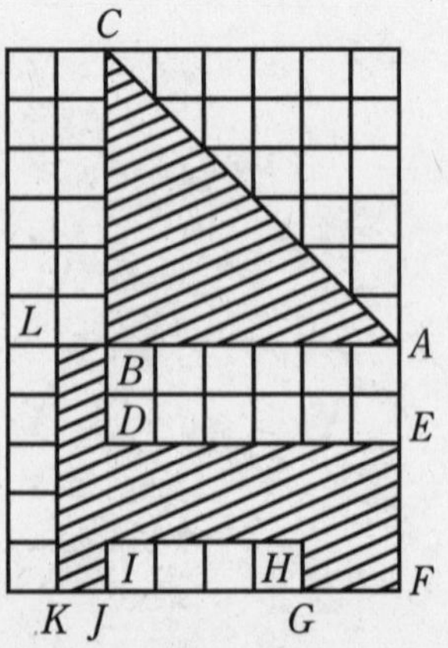

1. Choice C is correct.

Given: length of side of square = 1. [1]
Using [1], we get $AB = 6$, $BC = 6$ [2]

We know that

the Area of a triangle $= \frac{1}{2}$(base) (height) [3]

Substituting [2] into [3], we get

Area of shaded triangle $ABC = \frac{1}{2}(6)(6)$
$= 18$ [4]

We know that the area of a square $= (\text{side})^2$ [5]

Substituting [1] into [5], we have

Area of each square $= (1)^2 = 1$ [6]

Counting the number of squares in the other shaded figure (*BDEFGHIJKL*), we find 19. [7]

Multiplying [6] by [7], we have

Area of *BDEFGHIJKL* $= 19 \times 1 = 19$ [8]

(Use Strategy 3: The whole equals the sum of its parts.)

We know:

Total Shaded Area = Area of *ABC* + Area of *BDEFGHIJKL* [9]

Substituting [4] and [8] into [9], we get

$$\text{Total Shaded Area} = 18 + 19 = 37$$

(Math Refresher #303 and #307)

2. Choice C is correct. **(Use Strategy 17: Use the given information effectively.)**

Since the triangle is equilateral, all of its sides are equal. Thus,

$$5x - 2 = x$$
$$4x = 2$$
$$x = \frac{1}{2}$$
$$\text{Perimeter} = \text{Sum of 3 sides} = \frac{1}{2} + \frac{1}{2} + \frac{1}{2} = 1\frac{1}{2}$$

(Math Refresher #508 and #406)

3. Choice E is correct. **(Use Strategy 10: Know how to use units of time, distance, area.)**

The number of waves that pass through a certain point in t seconds

$$= \frac{w \text{ waves}}{s \text{ seconds}}(t \text{ seconds})$$
$$= \frac{wt}{s} \text{ waves}$$

(Math Refresher #121)

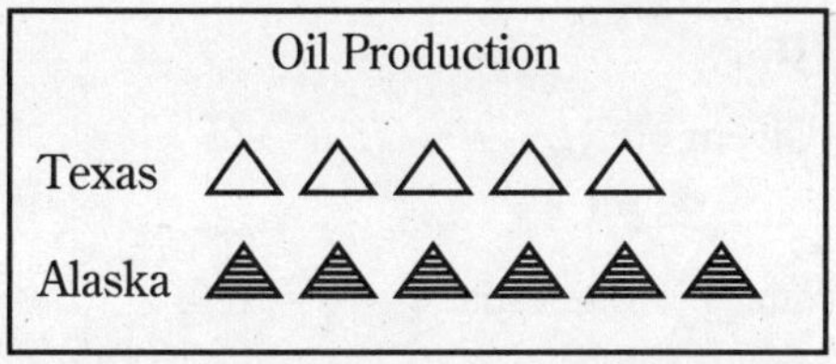

4. Choice C is correct. **(Use Strategy 2: Translate from words to algebra.)**

We are told ▲ = 3△

(Use Strategy 17: Use the given information effectively.)

$$\text{Texas total} = 5$$
$$\text{Alaska total} = 3(6) = 18$$

(Use Strategy 3: Know how to find unknown quantities from known quantities.)

$$\frac{\text{Alaska production}}{\text{total production}} = \frac{18}{5 + 18} = \frac{18}{23} = \text{required ratio}$$

(Math Refresher #200 and #431)

5. Choice C is correct. Probability is defined as

$$\frac{\text{number of favorable ways (coins)}}{\text{total number of ways (coins)}} = \frac{F}{N}$$

If the probability of selecting a nickel is $\frac{3}{8}$, then for nickels, $\frac{F}{N} = \frac{3}{8}$. But N [the total number of ways (or coins)] is 24.

So $\frac{F}{N} = \frac{3}{8} = \frac{F}{24}$; $F = 9$ (nickels)

The probability of selecting a dime is $\frac{1}{8}$, so for a dime, $\frac{F}{N} = \frac{1}{8} = \frac{F}{24}$; $F = 3$ (dimes)

Since there are 24 coins and there are 9 nickels and 3 dimes, $24 - 3 - 9 = 12$ quarters. **(Use Strategy 3: Subtract whole from parts.)**

(Math Refresher #614)

6. Choice C is correct. **(Use Strategy 17: Use the given information effectively.)**

Given:  [1]

In order for a given figure to have been formed from [1], it must have the same number of shaded and unshaded squares.

Choice I has 8 unshaded and 6 shaded squares. Thus, it could *not* be formed from [1].

Choice II has 5 unshaded and 6 shaded squares. Thus, it could *not* be formed from [1].

Looking at Choices A through E, we see that the correct choice must be Choice C: III only.

7. Choice D is correct. $f(x + 2) = (x + 2 - 1)^2 + (x + 2 - 2)^2 + (x + 2 - 3)^2 = (x + 1)^2 + x^2 + (x - 1)^2 = x^2 + 2x + 1 + x^2 + x^2 - 2x + 1 = 3x^2 + 2$.

(Math Refresher #616)

8. Choice D is correct. The procedure, as described, can be summarized in the following table:

Given Container	–	*Receiving Container*	=	*Excess to 50 cm³ Container*
25 cm³	–	16 cm³	=	9 cm³
16 cm³	–	9 cm³	=	7 cm³
9 cm³	–	4 cm³	=	5 cm³
4 cm³	–	1 cm³	=	3 cm³
		Total	=	24 cm³

(Use Strategy 2: Remember the definition of percent.)

Thus, $\frac{24 \text{ cm}^3}{50 \text{ cm}^3} \times 100 = 48\%$ of the 50 cm³ container is full.

(Use Strategy 3: The whole equals the sum of its parts.)

So, 100% − 48% = 52% of the 50 cm^3 container is empty.

(Math Refresher #107)

9. 10

Given: $ab = 40$ $\boxed{1}$

$\frac{a}{b} = \frac{5}{2}$ $\boxed{2}$

(Use Strategy 13: Find unknowns by multiplication.)

Multiplying $\boxed{2}$ by $2b$, we get

$$2b\left(\frac{a}{b}\right) = \left(\frac{5}{2}\right)2b$$

$$2a = 5b$$

$$\frac{2a}{5} = b \quad \boxed{3}$$

Substitute $\boxed{3}$ into $\boxed{1}$. We have

$$ab = 40$$

$$a\left(\frac{2a}{5}\right) = 40$$

$$\frac{2a^2}{5} = 40 \quad \boxed{4}$$

Multiplying $\boxed{4}$ by $\frac{5}{2}$, we get

$$\frac{5}{2}\left(\frac{2a^2}{5}\right) = (40)\frac{5}{2}$$

$$a^2 = 100$$

$$\sqrt{a^2} = \sqrt{100}$$

$$a = \pm 10$$

Since we were given that a is positive, we have $a = 10$.

(Math Refresher #406, #429, and #430)

10. 20

(Use Strategy 2: Translate from words to algebra.)

Given: Stephanie's earnings $= \$x$ $\boxed{1}$
Stephanie's time = 10 hours $\boxed{2}$
Evelyn's earnings $= \$y$ $\boxed{3}$
Evelyn's time = 20 hours $\boxed{4}$
$x + y = 60$ $\boxed{5}$

We know that hourly wage $= \dfrac{\text{total earnings}}{\text{total hours}}$ $\boxed{6}$

Substituting $\boxed{1}$ and $\boxed{2}$ into $\boxed{6}$, we get

Stephanie's hourly wage $= \dfrac{\$x}{10 \text{ hours}}$ $\boxed{7}$

Substituting $\boxed{3}$ and $\boxed{4}$ into $\boxed{6}$, we get

Evelyn's hourly wage $= \dfrac{\$y}{20 \text{ hours}}$ $\boxed{8}$

We are told that they have the same hourly wage. Using $\boxed{7}$ and $\boxed{8}$, we have

$$\frac{\cancel{\$}x}{10 \cancel{\text{ hours}}} = \frac{\cancel{\$}y}{20 \cancel{\text{ hours}}}$$

$$\frac{x}{10} = \frac{y}{20} \quad \boxed{9}$$

$$\overset{2}{\cancel{20}}\left(\frac{x}{\cancel{10}}\right) = \left(\frac{y}{\cancel{20}}\right)\cancel{20}$$

$$2x = y \quad \boxed{10}$$

Substituting $\boxed{10}$ into $\boxed{5}$, we get

$$x + 2x = 60$$

$$3x = 60$$

$$x = 20$$

(Math Refresher #200, #201, and #406)

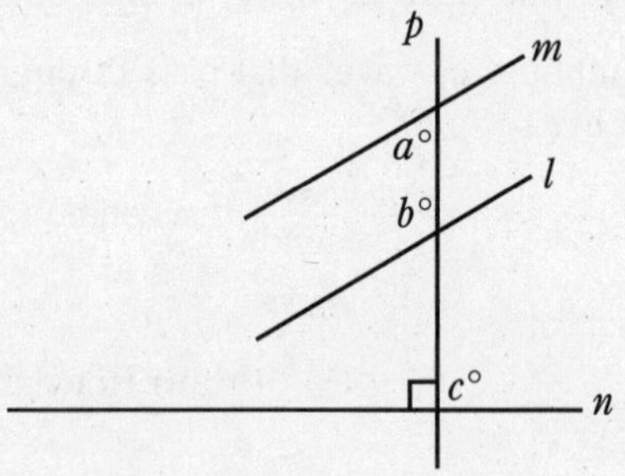

11. 270

Given: $m \parallel l$ $\boxed{1}$

$p \perp n$ $\boxed{2}$

From $\boxed{1}$ we get that $a + b = 180$, $\boxed{3}$
because when 2 lines are parallel, the interior angles on the same side of the transversal are supplementary.

From $\boxed{2}$ we get that $c = 90$ $\boxed{4}$
because perpendicular lines form right angles.

(Use Strategy 13: Find unknowns by addition.)

Add $\boxed{3}$ and $\boxed{4}$. We have

$$a + b + c = 180 + 90$$

$$= 270$$

(Math Refresher #504, #501, and #511)

12. 5

We know area of circle $= \pi(\text{radius})^2$ $\boxed{1}$

Given: radius of larger circle $= r + 3$ $\boxed{2}$
radius of small circle $= r$ $\boxed{3}$

Substitute $\boxed{2}$ into $\boxed{1}$. We have

Area of larger circle $= \pi(r + 3)^2$ $\boxed{4}$

(Use Strategy 4: Remember classic expressions.)

$$(r + 3)^2 = r^2 + 6r + 9 \qquad \boxed{5}$$

Substitute $\boxed{5}$ into $\boxed{4}$. We have

$$\text{Area of larger circle} = \pi(r^2 + 6r + 9) \qquad \boxed{6}$$

Substituting $\boxed{3}$ into $\boxed{1}$, we get

$$\text{Area of small circle} = \pi r^2 \qquad \boxed{7}$$

(Use Strategy 13: Find unknowns by subtraction.)

Subtract $\boxed{7}$ from $\boxed{6}$. We have

Difference of areas

$$= \pi(r^2 + 6r + 9) - \pi r^2 \qquad \boxed{8}$$

Given: Difference of areas $= 21\pi$ $\boxed{9}$

Substitute $\boxed{9}$ into $\boxed{8}$. We have

$$21\pi = \pi(r^2 + 6r + 9) - \pi r^2 \qquad \boxed{10}$$

(Use Strategy 13: Find unknowns by division.)

$$\frac{21\pi}{\pi} = \frac{\pi(r^2 + 6r + 9)}{\pi} - \frac{\pi r^2}{\pi}$$

$$21 = r^2 + 6r + 9 - r^2$$
$$21 = 6r + 9$$
$$12 = 6r$$
$$2 = r \qquad \boxed{11}$$

Substitute $\boxed{11}$ into $\boxed{2}$. We get

radius of larger circle $= 2 + 3$
$= 5$

(Math Refresher #409, #310, and #406)

13. 2

(Use Strategy 17: Use the given information effectively.)

The most favorable conditions for Team C would be the following:

	FIRST PLACE	SECOND PLACE	THIRD PLACE
	(8 points)	(4 points)	(2 points)
EVENT ③	TEAM C (4 + 8 = 12)	TEAM A (12 + 4 = 16)	TEAM B (12 + 2 = 14)
EVENT ④	TEAM C (12 + 8 = 20)	TEAM B (14 + 4 = 18)	TEAM A (16 + 2 = 18)

Thus, Team C has a total of 4 + 8 + 8 = 20 points after 2 more games. Team A has 12 + 4 + 2 = 18 points. Team B has 12 + 2 + 4 = 18 points. Thus, Team C will have to play at least 2 more games.

(Math Refresher #701)

14. 2

(Use Strategy 17: Use the given information effectively.)

Since $x = 15$, then

$$m\angle LMN = 90$$
$$m\angle JNK = 75$$
$$m\angle KNM = 15$$
$$m\angle JNM = 90$$

Thus, the figure, with dashed line extensions, follows:

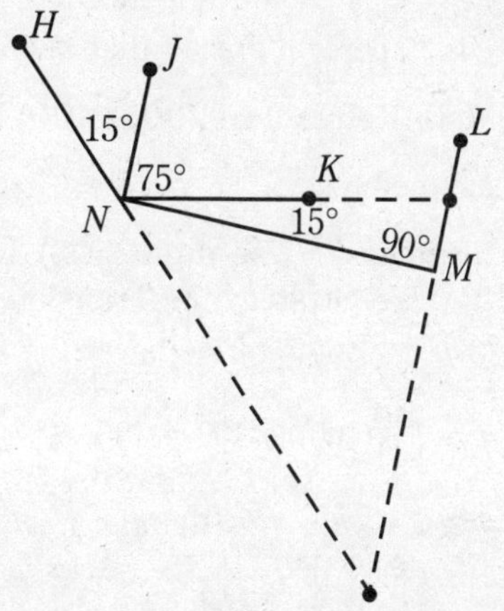

Clearly $\overleftrightarrow{JN} \parallel \overleftrightarrow{ML}$ and $\overleftrightarrow{JN}$ will not intersect $\overleftrightarrow{ML}$. $\overleftrightarrow{NK}$ and $\overleftrightarrow{NH}$ will each intersect $\overleftrightarrow{ML}$ exactly once. Thus, there will be exactly 2 more additional points of intersection.

(Math Refresher #504 and Logical Reasoning)

15. 20

(Use Strategy 2: Translate from words to algebra.)

We are told that

$$a = b + \frac{10}{100}b = \frac{11}{10}b \qquad \boxed{1}$$

$$ac = bd + \frac{32}{100}bd = \frac{33}{25}bd \qquad \boxed{2}$$

In equation $\boxed{2}$, reduce $\frac{32}{100}$ to $\frac{8}{25}$. Then combine: $ac = \frac{25}{25}bd + \frac{8}{25}bd = \frac{33}{25}bd$.)

(Use Strategy 13: Find unknowns by division.)

We divide $\boxed{2}$ by a

$$c = \frac{33}{25}\left(\frac{b}{a}\right)d \qquad \boxed{3}$$

(Use Strategy 13: Find unknowns by multiplication.)

Multiply $\boxed{1}$ by $\frac{1}{b}$, giving

$$\frac{a}{b} = \frac{11}{10}$$

or $$\frac{b}{a} = \frac{10}{11} \qquad \boxed{4}$$

Substituting $\boxed{4}$ into $\boxed{3}$, we get

$$c = \frac{33}{25}\left(\frac{10}{11}\right)d$$

$$c = \frac{\overset{3}{\cancel{33}}}{\underset{5}{\cancel{25}}} \times \frac{\overset{2}{\cancel{10}}}{\cancel{11}}d$$

$$c = \frac{6}{5}d$$

or $$c = d + \frac{1}{5}d$$

or $$c = d + \frac{20}{100}d$$

Thus, c is 20 percent greater than d.

(Math Refresher #200, #406, and #431)

Alternate method:

(Use Strategy 7: Use numerics.) Let $b = 100$, $d = 10$. **(Use Strategy 2: Translate words to algebra.)**

Then $a = \frac{10}{100}(100) + 100 = 110$

$$ac = \frac{32}{100}bd + bd = \frac{32}{100}(100)d + 100d$$

$$110c = 32d + 100d = 132d \qquad \boxed{1}$$

$$c = \frac{x}{100}d + d = \frac{xd + 100d}{100} = \frac{(x + 100)d}{100} \qquad \boxed{2}$$

Divide $\boxed{1}$ by 110:

$$c = \frac{132}{110}d \qquad \boxed{3}$$

Compare $\boxed{3}$ with $\boxed{2}$:

$$\frac{132}{110} = \frac{x + 100}{100}$$

$$\frac{13{,}200}{110} = x + 100$$

$$120 = x + 100$$

$$20 = x$$

(Math Refresher #200, #406, and #431)

16. $\frac{1}{48}$ or .020 or .021

(Use Strategy 2: Translate from words to algebra.)

Given:

$$1 \text{ gross} = 12 \text{ dozen}$$
$$1 \text{ dozen} = 12 \text{ (eggs)}$$

Thus,

$$1 \text{ gross of eggs} = (12 \cancel{\text{dozen}})\left(\frac{12 \text{ eggs}}{\cancel{\text{dozen}}}\right)$$
$$= 144 \text{ eggs}$$

$$3 \text{ eggs, expressed as a fraction of a gross} = \frac{3}{144}$$
$$= \frac{1}{48}$$

(Math Refresher #200 and #121)

17. 5

We are given that

Volume of 1 brick = 40 cubic inches $\boxed{1}$

Volume of the final pile of bricks = 8,000 cubic inches $\boxed{2}$

(Use Strategy 3: The whole equals the sum of its parts.) Logically, we know the number of layers in the final pile of bricks

$$= \frac{\text{volume of the final pile of bricks}}{\text{volume of each layer of bricks}} \qquad \boxed{3}$$

From the diagram in the question, we see that

1 layer of bricks = 40 bricks $\boxed{4}$

Thus, by using $\boxed{1}$ and $\boxed{4}$, we know that the volume of each layer of bricks

= volume of 1 brick
× number of bricks in 1 layer
= 40 cubic inches × 40
= 1,600 cubic inches $\boxed{5}$

Substituting $\boxed{2}$ and $\boxed{5}$ into $\boxed{3}$,
the number of layers in the final pile of bricks

$$= \frac{8{,}000 \text{ cubic inches}}{1{,}600 \text{ cubic inches}}$$

(Use Strategy 19: Factor and reduce.)

$$= \frac{8 \times 1{,}000}{16 \times 100}$$

$$= \frac{\cancel{8} \times 10 \times \cancel{100}}{\cancel{8} \times 2 \times \cancel{100}}$$

$$= \frac{10}{2} = 5$$

(Math Refresher #200 and #601)

18. 108

(Use Strategy 11: Use new definitions carefully.)

The first few 3-digit numbers are 100, 101, 102, 103, 104, etc.

Clearly, the smallest possible 3-digit number in which no digit is repeated is $x = 102$.

From the definition of y, y must be 210.

Thus, $y - x = 210 - 102 = 108$

Explanatory Answers for Practice Test 4 (continued)

Section 7: Critical Reading

As you read these Explanatory Answers, refer to "16 Verbal (Critical Reading) Strategies" (beginning on page 119) whenever a specific strategy is referred to in the answer. Of particular importance are the following Master Verbal Strategies:

Sentence Completion Master Strategy 1—page 120.
Sentence Completion Master Strategy 2—page 121.
Reading Comprehension Master Strategy 2—page 138.

Note: All Reading questions use Reading Comprehension Strategies 1, 2, and 3 (pages 135–140) as well as other strategies indicated.

1. Choice D is correct. See **Sentence Completion Strategy 4**. The words "in addition to" constitute a *support indicator*. We can then expect an additional favorable word to complete the sentence. That word is "dapper" (Choice D), meaning "neatly dressed." Choices A, B, C, and E are incorrect because they do not make good sense in the sentence.

2. Choice D is correct. See **Sentence Completion Strategy 2**. Examine the first word of each choice. We eliminate Choice C, motor, and Choice E, reciprocal, because motor curbs and reciprocal curbs do not make good sense in the opening clause of the sentence. Now we consider Choice A, profitable…drive, which does not make sense in the sentence; Choice B, flexible…produce, which also does *not* make sense in the sentence; and Choice D, import…ship, which *does* make sense in the sentence.

3. Choice A is correct. See **Sentence Completion Strategy 1 and 3**. Photographs of starving children must demonstrate something. If you tried to complete the sentence *before* looking at the five choices, you might have come up with words like "results" or "effects." Therefore, Choice A is correct. The other choices are incorrect because they do not make sense in the sentence.

4. Choice D is correct. See **Sentence Completion Strategy 2**. Examine the first word of each choice. We can eliminate Choice B, advantages, because it doesn't make sense in the sentence. The first words of the other four choices *do* make sense, so let us proceed to fill the two spaces for each of these remaining choices. Only Choice D, tensions… security, makes good sense in the sentence.

5. Choice B is correct. If you used **Sentence Completion Strategy 3**, you might have come up with any of the following words:

   refused   repudiated   shunned

   These words all mean about the same as the correct Choice (B) rejected.

6. Choice D is correct. See lines 5–7: "...individual attention...which creates...more efficient learning environment." Note that what is contained in Choice A (flexible standards), Choice B (parent and child), Choice C (travel time), and Choice E (conditions in learning environment) are all mentioned, but an effective learning condition is not based upon them.

7. Choice B is correct. Choice A is addressed in lines 10–12. Choice C is addressed in lines 14–16. Choice D is addressed in lines 13–14 (varied feedback). Choice E is addressed in lines 10–12 (diversity). For Choice B, multicultural ways are not mentioned in the passage, and even though there may be many students, those students may all be of one culture.

8. Choice E is correct. The criterion that appears in both passages is the learning experience. See lines 5–7 and lines 10–12.

9. Choice C is correct. What is missing in home-schooling is the interaction with other students, as stated in lines 10–14. Thus interaction with students on a regular basis would fill the void. Note in Choice B, the "occasional" work may not be adequate. In Choice D, spending one-half time at home and one-half time in school may make it difficult and awkward to coordinate or relate what is taught or developed at home and what is taught or developed at school.

10. Choice D is correct. See lines 16–17: "The cry for freedom...the birth of the New Man." Choice A is incorrect. Although the author may agree to what the choice says, he does not actually state or imply such. Choice B is incorrect because nowhere in the passage is Choice B stated or implied. Choice C is incorrect. See lines 25–27: "African-American literature rejects the despair and cynicism; it is a literature of realistic hope and life affirmation." Choice E is incorrect. See lines 36–37: "...life should not be a sedate waltz or foxtrot..."

11. Choice A is correct. See lines 32–36: "...life should be vivacious, exuberant, wholesomely uninhibited...and man should be loving." Choice B is incorrect because nowhere does the passage indicate that Choice B is true. Choice C is incorrect. Although lines 35–36 state that "life should be passionately lived and man should be loving," these lines do not mean that people should demonstrate their passions in public whenever the urge is there. Choice D is incorrect. Nowhere does the passage recommend Choice D. Choice E is incorrect. Although lines 6–10 state that "In African-American literature...there is...the rage of the oppressed," the passage does not state or imply that the descendants of those who have been oppressed should be enraged.

12. Choice D is correct. Let us consider each item. Item I is not true because the passage nowhere expresses the need for ***nonviolent*** opposition to racism. Item II is true. See lines 42–46: "Black literature in America [African-American literature] is...finding deep joy in his humanity." Item III is true. See lines 31–36: "African-American literature is a statement...and man should be loving." Accordingly, only Items II and III are true. Therefore, Choice D is correct, and Choices A, B, C, and E are incorrect.

13. Choice B is correct. See lines 23–27: "Like the spirituals...realistic hope and life-affirmation." Choice A is incorrect. See lines 6–15: "In African-American literature...the burden of protest." Although an indication of anger is present in the passage, it is not dominant. Moreover, nowhere in the passage is there evidence of vindictiveness. Choice C is incorrect because forgiveness and charity are not referred to in the passage. Choice D is incorrect. See lines 23–30: "Like the spirituals...goodness will prevail." Choice E is incorrect. Although the passage refers to *grief* in line 14 and also *cruelty* in line 38, grief and cruelty do not represent the tone of the passage.

14. Choice E is correct. See lines 20–23: "...for a human world."

15. Choice C is correct. It can be seen from the context of the sentence that the word "iniquity" must mean something bad (the word is preceded by "investigation" and is in contrast to "an investigation... potential godliness," which appears in the same sentence). See also **Reading Comprehension Strategy 5**.

16. Choice A is correct. See lines 71–72: "...as Dr. Skinner argues, that one can extrapolate from pigeons to people..." Choice B is incorrect because, though Skinner agrees that introspection may be of some use (lines 14–18), nowhere does the article indicate that he suggests wide use of the introspective method. Choice C is incorrect since Skinner, so the author says (lines 74–76), "has not satisfactorily rebutted the basic criticism that behaviorism 'is scientistic rather than scientific.'" Choice D is incorrect because lines 81–82 state that "Skinner predicts...impending disaster." Choice E is incorrect because there is nothing in the passage to indicate this statement. Incidentally, this point of view (Choice E) is held by Noam Chomsky of linguistics fame.

17. Choice E is correct. Choice A is incorrect; see lines 83–89: "Two key concepts…not so reassuring." Choice B is incorrect. See lines 11–14: "…an earlier stage of…influence of mentalism." Choice C is incorrect. See lines 60–64: "It is a veritable…to external stimuli." Choice D is incorrect since mentalism evolved before methodological and radical behaviorism. See lines 10–17: "What such people…its possible usefulness." Choice E is correct. The passage, from line 63 to the end, brings out weaknesses in Skinner's presentation.

18. Choice D is correct. Skinner, in lines 26–27, says "…few would contend that behavior is 'endlessly malleable.'" Also, see lines 35–42: "Contingencies of reinforcement…likely to occur." In effect, Skinner is saying that behavior cannot always, by plan or design, be altered or influenced; behavior must depend, to some extent, on the element of chance.

19. Choice D is correct. Skinner is known for his experiments with pigeons. Also, rats have been used frequently by behaviorists in experimentation. See lines 65–73. In addition, see lines 37–38: "In both natural…is crucial." The other choices are not relevant to Darwin or his work.

20. Choice A is correct. From the context in the rest of the sentence where "extrapolate" appears, Choice A fits best. Note that the word "extrapolate" is derived from the Latin "extra" (outside) and "polire" (to polish). See also **Reading Comprehension Strategy 5**.

21. Choice C is correct. Choice A is incorrect because Choice A is true according to lines 14–15. Choice B is incorrect because Choice B is true according to lines 65–70. Choice C is correct because Choice C is *not* true according to lines 68–72. Choice D is incorrect because Choice D is true according to lines 10–18. Choice E is incorrect because Choice E is true according to lines 57–61.

22. Choice B is correct. Choice A is incorrect; see lines 19–22: "…to those who object…Skinner expresses puzzlement." Choice B is correct because Skinner, a radical behaviorist, though believing that environmental influences are highly important in shaping human behavior, nevertheless states in lines 35–38: "Contingencies of reinforcement…[are] crucial." Operant conditioning is, according to behaviorists, a vital aspect of learning. Choice C is incorrect. Although Skinner accepts introspection (lines 16–18) as part of his system, nowhere does he place primary importance on introspection. Choice D is incorrect. Though Skinner may agree with this choice, nowhere in the passage does he state or imply this opinion. Choice E is incorrect. The word "malleable" means capable of being shaped or formed—from the Latin "malleare," meaning "to hammer." The quote in the stem of the question says, in effect, that few people would say that behavior can always be shaped.

23. Choice A is correct. I is correct; see lines 79–80. II is incorrect; don't be fooled by what is in lines 76–79. It does not refer to *scientistic* areas. III is incorrect; see lines 76–79.

24. Choice D is correct. Given the context of the sentence and the sentences preceding and succeeding it, "veritable" means "true." One may also note the "ver" in "veritable" and may associate that with the word "verify," which means "to prove to be true." This is the association strategy, which can be used to figure out clues to meanings of words. See also **Reading Comprehension Strategy 5**.

Explanatory Answers for Practice Test 4 (continued)

Section 8: Math

As you read these solutions, you are advised to do two things if you answered the Math question incorrectly:

1. When a specific Math Strategy is referred to in the solution, study that strategy, which you will find in "19 Math Strategies" (beginning on page 69).
2. When the solution directs you to the "Complete Math Refresher" (beginning on page 167)—for example, Math Refresher 305—study the 305 Math principle to get a clear idea of the Math operation that was necessary for you to know in order to answer the question correctly.

1. Choice D is correct.

Given:

$$5x = 3 \qquad \boxed{1}$$

(Use Strategy 12: Try not to make tedious calculations.)

Method 1: Add 3 to both sides of $\boxed{1}$

$$5x + 3 = 6 \qquad \boxed{2}$$

(Use Strategy 13: Find unknown expressions by multiplication.)

Square both sides of $\boxed{2}$

$$(5x + 3)^2 = 36 \qquad \boxed{3}$$

This method involves simpler arithmetic (no fractions) than the next method.

Method 2: This method is a bit slower. Solve $\boxed{1}$ for x to get

$$x = \frac{3}{5} \qquad \boxed{4}$$

Using $\boxed{4}$, calculate the unknown expression.

$$(5x + 3)^2 =$$
$$\left[5\left(\frac{3}{5}\right) + 3\right]^2 =$$
$$(3 + 3)^2 =$$
$$6^2 = 36$$

(Math Refresher #406 and #431)

2. Choice C is correct. **(Use Strategy 2: Translate from words to algebra.)**

$$\text{Let } 8n = \text{number of boys} \qquad \boxed{1}$$
$$7n = \text{number of girls} \qquad \boxed{2}$$

The ratio of $\frac{\text{boys}}{\text{girls}} = \frac{8n}{7n} = \frac{8}{7}$ and the given condition is satisfied.

(Use Strategy 3: The whole equals the sum of its parts.)

Total number of students = boys plus girls $\boxed{3}$

Substituting [1] and [2] into [3], we get

Total number of students = $8n + 7n = 15n$ [4]

[4] is a multiple of 15

Choices A, B, D, and E are multiples of 15:

(A) $15 = 15 \times 1$
(B) $45 = 15 \times 3$
(D) $60 = 15 \times 4$
(E) $90 = 15 \times 6$

Only Choice C, 50, is *not* a multiple of 15.

(Math Refresher #200 and #431)

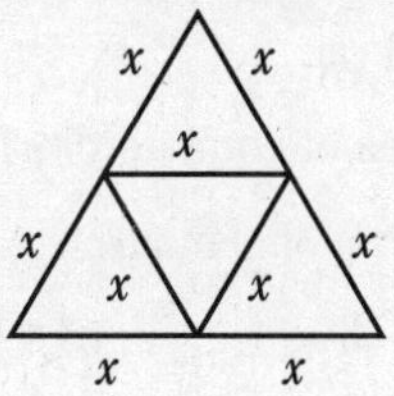

3. Choice A is correct. **(Use Strategy 2: Translate from words to algebra.)**

Let x = side of smaller triangles
Thus, $3x$ = perimeter of each smaller triangle
$6x$ = perimeter of largest triangle

We are told

$$3x = 1$$
$$x = \frac{1}{3} \quad \boxed{1}$$

(Use Strategy 13: Find unknowns by multiplication.)

Multiplying [1] by 6, we get

$6x = 2$ = perimeter of largest triangle

(Math Refresher #200 and #306)

4. Choice D is correct. **(Use Strategy 3: The whole equals the sum of its parts.)**

Amount left = Original amount − Amount spent
= \$15.25 − \$7.50
= \$ 7.75

5. Choice A is correct. **(Use Strategy 17: Use the given information effectively.)**

$$\text{Given: } \frac{4^3 + 4^3 + 4^3 + 4^3}{4^y} = 4$$
$$\frac{4(4^3)}{4^y} = 4$$
$$\frac{4^4}{4^y} = 4$$
$$4^{4-y} = 4^1 \quad \boxed{1}$$

In [1] each expression has base 4. Since the expressions are equal, the exponents must also be equal. Thus,

$$4 - y = 1$$
$$-y = -3$$
$$y = 3$$

(Math Refresher #429 and #406)

6. Choice C is correct. Cross multiply:

$$2(2x^2 + x - 5) = x^3 + 4x^2$$
$$4x^2 + 2x - 10 = x^3 + 4x^2$$

(Use Strategy 1: Cancel quantities to make the problem simpler.)

Cancel $4x^2$ from both sides:

$2x - 10 = x^3$ and so $x^3 - 2x = -10$.

(Math Refresher #406 and #120)

7. Choice D is correct. **(Use Strategy 2: Translate from words to algebra.)** Perhaps the best way to answer this type of question is to write a description of what occurs:

starting point	100	$t = 0$
after 8 yrs	200	$t = 8$
after 8×2 yrs	400	$t = 16$
after 8×3 yrs	800	$t = 24$

You can see that this is represented as population $= 100 \times 2^{\frac{t}{8}}$.

(Math Refresher #429)

8. Choice D is correct. **(Use Strategy 6: Know how to manipulate inequalities.)** $2x + 5 < 5$

Subtracting 5 from both sides, $2x < 0$.
Dividing both sides by 2, $x < 0$.
Since x must be a positive integer, that is, x is greater than 0, the solution set is the empty set or { }.

(Math Refresher #803 and #808)

9. Choice B is correct. $(a^b)^b = x^b = y$. $(a^b)^b = a^{b^2} = y$

(Math Refresher #429)

10. Choice A is correct. **(Use Strategy 17: Use the given information effectively.)** To find the coordinates of the intersection point, we must first solve the equations $y = x - 1$ and $2x + 5y = 9$. In the equation $2x + 5y = 9$, we substitute $y = x - 1$. We obtain

$$2x + 5(x - 1) = 9$$

Thus

$$2x + 5x - 5 = 9$$

and

$$7x = 14$$
$$x = 2$$

From the first equation, $y = x - 1$, so $y = 2 - 1 = 1$. Thus $x = 2$ and $y = 1$ so the coordinates of the point are (2,1).

(Math Refresher #417)

11. Choice B is correct. **(Use Strategy 13: Subtract equations)** Using $C = md + t$, if the business trip were increased by 5 days, $C' = m(d + 5) + t$. Subtracting equations, $C' - C = m(d + 5) + t - (md + t) = md + 5m + t - md - t = 5m$.

(Math Refresher #122)

12. Choice D is correct. **(Use Strategy 6: Know how to manipulate inequalities.)** Since $x - 3 \le 0$, $x \le 3$. Choice D represents x on the number line.

(Math Refresher #129 and #420)

13. Choice E is correct. **(Use Strategy 13: Find unknowns by multiplication and subtraction.)** If we multiply the first equation by 2, we get: $8x - 6y = 18$. Subtract this equation from the second equation in the question:

$$\begin{array}{r} 8x + ky = 19 \\ -[(8x - 6y) = 18] \\ \hline ky + 6y = 1 \end{array}$$

If $k = -6$, we would have: $-6y + 6y = 0 = 1$, which is not true. Thus if $k = -6$, there will be no solution to the equations.

(Math Refresher #407)

14. Choice D is correct.

Given: $r = 7a$ [1]

$5w = 7a$ [2]

From [2] we get $w = \frac{7a}{5}$ [3]

(Use Strategy 13: Find unknowns by subtracting.)

Subtract [3] from [1]. We get

$$r - w = 7a - \frac{7a}{5}$$

$$= \frac{35a}{5} - \frac{7a}{5}$$

$$r - w = \frac{28a}{5}$$

(Math Refresher #406)

15. Choice C is correct. **(Use Strategy 3: The whole equals the sum of its parts.)**

Total area = area of triangle + 3(area of semicircle) [1]

Given: Radius of each semicircle = 2 [2]

From [2] we know each diameter = 4

Thus, the triangle has three equal sides of length 4 and is equilateral. [3]

We know: Area of equilateral triangle $= \frac{S^2\sqrt{3}}{4}$ [4]

Area of semicircle $= \frac{\pi r^2}{2}$ [5]

Substituting [4] and [5] into [1], we get

$$\text{Total area} = \frac{S^2\sqrt{3}}{4} + 3\left(\frac{\pi r^2}{2}\right) \quad [6]$$

Substituting [2] and [3] into [6], we get

$$\text{Total area} = \frac{4^2\sqrt{3}}{4} + 3\left(\frac{\pi(2)^2}{2}\right)$$

$$= \frac{16\sqrt{3}}{4} + 3\left(\frac{4\pi}{2}\right)$$

$$\text{Total area} = 4\sqrt{3} + 6\pi$$

(Math Refresher #308, #310, and #311)

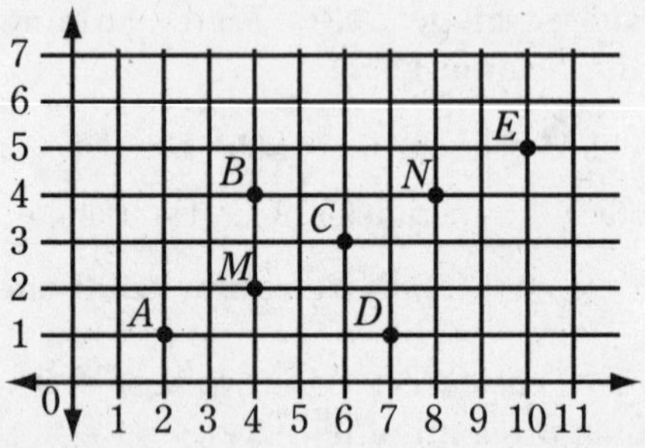

16. Choice E is correct. **(Use Strategy 8: When all choices must be tested, start with E and work backward.)**

In the diagram above, we have plotted each of the points given in the choices. From the diagram, it is clear that

$$MC = CN = NE$$

Thus, since $ME = MC + CN + NE$, then

$$3NE = ME$$

as required, so that point E is the answer.

(Math Refresher #410)

Explanatory Answers for Practice Test 4 (continued)

Section 9: Critical Reading

As you read these Explanatory Answers, refer to "16 Verbal (Critical Reading) Strategies" (beginning on page 119) whenever a specific strategy is referred to in the answer. Of particular importance are the following Master Verbal Strategies:

Sentence Completion Master Strategy 1—page 120.
Sentence Completion Master Strategy 2—page 121.
Reading Comprehension Master Strategy 2—page 138.

Note: All Reading questions use Reading Comprehension Strategies 1, 2, and 3 (pages 135–140) as well as other strategies indicated.

1. Choice E is correct. See **Sentence Completion Strategy 2**. Examine the first word of each choice. We eliminate Choice B, expedite (meaning "to speed up"), and Choice D, drench (which means "to wet through and through"), because the parked vehicles do not expedite or drench the flow of traffic. Now we consider Choices A, C, and E. The only word pair that makes good sense in the sentence is Choice E, impede…flout. The word "impede" means "to block up or obstruct," and the word "flout" means "scoff at or show contempt for."

2. Choice E is correct. See **Sentence Completion Strategy 2**. Examine the first word of each choice. We eliminate Choice D, recording, because the film rental business is not recording. Now we consider the four remaining word pairs. The only choice that makes sense in the sentence is Choice E, booming…leisure.

3. Choice E is correct. See **Sentence Completion Strategy 2**. Look at the first word of each choice. The first words in Choices B, C, and D do not sound right when inserted in the first blank of the sentence. Thus we can eliminate Choices B, C, and D. Now try both words in the remaining Choices, A and E. Choice E is the only one that works.

4. Choice E is correct. See **Sentence Completion Strategy 1**. Try each choice. The *apparent contradiction* of scarcity amidst plenty characterizes even a rich country in a time of inflation.

5. Choice C is correct. See **Sentence Completion Strategy 1**. The word "generate" (meaning "to produce") completes the sentence so that it makes good sense. The other choices don't do that.

6. Choice D is correct. See **Sentence Completion Strategy 1**. Try each choice. The sentence implies that he retained the belief until his death; hence he was *stubborn* or unchanging in his belief.

7. Choice C is correct. Throughout Passage 1, the author is bringing out the fact that violence is widely shown and well received on television. For example: Line 1: "Violence is alive and well on television." Lines 4–5: "…as a result of…the horror of violence." Lines 12–13: "Violence on TV…in recent years." Although Choices A, B, D, and E are discussed or implied in the passage, none of these choices summarizes the content of the passage as a whole. Therefore, these choices are incorrect.

8. Choice D is correct. See lines 29–33: "The simple gunfight…for hundreds to die." Accordingly, Choice A is incorrect. Choices B and C are incorrect because there is no violence shown on the screen in these choices. Choice E is incorrect because the violence of a double murder by a jealous husband hardly compares in intensity with the violence of a bomb exploding in a bus carrying a busload of innocent civilians.

9. Choice E is correct. See lines 29–33: "The simple gunfight of the past…for hundreds to die." Choice A is incorrect because, though the statement may be true, the passage nowhere indicates that TV programs generally are different today from what they were a generation ago. Choice B is incorrect. See lines 37–38: "Many people…the way of the world." Choice C is incorrect. See lines 12–14: "Violence on TV…and more action series," Choice D is incorrect. See lines 38–41: "It is high time… viewing televised violence." No mention is made in the passage that broadcasting stations are doing any warning or notifying about the dangers of showing violence on TV.

10. Choice C is correct. The cruelties of our prison system are referred to in lines 63–69: "…just as so much of our current violence is socially acceptable…classes of society." The horrors of our prisons were current at the time the author wrote this article, and they are current today. The violence spoken about in Choices A, B, and D were socially acceptable at the time they occurred in the past. The question asks for an illustration of *current* "socially acceptable" violence. Accordingly, Choices A, B, and D are incorrect. Choice E, though it refers to current violence, is *not* socially acceptable. See lines 70–74: "What we have now…familiar 'crime in the streets.'" Therefore, Choice E is incorrect.

11. Choice A is correct. The author's definition of violence is extremely broad—including not only acts of force but also the social infliction of harm as in "exploiting women and children in textile mills and sweatshops" (lines 58–59). Passage 2 refers to acts of violence other than those expressed in Choices B and C. Therefore, these choices are incorrect. One could easily cite illegal conduct on the part of the government or a citizen that is *not* of a violent nature. Therefore, Choice D is incorrect. The FBI could conceivably commit an act of violence. The author would not condone this. See lines 77–79: "But now, too, official violence… numerous sympathizers." Therefore, Choice E is incorrect.

12. Choice A is correct. The author of Passage 2 describes current violence as "acceptable neither to the authorities nor to the victims" [Item I]. Item II and Item III are not indicated anywhere in the passage. Therefore, only Choice A is correct.

13. Choice C is correct. It indicates the only form of violence that is *not* mentioned in Passage 2. The following line references are given to indicate that Choices A, B, D, and E represent forms of violence that *are* mentioned in the passage. Choice A—see lines 48–49: "…the lawlessness… during Reconstruction and after." Choice B—see lines 43–44: "…our almost…against the Indians." Choice D—see lines 44–45: "…and all the others… Mexicans in Texas." Choice E—see lines 46–47: "…the pervasive violence of slavery."

14. Choice D is correct. The author, throughout Passage 2, expresses opposition to any type of violence—whether one engages in violence or tolerates it. Therefore, Choice D is correct because the author would not approve of the violence practiced by football players. Accordingly, Choices A, B, C, and E are incorrect. Although Choice A involves violence, a person who tries to prevent a mugging is obviously opposed to the violence of the mugger.

15. Choice C is correct. In the context of the rest of the sentence in lines 2–3 and line 46, you can see that "pervasiveness" means "seeping through." Note that Choice A is incorrect because in lines 2–3, the word "variety" is used and would be redundant if repeated. This is also true for Choice B, "televised." See also **Reading Comprehension Strategy 5**.

16. Choice E is correct. See lines 17–18, 24, and 31.

17. Choice A is correct. The author's attitude in Passage 2 is that violence as shown historically is "a way of life." Thus if violence were curtailed on television, it would still exist elsewhere.

18. Choice D is correct. Only the author of Passage 1 proposes a direct resolution—lines 38–41. The statement in Choice A is *true*. See lines 70–89. The statement in Choice B is *true*. See lines 29–31 and 43–69. The statement in Choice C is *true*. The

author of Passage 1 primarily talks only about televised violence, whereas the author of Passage 2 refers to corporate violence, air pollution, prison violence, and the like. The statement in Choice E is *true.* See lines 38–41 and lines 42–69.

19. Choice C is correct. It can be seen from what precedes in Passage 2 that "polarization" must mean some very great opposing viewpoints. Don't be lured into Choice A, thinking that polarization has to do with electrical current; or Choice B, that polarization has to do with governments, since society was discussed; or Choice D, that polarization has to do with religion, because religious dissent was mentioned; or Choice E, that polarization has to do with climate, because we have a North and South Pole. See also **Reading Comprehension Strategy 5**.

Explanatory Answers for Practice Test 4 (continued)

Section 10: Writing

For further practice and information, please refer to Grammar and Usage Refresher starting on page 455.

1. **(C)** We are concerned here with the apostrophe use with a singular name ending in "s." We are also concerned with improper ellipsis. In Choice A, "James's" is correct but we must either say "to read than *the prose style* of James Joyce" or "to read than James Joyce's." In Choice B, "Jame's" is incorrect—his name is not "Jame." Choice C is correct. Choices D and E are incorrect for the same reason that Choice A is incorrect—improper ellipsis.

2. **(C)** Choice A is incorrect because in a "neither… nor" construction, the number of the verb is determined by the "nor" subject noun ("followers"). Since "followers" is plural, the verb must be plural ("know"). Choices B, D, and E are incorrect for the same reason. Moreover, Choice B is incorrect for another reason: the correlative form is "neither… nor"—not "neither…or." Choice C is correct.

3. **(A)** Choice A is correct. Choice B's passive verb ("was requested") interferes with the flow of the sentence. "It occurred" in Choice C is unnecessary. Choice D is too wordy for what has to be expressed. Choice E changes the meaning of the original sentence—the students did not "insist."

4. **(B)** Choice A is indirect. Choice B is correct. In Choice C, "as a prize" repeats unnecessarily the "Nobel Prize." Choice D is much too awkward. Choice E is incorrect—the scientists did not discover viruses.

5. **(D)** The important thing is not "promptness"; accordingly, Choice A is wrong. Choice B is incorrect because it is not the "loan" that must be returned. In Choice C, "You must understand" is unnecessary. Choice D is correct. Choice E changes the meaning of the original sentence.

6. **(E)** Choice A is incorrect. There has to be a parallel construction; "in addition to a fine scholastic record" has to relate to Bob, such as, "in addition to his having a fine scholastic record…" Choice E does relate to Bob, as it says "as well as a superior student." Choice B would be correct if it were preceded and followed by a dash in order to set the choice off from what goes before and after. Choice C is wrong because one does not "amass a scholastic record." Choice D is a complete sentence within a sentence, thus creating a run-on sentence situation. Choice E is correct.

7. **(E)** In Choice A, the use of the passive verb ("were trounced") reduces the effectiveness of expression. Choice B is indirect. Choice C is incorrect. The word "they" has an antecedent problem: Who won the World Series, the "odds" or the "Mets"? In Choice D, "which is hard to believe" is unnecessary. Choice E is correct.

8. **(E)** In Choice A, "are necessary" is not only not necessary, but the expression makes the sentence ungrammatical with the additional complete predicate ("are necessary"). There are too many "ands" in Choice B. Some grammarians call this an "Andy" sentence. In Choice C, "And other fruit...peaches" is an incomplete sentence—also called a sentence fragment. Choice D also suffers from sentence fragmentation: "Such as pineapples and peaches." Choice E is correct.

9. **(B)** In Choice A, it is unidiomatic to say "instruction to learn." Choice B is correct. Choice C is too wordy. Choice D is not as direct as Choice B. Choice E suffers from lack of parallelism.

10. **(B)** Choice A is incorrect because the words "not only...but also" should be placed immediately before the parallel terms, which are "of the Ways and Means Committee" and "of the Finance Committee." Choice B is correct. Choice C is too wordy. Choice D is incorrect because it does not place the words "not only...but also" directly before the parallel terms. Choice E is awkward.

11. **(D)** Choices A and B are incorrect because they both contain an unnecessary shift from active to passive voice, resulting in awkwardness. Choice C is too wordy. Choice D is correct. Choice E is a complete sentence, making the original a run-on sentence.

12. **(B)** Choice A is incorrect because "Buckley" and "him" are in apposition with "candidates," the subject of the sentence. Since the subject is nominative, the appositive must also be nominative; hence "he" should be used instead of "him." Choice B is correct. Choice C uses "him" incorrectly for "he." The use of the passive voice ("were made") makes Choice D unnecessarily indirect. Choice E omits "two candidates for the U.S. Senate" which is necessary to the meaning of the sentence.

13. **(E)** Choices A and B are incorrect because they are both misplaced as modifiers—it is not clear who is the student. Choice C is a complete sentence, making the original sentence a run-on sentence. Choice D is incorrect because "being that" is poor English. Choice E is correct.

14. **(C)** Choice A is not correct because the word "who" is incorrectly used; as the object of the preposition, the word "whom" should be used. In Choice B, the second "to" is redundant. Choice C is correct. Choice D uses the word "who" instead of "whom." Choice E does not include a reference to the book, which is in the original sentence.

What You Must Do Now to Raise Your SAT Score

1. a) Follow the directions on page 911 to determine your scaled score for the SAT Test you've just taken. These results will give you a good idea about how hard you'll need to study in order to achieve a certain score on the actual SAT.

   b) Using your Test correct answer count as a basis, indicate for yourself your areas of strength and weakness as revealed by the "Chart for Self-Appraisal" on page 916.

2. Eliminate your weaknesses in each of the SAT test areas (as revealed in the "Chart for Self-Appraisal") by taking the following Giant Steps toward SAT success:

Critical Reading Part

Giant Step 1

Take advantage of the Critical Reading Strategies that begin on page 119. Read again the Explanatory Answer for each of the Critical Reading questions that you got wrong. Refer to the Critical Reading Strategy that applies to each of your incorrect answers. Learn each of these Critical Reading Strategies thoroughly. These strategies are crucial if you want to raise your SAT Verbal score substantially.

Giant Step 2

You can improve your vocabulary by doing the following:

1) Study the SAT 3,400-Word List beginning on page 359.

2) Take the 100 SAT-type "tough word" Vocabulary Tests beginning on page 408.

3) Study the Gruber Prefix-Root-Suffix List beginning on page 348.

4) Learn the Hot Prefixes and Roots beginning on page 1049.

5) Read through A List of SAT Words Appearing More Than Once beginning on page 353.

6) Look through the Most Important Words and Their Opposites beginning on page 355.

7) Learn the 3 Vocabulary Strategies beginning on page 150.

8) Read as widely as possible—not only novels. Nonfiction is important too…and don't forget to read newspapers and magazines.

9) Listen to people who speak well. Tune in to worthwhile TV programs.

10) Use the dictionary frequently and extensively—at home, on the bus, at work, etc.

11) Play word games—for example, crossword puzzles, anagrams, and Scrabble. Another game is to compose your own Sentence Completion questions. Try them on your friends.

Math Part

Giant Step 3

Make good use of the 19 Math Strategies that begin on page 69. Read again the solutions for each Math question that you answered incorrectly. Refer to the Math Strategy that applies to each of your incorrect answers. Learn each of these Math Strategies thoroughly. We repeat that these strategies are crucial if you want to raise your SAT Math score substantially.

Giant Step 4

You may want to take the **101 Most Important Math Questions You Need to Know How to Solve** test beginning on page 31 and follow the directions after the test for a basic Math skills diagnosis.

For each Math question that you got wrong in the Test, note the reference to the Complete Math Refresher section beginning on page 167. This reference will explain clearly the mathematical principle involved in the solution of the question you answered incorrectly. Learn that particular mathematical principle thoroughly.

For Both the Math and Critical Reading Parts

Giant Step 5

You may want to take the **Strategy Diagnostic Test** beginning on page 1 to assess whether you're using the best strategies for the questions.

For the Writing Part

Giant Step 6

Take a look at Part 9, the SAT Writing Test, which describes the various item types in the Writing Section and sample questions with answers and explanations. Also make use of the Grammar Refresher—Part 8.

3. After you have done some of the tasks you have been advised to do in the suggestions, proceed to Practice Test 5, beginning on page 956.

   After taking Practice Test 5, concentrate on the weaknesses that still remain.

4. If you do the job *right* and follow the steps listed earlier, you are likely to raise your SAT score on each of the Verbal, Math, and Writing parts of the test substantially.

> I am the master of my fate:
> I am the captain of my soul.
>
> —From the poem "Invictus"
> by William Ernest Henley

Answer Sheet for Practice Test 5

SECTION 1

Begin your essay on this page. If you need more space, continue on the next page. Do not write outside of the essay box.

Continue on the next page if necessary.

Continuation of ESSAY Section 1 from previous page. Write below only if you need more space.

Start with number 1 for each new section. If a section has fewer questions than answer spaces, leave the extra answer spaces blank. Be sure to erase any errors or stray marks completely.

SECTION 2

1 A B C D E	11 A B C D E	21 A B C D E	31 A B C D E
2 A B C D E	12 A B C D E	22 A B C D E	32 A B C D E
3 A B C D E	13 A B C D E	23 A B C D E	33 A B C D E
4 A B C D E	14 A B C D E	24 A B C D E	34 A B C D E
5 A B C D E	15 A B C D E	25 A B C D E	35 A B C D E
6 A B C D E	16 A B C D E	26 A B C D E	36 A B C D E
7 A B C D E	17 A B C D E	27 A B C D E	37 A B C D E
8 A B C D E	18 A B C D E	28 A B C D E	38 A B C D E
9 A B C D E	19 A B C D E	29 A B C D E	39 A B C D E
10 A B C D E	20 A B C D E	30 A B C D E	40 A B C D E

SECTION 3

1 A B C D E	11 A B C D E	21 A B C D E	31 A B C D E
2 A B C D E	12 A B C D E	22 A B C D E	32 A B C D E
3 A B C D E	13 A B C D E	23 A B C D E	33 A B C D E
4 A B C D E	14 A B C D E	24 A B C D E	34 A B C D E
5 A B C D E	15 A B C D E	25 A B C D E	35 A B C D E
6 A B C D E	16 A B C D E	26 A B C D E	36 A B C D E
7 A B C D E	17 A B C D E	27 A B C D E	37 A B C D E
8 A B C D E	18 A B C D E	28 A B C D E	38 A B C D E
9 A B C D E	19 A B C D E	29 A B C D E	39 A B C D E
10 A B C D E	20 A B C D E	30 A B C D E	40 A B C D E

CAUTION Use the answer spaces in the grids below for Section 2 or Section 3 only if you are told to do so in your test book.

Student-Produced Responses ONLY ANSWERS ENTERED IN THE CIRCLES IN EACH GRID WILL BE SCORED. YOU WILL NOT RECEIVE CREDIT FOR ANYTHING WRITTEN IN THE BOXES ABOVE THE CIRCLES.

9	10	11	12	13
/ /	/ /	/ /	/ /	/ /
. . . .	. . . .	. . . .	. . . .	. . . .
0 0 0	0 0 0	0 0 0	0 0 0	0 0 0
1 1 1 1	1 1 1 1	1 1 1 1	1 1 1 1	1 1 1 1
2 2 2 2	2 2 2 2	2 2 2 2	2 2 2 2	2 2 2 2
3 3 3 3	3 3 3 3	3 3 3 3	3 3 3 3	3 3 3 3
4 4 4 4	4 4 4 4	4 4 4 4	4 4 4 4	4 4 4 4
5 5 5 5	5 5 5 5	5 5 5 5	5 5 5 5	5 5 5 5
6 6 6 6	6 6 6 6	6 6 6 6	6 6 6 6	6 6 6 6
7 7 7 7	7 7 7 7	7 7 7 7	7 7 7 7	7 7 7 7
8 8 8 8	8 8 8 8	8 8 8 8	8 8 8 8	8 8 8 8
9 9 9 9	9 9 9 9	9 9 9 9	9 9 9 9	9 9 9 9

14	15	16	17	18
/ /	/ /	/ /	/ /	/ /
. . . .	. . . .	. . . .	. . . .	. . . .
0 0 0	0 0 0	0 0 0	0 0 0	0 0 0
1 1 1 1	1 1 1 1	1 1 1 1	1 1 1 1	1 1 1 1
2 2 2 2	2 2 2 2	2 2 2 2	2 2 2 2	2 2 2 2
3 3 3 3	3 3 3 3	3 3 3 3	3 3 3 3	3 3 3 3
4 4 4 4	4 4 4 4	4 4 4 4	4 4 4 4	4 4 4 4
5 5 5 5	5 5 5 5	5 5 5 5	5 5 5 5	5 5 5 5
6 6 6 6	6 6 6 6	6 6 6 6	6 6 6 6	6 6 6 6
7 7 7 7	7 7 7 7	7 7 7 7	7 7 7 7	7 7 7 7
8 8 8 8	8 8 8 8	8 8 8 8	8 8 8 8	8 8 8 8
9 9 9 9	9 9 9 9	9 9 9 9	9 9 9 9	9 9 9 9

Start with number 1 for each new section. If a section has fewer questions than answer spaces, leave the extra answer spaces blank. Be sure to erase any errors or stray marks completely.

SECTION 4

1 A B C D E	11 A B C D E	21 A B C D E	31 A B C D E
2 A B C D E	12 A B C D E	22 A B C D E	32 A B C D E
3 A B C D E	13 A B C D E	23 A B C D E	33 A B C D E
4 A B C D E	14 A B C D E	24 A B C D E	34 A B C D E
5 A B C D E	15 A B C D E	25 A B C D E	35 A B C D E
6 A B C D E	16 A B C D E	26 A B C D E	36 A B C D E
7 A B C D E	17 A B C D E	27 A B C D E	37 A B C D E
8 A B C D E	18 A B C D E	28 A B C D E	38 A B C D E
9 A B C D E	19 A B C D E	29 A B C D E	39 A B C D E
10 A B C D E	20 A B C D E	30 A B C D E	40 A B C D E

SECTION 5

1 A B C D E	11 A B C D E	21 A B C D E	31 A B C D E
2 A B C D E	12 A B C D E	22 A B C D E	32 A B C D E
3 A B C D E	13 A B C D E	23 A B C D E	33 A B C D E
4 A B C D E	14 A B C D E	24 A B C D E	34 A B C D E
5 A B C D E	15 A B C D E	25 A B C D E	35 A B C D E
6 A B C D E	16 A B C D E	26 A B C D E	36 A B C D E
7 A B C D E	17 A B C D E	27 A B C D E	37 A B C D E
8 A B C D E	18 A B C D E	28 A B C D E	38 A B C D E
9 A B C D E	19 A B C D E	29 A B C D E	39 A B C D E
10 A B C D E	20 A B C D E	30 A B C D E	40 A B C D E

CAUTION Use the answer spaces in the grids below for Section 4 or Section 5 only if you are told to do so in your test book.

Student-Produced Responses ONLY ANSWERS ENTERED IN THE CIRCLES IN EACH GRID WILL BE SCORED. YOU WILL NOT RECEIVE CREDIT FOR ANYTHING WRITTEN IN THE BOXES ABOVE THE CIRCLES.

Grids 9, 10, 11, 12, 13, 14, 15, 16, 17, 18 — each grid:

	/	/	
.	.	.	.
	0	0	0
1	1	1	1
2	2	2	2
3	3	3	3
4	4	4	4
5	5	5	5
6	6	6	6
7	7	7	7
8	8	8	8
9	9	9	9

Start with numbe for each new section. If a section has fewer questions than answer spaces, leave the extra answer spa s blank. Be sure to erase any errors or stray marks completely.

SECTION 6

A B C D E	11 A B C D E	21 A B C D E	31 A B C D E
A B C D E	12 A B C D E	22 A B C D E	32 A B C D E
A B C D E	13 A B C D E	23 A B C D E	33 A B C D E
A B C D E	14 A B C D E	24 A B C D E	34 A B C D E
A B C D E	15 A B C D E	25 A B C D E	35 A B C D E
6 A B C D E	16 A B C D E	26 A B C D E	36 A B C D E
7 A B C D E	17 A B C D E	27 A B C D E	37 A B C D E
8 A B C D E	18 A B C D E	28 A B C D E	38 A B C D E
9 A B C D E	19 A B C D E	29 A B C D E	39 A B C D E
10 A B C D E	20 A B C D E	30 A B C D E	40 A B C D E

SECTI 7

1 A B C D E	11 A B C D E	21 A B C D E	31 A B C D E
2 A B C D E	12 A B C D E	22 A B C D E	32 A B C D E
3 A B C D E	13 A B C D E	23 A B C D E	33 A B C D E
4 A B C D E	14 A B C D E	24 A B C D E	34 A B C D E
5 A B C D E	15 A B C D E	25 A B C D E	35 A B C D E
6 A B C D E	16 A B C D E	26 A B C D E	36 A B C D E
7 A B C D E	17 A B C D E	27 A B C D E	37 A B C D E
8 A B C D E	18 A B C D E	28 A B C D E	38 A B C D E
9 A B C D E	19 A B C D E	29 A B C D E	39 A B C D E
10 A B C D E	20 A B C D E	30 A B C D E	40 A B C D E

CAUTION Use the answer spaces in the grids below for Section 6 or Section 7 only if you are told to do so in your test book.

Student-Produced Responses ONLY ANSWERS ENTERED IN THE CIRCLES IN EACH GRID WILL BE SCORED. YOU WILL NOT RECEIVE CREDIT FOR ANYTHING WRITTEN IN THE BOXES ABOVE THE CIRCLES.

Grids 9, 10, 11, 12, 13, 14, 15, 16, 17, 18 — each:

	/	/	
.	.	.	.
	0	0	0
1	1	1	1
2	2	2	2
3	3	3	3
4	4	4	4
5	5	5	5
6	6	6	6
7	7	7	7
8	8	8	8
9	9	9	9

Start with number 1 for each new section. If a section has fewer questions than answer spaces, leave the extra answer spaces blank. Be sure to erase any errors or stray marks completely.

SECTION 8

1 Ⓐ Ⓑ Ⓒ Ⓓ Ⓔ	11 Ⓐ Ⓑ Ⓒ Ⓓ Ⓔ	21 Ⓐ Ⓑ Ⓒ Ⓓ Ⓔ	31 Ⓐ Ⓑ Ⓒ Ⓓ Ⓔ
2 Ⓐ Ⓑ Ⓒ Ⓓ Ⓔ	12 Ⓐ Ⓑ Ⓒ Ⓓ Ⓔ	22 Ⓐ Ⓑ Ⓒ Ⓓ Ⓔ	32 Ⓐ Ⓑ Ⓒ Ⓓ Ⓔ
3 Ⓐ Ⓑ Ⓒ Ⓓ Ⓔ	13 Ⓐ Ⓑ Ⓒ Ⓓ Ⓔ	23 Ⓐ Ⓑ Ⓒ Ⓓ Ⓔ	33 Ⓐ Ⓑ Ⓒ Ⓓ Ⓔ
4 Ⓐ Ⓑ Ⓒ Ⓓ Ⓔ	14 Ⓐ Ⓑ Ⓒ Ⓓ Ⓔ	24 Ⓐ Ⓑ Ⓒ Ⓓ Ⓔ	34 Ⓐ Ⓑ Ⓒ Ⓓ Ⓔ
5 Ⓐ Ⓑ Ⓒ Ⓓ Ⓔ	15 Ⓐ Ⓑ Ⓒ Ⓓ Ⓔ	25 Ⓐ Ⓑ Ⓒ Ⓓ Ⓔ	35 Ⓐ Ⓑ Ⓒ Ⓓ Ⓔ
6 Ⓐ Ⓑ Ⓒ Ⓓ Ⓔ	16 Ⓐ Ⓑ Ⓒ Ⓓ Ⓔ	26 Ⓐ Ⓑ Ⓒ Ⓓ Ⓔ	36 Ⓐ Ⓑ Ⓒ Ⓓ Ⓔ
7 Ⓐ Ⓑ Ⓒ Ⓓ Ⓔ	17 Ⓐ Ⓑ Ⓒ Ⓓ Ⓔ	27 Ⓐ Ⓑ Ⓒ Ⓓ Ⓔ	37 Ⓐ Ⓑ Ⓒ Ⓓ Ⓔ
8 Ⓐ Ⓑ Ⓒ Ⓓ Ⓔ	18 Ⓐ Ⓑ Ⓒ Ⓓ Ⓔ	28 Ⓐ Ⓑ Ⓒ Ⓓ Ⓔ	38 Ⓐ Ⓑ Ⓒ Ⓓ Ⓔ
9 Ⓐ Ⓑ Ⓒ Ⓓ Ⓔ	19 Ⓐ Ⓑ Ⓒ Ⓓ Ⓔ	29 Ⓐ Ⓑ Ⓒ Ⓓ Ⓔ	39 Ⓐ Ⓑ Ⓒ Ⓓ Ⓔ
10 Ⓐ Ⓑ Ⓒ Ⓓ Ⓔ	20 Ⓐ Ⓑ Ⓒ Ⓓ Ⓔ	30 Ⓐ Ⓑ Ⓒ Ⓓ Ⓔ	40 Ⓐ Ⓑ Ⓒ Ⓓ Ⓔ

SECTION 9

1 Ⓐ Ⓑ Ⓒ Ⓓ Ⓔ	11 Ⓐ Ⓑ Ⓒ Ⓓ Ⓔ	21 Ⓐ Ⓑ Ⓒ Ⓓ Ⓔ	31 Ⓐ Ⓑ Ⓒ Ⓓ Ⓔ
2 Ⓐ Ⓑ Ⓒ Ⓓ Ⓔ	12 Ⓐ Ⓑ Ⓒ Ⓓ Ⓔ	22 Ⓐ Ⓑ Ⓒ Ⓓ Ⓔ	32 Ⓐ Ⓑ Ⓒ Ⓓ Ⓔ
3 Ⓐ Ⓑ Ⓒ Ⓓ Ⓔ	13 Ⓐ Ⓑ Ⓒ Ⓓ Ⓔ	23 Ⓐ Ⓑ Ⓒ Ⓓ Ⓔ	33 Ⓐ Ⓑ Ⓒ Ⓓ Ⓔ
4 Ⓐ Ⓑ Ⓒ Ⓓ Ⓔ	14 Ⓐ Ⓑ Ⓒ Ⓓ Ⓔ	24 Ⓐ Ⓑ Ⓒ Ⓓ Ⓔ	34 Ⓐ Ⓑ Ⓒ Ⓓ Ⓔ
5 Ⓐ Ⓑ Ⓒ Ⓓ Ⓔ	15 Ⓐ Ⓑ Ⓒ Ⓓ Ⓔ	25 Ⓐ Ⓑ Ⓒ Ⓓ Ⓔ	35 Ⓐ Ⓑ Ⓒ Ⓓ Ⓔ
6 Ⓐ Ⓑ Ⓒ Ⓓ Ⓔ	16 Ⓐ Ⓑ Ⓒ Ⓓ Ⓔ	26 Ⓐ Ⓑ Ⓒ Ⓓ Ⓔ	36 Ⓐ Ⓑ Ⓒ Ⓓ Ⓔ
7 Ⓐ Ⓑ Ⓒ Ⓓ Ⓔ	17 Ⓐ Ⓑ Ⓒ Ⓓ Ⓔ	27 Ⓐ Ⓑ Ⓒ Ⓓ Ⓔ	37 Ⓐ Ⓑ Ⓒ Ⓓ Ⓔ
8 Ⓐ Ⓑ Ⓒ Ⓓ Ⓔ	18 Ⓐ Ⓑ Ⓒ Ⓓ Ⓔ	28 Ⓐ Ⓑ Ⓒ Ⓓ Ⓔ	38 Ⓐ Ⓑ Ⓒ Ⓓ Ⓔ
9 Ⓐ Ⓑ Ⓒ Ⓓ Ⓔ	19 Ⓐ Ⓑ Ⓒ Ⓓ Ⓔ	29 Ⓐ Ⓑ Ⓒ Ⓓ Ⓔ	39 Ⓐ Ⓑ Ⓒ Ⓓ Ⓔ
10 Ⓐ Ⓑ Ⓒ Ⓓ Ⓔ	20 Ⓐ Ⓑ Ⓒ Ⓓ Ⓔ	30 Ⓐ Ⓑ Ⓒ Ⓓ Ⓔ	40 Ⓐ Ⓑ Ⓒ Ⓓ Ⓔ

SECTION 10

1 Ⓐ Ⓑ Ⓒ Ⓓ Ⓔ	11 Ⓐ Ⓑ Ⓒ Ⓓ Ⓔ	21 Ⓐ Ⓑ Ⓒ Ⓓ Ⓔ	31 Ⓐ Ⓑ Ⓒ Ⓓ Ⓔ
2 Ⓐ Ⓑ Ⓒ Ⓓ Ⓔ	12 Ⓐ Ⓑ Ⓒ Ⓓ Ⓔ	22 Ⓐ Ⓑ Ⓒ Ⓓ Ⓔ	32 Ⓐ Ⓑ Ⓒ Ⓓ Ⓔ
3 Ⓐ Ⓑ Ⓒ Ⓓ Ⓔ	13 Ⓐ Ⓑ Ⓒ Ⓓ Ⓔ	23 Ⓐ Ⓑ Ⓒ Ⓓ Ⓔ	33 Ⓐ Ⓑ Ⓒ Ⓓ Ⓔ
4 Ⓐ Ⓑ Ⓒ Ⓓ Ⓔ	14 Ⓐ Ⓑ Ⓒ Ⓓ Ⓔ	24 Ⓐ Ⓑ Ⓒ Ⓓ Ⓔ	34 Ⓐ Ⓑ Ⓒ Ⓓ Ⓔ
5 Ⓐ Ⓑ Ⓒ Ⓓ Ⓔ	15 Ⓐ Ⓑ Ⓒ Ⓓ Ⓔ	25 Ⓐ Ⓑ Ⓒ Ⓓ Ⓔ	35 Ⓐ Ⓑ Ⓒ Ⓓ Ⓔ
6 Ⓐ Ⓑ Ⓒ Ⓓ Ⓔ	16 Ⓐ Ⓑ Ⓒ Ⓓ Ⓔ	26 Ⓐ Ⓑ Ⓒ Ⓓ Ⓔ	36 Ⓐ Ⓑ Ⓒ Ⓓ Ⓔ
7 Ⓐ Ⓑ Ⓒ Ⓓ Ⓔ	17 Ⓐ Ⓑ Ⓒ Ⓓ Ⓔ	27 Ⓐ Ⓑ Ⓒ Ⓓ Ⓔ	37 Ⓐ Ⓑ Ⓒ Ⓓ Ⓔ
8 Ⓐ Ⓑ Ⓒ Ⓓ Ⓔ	18 Ⓐ Ⓑ Ⓒ Ⓓ Ⓔ	28 Ⓐ Ⓑ Ⓒ Ⓓ Ⓔ	38 Ⓐ Ⓑ Ⓒ Ⓓ Ⓔ
9 Ⓐ Ⓑ Ⓒ Ⓓ Ⓔ	19 Ⓐ Ⓑ Ⓒ Ⓓ Ⓔ	29 Ⓐ Ⓑ Ⓒ Ⓓ Ⓔ	39 Ⓐ Ⓑ Ⓒ Ⓓ Ⓔ
10 Ⓐ Ⓑ Ⓒ Ⓓ Ⓔ	20 Ⓐ Ⓑ Ⓒ Ⓓ Ⓔ	30 Ⓐ Ⓑ Ⓒ Ⓓ Ⓔ	40 Ⓐ Ⓑ Ⓒ Ⓓ Ⓔ

SAT PRACTICE TEST 5

SECTION 1

Time: 25 Minutes—Turn to page 950 of your answer sheet to write your ESSAY.

The purpose of the essay is to have you show how well you can express and develop your ideas. You should develop your point of view, logically and clearly present your ideas, and use language accurately.

You should write your essay on the lines provided on your answer sheet. You should not write on any other paper. You will have enough space if you write on every line and if you keep your handwriting to a reasonable size. Make sure that your handwriting is legible to other readers.

You will have 25 minutes to write an essay on the assignment below. *Do not write on any other topic. If you do so, you will receive a score of 0.*

Think carefully about the issue presented in the following quotations and the assignment below.

> One of the main purposes of education is to get students excited about the "process" behind problem solving instead of rushing into an answer and just concentrating on the final result. Often students can extract something from a problem that leads to the answer. Students can relax and think more clearly when they concentrate on the game or the wonderful process, if you will, of thinking.
>
> —Adapted from G. Gruber, "A Superlative Guide to the Hows and Wise," *Omni* Magazine

Assignment: Do you agree with the above quote? In many cases, is the problem solver concerned just about getting an answer, and not about concentrating on the "process" to get the answer? Do you agree that by not having faith in the process, he or she often does not arrive at the solution? In answering these questions, describe in your own experience, why you agree or disagree and what rewards are lost or gained when you just concentrate on an answer without being aware of or interested in the process in arriving at the answer.

DO NOT WRITE YOUR ESSAY IN YOUR TEST BOOK. You will receive credit only for what you write on your answer sheet.

BEGIN WRITING YOUR ESSAY ON PAGE 950 OF THE ANSWER SHEET.

If you finish before time is called, you may check your work on this section only.
Do not turn to any other section in the test.

SECTION 2

Time: 25 Minutes—Turn to Section 2 (page 952) of your answer sheet to answer the questions in this section.
20 Questions

Directions: For this section, solve each problem and decide which is the best of the choices given. Fill in the corresponding circle on the answer sheet. You may use any available space for scratchwork.

Notes:

1. The use of a calculator is permitted.
2. All numbers used are real numbers.
3. Figures that accompany problems in this test are intended to provide information useful in solving the problems. They are drawn as accurately as possible EXCEPT when it is stated in a specific problem that the figure is not drawn to scale. All figures lie in a plane unless otherwise indicated.
4. Unless otherwise specified, the domain of any function *f* is assumed to be the set of all real numbers *x* for which *f*(*x*) is a real number.

REFERENCE INFORMATION

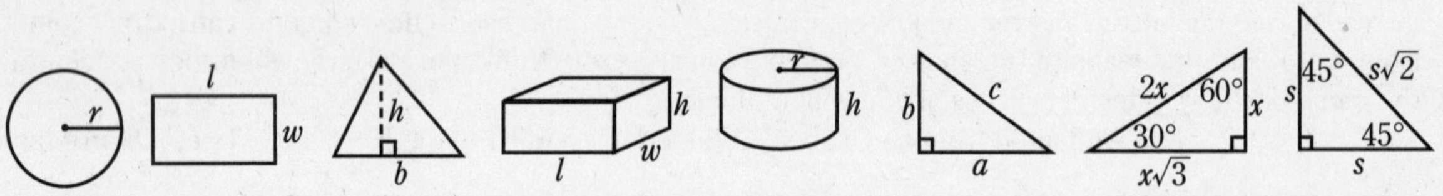

$A = \pi r^2$ $C = 2\pi r$ $A = lw$ $A = \frac{1}{2}bh$ $V = lwh$ $V = \pi r^2 h$ $c^2 = a^2 + b^2$ *Special Right Triangles*

The number of degrees of arc in a circle is 360.
The sum of the measures in degrees of the angles of a triangle is 180.

$$\begin{array}{r} 59\Delta \\ -293 \\ \hline \square 97 \end{array}$$

1. In the subtraction problem above, what digit is represented by the □?

(A) 0
(B) 1
(C) 2
(D) 3
(E) 4

2. If $\frac{a-b}{b} = \frac{1}{2}$, find $\frac{a}{b}$.

(A) $\frac{9}{2}$
(B) $\frac{7}{2}$
(C) $\frac{5}{2}$
(D) $\frac{1}{2}$
(E) $\frac{3}{2}$

GO ON TO THE NEXT PAGE

Number of pounds of force	Height object is raised
3	6 feet
6	12 feet
9	18 feet

3. In a certain pulley system, the height an object is raised is equal to a constant c times the number of pounds of force exerted. The table above shows some pounds of force and the corresponding height raised. If a particular object is raised 15 feet, how many pounds of force were exerted?

(A) $3\frac{3}{4}$
(B) 7
(C) $7\frac{1}{2}$
(D) 8
(E) 11

4. If $\frac{y}{3}$, $\frac{y}{4}$, and $\frac{y}{7}$ represent integers, then y could be

(A) 42
(B) 56
(C) 70
(D) 84
(E) 126

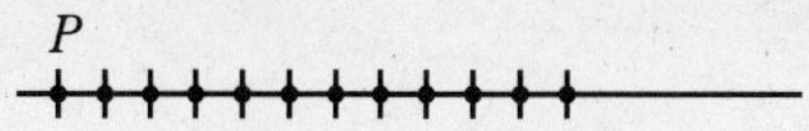

5. The above line is marked with 12 points. The distance between any 2 adjacent points is 3 units. Find the total number of points that are more than 19 units away from point P.

(A) 2
(B) 3
(C) 4
(D) 5
(E) 6

6. Given $(a + 2, a - 2) = [a]$ for all integers a, $(6, 2) =$

(A) [3]
(B) [4]
(C) [5]
(D) [6]
(E) [8]

GO ON TO THE NEXT PAGE

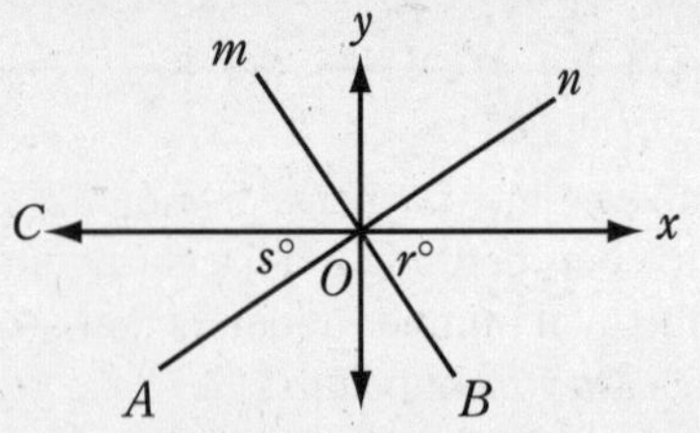

Note: Figure is not drawn to scale.

7. If $mB \perp nA$ in the figure above and COx is a straight line, find the value of $r + s$.

(A) 180
(B) 135
(C) 110
(D) 90
(E) The answer cannot be determined from the information given.

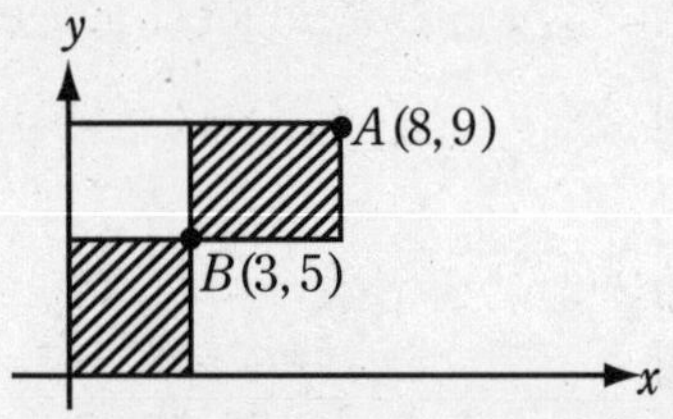

8. Points A and B have coordinates as shown in the figure above. Find the combined area of the two shaded rectangles.

(A) 20
(B) 26
(C) 32
(D) 35
(E) 87

9. One out of 4 students at Ridge High School studies German. If there are 2,800 students at the school, how many students do *not* study German?

(A) 2,500
(B) 2,100
(C) 1,800
(D) 1,000
(E) 700

10. The cost of a drive-in movie is $\$y$ per vehicle. A group of friends in a van shared the admission cost by paying \$0.40 each. If 6 more friends had gone along, everyone would have paid only \$0.25 each. What is the value of $\$y$?

(A) \$4
(B) \$6
(C) \$8
(D) \$10
(E) \$12

GO ON TO THE NEXT PAGE

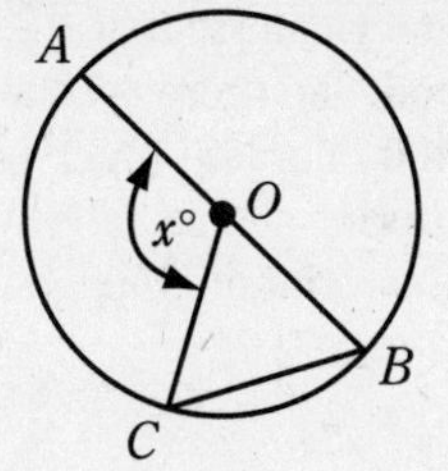

11. If AB is a diameter of circle O in the figure above, and $CB = OB$, then $\frac{x}{6} =$

(A) 60
(B) 30
(C) 20
(D) 10
(E) 5

12. A certain store is selling an $80 radio for $64. If a different radio had a list price of $200 and was discounted at $1\frac{1}{2}$ times the percent discount on the $80 model, what would its selling price be?

(A) $90
(B) $105
(C) $120
(D) $140
(E) $160

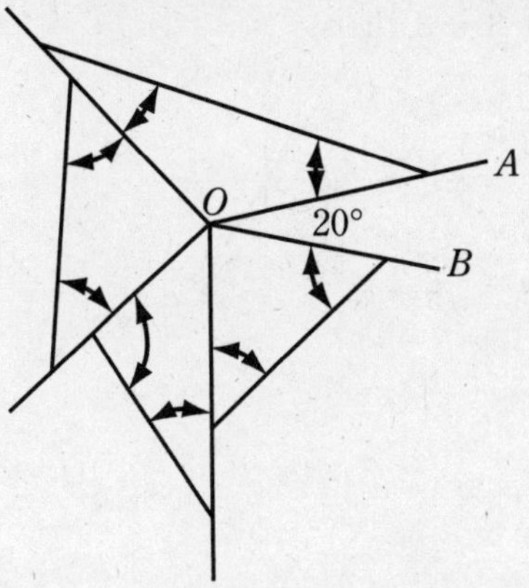

13. If $\angle AOB = 20°$ in the figure above and O is a common vertex of the four triangles, find the sum of the measures of the marked angles in the triangles.

(A) 380
(B) 560
(C) 740
(D) 760
(E) 920

14. Some integers in set X are odd.

If the statement above is true, which of the following must also be true?

(A) If an integer is odd, it is in set X.
(B) If an integer is even, it is in set X.
(C) All integers in set X are odd.
(D) All integers in set X are even.
(E) Not all integers in set X are even.

GO ON TO THE NEXT PAGE

15. If $|y + 3| < 3$, then

(A) $-6 < y < 0$
(B) $3 < y$
(C) $0 < y < 3$
(D) $y = -1$
(E) $y = -2$

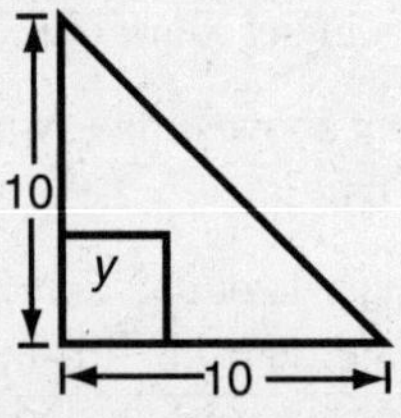

16. In the figure above, the area of the square is equal to $\frac{1}{5}$ the area of the triangle. Find the value of y, the side of the square.

(A) 2
(B) 4
(C) 5
(D) $2\sqrt{5}$
(E) $\sqrt{10}$

17. A certain printer can print at the rate of 80 characters per second, and there is an average (arithmetic mean) of 2,400 characters per page. If the printer continued to print at this rate, how many *minutes* would it take to print an *M*-page report?

(A) $\frac{M}{30}$
(B) $\frac{M}{60}$
(C) $\frac{M}{2}$
(D) $\frac{2}{M}$
(E) $\frac{60}{M}$

18. A certain satellite passed over Washington, D.C., at midnight on Friday. If the satellite completes an orbit every 5 hours, when is the next day that it will pass over Washington, D.C., at midnight?

(A) Monday
(B) Wednesday
(C) Friday
(D) Saturday
(E) Sunday

GO ON TO THE NEXT PAGE

19. The price of a car is reduced by 30 percent. The resulting price is reduced by 40 percent. The two reductions are equal to one reduction of

(A) 28%
(B) 42%
(C) 50%
(D) 58%
(E) 70%

20. In the figure above, the circle is inscribed in the equilateral triangle. If the diameter of the circle is 2, what is the total shaded area?

(A) $3\sqrt{3} - \pi$
(B) $3\sqrt{3} - 4\pi$
(C) $3\sqrt{3} - \frac{3\pi}{2}$
(D) $6\sqrt{3} - \frac{3\pi}{2}$
(E) $108 - \pi$

STOP

If you finish before time is called, you may check your work on this section only.
Do not turn to any other section in the test.

Take a 5 minute break

before starting section 3

SECTION 3

Time: 25 Minutes—Turn to Section 3 (page 952) of your answer sheet to answer the questions in this section.
20 Questions

Directions: For this section, solve each problem and decide which is the best of the choices given. Fill in the corresponding circle on the answer sheet. You may use any available space for scratchwork.

Notes:

1. The use of a calculator is permitted.
2. All numbers used are real numbers.
3. Figures that accompany problems in this test are intended to provide information useful in solving the problems. They are drawn as accurately as possible EXCEPT when it is stated in a specific problem that the figure is not drawn to scale. All figures lie in a plane unless otherwise indicated.
4. Unless otherwise specified, the domain of any function f is assumed to be the set of all real numbers x for which $f(x)$ is a real number.

REFERENCE INFORMATION

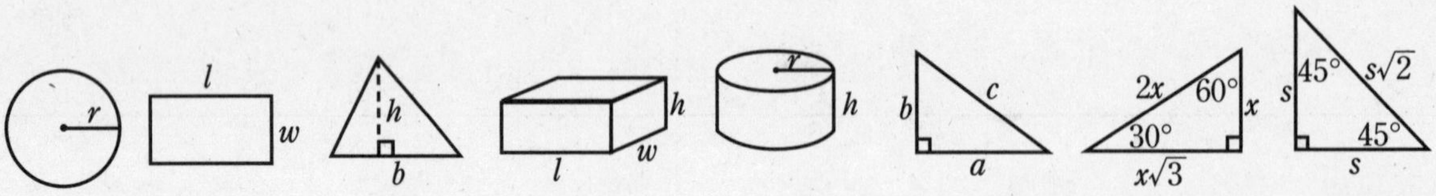

$A = \pi r^2$ $C = 2\pi r$ $A = lw$ $A = \frac{1}{2}bh$ $V = lwh$ $V = \pi r^2 h$ $c^2 = a^2 + b^2$ *Special Right Triangles*

The number of degrees of arc in a circle is 360.
The sum of the measures in degrees of the angles of a triangle is 180.

1. After giving \$5 to Greg, David has \$25. Greg now has $\frac{1}{5}$ as much as David does. How much did Greg start with?

(A) \$0
(B) \$5
(C) \$7
(D) \$10
(E) \$15

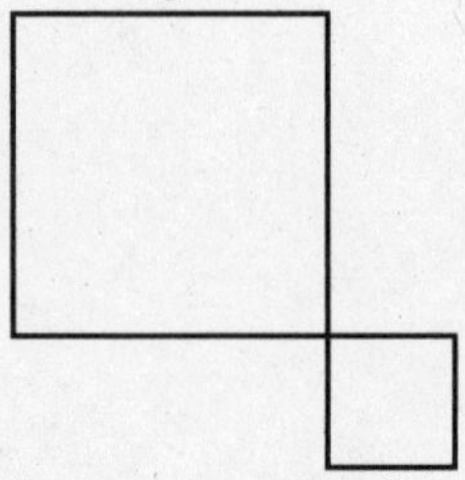

2. The figure above shows two squares with sides as shown. What is the ratio of the perimeter of the larger square to that of the smaller?

(A) 3 : 2
(B) 2 : 1
(C) 3 : 1
(D) 6 : 1
(E) 9 : 1

GO ON TO THE NEXT PAGE

3. A car travels 1,056 feet in 12 seconds. In feet per second, what is the average speed of the car?

(A) 98.0
(B) 78.8
(C) 85.8
(D) 84.0
(E) 88.0

4. If $2z + 1 + 2 + 2z + 3 + 2z = 3 + 1 + 2$, then $z + 4 =$

(A) 1
(B) 4
(C) 5
(D) 6
(E) 10

5. $2(w)(x)(-y) - 2(-w)(-x)(y) =$

(A) 0
(B) $-4wxy$
(C) $4wxy$
(D) $-4w^2x^2y^2$
(E) $2w^2x^2y^2$

6. What is an expression for 5 times the sum of the square of x and the square of y?

(A) $5(x^2 + y^2)$
(B) $5x^2 + y^2$
(C) $5(x + y)^2$
(D) $5x^2 + y$
(E) $5(2x + 2y)$

GO ON TO THE NEXT PAGE

7. If p and q are positive integers, x and y are negative integers, and $p > q$ and $x > y$, which of the following must be less than zero?

I. $q - p$
II. qy
III. $p + x$

(A) I only
(B) III only
(C) I and II only
(D) II and III only
(E) I, II, and III

8. If $a = 1$, $b = -2$ and $c = -2$, find the value of $\frac{b^2c}{(a-c)^2}$.

(A) $-\frac{8}{9}$
(B) $-\frac{2}{3}$
(C) $\frac{8}{9}$
(D) 8
(E) 9

9. If $y = 28j$, where j is any integer, then $\frac{y}{2}$ will always be

(A) even
(B) odd
(C) positive
(D) negative
(E) less than $\frac{y}{3}$

10. If $3a + 4b = 4a - 4b = 21$, find the value of a.

(A) 3
(B) 6
(C) 21
(D) 42
(E) The answer cannot be determined from the information given.

GO ON TO THE NEXT PAGE

11. If N is a positive integer, which of the following does *not* have to be a divisor of the sum of N, $6N$, and $9N$?

(A) 1
(B) 2
(C) 4
(D) 9
(E) 16

12. If $x = 3a - 18$ and $5y = 3a + 7$, then find $5y - x$.

(A) -11
(B) 11
(C) 18
(D) 25
(E) $6a - 11$

13. If $p + pq$ is 4 times $(p - pq)$, which of the following has exactly one value? $(pq \neq 0)$

(A) p
(B) q
(C) pq
(D) $p + pq$
(E) $p - pq$

14. If $2 + \frac{1}{z} = 0$, then what is the value of $9 + 9z$?

(A) $-\frac{9}{2}$
(B) $-\frac{1}{2}$
(C) 0
(D) $\frac{9}{2}$
(E) The answer cannot be determined from the information given.

GO ON TO THE NEXT PAGE

15. How many times does the graph of $y = x^2$ intersect the graph of $y = x$?

(A) 0
(B) 1
(C) 2
(D) 3
(E) 4

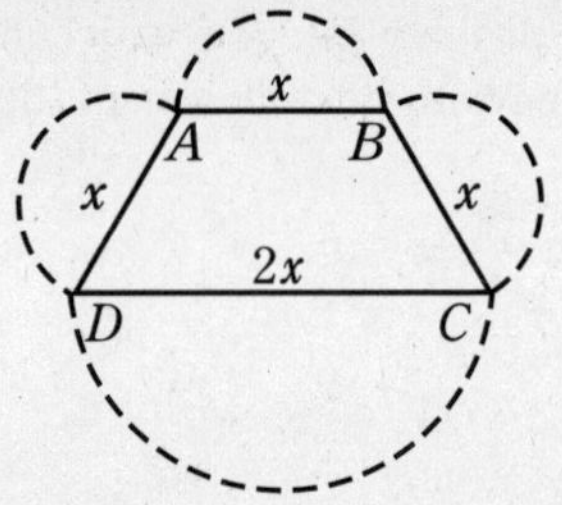

17. The quadrilateral *ABCD* is a trapezoid with $x = 4$. The diameter of each semicircle is a side of the trapezoid. What is the sum of the lengths of the 4 dotted semicircles?

(A) 8π
(B) 10π
(C) 12π
(D) 14π
(E) 20π

16. Let $wx = y$, where $wxy \neq 0$.

If both x and y are multiplied by 6, then w is

(A) multiplied by $\frac{1}{36}$
(B) multiplied by $\frac{1}{6}$
(C) multiplied by 1
(D) multiplied by 6
(E) multiplied by 36

18. $\frac{7x}{144}$ yards and $\frac{5y}{12}$ feet together equal how many inches?

(A) $\frac{7x}{12} + \frac{5y}{4}$
(B) $\frac{7x}{12} + 5y$
(C) $\frac{7x}{4} + 5y$
(D) $\frac{7x}{4} + 60y$
(E) $7x + \frac{5}{4}y$

GO ON TO THE NEXT PAGE

19. If $x < 0$ and $y < 0$, which of the following must always be positive?

I. $x \times y$
II. $x + y$
III. $x - y$

(A) I only
(B) I and II only
(C) I and III only
(D) II and III only
(E) I, II, and III

20. Given that $a + 3b = 11$ and a and b are positive integers, what is the largest possible value of a?

(A) 4
(B) 6
(C) 7
(D) 8
(E) 10

STOP

If you finish before time is called, you may check your work on this section only. Do not turn to any other section in the test.

SECTION 4

Time: 25 Minutes—Turn to Section 4 (page 953) of your answer sheet to answer the questions in this section.
24 Questions

Directions: For each question in this section, select the best answer from among the choices given and fill in the corresponding circle on the answer sheet.

Each sentence below has one or two blanks, each blank indicating that something has been omitted. Beneath the sentence are five words or sets of words labeled A through E. Choose the word or set of words that, when inserted in the sentence, best fits the meaning of the sentence as a whole.

EXAMPLE:

Hoping to ______ the dispute, negotiators proposed a compromise that they felt would be ______ to both labor and management.

(A) enforce...useful
(B) end...divisive
(C) overcome...unattractive
(D) extend...satisfactory
(E) resolve...acceptable

Ⓐ Ⓑ Ⓒ Ⓓ ●

1. Athens was ruled not by kings and emperors as was common among other ______ at the time, but by a citizenry, which ______ fully in the affairs of the city.

(A) committees...cooperated
(B) tribes...engaged
(C) cities...revolutionized
(D) populations...applied
(E) societies...participated

2. Fossils are ______ in rock formations that were once soft and have ______ with the passage of time.

(A) abolished...corresponded
(B) interactive...communicated
(C) preserved...hardened
(D) created...revived
(E) discounted...deteriorated

3. The social-cultural trends of the 1960s ______ not only the relative affluence of the postwar period but also the coming to maturity of a generation that was a product of that ______.

(A) dominated...movement
(B) reflected...prosperity
(C) accentuated...depression
(D) cautioned...decade
(E) accepted...revolution

4. Rotation of crops helps to ______ soil fertility and soil usefulness for a long period of time.

(A) conserve
(B) disperse
(C) employ
(D) research
(E) shorten

5. Some illnesses, such as malaria, that have been virtually eliminated in the United States are still ______ in many places abroad.

(A) discussed
(B) prevalent
(C) scarce
(D) unknown
(E) hospitalized

6. With lack of ______, almost anyone can develop the disease we call alcoholism, just as any of us can contract pneumonia by ______ exposing ourselves to its causes.

(A) advice...carefully
(B) control...foolishly
(C) opportunity...knowingly
(D) sympathy...fortunately
(E) conscience...happily

GO ON TO THE NEXT PAGE

7. Use of air conditioners and other electrical apparatus had to be ______ that summer because of the ______ of the generating system.

(A) postulated...reaction
(B) curtailed...inefficiency
(C) implemented...residuals
(D) augmented...responsiveness
(E) manipulated...intensity

8. The Bavarians consider beer their national beverage, yet at the same time they do not view it as a drink but rather as ______ bread—a staple food.

(A) fresh
(B) liquid
(C) stale
(D) bitter
(E) costly

GO ON TO THE NEXT PAGE

Each passage below is followed by questions based on its content. Answer the questions on the basis of what is stated or implied in each passage and in any introductory material that may be provided.

Questions 9–10 are based on the following passage.

Despite the many categories of the historian, there are only two ages of man. The first age, the age from the beginning of recorded time to the present, is the age of the caveman. It is the age of war. It is today. The second age, still only a prospect, is the age of civilized man. The test of civilized man will be represented by his ability to use his inventiveness for his own good by substituting world law for world anarchy. That second age is still within the reach of the individual in our time. It is not a part-time job, however. It calls for total awareness, total commitment.

9. The title below that best expresses the ideas of this passage is:

(A) The Historian at Work
(B) The Dangers of All-Out War
(C) The Power of World Anarchy
(D) Mankind on the Threshold
(E) The Decline of Civilization

10. The author's attitude toward the possibility of man's reaching an age of civilization is one of

(A) limited hope
(B) complete despair
(C) marked uncertainty
(D) complacency
(E) anger

Questions 11–12 are based on the following passage.

Readers in the past seem to have been more patient than the readers of today. There were few diversions, and they had more time to read novels of a length that seems to us now inordinate. It may be that they were not irritated by the digressions and irrelevances that interrupted the narration. But some of the novels that suffer from these defects are among the greatest that have ever been written. It is deplorable that on this account they should be less and less read.

11. The title below that best expresses the ideas of this passage is:

(A) Defects of Today's Novels
(B) Novel Reading Then and Now
(C) The Great Novel
(D) The Impatient Reader of Novels
(E) Decline in Education

12. The author implies that

(A) authors of the past did not use narration to any extent
(B) great novels are usually long
(C) digressions and irrelevances are characteristic of modern novels
(D) readers of the past were more capable
(E) people today have more pastimes than they formerly had

GO ON TO THE NEXT PAGE

Questions 13–24 are based on the following passage.

This passage describes the relationship between age and income throughout various periods of American history and the effects this trend will have on the various population groups in the future.

The relationship between age and income is only casually appreciated by recent theories on the purported redistribution of income. It is known, of course, that the average person's income begins to decline after he is fifty-five years of age, and that it declines sharply after sixty-five. For example, as early as 1957, 58 percent of the spending units headed by persons sixty-five years and older earned less than $2,000. The relationship between old age and low income has often been considered a reflection of sociological rather than economic factors—and therefore not to be included in any study of the economy. Actually, the character of the relationship is too integrated to be dissected. However, its significance is mounting with the increase in the number of older persons. The lowest-income groups include a heavy concentration of older persons—in 1957, one-third of all spending units in the $0–$2,000 class were headed by persons sixty-five years and older; in 1948, it was 28 percent.

But in economic planning and social policy, it must be remembered that, with the same income, the sixty-five-or-more spending unit will not spend less or need less than the younger spending unit, even though the pressure to save is greater than that on the young. The functional ethos of our economy dictates that the comparatively unproductive old-age population should consume in accordance with their output rather than their requirements. Most social scientists have accepted these values; they have assumed that the minimum economic needs of the aged should be lower than those of the younger family. But it is precisely at retirement that personal requirements and the new demands of leisure call for an even larger income if this period is to be something more enjoyable than a wait for death.

The relationship between age and income is seen most clearly in the unionized blue-collar worker. Except for layoffs, which his seniority minimizes, and wage increments for higher productivity, awarded in many industries, his income range is determined by his occupation. But within that income range, the deciding factor is the man's age. After forty-five, the average worker who loses his job has more difficulty in finding a new one. Despite his seniority, the older worker is likely to be downgraded to a lower-paying job when he can no longer maintain the pace set by younger men. This is especially true of unskilled and semiskilled workers.

The early and lower income period of a person's working life, during which he acquires his basic vocational skills, is most pronounced for the skilled, managerial, or professional worker. Then, between the ages of twenty-five and fifty, the average worker receives his peak earnings. Meanwhile, his family expenses rise, and there are children to support and basic household durables to obtain. Although his family's income may rise substantially until he is somewhere between thirty-five and forty-five, per capita consumption may drop at the same time. For the growing, working-class family, limited in income by the very nature of the breadwinner's occupation, the economic consequences of this parallel rise in age, income, and obligations are especially pressing. Many in the low-income classes are just as vulnerable to poverty during middle age, when they have a substantially larger income, as in old age. As family obligations finally do begin declining, so does income. Consequently, most members of these classes never have an adequate income.

Thus we see that, for a time, increased age means increased income, and therefore a probable boost in income-tenth position. Although there are no extensive data in the matter, it can be confidently asserted that the higher income-tenths have a much greater representation of spending units headed by persons aged thirty-five to fifty-five than do the lower income-tenths. This is demonstrably the case among the richest 5 percent of the consumer units. The real question is: To what extent does distribution of income-tenths within a certain age group deviate from distribution of income-tenths generally? Although information is not as complete as might be desired, there is more than enough to make contingent generalizations. Detailed data exist on income distribution by tenths and by age for 1935–36 and 1948, and on income-size distribution by age for the postwar years. They disclose sharp income inequalities within every age group (although more moderate in the eighteen-to-twenty-five category)—inequalities that closely parallel the overall national income pattern. The implication is clear: A spending unit's income-tenth position *within his age category* varies much less, if at all, and is determined primarily by his occupation.

In other words, in America, the legendary land of economic opportunity where any man can work his way to the top, there is only slight income mobility outside the natural age cycle of rising, then falling income. Since most of the sixty-five-and-over age group falls into the low-income brackets and constitutes the largest segment of the $0–$2,000 income class, it is of obvious importance in analyzing future poverty in the United States to examine the growth trends of this group. The sixty-five-and-over population composed 4.0 percent of the total population in 1900, 5.3 percent in 1930, and 8.4 percent in 1955 and will reach an estimated 10.8 percent in 2010. Between 1900 and 2010, the total national population is expected to increase 276 percent, but those from ages forty-five through sixty-four are expected to increase 416 percent, and those sixty-five and over are expected to increase 672 percent. Between 1990 and 2010, the population aged eighteen to twenty-five is also expected to grow far more rapidly than the middle-aged population. With the more rapid expansion of these two low-income groups, the young and the old, in the years immediately ahead, an increase in the extent of poverty is probable.

GO ON TO THE NEXT PAGE

13. According to the passage, most social scientists erroneously assume that

(A) personal expenses increase with the age of the spending unit
(B) the needs of the younger spending unit are greater than those of the aged
(C) the relationship between old age and low income is an economic and not a sociological problem
(D) members of the old-age population should consume in accordance with their requirements
(E) leisure living requires increased income

14. The word "appreciated" in line 2 most nearly means

(A) had artistic interest
(B) increased in value
(C) had curiosity
(D) had gratitude
(E) understood

15. It can be inferred that in the 35–55 age category

(A) income-tenth positions vary greatly
(B) income-tenth positions vary very little
(C) earning potential does not resemble the overall national income pattern
(D) occupations have little bearing on the income-tenth position
(E) there is great mobility between income-tenth positions

16. The author believes which of the following?

I. The aged will continue to increase as a percentage of the total population.
II. Income inequalities decrease with increasing age.
III. Managerial and professional workers have greater income mobility than blue-collar workers.

(A) I only
(B) II only
(C) III only
(D) I and II only
(E) I and III only

17. In the passage the term "functional ethos" in line 23 means

(A) national group
(B) ethnic influence
(C) prevailing ideology
(D) biased opinion
(E) practical ethics

18. The article states that the old-age population

(A) has increased because of longer life expectancy
(B) exceeds all but the 18–25 age group in growth rate
(C) is well represented among the higher income-tenths
(D) is increasing as a percentage of the low income-tenths
(E) has its greatest numbers among the middle-income group

19. According to the author, aside from the natural age cycle, economic opportunity in America is greatly limited by

I. occupation
II. income inequality within every group
III. class

(A) I only
(B) II only
(C) III only
(D) I and III only
(E) I and II only

20. The word "ethos" in line 23 most nearly means

(A) the character of a group of people
(B) economic–sociological ramifications
(C) the productivity of all age groups
(D) the management of large corporations
(E) the social scientists who deal with the economy

21. According to the passage, the older, unionized blue-collar workers are

(A) assured constant salary until retirement
(B) given preference over new workers because of seniority
(C) likely to receive downgraded salary
(D) more susceptible to layoff after 40
(E) encouraged to move to slower-paced but equal-paying jobs

GO ON TO THE NEXT PAGE

22. The article states that the average worker finds that

(A) as family obligations begin escalating, income begins to decline
(B) he reaches economic stability at middle age because of the parallel rise in age, obligations, and income
(C) he earns least while he is acquiring vocational skills
(D) he reaches peak earning power between the ages of 40 and 65
(E) his wage gains coincide with the decline of family needs

23. It can be inferred that one could most accurately predict a person's income from his or her

(A) age
(B) natural age cycle
(C) occupation
(D) occupation and age
(E) seniority position

24. Which lines in the passage illustrate the author's sarcasm?

(A) lines 19–23
(B) lines 45–48
(C) lines 64–66
(D) lines 86–89
(E) lines 104–107

STOP

If you finish before time is called, you may check your work on this section only.
Do not turn to any other section in the test.

Take a 1 minute break

before starting section 5

SECTION 5

Time: 25 Minutes—Turn to Section 5 (page 953) of your answer sheet to answer the questions in this section.
35 Questions

Directions: For each question in this section, select the best answer from among the choices given and fill in the corresponding circle on the answer sheet.

The following sentences test correctness and effectiveness of expression. Part of each sentence or the entire sentence is underlined; beneath each sentence are five ways of phrasing the underlined material. Choice A repeats the original phrasing; the other four choices are different. If you think the original phrasing produces a better sentence than any of the alternatives, select Choice A; if not, select one of the other choices.

In making your selection, follow the requirements of standard written English; that is, pay attention to grammar, choice of words, sentence construction, and punctuation. Your selection should result in the most effective sentence—clear and precise, without awkwardness or ambiguity.

EXAMPLE:

Laura Ingalls Wilder published her first book and she was sixty-five years old then.

(A) and she was sixty-five years old then
(B) when she was sixty-five
(C) at age sixty-five years old
(D) upon the reaching of sixty-five years
(E) at the time when she was sixty-five

Ⓐ ● Ⓒ Ⓓ Ⓔ

1. Joe couldn't wait for his return to his home after being in the army for two years.

(A) Joe couldn't wait for his return to his home
(B) There was a strong desire on Joe's part to return home
(C) Joe was eager to return home
(D) Joe wanted home badly
(E) Joe arranged to return home

2. Trash, filth, and muck are clogging the streets of the city, and that's not all, the sidewalks are full of garbage.

(A) that's not all, the sidewalks are full of garbage
(B) another thing: garbage is all over the sidewalks
(C) the garbage cans haven't been emptied for days
(D) in addition, garbage is lying all over the sidewalks
(E) what's more, the sidewalks have garbage that is lying all over them

3. Tired and discouraged by the problems of the day, Myra decided to have a good dinner, and then lie down for an hour, and then go dancing.

(A) Myra decided to have a good dinner, and then lie down for an hour, and then go dancing
(B) Myra decided to have a good dinner, lying down for an hour, and then dancing
(C) Myra decided to have a good dinner, lie down for an hour, and then dancing
(D) Myra decided to have a good dinner, lay down for an hour, and then dance
(E) Myra decided to have a good dinner, lie down for an hour, and then go dancing

4. I am not certain in respect to which courses to take.

(A) in respect to which courses
(B) about which courses
(C) which courses
(D) as to the choice of which courses
(E) for which courses I am

GO ON TO THE NEXT PAGE

5. The people of the besieged village had no doubt that the end was drawing near.

(A) that the end was drawing near
(B) about the nearness of the end
(C) it was clear that the end was near
(D) concerning the end's being near
(E) that all would die

6. There isn't a single man among us who is skilled in the art of administering first aid.

(A) who is skilled in the art of administering first aid
(B) who knows how to administer first aid
(C) who knows the administration of first aid
(D) who is a first-aid man
(E) who administers first aid

7. This is the hole that was squeezed through by the mouse.

(A) that was squeezed through by the mouse
(B) that the mouse was seen to squeeze through
(C) the mouse squeezed through it
(D) that the mouse squeezed through
(E) like what the mouse squeezed through

8. She soundly fell asleep after having finished the novel.

(A) She soundly fell asleep
(B) She decided to sleep
(C) She went on to her sleep
(D) She fell to sleep
(E) She fell fast asleep

9. This is one restaurant I won't patronize because I was served a fried egg by the waitress that was rotten.

(A) I was served a fried egg by the waitress that was rotten
(B) I was served by the waitress a fried egg that was rotten
(C) a fried egg was served to me by the waitress that was rotten
(D) the waitress served me a fried egg that was rotten
(E) a rotten fried egg was served to me by the waitress

10. Watching the familiar story unfold on the screen, he was glad that he read the book with such painstaking attention to detail.

(A) that he read the book with such painstaking attention to detail
(B) that he had read the book with such painstaking attention to detail
(C) that he read the book with such attention to particulars
(D) that he read the book with such intense effort
(E) that he paid so much attention to the plot of the book

11. If anyone requested tea instead of coffee, it was a simple matter to serve it to them from the teapot at the rear of the table.

(A) it was a simple matter to serve it to them
(B) it was easy to serve them
(C) it was a simple matter to serve them
(D) it was a simple matter to serve it to him or to her
(E) that person could serve himself or herself

GO ON TO THE NEXT PAGE

The following sentences test your ability to recognize grammar and usage errors. Each sentence contains either a single error or no error at all. No sentence contains more than one error. The error, if there is one, is underlined and lettered. If the sentence contains an error, select the one underlined part that must be changed to make the sentence correct. If the sentence is correct, select Choice E. In choosing answers, follow the requirements of standard written English.

EXAMPLE:

The other delegates and him immediately
A B C
accepted the resolution drafted by
D
the neutral states. No error.
E

(A) ● (C) (D) (E)

12. Since we first started high school, there has been
A B
great competition for grades between him and I
C D
No error.
E

13. Many people in the suburbs scarcely know about
A B
the transportation problems that city dwellers
C
experience every day. No error.
D E

14. The subject of the evening editorial was us
A
instructors who have refused to cross the picket
B C
lines of the striking food service workers.
D
No error.
E

15. After the contestants had completed their speeches,
A
I knew that the prize would go to he whom
B C
the audience had given a standing ovation.
D
No error.
E

16. Falsely accused of a triple murder and imprisoned
A B
for 19 years, Ruben (Hurricane) Carter, a former
boxer, was freed when a federal judge declared
C
him guiltless. No error.
D E

17. Your math instructor would have been happy to
A
give you a makeup examination if you would have
B
gone to him and explained that your parents were
C
hospitalized. No error.
D E

18. The child asking a difficult question was perhaps
A B
more shocking to the speaker than to the child's
C D
parents. No error.
E

19. Now that the pressure of selling the house and
A B
packing our belongings is over, we can look forward
C D
to moving to our new home in California.
No error.
E

20. My grandmother leads a more active life than
A B
many other retirees who are younger than her.
C D
No error.
E

21. I appreciate your offering to change my flat tire,
A B
but I would rather have you drive me to my meeting
C
so that I will be on time. No error.
D E

22. The novelists who readers choose as their
A B C
favorites are not always the most skilled writers.
D
No error.
E

GO ON TO THE NEXT PAGE

23. The problem of how to deal with all the
A
mosquitoes disturb many residents of the Tropics.
B C D
No error.
E

24. The family's only son could of gone to college, but
A B C
he decided to join the army after he graduated
from high school. No error.
D E

25. Yesterday at the racetrack, many people were
A B
fearful of betting on the horse who had fallen in the
C D
last race. No error.
E

26. If someone wants to buy all the antiques that I have
A B
for the rummage sale, then they should make me
C D
a reasonable offer. No error.
E

27. The man who Mexican authorities believe to be
A B
the country's number one drug trafficker has been
C D
arrested in a Pacific resort area. No error.
D E

28. While her mother was inside the house talking on
A B
the phone, the child fell off of the unscreened
C D
porch. No error.

29. The racehorse ran swifter in today's race than he
A B
had run in his practice sessions last week. No error.
C D E

GO ON TO THE NEXT PAGE

Directions: The following passage is an early draft of an essay. Some parts of the passage need to be rewritten.

Read the passage and select the best answers for the questions that follow. Some questions are about particular sentences or parts of sentences and ask you to improve sentence structure or word choice. Other questions ask you to consider organization and development. In choosing answers, follow the requirements of standard written English.

Questions 30–35 refer to the following passage.

[1]Lampe-Pigeon is the charming name for a tall kerosene lamp, more than nine and one-half inches in height, created more than 100 years ago for use in the wine caves of France. [2]Its diminutive size makes it suitable for being used on a mantel, as a centerpiece in lieu of candles, or even bracketed as a wall sconce. [3]The brass lamp, which contains within it a glass globe, is still being handmade by the same company, though one is more likely to see it in a French home these days than in a cave. [4]And, of course, it would be a handy source of light in the event of a power failure. [5]Other antique-type lamps have been manufactured and they do not have the elegance or simplicity of the Lampe-Pigeon. [6]Many people prefer more modern lamps especially those of the halogen variety.

30. What should be done with sentence 3?

(A) It should end after the word company.
(B) It should remain as it is.
(C) It should be placed after sentence 4.
(D) It should follow sentence 1.
(E) It should introduce the passage.

31. Sentence 1 would be more logical if it read, Lampe-Pigeon is the charming name for

(A) a tall kerosene lamp, measuring more than nine and one-half inches, created...
(B) a kerosene lamp, although more than nine and one-half inches tall, created...
(C) a more than nine-and-one-half-inch-tall kerosene lamp, created...
(D) a tall, more than nine-and-one-half inch kerosene lamp, created...
(E) a kerosene lamp, of a height of more than nine and one-half inches, created...

32. The phrase for being used in sentence 2 should be

(A) changed to for use
(B) left as it is
(C) changed to for one to use it
(D) changed to to being used
(E) changed to as a piece used on a mantel

33. Sentence 3 would read more smoothly were it to begin

(A) The glass globed brass lamp...
(B) The brass lamp with a glass globe...
(C) The glass globe, found in the brass lamp...
(D) as it does now
(E) The brass lamp, inside of which is a glass globe...

34. What should be done with sentence 6?

(A) It should be left as it is.
(B) It should be deleted from the paragraph.
(C) It should be placed before sentence 5.
(D) It should be placed before sentence 4.
(E) It should be placed before sentence 3.

35. In sentence 5,

(A) "manufactured" should be changed to "produced"
(B) "Lampe-Pigeon" should be changed to "lamp in question"
(C) "elegance and simplicity" should be changed to "modernization"
(D) "and" should be changed to "but"
(E) the sentence should remain as it is

STOP

If you finish before time is called, you may check your work on this section only. Do not turn to any other section in the test.

SECTION 6

Time: 25 Minutes—Turn to Section 6 (page 954) of your answer sheet to answer the questions in this section.
18 Questions

Directions: This section contains two types of questions. You have 25 minutes to complete both types. For questions 1–8, solve each problem and decide which is the best of the choices given. Fill in the corresponding circle on the answer sheet. You may use any available space for scratchwork.

Notes:

1. The use of a calculator is permitted.
2. All numbers used are real numbers.
3. Figures that accompany problems in this test are intended to provide information useful in solving the problems. They are drawn as accurately as possible EXCEPT when it is stated in a specific problem that the figure is not drawn to scale. All figures lie in a plane unless otherwise indicated.
4. Unless otherwise specified, the domain of any function *f* is assumed to be the set of all real numbers *x* for which *f*(*x*) is a real number.

REFERENCE INFORMATION

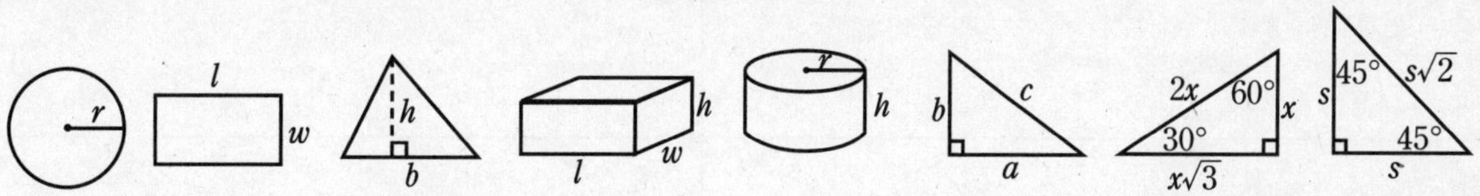

$A = \pi r^2$ $C = 2\pi r$ $A = lw$ $A = \frac{1}{2}bh$ $V = lwh$ $V = \pi r^2 h$ $c^2 = a^2 + b^2$ *Special Right Triangles*

The number of degrees of arc in a circle is 360.
The sum of the measures in degrees of the angles of a triangle is 180.

1. In the equation $5\sqrt{x} + 14 = 20$, the value of x is

(A) $\sqrt{\frac{6}{5}}$
(B) $\frac{34^2}{25^2}$
(C) $6 - \sqrt{5}$
(D) $\frac{6}{5}$
(E) $\frac{36}{25}$

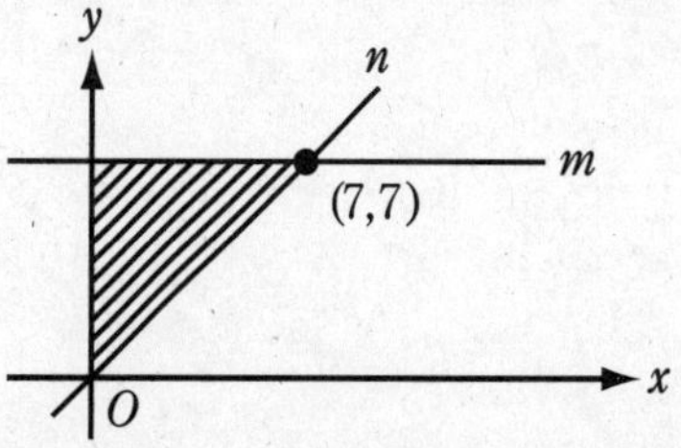

2. In the figure above, m is parallel to the x-axis. All of the following points lie in the shaded area EXCEPT

(A) (4,3)
(B) (1,2)
(C) (5,6)
(D) (4,5)
(E) (2,5)

GO ON TO THE NEXT PAGE

3. At Lincoln County High School, 36 students are taking either calculus or physics or both, and 10 students are taking both calculus and physics. If there are 31 students in the calculus class, how many students are in the physics class?

(A) 14
(B) 15
(C) 16
(D) 17
(E) 18

4. Mr. Simmons stated that if $a^2 > b^2$ where a and b are real, then it follows that $a > b$. Mr. Simmons's statement would be refuted if (a,b) =

(A) (2,3)
(B) (3,2)
(C) (4,−2)
(D) (−4,−2)
(E) (−2,−3)

5. Which of the following is always true for real numbers a, b, and c?

I. $\sqrt{a+b} = \sqrt{a} + \sqrt{b}$
II. $a^2 + b^2 = (a + b)^2$
III. $a^b + a^c = a^{(b + c)}$

(A) I only
(B) II only
(C) III only
(D) I, II, and III
(E) neither I, II, or III

Question 6 refers to the following:

$R = \{x : 1 \geq x \geq -1\}$
$S = \{x : x \geq 1\}$

6. The number of elements that is (are) common to both R and S is (are)

(A) 0
(B) 1
(C) 2
(D) 3
(E) infinite

GO ON TO THE NEXT PAGE

7. Two lines in a plane are represented by $y = x - 1$ and $2x + 5y = 9$. The coordinates of the point at which the lines intersect are

(A) (2,1)
(B) (1,2)
(C) (2,5)
(D) (5,2)
(E) (3,5)

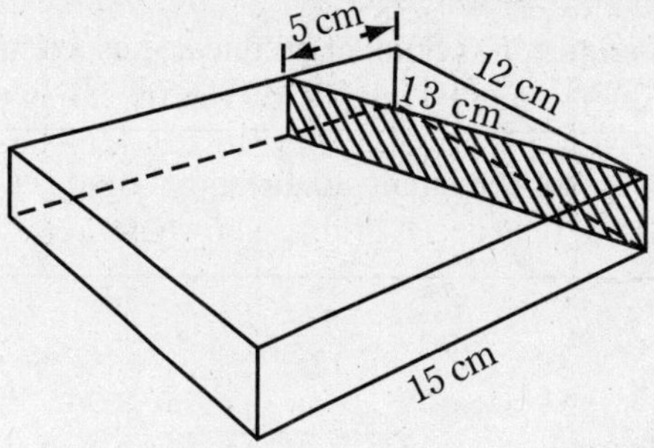

8. The rectangular box above has a rectangular dividing wall inside, as shown. The dividing wall has an area of 39 cm^2. What is the volume of the trapezoid-shaped box?

(A) 90 cm^3
(B) 180 cm^3
(C) 360 cm^3
(D) 450 cm^3
(E) 540 cm^3

GO ON TO THE NEXT PAGE

Directions: For Student-Produced Response questions 9–18, use the grids at the bottom of the answer sheet page on which you have answered questions 1–8.

Each of the remaining 10 questions requires you to solve the problem and enter your answer by marking the circles in the special grid, as shown in the examples below. You may use any available space for scratchwork.

Answer: $\frac{7}{12}$ or 7/12

Write answer in boxes. →

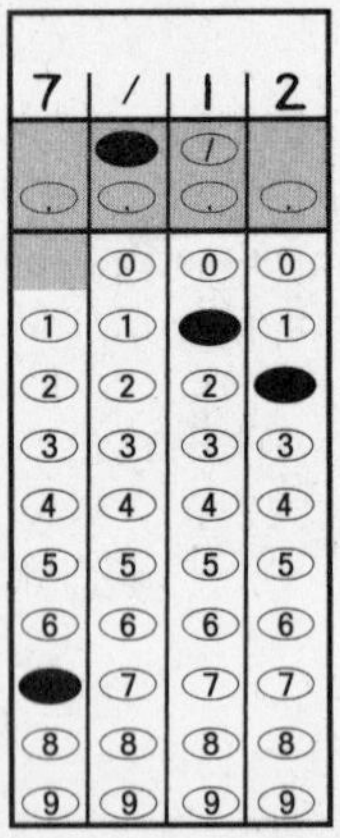

← Fraction line

Grid in result. →

Answer: 2.5

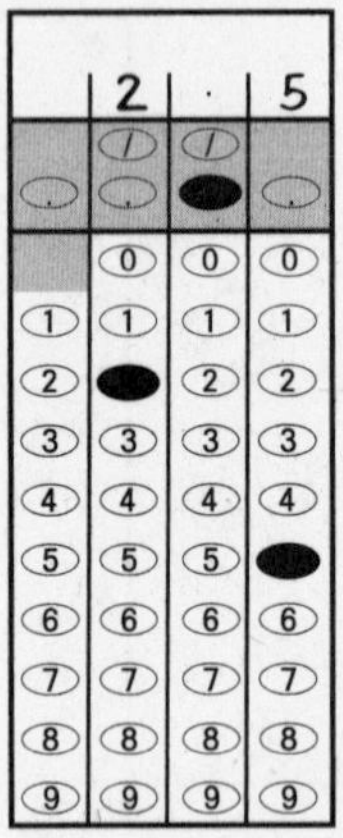

← Decimal point

Answer: 201
Either position is correct.

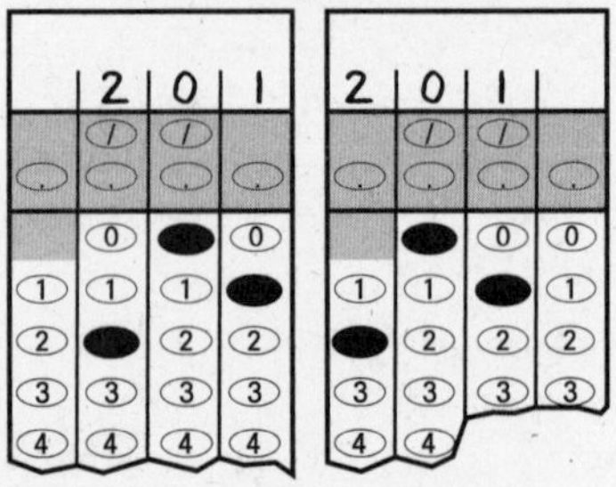

Note: You may start your answers in any column, space permitting. Columns not needed should be left blank.

- Mark no more than one oval in any column.
- Because the answer sheet will be machine-scored, **you will receive credit only if the ovals are filled in correctly.**
- Although not required, it is suggested that you write your answer in the boxes at the top of the columns to help you fill in the ovals accurately.
- Some problems may have more than one correct answer. In such cases, grid only one answer.
- No question has a negative answer.
- **Mixed numbers** such as $2\frac{1}{2}$ must be gridded as 2.5 or 5/2. (If  is gridded, it will be interpreted as $\frac{21}{2}$, not $2\frac{1}{2}$.)
- Decimal Accuracy: If you obtain a decimal answer, **enter the most accurate value the grid will accommodate.** For example, if you obtain an answer such as 0.6666..., you should record the result as .666 or .667. **Less accurate values such as .66 or .67 are not acceptable.**

Acceptable ways to grid $\frac{2}{3}$ = .6666...:

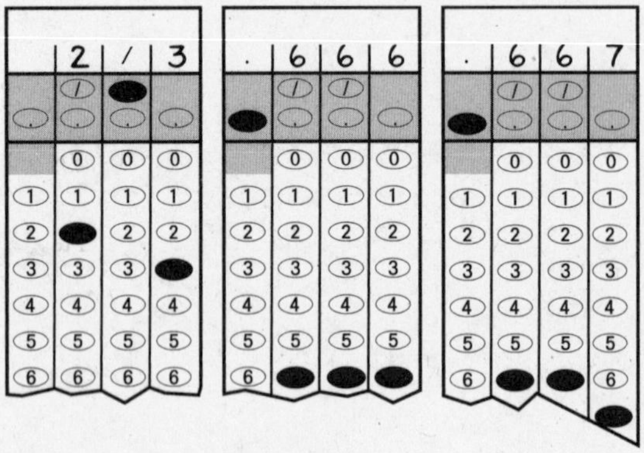

9. $\left(\frac{1}{2}-\frac{1}{3}\right)+\left(\frac{1}{3}-\frac{1}{4}\right)+\left(\frac{1}{4}-\frac{1}{5}\right)+\left(\frac{1}{5}-\frac{1}{6}\right)+\left(\frac{1}{6}-\frac{1}{7}\right)+\left(\frac{1}{7}-\frac{1}{8}\right)+\left(\frac{1}{8}-\frac{1}{9}\right)$ is equal to what value?

10. If the first two elements of a number series are 1 and 2, and if each succeeding term is found by multiplying the two terms immediately preceding it, what is the fifth element of the series?

GO ON TO THE NEXT PAGE

11. If p is $\frac{3}{5}$ of m and if q is $\frac{9}{10}$ of m, then, when $q \neq 0$, the ratio $\frac{p}{q}$ is equal to what value?

12. If the average (arithmetic mean) of 40, 40, 40, and z is 45, then find the value of z.

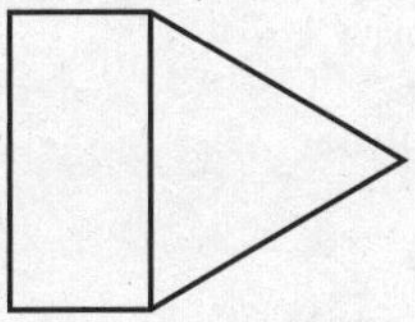

13. In the figure above, the perimeter of the equilateral triangle is 39 and the area of the rectangle is 65. What is the perimeter of the rectangle?

Game	*Darrin*	*Tom*
1	69	43
2	59	60
3	72	55
4	70	68
5	78	73
Totals	348	299

14. Darrin and Tom played five games of darts. The table above lists the scores for each of the games. By how many points was Tom behind Darrin at the end of the first four games?

15. A box contains 17 slips of paper. Each is labeled with a different integer from 1 to 17 inclusive. If 5 even-numbered slips of paper are removed, what fraction of the remaining slips of paper are even-numbered?

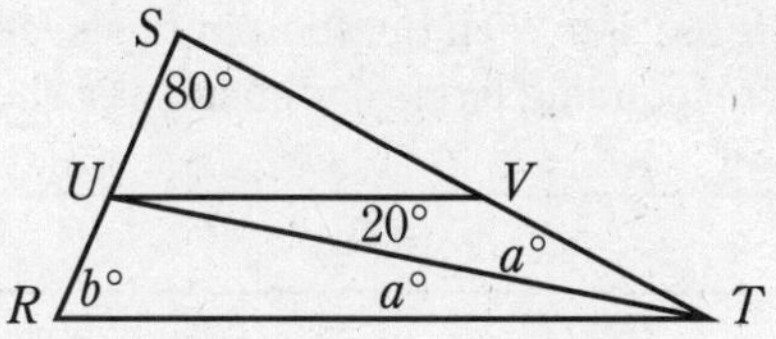

Note: Figure is not drawn to scale.

16. In ΔRST above, $UV \parallel RT$. Find b.

17. Rose has earned $44 in 8 days. If she continues to earn at the same daily rate, in how many *more* days will her total earnings be $99?

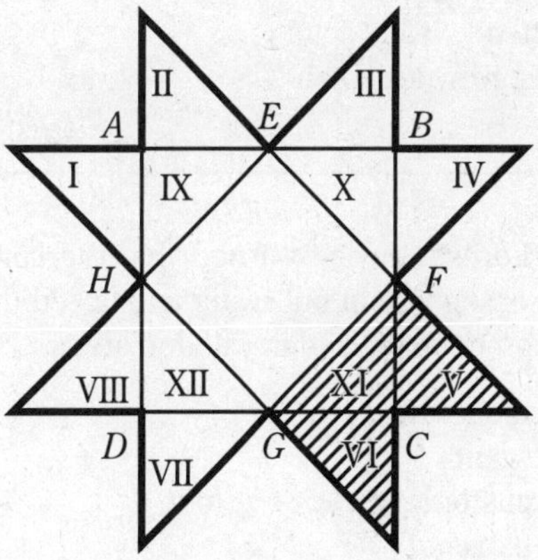

18. The areas of triangles I, II, III, IV, V, VI, VII, VIII, IX, X, XI, XII are the same. If the region outlined by the heavy line has area = 256 and the area of square $ABCD$ is 128, determine the shaded area.

STOP

If you finish before time is called, you may check your work on this section only.
Do not turn to any other section in the test.

Take a 5 minute break

before starting section 7

SECTION 7

Time: 25 Minutes—Turn to Section 7 (page 954) of your answer sheet to answer the questions in this section.
24 Questions

Directions: For each question in this section, select the best answer from among the choices given and fill in the corresponding circle on the answer sheet.

Each sentence below has one or two blanks, each blank indicating that something has been omitted. Beneath the sentence are five words or sets of words labeled A through E. Choose the word or set of words that, when inserted in the sentence, best fits the meaning of the sentence as a whole.

EXAMPLE:

Hoping to _______ the dispute, negotiators proposed a compromise that they felt would be _______ to both labor and management.

(A) enforce...useful
(B) end...divisive
(C) overcome...unattractive
(D) extend...satisfactory
(E) resolve...acceptable

Ⓐ Ⓑ Ⓒ Ⓓ ●

1. The Forest Service warned that the spring forest fire season was in full swing and urged that _____ caution be exercised in wooded areas.

(A) moderate
(B) scant
(C) customary
(D) extreme
(E) reasonable

2. The Classical Age of Greek art ended with the defeat of Athens by Sparta; the _____ effect of the long war was the weakening and _____ of the Greek spirit.

(A) cumulative...corrosion
(B) immediate...storing
(C) imagined...cooperation
(D) delayed...rebuilding
(E) intuitive...cancellation

3. Mary, bored by even the briefest periods of idleness, was _____ switching from one activity to another.

(A) hesitantly
(B) lazily
(C) slowly
(D) surprisingly
(E) continually

4. The bee _____ the nectar from the different flowers and then _____ the liquid into honey.

(A) consumes...conforms
(B) observes...pours
(C) rejects...solidifies
(D) crushes...injects
(E) extracts...converts

5. The plan turned out to be _____ because it would have required more financial backing than was available.

(A) intractable
(B) chaotic
(C) irreversible
(D) untenable
(E) superfluous

GO ON TO THE NEXT PAGE

The two passages below are followed by questions based on their content and on the relationship between the two passages. Answer the questions on the basis of what is stated or implied in the passages and in any introductory material that may be provided.

Questions 6–9 are based on the following passages.

Passage 1

All the arts contain some preposterous fiction, but the theatre is the most preposterous of all. Imagine asking us to believe that we are in Venice in the sixteenth century, that Mr. Billington is a Moor, and that he is about to stifle the much admired Miss Huckaby with a pillow; and imagine trying to make us believe that people ever talked in blank verse—more than that: that people were ever so marvelously articulate. The theatre is a lily that inexplicably arises from a jungle of weedy falsities. Yet it is precisely from the tension produced by all this absurdity that it is able to create such poetry, power, enchantment, and truth.

Passage 2

The theater is a venue for the most realistic and direct fiction ever imagined. So many of the contemporary plays make us realize how we are living our lives and perhaps how we should change them. From these "reality shows" we can feel all the poverty, despair, and unfairness in our world, which then affords us the opportunity for change for the better.

6. Which statement best illustrates the author's meaning when he says, "The theatre is a lily that inexplicably arises from a jungle of weedy falsities"?

(A) The theatre is the "flower" among the arts.
(B) The theatre helps to raise public taste to a higher level.
(C) The theatre can create an illusion of truth from improbable situations.
(D) The theatre has overcome the unsavory reputation of earlier periods.
(E) In the theatre, real acting talent can be developed from unpromising material.

7. The author's feeling toward contemporary plays is that they

(A) have no value for the spectator
(B) can be appreciated by everyone
(C) elicit the negative aspects of life
(D) have a long-lasting effect on us
(E) do not deal with poetry or truth

8. The two passages are similar in that

(A) both describe specific examples from specific plays
(B) both are completely objective in their respective arguments
(C) both authors believe that they depict the accuracy of the particular time
(D) both authors show the same intensity and passion in their arguments
(E) both show that something positive can come out of something negative

9. Which of the following is true?

(A) One author would not disagree with the other's premise.
(B) The author of Passage 1 despises all characters in 16th-century plays.
(C) The author of Passage 1 believes that people in the 16th century were very articulate.
(D) Analogies to objects and places are a literary device used in only one passage.
(E) The author of Passage 2 believes that the theater compromises reality.

GO ON TO THE NEXT PAGE

Questions 10–15 are based on the following passage.

The following passage deals with adjustment to one's surroundings and the terms and theory associated with such adjustment.

As in the case of so many words used by the biologist and the physiologist, the word acclimatization is hard to define. With increases in knowledge and understanding, meanings of words change. Originally, the term acclimatization was taken to mean only the ability of human beings or animals or plants to accustom themselves to new and strange climatic conditions, primarily altered temperature. A person or a wolf moves to a hot climate and is uncomfortable there, but after a time is better able to withstand the heat. But aside from temperature, there are other aspects of climate. A person or an animal may become adjusted to living at higher altitudes than those it was originally accustomed to. At really high altitudes, such as that which aviators may be exposed to, the low atmospheric pressure becomes a factor of primary importance. In changing to a new environment, a person may, therefore, meet new conditions of temperature or pressure, and in addition may have to contend with different chemical surroundings. On high mountains, the amount of oxygen in the atmosphere may be relatively small; in crowded cities, a person may become exposed to relatively high concentrations of carbon dioxide or even carbon monoxide and in various areas may be exposed to conditions in which the water content of the atmosphere is extremely high or extremely low. Thus in the case of humans, animals, and even plants, the concept of acclimatization includes the phenomena of increased toleration of high or low temperature, of altered pressure, and of changes in the chemical environment.

Let us define acclimatization, therefore, as the process by which an organism or a part of an organism becomes inured to an environment that is normally unsuitable to it or lethal for it. By and large, acclimatization is a relatively slow process. The term should not be taken to include relatively rapid adjustments such as those our sense organs are constantly making. This type of adjustment is commonly referred to by physiologists as "adaptation." Thus our touch sense soon becomes accustomed to the pressure of our clothes and we do not feel them; we soon fail to hear the ticking of a clock; obnoxious odors after a time fail to make much impression on us, and our eyes in strong light rapidly become insensitive.

The fundamental fact about acclimatization is that all animals and plants have some capacity to adjust themselves to changes in their environment. This is one of the most remarkable characteristics of living organisms, a characteristic for which it is extremely difficult to find explanations.

10. According to the reading selection, all animals and plants

(A) have an ability for acclimatization
(B) can adjust to only one change in the environment at a time
(C) are successful in adjusting themselves to changes in their environments
(D) can adjust to natural changes in the environment but not to artificially induced changes
(E) that have once acclimatized themselves to an environmental change can acclimatize themselves more rapidly to subsequent changes

11. It can be inferred from the reading selection that

(A) every change in the environment requires acclimatization by living things
(B) plants and animals are more alike than they are different
(C) biologists and physiologists study essentially the same things
(D) the explanation of acclimatization is specific to each plant and animal
(E) as science develops, the connotation of terms may change

12. According to the reading selection, acclimatization

(A) is similar to adaptation
(B) is more important today than it formerly was
(C) involves positive as well as negative adjustment
(D) may be involved with a part of an organism but not with the whole organism
(E) is more difficult to explain with the more complex present-day environment than formerly

13. By inference from the reading selection, which one of the following would *not* require the process of acclimatization?

(A) an ocean fish placed in a lake
(B) a skin diver making a deep dive
(C) an airplane pilot making a high-altitude flight
(D) a person going from daylight into a darkened room
(E) a person moving from Denver, Colorado, to New Orleans, Louisiana

GO ON TO THE NEXT PAGE

14. The word "inured" in line 31 most likely means

(A) exposed
(B) accustomed
(C) attracted
(D) associated
(E) in love with

15. According to the passage, a major distinction between acclimatization and adaptation is that acclimatization

(A) is more important than adaptation
(B) is relatively slow and adaptation is relatively rapid
(C) applies to adjustments while adaptation does not apply to adjustments
(D) applies to terrestrial animals and adaptation to aquatic animals
(E) is applicable to all animals and plants and adaptation only to higher animals and man

GO ON TO THE NEXT PAGE

Questions 16–24 are based on the following passage.

The following passage is about the Chinese Empire, the forces that kept the Empire together, its culture, and its philosophy.

First of all, it is important to note that the old China was an empire rather than a state. To the Chinese and their rulers, the word China did not exist and to them it would have been meaningless. They sometimes used a term which we translate "the Middle Kingdom." To them there could be only one legitimate ruler for all civilized mankind. All others were rightly subordinate to him and should acknowledge his suzerainty. From this standpoint, there could not, as in Europe, be diplomatic relations between equal states, each of them sovereign. When, in the nineteenth century, Europeans insisted upon intercourse with China on the basis of equality, the Chinese were at first amused and then scandalized and indignant. Centuries of training had bred in them the conviction that all other rulers should be tributary to the Son of Heaven.

The tie which bound this world-embracing empire together, so the Chinese were taught to believe, was as much cultural as political. As there could be only one legitimate ruler to whom all mankind must be subject, so there could be only one culture that fully deserved to be called civilized. Other cultures might have worth, but ultimately they were more or less barbarous. There could be only one civilization, and that was the civilization of the Middle Kingdom. Beginning with the Han, the ideal of civilization was held to be Confucian. The Confucian interpretation of civilization was adopted and inculcated as the norm. Others might be tolerated, but if they seriously threatened the Confucian institutions and foundations of society, they were to be curbed and, perhaps, exterminated as a threat to the highest values.

Since the bond of the Empire was cultural and since the Empire should include all civilized mankind, racial distinctions were not so marked as in most other parts of the world. The Chinese did not have so strong a sense of being of different blood from non-Chinese as twentieth-century conceptions of race and nation later led them to develop. They were proud of being "the sons of Han" or "the men of T'ang," but if a people fully adopted Chinese culture, no great distinction was perceived between them and those who earlier had been governed by that culture.

This helps to account for the comparative contentment of Chinese under alien rulers. If, as was usually the case, these invading conquerors adopted the culture of their subjects and governed through the accustomed machinery and by traditional Confucian principles, they were accepted as legitimate Emperors. Few of the non-Chinese dynasties completely made this identification. This probably in part accounts for such restiveness as the Chinese showed under their rule. For instance, so long as they were dominant, the Manchus, while they accepted much of the Chinese culture and prided themselves on being experts in it and posed as its patrons, never completely abandoned their distinctive ancestral ways.

The fact that the tie was cultural rather than racial helps to account for the remarkable homogeneity of the Chinese. Many different ethnic strains have gone to make up the people whom we call the Chinese. Presumably in the Chou and probably, earlier, in the Shang, the bearers of Chinese culture were not a single race. As Chinese culture moved southward, it encountered differing cultures and, almost certainly, divergent stocks. The many invaders from the north and west brought in more variety. In contrast with India, where caste and religion have tended to keep apart the racial strata, in China assimilation made great progress. That assimilation has not been complete. Today the discerning observer can notice differences even among those who are Chinese in language and customs, and in many parts of China Proper there are groups who preserve not only their racial but also their linguistic and cultural identity. Still, nowhere else on the globe is there so numerous a people who are so nearly homogeneous as are the Chinese.

This homogeneity is due not merely to a common cultural tie, but also to the particular kind of culture which constitutes that tie. Something in the Chinese tradition recognized as civilized those who conformed to certain ethical standards and social customs. It was the fitting into Confucian patterns of conduct and of family and community life rather than blood kinship or ancestry which labeled one as civilized and as Chinese.

16. The force that kept the Chinese Empire together was largely

(A) religious
(B) military
(C) economic
(D) a fear of invasion from the north and west
(E) the combination of a political and a cultural bond

17. The reason China resisted having diplomatic relations with European nations was that

(A) for centuries the Chinese had believed that their nation must be supreme among all other countries
(B) the Chinese saw nothing of value in European culture
(C) China was afraid of European military power
(D) such relations were against the teachings of the Son of Heaven
(E) the danger of disease was ever present when foreigners arrived

GO ON TO THE NEXT PAGE

18. Confucianism stresses, above all,

(A) image worship
(B) recognition of moral values
(C) division of church and state
(D) acceptance of foreigners
(E) separation of social classes

19. Han and T'ang were Chinese

(A) philosophers
(B) holidays
(C) dynasties
(D) generals
(E) religions

20. If the unifying force in the Chinese empire had been racial, it is likely that

(A) China would have never become great
(B) China would be engaged in constant warfare
(C) China would have become a highly industrialized nation
(D) there would have been increasing discontent under foreign rulers
(E) China would have greatly expanded its influence

21. A problem of contemporary India that does not trouble China is

(A) overpopulation
(B) the persistence of the caste system
(C) a lack of modern industrial development
(D) a scarcity of universities
(E) a low standard of living

22. The Manchus encountered some dissatisfaction within the empire because

(A) of their tyrannical rule
(B) they retained some of their original cultural practices
(C) they were of a distinctly foreign race
(D) of the heavy taxes they levied
(E) they rejected totally Chinese culture

23. The Chinese are basically a homogeneous people because

(A) different races were able to assimilate to a great degree
(B) there has always been only one race in China
(C) the other races came to look like the Chinese because of geographical factors
(D) all other races were forcibly kept out of China
(E) of their antipathy toward intermarriage

24. The word "restiveness" in line 48 means

(A) authority
(B) happiness
(C) impatience
(D) hyperactivity
(E) quietude

STOP

**If you finish before time is called, you may check your work on this section only.
Do not turn to any other section in the test.**

SECTION 8

Time: 20 Minutes—Turn to Section 8 (page 955) of your answer sheet to answer the questions in this section.
16 Questions

Directions: For this section, solve each problem and decide which is the best of the choices given. Fill in the corresponding circle on the answer sheet. You may use any available space for scratchwork.

Notes:

1. The use of a calculator is permitted.
2. All numbers used are real numbers.
3. Figures that accompany problems in this test are intended to provide information useful in solving the problems. They are drawn as accurately as possible EXCEPT when it is stated in a specific problem that the figure is not drawn to scale. All figures lie in a plane unless otherwise indicated.
4. Unless otherwise specified, the domain of any function f is assumed to be the set of all real numbers x for which $f(x)$ is a real number.

REFERENCE INFORMATION

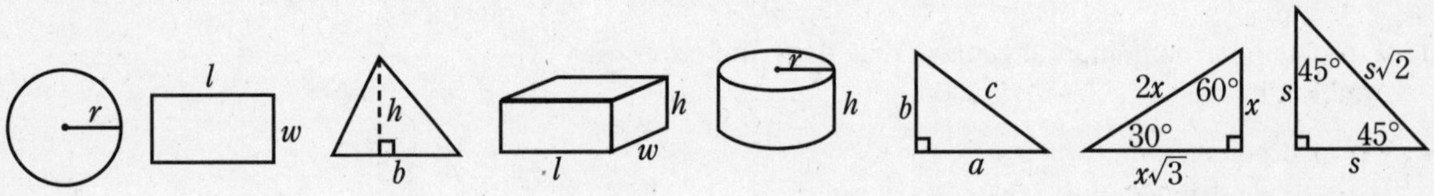

$A = \pi r^2$ $C = 2\pi r$ | $A = lw$ | $A = \frac{1}{2}bh$ | $V = lwh$ | $V = \pi r^2 h$ | $c^2 = a^2 + b^2$ | *Special Right Triangles*

The number of degrees of arc in a circle is 360.
The sum of the measures in degrees of the angles of a triangle is 180.

1. Johnny buys a frying pan and two coffee mugs for \$27. Joanna buys the same-priced frying pan and one of the same-priced coffee mugs for \$23. How much does one of those frying pans cost?

(A) \$4
(B) \$7
(C) \$19
(D) \$20
(E) \$21

2. A rectangular floor 8 feet long and 6 feet wide is to be completely covered with tiles. Each tile is a square with a perimeter of 2 feet. What is the least number of such tiles necessary to cover the floor?

(A) 7
(B) 12
(C) 24
(D) 48
(E) 192

GO ON TO THE NEXT PAGE

3. If 9 and 12 each divide Q without remainder, which of the following must Q divide without remainder?

(A) 1
(B) 3
(C) 36
(D) 72
(E) The answer cannot be determined from the given information.

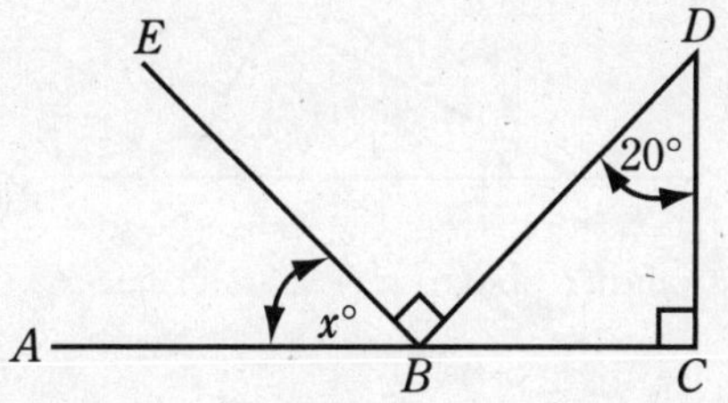

4. In the figure above, $DC \perp AC$, $EB \perp DB$, and AC is a line segment. What is the value of x? (*Note*: Figure is not drawn to scale.)

(A) 15
(B) 20
(C) 30
(D) 80
(E) 160

5. Given three segments of length x, $11 - x$, and $x - 4$, respectively, which of the following indicates the set of all numbers x such that the 3 segments could be the lengths of the sides of a triangle?

(A) $x > 4$
(B) $x < 11$
(C) $0 < x < 7$
(D) $5 < x < 15$
(E) $5 < x < 7$

6. Given three positive integers a, b, and 4, if their average (arithmetic mean) is 6, which of the following could *not* be the value of the product ab?

(A) 13
(B) 14
(C) 40
(D) 48
(E) 49

GO ON TO THE NEXT PAGE

7. If $mn \neq 0$, then $\frac{1}{n^2}\left(\frac{m^5n^3}{m^3}\right)^2 =$

(A) mn^4
(B) m^4n^2
(C) m^4n^3
(D) m^4n^4
(E) m^4n^5

8. From a party attended by 3 females and 3 males, 3 people at random enter a previously empty room. What is the probability that there are exactly 2 males in the room?

(A) $\frac{1}{4}$
(B) $\frac{3}{8}$
(C) $\frac{9}{20}$
(D) $\frac{2}{3}$
(E) $\frac{5}{6}$

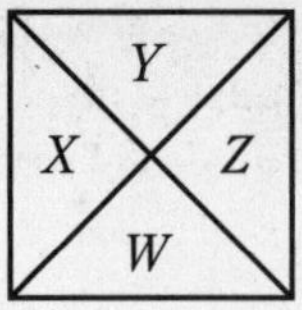

Question 9 refers to the figure above, where W, X, Y, and Z are four distinct digits from 0 to 9, inclusive, and $W + X + Y = 5Z$.

9. Under the given conditions, all of the following could be values of Z EXCEPT

(A) 1
(B) 2
(C) 3
(D) 4
(E) 5

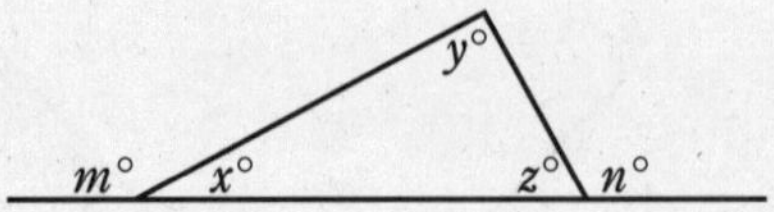

10. In the figure above, $m + n =$

(A) 90
(B) 180
(C) $180 + y$
(D) $90 + x + y + z$
(E) $2(x + y + z)$

GO ON TO THE NEXT PAGE

11. The volume of a cube is less than 25, and the length of one of its edges is a positive integer. What is the largest possible value for the total area of the six faces?

(A) 1
(B) 6
(C) 24
(D) 54
(E) 150

12. The ratio of females to males on a particular flight was 2 : 3. Females represented five more than $\frac{1}{3}$ of all the people aboard. How many people were on that flight?

(A) 15
(B) 25
(C) 30
(D) 45
(E) 75

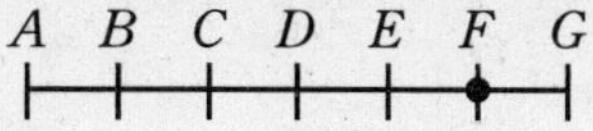

13. AG is divided into six equal segments in the figure above. A circle, not visible, with center F and radius $\frac{1}{5}$ the length of AG, will intersect AG between

(A) F and G
(B) E and F
(C) D and E
(D) C and D
(E) A and B

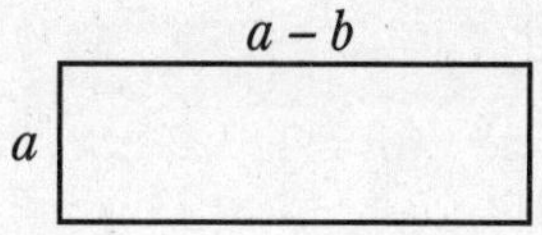

14. The figure above is a rectangle having width a and length $a - b$. Find its perimeter in terms of a and b.

(A) $a^2 - ab$
(B) $4a - 2b$
(C) $4a - b$
(D) $2a - 2b$
(E) $2a - b$

GO ON TO THE NEXT PAGE

$$\begin{array}{r} AB \\ +\,BA \\ \hline CDC \end{array}$$

15. If each of the four letters in the sum above represents a *different* digit, which of the following *cannot* be a value of A?

(A) 6
(B) 5
(C) 4
(D) 3
(E) 2

16. If $f(x) = x^2 + x$ and $g(y) = y^2$, then $f[g(-1)] =$

(A) 2
(B) −2
(C) 4
(D) −4
(E) −8

STOP

If you finish before time is called, you may check your work on this section only.
Do not turn to any other section in the test.

SECTION 9

Time: 20 Minutes—Turn to Section 9 (page 955) of your answer sheet to answer the questions in this section. 19 Questions

Directions: For each question in this section, select the best answer from among the choices given and fill in the corresponding circle on the answer sheet.

Each sentence below has one or two blanks, each blank indicating that something has been omitted. Beneath the sentence are five words or sets of words labeled A through E. Choose the word or set of words that, when inserted in the sentence, best fits the meaning of the sentence as a whole.

EXAMPLE:

Hoping to ________ the dispute, negotiators proposed a compromise that they felt would be ________ to both labor and management.

(A) enforce...useful
(B) end...divisive
(C) overcome...unattractive
(D) extend...satisfactory
(E) resolve...acceptable

Ⓐ Ⓑ Ⓒ Ⓓ ●

1. Joining ______ momentum for reform in intercollegiate sports, university presidents have called for swift steps to correct imbalances between classwork and ______ .

(A) a maximum...studies
(B) a rational...awards
(C) an increasing...athletics
(D) an exceptional...professors
(E) a futile...contests

2. Thinking nothing can be done, many victims of arthritis ignore or delay ______ countermeasures, thus aggravating the problem.

(A) tardy
(B) injurious
(C) characteristic
(D) weird
(E) effective

3. A strange and ________ fate seemed to keep him helpless and unhappy, despite occasional interludes of ________ .

(A) malevolent...conflict
(B) bizarre...disenchantment
(C) virulent...tension
(D) ineluctable...serenity
(E) intriguing...inactivity

4. Samuel Clemens chose the ________ Mark Twain as a result of his knowledge of riverboat piloting.

(A) protagonist
(B) pseudonym
(C) mountebank
(D) hallucination
(E) misanthrope

5. For years a vocalist of spirituals, Marian Anderson was finally recognized as ________ singer when the Metropolitan Opera House engaged her.

(A) a capable
(B) an unusual
(C) an attractive
(D) a cooperative
(E) a mediocre

6. Leonardo da Vinci ________ the law of gravity two centuries before Newton and also made the first complete ________ charts of the human body.

(A) examined...colorful
(B) anticipated...anatomical
(C) avoided...meaningful
(D) realized...explanatory
(E) suspected...mural

GO ON TO THE NEXT PAGE

The two passages below are followed by questions based on their content and on the relationship between the two passages. Answer the questions on the basis of what is stated or implied in the passages and in any introductory material that may be provided.

Questions 7–19 are based on the following passages.

The following two passages describe two views of the makeup and character of an artist.

Passage 1

The special quality which makes an artist of any worth might be defined, indeed, as an extraordinary capacity for irritation, a pathological sensitiveness to environmental pricks and stings. He differs from the rest of us mainly because he reacts sharply and in an uncommon manner to phenomena which leave the rest of us unmoved, or, at most, merely vaguely annoyed. He is, in brief, a more delicate fellow than we are and hence less fitted to prosper and enjoy himself under the conditions of life that he and we must face alike. Therefore, he takes to artistic endeavor, which is at once a criticism of life and an attempt to escape from life.

So much for the theory of it. The more the facts are studied, the more they bear it out. In those fields of art, at all events, which concern themselves with ideas as well as with sensations, it is almost impossible to find any trace of an artist who was not actively hostile to his environment and thus an indifferent patriot. From Dante to Tolstoy and from Shakespeare to Mark Twain, the story is ever the same. Names suggest themselves instantly: Goethe, Heine, Shelley, Byron, Thackeray, Balzac, Rabelais, Cervantes, Swift, Dostoevsky, Carlyle, Molière, Pope—all bitter critics of their time and nation, most of them piously hated by the contemporary 100 percenters, some of them actually fugitives from rage and reprisal.

Dante put all of the patriotic Italians of his day into Hell and showed them boiling, roasting, and writhing on hooks. Cervantes drew such a devastating picture of the Spain that he lived in that it ruined the Spaniards. Shakespeare made his heroes foreigners and his clowns Englishmen. Goethe was in favor of Napoleon. Rabelais, a citizen of Christendom rather than of France, raised a cackle against it that Christendom is still trying in vain to suppress. Swift, having finished the Irish and then the English, proceeded to finish the whole human race. The exceptions are few and far between, and not many of them will bear examination. So far as I know, the only eminent writer in English history who was also a 100% Englishman, absolutely beyond suspicion, was Samuel Johnson. But was Johnson actually an artist? If he was, then a kazoo player is a musician. He employed the materials of one of the arts, to wit, words, but his use of them was mechanical, not artistic. If Johnson were alive today, he would be a United States Senator, or a university president. He left such wounds upon English prose that it took a century to recover from them.

Passage 2

For the ease and pleasure of treading the old road, accepting the fashions, the education, the religion of society, he takes the cross of making his own and, of course, the self-accusation, the faint heart, the frequent uncertainty and loss of time, which are the nettles and tangling vines in the way of the self-relying and self-directed, and the state of virtual hostility in which he seems to stand to society, and especially to educated society. For all this loss and scorn, what offset? The artist is to find consolation in exercising the highest functions of human nature. The artist is one who raises himself from private consideration and breathes and lives on public and illustrious thoughts. The artist is the world's eye. He is the world's heart. He is to resist the vulgar prosperity that retrogrades ever to barbarism, by preserving and communicating heroic sentiments, noble biographies, melodious verse, and the conclusions of history. Whatsoever oracles the human heart, in all emergencies, in all solemn hours, has uttered as its commentary on the world of actions—these he shall receive and impart. And whatsoever new verdict Reason from her inviolable seat pronounces on the passing men and women and events of today—this he shall hear and promulgate.

These being his functions, it becomes the artist to feel all confidence in himself and to defer never to the popular cry. He and he alone knows the world. The world of any moment is the merest appearance. Some great decorum, some fetish of a government, some ephemeral trade, or war, or man, is cried up by half mankind and cried down by the other half, as if all depended on this particular up or down. The odds are that the whole question is not worth the poorest thought which the scholar has lost in listening to the controversy. Let her not quit her belief that a popgun is a popgun, though the ancient and honorable of the earth affirm it to be the crack of doom. In silence, in steadiness, in severe abstraction, let him hold by himself; add observation to observation, patient of neglect, patient of reproach, and bide his own time—happy enough if he can satisfy himself alone that this day he has seen something truly. Success treads on every right step. For the instinct is sure that prompts him to tell his brother what he thinks. The artist then learns that in going down into the secrets of his own mind he has descended into the secrets of all minds. He learns that the artist who has mastered any law in his private thoughts is master to that extent of all translated. The poet, in utter solitude remembering his spontaneous thoughts and recording them, is found to have recorded that which men in crowded cities find true for them also. The orator distrusts at first the fitness of his frank confessions, his want of knowledge of the persons he addresses, until he finds that he is the complement of his hearers—that they drink

GO ON TO THE NEXT PAGE

his words because he fulfills for them their own nature; the deeper he dives into his most private, most secret presentiment, to his wonder he finds this is the most acceptable, most public, and universally true. The people delight in it; the better part of every man feels. This is my music; this is myself.

7. Which of the following quotations is related most closely to the principal idea of Passage 1?

(A) "All nature is but art unknown to thee, All chance, direction which thou canst not see."
(B) "When to her share some human errors fall, Look on her face and you'll forget them all."
(C) "All human things are subject to decay, And, when fate summons, monarchs must obey."
(D) "A little learning is a dangerous thing, Drink deep or taste not the Pierian spring."
(E) "Great wits are sure to madness near allied, And thin partitions do their bounds divide."

8. The author of Passage 1 seems to regard the artist as

(A) the best representative of his time
(B) an unnecessary threat to the social order
(C) one who creates out of discontent
(D) one who truly knows how to enjoy life
(E) one who is touched with genius

9. It can be inferred that the author of Passage 1 believes that United States Senators and university presidents

(A) must be treated with respect because of their position
(B) are to be held in low esteem
(C) are generally appreciative of the great literary classics
(D) have native writing ability
(E) have the qualities of the artist

10. All of the following ideas about artists are mentioned in Passage 1 *except* that

(A) they are irritated by their surroundings
(B) they are escapists from reality
(C) they are lovers of beauty
(D) they are hated by their contemporaries
(E) they are critical of their times

11. Which of the following best describes the author's attitude toward artists in Passage 1?

(A) sharply critical
(B) sincerely sympathetic
(C) deeply resentful
(D) mildly annoyed
(E) completely delighted

12. It is a frequent criticism of the artist that he lives by himself, in an "ivory tower," remote from the problems and business of the world. Which of these below constitutes the best refutation by the writer of Passage 2 to the criticism here noted?

(A) The world's concerns being ephemeral, the artist does well to renounce them and the world.
(B) The artist lives in the past to interpret the present.
(C) The artist at his truest is the spokesman of the people.
(D) The artist is not concerned with the world's doings because he is not selfish and therefore not engrossed in matters of importance to himself and his neighbors.
(E) The artist's academic researches of today are the businessman's practical products of tomorrow.

13. The artist's road is rough, according to Passage 2. Which of these is the artist's greatest difficulty?

(A) The artist must renounce religion.
(B) The artist must pioneer new approaches.
(C) The artist must express scorn for and hostility toward society.
(D) The artist is uncertain of his course.
(E) There is a pleasure in the main-traveled roads in education, religion, and all social fashions.

14. When the writer of Passage 2 speaks of the "world's eye" and the "world's heart," he means

(A) the same thing
(B) culture and conscience
(C) culture and wisdom
(D) a scanning of all the world's geography and a deep sympathy for every living thing
(E) mind and love

15. By the phrase "nettles and tangling vines" (line 49), the author is probably referring to

(A) "self-accusation" and "loss of time"
(B) "faint heart" and "self-accusation"
(C) "the slings and arrows of outrageous fortune"
(D) a general term for the difficulties of a scholar's life
(E) "self-accusation" and "uncertainty"

GO ON TO THE NEXT PAGE

16. The various ideas in Passage 2 are best summarized in which of these groups?

I. truth versus society
the artist and books
the world and the artist

II. the ease of living traditionally
the glory of an artist's life
true knowledge versus trivia

III. the hardships of the scholar
the artist's functions
the artist's justifications for disregarding the world's business

(A) I and III only
(B) I only
(C) III only
(D) I, II, and III
(E) I and II only

17. In line 51, "seems to stand" means

(A) is
(B) ends probably in becoming
(C) gives the false impression of being
(D) is seen to be
(E) the quicksands of time

18. The difference between the description of the artist in Passage 1 as compared with the artist in Passage 2 is that

(A) one is loyal to his fellow men and women, whereas the other is opposed to his or her environment
(B) one is sensitive to his or her environment, whereas the other is apathetic
(C) one has political aspirations; the other does not
(D) one has deep knowledge; the other has superficial knowledge
(E) one could be proficient in a field other than art; the other could create only in his or her present field

19. Which of the following describes statements that refer to the *same* one artist (either the one in Passage 1 *or* the one in Passage 2)?

I. This artist's thoughts are also the spectator's thoughts.
This artist lives modestly and not luxuriously.

II. This artist admires foreigners over his own countrymen.
This artist reacts to many things that most people would be neutral to.

III. This artist is happy to be at his best.
This artist accepts society.

(A) I only
(B) II only
(C) III only
(D) I and III only
(E) I, II, and III

STOP

If you finish before time is called, you may check your work on this section only. Do not turn to any other section in the test.

SECTION 10

Time: 10 Minutes—Turn to Section 10 (page 955) of your answer sheet to answer the questions in this section.
14 Questions

Directions: For each question in this section, select the best answer from among the choices given and fill in the corresponding circle on the answer sheet.

The following sentences test correctness and effectiveness of expression. Part of each sentence or the entire sentence is underlined; beneath each sentence are five ways of phrasing the underlined material. Choice A repeats the original phrasing; the other four choices are different. If you think the original phrasing produces a better sentence than any of the alternatives, select Choice A; if not, select one of the other choices.

In making your selection, follow the requirements of standard written English; that is, pay attention to grammar, choice of words, sentence construction, and punctuation. Your selection should result in the most effective sentence—clear and precise, without awkwardness or ambiguity.

EXAMPLE:

Laura Ingalls Wilder published her first book and she was sixty-five years old then.

(A) and she was sixty-five years old then
(B) when she was sixty-five
(C) at age sixty-five years old
(D) upon the reaching of sixty-five years
(E) at the time when she was sixty-five

Ⓐ ● Ⓒ Ⓓ Ⓔ

1. He bought some bread, butter, cheese and decided not to eat them until the evening.

(A) some bread, butter, cheese and decided
(B) some bread, butter, cheese and then decided
(C) a little bread, butter, cheese and decided
(D) some bread, butter, cheese, deciding
(E) some bread, butter, and cheese and decided

2. The things the children liked best were swimming in the river and to watch the horses being groomed by the trainer.

(A) swimming in the river and to watch the horses being groomed by the trainer
(B) swimming in the river and to watch the trainer grooming the horses
(C) that they liked to swim in the river and watch the horses being groomed by the trainer
(D) swimming in the river and watching the horses being groomed by the trainer
(E) to swim in the river and watching the horses being groomed by the trainer

3. If an individual wishes to specialize in electrical engineering, they should take courses in trigonometry and calculus.

(A) they should take courses in trigonometry and calculus
(B) trigonometry and calculus is what he should take courses in
(C) trigonometry and calculus are what they should take courses in
(D) he or she should take courses in trigonometry and calculus
(E) take courses in trigonometry and calculus

4. If the dog will not eat its food, put it through the meat grinder once more.

(A) eat its food, put it through
(B) eat it's food, put it through
(C) eat its food, you should put it through
(D) eat food, put it through
(E) eat its food, put the food through

5. The bank agreed to lend Garcia the money, which made him very happy.

(A) Garcia the money, which made
(B) Garcia the money, a decision which made
(C) Garcia the money; this made
(D) Garcia the money, this making
(E) the money to Garcia and found

GO ON TO THE NEXT PAGE

6. Miami's daytime attire is less formal than New York.

(A) less formal than New York
(B) less formal then that in New York
(C) less formal than that in New York
(D) less formal than in New York
(E) less formal than the daytime attire we see in New York

7. As the fisherman explained that he wanted to hire a guide and row upstream in order to catch game fish.

(A) As the fisherman explained that he wanted to hire a guide and row
(B) The reason was as the fisherman explained that he wanted to hire a guide and row
(C) As the fisherman explained that he wanted to hire a guide and to row
(D) The fisherman explained that he wanted to hire a guide and row
(E) The fisherman explaining that he wanted to hire a guide and row

8. The speaker was praised for his organization, choice of subject, and because he was brief.

(A) for his organization, choice of subject, and because he was brief
(B) for his organization, his choice of subject and the speech having brevity
(C) on account of his organization and his choice of subject and the brevity of his speech
(D) for the organization of his speech, for his choice of subject, and because he was brief
(E) for his organization, his choice of subject, and his brevity

9. The fact that Charles did not receive a college scholarship disappointed his parents.

(A) The fact that Charles did not receive a college scholarship
(B) Because Charles did not receive a college scholarship was the reason he
(C) Being that Charles did not receive a college scholarship
(D) Charles not receiving a college scholarship
(E) Charles did not receive a college scholarship

10. The porch of a famous home collapsed during a party last week, which injured 23 people.

(A) which injured 23 people
(B) causing 23 people to be injured
(C) injuring 23 people
(D) damaging 23 people
(E) resulting in 23 people being injured

11. Jack's favorite summer supper includes barbecued chicken, grilled corn on the cob, sliced tomatoes, and he likes green salad.

(A) and he likes green salad
(B) in addition to green salad
(C) adding green salad
(D) including green salad
(E) and green salad

12. I want the best price I can get for my car.

(A) best price
(B) most highest price
(C) price which is the best
(D) most best price
(E) premium price

13. The injured man was taken to the hospital, where he was treated for facial lacerations and released.

(A) where he was treated for facial lacerations and released
(B) where he was treated and released for facial lacerations
(C) where his facial lacerations were treated and he was released from the hospital
(D) where his treatment was for facial lacerations and he was released from the hospital
(E) where he received facial lacerations treatment and was released

14. The wife of the new leader is tough, single-minded, and tries to be independent.

(A) tries to be independent
(B) acting in dependent
(C) independent
(D) an independent person
(E) an independent

STOP

If you finish before time is called, you may check your work on this section only. Do not turn to any other section in the test.

How Did You Do on This Test?

Step 1. Go to the Answer Key on pages 1004–1006.

Step 2. For your "raw score," calculate it using the directions on pages 1007–1008.

Step 3. Get your "scaled score" for the test by referring to the Raw Score/Scaled Score Conversion Tables on pages 1009–1011.

THERE'S ALWAYS ROOM FOR IMPROVEMENT!

Answer Key for Practice Test 5

Math

Section 2

	Correct Answer
1	C
2	E
3	C
4	D
5	D
6	B
7	D
8	D
9	B
10	A
11	C
12	D
13	A
14	E
15	A
16	E
17	C
18	B
19	D
20	A

____
Number correct

____
Number incorrect

Section 3

	Correct Answer
1	A
2	C
3	E
4	B
5	B
6	A
7	C
8	A
9	A
10	B
11	D
12	D
13	B
14	D
15	C
16	C
17	B
18	C
19	A
20	D

____
Number correct

____
Number incorrect

Section 6

	Correct Answer
1	E
2	A
3	B
4	D
5	E
6	B
7	A
8	D

____
Number correct

____
Number incorrect

Student-Produced Response Questions

9	7/18 or .388 or .389
10	8
11	2/3 or .667 or .666
12	60
13	36
14	44
15	1/4 or .25
16	60
17	10
18	48

____
Number correct

____
Number incorrect

Section 8

	Correct Answer
1	C
2	E
3	E
4	B
5	E
6	B
7	D
8	C
9	E
10	C
11	C
12	E
13	C
14	B
15	E
16	A

____
Number correct

____
Number incorrect

Critical Reading and Writing

Critical Reading

Section 4

	Correct Answer
1	E
2	C
3	B
4	A
5	B
6	B
7	B
8	B
9	D
10	A
11	B
12	E
13	B
14	E
15	A
16	E
17	C
18	D
19	D
20	A
21	C
22	C
23	C
24	D

Number correct

Number incorrect

Section 7

	Correct Answer
1	D
2	A
3	E
4	E
5	D
6	C
7	C
8	E
9	D
10	A
11	E
12	A
13	D
14	B
15	B
16	E
17	A
18	B
19	C
20	D
21	B
22	B
23	A
24	C

Number correct

Number incorrect

Section 9

	Correct Answer
1	C
2	E
3	D
4	B
5	A
6	B
7	E
8	C
9	B
10	C
11	B
12	C
13	B
14	C
15	E
16	C
17	C
18	A
19	E

Number correct

Number incorrect

Writing

Section 1

____

Essay score

Section 5

	Correct Answer
1	C
2	D
3	E
4	B
5	A
6	B
7	D
8	E
9	D
10	B
11	D
12	D
13	E
14	A
15	B
16	E
17	B
18	A
19	E
20	D
21	E
22	A
23	C
24	B
25	D
26	D
27	A
28	C
29	A
30	D
31	C
32	A
33	B
34	B
35	D

____

Number correct

____

Number incorrect

Section 10

	Correct Answer
1	E
2	D
3	D
4	E
5	B
6	C
7	D
8	E
9	A
10	C
11	E
12	A
13	A
14	C

____

Number correct

____

Number incorrect

Scoring the SAT Practice Test 5

Check your responses with the correct answers on the previous pages. Fill in the blanks below and do the calculations to get your Math, Critical Reading, and Writing raw scores. Use the table to find your Math, Critical Reading, and Writing scaled scores.

Get Your Math Score

How many Math questions did you get **right**?

Section 2: Questions 1–20 ________

Section 6: Questions 1–18 + ________

Section 8: Questions 1–16 + ________

Total = ________ **(A)**

How many Math questions did you get **wrong**?

Section 2: Questions 1–20 ________

Section 6: Questions 1–18 + ________

Section 8: Questions 1–16 + ________

Total = ________

× 0.25 = ________ **(B)**

A – B = ________

Math Raw Score

Round Math raw score to the nearest whole number.

____

Use the Score Conversion Table to find your Math scaled score.

____

Get Your Critical Reading Score

How many Critical Reading questions did you get **right**?

Section 4: Questions 1–24 ________

Section 7: Questions 1–24 + ________

Section 9: Questions 1–19 + ________

Total = ________ **(A)**

How many Critical Reading questions did you get **wrong**?

Section 4: Questions 1–24 ________

Section 7: Questions 1–24 + ________

Section 9: Questions 1–19 + ________

Total = ________

× 0.25 = ________ **(B)**

A – B = ________

Critical Reading Raw Score

Round Critical Reading raw score to the nearest whole number.

____

Use the Score Conversion Table to find your Critical Reading scaled score.

____

Get Your Writing Score

How many multiple-choice Writing questions did you get **right**?

Section 5: Questions 1–35 ________

Section 10: Questions 1–14 + ________

Total = ________ **(A)**

How many multiple-choice Writing questions did you get **wrong**?

Section 5: Questions 1–35 ________

Section 10: Questions 1–14 + ________

Total = ________

× 0.25 = ________ **(B)**

A – B = ________

Writing Raw Score

Round Writing raw score to the nearest whole number.

____

Use the Score Conversion Table to find your Writing multiple-choice scaled score.

____

Estimate your Essay score using the Essay Scoring Guide.

____

Use the SAT Score Conversion Table for Writing Composite to find your Writing scaled score. You will need your Writing raw score and your Essay score to use this table.

____

SAT Score Conversion Table

Raw Score	Critical Reading Scaled Score	Math Scaled Score	Writing Multiple-Choice Scaled Score*	Raw Score	Critical Reading Scaled Score	Math Scaled Score	Writing Multiple-Choice Scaled Score*
67	800			31	510	550	60
66	800			30	510	540	58
65	790			29	500	530	57
64	770			28	490	520	56
63	750			27	490	520	55
62	740			26	480	510	54
61	730			25	480	500	53
60	720			24	470	490	52
59	700			23	460	480	51
58	690			22	460	480	50
57	690			21	450	470	49
56	680			20	440	460	48
55	670			19	440	450	47
54	660	800		18	430	450	46
53	650	790		17	420	440	45
52	650	760		16	420	430	44
51	640	740		15	410	420	44
50	630	720		14	400	410	43
49	620	710	80	13	400	410	42
48	620	700	80	12	390	400	41
47	610	680	80	11	380	390	40
46	600	670	79	10	370	380	39
45	600	660	78	9	360	370	38
44	590	650	76	8	350	360	38
43	590	640	74	7	340	350	37
42	580	630	73	6	330	340	36
41	570	630	71	5	320	330	35
40	570	620	70	4	310	320	34
39	560	610	69	3	300	310	32
38	550	600	67	2	280	290	31
37	550	590	66	1	270	280	30
36	540	580	65	0	250	260	28
35	540	580	64	–1	230	240	27
34	530	570	63	–2	210	220	25
33	520	560	62	–3	200	200	23
32	520	550	61	–4 and below	200	200	20

This table is for use only with the test in this book.

* The Writing multiple-choice score is reported on a 20–80 scale. Use the SAT Score Conversion Table for Writing Composite for the total writing scaled score.

SAT Score Conversion Table for Writing Composite

Writing Multiple-Choice Raw Score	Essay Raw Score 0	1	2	3	4	5	6
–12	200	200	200	210	240	270	300
–11	200	200	200	210	240	270	300
–10	200	200	200	210	240	270	300
–9	200	200	200	210	240	270	300
–8	200	200	200	210	240	270	300
–7	200	200	200	210	240	270	300
–6	200	200	200	210	240	270	300
–5	200	200	200	210	240	270	300
–4	200	200	200	230	270	300	330
–3	200	210	230	250	290	320	350
–2	200	230	250	280	310	340	370
–1	210	240	260	290	320	360	380
0	230	260	280	300	340	370	400
1	240	270	290	320	350	380	410
2	250	280	300	330	360	390	420
3	260	290	310	340	370	400	430
4	270	300	320	350	380	410	440
5	280	310	330	360	390	420	450
6	290	320	340	360	400	430	460
7	290	330	340	370	410	440	470
8	300	330	350	380	410	450	470
9	310	340	360	390	420	450	480
10	320	350	370	390	430	460	490
11	320	360	370	400	440	470	500
12	330	360	380	410	440	470	500
13	340	370	390	420	450	480	510
14	350	380	390	420	460	490	520
15	350	380	400	430	460	500	530
16	360	390	410	440	470	500	530
17	370	400	420	440	480	510	540
18	380	410	420	450	490	520	550
19	380	410	430	460	490	530	560
20	390	420	440	470	500	530	560
21	400	430	450	480	510	540	570
22	410	440	460	480	520	550	580
23	420	450	470	490	530	560	590
24	420	460	470	500	540	570	600
25	430	460	480	510	540	580	610

Writing Multiple-Choice Raw Score	Essay Raw Score						
	0	1	2	3	4	5	6
26	440	470	490	520	550	590	610
27	450	480	500	530	560	590	620
28	460	490	510	540	570	600	630
29	470	500	520	550	580	610	640
30	480	510	530	560	590	620	650
31	490	520	540	560	600	630	660
32	500	530	550	570	610	640	670
33	510	540	550	580	620	650	680
34	510	550	560	590	630	660	690
35	520	560	570	600	640	670	700
36	530	560	580	610	650	680	710
37	540	570	590	620	660	690	720
38	550	580	600	630	670	700	730
39	560	600	610	640	680	710	740
40	580	610	620	650	690	720	750
41	590	620	640	660	700	730	760
42	600	630	650	680	710	740	770
43	610	640	660	690	720	750	780
44	620	660	670	700	740	770	800
45	640	670	690	720	750	780	800
46	650	690	700	730	770	800	800
47	670	700	720	750	780	800	800
48	680	720	730	760	800	800	800
49	680	720	730	760	800	800	800

Chart for Self-Appraisal Based on the Practice Test You Have Just Taken

The Chart for Self-Appraisal below tells you quickly where your SAT strengths and weaknesses lie. Check or circle the appropriate box in accordance with the number of your correct answers for each area of the Practice Test you have just taken.

	Writing (Multiple-choice)	*Sentence Completions*	*Reading Comprehension*	*Math Questions**
EXCELLENT	42–49	16–19	40–48	44–54
GOOD	37–41	13–15	35–39	32–43
FAIR	31–36	9–12	26–34	27–31
POOR	20–30	5–8	17–25	16–26
VERY POOR	0–19	0–4	0–16	0–15

* Sections 2, 6, 8 only.

Note: In our tests, we have chosen to have Section 3 as the experimental section. We have also chosen it to be a math section since we felt that students may need more practice in the math area than in the verbal area. Note that on the actual SAT you will take, the order of the sections can vary and you will not know which one is experimental, so it is wise to answer all sections and not to leave any section out.

SAT-I VERBAL AND MATH SCORE/PERCENTILE CONVERSION TABLE

Critical Reading and Writing

SAT scaled verbal score	Percentile rank
800	99.7+
790	99.5
740–780	99
700–730	97
670–690	95
640–660	91
610–630	85
580–600	77
550–570	68
510–540	57
480–500	46
440–470	32
410–430	21
380–400	13
340–370	6
300–330	2
230–290	1
200–220	0–0.5

Math

SAT scaled math score	Percentile rank
800	99.5+
770–790	99.5
720–760	99
670–710	97
640–660	94
610–630	89
590–600	84
560–580	77
530–550	68
510–520	59
480–500	48
450–470	37
430–440	26
390–420	16
350–380	8
310–340	2
210–300	0.5
200	0

Section 1—Essay

The following are guidelines for scoring the essay.

The SAT Scoring Guide

Score of 6	Score of 5	Score of 4
An essay in this category is *outstanding,* demonstrating *clear and consistent mastery,* although it may have a few minor errors. A typical essay	An essay in this category is *effective,* demonstrating *reasonably consistent mastery,* although it will have occasional errors or lapses in quality. A typical essay	An essay in this category is *competent,* demonstrating *adequate mastery,* although it will have lapses in quality. A typical essay
• effectively and insightfully develops a point of view on the issue and demonstrates outstanding critical thinking, using clearly appropriate examples, reasons, and other evidence to support its position	• effectively develops a point of view on the issue and demonstrates strong critical thinking, generally using appropriate examples, reasons, and other evidence to support its position	• develops a point of view on the issue and demonstrates competent critical thinking, using adequate examples, reasons, and other evidence to support its position
• is well organized and clearly focused, demonstrating clear coherence and smooth progression of ideas	• is well organized and focused, demonstrating coherence and progression of ideas	• is generally organized and focused, demonstrating some coherence and progression of ideas
• exhibits skillful use of language, using a varied, accurate, and apt vocabulary	• exhibits facility in the use of language, using appropriate vocabulary	• exhibits adequate but inconsistent facility in the use of language, using generally appropriate vocabulary
• demonstrates meaningful variety in sentence structure	• demonstrates variety in sentence structure	• demonstrates some variety in sentence structure
• is free of most errors in grammar, usage, and mechanics	• is generally free of most errors in grammar, usage, and mechanics	• has some errors in grammar, usage, and mechanics
Score of 3	**Score of 2**	**Score of 1**
An essay in this category is *inadequate,* but demonstrates *developing mastery,* and is marked by ONE OR MORE of the following weaknesses:	An essay in this category is *seriously limited,* demonstrating *little mastery,* and is flawed by ONE OR MORE of the following weaknesses:	An essay in this category is *fundamentally lacking,* demonstrating *very little* or *no mastery,* and is severely flawed by ONE OR MORE of the following weaknesses:
• develops a point of view on the issue, demonstrating some critical thinking, but may do so inconsistently or use inadequate examples, reasons, or other evidence to support its position	• develops a point of view on the issue that is vague or seriously limited, demonstrating weak critical thinking, providing inappropriate or insufficient examples, reasons, or other evidence to support its position	• develops no viable point of view on the issue, or provides little or no evidence to support its position
• is limited in its organization or focus, or may demonstrate some lapses in coherence or progression of ideas	• is poorly organized and/or focused, or demonstrates serious problems with coherence or progression of ideas	• is disorganized or unfocused, resulting in a disjointed or incoherent essay
• displays developing facility in the use of language, but sometimes uses weak vocabulary or inappropriate word choice	• displays very little facility in the use of language, using very limited vocabulary or incorrect word choice	• displays fundamental errors in vocabulary
• lacks variety or demonstrates problems in sentence structure	• demonstrates frequent problems in sentence structure	• demonstrates severe flaws in sentence structure
• contains an accumulation of errors in grammar, usage, and mechanics	• contains errors in grammar, usage, and mechanics so serious that meaning is somewhat obscured	• contains pervasive errors in grammar, usage, or mechanics that persistently interfere with meaning

Essays not written on the essay assignment will receive a score of zero.

Explanatory Answers for Practice Test 5

Section 2: Math

> As you read these solutions, you are advised to do two things if you answered the Math question incorrectly:
>
> **1.** When a specific Math Strategy is referred to in the solution, study that strategy, which you will find in "19 Math Strategies" (beginning on page 69).
>
> **2.** When the solution directs you to the "Complete Math Refresher" (beginning on page 167)—for example, Math Refresher 305—study the 305 Math principle to get a clear idea of the Math operation that was necessary for you to know in order to answer the question correctly.

1. Choice C is correct.

Given: $\begin{array}{r} 5\,9\,\Delta \\ -2\,9\,3 \\ \hline \square\,9\,7 \end{array}$ $\boxed{1}$

(Use Strategy 17: Use the given information effectively.)

From $\boxed{1}$ we see that $\Delta - 3 = 7$ $\boxed{2}$

From $\boxed{2}$ we get $\Delta = 10$ $\boxed{3}$

From $\boxed{1}$ and $\boxed{3}$ we get $\Delta = 0$ in $\boxed{1}$ and we had to borrow to get 10. Thus, we have

$$\begin{array}{r} 8 \\ 5\not{9}0 \\ -\ 293 \\ \hline \square 97 \end{array} \quad \boxed{4}$$

Calculating $\boxed{4}$, we get

$$\begin{array}{r} 8 \\ 5\not{9}0 \\ -\ 293 \\ \hline 297 \end{array}$$

We see that the digit represented by the $\square$ is 2.

(Math Refresher #406)

2. Choice E is correct.

Given: $\frac{a-b}{b} = \frac{1}{2}$ $\boxed{1}$

(Use Strategy 13: Find unknowns by multiplication.)

Multiply $\boxed{1}$ by $2b$. We have

$$2\not{b}\left(\frac{a-b}{\not{b}}\right) = \left(\frac{1}{\not{2}}\right)\not{2}b$$

$$2(a-b) = b$$

$$2a - 2b = b$$

$$2a = 3b \quad \boxed{2}$$

(Use Strategy 13: Find unknowns by division.)

Dividing $\boxed{2}$ by $2b$, we get

$$\frac{\cancel{2}a}{\cancel{2}b} = \frac{3\cancel{b}}{2\cancel{b}}$$

$$\frac{a}{b} = \frac{3}{2}$$

(Math Refresher #406)

3. Choice C is correct.

Number of pounds of force	Height object is raised
3	6 feet
6	12 feet
9	18 feet

$\boxed{1}$

(Use Strategy 2: Translate from words to algebra.)

We are given that:

$$\text{height raised} = c(\text{force exerted}) \quad \boxed{2}$$

Substituting the numbers from the first row of $\boxed{1}$ into $\boxed{2}$, we get

$$6 = c(3)$$
$$2 = c \quad \boxed{3}$$

Given: Height object is raised = 15 feet $\boxed{4}$

Substituting $\boxed{3}$ and $\boxed{4}$ into $\boxed{2}$, we have

$$15 = 2(\text{force exerted})$$
$$7\tfrac{1}{2} = \text{force exerted}$$

(Math Refresher #200 and #406)

4. Choice D is correct.

Given: $\frac{y}{3}, \frac{y}{4}, \frac{y}{7}$ are integers. $\boxed{1}$

(Use Strategy 17: Use the given information effectively.)

If all items in $\boxed{1}$ are integers, then 3, 4, and 7 divide y evenly (zero remainder). y must be a common multiple of 3, 4, and 7. Multiplying 3, 4, and 7, we get 84.

(Math Refresher #607)

5. Choice D is correct. **(Use Strategy 11: Use new definitions carefully.)**

We are told that the points are each 3 units apart, as indicated above. We are looking for all those points that are more than 19 units away from point P. By checking the diagram we find 5 such points (marked with arrow in diagram).

(Math Refresher #410a)

6. Choice B is correct.

Given:

$(a + 2, a - 2) = [a]$ for all integers a. $\boxed{1}$

We need to find (6,2) $\boxed{2}$

(Use Strategy 11: Use new definitions carefully.)

Using $\boxed{1}$ and $\boxed{2}$, we have

$$a + 2 = 6 \quad \text{and} \quad a - 2 = 2$$
$$a = 4 \qquad\qquad a = 4 \quad \boxed{3}$$

Using $\boxed{1}$, $\boxed{2}$, and $\boxed{3}$, we get

$$(6,2) = [4]$$

(Math Refresher #431 and #406)

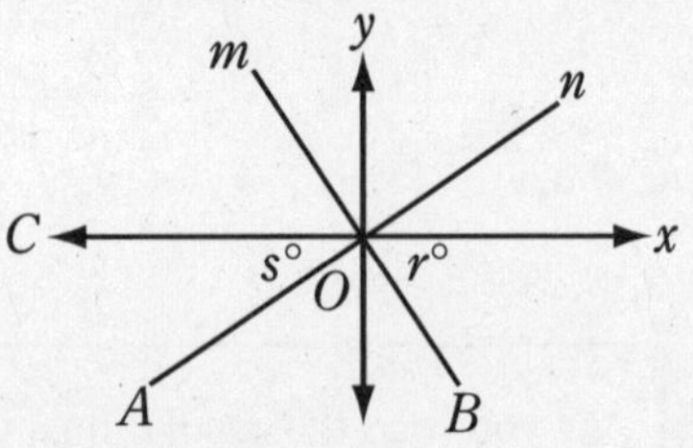

7. Choice D is correct.

Given: $mB \perp nA$ $\boxed{1}$

From $\boxed{1}$ we know that $\angle AOB$ is a right angle. Thus $\angle AOB = 90°$ $\boxed{2}$

From the diagram, we see that $\angle COx$ is a straight angle.

Thus $\angle COx = 180°$ $\boxed{3}$

(Use Strategy 3: The whole equals the sum of its parts.)

We know that

$\angle COA + \angle AOB + \angle BOx = \angle COx$ $\boxed{4}$

Given: $\angle COA = s°$ $\boxed{5}$

$\angle BOx = r°$ $\boxed{6}$

Substituting $\boxed{2}$, $\boxed{3}$, $\boxed{5}$, and $\boxed{6}$ into $\boxed{4}$, we get

$$s + 90 + r = 180$$
$$s + r = 90$$
$$r + s = 90$$

(Math Refresher #501, #511, and #406)

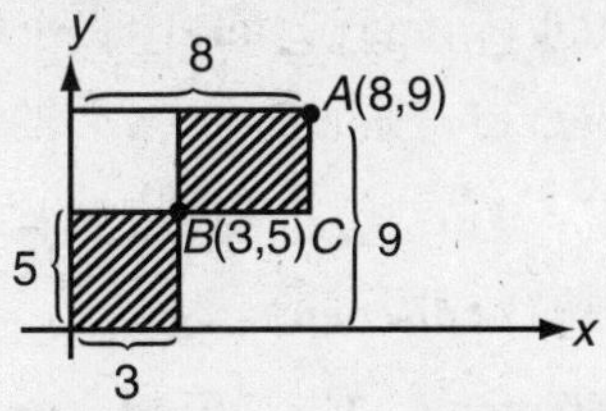

8. Choice D is correct. **(Use Strategy 17: Use the given information effectively.)**

From the given coordinates, we can find certain distances, as marked above.

Using these distances we find:

$BC = 8 - 3 = 5$ [1]
$AC = 9 - 5 = 4$ [2]

We know that area of a rectangle = length × width [3]

Using the diagram and [3], we have

Area of lower rectangle = $5 \times 3 = 15$ [4]

Substituting [1] and [2] into [3], we get

Area of upper rectangle = $5 \times 4 = 20$ [5]

(Use Strategy 13: Find unknowns by addition.)

Adding [4] and [5] together, we get

Total area = $15 + 20 = 35$

(Math Refresher #410 and #304)

9. Choice B is correct.

Given: Total number of students = 2,800 [1]

(Use Strategy 2: Translate from words to algebra.)

Number of German students $= \frac{1}{4} \times 2{,}800$

$= \frac{2{,}800}{4}$

$= 700$ [2]

(Use Strategy 13: Find unknown by subtraction.)

Subtracting [2] from [1], we get

Number of students not studying German = $2{,}800 - 700 = 2{,}100$

(Math Refresher #200 and #111)

10. Choice A is correct. **(Use Strategy 2: Translate from words to algebra.)**

Given: cost per vehicle = \$$y$ [1]
Let x = number of students paying \$0.40 [2]

Then $x + 6$ = number of students paying \$0.25 [3]

Using [1], [2], and [3],

We are told that: $x(\$0.40) = \$y$ [4]
$(x + 6)(\$0.25) = \$y$ [5]

From [4] and [5] we get

$$x(\$0.40) = (x + 6)(\$0.25)$$
$$.40x = .25x + 1.50$$
$$.15x = 1.50$$
$$x = 10 \quad [6]$$

Substitute [6] into [4]. We have

$$10(\$0.40) = \$y$$
$$\$4.00 = y$$
$$\$4 = y$$

(Math Refresher #200, #406, and #431)

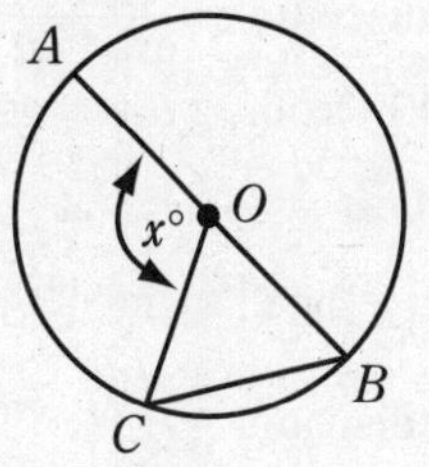

11. Choice C is correct.

Given: AB is a diameter [1]
O is the center of the circle [2]
$CB = OB$ [3]

Using [2], we know that OB and OC are radii [4]

From [4] we get that $OB = OC$. [5]

Using [3] and [5] together, we have

$OB = OC = CB$ [6]

(Use Strategy 18: Remember the equilateral triangle.)

From [6], we have ΔOBC is equilateral [7]

From [7], we get that $\angle B = \angle C = \angle COB = 60°$ [8]

From [1], we get $\angle AOB$ is a straight angle. [9]

From [9], we have $\angle AOB = 180°$ [10]

(Use Strategy 3: The whole equals the sum of its parts.)

From the diagram we see that:

$\angle AOC + \angle COB = \angle AOB$ [11]

Given: $\angle AOC = x°$ [12]

Substituting [8], [10], and [12] into [11], we get

$x + 60 = 180$

$x = 120$ [13]

(Use Strategy 13: Find unknowns by division.)

Divide [13] by 6. We have

$\frac{x}{6} = \frac{120}{6}$

$\frac{x}{6} = 20$

(Math Refresher #501, #508, #524, and #406)

12. Choice D is correct.

Given: Selling price of radio = \$64 [1]

Regular price of radio = \$80 [2]

(Use Strategy 2: Remember how to find percent discount.)

$\text{Percent discount} = \frac{\text{amount off}}{\text{original price}} \times 100$ [3]

Subtracting [1] from [2], we get

Amount off = \$80 − \$64 = \$16 [4]

Substituting [2] and [4] into [3], we have

$\text{Percent discount} = \frac{\$16}{\$80} \times 100$

$= \frac{\$16 \times 100}{\$80}$ [5]

(Use Strategy 19: Factor and reduce.)

$\text{Percent discount} = \frac{\cancel{\$16} \times \cancel{5} \times 20}{\cancel{\$16} \times \cancel{5}}$

Percent discount = 20 [6]

Given: Regular price of different radio = \$200 [7]

New percent discount

$= 1\frac{1}{2} \times$ Other radio's percent discount [8]

Using [6] and [8], we have

$\text{New percent discount} = 1\frac{1}{2} \times 20 =$

$= \frac{3}{2} \times 20$

$= 30$ [9]

(Use Strategy 2: Remember how to find percent of a number.)

Percent of a number = percent × number. [10]

Substituting [7] and [9] into [10], we have

Amount of discount = 30% × \$200

$= \frac{30}{100} \times \$200$

Amount of discount = \$60 [11]

(Use Strategy 13: Find unknowns by subtraction.)

Subtracting [11] from [7], we have

Selling price of different radio = \$200 − \$60

= \$140

(Math Refresher #200 and #114)

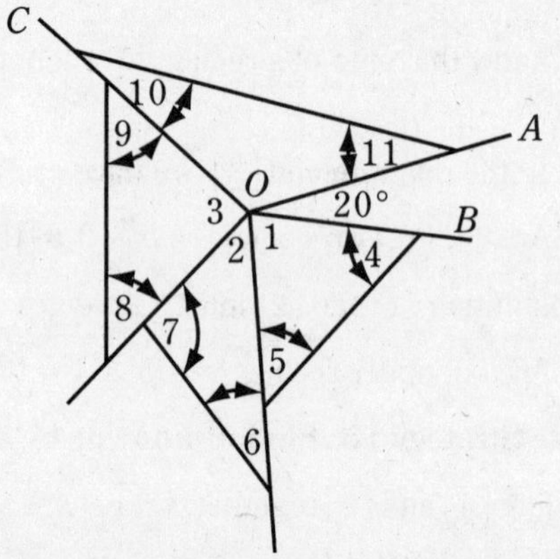

13. Choice A is correct.

Given: $\angle AOB = 20°$ [1]

(Use Strategy 3: The whole equals the sum of its parts.)

We know that the sum of the angles of a triangle = 180° [2]

For each of the four triangles, applying [2] yields:

$\angle 8 + \angle 9 + \angle 3 = 180$ [3]

$\angle 6 + \angle 7 + \angle 2 = 180$ [4]

$\angle 4 + \angle 5 + \angle 1 = 180$ [5]

$\angle 10 + \angle 11 + \angle COA = 180$ [6]

We know that the sum of all the angles about a point = 360° [7]

Applying [7] to point O, we have

$\angle 1 + \angle 2 + \angle 3 + \angle COA + \angle AOB = 360°$ [8]

Substituting [1] into [8], we get

$\angle 1 + \angle 2 + \angle 3 + \angle COA + 20 = 360$

$\angle 1 + \angle 2 + \angle 3 + \angle COA = 340$ [9]

(Use Strategy 13: Find unknowns by addition.)

Adding $\boxed{3}$, $\boxed{4}$, $\boxed{5}$, and $\boxed{6}$, we have

$$\angle 4 + \angle 5 + \angle 6 + \angle 7 + \angle 8 + \angle 9 + \angle 10 + \angle 11 + \angle 1 + \angle 2 + \angle 3 + \angle COA = 720° \quad \boxed{10}$$

(Use Strategy 13: Find unknowns by subtraction.)

Subtracting $\boxed{9}$ from $\boxed{10}$, we get

$$\angle 4 + \angle 5 + \angle 6 + \angle 7 + \angle 8 + \angle 9 + \angle 10 + \angle 11 = 380° \quad \boxed{11}$$

Thus, the sum of the marked angles = 380°

(Math Refresher #505 and #406)

14. Choice E is correct. **(Use Strategy 8: When all choices must be tested, start with choice E.)** If some of the integers in the set are odd, then not all are even. Note the other choices are not correct. For (D), all integers cannot be even since some are odd. For (C), since *some* integers are odd we cannot imply that all integers are odd. For (B), if an integer is even, it may not be in set X. Similarly for (A) if an integer is odd, it may not be in set X.

(Math Refresher #801 and #603)

15. Choice A is correct. **(Use Strategy 6: Know how to manipulate inequalities.)** Since the absolute value of $y + 3$ must be less than 3, y must be less than 0 but greater than -6.

(Math Refresher #615)

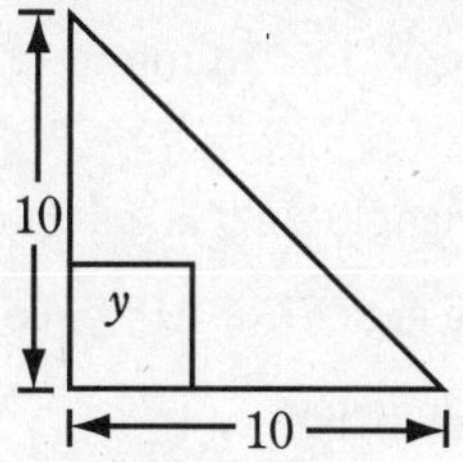

16. Choice E is correct.

We know that area of a triangle =

$$\frac{1}{2} \times \text{base} \times \text{height} \quad \boxed{1}$$

Using the diagram and substituting into $\boxed{1}$, we get

$$\text{Area of triangle} = \frac{1}{2} \times 10 \times 10$$
$$= 50 \quad \boxed{2}$$

(Use Strategy 2: Translate from words to algebra.)

We are told:

$$\text{Area of square} = \frac{1}{5} \times \text{area of triangle} \quad \boxed{3}$$

We know that

$$\text{Area of a square} = (\text{side})^2 \quad \boxed{4}$$

Using the diagram, and substituting into $\boxed{4}$, we get

$$\text{Area of square} = y^2 \quad \boxed{5}$$

Substituting $\boxed{2}$ and $\boxed{5}$ into $\boxed{3}$, we have

$$y^2 = \frac{1}{5} \times 50$$
$$y^2 = 10 \quad \boxed{6}$$

Take the square root of both sides of $\boxed{6}$. We get

$$y = \sqrt{10}$$

(Math Refresher #200, #303, #307, and #430)

17. Choice C is correct.

$$\text{Given:} \quad \text{Print rate} = \frac{80 \text{ characters}}{\text{second}} \quad \boxed{1}$$

$$\frac{\text{number of characters}}{\text{page}} = 2{,}400 \quad \boxed{2}$$

(Use Strategy 13: Find unknowns by division.)

Dividing $\boxed{2}$ by $\boxed{1}$, we have

$$\frac{2{,}400 \text{ characters}}{\text{page}} \div \frac{80 \text{ characters}}{\text{second}} =$$

$$\frac{2{,}400 \text{ characters}}{\text{page}} \times \frac{\text{second}}{80 \text{ characters}} =$$

$$\frac{2{,}400 \text{ seconds}}{80 \text{ pages}}$$

$$= \frac{30 \text{ seconds}}{\text{page}} \quad \boxed{3}$$

The time for an M-page report will be

$$\frac{30 \text{ seconds}}{\text{page}} \times M \text{ pages} =$$

$$\text{Time for } M\text{-page report} = 30M \text{ seconds} \quad \boxed{4}$$

(Use Strategy 10: Know how to use units.)

To change time from seconds to minutes, we multiply by

$$\frac{1 \text{ minute}}{60 \text{ seconds}} \quad \boxed{5}$$

Applying $\boxed{5}$ to $\boxed{4}$, we get

$$\text{Time for } M\text{-page report, in minutes} = 30M \text{ seconds} \times \frac{1 \text{ minute}}{60 \text{ seconds}}$$

$$= \frac{30M \text{ minutes}}{60}$$

$$= \frac{M}{2} \text{ minutes}$$

(Math Refresher #201 and #121)

18. Choice B is correct.

Given: On Friday, the satellite passed over Washington, D.C., at midnight $\boxed{1}$
Complete orbit = 5 hours $\boxed{2}$

(Use Strategy 17: Use the given information effectively.)

Using $\boxed{2}$, we see that five complete

orbits = $5 \times 5 = 25$ hours = 1 day + 1 hour $\boxed{3}$

From $\boxed{1}$ and $\boxed{2}$ we know that

DAY	TIME PASSING OVER D.C.	
Friday	7:00 P.M., midnight	$\boxed{4}$

Applying $\boxed{3}$ to $\boxed{4}$, and continuing this chart, we have

Saturday	8:00 P.M., 1:00 A.M.
Sunday	9:00 P.M., 2:00 A.M.
Monday	10:00 P.M., 3:00 A.M.
Tuesday	11:00 P.M., 4:00 A.M.
Wednesday	midnight, 5:00 A.M.

19. Choice D is correct. **(Use Strategy 2: Know how to find percent of a number.)**

Let x = price of car $\boxed{1}$

Given: 1st reduction = 30% $\boxed{2}$

2nd reduction = 40% $\boxed{3}$

We know that the amount of discount = percent × price $\boxed{4}$

Using $\boxed{1}$, $\boxed{2}$, and $\boxed{4}$, we get

Amount of 1st discount = $30\% \times x$
$= .30x$ $\boxed{5}$

(Use Strategy 13: Find unknowns by subtraction.) Subtracting $\boxed{5}$ from $\boxed{1}$, we have

Reduced price = $x - .30x$

$= .70x$ $\boxed{6}$

Using $\boxed{3}$, $\boxed{6}$, and $\boxed{4}$, we get

Amount of 2nd discount = $40\% \times .70x$

$= .40 \times .70x$

$= .28x$ $\boxed{7}$

Subtracting $\boxed{7}$ from $\boxed{6}$, we have

Price after 2nd reduction = $.70x - .28x$

$= .42x$ $\boxed{8}$

(Use Strategy 16: The obvious may be tricky!)

Since $\boxed{8} = .42x$, it is 42% of the original price of x. This is *not* the answer to the question.

Since $\boxed{8}$ is 42% of the original, it is the result of a 58% discount.

The answer is 58%.

(Math Refresher #200 and #114)

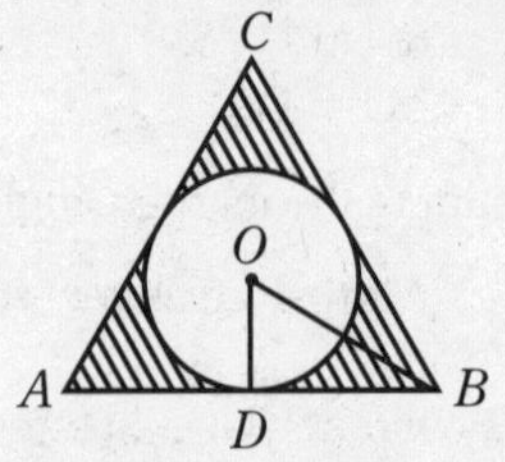

20. Choice A is correct. **(Use Strategy 3: Know how to find unknown quantities from known quantities.)**

The total shaded area = area of triangle ABC − area of the circle.

Given: Diameter of circle = 2 $\boxed{1}$

The radius, r, of the circle = 1. Thus the area of the circle is $\pi r^2 = \pi(1) = \pi$. $\boxed{2}$

Now we have to find the area of the equilateral triangle.

(Use Strategy 14: Draw lines to help find the answer.)

Draw radius OD, with D the point of tangency and OB as shown above. $\boxed{3}$

(Use Strategy 18: Remember the equilateral triangle.)

Given: Triangle ACB is equilateral $\boxed{4}$

From $\boxed{3}$ we get $OD \perp AB$, since radius $\perp$ tangent at point of tangency. $\boxed{5}$

From $\boxed{5}$, we get $\angle ODB = 90°$ $\boxed{6}$

From $\boxed{4}$, we get $\angle ABC = 60°$ $\boxed{7}$

From the geometry of regular polygons, we know that OB bisects $\angle ABC$. $\boxed{8}$

From $\boxed{7}$ and $\boxed{8}$ we get $\angle DBO = 30°$ $\boxed{9}$

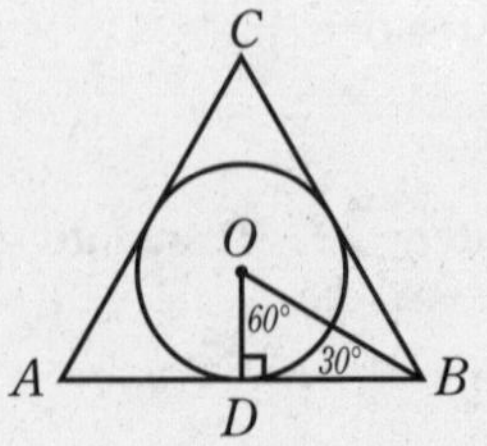

From [6] and [9], we have

ΔODB is a 30–60–90 triangle

From [1], we get $OD = 1$ [10]

(Use Strategy 18: Remember the special right triangles.)

Using [10] and the properties of the 30–60–90 right triangle, we get $OB = 2$, $DB = 1\sqrt{3} = \sqrt{3}$ [11]

We know $AB = 2 \times DB$ [12]

Substituting [11] into [12], we have

$$AB = 2\sqrt{3}$$ [13]

Let CD, the altitude of triangle ABC, be h.

The area of triangle ABC =

$\frac{1}{2}(CD \times AB) = \frac{1}{2}(h \times 2\sqrt{3}) = h\sqrt{3}$

Now $AD = \sqrt{3}$ and $AC = 2\sqrt{3}$.

By the Pythagorean Theorem,

$(2\sqrt{3})^2 - (\sqrt{3})^2 = h^2$

$(4 \times 3) - 3 = h^2$

$9 = h^2$

$3 = h$

So the area of the triangle $= 3\sqrt{3}$ [14]

(Use Strategy 13: Find unknowns by subtraction.)

Subtracting [2] from [14], we get

Shaded area $= 3\sqrt{3} - \pi$

(Math Refresher #308, #310, #508, #524, #525, and #509)

Explanatory Answers for Practice Test 5 (continued)

Section 3: Math

As you read these solutions, you are advised to do two things if you answered the Math question incorrectly:

1. When a specific Math Strategy is referred to in the solution, study that strategy, which you will find in "19 Math Strategies" (beginning on page 69).
2. When the solution directs you to the "Complete Math Refresher" (beginning on page 167)—for example, Math Refresher 305—study the 305 Math principle to get a clear idea of the Math operation that was necessary for you to know in order to answer the question correctly.

1. Choice A is correct. **(Use Strategy 2: Translate from words to algebra.)**

   Let x = Amount that Greg had to start.
   Then $x + 5$ = Amount that Greg has after receiving \$5 from David. [1]

   \$25 = Amount David has. [2]

   We are told that Greg now has $\frac{1}{5}$ as much as David does.

   This translates to:

   $$\text{Greg} = \frac{1}{5}(\text{David}) \quad \boxed{3}$$

   Substituting [1] and [2] into [3], we get

   $$x + 5 = \frac{1}{5}(25)$$
   $$x + 5 = \frac{1}{5} \times 5 \times 5$$
   $$x + 5 = 5$$
   $$x = 0$$

   (Math Refresher #200 and #406)

2. Choice C is correct. **(Use Strategy 17: Use the given information effectively.)**
   The ratio of the perimeter of the larger square to that of the smaller is

   $$\frac{6+6+6+6}{2+2+2+2} = \frac{24}{8} = \frac{3}{1} \text{ or } 3:1$$

   One can arrive at this result directly if one remembers that the ratio of the perimeters of two squares is the same as the ratio of the lengths of the sides of the two squares.

   (Math Refresher #303)

3. Choice E is correct. **(Use Strategy 9: Remember the rate, time, and distance relationship.)**
   Remember that rate × time = distance

   or $$\text{average rate} = \frac{\text{total distance}}{\text{total time}}$$

   or $$\text{average rate} = \frac{1{,}056 \text{ feet}}{12 \text{ seconds}}$$
   $$= 88 \text{ feet/second}$$

   (Math Refresher #201 and #202)

4. Choice B is correct.

Given: $2z + 1 + 2 + 2z + 3 + 2z = 3 + 1 + 2$

(Use Strategy 1: Cancel numbers from both sides of an equation.)

We can immediately cancel the +1, +2, and +3 from each side. We get

$$2z + 2z + 2z = 0$$
$$6z = 0$$
$$z = 0$$

Thus, $z + 4 = 0 + 4 = 4$

(Math Refresher #406 and #431)

5. Choice B is correct.

$$2(w)(x)(-y) - 2(-w)(-x)(y) =$$
$$-2wxy - 2wxy =$$
$$-4wxy$$

(Math Refresher #406)

6. Choice A is correct. **(Use Strategy 2: Translate from words to algebra.)**

The sum of $\underbrace{\text{the square of } x}_{x^2}$ and $\underbrace{\text{the square of } y}_{y^2}$ ($x^2 + y^2$)

So, five times that quantity is

$$5(x^2 + y^2)$$

(Math Refresher #200)

7. Choice C is correct. **(Use Strategy 2: Translate from words to algebra.)** We are given

$p > 0$ [1]

$q > 0$ [2]

$x < 0$ [3]

$y < 0$ [4]

(Use Strategy 6: Know how to manipulate inequalities.)

$p > q$ or $q < p$ [5]

$x > y$ or $y < x$ [6]

For I: Add $-p$ to both sides of inequality [5]:

$$q - p < 0$$

Thus, I is less than zero.

For II: From inequalities [2] and [4], $qy < 0$, and II is less than zero.

For III: The value of p and x depends on specific values of p and x.

(Use Strategy 7: Use numerics to help decide the answer.)

EXAMPLE 1

$p = 3$ and $x = -5$

Thus, $p + x < 0$

EXAMPLE 2

$p = 5$ and $x = -3$

Thus, $p + x > 0$

Thus, III is not always less than zero. Choice C is correct.

(Math Refresher #420, #421, and #431)

8. Choice A is correct.

Given: $a = 1, b = -2, c = -2$ [1]

$\dfrac{b^2c}{(a-c)^2}$ [2]

Substitute [1] into [2]. We get

$$\frac{(-2)^2(-2)}{(1-(-2))^2} =$$
$$\frac{4(-2)}{(3)^2} =$$
$$\frac{-8}{9}$$

(Math Refresher #429 and #431)

9. Choice A is correct.

Given: $y = 28j$ [1]

j is any integer [2]

(Use Strategy 13: Find unknowns by division.)

Divide [1] by 2. We have

$$\frac{y}{2} = \frac{28j}{2}$$

$\dfrac{y}{2} = 14j$ [3]

(Use Strategy 19: Factor.)

Factor the 14 in [3]. We get

$\dfrac{y}{2} = (2)(7)(j)$ [4]

Using [2] and [4], we see that $\frac{y}{2}$ is an integer with a factor of 2.

Thus, $\frac{y}{2}$ is even.

(Math Refresher #603 and #605)

10. Choice B is correct.

$$\text{Given: } 3a + 4b = 4a - 4b = 21 \quad \boxed{1}$$

From $\boxed{1}$, we get

$$3a + 4b = 21 \quad \boxed{2}$$
$$4a - 4b = 21 \quad \boxed{3}$$

(Use Strategy 13: Find unknowns by addition.)

Add $\boxed{2}$ and $\boxed{3}$ together. We get

$$\begin{aligned} 3a + \cancel{4b} &= 21 \\ +\ 4a - \cancel{4b} &= 21 \\ \hline 7a \quad &= 42 \\ a \quad &= 6 \end{aligned}$$

(Math Refresher #407)

11. Choice D is correct. **(Use Strategy 2: Translate from words to algebra.)**

$$N + 6N + 9N = 16N$$

Any divisor of 16 or of N will divide $16N$.

(Use Strategy 8: When all choices must be tested, start with Choice E and work backward.) Starting with Choice E, we see that 16 divides $16N$ evenly. Choice D, however, does *not* divide $16N$ evenly. Thus we have found the answer.

(Math Refresher #200 and #431)

12. Choice D is correct.

$$\text{We are given: } x = 3a - 18 \quad \boxed{1}$$
$$5y = 3a + 7 \quad \boxed{2}$$

We need $5y - x$. $\boxed{3}$

(Use Strategy 13: Find unknown expressions by subtracting equations.) Subtracting $\boxed{1}$ from $\boxed{2}$, we get

$$\begin{aligned} 5y - x &= 3a + 7 - (3a - 18) \\ &= 3a + 7 - 3a + 18 \\ 5y - x &= 25 \end{aligned}$$

(Math Refresher #406)

13. Choice B is correct. **(Use Strategy 2: Translate from words to algebra.)**

Given:

$$p + pq = 4(p - pq) \quad \boxed{1}$$

(Use Strategy 13: Find unknown expressions by division.) Since $pq \neq 0$, divide $\boxed{1}$ by p.

$$1 + q = 4(1 - q) \quad \boxed{2}$$
$$\text{or } 1 + q = 4 - 4q$$
$$\text{or } 5q = 3$$
$$\text{or } q = \frac{3}{5}$$

Thus, q has exactly one value.

Since p cannot be determined from equation $\boxed{1}$, none of the other choices is correct.

(Math Refresher #406)

14. Choice D is correct. **(Use Strategy 17: Use the given information effectively.)**

Since $2 + \frac{1}{z} = 0$, we have

$$\frac{1}{z} = -2$$
$$z = -\frac{1}{2} \quad \boxed{1}$$

We need $9 + 9z$. $\boxed{2}$

Substituting $\boxed{1}$ into $\boxed{2}$, we get

$$9 + 9\left(-\frac{1}{2}\right) = 9 - 4\frac{1}{2} = 4\frac{1}{2} = \frac{9}{2}$$

(Math Refresher #406 and #431)

15. Choice C is correct. **(Use Strategy 17: Use the given information effectively.)** We set $y = x^2 = x$.
$x = 1$ or $x = 0$
Thus they intersect twice.

(Math Refresher #417)

16. Choice C is correct.

$$\text{We are given: } wx = y \quad \boxed{1}$$
$$\text{or } w = \frac{y}{x} \quad \boxed{2}$$

(Use Strategy 2: Translate from words to algebra.) If x and y are multiplied by 6, in $\boxed{1}$, we have

$$w(\cancel{6})(x) = (\cancel{6})(y)$$
$$wx = y$$
$$w = \frac{y}{x} \quad \boxed{3}$$

$\boxed{2}$ and $\boxed{3}$ are the same.

$$\text{Therefore } \frac{y}{x} = 1\left(\frac{y}{x}\right)$$

The answer is now clear.

(Math Refresher #200 and #406)

17. Choice B is correct. **(Use Strategy 3: The whole equals the sum of its parts.)** The path is made up of 4 semicircles, three of diameter 4 and one of diameter 8.

Diameter (d) = 2 × radius (r) or $r = \frac{d}{2}$. Remember circumference is $2\pi r$. Thus,

$\frac{1}{2}$ circumference $= \frac{1}{2}(2\pi r)$.

Therefore, the length of the path is

$$\frac{1}{2}(2\pi)\left(\frac{4}{2}\right) + \frac{1}{2}(2\pi)\left(\frac{4}{2}\right) + \frac{1}{2}(2\pi)\left(\frac{4}{2}\right) + \frac{1}{2}(2\pi)\left(\frac{8}{2}\right)$$
$$= 10\pi$$

(Math Refresher #310 and #311)

18. Choice C is correct. **(Use Strategy 10: Know how to use units.)**

$$\frac{7x}{144}\text{ yards} = \left(\frac{7x}{144}\text{ yards}\right)\left(\frac{36\text{ inches}}{\text{yards}}\right) =$$

(Use Strategy 19: Factor and reduce.)

$$= \frac{7x}{\cancel{12} \times 12} \times \cancel{12} \times 3\text{ inches}$$

$$= \frac{7x}{\cancel{3} \times 4} \times \cancel{3}\text{ inches}$$

$$\frac{7x}{144}\text{ yards} = \frac{7x}{4}\text{ inches} \quad \boxed{1}$$

$$\frac{5y}{12}\text{ feet} = \left(\frac{5y}{\cancel{12}}\cancel{\text{feet}}\right)\left(\cancel{12}\frac{\text{inches}}{\cancel{\text{foot}}}\right) =$$

$$\frac{5y}{12}\text{ feet} = 5y\text{ inches} \quad \boxed{2}$$

(Use Strategy 13: Find unknown expressions by addition of equations.) Adding $\boxed{1}$ and $\boxed{2}$, we have

$$\frac{7x}{144}\text{ yards} + \frac{5y}{12}\text{ feet} = \left(\frac{7x}{4} + 5y\right)\text{ inches}$$

(Math Refresher #121 and #431)

19. Choice A is correct.

Given: $x < 0$ $\boxed{1}$

$y < 0$ $\boxed{2}$

(Use Strategy 6: Know how to manipulate inequalities.)

Multiplying $\boxed{1}$ by $\boxed{2}$, we get

$$x \cdot y > 0 \quad \boxed{3}$$

Thus I is always positive.

Adding $\boxed{1}$ and $\boxed{2}$, we get

$$x + y < 0 \quad \boxed{4}$$

Thus II is not positive.

(Use Strategy 7: Use numerics to help find the answer.)

Let $x = -2, y = -3$

III becomes $x - y = -2 - (-3)$

$= -2 + 3$

$= 1$ $\boxed{5}$

Now let $x = -3, y = -2$

III becomes $x - y = -3 - (-2)$

$= -3 + 2$

$= -1$ $\boxed{6}$

From $\boxed{5}$ and $\boxed{6}$, we see that III is not always positive.

Using $\boxed{3}$, $\boxed{4}$, and $\boxed{6}$, we find that only Choice A, I only, is correct.

(Math Refresher #419, #420, and #424)

20. Choice D is correct.

Given: $a + 3b = 11$ $\boxed{1}$

a and b are positive integers $\boxed{2}$

(Use Strategy 17: Use the given information effectively.)

From $\boxed{1}$, we get

$$a = 11 - 3b \quad \boxed{3}$$

From $\boxed{3}$, we see that a will be largest when b is smallest. Using $\boxed{2}$, we get

$$b = 1 \text{ is its smallest value} \quad \boxed{4}$$

Substituting $\boxed{4}$ into $\boxed{3}$, we have

$a = 11 - 3(1)$

$a = 11 - 3$

$a = 8$

(Math Refresher #406)

Explanatory Answers for Practice Test 5 (continued)

Section 4: Critical Reading

As you read these Explanatory Answers, refer to "16 Verbal (Critical Reading) Strategies" (beginning on page 119) whenever a specific strategy is referred to in the answer. Of particular importance are the following Master Verbal Strategies:

Sentence Completion Master Strategy 1—page 120.
Sentence Completion Master Strategy 2—page 121.
Reading Comprehension Master Strategy 2—page 138.

Note: All Reading questions use Reading Comprehension Strategies 1, 2, and 3 (pages 135–140) as well as other strategies indicated.

1. Choice E is correct. See **Sentence Completion Strategy 2.** Examine the first word of each choice. Choice A, committees, and Choice B, tribes, are incorrect because it is clear that committees and tribes cannot be equated with cities such as Athens. Now consider the other choices. Choice E, societies...participated, is the only choice with a word pair that makes sense in the sentence.

2. Choice C is correct. See **Sentence Completion Strategy 2.** Examine the first word of each choice. Choice A, abolished, and Choice E, discounted, do not make sense because we cannot say that fossils are abolished or discounted in rock formations. Now consider the other choices. Choice C, preserved...hardened, is the only choice with a word pair that makes sense in the sentence.

3. Choice B is correct. See **Sentence Completion Strategy 2.** Examine the first word of each choice. We eliminate Choice A, dominated, and Choice D, cautioned, because the trends do *not* dominate or caution affluence. Now consider the other choices. Choice C, accentuated...depression, and Choice E, accepted...revolution, do *not* make sense in the sentence. Choice B, reflected...prosperity, *does* make sense in the sentence.

4. Choice A is correct. See **Sentence Completion Strategy 1.** The word "conserve" (meaning "to protect from loss") completes the sentence so that it makes good sense. The other choices don't do that.

5. Choice B is correct. See **Sentence Completion Strategy 1.** The word "prevalent" (meaning widely or commonly occurring) completed the sentence so that it makes good sense. The other choices don't do that.

6. Choice B is correct. Since this question has two blanks, let us use **Sentence Completion Strategy 2.** When we use Step 1 of Strategy 2, we find a very unusual situation in this question—the first words in all five choices make sense: "With lack of" *advice* or *control* or *opportunity* or *sympathy* or *conscience*,

"anyone can develop the disease of alcoholism..." Accordingly, we must go to Step 2 of Strategy 2 and consider *both* words of each choice. When we do so, we find that only Choice B, control...foolishly, makes good sense in the sentence.

7. Choice B is correct. See **Sentence Completion Strategy 4.** "Because" is a *result indicator*. Since the generating system was not functioning efficiently, the use of electricity had to be *diminished* or *curtailed*.

8. Choice B is correct. See **Sentence Completion Strategy 1.** Something staple, such as bread, is in constant supply and demand. Beer, then, is considered a liquid bread by the Bavarians. Choices A, C, D, and E do not make good sense in the sentence.

9. Choice D is correct. One can see from the gist of the whole passage that the author is warning the reader of the dangers of anarchy and war. See line 4, "It is the age of war," and line 5, which speaks of the need for "the age of civilized man." Thus Choice D would be best.

10. Choice A is correct. See line 10 where the author says that "It calls for total awareness, total commitment," indicating limited hope.

11. Choice B is correct. It can be seen that the author contrasts novel reading in the past with novel reading in the present throughout the passage. Although the author does mention a "defect in today's novels" (Choice A), that is not the main consideration in the passage.

12. Choice E is correct. See lines 2–6: "there were few diversions...not irritated by the digressions and irrelevances..." Do not be lured into Choice B: Although some great novels are long, not all are.

13. Choice B is correct. See lines 26–29: "Most social scientists...have assumed that the minimum economic needs of the aged should be lower than those of the younger family."

14. Choice E is correct. Choice A does not make sense because artistic interest has nothing to do with the relationship between age and income. Choices C and D do not make sense because theories cannot casually have curiosity or gratitude. Of the remaining choices, Choice (E) understood is the only one that makes sense in the sentence. See also **Reading Comprehension Strategy 5.**

15. Choice A is correct. See lines 79–82: "[The data] disclose sharp income inequalities within every age group..."

16. Choice E is correct. For I, see lines 100–101: "...those sixty-five and over are expected to increase 672 percent." For III, see lines 54–58: "For the growing working-class family, limited in income by the very nature of the breadwinner's occupation..."

17. Choice C is correct. See lines 26–29: The sentence after the "functional ethos" sentence refers to "these values." See also **Reading Comprehension Strategy 5.**

18. Choice D is correct. See lines 104–107: "With the more rapid expansion of these two low-income groups, the young and the old..."

19. Choice D is correct. For I, see lines 83–85: "A spending unit's income-tenth position *within his age category* varies much less, if at all, and is determined primarily by his occupation." For III, see lines 54–58: "For the growing, working-class family, limited in income by the very nature of the breadwinner's occupation..."

20. Choice A is correct. Notice that "ethos" sounds a lot like "ethics," which has to do with moral principles, or character. See also **Reading Comprehension Strategy 5 and Vocabulary Strategy 3.**

21. Choice C is correct. See lines 40–43: "Despite his seniority, the older worker is likely to be downgraded to a lower-paying job..."

22. Choice C is correct. See lines 45–48: "The early and lower income period of a person's working life, during which he acquires his basic vocational skills..."

23. Choice C is correct. See lines 83–85: "A spending unit's income-tenth position is...determined primarily by his occupation."

24. Choice D is correct. The phrase "the legendary land of economic opportunity where any man can work his way to the top" (lines 86–88), in contrast to what the author really believes, represents *sarcasm*.

Explanatory Answers for Practice Test 5 (continued)

Section 5: Writing

For further practice and information, please refer to Grammar and Usage Refresher starting on page 455.

1. (C) Choice A is awkward and wordy. Choice B is indirect. Choice C is correct. Choice D is unacceptable idiomatically even though the meaning intended is there. Choice E changes the meaning of the original sentence.

2. (D) Choice A has incorrect punctuation. A dash (not a comma) is required after "that's not all." In Choice B, the expression "another thing" is too general. Choice C changes the meaning of the original sentence. Choice D is correct. Choice E is too indirectly expressed.

3. (E) Choice A suffers from too many "ands" (anditis). Choices B and C are incorrect because they lack parallel construction. In Choice D, the correct form of the infinitive meaning "to rest" is "(to) lie"—not "(to) lay." Choice E is correct.

4. (B) Choice A is awkward. Choice B is correct. Choice C is ungrammatical—"courses" cannot act as a direct object after the copulative construction "am not certain." Choice D is too wordy. Choice E does not make sense.

5. (A) Choice A is correct. Choice B is too indirectly stated. Choice C is verbose—since the people "had no doubt," there is no need to use the expression "it was clear." Choice D is indirect and awkward. Choice E changes the meaning of the original sentence.

6. (B) Choice A is too wordy. Choice B is correct. Choice C is indirectly stated. Choices D and E change the meaning of the original sentence.

7. (D) Choice A is indirectly stated. Choice B deviates from the original statement. Choice C makes the sentence a run-on. Choice D is correct. Choice E changes the meaning of the original sentence.

8. (E) Choice A is awkward. Choice B has a meaning which differs from that of the original sentence. Choices C and D are unidiomatic. Choice E is correct.

9. (D) The clause "that was rotten" is misplaced in Choices A, B, and C. Choice D is correct. Choice E is incorrect because the passive use of the verb is not as effective as the active use, in this context.

10. (B) Choice A uses the wrong tense sequence. Since the reading of the book took place before the watching of the picture, the reading should be expressed in the past perfect tense, which shows action prior to the simple past tense. Choice B corrects the error with the use of the past perfect tense, "had read," instead of the past tense, "read." Choices C, D, and E do not correct the mistake, and Choice E also changes the meaning.

11. **(D)** Choice A is wrong because the word "them," being plural, cannot properly take the singular antecedent, "anyone." Choices B and C do not correct this error. Choice D corrects it by substituting "to him or to her" for "to them." Choice E, while correcting the error, changes the meaning of the sentence.

12. **(D)** "...between *him* and *me*." The object of the preposition *between* must be an objective case form (*me*—not *I*).

13. **(E)** All underlined parts are correct.

14. **(A)** "The subject...was *we*..." The predicate nominative form is *we*—not *us*.

15. **(B)** "...the prize would go to him..." The object of the preposition *to* must be an objective case form (*him*—not he).

16. **(E)** All underlined parts are correct.

17. **(B)** "...if you *had gone to him*..." In the "if" clause of a past contrary-to-fact condition, one must use the past perfect subjunctive form *had gone*—not the future perfect subjunctive form *would have gone*.

18. **(A)** "The *child's* asking..." A noun or pronoun that precedes a gerund is in the possessive case. We, therefore, say *child's asking*—not *child asking*.

19. **(E)** All underlined parts are correct.

20. **(D)** "...who are younger than *she*." The nominative case (*she*—not *her*) must be used after the conjunction *than* when the pronoun is the subject of an elliptical clause ("than she is").

21. **(E)** All underlined parts are correct.

22. **(A)** "The novelists *whom* readers choose..." The direct object of the verb (choose) must be the objective case form (*whom*—not *who*).

23. **(C)** "The problem...disturbs..." The subject (*problem*) is singular. Therefore the verb (*disturbs*) must be singular.

24. **(B)** "...son *could have* gone..." The phrase *could of* is always incorrect, as it is a speech-based error from could have. Do not use *of* for *have*.

25. **(D)** "...the horse *which* had fallen..." The pronoun *which* should be used to refer to animals and things; *who* should be used to refer only to people.

26. **(D)** "...then *he or she* should make..." A pronoun must agree with its antecedent (*someone*) in number. Since *someone* is singular, the pronoun must be singular (*he or she*—not *they*).

27. **(A)** "The man *whom* Mexican authorities believe to be..." The subject of an infinitive must be in the objective case. The pronoun "whom" in the objective case—not "who" in the nominative case—is the subject of the verbal infinitive "to be."

28. **(C)** "...the child fell *off* the unscreened porch." The correct preposition is simply "off"—not "off of"—to introduce a noun or pronoun.

29. **(A)** "...ran *more swiftly*..." We must use an adverb—not an adjective—to modify a verb. Therefore, we use the adverbial comparative construction "more swiftly" instead of the comparative adjective "swifter" to modify the verb "ran."

30. **(D)** Choice A is incorrect because ending the sentence after company would destroy the charming contrasting idea which follows. Choice B is incorrect because sentence 3 clearly interrupts the flow of thought between sentences 2 and 4. Choice C is incorrect because sentence 3 relates closely in structure and content to sentence 1, especially in the reference to the caves of France, and should follow sentence 1. Choice D is correct. Choice E is incorrect because the explanation for Lampe-Pigeon which now introduces the passage is the best opening sentence. Sentence 3 clearly needs prior information to explain its references to the lamp and to the caves of France.

31. **(C)** Choices A and D are incorrect because they create a contradictory impression by equating tall with more than nine and one-half inches, even though Choice D is preferable because it is more concise. Choice B is incorrect because it conveys an unwarranted apologetic note for the height of the lamp by using the conjunction although. Choice C is correct because it concisely and clearly describes the height and type of lamp being described. Choice E is incorrect because it is wordy and therefore awkward.

32. **(A)** Choice A is correct because the simple prepositional phrase is preferable to the more awkward gerund form of the incorrect Choice B. Choice C is incorrect because it is too wordy and awkward. Choice D, in addition to being the above-mentioned more awkward gerund form, is incorrect also because of the inappropriate use of the preposition to after the adjective suitable. Choice E is incorrect because it is overly long and also would create an inappropriate repetition with the word centerpiece, which is used in the next phrase.

33. **(B)** Choice A is incorrect because glass globed is an awkward descriptive phrase. Choice B is correct because it is more concise than the repetitive clause which contains within it a glass globe. Choice C is incorrect and completely changes the focus of the sentence from the lamp to the globe. Choice D is incorrect because it is wordy and repetitive. Choice E is incorrect because it is too verbose.

34. **(B)** Sentence 6 contradicts and is not consistent with the paragraph and should be deleted. It would also make no sense to include that sentence in any other part of the paragraph.

35. **(D)** Since the author of the paragraph wants to show the beauty of the Lampe-Pigeon, he would contrast that lamp with the modern lamps and use the word "but" not "and." Therefore, Choice D is correct and Choice E is incorrect. For Choice A, "manufactured" is appropriate and it is not necessary to change the word to "produced." For Choice B, "Lampe-Pigeon" sounds better than "lamp in question." After all, this is not a legal document! For Choice C, "modernization" would contradict the antiquity of the lamp.

Explanatory Answers for Practice Test 5 (continued)

Section 6: Math

As you read these solutions, you are advised to do two things if you answered the Math question incorrectly:

1. When a specific Math Strategy is referred to in the solution, study that strategy, which you will find in "19 Math Strategies" (beginning on page 69).
2. When the solution directs you to the "Complete Math Refresher" (beginning on page 167)—for example, Math Refresher 305—study the 305 Math principle to get a clear idea of the Math operation that was necessary for you to know in order to answer the question correctly.

1. Choice E is correct. **(Use Strategy 1: Cancel quantities to make the problem simpler.)** Subtract 14 from both sides of the equation:

$$5\sqrt{x} + 14 = 20$$

$$5\sqrt{x} = 6$$

Divide by 5:

$$\sqrt{x} = \frac{6}{5}$$

Square both sides:

$$x = \frac{36}{25}$$

(Math Refresher #430)

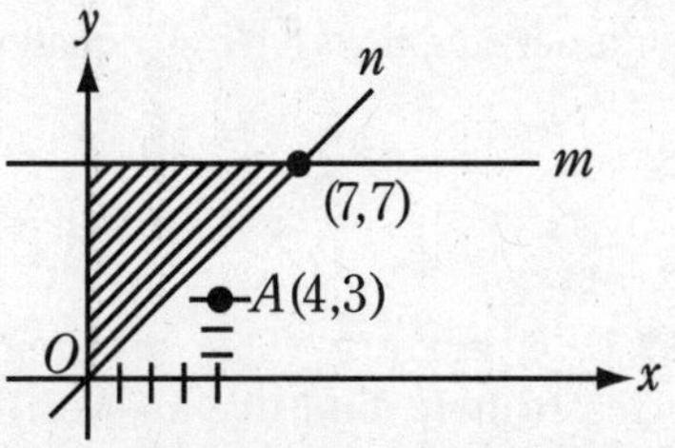

2. Choice A is correct. **(Use Strategy 17: Use the given information effectively.)** Since n goes through point O, the origin, whose coordinates are (0,0), and through (7,7), all of the points on n have x- and y-coordinates that equal each other. Choice A, (4,3), is 4 units to the right of O but only 3 units up. It is below n and not in the shaded area.

(Math Refresher #410)

3. Choice B is correct. **(Use Strategy 2: Translate from words to algebra.)** This problem tests the concepts of set union and set intersection. We can solve these types of problems with a diagram.

Thus, draw the diagram:

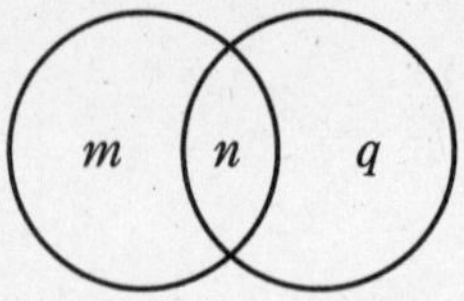

Where

m = number of students taking *only* calculus
q = number of students taking *only* physics
n = number of students taking *both* calculus and physics

Thus,

$m + n$ = number of students in calculus class
$n + q$ = number of students in physics class
$m + n + q$ = number of students taking either calculus or physics or both

We are given that

$$m + n + q = 36 \quad \boxed{1}$$
$$n = 10 \quad \boxed{2}$$
$$m + n = 31 \quad \boxed{3}$$

We want to find

$$n + q \quad \boxed{4}$$

(Use Strategy 13: Find unknowns by subtracting equations.) Subtract equation $\boxed{2}$ from equation $\boxed{3}$ to get

$$m = 21 \quad \boxed{5}$$

Now subtract equation $\boxed{5}$ from equation $\boxed{1}$ to get

$$n + q = 15$$

(Math Refresher #406)

4. Choice D is correct. **(Use Strategy 7: Use numerics to help find the answer.)** In order to show a counterexample to refute Mr. Simmons's argument, we must come up with two numbers a and b such that $a^2 > b^2$ but a is not greater than b. Choice A is incorrect since it is not true that $a^2 > b^2$ in this case. Choice B is incorrect since it is true that $a^2 > b^2$ and that $a > b$. Choice C is incorrect because $a^2 > b^2$ and $a > b$. Choice D is correct: a^2 is greater than b^2 since $(-4)^2 > (-2)^2$. But it is not true that $a > b$ since -4 is *not* greater than -2. Choice E is incorrect since it is not true that $a^2 > b^2$ in this case.

(Math Refresher #429, #424)

5. Choice E is correct. **(Use Strategy 7: Use specific numerical examples to prove or disprove your guess.)**

$\sqrt{2+2} \neq \sqrt{2} + \sqrt{2}$

$2^2 + 2^2 \neq (2 + 2)^2$

$2^1 + 2^2 \neq 2^{1+2}$

Therefore, neither (I) nor (II) nor (III) is generally true.

(Math Refresher #429 and #430)

6. Choice B is correct. The only element common to R and S is $x = 1$.

(Math Refresher #803)

7. Choice A is correct. To find the coordinates of the intersection point, we must first solve the equations $y = x - 1$ and $2x + 5y = 9$. In the equation $2x + 5y = 9$, we substitute $y = x - 1$. We obtain

$$2x + 5(x - 1) = 9$$

Thus

$$2x + 5x - 5 = 9$$

and

$$7x = 14$$
$$x = 2$$

From the first equation, $y = x - 1$, so $y = 2 - 1 = 1$. Thus $x = 2$ and $y = 1$, so the coordinates of the point are (2,1).

(Math Refresher #417)

8. Choice D is correct. **(Use Strategy 3: The whole equals the sum of its parts.)**

Volume of rectangular solid
= Volume of triangular box
+ Volume of trapezoid-shaped box $\boxed{1}$

Area of rectangular dividing wall
$= l \times w$
$39 \text{ cm}^2 = 13 \text{ cm} \times w$
$3 \text{ cm} = w$ $\boxed{2}$

$\boxed{2}$ is the height of the rectangular solid as well.

Volume of
rectangular solid $= l \times w \times h$
$= 15 \text{ cm} \times 12 \text{ cm} \times h$ $\boxed{3}$

Substituting $\boxed{2}$ into $\boxed{3}$, we get

Volume of rectangular solid =
$15 \text{ cm} \times 12 \text{ cm} \times 3 \text{ cm}$
Volume of rectangular solid $= 540 \text{ cm}^3$ $\boxed{4}$

Volume of triangular box

$= $ Area of base $\times$ height

$= \frac{1}{2} \times 12 \text{ cm} \times 5 \text{ cm} \times 3 \text{ cm}$ $\boxed{5}$

Volume of triangular-shaped box = 90 cm^3

Substitute $\boxed{4}$ and $\boxed{5}$ into $\boxed{1}$. We get

$540\text{ cm}^3 = 90\text{ cm}^3 + \text{Volume of trapezoid-shaped box}$
$450\text{ cm}^3 = \text{Volume of trapezoid-shaped box}$

(Math Refresher #312 and #306)

9. $\frac{7}{18}$ or .388 or .389

(Use Strategy 1: Simplify by cancelling.)

$$\left(\frac{1}{2}-\frac{1}{3}\right)+\left(\frac{1}{3}-\frac{1}{4}\right)+\left(\frac{1}{4}-\frac{1}{5}\right)+$$
$$\left(\frac{1}{5}-\frac{1}{6}\right)+\left(\frac{1}{6}-\frac{1}{7}\right)+\left(\frac{1}{7}-\frac{1}{8}\right)+$$
$$\left(\frac{1}{8}-\frac{1}{9}\right)=$$
$$\frac{1}{2}+\left(-\frac{1}{3}+\frac{1}{3}\right)+\left(-\frac{1}{4}+\frac{1}{4}\right)+$$
$$\left(-\frac{1}{5}+\frac{1}{5}\right)+\left(-\frac{1}{6}+\frac{1}{6}\right)+\left(-\frac{1}{7}+\frac{1}{7}\right)+$$
$$\left(-\frac{1}{8}+\frac{1}{8}\right)-\frac{1}{9}=$$
$$\frac{1}{2}+0+0+0+0+0+0-\frac{1}{9}=$$
$$\frac{1}{2}-\frac{1}{9}=$$
$$\frac{9}{18}-\frac{2}{18}=$$
$$\frac{7}{18}$$

(Math Refresher #110)

10. 8

(Use Strategy 11: Use new definitions carefully.) The first five elements of the series, calculated by the definition, are

1, 2, 2, 4, 8

11. $\frac{2}{3}$ or .667 or .666

(Use Strategy 2: Translate from words to algebra.)

$$p = \frac{3}{5}m \qquad \boxed{1}$$

$$q = \frac{9}{10}m \qquad \boxed{2}$$

(Use Strategy 13: Find unknowns by division of equations.)

$$\text{Thus, } \frac{p}{q} = \frac{\frac{3}{5}m}{\frac{9}{10}m}$$

$$= \frac{\frac{3}{5}}{\frac{9}{10}}$$

$$= \frac{3}{5}\times\frac{10}{9} = \frac{\overset{1}{\cancel{3}}}{\underset{1}{\cancel{5}}}\times\frac{\overset{2}{\cancel{10}}}{\underset{3}{\cancel{9}}}$$

$$\frac{p}{q} = \frac{2}{3}$$

(Math Refresher #200 and #112)

12. 60

(Use Strategy 5:

$$\textbf{Average} = \frac{\textbf{sum of values}}{\textbf{total number of values}}\textbf{)}$$

$$\text{Given: } \frac{40+40+40+z}{4} = 45 \qquad \boxed{1}$$

Multiplying $\boxed{1}$ by 4,

$$40 + 40 + 40 + z = 180$$
$$120 + z = 180$$
$$z = 60$$

(Math Refresher #601 and #406)

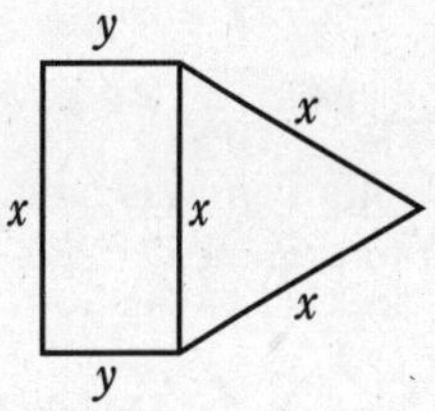

13. 36

(Use Strategy 2: Translate from words to algebra.) When the given diagram has been labeled as above, then we know

$$3x = 39 \qquad \boxed{1}$$
$$xy = 65 \qquad \boxed{2}$$

From $\boxed{1}$, we have

$$x = 13 \qquad \boxed{3}$$

Substituting $\boxed{3}$ into $\boxed{2}$, we have

$$13y = 65$$

$$\text{or} \quad y = 5 \qquad \boxed{4}$$

The perimeter of the rectangle

$$= 2x + 2y$$
$$= 2(13) + 2(5)$$
$$= 36$$

(Math Refresher #200, #304, #308, and #431)

14. 44

(Use Strategy 17: Use the given information effectively.)

Game	*Darrin*	*Tom*
1	69	43
2	59	60
3	72	55
4	70	68
5	78	73
Totals	348	299

We need the scores at the end of the first four games. We have been given the totals for all five games.

(Use Strategy 13: Find unknowns by subtraction.)

Darrin's Total = 348 $\boxed{1}$
Darrin's Game 5 = 78 $\boxed{2}$
Tom's Total = 299 $\boxed{3}$
Tom's Game 5 = 73 $\boxed{4}$

Subtract $\boxed{2}$ from $\boxed{1}$. We get

Darrin's total for 1st four games = 348 − 78
= 270 $\boxed{5}$

Subtract $\boxed{4}$ from $\boxed{3}$. We get

Tom's total for 1st four games = 299 − 73
= 226 $\boxed{6}$

Subtracting $\boxed{6}$ from $\boxed{5}$, we have

Number of points Tom was behind Darrin after the first four games = 270 − 226
= 44

(Math Refresher #702)

15. $\frac{1}{4}$ or .25

(Use Strategy 17: Use the given information effectively.)

The 17 slips, numbered from 1 to 17, consist of $\boxed{1}$
8 even numbers (2, 4, 6,...16) and $\boxed{2}$
9 odd numbers (1, 3, 5,...17). $\boxed{3}$

Subtracting 5 even-numbered slips from $\boxed{2}$ leaves

8 − 5 = 3 even-numbered slips. $\boxed{4}$

Adding $\boxed{3}$ and $\boxed{4}$, we have

9 + 3 = 12 slips remaining $\boxed{5}$

We need $\frac{\text{even-numbered slips}}{\text{total numbered slips}}$ $\boxed{6}$

Substituting $\boxed{4}$ and $\boxed{5}$ into $\boxed{6}$, we have

$$\frac{3}{12} = \frac{1}{4}$$

(Math Refresher #603)

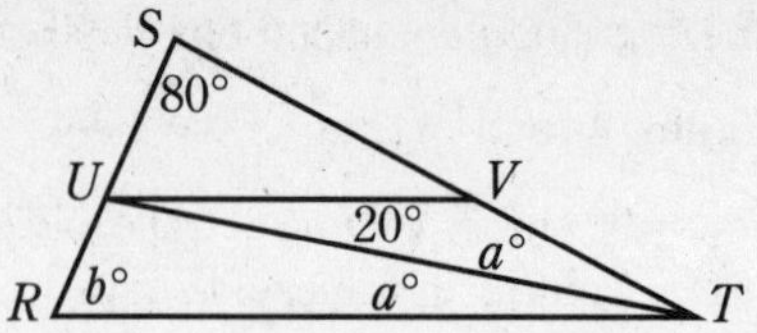

16. 60

Given: $UV \parallel RT$ $\boxed{1}$

From $\boxed{1}$, we get $a = 20$, since alternate interior angles are equal $\boxed{2}$

(Use Strategy 3: The whole equals the sum of its parts.) From the diagram we see that

$\angle STR = a + a$ $\boxed{3}$

Substituting $\boxed{2}$ into $\boxed{3}$, we have

$\angle STR = 20 + 20 = 40$ $\boxed{4}$

We know that the sum of the angles in a triangle = 180, thus

$\angle R + \angle S + \angle STR = 180$ $\boxed{5}$

We are given, in the diagram, that

$\angle R = b$ $\boxed{6}$
$\angle S = 80$ $\boxed{7}$

Substituting $\boxed{6}$, $\boxed{7}$, and $\boxed{4}$ into $\boxed{5}$, we get

$$b + 80 + 40 = 180$$
$$b + 120 = 180$$
$$b = 60$$

(Math Refresher #504, #505, and #406)

17. 10

(Use Strategy 2: Translate from words to algebra.)

Given: Rose's earnings = \$44 $\boxed{1}$
Rose's time worked = 8 days $\boxed{2}$

(Use Strategy 13: Find unknowns by division.)

Dividing $\boxed{1}$ by $\boxed{2}$, we have

Rose's daily rate = $\frac{\$44}{8 \text{ days}}$

Rose's daily rate = $\frac{\$11}{2 \text{ days}}$ $\boxed{3}$

Given: Total earnings to equal \$99 $\boxed{4}$

Subtracting $\boxed{1}$ from $\boxed{4}$, we get

Amount left to be earned = \$55 $\boxed{5}$

We know
(daily rate) (days worked) = money earned $\boxed{6}$

Substituting $\boxed{3}$ and $\boxed{5}$ into $\boxed{6}$, we get

$\left(\frac{\$11}{2 \text{ days}}\right)$(days worked) = \$55 $\boxed{7}$

Multiplying [7] by $\frac{2 \text{ days}}{\$11}$, we have

$$\frac{\cancel{2 \text{ days}}}{\cancel{\$11}}\left(\frac{\cancel{\$11}}{\cancel{2 \text{ days}}}\right)(\text{days worked}) = (\overset{5}{\cancel{\$55}})\,\frac{2}{\cancel{\$11}} \text{ days}$$

days worked = 10 days

(Math Refresher #200, #406, and #121)

18. 48

Given: Areas of all 12 triangles are the same [1]
Area of outlined region = 256 [2]
Area of square *ABCD* = 128 [3]

(Use Strategy 3: The whole equals the sum of its parts.)

By looking at the diagram, we observe

Area of 8 triangles (I, II, …, VIII) = Area of outlined region − area of square *ABCD*.

Substituting [2] and [3] into the above, we get

Area of 8 triangles (I, …, VIII)
= 256 − 128
= 128 [4]

Using [1], we get

Area of each of the 12 triangles = $\frac{\text{area of 8 triangles}}{8}$

Substituting [4] into the above, we get

Area of each of the 12 triangles = $\frac{128}{8}$

Area of each of the 12 triangles = 16 [5]

(Use Strategy 3: The whole equals the sum of its parts.)

Shaded area = Area ΔV + area ΔVI + area ΔXI [6]

Substituting [1] and [5] into [6], we get

Shaded area = 16 + 16 + 16 = 48

(Math Refresher #301)

Explanatory Answers for Practice Test 5 (continued)

Section 7: Critical Reading

As you read these Explanatory Answers, refer to "16 Verbal (Critical Reading) Strategies" (beginning on page 119) whenever a specific strategy is referred to in the answer. Of particular importance are the following Master Verbal Strategies:

Sentence Completion Master Strategy 1—page 120.
Sentence Completion Master Strategy 2—page 121.
Reading Comprehension Master Strategy 2—page 138.

Note: All Reading questions use Reading Comprehension Strategies 1, 2, and 3 (pages 135–140) as well as other strategies indicated.

1. Choice D is correct. See **Sentence Completion Strategy 1.** The word "extreme" is the most appropriate among the five choices because the forest fire season is in *full swing*. The other choices are, therefore, not appropriate.

2. Choice A is correct. See **Sentence Completion Strategy 2.** Examine the first word of each choice. We eliminate Choice C, imagined, and Choice E, intuitive. Reason: The effect of the long war was *not* imagined or intuitive (meaning knowing by a hidden sense). Now we consider Choice B, immediate...storing, and Choice D, delayed...rebuilding. Neither word pair makes sense in the sentence. Choice A, cumulative...corrosion, *does* make sense in the sentence.

3. Choice E is correct. See **Sentence Completion Strategy 3.** If you had tried to complete the sentence *before* looking at the five choices, you might have come up with any of the following words meaning "continually" or "regularly":

   constantly — always
   perpetually — persistently
   habitually

   The other choices are, therefore, incorrect.

4. Choice E is correct. See **Sentence Completion Strategy 2.** Examine the first word of each choice. Choice D, crushes, is eliminated because it is not likely that the bee will crush the nectar from different flowers. Now consider each pair of words in the other choices. We find that Choice E, extracts...converts, has the only word pair that makes sense in the sentence.

5. Choice D is correct. See **Sentence Completion Strategies 1 and 4.** The plan turned out to be impractical, unable to be logically supported. Note the root "ten" *to hold*, so "untenable" means *not holding*. Also note that the word "because" in the sentence is a *result indicator*.

6. Choice C is correct. In lines 8–11, the author is showing that through the "weedy falsities," truth can be created.

7. Choice C is correct. See the last lines, 15–18: "we can feel all the poverty, despair, and unfairness in our world..." For Choice A, there may be value for the spectator: see lines 14–15, "and perhaps how we should change them."

8. Choice E is correct. See lines 8–11, 13–15, and 15–18. This describes how something positive can come out of something negative. In Choice A, although specific references (lines 4 and 5) are made, there are no specific references in Passage 2. In Choice B, there is no indication of both being completely objective, especially in Passage 1 line 2 where the author states that the theater is the "most preposterous of all." Choice C is incorrect in that in Passage 1, the author certainly does not believe in the accuracy of the time (16th century), whereas in Passage 2, the author does believe in the accuracy of the time. Choice D is incorrect in that it appears that the intensity and passion of the author's arguments in Passage 1 is far greater than that of the author's in Passage 2.

9. Choice D is correct. In lines 8 and 9, note the words "lily" (a flower) and "jungle" (a place), which are used as analogies. We do not see such analogies in Passage 2. In Choice A, both authors would disagree, as the author in Passage 1 states that theater is fiction, not reality, and the author in Passage 2 states that the theater is real. In Choice B, see line 5: "the much admired Miss Huckaby." In Choice C, in lines 7–8, the author is sarcastic when he says that "people were ever so marvelously articulate." In Choice E, see lines 13–14: the author believes the contrary, that the theater is quite realistic.

10. Choice A is correct. See lines 42–44: "The fundamental fact.... in their environment." Choices B, D, and E are incorrect because the passage does not indicate that these statements are true. Choice C is incorrect because it is only partially true. The passage does not state that *all* animals and plants are successful in adjusting themselves to changes in their environments.

11. Choice E is correct. See lines 4–7: "Originally, the term acclimatization...altered temperature." Also see lines 9–12: "But aside from temperature... originally accustomed to." Choices A, B, C, and D are incorrect because one *cannot* infer from the passage what any of these choices state.

12. Choice A is correct. Acclimatization and adaptation are both forms of adjustment. Accordingly, these two processes are similar. The difference between the two terms, however, is brought out in lines 32–36: "By and large...as adaptation." Choice D is incorrect because the passage does not indicate what is expressed in Choice D. See lines 29–32: "Let us define acclimatization...lethal for it." Choices B, C, and E are incorrect because the passage does not indicate that any of these choices are true.

13. Choice D is correct. A person going from daylight into a darkened room is an example of adaptation—not acclimatization. See lines 32–36: "By and large...as 'adaptation.'" Choices A, B, C, and E all require the process of acclimatization. Therefore, they are incorrect choices. An ocean fish placed in a lake (Choice A) is a chemical change. Choices B, C, and E are all pressure changes. Acclimatization, by definition, deals with chemical and pressure changes.

14. Choice B is correct. Given the context in the sentence, Choice B is the best. By describing the environment as "normally unsuitable to it or lethal for it" (lines 31–32), the author implies that the organism will survive, and the only way to do that is to grow accustomed to it. See also **Reading Comprehension Strategy 5**.

15. Choice B is correct. See lines 33–36: "The term [acclimatization] should not be taken...as 'adaptation.'" Choices A, D, and E are incorrect because the passage does not indicate that these choices are true. Choice C is partially correct in that acclimatization does apply to adjustments, but the choice is incorrect because adaptation also applies to adjustments. See lines 35–36: "This type of adjustment... as 'adaptation.'"

16. Choice E is correct. See paragraph 2 (beginning): "The tie which bound this world-embracing empire together...was as much cultural as political."

17. Choice A is correct. See paragraph 1 (end): "Centuries of training had bred in them the conviction that all other rulers should be tributary to the Son of Heaven."

18. Choice B is correct. See the last paragraph about the close relationship between "ethical standards" and "Confucian patterns."

19. Choice C is correct. The reader should infer from paragraphs 3 and 4 that Han and T'ang were dynasties—just as there was a Manchu dynasty.

20. Choice D is correct. The passage points out that since more emphasis was placed on being members of the same culture, rather than on being members of the same race, there was a

"comparative contentment of Chinese under alien rulers" (paragraph 4: beginning).

21. Choice B is correct. See paragraph 5 (middle): "In contrast with India, where caste and religion have tended to keep apart the racial strata, in China assimilation made great progress."

22. Choice B is correct. Paragraph 4 (end) points out that the Manchus never gave up some of their ancestral ways, and this disturbed segments of the population.

23. Choice A is correct. The passage states that assimilation made great progress in China. (See the answer to question 21.)

24. Choice C is correct. From the context of the sentence and the sentence before and after it, it can be seen that "restiveness" must mean impatience or restlessness. See also **Reading Comprehension Strategy 5**.

Explanatory Answers for Practice Test 5 (continued)

Section 8: Math

As you read these solutions, you are advised to do two things if you answered the Math question incorrectly:

1. When a specific Math Strategy is referred to in the solution, study that strategy, which you will find in "19 Math Strategies" (beginning on page 69).
2. When the solution directs you to the "Complete Math Refresher" (beginning on page 167)—for example, Math Refresher 305—study the 305 Math principle to get a clear idea of the Math operation that was necessary for you to know in order to answer the question correctly.

1. Choice C is correct. **(Use Strategy 2: Translate from words to algebra.)** The key is to be able to translate English sentences into mathematical equations.

Let p = price of one frying pan
m = price of one coffee mug

We are given:

$$p + 2m = \$27 \qquad \boxed{1}$$
$$p + m = \$23 \qquad \boxed{2}$$

Subtract equation $\boxed{2}$ from equation $\boxed{1}$ to get

$$m = \$4 \qquad \boxed{3}$$

Substitute equation $\boxed{3}$ into equation $\boxed{2}$ to get

$$p + \$4 = \$23$$

Subtract \$4 from both sides of the above equation to get

$$p = \$19$$

(Math Refresher #200, #406, and #407)

2. Choice E is correct. **(Use Strategy 2: Translate from words to algebra.)**

Each tile is a square with perimeter = 2 feet

Each side of the tile is $\frac{1}{4}$(2 feet) $= \frac{1}{2}$ foot $\boxed{1}$

The area of each tile is (side)^2.

Using $\boxed{1}$, we get the area of each tile

$$= \left(\frac{1}{2}\right)^2 \text{ square foot} = \frac{1}{4} \text{ square foot} \qquad \boxed{2}$$

The area of the floor is $b \times h$ =
8 feet $\times$ 6 feet =
48 square feet $\boxed{3}$

(Use Strategy 17: Use the given information effectively.)

The number of tiles necessary, at minimum, to cover the floor

$$= \frac{\text{area of floor}}{\text{area of 1 tile}} \qquad \boxed{4}$$

Substituting $\boxed{2}$ and $\boxed{3}$ into $\boxed{4}$, we get:

$$= \frac{48}{\frac{1}{4}} = 48 \times \frac{4}{1}$$
$$= 192$$

(Math Refresher #200 and #303)

3. Choice E is correct.

The only restriction is that 9 and 12 must each divide Q without a remainder. [1]

(Use Strategy 7: Use numerics to help find the answer.)

Choose specific values for Q that satisfy [1].

EXAMPLE 1

$Q = 36$

Then, Q will divide 36 and 72.

EXAMPLE 2

$Q = 108$

Then, Q will divide neither 36 nor 72. Clearly, the answer to this question depends on the specific value of Q.

(Math Refresher #431)

4. Choice B is correct. Since $DC \perp AC$, $\angle DCB$ is a right angle and has a measure of 90°. **(Use Strategy 3: The whole equals the sum of its parts.)** Since the sum of the angles of a Δ is 180°, we have

$$\angle DBC + 90 + 20 = 180$$
$$\angle DBC = 70 \quad [1]$$

Since $EB \perp BD$, $\angle DBE$ is a right angle and has a measure of 90° [2]

(Use Strategy 3: The whole equals the sum of its parts.) The whole straight $\angle ABC$ is equal to the sum of its parts. Thus

$$\angle DBC + \angle DBE + x = 180 \quad [3]$$

Substituting [1] and [2] into [3], we have

$$70 + 90 + x = 180$$
$$x = 20$$

(Math Refresher #501, #505, #406, and #431)

5. Choice E is correct. **(Use Strategy 17: Use the given information effectively.)**

Given: x [1]
$11 - x$ [2]
$x - 4$ [3]

as the lengths of the three sides of a triangle.

(Use Strategy 18: Know and use facts about triangles.) We know that the sum of any two sides of a triangle is greater than the third side. [4]

First, we use [1] + [2] > [3]. We have

$$x + 11 - x > x - 4$$
$$11 > x - 4$$
$$15 > x \quad [5]$$

Next, we use [2] + [3] > [1]. We have

$$11 - x + x - 4 > x$$
$$7 > x \quad [6]$$

To satisfy [6] and [5], we choose [6].

$7 > x$, or $x < 7$ satisfies both [7]

Finally, we use [1] + [3] > [2]. We have

$$x + x - 4 > 11 - x$$
$$2x - 4 > 11 - x$$
$$3x > 15$$
$$x > 5, \text{ or } 5 < x \quad [8]$$

(Use Strategy 6: Know how to manipulate inequalities.) Combining [7] and [8], we get

$$5 < x < 7$$

(Math Refresher #516, #419, and #420)

6. Choice B is correct.

Given: a, b are integers [1]
Average of a, b, and 4 is 6 [2]

(Use Strategy 5:

$$\textbf{Average} = \frac{\textbf{sum of values}}{\textbf{total number of values}}\textbf{)}$$

Using [2], we have

$$\frac{a + b + 4}{3} = 6 \quad [3]$$

(Use Strategy 13: Find unknowns by multiplication.)

Multiply [3] by 3. We get

$$3\left(\frac{a + b + 4}{3}\right) = (6)3$$
$$a + b + 4 = 18$$
$$a + b = 14 \quad [4]$$

Using [1] and [4], the possibilities are:

$a + b$	ab	
1 + 13	13	Choice A
2 + 12	24	
3 + 11	33	
4 + 10	40	Choice C
5 + 9	45	
6 + 8	48	Choice D
7 + 7	49	Choice E

Checking all the choices, we find that only Choice B, 14, is not a possible value of *ab*.

(Math Refresher #601 and #406)

7. Choice D is correct. **(Use Strategy 17: Use the given information effectively.)**

$$\frac{1}{n^2}\left(\frac{m^5n^3}{m^3}\right)^2 = \frac{1}{n^2}\left[(m^2n^3)^2\right] = \frac{m^4n^6}{n^2} = m^4n^4$$

(Math Refresher #429)

8. Choice C is correct. Label the females F_1, F_2, and F_3 and the males M_1, M_2, and M_3. The total number of combinations of three people (such as F_1–F_2–M_1 or F_1–M_2–M_3) is 6 combinations taken 3 at a time, or ${}_6C_3$, which is equal to $(6 \times 5 \times 4)/(3 \times 2 \times 1) = 20$. There are 9 favorable combinations (trios that include exactly two men): M_1–M_2–F_1, M_1–M_2–F_2, M_1–M_2–F_3, M_1–M_3–F_1, M_1–M_3–F_2, M_1–M_3–F_3, M_2–M_3–F_1, M_2–M_3–F_2, and M_2–M_3–F_3. The probability of exactly two males in the room is:

$$\frac{\text{favorable combinations}}{\text{total combinations}} = \frac{9}{20}$$

(Math Refresher #613 and #614)

9. Choice E is correct. **(Use Strategy 8: When all choices must be tested, start with Choice E and work backward.)** In Choice E, if $Z = 5$, then $5Z = 25$. Thus $W + X + Y = 25$. Note that even if you used the highest ("distinct," which means "different") values of W, X, and Y, we would get $7 + 8 + 9 = 24$ as a maximum value. So Choice E could not be a value of Z. Now go to Choice D: If $Z = 4$, then $5Z = 20$, and you would have $W + X + Y = 20$. An example that would work in that equation is $W = 9$, $X = 8$, and $Y = 3$. You can also see that for Choices C, B, and A, $W + X + Y$ could equal 5×3, or 5×2, or 5×1, by easily adjusting the values of W, X, and Y. Don't forget, you can use 0 for any one (but just one) of the variables W, X, or Y.

(Math Refresher #431)

10. Choice C is correct. **(Use Strategy 3: The whole equals the sum of its parts.)** From the diagram, we see that each straight angle is equal to the sum of two smaller angles. Thus,

$$m = 180 - x \quad \boxed{1}$$
$$n = 180 - z \quad \boxed{2}$$

(Use Strategy 13: Find unknown expressions by addition of equations.) Adding $\boxed{1}$ and $\boxed{2}$, we have

$$m + n = 180 + 180 - x - z \quad \boxed{3}$$

We know that the sum of the angles of a triangle = 180

Therefore, $y + x + z = 180$ or

$$y = 180 - x - z \quad \boxed{4}$$

Substituting $\boxed{4}$ into $\boxed{3}$, we have

$$m + n = 180 + y$$

Accordingly, Choice C is the correct choice.

(Math Refresher #406, #505, and #501)

11. Choice C is correct. **(Use Strategy 2: Translate from words to algebra.)**
We know that the volume of a cube = e^3
We are told that $e^3 < 25$

(Use Strategy 17: Use the given information effectively.)

Since e is a positive integer (which was given),

e can be: $1 \rightarrow 1^3 = 1$
$2 \rightarrow 2^3 = 8$
$3 \rightarrow 3^3 = 27$
etc.

For $e = 2$, the volume is 8, which is < 25
Any larger e will have a volume > 25
Thus, area of one face $= e^2 = 2^2 = 4$
Total area $= 6(4) = 24$

(Math Refresher #202 and #313)

12. Choice E is correct. **(Use Strategy 2: Translate from words to algebra.)**

Let s = number of females
n = number of males
Then $s + n$ = total number of people.

$$\text{We are given: } \frac{s}{n} = \frac{2}{3} \text{ or } s = \frac{2}{3}n \quad \boxed{1}$$

$$\text{and: } s = \frac{1}{3}(s + n) + 5 \quad \boxed{2}$$

Substituting $\boxed{1}$ into $\boxed{2}$, we have

$$\frac{2}{3}n = \frac{1}{3}\left(\frac{2}{3}n + n\right) + 5$$
$$\frac{2}{3}n = \frac{1}{3}\left(\frac{2}{3}n + \frac{3}{3}n\right) + 5$$
$$\frac{2}{3}n = \frac{1}{3}\left(\frac{5}{3}n\right) + 5$$
$$\frac{2}{3}n = \frac{5}{9}n + 5 \quad \boxed{3}$$

Multiplying both sides of $\boxed{3}$ by 9, we get

$$9\left(\frac{2}{3}n\right) = 9\left(\frac{5}{9}n + 5\right)$$
$$\frac{18}{3}n = 5n + 45$$
$$6n = 5n + 45$$
$$n = 45$$

$s = \frac{2}{3}(45) = 30$

$s + n = 75$

(Math Refresher #200 and #406)

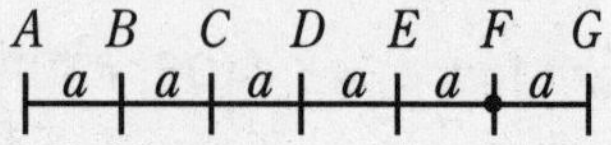

13. Choice C is correct.

Given:

AG is divided into 6 equal segments. [1]

Radius of circle, centered at $F = \frac{1}{5}AG$ [2]

(Use Strategy 14: Label unknown quantities.)

Label segments with "a" as shown in above diagram.

Using [2], radius of circle centered at $F = \frac{1}{5}(AG)$

$= \frac{1}{5}(6a)$

$= 1\frac{1}{5}a$

This means from the center at F, the left tip of the radius of the circle is $1\frac{1}{5}a$ from point F. Thus the circumference hits the line between D and E.

(Math Refresher #200 and #524)

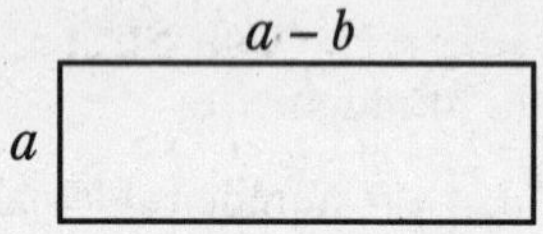

14. Choice B is correct. **(Use Strategy 2: Translate from words to algebra.)**

Perimeter of a rectangle

= 2(length) + 2(width) [1]

Substituting from the diagram into [1], we have

$\text{Perimeter} = 2(a - b) + 2(a)$

$= 2a - 2b + 2a$

$\text{Perimeter} = 4a - 2b$

(Math Refresher #200, #304, and #431)

15. Choice E is correct.

$$\begin{array}{r} AB \\ +\ BA \\ \hline CDC \end{array}$$

Given: A, B, C, and D are different digits. [1]

(Use Strategy 8: When testing the choices, start with Choice E.)

Let's see if $A = 2$ will work.

We get:

$$\begin{array}{r} 2B \\ B2 \\ \hline CDC \end{array}$$

Now for the range $B = 1, 2, 3, 4, 5, 6, 7$, the left C won't equal the right C. So we try $B = 8$. (Note we can't use $B = 2$ because A would equal B, which is incorrect.)

We would get:

$$\begin{array}{r} 28 \\ 82 \\ \hline 110 \end{array}$$

Also, the left C doesn't equal the right C.

The only digit left for B is 9. We then get:

$$\begin{array}{r} 29 \\ 92 \\ \hline 121 \end{array}$$

But then $D = A$, which is incorrect.

Thus $A = 2$ doesn't work.

16. Choice A is correct. $g(-1) = 1$, $f[g(-1)] = f(1) = 1^2 + 1 = 2$.

(Math Refresher #616)

Explanatory Answers for Practice Test 5 (continued)

Section 9: Critical Reading

As you read these Explanatory Answers, refer to "16 Verbal (Critical Reading) Strategies" (beginning on page 119) whenever a specific strategy is referred to in the answer. Of particular importance are the following Master Verbal Strategies:

Sentence Completion Master Strategy 1—page 120.
Sentence Completion Master Strategy 2—page 121.
Reading Comprehension Master Strategy 2—page 138.

Note: All Reading questions use Reading Comprehension Strategies 1, 2, and 3 (pages 135–140) as well as other strategies indicated.

1. Choice C is correct. See **Sentence Completion Strategy 2.** Examine the first word of each choice. Choice E, a futile, does *not* make good sense because we do not refer to momentum as futile. Now consider the other choices. Choice C, an increasing…athletics, is the only choice that makes sense in the sentence.

2. Choice E is correct. See **Sentence Completion Strategy 1.** The word "effective" (meaning "serving the purpose" or "producing a result") makes good sense in the sentence. The other choices don't do that.

3. Choice D is correct. See **Sentence Completion Strategy 4.** The word "despite" is an *opposition indicator.* A strange and inevitable, or *ineluctable* fate seemed to keep him helpless and unhappy, despite occasional periods of calm peacefulness, or *serenity.*

4. Choice B is correct. See **Sentence Completion Strategies 1 and 4.** Try each choice, being aware that "result" is, of course, a *result indicator*: Samuel Clemens chose the pseudonym (pen name) Mark Twain.

5. Choice A is correct. See **Sentence Completion Strategy 1.** The word "capable" means "skilled" or "competent." Clearly, Choice A, a capable, is the only correct choice.

6. Choice B is correct. See **Sentence Completion Strategy 2.** Examine the first word of each choice. We eliminate Choice C, avoided, and Choice D, realized, because it does not make sense to say that Leonardo realized or avoided the Law of Gravity. Now we consider Choice A, examined…colorful, and Choice E, suspected…mural, neither of which makes sense in the sentence. Choice B, anticipated…anatomical, is the only choice that makes sense in the sentence.

7. Choice E is correct. The author is stressing the point that the true artist—the person with rare

creative ability and keen perception, or high intelligence—fails to communicate well with those about him—"differs from the rest of us" (line 4). He is likely to be considered a "nut" by many whom he comes in contact with. "Great wits" in the Choice E quotation refers to the true artist. The quotation states, in effect, that there is a thin line between the true artist and the "nut." Choices A, B, C, and D are incorrect because they have little, if anything, to do with the main idea of the passage.

[Note: Choices C and E were composed by John Dryden (1631–1700), and Choices A, B, and D by Alexander Pope (1688–1744).]

8. Choice C is correct. See lines 8–10. The artist creates because he is "less fitted to prosper and enjoy himself under the conditions of life which he and we must face alike." Choices A and E are incorrect. Although they may be true, they are never mentioned in the passage. Choice B is incorrect because, although the artist may be a threat to the social order, he is by no means an unnecessary one. The author, throughout the passage, is siding with the artist against the social order. Choice D is incorrect. See lines 10–11: "Therefore he takes... attempt to escape from life." A person who is attempting to escape from life hardly knows how to enjoy life.

9. Choice B is correct. The author ridicules Samuel Johnson, saying that he is as much a true artist as a kazoo player is a musician. He then says that if Johnson were alive today, he would be a senator or a university president. The author thus implies that these positions do not merit high respect. Choice A is the opposite of Choice B. Therefore, Choice A is incorrect. Choice C is incorrect because, although the statement may be true, the author neither states nor implies that senators and university presidents are generally appreciative of the great literary classics. Choice D is incorrect. The fact that the author lumps Johnson, senators, and university presidents together as nonartistic people indicates that the author believes that senators and university presidents do not have native writing ability. Choice E is incorrect for this reason: The author believes that Johnson lacked the qualities of an artist. Johnson, if alive today, would be a senator or a university president. We may conclude, then, that the author believes that senators and university presidents lack the qualities of an artist.

10. Choice C is correct. Although a love of beauty is a quality we usually associate with artists, that idea about artists is never mentioned in the passage. All of the other characteristics are expressly mentioned in the first two paragraphs of the passage.

11. Choice B is correct. The author's sincere sympathy is shown toward artists in lines 17–24: "From Dante to Tolstoy...actually fugitives from rage and reprisal." There is no evidence in the passage to indicate that the author's attitude toward artists is Choice A, C, D, or E. Therefore, these choices are incorrect.

12. Choice C is correct. See line 69: "He and he alone knows the world."

13. Choice B is correct. See lines 54–61 and 64–66 in Passage 2.

14. Choice C is correct. From the context in Passage 2, we see that "world's eye" and "world's heart" refer to culture and wisdom, respectively. See lines 56–60: "...public and illustrious thoughts...resist the vulgar prosperity...by preserving and communicating...noble biographies...melodious verse..." This is all about *culture* and *wisdom*.

15. Choice E is correct. See the first sentence in Passage 2: "...the self-accusation, the faint heart, the frequent uncertainty and loss of time, which are the nettles and tangling vines..." Here "nettles and tangling vines" refers to "self-accusation" and "uncertainty." Nettles are plants covered with stinging hairs. Tangling vines give the impression of weaving all around in no particular or certain direction. So nettles can be thought of as "self-accusation"—something "stinging." And "tangling vines" can be thought of as "uncertainty." See also **Reading Comprehension Strategy 5**.

16. Choice C is correct. See Passage 2: The most appropriate groups are the hardships of the scholar, the scholar's functions, and the scholar's justifications for disregarding the world's business, as can be seen from the structure and content of the passage.

17. Choice C is correct. So far the tone of the passage is sympathetic toward the difficulties of the artist, so by placing "seems to be" in the context of the "virtual hostility" the artist feels from society, it is clear that the author is contrasting what the artist is and what he is perceived to be. The words "false impression" in Choice C fit best. See also **Reading Comprehension Strategy 5.**

18. Choice A is correct. See lines 91–98 and 54–56 in Passage 2 and lines 13–17 and 25–34 in Passage 1.

19. Choice E is correct. The statements in I can be seen to be associated with the artist in Passage 2 from lines 85–86 and 57–58, respectively. The statements in II can be seen to be associated with the artist in Passage 1 from lines 27–33 and 5, respectively. The statements in III can be seen to be associated with the artist in Passage 2 from lines 53–54 and 45–52, respectively.

Explanatory Answers for Practice Test 5 (continued)

Section 10: Writing

For further practice and information, please refer to Grammar and Usage Refresher starting on page 455.

1. **(E)** Choice A contains a "false series," meaning that the word "and" connects the three words in the series—bread, butter, cheese—with a wholly different clause, instead of with a similar fourth word. The series, therefore, needs its own "and" to complete it. Only Choice E furnishes this additional "and."

2. **(D)** Choice A violates the principle of parallel structure. If the first thing the children liked was "swimming" (a gerund), then the second thing they liked should be not "to watch" (an infinitive), but "watching" (the gerund). Choice B does not improve the sentence. Choice C repeats the beginning of the sentence with the repetitious words "that they liked." Choice D is correct. Choice E simply reverses the gerund and the infinitive without correcting the error.

3. **(D)** Choice A is incorrect because the pronoun must be singular ("he or she"—not "they") since the antecedent ("individual") is singular. Choice C is incorrect for the same reason. Moreover, this choice is roundabout. Choice B is incorrect because it is roundabout. Choice D is correct for the reason that Choice A is incorrect. Choice E is incorrect because its subject is "you" (understood). A third person subject is required to coincide with the third person of the antecedent "individual."

4. **(E)** Choices A, B, C, and D are incorrect because these choices do not make it clear whether the dog or the food ought to be put through the meat grinder. Moreover, "it's" in Choice B is wrong. Choice E is correct because it makes clear that the food—not the dog—is to be put through the meat grinder.

5. **(B)** Choices A, C, and D are incorrect because the word "money" is incorrectly the antecedent in these three choices. Choice B is correct because "a decision" correctly refers to the whole idea—"The bank agreed to lend Garcia the money." Choice E is incorrect because it does not retain the complete meaning of the original sentence.

6. **(C)** Choices A and D are incorrect because the expression "that in" is required to complete the comparison. Choice C is correct because it includes the required expression "that in." Choice B is incorrect because "then" is incorrect here for "than." Choice E is incorrect because it changes the meaning of the original sentence.

7. **(D)** Choices A, C, and E are incorrect because they do not fulfill the requirement of contributing to the composition of a complete sentence. Choice D is correct because it does complete that requirement. Choice B is incorrect because it is awkward.

8. **(E)** Choices A, B, and D are incorrect because they lack balance of grammatical structure. Choice C is incorrect because the "and-and" construction is frowned upon by grammarians. Choice E is correct because the grammatical structure is balanced. This choice consists of three well-formed prepositional phrases.

9. **(A)** Choice A is correct. The words which make up the choice act as the subject of the sentence. Choice B is incorrect because it is awkward. Choice C is incorrect because one should never begin a sentence with "Being that." Choice D is incorrect as it stands. If "Charles" were changed to the possessive "Charles'" or "Charles's" the choice would be correct. Choice E is incorrect because it, in itself, is a complete sentence which, as it stands, cannot act as the grammatical subject of the verb "disappointed."

10. **(C)** Choice A is incorrect because the pronoun *which* has an indefinite antecedent. Choices B and E are incorrect because they are too wordy. Choice C is correct. Choice D is incorrect because *damaging* is an inappropriate word choice.

11. **(E)** In this sentence we are looking for correct parallel structure in the last of a series of nouns. Choices A, B, C, and D are incorrect because they destroy the noun balance. Choice E is correct.

12. **(A)** Choice A is correct. Choices B and D are incorrect because the word *most* is unnecessary and incorrect here. Choice C is incorrect because it is wordy. Choice E is incorrect because *premium* is not the correct word for the meaning intended.

13. **(A)** Choice A is correct. Choice B is incorrect because the phrase *for facial lacerations* is misplaced. Choices C and D are incorrect because they are wordy. Choice C also contains the pronoun *it*, which has an indefinite antecedent. Choice E is incorrect because of the awkward use of *facial lacerations* as an adjective modifying *treatment*.

14. **(C)** In this sentence we must have an adjective to balance with *tough* and *single-minded*. Choices A, B, D, and E are incorrect because they do not maintain the required parallel structure. Choice C is correct.

What You Must Do Now to Raise Your SAT Score

1. a) Follow the directions on page 1007 to determine your scaled score for the SAT Test you've just taken. These results will give you a good idea about how hard you'll need to study in order to achieve a certain score on the actual SAT.

   b) Using your Test correct answer count as a basis, indicate for yourself your areas of strength and weakness as revealed by the "Chart for Self-Appraisal" on page 1012.

2. Eliminate your weaknesses in each of the SAT test areas (as revealed in the "Chart for Self-Appraisal") by taking the following Giant Steps toward SAT success:

Critical Reading Part

Giant Step 1

Take advantage of the Critical Reading Strategies that begin on page 119. Read again the Explanatory Answer for each of the Critical Reading questions that you got wrong. Refer to the Critical Reading Strategy that applies to each of your incorrect answers. Learn each of these Critical Reading Strategies thoroughly. These strategies are crucial if you want to raise your SAT Verbal score substantially.

Giant Step 2

You can improve your vocabulary by doing the following:

1) Study the SAT 3,400-Word List beginning on page 359.

2) Take the 100 SAT-type "tough word" Vocabulary Tests beginning on page 408.

3) Study the Gruber Prefix-Root-Suffix List beginning on page 348.

4) Learn the Hot Prefixes and Roots beginning on page 1049.

5) Read through A List of SAT Words Appearing More Than Once beginning on page 353.

6) Look through the Most Important Words and Their Opposites beginning on page 355.

7) Learn the 3 Vocabulary Strategies beginning on page 150.

8) Read as widely as possible—not only novels. Nonfiction is important too…and don't forget to read newspapers and magazines.

9) Listen to people who speak well. Tune in to worthwhile TV programs.

10) Use the dictionary frequently and extensively—at home, on the bus, at work, etc.

11) Play word games—for example, crossword puzzles, anagrams, and Scrabble. Another game is to compose your own Sentence Completion questions. Try them on your friends.

Math Part

Giant Step 3

Make good use of the 19 Math Strategies that begin on page 69. Read again the solutions for each Math question that you answered incorrectly. Refer to the Math Strategy that applies to each of your incorrect answers. Learn each of these Math Strategies thoroughly. We repeat that these strategies are crucial if you want to raise your SAT Math score substantially.

Giant Step 4

You may want to take the **101 Most Important Math Questions You Need to Know How to Solve** test beginning on page 31 and follow the directions after the test for a basic Math skills diagnosis.

For each Math question that you got wrong in the Test, note the reference to the Complete Math Refresher section beginning on page 167. This reference will explain clearly the mathematical principle involved in the solution of the question you answered incorrectly. Learn that particular mathematical principle thoroughly.

For Both the Math and Critical Reading Parts

Giant Step 5

You may want to take the **Strategy Diagnostic Test** beginning on page 1 to assess whether you're using the best strategies for the questions.

For the Writing Part

Giant Step 6

Take a look at Part 9, the SAT Writing Test, which describes the various item types in the Writing Section and sample questions with answers and explanations. Also make use of the Grammar Refresher—Part 8.

If you do the job *right* and follow the steps listed earlier, you are likely to raise your SAT score on each of the Verbal, Math, and Writing parts of the test substantially.

I am the master of my fate:
I am the captain of my soul.

—From the poem "Invictus"
by William Ernest Henley

Appendixes

Appendix A: Hot Prefixes and Roots

Here is a list of the most important prefixes and roots that impart a certain meaning or feeling. They can be instant clues to the meanings of more than 110,000 words.

PREFIXES THAT MEAN "TO, WITH, BETWEEN, OR AMONG"

PREFIX	MEANING	EXAMPLES
ad, ac, af, an, ap, as, at	to, toward	adapt—to fit into adhere—to stick to attract—to draw near
com, con, co, col	with, together	combine—to bring together contact—to touch together collect—to bring together coworker—one who works together with another worker
in, il, ir, im	into	inject—to put into impose—to force into illustrate—to put into example irritate—to put into discomfort
inter	between, among	international—among nations interact—to act among the people
pro	forward, going ahead	proceed—to go forward promote—to move forward

PREFIXES THAT MEAN "BAD"

PREFIX	MEANING	EXAMPLES
mal	wrong, bad	malady—illness malevolent—evil malfunction—poorly functioning
mis	wrong, badly	mistreat—to treat badly mistake—to get wrong

PREFIXES THAT MEAN "AWAY FROM, NOT, OR AGAINST"

PREFIX	MEANING	EXAMPLES
ab	away from	absent—not present, away abscond—to run away
de, dis	away from, down, the opposite of, apart, not	depart—to go away from decline—to turn down dislike—not to like dishonest—not honest distant—apart
ex, e, ef	out, from	exit—to go out eject—to throw out efface—to rub out, erase
in, il, ir, im	not	inactive—not active impossible—not possible illiterate—not literate irreversible—not reversible
non	not	nonsense—no sense nonstop—having no stops
un	not	unhelpful—not helpful uninterested—not interested

PREFIX	MEANING	EXAMPLES
anti	against	antifreeze—a substance used to prevent freezing antisocial—someone who is not social
ob	against, in front of	obstacle—something that stands in the way of obstinate—inflexible

PREFIXES THAT DENOTE DISTANCE

PREFIX	MEANING	EXAMPLES
circum	around	circumscribe—to write or inscribe in a circle circumspect—very careful
equ, equi	equal, the same	equalize—to make equal equitable—fair, equal
post	after	postpone—to do after postmortem—after death
pre	before	preview—a viewing that goes before another viewing prehistorical—before written history
trans	across	transcontinental—across the continent transit—act of going across
re	back, again	retell—to tell again recall—to call back, to remember
sub	under	subordinate—under something else subconscious—under the conscious

PREFIX	MEANING	EXAMPLES
super	over, above	superimpose—to put something over something else superstar—a star greater than other stars
un, uni	one	unity—oneness unanimous—sharing one view unidirectional—having one direction

ROOTS

ROOT	MEANING	EXAMPLES
cap, capt, cept, ceive	to take, to hold	captive—one who is held capable—to be able to take hold of things concept—an idea or thought held in mind receive—to take
cred	to believe	credible—believable credit—belief, trust
curr, curs, cours	to run	current—now in progress, running cursor—a moveable indicator recourse—running for help
dic, dict	to say	indicate—to say by demonstrating diction—verbal saying
duc, duct	to lead	induce—to lead to action aqueduct—a pipe or waterway that leads water somewhere
fac, fic, fect, fy	to make, to do	facile—easy to do fiction—something that has been made up satisfy—to make happy or to fulfill affect—to make a change in

PREFIX	MEANING	EXAMPLES
jec, ject	to throw	project—to put forward trajectory—a path of an object that has been thrown
mit, mis	to send	admit—to send in missile—something that gets sent through the air
pon, pos	to place	transpose—to place across compose—to put into place many parts deposit—to place in something
scrib, script	to write	describe—to write or tell about scripture—a written tablet
spec, spic	to look	specimen—an example to look at inspect—to look over
ten, tain	to hold	maintain—to hold up or keep retentive—holding
ven, vent	to come	advent—a coming convene—to come together

Appendix B: Words Commonly Mistaken for Each Other

Review the following lists of words quickly and use a pencil to mark the pairs that you have trouble remembering. This way, you'll be able to focus your attention on these on subsequent reviews.

AGGRAVATE/IRRITATE	—to make worse —to annoy
ALLUSION/ILLUSION	—reference —error in vision
ARBITER/ARBITRARY	—a supposedly unprejudiced judge —prejudiced
ASCENT/ASSENT	—upward movement —agreement; to agree
ASCETIC/AESTHETIC	—self-denying —pertaining to the beautiful
BAN/BANE	—prohibit —woe
CANVAS/CANVASS	—coarse cloth —examine; solicit
CAPITAL/CAPITOL	—excellent; chief town; money; punishable by death or life imprisonment —state house
CENSURE/CENSOR	—find fault —purge or remove offensive passages
COMPLACENT/COMPLAISANT	—self-satisfied; smug —kindly; submissive
COMPLEMENT/COMPLIMENT	—that which completes —praise
CONSUL/COUNCIL/COUNSEL	—diplomatic representative —group of advisors —advice
CONTEMPTIBLE/CONTEMPTUOUS	—despicable —scornful
COSMOPOLITAN/METROPOLITAN	—sophisticated —pertaining to the city

CREDIBLE/CREDITABLE	—believable —worthy of praise
DEMURE/DEMUR	—pretending modesty —hesitate; raise objection
DEPRECATE/DEPRECIATE	—disapprove regretfully —undervalue
DISCREET/DISCRETE	—judicious; prudent —separate and distinct
DISINTERESTED/UNINTERESTED	—unprejudiced —not interested
DIVERS/DIVERSE	—several —varied
ELICIT/ILLICIT	—extract —unlawful
EMEND/AMEND	—correct a text or manuscript —improve by making slight changes
EMINENT/IMMINENT	—high in rank —threatening; at hand
EQUABLE/EQUITABLE	—even-tempered —just
EXULT/EXALT	—rejoice —raise; praise highly
FORMALLY/FORMERLY	—in a formal manner —at a previous time
GORILLA/GUERRILLA	—large ape —mercenary
GOURMET/GOURMAND	—lover of good food —glutton
HAIL/HALE	—frozen pellets; to call; originate —strong, healthy
HEALTHY/HEALTHFUL	—possessing health —bringing about health
IMPLY/INFER	—indicate or suggest —draw a conclusion from
INCREDIBLE/INCREDULOUS	—unbelievable —unbelieving
INDIGENT/INDIGENOUS	—poor —native
INGENIOUS/INGENUOUS	—skillful; clever; resourceful —frank; naïve

INTERNMENT/INTERMENT	—imprisonment —burial
MAIZE/MAZE	—corn —confusing network
MARTIAL/MARITAL	—warlike —pertaining to marriage
MENDACIOUS/MERITORIOUS	—lying —possessing merit; praiseworthy
PERSONAL/PERSONABLE	—private —pleasant in appearance and manner
PERSPICACIOUS/PERSPICUOUS	—shrewd; acute —clear; lucid
PRACTICAL/PRACTICABLE	—sensible; useful —timely; capable of being accomplished
PRODIGAL/PRODIGIOUS	—wastefully lavish —extraordinarily large
PROPHECY/PROPHESY	—prediction —to predict
PROVIDED/PROVIDING	—on condition that —furnishing; giving
REGAL/REGALE	—royal —entertain lavishly
RESPECTFULLY/RESPECTIVELY	—with respect —in the order already suggested
SANCTION/SANCTITY	—authorize —holiness
SOCIAL/SOCIABLE	—pertaining to human society —companionable; friendly
STATUE/STATURE/STATUTE	—piece of sculpture —height —a law
URBAN/URBANE	—pertaining to the city —polished; suave
VENAL/VENIAL	—corrupt, mercenary —pardonable

Essentials from Dr. Gary Gruber

"Gruber can ring the bell on any number of standardized exams."
—*Chicago Tribune*

$16.99 U.S./£11.99 UK
978-1-4022-4308-0

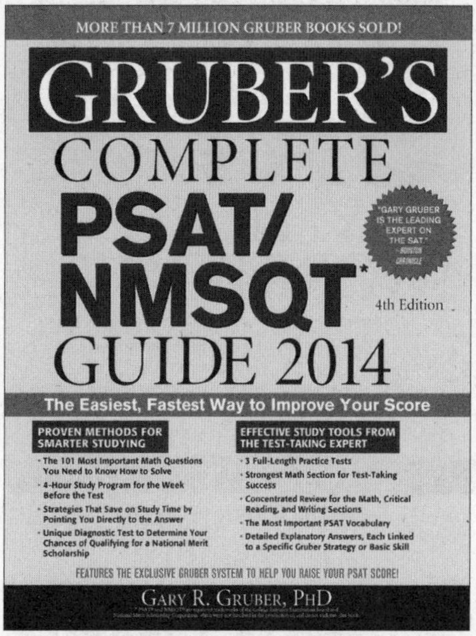

$13.99 U.S./£9.99 UK
978-1-4022-7976-8

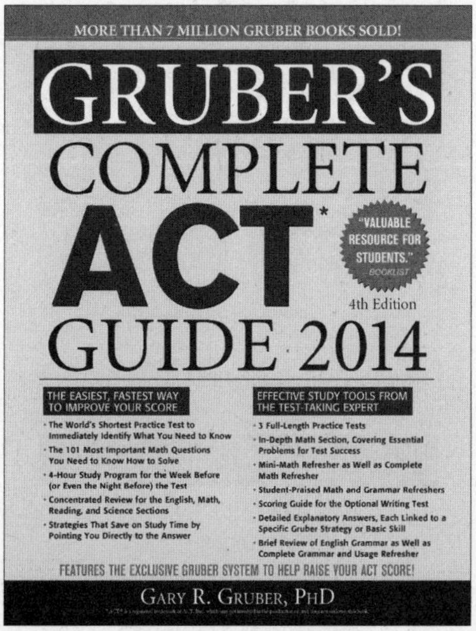

$19.99 U.S./£14.99 UK
978-1-4022-7970-6

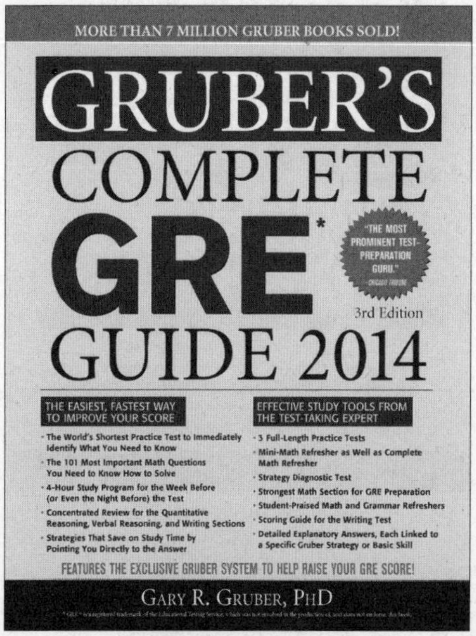

$20.99 U.S./£14.99 UK
978-1-4022-7967-6

Notes

Notes

Notes

Notes

Notes

Notes

Notes

Notes

Notes